shakespearean criticism

"Thou art a Monument without a tomb,
And art alive still while thy Book doth
   live
And we have wits to read and praise to
give."

*Ben Jonson, from the preface
to the First Folio, 1623.*

Mr. WILLIAM
SHAKESPEARES

COMEDIES,
HISTORIES, &
TRAGEDIES.

Published according to the True Originall Copies.

Martin Droeshout sculpsit London.

LONDON
Printed by Isaac Iaggard, and Ed. Blount. 1623.

Frontispiece to the First Folio (1623). By permission of the Folger Shakespeare Library.

Volume 34

shakespearean criticism

Excerpts from the Criticism of
William Shakespeare's Plays and Poetry,
from the First Published Appraisals
to Current Evaluations

Dana Ramel Barnes
Marie Lazzari
Editors

GALE

DETROIT • NEW YORK • TORONTO • LONDON

R
822.3309
SHA
SHA
v 34

STAFF

Dana Ramel Barnes, Marie Lazzari, *Editors*

Michelle Lee, *Assistant Editor*

Susan Trosky, *Managing Editor*

Marlene S. Hurst, *Permissions Manager*
Margaret A. Chamberlain, Maria L. Franklin,
Kimberly F. Smilay, *Permissions Specialists*
Diane Cooper, Edna Hedblad, Michele Lonoconus,
Maureen Puhl, Shalice Shah, *Permissions Associates*
Sarah Chesney, Jeffrey Hermann, *Permissions Assistants*

Victoria B. Cariappa, *Research Manager*
Julia Daniel, Tracie A. Richardson, *Research Associates*
Alfred A. Gardner, Sean R. Smith, *Research Assistants*

Mary Beth Trimper, *Production Director*
Deborah Milliken, *Production Assistant*
Sherrell Hobbs, *Macintosh Artist*
Randy Bassett, *Image Database Supervisor*
Mikal Ansari, Robert Duncan, *Imaging Specialists*
Pamela A. Reed, *Photography Coordinator*

∞™ This book is printed on acid-free paper that meets the minimum requirements of American National Standard for Information Sciences—Permanence Paper for Printed Library Materials, ANSI Z39.48-1984.

Library of Congress Catalog Card Number 86-645085
ISBN 0-8103-9980-6
ISSN 0883-9123

Printed in the United States of America
Published simultaneously in the United Kingdom
by Gale Research International Limited
(An affiliated company of Gale Research)
10   9   8   7   6   5   4   3   2   1

Gale Research

Contents

Preface vii

Acknowledgments ix

Twelfth Night

Preface

*S*hakespearean Criticism (SC) provides students, educators, theatergoers, and other interested readers with valuable insight into Shakespeare's drama and poetry. A multiplicity of viewpoints documenting the critical reaction of scholars and commentators from the seventeenth century to the present day derives from the hundreds of periodicals and books excerpted for the series. Students and teachers at all levels of study will benefit from *SC,* whether they seek information for class discussions and written assignments, new perspectives on traditional issues, or the most noteworthy analyses of Shakespeare's artistry.

Scope of the Series

Volumes 1 through 10 of the series present a unique historical overview of the critical response to each Shakespearean work, representing a broad range of interpretations. Volumes 11 through 26 recount the performance history of Shakespeare's plays on the stage and screen through eyewitness reviews and retrospective evaluations of individual productions, comparisons of major interpretations, and discussions of staging issues.

Beginning with Volume 27 in the series, *SC* focuses on criticism published after 1960, with a view to providing the reader with the most significant modern critical approaches. Each volume is ordered around a theme that is central to the study of Shakespeare, such as politics, religion, or sexuality. The topic entry that introduces the volume is comprised of general essays that discuss this theme with reference to all of Shakespeare's works. Following the topic entry are several entries devoted to individual works. Volume 34 is devoted to Appearance versus Reality, and provides commentary on that topic as well as on the plays *As You Like It, The Comedy of Errors,* and *Twelfth Night.*

SC also compiles an annual volume of the most noteworthy essays published on Shakespeare during the previous year. The essays, reprinted in their entirety, have been recommended to Gale by an international panel of distinguished scholars. The most recent volume, *SC Yearbook 1995,* Volume 32 in the series, was published in October 1996.

Organization of the Book

Each entry consists of the following elements: an introduction, critical essays, and an annotated bibliography of further reading.

- The **Introduction** outlines modern interpretations of individual Shakespearean topics, plays, and poems.

- The **Criticism** for each entry consists of essays that are arranged both thematically and chronologically. This provides an overview of the major areas of concern in the analysis of Shakespeare's works, as well as a useful perspective on changes in critical evaluation over recent decades.

- All of the individual essays are preceded by **Explanatory Notes** as an additional aid to students using *SC*. The explanatory notes summarize the criticism that follows.

- A complete **Bibliographical Citation** providing publication information precedes each piece of criticism.

- Each volume includes such **Illustrations** as reproductions of images from the Shakespearean period, paintings and sketches of eighteenth- and nineteenth-century performers, photographs of modern productions, and stills from film adaptations.

- The annotated bibliography of **Further Reading** appearing at the end of each entry suggests additional sources of study for the reader. Explanatory notes summarize each essay or book listed here.

- Each volume of *SC* provides a **Cumulative Index to Topics.** This feature identifies the principal topics in the criticism and stage history of each work. The topics are arranged alphabetically, and the volume and initial page number are indicated for each essay that offers innovative or ample commentary on that topic.

Citing *Shakespearean Criticism*

Students who quote directly from any volume in the Literature Criticism Series in written assignments may use the following general forms to footnote reprinted criticism. The first example pertains to material drawn from periodicals, the second to material reprinted from books.

[1]Gordon Ross Smith, "Shakespeare's *Henry V*: Another Part of the Critical Forest," in *Journal of the History of Ideas,* XXXVII, No. 1 (January-March 1976), 3-26; excerpted and reprinted in *Shakespearean Criticism,* Vol. 30, ed. Marie Lazzari (Detroit: Gale Research, 1996), pp. 262-73.

[2]Katherine Eisaman Maus, *Inwardness and Theater in the English Renaissance* (The University of Chicago Press, 1995); excerpted and reprinted in *Shakespearean Criticism,* Vol. 33, ed. Dana Ramel Barnes and Marie Lazzari, (Detroit: Gale Research, 1997), pp. 112-17.

Suggestions Are Welcome

The editors encourage comments and suggestions from readers on any aspect of the *SC* series. In response to various recommendations, several features have been added to *SC* since the series began, including the topic index and the sample bibliographic citations noted above. Readers are cordially invited to write, call, or fax the editors: *Shakespearean Criticism,* Gale Research, 835 Penobscot Building, Detroit, MI, 48226-4094. Call toll-free at 1-800-347-GALE or fax to 1-313-961-6599.

Acknowledgments

The editors wish to thank the copyright holders of the excerpted criticism included in this volume and the permissions managers of many book and magazine publishing companies for assisting us in securing reproduction rights. We are also grateful to the staffs of the Detroit Public Library, the Library of Congress, the University of Detroit Mercy Library, Wayne State University Purdy/Kresge Library Complex, and the University of Michigan Libraries for making their resources available to us. Following is a list of the copyright holders who have granted us permission to reproduce material in this volume of *SC*. Every effort has been made to trace copyright, but if omissions have been made, please let us know.

COPYRIGHTED EXCERPTS IN *SC*, VOLUME 34, WERE REPRODUCED FROM THE FOLLOWING PERIODICALS:

Ariel: A Review of International English Literature, v. 9, April, 1978 for "Shakespeare's Heroines: Disguise in the Romantic Comedies" by Peter Hyland. Copyright © 1978 The Board of Governors, The University of Calgary. Reproduced by permission of the publisher and the author.—*The CEA Critic*, v. 47, 1-2, Fall-Winter, 1984. Copyright © 1984 by the College English Association, Inc. Reproduced by permission.—*College English*, v. 25, April, 1964 for "Shakespearian Comedy in 'The Comedy of Errors'" by C. L. Barber. Copyright © 1964, renewed 1992 by the National Council of Teachers of English. Reproduced by permission of the publisher.—*Critical Quarterly*, v. 9, Autumn, 1967. Reproduced by permission of Basil Blackwell Limited.—*English Literary Renaissance*, v. 7, Spring, 1977; v. 23, Winter, 1993. Copyright © 1977, 1993 by *English Literary Renaissance*. Both reproduced by permission.—*Essays in Criticism*, v. II, April, 1952 for "Shakespeare and the Use of Disguise in Elizabethan Drama" by M. C. Bradbrook. Reproduced by permission of the Editors of *Essays in Criticism* and the author.—*Literature and Psychology*, v. XXIII, 1973. © Editor 1973. Reproduced by permission.—*The Modern Language Review*, v. 66, 1971 for "No Exit from Arden" by Ralph Berry; v. 69, July, 1974 for "Structure and Theme Through Separation and Union in Shakespeare's 'The Comedy of Errors'" by Vincent F. Petronella. Copyright © Modern Humanities Association 1971, 1974. Both reproduced by permission of the publisher and the authors.—*Philological Quarterly*, v. 59, Spring, 1980 for "Arm and Sleeve: Nature and Custom in 'The Comedy of Errors'" by Eamon Grennan. Copyright © 1980 by The University of Iowa. Reproduced by permission of the author.—*A Review of English Literature*, v. 5, October, 1964 for "'The Comedy of Errors' Rescued from Tragedy" by Gwyn Williams. Copyright © Longmans, Green & Co. Ltd. 1964. Reproduced by permission of the publisher and the author.—*Rocky Mountain Review*, v. 41, 1987. Reproduced by permission.—*The Sewanee Review*, v. LXXXIII, Spring, 1975 for "'Twelfth Night': Free Disposition on the Sea of Love" by Richard Henze. Copyright © 1975 by The University of the South. Reproduced with the permission of the editor of *The Sewanee Review* and the author.—*Shakespeare Quarterly*, v. XXI, Spring, 1970; v. 29, Summer, 1978; v. 43, Fall, 1992. Copyright © The Folger Shakespeare Library 1970, 1978, 1992. Reproduced by permission.—*Shakespeare Survey: An Annual Survey of Shakespearian Study and Production*, v. 32, 1979 for "Sexual Disguise in 'As You Like It' and 'Twelfth Night'" by Nancy K. Hayles; v. 34, 1981 for "Plays and Players in 'Twelfth Night'" by Karen Greif. Copyright © Cambridge University Press, 1979, 1981. Both reproduced with the permission of Cambridge University Press and the authors.—*Studies in English Literature, 1500-1900*, v. VIII, Spring, 1968 for "Shakespeare and Parmenides: Metaphysics of 'Twelfth Night'" by Walter N. King; v. 30, Spring, 1990 for "Dining Out in Ephesus: Food in 'The Comedy of Errors'" by Joseph Candido; v. 33, Spring, 1993 for "Slander in and Allow'd Fool: 'Twelfth Night's Crisis of the Aristocracy" by Karin S. Codden; v. 36, Spring, 1996 for "The Political Conscious of Shakespeare's 'As You Like It'" by Andrew Barnaby. Copyright © 1968, 1990, 1993, 1996 William Marsh Rice University. All reprinted by permission of *SEL Studies in English Literature 1500-1900*.—*Studies in Philology*, v. LXXXV, Winter, 1988 for "Shakespeare's 'Comedy of Errors' and the Nature of Kinds" by Arthur F. Kinney. © 1988 by the University of North Carolina Press. Used by permission of the publisher and the author.—*Texas Studies in Literature and Language*, v. XXIV, Summer, 1982 for "'Try in Time in Despite of a Fall': Time and Occasion in 'As You Like It'" by Donn Ervin Taylor; v. XXXVIII, Summer, 1996 for "On Not Being Deceived: Rhetoric and the Body in 'Twelfth Night'" by Lorna Hutson. Copyright © 1982, 1996 by the University of Texas Press.

Both reproduced by permission of the publisher and the authors.—*Theatre Journal*, v. 35, October, 1983. © 1983, University and College Theatre Association of the American Theatre Association. Reproduced by permission of The John Hopkins University Press.

COPYRIGHTED EXCERPTS IN *SC*, VOLUME 34, WERE REPRODUCED FROM THE FOLLOWING BOOKS:

Baldwin, T. W. From "Three Homilies in 'The Comedy of Errors'," in *Essays on Shakespeare and Elizabethan Drama in Honor of Hardin Craig*. Edited by Richard Hosley. University of Missouri Press, 1962. Copyright © 1962 by The Curators of the University of Missouri. Reproduced by permission.—Carlson, Susan. From *Women and Comedy: Rewriting the British Theatrical Tradition*. Essays in Literature, 1987. Copyright © Essays in Literature 1987. All rights reserved. Reproduced by permission.—Colie, Rosalie L. From *Shakespeare's Living Art*. Princeton University Press, 1974. Copyright © 1974 by Princeton University Press. All rights reserved. Reproduced by permission.—Cutts, John P. From *The Shattered Glass: A Dramatic Pattern in Shakespeare's Early Plays*. Wayne State University Press, 1968. Copyright © 1968 by Wayne State University Press. All rights reserved. Reproduced by permission of the publisher and the author.—Davis, Lloyd. From *Guise and Disguise: Rhetoric and Characterization in the English Renaissance*. University of Toronto Press, 1993. Copyright © University of Toronto Press Incorporated 1993. Reproduced by permission of University of Toronto Press Incorporated.—Desmet, Christy. From *Reading Shakespeare's Characters: Rhetoric, Ethics, and Identity*. Amherst: The University of Massachusetts Press, 1992. Copyright © 1992 by The University of Massachusetts Press. All rights reserved. Reproduced by permission.—Foakes, R. A. From an introduction to *The Comedy of Errors*, revised edition. Edited by R. A. Foakes. Methuen & Co. Ltd., 1962. Editorial matter © 1962 Methuen & Co. Ltd. Reproduced by permission.—Hart, John A. From *Dramatic Structure in Shakespeare's Romantic Comedies*. Carnegie-Mellon University Press, 1980. Copyright © 1980 by John A. Hart. Reproduced by permission of the author.—Hassel, R. Chris, Jr. From *Faith and Folly in Shakespeare's Romantic Comedies*. University of Georgia Press, 1980. Copyright © 1980 by the University of Georgia Press. All rights reserved. Reproduced by permission.—Kerrigan, William. From "Female Friends and Fraternal Enemies in 'As You Like It'," in *Desire in the Renaissance: Psychoanalysis and Literature*. Edited by Valeria Finucci and Regina Schwartz. Princeton University Press, 1994. Copyright © 1994 by Princeton University Press. All rights reserved. Reproduced by permission.—Manheim, Leonard F. From "The Mythical Joys of Shakespeare, or, What You Will," in *Shakespeare Encomium*. Edited by Anne Paolucci. The City College, 1964. Copyright © The City College of The City University of New York 1964, renewed 1992. Reproduced by permission.—Nevo, Ruth. From *Comic Transformations in Shakespeare*. Methuen & Co. Ltd., 1980. Copyright © 1980 Ruth Nevo. All rights reserved. Reproduced by permission.—Phialas, Peter G. From *Shakespeare's Romantic Comedy: The Development of Their Form and Meaning*. University of North Carolina Press, 1966. Copyright © 1966 by the University of North Carolina Press. All rights reserved. Used by permission of the publisher and the author.—Prouty, Charles Tyler. From "Twelfth Night," in *Stratford Papers: 1965-67*. Edited by B. A. W. Jackson. McMaster University Library Press, 1969. Copyright © McMaster University Library Press, Canada, 1969. Reproduced by permission.

PHOTOGRAPHS AND ILLUSTRATIONS APPEARING IN *SC*, VOLUME 34, WERE RECEIVED FROM THE FOLLOWING SOURCES:

Scene from "*The Comedy of Errors*," play by William Shakespeare. Folger Shakespeare Library. Reproduced by permission.—Scene from Royal Shakespeare Company's reproduction of "*Twelfth Night or What You Will*," play by William Shakespeare, photograph.—Scene from "*The Comedy of Errors*," play by William Shakespeare, engraving. Folger Shakespeare Library. Reproduced by permission.—Scene from "*Twelfth Night*," play by William Shakespeare, engraving. Folger Shakespeare Library. Reproduced by permission.—Scene ii of "*As You Like It*," play by William Shakespeare, engraving. Folger Shakespeare Library. Reproduced by permission.—Scene iii of "*As You Like It*," play by William Shakespeare, engraving. Folger Shakespeare Library. Reproduced by permission.

Explore your options!

Gale databases are offered in a variety of formats

The information in this Gale publication is also available in some or all of the formats described here. Your Gale Representative will be happy to fill you in. Call toll-free 1-800-877-GALE.

GaleNet ℠
your information community

GaleNet

A number of Gale databases are now available on GaleNet, our new online information resource accessible through the Internet. GaleNet features an easy-to-use end-user interface, the powerful search capabilities of BRS/SEARCH retrieval software and ease of access through the World Wide Web.

Diskette/Magnetic Tape

Many Gale databases are available on diskette or magnetic tape, allowing systemwide access to your most-used information sources through existing computer systems. Data can be delivered on a variety of mediums (DOS-formatted diskettes, 9-track tape, 8mm data tape) and in industry-standard formats (comma-delimited, tagged, fixed-field).

CD-ROM

A variety of Gale titles are available on CD-ROM, offering maximum flexibility and powerful search software.

Online

For your convenience, many Gale databases are available through popular online services, including DIALOG, NEXIS, DataStar, ORBIT, OCLC, Thomson Financial Network's I/Plus Direct, HRIN, Prodigy, Sandpoint's HOOVER, the Library Corporation's NLightN and Telebase Systems.

Appearance vs. Reality

INTRODUCTION

Critics have long noted a dichotomy between appearance and reality in Shakespeare's plays. Many of these works depend on the power of language and rhetoric to corrupt the truth, or on the fallibility of human perception: Iago deceives Othello, Macbeth and Lady Macbeth hallucinate, and the real and mythical worlds of *A Midsummer Night's Dream* intersect in a self-aware theatrical performance. Such dichotomies have been important touchstones in critical discussions of Shakespeare's oeuvre. Modern critics contend that Shakespeare delved deeply into the reflexive effect of language on the shaping of reality.

Commentators have also explored the ramifications of Shakespeare's plays as originally performed, considering the Elizabethan period and theatrical conventions. For example, the fact of male actors playing female characters, sometimes disguised as males, renders problematic issues of sexual identity and the nature of gender. Such role-playing also brings into question the nature of power and social status—whether power and status are dictated by a natural order or are discursively constructed. Shakespeare's plays thus manipulate appearance and reality to advance plot and character, and also to comment on broader issues of gender and power.

OVERVIEWS

M. C. Bradbrook (essay date 1952)

SOURCE: "Shakespeare and the Use of Disguise in Elizabethan Drama," in *Muriel Bradbrook on Shakespeare,* The Harvester Press, 1984, pp. 20-7.

[*In the following essay, Bradbrook discusses the dramatic conventions that may have influenced Shakespeare's frequent use of disguise.*]

Today disguise is a living part of the drama. Sir Francis Crewe of *The Dog beneath The Skin,* the mysterious stranger at *The Cocktail Party,* the intrusive little girls of Giraudoux's *Electra* do not bear the limited significance which naturalism and the set characters of the nineteenth century imposed. Disguise was then reduced to a subterfuge, restricted to the Scarlet Pimpernel, the hero of *The Only Way* or the heroine of *East Lynne* ('Dead! and he never called me mother!'). Ibsen and Chekhov transformed it. Those implications of self-deception and fantasy which are the stuff of *A Doll's House* and *The Cherry Orchard* lurk in a masquerade dress, or a few conjuring tricks at a ball. Yet even in its revival, disguise has not attained the manifold significance which it enjoyed in the Elizabethan theatre and which Shakespeare alone fully revealed.

A study of the subject was provided by V. O. Freeburg as long ago as 1915 and has not been superseded (*Disguise Plots in Elizabethan Drama,* Columbia University Press, New York). Dr Freeburg's conception of disguise belongs, however, to the nineteenth century: 'Dramatic disguise . . . means a change of personal appearance which leads to mistaken identity. There is a double test, change and confusion.' He eliminates the mere confusion of *The Comedy of Errors* and the substitution of Mariana for Isabella in *Measure for Measure,* where, as in the similar situation of *All's Well,* Shakespeare himself actually uses the word:

> So disguise shall, by the disguised,
> Pay with falsehood false exacting,
> And perform an old contracting.

> Only in this disguise I think't no sin
> To cosen him that would unjustly win.

I should prefer to define disguise as the substitution, overlaying or metamorphosis of dramatic identity, whereby one character sustains two roles. This may involve deliberate or involuntary masquerade, mistaken or concealed identity, madness or possession. Disguise ranges from the simple fun of the quick-change artist (*The Blind Beggar of Alexandria*) to the antic disposition of Edgar or Hamlet: it may need a cloak and false beard, or it may be better translated for the modern age by such terms as 'alternating personality'.

Dr Freeburg distinguishes five main types of disguise, all of which Shakespeare employs. These are the girl-page (Julia, Rosalind, Viola, Imogen), the boy-bride (*Taming of the Shrew* and *The Merry Wives*), the rogue in a variety of disguises (Autolycus) the spy in disguise (Vincentio) and the lover in disguise (Lucentio in *The Taming of the Shrew*). All go back to classical comedy, and except for the girl-pages they do not represent important aspects for Shakespeare. The boy-bride and the rogue are bound to lead to farce, and are handled better by Johnson in *Epicoene, Every Man In His Humour* and *The Alchemist.*

For the Elizabethans, 'disguise' still retained its primary sense of strange apparel, and 'disguising' was still the name for amateur plays. In Jonson's *Masque of Augurs* one player uses 'disguised' in the slang sense (to be drunk, as in *Antony and Cleopatra,* II vii 131) and is told 'Disguise was the old English word for a masque'. But it also carried the senses of 'concealment', and of 'deformity' ('Here in this bush disguised will I stand'; 'Her cheeks with chaps and wrinkles were disguised') from which the transition was easy to 'dissembling' ('disguise not with me in words'). The word thus retained a strong literal meaning yet also carried moral implications.

> Disguise, I see thou art an wickedness
> Wherein the pregnant enemy does much

says Viola, in the accents of Malvolio. New Guise and Nowadays, the tempters of *Mankind,* had been named from a dislike both of innovations and of that elaboration of dress which was so feelingly denounced by moralists from Chaucer to Tourneur.

The two archetypes were the disguise of the serpent and the disguise of the Incarnation. The devil's power of deceit furnished plots for many moralities. In Medwall's *Nature,* in *Republica* and in Skelton's *Magnifycence,* the vices take the virtues' names: in the last, Counterfeit Countenance becomes Good Demeanance, Crafty Conveyance becomes Sure Surveyance, Courtly Abusion becomes Lusty Pleasure and Cloaked Collusion becomes Sober Sadness. The two fools, Fancy and Folly, become Largesse and Conceit. The very names of such vices as Ambidexter and Hardy-dardy signify their power to juggle with appearance as they juggle with words. Slippery speech belongs with disguise:

> Thus like the formal Vice, Iniquity,
> I moralize two meanings in one word.

Both are combined in the great figure of the Marlovian Mephistopheles, disguised as a Franciscan friar. It is this tradition which lends such strength to Shakespeare's concept of the false appearance or *seeming.* There is no direct disguise in Angelo, Claudius, Iago, Iachimo or Wolsey, but an assumed personality. Miss Spurgeon has shown the force of the image of borrowed robes in *Macbeth.* The witches' invocation, recalling an important passage from Spenser on the fall of man, first states the theme: 'Fair is foul and foul is fair.' Lady Macbeth counsels her husband to look like the innocent flower but be the serpent under it. Macbeth himself speaks of 'making our faces vizards to our hearts, / Disguising what they are.' The clearest dramatic presentation of the theme occurs when the porter of Hell gate assumes a role which is no more than the mere truth. Here direct and planned concealment stirs pity and terror less than the disguise which is rooted in poetry and action, and perhaps not outwardly signified at all.

The diabolical villains, Richard III, Iago and the rest were, of course, not derived from any single original. Conscienceless Machievels such as Barabas, and Lorenzo of *The Spanish Tragedy* were behind them, as well as the Father of Lies; yet Donne's *Ignatius his Conclave* may serve as evidence that the old diabolism and new Machievellianism were linked in the popular mind.

Opposing infernal deceit was the heavenly humility of the Incarnation. The ruler of the world, concealed in humble garb, ministering to the needy, and secretly controlling every event is reflected in the disguised rulers (God's vicegerants), who wander among their subjects, living with them, and in the end distributing rewards and punishments in a judgement scene. Heavenly disguise enables Vincentio to test the virtue of his subjects, Henry to learn the secrets of his soldiers' feelings before Agincourt. Each of these roles has a long stage ancestry, but Shakespeare has strengthened the force of the disguise, which is in each case his own addition to the play. *Measure for Measure* contains a number of pronouncements upon disguising, and a wide variety of instances. The bride and the condemned prisoner have each their substitutes, 'Death's great disguiser', as the supposed Franciscan says to the Provost. Lucio, a direct descendant of the old Vice is 'uncased' in his own act of 'uncasing' the Duke. This is Shakespeare's fullest study of disguise.

Disguises generally mean a drop in social status (except in farce) and in comical histories came a whole series of rulers who wooed milkmaids, learnt home-truths from honest countrymen, stood a buffet with their subjects and finally revealed themselves with all graciousness. The exploits of King Edward in *George-a-Greene,* King Edward IV in Heywood's play, and King Henry VIII in *When You See Me You Know Me* foreshadow Henry V's jest with Williams. These jovial revellers seem related to the stories of Robin Hood and the King: Robin himself appears in some of the plays. Noble wooers in disguise often played a rustic part (as in *Friar Bacon, Mucidorus, The Shoemakers' Holiday* and *Fair Em*), and in his wooing, King Henry V again slips back into a rustic role, which, though it is not a disguise, is certainly an assumed part, and recalls such popular songs as:

> To marry I would have thy consent,
> But faith I never could compliment;
> I can say nought but 'Hoy, gee ho!'
> Words that belong to the cart and the plough.

Oh, say, my Joan, will not that do?
I cannot come every day to woo.

In the old chronicle play of *King Leir,* France wooed Cordella in such disguise. In his adaptation of this story, Shakespeare used another old tradition, that of the disguised protector. The tenderness and devotion of Kent to Lear, and Edgar to Gloucester are however but faintly suggested by Flowerdale of *The London Prodigal* or Friscobaldo of *The Honest Whore,* who in the guise of servants tend their erring children. In these plays, the disguise is comic as well as pathetic; yet the father who pities his children, like the husband who pities and succours his erring wife, must have had a biblical origin, and Shakespeare recalled this old tradition to its first significance.

Different aspects of the same disguise could be played upon (even Kent has his moments of comedy) because there was an 'open' or unresolved view of individuality behind Elizabethan character-drawing, which corresponded to the open use of words in Elizabethan poetry. Fixed denotation, which is encouraged by a standardised spelling and pronunciation, a dictionary definition, and controlling prose usage was still unknown. The great key-words had a radiant nimbus of association; they were charged with life, so that a writer could allow their significance to reverberate through a whole play. The meaning of poetry is not to be extracted but to be explored; and the creative uses of the pun, as illustrated in recent articles in this journal, are analogous to the use of multiple personality or disguise. Characters are fluid, and the role may vary from a specific or strictly individual one to something nearer the function of the Greek chorus. The antic disposition of Hamlet, or Edgar as Poor Tom, create an extra dimension for these plays as well as giving depth and fullness to the parts. Hamlet's coarseness and Edgar's wildness are parts of themselves, but they are more than merely that. Madness is a protective ruse, deriving in part at least from the disguise of Hieronimo, and of Antonio's disguise as a fool in Marston's *Antonio's Revenge.* Through this mask Hamlet penetrates the disguises of Polonius, Rosencrantz and Guildenstern, and Claudius. Edgar as madman has something of the insight of

the eternal eye
That sees through flesh and all.

The revengers, Hamlet and Vindice, have x-ray eyesight; their double roles of revenger and commentator correspond to the antinomy of their characters. Here again there is an easy gradation from the chronic to the individual. The Revenger was also both good *and* evil; for revenge was deadly sin, yet also the inevitable result of the greater sins which the hero so pitilessly anatomised. Such double roles had not only a verbal correspondence in the pun but a structural parallel in

the 'shadowing' of mainplot by subplot, most fully developed in *King Lear.* As Poor Tom, Edgar describes as his own the sins of Oswald and Edmund: his sinister disguise helps finally to turn the wits of the old king: he talks of the devils that inhabit him, till at Dover Cliff they are exorcised; finally he appears vizarded, the unknown challenger who executes a just vengeance, and forgives his dying enemy.

The Elizabethan theatre included a wide range of representation. Ghosts, spirits and visions appeared, or could even be used as disguise (as in *The Atheist's Tragedy,* where the hero dresses as a ghost). The appearance of Caesar's or Banquo's ghost also adds an extra dimension to the dramatist's world. Unearthly and almost unbearably poignant is Paulina's revival of the ghostly Hermione from dead marble to flesh and blood:

I'll fill your grave up: stir, nay come away,
To death bequeath your numbness, for from
  him
Dear life redeems you.

Leontes has but three words 'Oh, she's warm', and Hermione, save to Perdita, has none. It is the dream of all bereaved, handled with a sureness and delicacy that could come only from long mastery. In his last plays, Shakespeare makes disguise an essentially poetic conception, and varies the level of it more subtly than ever before. It is necessary only to think of Imogen, her brothers and Belarius, Posthumus as the poor soldier, Cloten in Posthumus' garments, the false seeming of the Queen and the vision of the ghosts and the gods; or of Perdita's contrast with Florizel, both of them with the more conventional muffling of his father and Camillo, and the many disguises of Autolycus. Perdita is seemingly a shepherdess, pranked up as a goddess for the May sports: Florizel is obscured as a swain. As they dance together, the disguised Camillo says:

He tells her something
That makes her blood look out: good sooth,
  she is
The queen of curds and cream.

Truly it is royal blood that rises, even as Florizel's youth shows 'the true blood which fairly peeps through it.' Here the threefold meaning of 'blood'—passion, descent, blushing—corresponds with the complex function of the disguises. Like those of Imogen and her brothers, they isolate the innocence and truth of the young, they are vestures of humility which disclose true worth; and yet they give the action a masque- or pageant-like quality which sets it apart from the rest of the play. In *The Tempest,* the varying of shapes belongs principally to Ariel, to Prospero, who can go invisible, and to the spirits of the masques. Yet Ferdinand and Miranda are in some sense obscured, and the anti-masque of Trinculo and Stephano with their frippery adds at least a further visual pattern.

The physical basis of disguise remained indeed of great importance. When the actors were so well known to the audience, it must have been easy for the spectators, like the playwright, to translate 'Enter Dogberry and Verges' into 'Enter Kempe and Cowley'. Costumes had to produce the stage atmosphere now given by scenery, lighting and make-up, and changes of costume must therefore have been valuable. Apparel was not thought of as concealing but as revealing the personality of the wearer. 'The apparel oft proclaims the man', and some of the most bitter and prolonged religious quarrelling of the age centred in the Vestarian controversy. Sumptuous clothing was a subject for satirists both off and on the stage; the Puritans attacked the theatre with the plea, based on the Mosaic injunction that for a man to put on the garments of a woman was an abomination. Hence there could be no such thing as a mere physical transformation. As the body revealed the soul, so appearance should reveal the truth of identity. A character could be really changed by the assumption of a disguise. The modern woman who restores her self-confidence with an expensive hat, the soldier who salutes the Queen's Commission and not the drunkard who happens to be wearing its insignia act in a manner familiar to Elizabethans. Hence Prospero's discarding of his magic robe symbolised most adequately his transformation from Magician back to Duke of Milan.

Such deepened power of guise and disguise did not prevent Shakespeare from using it in a practical and even thoroughly stagey fashion upon other occasions. His earliest plays are full of disguisings of a superficial kind: the complexities emerge in *The Merchant of Venice,* where he builds up a scale of contrast between Jessica's purely formal disguise, Nerissa's imitative one, and the significant robing of Portia. Viola's disguise, complicated by her likeness to her twin, is also contrasted with the literal dis-guise of Malvolio in yellow stockings and cross garters, and with the clown's assumption of Sir Thopas's part. Shakespeare on occasion used all the conventional tricks, as in *The Taming of the Shrew, The Merry Wives,* or Margaret's disguise as Hero, which leads to Claudio's pretended unmasking of the false semblant in the church scene, and to the final comedy of the masks.

The girl-pages, who would perhaps occur most readily to the mind as Shakespeare's favourite line in disguise, were already familiar from earlier narrative and drama. In comedy, there is less open characterisation than in tragedy: instead, the roles become stereotyped, based on sets of 'characteristics'. When the heroine is disguised as a boy, her two roles may be sharply contrasted, giving an effect as of shot silk, as the boyish wit or the feminine sensibility predominates. Shake-

speare allows some very stagey jests, such as the broad farce of Viola's duel with Sir Andrew: yet such parts as hers, with their obvious advantages for the boy-actors, also allowed Shakespeare to depict the relationship of men and women with a new ease and frankness. Rosalind enjoys her disguise and frankly exploits its possibilities, but even the most demure of the heroines is given a chance by indirection to find directions out. In spite of the clear contrast between appearance and reality, the disguised heroines owe the peculiar delicacy and felicity of their depiction largely to masquerade.

This particular convention remained popular, long after Shakespeare's day; Fletcher, in Bellario and Aspatia, drew a new and sophisticated version. Bellario's true sex is not revealed till the end, though by this time any theatrical page might be assumed to be a woman in disguise. In the later seventeenth and eighteenth centuries, 'breeches parts' were as popular with the actresses as they had been with the boys, and from the stage they re-entered the Romantic poem. Sir Walter Scott has two such characters, one the heroine of *The Lord of the Isles,* the other in *Harold the Dauntless,* where an utterly incredible Viking is attended for years by a devoted page, whose sex is finally revealed to the imperceptive warrior by no less a personage then Odin himself.

The deeper implications of disguise, however, did not long survive Shakespeare's day. Writers of today have rediscovered its possibilities for tragedy as well as comedy, and are no longer limited to the presuppositions governing *Charley's Aunt, Vice Versa,* or even *The Happy Hypocrite.* Yet the triple flexibility of language, characters and plotting which give the Elizabethans so strong and delicate a weapon belongs to them alone. Only occasionally in lyric verse, as in Yeats's sequence of *The Three Bushes*—where the old trick of *Measure for Measure,* the false bride, is put to new uses—disguise provides a statement of philosophic themes. The antithesis of Body and Soul, even of the One and the Many is symbolised in this folk story, written in ballad style and set to a popular tune. (Yeats's source, however, is actually a Provençal *tenzon,* which he may have learnt of from Ezra Pound; hence the mixture of courtly love convention with reminiscences of *Fair Margaret and Sweet William.*)

It may be that Shakespeare too drew some of his inspiration from popular literature, especially from ballads, where disguises of all kinds are of primary importance, both for comedy and for tragedy. Whilst disguise has been used in the drama, the pathos and depth of feeling in the ballads, dramatic in form as many of them are, far exceeds that of the pre-Shakespearean stage in general. Tom a Bedlam, Hind Horn, Fair Annie may have been the seed-plots for Edgar, Hamlet and Imogen, as the Robin Hood ballads were for the comical history plays. Shakespeare turned to the popular ballad in moments of deepest pathos for Ophelia and Desdemona, he turned to old wives' tales and riddles for the visionary horror of *Macbeth* and the visionary beauty of *The Winter's Tale,* as many times he drew his purest poetry from the diction of common life.

Nancy K. Hayles (essay date 1979)

SOURCE: "Sexual Disguise in *As You Like It* and *Twelfth Night,*" in *Shakespeare Survey: An Annual Survey of Shakespearian Study and Production,* Vol. 32, 1979, pp. 63-72.

[*In the following essay, Hayles compares Shakespeare's use of sexual disguise in* As You Like It *and* Twelfth Night, *concluding that his use of the device progressed from investigating the ramifications of role-playing to questioning the very nature of sex and gender.*]

In dealing with the female page disguise in Renaissance drama, one is invariably struck by the complexity of the double sex reversal implied by the presence of the boy actor. Lamb's remarks are typical: 'What an odd double confusion it must have made, to see a boy play a woman playing a man: one cannot disentangle the perplexity without some violence to the imagination.'[1] Perhaps because most of us share Lamb's perplexity, not much work has been done on the subject[2] other than a general acknowledgement that the device is both interesting and complex. Recently, however, sexual disguise has begun to attract attention from feminist critics because it seems to offer a way to combine Shakespearian criticism with contemporary social concerns.[3] Although more work is needed, and welcome, on this complex dramatic device, the tendency to regard it solely in terms of social and sexual roles seems to me misguided. While some aspects of the disguise are common to all the plays in which it appears, its dramatic function is shaped by the particular design of each play; and the differences are fully as important as the similarities in understanding the complexity of the device in Shakespeare's hands. In fact, Shakespeare's use of sexual disguise shows a definite progression: whereas in the early plays he uses it to explore the implications of sexual role-playing, in the later plays he seems increasingly interested in the metaphysical implications of the disguise, using it as a means to investigate, and eventually resolve, the disparity between appearance and essence. Although a study of all five plays that use sexual disguise is outside the scope of this essay, I hope to demonstrate the nature of the progression by comparing the use of the sexual disguise in *As You Like It* with its use in *Twelfth Night.*[4] The purpose of this essay is therefore not only to draw general conclusions about the nature of Shakespearian sexual disguise, but to do so in a way

that does justice to the uniqueness of each play. For that we turn now to the plays themselves.

As You Like It opens with scenes that emphasize rivalry and competition. Orlando has been mistreated by his brother Oliver, and Oliver in turn feels that Orlando has caused him to be 'altogether misprised' and undervalued by his own people. The rivalry that Duke Frederick still feels with the rightful Duke is also apparent. Moreover, the chief event of the opening scenes, the wrestling match between Charles and Orlando, is a formalized and ritualistic expression of male rivalry.[5] Against the backdrop of male rivalry, the female intimacy between Celia and Rosalind makes a striking contrast. It is an intimacy, however, maintained at some cost. When Duke Frederick peremptorily orders Rosalind into banishment, Celia's protest is countered by her father's attempt to transform intimacy into rivalry between the two girls, too:

> Thou art a fool; she robs thee of thy name,
> And thou wilt show more bright and seem
>   more virtuous
> When she is gone. Then open not thy lips.[6]
>   (I, iii, 76-8)

The opening scenes of the play, then, draw a society where intimacy among women is implicitly contrasted with the rivalry among men. When the scene changes to the forest, several incidents seem designed as signals that the forest is a world where co-operation rather than competition prevails. Orlando meets with civility instead of hostility when he seeks meat for the fainting Adam; Rosalind and Celia find the natives to be kind shepherds rather than would-be rapists; and the exiled Duke hails his followers as 'Co-mates and brothers'. But we soon discover that competition is not altogether absent from the Forest of Arden. Jaques accuses the Duke of himself usurping the forest from its rightful owners, the deer; Touchstone confronts and bests his country rival, William; and Silvius discovers that his beloved Phebe has fallen in love with a courtly newcomer. The situation is thus more complicated than a simple contrast between court competition and pastoral co-operation, or between female intimacy and male rivalry. The sexual disguise of Rosalind mirrors the complexities of these tensions.

We can consider the disguise as proceeding in two separate movements. First, the layers of disguise are added as Rosalind becomes Ganymede, and then as Ganymede pretends to be Orlando's Rosalind; second, the layers are removed as Ganymede abandons the play-acting of Rosalind, and then as Rosalind herself abandons the disguise of Ganymede. The layering-on movement creates conflict and the layering-off movement fosters reconciliation as the disguise confronts and then resolves the issue of competition versus co-operation.

In the most complex layering, Rosalind-as-Ganymede-as-Orlando's Rosalind, Rosalind presents Orlando with a version of his beloved very different from the one he imagines in his verses. When Rosalind-as-Ganymede insists that Orlando's Rosalind will have her own wit, her own will and her own way, implicit in the portrayal is Rosalind's insistence that Orlando recognize the discrepancy between his idealized version and the real Rosalind. In effect, Rosalind is claiming the right to be herself rather than to be Orlando's idealized version of her, as female reality is playfully set against male fantasy. In playing herself (which she can apparently do only if she first plays someone else)[7] Rosalind is able to state her own needs in a way she could not if she were simply herself. It is because she is disguised as Ganymede that she can be so free in portraying a Rosalind who is a flesh and blood woman instead of a Petrarchan abstraction. Rosalind's three-fold disguise is therefore used to accentuate the disparity between the needs of the heroine and the expectations of the hero.

Even the simpler layering of Rosalind-as-Ganymede accentuates conflict, though this time the couple being affected is Phebe and Silvius. Rosalind's guise as Ganymede causes Phebe to fall in love with her. Rosalind's on-layering, which inadvertently makes her Silvius's rival, causes Phebe's desires to be even more at variance with Silvius's hopes than before. It takes Ganymede's transformation into Rosalind to trick Phebe into accepting her swain, as the off-layering of Rosalind's disguise reconciles these two Petrarchan lovers. The Silvius-Phebe plot thus shows in simplified form the correlation between on-layering and rivalry, and off-layering and co-operation. It also gives us a standard by which we can measure the more complicated situation between Orlando and Rosalind.

Phebe and Silvius are caricatures of courtly love, and through them we are shown female manipulation and male idealization in a way that emphasizes the less pleasant side of the courtly love tradition. But it is important to see that this rustic couple merely exaggerates tendencies also present in Rosalind and Orlando. Rosalind's disguise creates an imbalance in her relationship with Orlando because it allows Rosalind to hear Orlando's love-confession without having to take any comparable risks herself. Rosalind's self-indulgence in demanding Orlando's devoted service without admitting anything in return could become a variation of the perversity that is anatomized for us in the relationship between Phebe and Silvius. Thus the expectations of Rosalind and the desires of Orlando are not only the responses of these two characters, but are also reflections of stereotypical male and female postures, familiar through the long tradition of courtly love. The layering of the disguise has served to accentuate the conflict between men and women; now the unlayering finally resolves that traditional tension between the needs of the female and the desires of the male.

The unlayering begins when Oliver appears to explain why Orlando is late. Oliver's tale reveals, in almost allegorical fashion, the struggle within Orlando when he sees his brother in peril, and the tale has as its point that Orlando put the needs of his brother before his own natural desire for revenge. More subtly, the tale with its depiction of the twin dangers of the snake and lioness hints at a symbolic nexus of male and female threats. The specificity of the imagery suggests that the details are important. The first beast is described as a lioness, not a lion; moreover, she is a lioness in suck, but now with teats sucked dry, her hunger presumably made more ferocious by her condition. The description thus links a specifically female animal, and a graphically specific female condition, with the threat of being eaten. The details, taken in sum, evoke the possibility of female engulfment. The snake about to enter the sleeping man's mouth, again a very specific image, suggests even to a non-Freudian the threat of phallic invasion. But perhaps most significant is simply the twinning of the threats itself, which suggests the presence of two different but related kinds of danger.

By overcoming the twin threats, Orlando conquers in symbolic form projections of both male and female fears. Rosalind responds to Oliver's account by swooning. Her faint is a literal relinquishing of conscious control; within the conventions of the play, it is also an involuntary revelation of female gender because fainting is a 'feminine' response. It is a subtle anticipation of Rosalind's eventual relinquishing of the disguise and the control that goes with it. The action surrounding the relation of the tale parallels its moral: Orlando performs a heroic and selfless act that hints at a triumph over threatening aspects of masculinity and femininity, and Rosalind responds to the dangers that Orlando faces with an unconscious gesture of sympathy that results, for a moment, in the loss of her conscious control over the disguise and with it, the loss of her manipulative control over Orlando. Rosalind's swoon thus provides a feminine counterpart to Orlando's selflessness.

Orlando's struggle and Rosalind's swoon mark a turning point. When they meet again, Rosalind tries at first to re-establish their old relationship, but when Orlando replies, 'I can live no longer by thinking', she quickly capitulates and re-assumes control only in order to be able to relinquish it. From this point on, the removal of the disguise signals the consummation of all the relationships as all four couples are married. The play suggests that control is necessary to state the legitimate needs of the self, but also that it must eventually be relinquished to accommodate the needs of another. Consummation is paradoxically achieved through an act of renunciation.

The way that sexual disguise is used reflects the play's overall concern with the tension between rivalry and co-operation. The disguise is first used to crystallize rivalry between the woman's self-image and the man's desires; in this sense it recognizes male-female discord and implicitly validates it. But because the disguise can be removed, it prevents the discord from becoming perpetual frustration. The workings of the disguise suggest that what appears to be a generous surrendering of self-interest can in fact bring consummation both to man and woman, so that rivalry can be transcended as co-operation brings fulfillment. In *As You Like It,* fulfillment of desire, contentment and peace of mind come when the insistence on self-satisfaction ceases. Duke Senior's acceptance of his forest exile and the subsequent unlooked-for restoration of his dukedom; the reconciliation between the sons of Rowland de Boys, in which Oliver resigns his lands to Orlando and finds forgiveness and happiness in love; the miraculous conversion of Duke Frederick by the old hermit and the voluntary abdication of his dukedom—all express the same paradox of consummation through renunciation that is realized in specifically sexual terms by the disguise.

When the boy actor who plays Rosalind's part comes forward to speak the epilogue, the workings of the sexual disguise are linked with the art of the playwright. The epilogue continues the paradox of consummation through renunciation that has governed sexual disguise within the play, as the final unlayering of the disguise coincides with a plea for the audience to consummate the play by applauding:

> My way is to conjure you, and I'll begin with the women. I charge you, O women, for the love you bear to men, to like as much of this play as please you. And I charge you, O men, for the love you bear to women—as I perceive by your simpering none of you hates them—that between you and the women the play may please. If I were a woman, I would kiss as many of you as had beards that pleased me, complexions that liked me, and breaths that I defied not. And I am sure, as many as have good beards, or good faces, or sweet breaths, will for my kind offer, when I make curtsy, bid me farewell.

At this moment the playwright relinquishes control of the audience. As with Rosalind and Orlando, his success is marked by a control that finally renounces itself, a control which admonishes only to release as the audience is asked to 'like as much . . . as please you'. Our applause is a gesture of acceptance which encompasses both the working of sexual disguise within the play, and the art whose operation parallels it as the play ends. At the same time, the boy actor alludes to the fact that he is not after all the woman he plays ('*if* I were a woman'), and so relinquishes the last level of the sexual disguise. For the last time, the unlayering of the disguise is linked with a reconciliation between the

sexes as the boy actor speaking the epilogue appeals separately to the men and women in the audience. Within the play these two perspectives have been reconciled, and the joint applause of the men and women in the audience re-affirms that reconciliation and extends it to the audience.

The sexual disguise in *As You Like It* therefore succeeds in interweaving various motifs. Many of the problems considered in the play (Duke Frederick's tyranny, Oliver's unfair treatment of Orlando, Phebe's exultation over Silvius) stem from excessive control, and the heroine exercises extraordinary control over the disguise. The removal of the disguise signals a renunciation of control on her part, and this in turn is linked with a voluntary renunciation of control by others, so that the unlayering and the resolution of problems neatly correspond. Moreover, the sexual reversal inherent in the disguise, which itself implicitly promises a reconciliation of male and female perspectives, is used to reconcile the men and women in the play. Since the key to reconciliation has been the renunciation of control, the playwright uses his relinquishing of control over the play to signal a final reconciliation between the men and women in the audience. Because of the correspondence between Rosalind as controller of the disguise, and Shakespeare as controller of the disguised boy actor who plays Rosalind's part, Rosalind's control over her disguise is paradigmatic of the playwright's control over the play. Both use their control creatively and constructively, but for both the relinquishing of control corresponds with the consummation of their art.

The means by which resolution is achieved in *As You Like It* says a great deal about the kinds of problems the play considers. By having Rosalind as surrogate playmaker, the playwright must not pose problems that are beyond her power to solve. There are a few hints that Rosalind's control exceeds the merely human; she tells Orlando she possesses magical powers, and Hymen mysteriously appears to officiate at the wedding. The playwright likewise allows himself some hints of supernatural intervention—witness Duke Frederick's miraculous conversion. But positing a human problem-solver almost necessitates limiting the problems to human scale. Moreover, because the disguise is the key to Rosalind's ability to solve problems, the emphasis on male and female perspectives inherent in the sexual disguise places the problems in the context of the social roles of each sex. The disguise thus gives the play artistic unity, but it also imposes limitations on the play's thematic scope. The brilliance of *As You Like It* is that it so perfectly matches what the play attempts to the inherent limitations of its techniques that it makes us unaware there are limitations.

In *Twelfth Night* the techniques, and the problems, are of a different order. Rather than conferring control upon the heroine, the disguise withholds it from her. Concurrently, the nature of the problems changes; in *Twelfth Night,* they cannot be solved by a renunciation of control, because part of the problem is an anxiety about who (or what) is in control. That the removal of the disguise is insufficient to achieve resolution implies an enlargement of the play's thematic scope. In *Twelfth Night* the problems—and the solution—are associated with forces more than human.

Joseph Summers has remarked that *Twelfth Night* has an unusual structure for a comedy, because there are no parents to erect obstacles for the lovers.[8] In the absence of parents, the ruling figures of the society could be expected to fill parental roles; but the Countess Olivia and the Duke Orsino are engaged in love problems themselves. As a result of the displacement of the ruling figures into the romantic plot, a vacuum exists at the top of the social hierarchy. This peculiarity of the play's structure is, I believe, related to the function of the sexual disguise in *Twelfth Night.* As we shall see, the disguise links ambiguity of sexual identity with a concern that this ambiguity can be exploited by super-human forces for evil ends. The absence of human controllers, because it creates a vacuum in which super-human forces can operate, facilitates the shift from the physical to the metaphysical implications of the disguise.

The ambiguous nature of the controlling forces arises first in the underplot. If (as Maria and her accomplices pretend) Malvolio really were possessed by devils, his acts would express not his spontaneous reactions but the desires of the controlling devils. In this sense he would be following a diabolical script, just as he earlier followed the script of the forged letter. The underplot thus introduces the idea that when Malvolio plays a role at odds with his real identity by appearing cross-gartered and smiling, he has unwittingly given diabolical forces the opportunity to usurp his identity for their own ends. Offsetting the seriousness of these implications is our knowledge that this is pretense, the festive revenge of the 'lighter folk' against Malvolio's self-righteous solemnity.[9]

The issues implicit in the playful exorcism of Malvolio are present in the main plot as well, but here the festive mockery that is the essence of the underplot is mingled with a more serious treatment. The connection between masking and the diabolical continues as a cluster of images associates the disguised Viola with the devil. For example, when Cesario first appears at Olivia's gate, Sir Toby in response to Olivia's query about the visitor replies, 'Let him be the devil and he will, I care not' (I, V, 129). Sir Toby again associates Cesario with the devil when he concocts the duel between the foolish Sir Andrew and Cesario. 'I have persuaded him the youth's a devil' (III, iv, 298) Sir Toby assures Fabian; and indeed, after Sir Andrew has

his head bloodied by Sebastian, he is convinced, when he happens upon Cesario again, that 'He's the very devil incardinate' (V, i, 179-80). Along with the misapprehensions of Sir Andrew are a related set of images in a more serious vein. Sir Toby's careless intimation that Cesario might be an aspect of the devil is echoed by Olivia after she has seen the visitor for herself. 'A fiend like thee might bear my soul to hell', she tells Cesario.

The evocation of the diabolical puts into a new context the word-play on divinity and divine texts in the initial meeting of Cesario and Olivia (I, V). If we are distracted from our delight in the wit-contest into a serious consideration, we see that the source of the wit is blasphemy. Thus our delight is being finely balanced against a suppressed recognition of moral ambiguity. Occasionally this recognition is almost allowed to surface; such a moment occurs when Olivia lifts her veil. In this moment of unmasking, the mock-adoration of Cesario's set speeches suddenly gives way to Viola's spontaneous reaction to Olivia's beauty. 'I see you what you are, you are too proud', she tells Olivia. 'But if you were the devil, you are fair' (I, V, 254-5).

The suppressed recognition of moral ambiguity is thus linked, in both main plot and underplot, with an ambiguity of identity. The two plots use different means to contain the moral ambiguities: in the underplot it is the allowed irreverence of festive mockery, while in the main plot it is our delight in the innuendoes and witty ambiguities that Viola's disguise creates. Both plots associate masking with a loss of control. In the underplot, we of course know that the controlling agents are not really devils but Sir Toby and his friends. In the main plot, however, it is not clear into whose hands control has fallen. Viola realizes in her speech near the beginning of act II (II, ii, 17-40) that the complications caused by the sexual disguise have surpassed her power to unravel them. But she cannot clearly see the end to which the disguise leads, or the nature of the controlling agents. If the agents are diabolical, then the end is evil, and wit and beauty are traps for the unwary, audience as well as character. In that case, the play's strategy of the witty containment of moral ambiguity is subverted, because wit, as the tool of diabolical agents, is itself morally ambiguous. Viola's speech is worth examining in detail, since it is the play's most explicit statement about the effect of her disguise and deals with the implications of her loss of control. Before looking closely at the speech, however, I want to mention a contemporary document that may throw some light on the issues being raised here.[10]

A principle support for the mounting Puritan attack on the stage during the last decade of Shakespeare's career was the Biblical prohibition against cross-dressing:

The woman shall not weare that which pertaineth
unto a man, neither shall a man put on a womans
garment: for all that doe so, are abominations unto
the Lord thy God.

                                        (Deuteronomy 22, 5)

Whether this passage applied to the transvestism of the
boy actors was exhaustively debated in an exchange of
letters between three Oxford dons, with Dr John
Rainolds, an eminent Puritan, arguing for a literal interpretation of the passage, and William Gager and his
friend Alberico Gentili attempting to defend the academic drama at Oxford. Six of these letters, two in
English and four in Latin, were printed in 1599 in a
volume entitled *Th' Overthrow of Stage-Plays.* The
debate between these formidably learned men became
widely known. J. W. Binns, writing on this controversy, notes that Prynne acknowledges his debt to
Rainolds in *Histriomastix,* and Thomas Heywood
praises Gager and Gentili in his *Apology for Actors.*[11]

In response to the claim from those defending the drama
that 'abomination' was too strong a term to apply to
the innocent disguises of the stage, Dr Rainolds, citing
the Bishop of Paris, forcefully argues for the potential
evil of sexual disguise:

> For the apparell of women (saith he) is a great
> provocation of men to lust and leacherie: because
> a womans garment being put on by a man doeth
> vehemently touch and moue him with the
> remembrance and imagination of a woman; and
> the imagination of a thing desirable doth stir up
> the desire . . . the law condemneth those execrable
> villanies, to which this change of raiment provoketh
> and entiseth.[12]

Sexual disguise, according to Dr Rainolds, is evil even
when done in play because the semblance of a woman
which the attire creates leads men to desire the boy wearing that attire; and this results in practices condemned by
Biblical law, practices which Rainolds in an earlier letter
calls 'beastlie filthiness, or rather more than beastlie'.[13]

Rainolds's comments on the effects of sexual disguise
are especially interesting (and relevant to *Twelfth Night*)
because they suggest a complex response that depends
upon the apprehension of the sexual ambiguity. The
male spectator, according to Rainolds, reacts erotically
to the female attire of the boy actor; yet at the same
time, the spectator has some apprehension that the actor
is in fact a boy, and so is led by degrees into being
inflamed with lust for the boy. The important point
here is that both elements—the maleness of the boy
actor and the femaleness of the womanly costume—
are necessary to lead the spectator into abomination.

In *Twelfth Night,* the sexual ambiguity of the disguise—
the male attire of Cesario and Viola's underlying femi-

ninity which both Olivia and Orsino sense—frees
Orsino and Olivia from their initial rigidity. C. L.
Barber's perceptive analysis of Olivia's and Orsino's
reactions to the disguise demonstrates how the disguise functions to release the two.[14] Olivia has refused
to admit suitors of any sort prior to Cesario's appearance; in particular, she has refused Orsino, the suitor
who by her own admission is a fine specimen of upright manhood. Yet when she sees the effeminate
Cesario, she immediately falls in love with 'him'. Thus
she is led by degrees to be able to love Sebastian, who
is masculine in person as well as in attire. 'So comes
it, lady, you have been mistook. / But nature to her
bias drew in that', Sebastian tells Olivia at the end of
the play. Meanwhile Orsino has been obstinately intent on pursuing a woman who rejects him. He admits
Cesario into his service, and quickly prefers this girl-
ish boy before all of his other attendants. As Cesario's
patron, he comes to love 'him'; and when it is revealed
that Cesario is in fact a woman, Orsino is content to
claim Viola as his bride. As C. L. Barber concludes, it
is the combination of masculinity and femininity in the
love-object that accomplishes what neither could by
itself. Thus the very sexual ambiguity which Dr
Rainolds claimed would lead the spectator into abomination, releases the characters in *Twelfth Night* from
frustration. Whereas Rainolds suggests that the fluidity
inherent in sexual disguise will lead to moral chaos,
the play shows that fluidity leading to fruition and
fulfillment.

It is of course not *necessary* to suppose that the use of
sexual disguise in *Twelfth Night* owes anything to the
Rainolds-Gager controversy. It was commonplace in
Puritan attacks on the stage to say that the theater in
general, and cross-dressing in particular, was the work
of the devil, so the play's association of sexual disguise with diabolical forces need not come from
Th'Over-Throw of Stage-Plays pamphlet, even assuming it is indebted to the Puritan attacks generally.[15] The
principal new element in the Rainolds-Gager controversy is the dynamic of sexual disguise, the suggestion
that the spectator apprehends the sexual ambiguity of
the actor, and that this apprehension affects the moral
state of the spectator. But it is just this dynamic which
illuminates the complex effects created by the disguise,
as an analysis of Viola's speech shows.

Let us turn now to that speech (II, ii, 17-40). Viola
prays, 'Fortune forbid my outside have not charm'd
her!' invoking the goddess of chance to intervene so
that her appearance is not mistaken for her essence. As
she thinks over Olivia's response, Viola convinces
herself that the lady does indeed love Cesario, and
concludes:

> Disguise, I see thou art a wickedness,
> Wherein the pregnant enemy does much.

                                        (II, ii, 26-7)

'Pregnant enemy' is invariably glossed as the devil, the 'dextrous fiend', as Dr Johnson called him, who uses any disruption of the established order to wreak havoc on man. Viola then imagines the matter that the 'pregnant enemy' forms to his ends:

> How easy is it for the proper false
> In women's waxen hearts to set their forms!
> Alas, our frailty is the cause, not we,
> For such as we are made of, such we be.
>
> (II, ii, 28-31)

The plasticity of the female heart, inherent in woman's flawed nature, allows a 'form' to be set there, and the form evokes love, even when the essence may be at odds with the form. So far the progression Viola describes is similar to that in Dr Rainold's letter, and, like his prediction, carries the sense of a sequence of association exploited by a diabolical agent to lead fallible mankind into damnation. Viola ends the speech by resigning the complexity of the situation to time:

> O time, thou must untangle this, not I
> It is too hard a knot for me t' untie.
>
> (II, ii, 39-40)

Ultimately, the sexual disguise in *Twelfth Night* leads to happiness rather than abomination because the metaphysical entities being invoked—fortune, nature and time—are benign. The plasticity of Olivia's female nature allows her heart to receive Cesario's form. When she sees Cesario again and is refused by 'him', she despairs; but the disguise has already begun to release Olivia from frustration by impressing on her heart the twin's form. Fortune lends its aid by arranging events so that Sebastian is there to take Cesario's place with Olivia when the proper time comes and, by becoming Sebastian's wife, Olivia 'reaps a proper man' she never could have had in Cesario. The discrepancy between appearance and essence, which could have been exploited by diabolical agents for evil ends, has instead allowed Olivia to find fulfillment.

The claim for the beneficial effects of the disguise thus rests on the assumption that the control has been put into the hands of benign entities (fortune, nature, time) rather than diabolical agents. Such a disposition of control still does not resolve all the ambiguities, however, because these entities, although not evil, can nevertheless be ambiguous. For Malvolio, for example, time brings in its revenges. Antonio too is disillusioned rather than freed by disguise. When Cesario is confused with Sebastian, Antonio feels the confluence of this unknown element with his beloved Sebastian as a betrayal. For Antonio, the proper love-object *is* Sebastian, so the ambiguities introduced by Viola's disguise cannot lead him to a more appropriate choice; they only cause him pain. When Cesario denies Antonio his purse, Antonio uses imagery which again sets

into opposition the diabolical and the divine, but now there is no redeeming potential in the confusion. Instead Antonio reacts to the ambiguity as if a true god had been transformed into an idol:

> O how vile an idol proves this god!
> Thou hast, Sebastian, done good feature
>   shame.
> In nature there's no blemish but the mind:
> None can be call'd deform'd but the unkind.
> Virtue is beauty, but the beauteous evil
> Are empty trunks, o'er-flourish'd by the devil.
>
> (III, iv, 374-9)

Antonio sees the discrepancy between appearance and essence, which allowed Orsino and Olivia to be freed, as a diabolical trap designed to lure the unwary into worship. The ambiguity of the disguise, helpless to release Antonio from the anguish of his love, can at most restore the loved one to him, as it does when he meets Sebastian again at the end of the play.[16]

Perhaps Antonio's worship explains why Sebastian at the end uses language which denies the claim of godhood and places him firmly in the world of the flesh. When he first sees Cesario, Sebastian says,

> Do I stand here? I never had a brother;
> Nor can there be that deity in my nature
> Of here and everywhere.
>
> (V, i, 224-6)

And then, when Viola takes him for a spirit, he replies,

> A spirit I am indeed,
> But am in that dimension grossly clad
> Which from the womb I did participate.
>
> (V, i, 234-6)

Sebastian's statements imply a reintegration of form and essence when he presents himself not as a god (or a devil) but as a man, a spirit in a corporeal body. There is indeed an ambiguity in this union of spirit with flesh, but it is an ambiguity which defines the essence of man, as Sebastian proclaims himself a man, and one which is finally cause for celebration and happiness rather than temptation. The closing scenes, which resolve some of the ambiguities, reassure us that the ambiguities which cannot be resolved will nevertheless lead to good rather than evil. Gaiety, not melancholy, is finally the appropriate response to an ambiguous world.

Sexual disguise is thus a multifaceted device in Shakespeare. The progression from *As You Like It* to *Twelfth Night* shows a shift in emphasis from a *sexual* disguise to a sexual *disguise*. In *Cymbeline,* the last play where Shakespeare uses the device, the emphasis is almost entirely metaphysical rather than social. The growing sense of wonder that accompanies the removal of the disguise in the later plays is possible only because its implications transcend the merely social, or even the human. It would be unfortunate if our modern preoccupations blind us to this sense of wonder, or to an appreciation of the rich diversity with which Shakespeare uses the device. In Shakespeare's hands, sexual disguise illuminates not only the relationship of woman to man, but also the relation of appearance to reality and human beings to forces more than human. The multiplicity of meanings with which Shakespeare invests the disguise does not really 'disentangle the perplexity [of seeing] a boy play a woman playing a man', but it provides a thematic counterpart to that complexity of vision, and so orders it into one aesthetic whole.

Notes

[1] Charles Lamb in remarks on *Philaster,* quoted in V. O. Freeburg, *Disguise Plots in Elizabethan Drama* (New York, 1915), p. 22.

[2] The principle book length study is V. O. Freeburg's *Disguise Plots in Elizabethan Drama,* in which he undertakes an anatomy of disguise plots, classifying them according to kinds of disguises. M. C. Bradbrook in 'Shakespeare and the Use of Disguise in Elizabethan Drama', *Essays in Criticism,* 2 (1962), 159-68, after taking exception to Freeburg's definition of disguise as a change in physical appearance, considers psychological poses as well as physical masking. In trying to cover the whole range of possible disguises, Bradbrook is forced to be suggestive rather than comprehensive, and although she comments perceptively on the interconnections between disguise and identity—the area Freeburg most neglects—her conclusions remain interesting but vague. F. H. Mares in 'Viola and Other Transvestist Heroines in Shakespeare's Comedies', *Stratford Papers, 1965-1967,* ed. B. A. W. Jackson (McMaster Univ. Library Press, 1969), pp. 96-109 gives an urbane and sensible, if not deeply reasoned, perspective on the disguised heroine in four plays. Mares considers *Tweifth Night* and *As You Like It* to be the most dramatically economical uses of the disguise, *Two Gentlemen of Verona* simplistic in its responses, and *Cymbeline* complex but not integrally related to the theme. Two dissertations have appeared on the subject. Doris Feil in 'The Female Page in Renaissance Drama' (Arizona State University, 1971) gives a statistical overview of the female page in Renaissance drama from 1592-1642. In 'The Disguised Heroine in Six Shakespearean Comedies' (Univ. of Connecticut, 1970), James P. O'Sullivan discusses *Merchant of Venice, As You Like It, Twelfth Night, Two Gentlemen of Verona, All's Well* and *Cymbeline.* His analysis is not concerned specifically with sexual disguise.

[3] Examples are Carolyn Heilbrun, *Toward a Recognition of Androgyny* (New York, 1973), and *Shakespeare and the Nature of Women,* Juliet Dusinberre (New York, 1975).

[4] The other plays using female sexual disguise are *Two Gentlemen of Verona, Merchant of Venice,* and *Cymbeline. Two Gentlemen of Verona* shows in rudimentary form what the later plays show more fully (see Harold Jenkins, 'Shakespeare's *Twelfth Night', Rice Institute Pamphlet,* 45, No. 4 (1959), 19-42 for a discussion of *Two Gentlemen of Verona* as an anticipation of *Twelfth Night*). In *Merchant* of *Venice,* the disguise is more obviously functional and less explored in itself than in either *As You Like It* or *Twelfth Night.* The case of *Cymbeline* is complex, and is the subject of an article in preparation. Two plays contain instances of male sexual disguise, the Induction to *Taming of the Shrew* and *Merry Wives of Windsor,* both of which use boy brides. Male transvestism is mentioned as well in *Antony and Cleopatra,* but not shown on stage. Male disguise is not discussed because it seems clear that Shakespeare was mainly interested in the possibilities of sexual disguise offered by the female page.

[5] Ralph Berry in *Shakespeare's Comedies: Explorations in Form* (Princeton, 1972), comments on the need to control others in *As You Like It,* and remarks in passing that the wrestling match may be symbolic of what he sees as the dominant theme (p. 177). We part company in our interpretation of the play's later scenes. Berry singles out for attention the discordant elements, even in the final scene, whereas my emphasis is on the final resolution and reconciliation.

[6] Quotations are from the New Arden: *As You Like It,* ed. Agnes Latham (1975); and *Twelfth Night,* ed. J. M. Lothian and T. W. Craik (1975).

[7] A felicitous phrase supplied by a private communication with Ellen Cronan Rose.

[8] Joseph Summers, 'The Masks of *Twelfth Night,* in *Shakespeare: Modern Essays in Criticism,* ed. Leonard F. Dean (Oxford 1967), pp. 134-5.

[9] C. L. Barber's important book *Shakespeare's Festive Comedy: A Study in Dramatic Form and its Relation to Social Custom* (Princeton, 1959), discusses the functions of festive misrule in Shakespeare's comedies. Barber's general formula for festive comedy is a movement through release to clarification, a formulation that does much to illuminate *Twelfth Night.*

[10] For much of the information that follows I am indebted to J. W. Binns's excellent article, 'Women or Transvestites on the Elizabethan Stage?: An Oxford Controversy', *Sixteenth Century Journal,* 2 (1974), 95-120. Besides drawing attention to the Rainolds-Gager

controversy, Binns supplied translations and summaries of hitherto unpublished letters in the controversy.

[11] Binns, p. 119.

[12] Binns, p. 103.

[13] Binns, p. 102.

[14] See 'You are betroth'd both to a maid and man', *Shakespeare's Festive Comedies,* pp. 245-7.

[15] For an overview of Puritan rhetoric against the stage, see Elbert Nevius Sebring Thompson, *The Controversy Between the Puritans and the Stage,* Yale Studies in English, 20 (New York, 1903), especially pp. 102-9 for theaters as purveyors of sin.

[16] I take Antonio's dilemma in *Twelfth Night* to be another version of the dilemma of that other Antonio in *Merchant of Venice:* both Antonios love another man, and both are forced to come to some kind of accommodation when the man they love takes a wife. The pain that surrounds both Antonios seems to me an expression of the consequences of a homoerotic love in a heterosexual society. The men that the Antonio figures love (Bassanio, Sebastian) may return the love, but both ultimately marry women and give their allegiance to their wives.

SEEING / (DIS)BELIEVING

Alex Aronson (essay date 1970)

SOURCE: "Shakespeare and the Ocular Proof," in *Shakespeare Quarterly,* Vol. XXI, No. 4, Autumn, 1970, pp. 411-29.

[*In the following essay, Aronson surveys Shakespeare's plays and concludes that "the choice between the eye and the mind, between the ocular proof and spiritual awareness which Shakespeare's characters are compelled to make, is of the very essence of his tragic vision."*]

I

If there is any psychological validity in Blake's dictum—"As a man is, so he sees"—and if it is true not only of the ordinary man, for instance the reader of Shakespeare's plays and the spectator in the theater, but also of the characters he created, then it suggests a criterion by which to judge the thoughts, speeches, and actions of men and women on the stage. For "as a man sees, so he is" seems the natural corollary to Blake's dictum. A man's sense-perceptions, his responsive contact with the outside world through his eyes, will determine his "outlook" on the world and its inhabitants, which in turn, will give rise to forms of behavior open to moral judgment. This dependence of *being* on *seeing* will color man's knowledge, not only of others, but of himself as well. Man "is" not merely *how* he sees, but *what* he sees, as well as *when* he sees, and, not least of all, *because* he sees what he thinks he sees.

The spectator in the theater (and even more so the reader of plays) may, as a rule, be supposed to possess a greater degree of "insight" than the actor on the stage, involved as the latter is in intensely emotive situations. The onlooker, in his twofold function as passive recipient, on the one hand, yet carried along by the intensities of the action on the stage, on the other, and quite ready to identify himself with those characters who "see" rather than "are seen"—this sympathetic witness of so frequently distorted vision and short-sighted violence need not necessarily be aware of the archetypal nature of the conflict between "sight" and "insight" arising from it. He may refer what *he* sees on the stage merely to the personal tortuosities of the characters concerned. Though the metaphor may seem to him psychologically significant, it may not convey that generalized truth which an archetypal pattern of experience is meant to imply.

The purpose of this paper, however, is to show how, with the growing maturity of his art, Shakespeare lifted the conflict and the tension out of the realm of the merely personal and idiosyncratic. He, as it were, universalized it by emphasizing the ever-repeated, legendary, indeed mythical nature of man's distorted vision that leads from spiritual to actual blindness. The archetype of evil is not necessarily expressed in terms of this or that "character", the outcast, the alien, the envious, the greedy, the ambitious, the voluptuous, not in Iago, in Lady Macbeth, in Edmund, not even in Caliban—all of them being undoubtedly projections of what the artist apprehended as evil in human nature. The archetypal essence of evil is so often conveyed through the metaphor of blindness itself that the many varieties of evil that men are capable of may be said to be not "as you are", but "as you see"—or rather as you believe you see. Spiritual blindness—being the result of distorted vision—induced either voluntarily or by compulsion, is one of Shakespeare's most recurrent themes. In the drama of the human soul, it leads from the conventional "lover's eye" of his early comedies, the magic of Helena's "triple eye" in *All's Well,* to Miranda's regained innocence of vision in *The Tempest.* It includes a large diversity of blindnesses each one the result of the same archetypal inability to come to terms with visual reality—Othello's pitiable lack of awareness in the face of the "ocular proof", Macbeth's self-blinding ambition, Lear's and Gloucester's initial *hubris* when confronted by the spectacle of life—nasty, brutish, and short as well as largely incomprehensible.

The evil that Shakespeare expresses through this metaphor lies in men's belief that what they see is a "true" image of life, even when what they see is manifestly impossible. Accepting the most absurd ocular proof at its face-value, they choose the illusory reality of a fool's paradise where "nothing is but what is not". This is why Othello calls Iago "honest", Gloucester trusts Edmund rather than Edgar, Lear banishes Cordelia, and Macbeth relies on the Witches' ambiguous prophecies. By applying a distorted vision to others they also misjudge themselves. Theirs is a surrender to the destructive elements residing in man's unconscious, a return to some primordial darkness of which blindness, in Shakespeare's plays, is the most adequate symbol. Redemption, in the form of insight, if and when it comes, as a rule arrives too late. The price to be paid for re-established vision which enables you to come to terms with reality as it is rather than as it "looks" is always death. The main difference between the actor on the stage and the spectator in the theater seems to be that the former is aware of the evil and therefore "suffers" his blindness, while the latter is content with the knowledge that what he sees on the stage is merely a form of make-believe and therefore requires no commitment on his part. The spectator's prerogative, one may assume, is to be blind without having to suffer the agonies of redemption.

The universe of Shakespeare's early plays takes for granted the visual existence of beauty aesthetically perceivable to the lover only. This alone gives shape and meaning to life. Following the conventional pattern of Renaissance love poetry, Shakespeare makes his youthful heroes and heroines love "through the eye". Whatever obstacles there may be are the result of mistaken identities, external circumstances, or the whims and moods of uncomprehending and frequently unsympathetic male adults (on more than one occasion afflicted with myopic vision), fathers, uncles, brothers, and such like. This is true of Orlando no less than of Romeo, of Hero no less than of Juliet. The rule of the eye over the mind in these plays is constantly stressed as a prerequisite to the achievement of human happiness. To see beauty where and when it exists and to be seen by beauty provides man with a gratifying stimulus to living which no book-learning can supply. The contrast established between the two kinds of truth resulting either from studying books (through the mind) or from looking at beauty (through the eyes) is significant: for it introduces the archetype, the evil of blindness, into a universe where man's proudest attribute is his eyesight, a universe of eternal daylight where happiness is granted to those alone who "keep their eyes open":

> Why! all delights are vain, but that most vain,
> Which with pain purchas'd doth inherit pain:
> As, painfully to pore upon a book
> To seek the light of truth: while truth the
>   while
> Doth falsely blind the eyesight of his look:
> Light seeking light doth light of light beguile:
> So, ere you find where light in darkness lies,
> Your light grows dark by losing of your eyes.
> Study me how to please the eye indeed,
> By fixing it upon a fairer eye,
> Who dazzling so, that eye shall be his heed,
> And giving him light that it was blinded by.
>   (*Love's Labour's Lost* I. i. 72)

The ability to see beauty and to recognise it for what it is is love's only test of truth. One who knows "love's truth", then, has learned to see. Berowne, the most articulate spokesman for this simplified doctrine of "ocular proof", goes as far as this kind of argument will lead him. Love, he says,

> Adds a precious seeing to the eye;
> A lover's eye will gaze an eagle blind—
>   (IV. iii. 334)

and, consistent to the very end, calls his eye "the window of my heart", thereby implying, as so many legends, beliefs, and myths did before him, that the organ of the soul is indeed the eye and that the lover looking into the eye of his beloved will perceive the innermost recesses of her being.

As long as love exists in the largely illusory daylight world of Shakespeare's comedies, "seeing" is liable to lead to partial if not distorted "truth". The risk that the lovers take when gazing into each other's eyes is that of neglecting the presence of moral evil among them. Whenever such evil makes its appearance, the spectator is as a rule taken into confidence. The characters on the stage remain oblivious of its threatening existence. Whether, for instance, Don John's intentions, in *Much Ado,* are due to motiveless or motivated malignity, the possible consequence of scorned ambition or of a general hatred of mankind, he certainly distracts the vision of one of these thoughtless lovers. We are not told how often and how deep Claudio gazed into Hero's eyes. We may have our doubts as to whether he discovered—or was even capable of discovering—her soul within them. In effect Don John wins an easy victory over Claudio's eyes. Calumny is unquestioningly taken for truth, on the basis of what other people have overheard or "seen" and, at that, indistinctly, at night, and from quite some distance. Hero must first die an artificial, an "untrue" death to be resurrected again so that Claudio may learn to see beyond appearances. For the first time, and in a context of potential tragedy, Shakespeare makes us face the conflict and the resulting tension: sight must be replaced by insight, and imaginative awareness must serve as a necessary substitute for the ocular proof if truth is to be established. For this is what Shakespeare tells us through the mouth of Friar Francis: the only truth worth knowing is that which is reached through the creative effort of the conscious mind. The Friar, like most holy men in Shakespeare, is merely a *deus ex machina*. Yet he, at the very last moment, teaches Claudio how not to stumble with his eyes wide open. In a way, he teaches him to look into the mirror of his own eyes, and to discover there what we in the theater knew all along, Hero's innocence:

> When he shall hear she died upon his words,
> Th' idea of her life shall sweetly creep
> Into his study of imagination,
> And every organ of her life,
> Shall come apparelled in more precious habit,
> More moving delicate, and full of life,
> Into the eye and prospect of his soul,
> Than when she lived indeed.
>
> (IV. i.225)

II

In Shakespeare's tragic universe of formless ambiguities and indistinct shapes, man inevitably and consistently is made to face the most questionable reality of all, his own soul. This is no longer the daylight universe of lovers looking for the soul in their "lady's eyes". Man's increasing isolation in an unfriendly universe makes him search for self-knowledge and the meaning of his identity beyond his emotional involvements. That this identity appears to him as if seen in a distorting mirror, in the form of a shadow, his *alter ego* or his double, is quite in the nature of things. For human isolation and the suffering it entails prevent clear vision. Shakespeare, as early as in *Richard II,* defines that kind of blindness which concerns man most of all because it refers to his loss of identity in a moment of anguish:

> Each substance of a grief hath twenty
>   shadows,
> Which shows like grief itself, but is not so.
> For sorrow's eye, glazed with blinding tears,
> Divides one thing entire to many objects,
> Like perspectives, which, rightly, gaz'd upon,
> Show nothing but confusion. . . .
>   'Tis with false sorrow's eye,
> Which, for things true, weeps things
>   imaginary.
>
> (II. ii. 14)

Richard himself is a victim of this confusion between substance and shadow. He realizes the fundamental distinction between what *is* and what is *seen* in a way that no lover in Shakespeare's early comedies would have been capable of. Thus Richard breaks the looking

glass in which he discovered his own shadow, the unsubstantial reflection of his own eyes gazing back at him, and knowing at last that the "substance" is elsewhere:

> The shadow of my sorrow? ha! let's see:—
> 'Tis very true, my grief lies all within;
> And these external manners of lament
> Are merely shadows to the unseen grief
> That swells with silence in the tortured soul:
> There lies the substance.
>
> (IV. i. 294)

Lear's looking glass is the Fool. Searching for his own identity, as Richard II had done before him, he asks him:

>   Where are his eyes?
> Either his notion weakens, or his discernings
> Are lethargied—Ha! Waking? 'tis not so.
> Who is it that can tell me who I am?

To which the Fool replies,

>   "Lear's shadow."
>
> (I. iv. 249)

Macbeth is his own Fool. His looking glass is his own soul. Looking into it he discovers the unsubstantial nature of his vaulting ambition. His realization that the "walking shadow" and the "poor player" are projections of his own inner hollowness is the only kind of self-knowledge that is available to him. Does he dare face that knowledge? It signifies as little to him as did the looking glass to Richard or the Fool's caustic remark to Lear. It is broken, fragmentary knowledge "signifying nothing". None of Shakespeare's great tragic heroes exhibit that kind of spiritual courage which is required when you stand face to face with your own shadow, your eyes open without flinching.

Yet self-knowledge is what they are after. And if the eye is indeed the "window of the heart", your own reflection in the eye of someone else may reveal your own meaning to you. Perhaps Blake's dictum should not have been "As a man is, so he sees", but "As a man is, so he sees himself" in or through the eyes of others. The argument is, of course, fallacious. For if a man's eyesight is deficient and therefore indistinct, there is little likelihood that the image of himself reflected in the eyes of others will help him towards self-knowledge. It is no accident, therefore, that Shakespeare puts this kind of argument into the mouths of two characters whose purity of motive is open to question. The first, Achilles, in *Troilus and Cressida,* is shown to be a self-centered and pompous fool, who adds his own interpretation to the meaning of a book (generally assumed to be Plato) that Ulysses is reading. According to Ulysses, Plato meant to say that man, whether rich or poor in material wealth or wisdom,

> Cannot make boast to have that which he has;
> Nor feels not what he owns, but by reflection;
> As when his virtues shining upon others,
> Heat them, and they retort that heat again
> To the first giver.
>
> (III. iii. 98)

Achilles readily agrees. What the writer of the book here said about virtue, is, he thinks, even more applicable to the beauty of a face and, no doubt, of the spirit as well:

> The beauty that is borne here in the face,
> The bearer knows not, but commends itself,
> To others' eyes, nor doth the eye itself,
> That most pure spirit of sense, behold itself
> Not going from itself: but eye to eye oppos'd,
> Salutes each other with each other's form.
> For speculation turns not to itself,
> Till it hath travell'd, and is mirrored there
> Where it may see itself.
>
> (III. iii. 103)

Is Achilles, who otherwise shows little sense throughout the play, quoting Socrates?[1] Possibly he is merely repeating a commonplace in Elizabethan psychology which offered a kind of short-cut to self-knowledge. Accordingly, all you have to do is to look for the "shadow" without rather than within. Cassius who may be said to possess all the political shrewdness that Achilles lacks—though similarly self-centered and unaware of the spiritual implications of his actions—asks Brutus to use him, his friend, as a mirror wherein he may discover his true self:

> And it is very much to be lamented, Brutus,
> That you have not such mirror as will turn
> Your hidden worthiness into your eyes,
> That you might see your shadow. . . .
> And since you know you cannot see yourself
> As well as by reflection, I, your glass,
> Will modestly discover to yourself
> That of yourself which you yet know not of.
>
> (*Julius Caesar* I. ii. 54)

The spiritual analogy implied in both passages, however, is morally questionable. For those that draw the parallel between eye and soul are hardly qualified to do so. To neglect the ironic implications of these two passages is to miss the ambiguity of the situation: for though Shakespeare makes Achilles and Cassius philosophize about the eye as a "mirror of the soul", there is little enough soul in either of them. Ulysses is not fooled by Achilles. But Brutus having looked into Cassius' eyes, discovers his shadow there. And his

>   state of man,
> Like to a little kingdom suffers then,
> The nature of an insurrection.
>
> (II. i. 67)

There are other, subtler ways in which Shakespeare's heroes become aware of the existence of their shadow. They may, especially in times of spiritual anguish, project it outside themselves, by turning their defective spiritual eyesight into visual self-deception. Their blindness acquires, as it were, corporal shape: out of the dimness of their vision arise forms of non-being, "false" shadows yet visible to their eye, compelling them to assume the existence of the physically unsubstantial, an assumption liable to annihilate any rationally valid distinction between the real and the unreal, the visible and invisible. The shadow-image of your own soul, in the words of Achilles and Cassius, should reflect your own true self. Yet man can bear a limited vision of truth only: instead of leading to self-knowledge, the "shadow" comes in the terrifying shape that man's unconscious creates. The confrontation of shadow and eye is of little help: the dividing line between the spiritual and the physical disappears, and the hero is left wondering on which side of the line reality lies.

Brutus' realization of defeat at the end of the play is in part due to the "weakness of mine eyes" (IV. iii. 275) which showed him the shadow of his own soul in the form of a "monstrous apparition". Though his eyes may falter at first, they adjust themselves soon enough to his "evil spirit". What he sees is, indeed, a form of non-being, yet he never doubts the "reality" of its existence: "Why, I will see thee at Philippi then" (IV. iii. 285), he says, knowing at last that there is no escape from your own shadow, however unsubstantial the nightmare-image of your self may be.

Hamlet is no less willing, indeed eager, to hold converse with his father's Ghost. Once before, in a conversation with Horatio, he had seen his father in his "mind's eye" (I. ii. 185). Now he stands face to face with the shadow of his own mind. He, as it were, receives an ocular proof of the impossible, because the non-existing, and perceives the invisible. His friend Horatio, who first doubts the reality of the Ghost, as indeed any sensible man would do who knows how defective and indistinct eyesight can be, later on accepts the apparition but only in so far as his senses, and especially his sense of sight, have "approved" it:

> I might not this believe
> Without the sensible and true avouch
> Of mine own eyes.
>
> (I. i. 56)

That Horatio should at all be able to "see" the Ghost reveals his integrity of mind. "Blood and judgement" are so well "commingled" in his nature that he is capable of seeing beyond himself, realizing, in his own limited way, that the time is out of joint and that much insight will be required to set it right. Gertrude lacks that integrity and, therefore, is "blind" to anything that is not corporal:

> Alas, how is't with you,
> That you do bend your eye on vacancy,
> And with the incorporal air do hold
>   discourse?
>
>   (III. iv. 115)

she asks Hamlet when he meets his father's Ghost for the second time and in her presence.

Banquo is a worthy cousin to Horatio. He questions the Witches, assuming immediately that their essential nature is different from

>   that indeed
> Which outwardly you show.
>
>   (I. iii. 54)

In addition, he doubts the reliability of his and Macbeth's eyesight, concluding that they must have been mistaken and what they thought they had seen was the result of their having eaten

>   Of the insane root
> That takes the reason prisoner.
>
>   (I. iii. 85)

Macbeth's attitude is necessarily different. He not only "sees" the Witches, the floating dagger, and Banquo's Ghost, but recognizes them as belonging to him, variations on the theme of his own shadow—in a way, the looking glass in which he perceives his own soul. He also realizes, and more clearly and overwhelmingly than any other character in Shakespeare's plays, that the organ with which one perceives one's own shadow is not the eye, but the imagination. The apparition of the dagger evokes from Macbeth some of the most revealing remarks about the phenomenon of "double vision" to which intense suffering exposes man at a moment of spiritual crisis:

> Art thou not, fatal vision, sensible
> To feeling as to sight? or art thou but
> A dagger of the mind . . . ?
> Mine eyes are made the fools of th' other
>   senses
> Or else worth all the rest. . . .
> It is the bloody business which informs
> Thus to mine eyes.
>
>   (II. i. 36)

The world of shadows which Macbeth inhabits is made fairly explicit by constant references to the ambiguity of the very concept of reality. Macbeth's agony consists in his having to face the shadow of his own inner self without being equipped with the emotional reserves that would make such a confrontation in any way meaningful. He therefore dismisses Banquo's Ghost:

> Hence, horrible shadow!
> Unreal mockery, hence!
>
>   (III. iv. 106)

not realizing that this self-created shadow is merely one out of many: for the shadows multiply in his soul in proportion to the ever-thickening darkness around him. When he requests the Witches, on his second visit to them, to reveal his future to him, they even perform a shadow-show for him:

> Show his eyes, and grieve his heart:
> Come like shadows, so depart.
>
>   (IV. i. 110)

That his wife should consistently refuse to grasp the meaning of all these various shadows for Macbeth is in keeping with her obsession with what she believes to be "real" and therefore accessible to sight. All the rest is foolishness or, at best, self-deception:

> 'Tis the eye of childhood
> That fears a painted devil. . . .
>
>   (II. ii. 54)

she exclaims in answer to Macbeth's compulsive fear to look again at dead Duncan. On a later occasion when faced by the shadow of Banquo which his own mind had created, he answers his wife's question, "Are you a man?", with the doubtful affirmation:

> Ay, and a bold one, that dare look on that
> Which might appal the devil.
>
>   (III. iv. 59)

Macbeth is quite ready to look at the evil without, perceivable to the eye as part of "objective" reality; yet he wilfully blinds himself to the existence of the evil within, claiming to be "bold" when he should have been human.

Lady Macbeth, fully realizing her power over her husband's mind, provides him with a kind of distorting mirror. At the end of the first Act, Macbeth believes that what her eyes see must be the truth. And since the ocular proof of Duncan's death is all that matters, the "sightless substances" of which she is as aware as Macbeth pertain to the "spirits that tend on mortal thoughts", not to the reality of human life. In her own simplified way, she constantly tries to correct her husband's faulty vision:

When all's done
You look but on a stool.

(III. iv. 66)

When the shadow disappears, the mockery gone, the imaginary looking glass broken, Macbeth is "a man again". The "substance" of his manhood, however, we know, will never be regained. The real mockery is still to come.

III

In a patriarchal society—the one that Shakespeare represented on the stage—in which masculine forms of conduct are taken for granted and the emotional and intellectual habitus of both men and women is determined by a predominantly masculine code of behavior, women are objects of choice rather than choosers. When Shakespeare shows some of them as free agents, choosing their mate without any external compulsions, in a love-relationship or in marriage, their eyesight is liable to lead them astray. By committing themselves "through the eye" only, they are "blinded" by inadequate vision leading to faulty judgment. The involvement being colored by violent erotic impulses, they act against reason and common sense. Inhibitions that had formerly been freely accepted as guides towards honorable living and on which such conceptions as chastity, virginity, fidelity in marriage, or respectable widowhood were founded, are thrown overboard. When "compulsive ardour gives the charge" and "reason panders will", desire becomes a slave to the sense of sight and the blind violence of lust rules supreme.

This does not mean to say that woman's "eye" is incapable of self-analysis and self-knowledge. In Shakespeare's mature comedies, the women—Portia, Rosalind, Viola—are indeed the ones who choose. And though we may be surprised at the object of their choice, we can hardly accuse them of faulty eyesight. Yet, whenever Shakespeare portrays women in the frailty of their flesh, they are usually shown to be aware of their transgression of a code of conduct which made conscious masculine choice the very basis upon which their civilization was built. The eye which in ancient mythology always symbolized the light of consciousness is here the tempter. Olivia, in *Twelfth Night,* is the first to hint at this peculiarly feminine "frailty":

Even so quickly may one catch the plague?
Methinks I feel this youth's perfections
With an invisible and subtle stealth
To creep in at mine eyes. . . .
I do I know not what; and fear to find
Mine eye too great a flatterer for my mind.

(I. v. 314)

The plague that Olivia catches is that of blindness. Yet she knows that she is acting against the principles of conduct that she had set herself in accordance with the admittedly rather far-fetched dictates of the social group of which she is a part. Her implied self-mockeiry lacks the intensity of later plays. One is out of sympathy with Olivia because she constantly fools herself, or rather lets herself be deceived by her eyes, willingly and knowingly. Eventually she even achieves happiness—in terms of an imaginary ocular proof. Her choice is founded on the inability of her eyes to distinguish between a girl dressed in boy's clothes and the girl's very real brother. It is happiness experienced through indistinct vision.

One is similarly out of sympathy with Gertrude. The fact that we hardly ever see her through her own eyes but through the eyes of others, her former husband and her son, undoubtedly determines our attitude towards her. Her "frailty", Hamlet implies, is that of visual lust. It is this fascination "through the eye" that leads to the paralysis of judgment. The more uncontrolled the lust, the greater the blindness that follows:

Have you eyes?
Could you on this fair mountain leave to feed,
And batten on this moor? Ha! have you eyes?
. . . Sense, sure, you have,
Else could you not have motion: but sure, that sense
Is apoplex'd: for madness would not err,
Nor sense to ecstasy was ne'er so thrall'd
But it reserv'd some quantity of choice,
To serve in such a difference. What devil was't
That thus hath cozen'd you at hoodman-blind?
Eyes without feeling, feeling without sight,
Ears without hands or eyes, smelling sans all
Or but a sickly part of one true sense
Could not so mope.

(III. iv. 65)

Gertrude responds to her son's arguments with surprising eagerness. Hamlet opens his mother's eyes and lets her "see" her soul. What she sees there is a reflection of her disordered appetite:

Thou turn'st mine eyes into my very soul;
And there I see such black and grained spots
As will not leave their tinct.

(III. iv. 89)

Cressida's story is a variation on the same theme. Her intrinsic shallowness, which she seems to share with Gertrude, is the only excuse for her conduct. She had previously made her choice. Pandarus had helped her by "opening" her eyes to Troilus' presence: "Why, have you any discretions? Have you any eyes? do you know what a man is?" (I. ii. 209). When Cressida shows herself to be "frail" and, incidentally, fully realizes the implications of what she is about to do, she blames her eyes for having mis-directed her mind:

> Troilus farewell; one eye yet looks on thee;
> But with my heart, the other eye, doth see;
> Ah, poor our sex: this fault in us I find:
> The error of our eye, directs our mind.
> What error leads, must err: O then conclude,
> Minds sway'd by eyes, are full of turpitude.
> (V. ii. 104)

Self-mockery has turned into anguish, deficient eye-sight into moral evil. Both Hamlet and Troilus per-ceive the same "turpitude" in the eyes of those they love. For Hamlet this discovery is part of a larger rec-ognition, that time is out of joint and visual lust has taken over, destroying the precarious balance between blood and judgment.

Shakespeare's treatment of the metaphor of distorted vision acquires in his tragedies an archetypal charac-ter. Men and women alike are born into an alien uni-verse which neither their mind nor their senses can fully explore. Knowledge through bodily senses is swayed by "affections"—by which the Elizabethans meant appetites, desires, and lusts—which prevent men from perceiving the true nature and meaning of the world they inhabit. What we "see" is always open to a variety of interpretations. Nothing ever is that it seems to be. It is no accident that Shakespeare puts the fol-lowing lines into the mouth of Antony:

> Sometime we see a cloud that's dragonish,
> A vapour sometime, like a bear, or lion,
> A tower'd citadel, a pendent rock,
> A fork'd mountain, or blue promontory
> With trees upon't, that nod unto the world,
> And mock our eyes with air. . . .
> That which is now a horse, even with a
>   thought
> The rack dislimns, and makes it indistinct
> As water is in water.
> (*Antony and Cleopatra* IV. xii. 2)

What is true of the physical universe applies in an even greater measure to human relationships. If what is corporal in man is at all times subject to uncontrol-lable emotions, how much greater must the intensity of spiritual surrender be when man finds himself ruled by those same "appetites". The eye as the "window of the heart" is forever liable to reflect a distorted image of people and things. The moral evil resulting from such a lack of insight, Shakespeare implies, does not neces-sarily reside in "nature". Neither the body nor the mind is *a priori* evil. It is "man-made" and can be explained as originating in a false sense of security ("I see, there-fore I am"), an inflated self-confidence that puts all trust in the physical ability to perceive, to measure, to calculate, to establish an ocular proof of "truth" which

in effect is not open to such visual measurements at all. The refusal to face a truth that ought to be con-fronted in terms of imaginative awareness only is the undoing of the tragic hero. This is what Tiresias meant when he warned Oedipus of a false clear-sightedness:

> Have you eyes,
> And do not see your own damnation? Eyes,
> And cannot see what company you keep?
>   . . . Those now clear-seeing eyes
> Shall then be darkened. . . .
> He that came seeing, blind shall he go.[2]

Greek philosophy as well as mythology provides us with an instance of archetypal polarity implied in the eye-metaphor as used by Shakespeare. Being a defi-cient instrument of sight, the eye may take the shadow for the substance and thereby falsify the meaning of reality. On the other hand, blindness, that is the physi-cal inability to see, may force man to turn the eye inward and reveal there a wisdom which is beyond the reach of sight. This is why Plato warns men not to introduce "in the act of thought sight or any other sense"[3] if he wishes to attain knowledge which in-cludes self-knowledge. His *Phaedo* expresses a subtle contempt for the body, a kind of ironic aloofness which, across the centuries, contrasts in a strange and reveal-ing manner with Shakespeare's frantically violent out-bursts against visual lusts in his darkest plays. The body, explains Socrates,

> fills us full of loves, and lusts, and fears, and
> fancies of all kinds, and endless foolery, and, as
> men say, takes away from us the power of thinking
> at all. Whence come wars, and fightings and
> factions? whence but from the body and the lusts
> of the body?[4]

Plato's imaginary heaven can be found only when man succeeds in breaking through "the exterior limit" of his sense-perceptions, divests himself of his body; thus "he would see a world beyond", which is a place of "the true light and the true earth". Plato, however, expresses his doubts whether "the nature of man could sustain the sight".[5] He admits that only too often, instead of this voluntary rejection of the body as an instrument of perception, "the soul too is then dragged . . . into the region of the changeable, and wanders and is confused."[6]

Aristotle supplies the finishing touch to the polarity inherent in the eye-metaphor. The separation of body from soul seems to him an artificial withdrawal from reality. Man's unending desire to explore this alien universe with whatever limited instruments nature may have endowed him is the main challenge. These instru-ments used by men in search of the meaning of what is most alien, his own soul, are viewed differently by Aristotle:

All by nature desire to know. An indication of this is the delight we take in our senses; for even apart from their usefulness they are loved for themselves; and above all others the sense of sight. For not only with a view to action, but even when we are not going to do anything we prefer seeing to everything else. The reason is that this, most of all senses, makes us know and brings to light many differences between things.[7]

One of the many differences that our sense of sight should bring to light is that between appearance and reality, seeming and being, between what we think we see and what *is*. And though doubts may arise in our mind as to whether anything ever *is* at all or merely appears to be *because* we see it in a certain way, Shakespeare's most tragic heroes, Othello, Macbeth, and Lear, are victims of the same visual deception: they take the shadow for the substance. They stumble when they see.

If Aristotle were right, all that would be required to achieve self-knowledge, is some ocular proof providing us with knowledge that gives pleasure and wisdom. Othello demands such a visual experiment. He wants to "see" in order to set his mind at rest. That Iago manipulates the show, prepares the setting for the experiment, and deceives Othello, is relevant only in so far as he exploits Othello's "blindness" to the full. Othello, who was only too eager to believe what his eyes showed him, was ready to let himself be fooled. Did he not see Desdemona's handkerchief in Cassio's hand? "I'll see before I doubt, when I doubt, prove" (III. iii. 190). An absolute Aristotelian proof, however, is hard to come by. Othello, unconsciously following Brabantio's advice "Look to her, Moor, have a quick eye to see" (I. iii. 292), and accepting Iago's warning,

Look to your wife; observe her well with
  Cassio;
Wear your eye thus, not jealous but
  secure—

(III. iii. 197)

demands the "ocular proof" of his wife's infidelity. The Aristotelian "delight" in the sense of sight is here carried to its ultimate absurdity:

Would you, the supervisor, grossly gape on,
Behold her topp'd? . . .
It is impossible you shall see this,
Were they as prime as goats, as hot as
  monkeys,
As salt as wolves, in pride; and fools as
  gross
As ignorance made drunk. . . .

(III. iii. 395-405)

This *is* the proof. Let imagination do the rest. As for Desdemona, Iago has only to remind Othello of her conduct towards her father,

She that so young could give out such a
  seeming,
To seal her father's eye up, close as oak,

(III. iii. 213)

to evoke in Othello's mind Brabantio's own words when he called Desdemona's choice a preposterous error of nature. For, "Being not deficient, blind, or lame of sense" (I. iii. 63), she surely could have chosen a more suitable husband from among the young noblemen of Venice. Is this not an "ocular proof" of Desdemona's *blindness*, thinks Othello, "And yet, how nature erring from itself . . ." (III. iii. 231)—and leaves the sentence unfinished. On the other hand, Desdemona must have "seen" whom she was marrying, whatever Brabantio or Iago may say, "For she had eyes, and chose me" (III. iii. 193). Desdemona's "insight", however, is that of a simple and unschooled soul. Her way of "apprehending" Othello was, one is tempted to say, Platonic rather than Aristotelian. "I saw Othello's visage in his mind" (I. iii. 253), and this, in all the simplicity of her soul, determined her choice. The "error" does not lie in nature, but in Othello's own blindness. What is at stake is not only his love for Desdemona but the integrity of his own self. Othello's disintegration before his own "shadow", so forcefully projected by Iago on the screen of his imagination, turns substance into a mockery and the Aristotelian "delight" in the sense of sight into unbearable anguish. When his eyes are finally "opened", Desdemona is dead, an innocent victim of the ocular proof. Blake's dictum, as applied to Othello, should read, "As a man sees, so he destroys". Othello looked into the distorting mirror held up by Iago for him to see himself. What he saw was the chaos within. Only by breaking the mirror could he free himself of the nightmare-vision. The return from the shadow to the substance is a return from life to death. Othello's conscious mind is never really involved. For had it been, he would have "seen through" Iago's machinations and corrected his vision accordingly.

Macbeth, on the other hand, is the most conscious of Shakespeare's "blind" heroes: his eyes tell him the truth, his imagination elaborates it, his mind interprets what eye and imagination so vividly perceive. Macbeth is only momentarily deceived by his wife's vision of ultimate success. Both before and after the murder of Duncan he prays for darkness. He admits to himself (and to his wife) that he is afraid of facing the ocular proof ("Look on't again I dare not"), because he knows that, in the words of Macduff, it might

destroy your sight
With a new Gorgon.

(II. iii. 77)

The darkness which accompanies us throughout the play is indeed an embodiment of evil. Macbeth's mind remains frighteningly lucid, analytical, Aristotelian. His prayer before the murder—

> The eye wink at the hand; yet let that be
> Which the eye fears, when it is done, to see—
>
> (I. iv. 52)

remains unfulfilled. One cannot impose blindness if the mind's eye compels one to see. The murder having been commited, Macbeth looks at his hands and exclaims, "This is a sorry sight" (II. ii. 20), while a few lines later he realizes with a shock of recognition that, even away from Duncan's bedroom, the ocular proof will always be with him, constantly reminding him of what his eyes have seen: "What hands are here? ha! they pluck out mine eyes" (II. ii. 58). What the eye "fears to see", the murder committed with those hands which are the true instruments of darkness, attracts and hypnotizes Macbeth beyond human endurance. Before the murder he could still visualize the universal effects of shedding Duncan's innocent blood. He knew then that even if his own eye could "wink" at his hand, other eyes would be open and then

> Pity, like a naked new-born babe . . .
> Shall blow the horrid deed in every eye
> That tears shall drown the wind.
>
> (I. vii. 24)

And if the winds are "drowned" by tears, what will the eyes see but a world of shadows where nothing is real any more, and the "tender eye of pitiful day", Helios-Hyperion, the all-knowning and the all-seeing sungod, will be darkened by the "bloody and invisible hand" of man. For truly, "Never shall sun that morrow see" (I. v. 60). All this Macbeth knows, and this knowledge "opens his eyes" in ever-increasing measure, until life itself, which had given him ocular proof of hell, is "but a walking shadow" seen by the light of a "brief candle" which, like a mirror in Macbeth's consciousness, only shows the absurdity of all human effort at "seeing" and at giving meaning to what "the eye fears to see". The archetype of evil Shakespeare is concerned with in his tragedies is, indeed, lack of insight and imaginative apprehension. The greater evil, however, is when you "see" and pray for the "blanket of the dark" to hide your soul behind a protective wall of blindness. Lady Macbeth, who suffers from no hallucinations, sees no ghosts, and contemptuously refers to Macbeth's "sights" as created by "the eye of childhood", symbolizes the ultimate evil:

> *Doctor:* You see, her eyes are open.
> *Gentlewoman:* Ay, but her sense is shut.
>
> (V. i. 24)

She, like Banquo's Ghost, has "no sepculation" in her eyes. Not only the substance, even the shadow eludes her.

IV

To see is to perceive evil. Not to see is to be at the mercy of evil. The one who sees too well but not wisely, and the one who sees not enough are equally doomed to blindness. Innocence and guilt are similarly punishable before the gods. To commit evil in ignorance of it is no less a crime than to know evil and to do it. Gloucester's crime is ignorance of evil: he committed it in the unawareness of lust. He "saw" well enough where he was going, but did not associate visual lust and all that it implies with moral evil. Edgar, undoubtedly with his father in mind, paraphrases his father's fundamental "innocence". For Gloucester's lust was not guilt-ridden. He "served the lust of my mistress' heart, and did the act of darkness with her"; he "slept in the contriving of lust, and wak'd to do it" (III. iv. 87). The moral evil of adultery is passed over in silence. If Gertrude and Cressida are condemned for their "frailty", Gloucester is unrepentant and, if anything, proud of his achievements. Anyway, "There was good sport at his making, and the whoreson must be acknowledged" (I. i. 23). The gods think otherwise. At least that is what Edgar declares when confronting Edmund at the end of the play:

> The gods are just, and of our pleasant vices
> Make instruments to plague us:
> The dark and vicious place where thee he got
> Cost him his eyes.
>
> (V. iii. 170)

Gloucester's visual lust, however, is only one aspect of his spiritual blindness. By light-heartedly ignoring the meaning of Lear's choice at the beginning of the play and by being blind to the presence of evil, he fails to see what the spectator in the theater has grasped during the very first conversation between him and Edmund. His distroted vision belongs to the same symbolic pattern as Lear's madness, the eye of the one reflecting the mind of the other, so that Gloucester's actual blindness appears merely as a climax of a process that started before the play began. The ironical implications of Cornwall's exclaiming, when putting out Gloucester's second eye, "Lest I see more, prevent it" (III. vii. 82), are not lost on us. Gloucester's eyes have "seen" little enough before his blindness. What moral mischief, corruption and evil does Cornwall wish to prevent his one remaining eye from seeing? What ocular proof should be kept secret from Gloucester? Yet his false sense of security based on his faulty eyesight will be replaced by a new and more precious "commodity". Othello and Macbeth only began seeing—if indeed they ever did—with their inner eye after they had "stumbled" into disaster. Gloucester's gift of insight comes to him like the agonizing birth-pangs of consciousness itself:

> I have no way, and therefore want no eyes;
> I stumbled when I saw: for oft 'tis seen,
> Our means secure us, and our mere defects
> Prove our commodities.

> (IV. i. 18)

His ultimate moral realization of the evil implied in his former innocence comes shortly after. Blindness shows the way from seeing to feeling, that is, from ignorance to knowledge. The pattern that Shakespeare follows is once more the archetypal process from the ocular proof and the evil associated with it, to the moral good that results from insight. It is his not-seeing that redeems him of unconscious evil. Gloucester seems to echo Oedipus' words

> What should I do with eyes
> Where all is ugliness?

Yet Gloucester goes a step further when he describes "the superfluous and lustdieted man", the innocently evil man, that is himself, as one

> That will not see
> Because he doth not feel.

> (IV. i. 68)

Neither Othello nor Macbeth could arrive at such an ultimate conclusion. For what Gloucester compares in this passage is the meaninglessness of the ocular proof, on the one hand, and the significance of imaginative awareness, which he calls "feeling", on the other. Such an awareness, however, requires more than usual moral integrity: for the truth that your imagination lets you see smells of mortality. It may conceivably be an even deeper evil than the one that the ocular proof revealed to you. When blindness and insanity meet on the heath, their conversation develops this contrast between seeing and feeling still further. Lear's madness is, in a manner of speaking, in advance of Gloucester's blindness. His sarcasm, when speaking of the "scurvy politician", is indeed an "insight" which, ironically enough, only madness could have supplied:

> *Lear:* . . . Yet you see how this world goes.
> *Gloucester:* I see it feelingly.
> *Lear:* What, art mad? A man may see how
>   this world goes with no eyes.
> Look with thine ears. . . .

> Get thee glass-eyes
> And, like a scurvy politician, seem
> To see the things thou dost not.

> (IV. vi. 151 ff.)

The reference to glass-eyes carries the archetypal metaphor still further. For they will substitute one distortion for another. They are, indeed, the ultimate symbol of the deceptive nature of all knowledge through ocular proof. They stand for the antithetical core hidden in all human experience when based on the senses rather than on spiritual awareness—symbolized in *Othello* by the contrast between Iago's seeming honesty and actual dishonesty, between Desdemona's apparent guilt and real innocence, and in *Macbeth* between his "hands" as instruments of action and his "eyes" as a means of becoming aware of the consequences of his action. We also remember Gloucester's mocking reference to spectacles at the beginning of the play:

> The quality of nothing hath not such need to hide itself. Let's see: come: if it be nothing, I shall not need spectacles.

> (I. ii. 32)

Gloucester's eyes do not help him to see beyond the "quality of nothing", to distinguish between seeming and being. Not spectacles but blindness makes him see "feelingly", just as Cordelia's love and humility enable Lear to see her as "a soul in bliss". What indeed Lear "sees" when he rediscovers the true Cordelia cannot be judged by the criteria established by the sense of sight as applied to the ocular proof. Evidently, Lear's recognition of Cordelia in terms of mutual suffering and compassion does not require the help of mirrors or spectacles. Man's sense of sight, Shakespeare constantly implies in *King Lear,* may, at best, become aware of the forms of beauty only: beauty's spiritual essence can be apprehended by the mind alone. It is the organ of this apprehension that we call insight.

The choice between the eye and the mind, between the ocular proof and spiritual awareness which Shakespeare's characters are compelled to make, is of the very essence of his tragic vision. Choosing wrongly, for the wrong reason, and deliberately, leads to evil, while an unconscious surrender to evil leads to suffering. Yet, within the total context of Shakespeare's work, compassion and love, allied to beauty, have the last word. The ultimate choice is always between Caliban's sense-perceptions (for, "As Caliban is, so he sees"), his visual lust, and Miranda's innocence of mind. In Sonnet 114 Shakespeare speaks of "love's alchemy", an alchemy of seeing. If what we see is found to be "poison", it is merely an additional variation on the theme of knowledge and the way we come by it. Beauty, by "flattering" the eye, "poisons" the understanding. Deformity appears as perfection. Caliban seems an Ariel, evil is no longer recognized as such:

> Or whether doth my mind, being crown'd with
>   you,
> Drink up the monarch's plague, this flattery?
> Or whether shall I say, mine eye saith true,

And that your love taught it this alchemy,
To make of monsters and things indigest
Such cherubins as your sweet self resemble,
Creating every bad a perfect best,
As fast as objects to his beams assemble?
O, 'tis the first: 'tis flattery in my seeing,
And my great mind most kingly drinks it up:
Mine eye well knows what with his gust is
    'greeing,
And to his palate doth prepare the cup:
        If it be poison'd, 'tis the lesser sin
        That mine eye loves it and doth first
            begin.

Neither Ferdinand nor Miranda could have spoken these lines: for this sonnet takes for granted a degree of sophistication that neither of them possesses. Yet, "love's alchemy" is with them, and even if—in the ignorance of their seeing—*they* are not conscious of the poison, Prospero *is*. It is he, then, who prevents the poison from infecting Miranda's mind. When she "sees" beauty in the shape of Ferdinand for the first time, her eye is "flattered" by the ocular proof of perfection. Prospero chides Miranda for judging by sight only. In a few lines he disposes of what has troubled the minds of many a Shakesperian hero before; the bewildering sameness of beauty perceived through the eye and evil perceived through the mind. Gifted with deeper insight, he demolishes once and for all the false sense of security associated with the ocular proof in Shakespeare's previous plays:

Thou think'st there is no more such shapes as
    he,
Having seen but him and Caliban: foolish
    wench!
To th' most of men this is a Caliban,
And they to him are angels.

                              (I. ii. 475)

Prospero knows that innocence supporting evil, though unconsciously, becomes a partner in crime. His daughter's naive acceptance of a world of evil when it comes into her sight must have filled him (as certainly it did Shakespeare) with a sense of frustration. Never having met mankind "in the raw" and, therefore, never having received the ocular proof of good and evil beyond the confines of the island, she exclaims in the face of an incomprehensible reality:

            O, Wonder,
How many goodly creatures are there here!
How beauteous mankind is! O brave new
    world,
That has such people in't!

                              (V. i. 181)

To which Prospero, rather drily, replies, "'Tis new to thee."

Can Prospero help us to reach an adequate response to Miranda's "flattery in her seeing"? His position is not without ambiguities: having discarded his "Art" he will now return to the ordinary life of men from which he had been exiled for so long a time. He will return to a world of evil, where seeming is taken for being, and the ocular proof alone is taken for evidence of truth. The story he told his daughter at the beginning of the play, we remember, is not only characterized by evil done to him by others in the past, but it also tells us of his own lack of insight and his blindness to evil. It is the archetypal story of the fair and the foul brother, the latter judging reality by the ocular proof that his eyes so amply supply, the former cultivating his blindness in all "innocence", unable to grasp the extent of evil which his eyes must have shown him so plainly. Prospero's exile on the island frees him from the ambiguities of the past: it is devoted to the training of consciousness, the disciplining of his mind, and the art of controlling nature. His "magic" is that of consciousness making him "see" and "know" beyond the limitations of the ocular proof. His training in self-discipline is really a training in the art of seeing and of responding to the light of knowledge unaffected by motivations born of "appetite". Prospero, at the end of the play, is a giver of light—Hyperion—who by forgiving others teaches them to see, to discriminate with their eye and their mind, reason no longer "pandering" will, but the one in complete harmony with the other.[8]

The victory of consciousness over the chaos created by man's appetites and lusts, that is to say, the victory of awareness over ocular proof, seems to be at the very core of *The Tempest*. Yet the act of seeing without the pitfalls of self-deception may give but little delight to Prospero. The insight he acquired on the island does not lead to the redemption of those whose success in life was achieved by evil means, such as his brother Antonio. All the ambiguities that result from too strong a reliance on the life of the senses remain intact. For Prospero himself may be taken to be a victim of his own Art, a fact which—if it proves anything at all—points at the intrinsic absurdity of the human condition. For what Prospero "sees" when he confronts the world of his evil-thinking and evil-doing brother and his associates is neither brave nor new. It is the archetypal world of beautiful shapes and evil intentions. They neither are "insubstantial" nor "such stuff as dreams are made on". They are of Caliban's family even if externally polished and using the language of civilized life. Prospero's forgiveness means little or nothing to them.

Will he be able to face the "Caliban within" having failed to give light to that "thing of darkness"? The contemporary spectator may well ask himself the question when he reaches the end of *The Tempest* and looks for the substance beyond the shadow in the looking-glass. He may well ask himself what good Prospero's disciplined consciousness may do to him if all that it reveals to him is a civilization of the worldly-wise, those who look at evil with their eyes open and whose natural habitat is the dark chaos of hell rather than the clear, all-seeing light of the mind. What does Hyperion do in the company of these petty evil-doers who "see" what they want to see—the ocular proof of Prospero's weakness—and are blind to his strength, which lies in his virtue of compassion, "who do not see because they do not feel"?

The contemporary spectator, having experienced an anguish and an exile the frightfulness of which far surpasses anything Shakespeare could have known, may be excused if he attempts to refer Prospero's predicament to his own. For Prospero's tale translated into a contemporary idiom appears to be an attempt at interpreting the human mind in terms of its power to contemplate the senseless. The following may not be Prospero's voice, but it speaks in his spirit:

> No one will live his fate, knowing it to be absurd, unless he does everything to keep before him that absurd brought to light by consciousness. . . . Living is keeping the absurd alive. Keeping it alive is, above all, contemplating it.[9]

The myth of the absurd is, to a considerable extent, the myth of the ocular proof. Oedipus, blind, anguished, and exiled, is the archetype. His suffering stands for man's struggle out of the false security of the ocular proof towards the life-creating light of consciousness, man stumbling "when he saw" and gaining insight by defeating the urges of the unconscious. It is the absurdity of his suffering, the gradually dawning recognition that "there is no sun without shadow" and that "it is essential to know the night" that relates Oedipus to Prospero no less than to the contemporary spectator. By dispensing with his "Art" when confronting reality in the shape of Miranda's "brave new world", Prospero accepts nature, human nature, and his own awareness of it, as his only guides. Knowing of the absurdity of all effort and aspiration that is merely human and therefore limited by the ocular proof that guides them, Prospero, a "blind man eager to see who knows that the night has no end",[10] joins those whose evil he had forgiven in an attempt at "nobler reason" on their return-journey to civilization.

Ferdinand and Miranda will accompany him on his voyage. Their innocent presence will keep that precarious balance between the absurd and the beautiful from toppling. It will help Prospero, if not to forget, at least to circumvent his awareness of imminent chaos. The two young lovers, ignorant of the distinction between shadow and substance, will be nature's ocular proof of love's alchemy: a return to the primeval myth of manking before their eyes began to "see"—and knew the meaning of evil.

Notes

[1] The reference here may be to the *First Alcibiades* (132, 133). In Jowett's translation: "If the eye is to see itself, it must look at the eye, and at that part of the eye where sight which is the virtue of the eye resides." For a further discussion of this theme in *Troilus and Cressida* see L. C. Knights, *Some Shakespearean Themes* (London: Chatto and Windus, 1959), p. 70.

[2] *King Oedipus,* translated by E. F. Watling (Penguin Books, 1947).

[3] Plato, *Phaedo,* Jowett's translation (Pocket Books, Inc., 1950), p. 79.

[4] *Phaedo,* p. 80.

[5] *Phaedo,* p. 148.

[6] *Phaedo,* p. 102. See also Edith Sitwell, *A Notebook on William Shakespeare* (London: Macmillan, 1950), especially the chapter on *King Lear,* p. 47 et seq.

[7] *Metaphysics,* Book A, I, 980a, 21.

[8] Modern depth-psychology has a good deal to say about the sun-symbolism with reference to consciousness. Myths make use of this primeval image of the eye giving and receiving light, seeing as well as seen, discriminating as well as being an object of discrimination. See Erich Neumann, *The Origins and History of Consciousness* (New York: The Bollingen Library, 1954), II, 311 ff.

[9] Albert Camus, *The Myth of Sisyphus* (New York: Vintage Books, 1959), p. 40.

[10] Camus, p. 90.

Lloyd Davis (essay date 1993)

SOURCE: "The Figure of Woman," in *Guise and Disguise: Rhetoric and Characterization in the English Renaissance,* University of Toronto Press, 1993, pp. 129-66, 204-11.

[*In the essay that follows, Davis examines Shakespeare's use of transsexual disguise.*]

> A woman's face with Nature's own hand painted
> Hast thou, the master mistress of my passion;
>
>   William Shakespeare, Sonnet 20

Thus is the manifest and exalted, even as she is masked and lost, in discursive parades that set her outside her self; ideally offered to the oratorical disputes between men.

Luce Irigaray
The Speculum of the Other Woman

I

Near the end of her essay on disguise in Elizabethan drama, M.C. Bradbrook asserts that after Shakespeare stopped writing for the stage the 'deeper implications of disguise . . . did not long survive,' suggesting that dissembling characters could no longer aptly represent issues of selfhood and identity. Even by 1609 a certain predictability is found in the motif. The example is taken from Beaumont and Fletcher's *Philaster*. 'Bellario's true sex is not revealed till the end, though by this time any theatrical page might be assumed to be a woman in disguise.'[1] In this view it seems that an audience accustomed to stage effects and plot twists, its sophistication registered in the exclusive cost of attending the private theatres, automatically expects such reversals of appearance and persona. Many plays in the period show the donning of transvestite garb and include complaints against the distresses of sexual disguise. The heroine of Lyly's *Gallathea* laments, 'O woulde the gods had made mee as I seeme to be, or that I might safelie bee what I seeme not'; Shakespeare's Viola declaims, 'Disguise, I see thou art a wickedness.'[2] In these confessional asides, the process of sexual dissemblance is made a thematic issue. With the recurring treatment of the processes and dilemmas of cross-dressing, even for plays like *Epicoene* and *Philaster* where the cross-dresser is disguised from the start, the impact seems to reside less in startling revelations than in a gradual build-up and complication of familiar issues and theatrical tropes.

In performance a 'theatrical competence' shared by spectator and actor could emphasize such themes and consider gender as a key part of the dramatic process.[3] Transvestite roles could be exaggerated to remind the audience who is and isn't wearing the pants. Numerous scenes allow for such emphasis: Lyly has Gallathea and Phillida try to learn from each other how boys behave; Shakespeare provides the comic duel between Cesario and Aguecheek; Ganymede embarrassingly faints when hearing of Orlando's wound; and Epicoene could swagger every now and then. No doubt there were extra insights and pleasures to be gained for those who watched and didn't suspend disbelief. And perhaps the more readily these insights were had, the more they were to be enjoyed: in recognizing the male actor beneath a female character impersonating a man, or beneath a male character who pretends to be a woman; glimpsing roles and identities baroquely but not opaquely layered on top of and relativizing each other. On account of these frequently compounding theatrical cues—the sort of plot and character reversals that Virginia Woolf wryly uses to exemplify the Elizabe-

than period in *Between the Acts*—Bradbrook infers that androgynous disguise was, if not passé, a generic commonplace that audiences anticipated, understood, and were satisfied to see again.[4]

The period's continuing religious and moral debates over theatricality, disguise, and 'excesse of Apparrell,'[5] especially in reference to sexuality and gender, undermine this thesis of pervasive acceptance of dramatic cross-dressing. The plays' cultural context informs their critical perception. As Jean Howard has recently noted, theatricality and dress were often seen to challenge an 'official ideology of social stasis' that sought to reinforce gender and class distinctions.[6] A well-known Elizabethan exchange over theatrical cross-dressing had pitted Rainolds against Gager and Gentili, the former arguing that 'even the shortest use of women's clothing is sufficient to stir up unclean passions' in both actors and audience. Rainolds combines homophobic and misogynist themes to attack a 'lust' compounded by seeing boys dressed as women.[7]

This dispute over theatrical costume exemplifies conservative religious-moral disapproval and suspicion towards fashion in the period. The 'Homilie against Excesse of Apparrell' warns of the threats to social rank: 'that euery man behold and consider his owne vocation, in as much as GOD hath appointed euery man his degree and office, within the limittes whereof it behoueth him to keepe himself. Therefore all may not looke to weare like apparell, but euery one according to his degree, as GOD hath placed him' (103). It goes on to reveal both a specific focus against women's dress and sexual desire, citing the patristic source of Tertullian, and an anxious concern over the blurring of gender distinctions through the disguisings of fashion: 'For the proude and haughtie stomacks of the daughters of England, are so maintained with diuers disguised sortes of costly apparell, that as *Tertullian* an auncient father saith, there is left no difference in apparell betweene an honest matrone and a common strumpet. Yea many men are become so effeminate, that they care not what they spend in disguising, euer desiring new toyes and inuenting new fashions' (105). The disputes over costume and fashion were to grow in number and intensity under the Stuarts, less on account of a rising tide of puritanism than, as Margot Heinemann points out, because of the increasingly complex array of cultural, political, and religious attitudes that theatre and fashion were taken as signifying.[8] Though cross-dressing may have begun to lose dramatic surprise, perhaps to the point of being predicted by theatre audiences, it retained an urgent social significance that could circumscribe the throne, with Prynne being punished for slandering the queen in *Histriomastix*.

These opposing social functions and effects of dress, cross-dressing, and theatricality reveal their complicated relation to the period's sexual politics. On the one hand, dramatic transvestism might be seen to challenge cultural impositions of gender and identity. Such is Phyllis Rackin's view that in 'inverting the offstage associations, stage illusion radically subverted the gender divisions of the Elizabethan world.'[9] In these critical terms, the attacks and pronouncements against theatricality and dress respond to such subversive gestures. On the other hand, gender divisions may not have been as rigid as some critics might suggest; the concerns of the homilies seem to acknowledge that more flexible images of sexual identity were in social circulation outside the theatre. In addition, the place of the stage was shifting from the liberties of 'whatever could not be contained within the strict bounds of the community'[10] to a more central, fixed locus, with the opening of private theatres complementing court performances, shows at the Inns of Court, and royal and mayoral processions. Along with this shift, images of transsexual disguise seem to have been being accommodated if not co-opted by an urban ideology that was starting to fragment and limit rituals of inversion and misrule[11] and to reconsider the social roles of women as attitudes towards marriage and the family began to alter.[12]

Despite definitive interpretations by modern critics, then, dramatic cross-dressing frequently evades univocal readings as either subversive or stabilizing. It may work normatively or transgressively, within the theatre and without, representing the range of cultural functions that gender performs. Specific attitudes towards androgyny as a type of worrying deviance are doubtless being worked through in the hybrid figures of dramatic cross-dressing. Yet as the contradictory evaluations of these androgynous images suggest, they also serve to convey and question general myths and concerns about sexuality. As Harold Garfinkel affirms in his study of sexual passing, the 'intersexed' figure discloses the 'omnirelevance of sexual statuses to affairs of daily life' by compressing, juxtaposing, and disturbing a 'community of understandings' that would envisage sexuality as 'a natural fact of life,' and in so doing efface it 'as a natural and *moral* fact of life.'[13] Dramatic androgyny, which Bradbrook and others seem to consider a predictable reversal of either dramatic or social personae, is more interestingly used to stage the complex ambiguities of sexuality and the social construction of gender. It interrogates conventionalized cultural and literary discourses through which apparently straight male and female characters can be depicted.[14]

In introducing practices of expedient change that are socially and personally motivated, transvestite disguise undermines commonsense presumptions of gender as a 'temporally identical thing over all historical and prospective circumstance and possible experiences . . . the self-same thing in essence.'[15] It relates sexual identity to the ethopoetic processes of characterization and so opens up questions concerning the motives that underlie sexuality and the desires that interact with gender. The juxtaposing of a 'natural' and a disguised sexual ethos suggests the dialogic conflict between essentialist and sophistical notions of selfhood. Particularly in plays of the period, where confusions among characters are commonly reconciled by confessions of 'true' selfhood, the interpersonal and social stakes of gender are highlighted. Reviled and accepted, socially marginalized and enclosed, androgynous disguise concentrates a contested ideology of sexual identity. In so doing, and as the repeated references of the homily on apparel to the Bible and to Tertullian suggest, it rehearses feminist and misogynist themes from the classical and Christian canons and enables many Renaissance texts to engage this discursive context. As well as being a familiar theatrical device and social concern, cross-dressing figures in a textual tradition of gendered characterization and the rhetorical construction of sexuality. This tradition will be examined in this chapter by considering the connections dramatic cross-dressing has, first with the rhetorical practices of epideixis and misogyny, both of which seek to presume and construct unambiguous gender roles, and then with an androgynous ethos that emerges in a range of Renaissance texts through the speech act of confession. A text's confessional revelation may serve more to question the determined gender that its preceding discourse of character has already presumed than finally to confirm its characters' sexual identities.

The structure of the androgynous figure is metonymic. It represents the interchange of parts and names of identities. The deep ethopoetic reference of rhetoric, implicit in the conception of the 'proper' as that which is self-sufficient and self-possessed, re-emerges in the disruptions to univocal meaning and identity that Elizabethan definitions of metonymy note:

> when a word hath a proper signification of the owne, and being referred to an other thing, hath an other meaning.[16]

> Metonimia, when of things that be nigh together, wee put one name for another.[17]

Through these definitions, metonymy may either exchange meanings or, by virtue of its marked rhetoricity, reaffirm 'proper' meaning.[18] It inscribes the dialogic process of androgyny, for in terms of gender, cross-dressing relocates social-sexual roles, parts, and names, with similarly ambiguous effects of stabilization and subversion.

In the deeper rhetorical logic that informs many Renaissance texts, however, the conventional, naturalized order of gender and discourse is based on man, and woman signifies a deviation from masculine essence.

Ian Maclean has traced this order to the hierarchical thinking of Aristotelian metaphysics:

> In the distinction of male and female may be discerned Aristotle's general tendency to produce dualities in which one element is superior and the other inferior. The male principle in nature is associated with active, formative and perfected characteristics, while the female is passive, material and deprived, desires the male in order to become complete. The duality male/female is therefore paralleled by the dualities active/passive, form/matter, act/potency, perfection/imperfection, completion/incompletion, possession/deprivation.[19]

We might add a further parallel, the rhetorical duality of the proper and the figurative, with its implications for self-representation. In this opposition, woman embodies figurative speech; she is the rhetorically improper persona who may disrupt or confirm the categories of gendered ethos.

Typically, this metonymic femaleness structures androgyny in two ways. First, it may disguise maleness and cause androgyny, as in the induction to *The Taming of the Shrew*. 'if the boy have not a woman's gift / To rain a shower of commanded tears, / An onion will do well for such a shift' (Ind i.124-6). Here the onion is not only an external prop that enables the boy to act like a woman; it also signifies the dissembled guise of crying that women characteristically assume to produce certain emasculating effects upon men. Secondly, femaleness emerges through the guise of 'masculine usurp'd attire' and forms the end point of androgyny.[20] In each case, a prior male ethos is corrupted by a belated feminizing that metonymically constructs androgyny.[21] Femaleness can be the cause of androgyny, as in *Taming,* or its effect, as in *Twelfth Night* and *Philaster.* In both cases, the possibility of corruption confirms the prior presence and wholeness of the male ethos. The causal exchange in these examples reifies an original maleness and woman's belated figural function. Such logic is also metonymic in structure, as one of Peacham's examples of the trope suggests: 'when the efficient cause is understood of the effect . . . when the effect is gathered by the efficient.' This interchangeable causality reinforces the function of androgyny as a rhetorical motif in texts of the period, one that affects their discursive logic and tropes.[22]

The metonymic structure engenders the proper order of meaning, wherein a privileged 'male' tenor holds an essential priority as 'the underlying idea or principal subject which the vehicle or figure means.'[23] This order posits the representing female figure as a supplement to the 'principal subject.' The underlying meaning of maleness is displaced into a feminized and feminizing figural discourse and acquires a consequent androgyny in its characterization. The logic intrinsic to

this rhetoric again works with ambiguous cultural effects. On the one hand, it may envisage an original male ideal as threatened by the figural self-difference introduced through an emasculating vehicle or trope. On the other hand, this rhetorical logic may also function to grant masculinist discourse a presence and an influence that are based upon the absence of an archetypal androgynous figure. Such seems to be the moral of Aristophanes' myth of the hermaphroditic origins of sexual love in the *Symposium*: 'So you see, gentlemen, how far back we can trace our innate love for one another, and how this love is always trying to redintegrate our former nature, to make two into one, and to bridge the gulf between one human being and another.'[24] Aristophanes' lost third sex explains and naturalizes the existing hierarchical relationship between the sexes; it is this relationship's origin and its eternal goal. Through a similar mythic structure, figurative language was often seen as the archetypal norm that originates and justifies social institutions. Cicero's classic statement in *De Oratore* on 'the highest achievements of eloquence' was picked up by rhetoricians like Wilson and Puttenham, who held that poets 'were the first law-makers to the people, and the first politicians, devising all expedient means for th' establishment of Common wealth.'[25] Through these interconnected myths of rhetorical, sexual, and social origin and reunion, the threat to patriarchal discourse of a figurative androgyny that emerges in other contexts may be defused, again with a suggestion of the social ambiguity of the androgynous image.

This mythic discourse underlies the dramatistic motif of transvestite disguise. The essentialist ethopoetic tradition, re-envoiced by male speakers in patriarchal contexts, may be interrogated rather than simply inverted by the androgynous figures. Androgyny conveys neither an antithetical nor a confirming social deviance; rather the figure may confound cultural priorities and systems of gender and identity by revealing their ambiguous interdependence. As a kind of femininized masculinity, androgyny exemplifies the uncertain ethopoetic effects of the trope of disguise, which sets up various categories of identity like the prince and the subject and then calls them into question through the equivocal terms that constitute them. The rhetorical means of establishing and expressing these categories exposes them to dialogic challenge.

As a tragicomedy, a hybrid genre that 'combines old sexual discourses in new ways,'[26] a sexual-disguise play like *Philaster* stages a similar disruption of notions of gender and identity and their function in social order. Indeed, Beaumont and Fletcher's text seems a particularly significant example of the ethopoetic issues raised by an androgynous rhetoric. With many similar texts it can be considered 'as a play about masking, about the conscious and unconscious assumption of false identities and about levels of self-knowledge and self-deception,' as Coppélia Kahn observes of *Twelfth Night*.[27] Yet in contrast to such Shakespearean versions, *Philaster* does not conclude with sociosexual order seemingly restored, even though the protagonist regains his throne and wins his beloved. The androgynous figure Bellario/Euphrasia remains outside the political-marriage finale, a reminder of social limits imposed on and by orthodox sexuality and proper selfhood. The character exceeds the return to the norms of gender and identity, the restoration of 'personal and interpersonal "oneness" ' that often seems central to the dénouement of Shakespearean romantic comedy.[28] Such exclusion foregrounds questions about the neat closure of events in *Twelfth Night* that are half-hinted at in Orsino's final speech, which registers Viola's continuing androgyny, the constant dependence of gender on guise, and his own ambiguous desire. Like Rosalind's epilogue to *As You Like It,* these words toy with the idea of transvestism, sustained beyond the theatrical frame, while seeming to reject it: 'Cesario, come— / For so you shall be while you are a man; / But when in other habits you are seen, / Orsino's mistress, and his fancy's queen' (V.i.385-8).

A marked supernumerary within the play's social world, Bellario also serves to focus the stylistic excess often attributed to Beaumont and Fletcher's work onto questions of gender and self-representation. This excess is often contrasted unfavourably with Shakespearean discourse. As Bradbrook's comments suggest, Beaumont and Fletcher are seen to be flawed, their defects due to their relative belatedness to Shakespeare. Indeed, against Shakespeare's prior, proper, and singular corpus, their collaborative work is constructed in terms of a discursive deviance not dissimilar to that of androgyny. It offers no univocal image of the author. Its unresolved ambiguities can be seen as signs of incompletion in comparison to the late romances, typically considered as 'genres of wish-fulfillment' and of personal synthesis.[29] It is also regarded as a kind of decadence that parasitically threatens the integrity of Shakespeare's text, either by corrupting earlier masterpieces and paragons of characterization, or, as when Fletcher worked with Shakespeare on *The Two Noble Kinsmen,* by vitiating the bard's efforts and very identity: 'He and Beaumont had pulled Hamlet down to the comic level of Philaster; now Shakespeare's Palamon and Arcite could be irreverently handled in the same play as Shakespeare was presenting.'[30] If not decadent, Beaumont and Fletcher's style is regarded as 'rhetorical' in a merely figural sense, where 'we consciously follow the ebb and flow of Philaster's passion, responding to his diatribes and laments as declamatory exercises.'[31] In this view, the text's 'spatial design' formalizes its characterization, placing 'ultimate stress . . . less upon the nature of the participants than upon the artifice which employs them.'[32] Just as androgyny may concentrate key notions of gender and identity, the intensity of this 'artifice,' rather than leading away

from characterization, may test the ethopoetic process through which generically and socially standard characters, especially the heroic male protagonist, are portrayed. The rhetorical rhythms of Beaumont and Fletcher's work put into question both the subjective investments that motivate self-representation, and perhaps the not-unrelated critical investments that motivate the icon of Shakespeare. For running through and determining these criticisms of their work is a consistent psychological essentialism that derives from early-nineteenth-century celebrations of the Shakespearean rhetoric of character, a tradition exemplified by Schlegel's contrasting comment that Beaumont and Fletcher's 'poetry was not an inward devotion of the feeling and imagination, but a means to obtain brilliant results. Their first object was effect.'[33]

The political and sexual dilemmas in *Philaster* that are concentrated in the triangle of Philaster, Arethusa, and Bellario rest on the identity of the last. The androgynous woman is here central to personal and social certainty. Her characterization seems to reveal both the discursive presuppositions of gender and the inconsistencies of identity that these presuppositions would suppress. The discontinuity of selfhood and gender emerges most tellingly in the impassioned speeches of the protagonist, Philaster. In their extreme fervour, and indeed through their resounding misogynistic echoes of Hamlet, his complaints against Arethusa and Bellario soar beyond the 'proper' norms of the heroic male. In her pivotal and inconstant role, Bellario both triggers this androgynous rhetoric and then seems to restore its gendered balance at the play's end. Her word discloses the instabilities of a masculinist discourse that pursues its ethopoetic goals through the figure of woman, its rhetorical 'master mistress.' For this project inevitably deconstructs the masculine ideal it aims to realize through revealing the figure of woman within that ideal. Woman is the figural difference that both guarantees and denies the *telos* of masculine characterization.[34] The significance of Bellario's androgynous disguise lies, then, not only in its display of themes of sexual self-knowledge and deception but in its revelation of the discursive means through which sexual selves can be known and deceived. Citing dramatic and non-dramatic precursors through the over-determined trope of androgyny and a familiar story-line of usurpation, restoration, and sexual politics, *Philaster* replays a rhetorical tradition of gendered ethopoesis.

II

The main features of this ethopoetic tradition can begin to be seen in the classic rhetorical texts of male praise for woman, Gorgias' and Isocrates' encomia on Helen. Their well-wrought styles disclose a paradoxical relationship between the speaking male and the spoken female, the two figures that the encomia necessarily depict. The man's praise, which begins by presuming his separate perspective upon woman, gradually intertwines them, as he becomes reliant on her figure or image to portray himself and so fulfil what Joel Fineman calls 'the *cogito* of praise . . . "I praise therefore I am." '[35] This interdependence destines the loss of an original ethos that the speaker would understand as uttering his words of praise and then being reinforced by them. Androgynous disguise constructs a similar ambiguity regarding a prior ethos, not only for the disguised figure but for others who find their own gender and identity being disturbed by his or her presence. If the paradox of praise is 'not simply the negation of straightforward praise but, instead, its peculiar imitative double, a rhetorical doubling,'[36] then androgyny is, like misogyny, an analogue of praise, as the ethopoetic doubling of straight gender. The classical encomia instigate this sexual doubling in a rhetoric of characterization that later works will both imitate and revise.

Gorgias' text initially reacts to the canonical dominance of a proper, heroic, male ethos that derives from the Homeric works and that casts Helen antithetically as a perpetual 'reminder of the calamities.'[37] The orator will conclude by claiming 'I have removed by my speech a woman's infamy' (31), construing the speech as his own heroic rescue of the fair sex.[38] Though saving Helen from cultural blame, the *Encomium* deprives her of any agency, characterizing her as the object of male strength, speech, and desire—'she was seized by force, or persuaded by speeches, (or captivated by love)' (23)—all of which are seen as functions of each other and are reproduced by the speaker's own powerful rhetoric:

> the persuader, because he compelled, is guilty; but the persuaded, because she was compelled by his speech, is wrongly reproached . . . The power of speech bears the same relation to the ordering of the mind as the ordering of drugs bears to the constitution of bodies . . . Things that we see do not have the nature which we wish them to have but the nature which each of them actually has; and by seeing them the mind is moulded in its character too . . . So if Helen's eye pleased by Alexander's [ie, Paris'] body, transmitted an eagerness and striving of love to her mind, what is surprising?
>
> (27-9)

This ancient, mechanistic account of perception empowers Paris' sexual identity and weakens Helen's. Her love is an effect of perception, and her perception is an effect of Paris' original presence. She experiences the same kind of passive sight and selfhood that Shakespeare's Cressida complains about—'The error of our eye directs our mind' (V.ii.106)—where woman's random gaze is cognitively overpowering, subjecting her emotionally and sexually to the masculine presence she observes.[39] Paris' persuasive mastery thus forms a rhetorical parallel to his pre-verbal, visual

essence. Together they construct a discourse of masterful desire and sexuality that reifies male speech on the basis of female *pathos*.

Gorgias' self-congratulatory closing consolidates this pattern. He assumes a rhetorical control analogous to Paris'. Helen, the apparent topic, is overshadowed by a speaker whose own discursive pleasure emerges as the ultimate motive of the *Encomium*: 'I have removed by my speech a woman's infamy, I have kept to the purpose which I set myself at the start of my speech; I attempted to dispel injustice of blame and ignorance of belief, I wished to write the speech as an encomium of Helen and an amusement for myself' (31). The confessional statement of intentions reveals a self-reflexive aim that realizes satisfaction more from its own words than from women and that represents itself metonymically through the figure of Helen. She is the occasion for a rhetorical narcissism to exercise and enjoy itself by declaiming upon favourite topoi, which, as E.R. Curtius suggestively defines, generally work as 'intellectual themes, suitable for development and modification at the orator's pleasure.'[40]

In this view, Helen is an effect of praise that reveals and satisfies the male ethos. As Lauren Silberman has noted, Spenser seems to criticize this reductive transposition of female character through the legend of Britomart: 'Here haue I cause, in men iust blame to find, / That in their proper prayse too partiall bee, / And not indifferent to woman kind.'[41] Men's 'proper prayse' of the other is a process of self-praise and definition, that also erases woman's role in history. Gorgias' *Encomium* at first seems to acknowledge Helen's historical causality. Through her beauty she produces, though not the Trojan war itself (caused by 'great reasons'), the rhetorical tradition of the Trojan war: 'In very many she created very strong amorous desires; with a single body she brought together many bodies of men who had great pride for great reasons' (21). If the physical and martial priority of the men seems momentarily displaced by and dependent on Helen's 'amorous' influence, this inspirational effect is in turn eclipsed by the history of their discourse and action. Her causal role is used to undermine her own agency.

These historical and subjective transpositions between cause and effect also appear in Isocrates' 'Encomium on Helen.' Early in the text, Helen is the vehicle through which men's great deeds can be spoken of: 'I think this will be the strongest assurance for those who wish to praise Helen, if we can show that those who loved and admired her were themselves more deserving of admiration than other men.'[42] As topos, Helen allows these male feats to be eternally replayed in oratorical arenas and verbal battles—masculinist rhetoric as warfare.[43] Isocrates' title echoes Gorgias' title, and he vigorously attacks his rivals: 'They ought to give up the use of this claptrap, which pretends to prove things by verbal quibbles, which in fact have long since been refuted, and to pursue the truth' (4). 'Helen' figures the truth of Isocrates' speech as opposed to the 'erstic disputations' of others (6), and he glorifies her beauty as a sign of virtue, which is 'the most beautiful of ways of living' (59). As sign, Helen is then precluded from the virtue won by men and seems only to serve as a pretext to man's utterance, which circulates among a closed male audience: 'while it is partly because of Homer's art, yet it is chiefly through her that his poem has such charm and has become so famous among all men' (65).

Despite her rhetorical effacement, Helen assumes a responsibility for male discourse through both the metonymic interchange of cause for effect and the paradox of praise. As figurative vehicle she allows her praisers not merely to talk of her but to speak. Only on the basis of her metonymic effect—that is, on the basis of her silence—can the linked ideals of male sexual, military, and oratorical performance and pre-eminence be represented, as the orator tries to display his own archetypal ethos. However, Helen's figural function as a metonym of male virtue sets up a rhetorical process that from the start defers this singular ethopoetic goal. The male speaker is reliant upon her. The encomia necessarily employ an androgynous rhetoric, with woman as vehicle, that undermines the hierarchy of univocal gender and masculine identity that the epideictic structure presumes to reinforce.

This ambiguous rhetorical relation between man and woman continues and intensifies in the Renaissance reproduction of the classical topoi. The subservient discursive function of woman appears in various texts, quite strikingly in *Cymbeline* for example, where it motivates the bet between Posthumus Leonatus and Iachimo on Imogen's virtue, a bet that is in effect an 'oratorical dispute' at her expense, and one that values its own words above her. If, Posthumus says, Iachimo wins, 'I am no further your enemy; she is not worth our debate' (I.iv.165-6). On the other hand, what Thomas Greene calls the 'heuristic' form of Renaissance *imitatio,* which emphasizes derivation plus distance from the original,[44] seems to draw out questions concerning woman's rhetorical place and the hierarchy of gender it is used to represent in the classical works. Marlowe's 'interrogative text' *Doctor Faustus* uses Helen to dramatize the fall of the protagonist's essential Christian ethos. Rather than confirming his selfhood, she marks its sexual loss, an ironic inversion of the neo-Platonic soul's union with the godhead: 'Sweet Helen, make me immortal with a kiss: / Her lips suck forth my soul, see where it flies. / Come, Helen, come, give me my soul again' (xviii.101-3).[45] In *Troilus and Cressida,* masculine ideals of virtue, figured in the encomia through Helen's incomparable beauty, are challenged by Thersites' cynicism, which

would rewrite the Trojan war as a discourse of male jealousy, 'All the argument is a whore and a cuckold' (II.iii.68). He demythologizes the tradition of martial masculinity given to the Renaissance through the classical tradition, as does La Rochefoucauld in his seventh maxim on the rivalry of Augustus and Antony, by affirming that its motive lies in a jealous desire for absolute, heroic selfhood that nonetheless is determined by its mediation through the sexual other and rivalry with other men.[46]

These Renaissance revisions of classical plots and personae represent a fractured structure of gender. The hierarchical order of male and female, with its attendant oppositions of whole and part, tenor and vehicle, is not simply reversed; instead the possibilities of their dialogic relationship are raised. The essentialism that underlies the encomia is complicated as the male ethos reveals its interdependence with woman even when, as in misogynistic texts, she is openly repudiated. Although it is the negative form of epideixis, misogynist rhetoric reproduces the structural paradoxes of gender inscribed in the encomia. Within the recurring disclaimers and criticisms of female character and the implicit justifications of male identity sounds a discourse of androgynous ethopoesis.[47]

III

Thomas Wilson's *Arte of Rhetorique* adopts a consistently misogynistic tone that both rehearses the masculinist premises of the rhetorical tradition and exposes them to the paradox of ethopoetic gender. It opens with an epistle to Lord Dudley that expresses themes of rhetorical domination and desire. The epistle is epideictic; yet unlike the encomia on Helen and more like a love sonnet, it seeks to woo its addressee—to persuade Dudley to offer support and patronage. As well as stroking the noble ego, the letter reveals a conflict of desire between praiser and praised, in the request and rejection, superiority and inferiority, that underlie its address: 'If pleasure maie provoke vs, what greater delite doe wee knowe, then to see a whole multitude, with the onely talke of man, rauished and drawne which way he liketh best to haue them?'[48] Wilson makes explicit the rhetorical desire that was noted in narcissistic form in Gorgia's speech. He gives a sensual twist to the conventional description of the orator's aims to 'instruct, move and charm his hearers,'[49] depicting the interaction between the wills and passions of speaker and audience in terms of sexual domination that were not unfamiliar in the Renaissance. Relations between the passions and the will were commonly coded into terms of gender and power, with the will sometimes being stereotyped as an empowered female, because of its exceptional sway. Thus in *A Helpe to Discovrse,* a sort of everyman's commonplace book, the anonymous authors instruct that 'Will is as free as Emperor, cannot be limited, barred of her liberty, or made will by any coaction, when she is vnwilling.'⁵⁰ Here a misogynist trope, suggesting the inversion of the patriarchal body politic that Elizabeth could represent, underlies the explanation of the will's power and forms the basis of a common image of psychological affect.

Wilson's model of rhetorical pleasure reproduces a visual, verbal, and sexual hierarchy of provocation and stimulation. 'Wee' watch the male orator watching the results of his words; and in each case watching is full of knowing delight. The masterful orator moves and positions the passive audience, taking them 'which way he liketh best to have them.' Their multitude increases his mastery and 'our' voyeuristic pleasure. This appreciation vicariously connects 'vs' to him within his system of pleasure, for we enjoy what he enjoys even if we don't do it ourselves. The implication is that, having watched and entered this visual order, we could do it too. Wilson himself assumes a double role as the virile orator and the aroused observer, his company with 'vs' removing any offensive hint of emasculation for Lord Dudley.

The sexually loaded description feminizes the orator's audience, subjecting its passion to his will. The monologic rhetorical address that derives from Aristotle, with its effects of *pathos,* is sexualized. The audience's pleasure in its ravishment remains dependent on the speaker's primary, causal desire. The imagery of ravishment indicates the gendered presumptions of the rhetoric: an opposed audience and speaker, with 'maleness' supposedly precluded from the former and fixed within the speaking function. Yet a male presence reappears in the specular *pathos* of 'delite' that 'wee'—a second audience including the author, Lord Dudley, and other would-be rhetoricians—feel from watching and hearing the speaker's still-primary verbal desire. This second male function, although it is not the addressed, feminized audience but one that voyeuristically observes and listens to the masterful speaker, reflects the impressed passivity and pleasure of that first audience. The resultant ambiguity of male pleasure as ravisher and ravished—the ravisher ravished—inheres most strongly in the paradoxical role of 'Wilson' himself, who as the enjoyer of this rhetoric is, like Gorgias, the narcissistic object of his own discourse.

The epistle tries simultaneously to establish a conventional hierarchy of verbal gender and to suppress the androgynous ethos that thereby emerges. As the *Arte* continues, the system of macho rhetorical pleasure is reinforced by the transfer of the male audience's passive pleasure to woman. This stereotyping builds to a clichéd misogynist joke that would preclude woman from speech. Tracing this development through Wilson's text reveals the metonymic structure of androgyny implicit in its masculinist rhetoric.

Explaining what he calls the first kind of oratory, 'praise, or dispraise,' and thus again suggesting the importance of epideixis, Wilson notes that when speaking about people their sex is an important theme: 'To bee born a manchilde, declares a courage, grauitie, and constancie. To be borne a woman, declares weaknesse of spirit, neshnesse of body, and ficklenesse of mind' (13).⁵¹ Gender is an essential sign of one's physical, emotional, and cognitive self. The emphasis on birth suggests a pre-social fixedness to these traits. Since gender 'declares' them, it becomes a discursive form that, through an apparently natural priority, presents a zero degree of social contingency. And as the truths of character uttered at birth by gender seem incontrovertible, they may function rhetorically as commonplaces.

Nature and gender reinforce each other to establish a uniform type of encomiastic speech that becomes the model for other rhetorical genres. Uniformity exerts a certain pressure upon the way in which topics are to be represented. A predilection for similarity and consistency is a function not only of content but of rhetorical form, as Wilson demonstrates in an example from a set piece on love: 'Naturall love, is an inward good will, that we beare to our parents, wife, children, or any other that be nigh of kinne to us, stirred thereunto not onely by our flesh, thinking that like as we would loue ourselues, so wee should loue them, but also by a likenesse of minde' (33). This homogenization of love into terms of nature and inwardness is achieved through the use of 'similitude,' which is later defined as 'a likenesse when two thinges, or more then two, are so compared and resembled together, that they both in some one propertie seeme like' (188). In this scheme, similitude is a figure of comparison that does not deviate from proper meaning as does metonymy ('when a word hath a proper signification of the owne, and being referred to an other thing, hath an other meaning' [175]). Through the visual notion of resemblance, similitude revises difference as a unitary 'likenesse,' recalling the narcissistic ethos that would structure masculinist rhetoric. The slippage between the discursive functions of likeness is then exemplified by its rhetorical pressure on the topic of love. Likeness bases different types of love on self-love, 'like as we would loue ourselues, so wee should loue them,' and then locates this 'Naturall love' in an 'inward good will' that preserves the patriarchal family of 'parents, wife, [and] children.' The narcissistic motive translates love into a unity founded on the intrinsic identity of male selfhood and its 'inward' will. On this basis, love's place in a reflexive order of masculine identity and desire is established.

As a rhetorical form, likeness represents a number of culturally valued relationships. In its construction of love, it inscribes rules of personal interaction that seem to foster altruism and direct desire outwards. The premise of this orientation to the other, however, is a masculine self-identity, perhaps not so much assumed as sought, that remains as the object of desire. Thomas Wright suggests the presence of this specular self-identification within love, prior to one's male self turning to another, when it seems that the narcissism is projected: 'The ground of every man's love of himself is the Identity of a man with himself, for the lover and beloved are all one and the same thing.'[52] Likeness determines the relations between self and other by structuring their difference through the essential identity of selfhood.

In this visual construct, women are conceived as complementary to male identity for the sake of social and sexual harmony. As an example of exhortation, Wilson quotes a letter by Erasmus that urges his male correspondent to marry: 'leauing to liue single, whiche both is barraine, and smally agreeing with the state of mans Nature . . . giue your selfe wholy to most holy Wedlocke' (40). The letter's implied program is that woman is to give herself to 'mans Nature,' a primary 'state' that determines the social and religious orthodoxy symbolized by 'holy Wedlocke.' Yet since man requires woman to realize this 'state,' his incompleteness and dependence on her are also intimated. It is woman's faithfulness to this structure that sustains society and raises marriage above other personal relationships. Erasmus distinguishes the wife by her unequivocal identity—her intrinsic opposition to any kind of dissimulation—which allows for her full union with man: 'when others are matched together in friendship, doe we not see what dissembling they vse, what falshood they practice, & what deceiptful parts they play . . . whereas the faithfulness of a wife is not stained with deceit, nor dusked with any dissembling' (54). Implicitly attacking traditions of male bonding, these remarks intimate the inauthenticity and incompletion of the masculinist ethos. They try to construct a univocal role for woman in order to salvage the naturalized image of cultural continuity and male identity, and in so doing paradoxically note that identity's dependence upon her.

This dependence is suppressed and revealed as Wilson's text continues. At one point the male speaker is instructed on the effectiveness of contrast. The notion does not, however, suggest a heterogeneous rhetorical principle that would subvert the valued order of likeness that has already been established. Contrast is figured through woman's appearance and morality, social indices of her sexuality that deviate from the ideal norm of a homoeostatic ethos. As likeness signifies man, contrast or inconstancy becomes the sign of woman within a code of cultural tropes. The speaker's control over contrast, its availability as a figure to be used by him, contrasts him to it. This control implies his discursive status and the fixed order in which contrast, like Spenser's Mutabilitie, is conceived, as an antithesis subsequent to natural likeness: 'By contrar-

ies set together, things oftentimes appeare greater . . . set a faire woman against a foule, and she shall seeme much the fairer, and the other much the fouler . . . if any one be disposed to set forth chastitie, he may bring in of the contrary part whoredome, and shewe what a foule offence it is to liue so vncleanly, and then the deformitie of whoredome, shall much set forth chastitie' (125).[53]

Once again, within a logic of juxtaposed appearances, contrast's, and thus woman's, difference is constrained by certain priorities. This visual hierarchy both establishes woman's threat to homoeostatic character and seeks to control it through a misogynist attack against dissembled and mutable sexuality, imaged here as elsewhere in denunciations of her beauty and make-up.[54] The female trope of contrast—'she can turn, and turn; and yet go on / And turn again'—is subject to the discursive norm of male likeness.[55] Her sophistical inconstancy offends the male speaker's verbal and rational consistency. In Wilson's example, the contrasted term reinforces the patriarchally valued first term and affords it a moral priority. The orator would order woman's character, and thereby his own, through a hierarchy of the verbally, sexually, and ethically proper.

It is a hierarchy that includes linguistic form. The values of the proper are perceived in a masculinist grammar that would synthesize nature and culture: 'yet in speaking at the least, let vs keepe a naturall order, and set the man before the woman for maners sake' (167). The passage from 'naturall order' to 'maners sake' suggests the mythicizing of rhetoric, as the order of gender becomes the grammatical structure of speech. The formal limitations of woman's discursive place are 'naturall' conditions that seek to control her unnatural volubility, 'that endless daily talk frequented by women.'[56] At their extreme they preclude her from utterance: 'What becometh a woman best, and first of all? silence. What second? silence. What third? silence. What fourth? silence. Yea, if a man should aske me till Domes daie, I would still crie silence, silence: without the which no woman hath any good gift, but hauing the same, no doubt she must have many other notable gifts, as the which of necessitie, doe euer followe such a vertue' (202). Silence, the lack of speech, would ideally characterize woman and, as it does for Jonson's Morose, denote her possession of other traits—'gifts' granted to her by man—that are socially valued.

Wilson's views disclose the silence that the encomiasts implicitly valued in their portraits of Helen's physical beauty. It signifies a symbolic passivity that has two related consequences. First, woman's silence would restrict her to a cultural role as audience, unable to speak or act socially except to facilitate the speech of men, as Duchess Elisabetta and Emilia Pia do for Castiglione's courtiers.[57] Secondly, the constraints of silence limit her speech to the rules of a masculine hermeneutic, and she is cast, using Cixous's terms, ' "within" the discourse of man, a signifier that has always referred back to the opposite signifier.'[58] A visual structure of rhetoric that sees the male ethos as the proper origin of speech, from the rules of grammar to the conventions of epideixis, is enjoined upon woman. She is openly to reflect male speech. A discursive ethos that might express a hidden motive is explicitly proscribed in her social discourse and demeanour, as John Donne emphasizes in the Christmas sermon of 1624. Citing Saint Cyprian, and so recalling the misogynistic rhetoric of the church fathers, he announces: "It is not enough for a virgin to bee a virgin in her owne knowledge, but she must governe her selfe so, as that others may see, that she is one, and see, that shee hath a desire, and a disposition, to continue so still . . . She must appear in such garments, in such language, and in such motions . . . as they that see her, may not question, nor dispute, whether she be a maid or no.'[59] The onus on woman's utterance and action is that it be overtly perceptible to 'others,' precluding the interpersonal inconstancy of 'dissembling' that Erasmus had feared. Donne's emphasis on the virgin intimates the urgency of univocal female ethopoesis for elementary social structures. Cultural truth depends on woman's words about herself, as Castiglione's Lord Gasper graphically emphasizes in describing the dangerous consequences of woman's sexuality, dangers that may lie not so much in her actions themselves but in what she may say about them: 'they may apply their force to keepe themselves in this one vertue of chastitie, without the which children were uncertain, and the bond that knitteth all the worlde together by bloud . . . should be loosed.'[60] 'Chastitie' is a symbolic rather than a natural category, applied here to woman's speech as well as her actions. It works to characterize her sexuality univocally, in the fixed and certain terms favoured by masculinist rhetoric.

In spite of the limits imposed on woman's speech, actions, and rhetorical role, her word assumes a central function in defining cultural truths. It can form the basis of interconnecting and reinforcing networks of personal, familial, and sociopolitical structures, as an early exchange in *The Tempest* between Prospero and Miranda suggests:

> Thy father was the Duke of Milan and
> A prince of power.
> *Mir.*   Sir, are not you my father?
> *Pros.* Thy mother was a piece of virtue, and
> She said thou wast my daughter; and thy
>   father
> Was Duke of Milan, and his only heir
> And princess no worse issued.
>
>   (I.ii.54-9)

It is the word of Prospero's wife that constructs these reciprocal relationships of paternal and patriarchal identity.[61] Though marginalized by encomiastic rhetoric and,

as Prospero's sceptical tone intimates, easily positioned within misogynistic speech, the figure of woman assumes a pivotal function in a potentially unstable masculinist discourse of social and personal values. She is the antithesis—contrast—that can anchor male speech and selfhood in the truth of likeness; or, through her inconstancy, she can undermine the structure of properness she is used to shore up. As Donne's, Gasper's, and Prospero's emphasis on admissions of chastity suggests, this ambiguity radiates from woman's sexual identity within the ethopoetics of gender.

In the third book of the *Institutes,* Calvin also warns against this ambiguity, perceiving its effects in the connections between the instability of woman's speech, identity, and sex and a subversively dramatistic reality. He is dismissing the practice of confession as a mere show of truth-telling. Three times the commentary notes the eclipse of univocal gender through the androgynous effects of woman's confession. It seems that because of its traditional function as 'the true discourse on sex,' confession is also empowered to disguise this truth, to conceal it at the supposed moment of revelation.[62] Such concealment is represented here as an effect of a feminizing speech. In arguing against confession, Calvin seeks to preclude this disruption of words and gender, where confession functions as an androgynous speech act. These remarks extend the implications of confession from a specifically religious ritual to a wider genre of sexual self-revelation. Calvin's dicta were of course central to arguments against the stage, particularly on questions of gender and cross-dressing.[63] Although discussing the practice of confession, he touches on the same theme, the dramatistic relation of truth to gender. And in a work as relentlessly serious as the *Institutes,* this section's use of (or attempt at) sarcastic humour seems to highlight this concern and the incredulity with which Calvin contemplates the possible confusion of sexual identity.

Calvin begins his remarks on confession by typically attacking the medieval theologians. His caustic tone recalls the agonistic efforts of Gorgias and Isocrates in using the figure of Helen against their rivals: 'when these worthy fathers enjoin that every person of *both sexes* (*utriusque sexus*) must once a-year confess his sins to his own priest, men of wit humorously object that the precept binds hermaphrodites only, and has no application to any one who is either a male or a female.'[64] Confession triggers a blurring of sexual differences in what is depicted as a wholly male ritual: the male penitent addresses a priest, according to rules that are either enjoined by 'fathers' or ridiculed by 'men of wit.' Confession is both the pretext of this scene of male discourse and that which disrupts it, by introducing a feminizing hermaphroditism. The confessional revelation of sexuality does not reinforce this masculinist order and the discrete roles of those who envoice it, but serves generally to androgynize them, as occurs in the ideal scene of oratory that Wilson depicts.

These traces of equivocal gender emerge only when confessional truth is represented. Calvin does not object to revelations that are not verbalized but remain unmediated disclosures to God and so recognize his transcendent presence: 'the surest rule of confession is, to acknowledge and confess our sins to be an abyss so great as to exceed our comprehension' (549). The unspoken confession redefines the self in its original submission to God. Its truthfulness lies in the 'abyss,' an absence of human speech and 'comprehension,' which in turn signifies the pure presence of selfhood prior to discourse. In contrast, the uttered form of 'auricular confession . . . a thing pestilent in its nature' (550) disrupts man's submissive essence. The popish rhetoricity and staging of confession corrupt the inner identity of man as determined by God, and suggest the links between Calvin's antitheatricalism and its misogynistic premise. For this order of unspoken confession to God is also the model for woman's discursive relation to man, a silent subjection whose 'auricular' transgression recalls her natural talkativeness.

The clearest signs of the corruptions caused by confession emerge for Calvin in a sort of feminized sexual theatre: 'a certain matron, while pretending to confess, was discovered to have used it as a cloak to cover her intercourse with a deacon' (541). Confession becomes a motivated sexual disguise that is both worn 'as a cloak' and enacted by a noticeably eager woman. It then generates a larger confusion of sexuality that ranges from the hermphroditism noted above, to the implied passivity of the deacon's male sexuality, to the traditional prohibitions in 'the innumerable acts of prostitution, adultery, and incest, which it produces in the present day' (551). The portrayal of the matron and the emphasis on her desire weight Calvin's denunciation of confession against the sexual duplicity of woman's speech. However, her performance provokes his own voyeuristic pleasure at the popish ritual. His criticisms reflect the suppression of self-threatening pleasure in Rainolds' attack on theatricality[65] and anticipate Wilson's scene of passive, narcissistic delight at rhetorical expertise. The matron's theatrically disguised word undermines the truth of male sexuality. It is analogous to the verbalized confession that taints the penitent male. In this scheme of confessional, religious discourse, woman represents the corruption of the soul through speech. She embodies a sexualized rhetoric that may threaten the intrinsic male ethos.

The figure of woman, though widely conceived as secondary and external to the primary ethos, suggests this internalized confusion to other authors during the Renaissance. Even the passion of heterosexual love may realize androgynizing effects, as it fragments es-

sential male character. In the long section on love melancholy, Burton writes of lovers' loss of humanity and *ratio,* which he conceives as male virtues: 'at last *insensati,* void of sense; degenerate into dogs, hogs, asses, brutes; as Jupiter into a bull, Apuleius an ass . . . For what else may we think those ingenious poets to have foreshadowed . . . but that a man once given over to his lust . . . is no better than a beast.'[66] The divine mutability that Vives saw as epitomizing human nature here signifies the sexual loss of man's identity. The sort of 'interinanimation' that a younger Donne could celebrate in 'The Ecstasy' assumes a self-negating potency for Thomas Wright when 'hearts were more present, in thoughts and desires, with such bodies where they liked and loved than with that wherein they sojourned and lived.'[67] Donne himself preached on Easter Day 1625 that 'no outward enemy is able so to macerate our body, as our owne licentiousnesse.'[68] This image of the crossover between outwardness and inwardness implies a sexual deconstruction of essentialist or proper selfhood. The sermon's ensuing comments on the 'licentious man's' self-induced ruin can either suggest that the female inconstancy which threatens maleness from without is a figure for man's own inconstancy, his intrinsic androgyny, or imply the reverse, that man's internal ruin is a metonym for the extrinsic threat of woman.[69]

This confounding of the 'true' relation of the sexes, and of individual male identity, recalls the collapse of the imaginary structure of praise that the narcissistic reference of the encomia had implied but not acknowledged. The rhetorics of praise and of confession form a dialogic complex. Both may undermine the masculinist ethos, by revealing the sexual and discursive paradoxes of its essentialist premises. Yet where the epideictic structure would seek to displace this disclosure onto the figure of woman, by making her the object of praise or of attack, confessional rhetoric unveils such strategies and undermines the proper ethos that they represent. The attempt to displace self-subversion is most frequently inscribed through the epideictic switch from praise to misogyny. Misogyny seeks to preserve selfhood by denouncing woman, but in doing so admits its rhetorical interdependence with the other. In *Cymbeline,* for example, having boastingly praised Imogen's virtue, as Collatine did of Lucrece, Posthumus later denounces both himself and her in a generalized attack against the figure of woman. The change from praise to misogyny leads him first to imitate the discursive inconstancy that is the mark of woman, and then to confess that what corrupts the male tenor, his archetypal self-image, is an imperceptible, inner, female trace. It contradicts the visual ideal of the masculine ethos and already resides within: 'Could I find out / The woman's part in me' (II.v.19-20). Posthumus' rhetorical progression through praise, misogyny, and confession reproduces the determined discursive path that androgynizes masculine self-representation.

The rhetorical function of woman is that of an ethopoetic metonym for a male identity that is endlessly incomplete. Rather than merely serving his self-portrayals, woman names the continual disruption of male ethos and desire. Montaigne laments this process in 'Sebond' in terms of 'The lustfull longing which allures us to the acquaintance of women, seekes but to expell that paine, which an earnest and burning desire doth possesse us with, and desireth but to allay it thereby to come to rest, and be exempted from this fever.'[70] The sequence of desire, pain and fever, and 'lustfull longing' that drives 'us' to women, suggests a continuing metonymic deferral of desire.[71] It locates 'woman' as the ultimate effect of this desire rather than its cause. She externalizes masculine dissatisfaction, giving it a verbal and personal goal—'woman'—that may then be construed as its origin.

The external placement displaces cause and effect. While subjecting woman to man's discourse, and making her its misogynist target, this metonymic shift also grants her a figural potency. Her externalization as the goal of man's desire realizes, through 'the irony of the "peripety," ' her internalization as his motive. She functions as the 'synecdochic representative' of his discursive desire, 'represent[ing] the *end* or *logic* of the development as a whole.'[72] Despite her secondary function as the object rather than the speaker of traditional rhetorical pieces, woman is the 'master-mistress,' androgynous key to the representation of man and herself. The metonymic logic that structures these forms of rhetoric inscribes the splitting of the male ethos and tenor that occurs through the attempt at self-representation. The figure of woman is an ambiguous trope of masculine ethopoesis. She unsettles his own modes of characterization, exemplified by the epideictic inversions between himself and her, and shifts the place of her own speech in the verbal structure, through the androgynous effects of confessional truth.

IV

Theatrical versions of androgynous disguise in the Renaissance frequently portray this ambiguity in social dramas where the male ethos is initially idealized. A number of plays by Beaumont and Fletcher depict the androgynous process and its effects on exemplary male identities such as the brave prince and the loyal subject. In works like *A King and No King* and *The Maid's Tragedy* these topics are addressed through pairs of characters, who represent male and female ethopoetic processes in conflict. In *Philaster* the conflict is compressed within the androgynous characterization of Bellario and Philaster. As noted earlier, the heightened rhetoric of these plays serves to foreground the ethopoetic discourse through which the characters confront each other and the conflicts of gender and identity within themselves. There is a rhetorical rhythm, frequently developed through the alternation between epideixis and confession, whereby male characters first imply the imaginary structure of their own identity in its relation to others before having the presumptions of this structure undermined and being in effect 're-characterized.'

A King and No King begins after the conquest by Arbaces, king of Iberia, of his Armenian foe Tigranes. The classical ethopoetic trope of military virtue and self-realization is immediately cited. Arbaces orders Tigranes to marry his sister, and though not naming her, he praises her highly. Her beauty is the counterpart of his martial prowess, and the encomiastic strains and images reflect his opinion of himself: 'shee can doe as much / In peace, as I in Warre; sheele conquer too / You shall see, if you have the power to stand / The force of her swift lookes.'[73] These lines reiterate many of the themes of masculinist rhetoric. Arbaces reflexively praises himself and uses his sister to show his own qualities. She is unnamed, since her identity is irrelevant to his self-portrait; however, it later becomes ironically apparent that she is not named because Arbaces is wholly ignorant of her identity, and of his own, and of the relationship between them.

The common love-war conflation also suggests the place of woman in man's martial rhetoric. As Helen's beauty did for the ancient heroes and orators, his sister's beauty figures Arbaces' archetypal power, which is military and rhetorical, a fusion of body and spirit. Unlike Helen, whose passivity was strongly implied, in this play the woman is a rival to active male power. Her 'swift lookes' have the physical 'force' that Arbaces displayed on the battlefield, and while her character seems dependent on his report, it is soon to realize effects that will overturn his speech and thought. Nonetheless, for the moment Arbaces presumes a priority that his sister, Panthaea, initially reinforces, through her first selfless words, inquiring into 'My brothers health' (II.i.78), and then in her comments on the language of his letter to her: 'The kindest words, Ile keepe um whilst I live / Here in my bosome; theres no art in um, / They lie disordered in this paper, Just / As hearty Nature speakes um' (II.i.201-4). She internalizes the naturalized guise with which her brother's words invest themselves and imprints his fashioned ethos upon her own body. Yet as the following scenes reveal, and in a similar way to that in which Campaspe affected Alexander in Lyly's play, her subjected body and beauty subvert his social persona, revealing its ethopoetic inconstancy.

Having returned to the court, Arbaces sets about making the match between Tigranes and Panthaea, despite his sister's taking it 'Something unkindly . . . To have her Husband chosen to her hands' (III.i.2-3). He does so by proclaiming his absolute authority, a speech act that would decree his univocal will: 'I must have her know / My will, and not her owne must governe her . . . Shee should be forcst to have him, when I know / Tis fit: I will not heare her say shee's loth' (III.i.4-20). Arbaces' illocutionary power forecloses Panthaea's opposition, subjecting her discursive will, anticipated in her spoken 'lothness,' to his. He outlaws her speech and imposes the cultural regimen of woman's chaste silence.

This rhetorical authority is soon undermined. On seeing Panthaea, Arbaces silently struggles against his rapid falling in love. The sight of her disrupts the discourse of praise he had formerly controlled. In a confessional aside he notes his own self-loss—'Speak, am I what I was?' (III.i.80)—which he then tries to counter by invoking solidly male, military imagery. In confusion at his incestuous desire, he threatens anyone who says that the woman standing before him is his sister, decreeing that 'Shee is no kinne to me, nor shall shee be; / If shee were any, I create her none' (III.i.161-2). While the overt royal word strives to master the personal passion and the social identities that have produced this dilemma, his further asides emphasize the onset of deep pain similar to that acknowledged by Montaigne. Though addressed to the self as a type of inner speech, these asides do not reinforce Arbaces' identity but express its social, moral, and spiritual loss:

> . . . you are naught to me but a disease,
> Continuall torment without hope of ease;
> Such an ungodly sicknesse I have got,
> That he that undertakes my cure, must first
> Overthrow Divinity, all morall Lawes,
> And leave mankinde as unconfinde as
>   beasts . . .
>
> (III.i.190-5)

In commanding Panthaea and her supporters' silence with Lear-like obstinacy—'Let me not heare you speake againe . . . No man here / Offer to speake for her' (III.i.198-201)—he indicates the failure of his command, and ironically admits her significance and power in his discourse. Panthaea becomes an externalized sign of his inner sexual confusion: 'Incest is in me / Dwelling alreadie' (III.i.330-1). She is blamed by him as the cause of his internal distress, a female figure who concentrates the conflicts between his individual desire and social order. Panthaea becomes a synecdoche for the play's paradoxical title, whose male, political categories—king / no king—hinge on her equivocal role.

We see this kind of social and personal dependence on woman elsewhere in Beaumont and Fletcher's work. In *The Maid's Tragedy,* Amintor's response to his new wife Evadne's confession of her affair with the king not only challenges his self-conception—'What a strange thing am I?' he asks (II.i.318)—but also threatens the reciprocal, masculinist code of honour that supposedly sustains the social relationship between sovereign and subject: 'The thing that we call honour

beares us all / headlong unto sinne' (IV.ii.316-17). Evadne's actions disrupt Amintor's conception of obedience, driving him to a confused contemplation of regicide. Similarly, in the scene where Arbaces and Panthaea meet alone, her admission of love for him brings them closet to transgression, as they alternately embrace and fly from each other (IV.iv.1ff), and in his next speech we see Arbaces resigned to a life of sin and hell (V.iv.1-11).

However, in *A King and No King* such catastrophe is avoided by the further revelation that Arbaces and Panthaea are not brother and sister. Their love, having threatened the social order, finally restores it. Following the pattern of Shakespearean resolutions, the unravelling of the secrets of identities and birthrights stabilizes a confusion of personal and social positions, in which the loss of kingship and selfhood had threatened—'the whole storie / Would be a wildernesse to loose thy selfe / For ever' (V.iv.286-8). Arbaces' loss of royal preeminence translates into personal happiness, while Panthaea gains crown and husband. The characters' relations are co-ordinated by a benevolent cultural system that reconciles social and individual personae and is celebrated in the final lines: 'Come every one / That takes delight in goodnesse, helpe to sing / Loude thankes for me that I am prov'd no King' (V.iv.351-3).

The removal of the incest threat is based on the reassertion of Arbaces' and Panthaea's familial and personal difference. The play's conclusion is prepared through a separation of identities that enables order and relationships to be reimposed. Although Arbaces loses his dominant role, the structure of character is reaffirmed through the distinctions between man and woman, sovereign and subject, which grant everyone their social place.

Philaster, however, lacks this final and total ordering. Despite the betrothal of prince and princess and the restoration of the Sicilian crown, someone is left out. The androgynous character Bellario/Euphrasia exceeds the conventional resolution. She cannot be fitted into the ideal pattern of youthful consummation and cultural continuity: 'I grieve such vertue should be laied in earth / Without an Heyre' comments Philaster (V.v.197-8). This ending gains further significance as it differs in the two quarto versions. In the first quarto of *Philaster* (the second is the copy-text), Bellario is set to marry the courtier Trasiline, thus fulfilling the narrative pattern of plays like *As You Like It* and *Twelfth Night,* where marriage serves to close the plot on a note of social renewal. Bellario's isolation in the second ending seems to recall the exclusion of troubling characters like Jacques and Malvolio from the romantic endings of those plays, figures who question the ideal prospect of sociosexual regrowth. Robert K. Hunter has simply suggested that the first ending of

Beaumont and Fletcher's play is either 'authorial early drafts later recast into dramatically superior Q2 form,' or 'not authorial.'[74] These claims need to be reconsidered in view of the later ending's overt rejection of the conventional romance conclusion. In re-marking its later deviation from the generic norm it initially upholds, *Philaster* highlights the equivocal function of androgyny in both constructing and challenging the social system.

The significance of Bellario's exclusion may seem arbitrary, especially as she rejects the king's offer to find a noble match for her and pay her dowry. Her refusal and the plot's thematic remainder momentarily appear idiosyncratic:

> Never sir will I
> Marry, it is a thing within my vow,
> But if I may have leave to serve the
>   Princesse,
> To see the vertues of her Lord and her,
> I shall have hope to live.
>
> (V.v.187-91)

However, Bellario's personal wilfulness masks a broader social process that relies on and constructs her metonymic role. To apply Girard's terms to this dramatic resolution, Bellario functions as a scapegoat, a *'surrogate victim,'* whose final isolation is a relatively non-violent sacrifice in order 'to restore harmony to the community, to reinforce the social fabric.'[75] She rights a society disrupted, before the play's events commence, by the deposition of Philaster's father from 'his fruitfull *Cicilie*' (I.i.24). Along with her chastity, which retains a strongly positive symbolic value (and is crucial to the dénouement), Bellario's androgyny is the central element that affords her scapegoat function. Through doubled gender, she may represent all the other characters, a sociosexual vehicle that works through the similarities between her ambiguous self and them. At the same time, her hybrid but abnormal likeness to everyone also represents the degree of difference and distance that is required for the scapegoat figure to be cast out and social synthesis to take place. Bellario is alternately similar to man or woman; her similarity to both makes her different from each; and she also signifies the hermaphroditic links between them—'the persistent doubleness, the inherent twinship'—that could underlie Renaissance conceptions of sexual selfhood.[76] In *Philaster,* it is this sort of symbolic flexibility that makes the androgynous woman suitable for the sacrificial role. The metonymic complexity marks Bellario as the central figure in the text's sociosexual thematics. The symbolic power of her persona is further strengthened by the mystery of her disappearance and return, which, in effect, doubly charges her identity, since she returns twice, once in each gender.[77]

The other characters come to understand Bellario's androgyny in these constructive terms, as the key to their drama's stabilizing conclusion. By emphasizing her individual role in events, they naturalize the sociosexual structure of their community as that which she has disrupted. Her disguise seems to them first to have created the social danger, and the confession of her 'true' sex then restores harmony, exemplifying Donne's conception of the cultural centrality of woman's unequivocal persona, 'as they that see her, may not question, nor dispute, whether she be a maid or no,' with 'maid' marked for Philaster and the others as female *and* chaste:

> tell me why
> Thou didst conceale thy sex; it was a fault,
> A fault *Bellario,* though thy other deeds
> Of truth outwaigh'd it: All these Jealousies
> Had flowne to nothing, if thou hadst
>   discovered,
> What now we know.
>
> (V.v.146-51)

Philaster makes Bellario's disguise the pivotal factor for the events. In so doing, he ignores the social and sexual causes of her disguise, the differences between royalty and nobility, male and female, and the conflict between personal and social desires, that she explains prompted her action: 'I knew / My birth no match for you, I was past hope of having you' (V.v.174-6). His interpretation replays the metonymic transposition of woman's actions from social effect to social cause.

Bellario gives what Othello would call 'ocular proof' of her femaleness when she *'discovers her haire,'* a euphemized bodily token of her sex, to her incredulous father (V.v.112). She is thereby relocated as an object of a controlling masculinist gaze. Through observing her sex, the group recognizes and sorts itself out. Her revealed body, in its gender and overtness, is immediately fixed within the social hierarchy and has that hierarchy inscribed and imposed on itself. Its ambiguous gender becomes a cultural synecdoche, with 'the powers and dangers credited to social structure reproduced in small on the human body.'[78] This multiple function of the body as personal, social, and textual, recurs through the play. The subtitle, *Love Lies a-Bleeding,* connotes the social, personal, and sexual disintegration that seems about to begin when Philaster turns on both Bellario and his beloved Arethusa.[79] As noted, the drama seems to avoid this dissolution through sacrificing the androgynous scapegoat in order to represent what Andrew Gurr has called 'the orthodoxy of selfhood.'[80] This interpretation, the one that the characters themselves wish to accept, sacrifices or ignores Bellario's desire for the sake of social, moral order and of an orthodox ethos conceived in masculinist terms. Bellario's heroism typically involves the chastening of her sexuality.[81] Her double scapegoat function as cause and effect serves finally to conceal the extremes of collapse to which order has been stretched at the expense of her sexuality.

The ambiguous processes of gendering are not restricted to this overtly androgynous character but, as Gurr suggests, apply equally to the orthodoxy of selfhood that seems finally to be reinforced for all the characters. Bellario's self-exposure serves not only to settle the dilemma but, more subtly, to disrupt it, through implying the continuing ambiguity of Philaster's character, the exemplary ethos represented by the play. Her confession, as the sort of androgynous speech act abhorred by Calvin, registers the confusion of his desire and identity. For in announcing the truth of her own gender, Bellario reveals the androgynous truth of Philaster's, which underlies his heroic male ethos and echoes equivocally throughout the play and the closing scene. The apparent realization of this ideal masculine ethos in the betrothal to Arethusa and the restoration of the throne is undermined, as we will see, by his final muted admission of a split desire for an androgynous ideal. An interpretive response based on the ethopoetic synthesis of the conclusions of Shakespearean romance seems unable to account for the hero's 'schizophrenic unity,' which emerges in the course of the play.[82]

Like *Hamlet, Philaster* opens amidst an ongoing political intrigue that seems to set the stage for a tale of brave and decisive action. The king of Calabria has usurped the Sicilian throne from Philaster's father yet remains unable to have the prince killed because of the masses' love for him. Three courtiers inform us of this and of their secret support for Philaster, whom they praise as a heroic figure. They themselves are, however, compromised by having helped the usurper: 'My selfe drew some blood, in those warres, which I would give my hand, to be washed from,' admits their leader Dion (I.i.24-6). Because of this uneasy situation the king hopes to arrange his daughter Arethusa's marriage to a foreign prince, Pharamond of Spain, in order to produce a legitimate heir and, through machiavellian policy, 'to bring in the power of a forraigne Nation, to awe his owne with' (I.i.38-9). The drama concentrates key cultural ideas in a situation that rapidly includes marriage, sex, and the fates of Arethusa, Philaster, and all of Sicily.

Philaster's confused situation is politically and personally interwoven. The object of the people's and the courtiers' admiration, he is a much eulogized figure, the model of male virtue, 'the bravery of his age' (III.i.6). The paradox of this praise is its disabling effect upon him. The fine words of others make him a passive figure, incapable of acting in the very way that his praisers envisage. Like the object of the classical encomia, Philaster is used to signify masculinist ideals and, because he is so used, is cut off from them. His

character is androgynized, being reduced to a traditionally feminized passivity through the praise of his ideal maleness.

This encomiastic paradox works most strongly through the words of the prince's dead father. Philaster feels possessed by his father's spirit, which urges him heroically to seize power:

> now he tells me King,
> I was a Kings Heire, bids me be a King,
> And whispers to me, these are all my subjects:
>   . . . dives
> Into my fancy, and there gives me shapes,
> That kneele, and doe me service, cry me
>   King:
> But I'le suppresse him, he's a factious spirit,
> And will undoe me:
>
>   (I.i.269-76)

The spirit echoes at the deeper levels of Philaster's mind, filling his consciousness with past, present, and future possibilities for selfhood. He struggles to fulfil these discursive images of himself, the *ethoi* that others have constructed for him and that he has only partly internalized. His dilemma is to reconcile these images with those that he makes for himself. The command to fill the father's place arises from Philaster's uncertain and reluctant interiorization of his father's word, a word he wishes both to obey and to resist—obeying through regaining the throne, but resisting through his love for the daughter of his enemy. His contradictory response reveals the effects of confounded desire in his own inaction.[83] This inner dialogue between the positive and negative sides of his encomiastic image is then opposed externally by the word of the present king, who commands Philaster's obedience: 'Be more your selfe, as you respect our favour' (I.i.257). The tension between 'your selfe' and 'our favour' inscribes Philaster's struggle with an internally conflicted subjectivity in the face of an externally imposed subjection.

A stable point within this conflict soon emerges in his relationship with the princess Arethusa. Although she embodies his rejection of the father's word, the king's daughter is also a political and personal foil to Philaster and enables him to grasp a sense of self through these contrasts: 'Nature, that loves not to be questioned / Why she did this, or that . . . never gave the world / Two things so opposite, so contrary, / As he and I am' (I.ii.23-7). Her idealizing love for him, though starting from the encomiastic perspective of others, seems to allow him to accept the image of selfhood presented in their words. The sense of oppositeness allows Philaster to feel a stability of self. He can then act positively for the first time, as he expediently suggests that they employ his 'trustiest, lovingst, and . . . gentlest boy / . . . To waite on you, and *beare* our hidden love' (I.ii.138-40; emphasis added). The boy, a sign-vehicle of Philaster's secret, intrinsic desire, will ground him in an externalized selfhood and emotion, a process that has commenced already, through the reflexive effects of the praise of the boy that he expresses to Arethusa.

This 'boy' is of course Bellario, who, from the start, is thus loaded with the meanings, intentions, and desires of others. When Philaster relates the circumstances in which they met, he casts Bellario as the object of perception and language, asserting his own active masculine status through speaking of him, 'I have a boy . . . Hunting the Bucke / I found him' (I.ii.111-14).[84] Bellario's persona, however, is a complex figure. His gender seems constantly to undermine the maleness that it signifies, and Philaster is taken mainly with his 'pretty helpelesse innocence' (I.ii.123). Rather than simply feminizing the boy, Philaster's perception suggests the interplay of gender and desire in himself through his reaction to Bellario's attention to him: 'The love of boyes unto their Lords, is strange' (II.i.57). Again we might see Beaumont and Fletcher's play taking up a submerged theme of Shakespearean romance and revealing it as a central topos in the sexual discourse of selfhood. Philaster's words and later actions make overt Orsino's ambiguous recognition of Viola through Cesario, which the courtier Valentine wryly notes—'he hath known you but three days, and already you are no stranger' (I.iv.2-4)—and which Orsino himself equivocally admits: 'thy small pipe / Is as the woman's organ, shrill and sound, / And all is semblative a woman's part' (I.iv.32-4). While Philaster would attribute the love all to the boy, and distance himself from its homoerotic aim, his response to its strangeness intimates his own part in their androgynous rapport. Subsequently, he will love Arethusa only indirectly, through the love of a boy for himself, a love whose activeness once again ironically casts him passively as its object.

This sensed androgyny in Bellario seems to make him the ideal go-between, as one who always metonymically signifies the other. At the same time, Bellario's mediation disrupts the course of desire between lover and beloved, most obviously by detouring their discourse through himself and his passion for Philaster, which makes his accounts of their love vehicles for his own wish-fulfilling romance. This role as messenger also inscribes the androgynous and narcissistic doubling of the lovers' desire, which, while seeking out the other, also chooses its own image in the hermaphroditic envoy. Such messages of doubled desires are similarly sent in *Twelfth Night,* as Viola observes, 'My master loves her dearly, / And I (poor monster) fond as much on him; / And she (mistaken) seems to dote on me' (II.ii.33-5). As Derrida has noted, these repetitive and redoubling effects lie deep within the discursive function of the archetypal love-messenger, 'the son of Hermes and Aphrodite,' Hermaphrodite, who represents the self-deferring course of desire.[85] When he

sends Bellario to Arethusa, Philaster admits that 'Thy love doth plead so prettily to stay, / That (trust me) I could weepe to part with thee' (II.i.40-1). He mourns the loss of the androgynous boy and his ideal love, and like Orsino 'finds himself in the position of not being the object of desire but the desiring subject.'[86] In her turn, Arethusa learns of Philaster's affection through Bellario's reports of his distracted behaviour (II.iii.50-62). She enjoys imagining herself as wholly reliant on these accounts, delighting in their figural representation more than the 'truth' they might signify: 'thou knowest, a lie / That beares this sound, is welcomer to me, / Then any truth that saies he loves me not' (II.iii.64-6).

An ambiguous process of homosexual, heterosexual, and narcissistic desire is thus in train before Megra, caught sleeping with the Spanish prince Pharamond, accuses Bellario and Arethusa of having sex. Megra's charge translates the unasked but already disruptive questions of Bellario's gender and the others' desire into social effect, setting the sexual plot off on an even more convoluted course. At this point, too, the apparent revelation of Bellario's identity becomes linked to wider social events. The three lords, scheming for Philaster's return to power, seize upon the news, believing that ''Twill move him' to assail the king (III.i.35). They anticipate the sublimation of his disappointed desire into direct political action. However, Philaster's desire implodes, the cataclysmic images with which he responds to the courtiers' revelation signifying the upheaval of his own body politic and the fracturing of the princely ethos (III.i.67-149). The loss of a heroic masculine identity that motivates Hamlet's speeches against Ophelia and Gertrude becomes one of the later play's key motifs.

Megra's accusation is immediately accepted, suggesting the social investment in woman's sexual word. Acts three and four comprise a sequence of speeches among Philaster, Arethusa, and Bellario, through which the effects of their deceived and deceiving claims reverberate. The discursive dependence on Bellario's guise is compounded by the effects of Megra's lie. Whereas before the lovers had unwittingly responded to the redoubling of their desire through Bellario, they now react deliberately but no less emotively, assuming that they know the full significance of their personal and sexual relationships. Their images of each others' deceptions underpin a sense of pained selfhood. Philaster's violent threats against the others might suggest that this knowledge reinforces his own identity, granting it a masculinist power. Yet Bellario's mysterious guise continues to call forth a response that undermines as it determines this imagined male ethos: 'Tell me thy thoughts; for I will know the least / That dwells within thee, or will rip thy heart / To know it; I will see thy thoughts as plaine, / As I doe now thy face' (III.i.226-9). Through the violence of his rhetoric, Philaster believes that the truth of Bellario can be seen and known, and that this truth, tested in combat with his rival, would prove the independence of the 'I.' Yet his admitted misperception of Bellario's face undermines the motivated urge to see himself through this anatagonist. In the face of the other he perceives not a self-defining rival but his lover's desire, which calls forth his own self-confounding love.

The ensuing exchanges record a chain reaction of misrecognition that spreads from one character to the next, investing each through the illusory guise of the others. Despite his vengefulness, Philaster is unable to strike Bellario, as his anger gives way to his homoerotic vision: 'I must love / Thy honest lookes, and take no revenge upon / Thy tender youth' (III.i.273-5). Though stopping short of physical action, he still derives a narcissistic pleasure from his rhetorical despair and, like Hamlet, uses the misogynistic topoi he fires at Arethusa to consolidate the truth of his male persona against her falseness: 'that foolish man, / That reads the story of a womans face, / And dies beleeving it, is lost for ever' (III.ii.117-19). In a bitter soliloquy, he denounces 'the dissembling traines / Of womens lookes' (IV.iii.3-4), as well as Bellario's 'misbeseeming' and 'dissembling trade' (IV.iii.27,33). His accusations against them seek to reaffirm his own 'authentic' ethos. Arethusa, shocked by his outbursts, appeals to Philaster for 'constancy,' and then introjects his misogyny, doubting herself but at the same time trying to defend her desire through turning on Bellario as a 'dissembler' (III.ii.134-6).

In his despair Philaster focuses on first one figure and then another. His passion wildly substitutes different personae, including himself, as the cause of his dilemma but is satisfied with none. He swings from asking Arethusa to slay him, to stabbing Arethusa and Bellario, to bitter self-reproach at his cowardice for doing so. In focusing first on himself, he wishes to cast himself as the victim of his own heroism, a stoic self-assertion. He then turns on Arethusa and Bellario, aiming to kill each of them to save his identity.[87] The irony of these acts of masculinist violence is deepened by the willingness of his female victims, who bare their bodies to his dagger. As they seek to fulfil their desire for him, their passivity prevents him from attaining the active ethos he seeks. In these coital scenes of stabbing and of love 'lying a-bleeding,' the heroic persona is all but eclipsed. (As comic relief, a country naïf enters and, his rustic sense of honour shocked, tries to defend Arethusa.)

It is only after this impassioned violence starts to subside that Philaster begins to recognize the absence of the ethos he has been seeking. His madness figures a rhetorical passage towards selfhood, leading him through epideictic images of the other to the confessional realization of his own intrinsic lack and a sub-

dued 'equilibrium' that emerges from 'beneath the cloud of illusion, beneath feigned disorder.'[88] When the king asks Arethusa whether her attacker was Philaster, she answers, 'Sir, if it was he, / He was disguised.' Her remark strikes Philaster as totally enlightening, suggesting the deeper nature of his self-confusion: 'I was so: oh my stars! / That I should live still' (IV.vi.127-9). The uncovering of a disguise he has not controlled explains for him the inconstancy of selfhood through these events. At the same time, and beneath his awareness, these terms link him to the inconstant rhetorical image of woman and disclose the androgynous structure of his identity and behaviour to this point.[89]

As Bellario had done, Philaster now functions as a surrogate victim, a crucial sign in the social system whose value is contested by others. The king wishes to kill him so as to end the political turmoil, but the courtiers foresee that Philaster's death would spark another round of reciprocal violence. Instead of executing him, the king sends Philaster to quell the rioting citizens (V.iv.1ff). Social (dis)order, like his father's spiritualized word, speaks through him, granting him roles that he does not control but that determine his identity. Finally, his heroic ethos is set up through the ideal reciprocity between himself and society, symbolized in the restoration of the crown and his marriage to Arethusa, which together form an image of sociosexual completion: 'enjoy *Philaster* / This Kingdome which is yours' (V.v.210-11). The political equation between the state and the prince seems to figure the resolution of the dilemmas of selfhood and identity that have plagued the whole community.

These forms of closure are, however, realized only when the figure of Euphrasia is revealed through Bellario's identity. Philaster's self-realization and the parallel restoration of social harmony depend on this discovery. Euphrasia is brought into the resolution by the other characters, who first threaten Bellario with death and torture if he doesn't reveal the truth, and then reconcile her disguise through their sense of the events' happy ending, inviting her participation in it. Arethusa, who alone might now find this androgynous figure a threat, herself issues the invitation: 'I, *Philaster,* / Cannot be jealous, though you had a Lady / Drest like a Page to serve you, nor will I / Suspect her living heere: come live with me, / Live free as I do; she that loves my Lord, / Curst be the wife that hates her' (V.v.191-6). Exemplifying Erasmus' ideal of womanly certitude, Arethusa locates the previously disruptive signs of sexual ambiguity within the heterosexual order of marriage, where Bellario's love for Philaster is simply evidence of his desirability. The power of the reordered society to absorb these signs reveals its reinforced strength and the sureness of the characters' renewed identities. In hindsight, the disruptions seem to have been necessary to realize this return to political and personal ideals. Bellario has purged the system and proven its ethopoetic integrity and propriety, which are rehearsed in the play's closing maxim: 'Let Princes learne / By this to rule the passions of their blood, / For what Heaven wils can never be withstood' (V.v.216-18).

The secret of the woman behind Bellario's guise seems to reassert Philaster's maleness and explain the disruptive attraction the androgynous figure had held for him. The female tenor of this figure would thus reveal the constancy of his character, which instinctively recognized in the disguised identity before him the sociosexual subjection of Euphrasia and so all along was seeking to assert his natural mastery:

> I was past hope
> Of having you. And understanding well,
> That when I made discovery of my sex,
> I could not stay with you, I made a vow,
>   . . . never to be knowne
> Whilst there was hope to hide me from men's
>   eyes
> For other then I seem'd; that I might ever
> Abide with you . . .
>
>   (V.v.175-83)

The hopeless love, a desire that is forsaken as it longs to be 'discovered' (first by herself and then by Philaster), the virgin's vow, and the determination of her persona by 'men's eyes'—all these responses comprise a chain of disguises that Euphrasia is compelled to fashion anew within the masculinist discourse of desire. Her final revelation continues to represent the operation of this discourse; rather than allowing her selfhood to be realized, it imposes the cultural paradigms of sexual character upon her, in chaste service to Philaster.

Beaumont and Fletcher's text thus dramatizes in broad social terms the subversive and the stabilizing effects of identity and gender upon the representation of selfhood. The disguise of Bellario metonymically inscribes the conflicts between recognized and suppressed dimensions of sexuality, as other characters bewilderingly respond to the ambiguous signs of her androgyny. Their confusion is expressed in the sudden reversals of knowledge and emotion triggered by a series of set rhetorical speeches, the encomium and the confession, through which characters first presume the relationship between themselves and others and then reveal the 'truth' of these relationships. The formality of this rhetorical structure does not, however, efface the dramatic 'personality' of the characters, as many critics of Beaumont and Fletcher claim, but suggests the restrictions and conflicts of a discourse through which characters attempt to construct themselves and to interact with each other. The use of the encomium and the confession refers Beaumont and Fletcher's characterization to the rhetorical traditions in which relations between man and woman, and the process of sexual identity itself, were often depicted.

Bellario's revelation of her true gender is, then, the confessional speech act that seems to revise the relationships between the characters, allowing the social and discursive hierarchy of proper meaning and identity to be reaffirmed. As woman, she seems to reveal that the difference between male and female lies first in the intrinsic identity of each as a separate sexual being, and then in the subjection of woman to a masculinist ethos. At the same time, Bellario's confession is a revelation of androgyny, and of ambiguous identity not only in herself but in those who perceived her as a boy and responded to her disguised love. Such a one, of course, is the heroic Philaster. He resumes his identity on the revealed image of Bellario's femaleness, reproducing the essentialist structure of praise. Yet even as he seems to realize and resume this character, Philaster confesses to an ethos that resides within and breaks through the proper:

>   But *Bellario*,
> (For I must call thee so still) tell me why
> Thou didst conceale thy sex . . .
>
>   (V.v.145-7)

The inexplicable compulsion of his parenthetic 'must call' registers the excess of androgynous disguise, an ethopoetic trope that reveals the sex it conceals and rejects the identity it envoices.

V

The interplay of personal and interpersonal identities in androgynous disguise stages the conflicting effects of the ethopoetics of gender. Through this rhetorical and dramatistic trope Renaissance texts may articulate conservative cultural and historical concepts of sexual selfhood. The objectifying, self-defining genres of encomium and misogyny are prominently used in such conventional representations. At the same time, the confessional speech act functions recurrently through this discursive tradition to undermine the epideictic pairing of sexual self and other, male and female. An ambiguous ethos emerges in the process of self-revelation, even where such confession presumes its own univocal utterance through the shedding of past disguises. The rhetoric of confession defers sexual self-presence.

In this way androgynous disguise complements the ethopoetic process that marks the rhetorics of sovereignty and subjection. Strategies of disguise and character-making reveal and challenge the political and sexual motives of power, obedience, and desire that structure and underlie Renaissance discourses of essentialist selfhood. It is therefore significant that the three dramatic genres and corresponding figures that have been considered—satire, allegory, and tragicomedy; malcontent/prince, courtier, and androgyne—all function dialogically by both invoking and interrogating the tropes of discursive selfhood. Such dialogism is the key to the hybrid ethos that is fashioned by disguise. Each of these genres is also marked by a certain thematic undecidability or unfinishedness, which reflects the paradoxical impossibility of removing a disguise and ending its social significance, once it has been knowingly or even unknowingly assumed.

This complex of rhetorical functions makes disguise a critical trope for the Renaissance discourse of selfhood. Within specific ideological contexts, it figures the limits of images of selfhood and of genres of self-representation. Or perhaps it is better to say that disguise figures the limits to the limits that such images and genres would set up. For in always anticipating, even as it defers or denies, its final divestment, disguise reveals the ongoing process of selfhood. It is a process that, though framed by presumptions of origin and completion, enacts a dialogic, unfinished, and hybrid identity.

Notes

[1] M.C. Bradbrook 'Shakespeare and the Use of Disguise in Elizabethan Drama' *Essays in Criticism* 2 (1952) 167.

[2] *The Complete Works of John Lyly* 3 vols ed R. Warwick Bond (Oxford: Clarendon 1902) II.i.4-5, *Twelfth Night* II.i.27.

[3] Cf Keir Elam *The Semiotics of Theatre and Drama* (London: Methuen 1980) 87.

[4] Virginia Woolf *Between the Acts* (New York: Harcourt, Brace and World 1941) 88: ' "About a false Duke; and a Princess disguised as a boy; then the long lost heir turns out to be the beggar, because of a mole on his cheek; and Ferdinando and Carinthia—that's the Duke's daughter, only she's been lost in a cave— falls in love with Ferdinando who had been put into a basket as a baby by an aged crone. And they marry. That's I think what happens," she said, looking up from the programme.'

[5] 'An Homilie against excess of Apparell' in Mary Ellen Rickey and Thomas B. Stroup eds *Certaine Sermons or Homilies Appointed to be Read in the Time of Queen Elizabeth I (1547-1571)* (Gainesville: Scholars' Fascimiles 1968) 102-9. Further references will be included in the text.

[6] Jean E. Howard 'Renaissance Antitheatricality' in Jean E. Howard and Marion F. O'Connor eds *Shakespeare Reproduced: The Text in History and Ideology* (New York: Methuen 1987) 167.

[7] J.W. Binns 'Women or Transvestites on the Elizabethan Stage?: An Oxford Controversy' *Sixteenth Century Journal* 5 (1974) 113.

[8] Margot Heinemann *Puritanism and Theatre: Thomas Middleton and Opposition Drama under the Early Stuarts* (Cambridge: Cambridge University Press 1980) 21, 200-36; cf Jean E. Howard 'Crossdressing, the Theatre, and Gender Struggle in Early Modern England' *Shakespeare Quarterly* 39 (1988) 422: 'Dress, as a highly regulated semiotic system, became a primary site where a struggle over the mutability of the social order was conducted.'

[9] Phyllis Rackin 'Androgyny, Mimesis, and the Marriage of the Boy Heroine on the English Renaissance Stage' *PMLA* 102 (1987) 38; cf Michael D. Bristol *Carnival and Theater: Plebeian Culture and the Structure of Authority in Renaissance England* (New York: Methuen 1985) 167, Jonathan Dollimore 'Subjectivity, Sexuality, and Transgression: The Jacobean Connection,' *Renaissance Drama* 17 (1986) 77.

[10] Steven Mullaney *The Place of the Stage: License, Play, and Power in Renaissance England* (Chicago: University of Chicago Press 1988) 22.

[11] Cf Natalie Zemon Davis 'The Reasons of Misrule' in *Society and Culture in Early-Modern France* (Stanford: Stanford University Press 1975) 116, Jonathan Haynes 'Festivity and the Dramatic Economy of Jonson's *Bartholomew Fair' ELH* 51 (1984) 654-68, Richard Wilson ' "Is this a holiday?"': Shakespeare's Roman Carnival' *ELH* 54 (1987) 31-44.

[12] Cf Lawrence Stone *The Family, Sex and Marriage in England 1500-1800* (London: Weidenfeld and Nicolson 1977) 135 and *passim,* Mary Beth Rose *The Expense of Spirit: Love and Sexuality in English Renaissance Drama* (Ithaca: Cornell University Press 1988) 3 and *passim.*

[13] Harold Garfinkel 'Passing and the Managed Achievement of Sex Status in an Intersexed Person, Part 1' in *Studies in Ethnomethodology* (Cambridge: Polity 1989) 118-24 (original emphasis).

[14] Cf Stephen Orgel 'Nobody's Perfect: Or Why Did the English Stage Take Boys for Women' *South Atlantic Quarterly* 88 (1989) 7-29; Howard 'Crossdressing, the Theatre, and Gender Struggle' 428, 439-40.

[15] Garfinkel 'Passing' 133.

[16] Thomas Wilson *The Arte of Rhetorique* ed G.H. Mair (Oxford: Clarendon 1909) 175.

[17] Henry Peacham *The Garden of Eloquence* ed R.C. Alston (Menston: Scolar Press 1971) c.ii.

[18] As suggested in ch 1, in its distinction between the 'proper' and the figurative, the old rhetoric initiated more recent theories of the relation of metaphor and metonymy to the subject's speech—for example, the speculations of Roman Jakobson ('Two Aspects of Language and Two Types of Aphasic Disturbances' in *Fundamentals of Language* ['S-Gravenhague: Mouton 1956]) on their role in Freud's work on dreams and the language process generally (notions developed by Lacan).

[19] Ian Maclean *The Renaissance Notion of Woman: A Study in the Fortunes of Scholasticism and Medical Science in European Intellectual Life* (Cambridge: Cambridge University Press 1980) 8; Michel Foucault, in *The Use of Pleasure* (vol 2 of *The History of Sexuality* trans Robert Hurley [New York: Vintage 1990]), notes the importance for masculine self-formation of ensuring the oppositions remain intact (47).

[20] *Twelfth Night* V.i.250.

[21] Carla Freccero, in 'The Other and the Same: The Image of the Hermaphrodite in Rabelais' in Margaret Ferguson, Maureen Quilligan, and Nancy J. Vickers eds *Rewriting the Renaissance: The Discourses of Sexual Difference in Early Modern Europe* (Chicago: University of Chicago Press 1986), traces depictions of woman's belated androgynizing effect on man to the *Metamorphoses:* 'in Ovid's account, hermaphroditism becomes a curse, the reduction of an essentially masculine nature' (150).

[22] Peacham *Garden of Eloquence* C.ii. On the related metonymic function of woman in medieval discourse, see R. Howard Bloch 'Medieval Misogyny' *Representations* 20 (1987) 10.

[23] I.A. Richards *The Philosophy of Rhetoric* (New York: Oxford University Press 1965) 97.

[24] Plato *The Symposium* 191c-d in *The Collected Dialogues of Plato* ed Edith Hamilton and Huntington Cairns (Princeton: Princeton University Press 1985); cf Freccero 'The Other and the Same' 145-6.

[25] Cicero *De Oratore* trans E.W. Sutton and H. Rackham (Cambridge: Loeb 1975) I.viii.34, George Puttenham *The Arte of English Poesie* ed Gladys Doidge Willcock and Alice Walker (Cambridge: Cambridge University Press 1936) 7.

[26] Rose *Expense of Spirit* 9-10.

[27] Coppélia Kahn 'The Providential Tempest and the Shakespearean Family' in Murray M. Schwartz and Coppélia Kahn eds *Representing Shakespeare: New Psychoanalytic Essays* (Baltimore: Johns Hopkins University Press 1980) 227.

[28] Joel Fineman *Shakespeare's Perjured Eye: The Invention of Poetic Subjectivity in the Sonnets* (Berkeley: University of California Press 1986) 301.

[29] Coppélia Kahn 'The Absent Mother in *King Lear*' in Ferguson et al eds *Rewriting the Renaissance* 49. This reading of romance seems to derive from Northrop Frye *The Anatomy of Criticism: Four Essays* (New York: Atheneum 1967): 'Translated into dream terms, the quest-romance is the search of the libido or desiring self for a fulfillment that will deliver it from the anxieties of reality' (193). On the critical dismissal of Fletcherian tragicomedy as 'decadent,' cf Rose *Expense of Spirit* 181-5 and Dollimore 'Subjectivity, Sexuality, and Transgression' 73.

[30] Clifford Leech 'Introduction' to *The Two Noble Kinsmen* in *Pericles, Prince of Tyre, Cymbeline, The Two Noble Kinsmen* (New York: Signet 1986) xxxi.

[31] Arthur C. Kirsch *Jacobean Dramatic Perspectives* (Charlottesville: University Press of Virginia 1972) 41.

[32] Kirsch *Jacobean Dramatic Perspectives* 47; cf Eugene M. Waith *The Pattern of Tragicomedy in Beaumont and Fletcher* (New Haven: Yale University Press 1952) 42, 184; Andrew Gurr 'Introduction' in *Philaster or Love Lies a-Bleeding* (London: Methuen 1969) xxx.

[33] Augustus William Schlegel *A Course of Lectures on Dramatic Arts and Literature* trans John Black (London: Henry G. Bohn 1846) 468. This psychological essentialism often turns sexual; see Simon Shepherd's discussion of efforts to establish a suitable male heterosexuality for the bard and his work, 'Shakespeare's Private Drawer: Shakespeare and Homosexuality' in Graham Holderness ed *The Shakespeare Myth* (Manchester: University of Manchester Press, 1988) 96-110, and Joseph Pequigney *Such Is My Love: A Study of Shakespeare's Sonnets* (Chicago: University of Chicago Press 1985) 49-51.

[34] Cf Joel Fineman 'The Turn of the Shrew' in Patricia Parker and Geoffrey Hartman eds *Shakespeare and the Question of Theory* (New York: Methuen 1985) 153, Terry Eagleton *William Shakespeare* (Oxford: Basil Blackwell 1986) 65, Laura Levine 'Men in Women's Clothing: Anti-theatricality and Effeminization from 1579 to 1642' *Criticism* 28 (1986) 135-6; in 'Subjectivity, Sexuality, and Transgression,' Dollimore suggests a related reading of Fletcher's *Love's Cure:* 'a relegitimation of masculinity coexists with an ironic critique of it' (73).

[35] Fineman *Shakespeare's Perjured Eye* 267.

[36] Ibid 65.

[37] Gorgias *Encomium of Helen* ed and trans D.M. MacDowell (Bristol: Bristol Classic 1982) 21. Further references will be included in the text.

[38] Like Eve, the betrayer *or* mother of mankind, Helen was also used to defend women. In *Women and the English Renaissance: Literature and the Nature of Womankind, 1540-1620* (Brighton: Harvester 1984), Linda Woodbridge notes that Helen served as 'one of the frequentest *exempla* of both formal defenders and attackers' (127). This reversibility again suggests the figural ambiguity of woman.

[39] Cf Rose *Expense of Spirit* 206. Note Frank Lentricchia *Criticism and Social Change* (Chicago: University of Chicago Press 1983) 114 on philosophy's parallel deconstruction of the female subject through privileging a rhetoric of reason over 'feeling.'

[40] Ernst Robert Curtius *European Literature and the Latin Middle Ages* trans Willard Trask (New York: Pantheon 1953) 70. The humorous tone of Gorgias' conclusion may not mock Helen. As Maclean comments on Cornelius Agrippa's *De nobilitate et praecellentia foemini sexus* (1529), 'the humour may indicate the impossibility of discussing in serious terms the proposition of woman's equality, and therefore represents a strategy of discourse which is subversive in intention' (*Renaissance Notion of Women* 91). Woodbridge, however, emphasizes that the majority of misogynist Renaissance texts do adopt a jesting tone (*Women and the English Renaissance* 31 and *passim*).

[41] Edmund Spenser *The Faerie Queene* III.ii.1 in *Spenser: Poetical Works* ed J.C. Smith and E. de Selincourt (Oxford: Oxford University Press 1979); Lauren Silberman 'Singing Unsung Heroines: Androgynous Discourse in Book 3 of *The Faerie Queene*' in Ferguson et al eds *Rewriting the Renaissance* 259-71.

[42] Isocrates 'Encomium on Helen' in *Isocrates* 3 vols trans George Norlin and Larve van Hook (Cambridge: Loeb 1961-6) III:22. Further references (to paragraph numbers) will be included in the text.

[43] Cf Cicero *De Oratore* II.lxxx.325, Richards *Philosophy of Rhetoric* 24, Kenneth Burke *A Rhetoric of Motives* (Berkeley: University of California Press 1969) 52. Recalling Puttenham, we might note that his switch in the rhetoric of rhetoric, from warfare to courtly diplomacy, reflects a change in late-Renaissance ideals for male aristocratic behaviour; see Lawrence Stone *The Crisis of the Aristocracy* (Oxford: Clarendon 1965) 244.

[44] Thomas M. Greene *The Light in Troy: Imitation and Discovery in Renaissance Poetry* (New Haven: Yale University Press 1982) 40.

[45] Jonathan Dollimore *Radical Tragedy: Religion, Ideology and Power in the Drama of Shakespeare and His Contemporaries* (Chicago: University of Chicago Press 1984) 109.

[46] La Rochefoucauld *Maxims* trans Leonard Tancock (Harmondsworth Middlesex: Penguin 1986) 37-8; cf Rose *Expense of Spirit* 200-1, and René Girard 'The Politics of Desire in *Troilus and Cressida*' in Parker and Hartman eds *Shakespeare and the Question of Theory* 188-209.

[47] On the interrelation of encomium and misogyny, cf Paolo Valesio *Novantiqua: Rhetorics as a Contemporary Theory* (Bloomington: Indiana University Press 1980) 271 n15; Dympna Callaghan *Woman and Gender in Renaissance Tragedy: A Study of King Lear, Othello, The Duchess of Malfi and The White Devil* (New York: Harvester 1989) 125; R. Howard Bloch 'Chaucer's Maiden's Head: "The Physician's Tale" and the Poetics of Virginity' *Representations* 28 (1989) 127.

[48] Wilson *Arte of Rhetorique* A.iii. Further references will be included in the text.

[49] Quintilian *Institutio Oratio* trans E.H. Butler (London: Loeb 1969) III.v.2.

[50] W.B. and E.P. *A Helpe to Discourse, or A Miscelany of Merriment* (London: 1619) 119; cf Lily B. Campbell *Shakespeare's Tragic Heroes: Slaves of Passion* (New York: Barnes and Noble 1967) 99.

[51] In *The Book of the Courtier* (trans Thomas Hoby [London: Dent 1948]), Lord Gasper, Castiglione's 'aggrieved misogynist' (Joan Kelly *Women, History, and Theory* [Chicago: University of Chicago Press 1984] 39), makes a similar observation: 'when a woman is borne, it is a slacknesse or default of nature' (196).

[52] Thomas Wright *The Passions of the Mind in General* ed William Webster Newbold (New York: Garland 1986) 242; cf La Rochefoucauld's maxim 262: 'There is no passion in which love of self rules so despotically as love' (*Maxims* 72).

[53] See Spenser *Faerie Queene* VII.lviii

[54] For example, *Campaspe* II.ii.31-57, *Epicoene* I.i.109-44, *Hamlet* III.i.106-49, *Othello* II.i.100-66, Castiglione *The Courtier* 66-7, Michel de Montaigne *Essays* 3 vols trans John Florio (London: Dent 1965) II:193, Wright *Passions of the Mind* 188, *The Sermons of John Donne* ed Theodore A. Gill (New York: Meridian 1961) 154;

cf Callaghan *Woman and Gender* 118, Bloch 'Medieval Misogyny' 9-15.

[55] *Othello* IV.i.254-5; cf Peter Stallybrass 'Patriarchal Territories: The Body Enclosed' in Ferguson et al eds *Rewriting the Renaissance* 137, Catherine Belsey *The Subject of Tragedy: Identity and Difference in Renaissance Drama* (London: Methuen 1985) 149.

[56] Wright *Passions of the Mind* 120; cf I Corinthians 14:34, Belsey *Subject of Tragedy* 191, and Parker *Literary Fat Ladies* 106-17, 125, especially 112, where Parker notes a similar deployment of nature in Peacham's *Garden of Eloquence* and Richard Sherry's *Treatise of Schemes and Tropes* (1550).

[57] Cf Kelly *Women, History, and Theory* 34-5.

[58] Hélène Cixous 'The Laugh of the Medusa' *Signs* 1 (1976) 887

[59] *Sermons of John Donne* 104

[60] Castiglione *The Courtier* 219; cf Howard 'Cross-dressing, the Theatre, and Gender Struggle' on the 'strong discursive linkages . . . between female cross-dressing and the threat of female sexual incontinence' (420).

[61] Cf Stephen Orgel 'Prospero's Wife' *Representations* 8 (1984) 1-13.

[62] Michel Foucault *History of Sexuality* vol 1 *An Introduction* trans Robert Hurley (Harmondsworth Middlesex: Penguin 1981) 61; cf Elizabeth Hanson 'Torture and Truth in Renaissance England' *Representations* 34 (1991) 67 on the potential ambiguity of sworn speech in criminal trials.

[63] E. K. Chambers *The Elizabethan Stage* 4 vols (Oxford: Claredon 1923) 1:248; cf Howard 'Renaissance Antitheatricality' 169 on the links between women and acting.

[64] John Calvin *The Institutes of the Christian Religion* 2 vols trans Henry Beveridge (Grand Rapids Mich: Wm B. Eerdmans 1966) 1:540. Further references, all to vol 1, will be included in the text.

[65] Cf Dollimore 'Subjectivity, Sexuality, and Transgression': 'For John Rainolds the boy transvestite destroyed the fragile moral restraint containing an anarchic male sexuality' (65).

[66] Robert Burton *The Anatomy of Melancholy* 3 vols (London: Dent 1968) III:154-5; in 'Nobody's Perfect' Orgel suggests that heterosexuality was generally conceived as more of a cultural threat than homosexuality (26).

[67] Wright *Passions of the Mind* 249.

[68] *Sermons of John Donne* 151.

[69] Cf the two conclusions Levine draws from her study of antitheatrical texts—either 'there is no such thing as a masculine self' or there is 'something horrendously "other" at the core of the self': 'Men in Women's Clothing' 136.

[70] Montaigne 'Apologie of Raymond Sebond' in *Essays* II:193.

[71] Cf Jacques Lacan *The Four Fundamental Concepts of Psycho-Analysis* trans Alan Sheridan (New York: Norton 1981) 154.

[72] See Kenneth Burke *A Grammar of Motives* (Cleveland: Meridian 1962) 516-17.

[73] Beaumont and Fletcher *A King and No King* I.i.188-91. All references to Beaumont and Fletcher are to *The Dramatic Works in the Beaumont and Fletcher Canon* 10 vols ed Fredson Bowers (Cambridge: Cambridge University Press 1966). *A King and No King* and *The Maid's Tragedy* are in vol 2; *Philaster* is in vol 1. Further references will be included in the text.

[74] Robert K. Hunter 'Introduction' to *Philaster* in *Dramatic Works* 1:383, 385.

[75] René Girard *Violence and the Sacred* trans Patrick Gregory (Baltimore: Johns Hopkins University Press 1977) 79, 8.

[76] Greenblatt *Shakespearean Negotiations: The Circulation of Social Energy in Renaissance England* (Berkeley: University of California Press 1988) 78.

[77] On this motif, see Mary Douglas *Purity and Danger: An Analysis of Conceptes of Pollution and Taboo* (London: Routledge 1966) 95.

[78] Ibid 115.

[79] The publisher's address to the reader before the second quarto of 1622 uses this complex of bodily imagery to justify itself as the true edition: 'Courteous Reader. *Philaster,* and *Arethusa* his love, have laine so long a bleeding, by reason of some dangerous and gaping wounds, which they received in the first Impression . . . assuredly they will now find double favour, being reformed, and set forth suteable, to their birth, and breeding' (1:375).

[80] Gurr 'Introduction' *Philaster* lxvi.

[81] Cf Lisa Jardine *Still Harping on Daughters: Women*

and Drama in the Age of Shakespeare (Brighton: Harvester 1983) 186.

[82] John F. Danby *Poets on Fortune's Hill: Studies in Sidney, Shakespeare, Beaumont and Fletcher* (Washington: Kennikat 1962) 201-2.

[83] Cf Lacan's notion of 'the drama of Hamlet as the man who has lost the way of his desire': 'Desire and the Interpretation of Desire in *Hamlet*' in Shoshana Felman ed *Literature and Psychoanalysis: The Question of Reading—Otherwise* (Baltimore: Johns Hopkins University Press 1982) 12.

[84] On masculinist self-fashioning through hunting and love, cf sonnet 67 in Spenser's *Amoretti*.

[85] Jacques Derrida *The Postcard: From Socrates to Freud and Beyond* trans Alan Bass (Chicago: University of Chicago Press 1987) 145.

[86] Tennenhouse *Power on Display* 63.

[87] Cf Dollimore 'Subjectivity, Sexuality, and Transgression': 'Masculinity is rooted in a sexual violence performed inseparably against both men and women' (75).

[88] Michel Foucault *Madness and Civilization: A History of Insanity in the Age of Reason* trans Richard Howard (New York Vintage 1973) 34. Foucault also notes the revelatory function of madness in 'the tragicomic structures of preclassical literature' (34).

[89] Cf Lear's continuing struggle against the feminizing *Hysterica passio, King Lear* I.iv.296-9, II.iv.56-8, II.iv.296-9.

THEATRICAL DECEPTION

Susan Baker (essay date 1992)

SOURCE: "Personating Persons: Rethinking Shakespearean Disguises," in *Shakespeare Quarterly,* Vol. 43, No. 3, Fall, 1992, pp. 303-16.

[*In the following essay, Baker discusses Shakespeare's treatment of rank and power in terms of his characters' changing personages, concluding that the grounds of power remain fixed within a natural hierarchy.*]

I want to borrow an old word and its inflections. Shakespeare's contemporaries used the verb *personate* for the theatrical activity we designate as *acting a part* or *creating a role,* and this obsolete word has at least two advantages over those in current use: first, it sug-

gests "character" as activity; second, its invention in early modern England hints at a changing view of subjectivity. The first recorded appearance of *personation* occurs in the Induction to John Marston's *Antonio and Mellida* (probably 1599-1600), and, as Andrew Gurr argues,

> It is not stretching plausibility too far to suggest that the term was called into being by the same developments—in the kinds of part given the actors to play and their own skill in their parts—that made two great tragedians succeed the extemporising clowns on the pinnacle of theatrical fame. By 1600 characterisation was the chief requisite of the successful player.[1]

I suspect Gurr is right about this alteration in actors' goals and audiences' tastes; indeed, I suspect further that an increasing interest in characterization over improvisation was culturally significant. At this point, however, I shall simply borrow the term *personation* to indicate an activity frequently undertaken by characters in Shakespearean drama, the activity of *personating* someone else.[2] That is, I shall use *personation* to refer to onstage figures behaving as actors (rather than to actors carrying out their profession).[3]

It may be necessary to distinguish immediately between what I am calling *personation* and the broader term *disguise.* First, as I shall argue in more detail, personation requires disguise, but not all disguises are personations, at least not to the same degree. And second, I want to ask questions different from those often asked about disguise in the drama. Most studies of Shakespearean disguise have stressed either the thematics of illusion or a self-discovery presumably enabled by disguise.[4] Rather than dismissing disguise on the stage as merely (uninterestingly) conventional, or considering what the act and actions of disguising tell us about the represented disguisers as "individuals," or pondering what metatheatrical effects disguises create, I want to look at what the plays tell us about the people Shakespearean disguisers *personate.* By asking what happens when Shakespearean characters don disguises, I want to ask how Shakespearean personators insert themselves (their alternate, invented selves) into a (putatively) preexisting social order.

Although in literature the act of disguising most often functions primarily as a plot device, as a factor of narrative necessity, I would argue that representations of the process and consequences of disguising—as a sort of secondary elaboration—inevitably incorporate local detail and historically specific practices. Extrapolations from drama to "real life" are surely fraught with difficulties, even as we increasingly interpret such life as itself theatrical. Generally, this theoretical tangle doesn't bother me much; I am more concerned with the prospect of intervening in the ways today's readings of Shakespearean drama inform today's selves than with retrospectively reconstructing early modern personhood. The two projects are, however, not unrelated, and to the extent that I want to grasp something of what it meant to be an early modern person, personations *within* the plays can suggest what their original audiences assumed about human interactions, about what people needed or wanted to know about each other.

A contemporary example may be useful. In the United States today, new acquaintances generally ask each other "What do you do?"—a question that everyone understands as "What do you do for a living? What is your job?" Were I to decide to pass myself off as someone (anyone) else, I would have to be prepared to answer this question and to conduct myself accordingly. Similarly, a dramatic representation of someone pretending to be someone else—for whatever reason— would be likely to include such exchanges.[5] The point is that employment information need not be diegetically relevant, but the dramatization of plausible chat would reveal it. To my mind it is the very offhanded quality of such revelation that suggests its ideological importance.

Folktales provide another instructive example: no matter how similar the several versions of a widespread tale, specific renderings inevitably take on some local color. So too, although Arden, Belmont, and Illyria are never-never lands of romantic comedy, where Jack shall have Jill and nought shall go ill, they are also Shakespeare's England. Never-never lands, lands of Cockaigne, and big rock-candy mountains can only be imagined in terms of environments already known. And I would suggest that the homely particularities embedded in tales uninterested in naturalistic representation may well be ideologically revealing, may well signal attitudes and practices so taken for granted as to be invisible to tellers and their auditors as anything but "natural," or "inevitable," or "universal." It is to learn something of "what goes without saying" that I want to examine practices of disguise in Shakespeare's plays.

It will be useful to distinguish among four broad classes of disguise that appear in Shakespearean drama and the relations to which each answers. In choosing a disguise, characters may do any of the following: hide their own identities without asserting any other; substitute another, already existing identity for their own; invent a specific role or persona for a specific and limited purpose; or, finally, adopt a role—personate an invented, particular identity—to be played in multiple circumstances and for multiple audiences. This last category is the most interesting for the purposes of this essay, partly because it outlines for us what attributes seem to add up to a human being, what one needs to know and to present about oneself in order to interact with other people, what is required to act as a person.

More important, it allows us to track interactions through which a "self-conscious" personator maintains a fiction of identity. In other words, although personation involves disguisings, not all disguises are personations in the sense that they make up a new person. Still, each of the four categories of disguise offers some clues about the construction of early modern personhood.

The first sort of disguise, one that requires a minimum of personation, could be called that of the cloak, the mask, the vizard, or the veil. These are devices for allowing the disguise *of* without asserting any particular disguise *as*. Each of the various coverings hides whoever is behind it without asserting a specific (alternative) personage. However we evaluate Hal and Poins vizarded for robbery, Coriolanus in Antium, Polixenes and Camillo attending the sheepshearing festival, even Edgar armored to challenge Edmund, such disguises insist upon the hiding of a particular person rather than on the personation of someone new. Dialogically, cloaks and masks often enable an evasion of responsibility. As devices of concealment, these disguises seek either to evade one's own responsibility or to evoke in others responses that appearing in one's own guise would preclude. By hiding someone, these disguises allow for crimes (Hal), for spying (Polixenes), and for movement into enemy territory (Coriolanus, Edgar). In many cases disguise-by-cloaking acts as the antithesis of personation: if personation requires preparing a response, cloaking interposes a barrier that allows the disguisers to avoid answering for their actions.

In other cases disguise-by-cloaking lures the witnesses (or victims) of such disguise into statements that would never be pronounced in the acknowledged presence of the disguiser—Florizel's "One being dead" speech (4.4.387 ff.) is a clear example, as are those of participants in Shakespeare's various masked-ball scenes.[6] Frequently these disguises function both dramaturgically and diegetically as techniques of deferral, tactics that delay recognition in order to intensify the strategic power of recognition. Indeed, one could almost say that the represented people in these maskings are complicit with the playwright; for example, Hal, Polixenes, Edgar in knight's garb—all withhold their identities toward a moment of revelation, a moment of recognition prepared to astound its onstage audience and move the theater audience as witness to this astonishment. This deferral by disguise is most obvious in two cases on the borderline between cloaking and impersonation: a veiled Hero pretends briefly to be her own cousin in *Much Ado,* and the Provost of *Measure for Measure* presents a muffled Claudio as an anonymous prisoner saved from beheading. In both these instances the figures impersonated (briefly) remain mysterious to the assembled group or to a significant part of it, and the disguise exists only to be discarded. That is, the hiding exists only as a precondition for revelation, and the revelation is explicitly dialogic, explicitly designed to evoke a response. Of course, to hide one's face is always to open the possibility of being taken for someone else, but in Shakespearean disguises of cloak or vizard, the pertinent move is the hiding of one identity rather than the active assertion of another. It is worth noting, however, that most often the impulse for cloaking or masking marks some distortion, disruption, or dislocation of *reciprocal* relations, of mutually implicating bonds—working either to evade the obligations attending such bonds or, more often and more obliquely, to enforce them.

One may, perhaps, endorse Hero's claims on Claudio, dispute Polixenes' demands on Florizel, and puzzle over Hal's casual theft from those he owes good governance; but in each case we can see that reciprocal claims are at stake. Taken in aggregate, the cloaking and masking disguises in Shakespearean drama seem to argue for a connection between the disruption of mutual bonds and the obscuring of personal identity. Like x in an algebraic formula, the vizard or veil inscribes an absence and an ignorance—a "meaning" that becomes singular and visible only within a network of orderly relations. Where reciprocal relations are somehow violated, persons are no longer themselves; when persons are no longer themselves, reciprocal relations are distorted. And as we shall see, relations are at stake as well when one Shakespearean character usurps another's identity.

Shakespearean drama includes only a few instances of this second form of disguise, of one character directly impersonating another, deliberately assuming someone else's identity. As I have already noted, for my purposes these substitutive disguises are less noteworthy than those for which a new "person" must be invented. To pretend to be a particular someone is an act of imitation (mimesis) rather than construction. (One might compare current inflections of *impersonate:* stand-up comedians do impersonations; variety performances include female impersonators; one may be arrested for impersonating an officer.) Imitative disguise requires simply adopting (wherever relevant) already established status, attributes, history, behavioral quirks, and so on—knowledge of which is shared in advance by both the disguisers and those they delude. Such disguises—substitutions—are acts of appropriation rather than invention and often tend toward the exaggeration of caricature.

Although substitutive disguises offer little useful information about precisely what in the early modern period was seen as constituting a person, they do suggest reasons (motives) for the social demand that people be constituted as singular. With one minor exception, all substitutive impersonations in Shakespearean drama involve illegitimate sexuality; they either accompany attempts to evade responsible relations or serve as

protective reactions to such attempts. (The exception occurs when assorted soldiers in *1 Henry IV* dress as the king, offering their lives and bodies as decoys to preserve his.) In the bed-tricks of *Measure for Measure* and *All's Well,* the substitution of one woman for another foils a man's illicit desire and legitimates a marriage of otherwise dubious status. In *Merry Wives,* Falstaff's will toward adulterous seduction leads to his disguises as the fat old woman of Brainford and as Herne the Hunter; this play uses impersonation to accomplish the comic humiliation of a braggart-lecher who presumes too far on the sexual privileges of his class. In *Much Ado About Nothing* and *Cymbeline,* on the other hand, the impersonations are calculated to humiliate innocent women: Don John's plot to have Margaret (offstage) taken for Hero implies sexual misconduct and provokes Claudio to sexual slander; Cloten dons Posthumus's clothing so that his intended rape of Imogen may be all the more painful to her. Even in *The Taming of the Shrew,* Tranio's impersonation of Lucentio and the Pedant's of Vincentio (at Tranio's instigation) work to sidestep the legitimating process of premarital negotiations. It is no wonder Bianca turns pale when the right Vincentio is recognized (5.1.138); she has married without securing any dower rights. If we are to read Bianca's petulance in the final scene as anything beyond a farcical reversal of expectations, we might think of it less as revealing some previously concealed nature, some long-term hypocrisy, than as symptomatic of a not unreasonable anger at an unsatisfactory marriage settlement.[7] (Whatever Vincentio might mean when he tells Baptista "we will content you" [1. 135], it is probable that the arrangements would be less lavish than those Tranio—disguised as Lucentio—had promised.)

At any rate, it seems clear enough that, in Shakespearean drama, impersonation is most often a sexual ploy, specifically designed either to evade or to enforce social sanctions on sexuality. In such instances we may be reminded of the extent to which the social order *is* sexual positioning, of the extent to which subjectivity is marked by limits on desire. At this point, it is worth emphasizing how the circumstances and consequences of both types of disguise—masking and substituting—define subjectivity as thoroughly social. In all these instances, to alter one's relations to other people is to alter oneself as a person.

Of the varieties of disguise, I am most interested in the declarations and practices of those who are represented as inventing—creating, personating—a new identity. In these instances characters not only obscure who they have been but also must take pains to signal who they have become. When a new identity is to be personated, it has no preexisting relationships: no bonds, no reciprocal obligations, no legitimated sexual or other status. Yet the personator will be required to interact with other people; disguise is pointless without an audience. To watch and listen to characters undertaking personations, then, is to get some sense of what Elizabethans needed to know about each other. (I should perhaps stress that I take this information to be all the more telling in that it is *not* directly tied to authorial meditations on selfhood; rather, it appears as secondary elaboration of a plot device. As such secondary fleshing out, the details that accumulate around personations seem likely to point to what is taken for granted as constituting the identity of persons.)

Looking at the several occasions in Shakespearean drama when a character deliberately enacts a new persona, makes up a new person, we can divide them roughly into two types. Personations of the first sort are undertaken for one specific purpose; they are created for a limited and determinate audience and for a limited period of time, as when Feste personates Sir Topas to torment Malvolio, or Jessica dresses as a page to flee Venice. Such one-off personations can be thought of as task-oriented, as *ad hoc*. Most often this version of personation requires disguise as a *type*, generally an "occupational" type, visually marked for a predetermined slot in a socioeconomic hierarchy: priest, page, peasant, lawyer's clerk. The other sort of personations, which I shall refer to as "improvisational," are prepared for multiple audiences and for an indefinite period of time; that is, neither the audience nor the duration of the personation can be predicted at the moment of its adoption: think of Ganymede, Cesario, Caius, for example.

This division into task-oriented and improvisational disguises is, inevitably, somewhat arbitrary, and the resulting categories are impure. Portia, for example, invents the task-oriented role of Balthazar in order to save Antonio's life, but she quickly becomes improvisational—opportunistic even—when Bassanio insists that Balthazar accept a reward. In the case of *Cymbeline*'s Posthumus Leonatus, it is dramatically irrelevant how long he's to play a peasant; his disguise is improvisational in terms of the play's imitated action but effectively task-oriented in its brevity and its limited audience. Where personations are more extended, however, the figures being personated must be more developed. And in the representation of such figures, practical demands of dramaturgy intersect with custom, with what might be called everyday life.

Among the many early modern tracts debating women's roles are two with bastard-Latin titles, *Hic Mulier* and *Haec Vir*.[8] *Hic Mulier* attacks as unnatural the spectacle of women wearing men's clothes, and in *Haec Vir* a figure named "Hic Mulier" defends women's crossdressing on several grounds, including the arbitrariness of custom, an arbitrariness demonstrated through examples. In the midst of assorted Roman and other non-English practices, one specifically English practice is included:

even at this day it is a general received custom amongst our English that when we meet or overtake any man in our travel or journeying, to examine him whither he rides, how far, to what purpose, and where he lodgeth. Nay, and with that unmannerly boldness of inquisition that it is a certain ground of a most insufficient quarrel not to receive a full satisfaction of those demands which go far astray from good manners or comely civility.[9]

The syntax is convoluted, but the import is clear enough: custom requires travelers to answer specific questions that would be rude if asked under other circumstances. The writer seems to find this interrogation of travelers as notably odd as bathing in oils, delivering orations from a bed, or wearing white to signify mourning—strange practices that "Hic Mulier" cites from Latin literature. I doubt that we can recover the extent to which journeys in early modern England actually mandated interactions contrary to those appropriate for other settings, but the pamphleteer indeed describes exactly what happens when Shakespearean travelers first encounter other people.[10] They are asked questions.

This practice is certainly handy for dramatic exposition in general and specifically for letting an audience know the particulars of a personation. For example, Lear asks Caius:

> How now, what art thou? . . .
> What dost thou profess? . . .
> Who wouldst thou serve? . . .
> What services canst do? . . .
> How old art thou? . . .
>
> (1.4.9, 11, 24, 31, 36)

I would stress that such exchanges are not expository in quite the same way as "This is Illyria, lady," or "Well, this is the forest of Arden." That is, at the moments when travelers are questioned, the audience already knows all it needs to about setting and situation. Rather, these interrogations index salient information about any given person. Indeed, Shakespeare's personators are repeatedly offered the opportunity to present their new identities through a series of questions.

Frequently, questions are asked about one's current dwelling-place. In *As You Like It,* for example, Orlando asks Ganymede, "Where dwell you, pretty youth?" (3.2.334). Throughout this play people seem interested in each other's residences. Immediately on entering the Forest of Arden, Rosalind and Celia, seeking food and shelter, are, conveniently enough, able to buy from Corin's master "his cote, his flocks, and bounds of feed" and to hire Corin at better wages than the previous owner had paid him (2.4.83, 94). Their new house and grazing rights provide more than shelter and sustenance; they serve to demarcate the identities of Ganymede and Aliena. Indeed, it is specifically a discrepancy between dwelling-place and accent that prompts the invention of a biography for Ganymede:

> ORLANDO Your accent is something finer than you could purchase in so remov'd a dwelling.
>
> ROSALIND I have been told so of many; but indeed an old religious uncle of mine taught me to speak.
>
>   (3.2.341-44)

Once this disjunction is accounted for, Ganymede and Aliena are identified throughout with the sheepcote, even to the point that, for no immediately apparent reason, Ganymede volunteers information about their dwelling-place to Phebe. Additionally, when Oliver is seeking Ganymede and Aliena, he first asks if they are the owners of the sheepcote and only afterwards comments on the garments, age, features, and deportment by which Orlando has said Ganymede could be recognized. And Oliver couches the announcement of his plans to marry Aliena as a decision to become a shepherd, to adopt her occupancy as his occupation.

Although other plays share *As You Like It*'s concern with current dwellings, the single question most frequently asked of Shakespearean travelers is "Where do you come from?" And the question "From whence?" can be answered almost indifferently with information about regional or paternal origins, with a doubleness that perhaps sounds odd to our ears.[11] Some examples follow:

> BAPTISTA Whence are you, sir? What may I call your name?
>
> PETRUCHIO Petruchio is my name, Antonio's son,
> A man well known throughout all Italy.
>
> BAPTISTA I know him well; you are welcome for his sake.
>
>   (*Taming of the Shrew*, 2.1.67-70)

> BAPTISTA Lucentio is your name, of whence, I pray?
>
> TRANIO Of Pisa, sir, son to Vincentio.
>
> BAPTISTA A mighty man of Pisa; by report
> I know him well. You are very welcome, sir.
>
>   (*Taming of the Shrew*, 2.1.102-5)

> TIMON Whence are you?
>
> CAPHIS   Of Athens here, my lord.
>
>   (*Timon of Athens*, 2.2.17)

> THAISA And further, he desires to know of you
> Of whence you are, your name, and parentage.

> PERICLES A gentleman of Tyre, my name, Pericles,
> My education been in arts and arms.
>
>   (*Pericles*, 2.3.79-82)

> CYMBELINE   'Tis now the time
> To ask of whence you are. Report it.
> BELARIUS   Sir,
> In Cambria are we born, and gentlemen.
>
>   (*Cymbeline*, 5.5.15-18)

And—as we might expect—*Measure for Measure* works a twist on the usual responses:

> ESCALUS Of whence are you?
> DUKE Not of this country, though my chance is now
> To use it for my time. I am a brother
> Of gracious order, late come from the [See],
> In special business from his Holiness.
>
>   (*Measure for Measure*, 3.2.216-20)

Tentatively, I would suggest that the importance of answers to "From whence?" signals a double sense of *nativity* as one of several related terms that conjoin inconsistencies in theories of origin. At this point, I want to consider another of these double-edged words: *breeding*.

Two words associated with breeding recur in the descriptions of Shakespearean personators: *carriage* and *comportment*. Some sort of reference to the way one carries oneself often accompanies the decision to don a disguise. And the young women can be quite amusing on the topic of assuming a swaggering manliness. Thus Shakespearean personators are frequently shown to be aware that they must change their manners along with their clothing. Roughly as often, however, their "breeding" is revealed by their comportment, as when Proteus tells Sebastian (Julia) that his/her face and behavior "witness good bringing up" (*The Two Gentlemen of Verona*, 4.4.69). Such remarks have been read as evidence of Renaissance snobbery, of a belief that the innate superiority of those born to high rank will shine through the most humble clothing.[12] Yet the plays' stress on such terms as *comportment* opens a way to challenge the essentialism of such snobbery. Carriage, after all, is learned behavior. One's breeding, in the sense of rearing rather than of genetics, determines deportment, although the term *breeding* itself ordinarily works to occlude this distinction. Keith Johnstone claims that he teaches master/servant scenes as ones "in which both parties act as if all the space belonged to the master."[13] And indeed Ganymede, Cesario, Balthazar, Sebastian, Fidele, Caius, Friar Lodowick, Morgan, and perhaps even Poor Tom seem to comport themselves in ways characteristic of people accustomed to "owning" much of the space around them. Further, other characters in the plays often acknowledge the possessive rights of the personator. Again, however, visible behavior rather than some (intuited) intrinsic merit coordinates the interactions.

Similar conditions account for even the extreme cases of characters who are disguised without knowing it themselves. I am thinking of Perdita, Polydore/Guiderius, and Cadwal/Arviragus: royal children reared in ignorance of their true parentage. Apparently their noble blood prevails despite their humble upbringing. Camillo tells Polixenes that a certain shepherd "hath a daughter of most rare note" (*The Winter's Tale,* 4.2.41-42), and Imogen says the following of Polydore and Cadwal:

> Great men,
> That had a court no bigger than this cave,
> That did attend themselves and had the
>   virtue
> Which their own conscience seal'd them,
>   laying by
> That nothing-gift of differing multitudes,
> Could not outpeer these twain. . . .
>   (*Cymbeline,* 3.6.81-86)

Although these two romances seem to promote notions of innate nobility, they can as easily support a counterview. Neither play pretends that these children were reared in typically rustic circumstances. According to Polixenes, Perdita's shepherd father "from very nothing, and beyond the imagination of his neighbors, is grown into an unspeakable estate" (*The Winter's Tale,* 4.2.38-40), and we witness the Old Shepherd presiding over the sheepshearing festival, an important man in his own, albeit small, world. Indeed, Perdita's social status resembles that of Ganymede and Aliena in Arden. Strictly speaking, in terms of verisimilitude it would be difficult to imagine what models Perdita could have had for courtly deportment; but given her foster parents' standing in their neighborhood and their knowledge that her origins were rich and mysterious, it is only logical that she should bear herself in a manner suggesting high status. Similar arguments apply—even more strongly—to Polydore and Cadwal. Morgan/Belarius has always known they are princes and has reared them on tales of noble valor. Of Polydore, Belarius directly tells the audience:

> When on my three-foot stool I sit and tell
> The warlike feats I have done, his spirits fly
>   out
> Into my story; say, "Thus mine enemy fell,
> And thus I set my foot on 's neck," even then
> The princely blood flows in his cheek, he
>   sweats,
> Strains his young nerves, and puts himself in
>   posture
> That acts my words. . . .
>   (*Cymbeline,* 3.3.89-95)

However lowly their surroundings, Belarius has taught Guiderius and Arviragus the posture of princes. Indeed, he so often tells the audience how royally these boys behave that one begins to suspect the play of protesting too much. And when he claims that "nature prompts them / In simple and low things to prince it much / Beyond the trick of others" (ll. 84-86), we may well be tempted to counter, "No—it is Belarius that prompts them. . . . " In other words, these plays argue at least as strongly for nobility as learned as they do for its being innate. We might well look again at Imogen's description of Polydore and Cadwal:

> Great men,
> That had a court no bigger than this cave,
> That did attend themselves and had the virtue
> Which their own conscience seal'd them,
>   laying by
> That nothing-gift of differing multitudes,
> Could not outpeer these twain. . . .

If the modifying phrases are removed, this speech reads "Great men . . . Could not outpeer these twain," but the conditions under which great men would be the equals of the rustic brothers are explicit: no court, no attendants, no flatterers, no followers. If read as a description of great men, this speech suggests that "greatness" is the consequence of circumstances and deference rather than of any virtue one's own conscience seals. Greatness is a visible circumstance rather than an inner or autonomous attribute, a set of practices rather than an essence.

Matters of relative "greatness," of rank and power, extend across all categories of Shakespearean disguise, and a discussion of rank and power might usefully begin with the fact that, most obviously and most visibly, disguisers change their clothes. Recent attention to sumptuary laws and crossdressing reminds us that Renaissance clothing participated in an elaborate system for signifying rank, gender, occupation, allegiance (household)—in sum, one's place in the social order. Given, however, that the much cited sumptuary laws seem never to have been enforced very effectively,[14] I suspect they fall into that category of laws referred to by Kenneth Burke as "secular prayer." Burke writes that, although law is often "the efficient codification of custom," in its accumulation of abstractions by analogy, law is also a resource that can be "cashed in on . . . when the authority of customs threatens to wane. . . . Law then becomes a form of 'secular prayer.'" (A recent example would be laws forbidding drug abuse.) Burke then adds, "The attempt to pray by legislative fiat is particularly stimulated by distinctions in occupational and property relationships ('class struggle') as those who command the loyalty of the legislators encourage them to 'take up the slack,' between what is desired and what is got, by legal exhortations."[15] I believe it was so with sumptuary laws.

Interesting in many ways, they are perhaps most interesting as symptoms of anxiety about stability in the social hierarchy, particularly about a disjunction between rank and income, about the possibility of social mobility.

Something of the same anxiety that engendered sumptuary laws may account for the remarkable fact that when characters in Shakespeare's plays change their clothes, and hence their status, they never of their own (represented) volition disguise *up* the social scale. (They occasionally do so at the behest and to the benefit of someone who outranks them—Tranio, King Henry's men at Shrewsbury, Autolycus in Florizel's clothing, for example.) To my mind, this absence of upwardly mobile personation suggests a potent taboo, all the more powerful in that it seems to have operated tacitly rather than through direct censorship.[16] Although the stage itself was obviously exempt from sumptuary laws (not without objection), it seems to have been impermissible to *represent* the breaking of such laws. Apparently actors could with impunity dress as kings and dukes, but they could not play the parts of people successfully impersonating kings and dukes—or anyone who outranks the disguisers. (Think of the trouble Mosca gets into when—of his own volition rather than on Volpone's orders—he impersonates a magnifico. And note that the one decoy for Henry IV we actually see onstage—Sir Walter Blunt—also dies onstage.) One way to restate this apparent contradiction: the Shakespearean stage seems to have been free to imitate people exercising legitimated power but not to imitate the successful usurpation of power through any sort of disguise or impersonation.[17] And I would stress that this taboo seems to have applied not simply to royal power but also to the more dispersed relations of power that accompany various ranks and degrees. Indeed, rather considerable care seems to have been taken to protect against representing personation as permitting *any* appropriation of power.

The cases of an unwitting Christopher Sly and a calculating Autolycus are instructive. Here are the lord's instructions for his joke on the drunken tinker:

> What think you, if he were convey'd to bed,
> Wrapp'd in sweet clothes, rings put upon his
>   fingers,
> A most delicious banquet by his bed,
> And brave attendants near him when he
>   wakes,
> Would not the beggar then forget himself?
>   (*Taming of the Shrew,* Ind.1.37-41)

The fantasy outlined here is one of physical comfort: a soft bed, fresh clothing, music, bountiful food, bodily care by deferential servants. (Compare the fairies' quite similar treatment of Bottom in *A Midsummer Night's Dream*.) The appeal of such fantasy is underscored when we remember that soft bedding, changes of clothing, and ample food were all luxuries reserved to the wealthy in the sixteenth and seventeenth centuries.[18] Sly himself tells us he has "no more doublets than backs, no more stockings than legs, nor no more shoes than feet" (*Taming of the Shrew,* Ind.2.9-10).[19] It is no wonder that in the anonymous *Taming of a Shrew* Sly exclaims to the tapster who wakes him at the play's end, "I have had the bravest dream tonight that ever thou heardest in all thy life."[20] Notably, however, the perquisite of wealth and rank *not* provided to Sly is power—even the servants who pamper him are in on the joke. (We might compare Malvolio, whose once considerable power in Olivia's household evaporates when he apes the dandified apparel of his social superiors.)

The case of Autolycus is also telling. Having snapped up more than unconsidered trifles in exchanging clothes with Florizel, the professional swindler is quick to recognize opportunities his new guise offers, and he immediately cons gold from the shepherds as a bribe for promises to persuade the king in their favor. In his borrowed robes, the quondam peddler of ribbons and gloves becomes an influence peddler. The plot of *The Winter's Tale,* however, transforms Autolycus's fraud, and the rogue's usurped power works toward the good of all concerned—particularly, one might note, the good of Perdita and Florizel, whose rights to royal power are restored through the revelation of her origins. The usurpation of a courtier's power to corrupt ultimately serves here to confirm royal authority.

If Shakespearean drama indeed acknowledged some sort of public taboo against representing upward mobility through disguise, it also seems to have resisted staging the implications of downward mobility. The plays frequently represent disguised characters, despite the downward direction of their personations, either as relatively powerful or as compensated for their loss of status. Certainly the young women who dress as men gain a freedom of movement denied them in their women's weeds, and in some cases at least, they quickly accrue perquisites of status and power in their new environments. Portia's bravura rhetoric makes her the most powerful figure in the Venetian courtroom; she is able to do what the Duke of Venice cannot (or will not). Further, she is able to manipulate Bassanio's dawning sense of obligation toward securing the sort of marital relationship she wants. Viola, too, quickly becomes more powerful in Illyria than her status as page would seem to warrant. When Olivia falls in love with Cesario, she vests him/her with a degree of power (marked by the envy manifested by the members of Olivia's household), and, perhaps more important, Cesario exposes limits to Duke Orsino's power. Some sort of cultural logic may demand that Olivia be chastened for her independence, and we may see her humiliation in loving a man/woman as resembling that with which Oberon designs to punish Titania. Equally, however, in *Twelfth Night* it is the dispossessed woman, not the independent one, who loves Orsino. (Perhaps, like Phebe, he is not for all markets.) In *As You Like It,* Ganymede and Aliena seem to be acknowledged by other denizens of the forest as superiors. Although the sheepcote's previous owner is referred to as a "carlot" (3.5.108), or peasant, Ganymede and Aliena are treated deferentially. They may no longer be recognized as princesses, but they do outrank those in their immediate vicinity.

Speculatively I can offer two explanations for this insistence that power is retained even as status is lost. First, Shakespeare may well have suffered effects of his own father's downward mobility.[21] Second, a considerable body of recent research indicates that in early modern England downward mobility was an ever-present threat.[22] It seems plausible, then, that the repeated pattern of a disguised character's retaining or regaining power served first to arouse and then to assuage a potent anxiety, one Shakespeare may have shared with members of his audience. If so, it makes all the more interesting the few instances where disguise involves a clear diminution of power accompanying a step down in rank. Duke Vincentio, Kent (with Oswald), Coriolanus at the house of Aufidius, and (I would argue) Henry V as he moves in Erpingham's cloak among the soldiers all seem surprised—testy even—when they don't receive the automatic respect and obedience to which their offices have accustomed them. And I take it as significant that the disguisers who experience a disturbing loss of power all appear in plays where questions of power, authority, and office are explicitly thematized: *Measure for Measure; Henry V; Coriolanus;* and, most acutely, *King Lear.* Indeed, Edgar's disguise may be the most disturbing in the canon in that he not merely drops in rank but rather drops out of the social order altogether. We might say that for his onstage witnesses Edgar personates demonized otherness, and what power he then possesses is that of the outcast, the shaman, the madman, the devil. And—unlike those of other Shakespearean personators—Edgar's one disguise fractures into multiple personations, and this multiplicity is stabilized only through the donning of another disguise. (It is surely no coincidence that Edgar reestablishes his singularity by defeating his brother and thus relegating Edmund once again to the position of outsider.)

In sum, although disguise usually involves a change in rank and hence in automatic power, Shakespearean personae in disguise nonetheless seem to preserve power and status relative to those around them—except in those plays that explicitly interrogate the grounds of power and authority. We might say that rank and its perquisites tend to be taken for granted as "natural" properties, securely possessed by those who inherit them, unless a play specifically scrutinizes the conditions (and conditionality) of power. We might say as well, however, that the plays represent rank as a system, constitutive of persons. Indeed, this survey of what happens when Shakespearean characters go into disguise suggests a range of discourses pertinent to early modern subjectivity. Bonds, reciprocal obligations, sexual positionings, dwelling-places, regional and paternal origins, hierarchies of comportment and deference, the distribution of power—*all* serve to define Shakespearean characters as represented persons.

Notes

[1] *The Shakespearean Stage 1574-1642* (Cambridge: Cambridge Univ. Press, 1980), p. 98.

[2] *Character* here should be understood as under erasure—i.e., it is a word still in use though the totalized concept to which it purports to refer is no longer considered valid. Despite the distance between early modern uses of this word and our own, it remains the only readily available term we have for "a represented person in a play." To my ear, all my efforts to replace *character* in this discussion were distracting and tended to focus attention on the figure represented as personating rather than on the figure personated.

[3] In suggesting this specialization for the term *personate,* I indicate as well my debt to J. Leeds Barroll, *Artificial Persons: The Formation of Character in the Tragedies of Shakespeare* (Columbia: Univ. of South Carolina Press, 1974). Also relevant is Amélie Oskenberg Rorty, "A Literary Postscript: Characters, Persons, Selves, Individuals," in the collection she edited, *The Identities of Persons* (Berkeley: Univ. of California Press, 1976), pp. 301-23.

[4] No doubt influenced by Muriel Bradbrook's important essay, "Shakespeare and the Use of Disguise in Elizabethan Drama," *Essays in Criticism,* 2 (1952), 159-68, most critics have defined *disguise* broadly to include all sorts of illusion and deception. I agree with Peter Hyland, however, that a narrower definition is more useful, an argument he makes in "Disguise and Renaissance Tragedy," *University of Toronto Quarterly,* 55 (1985/86), 161-71. Other important studies, broader and more thematic than mine, include Anthony B. Dawson, *Indirections: Shakespeare and the Art of Illusion* (Toronto: Univ. of Toronto Press, 1978), and Thomas F. Van Laan, *Role Playing in Shakespeare* (Toronto: Univ. of Toronto Press, 1978). Victor Oscar Freeburg's *Disguise Plots in Elizabethan Drama: A Study in Stage Tradition* (New York: Columbia Univ. Press, 1915) remains a helpful survey, especially for situating Shakespearean practices in the larger context of early modern drama.

[5] At one time this particular exchange would have been relevant primarily to men; women were much more likely to be asked "Are you married?" Today this question about marital status would be considered rude in many circles, and a movie character who asked it would thereby be signalled as sexually predatory. This change in patterns of "casual conversation" signals social change in process.

[6] All citations of Shakespeare refer to *The Riverside Shakespeare,* ed. G. Blakemore Evans (Boston: Houghton Mifflin, 1974).

[7] Jonathan Miller typifies the usual reading: "In contrast to Kate's rather graceful submission, the disagreeable behaviour of her sister Bianca becomes repugnant and you can then see that the real shrew is Bianca and not Katharina at all" (*Subsequent Perfomances* [London: Faber & Faber, 1986], p. 122).

[8] The 1620 texts are reprinted in *Half Humankind: Contexts and Texts of the Controversy about Women in England, 1540-1640,* ed. Katherine Usher Henderson and Barbara F. McManus (Urbana: Univ. of Illinois Press, 1985), pp. 264-89.

[9] Henderson and McManus, eds., p. 283.

[10] The author of *Haec Vir* draws so many examples from literature that it is not impossible that this description refers more explicitly to plays than to actual travel. Indeed, it seems to me thoroughly plausible that practices developed for drama's expository needs may have been taken as models for the very behavior *Haec Vir*'s anonymous author finds peculiar.

[11] The distance between our "Where do you come from?" and that of early modern England can be highlighted by imagining a typical conversation with one's airplane seatmate. For us "Where do you come from?" asks where one currently lives; questions about where one was *born* or who one's *father* is would be discomfiting—despite the obvious relevance of such matters to who we are.

[12] A recent instance appears in Stephen Greenblatt, *Shakespearean Negotiations: The Circulation of Social Energy in Renaissance England* (Berkeley: Univ. of California Press, 1988): "Yet in Renaissance stories, paradoxically, the apparently fragile and mutable social codes are almost always reinscribed—despite his savage upbringing, the true prince reveals his noble nature" (p. 76).

[13] *Impro: Improvisation in the Theatre* (New York: Theatre Arts Books, 1981), p. 63.

[14] See Frances Elizabeth Baldwin, *Sumptuary Legislation and Personal Regulation in England* (Baltimore: Johns Hopkins Univ. Press, 1926). It should be noted that sumptuary laws regulating clothing had a long history in England; such laws were enacted at least as early as 1362. Still, the sheer number of acts and proclamations regulating clothing increased during the reign of Elizabeth. Baldwin offers three kinds of evidence for her view that sumptuary laws were largely unenforced: few records of their enforcement survive (pp. 54, 82, 86, 117, 167); numerous writers rail against extravagances in dress which effective enforcement would have prevented (pp. 34, 67, 166, 196, 204); the many acts and proclamations themselves decry laxity in the enforcement of their predecessors (pp. 141, 150, 164, 207, 214, 220-24). Sporadic efforts at enforcement are noted on pages 107, 113, 152, 167, 234, 237. For a helpful survey and bibliography of work on crossdressing, see Jean E. Howard, "Crossdressing, The Theatre, and Gender Struggle in Early Modern England," *Shakespeare Quarterly,* 39 (1988), 418-40. In *Vested Interests: Cross-Dressing and Cultural Anxiety* (New York and London: Routledge, 1992), Marjorie Garber emphasizes Tudor sumptuary laws as symptoms of cultural anxiety (pp. 21-32).

[15] *Attitudes Toward History* (1937; rpt. Boston: Beacon, 1961), p. 291.

[16] In *Censorship and Interpretation: The Conditions of Writing and Reading in Early Modern England* (Madison: Univ. of Wisconsin Press, 1984), Annabel Patterson stresses the self-censorship practiced by writers subject to official censorship.

[17] Leeds Barroll presents evidence that after the performance of *Richard II* on the eve of the Essex Rebellion "not the play but the persons involved in the production—both players and those who commissioned the performance—were deemed dangerous because they were doing something they *thought* to be seditious" ("A New History for Shakespeare and His Time," *SQ,* 39 [1988], 441-64, esp. p. 454). The "taboo" I am discussing may have operated in a similar fashion.

[18] For information about famine and hunger in Shakespeare's England, see Keith Wrightson, *English Society 1580-1680* (New Brunswick: Rutgers Univ. Press, 1982), pp. 142-46.

[19] While too many people today live in Sly-like poverty, playgoers and readers of Shakespeare are unlikely to be among them. Although Sly himself is described as never having seen a play, more people at the Globe than at Ashland or the Barbican would recognize or remember pangs of hunger and the itchy discomfort of straw bedding.

[20] Cited from excerpts given in the Oxford edition of *Taming of the Shrew,* H. J. Oliver, ed. (Oxford: Clarendon Press, 1984), p. 235.

[21] A recent account of John Shakespeare's rise and fall can be found in Russell Fraser, *Young Shakespeare* (New York: Columbia Univ. Press, 1988), pp. 42-49.

[22] For example, Keith Wrightson cites B. G. Blackwood's research on Lancashire, where of the 763 families identifiable as gentry in 1600, 278 had suffered serious economic and social decline by 1642 (p. 27). Similarly, Andrew Gurr notes that "In the wealthiest companies, such as the goldsmiths, nearly a third of apprentices were the sons of gentlemen. Gold was the principal alchemy for converting citizenry into gentry. Lack of it, for younger sons, worked the opposite way" (*Playgoing in Shakespeare's London* [Cambridge: Cambridge Univ. Press, 1987], p. 52).

Christy Desmet (essay date 1992)

SOURCE: "'Who Is't Can Read a Woman?': Rhetoric and Gender in *Venus and Adonis, Measure for Measure,* and *All's Well That Ends Well*," in *Reading Shakespeare's Characters: Rhetoric, Ethics, and Identity,* Amherst: The University of Massachusetts Press, 1992, pp. 134-63, 196-203.

[*In the excerpt that follows, Desmet examines Shakespeare's treatment of disguised female characters in* Venus and Adonis, Measure for Measure, *and* All's Well That Ends Well. *The editors have included only those footnotes that pertain to the excerpted portion of the essay.*]

Encouraged to impersonate exotic female characters even while the bulk of their rhetorical training makes communication with women problematic, young Renaissance rhetors enjoy an ambivalent relationship with women as fictional speakers and characters.

In the rhetorical tradition as in controversy over the theater, woman is associated with language's more disturbing effects. Discussions of the proper use of language tend to anthropomorphize style, and in this way ostentatious rhetoric gradually becomes identified with woman. Plato sets the terms for later discussions of style by associating rhetoric with pleasure and with the metaphor of clothing. In the *Gorgias,* Socrates makes a tentative connection between a beautiful and well-dressed body (which can mask an ugly soul) and rhetoric (which can mask base intentions with pleasurable effects). Each distorts the truth in its own way.[1] Seneca, in the 114th epistle of his *Epistulae Morales,* connects the lascivious pursuit of pleasure, fancy dress, and florid rhetoric more explicitly. According to Seneca's argument, not only a man's speech but all aspects of his life—habits, attendant, house, and even wife—will inexorably reveal his inner self. Thus we may expect a general effeminacy from the man of immoral character. He will wear loose robes and walk like a woman. When speaking, he will also indulge shamelessly in metaphor, trot out old-fashioned words, coin new ones, ramble on at length, or speak obscurely for fashion's sake.[2]

For Seneca, ornate speech, like ornate dress, specifically characterizes the effeminate man. In the history of style, however, showy rhetoric comes to be associated less with dissolute men than with richly clad women. Cicero, in the *Orator,* metaphorically equates rhetoric's tropes and schemes with jewels and cosmetics, the ornaments of women.[3] The plain style avoids excessive decoration, says Cicero. "Just as some women are said to be handsomer when unadorned," so the plain style is most pleasing when unembellished: "All noticeable ornament, pearls as it were, will be excluded; not even curling-irons will be used; all cosmetics, artificial white and red, will be rejected."[4] In the Renaissance, *Orator*'s sketchy personification of Rhetoric, with her curled hair and pink and white complexion, becomes a familiar figure. George Puttenham's *Arte of English Poesie,* for instance, argues that ornament makes poetry more decorous and agreeable to both ear and understanding. Poetry must show itself either "gallant or gorgious," according to Puttenham, leaving no limb naked and bare. For poems are like "great Madames of honour," whose beauty must be clothed in rich costumes—"silkes or tyssewes & costly embroideries"—that will not shame them at court.[5] In *The Arte of English Poesie,* rhetoric and gorgeous garments serve the general good by encouraging "decency" and social decorum. On the other hand, George Herbert, who wishes to address God directly, shuns decorative rhetoric as he would a painted woman. In "Jordan I" he asks aggressively, "Who says that fictions only and false hair / Become a verse?" Herbert prefers to address his lord "plainly"—that is, in the plain style—as "*My God, My King.*"[6] Not all love poetry needs wanton ornament, is Herbert's point.

Puttenham and Herbert explore the ethics of language through feminine personification, taking opposite positions. Herbert, following a Platonic line, finds rhetoric deceitful and emasculating; his Rhetoric is a whore. Puttenham, equating social decorum with the "good," adheres to a courtly ethic; his Rhetoric is an elegant but noble lady. Their opposed attitudes toward ornamental rhetoric could be traced to subject matter, but as Daniel Javitch has suggested, the difference between humanist and courtly rhetoric in the sixteenth century can be figured in terms of gender. The humanist orator has experience, learning, and above all good character. Despite his manifest virtue, however, his profession involves him in confrontation and struggle. Operating in the sphere of public affairs, he is isolated and beleaguered unless he persuades the populace to his point of view. As Javitch points out, Cicero's discussions of the orator often resort to martial imagery; according to Crassus in *De Oratore,* after his preparatory years the orator must move "right into the action, into the dust and uproar, into the camp and the fighting-line of public debate."[7]

Within the courtly tradition to which Puttenham belongs, by contrast, women and rhetoric can help to civilize the world of men. Castiglione's *Courtier* grants rhetoric a central role in the courtier's education. Javitch notes also that the courtier, unlike Cicero's perfect orator, "lives in a milieu remarkable for the prominent role it accords to women."[8] At Urbino the nobles play elaborate language games under the tutelage of elegant ladies, discussing topics more fit for poetry than for politics. They learn to act and especially to talk well, coping successfully with whatever twists and turns the witty conversation takes. In fact, the courtier strives to mold himself as a rhetorical artifact. The connection between women and rhetoric in the courtly tradition is strengthened by the fact that "many of the artifices recommended in the *Cortegiano* for appearing graceful are derived from or resemble the figuration of language and thought that the orator employs to beautify his discourse," the same kind of ornament that has been linked metaphorically to feminine jewels and cosmetics.[9]

Courtly rhetoric, like the courtier himself, achieves *grazia* through dissimulation, which becomes more troublesome when the connection between woman and ornamental language is "un-metaphored." For much of what is said in praise of courtly rhetoric is also used to censure woman. Platonic attacks on the art of rhetoric have traditionally criticized it for encouraging loquacity and dissimulation. Renaissance antifeminist literature links women to such abuses of language by accusing them of the same vices.[10] Woman's talkativeness often signals some deeper flaw—pride, vanity, or deceitful cunning. When a woman entertains a man with "long & vayne confabulation," warns educator Juan Luis Vives, it "is eyther folish or filthy."[11] C. Pyrre's poem, "The Praise and Dispraise of Women," succinctly numbers the vices of a talkative woman:

> Inconstancie in her doth raigne,
> She waverith full of chaunge,
> Oft blabbing, talkative and vaine
> Double tounged which semeth straunge.[12]

Being "double tounged," loquacious women not only babble incessantly but pose a moral danger to their male auditors. Rhetorically sophisticated women, to borrow a phrase from Bishop Jewel's "Oration against Rhetoric," devise "snares for captivating our ears" and through them our hearts and souls.[13]

The subject of this [essay] is what we might call Shakespeare's "cross-identification" with his female characters. A substantial amount of work has been done on the subversive effects of "cross-dressing" in

Shakespeare's plays, but the problem of identification is most interesting not in those plays that put their heroines into breeches but in those featuring female characters who exhibit erotic and verbal power without changing costume or sexual identity.[14] *Venus and Adonis, Measure for Measure,* and *All's Well That Ends Well* all feature female characters who combine sexual appeal with a command of oratory, and all examine the equivocal effect of female rhetoric on men.

Venus, from the poem bearing her name, is the earliest Shakespearean woman to have beauty, passion, and a golden tongue; for this reason, *Venus and Adonis* provides a good starting point for our examination of Shakespeare's female impersonations. Venus appears in a number of schoolboy rhetorical exercises: Rainolde, for instance, includes a "poetical narrative" about the love of Venus and Adonis that derives from Aphthonius. Shakespeare's Venus has never been a popular character. Larger than her boy lover, she can tuck Adonis under one arm and manage his horse's reins with the other. Too enthusiastic, too physical, she threatens to "smother" him with kisses: "And this flushed, panting, perspiring, suffocating, loquacious creature is supposed to be the goddess of love herself, the golden Aphrodite. It will not do," C. S. Lewis complains.[15]

Although Venus is remembered for her amorous acrobatics, for most of the poem she talks. The moments in which Venus wrestles Adonis to the ground or snatches kisses from him are welcome breaks in their one-sided verbal contest. At a low point in her attempted seduction, when she and Adonis awkwardly make the beast with two backs, the narrator uncharacteristically softens his tone to apostrophize Venus and offer his condolences:

> But all in vain, good queen, it will not be;
> She hath assay'd as much as may be prov'd.
> Her pleading hath deserv'd a greater fee;
> She's Love, she loves, and yet she is not
>   lov'd.
>
> (607-10)

As an underpaid lawyer as well as the judge who enforces Love's laws, Venus is an orator, and her weapons are those commonly found in the schoolboy's arsenal; she starts out as a Petrarchan poet but later employs the proverb and allegory to persuade her reluctant lover.

The narrator, whose loyalties shift throughout the poem, alternately identifies with Venus and competes with her for control of their shared story.[16] For the first half of the poem he competes with her directly, undermining Venus's arguments to Adonis by parodying them. As allegorists, Venus and the narrator both dissimulate, using what George Puttenham called the "figure of false semblant."[17] The narrator turns a piece of scene painting into allegory by making Titan, the "hot sun," into a voyeuristic surrogate for himself and a rival for Adonis's attentions (175-80). Venus offers to Adonis a more pointed allegory or extended metaphor, in which she is a park and Adonis the deer whom she invites to "graze" on her and to "stray lower, where the pleasant fountains lie" (229-34). Venus's allegory is succeeded by another from the narrator, a seductive rather than a parodic one this time. Venus had described her arms, which encircle Adonis desperately, as an "ivory pale"; the narrator, picking up on this cue, describes Adonis's hand, which is entrapped by Venus's own, as

> A lily prison'd in a jail of snow,
> Or ivory in an alabaster band,
> So white a friend engirts so white a foe:
>   This beauteous combat, willful and
>   unwilling,
>   Showed like two silver doves that sit a-
>   billing.
>
>   (362-66)

Unlike Venus, the narrator conducts his allegory to a romantically successful conclusion with the final simile comparing the two hands to billing doves. The narrator's formal success highlights Venus's amorous shortcomings.

The interplay between Venus and the narrator involves a constant shift of figure and ground that complicates the relationship between them. Venus is often criticized for her aggressive behavior, but most of it is attributed to her by the narrator. The hostile narrator of the poem's first half undermines Venus with unflattering epic similes: She is an "empty eagle" gorging herself on her young prey, while poor Adonis is a bird tangled in a net or a dive-dapper ducking beneath the waves (55-60, 67-72, 85-90). By relying on simile, the narrator emphasizes the self-serving motives behind Venus's rhetoric; he combats her flamboyant rhetoric with his own, more "reasonable" version of events by distinguishing insistently between *res* and *verba*. The narrator also manipulates Venus herself. At times he ridicules her by casting her in distasteful allegories. For instance, when she is "in the very lists of love, / Her champion mounted for the hot encounter" (595-96), Venus is mocked doubly by the martial metaphor and the couplet's concluding jibe, which compares her to Tantalus. The sudden shift of metaphor makes Venus not only ridiculous but morally reprehensible. But the narrator's sentiments are quixotic and can shift even within a stanza. For Adonis's pleasure, Venus offers, "like a fairy," to

>   trip upon the green,
> Or like a nymph, with long dishevelled hair,
> Dance on the sands, and yet no footing seen.
>   Love is a spirit all compact of fire,
>   Not gross to sink, but light, and will
>   aspire.
>
>   (146-50)

The wit of this stanza depends on the ambiguity inherent in the connective "like," which suggests but does not confirm Venus's ability to metamorphose into different shapes. It is not clear whether Venus is offering to dance in the guise of a nymph or fairy or whether she will just dance with the delicacy of those mythological creatures; in the same vein, it is uncertain whether her claim that she dances on sand without leaving footprints is meant to be taken literally or accepted as passionate hyperbole. Paul Fussell notes that often in this poem quatrain and couplet inhabit entirely separate worlds, and such is the case here.[18] For though Venus's desire makes her speech sound self-serving, the couplet translates her self-representation into a Neoplatonic vocabulary, dignifying her boasts by allegorizing them. The result is a bifurcated perspective on Venus and her motives.

Although Venus and the narrator are engaged in a battle of wits, Venus's status as a goddess helps her withstand the repressive rejoinders of both Adonis and the narrator. As Nancy Lindheim puts it, "The identification of Venus and love lies at the heart of Shakespeare's conception of the poem, though this identification is neither allegorical nor doctrinal. Venus is not 'Love' in the abstract way the Neoplatonists conceive it, but in the contradictory way it is experienced."[19] When Adonis first rejects her advances, Venus admonishes him with the mythological tale of Mars's love for her, which culminates in her leading him, as her prisoner, in a "red rose chain." Venus has an uncommon advantage here, because her mythological tale, unlike that of the red rose in Richard Rainolde's *Foundation of Rhetoric,* has no didactic point. Because she *is* the goddess of love, the anecdote involves reminiscence as much as storytelling, and the only lesson it offers is a radically amoral one: Carpe diem.[20] Venus's narrative therefore exceeds the limits of allegory to become myth, establishing a kinship between Venus and Shakespeare, the author of her narrative.

Ernst Cassirer locates in "metaphoric thinking" a common source for language and myth. Like metaphors, myths do not simply substitute fictions for concepts. Rather, the myth-making consciousness conflates name and essence, just as metaphor asserts an identity between frame and focus in Ricoeur's scheme.[21] Kenneth Burke complains that Cassirer, in spite of himself, considers myth's "word magic" a primitive prototype of scientific thought. Myth, Burke says by way of correction, is built on poetic rather than semantic meaning, on language that is overdetermined and weighted with attitude; the result is not an identity between name and essence but a wealth of perspectives, many of them conflicting with one another.[22]

Venus's "word magic" works by accumulating rather than eliminating different perspectives on her tales; like Shakespeare, she invites varied, often incompatible readings of her personal myth.[23] Her speech is weighted with attitude: She questions Adonis, exhorts him, and, most important, through her endless amplification sets the terms in which he finally speaks. Venus exploits the impersonal authority of proverbial sayings which, as Quintilian says, enhance a speaker's ethos:

> "Torches are made to light, jewels to wear,
> Dainties to taste, fresh beauty for the use,
> Herbs for their smell, and sappy plants to
>   bear:
> Things growing to themselves are growth's
>   abuse."
>
>   (163-66)

Somewhat later, Adonis replies to Venus's argument in similar language:

> "Who wears a garment shapeless and
>   unfinish'd?
> Who plucks the bud before one leaf put forth?
> If springing things be any jot diminish'd,
> They wither in their prime, prove nothing
>   worth."
>
>   (415-18)

Venus also recounts a fantastic etiological myth, in which Nature steals heaven's molds to forge a perfect Adonis, prompting Cynthia to hide her face in shame and make the night unnaturally dark. Adonis responds with his own myth of sedition, in which "Love to heaven is fled, / Since sweating Lust on earth usurp'd his name" (793-94). Coppélia Kahn, writing from a psychoanalytic perspective, argues that Adonis "is deeply alienated from his own kind, determined not to love even at the expense of being perverse."[24] On the level of language, as well, Adonis is alienated, having no voice of his own and no choice but to adopt Venus's style or stay silent: The text is too old, the orator too green.

The narrator makes Venus seem large, sweaty, and overbearing, while Adonis's rhetorical immaturity forces her to be garrulous. As Venus's voice begins to subdue others in the poem, however, the identification between her and the narrator solidifies and her speeches seem less sophistical; at the same time, paradoxically, she is forced into a more traditionally feminine role. Venus's drawn-out search for Adonis is filled with discussion: between Venus and the dogs, between Venus and Death, and finally between Venus and herself, when she muses about why Death cannot die. The second half of the poem is also dominated by descriptive narratives such as Venus's own cautionary tale of Wat the hare. The story of Wat is usually considered to be Venus's most charming and sincere rhetorical performance; in it she identifies emotionally with the hare, representing her own fears for Adonis rather than providing a real argument against boar hunting. What

has traditionally been considered the strength of this episode, its verisimilitude and the effect of pathos, nevertheless becomes a strategic weakness for Venus as an orator. The narrative is digressive: It lacks a direct application to Adonis's determination to hunt the boar and ends inconclusively when Venus loses the thread of her thought.

Venus's ethos is therefore redeemed at the expense of her rhetoric, for her later speeches are based more on direct appeals to pathos than on persuasive argument. As Heather Dubrow notes, in the second half of the poem Venus is described as a victim.[25] For instance, the narrator reverses earlier, unflattering comparisons between Venus and birds when,

> As falcons to the lure, away she flies,
> The grass stoops not, she treads on it so light,
> And in her haste unfortunately spies
> The foul boar's conquest on her fair delight,
>   Which seen, her eyes [as] murd'red with
>   the view,
>   Like stars asham'd of day, themselves
>   withdrew.
>
>   (1027-32)

No longer a predatory eagle or a vulture, Venus—like Kate in *The Taming of the Shrew*—becomes a tamed falcon. In a generous gesture, the narrator credits as well Venus's earlier claim that she can dance on sand without leaving footprints; pointing out that the grass does not "stoop" as she races over it, he resists the temptation to undercut Venus by unpacking the metaphor. The next epic simile, comparing Venus's wounded eyes to a snail's wounded horns, is even more pathetic. Both similes, however, circumscribe Venus's sphere of action, since the first domesticates her and the second imprisons her within the snail's shell. The story of Wat, like the epic similes, gives the narrator power over Venus by prefiguring her fate. Whereas Venus interpreted the narrator's story of the horse according to her own design, as a lesson in natural love, the narrator models Venus's flight on her own story of Wat the hare: Venus, like Wat, runs in terror, snatched at by brambles as she searches for the wounded Adonis. In this way, Venus is absorbed into the narrator's story, so that her emotions, like those of Niobe in Aphthonius's ethopoeia, provide an occasion and a pattern for the narrator's histrionics.[26]

The poem concludes with Venus's funeral elegy for Adonis and her prophecy of love's future ills. In the ethopoeia Venus and the narrator finally speak with one voice. The merger of their voices empowers Venus's rhetoric, for as Adonis's eulogist she generalizes her grief into a public lament. In the prophecy, Venus's voice becomes even more detached from her personal situation, for she speaks *ex cathedra*. Because the ills she predicts for future lovers—jealousy, folly, weakness, and sorrow—have all been portrayed within the poem, the prophecy is often read ironically. But Venus, like Ophelia in *Hamlet,* looks from the perspective of prudential wisdom. She might well say, with Ophelia, "O, woe is me / T' have seen what I have seen, see what I see!" (*Hamlet,* 3.1.160-61). By giving formal shape to her experience, Venus makes her own story universal. Thus, even as the narrator begins to impersonate rather than debate with Venus— when he becomes the ventriloquist behind her voice— Venus remains an authoritative speaker.

The paradoxical relationship between Venus and her narrator is not fully resolved, even at the poem's conclusion. After her prophecy, Venus apostrophizes the flower that springs up from Adonis's blood. Her speech, like the gesture of uprooting the flower, is purely ceremonial. Although Coppélia Kahn describes Venus as the nurturing mother who allows Adonis to regress into a state in which he has no separate identity, Venus represents the flower as Adonis's heir.[27] Since she determines its meaning, the flower is also the "heir" of Venus's invention. As a flower of rhetoric, it is analogous to *Venus and Adonis,* the "deformed heir" of Shakespeare's invention. In this way, Venus seems both to exemplify and to exceed feminine stereotypes, for she is simultaneously Adonis's mother and Shakespeare's peer. Venus's oratorical triumph is never complete, however, for the narrator supervises the act of plucking the flower by framing Venus's speech with reported discourse. Venus represents picking the flower as a maternal act, conferring Adonis's rights on his only heir by putting the flower in her bosom; the masculine narrator, by contrast, represents it as a murder in which Venus "crops" the flower's stalk and indifferently compares its bleeding "sap" to tears. At the end of her poem and her action, then, Venus is at last subjected to the narrator, who exiles her to Paphos to play the lamenting lover.

Venus's penchant for amplification and the rhetorical restraints imposed on her speech have parallels in the problem plays. Isabella from *Measure for Measure* and Helena from *All's Well That Ends Well* are both accomplished orators. Both, however, have also been accused of dissimulation. Both, accordingly, are subjected to patriarchal hierarchies at the end of their plays. While a number of critics have commented on the importance of rhetoric to *Measure for Measure,* Wylie Sypher thinks of the entire play as an exercise in Jesuitical casuistry. *Measure for Measure*'s plot also has a kinship with one of the more sensational controversiae. In the case of "the man who raped two girls," the law states that "a girl who has been raped may choose either marriage to her ravisher without a dowry or his death." The man in question, however, raped two girls on a single night. One seeks his death, the other marriage.[28] Although Angelo does not actually succeed in violating two girls, when Mariana and Isabella join forces to accuse him before the Duke, the rhetorical exercise's Byzantine circumstances are replicated. Shakespeare, however, gives his women, particularly Isabella, the job of judging Angelo's case. In this way a situation that calls for deliberative rhetoric is conducted by a figure who, as we will see, argues with the rhetorical ornament associated with seductive sophistic.

Isabella, along with the Duke, is at the oratorical center of *Measure for Measure.* Her identity is defined by her talent for public speaking, since Angelo's fall from grace proves Claudio's belief that she can "play with reason and discourse" (1.2.185). Isabella is the only woman in the play who controls her own voice and therefore contributes to the shaping of her identity. Mistress Overdone's character, like that of Mistress Kate Keepdown, is written in her very name; after nine husbands, she is overdone by the last. Juliet, too, has her identity written on her body with "character too gross" (1.2.155). Mariana, as Isabella's alter ego, endures the silence and emotional restraints that Isabella desires; Mariana is defined as a listener rather than a speaker, one whose "brawling discontent" is stilled by music and the friar's counsel.

R. G. Hunter sees *Measure for Measure* as a secular allegory in which Angelo as Justice persecutes Claudio, while Isabella, or Mercy, pleads for his release.[29] But although the participants in this debate take strong ethical stands, the play subverts the allegory by exposing the role rhetoric plays in matters of justice. Angelo condemns Claudio, at least according to Lucio, to make an example of him; representing a legal and moral category, Claudio will become a negative model for potential fornicators. Isabella, by contrast, insists on the mitigating circumstances that make Claudio an individual rather than an ethical type. Her defense turns on the quality of his act. She asks not "Did Claudio commit fornication?" but "Was Claudio condemned justly?" By giving Isabella a prominent voice in the debate, Shakespeare complicates the opposition of Justice and Mercy by making woman, whose decorative rhetoric is suspect, his eloquent spokesperson for mercy. Isabella brings *Measure for Measure* to a satisfactory end, but the play also subjects her to social norms, barring Isabella from the realm of moral agency by literally putting her, along with Mariana, in her proper place.

Isabella's rhetoric, like that of Portia in her courtroom scene, depends not only on the topics of argument but also on metaphors and allegories. Her proofs are often poetic rather than judicial. Nevertheless, Isabella's pathetic appeals mask a sophist's parasitic talent for rhetorical mimicry. In Plato's *Gorgias,* Gorgias claims that he can persuade patients to take their medicine more readily than a physician can; Isabella, playing with reason and discourse, is persuasive on subjects that belong properly to the judge's domain. Unlike Portia in *The Merchant of Venice,* she argues the law while dressed in woman's garb and has no male mentor; so although Sister Miriam Joseph has justly called Isabella one of Shakespeare's finest logicians, doubt is cast on the legitimacy of her ethical arguments because Isabella's gender automatically excludes her from the male-dominated institutions of Viennese justice.[30]

Isabella and Angelo nevertheless begin their debate in the judicial sphere, considering whether Claudio's case should be treated as a "legall" or "juridiciall" issue. In the first case, determining whether the deed was done is paramount; in the second case, defining the deed's nature is important. The Provost thinks that Claudio has offended "in a dream" (2.2.4), without intending to commit a crime.[31] Angelo, telling Isabella that it would be wrong to "condemn the fault, and not the actor of it" (2.2.37), insists that the only issue under consideration is the fact of Claudio's offense: He has committed fornication and must die. But although Isabella shares Angelo's frame of reference—she never questions for a moment the criminality of Claudio's offense—she does exploit for her own purposes Angelo's assumptions and his argumentative strategies. In her first encounter with Angelo, Isabella, like Portia, draws on the potential identification of judge and accused. Her position is fortified dramatically by the fact that Angelo has already proposed a reciprocal relationship between the judge and those he judges: When he offends in the manner of Claudio, Angelo tells Escalus, "Let mine own judgment pattern out my death, / And nothing come in partial" (2.1.30-31). Such an identification has also been suggested in the case of Pompey and Elbow when Escalus asks, "Which is the wiser here: Justice or Iniquity?" (2.1.172).

Although thematic repetition gives her arguments credibility, Isabella's imitative style of argument remains problematic; for, like Plato's Gorgias, she achieves her power by usurping the language of established authorities. Isabella's rhetorical strength is her ability to adopt the formal patterns of her adversary and to wield them agonistically.[32] In her first formal appeal, Isabella uses Angelo's supposition that act and actor are inseparable to suggest that a speaker and his words are coextensive. Arguing by analogy, she implies that, just as Claudio is accountable for his crime, so Angelo as judge must take responsibility for the sentence he levies on Claudio. Using the premise that exterior and interior are connected, Isabella then defines the judge's peculiar virtue with a series of synecdoches, arguing by analogy to privilege the interior quality of mercy over the external trappings of justice:

No ceremony that to great ones 'longs,
Not the king's crown, nor the deputed sword,
The marshal's truncheon, nor the judge's robe,

Become them with one half so good a grace
As mercy does.

                            (2.2.59-63)

Analogy becomes a master trope for Isabella, allowing her to argue that Angelo as judge and Claudio as malefactor are alike because both have the potential to fall. If Angelo had "slipped," Claudio would have forgiven him; by extension, Angelo should pardon Claudio. Since the exterior and interior of the judge are continuous, synecdoche makes Claudio's potential pardon imperative by converting the possibility that Angelo and Claudio might trade places into an affirmation of their consubstantiality: All men are equally sinful under God's judgment. Through Isabella's revisionary rhetoric, Angelo has metamorphosed from a judge into a sinner. Only by showing mercy to Claudio can he become man "new made" (2.2.79).

Angelo and Isabella continue to spar with analogy. Angelo, elaborating on Isabella's buried image of Claudio as a mirror in which Angelo sees his own likeness, represents the law as a prophet, who

Looks in a glass that shows what future evils,
Either now, or by remissness new conceiv'd,
And so in progress to be hatch'd and born,
Are now to have no successive degrees,
But here they live, to end.

                            (2.2.95-99)

Isabella responds by translating the "law" into "proud man," who sees not the future but his own image in the glass. "Like an angry ape," he "plays such fantastic tricks before high heaven / As makes the angels weep" (2.2.120-22). With this "peculiarly masculine" insight into the illusion of virtue, Isabella challenges Angelo's self-representation of himself as the law and implicitly accuses Angelo, as the ape who preens in his mirror, of being tainted with feminine vanity.[33]

Isabella speaks such "sense" that Angelo's long-repressed sexual "sense breeds with it" (2.2.141-42). Though Isabella uses analogy as a figure of thought, to illustrate the concept of mercy, Angelo treats her comparisons as figures of speech; perhaps more accurately, he treats her comparisons as tropes, in which his own sexual meaning readily replaces her legal one.[34] He attends to the ornamental pearls and cosmetic adornment of the oratory rather than to her argument, just as he perceives a sensuous beauty beneath her austere nun's habit. Employing imagery that applies equally to alluring women and sophistic rhetoric, Angelo marvels that

Never could the strumpet,
With all her double vigor, art and nature,

Once stir my temper; but this virtuous maid
Subdues me quite.

(2.2.182-85)

Isabella, as a speaker, persuades and "moves" Angelo by mirroring him. As Aristotle says, it is easy to praise Athenians among Athenians. Angelo and Isabella, as ascetics cut from the same cloth, are from the start identified with one another. Just as Angelo, in Lucio's flippant phrase, scarce confesses that his blood flows, so Isabella demonstrates a modest reticence in pleading for her worldly brother:

> There is a vice that most I do abhor,
> And most desire should meet the blow of
>   justice;
> For which I would not plead, but that I must;
> For which I must not plead, but that I am
> At war 'twixt will and will not.

(2.2.29-33)

Isabella makes herself into a paradox of one who pleads without pleading, rather like Venus, who is "Love" and "loves" but is not loved in return. Isabella's representation of her own ethos, however sincere, is perturbing because it makes her an impenetrable riddle. On the surface, the self-portrait makes her sound like Octavia in *Antony and Cleopatra,* of whom her brother says,

> Her tongue will not obey her heart, nor can
> Her heart inform her tongue—the swan's
>   down feather,
> That stands upon the swell at the full of tide,
> And neither way inclines.

(3.2.47-50)

But Octavia's behavior, we should remember, is screened through the political rhetoric and ambitions of her brother; Isabella's ability to verbalize proper sentiments without actually manifesting them makes her an independent agent and raises the possibility that she manipulates Angelo without really sharing his interests.

Exhibiting modesty by being voluble, Isabella is a living paradox who would have troubled others beside Angelo. Although *Measure for Measure* has no narrator to supervise its heroine's behavior, Isabella's performance is framed by commentary from the Provost and Lucio, whose contributions place her in a sexual psychomachy. The Provost prays for heaven to give Isabella "moving graces," but Lucio, by urging her to be less cold, emphasizes her potential kinship with women such as Elbow's wife and Mistress Overdone. Structural parallels also suggest unflattering dimensions of Isabella's oratory. As a manipulator of words, Isabella resembles Elbow, who like her can create a situation in which "malefactors" and "benefactors,"

"respected" and "suspected" persons, are interchangeable. Less lighthearted is the connection between Isabella's smooth tongue and Lucio's, for both advocate leniency for rebellions of the codpiece. Isabella, in other words, is placed somewhere between the unconscious users of language and Lucio, the play's archetypal sophist.

In her second appearance before Angelo, Isabella's paradoxes are intensified, for both her innocence and the provocative effect of her rhetoric are heightened. Angelo begins the discussion with an enthymeme:

>   It were as good
> To pardon him that hath from nature stol'n
> A man already made, as to remit
> Their saucy sweetness that do coin heaven's
>   image
> In stamps that are forbid.

(2.4.42-46)

Isabella feels herself to be in familiar territory where, as before, she and Angelo debate Claudio's case theoretically. But Angelo, having learned from Isabella's rhetorical practice, poses a *quaestione definita;* he asks not about chastity in general but whether Isabella, to redeem her brother, would give herself up to "such sweet uncleanness" as "she that he hath stain'd" (2.4.54-55). While Angelo urges Isabella to identify with Juliet, using the strategy Isabella adopted in the earlier scene, Isabella takes refuge in a technical *divisio* that limits their discussion to the martyrdom of the body rather than the soul.

Angelo complains that Isabella's "sense" does not follow his, surmising that she is either "ignorant" or seems so "craftily" (2.4.74-75). Because Isabella is a sophist playing with reason and discourse, both statements are true. Although she wants to save her brother, she speaks passionately in a cause that she cannot fully sanction. As Isabella rightly tells Angelo, "it oft falls out, / To have what we would have, we speak not what we mean" (2.4.117-18). In her second meeting with Angelo, however, Isabella is so submerged in her role as Claudio's advocate that, as she tells Angelo, they no longer speak the same language. Isabella's distaste for her task, combined with her verbal facility and her complete absorption in her role, makes her an unsettling character.

Even Isabella's virtuous ethos becomes problematic. When Angelo suggests that women are frail, Isabella responds, "Ay, as the glasses where they view themselves, / Which are as easy broke as they make forms" (2.4.125-26). Ironically, it is Isabella's casual acceptance of antifeminist commonplaces, her peculiar combination of eloquence and conventional modesty, that makes Angelo command her to put on the "destin'd livery" of sexuality. Whereas Adonis, the green orator, found Venus's old texts tedious, Angelo lusts after Isabella even while he acts tyrannically toward her. The logic of his response provides a model for understanding Isabella's fate in this play. Angelo finds Isabella's speech seductive because she speaks in an acceptable female idiom, the passionate plea of a virtuous woman. Angelo desires Isabella for the things that make her good, or because her projected ethos is effective. It is worth remembering that in *Venus and Adonis* the narrator begins to sympathize with Venus only when she abandons argument for pathetic narrative and then passionate lament. In both cases, male auditors respond to women speakers when pathos overshadows ethos in their speech.

Isabella, however, trespasses into the male domain of judicial debate and for this reason threatens both masculine rhetoric and the masculine political prerogative. Angelo himself figures his fall in terms of language use when he says, "Heaven hath my empty words, / Whilst my invention, hearing not my tongue, / Anchors on Isabel" (2.4.2-4). No longer capable of invention, the first part of rhetorical composition that deals with the "matter" rather than the "manner" of speaking, he is lost in empty words.[35] Although the Duke's motives are often questioned, a real difference in political effect distinguishes Isabella's sophistry from the Duke's when he prepares Claudio for death. As Sister Miriam Joseph notes, the Duke's speech is a well-constructed *sententia,* supported by the minor premise of an enthymeme and confirmed by a number of arguments; the speech "proves" to Claudio that life is brief, lonely, and less congenial than death, which offers the comfort of an "after-dinner's sleep" (3.1.33).[36] Willing to usurp the confessional's privileges with Claudio and later with Barnardine, the Duke of dark corners is an impersonator. His authenticity, however, is assured not only by his symbolic connection to the heavenly judge but by his alliances with other male authority figures, particularly Friar Thomas and Escalus. Appealing to Escalus when he is shaken by Lucio's casual slanders, the disguised Duke reminds us that men in this play construct themselves in response to one another. In this sense, the male bonding that figures prominently in Shakespeare's early comedies as a protection against woman's disruptive influence is also operative in *Measure for Measure.*[37]

Isabella, unlike the Duke, is a social anomaly—a novice who is not yet a nun, a nun out of her cloister, a woman who seeks silence but speaks in public. As Stephen Greenblatt shows through the case of Arnaud de Tilh, who for a time successfully appropriated the identity, wife, and property of Martin Guerre, Renaissance identity can be conferred from without by a judicial body representing community interests. Arnaud's conviction and execution deprive him of the identity he had usurped, but as becomes clear from Natalie Zemon Davis's *Return of Martin Guerre,* Arnaud im-

personated Martin successfully for as long as he did because he was a more pleasant and profitable Martin than the original; not only Martin's wife but an entire community unconsciously conspired to support the impersonation.[38] In the Duke's case as well, the ends formally justify his means, and we as audience support his impersonation. Isabella's impersonation is a different case altogether, for her assumption of male speech and logic violates social norms. Although not a *haec vir* or manly woman in her dress and appearance, Isabella does have affinities with that particular monster. When she lashes out against Claudio for begging his life at the expense of her chastity, Isabella expresses her rage by questioning her mother's chastity; she shares this form of invective with Lear and Posthumus Leonatus from *Cymbeline.* Isabella's righteous anger therefore entails an unusually strong identification with a male point of view.[39]

Like Shakespeare's Venus, Isabella is eventually subjected to Vienna's patriarchy. As Kathleen McLuskie has demonstrated, *Measure for Measure* constructs its women from a masculine point of view.[40] When Angelo feels his chastity threatened by Isabella's beauty, he resorts to the traditional division between virgins and strumpets; his vision gains wider currency as the play progresses. Once Isabella's tryst with Angelo is fixed, she becomes increasingly aligned with Mariana, an affiliation that domesticates Isabella and tames her tongue. *Measure for Measure*'s exercise in feminine identity fashioning exposes Isabella and Mariana to comic irony, then to more heavily satiric invective when they petition the Duke and find themselves put on trial along with Angelo. The ethics of the Duke's bed trick have been discussed at length.[41] Although appeals to dramatic convention are ultimately unsatisfactory, when Isabella repeats Angelo's elaborate instructions for their meeting—involving two keys for opening two separate doors into a brick-walled garden—the sanctity of Mariana's *hortus conclusus* is already invaded by phallic imagery. Isabella and Angelo become the butts of a joke they themselves create in earnest. Like the narrator of *Venus and Adonis,* then, we indulge in a moment of voyeurism, enticed by the hyperbolic detail recounted in all innocence by Isabella.[42]

In *Measure for Measure*'s trial scene, the Duke completes the humiliation of Isabella and Mariana by subjecting them to his secular authority; in this way he fulfills Angelo's attempted violation by forcing each in turn to put on metaphorically but publicly the "destin'd livery" of female sexuality. The scene, as a variant on the Parliament of Heaven, should provide the women with allegorical immunity, since the debate between Justice and Mercy proceeds in an orderly way and ends with mankind's redemption.[43] Yet in Shakespeare's version Isabella and Mariana must plead for themselves before Angelo. The Duke forces Isabella to present herself as a new kind of paradox, the unchaste nun; Mariana, who obediently accepts the bed trick, is paraded about as a monster beyond the normal matrix of sexual roles. The substitution of one woman for another in the bed trick is completed here in a way that denies both women their individuality and reduces them to misogynistic stereotypes.[44] As Jonathan Dollimore has suggested, the Duke's strategy in this scene is political.[45] Though Dollimore argues that the Duke stages Angelo's trial in order to demonstrate his own integrity as a ruler, sexual politics motivate the Duke as well; for although he takes back from Angelo his seat and authority, their common political role identifies them with one another. The Duke identifies less directly with the women. Although he has assured Mariana that her marriage to Angelo is legal, in the trial she is treated more as a sinner than an abused citizen. Safe in her moated grange, Mariana was supremely virginal; but in the trial scene, when she kneels to the Duke, Mariana also begins to resemble the Virgin's theological alter ego, the penitent Magdalene, who since the Middle Ages had been represented as a beautiful hermit.[46] Like the Magdalene, whose legend highlights her close relationship with Christ, Mariana turns to patriarchal authority to still her "brawling discontent" (4.1.9). When she enters Angelo's hortus conclusus, however, Mariana reverses the Magdalene's retreat from sexuality to spiritual grace. Marina Warner notes that a figure like the Magdalene ultimately "strengthens the characteristic Christian correlation between sin, the flesh, and the female."[47] Angelo, not the Virgin, inhabits the closed garden, and Mariana makes a pilgrimage from lonely but controlled chastity into that sinister garden. Through these inversions of traditional iconography, *Measure for Measure* ironically suggests the fragility of female chastity. At this point the opposition between virgin and whore has broken down completely. Mariana, as one who is "neither maid, widow, nor wife," easily becomes the object of Lucio's joke: "My lord, she may be a punk; for many of them are neither maid, widow, nor wife" (5.1.177-80).

Isabella is also reduced to a misogynistic stereotype. Joining hands with Mariana to plead for Angelo's life, she retains her characteristic grasp of equity. While Mariana argues that "best men are moulded out of faults" (5.1.439), Isabella pardons Angelo, as she would have pardoned Claudio, on the basis of his intention: "I partly think / A due sincerity governed his deeds, / Till he did look on me" (5.1.445-47). Isabella's identification with Mariana, although it demonstrates a more healthy acceptance of woman's perspective than Isabella has shown before, also links her visually and conceptually with the woman who is neither maid, widow, nor wife. Isabella, who prides herself on her chastity and her truthful tongue, has now lied and publicly proclaimed herself unchaste. In the scenario assigned her by the Duke, Isabella has experienced, if only in play, the public shame of feminine frailty. The act of

kneeling therefore deprives Isabella as well as Mariana of autonomy and control over her body.[48] Although both women kneel freely, Mariana to redeem her husband and Isabella in a gesture of solidarity with her, the Duke's script determines the range of action available to them. Put in her place as Mariana has been put in hers, Isabella leaves the stage in silence, as a proper but ordinary woman who will be tamed by marriage—and, we presume, cease to play with reason and discourse.

Helena of *All's Well That Ends Well,* like Isabella, is both an accomplished orator and a social anomaly. While Isabella is on the verge of taking religious orders, Helena, whose "Dian" is "both herself and Love" (1.3.212-13), stands on the threshold of sexual maturity. Helena also shares some of Isabella's verbal facility. Although she seems to speak "sensibly" or wisely when she cures the French King, her male auditors respond either with revulsion or with their physical "senses." The social context of Helena's rhetoric, however, differs from that of the other female Shakespearean orators, so that her verbal triumph and subsequent repression follow another pattern. Rossillion and France both have noble pasts that live in their collective social memories. Eulogizing the elder Rossillion for his son's benefit, the French King recounts how

> like a courtier, contempt nor bitterness
> Were in his pride or sharpness; if they were,
> His equal had awak'd them, and his honor,
> Clock to itself, knew the true minute when
> Exception bid him speak, and at this time
> His tongue obey'd his hand. Who were below him
> He us'd as creatures of another place,
> And bow'd his eminent top to their low ranks,
> Making them proud of his humility,
> In their poor praise he humbled.
>
>   (1.2.36-45)

In this ethical centerpiece, the elder Rossillion acts according to a courtly decorum that makes him temperate, gracious toward inferiors, and a master of proper timing, so that he knows exactly when to vindicate his honor; he even hopes to die decorously, without lingering beyond the time of his social usefulness. Rossillion also behaves courteously to his inferiors, acting as an emblem of humility to boost their collective pride.

The community supported by paragons such as Bertram's father seems to be structured as an extended family of the kind described by Lawrence Stone in his studies of English aristocratic society of this period.[49] Since Rossillion is dead, according to Lafew, the Countess will find a second husband, Bertram a new father, in the French King (1.1.6-7). The Countess, also sensitive to social obligations, keeps the "shrewd" and "unhappy" Clown because her dead husband had enjoyed him. Helena, too, has been "bequeathed" to the Countess by her father.[50] Antique communal values are espoused regularly in Rossillion and in France, but they remain powerful in theory rather than practice. The French King denies the Florentines his troops in their war against Siena simply because his Austrian ally asks him to withhold aid. Even though Florence's quarrel is "holy" and the Sienese are "black and fearful," the King of France lets his youths serve whom they will, with the Machiavellian hope that the restless gentry will find "breathing and exploit" in foreign wars (3.1.4-6; 1.2.15-17). Furthermore, Bertram's sullen refusal to play his assigned part at court, if the King's word can be accepted, typifies the new generation's lack of values.

Because Helena lives in a decaying society, clever wenches and unscrupulous parasites can easily advance themselves beyond their station. Under such conditions, the rhetoric of selfhood does not describe adequately the practice of self-fashioning. Ideally, in the closed world of Rossillion's aristocracy, inherited position and innate virtue go together. Blessing Bertram at his departure for France, the Countess prays that he will succeed his father in "manners" as in "shape" and that his "blood and virtue" will "contend for empire" within him (1.1.61-63). At the same time, according to the play's authority figures, virtue earns its own reward. When Bertram refuses to marry Helena, the King tells him that "good alone / Is good, without a name," and that "honors thrive, / When rather from our acts we them derive / Than our foregoers" (2.3.128-29, 135-37). The Countess echoes the King's attitude, rejecting Bertram for Helena when he flees the marriage. She counters Bertram's curse on Helena with her own "dreadful sentence," assuring Helena that "He was my son, / But I do wash his name out of my blood, / And thou art all my child" (3.2.66-68).

Since the symmetry between virtue and blood, manners and shape, or exterior and interior is often skewed in *All's Well That Ends Well,* human relations lack an ethical logic. Although virtue should be loved for itself, the characters often seem to form bonds on less analytical grounds. The Countess's spontaneous acceptance of Helena as her daughter, though based on a duty to Helena's father, is also supported by the Countess's memories of her own youth:

> Even so it was with me when I was young.
> If ever we are nature's, these are ours. This
>   thorn
> Doth to our rose of youth rightly belong;
> Our blood to us, this to our blood is born.
> It is the show and seal of nature's truth,

> Where love's strong passion is impress'd in
>   youth.
> By our remembrances of days foregone,
> Such were our faults, or then we thought them
>   none.

>   (1.3.128-35)

The prevalence of indefinite pronouns in this passage—the Countess does not identify "love's strong passion" as the "thorn" that pricks youth's rose until six lines have passed—strengthens the sense of memory in motion. The Countess, it seems, struggles to remember not only love but the language of love. The King, as well, is indirectly moved to accept Bertram by memories of a past he shared with Bertram's father. But other liaisons seem merely quixotic. Bertram's affiliation with Parolles is honored although not explained, for Parolles is not exposed until he betrays Bertram; and at the end of the play, Lafew accepts without demur Parolles' claim on his charity. But while a benign charity keeps the peace, intimate relations are often governed by mechanical matching of person to role. It is the French King who says, self-deprecatingly, that he merely "fill[s] a place" (1.2.69), but his phrase rings true for other relationships. For Bertram, Diana is only an erotic substitute for his despised wife; even in Helena's case, one affection mechanically drives out another when passion for Bertram makes her forget her father. In Lavatch's fantasy of social relations, the man who cuckolds him becomes his drudge and finally his friend, since "he that kisses my wife is my friend" (1.3.49-50). In his adulterous version of community relations, Lavatch pinpoints the ultimate source of all affection: "I am driven on by the flesh, and he must needs go that the devil drives" (1.3.28-30).

Given the unstable relation between status and merit in this play, Helena's behavior becomes ethically more complicated than her folk origins as the "clever wench" would suggest. *Measure for Measure*'s Isabella speaks only one language, but it is admirably suited for the problems she encounters. Helena, on the other hand, is emotionally and rhetorically immature, and her syntax and vocabulary change constantly. For this reason, she often seems to have no private voice or thoughts; what she says in soliloquy can be trusted no more than what she tells the Clown, and so she contradicts herself at every turn. In fact, Helena must speak every thought aloud, for the Countess first hears of her love for Bertram when the Clown overhears and reports her virginal laments. Increasing the opacity of Helena's character is the fact that she, like many characters in this play, talks about herself through abstractions that interact of their own volition and so bring with them prefabricated conclusions. When describing her hopeless love for Bertram, Helena figures him as a star far above her, in whose "bright radiance and collateral light" she must be content to take comfort (1.1.88). She is the hind who would mate with the lion and so must die for love. In a second soliloquy within this same scene, however, Helena has completely reversed her decision; asking generally "who ever strove / To show her merit, that did miss her love?" (1.1.226-27), she assumes the impersonal tone of a purveyor of proverbs, asserting that "our remedies oft in ourselves do lie, / Which we ascribe to heaven," and concluding that "the mightiest space in fortune nature brings / To join like likes, and kiss like native things" (1.1.216-17, 222-23).

Helena's self-examinations seem radically inconsistent because her speeches are made from the stuff of rhetorical debate; she constructs her self according to the rules of argument *in utram partemque.* The two soliloquies discussed above are separated by Helena's conversation with Parolles. When she and Parolles discuss the merits and demerits of chastity, they re-create in dialogue the *suasoria,* which considers issues such as whether one should marry without reference to any particular person. Parolles assumes a familiarity with Helena by asking if she meditates on virginity. She depersonalizes the question by rephrasing it: "Man is enemy to virginity; how may we barricado it against him?" (1.1.112-13). He responds that no defense exists against men, initiating an exchange of puns on the phrase "to blow up." Parolles insinuates that man, having "undermined" woman's will in the psychological as well as the physiological sense, then "blows her up" with child. In an effort to restore the military metaphor, Helena asks whether there is "no military policy how virgins might blow up men" (121-22). Parolles beats her back with her own weapon, closing off all avenues of escape with a metaphor based on their shared pun. "Virginity being blown down," the maidenhead broken, "man will quicklier be blown up" with sexual desire (123-24). To "blow down" his erection, woman loses her "city," letting her virginity be "blown down" once again. In Parolles' neat formulation, woman's domination of man logically entails her submission to him.

In her first soliloquy, Helena had constructed a hierarchy of love reinforced by natural analogies. Parolles undermines her idealism with his intimate puns and paradoxical metaphors, which draw man and woman into sexual combat. Unfolding virginity's paradox, that it depreciates with time, Parolles breaks down the careful distance Helena has set between herself and Bertram with a prosopopoeia of ancient Virginity. "Virginity, like an old courtier, wears her cap our of fashion," he preaches, "richly suited, but unsuitable—just like the brooch and the toothpick, which [wear] not now. Your date is better in your pie and your porridge than in your cheek; and your old virginity, is like one of our French wither'd pears, it looks ill, it eats drily, marry, 'tis a withered pear" (1.1.156-62). Parolles makes a shambles of Helena's analogical arguments, ridiculing the "great chain of being" that justifies her pious re-

nunciation of Bertram. If Bertram is like a distant star, a pear can with equal justice represent virginity. Thus Parolles ends triumphantly with a tautology: A withered pear *is* a withered pear. In this strophic suasoria, Parolles' ostentatious wit protects his fallacies from rebuttal so that Helena finds herself automatically on the defensive, sniped at from behind a stockade of masculine bawdry.[51]

Trapped in Parolles' seamy world, where a virgin can choose only between sexual violence or the lonely decrepitude of old age, Helena resolves their combative suasoria by vowing to pursue Bertam to France. In France, she demonstrates a new sense of rhetorical sophistication, for in order to cure the King she must represent herself as powerful but humble; she achieves her purpose by appealing furtively to his long-dormant sexual desire. When the Renaissance educator Juan Luis Vives argues that rhetorical training only leads women astray, he confronts a number of classical exemplars who combine private virtue with public eloquence. Vives contends, however, that these women never learned the art of rhetoric but "receaved it by the familiar custome of their fathers without any paine or labour."[52] Helena, who derives her authority from her physician father, claims to have no knowledge of her own; her speech, like her prescription, is acquired without labor from her father. Helena is therefore the perfect female speaker, eloquent through instinct and divine inspiration rather than art. Yet a skeptical analysis of Helena's encounter with the French King, one that keeps in mind her romantic goal, suggests that she insinuates herself into a male political hierarchy by adopting and transforming its discourse.

Helena comes to offer the King her secret prescription. But the King, like a patronizing father, insists gently that a young girl cannot help him:

> I say we must not
> So stain our judgment, or corrupt our hope,
> To prostitute our past-cure malady
> To empirics, or to dissever so
> Our great self and our credit, to esteem
> A senseless help when help past sense we
> deem.
>
> (2.1.119-24)

The King would lose much credit, he reminds Helena, if he were misled by a charlatan. A chiasmus in the final phrase here, "A *senseless help* when *help past sense* we deem," firmly locks Helena's proffered "help" between the King's good "sense" and the senselessness of her project, so that she cannot possibly act within his rhetorical coordinates. Helena counters the King's argument by deferring to his premise that he lacks hope and she lacks art. In Frank Whigham's terms, whereas he employs the "trope of self-deprecation," she uses the "trope of deference," paradoxically demanding recognition by deferring to the King.[53] Playing on the King's Stoic piety, Helena restates her case with a string of *sententiae*:

> He that of greatest works is finisher
> Oft does them by the weakest minister:
> So holy writ in babes hath judgment shown,
> When judges have been babes; great floods
>   have flown
> From simple sources; and great seas have
>   dried
> When miracles have by the great'st been
>   denied.
>
> (2.1.136-41)

Casting herself as the simple source from which a great flood flows, or the babe who makes wise judgments, Helena exploits the King's opinion of her youth and ignorance. From a rhetorical point of view, Helena's improvisatory performance not only capitalizes on the cultural association of woman with emotion but covertly testifies to her authenticity; spontaneous and unrehearsed, her speech *must* be sincere.[54] At last she preempts the King's style altogether, meeting his pessimistic chiasmus with an optimistic one of her own to confirm her credentials: "But *know* I *think,* and *think* I *know* most sure, / My art is not past power, nor you past cure" (2.1.157-58; my emphases). Within the chiasmus, the King's skeptical "thought" is contained by Helena's sure "knowledge."

Relenting, the French King responds less to Helena's vows than to her voice. He hears "some blessed spirit . . . speak / His powerful sound within an organ weak" (2.1.175-76). Proud of his own common sense, the King actually capitulates, as Angelo does in *Measure for Measure,* to his physical senses, for Helena influences him through his ears rather than his reason: "What impossibility would slay," the King's hope of cure, "sense saves another way" (2.1.177-78). There is a pun here on the difference between physical and common sense. Like the seductive rhetorician denounced by Bishop Jewel's *Oration against Rhetoric,* Helena can entice men with pleasing verse. Thus she cures the King with verbal rather than visual ornaments and cosmetics.

Lafew implies rather pruriently that Helena's medicine is sexual, since her simple touch might raise up impotent King Pippen, inspiring him to write love poetry and, by implication, to attempt more vigorous gestures of sexual appreciation (2.1.75-78). Helena cures the French King by relying on the very feature of rhetoric that Plato feared—its power to arouse pleasure in the listener. Appropriately, the King awards Helena with a choice of husband. Although, as "Doctor She," Helena provides the court with a welcome diversion as well as a medical miracle, when her verbal license translates into real authority over the lords she becomes more

threatening. When Helena goes through the ritual of selecting her husband, Lafew's framing commentary injects a note of comedy into the proceedings and invites skepticism about the sincerity of the French lords' enthusiasm for marrying her. While the lords vie with one another for the honor of Helena's hand, Lafew thinks that they reject her and rages against their lack of sexual spirit. But as Bertram's response to the King's remonstrance reminds us, the lords' courtesy to Helena is not entirely voluntary; when Bertram bridles at having his wife chosen for him and the royal honor is at stake, the King quickly produces his power.[55]

Because "he must needs go whom the devil drives," Helena's sexuality is disruptive. But her oratorical prowess is what makes her a real social threat. Helena's kinship with Parolles, the play's other sophistic orator, suggests why her rhetoric can be threatening to *All's Well*'s patriarchy. Parolles serves no man and any man, as he makes clear to Lafew, yet for a time he is secure in his role as Bertram's companion. In a similar way, Helena's meteoric rise into the Rossillion aristocracy demonstrates her ability to evade quietly the traditional categories of class and gender; in her disguise as an errant pilgrim, she is equally autonomous and resistant to patriarchal control. Unlike Parolles' facade, however, Helena's facade is impenetrable. Despite her anomalous social position, Helena so thoroughly adopts the language and values of the King and of Bertram's mother that her marriage to Bertram helps to emasculate and infantilize him. By the time he tries to seduce Diana, he has degenerated into a petulant, "ruttish" boy not unlike Venus's Adonis.[56]

At the end of *All's Well,* Helena is tamed, just as Isabella is, through her alliance with another woman. In this play, the bed trick and mock trial of the women are more perfunctory than in *Measure for Measure,* but the pattern is the same. Josephine Waters Bennett notices that, in act 5, first the Clown and then Lafew subject Parolles to a "verbal hazing, or masculine joshing."[57] The King treats his female supplicants with less permissiveness because, although Parolles' character is well known, the women's motives are opaque. Women in *All's Well* identify strongly with one another, but the trio of Diana, Helena, and the Widow is particularly potent. As Carol Thomas Neely aptly puts it, together they are "maid, widow, and wife," illustrating the range of acceptable roles for women.[58] Ironically, in this play even women who embrace sexual strictures are suspect. Diana, who has vowed to remain a maid, is treated first as a "fond" and "desperate" creature, then as a whore who has the presence of mind to keep bail on hand. The King's vituperative epithets recall both Helena's willingness to risk "searing" her maiden's name (2.1.172-73) when she cures the King and the fact that the Widow, like a "professional madam," has accepted Helena's money as payment for the bed trick.[59]

Describing *The English Gentlewoman* in 1631, Richard Brathwait suggests that "Silence in a *Woman* is a moving Rhetoricke, winning most, when in words it wooeth least."[60] In *Venus and Adonis, Measure for Measure,* and *All's Well That Ends Well,* Shakespeare in the end concurs. In *Venus and Adonis* Venus must retreat to lonely bereavement on Paphos, and in *All's Well That Ends Well* Bertram reserves the right to test Helena's improbable account of how she won his ring and conceived his child. Bertram controls the terms of their reconciliation as he did those of their separation. Isabella of *Measure for Measure* also loses her voice, since she leaves the stage without responding to the Duke's abrupt marriage proposal. In the end, Shakespeare silences the decorative rhetoric through which some of his boldest heroines, and he himself as actor and playwright, have won power for themselves.

Yet this conclusion calls for qualification, for these Shakespearean women are not completely stereotyped and confined to their narratives. Although in *Venus and Adonis* the masculine narrator has the final word, even here Shakespeare refuses to validate the narrator's perspective completely. In the beginning of the poem Venus, Adonis, and the narrator are locked in a triangle that replicates another triangle established in the dedication, which involves Shakespeare, the "deformed" heir of his invention, and its recipient, the Earl of Southampton. It is impossible to align neatly the figures in these two triangles, for Shakespeare is at once analogous to the narrator and to Venus: He petitions the Earl of Southampton as she pleads to Adonis. The sexual ambiguities involved in these analogies between characters within and outside the poem intensify the confusion of identities. Reading *Venus and Adonis,* then, demands a willingness to indulge in critical transvestism. *Measure for Measure,* as well, both invites and frustrates conventional responses.[61] And finally, in *All's Well That Ends Well,* Helena leaves the stage with her riddle intact. As one who is both "dead" and "quick" with child—or in dramatic terms, both a female character and a boy actor—she is a paradox whose potency will not be diffused.

Recent feminist criticism of Shakespeare has debated the question of Shakespeare's own sexual politics. One group treats Shakespeare as a perceptive and sympathetic creator of female characters, a Renaissance male feminist awaiting recovery. The other group, recognizing that his characters are constructed from a masculine perspective, perform resistant readings on the plays.[62] Both positions must be accepted, however, if we take into account the nature of identification, which seeks resemblance in difference. "Who is't can read a woman?" Cymbeline asks at the end of his play. Perhaps, as he claims, no man can read a woman successfully. But in Shakespeare's works, to attempt cross-gender identification means putting oneself temporarily in the place of the other. To this extent, trying to read woman as Other is representative of all attempts to read and write literary characters.

Notes

[1] Plato, *Gorgias,* 502b-e and 523a-524d, in *The Collected Dialogues of Plato,* ed. Edith Hamilton and Huntington Cairnes (Princeton: Princeton University Press, 1961).

[2] Seneca, *Ad Lucilium Epistulae Morales,* trans. Richard Gummere, Loeb Classical Library (Cambridge, Mass.: Harvard University Press, 1920), 3:300-319.

[3] Elsewhere Cicero uses the clothing metaphor without specifically feminizing it. See *Brutus,* trans. G. L. Hendrickson, Loeb Classical Library (Cambridge, Mass.: Harvard University Press, 1971), 75.262, 79.274; *De Oratore,* trans. E. W. Sutton and completed by H. Rackham, Loeb Classical Library (Cambridge, Mass.: Harvard University Press, 1948), 1.54.235, 2.28.123-24.

[4] Cicero, *Orator,* trans. H. M. Hubbell, Loeb Classical Library (Cambridge, Mass.: Harvard University Press, 1971), 23.78-79.

[5] George Puttenham, *The Arte of English Poesie,* ed. Gladys Doidge Willcock and Alice Walker (Cambridge: Cambridge University Press, 1936), 137.

[6] George Herbert, *George Herbert and the Seventeenth-Century Religious Poets,* ed. Mario A. Di Cesare (New York: Norton, 1978), 25-26.

[7] Cicero, *De Oratore,* 1.34.157. Daniel Javitch, *Poetry and Courtliness in Renaissance England* (Princeton: Princeton University Press, 1978), 25 and chap. 1, passim. On the humanist orator's ethical character, see Hanna H. Gray, "Renaissance Humanism: The Pursuit of Eloquence," *Journal of the History of Ideas* 24 (1963): 497-514. On the relationship between the courtly tradition and rhetorical construction of the self, see Richard A. Lanham, "The Self as Middle Style: *Cortegiano,*" in *The Motives of Eloquence: Literary Rhetoric in the Renaissance* (New Haven: Yale University Press, 1976), 144-64; and on the relationship between *The Courtier*'s self-examination and the debate structure of Cicero's *De Oratore,* plus the equivocal role played by woman, see Thomas M. Greene, "*Il Cortegiano* and the Choice of a Game," in *The Vulnerable Text: Essays on Renaissance Literature* (New York: Columbia University Press, 1986), 46-60.

[8] Javitch, *Poetry and Courtliness,* 27.

[9] Ibid., 37.

[10] For a bibliography of Renaissance antifeminist literature, see Suzanne W. Hull, *Chaste, Silent, & Obedient: English Books for Women, 1475-1640* (San Marino, Calif.: Huntington Library, 1982). Other useful works include *Half Humankind: Contexts and Texts of the Controversy about Women in England, 1540-1640,* ed. Katherine Usher Henderson and Barbara F. McManus (Urbana: University of Illinois Press, 1985); Lisa Jardine, *Still Harping on Daughters: Women and Drama in the Age of Shakespeare,* rev. ed. (New York: Columbia University Press, 1989); Patricia Parker, "Motivated Rhetorics: Gender, Order, Rule," in *Literary Fat Ladies: Rhetoric, Gender, Property* (London: Methuen, 1987), 97-125; and Linda Woodbridge, *Women and the English Renaissance: Literature and the Nature of Womankind, 1540-1620* (Urbana: University of Illinois Press, 1984).

[11] Johannes Lodovicus Vives, *The Office and Duetie of an Husband,* trans. T. Paynell (London, [1553]), Q2v-Q3r.

[12] C. Pyrrye, "The Praise and Dispraise of Women" (London, [1569]), A5v-A6r.

[13] Hoyt H. Hudson, "Jewel's Oration against Rhetoric: A Translation," *Quarterly Journal of Speech* 14 (1928): 383. Relevant to the entire discussion of woman's connection to rhetoric's disruptive powers is the excellent essay by Patricia Parker, "Motivated Rhetorics," in *Literary Fat Ladies,* 97-125.

[14] For the argument that Renaissance theatrical representations of femininity can not only encourage a metatheatrical awareness of the boy actor beneath his female role but also engage with moral and social definitions of woman, see Kathleen McLuskie, *Renaissance Dramatists* (Atlantic Highlands, N.J.: Humanities Press, 1989), 100-122.

[15] C. S. Lewis, *English Literature in the Sixteenth Century, Excluding Drama,* Oxford History of English Literature (Oxford: Clarendon Press, 1954), 499.

[16] Huntington Brown, "*Venus and Adonis*: The Action, the Narrator, and the Critics," *Michigan Academician* 2, no. 2 (1969): 73-87, makes the case for the narrator as an objective chorus. Most critics consider the narrator as an objective observer, but Richard A. Lanham thinks that he is satirized along with Venus and Adonis (*Motives of Eloquence,* 90). Besides Lanham, critics who have considered the poem from the standpoint of its rhetoric are Heather Dubrow, *Captive Victors: Shakespeare's Narrative Poems and Sonnets* (Ithaca, N. Y.: Cornell University Press, 1987); Clark Hulse, *Metamorphic Verse: The Elizabethan Minor Epic* (Princeton: Princeton University Press, 1981); John Doebler, "The Many Faces of Love: Shakespeare's *Venus and Adonis,*" *Shakespeare Studies* 16 (1983):

33-43. Lucy Gent, "*Venus and Adonis*: The Triumph of Rhetoric," *Modern Language Review* 69 (1974): 721-29, calls Venus an "arch-sophist."

[17] Puttenham, *Arte of English Poesie,* 186.

[18] Paul Fussell, Jr., *Poetic Meter and Poetic Form* (New York: Random House, 1965), 142.

[19] Nancy Lindheim, "The Shakespearean *Venus and Adonis,*" *Shakespeare Quarterly* 37 (1986): 193.

[20] Interpretations of this scene vary. Robert P. Miller's heavily moralistic reading suggests that Venus cleverly turns the story of her adulterous shame into proof of her sexual attractiveness in "The Myth of Mar's Hot Minion in *Venus and Adonis,*" *ELH* 26 (1959): 470-81. For a more positive allegorical reading of Venus's union with Mars as a *discordia concors,* see Edgar Wind, *Pagan Mysteries in the Renaissance,* rev. ed. (New York: Norton, 1968), 81-96, and Raymond B. Waddington, "*Antony and Cleopatra*: 'What Venus Did with Mars,'" *Shakespeare Studies* 2 (1966): 210-27.

[21] Ernst Cassirer, *Language and Myth,* trans. Susanne K. Langer (New York: Harper, 1946), 92-99.

[22] Kenneth Burke, *A Rhetoric of Motives* (1950; rpt., Berkeley: University of California Press, 1969), 40-42. In a slightly different argument based on Claude Lévi-Strauss's definition of myth, Clark Hulse suggests that *Venus and Adonis*'s ability to reconcile opposites in paradox is mythic (*Metamorphic Verse,* 172-73).

[23] The allegorical readings of this poem, which depend on sources ranging from Neoplatonic philosophy to the Ovid moralisé tradition, are too numerous to mention. For a recent summary of the criticism and its sources, see Lennet J. Daigle, "*Venus and Adonis*: Some Traditional Contexts," *Shakespeare Studies* 13 (1980): 31-46.

[24] Coppélia Kahn, *Man's Estate: Masculine Identity in Shakespeare* (Berkeley: University of California Press, 1981), 40.

[25] Dubrow, *Captive Victors,* 68-69. Dubrow's is the best recent treatment of the poem; however, she stresses the ethical judgments passed on Venus more than I do, tending to see her as more self-centered and the narrator as more balanced than I do.

[26] On the "proleptic" qualities of *Venus and Adonis*'s plot, see Hulse, *Metamorphic Verse,* 171.

[27] Kahn, *Man's Estate,* 45-46. For the idea that *Venus and Adonis,* by stressing Venus's maternal urges, works out a Renaissance ambivalence toward women that is especially notable in the courtly tradition of

Castriglione, see Wayne A. Rebhorn, "Mother Venus: Temptation in Shakespeare's *Venus and Adonis,*" *Shakespeare Studies* 11 (1978): 1-19.

[28] Wylie Sypher, "Shakespeare as Casuist: *Measure for Measure,*" *Sewanee Review* 58 (1950): 262-80; Elder Seneca, *Controversiae, Books* 1-6, vol. 1 of *Declamations,* trans. M. Winterbottom, Loeb Classical Library (Cambridge, Mass.: Harvard University Press, 1974), 1.5. A variant on the case of the man who raped two women can be found in Alexander Silvayn, *The Orator,* trans. Lazarus Piot (London, 1596), 276-80. Silvayn's version concerns "a maiden who being ravished, did first require her ravisher for her husband, and afterwards requested his death" (276). Interestingly, this story matches the scenario the Duke proposes at the end of *Measure for Measure,* when he marries Angelo to Mariana, then orders his death. For a thorough analysis of *Measure for Measure*'s pervasive interest in decorative rhetoric, which permeates even the language of seamy sexuality, see Joanne Altieri, "Style and Social Disorder in *Measure for Measure,*" *Shakespeare Quarterly* 25 (1974): 6-16.

[29] Robert Grams Hunter, *Shakespeare and the Comedy of Forgiveness* (New York: Columbia University Press, 1965), 206-7.

[30] Sister Miriam Joseph, *Shakespeare's Use of the Arts of Language* (New York: Columbia University Press, 1947), 232.

[31] On these distinctions, see Thomas Wilson, *Arte of Rhetorique,* ed. Thomas J. Derrick (New York: Garland, 1982), 189-92.

[32] Marion Trousdale, "Recurrence and Renaissance: Rhetorical Imitation in Ascham and Sturm," *English Literary Renaissance* 6 (1976): 156-79, argues that the practice of imitation in rhetorical education not only affected literary practice but also encouraged a general preoccupation with formal patterning. Some Renaissance accounts define imitation in terms of competition with an original. See G. W. Pigman, III, "Versions of Imitation in the Renaissance," *Renaissance Quarterly* 33 (1980): 1-32.

[33] Lawrence Sargent Hall links Isabella's use of the mirror image to the mirror Richard II uses to analyze his lack of self and to Hamlet's use of a mirror to show "unreflecting Gertrude" her essential self ("Isabella's Angry Ape," *Shakespeare Quarterly* 15, no. 3 [1964]: 157-65).

[34] On the distinction between figures of thought and of speech, which depend on words rather than ideas, see Quintilian, *Institutio Oratoria,* trans. H. E. Butler, Loeb Classical Library (Cambridge, Mass.: Harvard University Press, 1921), 9.1.

[35] This point is made by John L. Harrison, "The Convention of 'Heart and Tongue' and the Meaning of *Measure for Measure,*" *Shakespeare Quarterly* 5 (1954): 7.

[36] Miriam Joseph, *Shakespeare's Use of Language,* 182-83. T. W. Baldwin remarks that this argument follows the rules for a sententia, as prescribed by, Aphthonius (*William Shakspere's Small Latine and Lesse Greeke* [Urbana: University of Illinois Press, 1944], 2:88).

[37] For a psychoanalytic reading of this phenomenon, see Janet Adelman, "Male Bonding in Shakespeare's Comedies," in *Shakespeare's Rough Magic: Renaissance Essays in Honor of C. L. Barber,* ed. Peter Erickson and Coppélia Kahn (Newark: University of Delaware Press, 1985), 73-103. Much recent criticism stresses the Duke's inadequacy as a ruler and father figure. See David Sundelson, *Shakespeare's Restorations of the Father* (New Brunswick, N. J.: Rutgers University Press, 1983); Richard P. Wheeler, *Shakespeare's Development and the Problem Comedies: Turn and Counter-Turn* (Berkeley: University of California Press, 1981); and Leonard Tennenhouse, "Representing Power: *Measure for Measure* in Its Time," *Genre* 15 (1982): 139-56, who sees the Duke as a trickster. Other critics see the Duke, despite his shortcoming, as a truly providential figure. See Arthur C. Kirsch, "The Integrity of *Measure for Measure,*" *Shakespeare Survey* 28 (1975): 89-105; Darryl J. Gless, "*Measure for Measure,*" *the Law, and the Convent* (Princeton: Princeton University Press, 1979); and Muriel Bradbrook, "Authority, Truth, and Justice in *Measure for Measure,*" *Review of English Studies* 17 (1941): 385-99. However, it becomes possible to bridge the gap between these two readings of the Duke if we acknowledge that in this play authority is won by persuading others rather than derived from established hierarchies.

[38] Stephen Greenblatt, "Psychoanalysis and Renaissance Culture," in *Literary Theory / Renaissance Texts,* ed. Patricia Parker and David Quint (Baltimore: Johns Hopkins University Press, 1986), 210-24; Natalie Zemon Davis, *The Return of Martin Guerre* (Cambridge, Mass.: Harvard University Press, 1983).

[39] For the role played in masculine identity crisis by the absent mother, see Coppélia Kahn, "The Absent Mother in *King Lear,*" in *Rewriting the Renaissance: The Discourses of Sexual Difference in Early Modern Europe,* ed. Margaret W. Ferguson, Maureen Quilligan, and Nancy J. Vickers (Chicago: University of Chicago Press, 1986), 33-49. Also related to my discussion of Isabella's "masculine" dimension is David Sundelson's discussion of the discomfort created in *Measure for Measure* when androgyny yields to female sexuality in the absence of a powerful father figure (*Shakespeare's Restorations of the Father,* 89-102).

[40] Kathleen McLuskie, "The Patriarchal Bard: Feminist Criticism and Shakespeare: *King Lear* and *Measure for Measure*," in *Political Shakespeare: New Essays in Cultural Materialism,* ed. Jonathan Dollimore and Alan Sinfield (Ithaca, N. Y.: Cornell University Press, 1985), 88-108.

[41] For a recent summary of commentary on the bed trick and the unusual argument that the bed trick demonstrates the women characters' control and resourcefulness, see Eileen Z. Cohen, "'Virtue Is Bold': The Bed-trick and Characterization in *All's Well That Ends Well* and *Measure for Measure*," *Philological Quarterly* 65 (1986): 171-86.

[42] Marilyn L. Williamson, quoting a passage from Philip Stubbes's *Anatomy of Abuses,* suggests that Shakespeare may have wanted to tie this passage to Puritan attacks on sexual license. Stubbes describes secluded gardens like Angelo's as convenient locations for sexual assignations (*The Patriarchy of Shakespeare's Comedies* [Detroit: Wayne State University Press, 1986], 84-85).

[43] For the Parliament of Heaven, which involves a debate between female personifications of Justice and Mercy, see Samuel C. Chew, *The Virtues Reconciled: An Iconographic Study* (Toronto: University of Toronto Press, 1947), 35-68. Following Muriel Bradbrook's suggestion that *Measure for Measure* enacts the Parliament, John D. Cox finds medieval antecedents in several kinds of plays, particularly *The Woman Taken in Adultery* and *Mary Magdalene;* both involve a female figure who pleads for mercy. Interestingly, both medieval plays, like *Measure for Measure,* define women in terms of their sexuality. See John D. Cox, "The Medieval Background of *Measure for Measure*," *Modern Philology* 81, no. 1 (1983): 1-13.

[44] For the argument that substitution in the problem comedies is used to deny characters individuality, see Nancy S. Leonard, "Substitution in Shakespeare's Problem Comedies," *English Literary Renaissance* 9 (1979): 281-301. Leonard is more interested in Angelo, but her remarks are germane to Isabella as well.

[45] Jonathan Dollimore, "Transgression and Surveillance in *Measure for Measure*," in Dollimore and Sinfield, *Political Shakespeare,* 72-87.

[46] For a discussion of the Magdalene's history and her symbolic relationship to the Virgin Mary, see Marina Warner, *Alone of All Her Sex: The Myth and the Cult of the Virgin Mary* (New York: Knopf, 1976), 224-35.

[47] Ibid., 234.

[48] Irene Dash, *Wedding, Wooing, and Power: Women in Shakespeare's Plays* (New York: Columbia University Press, 1981), 251. See also Marcia Riefer, "'Instruments of Some Mightier Member': The Constriction of Female Power in *Measure for Measure*," *Shakespeare Quarterly* 35 (1984): 157-69.

[49] Stone, *Family, Sex, and Marriage;* and Lawrence Stone, *Crisis of the Aristocracy, 1558-1641* (Oxford: Oxford University Press, 1965).

[50] The play also depends on folk motifs, most notably in the circumstances surrounding the King's fistula and its cure. For a sociological analysis of the interaction between aristocratic politics and communal values derived from folk drama in Elizabethan drama, see Robert Weimann, *Shakespeare and the Popular Tradition in the Theater: Studies in the Social Dimension of Dramatic Form and Function,* ed. Robert Schwartz (1967; Baltimore: Johns Hopkins University Press, 1978).

[51] Helena's rhetorical situation resembles that of Venus at the beginning of *Venus and Adonis,* where the narrator's opening simile of the sun leaving the weeping morn at daybreak creates a martial world with no place in it for Venus.

[52] Vives, *Office and Duetie,* Q2v; see also Ruth Kelso, *Doctrine for the Lady of the Renaissance* (Urbana: University of Illinois Press, 1956), 72-73.

[53] Frank Whigham, *Ambition and Privilege: The Social Tropes of Elizabethan Courtesy Theory* (Berkeley and Los Angeles: University of California Press, 1984), 102-12, 130-36.

[54] See the excellent discussion of improvisatory *copia* and its association with inspiration in Terence Cave, *The Cornucopian Text: Problems of Writing in the French Renaissance* (Oxford: Clarendon Press, 1979), 125-56.

[55] Robert Ornstein makes an interesting comparison between Bertram and Hermia of *A Midsummer Night's Dream,* a woman forced to marry against her will, which emphasizes Helena's usurpation of the masculine role in courtship (*Shakespeare's Comedies: From Roman Farce to Romantic Mystery* [Newark: University of Delaware Press, 1986], 183).

[56] For Bertram as a prodigal son, see Williamson, *Patriarchy,* 66-67; on the emasculating incestuous overtones in Bertram's forced marriage to a woman so closely allied with his mother and on the Oedipal implications of Bertram's struggle against the King, see Richard P. Wheeler, *Shakespeare's Development,* 34-45.

[57] Josephine Waters Bennett, "New Techniques of Comedy in *All's Well That Ends Well*," *Shakespeare Quarterly* 18 (1967): 349.

[58] Carol Thomas Neely, *Broken Nuptials in Shakespeare's Plays* (New Haven: Yale University Press, 1985), 75.

[59] This phrase is used by Ian Donaldson, "*All's Well That Ends Well*: Shakespeare's Play of Endings," *Essays in Criticism* 27 (1977): 48.

[60] Richard Brathwait, *The English Gentlewoman* (London, 1631), 90.

[61] Jean E. Howard, "*Measure for Measure* and the Restraints of Convention," *Essays in Literature* 10 (1983): 149-58.

[62] For an account of the debate and its participants, see McLuskie, "Patriarchal Bard," and Martha Andresen-Thom, "Thinking about Women and Their Prosperous Art: A Reply to Juliet Dusinberre's *Shakespeare and the Nature of Women*," *Shakespeare Studies* 11 (1978): 259-76.

FURTHER READING

Ewbank, Inga-Stina. "Shakespeare's Liars." In *British Academy Shakespeare Lectures 1980-89*, pp. 85-116. Oxford: Oxford University Press, 1993.

  Examines Shakespeare's commentary on the simultaneous power of language to communicate and disguise intentions, to mislead, and to betray.

Howard, Jean E. "Cross-Dressing, the Theatre, and Gender Struggle in Early Modern England." *Shakespeare Quarterly* XXXIX, No. 4 (Winter 1988): 418-40.

  Explores attempts in Renaissance England to bolster a disintegrating hierarchy of gender and a "normative social order," considering Shakespeare's comedies to be conservative approaches to gender and class issues.

Weimann, Robert. "Representation and Performance: The Uses of Authority in Shakespeare's Theater." *PMLA* CVII, No. 3 (May 1992): 497-510.

  Discusses Shakespeare's simultaneous troubling of unitary power structures and of the authority of discourse within the context of Renaissance theatrics.

As You Like It

For further information on the critical and stage history of *As You Like It*, see *SC*, Volumes 5 and 23.

INTRODUCTION

Generally believed to have been written and first performed sometime between 1598 and 1600, *As You Like It* is largely a dramatic adaptation of Thomas Lodge's pastoral romance *Rosalynde* (1590). And, while Shakespeare mined this earlier work for most of the play's plot and many of its major characters, its sources are thought to also include such texts as Sir Philip Sidney's *Arcadia*, the anonymous *Historie of Sir Clyomen and Clamydes*, and Ovid's *Metamorphoses*. The work is typically seen as a light-hearted comedy, filled with the requisite misunderstandings and farcical happenings, but scholars have nonetheless observed that the play engages several serious subjects. Its principal actors are the virtuous Orlando de Boys and his beloved Rosalind, both of whom are banished from Duke Frederick's court to the near-mythical rural setting of the Forest of Arden. In these two characters Shakespeare personifies two of the work's leading themes: Orlando represents dishonored virtue restored, while Rosalind—who is disguised as Ganymede, a young man, for the majority of the play—inaugurates the theme of illusory appearance that questions the fabric of perception and reality.

As You Like It is often seen as a grand pastoral romance, tinged with an ironic commentary on the illusion of its ideals. As a pastoral comedy, its plot follows the classic three-part pattern, featuring an exile from court, followed by a renewal of character and social standing in a rural setting, and culminating in an exultant return to court. The two settings in the play, the natural world of Arden and Duke Frederick's court, are seen as analogous to the work's contrasting tensions of romantic idealism and ironic realism, respectively. Views of these contrasting worlds and the perspectives they represent have become commonplace in criticism on the play. Rosalie L. Colie, for example, has outlined many of the major pastoral themes and motifs reflected in the work, including its emphasis on dialogue, its mixture of comedy and tragedy, and its concern with the clash between art and nature and between court and country. Eamon Grennan, likewise, has approached the play as a pastoral comedy, but sees the work as a combining of pastoral and antipastoral elements. For Ralph Berry, the site of the anti-romantic rests in the character of Rosalind and in Touchstone, a professional fool from Duke Frederick's court who presumably acts as a mouthpiece for Shakespeare, allowing him to interject an ironic voice into the play. Other pastoral elements, such as the foolish shepherdess Phebe and her jilted Petrarchan lover, Silvius, are presented as stock characters, included to elicit mirth from the audience and to parody the limitations of the romantic genre.

Shakespeare's use of folly is another topic that attracts continual interest among critics of *As You Like It*. The play's humor, which pokes fun at human limitations and foolishness, has been perhaps most closely observed by R. Chris Hassel, who sees the work as a celebration of human folly, the absurdity of life, and the wisdom that comes with the apprehension of both. Hassel, along with several earlier commentators, has given significant attention to the play's fools Jaques and Touchstone. The character of Jaques has long been a compelling figure for audiences and critics. By the nineteenth century he had become a favorite subject of many, including William Hazlitt, who essentially cast him as a melancholic malcontent and a personification of self-indulgence and superficiality. This assessment has persisted, and Jaques is very consistently seen as striving to maintain the pretense of his aristocratic breeding, while only succeeding in demonstrating his foolishness. To a great degree, Jaques is contrasted with Touchstone who, despite his occupation, displays an intelligence, wit, and occasional profundity that equals or surpasses that of any other character in the play.

The depth of Touchstone's perceptions, however, are only rivaled by those of *As You Like It*'s chief protagonist, Rosalind. For many commentators, including Charles Brooks and Peter Hyland, Rosalind—in disguising herself as a man before she enters the Forest of Arden—draws attention to the work as self-conscious drama or metatheater, concerned with the consequences of acting and role-playing as part of the quest for self-knowledge. She is considered the locus of inversion in the play, and her character stirs a deeper understanding of the human condition by questioning the nature of observed reality. Rosalind is thought to forge her own identity throughout the course of the play through her adoption of a new appearance. Her disguise also draws attention to the Forest of Arden as a liminal space, where the ordinary perspectives—including commonly accepted gender and power structures both in and beyond the world of the play, such as the patriarchal status quo and the misdirected power of Duke Frederick that has banished Orlando from his rightful place as Duke—are turned upside down in order that they might be examined more closely. One of Shakespeare's most inventive and intelligent heroines, Rosalind also is the focus of the play's movement toward the reconciliation of opposites—realism and idealism, wisdom and folly, high and low, male and female. And, while many critics see Rosalind as this synthesizing figure, most concur that the underlying tensions in this play resist definite resolution, making *As You Like It* one of Shakespeare's most successful and compelling comedies.

OVERVIEWS

Ralph Berry (essay date 1971)

SOURCE: "No Exit from Arden" in *The Modern Language Review*, Vol. 66, 1971, pp. 11-20.

[*In the following essay, Berry outlines the anti-romantic elements of hostility, conflict, and debate that exist in* As You Like It *beneath the surface of romance.*]

The structure of *As You Like It* I take to be a synthesis of two structures, that of romance and anti-romance. The romantic elements need no recapitulation here; they compose, quite simply, the plot. Of the anti-romantic elements, much has already been commented on. For example: Rosalind, Touchstone, and Jacques provide a running fire (within the spectrum realism-satire) on the posturing of the romantics. There are plenty of overt hints that Arden is no paradise. Touchstone's 'Ay, now I am in Arden: the more fool I' (II.4.13)[1] shades into the evocation, which Kott has noted,[2] of an agrarian system governed by the capitalist laws of hire:

> But I am shepherd to another man,
> And do not shear the fleeces that I graze.
> My master is of churlish disposition . . .
>
>   (II.4.73)

And the play's conclusion, a set of major cadences rung to wedding bells, has already been consistently minored by the many references—obsessive, even for an Elizabethan comedy—to the traditional aftermath of marriage. The dwellers in Arden hear ever at their back the sound of horns.[3]

As You Like It's discordant music can be viewed as complementary to the play's evolving debate. It has become habitual to see the play's form as a set of debates. This is obviously true up to a point, though one should distinguish between the subject of the debate—usually court versus country—and the grand theme, which is the romantic ideal challenged by the probings of realism, commonsense, and satire. And yet the term 'debate', useful though it is in identifying an aspect of the play's tradition and form, masks a trap. The word tends to connote a balanced, objective inquiry into truth, an analysis conducted under conventional rules of a subject in which the allocation of sides to speakers is without psychological commitment, an opportunity to display dexterity. Such an implication is misleading here; for Shakespeare presents the 'debate' invariably as a struggle for mastery between two human beings, each of whom is determined to impose his or her values on the other. The constant human drive to dominate another is the underlying theme of much of the dialogue; and it is codified in Touchstone's haughty (and instant) response to Corin's 'Who calls?' 'Your betters, sir' (II.4.63). The power struggle, in muted form, is quite as present in Arden as at court; and we should look for its presence throughout the play following its overt presentation in Act I, the usurpation and defence of power. In view of the Shakesperian capacity for fusing literal and symbolic, I would not dismiss the wrestling-match as a mere concession to the groundlings. On the contrary, the wrestling-match is no bad figure for much of the play's substance. And I incline to regard the succession of covert struggles (to which we can return, in detail, later) as an extension of the play's anti-romantic structure.

But we can go further than this in our recognition of the play's anti-romantic possibilities, and I wish here to examine the relationships in *As You Like It*. Virtually all the relationships are governed by a sense of unease, irritation, or hostility. The impression we receive from the two major lovers in the foreground is quite different from that derived from all the other relationships (which include Rosalind and Orlando when confronted by any but each other). Indeed, if we disregard these lovers, we can perceive that the keynote of the relationships is a subdued or overt irritation. the reasons for this groundswell of hostility I take to be threefold: an underlying recognition that other people's qualities parallel and subtly menace one's own; an open clash of temperament and of values; a simple will to dominate. Let us consider the relationships in the light of these categories.

The opening Act provides us with the essence of the matter. Act I of *As You Like It* is sometimes viewed as a mere necessity of plot construction, yet it is almost the fundamental error of Shakespeare interpretation to write off any aspect of his work as being imposed by external necessity of stagecraft. We encounter two figures who find certain relationships intolerable: Oliver, and Duke Frederick. They present, obviously, the idea of conflict, but also prefigure the situation of insupportable relationship. Oliver, vis-á-vis Orlando, presents the first of these situations. His hatred is located in no known cause: '. . . for my soul, yet I know not why, hates nothing more than he' (I.1.148). And then, as Oliver continues to brood on the matter, the truth tumbles involuntarily out—this is a soliloquy, the repository if not the bill-board of truth in Shakespeare:

> Yet he's gentle; never school'd and yet learned; full of noble device; of all sorts enchantingly beloved; and, indeed so much in the heart of the world, and especially of my own people, who best know him, that I am altogether misprised.
>
> (I.1.149)

It looks forward to Iago's muttered charge against Cassio, 'He hath a daily beauty in his life / That makes me ugly' (*Othello,* V.1.19). It is possible to dislike others because they caricature oneself; Oliver hates Orlando because *he* seems an inferior version of his golden brother. And Adam commits the unforgivable sin, not of supporting Orlando, but of witnessing the two brothers' confrontation: hence 'Get you with him, you old dog' (I.1.73). Whereupon Adam doubles his offence by pointing out that Oliver is also an inferior copy of his father. The trouble, for Oliver, is the audience: hell is other people.

Orlando, then, is hated for his excellence, a situation which Adam sees very clearly:

> Your praise is come too swiftly home before
> you.
> Know you not, master, to some kind of men
> Their graces serve them but as enemies?
>
> (II.3.9)

Duke Frederick, the Oliver parallel, may well be assumed to share this hatred of his civilized and urbane brother. But his prevailing state of mind, as revealed, is characterized by suspiciousness and insecurity. A usurper himself, he sees threats everywhere. For him, the mere presence of people who recall his past is intolerably disturbing. Orlando, son of Sir Rowland, evokes only

> I would thou hadst been son to some man
> else.
> The world esteem'd thy father honourable,
> But I did find him still mine enemy . . .
>
> (I.2.203)

Similarly, for Rosalind: 'Thou art thy father's daughter; there's enough' (I.3.54). The Duke is able to rationalize his dislike for Rosalind into

> She is too subtle for thee; and her
> smoothness,
> Her very silence and her patience,
> Speak to the people, and they pity her.
> Thou art a fool. She robs thee of thy name.
>
> (I.3.73)

No doubt this situation objectively exists, but the Duke is clearly oppressed by a sense of comparisons, fatal to himself, suggested by the names of Sir Rowland, Orlando, Rosalind, Duke Senior. We should expect that this awareness of self-comparison is continued into his relationship with Oliver; and this is so. For obvious social reasons, Oliver has no opportunity of expressing his opinion of his 'semblable, son frère', the Duke; but the Duke has: 'More villain thou' (III.1.15).

The matter is analysed more acutely in Act II, in the relationships radiating out from Jacques. We need for the moment to note two—with Duke Senior, and with Touchstone. Now Duke Senior is the only character who has established a position in which he is, psychologically, immune to threats. he is equable, urbane, an ideal philosopher. He is, however, presented as an incorrigible moralizer; he is not to be restrained from sermonizing on stones. he sees the exterior world as a series of emblems. But this is precisely the bent of Jacques's mind. Independently he and the Duke arrive at the same metaphor: they perceive the natural kingdom of Arden as a power-struggle where man usurps the beasts' place, just as he himself is the victim of usurpation (Act II, Scene I). The point is not only that they agree—thus helping to establish the theme of natural conflict—but that they parallel each other, thus creating a tension. This is not apparent in the Duke's words; he is, after all, the overlord, and a man of rare mental equilibrium. For him, Jacques is an object of instruction and diversion: 'I love to cope him in these sullen fits, / For then he's full of matter' (II.1.67). Jacques, however, resents the patronage of a social superior whose mind inclines the same way as his: 'And I have been all this day to avoid him. He is too disputable for my company. I think of as many matters as he; but I give heaven thanks, and make no boast of them' (II.5.29). A palpable hit: Jacques, as we shall see, always flinches when touched. Here, at all events, we can note that the affinity between the Duke and Jacques (the tendency to dispute and moralize) results in the discomfort of the weaker man.

The mechanism of Jacques's relationships is detailed to us in Act II, Scene 7. I find in it one of the central passages of the play. Jacques has just entered, crowing of his encounter with Touchstone ('A fool, a fool! I met a fool i'the forest . . . ') and goes on to describe it (II.7.12-34). We should note that the Touchstone reported here is unrecognizable as the Touchstone we encounter before our eyes. Jacques presents Touchstone to us as a 'fool' in the double sense ('lack-lustre eye . . . Says very wisely . . . ') whereas it is perfectly clear elsewhere that Touchstone is an extremely intelligent man. Jacques's note is one of sour disdain, of scorn for the object that dares to 'moralize' (as he does). The word 'fool' occurs twelve times in this speech; and the *idea* of the speech is the tension between the two senses of 'fool', jester and simpleton.

And why? The why, as Jacques would say, is plain as way to parish church. He goes on to generalize—and as usual, when he generalizes, he talks of himself. The connexion between generality and application is perfectly plain, if implicit:

> He that a fool doth very wisely hit
> Doth very foolishly, although he smart,
> Not to seem senseless of the bob . . .
>
> (II.7.53)

The Duke's strong riposte (II.7.64-9) asserts that Jacques's generalizations have a personal origin and application; it must be so with 'He that a fool doth very wisely hit' as well. We need this passage to explicate the major preceding speech, and much else in *As You Like It*. Jacques's relationship with Touchstone depends on this admission:

> When I did hear
> The motley fool thus moral on the time,
> My lungs began to crow like chanticleer
> That fools should be so deep-contemplative . . .
>
> (II.7.28)

Touché: two fools together. Only Jacques does not say as much; he oscillates between a scornful wish (to the Duke) to be a fool ('Invest me in my motley', II.7.58) and a consistent attempt to patronize Touchstone when they meet. He does not say to *Touchstone* 'Motley's the only wear . . . ' (II.7.34). It is far more important to Jacques to maintain the position of mental superiority—if he can.

Jacques, in short, finds himself caricatured by the moralizing Fool. That Touchstone is a thoroughgoing professional adds to his offence. His response is a strategy of alternately deriding and patronizing Touchstone, which he pursues right up to the final scene: 'Is not this a rare fellow, my lord? He's as good at any thing, and yet a fool' (V.4.98). Jacques is exhibiting his good taste as a connoisseur of virtuosi, not genuinely commending Touchstone. The real man breaks out in the sudden stab of rancour at the end. To only one couple does Jacques fail to be civil, and offer the conventional good wishes:

> And you to wrangling; for thy loving voyage
> Is but for two months victuall'd.
>
> (V.4.184)

There remains a final instance in this category. Rosalind, overhearing Phebe's rejection of Silvius, interrupts the conversation with quite astonishing warmth—and rudeness. Why so much heat? The point of Phebe's speech (III.5.8-27) is a ruthless exposition of the banal conceit advanced by Silvius:

> 'Tis pretty, sure, and very probable,
> That eyes, that are the frail'st and softest things,

> Who shut their coward gates on atomies,
> Should be call'd tyrants, butchers, murderers!
>
> (III.5.11)

But this is no more than the Princess and her retinue do to retarded Petrarchans of *Love's Labour's Lost*— and the lesson is presented as a highly laudable operation in that play. Phebe voices the anti-romantic viewpoint so necessary to the play; and she administers a well-deserved beating to a ninny who, it seems, thrives on the diet. Why, then, the excited interruption of Rosalind, 'And why, I pray you?' followed by nearly thirty lines of abuse (III.5.35-63) which assert the simple point that Phebe's looks are not so stellar, at that? Because Rosalind's diatribe—a disgrace to a lady, however salutary it may be for Phebe—is again the equivalent of 'touché'. Phebe is a minor anti-romantic voice; Rosalind is the major. Phebe is a domineering woman who, reversing the sexual roles, has mastered her man; so is Rosalind. And, subtlest, Silvius appears before Rosalind as a rather poor creature; so, therefore, does Orlando. (What does Orlando say in the final scene when confronted with the news that his wife-to-be has been making a fool of him?) And Rosalind's response in crying up Silvius is in effect to cry up Orlando: 'Down on your knees, / And thank heaven, fasting, for a good man's love' (III.5.57).

Rosalind's part, in general, is one that affords consistent possibilities of an anti-romantic interpretation in keeping with the open-ended invitation extended by the play's title. She can perfectly well be played à la Angela Brazil; equally, one can seize on the clues of her opening lines. She enters not so much depressed as morose; and her complaint is 'the condition of my estate' (I.2.12)—in other words, a diminution of social status and power. She cannot 'forget a banished father' (I.2.4), but these ambivalent words can include a sense of personal loss, and a sense of being thrust unjustly into the shadows at Court. When she does meet her father, her impulse is not to fall upon his bosom, but to retain her independence and secret identity: 'I met the Duke yesterday, and had much question with him. He asked me of what parentage I was; I told him, of as good as he; so he laugh'd and let me go. But what talk we of fathers when there is such a man as Orlando?' (III.4.31). We are entitled to draw the perfectly obvious conclusion, well borne out by her conduct throughout the play. Rosalind misses not her father, but the status his presence conferred; and she is motivated above all by a will to dominate. For all Rosalind's brilliance, the generous Celia—one of life's givers—is an implied comment on her that one returns to.

An important category of relationship, then, is represented by Oliver, Duke Frederick, Jacques, and Rosalind. Each of them gives convincing testimony of being disturbed by the presence of certain others. The common element of disturbance is this: the other parallels self, and therefore subtly threatens self.

I now turn to a simple and obvious category, those relationships characterized by a direct clash of values. There are two such: Rosalind-Jacques, and Orlando-Jacques. They supply variations on the theme of romance challenged by anti-romance. The matter is initiated theatrically when Orlando bursts into the clearing, resolved to commit some high deed in the name of a meal for Adam, and with sword bared cries 'Forbear, and eat no more' (II.7.88). Jacques's retort (anticipating Alice's at the Mad Hatter's tea-party) is a classic deflation of romantic posturing: 'Why, I have eat none yet'. Soon the key word in such a clash, 'reason', makes itself heard: Jacques's 'An you will not be answered with reason, I must die' (II.7.100). This, coupled with the imperturbable good manners of the Duke, makes Orlando look a fool. That he is conscious of this is implicit in his later exchange with Jacques, which redresses the balance of debating advantage. It is the only occasion in the play when Orlando exhibits any venom; he draws on his considerable reserves of intelligence to defeat Jacques. The issue between them is formalized into their parting shots: 'Farewell, good Signior Love . . . Adieu, good Monsieur Melancholy' (III.2.275). Each, for the other, is an affected fool. But this is open contention: Jacques and Orlando bicker because they are quite unlike each other, not because they shadow each other.

The argument is carried on into the clash between Jacques and Rosalind in Act IV, Scene 1. This is a shrewder debate. Rosalind (in her persona of the anti-romantic Ganymede) opposes to melancholy not the open assertion of love, but the scrutiny of the realist. She asks, what good comes of melancholy? What are its benefits? And she fastens on to Jacques's lame answer of 'experience' with 'And your experience makes you sad. I had rather have a fool to make me merry than experience to make me sad' (IV.1.24). Here again the confrontation is open; it is sterility versus the life-force.

The passages in *As You Like It* which oppose Rosalind and Orlando with Jacques are central, but could not be expanded without making the play simpler and duller. The open clash of temperament and attitude lends itself to the debate principle, but would, if extended, speedily lose hold upon the audience. It is the essential principle of *Love's Labour's Lost*—debate between two clearly defined camps—and one that Shakespeare never repeats in such simple form. The debate-emphasis within *As You Like It* is shifted on to the brilliant device of making Rosalind a dual figure, *pour et contre,* a resort in which the conventional stage device takes over and assimilates a profound structural role. Rosalind/Ganymede *is* the debate: Rosalind/Ganymede *is* the 'other' expressing self. And it merges into the conflict of personality and attitude which does not express itself in such overt terms as 'love' and 'melancholy'. Harold Jenkins's statement of 'the play's principle of countering one view with another . . . the readjustment of the point of view'[4] goes far towards explaining the technique of *As You Like It*. But references to 'attitude', 'point of view', 'values' leave out of account the remorseless personal struggles through which these agreeable abstractions are presented. And the focus for these struggles—the core of the debate, the conflict—is Touchstone.

John Dover Wilson is, I believe, entirely right in according Touchstone's name a symbolic significance: 'As his name implies, he *tests* all that the world takes for gold, especially the gold of the golden world of pastoralism.' His realism, or even 'materialism', is a touchstone to keep the balance of the play.[5] We can agree that Touchstone supplies an essential ingredient in the play's composition, and that his comments—pungent, witty, realistic—on Court, Arden, and love provide a welcome leavening. I would, however, go further than this, and assert that Touchstone in his relationships advances a standard by which we are invited to measure the other relationships in the play.

The point about Touchstone is that he has no equals. He moves in a world in which there are superiors, and inferiors; he makes this categorization in all cases, and leaves his inferiors in no doubt whatever about their status. He appears first at Court, a supple entertainer making himself agreeable to the young ladies. Even so, a reference to Duke Frederick calls forth a warning in none too gentle terms from Celia: 'Speak no more of him; you'll be whipt for taxation one of these days' (I.2.76). Touchstone's response—'The more pity that fools may not speak wisely what wise men do foolishly'—and his sardonic commentary on Le Beau's scale of values establish his true credentials. This is a man of intelligence and insight, under no illusions about the Court, or Arden, for that matter. We should, therefore, receive with scepticism Jacques's account of his meeting with him. Touchstone, clearly, has been playing up to Jacques's evident assumption that a Fool is a fool; or simply over-acting, to take in an amateur of the trade.

Touchstone develops in Arden; the man grows before our eyes. Each of the locals encounters a Touchstone determined to enforce his moral (if not social) superiority. His entry into local society immediately signalizes this fact:

Touchstone Holla, you clown!
Rosalind Peace, fool; he's not thy kinsman.
Corin Who calls?
Touchstone Your betters, sir.

(II.4.62)

This is an unequivocal sketch of a situation to be repeated several times later. Act III, Scene 2 sees Touchstone at greater leisure take on the task of putting Corin in his place. Their discussion is interesting because it is a clear instance of the power-struggle (on Touchstone's side). Basically they are men of the same stamp, realists. Shakespeare's clowns and Fools invariably are. They have, therefore, nothing really to argue about, except Humpty Dumpty's question: who is to be top. Corin's exposé of 'properties' (III.2.22-9) has a hard common sense that Touchstone has no desire to attack frontally: 'Such a one is a natural philosopher'. So he shifts his ground, and wins his battle through verbal quibbles. It is a wit-contest that Touchstone easily wins, not a true contest of values.

There are direct echoes of this scene. The unfortunate William finds Touchstone in terrible mood, and his cadenza on the means whereby William is to be destroyed (V.1.45-53) effectively exposes William's pretensions to the hand of Audrey. It is a complete demolition of an inferior. Again, the penultimate scene— almost a mere excuse for a song—finds Shakespeare shading in his point. Touchstone never misses a chance to patronize whom he can; so the pages, for their pains, receive 'Truly, young gentlemen, though there was no great matter in the ditty, yet the note was very untuneable . . . I count it but time lost to hear such a foolish song' (V.3.32). We cannot speak of the 'real' Touchstone emerging only when his masters are absent; but it is certainly true that the Duke, before whom Touchstone displays his set-pieces (Act V, Scene 4) so skilfully, sees only a part of the man.

Touchstone must, however, be judged principally on his relations with Audrey and Jacques. The contributory evidence, which I have just cited, is necessary to establish the bent of his mind and the true facts of his relationships. These are demonstrated chiefly in Act III, Scene 3. Audrey and Touchstone have already come to an understanding—'And how, Audrey, am I the man yet? Doth my simple feature content you?' (III.3.2)— and it is plain that Touchstone's simple feature does. Now why does a man of Touchstone's stamp single out Audrey for a permanent liaison? Critics, suspecting the worst, have rushed in with their explanations. For Helen Gardner, 'Touchstone's marriage to Audrey is a mere coupling'.[6] For Harold Jenkins, it is the 'animal lust which propels him towards Audrey'.[7] James Smith's extraordinary view of Touchstone's motives is: 'Touchstone is on the way to tragedy because he has allowed desire to get out of control'.[8] Sex, the consensus asserts, is certainly at the bottom of it. But there are some caveats to be lodged. First, Touchstone is a character who is stated, not explained. We have no formal means of opening up his mind; he has no soliloquies, is never on stage alone. Second, sex is quite unsatisfactory as the sole motive for Touchstone's marriage. The Audreys of this world do not demand a price; the Audrey of this play does not ask it. She is perfectly ready to be married by a hedge-priest: 'Faith, the priest was good enough, for all the old gentleman's saying' (V.1.3). The critics who pounce on Touchstone for his bottomless cynicism in considering an illegal marriage to Audrey—so that he can leave her thereafter—customarily omit to add a detail of some consequence: Touchstone does, in fact, marry Audrey perfectly properly. He insists on it. Audrey is well satisfied with something less, but it is Touchstone who resists her: 'We shall find a time, Audrey; patience, gentle Audrey' (V.1.1). It is, as usual, necessary to pay attention to what people *do* as well as what they say. Touchstone would have had a better press had he taken over some of Orlando's cast-off sentiments to clothe his 'coupling'.

But the question of motivation remains. We can only take Touchstone's action at face value, the ironic acceptance of a slut by a man who will always be her superior. In the context of Touchstone's other relationships, it is a likely guess that the certainty that he will remain the dominant partner is uppermost in his mind. He undoubtedly likes to demonstrate his mastery in a series of brisk imperatives: 'Come, sweet Audrey' (III.3.83); 'Patience, gentle Audrey' (V.1.1.); 'Trip, Audrey, trip, Audrey' (V.1.69); 'Come, Audrey' (V.2.38); 'Bear your body more seeming, Audrey' (V.4.66). The dulcet adjectives fade before the end; she is an object to be possessed. Doubtless sex enters into the matter—this is customarily so with marriages, even those of Silvius, Oliver, and Orlando—but to accept it as the sole motive is to take Touchstone at his own word (precisely what he wishes the company to do) and to ignore the gap between the word and action. The version that Touchstone presents to the Duke is a double bluff that obliquely but justly indicates the truth of the matter: 'A poor virgin, sir, an ill-favour'd thing, sir, *but mine own*' (V.4.53).

Still, the matter is entangled with Jacques's presence, and the Jacques-Touchstone relationship must now be re-opened. Jacques, I have suggested, is both envious and disdainful of the Fool that caricatures him. Touchstone, for his part, is wary of a social superior who patronizes him insufferably but might put in a good word for him with the authorities (as Jacques does, in the final scene). It is, of course, quite misleading to allude to Touchstone and Jacques as 'usually allies'.[9] Theirs is the tension between amateur and professional, with a social gulf unconfirmed by the allocation of talent. The confrontation takes place in Act III, Scene 3, Jacques discovering himself as Audrey and Touchstone are about to make use of Sir Oliver's irregular services. Touchstone is caught at a disadvantage but rallies well: 'Good even, good Master What-ye-call't; how do you, sir? You are very well met. Goddild you for your last company. I am very glad to see you. Even a toy in hand here, sir. Nay;

pray be cover'd' (III.3.63)—a brave attempt at counter-patronage. Jacques instantly reminds Touchstone of his social function and status: 'Will you be married, *motley*?' And Touchstone parries the sneer with an apparently complacent account of man and his desires: 'As the ox hath his bow, sir, the horse his curb, and the falcon her bells, so man hath his desires; and as pigeons bill, so wedlock would be nibbling' (III.3.68). When, however, Jacques turns the knife again—'And will you, *being a man of your breeding*, be married under a bush, like a beggar?'—Touchstone advances the crux by which we are to judge him: 'I am not in the mind but I were better to be married of him than of another; for he is not like to marry me well; and not being well married, it will be a good excuse for me hereafter to leave my wife' (III.3.78). Now this speech is normally rendered as an 'aside' by modern editors. It is not so indicated in the Folio (which is, of course, not given to stage directions) and the relegation—I should say promotion—of the speech to 'aside' status is pure editorial conjecture. I contend that we have no reason for accepting the conjecture. There is no soliloquy of Touchstone's elsewhere; there is no other reasonable opportunity for an aside, or parenthetic soliloquy.[10] This is a character designed to be presented solely in terms of dialogue. The speech makes excellent sense if it is regarded as whispered to Jacques; in which case it becomes a pseudo-motive, a piece of man-of-the-world's cynicism put up to protect the gap in Touchstone's armour against the sneers of Jacques. He *must* defend himself. Touchstone has no intention, however, of allowing Jacques a permanent sneer at his sub-wedding; so after the face-saving formula of 'a flaw in the procedure may be useful later' he allows himself to be persuaded into a proper wedding. Touchstone is a much cleverer fellow than Jacques. No one ever knows when *he* is hit. Nor could we even guess it, without reviewing the whole pattern of his behaviour.

Touchstone, then, seems to me an early cameo of a type of character-portrayal that (since Bradley's day) has come to be recognized as a Shakespearian crux, located classically in the problem of Iago.[11] That is, he compels us to look for motives that are not stated in the text, which does however contain part-motives or pseudo-motives. I find the missing motive here to be the drive to power, because that is of a piece with Touchstone's relationships with his un-superiors; and because it embodies the drift of the whole play.

Touchstone, in fact, is the reduction of the ideas latent in *As You Like It*. He exhibits in gross form the will to mastery that is discernible in the actions of his betters. The play is set into a formal framework of political struggle, the usurpation by Duke Frederick; it focuses on the mating dance of a masterful female round her captive male, 'my child's father' as Rosalind herself

elegantly epitomizes him (I.3.11); it presents a running debate, ostensibly on values, in effect to protect the egos of the debaters; it etches in relationships with a controlled quantum of acid. The latent motivation of the characters is an impulse to protect themselves against the psychological threats from without. And this accounts for the sudden conversions of Duke Frederick and Oliver, who have earlier given indications that Duke Senior and Orlando represent threats to their psyches, not their persons. Of the others, Jacques finds intolerable the presence of Duke Senior and Touchstone, because *he* caricatures them. Rosalind finds Phebe's behaviour to Silvius an affront, for the same reason. Even the gentle Orlando has a flash of an intolerable presence: 'But, O, how bitter a thing it is to look into happiness through another man's eyes' (V.2.40). Virtually all the relationships manifest a sense of unease, of latent or open hostility. There is little true accord in Arden, prior to the final scene: and the audience is entitled, if it wishes, to its reservations even then. The idyll of Arden is an idea as much under fire as the denizens of the forest; and the final path that leads away from forest to court is a change of milieu, not a way out of those problems.

Notes

[1] Quotations are from Peter Alexander's edition of the complete works (1951).

[2] Jan Kott, *Shakespeare Our Contemporary,* Second edition (1967), p. 225.

[3] In sum: 'Arden is not a place where the laws of nature are abrogated and roses are without their thorns' (Helen Gardner, *'As You Like It', More Talking of Shakespeare,* edited by John Garrett (1959), 17-32 (p. 25)).

[4] Harold Jenkins, *'As You Like It', Shakespeare Survey,* 8 (1955), 40-51 (p. 49).

[5] John Dover Wilson, *Shakespeare's Happy Comedies* (1962), pp. 156, 158.

[6] Helen Gardner, *'As You Like It',* p. 28.

[7] Harold Jenkins, *'As You Like It',* p. 49.

[8] James Smith, *'As You Like It', Scrutiny,* 9 (1940), 9-32 (pp. 31-2).

[9] James Smith, p. 26.

[10] I take it as indicative of Shakespeare's overall concept of *As You Like It* that there are virtually no soliloquies save for Oliver, whose hatred is technically indispensable yet requiring internal explanation. There are,

therefore, very few points that are psychologically 'fixed'. This is a play exceptionally open to diversity of interpretation.

[11] See A. C. Bradley, *Shakespearean Tragedy* (1904), 222-32.

John A. Hart (essay date 1980)

SOURCE: "*As You Like It:* The Worlds of Fortune and Nature," in *Dramatic Structure in Shakespeare's Romantic Comedies,* Carnegie-Mellon University Press, 1980, pp. 81-97.

[*In the following essay, Hart examines the disparate worlds of Frederick's court and the Forest of Arden, exploring the contrasting qualities displayed by characters in each of these settings.*]

As You Like It presents an ideal world, just as *The Merchant of Venice* did. The Forest of Arden has as much romance, as many delightful lovers, more laughter and joy. Like *A Midsummer Night's Dream* and *The Merchant of Venice,* it is built by means of two worlds: the world ruled by Duke Frederick and the world of the Forest of Arden. The effect is not the "separate but equal" envelope structure of *A Midsummer Night's Dream,* nor the interlocking and necessary alternation of *The Merchant of Venice;* instead, Frederick's world first seems dominant and then dissolves and disappears into the world of Arden. Its life seems to be in the play not so much for itself as to help us understand and read its successor.

There is a set of contrasts between the two worlds of this play, but the contrasts are describable not in terms of opposition of power, as in *A Midsummer Night's Dream* and *The Merchant of Venice,* but in terms of attitudes of the dominant characters, as in *Much Ado About Nothing,* and in terms of differences in the settings and of changes in behavior for those characters who are part of both worlds. These contrasts are easy to describe because Shakespeare points the way clearly, making each world an extreme. Our approach will be to examine the qualities of Frederick's world, then to examine the qualities of Arden, and finally out of this contrast to see how the characters behave in each world.

1.

We have seen power presented in *A Midsummer Night's Dream* and *The Merchant of Venice.* In the former, Theseus rules according to judgment or reason; in the latter the Duke of Venice rules according to the laws of the city. Frederick's world is like neither of these. Frederick is in complete command of his court. He has taken his brother's place as Duke, exiled him with many of his followers, seized their lands for his own,

and now rules. His high-handed behavior is illustrated by his usurpation of his brother's dukedom, his immediate displeasure at Orlando, the sudden dismissal of Rosalind, the quick seizure of Oliver's lands. What is most characteristic of his power is that it is arbitrary; neither reason nor law seems to control it.

When we look for his motives, we discover two kinds. His greed for power and possessions is obvious. But personal attitudes are just as strong. He treats Orlando rudely because he is the son of Sir Rowland de Boys, an old enemy of his. He comes to hate Rosalind, giving as his reasons that he does not trust her, that she is her father's daughter, that his own daughter's prestige suffers by comparison; all these are half-hearted rationalizations rooted in jealousy and envy.

Frederick's behavior is echoed if not matched by Oliver's treatment of his brother Orlando and of his servant Adam. Oliver demeans and debases his younger brother; he plots his serious injury and later his death. He acts ignobly toward his faithful household servant Adam. Again, the motivations are mixed. He states explicitly that he wants Orlando's share of their father's bequest. But, beyond that, he wants to get rid of Orlando out of envy, out of fear of comparison made by others:

> . . . my soul (yet I know not why) hates nothing
> more than he. Yet he's gentle, never school'd and
> yet learned, full of noble device, of all sorts
> enchantingly belov'd, and indeed so much in the
> heart of the world, and especially of my own people,
> who best know him, that I am altogether mispris'd.

> (I, i, 165-171)

Thus, "tyrant Duke" and "tyrant brother" are described in tandem, public and private images of the same behavior. They have the power; they control their world; they do not fear disapproval or reprisal. Charles the wrestler, Lebeau and other lords surrounding Frederick, however many reservations they may have about the morality of their leaders, do not dare to question their authority. They have their own positions to protect.

Those chiefly harmed by the ruthless domination of these men are Orlando and Rosalind. They have committed no fault but they are hated. Their presence too gives definition to Frederick's world. Orlando has virtue, grace, beauty, and strength. Rosalind is beautiful, intelligent, virtuous, honest. Their actions, their reputations, the loyalty they command all testify to these wonders.

Yet both of them are conscious of what they do not have—their proper place and heritage in this world. Orlando feels deeply his brother's injury in depriving him of his education and his place in the household. Rosalind is sad at her father's banishment and then indignant at her own dismissal. Both are too virtuous to think of revenge; but they are fully aware that they are being wronged. Having all the graces, they are nevertheless dispossessed of their rightful positions.

Yet, these two have their own power. When they leave Frederick's world, they draw after them others, too loyal, too loving to remain behind. Celia, meant to profit from her cousin's departure, follows Rosalind into banishment without question or remorse. She has already promised that what her father took from Rosalind's father by force, "I will render thee again in affection." And when the test occurs soon after, she meets it at once. In her, love triumphs hands down over possession and prestige.

Her example is followed by the Clown. Not only will he "go along o'er the wide world" with Celia out of loyalty to her; he has also, in Frederick's world, lost place just as Rosalind has. There "fools may not speak wisely what wise men do foolishly" (I, ii, 86-87). Since he has lost his usefulness as a fool, he may as well leave with Celia and Rosalind. And Adam is in comparable situation. To Oliver, he is an "old dog," to be thrust aside. But so strong is his loyalty to Orlando that he will give him his savings, serve him, accompany him wherever he goes.

These gifted models of humanity, Rosalind and Orlando, draw out of Frederick's world the loving, the truthful, the loyal. Frederick and Oliver, seeking to control and ultimately to crush their enemies, only succeed in driving away other worthwhile characters with them.

The world of Frederick is simple in structure. The powerful control, but they envy the virtuous; the virtuous attract, but they want to have their rightful place. Those in authority triumph in their own terms, but things happen to them in the process. They turn against each other—Frederick would devour Oliver as he has so many others. Their world, as it grows more violent, diminishes in importance until it disappears altogether. The virtuous are undefeated though displaced.

2.

In contrast to the specific placing of Frederick's world, the Forest reaches beyond the bounds of any particular place, any specific time. Its setting is universalized nature. All seasons exist simultaneously. Duke Senior speaks of "the icy fang And churlish chiding of the winter's wind" (II, i, 6-7); but Orlando pins verses to "a palm tree," "abuses our young plants with carving," and "hangs odes upon hawthorns, and elegies on brambles" (III, ii, 360-362); and Rosalind and Celia live at the "tuft of olives." Again, Orlando does not wish to leave Adam "in the bleak air"; but in the next scene Jaques has met a fool who "bask'd

him in the sun." The songs continue this mixture: "Here shall he see No enemy But winter and rough weather" (II, v, 6-8) alongside "the greenwood tree" and "the sweet bird's throat" (II, v, 1, 4) both in the same song, or the alternation between the "winter wind" (II, vii, 174) and the "spring time, the only pretty ring time" (V, iii, 19), dominant notes in two other songs. If the Forest is not to be defined in season, neither is it limited to any particular place. The variety of trees already indicates this; the variety of creatures supports it: sheep, deer, a green and gilded snake, a lioness. Meek and domestic creatures live with the untamed and fierce.

Yet the Forest is more than an outdoors universalized, which largely accommodates itself to the mood and attitude of its human inhabitants. It is a setting in which the thoughts and images of those who wander through it expand and reach out to the animate, as if the Forest were alive with spirits taken for granted by everyone. Even so mundane a pair as Touchstone and Audrey, discussing her attributes—unpoetical, honest, foul—assign these gifts to the gods. Orlando, who is able at first meeting Rosalind only to utter "Heavenly Rosalind," is suddenly released to write expansive verses in praise of her, some of which place her in a spiritual context:

> . . . heaven Nature charg'd
> That one body should be fill'd
> With all graces wide-enlarg'd. . . .
> Thus Rosalind of many parts
> By heavenly synod was devis'd. . . .
> (III, ii, 141-143, 149-150)

Phoebe seconds his view by giving Rosalind qualities beyond the human:

> Art thou god to shepherd turn'd,
> That a maiden's heart hath burn'd? . . .
> Why, thy godhead laid apart,
> Warr'st thou with a woman's heart?
> (IV, iii, 40-41, 44-45)

And Rosalind, replying to Celia's finding Orlando under a tree, "like a dropp'd acorn," says, "It may well be call'd Jove's tree, when it drops such fruit" (III, ii, 235-237). Elsewhere he is "most gentle Jupiter." And she herself takes the name of Ganymed, cupbearer to Jupiter. Further, in her games with Orlando, she describes "an old religious uncle" who taught her (or him, for she is then playing Ganymed) how to speak well and who imparted knowledge of love, of women's faults, of the forlorn look of the true lover. To this fiction, she joins the later story of how, "since [she] was three year old, [she has] convers'd with a magician, most profound in his art, and yet not damnable" (V, ii, 60-61). She improvises, but it fits the expansive attributes of the Forest.

But in addition to mind-expanding qualities, the Forest produces some real evidence of its extraordinary powers. Oliver, upon his first appearance in the Forest, is beset by the green and gilded snake (of envy?) and by the lioness (of power?), but when these two are conquered, his whole behavior changes. And Frederick, intent on destroying his brother, meets an "old religious man" and

> After some question with him, was converted
> Both from his enterprise and from the world.
>
> (V, iv, 161-162)

And these events harmonize with Rosalind's producing Hymen, the god of weddings, to perform the ceremony and bless the four pairs of lovers. The Forest is a world of all outdoors, of all dimensions of man's better nature, of contact with man's free imagination and magical happenings.

The Forest has still another quality in its setting. It is not timeless but it reflects the slow pace and the unmeasurable change of the earth. The newcomers notice the difference from the world outside. Orlando comments that "there's no clock in the forest" (III, ii, 300-301); Rosalind tells us "who Time ambles withal, who Time trots withal, who Time gallops withal, and who he stands still withal" (III, ii, 309-311). And Touchstone, as reported by Jaques, suggests the uselessness of measuring changes in the Forest by the clock:

> 'Tis but an hour ago since it was nine,
> And after one hour more 'twill be eleven,
> And so from hour to hour, we ripe and ripe,
> And then from hour to hour, we rot and rot;
> And thereby hangs a tale.
>
> (II, vii, 24-28)

But he does notice, too, the withering away of man at the Forest's slow changes, a truism later elaborated by Jaques in his seven-ages-of-man speech.

But the qualities of the setting are only part of what goes into the definition of the Forest world. The natives to the Forest make their contributions as well. Corin and Silvius and Phoebe, Audrey and William and Sir Oliver Martext all appear, without seeming consequence or particular plot relevance, put there to show off different dimensions of the Forest, to strike their attitudes, to stand in contrast with the characters newly come from another world, and then, like the deer and the sheep and the snake and the lioness, to retire into the Forest again until or unless called upon by their visitors.

These characters have their separate occupations. Corin is an old shepherd, Silvius a young one, Phoebe—his beloved—a shepherdess, Audrey a goat girl, William a country bumpkin, Martext a clergyman. But these assignments are vaguely expressed. Martext, for instance, has professional status but mainly in his own eyes: "ne'er a fantastical knave of them all shall flout me out of my calling" (III, iii, 106-107). But Jaques dismisses him as a phony and Touchstone wants him to officiate at his marriage to Audrey because he believes him to be a fake. They all seem satisfied to have the name of an occupation rather than the function itself.

But their thoughts are also dissociated from ownership, ambition, achievement. Corin, wanting to help Rosalind and Celia, says:

> [I] wish, for her sake more than for mine
> own,
> My fortunes were more able to relieve her;
> But I am shepherd to another man,
> And do not shear the fleeces that I graze.
>
> (II, iv, 76-79)

The man who owns the sheepcote is not hospitable, is not even there, and has his land up for sale. Silvius, who is supposed to be buying the flock and pasture, "little cares for buying any thing" (II, iv, 90). Ownership is several steps removed from Corin, and until Rosalind offers to make the purchase he is uncertain who the landlord employing him is; nor does he particularly care.

Later, he generalizes his attitude toward life:

> I am a true laborer: I earn that I eat, get that I wear,
> owe no man hate, envy no man's happiness, glad of
> other men's good, content with my harm, and the
> greatest of my pride is to see my ewes graze and
> my lambs suck.
>
> (III, ii, 73-77)

The other natives share his view. William, Audrey's country lover, confesses to his name, to a certain unspecified amount of wealth, to having "a pretty wit," to loving Audrey, and to lack of learning; but when he is threatened by Touchstone and told to stay away from Audrey, he departs with "God rest you merry, sir" (V, i, 59), and we see no more of him or his love for Audrey. If it is love, it is love detached, without passion or claims.

Silvius dedicates himself entirely to love, Phoebe to being the scornful beloved and later the impassioned wooer of Ganymed. They do not express conflict or even action so much as attitude, as pose. "Loose now and then A scatt'red smile," Silvius says to Phoebe, "and that I'll live upon" (III, v, 103-104).

Audrey would be an honest woman, "a woman of the world," but she will not choose between lovers, she will not question Martext's legitimacy, she will be led by Touchstone wherever he wishes. Her future with Touchstone is not bright, as Jaques points out, but she doesn't question it.

In all these natives there is a non-critical quality, an innocence, a lack of competitiveness that suits well with the Forest world and helps to describe it. But Shakespeare gives us still other ways of distinguishing this world from Frederick's. Early in the play Celia and Rosalind engage in idle banter about the two goddesses, Fortune and Nature, who share equally in the lives of men. Fortune "reigns in gifts of the world," Rosalind says, "not in the lineaments of Nature" (I, ii, 41-42). It is a shorthand way of distinguishing the Forest world from Frederick's. Frederick's world is a world of Fortune, from which the children of Nature are driven. Power, possession, lands, titles, authority over others characterize that world, and men to live there must advance their careers or maintain their positions in spite of everything. The Forest world is completely Nature's. In its natives the idleness, the lack of ambition and combativeness, the carelessness about ownership and possession, the interest in the present moment without plan for the future, all are signs of a Fortuneless world. Instead there is awareness of the gifts inherent from birth in the individual, no matter how untalented or unhandsome (Audrey's response to her foulness or William's self-satisfaction, for instance). These are "the lineaments of Nature," the basic materials of one's being. In the Forest, the natives neither can nor aspire to change them. And the qualities of the setting—universality, gradual rather than specific change, a linkage between the outdoors world and a projected though perhaps imaginary supernatural, these too are compatible with the world of Nature, Fortune having been removed. Both Fortune and Nature, then, are abbreviated terms to epitomize the kinds of worlds represented by Frederick's on the one hand and the Forest's on the other.

One further means of defining the Forest world emerges with the character of Jaques. He has been in the outside world, but he has chosen the Forest and he is its most eloquent spokesman. He is the personification of the speculative man. He will not react when Orlando threatens his life: "And you will not be answer'd with reason, I must die" (II, vii, 100-101). He will not dance or rejoice in the final scene. He would prevent action in others if he could. He weeps that the Duke's men kill the deer, he would keep Orlando from marring the trees with his poems, he advises Touchstone not to "be married under a bush like a beggar" (III, iii, 84). He is like the natives of the Forest, ambitionless, fortuneless, directionless.

Instead, he gives his attention to the long view and the abstract view. He is delighted when he overhears Touchstone philosophizing about time; he projects human neglect in the deer at the coming of death for

one of their company; he argues the innocent indifference of the deer to corruption and inhumanity in man:

> Thus most invectively he pierceth through
> The body of the country, city, court,
> Yea, and of this our life, swearing that we
> Are mere usurpers, tyrants, and what's worse,
> To fright the animals and to kill them up
> In their assign'd and native dwelling-place.
> (II, i, 58-63)

When he would invoke the privilege of the fool to "Cleanse the foul body of th' infected world" (II, vii, 60) the Duke replies that with his past experience of evil he would succeed only in doing "Most mischievous foul sin" (II, vii, 64). In the abstract (in the Forest), his proposal sounds good; in the world of action it would be damaging.

But his greatest eloquence is saved for his seven-ages-of-man speech (II, vii, 139-166). It is an official acknowledgement of Nature's supremacy over man and the insignificance of man's affairs on the stage of the world. The movement of the speech is circular, from Nature through the efforts to shape natural gifts in man, to Fortune's world, and back to Nature again. Thus, the helplessness of infancy gives way to "the whining schoolboy" which in turn is followed by "the lover, Sighing like furnace, with a woeful ballad Made to his mistress' eyebrow." In the first three, we find pleasantly humorous recognition of the supremacy of Nature and the attempts to shape and apply natural gifts in man. The fourth and fifth, the soldier and the justice, suggest the ascendancy of Fortune in man's life—the soldier seeking the "bubble reputation," the justice "Full of wise saws and modern instances." But these temporary achievements disappear as Nature reclaims her own, first in the "slipper'd pantaloon" whose "big manly voice" turns "again toward childish treble" and finally in frightening second childishness, "Sans teeth, sans eyes, sans taste, sans every thing." In such a view, and in the view most congenial to the Forest world, "All the world's a stage, And all the men and women merely players." There are no consequences that matter.

3.

Duke Senior, like Jaques, has had experience in both worlds. He too is being "philosophical." Their life in the Forest

> Finds tongues in trees, books in the running
>   brooks,
> Sermons in stones, and good in every thing.
> (II, i, 16-17)

He and his men "fleet the time carelessly, as they did in the golden world" (I, i, 118-119). But for the Duke and his men, it is only play-acting. They appear in one scene as Foresters, in another as outlaws. He himself has lost his name: he is Duke Senior, not specifically named like Frederick. More than that, he has nothing serious to do. While his brother is seizing Oliver's lands and organizing a search for his daughter and seeking to destroy him, he is contemplating a deer hunt or asking for Jaques to dispute with or feasting or asking someone to sing. Duke Senior has no function to perform; he cannot be a Duke except in title. All the philosophical consolations he may offer himself and his men cannot alleviate the loss he feels at being usurped and banished by his brother. When Orlando reminds him of the outside world, he confesses: "True is it that we have seen better days" (II, vii, 120) and reinforces this reminiscence of the past by commenting on his present condition:

> Thou seest we are not all alone unhappy:
> This wide and universal theatre
> Presents more woeful pageants than the scene
> Wherein we play in.
>
> (II, vii, 136-139)

He is remarking on shared misery; he is using the same imagery of playing used by Jaques. But for Jaques it is made speculative, objectified; for Duke Senior, he and his fellows are participating in a play. His longings are elsewhere. It is not surprising that at the end, he resumes leadership over everyone and plans to return to active rule of his dukedom.

What is true of him is true with more immediacy of others newly arrived in the Forest. The clown, who assumes the name Touchstone, undergoes the same ambivalence. His first reaction to the Forest is negative: "Ay, now am I in Arden, the more fool I. When I was at home, I was in a better place" (II, iv, 16-17). He is no longer practicing his profession of fool, since he is in a fortuneless world: "Call me not fool till heaven hath sent me fortune" (II, vii, 19). Instead, he assumes several other roles, a liberating exercise for him; the Forest allows him to become expansive, imaginative, to take on the personage of the courtier, of the philosopher, of the wit, of the lover, to condescend to others at random and without consequence. To be able to speak his mind, to express himself, is the Forest's gift to him.

On the other hand, in all these poses, he undercuts the natives of the Forest. He mocks the passionate outbursts of Silvius in praise of his mistress by making the extravagant claim but changing the imagery to mundane and sensual terms: "I remember the kissing of her batler and the cow's dugs that her pretty chopp'd hands had milk'd" (II, iv, 48-50). He further shows off the silly self-absorption of Nature's pastoral lovers: he himself plays the lover in the Forest. The object of his love, Audrey the goat girl, has neither understanding nor beauty. He sees the disparity between his wit and her simplicity; he would have her poetical, "for the truest poetry is the most feigning" (III, iii, 19-20); he would not have her honest; he is glad she is foul. He strongly suspects that marriage to her would mean cuckoldry, yet he will have her at whatever cost: "man hath his desires; and as pigeons bill, so wedlock would be nibbling" (III, iii, 80-82). He joins the others in the rush to be married at the end of the play:

> I press in here, sir, amongst the rest of the country copulatives, to swear and to forswear, according as marriage binds and blood breaks.
>
> (V, iv, 55-57)

At other times he has confrontations with Corin and with William, the two natives seemingly most attuned to Nature's laws. Touchstone condescends to them, playing the courtier and the man of the world to men he treats as simpletons and inferiors. William, the rival for Audrey's hand, he questions as one would a child, and then threatens as one would an inferior being, and William, with no knowledge of position, with no wit, with no competitiveness, is easily routed. Touchstone challenges Corin too. Having never been in court, Corin is damned, says Touchstone. When Corin tries to defend life in the Forest, claiming that the manners of the court are not suitable to life in the country, Touchstone parries every explanation Corin gives with a witty rationalization. By measuring the life of the Forest against life at court, he brings together separate standards in the light of which either life by itself is preposterous. The Forest, which is the only way of life for all six of these natives, is by other values extremely limited. The importance of physical desire (the love affair with Audrey), of competitive relationships (the rivalry with William), of realistic appraisal (the reduction of Silvius's outbursts) is inherent in Touchstone's behavior; finally, the need for place, for function, for relationships with others runs throughout his criticism of Forest life:

> *Corin.* And how like you this shepherd's life, Master Touchstone?
> *Touch.* Truly, shepherd, in respect of itself, it is a good life; but in respect that it is a shepherd's life, it is naught.
>
> (III, ii, 11-15)

Touchstone's is the outsider's view of the Forest. His responses are the touchstones which set off the Forest natives most clearly. As Jaques is the "official" voice of the Forest, Touchstone is the "official" voice of the world outside.

The Forest is liberating for the newly arrived lovers, too. Oliver is freed from the burden of envy and absorption with power; and as a consequence he and Celia can fall immediately in love. So satisfying is it that Oliver would give up his possessions to Orlando and live a shepherd's life forever. Celia has assumed the name Aliena, left her father's court so completely that she never thinks of him again, and falls utterly in love when she meets the reformed Oliver. She has never been tied to the idea of possession or prestige and so she is easily open to the lures of the Forest.

Whereas Oliver's and Celia's love experience is muted, described rather than dramatized, Orlando's and Rosalind's is the heart of the play. Orlando, idle in the Forest and "love-shak'd," expresses his love for the lost Rosalind by writing passionate verses for her and hanging them on the trees; later he plays the game of wooing the young man Ganymed as if he were his Rosalind. He makes his protestations of love, he makes pretty speeches of admiration, he takes part in the mock-marriage ceremony, he promises to return to his wooing by a certain time. But his playing the game of courtship is as nothing compared to the game of deception and joyful play that Rosalind, safe in her disguise as Ganymed, engages in when she is with him. Her spirits soar and her imagination and wit expatiate freely and delightedly on the subject of men in love, on their looks, on their behavior, on the cure of their disease, and then specifically on Orlando's mad humor of love, on how he should woo, on how he can be cured through the lore she (he) acquired from the "old religious uncle." The Forest gives both of them an opportunity to play parts free of the restraints that might accompany acknowledged wooing.

But though their fanciful indulgence leads them to forget the rest of the world—Rosalind cries out, "But what talk we of fathers, when there is such a man as Orlando?" (III, iv, 38-39)—the play is only play and basically incompatible with their real natures.

Orlando's behavior outside and in the Forest suggests responsibility, suggests need for significant action. To him the Forest is a "desert inaccessible" and those in it "Lose and neglect the creeping hours of time" (II, vii, 110, 112); he himself will keep appointments with Duke Senior, he will care for his loyal servant Adam, he will save his brother's endangered life. He has a general distaste for the company of the speculative Jaques, and he finally gives up the wooing game entirely: "I can live no longer by thinking" (V, ii, 50). He is Nature's child, but he insists on living by Fortune's standards.

And Rosalind is even more emphatic in the attitudes founded in the outside world. Her first act in coming into the Forest is to buy a sheepcote; she uses the imagery of the market place when she is judging others: "Sell when you can, you are not for all markets" (III, v, 60), she says to Phoebe; "I fear you have sold your own lands to see other men's; then to have seen much, and to have nothing, is to have rich eyes and

poor hands" (IV, i, 22-25), she says to Jaques. With Silvius and Phoebe, she has small patience. To him she says, "Wilt thou love such a woman? What, to make thee an instrument, and play false strains upon thee? . . . I see love hath made thee a tame snake" (IV, iii, 67-68, 69-70). The natives receive short shrift from her, but she herself is in the depths of love for Orlando, and in her playing with Orlando partly mocks her own condition.

These two lovers, thoroughly based in the real world, are given the opportunity to exhibit, to spell out, a private love relationship thwarted or only implicit in earlier comedies. Portia and Bassanio, we pointed out, meet publicly and Bassanio has only begun to recognize the individuality of Portia at the end of the play; their public figures and their public relationships are the essential ones in *The Merchant of Venice*. In *Much Ado About Nothing* Beatrice and Benedick meet as private individuals, but they do not know or at least acknowledge their love for one another until very late in the play, and their recognition coincides with a discovery of the empty world in which they must live. But Rosalind and Orlando have a chance to meet and to play in a world where public cares are temporarily set aside, where each can express love for the other without embarrassment, where each can feel the presence and the personality of the other, and especially where we can watch these most gifted of Nature's children completely free and private with one another. Though the world of Fortune is part of their consciousness and their future, this holiday of love is a complement to the all-public relationship of Portia and Bassanio and an equal complement to the ever-present social pressures on Beatrice and Benedick.

4.

Given the characteristics of the Forest world, given the attachments of Duke Senior, Touchstone, Orlando, and Rosalind to the outside world, the resolution of the play can be foreseen. Under the spell of the Forest, pretended marriage takes place between Orlando and Rosalind (as Ganymed) with Celia officiating. Marriage almost takes place between Touchstone and Audrey with Martext officiating. In the last scene, all four couples are married in the only way possible in the Forest, by the appearance of Hymen, god of marriage, to perform the ceremony: "Then is there mirth in heaven, When earthly things made even Atone together" (V, iv, 108-110). Hymen joins the lovers and reintroduces the Duke to his daughter: "Good Duke, receive thy daughter, Hymen from heaven brought her . . ." (V, iv, 111-112). He thus re-establishes the father-daughter relationship first devised through his means at Rosalind's birth. The hiatus caused by the Duke's exile and by the disguises in the Forest is broken and the societal structure of father and daughter is made clear once again.

With the appearance of Touchstone another relationship is given social standing. When he is introduced to Duke Senior by Jaques, Touchstone immediately resumes his professional position as fool. His comment on the life of the courtier, his long argument on "the quarrel on the seventh cause" is appreciated by the Duke: "I like him very well"; "By my faith, he is very swift and sententious"; "He uses his folly like a stalking-horse, and under the presentation of that he shoots his wit" (V, iv, 53, 62-63, 106-107). A rapport is established between them which suggests that Duke will be Duke and master again and Fool will be Fool and servant. Adam, nearing Jaques' seventh age of man, has disappeared into the world of nature. But a new loyalty and interdependence is about to begin.

A final relationship is re-established among the sons of Rowland de Boys. Through its magic the Forest has brought Orlando and Oliver together. Now a third brother appears, carrier of the news of Frederick's resignation—"His crown bequeathing to his banish'd brother" (V, iv, 163)—and agent for restoring his own brothers to the outside world. His coming not only reunites all three but makes a necessary link to the outside world for them. It also sounds an echo: Charles the Wrestler sought advancement and distinction by breaking the ribs of three of his victims, all brothers. That was a symbol of the way power broke blood relationships in Frederick's world—Frederick with his niece and daughter, Oliver with his brother. Now separated families are reunited and friends.

That he is a young Jaques is also significant, arriving as the melancholy Jaques prepares to go off to another part of the forest. This young man prepares the way to future life in the world outside; the older is bound to the inactivity and the speculation of the Forest world.

But they have not yet left the Forest. Duke Senior's speech assuming his authority shows that he is in command of both the Forest world and his former Dukedom and that each of them is part of his experience and momentarily under his perfect control. Duke Senior's reference to the lands which will be given to the brothers is balanced and ambiguous:

> Welcome, young man;
> Thou offer'st fairly to thy brothers' wedding:
> To one his lands withheld, and to the other
> A land itself at large, a potent dukedom.
> 　　　　　　　　　　　　　　(V, iv, 166-169)

To Oliver, the lands taken from him by Frederick are returned; to Orlando, his son-in-law, the heritage of his dukedom is given. Yet there is just a suspicion that the gifts might be directed the other way: to Orlando, whose lands have been taken from him by Oliver, will be returned his father's lands; to Oliver, the Forest world where he has determined to remain; for the Forest

is without a ruler and without bounds, a place where he who does not have to own or possess anything may feel himself a powerful ruler.

This distinction between the brothers is followed by a statement of the Duke's own intention in regard to the Forest and the world outside it:

> First, in this forest let us do those ends
> That here were well begun and well begot;
> And after, every of this happy number,
> That have endur'd shrewd days and nights
> 　　with us,
> Shall share the good of our returned fortune,
> According to the measure of their states.
> 　　　　　　　　　　　　　　(V, iv, 170-175)

By "those ends," presumably, he means the marriages which have been the contribution and the fruit of the Forest world. Then his attention will be turned to the world outside the forest, where they will enjoy their "returned fortune, According to the measure of their states." Place and prestige are implied here, possession a necessary element. Both Forest and his Dukedom are in his mind and paired. And the retention of both worlds continues right to the end when he repeats the words *fall* and *measure* once to apply them to Nature's world and once to apply them to Fortune's:

> Mean time, forget this new-fall'n dignity,
> And fall into our rustic revelry.
> Play, music, and you brides and bridegrooms
> 　　all,
> With measure heap'd in joy, to th' measures
> 　　fall.
> 　　　　　　　　　　　　　　(V, iv, 176-179)

"New-fall'n" applies to his returned Dukedom, "fall" applies to the current Forest life. "Measure heap'd in joy" could apply to both worlds, but it recalls for us "the measure of their states" and the assumption of rank and position looked upon as normal in Fortune's world; the final "measures" refers to the dance they will do in the Forest. We are left, after this balanced holding of both worlds at once, with the departure of Jaques and with the dance which is the sign of the harmony of the moment.

The Epilogue is all that marks the return to the workaday world, spoken by the boy who has played Rosalind. He has gone from the heights of role-playing—this boy playing Rosalind playing Ganymed playing Rosalind—step by step back down the ladder of fantasy to speak directly to the men and women in the audience before him. He speaks of attraction between the sexes, of possible kisses, of the need for appreciation and applause. It is not the Forest nor the Duke's realm. It is the theater, the living reality of the image used so extensively in the play.

What is left of the play? A dream of power and evil transmuted into a dream where power and evil have disappeared. The result has been joy, romance, and various dimensions of love. The lovers of the earlier plays are translated in *As You Like It* into a world which suggests they can combine completeness of personality with private expression of love; but the world is a dream, a play world. *As You Like It* is the closest Shakespeare gets to the realization of such a dream; *Twelfth Night* explores its comic failure.

R. Chris Hassel (essay date 1980)

SOURCE: " 'Most Faining': Wits and Wise Fools in *As You Like It*," in *Faith and Folly in Shakespeare's Romantic Comedies,* The University of Georgia Press, 1980, pp. 110-48.

[*In the following essay, Hassel concentrates on Shakespeare's comic vision in* As You Like It, *describing it as an "affirmative celebration of man's follies and his potentialities."*]

As You Like It is a banquet of the follies of human perception and human behavior. But unlike *Much Ado about Nothing* the emphasis is decisively on the celebration rather than the discovery and acknowledgment of this folly. Partly because of the uniqueness of Arden and its inhabitants, absurd behavior is readily acknowledged throughout the play by the lovers, the shepherds, and the courtiers. Paradoxically, only the fool and the would-be fool in Arden, Touchstone and Jaques, seem to lack this humility. Their naiveté is especially amusing not only because it is their profession to know themselves to be fools, but also because they so frequently allude to Erasmian and Pauline statements of this wisdom. That strange and delightful absence of humility in these Erasmian fools, like its unusual presence among the rest of the characters in Arden, can deepen our understanding of the wisdom of folly in Shakespeare's romantic comedies.

As You Like It is also unique in its treatment of epistemological folly. Like *A Midsummer Night's Dream* it persistently involves us in romantic and aesthetic truths which surpass all knowledge. But *A Midsummer Night's Dream* focuses most of its attention on Bottom, the four lovers, Theseus, and the audience as beholders or interpreters of the transcendental. *As You Like It,* on the other hand, deals more with its expressive side, with the attempts of the lover or the artist, Orlando or Rosalind or Shakespeare himself, to convey transcendental truths. Like *A Midsummer Night's Dream,* but with more subtlety, *As You Like It* simplifies and enriches these rather esoteric aesthetic and epistemological themes with their analogies to attempts to convey the insights of religious faith. Religious rituals thus become the metaphoric counterpart in *As You Like It* to the observances and conventions of lovers and artists.

But all such conventions inevitably risk the folly of expressing the inexpressible, a folly familiar to both St. Paul and Erasmus.[1] Shakespeare thus joyously and ingeniously links fool, lover, artist, and priest in *As You Like It* into a common bond. They are all fools, and unless they acknowledge that folly they will never be wise. The foolish wits of Arden never quite grasp this wisdom. But the lovers, like the playwright, seem to know or to learn that their great feignings, the conventions they both must use to say what they so deeply feel, might also be great follies. For what they have to express may transcend both their art and human understanding. In an age that was unusually interested in sectarian controversies concerning the nature and efficacy of religious rituals,[2] such a comic interest in the rituals of lovers and artists could have seemed quite timely.

i. The Folly of the Fools

In *Twelfth Night,* it can be demonstrated that Feste is a truly wise fool. By "venting" a folly that is virtually universal in Illyria, he leads his victims to acknowledge and rejoice in their own absurdities, and he leads some out of their self-love. Viola praises his folly in precisely these terms at the beginning of Act III: "For folly that he wisely shows, is fit" (III.i.65). Feste's catechism of Olivia (I.v.52-67) early in the play and his late conversation with Orsino (V.i.10-20) reveal Feste's own awareness of this role of proving others to be fools, playing their enemy but being their friend. As he says, we are all patched men, some "patched with virtue," some "patched with sin." If we cannot mend ourselves, we must "let the botcher mend" us (I.v.40-44). His work with Toby, Andrew, and Malvolio is a similar if sillier tailoring. Through all of this wisdom, however, Feste never loses sight of his own patched clothes or of the folly that they represent. He always knows that he is a fool. And in that knowledge he is, like Viola in her foolish disguise, most healthy and most wise.

Touchstone and jaques have quite another role to play in *As You Like It.* Both of them seem superficially aware of the same Pauline and Erasmian commonplaces that Feste and Viola know so well. But though one is clearly an amateur fool and the other both a natural and a professional, neither can consistently admit that he is foolish. Jaques seems completely unaware that the motley coat he desires signifies first and foremost his certain knowledge that he is a fool. Touchstone, though more often aware of his patches, is just as likely to praise the wisdom of his own folly. Their lack of the wisdom of humility is almost always silly rather than sinister. Only Jaques occasionally tries our patience, along with that of Duke Senior and Rosalind, in his not-so-blissful ignorance. But we remain fond of both fools in the forest; we do not blame them too much for their folly.

In fact, their delightful naiveté about their own folly actually highlights the unusual degree of humility elsewhere in Arden.[3] Outcasts all, all seem aware of a common folly, personal and social if not cosmic as well. Duke Senior articulates this philosophy in his "sweet are the uses of adversity" speech, but in fact his attitude runs throughout the forest in courtiers and shepherds as well as lovers. With few exceptions, its inhabitants know their folly or readily learn of it, and they rejoice in the lesson. In one of his rare glimpses of this truth, Touchstone announces a lesson that most of the lovers in Arden would readily agree to: "We that are true lovers run into strange capers; but as all is mortal in nature, so is all nature in love mortal in folly" (II.iv.49-51). Orlando is delighted to be a fool in love: "'Tis a fault I will not change for your best virtue" (III.ii.270-71). Rosalind, in the same scene and also madly in love, can proclaim as Ganymede:

> Love is merely a madness, and, I tell you, deserves as well a dark house and a whip as madmen do; and the reason why they are not so punished and cured is that the lunacy is so ordinary that the whippers are in love too.
>
> (III.ii.376-80)

Look at Oliver and Celia, or Orlando and Rosalind, or even Silvius and Phebe to see how variously this madness is exhibited and finally also embraced. The fools in Arden are those who would make fun of this strange love. The lovers are merely mad, and they know it and love it.

As a result of the unusually widespread humility and self-knowledge in Arden, the fools are consistently rendered foolish by trying to expose a folly that is already acknowledged, or a simplicity that is equally aware of itself. Touchstone glories in confounding the foolish rather than the wise. And while we enjoy his silliness with, say, the shepherd, we know at the same time that Corin is not damned for bringing his sheep together or for his lack of courtly manners. The shepherd's words of simple duty, absolute self-knowledge, and humility render the fool's role useless and elicit our admiration. In fact, he is wiser than the fool who is trying to demonstrate his folly:

> Sir, I am a true laborer; I earn that I eat, get that I wear, owe no man hate, envy no man's happiness, glad of other men's good, content with my harm; and the greatest of my pride is to see my ewes graze and my lambs suck.
>
> (III.ii.69-73)

William near the end of the play is similarly impervious to Touchstone's assault. He may be dumbfounded but he is not frightened by either the false learning or the silly blustering of Touchstone's challenge:

> To wit, I kill thee, make thee away, translate thy life into death, thy liberty into bondage. I will deal in poison with thee, or in bastinado, or in steel; I will bandy with thee in faction; I will o'errun thee with policy; I will kill thee a hundred and fifty ways. Therefore tremble and depart.
>
> (V.i.51-56)

William leaves, but hardly gasping for fear: "God rest you, merry sir" (V.i.58). For again Touchstone has delightfully proven only himself a fool. These humble innocents are beyond his wit and his wisdom. So is most of the assemblage in Arden.

Touchstone proves his own folly most decisively when he refers naively to Pauline and Erasmian commonplaces about folly and wisdom. The wise fool would use his humility to demonstrate the folly of the proud, the wise, and the powerful, but Touchstone exposes the humility of his quarry by proving his own foolish pride. First he thinks that William is a clown and he, the clown, is a wise man:

> It is meat and drink to me to see a clown; by my troth, we that have good wits have much to answer for. We shall be flouting; we cannot hold.
>
> (V.i.10-12)

Then he responds to William's relatively innocent "Ay, sir, I have a pretty wit" with this:

> Why, thou say'st well. I do now remember a saying, "The fool doth think he is wise, but the wise man knows himself to be a fool."
>
> (V.i.29-31)

The paradox, of course, is St. Paul's, filtered perhaps through Erasmus's *The Praise of Folie*.[4] But though Touchstone remembers it well, he understands or applies it poorly: "You are not *ipse*, for I am he" (V.i.43). He is proud of his wisdom rather than his folly. When William asks, "Which he, sir?" we know that he has proven Touchstone the fool in his own confounding innocence. The professional fool just doesn't have a chance in Arden.

Neither does the amateur. Jaques is just as adept as Touchstone at proving himself a fool, and just as unaware of the lessons of humility he might be learning. His first scene depicts Jaques as a melancholy fool who has no sense of the absurdity others enjoy in him. Of Amiens' song, he moans as painfully as any lover,

More, I prithee more! I can suck melancholy out of
a song as a weasel sucks eggs. More, I prithee more!

(II.v.10-12)

Duke Senior and his brothers in exile love these sullen
fits of folly; in fact they encourage them, though without sarcasm or bitterness:

I love to cope him in these sullen fits,
For then he's full of matter

(II.i.67-68)

But Jaques, like Touchstone, is unaware of his own
absurdity. Worse, he is therefore more scornful of that
folly which he assumes lies only outside of himself.
We see this naiveté throughout the play. But nowhere
is it more obvious than in the scene with Amiens.

This is the scene in which Jaques sings his "ducdame"
refrain about the universal folly in Arden:

If it do come to pass
That any man turn ass,
Leaving his wealth and ease
A stubborn will to please,
Ducdame, ducdame, ducdame.
Here shall he see gross fools as he.
An if he will come to me.

(II.v.44-50)

Throughout the play Jaques evidences this frustrated
desire to demonstrate the folly in others. Paradoxically,
whenever he tries, he most clearly exposes his own.
The Duke will indeed see a gross fool, Jaques, "if he
will come to me." In explaining "ducdame," his mysterious invocation of fools, Jaques experiences the same
paradoxical proof of his own folly. But again he will
not accept it:

'Tis a Greek invocation to call fools into a circle.
I'll go sleep, if I can; if I cannot, I'll rail against all
the first-born of Egypt.

(II.v.52-54)

The conjurer Jaques must be in the center of the circle,
and therefore at the center of its folly. The railing
Herod is the most obvious exemplar of the folly of
pride in all of the mysteries; to our delight, Jaques
completely misses the connection.

This blindness to his considerable folly continues
throughout the play. With Duke Senior, in his next
appearance, Jaques exults over seeing a fool in the
forest:

A fool, a fool! I met a fool i' th' forest,
A motley fool! a miserable world!
As I do live by food, I met a fool.

(II.vii.12-14)

We know that Jaques could have seen himself in the
fool's edifying glass. Touchstone is aping his melancholy, "deep-contemplative" moralizing "on the time."
But characteristically, all Jaques can see is the folly of
the fool:

When I did hear
The motley fool thus moral on the time,
My lungs began to crow like chanticleer
That fools should be so deep contemplative;
And I did laugh sans intermission
An hour by his dial. O noble fool,
A worthy fool! Motley's the only wear.

(II.vii.28-34)

He is already wearing it, of course, already being
measured by the fool's dial. But he will not admit it.

As William asks of Touchstone, so Duke Senior asks
of Jaques, which fool he refers to. We hear echoes of
Feste trying to get Malvolio to acknowledge his share
of universal folly in *Twelfth Night*: "Are you not mad
indeed? or do you but counterfeit?" (IV.ii.110-11). But
like Malvolio, albeit with more humor, Jaques remains
naive: "O that I were a fool! / I am ambitious for a
motley coat" (II.vii.42-43). With "thou shalt have one,"
the Duke prods to Jaques to acknowledge the patches
that are his birthright. But against all of the Pauline
and Erasmian precepts to which he is at this very
moment alluding, Jaques still assumes his wisdom
obvious, and has little sense of his folly:

Provided that you weed your better judgments
Of all opinion that grows rank in them
That I am wise.

(II.vii.45-47)

He would be a wise physician to the "foul body of th'
infected world" (II.vii.60), yet he cannot even diag-
nose his own sickness. The exasperated but still charitable Duke finally assaults his blindness directly. "Physician, heal thyself," is the thrust of his remonstrance:

Most mischievous foul sin, in chiding sin.
For thou thyself hast been a libertine.

(II.vii.64-65)

Again Jaques evades the Duke's obvious lessoning.
By taking the Duke's thrust as an attack on satire,
rather than on his own lack of humility, he can go on
pridefully playing one who "cries out on pride"
(II.vii.70). His quick wit often allows Jaques to evade
edifying humiliation. But this is a comic curse, as it
was to Berowne and Beatrice, not a blessing. For it
deprives them all of the greater wisdom of humility.

The two most familiar examples of the liabilities of his
witty pride occur in exchanges' between Jaques and
the lovers Rosalind and Orlando. As soon as we see

Orlando absurdly tacking up verses all over the trees in Arden we acknowledge the silliness of his love, but also its attractiveness. Nowhere is the ambivalence more obvious than in Rosalind's mixed delight and amusement over his actions. But Jaques, like Touchstone, can only see the lover's folly, and must try again to prove it. Instead, he is again the inevitable victim of his proof. For in his relative humility Orlando is almost fool-proof, as in his witty pride Jaques is always in absolute jeopardy.

> ORLANDO. I will chide no breather in the world but myself, against whom I know most faults.
> JAQUES. The worst fault you have is to be in love.
> ORLANDO. 'Tis a fault I will not change for your best virtue. I am weary of you.
> JAQUES. By my truth, I was seeking for a fool when I found you.
> ORLANDO. He is drowned in the brook. Look but in and you shall see him.
> JAQUES. There I shall see mine own figure.
> ORLANDO. Which I take to be either a fool or a cipher.
>
> (III.ii.267-77)

Like Malvolio, Jaques will accept neither humbling alternative, even if he must therefore ignore what everyone else can see. Monsieur Melancholy is for this reason far more fool than Monsieur Love. For the latter knows himself to be a fool, and loves it.

With Rosalind, Jaques is again proven a fool for refusing to admit his folly and its universality. All other melancholies may be foolish—the scholar's, the musician's, the courtier's—but his is not (IV.i.10-18). He similarly evades her exposure of the folly of his travels. And then by sarcastically responding to Orlando's euphoric line of blank verse ("Good day and happiness, dear Rosalind" [IV.i.27]) he slips away from further proof. We can assume that Rosalind's parting shots also fall on deaf ears, for Jaques cannot yet embrace this essential comic lesson. Even Touchstone wears some humility in his tattered suit, his foolish antics, and his foul wife Audrey, though he would not be too well-married. But Jaques still finds the patched suit unbearable. As a result, he cannot share the experiences of marriage or festivity which conclude the play. Hymen implies in his final blessing of the fools and lovers that Touchstone's marriage with Audrey will not last long. But Jaques, who will hazard neither love nor folly, will therefore lose this chance at festive joy. His departure from the revellers suggests his inability to celebrate the wisdom of their mutual folly; he thus remains alien to their paradoxical happiness. Our response to his departure is not satisfaction, however, but a Jaques-like melancholy of our own. For we like him still, and we wish him well. After all, he is our fellow in folly, even if he does not know it yet.

ii. The Follies of the Play

Uniquely, then, most of the follies that Jaques and Touchstone expose are their own. The few follies they do hit upon in Arden are usually either the unpretentious silliness of innocents and simpletons or the assorted madnesses the lovers have already joyously acknowledged. But the play contains over sixty references to "fool," "folly," "foolish," and related morphemes. Where is the rest of this folly? Oddly, much of it lies outside of Arden, and even outside the world of the play, providing these two fools with some "matter" for their flouting wits in spite of the unusual humility of Arden's inhabitants. The rest lies in the romantic and pastoral fabric of the play itself. Because Shakespeare allows these fools to expose the follies of his dramatic medium and its sources along with their anatomies of general behavioral absurdities, he leads us to understand how the folly of the play and the folly of the players coalesce in *As You Like It*. If the Forest of Arden is an unusually humble place, so is the play itself. For it fosters in Jaques and Touchstone its own worst critics, and smiles like the lovers at the acknowledged follies they persistently try to expose.

Though anatomies of universal follies are among their most familiar moments in the play, few readers have noticed that Jaques and Touchstone are exposing follies that lie for the most part outside of Arden. Touchstone's anatomy of the courtier is in this category (v.iv.42-46), as is his subsequent analysis of the seven "degrees of the lie" (v.iv.65-97), the "Retort Courteous," the "Quip Modest," the "Lie Direct," and the rest. So is his earlier proof that the knight "that swore by his honor they were good pancakes, and swore by his honor the mustard was naught" was not forsworn (I.ii.59-63). Jaques's anatomy of the seven ages of man (II.vii.139-66) and his explosion against pride in the same scene also anatomize universal or general follies that lie largely outside of the boundaries of Arden. Both of them are rather successful with this abstract kind of foolery, and Touchstone probably deserves the Duke's praise, "He uses his folly like a stalking horse, and under the presentation of that he shoots his wit" (V.vi.100-101). But while Touchstone and Jaques make us mark the universal pageant of man's general folly, they also emphasize its relative absence in Arden, except among themselves. Jaques's seven ages, like Touchstone's seven degrees of the lie, is a conventional set-piece, a "progress" leading nowhere, a denial of value. So when they try to expose specific and widely acknowledged follies among the lovers, the country-folk, and the exiled court, they expose more of their own absurdity.

But the fools also expose the follies of the play, follies inherent in its pastoral and romantic sources as well as follies unavoidable in the conventions of drama. That Shakespeare gives his fools this latitude suggests that his comic attitude toward folly has grown to include the work itself and its author. As in *A Midsummer Night's Dream* this humility also includes the audience, which is willing to be taken in by these aesthetic follies even after having been made aware of them. We find a similar attitude in *Twelfth Night,* and see its culmination in *The Winter's Tale.* Shakespeare exhibits this aesthetic humility in various ways in *As You Like It,* with implications that are finally epistemological too. In fact, many critics—C. L. Barber, John Russell Brown, T. M. Parrott, and Sylvan Barnet, among others—have noticed the play's fascination with itself as a strangely conventional, pastoral, romantic, and dramatic creature. [5] Because its unusual self-criticism is so widely accepted, we need to review only a few of the most vital moments when the fools, or the play itself, exposes the strange tactics a play sometimes has to use to imitate reality.

We have already mentioned some examples of the fools' exposures of this aesthetic folly. Some of it simultaneously exposes the folly of the lovers. Jaques responds to Orlando's line of verse in the midst of a prose exchange with, "Nay then, God b' wi' you, an you talk in blank verse" (IV.i.28-29). Earlier Touchstone has his own go at Orlando's verse (and Rosalind's charming sentimentality) with parody as well as direct criticism:

Sweetest nut hath sourest rind,
Such a nut is Rosalinde.
He that sweetest rose will find
Must find love's prick, and Rosalinde.
(III.ii.104-7)

Admittedly Orlando's verse is not good: "This is the very false gallop of verses. Why do you infect yourself with them?" To Rosalind's response, "Peace, you dull fool! I found them on a tree," he responds, "Truly, the tree yields bad fruit." It does indeed. But both Rosalind and Orlando can smile good-naturedly at the inevitable folly of this conventional expression of their love, even while they are earnestly committing it. The feelings of Orlando are as true as the verse or the courtly pose is false. It takes a bright fool, a Rosalind or a Shakespeare, to know and to cherish this inner truth as she smiles at its outer folly, and to learn how to pick the meat out of the shell.

Touchstone has another go at romance after Silvius describes his love for Phebe in hopelessly conventional terms: "as true a lover / As ever sighed upon a midnight pillow" (II.iv.23-24). Witness Silvius's inexpressible passion:

Or if thou has not broke from company
Abruptly, as my passion now makes me,
Thou hast not loved. O Phebe, Phebe, Phebe!
(II.iv.37-39)

This too is textbook stuff, hack work, both the cardboard lover and his verse. But they remind Rosalind of a truer love not all that far removed from this highly conventional one:

Alas, poor shepherd! Searching of thy wound,
I have by hard adventure found mine own.
(II.iv.40-41)

Lest we be swept up by her passion, however, Touchstone offers his fool's version of romantic ecstasy. It smacks of love's prick rather than its spirit, and it therefore serves as a vital corrective for the absurdities which true lovers, not to mention their portrayers and viewers, can commit:

I remember, when I was in love . . . the kissing of her batler, and the cows' dugs that her pretty chopt hands had milked; and I remember the wooing of a peascod instead of her, from whom I took two cods, and giving her them again, said with weeping tears, "Wear these for my sake." We that are true lovers run into strange capers; but as all is mortal in nature, so is all nature in love mortal in folly.

(II.iv.42-51)

This little ritual or sacrament of the cods fleetingly suggests the Communion words, "He toke the cuppe, and when he had geven thankes, he gave it to them, saying, . . . drinke it in remembraunce of me" (p. 103). With Touchstone's odd fetishes, it reminds us that the follies of mortal lovers are indeed rich and strange. Such a silly moment corrects a romantic atmosphere that had briefly become too sentimental and too conventional with a healthy dose of comic realism.

The pastoral's tendencies towards philosophising and sentimentality are other conventions both Touchstone and Jaques assault through parody and direct criticism. Touchstone must be mocking Jaques's melancholy philosophizing when he "morals on the time" in front of him. Less consciously, Jaques is Shakespeare's agent of a criticism of similar extremes directed against Duke Senior and his fellow pastoral exiles. To lament the "poor dappled fools" who "should in their own confines . . . have their round haunches gored" (II.i.22-25) is silly stuff all by itself. Jaques's moralizing of this spectacle "into a thousand similes" carries it beyond the brink of absurdity. He stands on the bank, "weeping and commenting / Upon the sobbing deer" (II.i.64-65). When the first lord describes the weeping of the wounded deer, whose "big round tears / Coursed one another down his innocent nose / In piteous chase" (II.i.38-40) he could as well have been describing

Jaques's compassion for the deer as the deer's self-pity. Such extremes are unfortunate characteristics of the pastoral mode. By exaggerating them in Jaques, Shakespeare makes the exiles' folly and that of the genre obvious and funny to all of us.

Similar is Touchstone's confrontation with Corin right after we have heard the first of Orlando's poetical efforts. Its foolish anatomy of the shepherd's life is nonsense on the one hand, but good sense too. Pastorals tend to praise the outdoor life too uncritically. But in truth, whether we are selecting ways of living or dramatic modes, most of our choices are teasingly relative. So is the reality these choices seek to achieve or express:

> Truly, shepherd, in respect of itself, it is a good life; but in respect that it is a shepherd's life, it is naught. In respect that it is solitary, I like it very well; but in respect that it is private, it is a very vile life. Now in respect it is in the fields, it pleaseth me well; but in respect it is not in the court, it is tedious. . . . Hast any philosophy in thee, shepherd?

> (III.ii.13-21)

Literary genres, ways of living, the conventions of artists or lovers games, rituals, and disguises—all are partly true and partly false, too sentimental or not sentimental enough, adequate in this respect, and inadequate in that. Only a pastoral or a romantic vision that accepts and celebrates the folly of this relativity has achieved the Pauline and Erasmian humility that underlies so much of Shakespeare's comic wisdom. Neither Touchstone nor Jaques has this wisdom, at least not consistently. But during this momentary wit-strike, and while they parody and criticize the pastoral and romantic conventions of their play, they at least suggest it to us.

In the scene that follows this one, Touchstone makes the play's most important statement about the relative truth of its aesthetic conventions. Characteristically, he doesn't understand what he has said. But if we listen to him we will realize that the folly of the play is analogous to that of the lovers. The reason is that the conventionality of art, like that of courtship (or religious ritual), is a great feigning that can express great truths, so long as it doesn't take itself too seriously. In making this important connection for us, albeit absurdly, Touchstone leads us, Bottom-like, to sense the epistemological as well as the aesthetic dimensions of the themes of faith and folly in Shakespeare's romantic comedies.

The scene is well-enough known. Touchstone is trying to explain to Audrey the concept "poeticall." In this role he is intriguingly like Bottom blundering into his appropriate paraphrase of St. Paul when he needs to express the inexpressible. Jaques betrays his continuing misunderstanding of the paradoxical wisdom of folly when he comments on this vehicle of truth: "O knowledge ill-inhabited, worse than Jove in a thatched house!" (III.iii.7-8). Audrey then sets Touchstone up with one of the great straight lines in comedy: "I do not know what poetical is. Is it honest in deed and word? Is it a true thing?" (III.iii.14-15). Touchstone replies with unknowing Sidneyan and Platonic sublimity: "No, truly; for the truest poetry is the most faining." We are all familiar with Plato's indictment of poetry as an imitation, "three removes . . . from the truth," which "tends to destroy the rational part."[6] Where Touchstone picked up this piece of Platonic lore is anyone's guess; but that he is about to abuse it is a sure bet.

A logical progression of this warped Platonism is his assumption that only foulness guarantees honesty: "Praised be the gods for thy foulness" he tells Audrey. And later he tells Duke Senior, "Rich honesty dwells like a miser, sir, in a poor house, as your pearl in your foul oyster" (V.iv.57-59). Beauty, like poetry, is most feigning. Touchstone will therefore trust only the opposites of the appearance of truth. The kernel of truth must be distinguished from the chaff and the husk. But the figure of the pearl is much more appropriate to Touchstone in *As You Like It* than that of wheat and chaff, for with it Shakespeare exploits the unexpectedness of imaginative insight, the suddenly perfect, polished shape out of the rough barnacled mass, the pearl out of the mouth of the philosophic oyster Touchstone. Erasmus and St. Paul would have found him a fit spokesman.

For there is wisdom here as well as absurdity. If we look closer at Touchstone's indictment of poetry as "most faining," we will see that his sloppy syntax has caused him to proclaim the value of poetry, its truth rather than its folly. "For the truest poetry is the most faining," is what he actually says. The husk and the chaff are the stuff of the shadow world, the specific moment, *scientia,* accidence. The wheat, the pearl, is the kernel of truth, *sapientia.* The unique capacity of art and of ritual is to capture the primary, the sapiential, in an enduring form. As Sidney says, great poetry does not affirm accident; therefore it never lies. It is not "labouring to tell you what is, or is not, but what should or should not be."[7]

The greatest truth requires as its only adequate vehicle the most elusive and imaginative aesthetic conventions. The truest poetry must therefore always be the most feigning. This is why the great poets must always walk on Ferlinghetti's tightrope across the abyss of folly ("Constantly Risking Absurdity"). In case we are not following the gist of his banter with Audrey, Touchstone then relates this paradox about the reality of artistic conventions to the truth of the feigning conventions of lovers. Again he stumbles upon the wisdom: "and lovers are given to poetry, and what they swear in poetry may be said, as lovers, they do feign" (III.iii.17-18). When Audrey asks him, "Do you wish then that the gods had made me poetical?" he replies incongruously, "I do truly; for thou swear'st to me thou art honest. Now, if thou wert a poet, I might have some hope thou didst feign." His apparent contradiction must go in this direction: if Audrey were poetical, her swearing of honesty would mean lightness, and the shortsighted Touchstone could seduce her on the spot. He would gain then a goat-woman indeed, tarnished physically as well as spiritually, a foul pearl in a foul oyster, the least poetical woman possible. Luckily for him, she is not quite that.

Related types of true if foolish feigning in *As You Like It* are games and similar moments of playing and fantasizing. These frivolities remind us on the surface of childishness and of unsophisticated literary modes. At the same time they can also express and enact complex relationships among characters, and complex epistemological insights. The wrestling, for example, so obviously symbolic as a clash of values and perspectives, is also an image of Orlando's lovelessness and Frederick's loveless society. Grown men should not have to wrestle with such pretty women looking on and wanting to join the fray ("The little strength that I have, I would it were with you" [I.ii.178]). Running away from home, the courtship game, aimless philosophizing about nature and fortune, playing Robin Hood, carving on trees, saving a brother from a snake or a lion, and then forgiving him and finding him regenerated, love at first sight, oaths, magicians, the rituals and miracles of love—all of these beautifully childish and dreamlike feignings are facets of "inscape" which become almost literal in Arden. The reason is Shakespeare's genius, of course, but also the fact that games and related feignings and follies are natural to the human condition. Literalness is no more natural than figurativeness, nor is work more real than play, or reason than fantasy.[8] Only severely limited perspectives like those of a single-minded individual or a single literary mode would categorically prescribe one reality and exclude the others. Shakespeare keeps all of his options open in *As You Like It* by simultaneously enjoying and exposing the folly and the loveliness, the artificiality and the naturalness of all of these conventional games and rituals, these related feignings of man and of art.

Nowhere is this attitude more obvious than in the play's own amused self-criticism. Jaques and Touchstone have pointed out some of its aesthetic follies, but they have characteristically assumed that they shared none of them. In contrast to their uninvolved parody, and more like Rosalind's spirited role-playing, *As You Like It* gamely tries on the foolish, conventional, ritualistic garb of the comic and the romantic and even the satiric stage, and seeks to incorporate all of their shreds and patches into a new, comprehensive comic vision. Since the form of burlesque suggests that no single perspective—be it romantic, pastoral, idyllic, melodramatic, satiric, ironic, mythic, or what you will—can adequately express the complexity of reality, perhaps a blend of them, a comprehensive comic vision to match the comprehensiveness of reality itself, is the only adequate perspective. Shakespeare seems in *As You Like It* to be confirming his belief in the truth of the feignings of composite artistic conventions and modes by exposing the relative dishonesty of each of them individually, and then including valid parts of each perspective into his larger vision. This is so widely acknowledged a characteristic of the play that only a brief survey of its pertinence to our thesis will be presented here.

The play is full of aesthetic follies so grotesque and obvious that they must be calling attention to their own absurdity. It flaunts its folly by exaggerating its conventionality. The first scene, for example, begins and ends with a long, dreary piece of prose exposition, much like Prospero's speeches to Miranda in Act I, Scene ii of *The Tempest*. Rosalind's epilogue makes fun of this inauspicious beginning. The whole play is also strangely devoid of developing action, as the series of tableaux in Act II makes clear. Time stands still in the forest for more reasons than the lack of a clock. Further, characters like Duke Frederick and Oliver are so unabashedly villainous as to be mere humors of jealous ambition. Perhaps that is why they can be so easily converted when they enter the forest of Arden. The pastoral excesses in Duke Senior's first scene ("Sweet are the uses of adversity") are equally obvious as flauntings of the follies of the dramatic and pastoral modes. The bathetic responses to the sobbing, sentient deer, whose "big round tears / Coursed one another down his innocent nose / In piteous chase" (II.i.38-40), like the moralizing on those "native burghers," is foolish enough for many readers to catch a jangling note of absurdity before Jaques's obvious parody to come. But if this sentimental moralizing is pretty foolish, so is the overblown ideality, language, and sentiment of the prelapsarian Adam, the perfect pastoral servant, talking to his equally perfect master Orlando: "O my gentle master, O my sweet master, O, . . ." etc. (II.iii.2-4). He will follow Orlando "to the last gasp." We may also gasp at this, but not for admiration alone. Still, with many of these pastoral and dramatic excesses there is delight in indulging our sentimentality and our pastoralism, even while we recognize its folly. We relish the "tongues in trees, books in the running brooks, sermons in stones, and good in everything" even as we know that it is not quite true, a pastoral feigning in style and content. The same might be said of the anaphoric exchange of Orlando and Duke Senior in Act II, Scene vii (ll. 113-23). Part of the magic of *As You Like It* is that we can have it either way, critically or conventionally, or even both ways at once.

In a similar celebration of its aesthetic folly, the play just stops for Jaques's oration "All the world's a stage" in Act II, Scene vii. For all of its rhetorical beauty it is a thoroughly conventional set-piece expressed with a naive cynicism. But at the same time, Jaques's evocation of the trope of the theater of the world, however accidentally, can reinforce our understanding of man's inevitable folly and his ultimate need for humility, his position as actor in a moral universe before an eternal auditor. The theme of humility in *The Tempest* derives from a similar use of the same trope by Prospero. Such aesthetic follies are legion in *As You Like It,* and they have been often observed. They parody the pastoral romance from which the play is descended while simultaneously including *As You Like It* securely within that genre and also securely within the community of folly.

In a similar combination of parody and celebration, Touchstone and Audrey and then Silvius and Phebe parody the romantic love of Rosalind and Orlando, but they also expand our understandings of its dimensions. For the extreme physicality of the clowns and the extreme conventionality of the pastoral figures are both true if feigning (and faining) aspects of the richer relationship of the primary pair. Like the love at first sight which we like in Orlando and Rosalind, and Oliver and Celia, but howl at in Phebe and Touchstone (or Olivia and Viola, or Bottom and Titania in related situations), we are forced to be aware of the "most feignings" of character, action, theme, and verse before we are allowed to celebrate their great truths as well. If we like it we can laugh at the follies and love the profundities at once. "For ever and a day" cannot be accepted uncritically into this vision. But it can be included, if it is willing to be criticized: "Say 'a day,' without the 'ever'" (IV.i.133). And so as audience we must always be *en garde* as well, lest we enjoy one of these conventional phrases, actions, sentiments, philosophies, too uncritically. This is a strenuous aesthetic vision that involves us in its wise humility. But it is also a joyous one.

Three of its cleverest manifestations come when Shakespeare connects the conventions of romance with highly conventional and ostensibly dramatic religious forms. We have already mentioned the faint echo of Communion in Touchstone's "sacrament" of the cods. Orlando and Rosalind also occasionally talk like the Student and Master of the Catechism during his instruction as a lover. Later they join Silvius and Phebe in an elaborate litany of love. These last two parallels deserve closer attention.

When Rosalind instructs Orlando "who Time ambles withal, who Time trots withal, who Time gallops withal," etc. (III.ii.294-96), the style of questions and answers is clearly a parody of the catechism. The Master-Student relationship is part of that parody, but more important is the imitation of the unnatural style of the genre, a style itself based on the feigning of a dramatic situation. Orlando's lifeless questions about time ("Who doth he trot withal?," etc. (III.ii. 297, 303, 309, 313)) are met by Rosalind's equally repetitive and unimaginative answers, paradoxically livelier here because they are so dull. Also like the catechism is the analysis of each answer into four- or six-part responses. They recall the familiar "How many parts hath the Lord's Prayer?" or "Into how many parts dost thou divide this whole confession of faith?"[9] One can imagine the frustration of schoolboys and girls trying to memorize such abstract and repetitive material. That experience is not likely to have been forgotten, or to have been remembered too fondly, either. "To answer in a catechism" is to answer predictable questions in dull and lifeless responses. Celia herself refers to this unpleasant if necessary conventionality during the same scene (III.ii.216-17), making sure that no one misses the parody to come. Paradoxically, even the flatness of this conventional religious form edifies and orders, and thereby justifies its own stilted aesthetic existence.

The highly conventional litany to love is sung by the four lovers just after Rosalind-Ganymede has promised to resolve all of the complexities that their feignings have wrought (V.ii.79-109).[10] Its hyperbolic conventionality, as well as its antiphonal form ("And I for Ganymede. / And I for Rosalind. / And I for no woman") is again grotesquely contrived. Can love possibly be all of these things, this incredible combination of outward signs and inward qualities? Could any lover be so dedicated? They are all posing, or lying, or exaggerating. And yet even the one who is consciously feigning, Rosalind Ganymede, is only literally feigning. Secretly she is rejoicing with the rest, rejoicing even more because of her secret and the joy that she holds for them all. What of the conventionality of their litany? Is it so patently conventional? Notice the gradual transition from the artificial into the genuine, from the mechanical into the fluid. Notice the lovely crescendo as Silvius moves into the spirit of his hymn. It builds to "observance" and to "humbleness" and then the decrescendo begins, out of that moment of ultimate reality and ultimate convention, back to the conventionally juxtaposed "patience and impatience," back to the pure and passionless "trial" and the repeated "observance." That repetition combined with the awful, fourfold, later refrain ("If this be so, why blame you me to love you?") suggests on the one hand that the litany is running down. But simultaneously, repeating "observance" emphasizes the importance of observance not only to love but to any type of ritualized celebration. Observance makes the abstract concrete, expresses the inexpressible, like art, like ritual, like these words of Silvius. The conflicting and hyperbolical qualities of love are qualities confirmed by and contained in his litany. Likewise the direction of the celebration is carefully contrived: from sighs and tears to faith and service; from symptom to symbol; from fantasy to faith; from belief to worship; from protestation to celebration, the observance of belief, its manifestation. This characteristic moment has much to say of romantic faith and romantic folly, of the truth as well as the falsehood of the rituals and the conventionality of humankind.

One of the most outlandish of all the aesthetic conventions in *As You Like It* is the appearance of Hymen, a *deus ex machina,* in the final scene. The natural magic of Rosalind would have been quite sufficient, thank you, for the resolution of the plot. Like our first reaction to Adam's praise of his master, Orlando's catechism, or the lovers' litany, we may want to gasp or laugh out loud at the audacious folly of this moment. But while the appearance of such a figure makes fun of all conventionally contrived romantic endings, it also leads the audience, in the spirit of humility that permeates *As You Like It,* through its own ritual of romantic celebration, just as Silvius earlier led the lovers' litany. This most conventional dramatic creature, a feigning, a mere symbol, a figure of speech upon the stage, encourages us to celebrate the reality that we have learned to perceive in conventionality, games, and all of the playlike ritualistic qualities that enrich and direct human life. Laughable as Hymen is, a patent feigning, he still represents and embodies the audience's common and charitable wish for successful love and general comic happiness.[11] Such an "embodiment," such a "representation," might be all Hymen was ever supposed to stand for, as a god or a dramatic character. The greatest feigning is again the truest. Placing as it does the audience's most festive and charitable wishes before them on the stage, it merges stage and audience, confirming again the frequency of romantic and dramatic miracles, and the impossibility of expressing great truths without little lies.

But best of all of these moments of aesthetic self-criticism is Rosalind's epilogue, which once and for all explicitly admits the play's folly and its feignings and rejoices in it. First, it bluntly reminds us that the play also started with Orlando's long, undramatic prose passage, and criticizes both conventions: "It is not the fashion to see the lady the epilogue, but it is no more unhandsome than to see the lord the prologue" (ll. 1-3). She continues in this vein with her analogy between good wines and good plays: "If it be true that good wine needs no bush, 'tis true that a good play needs no epilogue; yet to good wine they do use good bushes, and good plays prove the better by the help of good epilogues." From the obvious humility of considering the play no better than a good wine, Rosalind goes even further into the play's folly. It is neither a good epilogue nor a good play: "What a case am I in then, that am neither a good epilogue nor cannot insinuate with you in the behalf of a good play!" Still, she will not be a beggar on behalf of this foolish play.

Rather she will be true to its title by asking her audience merely to like as much of it as pleases them. Playfully, she suggests that the play, and the pleasure, can be understood in more than one way when she asks that "between you and the women the play may please" "for the love you bear to women." And then comes that most magical moment of all, when Rosalind exposes the play's last and best "feigning" and admits the folly of her pretended womanhood: "If I were a woman I would kiss as many of you as had beards that pleased me, complexions that liked me, and breaths that I defied not." But she is not a woman, in spite of our belief in that most faining, a belief that has ripened almost into love by the magic of Shakespeare's conjuring. She is a boy actor who has been playing a woman playing a young man, and now she is a boy actor again. And so we must bid farewell to her false "case" with the rest of the dramatic illusions. This last piece of dramatic self-criticism is also the best. For it takes us right to the center of the folly and the wisdom of the imaginative contract between the audience and the play. Rosalind's final, literal stripping away of dramatic conventions confirms and celebrates the intricate conventionality of man, in love, in art, in society. Her profound foolishness, like Touchstone's, encourages us to understand how the rituals of any society may contain their most elusive truths. If they are sometimes the "most faining" it is because they are intricately allied to the least.

It is a paradox with Erasmian and Pauline precedent that characters like Bottom and Touchstone stumble forth in Shakespearean comedy to lead us to its profoundest truths. In *A Midsummer Night's Dream* the lovers are all mad, but they are also divinely mad. In *As You Like It* the lovers and the poet are all liars, but the audience is gladly fooled. In *The Praise of Folie* Erasmus cites St. Paul's authority when he reminds us that romantic dreamers and religious visionaries are "nere sybbe" in their madness and in their bliss. Harry Caplan suggests that like other Neoplatonists, Pico della Mirandola knows the possible folly of the imagination. But he also acknowledges its occasional necessity: "Higher faculties . . . cannot do without it; only let them guide it therefore, and it may act as the lens through which the intellect beholds the truth, it may prove to be the instrument of good prophesy, it may have part in the revelations of faith, and on it, as on wings, the mind may rise to contemplation of things divine."[12]

Touchstone has tried to tell us something like that in *As You Like It.* The lovers and the play itself are the imaginative pearls within the foul oysters of romantic and pastoral conventions. The audience is asked to share this humility by knowing how much it needs such feignings to understand such truths. But however we respond to the follies the play parades before us, we cannot criticize them condescendingly. For the play's aesthetic humility disarms that criticism by anticipating it, much as a character's ethical humility disarms the arsenal of the fool. Only the observer who must be condescending, like Jaques, remains immune to its festive happiness. And even Jaques is included in its wide-armed embrace of folly.

iii. The Folly of the Lovers

Touchstone's blundering philosophizing and Rosalind's epilogue leave little doubt that *As You Like It* is intensely interested in the realities that transcend the greatest feignings of fools, lovers, and artists. Man requires conventional rituals and roles to embody otherwise inexpressible feelings and truths, and to convey them to others.[13] But absurdity can result from an inadequate understanding of this conventionality. Touchstone is one extreme exemplar of such folly. He tries on as many roles as he has observed—lover, traveller, courtier, scholar, literary critic, philosopher, duellist, husband—but he can only be an insensitive parodist, a fool, a stone, in each of them. On the other extreme is the contemplative Jaques, who anatomizes but resists all roles. As a result he remains a mere observer of life, uninvolved in most of the follies and the joys of its earnest if foolish conventionality. He is even more a fool, as Rosalind tries to tell him, for this uninvolvement. But he recognizes his folly even less than Touchstone, and he would not change it.

Unlike Touchstone, the other characters, according to their capacities, reveal even while they experience it the complex truth which underlies their conventional feignings. The vision of *As You Like It* is not the satiric *Narrenschiff* Jaques might have presented but an affirmative celebration of man's follies and his potentialities. The widespread role playing that goes on among most of them heightens the positive, creative connections, between psychological and aesthetic conventions. And these connections, paradoxically, are highlighted by the character, Jaques, who seems to understand them least, during his cynical anatomy of the world as a stage. The others discover what he may never know, that all of the roles people (or artists) play can be creative as well as static, profound as well as foolish, and are often both at once. But when they work, these aesthetic or romantic conventions, these rituals and roles of artists and lovers, can lead to expressions and understandings of otherwise inaccessible truths. Their mutual feignings thus emerge from the comic vision of *As You Like It* as legitimate and essential ways to understand and cope with the humbling reality of man's finitude.

Orlando and Rosalind are the most realistic pair of characters in the play, but they engage us also as the most feigning. That their elaborately conventional behavior both edifies them and enriches their characterization illustrates how central the concept of "most

faining" is to the play's vision of the wisdom of folly. It is precisely because the emotions and impulses of love are so erratic, so powerful, and so confusing that love's seemingly foolish rituals and conventions, like those of art and religion, can serve such vital functions. Each of these feignings channels chaotic impulses into creative, acceptable, and comprehensible patterns, patterns which do not have to be rediscovered by each new lover, but which rather are the common legacy of all. Their gamelike, ritualized behavior in Arden thus frees Orlando and Rosalind from the stumbling, tongue-tied attempts at communication that they undergo at their first meeting. It simultaneously frees them from embarrassing frankness, from the "base truth" of their physical impulses, and from the threat of its direct, nonfigurative, sexual gratification. Orlando is given a voice by these formal and prescribed rituals and games, even if for a while it is a foolish voice. Rosalind as Ganymede is given a protective if foolish disguise against her lover and herself. Their feignings, their romantic rituals, are therefore true in many ways. They control their love, making it more formal than it really is—more orderly—giving it a prescribed, repeatable, and socially acceptable form of expression. They direct their intensely personal, even idiosyncratic emotion into a universalized form, which grants it dignity and importance. And they remind the lovers of their continuing folly while allowing them to express and refine their enduring love.

That they can embrace the folly of this feigning as well as its exhilarating joy attests to their unusual comic wisdom. It also points to their role in the play's analogous aesthetic vision. Like the play, and unlike Jaques, both Rosalind and Orlando are fully aware of their own folly and of the inescapable folly of love. Also like the play, as Mark Van Doren notices, both of them delight in that folly without ever becoming cynical about it.[14] J. D. Palmer has recently suggested that the lovers' unusual awareness of their own folly is connected to the play's theme of universal feigning: "There is a general agreement in the play that, as the song puts it, 'most loving is folly,' and accordingly Rosalind's counterfeit wooing is intended not merely to ridicule the foolishness of lovers, herself included, but to make it fully aware of itself in terms of a charade, a pretense, in which it is foolish to be wise."[15] Orlando "will chide no breather in the world but myself, against whom I know most faults" (III.ii.267-68). Rosalind knows that if "love is merely a madness . . . the lunacy is so ordinary that the whippers are in love too" (III.ii.376-80). They obviously share a joyous understanding that love, like faith, is a manner of madness. That understanding is surely related to Erasmian and Pauline paradoxes.

Orlando loves Rosalind at first sight, and he continues to love her throughout the whole play. The "heavenly Rosalind" of their first meeting is a faith from which he never substantially wavers, through all of the tests his love must encounter. But that first faith is strengthened by the conventional postures, the feignings, that both Orlando and Rosalind go on to assume. On their first meeting he can say nothing:

> Can I not say 'I thank you'? My better parts
> Are all thrown down, and that which here
>   stands up
> Is but a quintain, a mere lifeless block.
>
> (I.ii.230-32)

By the time he has reached Arden, he says far too much, in bad verses pasted upon every tree:

> O Rosalind! these trees shall be my books,
> And in their barks my thoughts I'll character.
>
> (III.ii.5-6)

But this howling, love-struck, tree-carving Petrarchan lover, like the earlier speechless one, will be laughed out of his excessive conventionality by the criticism of Touchstone and Jaques as well as Celia and Rosalind, so that by the beginning of Act IV he will have only a single line of blank verse: "Good day and happiness, dear Rosalind" (IV.i.27). This is still too much for Jaques, but it represents a considerable moderation in Orlando's excessively conventional and foolish behavior.

Orlando's sudden change into the humor of a Patrarchan lover continues to parody the play's literary heritage and its own conventionality. But it also reveals a momentary narcissism and a reluctance to grow up that Orlando must overcome. Like the antics of the gentlemen of *Love's Labor's Lost,* Orlando's false pose is too much surface and too little substance, therefore an impediment to both growth and self-expression. Orlando must learn that he can "live no longer by thinking" (V.ii.48), at least like this, too conventionally, in ways that obscure emotions and spirit rather than expressing them. Certainly the courtly pose is far less deeply ingrained in Orlando than it is in Berowne, and therefore more easily cured by Rosalind. But Orlando's immaculate dress, like his belief that a perfect woman loves him, must bother Rosalind; both excesses betray too much self-love, not just a conventional posture. Paradoxically, Rosalind's disguise, her feigning as Ganymede, functions to erode the false surface of Orlando's courtly humor and his narcissism at once, and thus frees him to love her more truly. This contrast between productive and unproductive folly, like the change finally effected in Orlando, is nicely opposed to Jaques's static anatomy of the seven ages of man. Man is not doomed to be the lover, though he may have to learn just how much of the lover to avoid and how much to keep by trying on the whole role briefly. Folly like Orlando's can free as well as enslave, especially if a Rosalind is around.

Much like his satiric counterpart, Silvius, Orlando is also something less than a man in his courtly pose. As Rosalind justly asks Celia of his versifying, "Is it a man?" Celia's answer, "And a chain that you once wore, about his neck" (III.ii.172), reminds us that Orlando is, indeed, a man, victorious over both Charles and Rosalind. But it also suggests distressing if amusing changes since then. Even before his effeminate and immature courtliness, Orlando's love of Rosalind seems to have cost him some manliness. If he has overthrown more than his enemies, he is also left somewhat impotent in Rosalind's presence after the wrestling:

> My better parts
> Are all thrown down, and that which here
>   stands up
> Is but a quintain, a mere lifeless block.
>
> (I.ii.230-32)

Silvius is similarly emasculated by Phebe's scorn. As Rosalind admonishes him, "Well, go your way to her, for I see love hath made thee a tame snake" (IV.iii.70-71). That both of them finally become better men through Rosalind's feigning intervention as a man, and that Rosalind and Phebe also become less masculine through the same contrivance suggest that Shakespeare is having a bit of fun with their androgynous relationships. A similar interest in shifting sexual roles in Rosalind's epilogue suggests its relationship to the whole play. Like the other roles and elements the play depicts and satirizes—fools, philosophers, the artistic form—so even the most basic human roles of male and female are never absolute. On the most basic physiological level of Touchstone's relationship to Audrey, the man needs the woman, the woman the man, for sexual satisfaction. In another sense, there is some yin and yang, some *res extensa* and some *res cogitans,* some dominance and some submissiveness, in all of us. Especially is this ambivalence true during adolescence, "as a squash is before 'tis a peascod, or a codling when 'tis almost an apple" (*Twelfth Night,* I.V.151-52). Having to court another man—an effeminate one at that, appropriately called "Ganymede"—is the perfect purgative to drive out Orlando's excessive courtliness and his immaturity, along with his sexual ambivalence. But neither Orlando nor Rosalind can reject all such ambivalence, or they would both become as simplistic as a Charles or an Audrey, a virtuous Adam or a villainous Frederick. The sorting out, the juggling, never completely end. One can never be completely male, or mature, or natural, without becoming as static as the frozen portraits of Jaques's ages. If such ambivalence, social or sexual, is embarrassing, it is also an inevitable folly of the maturing personality. Shakespeare has ingeniously woven these ideas into the roles and disguises in *As You Like It.*

Orlando's related conventional assumptions about "the beloved" are also moderated by the edification of

Rosalind-Ganymede, who has more than academic reasons for wanting to dispel his extremist expectations of his lover. Even Rosalind could never live up to his image of her perfection, and she would reject it if she could. For such a static posture of Platonic perfection is really no role at all for her; it is rather a non-role, another meaningless convention. Nor could Rosalind ever live with a rhapsodic sap who thinks that people die for love. So she tells Orlando, "Men have died from time to time, and worms have eaten them, but not for love" (IV.i.96-98). The stories to the contrary are "all lies," most feignings. Still, it must be pleasant and flattering for Rosalind to have a lover who momentarily believes in them, or one who would not be cured of his love except to prove his faith (III.ii.449). It is likewise both silly and exciting for her to find those verses everywhere. Orlando is proving himself a good Petrarchan lover and a good man even as he is being cured of the worst excesses of his tribe. And Rosalind, in spite of her own good taste, rather likes it.

Another important lesson for them both is the lesson of the horns that Benedick and Beatrice also grapple with in *Much Ado about Nothing*. No woman is perfect; many are quite imperfect. Orlando must at least acknowledge the possibility of imperfection in Rosalind before his edification is complete. Their love-game will dispel his excessively conventional faith in all women; but at the same time it will intensify his faith in one woman, Rosalind. We never seriously think, despite her warnings, that he will have any reason to repent this faith.

She begins her lesson during their first meeting in the forest. Women are "touched with so many giddy offenses" (III.ii.330) that they can hardly be recounted. Among them are many of the roles Rosalind-Ganymede will play in the courting game:

> changeable, longing and liking, proud, fantastical, apish, shallow, inconstant, full of tears, full of smiles; for every passion something and for no passion truly anything, as boys and women are for the most part cattle of this color; would now like him, now loathe him; then entertain him, then forswear him; now weep for him, then spit at him.

> (III.ii.385-91)

Of Rosalind's actual relationship to these roles we shall have more to say later, but we can see that their catalogue here is designed to disillusion the excessively trustful Petrarchan lover of his naive image of the beloved. She is likely to prove less than perfect, if better than this.

Specifically, she is likely to cuckold him. This threatening imperfection is the focus of Ganymede's assault on Orlando's continued faith in their next meeting.

The destiny of any husband is "horns; which such as you are fain to be beholding to your wives for" (IV.i.54-55). Orlando is sure to meet "your wife's wit going to your neighbor's bed" (IV.i.155). And he will find her ever changeable:

> Maids are May when they are maids, but the sky changes when they are wives. I will be more jealous of thee than a Barbary cock-pigeon over his hen, more clamorous than a parrot against rain, more newfangled than an ape, more giddy in my desires than a monkey. I will weep for nothing . . . when you are disposed to be merry; I will laugh like a hyen, . . . when thou art inclined to sleep.

> (IV.i.135-42)

In short, she might be jealous, henpecking, fashion-conscious, lecherous, opposite in all things—the perfect shrew. Of course she will not, but she could be any or all of these things at one time or another, and Orlando no less than Benedick must at least be aware of the possibilities to appreciate what he actually gets, and to be forewarned of what could be his. If Benedick fears too much of this, Orlando fears it too little, and Rosalind's game is an important corrective for his naiveté. The song of the foresters about horns (Act IV, Scene ii), the constant, blessed state of cuckoldry, is a conventional statement of the same truth about human imperfection.[16] Without that awareness, Orlando will never be ready to wed, for he will be unable to expect, let alone cherish, the imperfection that is his, hers, and everyone's.

Rosalind also becomes more worthy of love and more aware of herself as a result of the games that she plays with Orlando and the Petrarchan masks that she tries on. In fact, there is an extremely complex character behind the feignings of her role. Her disguise as Ganymede results from expediency, to be sure. It also betrays to a degree her own reluctance to mature and a decided enjoyment of controlling the action, of dominating events and people. She looks forward, for example, to playing a man:

> Were it not better,
> Because that I am more than common tall,
> That I did suit me all points like a man?
> A gallant curtal-axe upon my thigh,
> A boar-spear in my hand.

> (I.iii.111-15)

She has also promised Orlando that she will try to dominate him once they are wed. There is some truth in her role and her promise, and Orlando had better heed it.

The ritualized courting of Rosalind and Orlando, while certainly a game they both enjoy, grants her the proper courting she deserves as the daughter of the Duke. It also provides a civilized context she can control even though she is in Arden. For while they go through those conventional, even silly paces of boy courting boy, she is truly well-courted and Orlando well-trained in courting. Both are also thus protected from the potential folly of their unchecked passion. Further, as Rosalind enacts the conventions and rituals of the disdainful maiden—scorn, indifference, impatience, haughtiness, jealousy, spite, sarcasm, cynicism, and most of the others—she is doing more than parodying the conventional Petrarchan woman, though she is certainly doing that. She is also trying those postures on in a context in which she cannot be held accountable, much as the lovers in *A Midsummer Night's Dream* can behave madly, violently, and cruelly without personal blame because of Puck's magic potion. Rosalind is evaluating, like Orlando, the excessive postures of the courted woman, and approaching womanhood and the *via media* as a result of their game.

A good example of the complexity of her feigning occurs during her response to Orlando's verses. Though she can lament the lame feet and the tedious homily of his words as she plays the traditionally disdainful maid, she can also be secretly delighted that they are written to her. Thus Touchstone's assault on their "false gallop" and their "bad fruit" is aimed more at Rosalind's edification than at Orlando's: "If the cat will after kind, / So be sure will Rosalinde." Her kind, Touchstone is saying, is the nutty fool of love: "Sweetest nut hath sourest rind, / Such a nut is Rosalinde" (III.ii.98-99, 104-5). Her folly in loving the verses while she pretends to criticize them is especially clear when she tries lamely to defend them and herself against Touchstone's criticisms: "Out, fool! . . . Peace, you dull fool! I found them on a tree" (III.ii.94, 110). As the fool says of these attempts to avoid embarrassment, "You have said; but whether wisely or no, let the forest judge" (III.ii.116-17). This is one of his few chances to expose unacknowledged folly in the play, and he does it brilliantly. For the nuts who read and secretly love such bad verses are of the same kind as the nuts who write them. And "truly, the tree yields bad fruit" (III.ii.111). Though that is momentarily an embarrassing folly for Rosalind to bear, it is also a joyous one.

Its joy becomes obvious in her later exchange with Celia, which she begins by feigning indifference and scorn towards the poet. But after Rosalind's criticism of the tedious and lame verses ("I was never so berhymed since Pythagoras' time that I was an Irish rat, which I can hardly remember" (III.ii.168-69), she is soon beside herself to find out who wrote them, and to confirm her hope that it is Orlando:

> I prithee tell me who is it quickly, and speak apace.
> I would thou couldst stammer, that thou mightst
> pour this concealed man out of thy mouth. . . . Is

he of God's making? What manner of man? Is his head worth a hat? or his chin worth a beard?

> (III.ii.188-96 passim)

And then when it is confirmed, this recently and soon-again-to-be disdainful maiden sputters out her joy and her love in a foolish and delightful explosion of questions too many for Gargantua's mouth to answer:

> Alas the day! what shall I do with my doublet and hose? What did he when thou saw'st him? What said he? How looked he? Wherein went he? What makes he here? Did he ask for me? Where remains he? How parted he with thee? and when shalt thou see him again? Answer me in one word.

> (III.ii.208-13)

Because this delicious exuberance, this high folly, this near madness of her womanly love bursts quite through her feignings both as Ganymede and as the haughty mistress, we are never in any doubt that Rosalind is truer than Ganymede: "Good my complexion! Dost thou think, though I am caparisoned like a man, I have a doublet and hose in my disposition?" (III.ii.185-87). Fortunately for us and for Orlando, even her most feigning is never that true. Here, and when she faints at the sight of the handkerchief, the true folly of her great love is most manifest. The folly and the joy are both conveyed again just after this exchange by the continued images of nuts and fruits. Celia answers Rosalind, "I found him under a tree, like a dropped acorn." And though Rosalind can hardly have forgotten Touchstone's recent chiding, she has little doubt about the quality of the fruit this oak tree bears: "It may well be called Jove's tree when it drops forth such fruit" (III.ii.225-26). When she later says in the most horribly conventional Petrarchan style, "he comes to kill my heart," we see that Rosalind and Orlando are nuts of the same tree, and we smile and are delighted.

There are other brilliant glimpses of the true Rosalind through her feigning with Orlando, and we consistently see her womanhood better because she is playing the man. When, for example, she questions Orlando's lack of the proper symptoms of love, "lean cheek," sunken eye, "beard neglected," "shoe untied" and the rest (III.ii.352ff.), she is reciting romantic conventions that don't always represent reality. But she is also a bit distressed that Orlando does not conform more exactly with the textbook lover, and voices that distress through her feigning. She is still a little unsure of him; do those neat clothes suggest vestiges of narcissism? In a similar way her test of his faith is a real test as well as a game. She enjoys the excuse to be around Orlando, but she would also like to be as sure of his love as possible. Of course absolute surety is not vouchsafed to the true lovers in Shakespearean comedy. Hazard is a major ingredient of love's folly and its faith. And

Rosalind always has some sense of hazard, though Orlando is as sure a bet as Shakespeare will depict.

Rosalind's distrust, her fear of imperfection, surfaces more clearly when we see Rosalind-Ganymede again. She "will weep," even if "tears do not become a man," because Orlando is late. "His very hair is of the dissembling color" she says, and yet, "I'faith, his hair is of a good color." Celia chides her with more of the nut joke: "An excellent color. Your chestnut was ever the only color. . . . But why did he swear he would come this morning, and comes not?" A question to be asked. For Rosalind, no less than Orlando, must learn of her mate's possible imperfections as she tests his faith in her. Perhaps he is a "worm-eaten nut," without "verity in love" (III.iv.1-23 passim). As Celia says, you are a fool to believe in a brave young man, especially in Arden:

> O, that's a brave man; he writes brave verses, speaks
> brave words, swears brave oaths, and breaks them
> bravely, quite traverse, athwart the heart of his lover,
> as a puisny tilter, that spurs his horse but on one
> side, breaks his staff like a noble goose. But all's
> brave that youth mounts and folly guides.

> (III.iv.36-41)

But Rosalind chooses to be that fool, despite her doubts; so later does Celia with the tarnished but redeemed Oliver. Their choice of such folly represents a faith in more than feigning, and it is destined to end happily for both of them.

C. L. Barber comments best on this paradoxical lesson on their mutual fallibility that Orlando and Rosalind must both undergo:

> As Rosalind rides the crest of a wave of happy
> fulfillment, . . . we find her describing with delight,
> almost in triumph, not the virtues of marriage, but
> its fallibility. . . . Ordinarily, these would be strange
> sentiments to proclaim with joy at such a time. But
> as Rosalind says them, they clinch the achievement
> of the humor's purpose. Love has been made
> independent of illusions without becoming any the
> less intense; it is therefore inoculated against life's
> unromantic contradictions.[17]

That they can both learn so much of their folly and simultaneously strengthen their faith in one another through the charade Rosalind-Ganymede conjures for them in the forest is one of the great achievements of Shakespeare's art. It continues to draw strength from the Erasmian and Pauline paradoxes about faith and folly that lie behind it, even though those paradoxes are more deeply submerged than they were in *Love's Labor's Lost, A Midsummer Night's Dream,* or *Much Ado about Nothing.*

Rosalind's upbraiding of Orlando for being an hour late is also more than a mere feigning, though she quickly enough forgives him for his snail's pace. After all, he has only stood up a stand-in, and so he can hardly be blamed for making light of the transgression. Though we know better, this whole relationship seems to him a feigning pure and simple, and it is one that he will increasingly tire of. In the sequence that follows, Rosalind directs her own courting, and edifies Orlando as well as she can concerning the Petrarchan excesses he still exhibits, especially his naiveté about perfect women. Her playful feigning ends with another promise to meet in the forest. After Orlando's departure, she reminds us again of the true love that lies behind her feigned cynicism: "O coz, coz, coz, my pretty little coz, that thou didst know how many fathom deep I am in love!" (IV.i.189-90).

Then she almost destroys her cover by swooning over the bloody napkin (IV.iii.157). And Orlando finally does tire of the feigning: "I can live no longer by thinking" (V.ii.48). The conventions of lovers are supposed to free as well as restrict. Their rituals are supposed to allow the lovers to express inexpressible feelings, to perceive imperceivable truth, and to sense their communion with all past and future lovers. Like the conventions of religion or of art, the lovers' observances can make them larger than themselves, at least momentarily. But they are also feignings that are less than life, and finally their celebrants must return to the world of the body as well as the mind. For none of us can live forever by thinking, and least of all can lovers, unless they are of the hopelessly ethereal kind (like Orsino through most of *Twelfth Night*). Even he must finally see Viola in her woman's weeds, as must Orlando now in *As You Like It.* His feignings, like Rosalind's, were "most true"; but because of that they must finally be superseded by that elusive experience we like to call "real life." That return to the literal is also the thrust of Rosalind's epilogue. The fools have paradoxically deprived themselves of this joy by remaining oblivious to their own folly. The play has revelled in its absurd conventionality, and found there its "greatest poetry." The lovers, by embracing the follies of their feignings with an analogous joy, have evidenced the spiritual health they share with the play's attitude toward itself. They have also equipped themselves for the vicissitudes, as well as the joys, of life ever after. Their delicious balancing of play and seriousness, artifice and realism, folly and profundity, defines and emphasizes the atmosphere of humility in which the whole play must be understood.

Again, this strenuous comic vision demands an unusual degree of assent from the audience. Shakespeare and his audience must share a healthy sense of their mutual inabilities to express or understand the inexpressible and the inconceivable for the play to work fully. J. D. Palmer has already suggested that the self-conscious role-playing of the lovers and Shakespeare's playfulness with his art both involve the audience in "the equivocal relations between fiction and reality, game and earnest, folly and wisdom."[18] The blundering foolery of Touchstone and Jaques also contributes to this vision, especially when Touchstone discusses the "most faining" of artists and lovers. So, we will recall, did Bottom's Pauline allusions and the lovers' Erasmian ones as they awoke to a new wisdom in *A Midsummer Night's Dream*. Both plays, because they display an interest in the limits of human understanding and expression, would naturally have drawn upon and suggested such familiar and analogous Erasmian and Pauline paradoxes about foolish wits and wise fools.

iv. The Folly of the Liturgy

We have seen, through the folly of the fools, the lovers, and the play itself, how completely *As You Like It* investigates the realities that lie behind the conventions and rituals of human behavior and the aesthetic experience. We have suggested the epistemological dimensions of these interests and their Pauline and Erasmian contexts. But David Bevington, Jonas Barish, and Russell Fraser have also argued that the play touches, however obliquely, a heated Renaissance liturgical controversy. All three of them understand the play, partially, in terms of the contemporaneous Puritan-Anglican conflict between asceticism and artifice. To them, and to me, this widely fought controversy seems analogous to the distrust of artistic and psychological "feignings" we have found expressed so overtly and so ironically by Touchstone in the middle of *As You Like It*. We lack the numerous explicit allusions which invited us to pursue and understand the pertinence of another doctrinal controversy in *Love's Labor's Lost*. But in *As You Like It* a persistent interest in the ritualism that characterizes so much human activity, be it romantic or aesthetic, plus Touchstone's glance at a central issue of the controversy, the concept of "most faining," encourage us to pursue at least a few general parallels.

Fraser argues that the Puritans distrust the religious rituals and rites of the Anglican church (music, vestments, candles, crosses, genuflection, and the like) because they, like Touchstone, are unimaginative Platonists. They cannot see that these "most fainings" might be attempts to express or represent the "greatest poetry" of faith, as something "more than pure reason ever comprehends." To the Puritan mind any concrete representation of spiritual or abstract truth must be suspect because it feigns man's ability to perceive the ineffable.[19] David Bevington suggests how broadly such a dispute could have applied to the age and the play:

> Shakespeare insists . . . on the fallacy of oversimplifying the appeal to withdrawal, whether to courtly artifice or to ascetic plainness. . . . Man cannot turn his back on social rituals of legal contract, hierarchy, and divine worship. The

appearance of the outcast Orlando in the forest prompts Duke Senior to think not of society's ingratitude, but of their joint need for the dignified forms of civilization that must be reclaimed.[20]

And so the duke invites Orlando, and Old Adam too, to share their communal feast: "Sit down and feed, and welcome to our table" (II.vii.104). Such sharing reminds both of them of similar shared social rites and rituals in better times. Both Duke Senior and Orlando have

> with holy bell been knolled to church,
> And sat at good men's feasts, and wiped our eyes
> Of drops that sacred pity hath engend'red.
> (II.vii.121-23)

Barish takes this demonstration one important step further by showing that the distrusted religious ritual is often explicitly compared by the Puritan controversialists to the equally abhorred feignings of the stage:

> From Tyndale onward, through the writings of the anti-vestiarian polemicists, the controverters of the mass, the anti-episcopal satirists, the admonishers and apologists and animadverters, expounders of doctrine and compilers of cases of conscience, popish liturgy is scornfully likened to the theater, and much picturesque invective mustered to drive the point home. For Thomas Becon, the priests come to the altar like "game-players" to a stage, in "Hickscorners apparrell," in "gay, gawdie gallant, gorgious game-players garments." For the conciliatory Bishop Jewel, the "scenic apparatus of divine worship" is a "tawdry" thing which Christians should be able to do without; the sacraments should cease to be ministered "like a masquery or a stage play." For John Foxe, the decay of the primitive church meant that Christ's true votaries were supplanted by "a new sort of players, to furnish the stage, as school-doctors, canonists, and four orders of friars." Ridley informed his superiors that the prescribed ministering garments were "abhominable and foolishe, & to fonde for a vice in a playe," and when Hooper, in 1551, to the disgust of the zealous, consented to preach in them, he was said to have come forth "as a new player in a strange apparel . . . cometh forth on the stage." . . . And John Rainolds, inveighing against the stage, finds room for particular censure of "the profane and wicked toyes of *Passion-plays*, . . . procured by *Popish Priests*," who, "as they have transformed the celebrating of the Sacrament of the *Lords supper* into a *Masse-game,* and all other partes of the *Ecclesiasticall service* into *theatricall sights;* so, in steede of *preaching the word,* they caused it to be played."[21]

His vivid details illustrate both the customary outrage of the Puritan controversialists and their repeatedly pejorative references to the "playing," the feigning rituals, the games that mar the pure worship of God. In this contemporaneous play that is persistently interested in both the truth and the folly that underlies the "playing" of lovers and artists, Touchstone talks to Audrey about the feignings of both groups, and tells her that "the greatest poetry is the most faining." And Jaques tells us in a set-piece that "all the world's a stage." Such interests at a moment when drama as well as ritual was under severe Puritan attack suggest intriguing if elusive parallels between the play and the controversy. Speaking of such parallels, Fraser sees *As You Like It* only as a "bucolic lament for an age already and irremediably past."[22] But Bevington finds the play tactfully committed to the preservation and defense of many "social rituals." The play argues through being rather than through rhetoric that a man, like a work of art, needs psychological, social, political, legal, and religious rituals if he is to remain fully a man, and fully civilized.[23] I am persuaded by his argument and by the argument of the play that Bevington is correct. If he is, the religious dimensions of Shakespeare's treatment of faith and folly in *As You Like It* would have been all the more visible for his audience.

A discussion of general relationships between art and liturgy by Romano Guardini in *The Spirit of the Liturgy* suggests in conclusion how natural it would be for a play like *As You Like It* to reflect issues of the liturgical discussion through the paradox of the wisdom of folly. Appropriately, his discussion begins with the intuitive wisdom of the child. Child-play at its spontaneous, affirmative best is analogous to art or ritual, but precedes them both in time. It is a type of prelapsarian art or ritual, "purposeless but full of meaning nevertheless." "Because it does not aim at anything in particular, because it streams unbroken and spontaneously forth, its utterance will be harmonious, its form clear and fine; its expression will of itself become picture and dance, rhyme, melody and song. That is what play means; it is life, pouring itself forth without an aim, seizing upon riches from its own abundant store, significant through the fact of its existence" (p. 179). Art and liturgy, to Guardini, must try to recreate this intuitive wisdom of the child. To do so they would both teach profound truths indirectly rather than directly, by "being," in Bevington's term. They would immerse the audience, like the child at play, in the aura of truth itself: "The liturgy wishes to teach, but not by means of an artificial system of aim-conscious educational influences; it simply creates an entire spiritual world in which the soul can live according to the requirements of its nature. . . . [Like art] it is not a means which is adapted to attain a certain end—it is an end in itself" (p. 177).

But art, finally, can only attempt to represent "the higher life of which [man] stands in need, and to which in actuality he has only approximately attained. The artist

merely wants . . . to give external form to the inner truth." The liturgy, though it uses many of the forms and methods of art, can actually re-create something of the lost wisdom of the child:

> In it man, with the aid of grace, is given the opportunity of realizing his fundamental essence, of really becoming that which according to divine destiny he should be . . . a child of God. . . . Because the life of the liturgy is higher than that to which customary reality gives both the opportunity and form of expression, it adopts suitable forms and methods from that sphere in which they are to be found, . . . from art. It speaks measuredly and melodiously; it employs formal, rhythmic gestures; it is clothed in colours and garments foreign to everyday life; it is carried out in places and at hours which have been coordinated and systemised according to sublimer laws than ours. It is in the highest sense the life of a child, in which everything is picture, melody and song.

> Such is the wonderful fact which the liturgy demonstrates; it unites art and reality in a supernatural childhood before God.

(Pp. 180-81)

This analysis of the relationships between art and liturgy inevitably brings to mind the vision of both of Shakespeare's epistemologically oriented comedies, *A Midsummer Night's Dream* and *As You Like It*. What Mircea Eliade has said of religious symbols is equally true of the feignings of these two plays: "They unveil the miraculous, inexplicable side of life, and at the same time the sacramental dimensions of human existence."[24] Hymen is as useful in the latter as the fairies are in the former in representing this miraculous dimension of human experience. Bottom and Touchstone help us understand our epistemological folly in relationship to it. For man's imagination can be as erratic and as undisciplined as his behavior, as Pico, Erasmus, and St. Paul all suggest.[25] But that imagination, for all its madness, is also partly divine. Through this faculty man can contemplate the transcendental, and devise liturgical and artistic rituals to aid that contemplation. In such a context Jaques's "all the world's a stage," and Touchstone's "the truest poetry is the most faining," like Bottom's "most rare vision," are as relevant as they are naive. If they are obviously foolish as they grope toward these profoundest awarenesses, so are we all most foolish when we attempt to transcend our own finitude. At such moments our epistemological kinship to these Erasmian fools is almost inescapable.

A recent critic of relationships between comedy and Christianity, Nelvin Vos, reminds us how traditional and how timeless this Erasmian and Pauline identification of such folly and such wisdom really is. He asserts that comedy has always combined the incarnational view of man (only human) with the eschatological one (more than human). We laugh both at and with the comic victor/victim because he is "the image of dignity intermingled with frailty." He both unmasks "the incongruous involvement of the finite and the infinite" and also affirms it. In so doing, the fool—the Touchstone and the Jaques, the Feste, the Falstaff, the Bottom—helps us see "that the grossly human and the grandly sublime" are "wonderfully and repugnantly mixed" within us.[26] The wisdom of such folly is not the whole truth of *As You Like It*. But it is an important part of that truth. We have ignored the play's Erasmian Touchstones long enough.

Notes

[1] See ch. 1, pp. 9-15; ch. 3, pp. 53-63.

[2] Richard Hooker, for example, devotes an entire book of his *Laws of Ecclesiastical Polity* (Book 4) to this topic. See Davies, *Worship and Theology in England,* chs. 1-3; and George and George, *The Protestant Mind of the English Reformation,* pp. 348-63, on the importance of this controversy.

[3] Agnes Latham, among many others, notices this unusual humility in the green world in her introduction to *As You Like It*. She attributes it to the forest's magic (pp. lxx-lxxi), but banishment is itself humiliating enough to have achieved some natural magic among the foresters. Surprisingly little has been made of the important effects of this humility on the fools.

[4] Morris Palmer Tilley cites 128 proverbs concerning fools and folly. That none of them contains this Pauline and Erasmian paradox illustrates its unique biblical context. See *A Dictionary of the Proverbs in England* (Ann Arbor: University of Michigan Press, 1950), pp. 226-34.

[5] See Barber, *Shakespeare's Festive Comedy,* pp. 233-39; Kreider, "Genial Literary Satire," p. 222; Peter G. Phialas, *Shakespeare's Romantic Comedies,* pp. 219, 254; Brown, *Shakespeare and His Comedies,* pp. 145-50; T. M. Parrott, *Shakespearean Comedy,* p. 168; and Sylvan Barnet, "Strange Events: Improbability in *As You Like It*," p. 120.

[6] Plato *Republic* Book 10, 598e, 605b, trans. Paul Shorey, Loeb Classical Library.

[7] Sir Philip Sidney, *An Apology for Poetry,* in *Criticism: The Major Texts,* ed. Walter Jackson Bate (New York: Harcourt, Brace & World, 1952), p. 97.

[8] D. J. Palmer has written two excellent articles on this theme in *As You Like It:* "Art and Nature in *As You Like It*," and "*As You Like It* and the Idea of Play."

[9] Nowell, *A Catechism,* pp. 142, 191.

[10]
> PHEBE. Good shepherd, tell this youth what 'tis
>   to love.
> SILVIUS. It is to be all made of sighs and tears;
> And so am I for Phebe.
> PHEBE. And I for Ganymede.
> ORLANDO. And I for Rosalind.
> ROSALIND. And I for no woman.
> SILVIUS. It is to be all made of faith and
>   service;
> And so am I for Phebe.
> PHEBE. And I for Ganymede.
> ORLANDO. And I for Rosalind.
> ROSALIND. And I for no woman.
> SILVIUS. It is to be all made of fantasy,
> All made of passion, and all made of wishes,
> All adoration, duty, and observance,
> All humbleness, all patience, and impatience,
> All purity, all trial, all observance;
> And so am I for Phebe.
> PHEBE. And so am I for Ganymede.
> ORLANDO. And so am I for Rosalind.
> ROSALIND. And so am I for no woman.
>   (V.ii.78-97)

[11] G. Wilson Knight, *The Burning Oracle*, p. 21, intuits this metaphoric phenomenon when he suggests that dramatic action becomes sacramental when the audience participates in it.

[12] Pico della Mirandola, *On the Imagination*, p. 6.

[13] Although many critics mention role-playing as a motif in *As You Like It,* few consider it as central as I do. See especially Palmer, "Idea of Play," pp. 237-38. For other prominent statements see Bradbrook, *Shakespeare and Elizabethan Poetry,* p. 220; Kreider, "Genial Literary Satire," p. 212.

[14] Mark Van Doren, *Shakespeare,* pp. 127-35.

[15] Palmer, "Art and Nature," p. 38.

[16] Peter J. Seng, "The Forester's Song in *As You Like It*," p. 249.

[17] Barber, *Shakespeare's Festive Comedy,* p. 236.

[18] Palmer, "Idea of Play," p. 235.

[19] Fraser, *The War against Poetry,* pp. 40-44.

[20] Bevington, *Tudor Drama and Politics,* p. 298.

[21] Jonas A. Barish, "Exhibitionism and the Antitheatrical Prejudice," pp. 6-7.

[22] Fraser, *The War against Poetry,* p. 79.

[23] Bevington, *Tudor Drama and Politics,* p. 302. Jackson Cope's *The Theater and the Dream,* pp. 172-218, also comments on connections between drama and liturgy. He suggests that *As You Like It,* like Thomas Heywood's *Apology for Actors* (1612), defends theatrical illusion through the use of the theological topos of the theater of the world (pp. 173-74).

[24] Mircea Eliade, "Methodological Remarks on the Study of Religious Symbolism," in *The History of Religions,* p. 98.

[25] For Erasmian and Pauline statements, see chs. 1 and 3. See Pico della Mirandola, *On the Imagination,* pp. 5-6.

[26] Vos, *The Drama of Comedy,* p. 114.

Donn Ervin Taylor (essay date 1982)

SOURCE: " 'Try in Time in Despite of a Fall': Time and Occasion in *As You Like It,*" in *Texas Studies in Literature and Language,* Vol. XXIV, No. 2, Summer, 1982, pp. 121-36.

[*In the following essay, Taylor argues that rather than presenting contradictory descriptions of time-typified by the timelessness of the forest and the time consciousness of court—*As You Like It *evinces a unified vision of time as the seizing of fortune and occasion.*]

One of the more provocative interpretive problems of *As You Like It* is presented by the coexistence of two obvious but apparently contradictory facts. Under normal standards of rhetorical emphasis, the frequency with which time and the effects of time are mentioned throughout the play attests that time is one of the play's fundamental concerns, and thus that understanding the dramatist's vision of time is essential to interpreting the play. At the same time, however, the contradictory descriptions of time voiced by different characters at various points in the play make it extremely difficult for the modern audience to determine just what the dramatist's vision of time may be.

Indeed, recent inquiries into this problem have held that Shakespeare portrayed not one view of time, but two: that a relationship of unresolved contrast, perhaps of dialectic, exists between the threatening time associated with Duke Frederick's court and a strangely benevolent time found in the Forest of Arden. Accepting at face value Orlando's statement that "there's no clock in the forest,"[1] Jay L. Halio has argued that "Shakespeare throughout the play contrasts the timelessness of the forest world with the time-ridden preoccupations of court and city life," concluding that the forest is "the repository of natural life devoid of artificial time barriers."[2] More recently, Rawdon Wilson

has described the problem in Aristotelian terms, holding that an "internal dialectic . . . arises from the constant play between the objectivity of time (as the correlation of motion) and its relativity (as the correlation of a knowing mind)."[3] Wilson holds that the chief characters' perception of the objective, threatening time of Frederick's court undergoes gradual change to "a sense of interior time which becomes possible in Arden" and which "can exist, as a particular reflection of consciousness, only when objective time loses its importance and is no longer marked."[4]

I should like to argue that, on the contrary, *the dramatist* consistently envisions time as a phenomenon which exists objectively, independent of the individual characters' perception of it and independent of the place in which it is perceived, whether court or Forest of Arden. This vision becomes more apparent when primary attention is focused on the dramatic structures of the play, especially emblematic elements, and when the conflicting opinions of time expressed during the play are understood in terms of the pronounced changes of viewpoint which the chief characters experience during their stay in Arden.

This last consideration is particularly important, for recent interpretations have emphasized the chief characters' growth toward maturity in attitude and understanding during their passage through the forest. Albert R. Cirillo, for example, explains that those who enter Arden "emerge with a new perspective on life,"[5] and Helen Gardner views Arden as "a place of discovery . . . where each man finds himself and his true way."[6] In Arden, through experiences which critics have described variously as "encounters,"[7] confrontations with self[8] or "feignings," "disguisings," and "trial and error,"[9] youth grow to achieve understanding of themselves and their relationship to the world around them. This process of growth, with its attendant changes in viewpoint, is so pervasive in *As You Like It* that it must be considered in interpreting any part of the play. As we shall see particularly with Orlando, part of each character's growth to maturity involves discovery of his relationship to time, and his opinion of time at any given point reflects his state of growth. It is thus necessary to describe each character's progress through the growth process before his opinions of time can be properly interpreted, and for this reason it is best to approach the subject of time through dramatic structures.

The subject of time is introduced emblematically in the play's second scene through Rosalind's and Celia's conversation about the goddess Fortune. Fortune's bestowal of material rewards on her favorites is much in evidence in *As You Like It,*[10] but the present discussion is more concerned with her temporal attributes. The associations of Fortune with which the Elizabethan audience was familiar had been transmitted through a long tradition of the visual arts in which Fortune's attributes as bearer of rewards had become merged with those of *Occasio,* or Occasion, the bringer of opportunity, forming the composite figure which Howard R. Patch has termed the "Fortune of Time."[11]

This merging process has been described extensively in studies by Patch, Erwin Panofsky, and Samuel C. Chew.[12] According to Panofsky, the concept of the opportune moment which we now know chiefly as Occasio was in the ancient world represented by Kairos, a young male figure who carried the scales of decision balanced on the edge of a shaving knife, and whose momentary or fleeting character was portrayed by the wings on his heels and shoulders. In somewhat later representations, Kairos stood on a wheel, or two wheels, and (as Panofsky tells us) "his head often showed the proverbial forelock by which bald-headed Opportunity can be seized."[13] Shortly after the eleventh century, the image of Kairos merged with the feminine image of Fortune to become the "Fortune of Time."[14] Panofsky suggests that the impulse toward fusion was aided by the fact that Occasio, the Latin name for Kairos, was feminine in gender and thus led toward a feminine visual representation. The merger must also have been aided by the inherent similarity of the two concepts, for Fortune's notorious inconstancy is a function of time, while Occasio's fortunate moment brings the opportunity for good Fortune. But by whatever process of reasoning or association, the attributes of the two did become merged. Referring to this composite figure as "Fortune, standing for Occasio," Patch explains that because of the merged attributes "Fortuna is goddess of time in general and deity of the lucky moment."[15]

This merging of attributes may be observed visually in an emblem by Florentius Schoonhovius in which the goddess displays the prominent forelock of Occasio, yet identifies herself specifically as Fortune: *"Audentes Fortuna juvo"* ("I, Fortune, assist the daring"). The same merging is revealed by different means in a 1574 French language edition of Alciati's *Emblemata.* The emblem portraying the opportune moment is properly entitled Occasio, but as the heading at the top of the page indicates, Occasio is presented in a section entitled *FORTVNA.* And in the same manner, Vincenzo Cartari discusses Occasio under the heading *FORTVNA* in his mythological manual *Imagines Deorum,*[16] which was well known to the London literary world for which Shakespeare wrote.

Shakespeare's own use of this tradition of merged attributes is attested by a passage from *Julius Caesar,* a play nearly contemporaneous with *As You Like It.* The passage in question is the famous speech of Brutus:

> There is a tide in the affairs of men,
> Which, taken at the flood, leads on to fortune;

> Omitted, all the voyage of their life
> Is bound in shallows and in miseries.
>
>   (IV, iii, 218-21)

This speech assuredly describes the arrival of the fortunate moment, and the fact that only Fortune is named reflects the interchangeability of the two goddesses in the mind of the dramatist and, apparently, in the minds of the public for whom he was writing.

Similarly, the allusions by Rosalind and Celia to "the good housewife Fortune" in the second scene of the play (I, ii, 34) would have evoked for the Elizabethan audience associations of time and Occasion, and these temporal associations would have been reinforced before the end of the scene by the arrival of the fortunate but ethically critical moment in which Rosalind meets Orlando[17] and, more important, by Orlando's seizure of Occasion through his defeat of the churlish wrestler Charles. The wrestling match, of course, is the critical action which precipitates virtually all of the later actions in the play. Indeed, one of the prominent dramatic structures of the play is the succession of critical moments presented to the chief characters both before and during their passage through Arden, so that time threatens all the characters throughout the play, regardless of whether they are in court or in the forest. Most of the characters seize their Occasion, complete their growth to maturity, and are joined in good Fortune through the multiple marriage which concludes the play. But even in the seemingly benign environment of Arden, there exists the serious possibility that one may let his Occasion slip, and this potential for mis-Fortune is dramatized through such characters as the melancholy Jaques and the phlegmatic William.[18]

Although William is a minor character, his experience argues with particular eloquence against the existence of a special, nonthreatening time in Arden. William tells us that he was born in the forest (V, i, 24-25), but neither his origin nor his continued presence in the forest protects him from the loss of Audrey. Touchstone exclaims, "We shall find a time, Audrey" (V, i, 1). He and Audrey seize their Occasion, and William is dismissed: one may "lose his time" as easily in Arden as in Duke Frederick's court.

After its introduction through allusions to Fortune, the threat of time is reinforced by frequent references to time and its effects, and some of these references contain multiple meanings which link the narrative and symbolic levels of the play. An exchange of this kind occurs between Celia and Rosalind soon after Orlando's victory over Charles:

> *Celia*: Come, come, wrestle with thy
>   affections.
> *Rosalind*: O, they take the part of a better
>   wrestler than myself!

Celia: O, a good wish upon you! you will try
　　in time in despite of a fall.

　　　　　　　　　　　　(I, iii, 21-25)

As Richard Knowles has shown, Celia's first comment aids in allegorizing a traditional Renaissance theme, the conquest of the passions by the intellect.[19] Her second comment serves as the juncture of several meanings. First, it creates humor by conjoining the disparate acts of wrestling and loving. Through two senses of the word *try*—the senses of struggling and acting (or standing) in legal judgment—Celia states the condition of all men in their search for Occasion. At the same time, she evokes the Fall of Man, which was first suggested by the presence of an old man named Adam in the play's opening scene, so that through the shadow of the archetypal fall, the situation of Rosalind (and of mankind) becomes resonant with associations of love, sin, death, and man's inability to recover any potential for good—any Occasion—which he has let slip. In the same lines, the values of Adam's antique world are presented in implied contrast to the corrupt standards of Duke Frederick's court. And almost immediately after Celia's speech, Duke Frederick banishes Rosalind, underscoring the dramatist's vision of threatening time with the warning, "If you outstay the time . . . you die" (I, iii, 90-91).

The threat of time is further developed through Jaques's report of the scene in which Touchstone "rail'd on Lady Fortune" in the forest. The fool's vision of time is simplicity itself:

'Tis but an hour ago since it was nine,
And after one hour more 'twill be eleven;
And so, from hour to hour, we ripe and ripe,
And then, from hour to hour, we rot and rot.
　　　　　　　　　　　　(II, vii, 24-27)

This knowledge is, of course, quite literally what *any* fool knows, and it is amusing primarily because it omits the one fact that man must know in order to seize his Occasion, namely, the moment when time is fully ripe. Ironically, Jaques wastes an hour laughing at Touchstone (II, vii, 32-33), quite unaware that he continues to miss his own Occasion.

Touchstone's metaphor of growth to ripeness is used frequently during the play to reflect the proximity of Occasion. In the first such usage, the fool's directly sexual parody of Orlando's Platonic-Petrarchan love poetry provokes Rosalind's response, "You'll be rotten ere you be half ripe" (III, ii, 125). The second usage occurs in the Touchstone-Jaques encounter discussed above. Just before the account of his battle with the lioness, Orlando (through Oliver) portrays Rosalind's approach to Occasion by describing Ganymede as one who "bestows himself / Like a ripe sister" (IV, iii, 87-88). The metaphor receives its final

statement when Touchstone refers to William's twenty-five years as "a ripe age" (V, i, 22). William's unharvested ripeness represents an opportunity not taken, and he is banished from the possibility of love. In a similar metaphor, Celia and Rosalind describe Orlando as an acorn, a fruit dropped from Jove's tree (III, ii, 248-50), thus implying his growth toward mature status as an oak.

The threat of time is further developed by Orlando's love poetry, in which he claims for Rosalind "the touches dearest prized" from women renowned as patterns of feminine beauty. Rosalind's qualities include "Helen's cheek, but not her heart, / Cleopatra's majesty, / Atalanta's better part, / Sad Lucretia's modesty" (III, ii, 153-56). But these allusions convey more than conventional praise of the heroine's personal qualities, for their comparison of Rosalind to persons famous for suffering tragic ends implies the possibility of such an end for Rosalind.

And as these allusions suggest possibilities of misFortune for Rosalind, a second allusion to Atalanta suggests similar possibilities for Orlando. Atalanta's downfall began when she turned from her footrace to pursue three golden balls rolled across her path by Hippomenes, her would-be lover. This delay cost her both the race and the freedom of her maiden state, and it began the series of events which ended in her transformation into a beast.[20] The allusion linking Atalanta and Orlando occurs early in Orlando's development in the forest when the young lover rejects the melancholy company of Jaques. As Harold Jenkins and Peter G. Phialas have pointed out, this incident is significantly placed just before the first of the play's two major love scenes.[21] When Orlando deftly resists the old gentleman's attempts to detain him, Jaques remarks, "You have a nimble wit: I think 'twas made of Atalanta's heels. Will you sit down with me? and we two will rail against our mistress the world and all our misery" (III, ii, 292-95). The allusion seems to imply that tarrying to rail against misery would equate to Atalanta's turning from her goal. But Orlando does not let his Occasion slip: Signior Love dismisses Monsieur Melancholy and moves directly to his first forest-encounter with Rosalind.

Jaques, of course, has his own view of time, and it might be observed that one of his chief occupations in the play is delaying the completion of love. Ironically, delay is appropriate when he dissuades Touchstone from the fool's first attempt to marry Audrey (III, iii), for this delay prevents Touchstone's seizure of an unripe time. The fool is thus saved for the proper Occasion of the play's final scene, so that many varieties of love rather than his variety alone can simultaneously be joined in marriage. But Jaques's other attempts at delay would, if successful, prevent the seizure of Occasion. Having failed to delay Orlando, Jaques tries with equal lack of success to delay Rosalind (IV, i), and even as the couples gather for the multiple marriage, he delays Touchstone with a discussion of dueling, nearly the opposite of love (V, iv).

Jaques's view of time is in fact diametrically opposed to Orlando's view that "there's no clock in the forest." If Orlando speaks of immunity to time, Jaques in his Seven Ages of Man speech holds that time, not man, determines what man shall be, for in this melancholy vision there is no Occasion to be seized. In Jaques's view, infant gives way to schoolboy, and schoolboy is followed inexorably by lover, soldier, justice, shrinking old age, and, finally, complete incapacity "Sans teeth, sans eyes, sans taste, sans everything" (II, vii, 166). However, Jaques's speech is followed immediately by the scene in which the aged Adam receives in lavish quantity the love, care, and honor which hold no place in the melancholy outsider's scheme of things, and recent interpreters have tended to agree that the dramatist's juxtaposition of the two scenes signals his intention to refute Jaques.[22]

But if the dramatist rejects Jaques's extreme view of time, he also signals his rejection of the opposite extreme expressed by Orlando. And since Orlando is the chief exponent of Arden's timelessness, the development of his perception of time makes an excellent case study. Orlando begins as an unnurtured but naturally gifted youth and develops by Act V into a knowledgeable and confident young man who fully merits the "potent Dukedom" which is then announced as his heritage. But his development is by no means steady, for it contains several instances of regression. The play's opening scene reveals Orlando's sense of approaching crisis, and his seizure of Occasion through the defeat of Charles is the central event of the play's first two acts. But the time-conscious Orlando of these early scenes has begun to suffer the illusion of timelessness when, soon after his withdrawal to Arden, he describes Duke Senior's courtiers as men who "Lose and neglect the creeping hours of time" (II, vii, 112). As he is wrong in attributing savagery to these courtiers, he is also wrong in his perception of their relationship to time; and soon after this encounter, he begins to "fleet the time carelessly" in the manner which Charles had somewhat earlier attributed to the young men of Arden.[23]

This time-careless Orlando comes into conflict with a time-conscious Rosalind. Rosalind asks, "What is't o'clock?" (III, ii, 317), and he responds with his often quoted remark that "there's no clock in the forest" (III, ii, 318-19). Ironically, this exchange occurs immediately after the critical moment in which Orlando correctly used time by rejecting Jaques's invitation to tarry and rail against Fortune. Orlando's claim of timelessness prompts Rosalind's catalog of varied perceptions of time by people in differing situations, ending with

the sleeping lawyer who perceives no movement of time at all. Rosalind understands that one's *perception* of time does not slow the *actual passage* of time. Indeed, an important part of the courtship game between Orlando and Rosalind/Ganymede is devoted to the heroine's attempts to change her lover's view of time. Rosalind chides Orlando for his late arrival, while he feels it sufficient to come within an hour of his promise (IV, i, 42). When Orlando consents to the mock marriage, it is Rosalind who demands, "Ay, but when?" (IV, i, 133). And, echoing Celia's earlier reference to trial by time, Rosalind charges her lover to be on time for their next meeting: "Time is the old justice that examines such offenders, and let time try" (IV, i, 203-04).

Orlando's growth to maturity—including the development of his perception of time—appears to climax with his victory over the lioness. Although this scene has received several conflicting interpretations, virtually complete agreement exists that the lioness incident is the climactic event of the play, the decisive turning point which marks the beginning of the denouement.[24] This interpretive consensus is reinforced by the fact that the indecisive, time-careless Orlando who entered the battle emerges with the quiet confidence of a man who has attained maturity and self-knowledge. This newly confident Orlando, now more time-conscious than Rosalind, ends their inconclusive love-game with the temporally oriented statement, "I can live no longer by thinking" (V, ii, 55), and it is through ending the game that he again seizes Occasion by the forelock. Viewed in the overall context of the play, then, Orlando's belief in Arden's timelessness is merely an illusion held briefly during his passage through Arden and then abandoned as he achieves self-knowledge and maturity.

During the denouement which follows Orlando's victory, the dramatist's vision of threatening time is confirmed by the juxtaposition of dramatic actions and by the fact that no other view of time finds expression in the final act. The denouement is organized around a motif of convergence, a movement from the dissonance of the conflicting impulses which result from imperfect self-knowledge toward the individual and societal concord imaged by the multiple marriage of the final scene. In the scene immediately following Orlando's victory, Touchstone signals the movement toward Occasion with the double-edged remark, "We shall find a time, Audrey" (V, i, 1). He promptly banishes the ripe but phlegmatic William, who knows neither himself nor the passing of his Occasion. The next scene presents Oliver's and Celia's seizure of opportunity and Orlando's ending of the love game. Rosalind then arranges the multiple marriage, and her arrangements are followed immediately by the song which celebrates a lover and his lass who "take the present time" (V, iii, 31). Ironically, Touchstone fails to perceive the song's relevance to his own situation. The fool's conversation with the First Page reflects a marked difference in their range of vision, for Touchstone speaks only of the song, while the page speaks of the cosmic principle which the song celebrates.

> *Touchstone*: . . . though there was no great matter in the ditty, yet the note was very untuneable.
>
> *First Page*: You are deceived, sir: *we kept time, we lost not our time.*
>
> *Touchstone*: By my troth, yes; I count it but time lost to hear such a foolish song.
>
>   (V, iii, 35-41; emphases added.)

The irony of this exchange is deepened when Touchstone goes directly from this encounter to the marriage in which he not only achieves his victory over time but (with Audrey) acts out the very song whose relevance he has just denied. In the final scene, the movement to convergence is completed by the marriage in which eight of the central characters are shown to have "lost not our time," and immediately afterward the audience learns the fate of Duke Frederick and Jaques, the chief characters who did lose theirs. Thus, the design and emphasis of the play's denouement confirm the vision of threatening time introduced in Act I through the temporal connotations of the goddess Fortune.

In addition to establishing the consistency of the dramatist's portrayal of time, the preceding discussion should remind us just how pervasive the imaging of time is in *As You Like It*. As suggested earlier, time is certainly one of the play's fundamental concerns, and it is appropriate at this point to ask how the dramatist's portrayal of time should influence our understanding of the play. The chief effect of this portrayal is to require reexamination and redefinition of the nature of Arden. The knowledge that time's threat is present even in the idyllic world of the forest requires us to approach that world with much greater seriousness, and because of this seriousness we must view the play's fictional events and the individual characters' responses in a significantly different way. The threat of time, held constantly before the minds of the audience, provides a consistent background of cosmic reality against which the drama's moving pageant of human striving is to be viewed. The dramatic character may believe that in Arden he has world enough and time, but at his back the audience is always to hear the inexorable movement of time's winged chariot. And although we may wish to perceive Arden as a place "where each man finds himself and his true way," the background of threatening time and the examples of those characters who have "lost their time" remind us that not all who seek in Arden are destined to find. Shakespeare's Arden is not *necessarily* a place of discovery, but it *is* neces-

sarily a place of struggle. It is that liminal place where each man must strive to achieve mature understanding of himself and the world around him before the arrival of some fated moment whose approach is unknown to him during the course of his striving; it is a place where each man must as a descendant of Adam "try in time in despite of a fall."

But although Shakespeare holds this potentially tragic aspect of the human condition constantly before his audience, he does not allow it to dominate their response to the play. During the course of the play, the audience is made aware of many dire possibilities, but is not permitted to become overly concerned about them. With carefully modulated emphasis and balance, the dramatist has insured that the play's darker potential be *intellected* rather than *felt,* so that the tone and feeling of comedy predominate in governing the audience's response. And, most decisively, he has chosen to shape his potentially tragic materials into a comic resolution. As we have seen, the final act of *As You Like It* celebrates the chief characters' seizure of Occasion, and this comic resolution signals that in this play the dramatist's statement of man's relationship to time is one of qualified optimism. During the state of imperfect perception which youth experiences near the beginning of its passage through the forest, Orlando and Charles's young gentlemen may experience an illusion of freedom from the demands of time, and a person like Jaques, who has "lost his time" and is unable to come out of the forest, may experience the opposite illusion that man is the slave of time. But through the contrast afforded by these extreme views, Shakespeare brings his audience into contact with a more viable position of compromise: man is neither exempt from time nor is he, as Jaques would have it, a helpless victim. Although subject to the vicissitudes of Fortune, a man possessing the natural gifts of Orlando can complete his passage through Arden to the self-knowledge of mature manhood, can cooperate with time, can seize his Occasion by the forelock, and can claim both his bride and his rightful inheritance of "a land itself at large, a potent Dukedom."

Notes

[1] *As You Like It,* III, ii, 318-19. The edition used is *The Complete Works of Shakespeare,* ed. Hardin Craig and David Bevington, rev. ed. (Glenview, Ill.: Scott, Foresman, 1973). All references are to this edition and are hereafter given parenthetically following the citation.

[2] Jay L. Halio, "'No Clock in the Forest': Time in *As You Like It,"* *Studies in English Literature,* 2 (1962), 204, 207. Thomas Kelly, "Shakespeare's Romantic Heroes: Orlando Reconsidered," *Shakespeare Quarterly,* 24 (1973), 20-21, presents a similar view.

[3] Rawdon Wilson, "The Way to Arden: Attitudes toward Time in *As You Like It*," *Shakespeare Quarterly,* 26 (1975), 17.

[4] Ibid., p. 18.

[5] Albert R. Cirillo, *"As You Like It:* Pastoralism Gone Awry," *ELH,* 38 (1971), 21.

[6] Helen Gardner,"*As You Like It*," in *More Talking of Shakespeare,* ed. John Garrett (London: Longman, Green, 1959), p. 28.

[7] Harold Jenkins, *"As You Like It,"* *Shakespeare Survey,* 8 (1955), 50.

[8] D. J. Palmer, "Art and Nature in *As You Like It,"* *Philological Quarterly,* 49 (1970), 33.

[9] Gardner, p. 28.

[10] John Shaw, "Fortune and Nature in *As You Like It,"* *Shakespeare Quarterly,* 6 (1955), 45-50, develops the implications of Fortune as bringer of rewards, but does not pursue Fortune's temporal implications. Subsequent treatments have tended to follow Shaw. William S. Hecksher, "Shakespeare in His Relationship to the Visual Arts: A Study in Paradox," *Renaissance Drama: A Report on Research Opportunities,* 13-14 (1970-71), 57-58, addresses the dramatist's problem of communicating emblematic elements to the Elizabethan audience: " . . . whenever Shakespeare . . . merely alludes and leaves it to his reader to divine the existence of a pictorial source of inspiration, we may assume that he was confident that his audience (or at least those among his audience who were imbued with the Elizabethan and Jacobean culture) would respond almost automatically with recognition. . . . Where, however, Shakespeare went out of his way to hold up to us a work of art and where he used to this end all the devices of descriptive rhetoric, we can be fairly sure that no actual work of art was in his mind."

[11] Howard R. Patch, *The Goddess Fortuna in Medieval Literature* (Cambridge: Harvard Univ. Press, 1927), pp. 115-17.

[12] Erwin Panofsky, *Studies in Iconology: Humanistic Themes in the Art of the Renaissance* (1939; rpt. New York: Harper & Row, 1962), p. 72. Samuel C. Chew, "Time and Fortune," *ELH,* 6 (1939), 95-113, discusses both the Fortune-Occasio merger and a similar fusion of Fortune with the three fates: Fortune's wheel becomes a spinning wheel with which she spins the thread of life.

[13] Panofsky, p. 72.

[14] Panofsky, p. 72; Patch, p. 115; Chew, pp. 103-04.

[15] Patch, pp. 116-17.

[16] Vincenzo Cartari, *IMAGINES DEORVM, QVI ab antiquis colebantur* . . . (Lyons, 1581), pp. 303-22.

[17] Response to the sight of one's beloved is always ethically critical in the Platonic love theory of the 1590s. In this theory love is defined simply as the desire to possess beauty, but the attempt at possession may be either mental or physical. Properly understood, earthly beauty (beauty in material objects) is perceived to be the reflection of divine beauty (intelligible beauty without a physical body). As the only being created with both a rational soul and a physical body, man is the only creature to experience ethical conflict in attempting the possession of beauty. He has the moral obligation to choose the purely mental possession which leads toward God, but his body engenders impulses toward the physical possession which leads away from God. Consequently, each sighting of beauty is an ethically critical moment in which man must (as the Platonists saw it) will himself upward toward the life of the gods or allow himself to descend toward the life of the beasts.

Comparatively few of Shakespeare's contemporaries would have learned Renaissance love theory from its wellspring, Marsilio Ficino's *Commentary on Plato's Symposium* (c. 1485), but many would have been familiar with Ficino's ideas (in somewhat modified form) through Baldassare Castiglione's phenomenally popular *The Courtier* (1528), available to the London public in two English versions, both of which had been republished twice before 1588. Most reasonably well-read members of Shakespeare's audience would have been familiar with these ideas through English sources such as Sir Philip Sidney's *Astrophel and Stella,* the many other sonnet sequences, or Book III of Edmund Spenser's *The Faerie Queene.*

[18] Harry Morris, *"As You Like It:* Et in Arcadia Ego," *Shakespeare Quarterly,* 26 (1975), 269-75, focuses directly on the play's darker potential. Similar views are presented in Thomas McFarland, *Shakespeare's Pastoral Comedy* (Chapel Hill: Univ. of North Carolina Press, 1972), pp. 98-103, and René Fortin, "'Tongues in Trees': Symbolic Patterns in *As You Like It,"* *TSLL,* 14 (1972), 569-82.

[19] Richard Knowles, "Myth and Type in *As You Like It,"* *ELH,* 33 (1966), 4-5.

[20] Ovid, *Metamorphoses,* X, 560-704.

[21] Jenkins, p. 46, and Peter G. Phialas, *Shakespeare's Romantic Comedies: The Development of Their Form and Meaning* (Chapel Hill: Univ. of North Carolina Press, 1966), p. 232, emphasize the fact that Jaques is dismissed immediately before each of the play's two extended love scenes, once by Orlando and once by Rosalind.

Act III, scene ii. Rosalind as Ganymed, Touchstone, and Celia as Aliena. Frontispiece to the Rowe edition (1709).

[22] Gardner, p. 27, and Geoffrey Bullough, *Narrative and Dramatic Sources of Shakespeare, Vol. II, The Comedies, 1597-1603* (London: Routledge & Kegan Paul; New York: Columbia Univ. Press, 1958), p. 150.

[23] Charles's speech gives the audience its first information about the Forest of Arden, and thus the speech deserves a careful reading to determine the exact extent of this information. On the subject of time, Charles says only that "they say many young gentlemen flock to him [Duke Senior] every day, and fleet the time carelessly, as they did in the golden world" (I, i, 123-25). This statement asserts only that the young gentlemen *act as if* time were ineffective in Arden; Charles and his informants remain uncommitted as to the actual nature of time in Arden. In my view this passage serves two purposes: (1) it universalizes the forest experience by applying it broadly to many youths rather than allowing it to remain an unusual experience reserved for a chosen few and (2) it prefigures Orlando's illusion that "there's no clock in the forest."

[24] For varied interpretations, see Fortin, pp. 576-82; Halio, p. 206; Knowles, pp. 5-7, 12-13; McFarland, pp. 102-03; and John Doebler, "Orlando: Athlete of Virtue," *Shakespeare Survey,* 26 (1973), 114-17. Halio, Knowles, and Doebler emphasize the climactic nature of the incident.

William Kerrigan (essay date 1994)

SOURCE: "Female Friends and Fraternal Enemies in *As You Like It,*" in *Desire in the Renaissance: Psychoanalysis and Literature,* edited by Valeria Finucci and Regina Schwartz, Princeton University Press, 1994, pp. 184-203.

[*In the following essay, Kerrigan investigates the psychological underpinnings of* As You Like It, *including those associated with sibling rivalry, female friendship, and heterosexual love.*]

As You Like It is clearly less menacing than the dramas that surround it in the canon, including the comedies yet to come, and I treasure it for just this reason. Beginning with *Hamlet,* though of course with prior intimations, through to the *consummatum est* of *Timon of Athens,* plenty of stage time is given to what Wilson Knight used to call "the Shakespearean hate-theme"—poisoned idealism, anger at ingratitude and trust betrayed, misanthropy, world-hatred, sex-disgust, everything high and sweet collapsing into a chaos without distinction.[1] The Shakespearean hate-theme is a fearsome thing. Nothing and nobody stands in the way of it. As soon as triggered, it leaps from the particular to the global, and blasts away, in great pulsating tirades of poetic fury, at the very designs of nature and civilization. It speaks through Hamlet in most of the soliloquies, his enraged rejection of Ophelia's virginity, and the dagger-talk to his mother, through Othello, Lear, Coriolanus, and Timon, but finally it seems to be free of character or dramatic motive, hovering about the work of this period as an almost impersonal force, like pressure seeking outlets.

Fraternal rivalry, the "primal eldest curse" of *Hamlet,* is one of those outlets. Shakespeare writes the success story of a "band of brothers" in *Henry V,* then he relates the failure of a conspiracy of brothers in *Julius Caesar,* and then—assuming the correctness of the Evans chronology[2]—he writes *As You Like It,* which opens in a world torn by fraternal strife. The late Sir Rowland de Boys had three de Boys and has left the family lands and most of their money to Oliver, who now mistreats his youngest brother, Orlando, refusing him funds, denying him an education, and making him eat with the servants. So far as inheritance went, this was, as Louis Montrose has reminded us, the "courtesy of nations": primogeniture, the right of the firstborn to the family title and estates.[3] Younger sons of the aristocracy were indeed, like Orlando, resentful. Some became wastrels. Others became lawyers, clergymen, and civil servants. For such careers education was a prerequisite; hence Oliver's peculiar nastiness in refusing to educate his youngest brother.

Oliver de Boys even strikes Orlando de Boys while calling him a "boy" (1.1.52).[4] The blow precipitates a wrestling match. When next Orlando wrestles, the treacherous Oliver will have chosen a proxy—Charles, the Ultimate Warrior of the Normandy World Wrestling Federation, a brother-killer, who warms up for Orlando by tearing three of them to pieces.

Elder brothers despise younger brothers. When attention shifts to the dukedom, we learn that the direction of such hostility can be reversed. "What's the new news at the new court?" Oliver asks (1.1.96-97). Charles's reply is metadramatic: "There's no news at the court sir, but the old news. That is, the old Duke is banished by his younger brother the new Duke." The new news is the old news, a younger brother deposing his elder. The new news will go on being the old news as late as *The Tempest,* where younger brother Antonio usurps the dukedom of Prospero. Some things never change.

But villainy is a plodder in *As You Like It.* Oliver shows little agility in preparing Orlando's downfall. He simply gives Charles an account of his own character—envious of others, a backstabber, a plotter against his brother—and attributes it to Orlando. The height of his villainy is a plan to torch Orlando's bedroom; Richard III would have done better than that. Nor will Duke Junior put the murderous machiavel to school. When he realizes that Orlando is the son of Rowland de Boys, a great favorite with Duke Senior, his sibling hatred flares anew, and soon lights on his niece Rosalind, whom up to now he has appeared to love.

All of this is old news, business as usual in Shakespeare. Male aggression divides kingdoms, friends, lovers, and families. Passages of social criticism elsewhere in the play remind us of other typical symptoms of male contentiousness: the new self-interestedness with which men move upward in hierarchies, forgetting the antique bonds of service, as represented here by Adam; the ingratitude of friends; the pompous rigor with which insults are registered on the way to fighting a duel. Men seem to be making a mock of civilization. Old news.

What feels new, though it isn't quite, is the extraordinary closeness of Celia and Rosalind. Begun in the cradle, it has almost magically survived the hostility between their fathers. In *A Midsummer Night's Dream*, Hermia and Helena are "sweet playfellows," bosom companions, before love rivalry divides them.[5] But the friendship of Rosalind and Celia is presented as mysteriously exceptional: " . . . for the Duke's daughter her cousin so loves her, being ever from their cradles bred together, that she would have followed her exile, or have died to stay behind her. She is at the court, . . . and never two ladies loved as they do" (1.1.107-12). Their loves, a courtier remarks, "are dearer than the natural bond of sisters" (1.3.266). There does not appear to be, in other words, a standard model for this intimacy. No other women have loved this way. The love is dearer than that between sisters. Dearer, I wonder, because it is without rivalry?

For language such as this describing a bond between two people, begun in what is virtually a twinning in childhood, then continued into young adulthood, we have to jump ahead to Leontes and Polixenes in *A Winter's Tale*. That childhood friendship was broken by the "fall" of sexuality; women came between the two men, as they do again in the unfolding romance. Leontes' jealousy is a dark variant on the catfighting scenes in *A Midsummer Night's Dream:* narrative's sharpest way of dividing two friends is to have one of them suppose that the other has stolen his or her beloved. But the friendship between Celia and Rosalind, as we will see, is made exempt from this fate.

Rosalind has been called the wittiest woman in the canon. A wit can make do with a simpleton, but give a wit an answerably witty companion, as Shakespeare has in pairing Rosalind with Celia, and the result is a magnificent picture of great but unsentimental intimacy. The three or four scenes between Celia and Rosalind seem to me much the most beautiful things in the play. The way, never ceasing to score quips and quibbles, they still manage to adjust each other's emotions in benign directions, correct imbalances, get at the hard

truths behind circumlocutions—it's a marvel! Shakespeare, who had two sisters and two daughters, observed well. Did Touchstone train these female wits? It seems likely that they trained him, for they are completely his masters in the Shakespearean art of verbal fencing.

When they hit the road for Arden and Duke Senior, soon to be followed by Orlando and Adam, we feel that they really do go "To liberty, and not to banishment" (1.3.134). They are too fine for Duke Junior, with his ridiculous claim that Rosalind in her wit and grace makes Celia seem a "fool." In fact, a fool is too fine a thing for the vain and witless Duke Junior to understand. Celia reiterates the preciousness of their bond:

> If she be a traitor,
> Why so am I. We still have slept together,
> Rose at an instant, learn'd, play'd, eat
>   together,
> And whereso'er we went, like Juno's swans,
> Still we went coupled and inseparable.[6]
>
> (1.3.68-72)

And thus are born Ganymede and Aliena, brother and sister.

You have to make some choices in reading Shakespeare. The historical evidence is not decisive one way or the other, but the stakes are high, for on these choices depends the Shakespeare you experience and interpret. Some recent critics have made much of the fact that female roles were taken by men or boys on the English Renaissance stage.[7] They claim that there is always a certain metadramatic awareness of this; an aura of homoerotic flirtiness or knowingness surrounds feminine roles in Shakespeare, and comes to the fore with special intensity when cross-gender disguises are donned. It may seem to confirm this view that Rosalind takes the name of Ganymede, Zeus's cupbearer, the mythic prototype of the glamorous homosexual boy. But the historical evidence is never decisive, especially in the realm of myth. Maybe Shakespeare just kept the name from his source, Lodge's *Rosalynde,* where Ganymede was a better-motivated choice, since Rosalynde played the part of a page, not a brother. A male homosexual name could be thought appropriate to Shakespeare's Rosalind/Ganymede in the sense of "destined never to love a woman," the truth that she will stage for Phebe later in the play.

The larger question at stake is whether Shakespeare made good in dramatic terms on his mimesis of women—and whether, on the other side of the stage, his audience was willing to accept boy actors as women, even when these women in turn disguise themselves as boys.[8] Whipping up an artificial campiness around the feminine characters in *As You Like It* would erode the dramatic solidity of female friendship, to my mind a main source of the comedy's goodness.[9] The play does indeed accumulate a charge of homoerotic feeling, but it is not to be enjoyed as readily as some modern interpreters imagine. Work must be done before the epilogue, where "Rosalind" is clearly a male actor's female part, releases a homoeroticism kept largely in check during the comedy proper.

Though all the world's a stage, and men and women the players, Jacques's famous speech is about, narrowly, the ages of *man*. But in my view *As You Like It* is more profoundly concerned with the ages of woman, and with the place that might be assigned in the ages of woman to the radiant friendship (more than kin, and more than kind) of Rosalind and Celia.

But I have neglected to mention what happened before their exile to Arden. There would be no comedy without it: Rosalind and Orlando have fallen in love at first sight. The tongue-tied Orlando is "thrown down" and "overthrown": wrestling, with its fraternal rivalry and male violence, has been metaphorically transformed into love. The women in turn accept the metaphor, and it becomes part of their witty intimacy.

> *Celia.* Come, come, wrestle with thy
> affections.
> *Ros.* O they take the part of a better wrestler
> than myself.
>
> (1.3.20-22)

It is surely a portent that Orlando gets tongue-tied the moment he falls in love. Rosalind gives him a chain, perhaps actually places it around his neck, and Orlando finds himself transformed into "a mere lifeless block": "Can I not say, 'I thank you'?" (1.2.239). A moment later he has no difficulty in saying "I thank you sir" to Le Beau (1.2.257), yet the onslaught of love renders him speechless. It's the usual Petrarchan pattern, to be sure; but given his devotion to *this* woman, the fastest mouth in the play, Orlando's weighted tongue foretells that he will be the submissive partner in his love match. Maybe it also implies a degree of ingratitude due in part to his immaturity; since the death of his father, no one has given him anything. He has in particular complained of not receiving an education. Orlando will certainly be schooled in the discourses of courtship and marriage when Dr. Ganymede, the magical love counsellor of Arden, is finished with him.

The play is interested in time and how time can be divided, distinguished, and periodized. Jaques notes that "we ripe, and ripe, / And then from hour to hour, we rot, and rot. / Thereby hangs a tale" (2.7.26-28). Eventually the tale of ripening and rotting gets told, in Jaques's famous speech on the seven ages of man.[10] Rosalind is several times made to display the tradi-

tional lover's trait of impatience. In one of her wit lessons for Orlando she compares various subjective experiences of time to the gaits of a horse. A maiden rides the hours between her betrothal and her wedding at a "hard trot," because her impatience makes her uncomfortable. Orlando, in the end, is exhausted with delay: "I can live no longer by thinking" (5.2.50).

Yet we feel in Rosalind herself a drive contrary to this conventional impatience. She clings to her disguise and uses it more often and with more dedication than the plot itself requires. Why is she so concerned, when she faints over Oliver's presentation of the bloody handkerchief, that this feminine swoon will give her away? Beyond that, why does she swoon at all?[11] Because her anger at Orlando's lateness is instantly transformed, by the handkerchief, into anxious concern? It has crossed my mind that two things cross in the mind of Rosalind. The bloody handkerchief evokes both the violence done to Orlando and a sweeter violence that Orlando will do to her—the consummation of the wedding sheets: that which, in other words, she ought to be impatient for, but which in fact she appears to be warding off through the intrigues of her disguise. "O ominous!" Rosalind declared when first aware of Orlando's presence in the forest, "he comes to kill my heart!" (3.2.242). The handkerchief presents to her in one anamorphic image the pictures of killing her beloved and marrying (being killed by) her beloved, his blood spilt and her blood spilt. That conjunction knocks her out.

Comedies are mechanistic. Beloveds are found early in the play. They endure complications. Then, with some element of surprise, Jacks have their Jills, and the marriages crank into line. Viola in *Twelfth Night* is caught passively in her disguise, like patience on a monument smiling at grief, yet we never feel that her will is somehow resisting the mechanism of the plot. Her passivity can be viewed as a faith that "time," the comic plot, "must untangle this, not I" (*Twelfth Night* 2.2.39). But Rosalind seems freely to indulge in her disguise, to *explore* it, and for a time this indulgence acts as a drag on the destined resolution of the comedy.

Why? First of all, obviously, Orlando is undergoing a love test. Several Renaissance gender clichés operate in *As You Like It*. One of them is that women talk a lot, say whatever is on their minds—Rosalind mentions that one, and realizes how well it fits her. Another is a cliché about men, that they break vows made to women during courtship. This stereotype is alluded to early in the play, in one of Celia's speeches after Orlando's victory at the wrestling match: "If you do keep your promises in love / But justly, as you have exceeded all promise, / Your mistress shall be happy" (1.2.232-35). So Rosalind's doses of acid truth for Orlando are in part meant to test his fidelity. She induces him to make promises—that, for instance, he will appear at a certain time. Transgressions are punished, for they represent metaphorically the possibility of breaking love oaths. Perhaps, too, the charade of purporting to cure Orlando's love continues a pattern established the very first time she sees him; when they fell in love at first sight, she was also on a mission to dissuade him (from wrestling), and failed. Wrestling becomes courting: maybe she liked the fact that she failed to move him. Maybe she relishes, in Greenblatt's term, the friction.[12]

Usually we are meant to feel at the end of a comedy that the young have been freed from their complications and are now ready, with marriage, for a deeper happiness, something of great constancy. But Ganymede's scathing love cures feature some fairly chilling looks at the treacheries possible in marriage. Maybe Rosalind clings to her disguise because, as certain feminist readers have suggested, it removes her from the standard positions of the gender system. According to Catherine Belsey, devices such as the Ganymede disguise have "momentarily unfixed the existing system of differences, and in the gap thus produced we are able to glimpse a possible meaning, an image of a mode of being, which is not a-sexual, nor bisexual, but which disrupts the system of differences on which sexual stereotyping depends."[13] On this view, Rosalind/Ganymede enters a state of liminality, neither man nor woman, betwixt and between, and in this state enjoys the freedom to stock her spirit with novel perspectives.

I find a great deal to recommend this view, though I am not sure that Rosalind's state really is outside the Renaissance gender system, which is maybe not so pitiless or clear-cut as some feminists suggest. Courtship itself—which is certainly part of the gender system, and in comic drama has a whole genre given over to it (comedies end in marriage: another way of saying this is that comedies are typically about courtship)—is after all a liminal state, and is represented as such throughout Shakespearean comedy. During courtship some of the major dichotomies in life are experienced at the same time. The participants in a wooing may exchange vows and love tokens, at once married and not married; in the Renaissance this sort of doubleness flourished in the time between troth-plight (*sponsalia per verba de futuro*) and the exchange of performative vows completing the marriage (*sponsalia per verba de praesenti*).[14] Wooers are also chaste and sexual, settled and unsettled, adult and not fully adult, sane and mad.

Courtship, moreover, in Shakespeare as in our own day, can involve a feeling of being in disguise. Receiving a quick or sudden love puts one into a disguise: this person does not know you, and couldn't possibly love *you,* so it must be that some disguised version of yourself is loved. Even when love is gradu-

ally rather than suddenly declared, both parties often have a sense of slowly undisguising themselves as the relationship moves toward the ideal of full revelation. The true state of the courtship must also, for a time, be kept from other people. Thus Donne, in "Lecture upon the Shadow": "So whilst our infant loves did grow, / Disguises did, and shadows, flow, / From us, and our care; but, now 'tis not so." During courtship, then, identity can mutate into a series of pretenses.

Of course the ordinary liminality of courtship does not include female/male, as it does for Rosalind. Or does it?

There seem to be two conditions that must be met before, imaginatively, Rosalind will be ready to doff her disguise. One of them is satisfied when she encounters Phebe and Silvius acting out the familiar Petrarchan scenario of an extravagantly dogged male pursuing a coldly unyielding woman. Rosalind has no sympathy for this form of female superiority, though it is, in the abstract, not unlike what she has been imposing on Orlando. Maybe her chiding words to Phebe are in the manner of a self-repudiation. The content of her intervention, in any case, is a spirited attack on Phebe's self-love, which she interprets as the consequence of Silvius's misplaced devotion. Ganymede gives voice to an anger that the Petrarchan male, nourishing his obsession, keeps under wraps; this scolding induces Phebe's sudden crush on Ganymede. "It is a pretty youth," Phebe declares, "—not very pretty—/ But sure he's proud, and yet his pride becomes him. / He'll make a proper man. The best thing in him / Is his complexion; and faster than his tongue / Did make offence, his eye did heal it up" (3.5.113-17). Ganymede is not yet a man in the dazzled eyes of Phebe, and for this reason, the speech implies, is not enslaved by female beauty; Ganymede retains sufficient pride of his own to rebuke her feminine pride, rather than begging her to relent like the Petrarchan Silvius.[15] Phebe also senses a femininity in the body language of Ganymede, a friendliness of eye and gesture that "heals up" the sting of his rebuke. We might conclude that this crush somehow "completes" Rosalind, rounding out her liminality. She's looked at love from all sides now: as a woman, she enjoys the reciprocal love of a woman (Celia) and a man; as a man, she is loved by a woman (Phebe) and (in the game being played with Orlando) by a man.

The second condition for dropping the disguise seems to be the appearance of a male lover for her soul mate Celia.

Freud's recurrent problem in his four famous papers on female psychosexual development, and the main reason for the continual revisions of his theories, lies in his inability to understand how the little girl gets into an oedipal position.[16] For a heterosexual boy, the love object remains constant from cradle to grave: the mother, the sexualized mother of the Oedipus complex, and metaphorical derivatives of the mother in courtship and marriage. But the little girl, to emerge from childhood with a heterosexual disposition, has somehow to shift her love from the mother to the father. How can this happen without some traumatic disappointment with her mother, or with femininity itself? Throughout his life Freud kept trying to figure out how this shift might typically occur. Though the plot kept changing, the major scene remained the same. Somehow this shift must involve an injury to the girl's narcissism.

In *Paradise Lost* Milton anticipates Freud on this question. Eve's famous narrative of the first human courtship in Book 4 of the epic shows us that, even in Eden, the first suitor had a rival in Eve's own image, which is her first love. In loyalty to this primal affection, she does not fall in love at first sight, but rather turns and runs away.[17]

It is harder for a woman than it is for a man to realize that she needs the opposite sex to complete her. Here, I think, we are close to the heart of the Celia/Rosalind twinship. As in girlhood, so on the verge of courtship and marriage: the Rosalind/Celia relationship is puberty's renegotiation of the old attachment to the early mother. They jest about suitors, sexuality, having babies, but they are not, at the beginning of the play, courted. How could they be, when they are inseparable, waking together and eating together? Men will inevitably divide them. Their friendship is an attempt to achieve a completeness and self-sufficiency right on the threshold of mature sexuality—and as such this friendship does not really want to deal with the fact that maturity has to involve its dissolution. The moment Rosalind falls in love with Orlando, the friendship appears to receive its death notice. It has survived the violent rivalry of fathers, but now, with heterosexual love on the horizon, it seems to be doomed.

We see no signs of jealousy in Celia, though she is sometimes bored with Rosalind's Orlandoizing and appalled at her accounts of feminine treachery. In his book *The Theater of Envy: William Shakespeare,* René Girard concedes that the Rosalind/Celia relationship is a notable exception to his theories of mimetic desire.[18] There ought to be rivalry here. There ought to be rivalry the very moment that Rosalind tells Celia to "Let me love him for that [because he is deserving], and do you love him because I do" (1.3.34-35). Their friendship does not obey the ordinary laws of human relationship in Shakespeare.[19] But Girard, rather than interpreting this suspension of the ordinary, gets worried about his theory; instead of suffering the scandal of an exception, he blames the idiocy of the pastoral genre, too stupid to allow for conflict, devises a convoluted scheme in which mimetic desire governs the play after

all, and winds up with the exception proving the rule. But the plot of *As You Like It,* with the promise of goodwill evident in its title, moves to protect this friendship from internal as well as external disruptions. Celia need not be jealous; the plot will provide. With the appearance of a reformed Oliver, both women can simultaneously, in a twinned marriage ceremony, make the transition into adulthood, choose marriage over female friendship, yet at the same time elevate their cousinhood into sisterhood, becoming aunts to each other's children. A pair weds a pair. For the friendly cousins to marry brothers—and better than that, brothers who have settled their sibling rivalry—is the best-case situation for preserving their old oneness in the adult context of marriage. Resentments that divided their fraternal fathers have already been ironed out in their fraternal husbands.

Let me put this another way. Courtship is a time of liminal experimentation for a woman—both Shakespeare and Milton know this, and since they do, it cannot be altogether outside the gender wisdom of the Renaissance. Let's suppose that courtship in Renaissance culture has its own gender channels. Men declare their love openly, enjoying what Cressida terms "men's privilege / Of speaking first" (3.2.127-28); if they are tongue-tied and cannot speak, they as it were write poems and hang them on trees. They let women know. But women do not ordinarily profess their hearts. They are courted, and during this time remain ambiguous, disguised, undeclared, and undivulged. It is understood in these cultural arrangements that the resolution of the courtship, its success or failure, is a woman's call. Finally she declares her heart, and it is either at one with the man's declared love or it is not. Courtship is the time of woman's greatest power and liberty.[20] It is for her to decide *when the comedy will be over.* Moreover, this is probably the most important decision of her life. The comedy of courtship is a realm of female supremacy—she's the monarch of the play, as it were, and calls the shots.

Marriage, typically in Shakespeare, is a realm of male supremacy. But this comedy seeks to mediate courtship and marriage. Rosalind arranges a marriage that, so far as possible, will allow the liberty of courtship— whose main expression is the relationship with Celia— to survive the end of the comedy. The rebuke to feminine pride that Freud posited at the threshold of the female Oedipus complex, and the echo of that rebuke at the threshold of courtship, when feminine friends must partially give way to male lovers, are deflected onto Phebe. The play gives to *her* the castrating disillusionment of trying to make a woman do for a man. In Rosalind and Celia, Shakespeare builds a nest for feminine pride, bestows the gift of mutual wit to prevent that pride from becoming pathological, and in the end folds friendship into heterosexual marriage. When the forthcoming nuptial arrangements are repeated before Duke Senior, Rosalind and Celia leave the stage together, and soon return, Rosalind having discarded her hose and doublet, with the figure of Hymen, who then performs the only marriage ceremony wholly completed on Shakespeare's stage.[21] Their entrance with Hymen in tow is a crowning emblem of the comic transformation of their friendship. Hymen unites rather than severs them.

The absence of the hate-theme clears a space for this triumphant empathy. But a full analysis of the achievement must include the comedy's successful defensive measures for denying a purchase to wrath and rant.

In the plays that lead up to *As You Like It,* Shakespeare avoids serious conflict with the father. Precisely that avoidance is the watchword of Henry V's career. As a young man he acts a prodigal. But at the end of *Henry IV, Pt. 1,* he rescues his father in battle; at the end of *Pt. 2,* he repudiates Falstaff, assimilating his father's disapproval; finally, in *Henry V,* we see him fulfilling his father's political ambitions, right down to wooing Katherine with the thought that one of their sons might lead a crusade (5.2.206-10). As Shakespeare planned *Julius Caesar,* he edited out Plutarch's suggestion that Caesar was Brutus's father.[22]

Rosalind remarks at one point: "why talk of fathers, when there is such a man as Orlando?" (3.4.34-35). But in fact the paternity of Orlando is early on presented as the rationale for her love. Rosalind feels free to love Orlando because Duke Senior loved Rowland de Boys. This relayed affection also bears upon Oliver's hostility toward his brother. He professes to resent the younger man's natural gentility and charisma. But I think we can be certain that another way to describe his envy is that Orlando (but not Oliver) has inherited the bearing and the grace of his father; Orlando himself says that the "spirit of my father" (1.1.70) compels him to rebel against his ill-treatment by Oliver. So Rosalind, in loving Orlando, repeats in the sphere of heterosexual love her own father's love for Rowland de Boys. Duke Senior sanctions or, better, initiates her love.

The prominence of fraternal rivalry at the beginning of the play serves to close off the possibilities for cross-generation hostility. Oliver does not curse Sir Rowland for failing to transmit his natural endowment to him; all his aggression is subsumed in his hatred for Orlando. The one exception is Celia, who rejects Duke Junior in accompanying Rosalind to the forest of Arden. Shakespeare disposes of this conflict with the deus ex machina of Duke Junior's instantaneous fit of monastic penance, brought on by his encounter with an old religious man. This, combined with Oliver's abrupt submission to the spirit of his father as embodied in Orlando, squares things with the paternal generation. At the end of the play there is no reproach whatsoever

for fathers. We certainly sense that such themes are straining to get out, and they will, though somewhat disguised, in *Hamlet.* Reading the plays in sequence, it seems clear that Shakespeare, as Barber and Wheeler maintain, is laboring mightily to postpone *Hamlet.*[23] The paternal outlets of the hate-theme are sealed off by the end of *As You Like It.*

The escape from tragedy is of course embodied in a place, the forest of Arden. Early in the play, Rosalind and Celia debate the correct way of distinguishing between the realms of nature and fortune, that housewife at her wheel. Fortune is said to supply the gifts of the world, whereas nature bestows the "lineaments" (1.2.41) of one's fundamental endowment. Shakespeare will be preoccupied for the rest of his career with various conceptions of nature.

No doubt Arden to some extent is nature. The exiled courtiers talk about suffering weather and the changing seasons. They debate with Jaques about man's place in nature—about, for example, whether men should live on fruit or vension. But if we take Arden in this way, we must be struck by the fact that the exiles' relationship to this nature is transformed utterly by their literacy. The whole question of man's relationship to nature is a pastoral question—and thus a question whose precondition is literacy. In the "uses of adversity" speech, Duke Senior concludes that "our life, exempt from public haunt, / Finds tongues in trees, books in the running brooks, / Sermons in stones, and good in everything" (2.1.15-17). Arden is a text, something read. So is Jaques; Duke Senior now and then browses him: "I love to cope him in these sullen fits, / For then he's full of matter" (2.2.67-68). Indeed, there are poems on the trees.[24]

Arden is a forest of literacy, teeming with heteroglossia. Amiens sings a song celebrating the movement from corrupt court to nature; Jaques inserts a verse ridiculing the stupidity of anyone who would abandon wealth and ease to live in a forest. Song, mock-song. Orlando puts up his Rosalind poems; Touchstone proceeds to grind out mock-Rosalind poems. Even the vicar is named Martext. There's a resident satirist in Jaques, who has his own love affair with the resident fool. The horns of the deer inevitably, given language, are transferred from nature to culture, to branch out as the horns of the cuckold—horns that any married man must be prepared to wear. The comic and satirical scenes tend to assume the exhaustive structure of encyclopedia entries: on the kinds of melancholy, the strides of time, the seven varieties of insult, the seven ages of man. Philosophy and theology are sent up. There are burlesque versions of Caesar's "I came, I saw, I conquered," Troilus and Cressida, Hero and Leander. Ovid's myths are also burlesqued, as when Orlando tells Jaques to look at his image in a pond. There are lawyer jokes, priest jokes, rich-man jokes, lover jokes, simpleton jokes, women jokes, men jokes, fool jokes, and so on. "Nay then God buy you, and you talk in blank verse," says Jaques, talking in blank verse. The fool compares his state to Ovid's exile, and Phebe, a rustic shepherdess, quotes Marlowe: "Dear shepherd, now I find thy saw of might, / Who ever lov'd that lov'd not at first sight"—a heroic couplet, the form in which Marlowe wrote *Hero and Leander*. Arden is less nature than a heteroglossic rap on nature—an adventure in the forms and counterforms of literate life.

The followers of Jaques Lacan maintain that language is paternal, a system we are inserted into by virtue of oedipal castration. But of course that isn't true. Nothing that Jaques says is altogether true. Language is embryonically a part of the mother/infant dyad. Infants are bathed in language, and the first distinct signifiers are gradually differentiated from this global immersion in baby talk, body talk, clucks, goo-goos, coochie-coos, lullabies—the "blooming buzzing confusion" of William James.[25]

I almost hesitate to say it, because it is such an obvious point, and so comically open to any interpretation whatsoever, but this forest where maybe you should kill deer, and maybe you shouldn't. . . . Shakespeare's mother came from a prominent family of landowners in Stratford, and her name was Mary Arden.[26] Shakespeare's grandfather cultivated Arden forests as a tenant farmer. Can it be incidental that Shakespeare writes his mother's maiden name when Englishing Ardennes? With all the literacy in *As You Like It*'s Arden, does the play contact an early mother there, a set of problems that stand prior to conflict with the father?

Sibling rivalry must surely predate the Oedipus complex for Shakespeare. I think it has its roots in being displaced at the breast, as a new baby usurps the mother's central affections while her former darling stares in envy at the new arrival occupying his one-time place.[27] Duke Junior claiming the manor for himself might be read as the younger brother displacing the older. If we shift to the sibling feud in the de Boys family, Oliver forcing his younger brother to eat with the servants seems from this perspective an appropriate revenge. In the same spirit, one could read Duke Senior's migration to Arden as a wishful undoing of this primal usurpation. Junior has the dukedom, but Senior has the mother—Mother Earth, Mother Nature, Mother Arden.

Both sets of exiles discover that, in order to get to Arden, one must nearly starve; hunger in infancy is what calls forth the mother, transforming her absence into presence. These cues suggest that the flight to Arden is at some level a flight to the mother of infancy.

But this early mother also has her terrible aspects; she is a devourer, engulfer, smotherer. I see her in the "suck'd and hungry lioness" (4.3.126), more dangerous than the snake, who lies in wait for the sleeping Oliver:

> Under an old oak, whose boughs were moss'd
>   with age
> And high top bald with dry antiquity,
> A wretched ragged man, o'ergrown with hair,
> Lay sleeping on his back. About his neck
> A green and gilded snake had wreath'd itself,
> Who with her head, nimble in threats,
>   approach'd
> The opening of his mouth. But suddenly
> Seeing Orlando, it unlink'd itself,
> And with indented glides did slip away
> Into a bush, under which bush's shade
> A lioness, with udders all drawn dry,
> Lay crouching head on ground, with catlike
>   watch
> When that the sleeping man should stir; for
>   'tis
> The royal disposition of that beast
> To prey on nothing that doth seem as dead.
> This seen, Orlando did approach the man,
> And found it was his brother, his elder
>   brother.
>
>   (4.3.105-20)

An impotent father presides. The "old oak" overseeing this extraordinary scene evokes a very old man, like the oak in Jonson's "To the Immortal Memory and Friendship of . . . Sir Lucius Carey and Sir H. Morison" that falls "a log at last, dry, bald, and sere."[28] This is the father sans everything, reduced to an emblematic presence only. But men of such antiquity, according to the logic of the seven ages, reencounter their opposites in "second childishness" (2.7.165). Events transpiring beneath the tree bear the stamp of relived infancy. The oak is bald, the man beneath "o'ergrown with hair." Yet in the drama unfolding below, in the ground-level realm of second childishness, the "dry" of the treetop reappears as the "dry" udders of the lioness. Oliver has neither youth nor age, but a pre-dinner sleep of exhaustion, dreaming on both.

The scene bristles with maternal meance. All the players are dry and hungry. In this "wretched ragged man" we have for the third time confirmation that exiles to Arden arrive there in a state of near starvation. As he sleeps, ancient nightmares—the "indented" and "catlike" totem animals of the maternal hate-theme—seem to materialize about him. Choking or poisoning might be the aim of the female snake wound around Oliver's neck, reminiscent of the chain Rosalind gave to his younger brother after the wrestling match.[29] "Nimble in threats," she moves toward the mouth in a deadly assault on the first site of mother/infant merger, later the first site of ego boundaries, and still later the site of speech. What does the snake intend to do before it slithers away at the appearance of Orlando? Her prey is in need of nourishment; the maternal beast waiting in the bush is sucked and hungry. The blasts of the winter wind, in one of Arden's songs, are "not so unkind / As man's ingratitude" (2.7.176).[30] I think the snake threatens to enter his mouth and bite an ungrateful tongue, a tongue like Orlando's earlier in the play, that cannot say, when a woman puts the gift of a chain around his neck, "I thank you." Reimagining the chain as a snake, this scene projects that ingratitude back into the preliterate recesses of psychic time as a motive for maternal vengeance and therefore also as a deep motive for the speechless ingratitude of mature males, whose tongues are weighted with the unconscious stings of infantile revenge tragedies. Unlike the snake, who threatens a motionless prey and slinks off when distrubed by Orlando, the "royal disposition" of the beast crouching in the bush's shade—a regressive figuration of the classic *vagina dentata*—requires animated game, the pleasure of a kill. The lioness "with udders all drawn dry" is a nightmare out of Melanie Klein, a talionic mother who will devour her child because, in that child's primitive fantasy world, he has devoured her.[31]

Twice Orlando turns his back on the endangered brother. But "kindness" and "nature" defeat revenge and justice (4.3.128-30). Orlando saves his brother from the lioness, at the cost of being wounded himself, and immediately the sibling rivalry is over. They weep to hear each other's story; after a brief audience, Duke Senior formally assigns the duties of hospitality for the newcomer to his "brother's love" (4.3.144). As Oliver was excessive in hostility, so now he is excessive in beneficence: he will give Orlando the estates, and live in Ardenic bliss with his beloved Aliena.

In sum, the older brother forgives the younger brother because the younger has rescued him. I think this is a dramatic representation of one of the earliest checks against all-out sibling rivalry. That new brother has taken my place; see how Mother dotes on him, when she should be doting on me. But on the other hand, there is the counterthought we have come to expect in the reversible intellectual structures of Arden: it is good to be free of that mother, to mourn my losses and become an independent self. The usurper is also a liberator. I will no longer be engulfed. The new baby has pushed me toward my future.

The fear of being engulfed by a primeval mother might translate, on a much later plane of psychic development, into a dread of being overmastered by the wit and bossiness of a dominant wife. Maybe that is yet another reason why the wound ends the masquerade and rounds off the love test: by surviving the onslaught of the most savage early mother, the hungry dry-dugged lioness, Orlando has proven himself fit for marriage to a Rosalind.

After which, an epilogue of elaborate pointlessness:

> It is not the fashion to see the lady the epilogue; but it is no more unhandsome than to see the lord the prologue. If it be true that good wine needs no bush, 'tis true that a good play needs no epilogue. Yet to good wine they do use good bushes; and good plays prove the better by the help of good epilogues. What a case am I in then, that am neither a good epilogue, nor cannot insinuate with you in the behalf of a good play? I am not furnished like a beggar, therefore to beg you will not become me.

Strictly from hunger, Rosalind's epilogue seems condemned to offer and then to undermine rationales for itself. Yet the logic of the play is still subliminally at work in this self-thwarting appendage. An impulse to epilogue seems at war with an impulse to anti-epilogue. Rosalind is pretending to a great deal of trouble in asking for the audience's gratitude. By the end we realize that the epilogue cannot request this gratitude without first delivering to its audience the comedy's mixed sexual messages. Before the comedy can receive its due, theater must come clean.

As is conventional in epilogues, the play is reduced to an object of primitive judgment. Like wine, it is either good or bad, to be spit out with hisses or taken in with applause. And in fact things look bad for *As You Like It* in this suspended state between fiction and fact, performance and reception: Rosalind has neither a good epilogue for a bad play nor a good epilogue for a good play. It would certainly be a good epilogue for my interpretation if this lighthearted condemnation of the comedy could be associated with the primitive object encountered in the forest of Arden. Metaphorically a bush (the ivy sprig, traditional sign of the vintner) and a woman, the prologue may indeed remind us of "Into a bush, under which bush's shade / A lioness. . . . " That may seem a stretch. But when the epilogue discovers a raison d'être, it has to do with kissing, bringing mouths together without hatred or reproach:[32]

> My way is to conjure you, and I'll begin with the women. I charge you, O women, for the love you bear to men, to like as much of this play as please you. And I charge you, O men, for the love you bear to women—as I perceive by your simpering none of you hates them—that between you and women the play may please. If I were a woman, I would kiss as many of you as had beards that pleased me, complexions that liked me, and breaths I defied not. And I am sure, as many as have good beards, or good faces, or sweet breaths, will for my kind offer, when I make curtsy, bid me farewell.

This is *As You Like It*. What women like in the play, they should equate with the love they bear to men; what men like in the play, they should equate with the love they bear to women. Dr. Ganymede is on the audience's case: liking the play is equivalent to heterosexuality; the gravity of the genre produces marriages. But this heterosexual declaration is followed by an evocation of male fellowship.

The fear of being engulfed by a primeval mother might also translate, on a much later plane of psychic development, to a fear of being drawn into dangerous fantasies by a masterful work of art. The epilogue banishes this fear in jovial acceptance. Ganymede's insistence that Orlando treat him as Rosalind echoes the male actor's insistence throughout the performance that the audience treat him as Rosalind. Exposing this similitude, the epilogue balances the theme of female friendship with good spirits between men. There is one final undermining in the offer to kiss pleasing mouths: "If I were a woman. . . . " He is not. The woman-man that has been "Rosalind" here divides into a role and an actor; our lady the prologue is our lord the prologue. After heterosexuality has been linked to the liking of the play, after the male actor has expressly disengaged himself from the female role, homosexual desire surfaces in the kisses that he in playing she would plant on the audience's most attractive faces.[33] *As You Like It* has met and survived the hungry lioness; homosexuality holds no terror, since the imago that might compel it has been overcome. Written by a male, performed by males, and ultimately addressed to males, the play has as its bottommost wish the desire to cleanse and reaffirm the realm of the oral, blocking out the hate-theme at its source. Even if the good comedy is bad, it will be good. Even if the heterosexual desire celebrated in the play is homosexual desire, it will be good. As the comedy itself becomes a primitive object in its epilogue, the very idea of a primitive object becomes comic—a thing created by men for the entertainment of men. With a most flirtatious curtsy the actor exits to applause, having shown to the limits of Shakespeare's imagination that men can reconfigure their dread of women.

Notes

[1] G. Wilson Knight, *The Wheel of Fire* (rpt. London: Methuen, 1986), p. 236.

[2] I refer to the sequence given in G. Blakemore Evans et al., eds., *The Riverside Shakespeare* (Boston: Houghton Mifflin, 1974), pp. 47-56.

[3] Montrose, "'The Place of a Brother' in *As You Like It*: Social Process and Comic Form," *Shakespeare Quarterly* 32 (1981): 28-54. I have some local disagreements with Montrose. For example, I see no evidence that Orlando is bitter about the *principle* of primogeniture. His allusion to the "courtesy of nations" is not sarcastic (Montrose, 31, 32, 36); he instead resents the particular indignity of his treatment at the hands of Oliver. Stressing the social elevation of Orlando through his marriage to Rosalind, Montrose believes that the play appeals to the grudges of younger brothers. Moreover, he assumes that Renaissance attitudes toward primogeniture were governed by self-interest, younger brothers resenting it, eldest brothers favoring it. I therefore find it odd that he never mentions, even in passing, Shakespeare's own status as an eldest brother. This oversight may count as an aporia, since it is impossible to see how Shakespeare, given Montrose's belief in the necessary self-interestedness of social attitudes, could have sympathized so fully with younger brothers. But the major problem with the Montrose essay is that his approach via primogeniture all but ignores the heart of the play: the friendship between Celia and Rosalind. Orlando is actually a rather dull character, and the best bits in the first two acts (which Montrose admits are his primary focus) concern the radiant female friends. Toward the end of this essay I will offer some psychoanalytic suggestions about the treatment of fraternal rivalry in *As You Like It*.

[4] All citations of the play are from Agnes Latham, ed., *As You Like It* (Londo : Methuen, 1975).

[5] One also thinks of the female community gathered around the princess in *Love's Labour's Lost,* though Boyet is so prominent in their scenes that they have scant opportunity to converse with one another, the opening of 5.2 being the lone exception. Perhaps a better example of the power of female unity is *Richard III* 4.4, where the three queens make common cause against Richard, weave their curses together, and imaginatively put an end to the Wars of the Roses.

[6] The coupled swans recall Spenser's "Prothalamion," probably written in 1596. For other sources, consult *The Works of Edmund Spenser: The Minor Poems,* Vol. 2, ed. Edwin Greenlaw, Charles Osgood, Rederick Padelford, and Ray Heffner (Baltimore: Johns Hopkins University Press, 1947), pp. 667-73. The image foreshadows the union of friendship and marriage at the entrance of Hymen in Act 5.

[7] Examples may be found in Lisa Jardine, *Still Harping on Daughters: Women and Drama in the Age of Shakespeare* (New York: Columbia University Press, 1983), pp. 9-36; and Stephen Orgel, "Nobody's Perfect, or Why Did the English Stage Take Boys for Women?" *South Atlantic Quarterly* 88 (1989): 7-29.

[8] The alternative, as Robert Kimbrough suggests in "Shakespeare's Androgyny Seen Through Disguise" (*Shakespeare Quarterly* 33 [1982]): 17-33, is that al-

most all of the plays would have to have been treated as farce (p. 17).

9 A review of the early criticism of the play reveals that my main predecessor in this view is H. N. Hudson. An appreciation of the Rosalind-Celia friendship shines through the haze of his Wordsworthian prose. "Instinct with the soul of moral beauty and female tenderness, the friendship of these more-than-sisters 'mounts to the seat of grace within the mind.'" He finds sisterhood in the very serenity of Arden: "the graces of art and the simplicities of nature meet together in joyous, loving sisterhood." *Shakespeare: His Life, Art, and Characters,* 4th ed., rev.; 2 vols. (Boston: Ginn and Company, 1891), 1:346, 349.

10 C. L. Barber, *Shakespeare's Festive Comedy* (New York: Meridian Books, 1963), p. 226.

11 On swooning in medieval romance and Shakespearean comedy, see the interesting remarks of E. E. Stoll in *Shakespeare Studies* (New York: Macmillan, 1927), pp. 40-42.

12 Stephen Greenblatt, *Shakespearean Negotiations* (Berkeley: University of California Press, 1988), pp. 66-93. "And the effect of her humour," the foreshadowing Hudson writes of Rosalind, "is, as it were, to *lubricate* [his emphasis] all her faculties, and make her thoughts run brisk and glib" (*Shakespeare,* 1:345).

13 "Disrupting Sexual Difference: Meaning and Gender in the Comedies," in John Drakakis, ed., *Alternative Shakespeares* (London: Methuen, 1985), p. 190. See also, in the same volume, Jacqueline Rose's "Sexuality in the Reading of Shakespeare: *Hamlet and Measure for Measure.*" Belsey's view that something prototypically "feminist" emerges from woman-into-man disguises in Shakespeare runs counter to that of Linda Woodbridge in *Women and the English Renaissance: Literature and the Nature of Womankind, 1540-1620* (Urbana: University of Illinois Press, 1986), pp. 154-55. Robert Kimbrough discusses the controversy in *Shakespeare and the Art of Humankindness: The Essay toward Androgyny* (Highlands, New Jersey: Humanities Press, 1990), pp. 101-5.

14 On the oddities of marriage law, consult Frederick Pollock and Frederic Maitland, *The History of English Law,* 2 vols. (rpt. Washington, D.C.: Lawyers' Literary Club, 1959), 2:368-99.

15 In a comparable scene in *Twelfth Night* (1.5.238-58), Viola/Caesario first (unlike Rosalind/Ganymede) praises the beauty of Olivia, then (like Rosalind/Ganymede) indicts her pride. Like Phebe, Olivia clearly prefers this freedom from enamorment to Orsino's Petrarchan enslavement.

16 These essays, cited from James Strachey, ed. and trans., *The Standard Edition of the Psychological Works of Sigmund Freud,* 24 vols. (London: Hogarth Press, 1953-74), are "On the Sexual Theories of Children" (9:207-26); "The Dissolution of the Oedipus Complex" (19:172-79); "Some Psychical Consequences of the Anatomical Distinction Between the Sexes" (19:243-58); and "Femininity" (22:112-35). Scorned by the first generation of academic feminists, these papers have recently been hailed by some members of the second and third generations—an event so momentous as to have made the cover of *Newsweek* in 1991. See the introductory matter in Elisabeth Young-Bruehl, ed., *Freud on Women: A Reader* (New York: Norton, 1990).

17 Interpretations of Eve's courtship from a Freudian point of view may be found in Mark Edmundson, *Towards Reading Freud: Self-Creation in Milton, Wordsworth, Emerson, and Sigmund Freud* (Princeton: Princeton University Press, 1990), pp. 57-86; William Kerrigan and Gordon Braden, *The Idea of the Renaissance* (Baltimore: Johns Hopkins University Press, 1989), pp. 201-3; and my "Gender and Confusion in Milton and Everyone Else," *Hellas* 2 (1991): 195-220.

18 (New York: Oxford University Press, 1991), pp. 92-105.

19 So far is Celia from jealousy that she plays the priest in the mock wedding of 4.1.118-24.

20 Several points in this account of courtship are illustrated in one of Cressida's speeches:

> If I confess much you will play the tyrant.
>   . . . See, we fools!
> Why have I blabb'd? Who shall be true to us
> When we are so unsecret to ourselves?—
> But though I lov'd you well, I woo'd you not;
> And yet, good faith, I wish'd myself a man,
> Or that women had men's privilege
> Of speaking first.
>
>   (3.2.118-28)

Carol Thomas Neely, in *Broken Nuptials in Shakespeare's Plays* (New Haven: Yale University Press, 1985), pp. 6-22, offers a brief and historically informed account of the "deidealization" to which married women are subjected in Shakespeare. Recent generalization about this subject is too often guided by Lawrence Stone's *The Family, Sex and Marriage in England 1500-1800* (New York: Harper and Row, 1977); I suspect that the balanced views of Keith Wrightson, *English Society 1580-1680* (New Brunswick: Rutgers University Press, 1982), pp. 89-117, are more trustworthy.

21 Ann Jennalie Cook, *Making a Match: Courtship in Shakespeare and His Society* (Princeton: Princeton

University Press, 1991), p. 223. Cook also stresses the unreality of the marriage, its distance from contracts and settlements. Property came under English common law, which preferred that it be exchanged in public; thus brides were customarily endowed at the church door (Pollock and Maitland, *History of English Law,* 2:374-75).

22 Ernest Jones, *Hamlet and Oedipus* (New York: W. W. Norton, 1949), pp. 121-25.

23 C. L. Barber and Richard P. Wheeler, *The Whole Journey: Shakespeare's Power of Development* (Berkeley: University of California Press, 1986), pp. 237-42.

24 Dryden was dead wrong in supposing that Shakespeare "needed not the spectacles of Books to read Nature"—D. Nichol Smith, ed., *Shakespeare Criticism 1623-1840* (London: Oxford University Press, 1963), p. 16.

25 For a distinguished psychoanalytic discussion of this point, see Hans Loewald's "Primary Process, Secondary Process, and Language," in Joseph H. Smith, ed., *Psychoanalysis and Language* (New Haven: Yale University Press, 1978), pp. 235-70.

26 William George Clarke seems to have been the first to note, in his edition of 1864, that Arden "was the maiden name of his very own mother—Mary Arden, whose ancient family derived their name" from the forest of Arden in Warwickshire; see Richard Knowles, ed., *A New Variorum Edition of Shakespeare's* As You Like It (New York: MLA, 1977), p. 556. James Joyce includes the association in the great "Shakespeare chapter" (9) of *Ulysses,* ed. Hans Walter Gabler (New York: Random House, 1986): "—As for his family, Stephen said, his mother's name lives in the forest of Arden" (p. 171). Barbara Bono has also argued for this connection; see "Mixed Gender, Mixed Genre in Shakespeare's *As You Like It,*" in Barbara Lewalski, ed., *Renaissance Genres: Essays on Theory, History, and Interpretation* (Cambridge: Harvard University Press, 1986), p. 194. One should also consult the long note on "forrest of Arden" in H. H. Furness, ed., *As You Like It* (New York: Lippincott, 1890), pp. 16-18.

27 Gilbert would have been the usurping brother in Shakespeare's own childhood. Though one cannot rule out the possibility of a wet nurse, I strongly suspect that Mary Arden nursed her own children. The smothering fantasies discussed by Rothenberg (see note 29) might have resulted from Mary Shakespeare's feeling that, having lost Joan in 1559 or 1560 and Margaret in 1563, she would need to provide her next child with a great deal of nourishment in order for it to survive infancy. I will extend these comments in a forthcoming book, *Hamlet's Perfection.* The locus classicus for

the idea of a sibling rivalry originating in being replaced at the breast is Augustine's *Confessions* 1.7.

28 *Ben Jonson: The Complete Poems,* ed. George Parfitt (New Haven: Yale University Press, 1975), p. 213. "Under an old oak, whose bows were mossed with age" gives prominence to "old," which refuses to submit to metrical law. One commentator (see Furness, *As You Like It,* p. 241) "cannot believe that in an otherwise deftly wrought and perfectly rhythmical passage, Shakespeare would load a line with a heavy monosyllable, entirely superfluous to any purpose other than that of marring the description and making the verse halt."

29 Montrose, in "'The Place of a Brother'" (p. 50), connects the snake to the chain Rosalind gave to Orlando at their first meeting. Celia later recalls it when trying to identify for Rosalind the lyricist of her name: "And a chain, that you once wore, about his neck" (3.2.178). For infantile fantasies about choking and smothering in Shakespeare, see Alan Rothenberg, "Infantile Fantasies in Shakespearean Metaphor: (1) The Fear of Being Smothered," *Psychoanalytic Review* 60 (1973): 205-22; and "The Oral Rape Fantasy and Rejection of the Mother in the Imagery of Shakespeare's *Venus and Adonis,*" *Psychoanalytic Quarterly* 40 (1971): 447-68. Rothenberg does not suggest an etiology for this complex of fantasies in Shakespeare, but see note 27.

30 Wilson Knight (cited in note 1) always assumed that anger over ingratitude was at the heart of the Shakespearean hate-theme, in part because he was the only major critic of his generation to accept the centrality of *Timon of Athens* to Shakespeare's tragic phase. See Viola's contempt for ingratitude above all other vices in *Twelfth Night* 3.4.363-66.

31 One thinks here of the bear in *The Winter's Tale;* see Murray Schwartz, "*The Winter's Tale:* Loss and Transformation," *American Imago* 32 (1975): 158-59.

32 I have discussed some of the roles of kissing in Renaissance lyric poetry in "Kiss Fancies in Robert Herrick," *George Herbert Journal* 14 (1990/91): 155-71.

33 I am anticipated by, among others, Leslie Fiedler, *The Stranger in Shakespeare* (New York: Stein and Day, 1972), p. 47, and Stephen Dedalus in Joyce's *Ulysses,* p. 157: "But his boywomen are the women of a boy. Their life, thought, speech are lent them by males." On the female dislike of kissing men with beards and bad complexions see *Much Ado About Nothing* 2.1.26-28, Marston's *The Dutch Courtesan* 3.1.10ff., and the ninth lyric of Jonson's "The Celebration of Charis." The rejection of these men in the audience, the men that he in playing she would not

wish to kiss, might be taken as a comic version of the wound the lioness inflicts on Orlando.

Andrew Barnaby (essay date 1996)

SOURCE: "The Political Conscious of Shakespeare's *As You Like It,*" *Studies in English Literature, 1500-1900,* Vol. 36, No. 2, Spring, 1996, pp. 373-95.

[*In the following essay, Barnaby studies the ways in which* As You Like It *confronts and reflects the moral and political economies of late-Elizabethan culture.*]

> the purpose of playing . . . [is] to hold as 'twere the mirror up to nature: to show virtue her feature, scorn her own image, and the very age and body of the time his form and pressure.
>
> *Hamlet* (III.ii.20-4)

When in *As You Like It* the courtier-turned-forester Jacques declares his desire to take up the vocation of the licensed fool, he is immediately forced to confront the chief dilemma of the would-be satirist: the possibility that his intentions will be ignored and his words misconstrued as referring not to general moral concerns—the vices of humankind, for example—but rather to specific realities, persons, events (II.vii.12-87).[1] Given that Jacques has just demonstrated a laughable inability to grasp the barbs of a true practitioner of the satiric craft (Touchstone), we must be wary of taking him as a reflexive figure of Shakespeare's own vocation. But the lines undoubtedly show Shakespeare's discomfort with the recent censoring of satiric material (including a well-publicized burning of books in June of 1599),[2] and his own earlier experience with *Richard II,* as well as Ben Jonson's recent jailing for the "seditious and slanderous" content of the *Isle of Dogs,* had certainly made him familiar with the danger posed by those readers who misread the typical as the straightforwardly topical. Despite his simple-mindedness, then, Shakespeare's Jacques does in some way reflect a working playwright's continual anxiety that his works might be misconstrued as deriving meaning not from his intentions but from ideas and events beyond the signifying scope of his labors.

The modern equivalent of this reader-writer conflict resides not in the competing interpretations of author and court censor but in those of author and scholar-critic. But the necessity of facing up to such interpretative discrepancies has for the most part been obscured by the reigning critical methodology in Renaissance studies, New Historicism, and in particular by its inability to formulate a convincing explanatory model for the processes of acquisition by which texts come both to represent and to participate in the larger discursive systems that determine them. Although it would be counterproductive to dismiss the very im-

pressive critical achievements of New Historicism, we might yet need to consider what we are to make of writing itself as a purposeful and perspectively limited activity: what of writers as the agents of meaning within their own textual compositions? what do we do when what we can reconstruct of authorial intention runs counter to "cultural" evidence? and, more broadly, how precisely can any literary work be understood to signify historical reality?

In taking up these issues, Annabel Patterson has recently argued that it has become necessary to "reinstate certain categories of thought that some have declared obsolete: above all the conception of authorship, which itself depends on our predicating a continuous, if not a consistent self, of self-determination and, in literary terms, of intention." And she adds specifically of poststructuralist criticism of Shakespeare that the "dismissal of Shakespeare as *anybody,* an actual playwright who wrote . . . out of his own experience of social relations" has shown itself to be both incoherent methodologically and reductive at the level of historical understanding.[3] Such out-of-hand dismissal precludes the possibility of understanding how the early modern period actively conceptualized and debated its cultural forms or how an individual writer may have sought to engage in those debates.

The remainder of this essay will focus on how *As You Like It* (and so Shakespeare himself) does consciously engage in debate concerning the crises points of late-Elizabethan culture: the transformation of older patterns of communal organization under the pressures of new forms of social mobility, an emergent market economy, and the paradoxically concomitant stratification of class relations; the more specific problems of conflict over land-use rights, the enclosure of common land and its attendant violence, poverty and vagrancy.[4] In considering how modern historical understanding might itself seek to articulate this engagement, moreover, I shall be arguing that the play's meditation on the unsettled condition of contemporary social relations is precisely, and nothing more than, an interpretative response to the perceived nature of those conditions.

To recognize that what we have in Shakespeare's play can never be anything but a rather one-sided dialogue with social conditions then current is not to deny that the play is, in crucial ways, at once topical and discursively organized. But it is to acknowledge that such topicality and discursivity are necessarily transformed by the historical condition of writing itself. What we are left with, then, is not a symbolic re-encoding of the entire sweep of current circumstances (as if the play could encompass the full historical truth of even one element of Elizabethan culture in its own tremendous complexity). Shakespeare does indeed address the peculiar historical circumstances of late-Elizabethan culture, and that engagement is evidenced in the formal elements of his play (most particularly in its pastoral form, an issue that will be examined in greater detail in subsequent sections). But if *As You Like It* is historically relevant it is so primarily because it can be read as a rhetorical (and so intentional) act in which one writer's sense of things as part of history becomes available to his readers in the purposeful design of the play. It is to an understanding both of that design and of the limitations of current critical practice that the following discussion is directed.

I

The play begins with Orlando's complaining of his mistreatment at the hands of his older brother, Oliver, who has refused to fulfill the charge of their father, Sir Rowland de Boys: it was Sir Rowland's wish that his youngest son receive both a thousand crowns and sufficient breeding to make a gentleman of himself, despite being excluded from the much greater wealth of the estate because of the law of primogeniture. But Oliver has treated Orlando as a servant instead, and, in likening himself to the prodigal son (I.i.37-9), Orlando seeks both to remind Oliver that, unlike his gospel counterpart, *he* has yet to receive his promised inheritance and to register, for the audience as well as for Oliver, the discrepancy between his noble birth and his current circumstances.

In the course of rebuking Oliver for being so remiss in his fraternal duties, Orlando violently, if briefly, seizes his brother. In his finely nuanced reading of the play, Louis Montrose has argued that, in its explosive suddenness and aggressiveness, Orlando's action captures the essential tension caused by the culturally charged nature of the sibling conflict over primogeniture in Renaissance England, where younger sons of the gentry were excluded from the greater wealth of family estates in increasing numbers.[5] Moreover, the symbolic associations of the violence complicate the political inflections of the scene. For, in context, the violence does not just move from younger brother to older brother but also from servant to master and from landless to landowner, and these associations extend the cultural scope of the already politicized conflict. As Montrose suggests, in the broader discursive contextualization of the scene, Orlando's alienation from his status as landed gentleman serves "to intensify the differences between the eldest son and his siblings, and to identify the sibling conflict with the major division in the Elizabethan social fabric: that between the landed and the unlanded, the gentle and the base."[6]

Richard Wilson has recently elaborated on this argument by suggesting that the play's central conflicts reenact the particular tensions unleashed in Elizabethan society by the subsistence crisis of the 1590s.

According to Wilson, in its "discursive rehearsal" of the social hostilities generated out of the combination of enclosure and famine (especially severe in the years just prior to the play's composition and in Shakespeare's native Midlands), the play becomes complexly enmeshed in the "bitter contradictions of English agricultural revolution," a struggle played out in the various conflicting relations between an enervated aristocracy, a rising gentry, and a newly dispossessed laboring class and effected primarily by the emergence of a new market economy.[7]

As compelling and historically informed as Wilson's reading is, however, it is yet undermined by its vagueness concerning how the play actually represents these issues. That Wilson wants and needs to posit the dialogic encounter of text and context as the site of the play's (and his argument's) meaning is evidenced by his own critical rhetoric. As we have just noted, he refers to the play as a "discursive rehearsal" of a multifaceted sociocultural history; elsewhere he writes that "the play is powerfully *inflected* by narratives of popular resistance"; that "social conflict [over famine and enclosure] *sears* the text"; that Duke Senior's situation in the forest of Arden "*chimes* with actual projects" associated with the capitalist development of the woodlands; that the play "*engages in the discursive revaluation* of woodland" that emerged as part of the rise of a market economy in late-Renaissance England.[8] The problem with this type of phrasing is that it never renders intelligible the processes by which text and context come into contact. We are dealing, in short, with the theoretical problem of how precisely a literary work may be said to allude to, reflect, meditate on, or even produce the historical forces that form its enabling conditions.

To put the issue another way, Wilson's reading is stranded by its inability to assess what we might call the play's signifying capacity. While I am not disputing that the particulars of enclosure and famine (and more generally the social transformation of late-Elizabethan society) constitute the proper historical backdrop of the play, Wilson consistently scants the historical conditions of writing and reception, and he therefore has no means of assessing the work of the text as a site of meaning.[9] Eschewing any reliance on the text's own coherence or Shakespeare's possible intentions as explanatory models, Wilson's argument relies instead on the juxtaposition of select formal elements of the play (plot details, bits of dialogue, character motivation, etc.) with a dense evocation of historical details that appear circumstantially relevant to the play's action. While this mode of argumentation—what Alan Liu has recently termed a kind of critical *bricolage*[10]—yields some perceptive insights into the workings of the play, social reality, and the discursive networks connecting them, what it really produces is a series of strange allegorical encounters in which the play is said to provide shadowy symbolic re-encodings of a broad spectrum of historical realities: legal edicts, demographic statistics, anecdotes from popular culture, institutional practices, persons, events, and even vast structural changes in the organization of English culture.

To get a clearer sense of this method we might consider just a few of his more suspect interpretative findings. For example, according to Wilson, Rosalind's lack of "holiday humor" in I.ii stems not from her father's banishment but from her recognition of a broader crisis of the aristocracy (particularly centered on a new "aristocratic insolvency"), and this even though her own subsequent banishment is read as a symbol of the expulsion of tenant farmers from common lands; and later her cross-dressing becomes an "impudent challenge" both of rural poachers to "the keepers of game" and, more generally, of class and gender trespassers to the patriarchal hierarchy maintained by the Elizabethan upper orders. The "obscure demise" of Orlando's servant, Adam, figures the rising "mortality rate" in rural England due to the late-1590s dearth, even though Adam does not die (he merely disappears as a character—a point to which we shall return). Orlando's carving of his beloved Rosalind's name on the forest trees is said to symbolize a Stuart policy of marking trees as part of the surveying that preceded royal disafforestation; and this is so even though such a policy post-dates the composition of the play and even after Wilson has described Orlando as a gentleman-leader of popular resistance for whom the damaging of trees was a potent sign of protest.[11] In almost all of the examples he gives, the text is so overdetermined by contradictory historical realities that it becomes virtually unreadable; despite his historicizing efforts, Wilson seems to repeat the very argument of those he terms "idealist critics" who see the play as "free of time and place."[12]

The argument's lack of coherence appears to derive primarily from Wilson's attempt to analyze what he calls the play's "material meaning." Although he never says precisely how we are to understand the phrase, his one effort at glossing suggests that it is something known only in the negative, as that which is concealed or evaded by the text's explicit statements.[13] This is an odd notion, given the ease with which Wilson finds the text making explicit statements about the social situation;[14] indeed, given his practice, it makes more sense to take the term "material" in its traditional Marxist sense: the "historical" as located in a culture's dominant mode of production. In the case of *As You Like It* the "material" would then include the cultural struggle over agrarian rights, the conversion of woodland to arable land, and the broader movement of a regulated to a market economy (seen especially in the capitalization of land-use rights), and this "material" history would provide the base from which the mani-

festations of superstructure (including the play) would derive meaning.

The problem with this formulation is that it both reduces the play to a straightforward (albeit jumbled) allegory of "history as it really happened" and avoids the theoretical problem of how (or where) the play actually represents this history. Addressing precisely this hermeneutic problem in relation to the Shakespearean text (and so offering a different sense of "material meaning"), Patterson properly asks: "how do words relate to material practice?" And she notes that Shakespeare himself "used both 'abstract' and 'general' as terms to denote his own form of material practice, writing for a popular audience, the 'general,' and abstracting their experience and his own into safely fictional forms."[15] Such a critical stance depends on several related notions: that Renaissance writers were quite capable of comprehending the cultural situation of their own productions; that these productions must be read as forms, that is, as organized, fictionalized, and generically regularized abstractions of perceived realities; that any discussion of form must consider the representational practices by which historical situations are reproduced aesthetically; and that, as abstractions, forms take their meaning from a variety of interpretative exchanges—between author and world as an act of perception, author and reader/audience as a rhetorical act, reader/audience and world as an act of application—and therefore cannot be explained by recourse to the notion of a general, all-encompassing discursive field. To view fictional form as a significant material practice in its own right is to see that it at once signifies historical realities and constitutes its own reality, that it is both constantive and performative; it thus "both invite[s] and resist[s] understanding in terms of other phenomena."[16]

As texts such as Ben Jonson's Preface to *Volpone* suggest, for Renaissance writers this invitation and resistance is played out primarily (though not exclusively) in ethical terms.[17] The citation from *Hamlet* that stands as my epigraph makes a similar point: "to hold . . . the mirror up to nature" is to engage in moral discrimination, distinguishing virtue from vice in acts of praise and blame. Such acts might themselves be understood as historically relevant; indeed, Hamlet's earlier assertion that actors are "the abstract and brief chronicles of the time" (II.ii.524-5) suggests that dramatic representations were expected to speak to contemporary history (albeit in "abstract and brief" form). Leah Marcus takes this point even further in her claims that "local meaning was at the center" of Renaissance literary practices, and that what contemporaries "attended and talked about" concerning a literary work was its "currency . . . , its ability to . . . 'Chronicle' events in the very unfolding." But, as she also points out, Renaissance "poets and dramatists [typically] looked for ways to regularize and elevate topical issues so that they could be linked with more abstract moral concerns."[18] In *As You Like It* that ethical sensibility, "regularizing and elevating" a pressing cultural debate over current social conditions, is marked especially in the play's engagement with the traditions of pastoral, where pastoral must be understood as a form obsessively concerned with the related questions of social standing (the constant re-marking of distinctions between gentle and base) and moral accountability.[19] It is to an attempt to assess the moral and political commitments of the play, as well as the representational strategies it employs to render these commitments intelligible, that we now turn.

II

The three plays that Shakespeare wrote in 1599—*Julius Caesar, Henry V,* and *As You Like It*—are all variously concerned with aristocratic identity, an issue cited, probed, redefined in late-Elizabethan culture in "a vast outpouring of courtesy books, poetry, essays, and even epics," all directed toward "the fashioning . . . of the gentleman or the nobleman."[20] *Julius Caesar* looks at the issue as a crisis of aristocratic self-definition in the face of Tudor efforts at political and cultural centralization; the play examines this crisis and moralizes it in terms of a questioning of the continued possibility of aristocratic excellence (defined primarily in terms of humanist notions of virtuous civic action).[21] *Henry V* explores the relationship between aristocratic conduct and national identity in the context of militarist expansionism, but this focus is extended to an examination of the aristocratic capacity for responsible leadership of commoners and the popular response to that leadership.[22] As critics have recently argued, both plays are concerned with the nature of historical understanding itself, and especially with examining the possibilities and limits of applying knowledge of the past—already an interested rhetorical activity—to present concerns.[23] Like *As You Like It,* then, both plays are interested at once in the vexed relation between aristocratic culture and the broader workings of political society and in the representational and interpretative practices by which fictional accounts serve as mediatory sites of informed public concern over contemporary affairs.

As You Like It returns the meditation on aristocratic conduct to the domestic sphere where, as we have seen suggested, it focuses on the related issues of inheritance practices, agrarian social structure, and the current controversy over land-use rights. Right from its opening scene, in fact, the play introduces us to its particular interest in the problem of aristocratic definition. Indeed, despite Orlando's complaints against the system of primogeniture which denies him his brother's authority, the real source of his frustration is that his "gentlemanlike qualities"—the very marks of his class, so crucial in a deferential society—have been obscured

by his having been "trained . . . like a peasant" (I.i.68-70). Throughout the opening scene, in fact, what Orlando is most concerned with is the possibility that his status might be taken away simply by its not being properly recognized. In its particular locating of Orlando's predicament, then, the play's opening scene initiates a line of inquiry that will both inflect the rest of the play and share in a culturally charged debate: by what markings is it possible to identify the true aristocrat?

But the issues of status and its violation, of place, displacement, and recognition—all so central to the play's comic vision—are not confined to the interactions among the upper orders. For they are raised as part of an exploration of the customary bonds between the upper and lower orders as well. And, as the relationship between landowner and landless servant depicted in the opening suggests, the play also puts in question the nature and meaning of aristocratic conduct toward social inferiors. Shakespeare, we shall see, interlaces the depiction of violated noble status with a depiction of the displacement of laboring classes (represented in the opening scenes by both Orlando and Adam) from their traditional places in the service of the rural nobility.

The play's concern with the related issues of social standing and displacement, aristocratic conduct, and the moral bonds connecting high and low, is further developed in II.iii. Upon returning from Frederick's court, Orlando is secretly met by Adam who warns him of Oliver's villainous plot:

> this night he means
> To burn the lodging where you use to lie,
> And you within it.
>
> (II.iii.22-4)

Amidst the special urgency of the moment, Adam's warning is enveloped in a broader meditation on what has happened in the wake of Sir Rowland's passing. So he addresses Orlando:

> O unhappy youth,
> Come not within these doors! Within this roof
> The enemy of all your graces lives.
> Your brother—no, no brother, yet the son
> (Yet not the son, I will not call him son)
> Of him I was about to call his father—
>
> . . . . .
>
> This is no place, this house is but a butchery;
> Abhor it, fear it, do not enter it.
>
> (II.iii.16-28)

Marking the logical consequence of the sibling conflict set in motion in the opening scene, Oliver's "unbrotherly" act is viewed here as particularly hei-nous, totally unnatural, a kind of abomination; indeed, as Montrose notes, we hear in this struggle the echoes of the original fratricide, the elder Cain killing his younger brother Abel.[24] But the fratricide is clearly rewritten in the cultural context of Renaissance inher-itance practices, for we note that Oliver's "sin" is fig-ured particularly as a repudiation of the familial duties and obligations emanating from a line of inheritance between noble father and noble son. Sir Rowland's heir, in effect, perverts the very link between nature and human social order—the family—and thereby dis-avows the very foundation of his inheritance. Oliver's unbrotherly dealings mark the violation of more than just the person of his brother; they are symbolically broadened to assimilate the house itself, symbol of both the family and the larger estate as an extension of the family. In dishonoring his place within the family, Oliver threatens the very cultural inheritance that ex-tends a sense of place to those outside the family. Adam thus identifies Oliver's special villainy as a violation of kinship ties that both reenacts human history's pri-mal scene of violence and marks the loss of that "place"—the noble manor—whose very purpose is to locate the various lines of interaction defining the so-cial order.[25]

In II.iii, then, younger brother and elder servant are linked together in their experience of the psychically disorienting effects of displacement, a loss registered particularly in the feelings of estrangement they voice over their impending exile (II.iii.31-5, 71-4). There is something extremely conservative in this nostalgic evocation of tradition, of course, but it is important to insist that the image of "proper" social relations that Shakespeare depicts does not offer merely a moralized restoration of traditional cultural forms but provides rather an extended meditation on the political economy that should at once reveal and sustain the moral economy.

As an example of this concern, Shakespeare's complex adaptation of the gospel parable he so carefully etches into the opening scene deserves greater attention. We noted earlier that at the very outset of the play Orlando's self-figuration as the prodigal son is intended to regis-ter the discrepancy between his noble birth and his current circumstances. But the very lack of applicabil-ity of the parable to Orlando's case—unlike the prodi-gal son he has neither squandered his inheritance nor even received it—is even more significant within the play's moral and political vision. This discrepancy is critical primarily because it reconfigures the parable's central focus on the interaction of family members from how each of the two brothers interacts independently with the father to a direct confrontation between them. At the most obvious level, this change has the effect of politicizing the fraternal struggle by making it a con-flict over the now-deceased father's patrimony, whereas

in the parable the fraternal conflict is less about inher-itance per se than with the sibling rivalry over the attentiveness of the still-living father. Shakespeare, that is, transforms a story concerned with the nature of a future "heavenly" kingdom into a decidedly human, indeed, political affair.

More specifically, the retelling provides a completely different context for understanding the roles of the two brothers within the parable. For example, whereas the parable faults (even as it treats sympathetically) the elder brother's uncharitable attitude toward his younger brother, the play, by contrast, renders this animosity, and the behavior that attends it, unsympa-thetic; indeed, Shakespeare appears to conflate two different parts of the parable by rewriting the elder brother's (now perverse) behavior as the cause of the (now innocent) younger brother's degradation. Liv-ing among the hogs and eating husks with them, Orlando appears as the dutiful son, toiling long years without just recompense. Although the play never quotes the parable directly on this point, Shakespeare subtly borrows from the parable the elder brother's complaint to his father—"All these years I have slaved for you and never once disobeyed any orders of yours"—and reassigns the context to Orlando's frus-tration with Oliver's unfair treatment of him. And as Orlando is no longer responsible for his fallen cir-cumstances, so his situation ceases to represent a moral failing—a lapse in personal ethical responsibility—and comes instead to mark a political and economic awareness of the social mechanisms that lead one into such penury.

Oliver's role is thereby refigured (loosely to be sure) as "prodigal." In the parable, of course, it is the elder brother who laments that while he has never "disobeyed any orders" of the father, his prodigal brother enjoys all the special privileges even after "swallowing up [the father's] property." But Shakespeare makes the true bearer of privilege appear prodigal precisely be-cause, while he has done nothing to earn his portion of the estate (other than being the eldest son), he has enjoyed its benefits without sharing them with his hard-working brother. And even as the play merges the Judeo-Christian primal scene of violence—Cain's kill-ing of his younger brother Abel—with the Christian parable of the difficult demands of brotherly love, it also recontextualizes the elder brother's failure of char-ity in the political relations not just between elder and younger sons (already politicized in Renaissance cul-ture) but also between masters and servants, landed and landless, gentle and base. Moreover, while the opening scene stages, in the guise of Orlando's vio-lence, a threat to the overturning of traditional author-ity, the subsequent scenes stage a recognition of what is more precisely in need of transformation: the aristo-cratic figure who fails to fulfill the obligations of sta-tus and custom, and especially to maintain cultural stability by sustaining the moral (and political) value that accrues to social place.

It is within the context of such unbrotherly dealings and their symbolic affiliation with social injustice conceived on a broader scale that Duke Senior's praise of rural life at the opening of act II has its strongest resonance:

> Now, my co-mates and brothers in exile,
> Hath not old custom made this life more
>   sweet
> Than that of painted pomp? Are not these
>   woods
> More free from peril than the envious court?
> Here feel we not the penalty of Adam.
>
>   (II.i.1-5)

Exiled to Arden by his usurper-brother, Frederick, Duke Senior moralizes his own violated status as a paradoxically edifying experience, one in which the recovery of a communal (fraternal) ethic, in opposition to a courtly one, marks the return to a prelapsarian condition.

We must pause over such an idealization, of course. For it is possible to read the "pastoral" vision here as merely mystifying the class consciousness it appears to awaken. Montrose asserts, for example, that Renaissance pastoral typically "puts into play a symbolic strategy, which, by reconstituting the leisured gentleman as the gentle shepherd obfuscates a fundamental contradiction in the cultural logic: a contradiction between the secular claims of aristocratic prerogative and the religious claims of common origins, shared fallenness, and spiritual equality among . . . gentle and base alike."[26] For a modern reader especially, the very social structure maintained in Duke Senior's Arden weakens the political force of his claims for ethical restoration. From this limited perspective, that is, Duke Senior bears a remarkable resemblance to the gentleman-shepherd of so many Elizabethan pastorals, who, "in the idyllic countryside" is most determined to "escape temporarily from the troubles of court." As Montrose adds, "in such pastorals, ambitious Elizabethan gentlemen who may be alienated or excluded from the courtly society that nevertheless continues to define their existence can create an imaginative space within which virtue and privilege coincide."[27] The duke's idealization of the leisured life of the country would then, despite its egalitarian appeal, serve to re-emphasize the division between baseness and gentility and to celebrate aristocratic values in isolation from a broader vision of how those values serve as the foundation of an entire network of social relations.

We might note further how Duke Senior's aristocratic rhetoric appears to de-radicalize its own most potent political symbol: the image of a prelapsarian fraternal community. As Montrose and others have pointed out, from the Peasants' Revolt of 1381 onward popular social protest in England often challenged class stratification by appealing to a common Edenic inheritance. Powerfully condensed into the proverb, "When Adam dalf and Eve span, who was then the Gentleman?" such protest offered a radical critique of aristocratic privilege, both interrogating the suspect essentialism inherent in the notion of "degree" and reversing the valuation of labor as a criterion of social status.[28] Duke Senior's speech, however, does neither: it never questions the "naturalness' of his rank within the fraternal community (which never ceases to be hierarchically organized) nor does it champion labor as a morally edifying and communal burden. For Duke Senior, the retreat to a prelapsarian condition becomes rather the site from which to critique court corruption and decadence.

Nevertheless, we should not underestimate the reformist, populist impulse embedded in that critique. For, as act I depicts it, the condition of fallenness that exists in Frederick's court is defined primarily by its persecution of those members of the nobility—Orlando and Rosalind—most popular with the people (I.i.164-71, I.ii.277-83). Moreover, Orlando and Rosalind are conceptually linked to Sir Rowland himself, so universally "esteemed," as Frederick tells us, and so an enemy (I.ii.225-30). Frederick's function as the play's arch-villain is registered therefore, like Oliver's before him, by a lack of respect for the memory of that overdetermined father whose recurrent, if shadowy, presence in the play provides a "local habitation and name" to a broader cultural ideal: the forms of customary obligation that link gentle and base in pastoral fraternity, an evocation of religious communion that emphasizes social dependency and reciprocity even as it does not thereby reject society's hierarchical structure.

Much of the value (both moral and political) associated with that community is symbolized in Duke Senior's phrase "old custom" and its own associations with popular protest. As Patterson remarks, even when such protest did not advocate structural changes in the social order, an appeal to the authority of "origins" (again, often condensed into the recollection of a common Edenic origin) "was integral to the popular conception of *how* to protest, as well as providing theoretical grounds for the 'demands,' for the transformation of local and individual grievances into a political program."[29] *As You Like It* makes it clear that the duke's use of the phrase cannot be seen as privileging the rights of the nobility alone; indeed, Adam's subsequent lament over his exile (II.iii.71-4) is designed to set out the meaning of "old custom" from the perspective of the rural servant. Linking together a sense both of the immemorialness of custom and of its historical embeddedness by reference to his age and associating that further with the original Edenic dispensation through his name, Adam's speech marks how an appeal to customary practices could serve the interests of the lower orders.

In the tradition of popular protest, an idealization of the past could serve as the focal point of protesters' awareness of current social injustice, even as the perception of injustice was rarely separated from an appeal to the moral economy taken to subtend the political one. This ethical evaluation of the mutual interests of the upper and lower orders is powerfully figured in the tableau that closes act II: Duke Senior, Orlando, and Adam gathered together at a life-sustaining meal. Here, the problem of rural poverty (old Adam is starving to death) is answered in the nostalgic evocation of "better days," when paupers were "with holy bell . . . knoll'd to church, / And sat at good men's feasts" (II.vii.113-5). The meal, reimagined as a Sabbath-day feast, symbolizes the restoration of social communion especially as this is founded on those culturally sustaining lines of authority in which servants and masters properly recognize each other with reciprocal "truth and loyalty" (II.iii.70), the very qualities that were the hallmark of the days of Sir Rowland.[30]

In focusing on the paired plights of Orlando and Adam up through the end of act II, the play defines that perception of injustice, and of the moral obligations of the community, from the perspective of the lower orders and their first-hand experience of the effects of enclosure and eviction, dearth and hunger. Moreover, what Wilson misreads as Adam's subsequent "demise" (his disappearance from the play after act II) can be better understood as Shakespeare's attempt to give even more nuanced attention to the plight of the lower orders. In replacing Adam with the shepherd, Corin, as the play's test case, Shakespeare refocuses the issue of the condition of rural laborers in a character whose situation more obviously typifies such conditions in their particular relation to enclosure and eviction, especially in the face of the new commercialization of the land.

Significantly, Shakespeare puts the words describing the bleak prospects for rural living into Corin's own mouth; he thereby suggests a clear-sighted popular consciousness of the current situation. So Corin has earlier described his living in response to Rosalind's request for food and lodging:

> I am shepherd to another man,
> And do not shear the fleeces that I graze.
> My master is of churlish disposition,
> And little reaks to find the way to heaven
> By doing deeds of hospitality.
> Besides, his cote, his flocks, and bounds of feed
> Are now on sale, and at our sheep-cote now

> By reason of his absence there is nothing
> That you will feed on.

> (II.iv.78-86)

Hunger is again the central issue, but the exchange subtly shifts attention away from the almost incidental hunger of disguised aristocrats (who can afford to "buy entertainment" [line 72]) to the plight of the rural laborer whose suffering derives from the very condition of his employment (significantly, in the service of an absentee landlord). As Lawrence Stone summarizes the historical situation described here:

> the aristocracy suffered a severe loss of their landed capital in the late-Elizabethan period, primarily because of improvident sales made in order to keep up the style of life they considered necessary for the maintenance of status. When they abandoned sales of land and took to rigorous economic exploitation of what was left in order to maximize profits, they certainly restored their financial position, but at the expense of much of the loyalty and affection of their tenants. They salvaged their finances at the cost of their influence and prestige.

He adds that as part of a "massive shift away from a feudal and paternalist relationship" on the land, "these economic developments were dissolving old bonds of service and obligation," a process compounded by an "increasing preference [among the nobility] for extravagant living in the city instead of hospitable living in the countryside."[31] A figure for the current destruction of the manorial economy, Corin's master is guilty of all these charges simultaneously: he is absent from the estate; he exploits the (once commonly held) land for profit; he threatens to sell the estate with no concern for his workers' future prospects; he refuses the ethical responsibilities of his class—hospitable living, the sustenance of the customary culture, leadership of the countryside. The scene's concern with the immediate need to allay hunger becomes then a stepping-stone to a broader mediation on hunger's place in the complex socioeconomic transformation of late-Elizabethan culture. From the immediate perspective of the play, moreover, this transformation threatens to become a dangerous social upheaval, the blame for which must be assigned to the moral failure of well-to-do landowners.

As idealistic as it is, then, Celia and Rosalind's offer to purchase the "flock and pasture" and "mend" Corin's wages (II.iv.88, 94) retains an element of popular political consciousness; for it suggests that it is still possible for laborers to reap the rewards of faithful service to masters who know how to nurture traditional lines of authority.[32] Shakespeare's revision of his source text, Thomas Lodge's *Rosalynde,* is particularly relevant on this point, not the least for its demonstration of the deliberateness with which Shakespeare addresses the specific issue of economic hardship among the rural poor. In Lodge's romance, the shepherd (Coridon) offers Aliena and Ganimede the simple comforts of his lowly cottage as part of a traditional extolling of pastoral content:

> Marry, if you want lodging, if you vouch to shrowd your selves in a shepheardes cotage, my house . . . shalbe your harbour . . . [A]nd for a shepheards life (oh Mistresse) did you but live a while in their content, you would saye the Court were rather a place of sorrowe, than of solace. Here (Mistresse) shal not Fortune thwart you, but in meane misfortunes, as the losse of a few sheepe, which, as it breeds no beggerie, so it can bee no extreame prejudice: the next yeare may mend al with a fresh increase. Envie stirs not us, wee covet not to climbe, our desires mount not above our degrees, nor our thoughts above our fortunes. Care cannot harbour in our cottages, nor do our homely couches know broken slumbers: as we exceed not in diet, so we have inough to satisfie.[33]

The fact that the sheepcote is for sale (and so, by a stroke of good fortune, available as a home for the wandering noblewomen) is only incidental to Coridon's prospects; the simple pleasures of his life will hardly be affected by a change in masters. Shakespeare, by contrast, revalues Corin's poverty by tying it explicitly to his economic vulnerability in the new commercial market: as one who, as "shepherd to another," does not "shear the fleeces" he grazes. In associating Corin's straitened circumstances—his limited supply of food is not "inough to satisfie"—with his very lack of authority over the estate (and his master's unreliable ownership practices), Shakespeare's revision of the scene emphasizes the real threat of rural dispossession; he thus makes it clear that "pastoral content" can only result from a functional economic relation between servant and landowner: hence, Corin's concern that his new masters actually "like . . . / The soil, the profit, and this kind of life" (II.iv.97-8).

The conflicted relationship between leisured gentleman and base laborer is symbolically played out in the conversation between Corin and Touchstone in III.ii. Although the confrontation is humorous, it also includes a more serious evaluation of the attendant problems of social stratification, marked especially by the lack of respect shown toward common laborers. As Judy Z. Kronenfeld points out, Shakespeare here transforms the typical pastoral encounter in which an "aristocratic shepherd" (a gentleman pretending to be a shepherd) demonstrates courtly superiority by mocking the "clownish countryman" (or what is really a "burlesque version of the countryman").[34] What Shakespeare depicts instead is an encounter between a lowly court servant (now a pretended gentleman) and a sympathetically realistic shepherd. Touchstone's pretense to gentility in the scene hearkens back to his original meeting of Corin in II.iv. There, in the company of

Celia and Rosalind, Touchstone responds to Corin's "Who calls" with the demeaning "Your betters, sir" (lines 67-8): the response mockingly raises Corin to the level of the gentlewomen ("sir") only to reassert the difference in social standing ("your betters") and to place Touchstone in that higher circle.

Touchstone maintains the masquerade in III.ii when he attempts to flout Corin's baseness in a condescending display of courtly sophistication (lines 11-85). But, as Kronenfeld notes, the sophistication comes off as mere "court sophistry," and the emptiness of his claims to superiority is thereby exposed as nothing more than a witty social rhetoric covering over an absence of any clearly defined *essential* differences between gentle and base. Shakespeare thus uses the tradition against itself, for the typical encounter of aristocrat (pretending to be a shepherd) and countryman—where the contrast is meant to "reaffirm the social hierarchy"—is rewritten to suggest (albeit humorously) the mere pretense of that contrast.[35] It is possible to read the scene as positing that there are no differences between gentle and base, a position which might include the more radical recognition that class standing itself is merely the result of an ideological manipulation of cultural signs. Within the context of the play as a whole, however, it perhaps makes more sense to read it as a moral commentary on class division and especially on the meaning of aristocratic identity: if gentility is as much a social construct as it is a privileged condition of birth, its maintenance requires that it be continually reconstructed through meritorious signs, and these signs are to be made legible in the virtuous conduct shown toward those whose livelihood depends on how the "gentle" fulfill the obligations of their class.

III

In discussing George Puttenham's *Arte of English Poesie* in the context of Elizabethan pastoral discourse, Montrose cites Puttenham's claim that pastoral was developed among ancient poets "not of purpose to counterfait or represent the rusticall manner of loves and communication: but under the vaile of homely persons, and in rude speeches to insinuate and glaunce at greater matters, and such as perchance had not bene safe to have beene disclosed in any other sort."[36] Puttenham's related concerns with safety and the necessity of dissimulation in a dangerous social environment, the poet's self-awareness as a cultural commentator, and the struggle to make homely fiction serve the higher ends of instruction bring us back to Patterson's contention that Shakespeare's own "material practice" purposely seeks out "safely fictional forms" to achieve its ends. In *As You Like It*, moreover, Shakespeare's practice turns explicitly to pastoral form, which, we might surmise, is deliberately deployed to "glaunce at greater matters" "cleanly cover[ed]" (as Spenser puts it in the *Shepheardes Calender*) by a "feyne[d]" story.[37]

The precise nature of those "matters" and Shakespeare's specific ends may be debated, of course. But it is hard to imagine that they are any less comprehensive than those attributed by Montrose to Puttenham. Puttenham, Montrose writes, conceives "of poetry as a body of changing cultural practices dialectically related to the fundamental processes of social life"; and his "cultural relativism and ethical heterodoxy, his genuinely Machiavellian grasp of policy, are evident . . . in his pervasive concern with the dialectic between poetry and power."[38] It comes as some surprise, therefore, when Montrose later revises this estimation and gives us a Puttenham whose writing only serves the ends of personal aggrandizement within the confined circles of the court, whose sense of his culture's complexity is merely the sophistry of a "cunning princepleaser," and whose grasp of the political purposes of poetry never rises above its merely politic ends. And, as Montrose dismisses the narrowness of Puttenham's courtly orientation, so he dismisses pastoral discourse itself, whose power to "glaunce at greater matters" is suddenly reduced to courtliness in another form: thus, the "dominantly aristocratic" perspective of Elizabethan pastoral becomes but a reinscription of "agrarian social relations . . . within an ideology of the country," which is "itself appropriated, transformed, and reinscribed within an ideology of the court."[39] Pastoral's "greater matters," it seems, are only the matters of the great for whom the masks of rural encomium serve their own (narrowly defined) hegemonic interests. For Montrose, that is, despite pastoral writers' own recognition that their art form is "intrinsically political in purpose," pastoral's central concern with aristocratic identity only serves to mystify the issues of class standing and social relations it appears to raise.[40] As he argues, finally, because Renaissance pastoral "inevitably involve[s] a transposition of social categories into metaphysical ones, a sublimation of politics into aesthetics," it necessarily functions as "a weapon against social inferiors."[41]

Without denying pastoral's aristocratic orientation, we might note that it is only from the reductively binary perspective of the New Historicist that an "elite community" must be opposed to all "egalitarian ideas," or that its members could have "little discernible interest" in the condition of those who serve them.[42] *As You Like It* certainly suggests that such a critical perspective fails to register the possibility of the presence of dissenting voices within the dominant culture. Indeed, if the play is not in full support of the popular voice, it is yet concerned to link an aristocratic crisis of identity to the more vexing problems of the "base." Shakespeare's pastoral world is thus less concerned with celebrating nobles as virtuous than in reexamining the precise nature of aristocratic virtue. And lest we think Shakespeare is the exception that proves the rule, it is instructive to recall the aristocratic Sidney's own brief meditation on pastoral in his *Defence of Poesy*: "Is the poor pipe disdained, which sometimes out of Meliboeus' mouth can show the misery of people under hard lords and ravening soldiers and again, by Tityrus, what blessedness is derived to them that lie lowest from the goodness of them that sit highest?"[43] That "blessedness," moreover, is not presumed to be the reality of his culture but only a symbolic idealization challenging his aristocratic readers to a kind of creative, ethically oriented *imitatio*.

Montrose's Historicism cannot envision this possibility because he denies to Renaissance pastoral writers any critical distance from the courtly aristocracy from which they drew support (including occasional financial support). He goes even further in denying that "the mediation of social boundaries was [even] a *conscious* motive in the writing of Elizabethan pastorals," let alone that a cultural critique might have been leveled "in terms of a *consciously* articulated oppositional culture."[44] Such a dismissal of Renaissance writing as a purposeful, socially engaged activity is typical of New Historicist criticism more generally, which matches a methodological subordination of individual intention to larger "systems" of thought with a tonal condescension toward the capacity of earlier writers to comprehend their own cultural situations. Against this effacement of the subject, I would counter that an interest in the historical conditioning of texts is necessarily concerned with the conditions of their being written and being read, with the social processes by which meaning is formulated and communicated, with acts of knowledge as acts of persuasion, with the "rhetoricity" of texts as the essence of their historicity.[45] The reduction of historical criticism to the impersonal voice—to what Foucault once called the "it-is-said"[46]—precludes the possibility of understanding how the movement of ideas within discursive systems requires real readers and writers whose very activities help reveal to us the contours of historical existence.

Notes

[1] All references to Shakespeare's plays are to *The Riverside Shakespeare,* ed. G. Blakemore Evans (Boston: Houghton Mifflin, 1974).

[2] Celia's earlier remark to Touchstone—"since the little wit that fools have was silenc'd, the little foolery that wise men have makes a great show" (I.ii.88-90)—obliquely refers to this.

[3] Annabel Patterson, *Shakespeare and the Popular Voice* (Oxford: Basil Blackwell, 1989), pp. 4, 24.

[4] For a concise summary of these changing historical circumstances, see Lawrence Stone, *The Causes of the English Revolution, 1529-1642* (New York: Harper and Row, 1972), pp. 58-117.

[5] Louis Montrose, "'The Place of a Brother' in *As You Like It:* Social Process and Comic Form," *SQ* 32, 1 (Spring 1981): 28-54.

[6] Montrose, "'The Place of a Brother,'" pp. 34-5. That the exchange between Orlando and Oliver is more than just the struggle between younger and older brothers is emphasized by Orlando's response to Oliver's insulting question: "Know where you are, sir?" Orlando replies: "O sir, very well; here in your orchard" (I.i.40-1). The condition of "gentility" (marked in the mocking uses of "sir") is clearly tied to the question of who actually owns the property.

[7] Richard Wilson, "'Like the old Robin Hood': *As You Like It* and the Enclosure Riots," *SQ* 43, 1 (Spring 1992): 1-19, 3-5. For a historical overview of the broader cultural, political, and economic issues conditioning this hostility, see Roger B. Manning, *Village Revolts: Social Protest and Popular Disturbances in England, 1509-1640* (Oxford: Clarendon Press, 1988).

[8] Wilson, "'Like the old Robin Hood,'" pp. 4, 5, 9; my emphases.

[9] Wilson's lack of interest in what the text itself does to produce the meanings he finds in it is perhaps not so surprising given his attempt, formulated elsewhere, to theorize the fundamental irrelevance of literature to the forces of history and culture that must always supersede it. See his Introduction to *New Historicism and Renaissance Drama*, ed. Richard Wilson and Richard Dutton (London: Longman, 1992), pp. 1-18. It should be noted that Wilson considers himself a "Cultural Materialist" rather than a "New Historicist," and in that Introduction he seeks to differentiate the critical assumptions governing their respective practices. But the mode of argumentation employed in his essay on *As You Like It* does not bear out the differences he alleges.

[10] Alan Liu, "The Power of Formalism: The New Historicism," *ELH* 56, 4 (Winter 1989): 721-71, 721.

[11] Wilson, "'Like the old Robin Hood,'" pp. 4, 6, 9, 10-11, 13, 18.

[12] Wilson, "'Like the old Robin Hood,'" p. 3 and n. 15. Liu remarks that "the limitation of the New Historicism is that in its failure to carve out its own theory by way of a disciplined, high-level study of the evolution of historically situated language, its discoverable theory has been too assimilable to the deconstructive view of rhetoric as an a-, trans-, or uni-historical figural language" (p. 756). Although his own critical practice employs precisely this kind of formalism, Wilson himself makes much the same complaint about New Historicist critics, whose elision of historical referent in favor of the "textuality of history," he asserts, aligns them with New Critics (*New Historicism and Renaissance Drama*, pp. 9-10).

[13] Wilson first uses the phrase, without defining it, on p. 3 of "'Like the old Robin Hood'"; later he cites Foucault's observation that "in every society discourse is controlled and redistributed to avert its dangers and *evade its formidable materiality*." As an instance of this, Wilson notes that "pastoral discourse . . . *will conceal* the real revolution in the forest economy" (p. 17; my emphases). (Inexplicably, although in his Introduction to *New Historicism and Renaissance Drama* Wilson again notes Foucault's claim for the "'formidable materiality' of all discourse" [p. 9], he does so as part of his critique of the overly abstract post-Marxist practice of Foucault and other French intellectuals, especially as this tradition has become the philosophical foundation of American New Historicism.) For discussion of the trope of revelatory "concealment" within post-structuralist criticism, see Richard Levin, "The Poetics and Politics of Bardicide," *PMLA* 105, 3 (May 1990): 491-504, 493-4.

[14] One example: Touchstone's quip to the bumpkin, William, concerning their rival claims on Audrey—"to have, is to have" (V.i.40)—means, we are told, that a new concept of property ownership is now superseding traditional agrarian rights based on the notion of collective possession (Wilson, p. 18).

[15] Patterson, p. 14.

[16] Ibid.

[17] See Preface to *Volpone,* in *Ben Jonson,* ed. C. H. Herford and Percy and Evelyn Simpson, 11 vols. (Oxford: Clarendon Press, 1925-52), 5:18-9. Having been jailed again in 1604, along with Chapman and Marston, for the anti-Scottish sentiments of *Eastward Ho!,* Jonson used the Preface to chastise readers for their propensity for assigning topical meanings to his plays: by substituting local for more general meanings, Jonson thought, his readers would necessarily fail to appreciate the moral lessons of his writing and so not see how his meanings were to be used for their own edification and improvement.

[18] Leah Marcus, *Puzzling Shakespeare: Local Reading and Its Discontents* (Berkeley: Univ. of California Press, 1988), pp. 26, 41.

[19] For discussion, see Louis Montrose, "Of Gentlemen and Shepherds: The Politics of Elizabethan Pastoral Form," *ELH* 50, 3 (Fall 1983): 415-59, esp. 425, 433.

[20] Wayne A. Rebhorn, "The Crisis of the Aristocracy in *Julius Caesar*," *RenQ* 43, 1 (Spring 1990): 75-111, 81.

[21] For discussion, see Timothy Hampton, *Writing from History: The Rhetoric of Exemplarity in Renaissance Literature* (Ithaca: Cornell Univ. Press, 1990), pp. 198-236.

[22] For discussion, see Patterson, pp. 71-92.

[23] Hampton, pp. 210-4; Patterson, pp. 83-90.

[24] Montrose, "'The Place of a Brother,'" p. 46.

[25] On the importance of the noble manor to the aristocratic ethical ideal, see Don E. Wayne, *Penshurst: The Semiotics of Place and the Poetics of History* (Madison: Univ. of Wisconsin Press, 1984).

[26] Montrose, "Of Gentlemen and Shepherds," p. 432.

[27] Montrose, "Of Gentlemen and Shepherds," p. 427.

[28] Montrose, "Of Gentlemen and Shepherds," pp. 428-32; Patterson, pp. 39-46.

[29] Patterson, p. 41.

[30] For discussion of the cultural importance of the meal as a marker of "serviceable" authority in the Renaissance, see Michael Schoenfeldt, "'The Mysteries of Manners, Armes, and Arts': 'Inviting a Friend to Supper' and 'To Penshurst,'" in *"The Muses Common-Weale": Poetry and Politics in the Seventeenth Century,* ed. Claude J. Summers and Ted-Larry Pebworth (Columbia: Univ. of Missouri Press, 1988), pp. 62-79.

[31] Stone, pp. 68, 72, 84.

[32] The promise of increased wages for Corin recalls the 500 crowns Adam has saved under Sir Rowland (II.iii.38). Although Orlando goes on to extol Adam's virtue as "the constant service of the antique world, / When service sweat for duty, not for meed!" (lines 57-8), we see that dutiful service rightfully expects proper compensation.

[33] Thomas Lodge, *Rosalynde,* in *As You Like It* (A New Variorum Edition), ed. Howard H. Furness (Philadelphia, 1890), p. 338; spelling slightly modernized.

[34] Judy Z. Kronenfeld, "Social Rank and the Pastoral Ideals of *As You Like It*," *SQ* 29, 3 (Summer 1978): 333-48, 344.

[35] Kronenfeld, pp. 345, 344.

[36] Quoted in Montrose, "Of Gentlemen and Shepherds," p. 435.

[37] Edmund Spenser, *The Shepheardes Calender,* "September" (lines 137-9), in *Poetical Works,* ed. J. C. Smith and E. de Selincourt (Oxford: Oxford Univ. Press, 1970), p. 453.

[38] Montrose, "Of Gentlemen and Shepherds," pp. 435-6.

[39] Montrose, "Of Gentlemen and Shepherds," pp. 438-44, 426, 431.

[40] Montrose first makes this point in "'Eliza, Queene of shepheardes,' and the Pastoral of Power," *ELR* 10, 2 (Spring 1980): 153-82, 154.

[41] Montrose, "Of Gentlemen and Shepherds," pp. 446-7.

[42] Montrose, "Of Gentlemen and Shepherds," p. 427; for broader discussion, see Kevin Sharpe, *Politics and Ideas in Early Stuart England* (London: Pinter, 1989), esp. chaps. 1-2, 6, 10.

[43] Quoted in Kronenfeld, p. 334.

[44] Montrose, "Of Gentlemen and Shepherds," pp. 427, 432; my emphases.

[45] For discussion of the promise of this kind of "rhetorical" criticism, see Liu, p. 756.

[46] Michel Foucault, *The Archaeology of Knowledge,* trans. A. M. Sheridan-Smith (New York: Pantheon Books, 1972), p. 122.

APPEARANCE VS. REALITY

Peter Hyland (essay date 1978)

SOURCE: "Shakespeare's Heroines: Disguise in the Romantic Comedies," in *Ariel: A Review of International English Literature,* Vol. 9, No. 2, April, 1978, pp. 23-39.

[*In the following excerpt, Hyland emphasizes the metadramatic aspects of* As You Like It, *highlighted by Rosalind's pretense of being a man in the play.*]

Shakespeare clearly saw that to achieve the audience involvement that he wanted he had to allow the disguised heroine to dominate the play; even so, in *As*

You Like It, because he still feels the need to justify the act of disguising he does not bring Ganymede into the play until II.iv. As Ganymede, Rosalind does dominate the play, but it is significant that until she takes on her male disguise she appears to be weaker than Celia. Celia it is who suggests the idea of flight and disguise, while Rosalind can only raise somewhat fearful objections:

> Why, whither shall we go? . . .
> Alas, what danger will it be to us,
> Maids as we are, to travel forth so far!
>   (I. iii. 102, 104-5)

It is only when she gets the idea of disguising herself as a man that Rosalind becomes the stronger and more active of the two. So, at her first appearance as a man, Rosalind consciously takes the dominant position: "I could find it in my heart to disgrace my man's apparel, and to cry like a woman; but I must comfort the weaker vessel, as doublet and hose ought to show itself courageous to petticoat; therefore, courage, good Aliena" (II.iv.4-7). And as doublet and hose assert themselves here, so do they throughout the play, as all confusions relate directly to Rosalind's disguise.

Rosalind's primary, female persona steps quite consciously out of the action, leaving the secondary persona Ganymede to inhabit the same plane as the other characters. The effect of this is to put Rosalind in the position, shared by the audience, of acknowledging the artifice of the play. "I'll prove a busy actor in their play" (III.iv.54), she says as she decides to interfere in the affairs of Phebe and Silvius, and her words, in their self-consciousness, could well refer to her position in the play as a whole. For much of *As You Like It* is in effect created and stage-managed by Rosalind. When she persuades Orlando to pretend that Ganymede is Rosalind she puts herself in a position to play her own part and yet keep at a distance from it; the audience, at the same distance, appreciates fully the nature of her control. She is Rosalind watching Ganymede watching Rosalind, and fully aware of her own position and its relation to that of the audience. In projecting herself out into the audience in this way, she draws them further into the play. This is important, since it is Rosalind's point of view that balances and encloses all others, both romantic and satiric, and the use made of her disguise firmly aligns the audience with this point of view.

Rosalind's special consciousness of her position in relation to the artifice of the play is emphasized in the last act. In presenting the masque which resolves all the confusions of the play she is equating herself with the playmaker, who necessarily stands outside the action; while at the same time her participation in the masque returns her to the artifice of the action, since Ganymede disappears and Rosalind once again joins

the actors within the illusion. Not for long, however, for she soon steps out of the play once again in order to speak the Epilogue, and it is worth noting that this is the only occasion in Shakespearian drama where a female character speaks the Epilogue or even, indeed, the last word. It is most appropriate that she should, for in directly addressing the audience in this way she is acknowledging the intimate nature of the relationship they have shared throughout the play.

Wolfgang Iser (essay date 1983)

SOURCE: "The Dramatization of Double Meaning in Shakespeare's *As You Like It,*" in *Theatre Journal,* Vol. 35, No. 3, October, 1983, pp. 307-32.

[*In the following essay, Iser explores the dramatic representations of language in* As You Like It, *in terms of themes of doubling—double meanings, doublings of character through disguise, and doubled worlds.*]

I

As You Like It is a dramatic adaptation of a well-known pastoral romance, and as such it testifies to the irresistible wave of shepherds that engulfed the literary scene of the Renaissance.[1] The pastoral world embraced all genres of the age, and changed the system of genres by introducing a new one in the shape of the pastoral romance, which broke down the boundaries within which the eclogue had been confined. But even the traditional form of the eclogue had not used its shepherds merely to depict rustic life—they always served to designate something other than themselves. In the pastoral romance, this purpose was fulfilled by the representation of two different worlds: Arcadia would either reflect the social and political world, or be confronted by it. And as Arcadia was, from the very beginning, a product of art—with its origins in Virgil's *Eclogues*—the romance also made it possible for the reader to observe the relation of art to reality as well as the effects brought about by this relation. Furthermore, Renaissance pastoral was considered to be a product of the feigning process through which reality could be repeated as a game, allowing a sort of replay of those courses of action excluded by the real actions of the social and political worlds. Thus the pastoral world remained tied to one outside itself, and by linking the two the pastoral romance took on its generic pattern.

Now despite the interrelation of these two worlds, they in fact embody two very different semiotic systems, with a clearly marked boundary running between them. The far-reaching importance of this dividing line can be gauged from the fact that the central characters who cross from the socio-political into the pastoral world are split into two persons, and thus by doubling themselves are able to act out the difference between what they have been and what they have now become. Playing a double role reflects the duality of the two worlds represented by the characters themselves, and in speaking with two voices, they are able to exceed the limitations of each of those worlds.

Though Shakespeare took the plot of his comedy from Lodge's *Rosalynde,* his adaptation did not focus so much on action as on the *"double-voiced discourse"* given dramatic expression by the dialogue.[2] And as the different speeches are spoken in different worlds, they have to incorporate the distinction between these worlds; thus the political "voice" has to be different from the pastoral—what is hidden by the one will be revealed by the other.

One might say that the whole comedy is based on the principle of doubling. At the beginning the political world itself appears on two different, though parallel levels: Oliver has his double in his brother Orlando, who also has a claim to his father's inheritance, and Duke Frederick has his in his brother, the Old Duke, whose position he has usurped. In both cases the presence of the double is regarded as a threat which can be removed only by means of separation—the Old Duke is driven away, and Orlando is robbed of his rights. This separation, however, can be achieved only by breaking the code upon which the usurper depends for the stability of his own position: for Frederick it is government, for Oliver it is the family. Their protection of themselves through the very system they have violated entails the constant potential presence of their doubles, and herein lies the basic pattern of the political world.

The theme is made evident right from the start, through the eyes of Orlando, the rejected double. He is depressed by the miserable situation in which he is kept by his brother Oliver:

> My brother Jaques he keeps at school, and report speaks goldenly of his profit: for my part, he keeps me rustically at home, or, to speak more properly, stays me here at home unkept; for call you that keeping for a gentleman of my birth, that differs not from the stalling of an ox? His horses are bred better; for besides that they are fair with their feeding, they are taught their manage, and to that end riders dearly hired: but I, his brother, gain nothing under him but growth, for the which his animals on his dunghills are as much bound to him as I. Besides this nothing that he so plentifully gives me, the something that nature gave me his countenance seems to take from me.
>
> [I.i.5-18]

The word-play on *keep* and *unkept* lights up connotations which, in each case, are swiftly snuffed out. The individual meanings of the word must clash if Orlando's

sadness (I.i.4) is to find expression. Since he receives so much of the nothing, and since Oliver continually takes away the something nature (their common stock) gave him, the key words of Orlando's statement can only be understood by way of their opposites (e.g., *keep* means unkeep, and *give* means take away). Thus the speech incorporates another speech which is not articulated because it lies outside the words spoken, but is nevertheless present through the distortion of meanings.

Nothing and *something* here are dialogic words that yoke together meaning and contradiction in such a way that each cancels out the other. Obviously, this brings out the unnaturalness of the brother's behavior, but the opening of the play contains more than just this piece of exposition. It also introduces the theme which is to be orchestrated throughout the comedy. Orlando's speech is what Bakhtin called a "dialogized hybrid," for it is "precisely the fusion of *two* utterances into one", in which the speaker is present to the extent that he is there only to be displaced by a voice that is not speaking.[3] Thus the words incorporate the conflict between two voices, the dramatic point being that the silent voice prevails over that which is speaking.

The probability that Oliver will fail to suppress his double is already clear from the first dialogue between the brothers. After a short exchange, it leads very swiftly to violence, for Orlando continually doubles Oliver's words with their unsuspected implications, thus imposing on him the very double that he wishes to be rid of. The climax of this dialogue comes not with the actual violence but with a play on words. As the two of them scuffle, Oliver calls Orlando a *villain* (I.i.55), whereupon Orlando answers:

> I am no villain. I am the youngest son of Sir Rowland de Boys: he was my father, and he is thrice a villain that says such a father begot villains. Wert thou not my brother, I would not take this hand from thy throat till this other had pulled out thy tongue for saying so. Thou hast railed on thyself.
>
> [I.i.56-62]

Thus if Orlando is a villain—because he is fighting Oliver—then Oliver is not only insulting their father, whose blood is doubled in the two sons, but also himself, because he is Orlando's double. Oliver may well have been unconscious of this implication at the moment of speaking, and he would most certainly not have intended it. But the implication is by no means an arbitrary one, for it links the utterance to a code that is valid for both characters, thereby endowing it with a meaning that must either thwart Oliver's intention or show it to be a violation of the code. Oliver remains unaware of this duality, for it is a feature of the language of usurpation that it is monologic—it always seeks to equate language and reality, thereby expunging those connotations which even a denotative use of language cannot help evoking.

The implications, however, which remain unconscious in such pragmatic speech may have their repercussions if only through the fact that the listener must interpret his partner's words in order to understand them. There can never be an automatic transfer of intentions from one partner to the other; meaning is not integral to an utterance, but has to be ascribed to it by the listener, which entails a process of interpretation. This in turn depends upon the implications contained within the utterance, and these cannot always be fully controlled by the intention of the speaker. Thus the verbalization of the unspoken can lead to all sorts of surprises.

The dialogic character of language is thus evident from the very first lines of the very first scene: Oliver's injustice emerges through Orlando's irony, and Oliver's intentions fail through the implications of his utterances. This bracketing together of meanings that run counter to each other dramatizes the dialogic nature of the words.

For Oliver the best solution is a deliberately monologic use of words, and this is what he practices in the ensuing scene with Charles. Charles is a wrestler prepared to take on all challengers, but with the warning that the outcome of any match will be fatal. Charles is worried that Orlando wants to fight him and may therefore suffer a fate that Charles would rather not impose. Oliver, however, sees his chance to be rid of Orlando, and so he tells Charles about his brother's "villainous" nature and evil plots. Thus the two finally come to an understanding, but it is an understanding in which what is said (Orlando's alleged plotting) conceals what is meant.

The examples we have quoted at the beginning of the play reveal a conspicuous doubleness of the language, and although this varies in its nature, in all cases it is marked by the distinction between the manifest and the latent. The more the language negates itself, as in Orlando's speech, the more apparent is the latent meaning; the more exclusive the manifest seeks to be, the more illusory becomes the utterance. Orlando's speech appears to be negated as alien meanings insinuate themselves into what he says; although they are silent, they dominate the utterance. Orlando, then, is present in what he is not. Oliver's speech appears to be illusory, as he eradicates the interconnection between what is said and what is implied. Oliver, then, experiences this obliteration as a thwarting of his intentions. The difference which marks off the latent from the manifest may vary in degree, thereby requiring us to change our sense of the patterns of their relationship, but—whatever the relation—the difference can never be eradicated even if it is supposed to be. When difference is emphasized, negations abound; when it is wiped out,

the utterance becomes illusive. Whichever is the case, difference makes itself felt in one form or another, and consequently all language use is inevitably marked by it. Regardless of which element is dominant, the latent comes to the fore both in negation and illusiveness, spotlighting what has not been coped with in the respective instances.

The dialogue arises out of what needs to be mastered, and it is doubtful whether it can ever take on a finality other than the pragmatic; for it would seem that the latent can never be fully integrated into the manifest, in consequence of which the dialogue can only unfold varying relationships between the two. This at any rate is the situation of the dialogue in the political world at the start of the play.

If the very first dialogue in the comedy fails, this is because words for Orlando are dialogic and for Oliver monologic; for the former the spoken is doubled by the unspoken, which endows it with its meaning, while for the latter the spoken aims at an equation of language and object, with all implications being suppressed. For Orlando, however, the dialogic word is merely a weapon with which to strike Oliver, and so ultimately it is subjected to pragmatic ends; the monologic word, on the other hand, is an expression of power which—because it imposes univocal meanings—inevitably results in a split between utterance and intention. In the first instance the double meaning is pragmatized, and in the second it has to be suppressed, and so it becomes a negative foil to the array of possibilities that are unfolded in the Forest of Arden.

There is one further sense in which the language of the dialogue acts as a reflection of the political world. The latter is characterized by the theme of usurpation—Oliver in the context of family, Duke Frederick in that of government. Usurpation depends on the suppression of the double, and this is why the monologic words of the usurper are always calculated to establish the univocal meaning he desires. But this very requirement betrays the fact that behind his utterances lurks a 'latent' which cannot be banished if the cherished purpose is to be fulfilled. Thus the monologic word is also caught up by the inherent structure of language itself. The spoken is always impregnated with associations that cannot be dispensed with, and every object to which the spoken refers is one that has already been described in countless ways, so that whatever is said about it can only be a selection from the possibilities, thus defining itself by what it excludes. The dialogue in the political world of this comedy shows the extent to which the unspoken is always present alongside the spoken. In the example we discussed earlier, what is unspoken in the quarrel between Oliver and Orlando is the breaking of the code that is equally valid for both—though here the unspoken establishes its presence by an utterance which undoes its own intention. The dialogue brings home to us the continual presence of something that is absent, and this applies even when hypocrisy—at least to the spectator's eyes—makes the spoken appear to be the suppression of the true intention. Through the doubling process of the overt and the covert, language brings about a constant switch between the present and the absent, and in this way it runs counter to the pragmatic actions of the political protagonists.

Thus we have Duke Frederick banishing Rosalind from his court and telling his daughter Celia, who has pleaded on Rosalind's behalf:

> She is too subtle for thee, and her smoothness,
> Her very silence, and her patience
> Speak to the people and they pity her.
> Thou art a fool; she robs thee of thy name,
> And thou wilt show more bright and seem
>   more virtuous
> When she is gone.
>
> [I.iii.73-78]

Here the Duke projects his own fear onto the situation of his daughter, whom he sees as being threatened by her double in such a way that along with the loss of her name she might herself be obliterated. This may well have been the reason for his removing his own double. Yet what is spoken appears to be unreal the moment Celia reveals what has so far been concealed, namely that she and Rosalind are two in one ("thou and I am one" [I.iii.93]). This is why they now flee together to the Forest of Arden, although the whole point of the Duke's banishing Rosalind was to remove this "identity."

Thus failed speech-acts highlight the situation of the usurpers in the political world. They may be able to get rid of their doubles, but they cannot escape the doubleness of language. This endows the language of power with a touch of comedy, as the usurpers' removal of their respective doubles is imposed on language itself by eradicating its interplay between the manifest and the latent. Language, then, seems almost to defend itself against this manner of its use, re-establishing the doubleness between revealing and concealing by making the excluded strike back at the excluder. What has been suppressed now wrecks the plans that underlie the spoken, and this process turns language itself into a comic paradigm as it both undercuts the position of power and promises a resolution of the conflict. The pattern of restitution necessary for such an outcome is provided by the doubling of worlds that Shakespeare took over from the pastoral romance.

II

The Forest of Arden, to which the main characters run away, is a northern Arcadia. Although the shepherds

themselves become peripheral figures through the intrusion of the refugees from the political world, this does not affect their sign value, which invokes the traditional function of the pastoral world. This remains a creation of art which does not designate itself or exist in its own right, but refers to another world to which it is tied. No matter how different the rustic world may be from the political, this difference is never taken so far that the pastoral world can establish itself as a counter to the real one. If it did, it would have to carry its own definition with it, thus losing its true function: to mirror what is concealed in the world to which it is linked.

Although the usurpers force their doubles to take refuge in the Forest of Arden, this is neither conceived as a haven for the banished nor as a realm of escape. On the contrary, it is a place of freedom, as Celia points out when they are crossing the boundaries between the two worlds: "Now we go in content/To liberty, and not to banishment" (I.iii.133-134). Thus the relation of rustic to political is one of the counter-image rather than the counter-reality. Whatever may be the nature of the individual images, the rustic world as an image clearly represents something other than itself. Normally this 'other' is the political world, and so the conflicts and quarrels of this world constantly recur in the pastoral, but the image embodies, as Gadamer has put it, "an increase in being" of that which it pictures, and this is bound to result in a change of what is represented.[4]

Since the image changes the nature of the reality it depicts, clearly the change will be all the more fundamental in the case of a counter-image. This, like all images, takes an extract from reality, but turns it upside down, so that whatever may be the realities of the political world, in the pastoral they take on the character of a game. The Old Duke talks of them in terms of "the scene/Wherein we play in" (II.vii.138-139). Whatever the actual events, life in the Forest of Arden is put in brackets, thus providing an opportunity for the characters to bring out into the open what the code of the political world had denied them. The substance of the ensuing game is a repeat of the lives of the characters who, being released from the encroachments of reality, indulge in playing themselves. Turning themselves into actors allows them to stage their own other selves. The masks they have donned appear to be a mirror reflecting the reverse side of what they are, thereby making them aware of their own rear view, as it were. Thus they rehearse their actions as a test of reality in order, ultimately, to revolutionize the political world to which they will eventually return.

Furthermore, this constant staging and rehearsing of realities indicates that whatever is termed a world only reflects a state of affairs; it is one among many possibilities, and no single possibility can ever be equated with *the* world. Thus, the world mirrored in the counter-image is bound to undergo a change, simply because the state of affairs portrayed reveals itself as a particular form of world, highlighted by the fact that the pastoral counter-image has put the represented world in brackets. But since form is indispensable for the presentation of the world, only play allows for a depiction of the world as if it were such, thus avoiding the identification of the world with its form.

The game not only spotlights an aspect different from the world put in brackets, but it also represents the very conditions according to which a world may be assembled. This, however, is something which in the pragmatic world of political and social realities is always eclipsed, so that only the reality staged in the counter-image provides a glimpse into the circumstances that give rise to the organization of worlds. And this, in turn, can only be acted out in play, as any other means of objectifying would be tantamount to an explanation of origins, which play is forever subverting.

The distinction between the two worlds has certain repercussions on the language that may be seen on two widely differing levels. The first concerns the two extremes marked by Jaques and the fool, and the second is to be found in the characters who are disguised. The participation of Jaques and Touchstone in the two worlds is unbalanced in that Jaques only lives in the forest, whereas Touchstone lives in both worlds. Jaques and Touchstone also differ from the main characters in that they are not disguised and thus do not enter the play in the form of a counter-image.

Jaques' language is conspicuous through a feature which, in the political world, is only to be observed in Orlando's speeches. In the dialogue with Oliver, Orlando brought out the hidden implications in order to reverse the manifest meaning by uncovering the latent. In Jaques this tendency becomes virtually an obsession. Even before he comes on stage, we hear that:

> Thus most invectively he pierceth through
> The body of country, city, court,
> Yea, and of this our life. swearing that we
> Are mere usurpers, tyrants, and what's worse,
> To fright the animals and to kill them up
> In their assign'd and native dwelling-place.
> [II.i.58-63]

Jaques views all conventions as social disguises. They are for him fictions in which people wrap themselves in order to conceal the motives behind their behavior. This is why he regards himself as an outsider, living on the fringes of society. As conventions are merely a disguise, he continually pulls the rug from underneath all utterances in order to bring the speaker's overt behavior crashing down. In the political world, only

Orlando unmasked the latent behind the manifest, but in the Forest of Arden this linguistic self-defense heads off in a slightly different direction. In principle, Jaques does the same as Orlando, but within the counter-image the same can never be the same, for while the real world *is,* the image world reflects. Exposing the hidden aspects of utterances in order to show them up as disguises must in turn entail a hidden code which regulates all links between the manifest and the latent in terms of a determinate relationship. Jaques sees this code as being integral to language itself, and so for him double meaning simply reflects concealment: it is a semiotics of duplicity. But this brings him into difficulties with his melancholy, which he takes to be the only genuine reality that he has gained from experience—experience of which Rosalind remarks: "Then to have seen much and to have nothing is to have rich eyes and poor hands" (IV.i.22-23). If the manifest is only a disguise of the latent, then one cannot help suspecting that Jaques' identification of himself with melancholy can itself only be a disguise. Indeed, it could even be the expression of a hidden desire to belong to the very society that he appears to despise. If this were so, the double meaning that Jaques purports to have seen through might well rebound on him, for the code he keeps unmasking would also apply to himself. Excepting oneself from an otherwise universal law is indicative of a blindness which in turn may raise the possibility that the link between manifest and latent is *not* as automatically coded as Jaques' unmasking technique would seem to imply. But if it is not, then either there must be alternative structures of double meaning, or Jaques is guilty of double standards.

The political world makes double meaning appear to be a matter only of disguise and unmasking, but this is not due to the structure of double meaning so much as to the prevailing pragmatic pressures. Jaques does identify the relation between the manifest and the latent with these pressures, for he invokes as evidence the lessons of his experience. But that which orients the political world does not govern behavior in the Forest of Arden, for this is not a world of experience: it is a reflection of the world to which it is linked for the purpose of divulging what has hitherto been concealed in that world.

Now, to what extent does Jaques reflect the reverse side of what became obvious in the dialogue between Orlando and Oliver? In the latter, double meaning indicated that which escaped mastery, whereas for Jaques double meaning is reduced to a trope for universal duplicity. Through him, the underlying structure of dialogue pervading the political world is repeated in the pastoral world, reifying, however, one aspect of the relation between manifest and latent, and thereby blacking out the whole range of possibilities inherent in this relationship. And this makes him into an outsider not only for the society in which he finds himself, but also for the pastoral play world. Whoever is in the game, but cannot take part in it, will be overcome by melancholy.

This is why Jaques cannot stand the game, for to him it is not different from reality; on the contrary, "All the world's a stage" (II.vii.139), as he says at the beginning of the famous speech with which he equates the pastoral and political worlds. By cancelling out the semiotic difference between game and reality, Jaques only causes this difference to emerge again as a sort of split in his own behavior. What he takes to be the code of double meaning appears to be nothing but an oppositional relationship between showing and concealing which merely points toward the pragmatic function double meaning is meant to serve, at the same time indirectly drawing attention to its other potential functions. What Jaques regards as his identity is as deceptive an appearance as the masks of the other characters, for he does not recognize that the melancholy by which he defines himself is as much a definition by convention as that which he applies to them. Ultimately his speech-acts, which he regards as acts of unmasking, always fall on stony ground because the play world brackets off that very reality within which the disclosure of hidden implications takes on its pragmatic significance. If Jaques takes one particular mode of double meaning to be its nature, then the nature of double meaning emerges from the fact that what he takes to be insight is actually blindness. Nowhere is the difference between game and reality, which Jaques suppresses, more evident than in the language of Orlando which Jaques reflects; in the political world, Orlando's language was self-defense, and by mirroring this speech-act under the changed conditions of the Forest of Arden, Jaques' language turns out to be a defense against other possible forms of double meaning. What led in the first instance to revelation, here in the second becomes concealment of all the other potential structures inherent in the relation of manifest to latent. In the pastoral counter-image, then, Jaques' utterances serve to show—though involuntarily—not only that there is multifarious interplay between the manifest and the latent, but also that the form of this relationship changes according to context. If the hidden can be drawn forth from dialogue, this implies that every utterance is doubled by what remains unspoken, the articulation of which makes the utterance transparent. But this, in turn, requires a standpoint which is able to bring forth the unspoken, thereby itself being doubled by an unspoken which does not become transparent in that particular speech-act. And so on, ad infinitum.

This prevents Jaques from becoming a fool, though he would like to be one (II.vii.42). He has great admiration for the fool, but in fact he misunderstands him because he thinks that what is said and what is meant coincide in the fool's language, thereby eliminating double meaning (see especially II.vii.14-34). This im-

plies, however, that in such cases Jaques cannot help presuming that the eradication of difference between saying and meaning in the fool's speech arises out of an as yet unfathomed meaning. If that were so, the much admired speech of the fool would not just highlight the obliterated interplay between the manifest and the latent, which Jaques assumes to be the case, but would turn the fool's speech into a manifest meaning pointing to an undisclosed latent one. Thus Jaques falls prey to the structure of double meaning which—though he recognizes it—he has reduced to double-tongued duplicity. His failure to see what he already knows—i.e., the double meaning of language—is due to the fact that he thinks transparency removes double meaning. Although he shows an awareness which the characters from the political world lack, he nevertheless falls victim to this very awareness by making it the be-all and end-all and so failing to grasp that which gives rise to awareness. When he meets the fool, Jaques' failure to discern the difference between manifest and latent results in an admiration that amazes even himself; when he meets the other characters his awareness of the difference is all too strong, so that his idea of double meaning is itself a univocal meaning. Consequently his unmasking activity seems futile because in the play world the context for such speech-acts has changed, and therefore double meaning as he sees it appears to be distorted and thus serves to show up his own lack of awareness. Double meaning has, so to speak, caught Jaques out because he can only conceive of it in terms of the pragmatic conditions pertaining to the political world. If Jaques were not acting in a play world, he would be a figure of fun because his own consciousness dupes him. But in the play world, the man who thinks he knows everything becomes melancholic, because his certainty stops him from grasping the other possibilities which the game might add to those he already knows.

Unlike Jaques, Touchstone belongs to both worlds, though at the same time he remains an outsider to both. From the very start he has a double role which he can unite in his single person, in contrast to the other characters. In the political world, the protagonists suppress their doubles, and in the pastoral world they double themselves through their disguises. The fool, however, is always his own double without ever having to disguise himself. The Fool is traditionally a doubling figure, usually functioning as an inverted mirror-image of his master—the classic example being the Fool in *King Lear*. Touchstone also functions as a double, both in the world where the double is suppressed and in that where the characters provide their own doubles.

In Touchstone's first conversation with Celia and Rosalind, he swears by his honor that he is not a messenger from Duke Frederick. The dialogue continues as follows:

CELIA: Where learned you that oath, fool?

TOUCHSTONE: Of a certain knight, that swore by his honour they were good pancakes, and swore by his honour the mustard was naught. Now I'll stand to it, the pancakes were naught and the mustard was good, and yet was not the knight forsworn.

CELIA: How prove you that in the great heap of your knowledge?

ROSALIND: Ay marry, now unmuzzle your wisdom.

TOUCHSTONE: Stand you both forth now: stroke your chins, and swear by your beards that I am a knave.

CELIA: By our beards, if we had them, thou art.

TOUCHSTONE: By my knavery, if I had it, then I were. But if you swear by that that is not, you are not forsworn. No more was this knight, swearing by his honour, for he never had any; or if he had, he had sworn it away before ever he saw those pancakes or that mustard.

CELIA: Prithee, who is't that thou mean'st?

TOUCHSTONE: One that old Frederick your father loves.

[I.ii.58-76]

The logical proposition, the stringency of argumentation, and the linguistic precision are meant to substantiate the so-called honor that Touchstone has sworn by. Now honor is the highest value in courtly society and is therefore the prevailing convention in the political world of Duke Frederick. The argument itself is two-edged, for the social value is implicitly downgraded by being linked to culinary matters in order to provide a seemingly unmistakable reference that will consolidate its validity. Built into this logical argument is a sort of toppling effect which, while leaving the argument itself intact, nevertheless sets it against a background that totally trivializes the point it seeks to make. This foreshadows the basic fabric of double meaning which can now emerge from the dialogue in so many different guises.

In this example, honor is trivialized because the knight in question has none. In this respect, the trivialization does not entail a devaluation of the social norm. But the knight happens to be a trusted follower of Duke Frederick's, and so if a man whom the duke loves has no honor, then the social system which the duke represents is unmasked as dishonorable. Conversely, if the knight does have honor, then the fool must be a knave. But since the ladies swear by their beards that he is a knave, thus basing their oath on something that does not exist, it follows that the fool is not a knave, and so the manifested social values of the political world are indeed shown to be disguises. Furthermore, the fool endows his speech with a high degree of precision, but this precision is based on something that

does not exist. In this way the fool's language reflects the monologic speech of the usurpers, who not only make reality conform to what they say, but also invent states of affairs, in order to posit them as realities.

The fool's language explodes into multiple senses, each of which co-exists with the others and is controllable by the lexical meaning of the words, allowing for the comprehension of each of the individual significations. This multiplicity arises out of the fact that his utterances are always voiced in given situations which are themselves conditioned in many different ways. As the fool refrains from adopting any one permanent standpoint, he is in a position to bring out the many potential meanings inherent in a situation. He is therefore often misunderstood by his partners because they tend to extract a single sense from his utterances—a sense which may well have been intended but nevertheless is a misrepresentation insofar as this sense is only one among several and therefore takes its relevance from its relation to other senses and not so much from an understanding of the situation. The fact that his language is marked by multiple senses but is interpreted as if it were unequivocal points to the paradoxical structure of meaning itself. The multiplicity of senses is caused by the fact that every situation, brought about by interdependent actions and intersecting viewpoints, contains a plurality of voices. If this plurivocity is to be verbalized, the distinctions and differences of the various senses pertaining to and inherent in the situation have to be strictly observed. In order to accomplish this, the fool cannot have a personal language of his own, but must be able to speak all the "languages" of the situation without ever opting for just one, for if he did, he would then identify himself with that one and so exclude all the others. It is only because he has no language of his own that he can speak all these "foreign" languages. His partners, however, are bewildered by the apparent instability of his speeches, because what he says seems to be constantly switching over to other possible senses. And so when they misunderstand him or regard his utterances as nonsensical or opt for just one of the possible senses, they ought to realize that meaning only becomes meaning by way of the attitude adopted to what has been said. But this attitude is of a pragmatic and not a semantic nature; it reveals the use that is made of meaning, as well as the degree to which this practical function blots out the range of other possibilities. Thus the pragmatic meaning is doubled by that which it excludes; it becomes meaning because of its preciseness, and this depends on those elements which the language does not articulate.

The dialogues between the fool and the other characters continually illustrate this principle. Thus unlike Jaques, the fool does not pull out the double meaning of every utterance in order to expose its disguised motivations, but he twists every situation in such a way that its multifariousness reveals the extent to which meaning fulfills its pragmatic function by consolidating itself to the exclusion of other meanings.

Since the fool refrains from adopting any stance toward his own language, each of the emerging senses is made to topple over into another, and as this happens to all of them, they begin to parody one another. "Linguistic consciousness—parodying the direct word . . . its absurd sides . . . constituted itself *outside* this direct word and outside all its graphic and expressive means of representation. A new mode developed for working creatively with language: the creating artist began to look at language from the outside, with another's eyes, from the point of view of a potentially different language and style . . . The creating consciousness stands, as it were, on the boundary line between languages and styles. This is, for the creating consciousness, a highly peculiar position to find itself in with regard to language."[5] The fool has this creative mind insofar as he always stands on the boundaries of possible senses, toppling what has been hidden by one out into the openness of the others. There are always several languages intersecting in his speeches, and the point of their intersection is a kind of semantic blank which denotes that meaning is not to be deduced from meaning but from a source that is not in itself semantic. In the fool's language, difference itself is made visible as the generative matrix out of which the multiplicity of senses arises, and as they mutually encroach upon each other, they point to an origin which is non-semantic in nature.

The fool does not have to alter his linguistic behavior when he accompanies Rosalind and Celia to the Forest of Arden. As he is, so to speak, extraterritorial in relation to both worlds, his basic mode of speaking remains the same, though differently orchestrated in relation to the prevailing circumstances. If the mutual toppling of the multiple senses reveals what each one of them has excluded, then difference gives rise to a semiotic interplay between the overt and the covert. As the political world is dominated by pragmatic pressures of various kinds, this semiotic interplay is virtually endless; it reflects the never-ending exclusions brought about by the pressing demands pervading the political actions—demands which are counteracted by the plurivocity of the fool's speech. In the Forest of Arden everything turns into a game, allowing the fool to play with the toppling effect of his own plurivocal speech. In the political world, his language refers mainly to the norms of courtly society, whereas in the Forest of Arden its main concern is the game of love, but since the pastoral world is already a mirror of relationships as they existed in the political world, the fool's speeches go one better than this mirroring effect by bringing out the reverse side of the love-play, i.e., they reflect what even play tends to eclipse. This is clearly to be seen in the conversation between

Touchstone and Audrey, the shepherdess he is wooing:

> TOUCHSTONE: When a man's verses cannot be understood, nor a man's good wit seconded with the forward child, understanding, it strikes a man more dead than a great reckoning in a little room. Truly, I would the gods had made thee poetical.
>
> AUDREY: I do not know what 'poetical' is. Is it honest in deed and word? Is it a true thing?
>
> TOUCHSTONE: No truly; for the truest poetry is the most feigning, and lovers are given to poetry; and what they swear in poetry may be said as lovers they do feign.
>
> AUDREY: Do you wish then that the gods had made me poetical?
>
> TOUCHSTONE: I do truly. For thou swear'st to me thou art honest. Now if thou wert a poet, I might have some hope thou didst feign.
>
> [III.iii.9-23]

At best, Touchstone's speech seems to Audrey to be loaded with countersense, and in any case, what he tells her overtaxes her intellect. Audrey swears she is honest, and thus implicitly invokes a love code through which society has brought man's basically antisocial passion under control. Now, if the desire for love can find its expression in terms of a prevailing code, then clearly it has already been tamed by social convention. Despite this adverse effect, the code is necessary if passion is to be fulfilled within the desired context. That which appears to be mutually exclusive can only be brought together by poetry, for only poetry can give uninhibited expression to the desire for love. Whenever expression is verbalized, this very act is permeated by a basic ambivalence. "Expression in language. . . . like all codes, has a double status: it is both the necessary systematization of experience and a reification of that experience".[6] Consequently, an awareness of fictionalizing is to be inscribed into the very language which is designed to express the complexity of the passion, thus avoiding its reduction to the level of convention or killing off the desire altogether. Only through feigning—an act that crosses all the boundaries—can the boundlessness of passion find its expression.

At this point there occurs a new turn in the toppling effect, introduced by Audrey's question: "Would you not have me honest?" (III.iii.24). In his speech the fool had endowed feigning with a positive status, but Audrey interprets it according to the prevailing code as something dishonest which cannot therefore express her own passion. As she tries to clarify the fool's speech, the utterance takes on a double meaning she does not suspect. She is right to interpret feigning as lying, but her being right is the result of a selective interpretation of the fool's words; she has unwittingly closed off those possible meanings which he had brought into play and which now have their own repercussions on Audrey's words by making her correct interpretation appear trivial or even ridiculous. The exclusion of possible senses may have a stabilizing effect within the political world, but in the pastoral counter-image they show up the comic limitation of whatever meaning has been formed.

We have not yet by any means exhausted the range of possible senses connected with Touchstone's language. When he describes poetry as feigning, he uses a superlative: "the truest poetry is the most feigning," thereby opening up a new perspective on the poor verses that Orlando had written for Rosalind in the preceding scene. The verses are bad because they follow the Petrarchan code and so attempt to equate desire with its linguistic expression. They lack the feigning force that crosses all boundaries and alone is able to picture unrestrained desire. Instead, Orlando subjugates his passion to censorship practiced by the Petrarchan love code, with the result that in trying to describe his wings of passion he finally clips them.

Once again another sense emerges: against the background of such bad poetry, "true" poetry shows that passion must be something feigned. As a basic human impulse it can only achieve expression by way of existing conventions that govern human relations; but imposing a form on desire deprives it of its very nature. Consequently, only through distortion of forms can it burst out into the open, and such manifestations work best when desire discloses itself within the realm of conventions as something utterly fictional, mingling existing realities with that which they have negated. Passion cloaked in the trappings of pure invention is the adequate counter-image to the realities of existing conventions. The true lover must therefore always poeticize this passion, signalizing that whatever is said is meant to be outstripped. Only when he clothes his passion in the language of lies, according to existing conventions, can this passion be satisfactorily characterized through the distortion of the prevailing code. True poetry has absorbed the taint of untruth, because only in this way can expression be given to the truth of passion against the background of convention. It is therefore no accident that Jaques, who overhears the fool's conversation, is filled with admiration, for the fool succeeds in showing the falsity of poetry to be truthful, thereby achieving a balance that Jaques has sought in vain while penetrating the linguistic disguises of his fellow creatures.

What marks the fool off from all the other characters is the fact that his language differs from theirs. He does not identify himself with any one language, nor does he speak any one language that might be compared to the others. This is mainly because differentiation is a continually effective force within his own

speech, turning it into a rhetoric of double meaning. It certainly cannot be seen as a rhetoric of emphasis, for it does not set out to bring about whatever is said through it. Thus it differs from the rhetoric of persuasion that tries to obtain explicit agreement.[7] This is why the fool is frequently misunderstood by the other characters, for they do not understand his rhetoric but only that which is said *through* the rhetoric. This, of course, complies with normal expectations of dialogue. The fool's rhetoric renounces emphatic persuasion because for him the utterance is merely a medium to ensure the return of elements suppressed by what has been said. This deconstruction of conventional emphatic rhetoric makes it possible to penetrate through the pragmatic and semantic functions of the utterance in order to show that such functions are the reason for exclusion taking place in all speech. The rhetoric of double meaning brings the utterance and that which it has excluded into co-presence, thereby making the displaced rebound on what is said. This "carnivalization" of rhetoric, according to Bakhtin, parades all definite meanings produced by language—provisional, restricted and illusory as they are.[8] Hence the continual overturning of senses which ensue from the fool's speech.

This is evident in the dialogue about honor as well as in that about love. Each sense that emerges from the dialogue acquires its substance by excluding something equally pertinent, which in turn invalidates the first sense when it takes its own place in the foreground of the conversation. The one does not, however, establish ascendancy over the other; the process is rather one of reciprocal exclusion according to whatever elements have given rise to the respective sense. Carnivalization of rhetoric leads to a continual overturning of definitive meanings, and this spotlights the basic structure of meaning as a doubling of the overt by the covert.[9] Each definitive meaning, obtaining its position from pragmatic circumstances, is a resolution of the difference between the overt and the covert, but the fool's parade of topsy-turvy meanings continually re-inscribes difference into meanings, and the resultant deconstruction of them lays bare the conditions that give rise to meaning.

By toppling all the senses of his speech, the fool stresses difference as the mainspring of sense, and he is able to afford this "game," because double meaning as thematized by his utterances is not tied to pragmatic applications. On the contrary, he banishes all practical usages from meaning in order to show that double meaning is the precondition for any definitive meaning. In this respect he contrasts with all the other characters in the play and, consequently, provides the necessary counter-image for each of the two worlds. It is through this incessant mirroring of the proceedings that the dialogue of the characters takes on its dramatic dimension, for the difference that he continually reinscribes into definitive meanings is bridged by many speeches made by those characters whose pragmatic intentions require unequivocalness.

If the game of double meaning is cancelled for reasons of political power (Oliver and Duke Frederick), there is a corresponding increase in the degree of suppression, with the double meaning present as the displaced element. If the game is pragmatized, the revelation of implications serves to defend the disadvantaged party (Orlando), with double meaning present as a strategem (Orlando), or as the failure of intended speech-acts (Oliver). And if the game is seen as being regulated by a code of concealment inherent in language itself (Jaques), then double meaning is present in the guise of self-deception. However the difference may be bridged, double meaning cannot be obliterated, even though every pragmatic application of language has such obliteration as its aim.

This situation highlights an important consequence, the discussion of which will be deferred to the end of the essay. Each character assumes his or her own individuality through the way in which difference is overcome in the respective speech-acts. Thus bridging of difference turns out to be a basic condition for the act of representation which varies according to the individual mode in which difference is resolved. But from the standpoint of the fool, all the other characters' speech-acts appear merely as possibilities contained within the semiotic game of double meaning. This game is dramatic in that either one must act and therefore inevitably lose, or cancel out all actions, as does the master of the game, the fool himself.

This gap is always evident in the dialogues involving the fool. As a result, his partners find his speeches paradoxical, because he adapts himself to their expectations of dialogue only to elucidate double meaning on the semantic level, thereby undermining the vital precondition for the success of any linguistic interchange. On the surface he may appear to be making a concession to his partners, but in fact on the semantic level double meaning takes on the appearance of a failed speech-act, because at one moment the utterance is shown to be the suppression of something concealed, and the next what is concealed is shown to be the distortion of the utterance. The rhetoric of double meaning practiced by the fool can only be conveyed through the disintegration of semantics, which explodes into comedy. His language is comic because the utterance always has an annulling effect on what it says, while the replies to his speeches also appear comic because they try to reduce his words to an unequivocal meaning, the annulment of which gave rise to his speech in the first place. But this very process makes it possible for us to become aware of the losses and distortions that are the price of semantic clarity. Hence the dialogues involving the fool often result in failure,

though the comedy of this failure holds out the promise of restitution, amounting here to a reconciliation of what appears to be irreconcilable: the pragmatic purpose of a speech-act and the structure of double meaning. The pattern of restitution is unfolded by the protagonists in the Forest of Arden.

Rosalind and Celia disguise themselves when they cross over from the political world to the pastoral. Celia becomes Aliena, and Rosalind becomes Ganymede. Just as the pastoral world is the counter-image to the political, these two characters assume roles opposite to themselves. The very name Aliena is a clear indication of Celia's self-alienation, and Rosalind alienates herself from her own sex, thus doubling herself in two mutually exclusive ways. There are two basic effects here: first, the radical split between appearance and reality, and secondly the character's own awareness of the split in her person. This in turn is a doubling of the structure of the two different worlds. Consequently, Rosalind will not only speak with two voices, but she will also use both registers of this double-voiced language simultaneously. Whenever this happens, disguise and real character function as reciprocal reflections. However, if the real self is reflected in the disguised character, the original Rosalind cannot remain unchanged, as the mask—being Rosalind's own otherness—adds something to what she has been so far.

Now disguise is a fiction, and in Elizabethan eyes it constituted an illusory concealment of the reality hidden behind it. Therefore the disguise endowed that which was hidden with a higher status of reality than that represented by the disguise.[10] This process is a counter-image of the situation in the political world. Duke Frederick and Oliver were not in disguise, but their conduct *was* a disguise, concealing the reality which motivated their actions and with which they identified themselves. With Rosalind and Celia, the process is turned upside down in that the disguise is seen right from the start as something alienating— either through the name (Aliena) or through the change of sex—so that the character can direct herself as someone split apart from herself, thus enacting a play between the mutually exclusive selves.

When Rosalind speaks as Ganymede, Ganymede must constantly refer back to Rosalind because the disguise cannot be a true representation of herself. And so Rosalind always speaks through Ganymede as if she were someone else, and Ganymede, when he speaks, can only elucidate what Rosalind is. If Rosalind is the hidden reality behind Ganymede, Ganymede is a sort of guinea-pig through whom Rosalind can adapt to reality. Originally Rosalind and Celia assumed their disguises in order to protect themselves on the way to the forest, but the function of the disguise changes once they have entered the pastoral haven. Initially Rosalind became a man to defend her womanhood, but now in the guise of Ganymede she wishes to play the role of the reluctant lady, so that she can test Orlando's love. Thus the character again doubles herself behind the mask by playing the role of the cynic—a role in accordance with the highly elaborate Petrarchan love code.

When Rosalind discovers Orlando's verses on the trees, her reaction is split. At first she speaks ironically of the low standard of this conventional poetry, without thinking of the author. But when she learns that Orlando wrote the verses, and must therefore be in the neighborhood, her attitude changes. She is suddenly shocked by the vast difference between what she is and what she appears to be. She asks Celia: "Good my complexion! Dost thou think though I am caparisoned like a man I have a doublet and hose in my disposition? One inch of delay more is a South Sea of discovery" (III. ii. 191-194). She is afraid that as a woman playing the role of a man she will not have sufficient control over her own emotions: "Do you not know I am a woman? When I think, I must speak. Sweet, say on" (III. ii. 245-246). Here a conflict of language begins to emerge within the conflict of roles, for as a man Rosalind cannot say what she feels, even though it demands immediate expression. How can that be said which must not be said although such a mind must needs say it?

Ganymede begins the conversation with Orlando by making ironic comments on the bad verses which evidently he had placed on the trees. Orlando acknowledges that the verses are his, whereupon Ganymede feigns astonishment at the fact that Orlando has none of the classic symptoms of a lovesick poet:

> A lean cheek, which you have not; a blue eye and sunken, which you have not; an unquestionable spirit, which you have not; a beard neglected, which you have not . . . Then your hose should be ungartered, your bonnet unbanded, your sleeve unbuttoned, your shoe untied, and everything about you demonstrating a careless desolation.
>
> [III. ii. 363-371]

Ganymede criticizes Orlando because his appearance has so little in common with the code of convention that underlies his poetry. But through Ganymede's criticism we can discover Rosalind's own desire to provoke Orlando so that she can hear more about his love. For Ganymede's critique of the Petrarchan clichés in Orlando's verses expresses Rosalind's own dissatisfaction with a love that clearly regards the Petrarchan code as an adequate means of describing itself. The reproach that Orlando does not look like a Petrarchan lover turns into an appeal to make Orlando reveal the true nature of his love, and evidently this can only be done if the conventional code is now abandoned.

The dialogue in this scene is typical of the conversations between the lovers. The silent voice of Rosalind is always speaking through the utterances of Ganymede. This entails a switch from one language function to the other, but frequently they are present at the same time. What Ganymede says always represents something else, and this something may be Rosalind's expression of her love, or it may be an appeal to Orlando to reveal his innermost feelings; and when Ganymede's speech represents the Petrarchan code of love, the language of representation is meant to give presence to both expression and appeal simultaneously. What is said serves to say something else without actually having to say it, and thus the character communicates the unsayable. In accordance with the progress or regress of the dialogue, the language function which is dominant at each respective moment will either topple into or adumbrate another one, but as already stated they are frequently present at the same time, and it is the simultaneity that gives to Ganymede's speech its double meaning. The completed utterance does not exclusively point to what is intended, but at the same time reveals what is eclipsed by it, so that Ganymede's language "means one thing, at the same time means *another,* and yet at the same time does not cease to mean the first thing."[11]

If double meaning entails an alternating dominance of one language function over the other, this must of necessity have certain effects on the relation between character and disguise. Although representation, expression, and appeal constantly shade into each other, and so appear to be simultaneously present, each nevertheless dominates at a given moment and therefore all bring out varying identities of Rosalind. Sometimes she is Rosalind herself, sometimes she is Rosalind pretending to be Ganymede, and sometimes her double role of Rosalind/Ganymede serves to fictionalize Rosalind. And so whenever the expression of, or an appeal for, love takes over, the mask represents that which it is actually meant to conceal, but represents it without making it overt. When Rosalind, disguised as Ganymede, fictionalizes herself, she is at one and the same time herself and outside herself. At such moments she herself is almost pure difference, which manifests itself in a rapid change of roles, bringing about a co-presence of the three different language functions. Thus once again the unspoken speaks through what is said and indeed depends on the spoken for its presence. Even if every sentence has a definite reference, this always vanishes in order that the sentence may bear a different reference. And so when representation is uppermost, it ceases to portray the Petrarchan love code, the fading of which turns the sentence into a carrier for either expression or appeal.[12]

We have here two languages that continually interweave, establishing and obliterating differences. So long as Rosalind/Ganymede tries to sound out Orlando about his love, using the Petrarchan code, her own desire can only be articulated through the fictionalization of this code. For only when this ceases to be able to represent love can her love take on expression. If expression is made possible by the fictionalization of the code, then the code itself must be outstripped by something which in turn does not have a form specific to any code. Outstripping the code testifies to the overpowering desire that breaks up the differentiation inherent in the code, whose distortion is proportionate to the genuineness of the passion to be communicated.

This transgression of the code is different from that which is to be found in the political world. There the code was violated so that the suppressed could remain hidden; here it is violated so that the hidden may be expressed. Thus each language function in Rosalind's speech brings out another function, which in turn changes into another, in consequence of which there is a constant interplay between differentiation and dedifferentiation. As this process is synchronic, the meaning of her utterance is decentred, so that meaning may be traced to a source other than semantic. Double meaning arises out of the difference which permeates the language functions, annuls their standpoints and makes them coalesce. Thus the descriptive function of representative speech is annulled so that this can become the medium for a hidden desire; appearing either as unarticulated expression or as a wordless appeal to the lover. The manifest function is made to disappear in order to ensure the manifestation of the latent, though the suppressed function leaves behind its own traces in that it is the bearer of the now manifested unspoken. This is almost a direct reversal of the relation we discussed earlier between the manifest and the latent: here the overt becomes present by transforming the overt into the latent.

Despite its density, Rosalind's language does not itself have multiple meanings, even though what is said continually refers to something hidden, and every utterance is part of a disguise. The shifts and disguises do not spring from the wish to hide something, but signify that in the synchronic application of the different language functions, the dynamism of her passion is urging expression in the language in semantics. This is the reason why all the operations of the mask—to be conceived of as a structured focusing on existing challenges—are doubled by an operation of dedifferentiation carried out by the character underneath, reversing what the mask articulates. Each operation is doubled by a counter-operation, and the two operations in their simultaneity result in a depiction of change, catching it at the very moment of its happening. One might call this recurrent change the signified which, though ungraspable, burrows its way through the synchronic process of structured focusing (mask) and latent dedifferentiation (character underneath).

How is this process of constant change to be communicated? Rosalind/Ganymede seeks to produce in Or-

lando the same change of being that she has produced in herself. She wishes to cure him of his Petrarchism and so to penetrate below the surface of the code and bring forth the truer level that her love hopes to find. Therefore she arranges a game in which the male Ganymede plays the female role in the make-believe Petrarchan courtship. And as Ganymede knows that Orlando would do anything for love of Rosalind, he/she forces him to play the game:

> He was to imagine me his love, his mistress; and I set him every day to woo me. At which time would I, being but a moonish youth, grieve, be effeminate, changeable, longing and liking, proud, fantastical, apish, shallow, inconstant, full of tears, full of smiles, for every passion something and for no passion truly anything.
>
> [III. ii. 395-402]

As Ganymede, Rosalind plays the mistress's role and involves Orlando in a game which, had it taken place in the courtly world of Duke Frederick, would have been taken for reality, being in keeping with the prevailing conventions of courtly society. But what remains unconscious in the court is immediately observable in the Forest of Arden. Ganymede and Orlando are not playing roles that are accidentally thrust upon them by prevailing social conventions—they deliberately play what they are not or what they do not want to be. And so Orlando, being conscious of the fiction, can hint that Ganymede's acting is no true substitute for the real Rosalind. But while they are both playing their roles, they are also acting themselves. Rosalind is enacting her passion in order to test Orlando, and Orlando is enacting his and thereby leaving the Petrarchan code (as embodied by Ganymede) far behind. While Rosalind and Orlando each act their parts and at the same time play themselves, the game becomes a means of mastering that which is absent. Orlando enacts the fulfillment of his passion—and only the game makes it possible for him to express what is otherwise denied to him—and Rosalind experiences the love of Orlando, which assumes the desired form through the disintegration of the Petrarchan code which Ganymede represents.

Thus it turns out that only the game can be an adequate vehicle for double meaning, for it is understood within the play that whatsoever is enacted must be taken as if it were real. Consequently, the game mirrors the latent which is hidden behind the manifest. By mastering the absent, the game sets in motion a process of change, for it provides a form in which difference is simultaneously present and constantly bridged. Difference emerges as the constitutive matrix of play not least through the basic play movement of back and forth which is a constant effort to overcome difference, but it results only in an endlessly varied patterning of play structures. Obviously the dialogue achieves its ideality when speech loses its finality. But this is possible only in play, which alone can stage that which remains excluded from our everyday reality.

III

The variations we have observed so far in the relationship between manifest and latent all arise from and are conditioned by dialogue. This seems only natural as dialogue is *the* medium of drama, and is moreover governed by the basic rule of linguistic interaction: the interplay between the overt and the covert. This rule enables language to function and appears to be a property of language existing independently of the context and code which further condition it. Each dialogue attempts to achieve a purpose, and it is this final goal which regulates the interplay of the overt and covert both in everyday conversation and in drama. This may be a reason why Bakhtin views drama as a monologic form of speech, because the purpose to be accomplished by dramatic interchange impedes the unfolding of the "dialogic word," conspicuous for its multifarious allusions and references.[13] The prevailing pragmatics which govern the interplay between the overt and the covert are thematized in Shakespeare's comedy; consequently the pragmatic intentions permeating the dialogue are bracketed off in order to dramatize the basic rule of language use itself. Each purpose that arises in dialogue is only to be taken as if it were one—a fact borne out by the pastoral mode in which the whole interchange is cast. Instead of dialogues we have staged dialogues; and it is a distinctive feature of pastoral literature that it mirrors fundamental aspects of human life: in this particular instance, the aspect is the basic rule of language use itself.

If the interplay between the spoken and the unspoken is to be foregrounded or thematized, the purpose which normally regulates the relationship in question must fail, because otherwise our attention would focus on the purpose rather than on the relationship. But at the same time, if dialogue is to disclose its basic rule, clearly the disclosure cannot be separated from the dialogue, and this in turn has repercussions on the interplay itself. Even the rule governing dialogue requires language for its depiction, and since all speech is intentional, the presentation of the rule will never escape the pragmatics of dialogue. The rule cannot be presented by itself, and so the pragmatic intentions of dialogue will shape the interplay between the overt and the covert, in consequence of which none of the forms it takes will ever encompass all the possibilities inherent in it. Instead, it will be disclosed only in variations according to what the dialogue is designed to achieve, so that its many manifestations may, more often than not, be in direct conflict with one another.

Now, when the speech-acts of the usurpers fail, their attitudes reflect either an unawareness of the interplay between overt and covert, or—if they are aware—a perception of it as a pair of opposites to be manipulated according to the purpose pursued. Their use of language prevents them from controlling the implications of their words, because they fail to see how the unspoken can rebound on the spoken. They are usurpers not only because they have suppressed their doubles, but also because they believe the manifest to be the successful suppression of the latent.

The interplay, however, is most vividly illuminated only when it is reflected in the mirror of the pastoral world. Jaques regards the interrelation between manifest and latent as one of dissimulation, thereby revealing its negative side as practiced in the political world. But if the interplay is unmasked as one of disguise only, then it is reduced to a univocal allegorization which brings the semiotic interplay between the spoken and the unspoken to a grinding halt.

The deficiency of this univocal allegorization is shown up by the multiple senses of the fool's language; its plurivocity opens up what Jaques' reduction eclipses. He wrecks all frames of reference essential for Jaques in order to expose the conditions on which they hinge. Thus the simultaneity of overt and covert within the fool's speech brings about a sort of explosion of meanings.

What is split asunder by the multiple senses of the fool's speeches is drawn together in Rosalind's synchronous use of language functions. The intentions underlying her words must be covered up in order that her wordless passion may be given linguistic expression.

All these variations within the relationship between the spoken and the unspoken are nothing but paradigms of double meaning, and indeed double meaning can only emerge through paradigms, since by itself it cannot be grasped. The paradigms, in turn, are conditioned by the ineradicable pragmatic intentions prevailing in each dialogue, and that holds true not least for an elucidation of the actual rule that underlies dialogue. Even in the pastoral world, where the interrelation between overt and covert becomes the topic of a multifaceted play, it is nevertheless tied to dialogue, with the resultant paradox that elucidation of the rule of dialogue can never be fully achieved because elucidation is itself a pragmatic function.

Thus whatever the manner of elucidation, something is always going to be excluded. In the dialogue of the political world, it is the interplay between manifest and latent that is excluded, with the result that this world is marked by usurpation and failed speech-acts. In the pastoral dialogues, the interplay becomes the theme, but when conceived in terms of a univocal allegorization (Jaques), it excludes the multiple senses inherent in it, whereas when multiple senses are to be spotlighted (Touchstone), then there can be no telescoping of the overt and the covert. And even when the unspoken articulates itself through the spoken (Rosalind), there is still an exclusion, this time relating to the pragmatic function of dialogue itself. We have to keep in mind that dialogue in the pastoral world is already a staged dialogue, which is now turned into the subject of a game between Rosalind and Orlando, thus deliberately bracketing off the pragmatic function of what is spoken, in order for the unspoken to make its appearance through what is said. It is only the mutually agreed inconsequence of the Rosalind/Orlando dialogue that allows for the instantaneous presence of three different language functions: representation, expression and appeal—all undoing each other and using each other for what each of them intends but does not verbalize. If the pastoral world is a mirror-image revealing the reverse side of the political world, the staging of a play within this make-believe world constitutes a last chance of elucidating that which defies linguistic presentation. The play within the play is a form eminently suited to this process, for, as a heightened illusion it gives presence—albeit in the form of a fleeting semblance—to that which by its nature can never assume even the shape of a given.

The paradigms discerned gain their individuality from the way in which the overt and the covert interrelate. Yet whatever the relationship may be like, something is excluded in every instance. As the excluded rebounds, the effect of the absent on the present emerges as a rich source of comedy. What has been cut off by the intentional speech-act, re-appears and the resultant simultaneity of the mutually exclusive turns comedy into a potent medium for the dramatization of double meaning. But while the individual speech-acts become comic paradigms, their sequence also leads to another basic feature of comedy, which is the pattern of restitution. This, however, can only follow upon failure, and so the question arises, what exactly is it that fails here?

We have seen that double meaning takes on different forms according to the pragmatic function behind the dialogue. These forms are not double meaning itself, but are its representatives, whose difference denotes that double meaning can never be presented as itself. The moment it takes on a form through the finality of the dialogue, it establishes its presence through the fact that whatever is excluded from that form will strike back at it, subverting its claim to be truly representative. Consequently, the various representations of double meaning suffer the same fate as that which Freud attributed to the representation of drives—representations meant to make something present which they themselves are not and which hence cannot be equated with the drives. However, the continual formulation and failure of these representatives is necessary if one is to formulate a concept of that which can never be delineated.

Language, then, becomes the medium for comedy—not because it is comic in itself, but because the interplay between manifest and latent can only be conveyed through a form that seeks to represent something which cannot be conveyed through any form. Comedy as a string of failed actions indicates that the structure of double meaning itself can never be cast in any form, since it is the generative matrix of language which defies translation into the symbolic order of language.

Comedy is an ideal setting for the elucidation of this process, because every failed action bears with it the promise of restitution. This interdependence highlights double meaning as an ineradicable structure inscribed into language itself which gains visibility through the dramatization of its failed representations, the inexhaustible variety of which assures a resolution to every conflict arising. There is always an alternative to failure, and consequently double meaning itself cannot finally fail, thus testifying to the fact that it is an inalienable part of our anthropological makeup.

The spoken is constantly toppled by the unspoken, and this toppling movement is further differentiated by the switch that keeps taking place between the comedy of the characters and that of their use of language. The less the characters know about how language functions, the more they are caught up in comedy which makes their unconscious language use rebound on them. Unlike most of the other characters, the fool is not subject to this type of comedy which, however, enhances the comedy of his linguistic manipulations. For him everything spoken becomes a springboard for everything unspoken, so that he produces a form of language which wrecks the pragmatic finality of the dialogue. And finally, Rosalind's play within a play is the complete carnivalization of all utterances, which so accelerates the toppling movement that double meaning appears as a process of transformation. This is without doubt the most comprehensive (though, of course, still not all-encompassing) form of its representation.[14]

Our argument so far yields another completely different aspect of double meaning which also pertains to its dramatization, though it is not restricted to comedy. Whenever the manifest and the latent shade into each other and co-exist, their relation is one of double meaning, as a prevailing difference marks them off from one another; without difference, there could be no double meaning. The difference, however, is a continual propellant for its own removal and this leads to the creation of a gestalt. All the paradigms discussed arose out of an attempt to bridge difference, and their very differentness indicated the variety of possibilities inherent in difference as the constitutive matrix of double meaning. Removal of difference is therefore the impulse that gives rise to representation. This applies above all to the individuality of the characters, which establishes itself in accordance with the way they interweave the spoken and the unspoken. What they say is overshadowed either by what remains hidden or by what has been displaced through the utterance; this, in turn, reinscribes itself into what is spoken, thus delineating the individual contours of the characters. Each attempt at bridging difference has a unique feature, and so both the acknowledgement of difference and its removal turn out to be the origin of representation in literature.

If representation arises out of bridging difference, it can no longer be conceived of in terms of mimesis, but must be construed in terms of performance, for each act of difference-removal is a form of production, not of imitation. Furthermore, the fact that performance is a means of bringing something about suggests a process of staging, and this endows it with an intangible quality.

There is yet another even more comprehensive sense in which representation springs from the bridging of difference. Our individual paradigms showed that double meaning was revealed in ever-changing forms, culminating in Rosalind's play within the play turning transformation itself into a representative of double meaning. Now this constant switching, which becomes visible on all levels, thus emerges as the represented subject of the comedy. But this cannot possibly be mimetic; its performative starting-point lies in the removal of difference—a process which continually alters the positions which it has marked out.

Difference, then, inspires the attempt to remove it, and it is this attempt that leads to representation as performance. Yet difference inscribes itself into representation by revoking the assumed authenticity of representation with regard to that which it makes present, and in so doing it turns representation into aesthetic semblance. Thus difference, though the origin of representation, is present as deferral of knowing what origins are. Representation, therefore, has no original substance of its own, but is the imaginary capture of something that cannot be captured. Its transformation into aesthetic semblance is the price that representation must pay if it is to be successful. The compensation for such a price, however, is the ineluctable variety of depictions of something whose very nature prevents it from ever being conceived in terms of an object: in Shakespeare's comedy, this is transformation itself.

IV

The dramatization of double meaning reveals to what extent the semantics of language is left behind, though double meaning is still semantic to the extent that it has a form. But this serves primarily to focus on the processes whereby meaning is formed and to eluci-

date that fact that meaning cannot be its own origin. The question therefore arises as to how far this dramatization conditions its own reception. It is clear from the epilogue that it is meant to do so. The epilogue is delivered by Rosalind, who steps out of all her disguises to confront the audience as an actress—or, in Shakespeare's day, as a boy actor. What Rosalind has shown in the play is now to take effect on the audience. But how is she to address them? She decides: "My way is to conjure you" (V. iv. 208). *Conjure* has a striking double meaning—to charge, as she puts it a moment later, but also to produce through magic. Now by retreating to the pastoral world, Rosalind had alienated herself into her own otherness, and through her disguise she had undergone a transformation of what she had been. By the same means, she also worked a similar transformation in the other characters who had fled to the forest, and now that they have been transformed they may themselves produce equally magic changes in the political world. Thus the actor or actress ends the play by "conjuring" the audience, or charging them with a responsibility toward the play—that is, to like as much of it as pleases them and as perhaps their experience will allow ("for the love you bear to men, / women")—the implication being that the magic of the play might make them even capable of changing that experience; she asks them to make a decision about their response to the play.

Dramatized double meaning will give the audience the impetus for change through the problems they will have in registering it. These problems begin when the plurality of senses is interwoven in the form of mutual dissimulation or is condensed by telescoping; they continue whenever the utterance becomes merely the medium for the recurrence of what it has displaced; and finally, they occur when a particular sense says something definite in order to mean something else. Such a presentation of double meaning either scatters the audience's attention or demands their multiple attention.[15] But the latter is contrary to the normal mode of perception. It is true that perception is also marked by a form of doubling, since it bisects each field of perception into figure and ground, but this doubleness is always hierarchically organized, whereas double meaning is distinguished by the absence of any such hierarchy. Hence double meaning brackets off the basic structure underlying perception—its pragmatic orientation—and in doing so, it makes us aware of the schemata that guide perception. Multiple attention is even more provocative to our acts of comprehension, for whenever phenomena have to be linked up with each other, either a predicative or a passive synthesis is required. Double meaning, however, runs counter to any such dialectic solution, and so just as it delimits pragmatic semantics in relation to perception, so it delimits predicative semantics in relation to acts of comprehension.

All this becomes a dramatic experience when the spectator takes on the role of third party, being the only person in a position to perceive the presence of the absent in the present. Although it is the characters that produce this simultaneity, they are blinded to it by the pragmatic aims of their dialogue. But to this rule there are two exceptions: with the fool, the pragmatic element is wrecked, and with Rosalind it is put in brackets. These two exceptions sharpen our awareness that everything spoken is doubled by an unspoken. And once the spectator, as the third party, allows the dialogue to function as the bearer of double meaning, he or she may sense something of the nature of double meaning through the very exclusion of those principles which otherwise stabilize perception and comprehension.

Such an experience demands multiple attention, for the spectator has to grasp something that can emerge only through the suspension of established patterns of comprehension. And yet this demand is related to nothing in the least extraordinary, for the interplay of the overt and the covert is a basic principle of ordinary language. What happens here is simply that something is brought to the surface which normally remains hidden. But when double meaning translates itself into the production of multiple attention, it does run contrary to our everyday acts of perception and comprehension. Consequently the spectator must either transmute his multiple attention into acts of selective comprehension—thus reacting like those characters in the play who always foreshorten the double meaning—or he must maintain an awareness that will keep up with what is happening to him. Making someone aware of what had previously been closed to him entails conditioning him for a change. This is why Rosalind "conjures" the audience in the epilogue to link up their experience of the play with their own experience.

Since multiple attention cannot be maintained indefinitely, it triggers the demand for a semantic ordering of what has been given to experience. The meaning arrived at both in the reception of the text and in its subsequent interpretation turns out to be a semantic appropriation of an imaginary experience which in itself cannot be semantic, because the result cannot be its own origin. The imaginary, however, can only become an experience when moulded by something other than itself which allows it to assume a tangible form. Thus double meaning may be regarded as the medium of the imaginary. When multiple attention releases an activity of semantic ordering, the spectator bridges differences and thereby repeats the very act out of which representation as performance has arisen in the text. The direction such processings will take depends on whether the spectator's existing codes remain dominant or are suspended by the imaginary experience. Multiple attention opens up a path for an unfamiliar experience to travel along by delimiting both the division between figure and ground, which is basic to perception, and the relations operative in predicative judgments which are basic to comprehension. Such a decentering lays the spectator open to the imaginary experience, which establishes itself against the background of that which it has suspended.

Notes

[1] All quotations from *As You Like It* (The Arden Shakespeare), ed. by Agnes Latham, London 1975.

[2] For the terminology and its application, see M. M. Bakhtin, *The Dialogic Imagination. Four Essays,* (Slavic Series 1) ed. by Michael Holquist and transl. by Caryl Emerson and Michael Holquist (University of Texas Press: Austin and London, 1981), p. 324 ff.

[3] Bakhtin, p. 361.

[4] Hans-Georg Gadamer, *Truth and Method,* trans. Garrett Barden and John Cumming (New York, 1975) p. 124.

[5] Bakhtin, p. 60.

[6] This is a point developed by Nina Schwartz in her paper "As It Likens You: The Metamorphosis of Consciousness in the Fictional Order," submitted in my seminar in the winter quarter 1980 at the University of California, Irvine.

[7] See Hans Blumenberg, *Wirklichkeiten in denen wir leben* (Stuttgart, 1981) pp. 112f.

[8] For reference see the German translation of Bakhtin: Michail M. Bachtin, *Literatur und Karneval. Zur Romantheorie und Lachkultur* (Munich, 1969) pp. 47-60.

[9] See Dieter Henrich, "Freie Komik" in *Das Komische* (Poetik und Hermeneutik VII), ed. by Wolfgang Preisendanz and Rainer Warning (Munich, 1976) pp. 385 ff.

[10] See also Agnes Latham, "Introduction," *As You Like It,* p. xxii.

[11] Paul Ricoeur, *Hermeneutik und Strukturalismus. Der Konflikt der Interpretationen I,* German transl. by Johannes Rütsche (Munich, 1973) pp. 82 f.

[12] For the individual speech functions, see Felix Martínez-Bonati, *Fictive Discourse and the Structures of Literature. A Phenomenological Approach,* trans. Philip W. Silver (Ithaca, N.Y.: Cornell Univ. Press 1981) pp. 87 f.

[13] Bakhtin, *Dialogic Imagination,* p. 405, maintains, however: "To a certain extent comedy is an exception to this."

[14] The plot of the play sheds revealing light on this assumption. Those characters in the political world who have suppressed their doubles as well as the double meaning in their own speech, are never in a position to change into their own otherness. But at the end they are totally transformed. Duke Frederick and Oliver cease completely to be that which they had been before. In the political world they had constantly invoked—though always violated—the codes of government and family, and so they gave the impression that their conduct was regulated by these codes. However, they were not aware of the degree to which their conduct was in fact regulated by the breaking of these codes. Thus they had long since distanced themselves, unconsciously, from the selves associated with such codes, as a result of which they are now able to break radically with that which they had hitherto always claimed to be their guiding principles.

Duke Frederick comes to the forest, undergoes a religious conversion, and resolves to lead a monastic life. Oliver leaves the political world, and takes on a new identity in the pastoral world. And so the characters who had banished their doubles now change identities because they have never known what it was to play their own otherness.

Such a total transformation is fairytale in character, because what happens to Duke Frederick and Oliver is miraculous and unforeseen. In fairytales the miraculous is commonplace, since it offers "the only possible guarantee that the unmorality of reality has ceased to be" (André Jolles, *Einfache Formen,* Tübingen, 1956, p. 203). But even this fairytale transformation is marked by the simultaneity of the mutually exclusive. The miracle is miraculous because it is shot through with failure. In the fairytale, however, such a difference is bridged by miraculous transformations.

[15] On the problem of multiple attention, see Anton Ehrenzweig, *The Hidden Order of Art* (Berkeley and Los Angeles, 1971) pp. 22 f.

PASTORAL ELEMENTS

Rosalie L. Colie (essay date 1974)

SOURCE: "Perspectives on Pastoral: Romance, Comic and Tragic," in *Shakespeare's Living Art,* Princeton University Press, 1974, pp. 243-83.

[*In the following excerpt, Colie discusses* As You Like It *from the perspective of the classical pastoral—* *mixing comedy and tragedy, and recollecting themes of nature versus nurture, art versus nature, and country versus court.*]

I

By the end of the sixteenth century, the pastoral mode embraced many particular genres, offered rich options to writers interested in literary experimentation, particularly in mixed genres, and, furthermore, had become embroiled in one of the great literary quarrels which characterized Renaissance literary theory. The pastoral permitted and encouraged opportunities for mixing in one work "imitation" with "invention," art with artifice, the artless with the artful—and generated discussions of such mixes. Eclogues were the principal pastoral form, hallowed by antiquity, but other pastoral lyrics flourished: the love-lyric, the dialogue, the song. Pastoral episodes regularly offered relief in poems largely devoted to epic gests; an English poet wrote a heroic epic in prose entitled, in spite of its relatively scant preoccupation with shepherds, *Arcadia,* and set into this prose-epic a series of pastoral poems which are themselves a self-sufficient anthology of pastoral forms and themes. Following hints from Italian eclogue-writers and fulfilling medieval Latin literary traditions, Marot and Spenser presented unabashed models of Christian pastoral, enriching the imaginative possibilities for their successors; both poets also experimented successfully with satirical poems within the pastoral mode. Indeed, one can recognize anthologies of pastoral work—Sannazaro's *Arcadia* is one example; *The Shepheardes Calender* offers a survey of pastoral themes and topics, and Sidney's shepherds in the *Arcadia* offer a magnificent epideictic display of the eclogue's range of possibilities, formal and topical.[1]

From *commedia dell' arte* and other popular forms to the grand productions of Tasso and Guarini, drama exploited pastoral scenes, pastoral characters, and what might be called (in the Renaissance anyway) the lyric pastoral *pathétique.*[2] The way in which the pastoral locale was taken as an official site for love-play and for love-poetry can be illustrated by a late anthology of pastoral lyrics published in 1600, *England's Helicon;* that an English Arcadian rhetoric and a mildly Arcadian logic were produced at the turn of the century shows how powerfully the literary notion of Arcadia had come to operate across the spectrum of literary possibility in England's green and pleasant land. From one end to the other of the social and literary scale, pastoral myths and patterns were available: in Whitsun pastorals, pastoral interludes, pastoral romances, in narrative books and on the stage, pastoral masques and (even more common) pastoral episodes within masques, spectators could take their pastoral experience. The ways of pastoral, then, were many and varied; the mixtures of forms, conventions, devices in pastoral allowed a very wide range of decorums.

The richness of the mixture is not really surprising: the literary critical quarrel over the pastoral as *the* mixed dramatic genre, thus as the official locus of tragicomedy,[3] broke out over Guarini's *Il pastor fido* and culminated in the establishment of the pastoral play as the official mixture of comedy with tragedy (sometimes with satire as well), exemplified in such devices as double-plotting, mixed styles, and even interludes from the non-literary arts, such as music, dancing, and the visual arts.[4] Wherever one looked, one could find pastoral—and once-found, twice-found, for the generous, nearly boundless forms of pastoral offered immense opportunities for craft and for imagination.

From such a background, Shakespeare's sophisticated traffic with pastoral is hardly surprising; typically, he experimented with the mode in various ways, in both early and late plays. In *As You Like It,* a play with a remarkably tight thematic construction, he worked with many pastoral themes and motifs, to say nothing of pastoral types in the *dramatis personae,* in what is primarily a romantic love-story derived from a prose narrative. Although "romance" and its proper subject, love, dominate this play, with the shepherding and versifying rather its decoration than its psychological locus, nonetheless the skeletal structure of this romantic comedy *is* the standard dramatic pastoral pattern— a pattern of extrusion or exile, recreative sojourn in a natural setting, with ultimate return "homeward" from the exile, a return in moral strength reinforced by the country experience of kind and kindness.

As You Like It is, for once, about sheep, but this plot-form, from academic drama to *commedia dell' arte,* was so thoroughly identified with the pastoral that as a formula it could imply without overtly stating a great deal of standard pastoral thematics. Sheep, for instance, were often quite absent from such plays, which sometimes lacked even the pasture environment. But the *themes* associated with pastoral (court-country, art-nature, nature-nurture) could be counted on to inform plays with this plot-pattern. A plot on this plan, thus, was a recognizable vehicle for discourse on the pastoral themes, an abstraction designed to interpret problems of nature and nurture originally associated with more overtly pastoral topics.

Though it follows the pastoral dramatic plot and has to do with sheep and shepherds, *As You Like It* is by no means "officially" pastoral. It ignores, certainly, some of the major cruces of Italian pastoral dramatic theory: it has no double-plot, for instance, in the pure sense. Though the De Boys story is separate from the ducal story, nonetheless Orlando is early displayed at court, catching the attention of Rosalind; throughout, his situation is seen as a counterpart to hers. Although the country lovers overlap with their courtly parallel figures, they are in the play rather to round out the range of pastoral alternatives than to divert into a "plot" of

their own. Nor are there radical shifts of locale and of genre in *As You Like It:* the ducal and gentlemanly affairs, so to speak, are conveniently focused in one place, the forest, by means of the exile-device; though the breath of tragedy blows through the forest, the dominant tone is always, through Duke Senior's and Rosalind's efforts, kept lucidly "comic."

Duke Senior, Rosalind, Orlando: all are exiled, and in their company come the spiritual exiles who will not part from them, Celia, Touchstone, the Duke's men, Adam. In the forest these exiles, valiantly seeking some cheer, meet that symbolic, alienated, self-exiled figure, the melancholy Jaques, already located in the wood. All these victims—Jaques too—of the world find renewal in the simple culture of the Forest of Arden, and all, save Jaques and Touchstone, return triumphantly to reconstruct the social world from which they had been driven out. Against this basic construction, the play is rich in additional pastoral themes and motifs, many of them ultimately Theocritan and Vergilian, reworked throughout the Latin Middle Ages, reconceived in the Renaissance.

The play makes much of the dialogue and dialectic which so inform pastoral: the love-debates of Silvius and Corin, Silvius and Phebe; the discussion of court and country between Corin and Touchstone; the styles of courtship of Orlando and Rosalind; the dialogue on nature and nurture between Orlando and Oliver; and, as in Spenser's wonderful array of pastoral debates, *The Shepheardes Calender,* the themes so dialectically handled provide an enriching counterpoint to one another. Both the pastoral *agon* (Corin-Silvius) and the pastoral *paragone* of real sheep-herding versus literary sheep-keeping (Corin-Touchstone) are part of the play's thematic structure. Among the many things this play is, it is a *comparative* work about competing life-styles, among these the competition of shepherdly lives, with real shepherds who dip their sheep and lambs, whose hands smell of tar and of the oil from the sheep's wool, and others who live "poetically." We are asked to measure the real and literary shepherds against each other, not once but several times. Behind the prating of the shepherd's life, important thematically as it is in the play, lies a grander anthropological conception, the (pastoral) myth of the Golden World, "the antique world" in which there was perfect commerce and mutual service among men naturally well-disposed to one another, the myth, then, of the Golden Age.[5] In antiquity, the pastoral life had been assigned to the Age of Gold, when men lived in commutual confidence and kept their flocks and herds together, their natural characters attuned to the gentle world they inhabited, their goods held comfortably and easily in common. Such a world had no need for war and was therefore an ideologically pacifist community; such discomfitures as men suffered were not caused by human agency but by natural hazards (winter and rough weather) and by creatures not yet enrolled in the peaceable kingdom (wolves and snakes, in ancient pastoral; snakes and lions in *As You Like It;* metaphorical kites and wolves and real bears in *The Winter's Tale*). Insofar as this ideal theme bears upon the dialectic of pastoral, it implies the corruption of an imperfect world of men—*urbs,* the court—against which its perfections could be fully felt.

With the development of a pastoral *pathétique* by which men identified with the gentler creatures and, in the Renaissance, allowed themselves the luxury of self-cultivation, even of emotional self-exploitation,[6] love officially became the major pastoral occupation, taking precedence even over keeping sheep real or poetical. That is, the shepherd was naturally a poet in the pastoral genres, but before long was also a poet-lover. At first, the pastoral world was pleasant, natural, easy, and so was its love—although the shepherd's complaint about his cold, coy, or faithless mistress (with a corresponding saddening of his landscape to match his emotional situation) was the celebration of another kind of love, troublesome, upsetting, potentially destructive of the mutuality of pastoral society. Gradually shepherds and, later, shepherdesses began to die of love—even the pastoral landscape was not always sufficient to nourish the love-struck pastoralist through his emotional afflictions. Though the pastoral world with its celebration of timelessness and harmony would seem to have been created precisely to deny the efficacy of death, nevertheless death's shadow lay across even its green perfections to chill its warm airs.[7]

The pastoral elegy offers a marvelous rationale for death, with its classic expression of the wonderful comforts and assuagements for personal loss; it provides the pattern for the pastoral relation of man to nature, of creation to inspiration: there, the shepherd-singer, the shepherd-maker, is gathered into the pastoral artifice of nature's eternity, these two fused into one. At one with this imaginative and nutritive nature, the dead shepherd-poet becomes a part of the inspiration he had himself once drawn from nature's store. In life poetically competitive—shepherd, goatherd, and cowherd continually sang in *agon,* each praising his own particular life-style, ritualized into poetic activity—and in death tradition-preserving, the pastoralist invented a world of the imagination in which, depending on his temperament, he could live as he would. He might, then, live sparingly, in simple opposition to urban luxury, confident of nature's power to provide for him; or he might live richly, feasting from nature's endless store, recreating himself and his art thereby. Whichever "nature" he chose as his setting, that entity was expected to provide sufficiently for his aesthetic and emotional needs—in other words, to nurture him.[8]

Theocritus, with whom this all began,[9] was less concerned with the relative values of city and country

than with the positive recreations of the country: what court-country *agon* we find in him, we bring with us from reading subsequent pastoral writers. Vergil, however, made overt the *paragone* of city and country life; certainly implied in his eclogues and subsequently in the pastoral psychology is the sense of relief from the pressure of daily concerns (*negotium*) in a "liberty" and "freedom" (*otium*) consciously contrasted to the workaday round, a praise of simplicity (and, therefore, of "nature") as contrasted with the artificiality of urban life.[10] As needs no reminder, the inventors and practitioners of literary pastoral were not professional shepherds, but highly sophisticated city-dwellers, whose country life of the imagination was quite different from that enjoyed by the inhabitants of the real Arcadia or, after erosion, of the real Sicily. Thomas Rosenmeyer has put it well: Theocritus' Sicily is not so much a geographical place as a cartographical fiction. Even the country of Vergil's *Eclogues* is a mixed scene, by no means the recognizable North Italian locality of the *Georgics,* for instance.[11] To call such a locale "Arcadia," Rosenmeyer tells us, is precisely to rob it of its "real" geographical implications, to insist that, as a natural spot, it is a mental artifact, a concept, an image in itself.

The encroachments of the city on the green world—of *negotium* upon *otium*—are destructive not only of a simpler form of society, but also of the psychological symbol the pastoral world is. For the literary pastoral celebrates the glorious unrealities of the imagination, its necessary furlough from its assignment of work, obligation, and duty.[12] The iron, or at best brazen, world is man's normal portion: as Sidney put it, "poets only deliver a golden." In the literature with which we have here to deal, the literary opposition between *urbs* and *rus* shifted to become in the Renaissance a *topos* in itself, but with a particular fit to Renaissance literature and socio-economic notions—that is, it shifted its formulation from "city" to "court," and the court-country paradigm became one major focus of pastoral organization.[13] The naturalness, freedom, delightfulness of the pastoral ethos often criticized, overtly or by implication, the self-seeking, self-aggrandizing materialistic artificiality of any court—"court" a synechdoche for any artificial, programed social organization. "Sicily" and "Arcadia" were not measured merely against (as Poggioli believed) the megalopolis, Alexandria, Rome, Paris, but against *any* strict program of social forms, formalities, polite fictions, or flatteries. At Versailles, later, queen and courtiers carried crooks and passed their time as shepherdesses and dairymaids; consciously or not, they acted out the extreme solipsism of the pastoral fiction, so delicately self-referential that only the most sophisticated can comprehend its significations. In the ambivalent symbiosis of court and country, at least in Renaissance pastoral writing, it was the courtier who came for instruction of confirmation to the shepherd, from whom the courtier, an apprentice shepherd, could learn what natural "courtesy" was.

Since the poet's world could be reshaped according to the imagination, could reject conventional decorum to set queens in the dairy, eating bread and honey, poetic imagination could work what miracles it would with its pastoral situation. If queens are dairymaids, shepherdesses can just as well be queens, or at least princesses—and so they turned out to be, over and over again, in the wish-fulfilling satisfactions of pastoral myths. The "marvelous," that subject for endless discussion among Italian critics,[14] was commonplace in the pastoral environment, with social miracle one of pastoral's chief donations. Not least of these was the re-establishment in the pastoral environment of Golden Ageness ("poets only deliver a golden"), or (better) Golden Agelessness: in this generic country, there was no season's difference, in the forest no clock.[15] The landscape stood, at its best, at a perpetual spring, fruiting, and harvest; at worst, the season's round was characteristically benevolent. When the landscape was not at its rich mellowness, the pastoral *pathétique* was generally to blame—the landscape had fallen off to mirror its shepherd's disappointments or depression. In this fiction, then, a poet's triumph was complete: by its means, he could create a nature whose sole poetic obligation was to identify with his emotional state. Such a nature is entirely dependent upon imaginative art, is a nature openly, proudly artificial, a nature which inverts the usual system of imitation, by which art conventionally looks to nature as its model, to offer an art form on which nature might model itself for its own improvement. The pastoral, then, offered a paradigm for the creative imagination in which the doctrine of *mimesis* is questioned or rejected[16]—and so, really, is the idea of decorum. Not that the pastoral has not its own rules, conditions, and decorum—but its decorum is a conscious reversal of worldly decorus standards.

For these reasons, the art-nature question, another major critical topic of the period, was deeply tied to the pastoral mode, which became the debate's normal habitat. Poets played with the notion of pastoral nature, used as a stalking-horse against the artifices of another ethos—itself a magnificent, self-conscious artifact. From pastoral writing (often mixed with notions of education and cultivation generally classed as georgic),[17] men took a major metaphor, that of the "improvement" of natural things, especially the improvement of breeds by crossing or grafting. "Breeding," that most natural of procedures, became an area where art counted most. The question was delightfully debated: was a man entitled to use his wit to perfect nature, or did he, by interfering in natural processes ("The Mower against Gardens"), degrade and adulterate natural patterns and products?[18]

For agriculturalists as well as for poets speaking metaphorically, this is at once an aesthetic and a moral problem—involving, among other things, the rights of the arts (all the arts, not just poetry, certainly not just pastoral poetry) to do what art does: that is, to "improve" the nature it imitates. In the simplified and rigid scheme of styles and topics inherited by Renaissance theorists ("systematized" is surely the better word[19]), shepherds are honest people, as George Herbert put it: they speak in a simple, or low, style befitting the life they lead and the landscape in which they dwell. Should, then, kings and princesses masquerading as shepherds and shepherdesses undertake a simple style of life and of speech? What does such disguise do to a literary decorum based upon a hierarchy of values, with strict relations observed between social rank and level of style? Should those nobles who opt for the country learn, like Berowne, an uncourtly speech, doff, like Kent, the latinate orotundities of rank? Should they not, in short, suit their words to their new actions? Within the artifice of the pastoral frame, all this is made problematical, to be interestingly explored in many works. If, as countless Renaissance pastoralists demonstrate, the pastoral natural world is a complex imaginative artifice, why should not princes and princesses, with their sophisticated and fine-spun speech, be welcome in Arcadia, where their rhetorical finesse simply adds to the imaginative beauties in the pastoral ecology? And welcome they were—which meant that another mixture of decorums was made in this already most mixed of modes.

Such *genera mixta* bring their own contradictions. For instance, in this literary ethos so deceptively simple, the best of everything is selected: the best of genres, the best of styles, the best of solutions to human problems. No wonder then, when we seem to lose a major figure in Tasso's *Aminta* by suicide, we yet recover that figure alive by love's magic power and the accident of a convenient bush: Aminta is too valuable to be spared, and the landscape's marvels are sufficient to save even the most despairing shepherd. Art rescues men from the trials of their lives, and the pastoral makes no bones about it. No wonder, then, that as Guarini laboriously insisted against his fierce opponents and as Fletcher so gracefully observed, comedy and tragedy came so easily to dwell together in the nurturing environment of literary pastoral. Fletcher's comment on his own *Faithful Shepherdess,* written after *As You Like It* and well after the major documents of the Guarini quarrel, states the plain case for the mixture of comic and tragic modes:[20]

> A tragie-comedie is not so called in respect of mirth and killing, but in respect it wants deaths, which is inough to make it no tragedie, yet brings some neere it, which is inough to make it no comedie: which must be a representation of familier people with such kinde of trouble as no life be questiond, so

that a God is as lawfull in this case as in a tragedie,
and meane people as in a comedie.

Part of the reason for the tragicomic mix, then, is in
the nature of the action; another reason lies in the
mixture of ranks involved in most pastoral romances
and plays, where disguise of great ones is a principal
plot-device.

With these literary or generic and social mixes, comes
also moral mixture, a mixture of ways of life set in
actual or implied contradistinction or even contradiction.[21] Looking back to Theocritus, we can see that
some cultural distinction underlies the agonistic presentation of pastoral eclogues, in the competitions
between singers judged for their skill in singing—or,
to say it another way, between singers judged for their
success in defending their particular variant upon the
pastoral life. Neatherd, goatherd, shepherd challenged
one another, to be challenged in turn by fishermen and
mowers, sometimes even by hunstmen[22]—and, given
such a thoroughly country mixture, why not by a courtier as well, especially a courtier disguised as a countryman?[23] Of course, by the time we arrive at this
particular elaboration of pastoral *agon,* a radical discharge of original pastoral democracy has been effected:
when court invades country, rank, however
understressed, intrudes upon such egalitarian
commutuality as countrymen enjoy, alters the condition in which, as the Golden Age myth had it, social
class was irrelevant. Once the mixture of class is accepted in the pastoral system, then alienation may
become a conscious topic, too: perhaps this is Vergil's
point in the First Eclogue. So the melancholy Jaques
may not be all that out of place in the Forest of Arden,
even though he is "Monsieur Traveler" and, it would
seem, at the very least a university wit. He has, presumably, become disgusted and worn out by the conflicting sophistications he has seen and is, at least, true
to the Arden he criticizes, when alone of the cast he
declines to return to court. Celia's choice of pseud-
onym, Aliena, honors the reason for her voluntary exile
and is one token of her courtier-status within the forest. The pastoral world is not for the disappointed and
victimized alone, to relearn their integrity; it exists also
for those more seriously estranged from society, as the
early reference in *As You Like It* to Robin Hood suggests.

II

As You Like It[24] miraculously collects the major themes
of the pastoral, manipulating and juxtaposing them so
as to bring that rich mix under critical scrutiny. Not
only is the classic pastoral dramatic pattern its basic
fiction—exile from court; country restoration; triumphant return to court—but so also are the themes of
nature and nature, of art and nature, of art and artifice,
of court and country debated in eclogue-like exchanges
uttered by representatives of pastoral and non-pastoral
(sometimes even anti-pastoral) positions. The "parallel
and parody" of the play, so well analyzed by Jay Halio
and others,[25] works beautifully to undermine doctrinaire attitudes, social, moral, or literary. The play's
perspectivism is sufficient exposure of the implications
of the *vie sentimentale* for which pastoral had come so
masterfully to stand.

Even satire and folly, embodied in Jaques and Touchstone, in turn set into *agon,* come to challenge and to
reinforce the values of this pastoral. The love at the
center of the play is not a particularly pastoral love,
save in that the playwright works toward eliminating
the artificial and non-natural aspects and elements of
love; but the pastoral tradition, with its exquisite con-
centrations upon the emotional muances and values of
love, offered a superb literary opportunity for examining the love-subject.

Nor is love the only topic so scrutinized: Corin speaks
of his content in the life he leads, in open contrast to
Touchstone's obvious dependency upon his ladies, yet
we know from his own mouth that Corin is shepherd
to another man and not, in Fletcher's sense, one of the
true literary shepherds who are "owners of flockes and
not hyerlings."[26] Corin qualifies his own position: so
does Touchstone who, praising the court above the
shepherd's life, by his witty chop-logic lays open the
shabbiness of the court's customs. Shepherd and jester
are brothers, after all, under the skin: Touchstone, remembering Jane Smile, recalls that early love in the
generic language of the peasant Corin. The "country
copulatives" comment on each other, and on the courtiers: Orlando, courtly mock-shepherd genuinely disin-
herited, dotes on Rosalind; Silvius, a real shepherd
who has learned his love-role as thoroughly as Orlando has his, dotes upon Phebe; Phebe, a real shepherdess struck by the *coup de foudre* prescribed by
Marlowe (to whom they refer as "the dead shepherd,"
in pure literary idiom), dotes upon Ganymede; and
Ganymede dotes, as he insists, upon no woman.

All of them, even the trim Ganymede, smugly apart
from their encirclement, show some aspects of pastoral
loving; all of them, in turn, have been called (like all
fools) into a circle. Ganymede assumes with his disguise (Shakespeare's one-upmanship is manifest in this
boy-actor-disguised-as-a-girl-disguised-as-a-boy-acting-
the-part-of-a-girl) one proper pastoral love-attitude, that
conventionally assigned the shepherdess, of coolness
to the lover. Orlando may not have been given a
gentleman's education by his hard-hearted brother, but
he knows all the same that proper pastoral lovers hang
poems on trees. Silvius loves his lady totally, as if she
were perfectly beautiful, in spite of Rosalind's rebuke
to Phebe; and Phebe illustrates, before our very eyes,
how totally love can wipe out all other considerations,
particularly those of common sense.

Yet all shall be changed: though in the beginning each loves the wrong person, we see Phebe settle for Silvius; we see Touchstone, clad in his courtly aura as well as in motley, win the goat-girl Audrey from the well-to-do rural William—win her, then, by his courtly "rank." We see Aliena paired with the repentant Oliver, both of them struck as finally as Phebe by Marlovian love at first sight. And we see, by a magic attributable to her forest-character, Ganymede-Rosalind claim her lover Orlando. Only Silvius and Phebe, of the whole crowd, are what they seem and no more: the others, one way or another, have been disguised from others and from themselves. And all of them, save Silvius and Phebe, must cope with the undisguising: Audrey must be either taken to the court by her fool or brutally abandoned: Aliena-become-Celia at once threatens her lover's recent vow of shepherdhood, that sign of his reconciliation with kind nature; Orlando must learn what his beloved is to inherit.[27]

Desengaño does not rob the pastoral of its sweetness in *As You Like It*. These considerations do not intrude upon the play itself, in which, however much pastoral love is mocked, its sweet fidelities are rewarded, too. By making fun of Orlando's language, Rosalind jokes him into ever-increasing avowals of his love for her. She may seem to mock all lovers, but at the news of Orlando's hurt by the lion faints like a green girl. Touchstone does not want to be in Arden and contrasts Corin's life unfavorably with what he had known at the court, but he makes the best of his forest opportunities, and his logic actually recoils on him, to endorse the simplicities Corin embodies. The melancholy-satiric Jaques comes to scoff at pastoral sentimentalism, but he is scoffed at in his turn—and for pastoral sentimentalism at that. The data of various literary modes are mocked and yet, through all the mockery, reaffirmed: questioned, teased, tested, found wanting—and found valuable in spite of manifest weaknesses.

In this way, perspectivism is built into this play; it is the play's method, but it relies on traditional implications within the mode, by developing an inherent dialectical tendency in pastoral eclogues to an astonishing degree. Many contests question the traditions which ultimately they endorse: the lovers' fourfold catch suggests the merry-go-round illusion of the experience of loving; Corin and Silvius speak not just about love, but about the kinds of love appropriate to the different ages of man, and Jaques deals with love as developmental folly in his far more total indictment of man's ages and the illusions of each age. Touchstone and Corin debate the life of court and country to demonstrate the limitations of both. Jaques marches through the play, in his melancholy isolation a challenge to everyone's social assumptions and conclusions: like Philisides, Sidney's name for his symbolic self in the *Arcadia,* Jaques has retired to the forest in disappointment with the world's offerings. Though established in

Arden, Jaques is characterized as a traveler, a continentalized Englishman who (as the character-books assure us) can never find aught at home good again. He is also—a bit unexpectedly—the superpastoralist of the play, speaking out for the pathetic identification of creatural suffering with human unhappiness. He is who criticizes the Robin Hood band of gentlemen around Duke Senior for their unbrotherly attacks upon the deer-commonwealth, whose "fat burghers" are slaughtered for men's whims and pleasure; but all this while he is also unpastorally melancholy, unpastorally anti-social. As we look at him more narrowly, of course, we see the social role his melancholy fulfills, and how consistently Jaques acts the part the Duke's men expect of him. It is he who recognizes a freedom even greater than that of the forest in his cry, "Motley's the only wear!" He knows how to call all fools into a circle; he, in short, reminds us by most unpastoral means that Arden is a pleasaunce, that for all its rough weather, the forest is also Cockayne, where all is upside down to be set aright. He knows what his fellow-fool recognizes at sight: "Ay, now I am in Arden; the more fool I; when I was at home I was in a better place; but travellers must be content." And yet Arden is his home, as he chooses to remain in the forest now solitary enough for his nature.

What the forest is, is never made entirely clear, although it *is* obvious that, even with the season's difference, the forest is a better place than the usurper's court. In the forest there is no need for "new news o' the new court"; fashionable gossip is irrelevant to the fundamental constants of courtesy, civility, and humanity. And yet, for all the talk of the golden world, Arden is never "really" that—Corin's master was of churlish disposition and inhospitable, ready to sell his sheepfarm for gold. Unprofessional cleric that he is, Sir Oliver Martext is nonetheless at home in Arden; Duke Senior's fellow exiles do not hesitate to comment on the bitter wind, painful to them if less "unkind" than man's ingratitude. The moral arrangements of the golden world are, come wind come weather, scrupulously observed, together with the pastoral delusions. The melancholy Jaques is courteously received, his idiosyncrasies are respected, enjoyed, and even admired;[28] when Orlando, assuming the role of salvage man, bursts in upon the *fête champêtre,* he is welcomed, not repulsed, in spite of his words and his sword; the country lovers ultimately accept each other with grace. The Duke lives, "the Robin Hood of England" to whom young gentlemen flock "every day, and fleet the time carelessly," so that such rank as he has is, like Robin Hood's, only first among equals. To the forest come Rosalind and Celia, Touchstone faithfully in attendence; to the forest comes Jaques; to the forest comes the outlawed Orlando, with old Adam on his back.[29] In the forest Oliver de Boys and Duke Frederick make their moral recoveries and find their various rewards. In the forest, the fairy-tale world rules:

a serpent and a lion, hitherto inconceivable, threaten the only newcomer distinguished for his savagery: in token of his recognition of the beast within, Oliver had become a hairy man.[30] In Arden, an untaught innocent younger-brother-hero can save that newcomer from these creatures by the "kindness" of his "nature," which marks him as trueborn in spite of his deprivation of nurture. In the forest, whatever nature's natural drawbacks, nature makes written calendars irrelevant: there are no clocks in the forest, and there is time enough for everyone's inner and social needs: the forest, as C. L. Barber reassuringly claims, induces and confirms holiday humor.[31]

Time does not pass, theoretically at least, in the golden world—but this rule does not hold for our play, where we are endlessly made aware, both in earnest and in jest, of the passage of time: in the confrontation of generations (Silvius and Corin, dukes and daughters, Sir Rowland's sons and his aged servant Adam);[32] Orlando comes late to his appointments with Ganymede, who rates him for that—because she is a young girl in love, as she tells us in her psychological typology of time, time trots hard with her. A living emblem of the last age of man, the nearly dying Adam is brought in to emphasize Jaques' classic oration. In other words, this forest is at once ideal and real; the inhabitants of Arden insist that their life is unvaried, as in the Golden Age; but the play works in the rhythms of experience's human actuality. On one side, Arden *is* holiday, and thus timeless; it offers a chance for recovery and redemption, a parodic, exalted imitation of the real world, now corrected and purged. In Arden, fools are visibly in circles, men feast graciously on venison and wine— but time passes as they do so, as we are continually reminded, and men ripen and rot in spite of the lack of clocks.

What the forest offers is its liberties: love finds what it seeks; Jaques is allowed to criticize as he likes; Touchstone may mock, Corin may be threatened with impoverishment. But nothing untoward happens; the forest offers restitution to the dispossessed as well as the far more important imaginative freedom in which the natural spirits of men and women may expand. Duke Senior, Rosalind, and Orlando know that this forest is their goal; there they find a world where even real brothers can be brothers. For with the psychological flowering favored in Arden, we are reminded that all life is not so free: Cain and Abel patterns recur in the play, in each generation. Even in *that* pattern, indeed, one can find a pastoral analogue: the pastoral Abel is the contemplative man, Cain the cultivator, the active man, the man of violence prepared to defend the value of his way of life and its produce. In his underpopulated world, Cain felt he had to savage his brother, as Duke Frederick and Oliver seek to savage their brothers. When these romance-brothers enter the forest, however, reformation strikes at once; the virtuous

maintain and corroborate their gentility and their gentleness, and the evil recover or discover the gentleness in themselves they had denied. Orlando's lapse into savagery, so clearly motivated by his concern for old Adam, is immediately reversed by the gentleness with which his threat of violence is received. As is usual in these discussions of pastoral nature, we find throughout the play the terms which form its structure: nature, natural, kind, kindness, civil, civility, gentle, and gentleness. For nature is kind, and kindness: a recognition of one's kind, a response designed to protect and to strengthen whatever is mutually human.

Against this background, Orlando's complaint against his unnatural nurture makes full sense. His brother owed him, as kin, to raise him as the gentleman he is, but chose instead to rob him of his rights and to cast him, if he could, as a type of Prodigal Son. Finally, Oliver even tried to kill the boy, in an unmotivated gesture of the supreme unkindness. Oliver is presented, as Iago was to be, as simply evil—"simply" evil. The question of nature and nurture running through so much of the play is nowhere debated outright, but from the start the debaters are given real parts in the play. In contrast to his brother, Orlando is, as his behavior consistently confirms, preternaturally "gentle," even though he is also preternaturally strong. Actually, as he and we come to recognize, he has no need of that mysterious education he laments, and grows into a symbolic portion far grander than his inheritance would have been. Orlando assumes responsibility for Adam, grown old in his father's service, to the extent that he violates his own nature by attempting to steal for his sake. He cannot pass by on the other side and let the lion attack his sleeping brother, for all that his brother has done against him. His natural qualities caused him to fall in love with Rosalind, and her to fall in love with him. He speaks of his own gentility ("Yet am I inland bred")[33] and recognizes the same "inland" quality in Ganymede's speech, anomalously cultured for the child of the forest he claims to be. Folk hero that he is, Orlando, the youngest of three sons, is eminently suited to take his place at the head of his family and to marry the Duke's daughter at the end of the play, to return with daughter and Duke to the court, confident of exhibiting the courtliness he has always naturally displayed.

The debate between nature and nurture overlaps the problem of nature and art: nurture is education, altering, improving, grafting, conventionally taken as "good." In Orlando's case, it turns out that the art of which he laments the lack is in fact superfluous. He is what he is "by nature"—and when he assumes various stylized, courtly poses, such as in his role of pastoral lover, Rosalind makes fun of his efforts. As often happens in Shakespeare's versions of pastoral, the nature-nurture debate is skewed and ultimately denied, as received dialectical opposites are shown to be fused in the person (Orlando, Perdita, Arviragus, Guiderius) whose gentle birth marches with his courteous nature. Nurture is not necessary for such as these: all the education in the world had failed to improve Oliver, until he experienced his brother's miraculous assertion of kindness. In Jaques, we see that education has even weakened his feelings for his kind. Rosalind is not the nutbrown boy she pretends she is; her cultivated ancestry of magicians is a fiction to account for the cultivation of her nature and her breeding. In her case, indeed, the disguise which makes it possible for her to take her place in Arden is a fiction in itself. Though she is spokeswoman for what is natural, real, and psychologically sincere, and persuades Orlando to natural and unstylized love, she is of course always neither simple nor boy.

The forest, then, shelters a countersociety, idyllic and playful, offering a model of possibility to the real world,[34] a countersociety made up on the one hand by the fictions of a literary convention and on the other by the types of that convention, determined to express the goodness of their natures. The pastoral second chance offered by the Forest of Arden is not just a second chance for the people in the play; it is equally a second chance for the larger society of which the *dramatis personae* are representatives. As the procession troops courtward, men with antlers on their heads, girls dressed as country brother and sister, nutbrown from sun or dye, dukes and reconciled brothers, we believe in the escapade and in their unlikely return, believe in their capacity to maintain reform, because of the upright good sense they have demonstrated or learned in the forest, because of their natural courtesy, kindness, and radiant moral strength. But we believe in them also because the pastoral refuge has acknowledged the flawed realities of the workingday world; the holiday has recognized real experience. Touchstone is not the only character on whom the truth of experience can be proved: all of them try, assay, essay the pastoral myth, each from his own perspective, and all of them find at its heart the recreative values of nature, kind, and kindness promised by the tradition. The play's perspectivism insists also upon the convergence of all views at its central and controlling point, the symbolic, simple truth of this most artificial of literary constructs.

Notes

[1] Thomas G. Rosenmeyer, *The Green Cabinet* (Berkeley, 1969), is the most valuable analysis of pastoral thematics I have seen; see also Alice Hulubei, *L'Églogue en France au xvie siècle* (Paris, 1938); Mia I. Gerhardt, *Essai d'analyse de la pastorale* (Assen, 1950); W. Leonard Grant, *Neo-Latin Literature and the Pastoral* (Durham, N.C., 1965); W. W. Greg, *Pastoral Poetry and Pastoral Drama* (London, 1906); E. K. Chambers, *English Pastorals* (London, 1895); Frank

Kermode, ed., *English Pastoral Poetry* (London, 1952), Introduction; Jules Marsan, *La Pastorale dramatique en France* (Paris, 1905); Enrico Carrara, *La poesia pastorale* (Milano, n.d.); Hallett Smith, *Elizabethan Poetry* (Cambridge, Mass., 1952).

[2] See Rosenmeyer, pp. 77-85, who offers a corrective to the view of Renato Poggioli as expressed in "The Pastoral of the Self," *Daedalus,* LXXXVIII (1959), 686-99; see also Bruno Snell, *The Discovery of the Mind,* tr. T. G. Rosenmeyer (New York, 1960), Chapter 13.

[3] For this, see F. H. Ristine, *English Tragi-comedy* (New York, 1910); Marvin T. Herrick, *Tragicomedy* (Urbana, 1962), esp. pp. 125-71; Madeleine Doran, *Endeavors of Art,* pp. 182-215; Karl S. Guthke, *Modern Tragicomedy* (New York, 1966), pp. 3-5, 45-92; Cyrus Hoy, *The Hyacinth Room,* pp. 270-73.

[4] Cf. Rosenmeyer on the "mix" of pastoral, pp. 145-67; and K. M. Lea, *Italian Popular Comedy,* I, 196, for *commedia dell' arte* mixtures.

[5] For this topic, see the classic work of A. O. Lovejoy and George Boas, *A Documentary History of Primitivism and Related Ideas in Antiquity* (Baltimore, 1935); Harry Levin, *The Myth of the Golden Age in the Renaissance* (Bloomington, 1969); Rosenmeyer, pp. 220-24; Mia I. Gerhardt, *Het Droombeeld van de Gouden Eeuw* (Utrecht, 1956); and E. H. Gombrich, "Renaissance and Golden Age," *Norm and Form,* pp. 29-34.

[6] See Renato Poggioli, "The Oaten Flute," *Harvard Lib. Bull.,* XI (1957), 147-84; "Pastoral of the Self"; and Rosenmeyer, p. 223.

[7] The classic statement of this is Erwin Panofsky's "'Et in Arcadia Ego,'" in *Philosophy and History,* ed. R. Klibanksy and H. J. Paton (Oxford, 1936); reprinted in *Meaning in the Visual Arts* (Anchor, 1955), pp. 295-320. Cf. Rosenmeyer, pp. 224-31.

[8] Cf. Lovejoy and Boas, *passim;* Poggioli, "Flute" and "Pastoral of the Self."

[9] Rosenmeyer's book deals primarily with the Theocritan elements of the pastoral lyric tradition; for Virgil, see Michael Putnam, *Virgil's Pastoral Art* (Princeton, 1970); and Kermode, Introduction, pp. 14-15, for the city-country transition to court-country.

[10] Rosenmeyer, pp. 65-97, 98-129; and Barber, *Festive Comedy,* chapter 2 and pp. 223-29.

[11] Rosenmeyer on "place" p. 232; on chores, p. 25.

[12] Empson, *Versions of Pastoral;* Barber, *Festive Comedy;* Harry Berger, Jr., "The Ecology of the Mind,"

Centennial Review, VIII (1964), 409-34; "The Renaissance Imagination: Second World and Green World," *Cent. Rev.,* IX (1965), 36-78.

[13] An interesting instance of unawareness of generic traditions occurs in Charles Barber's discussion of *The Winter's Tale* in *Shakespeare in a Changing World,* ed. Arnold Kettle (London, 1964), pp. 233-52.

[14] Cf. Baxter Hathaway, *Marvels and Commonplaces* (New York, 1963), pp. 35-56.

[15] For the timelessness trope, see Rosenmeyer, 86-88; and above, footnote 5.

[16] Though the pastoral mode, utilizing the "low style," observed strict prescriptions of *mimesis* with respect to matching style to country matters and, in many cases, to primitive states of society, nonetheless (by the Renaissance anyway) part of its literary power lay in the ironies involved in portraying this kind of society for a courtly audience. With the development of a literary criticism centering on *maraviglia* (see Hathaway, op. cit., *passim*), as well as the theory of tragicomedy which accepted pastoral setting as requisite to the new genre, *mimesis* in the strict sense fell out of the debate, in spite of continued talk about decorum and "matching."

[17] In his forthcoming work, Dr. Alarik Skarstrom will lay out some of the "georgic" aspects of pastoral.

[18] This question, a topic in Pliny and Seneca, is discussed in *"My Ecchoing Song,"* pp. 36-38; see Edward A. Tayler, *Nature and Art in Renaissance Literature* (New York, 1964), pp. 16-17; and Charles Barber, "The Winter's Tale and Jacobean Society," *Shakespeare in a Changing World.*

[19] See Fred J. Nicholls' excellent (though oddly-titled) article, "The Development of the Neo-Latin Theory of the Pastoral in the Sixteenth Century," *Humanistica Lovanesia,* XVIII (1969), 95-114.

[20] Cited in Eugene M. Waith's valuable book, *The Pattern of Tragicomedy in Beaumont and Fletcher* (New Haven, 1952), p. 44.

[21] See Rosenmeyer, pp. 68-70, 86-88.

[22] J. C. Scaliger, *Poetics,* II, xcix.

[23] I.e., Florizel in *The Winter's Tale* fulfills the simple prescription, while the guileless Perdita's unconscious disguise as a shepherdess moves into the problematic realm. See Rosenmeyer, p. 103.

[24] See Edwin Greenlaw, "Shakespeare's Pastorals," *SP,* XIII (1916), 122-54; Mary Lascelles, "Shakespeare's Pastoral Comedy," *More Talking of Shakespeare,* ed.

John Garrett (London, 1959), pp. 70-86; Helen Gardner, "'As You Like It,'" ibid., 17-32; Peter G. Phialis, *Shakespeare's Romantic Comedies* (Durham, N.C., 1966), pp. 219-31; Harold Jenkins, "'As You Like It,'" *S. Stud.,* VIII (1955), 40-51; R. P. Draper, "Shakespeare's Pastoral Comedy," *Études anglaises,* XI (1958), 1-17; Waith, *Pattern,* pp. 80-83; Sylvan Barnet, "Strange Events: Improbability in *As You Like It,"* *S. Stud.,* IV (1968), 119-31; Marco Mincoff, "What Shakespeare did to *Rosalynde,"* *Sh. Jhrb.,* XCVI (1960), 78-89.

[25] Jay L. Halio, Introduction to *As You Like It: Twentieth Century Views* (Englewood Cliffs, 1968); and see Gardner, "'As You Like It,'" pp. 61-62.

[26] Waith, p. 44; Rosenmeyer, pp. 99-103.

[27] For the convention of disguise as written into pastoral drama and interlude, see Lea, I, 191. Also Walter R. Davis, "Masking in Arden," *SEL,* V (1965), 151-63. For love-in-a-circle, see Lea, I, 182.

[28] For the combination of satire and pastoral see Waith, 81-85 (citing Donatus' confusion of satire with satyr); Rosenmeyer, p. 25; Greg, p. 411; Ralph Berry, "No Exit from Arden," *MLR,* LXVI (1971), 11-20; and James Smith, *"As You Like It,"* Scrutiny, X (1932), comparing the satiric element with that of the tragedies.

[29] For this as an emblem of *pietas,* deriving from the *Aeneid,* see Nancy R. Lindheim, *"King Lear* as Pastoral Tragedy," *Some Facets.*

[30] See Richard Bernheimer, *Wild Men in the Middle Ages* (Cambridge, Mass., 1952).

[31] Barber, *Festive Comedy;* Berger, "The Renaissance Imagination."

[32] Jay L. Halio, "'No Clock in the Forest,'" *SEL,* II (1962), 197-207; Frederick Turner, *Shakespeare and the Nature of Time* (Oxford, 1971), pp. 28-44.

[33] Madeleine Doran, "'Yet Am I Inland Bred,'" *Shakespeare 400,* pp. 99-114.

[34] For countersociety, see Berger, "'The Renaissance Imagination."

Eamon Grennan (essay date 1977)

SOURCE: "Telling the Trees from the Woods: Some Details of *As You Like It,*" in *English Literary Renaissance,* Vol. 7, No. 2, Spring, 1977, pp. 197-206.

[*In the following essay, Grennan examines the means through which Shakespeare extends the pastoral con-*

ventions of his source material to create in As You Like It *a work that is allusive, ironic, and "pastoral in the fullest sense possible."*]

Some general assumptions about the nature of *As You Like It* tend to divert critical attention from certain of the play's specific details, either drawing them without distinction under the "pastoral" or the "anti-pastoral" umbrella or ignoring them altogether.[1] The aim of the present essay is to subject a few of these usually neglected details to a scrutiny more exact and speculative than they normally receive. Such a reading will establish, I trust, the precise manner in which the play *is* "pastoral" or "anti-pastoral." In different ways all of the details to be examined are connected with this generic affiliation. Looked at with a fresh eye, they confirm yet again our respect for the practical genius with which Shakespeare exploited his sources and influences in the creation of a work that, for all its conventional freight, is entirely and inimitably his own.

I

Since it is the manifesto of English pastoral poetry, it is odd that Spenser's *Shepheardes Calender* is rarely if ever mentioned in connection with *As You Like It.*[2] To look at the play by the light of Spenser's work, however, is to see more clearly certain elements in the drama that are common to all pastorals (Shakespeare's major source, Lodge's *Rosalynde,* among them) as well as to understand better a few details that cannot be accounted for by the principal source. Many of the components of *As You Like It,* for example, can be assigned to one or another of the "three formes or ranckes" into which the enigmatic E.K. divides the twelve eclogues of the *Calender.* According to the commentator the individual poems are "eyther . . . Plaintive . . . or recreative . . . or Moral." The plaintive includes elegies and laments, amorous and otherwise; the recreative deals with "matter of love, or commendation of special personages"; the moral may range from the status of poetry to the reverence due old age, and "for the most part be mixed with some Satyrical bitternesse."[3]

As lovers, Silvius and Orlando represent the amorous side of the plaintive mode. Orlando is the less serious, albeit more complex, version of the type, Silvius its complete embodiment. As "the shepherd that complain'd of love," caught in the act of "Praising the proud disdainful shepherdess / That was his mistress" (III.iv.50-51),[4] this despairing but irrepressible lover epitomizes the convention. As with all such conventional lovers, both men are poets. While Orlando merely writes his poems, however, and hangs them like pastoral fruit on the trees of Arden, Silvius' whole life is enacted in a language deliberately poetic, remote from the everyday tones of even his fellow shepherds. Like the laments of Spenser's shepherd-lovers, often pre-

sented as songs sung either by the lover himself or by a friend—"January" and "December," for instance—all of Silvius' utterances are in the nature of "performance," most obviously in the "pageant truly play'd" between him and his scornful lady (III, v).[5] The recitation of Orlando's poems by Rosalind, Celia, or Touchstone makes an allusion in a different key to this aspect of the convention.

The elegiac side of the plaintive mode is also fully represented in *As You Like It,* although, in tune with his practice throughout the play, Shakespeare alters in important ways the traditional model. As with Spenser's "November," the elegy of *As You Like It* must also be regarded as a performance. Its subject is that most indigenous of the forest's inhabitants, the deer. First, in an elaborate set-piece delivered by an anonymous lord, the expiring beast is set in a stylized landscape—"Under an oak, whose antique roots peep out / Upon the brook that brawls along this wood" (II.i.31-32)—attended by a single mourner, Jaques. In pathetic rhetoric the death of the animal and its implications are lingered over, with Jaques's moralizing in this part matching the meditation in "November" on the "trustlesse state of earthly things" (l.153). True to its conventional nature the closing lines of Spenser's poem achieve the apotheosis of its subject. "Carefull" is transformed into "joyfull" verse, and the dead Dido is translated into one who "lives . . . with the blessed Gods in blisse" (l.194). The conclusion of the deer episode in the play is an ironic reflection of this conventional transition from elegy to ecstasy. There, an unusually ebullient Jaques plans to present the slain deer to the Duke "like a Roman conqueror" (IV.ii.3-4). Whether this is the same animal he wept over earlier does not really matter. Together, the incidents compose a single, recognizable, pastoral event. The elegy begun in grief concludes in celebration, accompanied by a song that fulfills conventional requirements: the dead deer's horns become an emblem of the lusty living, and the slaughtered beast finds his apotheosis in a picture of continuous if illicit generation:

Take thou no scorn to wear the horn,
It was a crest ere thou wast born;
Thy father's father wore it,
And thy father bore it.
The horn, the horn, the lusty horn
Is not a thing to laugh to scorn.

(ll. 13-18)[6]

Just as certain of Spenser's eclogues display elements that belong to more than one category, the earlier part of Jaques's elegy for the deer, as well as pertaining to the plaintive mode, also falls into E.K.'s third "forme" or "rancke." The poems in this "moral" category (e.g. "Februarie," "Maye," and "August") often mine the pastoral world for metaphors and allegories to express certain spiritual truths; and although of a more secular

Act IV, scene iii. Oliver, Celia as Aliena, Rosalind as Ganymed. Frontispiece to the Bell edition (1773).

cast than those of the *Calender* the truths wrung from the landscape of Arden certainly belong to this group. Duke Senior's first speech, in fact, perfectly illustrates the workings of this kind of poetry: "And this our life, exempt from public haunt, / Finds tongues in trees, books in the running brooks, / Sermons in stones, and good in every thing" (II.i.15-17). Touchstone's brief lecture to Audrey on the nature of poetry (III.iii.18ff.) may also be placed in this category, both because of its subject matter and because it is in part "mixed with some Satyrical bitternesse."[7]

It is Jaques, of course, who speaks most consistently in the accents of moral pastoral. "Did he not moralize this spectacle?" asks the Duke of Jaques's response to the death of the deer, catching perfectly the melancholy observer's nature and function. As Spenser's shepherd-poets extract satirical human truths from beast fables (e.g. "Maye"), Jaques translates the abandoned deer into an allegorical anatomy of social life: "Thus most invectively he pierceth through / The body of the country, city, court" (II.i.58-59). Conventional pastoral can also account for the fact that Jaques's sour, satirical nature is attributable to his having been a traveler (IV.i.17ff.).[8] Spenser's Diggon, critic of the world's abuses, was also a traveler:

> In forrein costes, men sayd, was plentye:
> And so there is, but all of miserye.
> I dempt there much to have eeked my store,
> But such eeking hath made my hart sore.
> ("September," ll. 28-31)

While Jaques is not Diggon, certain similarities between them do emerge:

> *Rosalind:* A traveller! By my faith, you have
>   great reason to be sad. I fear you have sold
>   your own lands to see other men's; then to
>   have seen much, and to have nothing, is to
>   have rich eyes and poor hands.
>
> *Jaques:* Yes, I have gain'd my experience.
> *Rosalind:* And your experience makes you
>   sad.
> (IV.i.21-27)

Jaques's specifically pastoral nature may also help to explain another of Shakespeare's invented, and apparently "unpastoral," characters. The seventh and ninth eclogues of *The Shepheardes Calender* deal with "dissolute shepherds and pastours," with Diggon's "Satyrical bitternesse" in "September" directed mainly against ecclesiastical abuses and bad priests,[9] Unlikely as it may seem, Jaques's diatribe against the "dissolute pastour" of the forest, Sir Oliver Mar-Text, may be best understood through this conventional lens. Having dismantled the makeshift nuptials of Touchstone and Audrey, the irate Jaques gives them the following sound moral advice: "Get you to church, and have a good priest that can tell you what marriage is. This fellow will but join you together as they join wainscot; then one of you will prove a shrunk panel, and like green timber warp, warp" (III.iii.84-89). In his final action at the end of the play Jaques confirms himself in his role as the agent of moral pastoral. There he commits himself to "other than . . . dancing measures" (V.iv.193), leaving the enchanted circle of redeemed lovers for the company of the newly converted Duke Frederick, who "hath put on a religious life" (V.iv.181). Admittedly a device to erase all shadows from the play's sunny conclusions, it is nonetheless noteworthy that Shakespeare chooses just such an exit for his satirist. By doing so he seals the association between Jaques and the moral dimension of conventional pastoral, ironically enclosing him within the borders of a convention from which, from the start, he has sought to be excluded.[10]

The last of E.K.'s learned categories to be considered is the "recreative," to which belong the intensely lyrical inset songs of "Aprill" and "August." Since, as Book VI of *The Faerie Queene* and *As You Like It* illustrate clearly, the pastoral experience itself is essentially "recreative," such songs lie at its very heart; they celebrate both themselves (the experience of song) and the pastoral landscape from which they draw their lyrical sustenance. This dual function is well suggested by the following lines from "Aprill":

> Upon her head a Cremosin coronet,
> With Damaske roses and Daffadillies set:
>   Bayleaves betweene,
>   And Primroses greene
> Embellish the sweete Violet.
> (ll. 59-63)

Furthermore, these songs are presented also in the nature of explicit "performances," for the delight of a group of auditors within the poem's own world.

Interspersed through the dramatic action of *As You Like It* are musical interludes which clearly fall into this "recreative" category. Whether sung by Amiens, the two pert pages, or an anonymous lord, these songs are refreshing pauses in the play's progress. Each takes the pastoral landscape itself as its subject, whether to praise it directly ("Under the greenwood tree") or to employ its details metaphorically, as in the contrast between certain of its features and the norms of "civilized" behavior ("Blow, blow, thou winter wind"). Such songs translate both the rough and the smooth facts of their environment into what Amiens refers to as "so quiet and so sweet a style." And in the very act of doing so they serve as extended metaphors for the traditional pastoral experience itself.

Even in the songs, however, Shakespeare does not let us immerse ourselves in the pastoral dream. As always in *As You Like It,* celebration must coexist with irony, so that Jaques can taunt the naive optimism of "Under the greenwood tree" with a "verse" of his own, and even the sweetness and delicacy of that most beautiful of all pastoral lyrics, "It was a lover and his lass," are countered by the mockery of its auditor, Touchstone.[11]

Although in a graver mode, the masque of Hymen partakes of the recreative quality of the songs. Like Spenser's "Aprill" the masque stands in relation to the entire work as the perfect pastoral epiphany. It reveals the tendency of the whole form towards an idealized vision of that natural, human, and divine harmony which, embodied in the dance of the Graces, Calidore glimpses for a moment in Book VI of *The Faerie Queene.* Spenser would have understood Hymen's proclamation: "Then is there mirth in heaven, / When earthly things made even / Atone together" (V.iv.108-10). As Walter Davis says of this pastoral pattern, "The centre is always supernatural, usually either a shrine like the Cave of the Nymphs or the dwelling of a magician. It may be the actual dwelling place of the God."[12] This point must be qualified, and in a way that fits neatly into the scheme of the present argument, by the fact that at the heart of such a supernatural event stands a simple mortal: the "fayre Elisa" of "Aprill," though "sprong . . . of heavenly grace," is the living English queen; the Graces in Book VI surround a "jolly shepheards lasse," the poet's Rosalinde; and Hymen, to the supernatural accompaniment of "still music," presents to her father and her lover the very human Rosalind.

II

Besides bearing the marks of E.K.'s categories, *As You Like It* manifests other links with conventional pastoral as exemplified by *The Shepheardes Calender,* links that may help to explain even a few of the more curious features of the play. One of the most striking aspects of Spenser's work, for example, is its author's repeated allusions to Chaucer. Dressing him in Lydgate's fine phrase as "the Loadestarre of our Language," E.K. notes that "our Colin clout" calls him "Tityrus the God of shepheards, comparing hym to the worthines of the Roman Tityrus Virgile," and in a "Glosse" even refers to Chaucer as "the God of Poetes for hys excellencie" (pp. 416, 443). Spenser himself admits that he, as Colin Clout, "of Tityrus his songs did lere" ("December," l. 4).

This pastoral habit of invoking a famous poetic predecessor may explain an odd detail of *As You Like It*— the allusions both direct and oblique to Christopher Marlowe. For not only does Phoebe quote verbatim a well-known tag from *Hero and Leander,* but she also refers to its author as "Dead shepherd" (III.v.81-82). Implicit here is the suggestion that the dead Marlowe was the shepherds' poet-in-residence, while the words

may also be taken as "an expression of pity for Marlowe's sad & untimely end."[13] Marlowe's presence in the play may also confirm that, as many critics have claimed, an uncharacteristically grave remark of Touchstone's is in fact a reference to the poet's death: "When a man's verses cannot be understood, nor a man's good wit seconded with the forward child, understanding, it strikes a man more dead than a great reckoning in a little room."[14] That such allusions occur right after a punning reference to "the most capricious poet" Ovid adds to this whole sequence a specific literary density perfectly appropriate to conventional pastoral. Spenser's invocations of Chaucer and Vergil, for example, establish a literary pedigree for himself as well as underlining the intensely literary nature of the pastoral form itself as it self-consciously incorporates the author's literary ancestors. The examples from *As You Like It* fit these requirements. Both Marlowe and Shakespeare were indelibly associated in the literary mind with Ovid. Marlowe had translated the Elegies, his *Hero and Leander* was "steeped in Ovidian memories of the Amores and the Heroides,"[15] while, as Francis Meres put it, "the sweete wittie soule of Ovid lives in mellifluous and honey-tongued Shakespeare."[16] With Marlowe as Shakespeare's "God of shepheards," bound to Ovid as Spenser's Chaucer is to Vergil, the dramatist creates for himself a distinctly respectable (if ironically shaded) literary pedigree. By doing this he exploits in his own way yet another of the most characteristic features of conventional pastoral.

For the above assertions to hold good, of course, the dramatist's self would have to appear under some poetic disguise in his own pastoral world, the poet's autobiographical presence under a shepherd's mask being an obligatory element of conventional pastoral. Tityrus is Vergil; Tirsi in Tasso's *Aminta* is a version of the poet himself; Phillisides and Astrophel both serve as pastoral alter egos of Sidney; and under the person of Spenser's Colin Clout, as E.K. tells us, "the Author selfe is shadowed" (p. 418). The presence in *As You Like It,* then, of a character who bears the author's own name must surely be understood as a bow towards this common element of the convention and not merely as a "mild theatrical in-joke."[17] In tune with the mood of the play, however, this conventional feature, too, undergoes an ironic sea-change. Thus the incessantly loquacious poet-lover-shepherd of tradition has been transmogrified into William the silent, "a country fellow, in love with Audrey" as the *dramatis personae* tells us, whose name is consummately unpastoral, whose lengthiest utterance is all of seven small words long ("Ay, Sir, I have a pretty wit" [V.i.29]), and who accepts with (in conventional terms) unforgivable equanimity the loss of his lady. Although a very minor character, then, William is yet another example of how the dramatist can adapt the most recognizable (and hackneyed) features of conventional pastoral to his own more complex purposes.

III

A final indication of how Shakespeare turns Lodge's simple idyll into a rich compendium of the pastoral genre itself lies in the conversions to which he subjects his villains. Oliver's description of his transformation stresses its suddenness: "'Twas I; but 'tis not I. I do not shame / To tell you what I was, since my conversion / So sweetly tastes, being the thing I am" (IV.iii.135-37). Equally unprovided for is the entrance of the "Second Brother" with the news of Duke Frederick's spiritual metamorphosis. Pursuing his revenge, the Duke had come

> To the skirts of this wild wood . . .
> Where, meeting with an old religious man,
> After some question with him, was converted
> Both from his enterprise and from the world.
> (V.iv.159-62)

In both cases Shakespeare alters Lodge's narrative: Saladyne experiences his change of heart *before* he enters the forest, where he has come to seek forgiveness of his brother prior to a penitential pilgrimage to the Holy Land; Torismond, being "slaine in battaile," is granted no conversion at all.[18] By calling attention to the seemingly miraculous conversions of his villains, therefore, Shakespeare is deliberately emphasizing the power of the pastoral landscape itself to effect marvellous transformations.[19] In doing so he reveals the true nature of this pastoral world, a world whose green is gold, a protected environment that can absorb elements of the actual world and convert them into its own radiant and recreative fictions, translating the stubbornness of reality into the quiet, sweet style of visionary optimism.[20]

By incorporating so many aspects of the convention, and then by placing them in a context more complex and demanding than that of a normal pastoral, Shakespeare greatly extends and enriches the limited nature of his major source. But as the present argument has tried to show, *As You Like It* remains, for all its ironic highlights and extensions, pastoral in the fullest sense possible. In its most minute and apparently insignificant details as much as in its wonderfully worked out general design, the play bears brilliant witness to its author's capacious comprehension of the whole pastoral tradition. Most of all, perhaps, it demonstrates Shakespeare's ability to make practical use of the convention within which he had chosen to exercise, as he liked it, his genius.

Notes

1 See, for example, the essays in *As You Like It: Twentieth Century Views,* ed. Jay Halio (Englewood Cliffs, N.J., 1968). Agnes Latham's introduction to her new

Arden edition (London, 1975), however, is admirable for its patient scrutiny of and perceptive commentary upon the details; her scholarly elucidation of aspects of genre and character is indispensable to any serious study of *AYL.* In "*As You Like It: Et in Arcadia Ego,*" *Shakespeare Quarterly,* 26 (1975), 269-75, Harry Morris also enriches our understanding of the play's conventional nature by discussing in a usefully specific way the presence in *AYL* of motifs from the pictorial pastoral tradition.

2 In two of the most recent substantial discussions of the play, for example, *The Shepheardes Calender* receives only scant, passing reference. See David Young, *The Heart's Forest: A Study of Shakespeare's Pastoral Plays* (New Haven and London, 1972), pp. 13, 73; and Rosalie L. Colie, *Shakespeare's Living Art* (Princeton, 1974), p. 246. For my argument to be valid, of course, it is not necessary to claim the *Calender* as a "source," merely as a useful point of departure for a study of the play's pastoral nature.

3 In *The Poetical Works of Edmund Spenser,* ed. J. C. Smith and E. de Selincourt (London, 1912), p. 419. Subsequent references in the text are to the same edition.

4 The edition used for textual refs. to *AYL* is *The Riverside Shakespeare,* ed. G. B. Evans (Boston, 1974).

5 On the question of "performance" see Thomas G. Rosenmayer's excellent study of the tradition, *The Green Cabinet: Theocritus and the European Pastoral Lyric* (Berkeley and Los Angeles, 1969), pp. 119-21.

6 That such an incident is nowhere to be found in Lodge's *Rosalynde* may be taken as further evidence of how Shakespeare intensifies and comments upon the pastoral nature of his work.

7 Possibly Touchstone's remark that "the truest poetry is the most feigning" is a humourously barbed allusion to Sidney's famous discussion in his *Defence of Poesie,* his witty assertion that the poet "nothing affirmeth, and therefore never lieth," as well as his description of poetry as "faining notable images of vertues, vices, or what els." *The Prose Works of Sir Philip Sidney,* ed. Albert Feuillerat (Cambridge, 1962), III, 29, 11.

8 The more common way of understanding this is as a function of his melancholy or as proof of his being a portrait (or a caricature) of one or another contemporary satirist. See Latham, "Introduction," pp. xlvi-li, for a full discussion.

9 The attack that Milton's shepherd-poet launches against those "Blind mouths! that scarce themselves know how to hold / A Sheep-hook" is sufficient to show the bad priest as an integral element of the Eu-

ropean pastoral tradition. For, as Thomas Rosenmayer says, such Renaissance pastoralists as Petrarch, Mantuan, Spenser, and Ben Jonson "paved the way for Milton's treatment of the church in 'Lycidas'" (*The Green Cabinet,* p. 211).

[10] Latham's assertion that Jaques "can claim . . . to be most faithful to the pastoral ideal" can best be understood, it seems to me, if he is placed in the special category to which I am assigning him.

[11] In its imagery and rhythm this song is the counterpart not only of Spenser's bouncy roundelay in "August" ("It fell upon a holly eve, / hey ho hollidaye"), but also of "Coridon's song" ("A blyth and bonny country Lasse / heigh ho the bonny Lasse") in Lodge's *Rosalynde.*

[12] *A Map of Arcadia, Sidney's Romance in Its Tradition* (Yale, 1965), p. 35, quoted by Latham, p. lxxi. See also her "Introduction," pp. xxi-xxiii.

[13] The remark is Dyce's. See the New Variorum edition of *AYL,* ed. H. H. Furness (Philadelphia, 1890), p. 206.

[14] III.iii.12-15. The best account of this is in Frederick S. Boas, *Christopher Marlowe: A Biographical and Critical Study* (Oxford, 1940). See especially, for a history of the assumption, p. 283*n.* Latham (pp.xxxiii-xxxiv) agrees that "Marlowe was undoubtedly in Shakespeare's mind" when he wrote *AYL,* but is not convinced of the reference to his death, finding in it and the neighboring allusions to Ovid an echo of Chapman's *Ovid's Banquet of Sense* (1595). Neither argument can be proven conclusively, although my present discussion may tend to strengthen the arguments in favor of Marlowe.

[15] Boas, p. 225.

[16] *The Shakespeare Allusion Book* (London, 1932), p. 46.

[17] Latham, p. lxvii. She mentions the suggestion sometimes made that Shakespeare himself played this part. If he did, it gives even more point to my argument. In "William Shakespeare as William in *As You Like It,*" *Shakespeare Quarterly,* 11 (1960), 228-31, William M. Jones speculates, perhaps over-ingeniously, on the likelihood that the part of William was played by the dramatist himself. Convincing or not, his argument gains piquancy, possibility, and *formal* relevance in the light of the present essay.

[18] For *Rosalynde,* see Variorum *AYL,* pp. 358-60, 387. The subject of conversion is touched on by Latham, who refers it, however, to "the world of Shakespearian romance" (pp. lxx-lxxi).

[19] It is for this reason that one of Samuel Johnson's few negative observations on *AYL* is groundless. Had Johnson been more in sympathy with the pastoral form itself, he could not have objected to the fact that "Shakespeare suppressed the dialogue between the usurper and the hermit, and lost an opportunity of exhibiting a moral lesson" (*The Works of Samuel Johnson, LL.D.,* ed. Arthur Murphy, 12 vols. [London, 1806], II, 203-04), since in that very fact lies the required dramatic point about the benevolent nature of the pastoral landscape itself.

[20] Cf. the tone and substance of some of Sidney's remarks in the *Defence,* which seem to point especially towards poetry that is in the deepest sense 'pastoral': e.g., "Nature never set foorth the earth in so rich Tapistry as diverse Poets have done, neither with so pleasaunt rivers, fruitfull trees, sweete smelling flowers, nor whatsoever els may make the too much loved earth more lovely: her world is brasen, the Poets only deliver a golden" (p. 8). *AYL* is both celebration of and ironic commentary upon such an idealistic stance.

Judy Z. Kronenfeld (essay date 1978)

SOURCE: "Social Rank and the Pastoral Ideals of *As You Like It,*" in *Shakespeare Quarterly,* Vol. 29, No. 3, Summer, 1978, pp. 332-48.

[*In the following essay, Kronenfeld argues that* As You Like It, *rather than reaffirming the correctness of social hierarchies—as is typical among pastorals—presents a complex examination of the virtues of the high and the low in society.*]

Ever since William Empson suggested that the "old pastoral . . . was felt to imply a beautiful relation between rich and poor," there has been interest in pastoral as a kind of social myth.[1] But if pastoral "reinforces illusions of class harmony" and thus assuages "the anxiety and guilt of the dominant classes," as some critics have suggested,[2] it becomes a deliberately promulgated, self-consciously "false vision,"[3] "a specious, self-interested distortion of the truth."[4]

Such a view is irrelevant or simply wrong to most students of the pastoral, who might be supposed as saying, with Sydney: "the [pastoral] poet nothing affirmeth, therefore he never lieth." They deny that a symbol of a state of mind, "an imaginary alternative" which can be "held to fictive standards only,"[5] is meaningful only to a hypocritical "dominant class." They remind us that even if the imagined world of shepherd pastime is the courtier's, insofar as he acts the poet or the lover or the man of contemplation, the shepherd's social rank is of little significant concern.

But even if no literature, including pastoral, mirrors "reality" in any simple way, it is surely an error to assume that imaginative aims and achievements necessarily preclude social content or reference. Some pastoral does indeed portray or long nostalgically for "idyllic, feudal, patriarchal relations"[6] when "service sweat for duty, not for meed."[7] Through its appropriation of the topos of the Golden Age, moreover, pastoral may encompass the dream of economic and social justice. From Vergil's time on, pastoral has manifested an awareness of the ways in which economic and political realities (dispossession for a Meliboeus, wage-labor and a "churlish" master for a Corin) impinge on spiritual or social possibilities. To assume that writers of pastoral were totally oblivious of the social implications of the worlds they constructed, therefore, seems as mistaken as to assume that such social visions, where they exist, are simply self-serving creations of the rich or powerful.

The pastoral view of the social order may be essentially aristocratic, and its view of justice may be that justice is an "aristocratic obligation."[8] But it is important to observe, on the other hand, that the holders of non-democratic and non-economic views of social problems and solutions are not necessarily without genuine concern to "reconcile conflict between the parts of . . . society."[9] Sidney, thinking of Vergil, seems to have felt that the pastoral was indeed concerned with making moral sense of the relationship of the high and the low.

> Is the poor pipe disdained, which sometimes out of Meliboeus' mouth can show the misery of people under hard lords or ravening soldiers and again, by Tityrus, what blessedness is derived to them that lie lowest from the goodness of them that sit highest?[10]

The high and the low, the rich and the poor, may literally confront each other in those forms of pastoral in which the chivalric romance has combined with the eclogue to yield the pastoral romance plot of exile, sojourn in a pastoral place, and return to the court. "When court invades country, rank, however understressed, intrudes upon such egalitarian commutuality as countrymen enjoy, alters the condition in which, as the Golden Age myth has it, social class was irrelevant. . . . "[11] When courtiers playing shepherds or literary nymphs rub shoulders with more homespun countrymen, it is not necessarily only a countering of "imagination" by "reality" that we observe.[12] In such literary situations, we often see how pastoral works out its social vision, how it "attempts to reconcile conflict between the parts of . . . society." According to Humphrey Tonkin, this is indeed what happens, for example, in the Pastorella episode of *The Faerie Queene*, Book VI:

> [Pastoral's] workings suggest that the natural world itself approves and reinforces the social hierarchy:

for all that it may look otherwise, the social system *is* rooted in natural laws. The anxieties and doubts of its readers are mirrored in the structure of romance, but then dispelled. Disguises, sexual confusions, a distinct air of revolution in the hobnobbing of aristocrat and peasant—these resolve themselves as if by miracle into a conclusion which restates the social order.[13]

If literature "is a social process, and also an attempt to reconcile the conflicts of an individual in whom those of society will be mirrored,"[14] pastoral would seem to be fundamentally related, not only to the relationship between the high and the low, but to a tension between the values associated most strongly with the lowly and plain Christian (content, humility, dependence on God) and the values associated with rank and privilege, arts and eloquence, "nobility, magnificence, splendor, and majesty."[15] The tension between the egalitarianism of primitive Christianity and the hierarchical thinking of later Christianity and Tudor propaganda was not totally put to rest by the "Elizabethan world picture."[16] And the figure of the shepherd, so rich in its connotations, was ideally suited to deal with such tensions, because it could contain opposed meanings. As a figure of leisure, the shepherd may indeed be a gentleman, for whoever "professeth liberall sciences and . . . who can live idly and without manuall labour, and will beare the port, charge and countenaunce of a gentleman . . . shall be taken for a gentleman. . . . "[17] Or, the shepherd's idleness may be of quite a different sort: "The wisdom of a learned man cometh by opportunity of leisure: and he that hath little business shall become wise" (Ecclesiasticus xxxvii. 24). He may be as unbusy as the lilies of the field, relying, like the good shepherd Abel and like Spenser's Melibee, on God's providence alone.

I would like to consider *As You Like It*[18] in the context of pastoral's potential for reconciling the different parts of society and the values associated with them. I shall argue that Shakespeare treats, if gently and obliquely, a number of the tensions that separate the high and the low, the Christian and the courtly. In doing so, I think, he calls the pastoral idealizations of these relationships into question. The pressure he puts on the ideal visions, however, if corrective, is positively so. It ultimately serves to revitalize and reaffirm the pastoral vision of charitable relations among humans.

I

Although not precisely a noble shepherd (more a noble forester), Shakespeare's Duke seems to have learned the pastoral truth that "it is the mind that maketh good or ill"; he appears to have found "the paradise within." Addressing himself to his "co-mates and brothers in exile" (II. i. 1), he celebrates a rather penitential landscape. The equality and kinship felt here are possible because in the pastoral world men are made mindful of their basic kinship as Christians: they are all children of Adam and all fallen, all exiled from that first paradise.

The winter's wind tells the Duke that he *is* what others are: mere mortal flesh. And he appears happy for the knowledge. The Duke's behavior springs from Christian fellowship and charity; he is a civilized Robin Hood to the distressed Orlando and Adam and, later, to the wounded Oliver. Although he has been bereft of his dukedom by "stubborn Fortune," he shows the strength of his Nature; he appears to pass the test that pastoral romance is ideally suited to make of its noble heroes who turn shepherd or forester.

> So that if we will effectually comprehend the true essence of man, and with a right eie consider his qualities, he should cast off all his habilitie, deprive himselfe of honour, forsake the goodes of fortune, lay aside his costly apparel, and so we ought to behold naked, not his body, but his mind. . . . [19]

Whether raised "rustically" (I. i. 7) like Orlando, like Guiderius and Arviragus, and like Perdita, or subjected to rusticity, characters such as Duke Senior, essentially of the "royal foundling" type, have the best of Nature, but without the corruptions of Nurture. They thus imply the recognition that courtliness can be vicious at the same time that they reaffirm the idea of true blood nobility by suggesting that mere environment cannot produce it. Such characters address the courtesy book question about the nature of true nobility by presenting an ideal mixture of Christian virtue and noble rank.

A passage from the second book of *The Courtier* is, I think, worth quoting here, because it shows how self-conscious Renaissance writers could be about such strategies. The passage suggests that rusticity and equivalent masquerades were, at least on occasion, pretenses made to be seen through.

> [T]here is no better way of showing oneself in such things, at public spectacles . . . because masquerading carries with it a certain freedom and license, which . . . enables one to choose the role in which he feels most able, and to bring diligence and a care for elegance into that principal aim, and to show a certain nonchalance in what does not matter: all of which adds much charm; as for a youth to dress like an old man, yet in a loose attire so as to be able to show his vigor; or for a cavalier to dress as a rustic shepherd, but astride a perfect horse and gracefully attired in character; the bystanders . . . realizing that there is much more than was promised by the costume . . . are delighted and amused. . . . If on such occasions the prince puts off his identity as prince, and mingles with his

inferiors as an equal (yet so that he can be recognized), then in rejecting his own, he attains to a higher greatness, which is to seek to surpass others not by authority but by ability, and to show that his own worth is not the greater merely because he is a prince.[20]

When the wife of King René of Anjou appeared as a shepherdess in a fifteenth-century French tournament, she rode an elaborately caparisoned palfrey and carried a crook with silver metalwork.[21] In the *Arcadia*, Sidney describes a joust involving men "apparalled like shepherds, for the fashion." The contender has "furniture . . . drest over with wooll, so enriched with Jewels artificially placed, that one would have thought it a mariage between the lowest and the highest."[22] Henry VIII's royally rustic Mayings (for which he sometimes dressed all in green velvet) would also appear to have striven for such a symbolic marriage between humility and pomp, spareness and plenty, the low and the high. During one such occasion, Henry was invited by Robin Hood and his company of yeomen (all his own guard, of course) to see how they lived in the green wood. "Then said Robyn hood, Sir Outlawes brekefaste is venyson, and therefore you must be content with such fare as we use."[23] Such games appear to have been imitations of a kindly but elegant relationship between royalty and the people, paralleled later by Elizabeth's relations with her humbler subjects, such as the Cotswold shepherds, in her Progresses. Such entertainments show that majesty has ears for the words of simplicity. Yet one would have been made very much aware of the gap as well as of the effort to close it, just as one is made aware, in the description of entertainments that Castiglione's Frederico gives, that the prince can dress as a rustic precisely because he is not one.

Shakespeare does present the Duke as a model of pastoral virtue; at the same time, however, he underscores those aspects of the Duke's behavior that suggest a performance, a pastoral masquerade. Amiens' comment on the Duke's sentiments (I. iii. 18-20) hovers between genuine delight that the Duke can derive pleasure from a forced situation and an ironic recognition that the pleasure may be forced, that the Duke has indeed transformed ("translated") reality in the process of moralizing his situation. There is just enough of a note of bombast, of moral self-congratulation in the Duke's speech to make us think he may be compensating for felt discomforts, enjoying his own ability to celebrate a moral tonic somewhat more than he enjoys the tonic itself. Amiens is one of the "loving lords" (I. i. 101) who has left his "wealth and ease" (II. v. 52), but his "I would not change it" (II. i. 18) sounds a little like the indulgence of a kindly parent and marks his detachment from the Duke's vision and enthusiasm. The Duke has replaced the false flattering counselors of the court with the counselors of physical pain and adversity, but he still has his courtiers, who, unlike the wind, are not completely free of the need to flatter, or at least to compliment, his vision. Even among "co-mates and brothers," after all, there are vassals and lords. And it is somewhat easier to present a "show / of smooth civility" (II. vii. 95-96) when one is not quite on "the thorny point / Of bare distress" (II. 94-95).

When the Duke permits himself to utter some anti-hunting sentiments upon which he does not quite intend to act (II. i. 21-25), the hint of bombast in the "uses of adversity" speech begins to sound a bit more clearly. The theme of the hunter's usurpation is entertaining matter for the Duke, perhaps a subject for intellectual debate. The far more sentimentalizing Jaques has been expatiating on it in a "sullen fit" (II. i. 68), and the Duke looks forward to an encounter with him. Outside a specifically pastoral setting, hunting is a way to turn a noble's "banishment" into holiday "liberty" (I. iii. 138). For this reason, the Duke's remarks about hunting, seen in a specifically pastoral context, seem to point to a discrepancy between the social idealism of pastoral (which opposes hunting) and the reality of privilege (which licenses it). It is true that Robin Hood, the hunter who champions the poor, becomes a pastoral figure in Renaissance literature, but his hunting is surely in part a matter of *denying* noble privilege. In Arden hunting seems not clearly a necessity (in which case it might be excused), for fruit and wine are apparently available (II. vi. 98; II. v. 32). So it seems quite likely that Shakespeare is mildly questioning the Duke's position. And if this genuine questioning is muted by the self-indulgent sentimentality of Jaques' anti-hunting sentiments,[24] it is still important to remember that hunting is a specifically non-pastoral activity—the prototype of the exploitation of man by man and of war, and unknown in the vegetarian and communal Golden Age. As Arthur Golding phrased it in his influential translation of Ovid,

> The lavas earth dooth yeeld
> you plentiously
> Most gentle foode, and riches too content
> bothe mynd and eye.
> There needes no slaughter nor no blood too
> get your living by.
>
> . . . . .
>
> The nature of the beast that dooth delyght in
> bloody foode,
> Is cruell and unmercifull.
> Oh what a wickednesse
> It is to cram the mawe with mawe, and frank
> up flesh with flesh,
> And for one living thing too live by killing of
> another:

> . . . . .
>
> as if thou could not stawnche
> The hunger of thy greedye gut and evil
> mannerd pawnche,
> Onlesse thou stroyd sum other wyght. But that
> same auncient age
> Which wee have named the golden world,
> cleene voyd of all such rage,
> Livd blessedly by frute of trees and herbes
> that grow on ground,
> And stayned not their mouthes with blood.[25]

Thus the Duke enters into an exploitative relation with the forest—a relation to which our attention is called—by engaging in the specifically noble leisure-time sport of hunting, which is traditionally opposed to the peaceful activities of shepherds who live in harmony with nature.[26]

II

One would pay less attention to such subtle qualifications of the Duke's pastoral virtue were it not that Shakespeare also underlines the discrepancy between the pastoral virtues of the high and the low.

Although Celia is an excellent example of pastoral virtue in leaving her wealth and ease for love of Rosalind, and although the cousins, in good pastoral fashion, will "mock the good housewife Fortune from her wheel" (I. ii. 31-32), countering Fortune, who "reigns in the gifts of the world" (I. ii. 41), with Nature, they do of course take the "gifts of the world" with them to Arden. "Let's away, / And get our jewels and our wealth together" (I. iii. 133-34). This, in part, is Shakespeare's realism: Rosalind and Celia, like Orlando, expect a wood filled with vagabonds, not a hospitable court in exile. But there is more than realism involved here. Putting jewels in one's purse contrasts strongly with giving up one's purse, which, of course, is what the servant Adam does before departing for Arden. Nor does Adam's generosity stem from having nothing to lose; he knows that to want "money" and "means" (III. ii. 25) is indeed to be in difficult straits; for, as he says, "unregarded age" may be "in corners thrown" "when service should in [his] old limbs lie lame" (II. iii. 42-44). Whatever else they are, then, the "uses of adversity" and the fruits of winter are a matter of practice for the simple Adam, whose "age is as a lusty winter / Frosty, but kindly" (II. ii. 52-53).

Lacking the comforts of the hunt and of courtiers to set his table and seek out entertainment for him, Adam is unsurpassed as a model of pastoral virtue: he exemplifies that aspect of pastoral which comes closest to the evangelical. If the Duke's praise of the biting and blowing winter's wind puts us in mind of our common condition as fallen men, suffering the penalty of Adam and in need of grace, Adam is quite literally an example of that condition. Concerned with dying well (II. iii. 76), he *will* win the way to heaven by "deeds of hospitality" (II. iv. 82). He is the good shepherd whose condition approaches that of the lilies of the field. For, like Spenser's Melibee (whose little "growes dayly more / Without [his] care"²⁷), he discards all material helps and relies solely on God's providence:

> He that doth the ravens feed,
> Yea, providently caters for the sparrow,
> Be comfort to my age!
>
> (II. iii. 43-45)

As such he contrasts with our noble shepherd the Duke, whose peace of mind is somewhat less convincing and whose ease is at least in some measure the result of his gentlemanly status, even in exile. "The constant service of the antique world" that Adam exemplifies is well repaid by Orlando, who carries Adam on his shoulders as Aeneas carried his father Anchises on the way to the founding of a new society.²⁸ Orlando's support of his servant is also a somewhat clearer image of pastoral humility—and nobility—than the Duke's sententious celebration of equality in the wind and rough weather of Arden before an admiring audience.

III

As You Like It should be considered in the context of those English pastoral works that juxtapose the high and the low, masters and servants, rich and poor, court and country—with the result that the shepherd can no longer be simply a metaphor for the poet-lover, or for alternative kinds of experience, but must be placed within a social hierarchy. Such hierarchies frequently have three levels. Aristocratic shepherds come from the world of chivalric romance. Literary classless native Arcadians—poets and lovers such as Silvius and Phebe—come from the Italian pastoral drama and the eclogue tradition.²⁹ And "actual" rustics come most immediately from English traditions of the honest countryman or his comic counterpart, the country clown.³⁰ Edwin Greenlaw long ago remarked on the presence of such bumbling shepherds in an article³¹ on the structural affinities of the pastoral plots of *Daphnis and Chloe,* Sidney's *Arcadia, The Faerie Queene* VI (and one might add Greene's *Menaphon* to his list). In varying ways in each of these works, the "hobnobbing of aristocrat and peasant" finally results in a restatement of the social order.

In Spenser, the validation of rank, the proof of the necessity of leadership, emerges, as it were, in spite of the fact of Calidore's attraction to and praise of Melibee's estate. Shepherds may sing "layes of sweete love and youthes delightful heat" (VI. ix. 4), or, like Melibee, songs of content, but they need to be protected from brigands and similar threats; and prayer is

not enough. The bumpkin Coridon, comic counterpart of the honest countryman, balances, or should we say subverts, the praise of Melibee's mean and sure estate—reasserting the necessity of protection and rule by one's superiors. Coridon suffers from "cowherdize" (VI. x. 37) and thus can neither protect Pastorella from a tiger nor guard the pastoral place from the onslaughts of brigands. Thus the contentedness of pastoral inhabitants, even their ability to enjoy the spiritual satisfactions of limitation, becomes, as it were, a gift of noble duty. (This is very traditional and ancient: the poor may win merit for patience and humility because the rich and privileged take on the burden and potential corruptions of action.)

Somewhat similarly, in Sidney's *Arcadia,* the inappropriateness of pastoral retreat for nobles is indicated by the foolishness of the rustic clowns Dametas, Mopsa, and Miso. Ridiculous in love and war, Dametas is the comic foil for the princes Pyrocles and Musidorus. He hides in a bush while Musidorus kills a bear but emerges once it is dead to give it many a wound, very much as Falstaff might.

In Robert Greene's *Menaphon,* "style is the vehicle of the social distinctions which are . . . uniquely emphasized. . . . The high style is emblematic of high estate, the low style of the lower classes."³² "Plaine Dorone, as plaine as a packstaffe" (who incidentally had a brother Moron who "died of a surfet"³³) is in love with Carmela. They sing a burlesque eclogue, an absurd version of what W. Leonard Grant calls "pastoral cipher."³⁴

> Carmela.
> Ah, Doron, ah my heart, thou art as white,
> As is my mothers Calfe, or brinded Cow
>
> . . . . .
>
> Doron.
> Thy lippes resemble two Cowcumbers faire,
> Thy teeth like to the tuskes of fattest swine,
> Thy speach is like the thunder in the aire
> Would God thy toes, thy lips, and all were mine.
>
> (ll. 137-38)

Although the ecolgue, according to Greene, bespeaks a time "when a ring of a rush would tye as much Love together as a Gimmon of golde" (140), it shows what results when pastoral decorum is carried to a laughable extreme. (A similarly absurd poem is attributed to Dametas in Sidney.³⁵) Greene's attitude toward these "Countrey lovers" (139) is far more mocking than Shakespeare's attitude toward his rude mechanicals, who speak in a somewhat similar, if slightly more lyric, vein in *A Midsummer Night's Dream:*

These lily lips,
This cherry nose,
These yellow cowslip cheeks,
Are gone, are gone!
Lovers make moan;
His eyes were green as leeks.

(V. i. 330-35)

In Longus' pastoral romance, *Daphnis and Chloe,* the hero and heroine are aristocratic shepherds, but they are brought up unaware of this fact in the country. They behave like peasants, albeit charming ones, "noticeably better looking than ordinary country people."[36] Daphnis cares for real sheep, kissing them and swearing by them, and as a result he may smell of them, too. In Angel Day's Elizabethan version of Longus' romance, however, imitated from the French of Jaques Amyot (who seems to be fairly faithful to the original[37]), many opportunities are taken to emphasize the qualitative difference between Daphnis and Chloe (who are innately noble, refined, and virtuous) and their country companions. In particular, Day, building on some suggestions in Amyot, and to a lesser extent in Longus, and creating his own material where there is a hiatus in the manuscript Amyot used,[38] does much to create a noble/bumpkin dichotomy, contrasting the shepherd Daphnis and the cowherd Dorcon, his rival in love for Chloe. Although a somewhat brutish character in Longus, Dorcon is not really outranked socially by Daphnis there. In Day, however, Dorcon is consistently referred to as a "clown" and a base profit-seeker, "with a covetous regard of profit and husband-like desire," who cannot really love in a refined Neoplatonic, manner.[39]

In *As You Like It* the confrontation of highborn aristocratic shepherds and lowly countrymen transcends both courtly idealization (as with Melibee) and courtly mockery (as with Coridon, Dametas, Doron and Carmela, and Dorcon) of the country life. The conventions of ideal pastoral hospitality and, ultimately, the myth of those "idyllic, patriarchal, feudal relationships" that pastoral may assert are both qualified and revitalized. The pattern in Spenser is a common one: the wandering noble is greeted by a most polite Arcadian host and immediately given the hospitality of meager, but sweet because simple, food and lodging. Thomas Lodge's eloquent shepherd host immediately offers his poor shepherd's cottage as housing and goes on to extol pastoral content: "and for a shepheard's life (oh Mistresse) did you but live a while in their content, you would say the Court were rather a place of sorrowe, than of solace. . . . Care cannot harbour in our cottages. . . ." The fact that the sheepcote is going to be put up for sale is merely a fortunate accident, revealed *after* Coridon has offered his cottage, that allows Aliena to carry out her wish to "live low, and content me with a countrey life."[40] And in Spenser, as we have seen, the "blessedness derived to them that lie

lowest from the goodness of them that sit highest" is, by implication, protection, in return for which the ideal member of the mean and sure estate rests content with his place and offers the simple hospitality he can.

IV

In *As You Like It,* the parts are not played in accordance with either of these scripts. First, Celia and Rosalind do not count on the convention of pastoral hospitality. Celia immediately suggests that gold be offered for food, though Corin's apparent gentleness, if not courtly eloquence, causes Rosalind to add "love" (II. iv. 71) when she makes the request. Second, what in Lodge appears to be merely a fortunate accident is in Shakespeare the point, an economic one. Corin insists that he is in no position to offer hospitality, for he is "shepherd to another man" (II. iv. 78) whose sheepcote, now on sale, contains nothing for the nobles to "feed on" (II. iv. 86). We are deliberately confronted with a day-laborer who does not have the glamour or the self-sufficiency of the herd-owning shepherd, who may even be a villein who goes along with the sheepcote and flock to its new owner. (An allusion to the difficulties caused by enclosures is hard to miss here;[41] whatever their actual extent, enclosures were a potent symbol of the absence of idyllic, patriarchal, feudal relations.) It is as if Shakespeare had asked himself how it could be that Melibee, whether a hired hand or an impoverished herd-owner, could both offer hospitality to nobles *and* spurn their gold! Mutual benefits require a certain minimum standard unobtainable if masters are "churls" and relations with them far from familial or idyllic. Clearly, the "noble shepherds" in Shakespeare's play must immediately become owners and Corin their new servant. And Corin knows that owners are interested in the economic facts: "If you like . . . / The soil, the profit, and this kind of life . . ." (II. iv. 97-98). Patronage and service are now restored and both parts of society are happy again; the patron now has a livelihood to dispense and the servant an appropriate object for his service.

If this constitutes almost an "unmasking" of pastoral,[42] however, it is worth noting that Shakespeare does not finally reject its conventions and vision but revitalizes them, especially as regards the charitableness of the lowly. His Corin is not nearly as rough and gross as the plucky Corin of *Clyomon and Clamades,* who describes the "leisure" of actual shepherds in what appears a most ironic way ("But tis a world to zee what mery lives we Shepheards lead, / Why where Gentlemen and we get once a thorne bush over our head"), and who says that nobles who request hospitality do nothing more than travel "up and downe the country, thus to flout poore men."[43] His own dispossessed situation is genuinely distressing to Shakespeare's Corin, and not, as in Lodge, merely a matter of convenience for the nobles. Yet even in this situation Corin pities the "young maid with travel much oppress'd . . . for her sake more than for [his] own" and wishes that his "fortunes were more able to relieve her" (II. iv. 74, 76, 77). He virtually offers them nothing he has.

Shakespeare first defines the situation as unconventional, then finds within it the conventional virtues, thus revitalizing the idea of pastoral charity, of that "sacred pity" (II. vi. 123) that binds men together in a gentle community. But perhaps "the golden age of hospitality" endures longer in servants than in masters. Although it is often the humbler character who is accused of covetousness or baser desires (e.g., Dorcon in Day's *Daphnis and Chloe*), here the masters are the "churls" and the servants, once again, most hospitable. Churlishness, then, is not necessarily a matter of rank; a master who "little recks to find the way to heaven / By doing deeds of hospitality" (II. iv. 81-82) may well deserve the epithet.

Corin himself transcends the idealizing and the mocking stereotypes of the country. He is polite, but not eloquent or gently mannered like the traditional shepherd host (what Lodge's Corin attempts to be and what Melibee is). He may not complain unduly about his estate, but neither is he going to exult over the pleasures of penury, as Lodge's shepherd does, in his traditional role as praiser of the mean and sure. Corin is simple and straightforward, but not grossly clownish, as Lodge's Corin is when he is not being eloquent, and as are his namesakes: the Corin of *Clyomon* and the Coridon of Spenser's *Faerie Queene*.

V

As we have seen, in a significant number of pastoral romance plots, there is a juxtaposition of, or an actual confrontation between, aristocratic shepherd and clownish countryman—as, for example, Calidore vs. Coridon, Melicertus vs. Doron. Shakespeare re-focuses the tension between gentleman and clown, court and country, in the figures of Touchstone and Corin. The usual contrast between real gentlemen pretending to be shepherds and the burlesque version of the countryman, which tends to reaffirm the social hierarchy, here becomes a contrast between the pretended gentleman and the real shepherd—a contrast not disadvantageous to the real shepherd. Although he can make fun of the courtier's role on occasion (V. iv. 43 ff.), Touchstone plays it snobbishly and scornfully here; he appears to try to raise his own status by forcing his very marginal "inferiors" into a considerably lower position than they actually merit.[44] His scorn for a respectable if simple countryman contrasts with Calidore's attitude of *noblesse oblige* toward a truly ineffectual countryman. In court, Touchstone is the "roynish clown" or the "clownish fool" (I. iii. 13). Yet, as soon as he enters Arden he behaves as Corin in *Clyomon* says gentlemen be-

have toward poor men: he will "be flouting" (V. i. 12), enjoying the opportunity to call the first countryman he encounters a peasant: "Holla, you clown!" (II. iv. 66). While Rosalind's admonition, "Peace, fool; he's not thy kinsman" (l. 67), puns on *clown,* meaning court fool, it also inevitably applies the meaning Touchstone had intended for Corin to himself: "he's not a lout like you." But Touchstone is not silenced, for he answers Corin's "Who calls" with "Your betters, sir" (l. 68), adding the "sir" in a mockery of good grace, suggesting that he speaks not only for the nobles, but with them.

In giving Touchstone so transparent a game of social oneupsmanship to play, Shakespeare implies that the claims of some "nobles" to status are based merely upon such words of condescension. But if the gentleman must be distinguished from the countryman, even in Arcadia, it should be by the way he fulfills his part of the feudal contract—dealing nobly, not basely, with the limitations of the lowborn, with whom, after all, he need not compete! Touchstone's scornful "flouting" suggests failings in his courtly models. Orlando, by contrast, illustrates, in his treatment of Adam, the support that proper gentlefolk should offer those beneath them. By dealing obliquely rather than directly with the relations or tensions between high and low, gentleman and countryman, Shakespeare can reveal where and perhaps why some gentlemen's attitudes miss the truth without implicating gentlemen *per se*. The confrontation issues, not in the more usual reaffirmation of courtly superiority over country cloddishness, but in a reaffirmation, by implication, of what relationships between the high and the low should properly be like.

The debate between Corin and Touchstone is, then, an interesting version of the pastoral confrontation between high style and low, complexity and simplicity, as well as a variant on the debate between town and country values—as seen in Alexander Barclay's eclogues (e.g., the sixth), Anthony of Guevera's *A Dispraise of the Life of a Courtier, and a commendation of the life of the labouring Man* (1548; trans. Francis Briant), and such tracts as Nicholas Breton's *The Court and the Country, or, A Briefe Discourse between the Courtier and Country-man* (1618). It is also an amusing inversion of the "civil conversation" between high and low recommended in sixteenth-century "books for good manners" (V. iv. 95), such as Guazzo's.

In response to Corin's question, "And how like you this shepherd's life, Master Touchstone?" (III. ii. 11-12), Touchstone, of course, replies with his tour de force: "Truly, shepherd, in respect of it self it is a good life; but in respect that it is a shepherd's life, it is naught" (13-15 ff.). Touchstone's use of the pattern of thesis and antithesis indicates Shakespeare's awareness that pastoral attempts to reconcile the high and the low, to combine the best of two possible worlds (the best of the life of plenty, at the court, and of the life of spareness, the mean and sure estate, in the country).[45] But, in the dramatic context, Touchstone's speech emerges as a wordy nothing, pure tautology, court sophistry; he undoubtedly hopes that its overpowering tone will carry the message and obscure the fact that there is no content. Corin's turn at philosophy results in a low-style list of banal-sounding *sententiae,* undoubtedly funny. Yet, while Touchstone's talk is meant to sound impressive to country ears and yet say nothing at all, Corin's country simplicities do say something. Corin announces some of the simple facts that characters re-acquaint themselves with in Arden. "The property of rain is to wet, and fire to burn" (III. ii. 26-27) is reminiscent of the Duke's re-acquaintance with the elemental conditions of human life, the "penalty of Adam . . . the season's difference" (II. i. 5-6).

Were the conversation between Touchstone and Corin a courtesy-book model, it would perhaps do what pastoral attempts to do: pay homage to the Christian virtues of humility and content and to the Christian concept of the brotherhood of all men, while at the same time asserting the existence of a social hierarchy. The writers of Renaissance courtesy books did feel the weight of the "old egalitarian taunt 'When Adam dolf and Eve span, / Who was then the gentleman?'"[46] Thus, according to Guazzo, it is

> hatefull and hurtfull . . . for a brave gentleman to mocke and scorne a simple soule of the country. . . . [L]et him remember that Gentlemen were admonished by Christ that they should not be puft up with vain glorie, for so much as they ought to say with the common sort (Our father which art in heaven) which they can not say with a pure and unfaigned heart, if they take not yeomen and poore men for their brothers. . . .

This does not mean, however, that all brothers are equal.

> Nowe touching the unnoble or yeomen, they must not for all this, thinke them selves without imperfection, for many of them have an infirmitie more greevous and pernicious than any before rehearsed: which is, that they will not acknowledge and confesse themselves inferiour to Gentlemen, both by nature, fortune, and vertue: not knowing that amongst the seven degrees of superioritie, this is particularly set downe of Gentlemen over the baser sorte, who by all reason ought to submitte themselves to their will and pleasure.[47]

Touchstone does indeed mock and scorn, not going "by the book" (V. iv. 90), and Corin, in his own way, refuses to confess himself inferior. Touchstone starts out quite typically by advancing the court as the model of manners and morals—as do those Renaissance books for good manners that take the courtier, pursuing honor

via arms, the law, or learning, as the model, as contrasted with the countryman, often portrayed as pursuing mere wealth. In response, Corin, somewhat like Breton's countryman,[48] avows that staple of a society of "estates": "Those that are good manners in the court are ridiculous in the country" (III. ii. 45-46).

This entirely traditional cultural relativism is in fact what protects Corin from Touchstone's assaults. The simple and pragmatic Corin is unashamed to avow the most unglamourous of facts: for example, the hireling shepherd has greasy hands, and kissing them "would be uncleanly" (III. ii. 50). Because Corin does not accept Touchstone's verdict that he is "damned" for not having been to court, Touchstone is forced to change horses in mid-stream, which he unabashedly does. Having attempted to prove the court most moral, he now attempts to delude Corin by arguing that the court is, in fact, more base or perverse than the country. Indeed, he says, the civet which perfumes courtly hands that never touch labor of any sort is filthier than tar, being "the very uncleanly flux of a cat" (l. 68). The very act of perfuming hands to beautify them soils them more deeply. Now Touchstone is taking the usual position of the exponent of the country, arguing that court manners are the more perverse. (In Breton's tract, courtier and countryman each try to accuse the other of having the filthier habit, eating garlic and using tobacco respectively.) For all his pretensions of superiority, Touchstone now suggests the common humanity of court and country: "Why, do not your courtier's hands sweat?" (l. 55).

While clowns such as Doron and Carmela (in Greene) and Coridon (in Spenser) are presented as failures at the high style or in noble activity, Corin's very lack of compliance in a game of rivalry defeats Touchstone— even when the latter uses an egalitarian sentiment in an effort to be superior! Having forced Touchstone into a ridiculous and untenable position, Corin now refuses to play the game. Insulted for being "raw," however, he does feel a bit of pique: "Sir, I am a true labourer" (l. 73). He enjoys the spectacle of increase in his flocks. Touchstone, unable to resist the opportunity to impugn the innocence of God's preferred, the shepherd—that "most innocent" of persons, as the characterist John Stephens has it[49]—returns rather desperately but ineffectually to the original premise of the argument: that the country is more wicked, that Corin sins in bringing "the ewes and the rams together" and in getting his living "by the copulation of cattle . . ." (ll. 79-80). In pretending, preposterously, that "a she-lamb of a twelvemonth" (ll. 81-82) can be "betrayed," Touchstone betrays himself, for of all the "country copulatives" (V. iv. 55-56), he is most like the "crooked-pated, old, cuckoldy ram" (l. 82) he describes. Even if Touchstone's role in the play is the salutary one of emphasizing the animal component in all human love that is "mortal in folly," he overdoes it here. He treats Corin as if he were another kind of being, not merely one who is lower in rank. Corin, mean-while, has the wisdom the "noble" should have; he is wise enough to avoid trying to compete. This shepherd's content, then, is not the courtier's dream of content, nor is it content based merely on a recognition that it is best to accept limitation in return for not having to risk danger. It is the self-acceptance of an entirely separate and very English caste which would say that "comparisons are odious."

VI

Courtly and clownish lovers are not explicitly con-trasted in *As You Like It,* because *all* nature in love is mortal in folly[50] (unless Touchstone qualifies as coun-try clown!). But the relation between William and Touchstone is almost a parody of such a contrast—as for example, between Doron and Melicertus, or be-tween Coridon and Calidore. In courting Audrey, Touchstone assumes the role of the knight attempting to win a country maid. But while the social distance between the knight and the shepherdess in pastourelle is very great, in Touchstone's case the courtship be-comes parody, for he only pretends to a great differ-ence in rank. One of the frequent themes of pastourelle is the "baffling" of the knight by the country maid who prefers her country "Robin" and her country cates: "J'aime mieux mon fromages gras et mon pain et mes bonnes pommes que votre oiseau avec ses plumes."[51] But Audrey, who desires nothing more than to be "a woman of the world" (V. iii. 4-5), has undoubtedly decided that Touchstone is the better match, and so disavows her country lover William: "he hath no inter-est in me in the world" (V. i. 8-9).

William seems to be a true country clown. Yet, at the same time, he is a counter to all pastoral stereotypes, even to such bumpkins as Doron and Carmela. They are amusing, as Greene says, because their "country comparisons" are limited (*Menaphon,* l. 139); it is their imitation of courtly wooing in country style that al-lows noble condescension. William, on the other hand, is completely insensitive; he cannot be mocked as an unsuccessful imitator of high culture because he is unaware that he has been presented with superior skills, unaware, perhaps, that anything significant for him has even transpired. Having been duly bastinado'd by Touchstone's rhetoric, he departs with "God rest you merry, sir" (V. i. 59). In spite of Touchstone's conde-scending translations into the "vulgar" (l. 48), his abun-dant proof of his ability at the rhetorical skills of amplification and variation, and his "killing" William "a hundred and fifty ways" (l. 57) with tautologies, Touchstone is unable to penetrate William's dullness. In ridiculing William, Touchstone runs at an open door with a battering ram. This second confrontation be-tween pretended gentleman and clown suggests once again, then, that real countrymen have not been de-signed to flatter the egos of their superiors.

VII

As You Like It is unusual in the context of those pas-toral works that involve an actual confrontation be-tween the high and the low. Most such works reaffirm social hierarchy by giving the noble shepherd an ap-parent monopoly of virtue, suggesting that he does in fact combine the best of both possible worlds. In *As You Like It,* the Duke's sentimental attitudes and avail-able comforts may not ultimately detract from his char-ity, but if he, Celia, and the "loving lords" are to be regarded as examples of pastoral virtue, of Christian benevolence and love, Adam and Corin are possibly to be seen as even better examples. The connection be-tween baseness and nobility of spirit and baseness and nobility of rank is very much qualified. It is unusual to praise the lowly for their Christian virtues in a context in which the virtues of the wellborn are qualified, if ever so slightly. But of course, the lowly are not uni-formly wise, kindly, or honest either. The idealistic view of the mean and sure estate is qualified by Audrey's status-seeking and corruptibility. And Will-iam *is* a dolt. This mixture of types in all classes—and the rich complexity of their juxtaposition—distinguishes *As You Like It* from those pastoral works that exhibit noble shepherds and bumbling clowns in a more for-mulaic way.

Pastoral is concerned with reformation, not revolution.[53] Shakespeare, working within the tradition, does not really "unmask" pastoral; he merely puts pressure on its social vision in order to revivify it. Ultimately, Orlando is a noble shepherd combining the best of both possible worlds—particularly by contrast with Touchstone, the gentleman manqué, and, more subtly perhaps, by contrast with the Duke. Noble status must be justified both by noble deeds and by noble atti-tudes. Shakespeare's pastoral world, then, is one in which, instead of celebrating the virtues of the highborn, the playwright reaffirms what those virtues consist of. Indeed, Shakespeare seems to suggest that those "idyl-lic, patriarchal, feudal" relations must sometimes be restored—or even created—before they can be cel-ebrated.

Notes

[1] *Some Versions of Pastoral* (Norfolk, Conn.: New Directions, 1960), p. 11. See, for example, Laurence Lerner, *The Uses of Nostalgia: Studies in Pastoral Poetry* (London: Chatto and Windus, 1972); Raymond Williams, *The Country and the City* (London: Chatto and Windus, 1973); Humphrey Tonkin, *Spenser's Courteous Pastoral: Book VI of The Faerie Queene* (Oxford: Clarendon, 1972), esp. p. 115, pp. 290 ff.; Renato Poggioli, "Naboth's Vineyard or the Pastoral View of the Social Order," *Journal of the History of Ideas,* 24, (1963), 3-24; A. J. Sambrook, "The En-

glish Lord and the Happy Husbandman," *Studies on Voltaire and the Eighteenth Century,* 57 (1957), 1357-75; Nancy Jo Hoffman, *Spenser's Pastorals* (Baltimore: Johns Hopkins Univ. Press, 1977), esp. pp. ix-xi, 1-8; Leo Marx, "Susan Sontag's 'New Left' Pastoral: Notes on Revolutionary Pastoralism in America," *Literature in Revolution, TriQuarterly,* 23/24 (Winter-Spring, 1972), 552-75; John Seelye, "Some Green Thoughts on a Green Theme," *TriQuarterly,* 23/24 (Winter-Spring, 1972), 576-638; Harold Toliver, *Pastoral Forms and Attitudes,* esp. Ch. II, "Pastoral Hierarchy and Entelechy" (Berkeley: Univ. of California Press, 1971); *A Book of English Pastoral Verse,* ed. John Barrell and John Bull (New York: Oxford Univ. Press, 1975), Intro.; Richard Feingold, *Nature and Society: Later Eighteenth Century Uses of the Pastoral and Georgic* (New Brunswick, N. J.: Rutgers Univ. Press, 1978).

[2] Leo Marx summarizing Empson, "Susan Sontag's 'New Left' Pastoral," *TriQuarterly,* 23/24 (Winter-Spring, 1972), 555.

[3] Barrell and Bull, p. 4. "[P]astoral . . . posit[s] a simplistic, unhistorical relationship between the ruling, landowing class—the poet's patrons and often the poet himself—and the workers on the land; as such its function is to mystify and to obscure the harshness of actual social and economic organization. . . . At the outset, the Pastoral is a *mythical* view of the relationship of men in society, at the service of those who control the political, economic and cultural strings of society."

[4] Anonymous reviewer of Lerner, *Uses of Nostalgia, TLS,* 6 Oct. 1972, p. 1186, attributes this view to the book.

[5] David Young, *The Heart's Forest: A Study of Shakespeare's Pastoral Plays* (New Haven: Yale Univ. Press, 1972), pp. 27-28.

[6] Poggioli, "Naboth's Vineyard," quoting Karl Marx, p. 23.

[7] *As You Like It,* II. iii. 58 in *The Riverside Shakespeare* (Boston: Houghton Mifflin, 1974), p. 377. Further references to Shakespeare's plays are to this edition.

[8] Poggioli, p. 9.

[9] Empson, p. 19.

[10] Sidney, *Defence of Poesy,* ed. Dorothy M. Macardle (London: Macmillan, 1962), p. 24. Surprisingly, Poggioli is the only other writer on pastoral I know of who notes Sidney's statement, in which as he says, "pastoral poetry is viewed as an instrument of pity,

which is the prime mover of personal justice" ("Naboth's Vineyard," p. 9).

[11] Rosalie Colie, *Shakespeare's Living Art* (Princeton: Princeton Univ. Press, 1974), p. 253.

[12] Examples of works in which the introduction of coarser countrymen *is* primarily a way of juxtaposing "reality" and "imagination" might include Cervantes' *Dog's Colloquy* in *The Deceitful Marriage and Other Exemplary Novels,* trans. Walter Starkie (New York: New American Library, 1963)—see pp. 255-56—and some of the *maggi* described by Marvin T. Herrick in Chapter II of *Italian Comedy in the Renaissance* (Urbana: Univ. of Illinois Press, 1966). On the other hand, in Lorenzo de' Medici's *Altercazione,* the nobleman meets a real shepherd who asks if he has come to the country to gloat over his advantages when compared to the difficult life shepherds lead. See *Lorenzo de' Medici: Tutti Le Opere* (Milano, 1958), III, 11-15.

[13] Tonkin, *Spenser's Courteous Pastoral,* p. 291.

[14] Empson, p. 19.

[15] Thomas More, *Utopia,* trans. H. V. S. Ogden (Northbrook, Ill.: AHM Publishing Corp., 1949), p. 82. More comments ironically on those things "which public opinion commonly regards as the true ornaments of a nation."

[16] See Ernst Troeltsch, *The Social Teaching of the Christian Churches,* trans. Olive Wyon (London: George Allen & Unwin, 1931), I, 120-27, 280-328, for an account of the egalitarian and hierarchical strains in Christian thought. As Lila Geller notes, in "Spenser's Theory of Nobility in Book VI of the *Faerie Queene,*" *English Literary Renaissance,* 5 (1975), 56, the courtesy book literature frequently feels it necessary to deal with the conflict. See John Edward Mason, *Gentlefolk in the Making* (New York: Octagon, 1971), pp. 7, 36. Also see, for example, Robert Dudley, *The Tree of Commonwealth,* excerpted in *Tudor Economic Documents,* ed. R. H. Tawney and Eileen Power (1924; rpt. London: Longmans, Green & Co., 1951), III, 14-17.

[17] Thomas Smith, *De Republica Anglorum 1583* (Menston, Eng.: Scolar Press, 1970), p. 27. Spelling of this and subsequent quotations corresponds to the originals except that I have normalized *i* for *j, u* for *v, v* for *u,* and Elizabethan long *s.*

[18] Rosalie Colie, in *Shakespeare's Living Art,* lists most of the relevant criticism in the notes to pp. 253-60 of her chapter on pastoral; *Pastoral and Romance: Modern Essays in Criticism,* ed. Eleanor Terry Lincoln (Englewood Cliffs, N. J.: Prentice-Hall, 1969) prints

several major essays on *As You Like It*. Other critics writing on *As You Like It* and pastoral include David Young in *The Heart's Forest;* Thomas McFarland, *Shakespeare's Pastoral Comedy* (Chapel Hill: Univ. of North Carolina Press, 1972); and Charles W. Hieatt, "The Quality of Pastoral in *As You Like It,*" *Genre,* 7 (1974), 164-82.

[19] Giovanni Battista Nenna, *Nennio, or a Treatise of Nobility,* trans. Wm. Jones (1595), A Renaissance Library Facsimile Edition (Jerusalem: Israel Univ. Press; London: H. A. Humphrey, 1967), sig. 74ᵛ.

[20] Baldassare Castiglione, *The Book of the Courtier,* trans. Charles S. Singleton (Garden City, N. Y.: Doubleday, 1959), pp. 103-4. Harold Toliver has also drawn attention to this passage in *Pastoral Forms and Attitudes* (Berkeley: Univ. of California Press, 1971), pp. 27-28.

[21] Glynne Wickham, *Early English Stages: 1300-1600* (London: Routledge & Kegan Paul, 1963), I, 23.

[22] *The Prose Works of Sir Philip Sidney,* ed. A. Feuillerat (Cambridge: Cambridge Univ. Press, 1962), I, 284-85.

[23] Edward Hall, *Hall's Chronicle . . . 1548* (London, 1809), p. 582.

[24] See Judy Z. Kronenfeld, "Jaques and the Pastoral Cult of Solitude," *Texas Studies in Literature and Language,* 18 (1976), 451-73.

[25] *Shakespeare's Ovid, Being Arthur Golding's Translation of the Metamorphoses,* ed. W. H. D. Rouse (London: Centaur, 1961), pp. 296-97. Also see Arthur O. Lovejoy, et al., *A Documentary History of Primitivism and Related Ideas* (Baltimore: Johns Hopkins Univ. Press, 1935) I, 14 ff. and Claus Uhlig, "'The Sobbing Deer': *As You Like It* II. i. 21-66 and the Historical Context," *Renaissance Drama,* NS 3 (1970), 79-109.

[26] For relevant associations of shepherds vs. hunters see the anonymous play *The Maid's Metamorphosis* and Sidney's entertainment, *The Lady of May* (though in the latter neither shepherd nor hunter is really worthy).

[27] Spenser, *Faerie Queene,* VI. ix. 21 in *Poetical Works,* ed. J. C. Smith and E. de Selincourt (London: Oxford Univ. Press, 1965), p. 377. Further references to Spenser's *Faerie Queene* are to this edition.

[28] Nancy R. Lindheim, "*King Lear* as Pastoral Tragedy," in *Some Facets of King Lear,* ed. Rosalie Colie and F. T. Flahiff (London: Heinemann, 1974), p. 183, (n. 10) mentions the Aeneas/Anchises, Orlando/Adam parallel.

[29] Silvius' name, changed from "Montanus," echoes the many Silvias (Tasso), Sylvios (Guarini), and Sylvanuses (Montemayor) of Continental pastoral. He is the "faithful shepherd" (V. ii. 81), "this most faithful shepherd" (V. iv. 14), *il pastor fido*. Still, he has some economic standing, for he was going to buy the flock and pasture from Corin's master. Phebe has the petulant literal-mindedness of the coy maid of Italian pastoral and its English imitations, but her standing is less than totally literary, for, according to Rosalind, she has "a huswife's hand" (IV. iii. 27).

[30] Charles W. Hieatt classifies the pastoral ranks similarly in "The Quality of Pastoral in *As You Like It,*" but for him "actual" rustics are merely "anti-pastoral figures" as opposed to an intrinsic part of pastoral's social vision. See p. 167.

[31] "Shakespeare's Pastorals," *Studies in Philology,* 13 (1916), 122-54.

[32] Walter R. Davis, *Idea and Act in Elizabethan Fiction* (Princeton: Princeton Univ. Press, 1969), p. 174.

[33] *Menaphon,* in *Life and Complete Works of Robert Greene,* ed. Alexander B. Grosart (New York: Russell & Russell, 1964) VI, 68, 102. Further references to *Menaphon* are to this edition.

[34] *Neo-Latin Literature and the Pastoral* (Chapel Hill: Univ. of North Carolina Press, 1965).

[35] *Prose Works,* II, 18.

[36] Trans. Paul Turner (Harmondsworth, Eng.: Penguin 1968), p. 22.

[37] This judgment is based on a comparison of Amyot, *Daphnis et Chloé* (Paris: Librarie des Bibliophiles, 1872) with two modern translations of Longus, by George Thornley (London: Wm. Heinemann, 1916) and by Paul Turner.

[38] See the introductions to the George Thornley translation of Longus and to Daye's Elizabethan version: *Daphnis and Chloe,* the Elizabethan version from Amyot's translation by Angel Day, ed. Joseph Jacobs (London, 1890).

[39] Day, pp. 26-27, 20-21.

[40] Thomas Lodge, *Rosalynde,* in *As You Like It:* A New Variorum Edition, ed. H. H. Furness (1890; rpt. New York: Dover, 1964), p. 338.

[41] According to M. St. Clare Byrne, *Elizabethan Life in Town and Country* (London: Methuen, 1961), p. 136, the district known as Arden was well enclosed by this time.

[42] This is what Nancy Jo Hoffman terms it in *Spenser's Pastorals,* xi.

[43] *Clyomon and Clamades: A Critical Edition,* ed. Betty J. Littleton (The Hague: Mouton, 1968), ll. 1293-94, 1312.

[44] Ralph Berry, in "No Exit from Arden," *Modern Language Review,* 66 (1971), 11-20, sees the drive for dominance as central to the play.

[45] Compare, for example, Sidney's way of describing Arcadia: "As for the houses of the country . . . they were all scattered, no two being one by th'other, & yet not so far off as that it barred mutual succour: a shew, as it were of an accompanable solitarines, & of a civil wildnes." *Prose Works,* I, 14.

[46] Geller, "Spenser's Theory of Nobility"; see n. 16.

[47] *The Civile Conversation of M. Steeven Guazzo,* The First Three Books Translated by George Pettie, Anno 1581 and the Fourth Book by Barth. Young, Anno 1586 (London: Constable, 1925), pp. 194-95.

[48] See *The Court and the Country* . . . in W. C. Hazlitt, *Inedited Tracts* . . . (London, 1868), p. 196. "Truly, Cousin, I thinke every thing is best in his owne nature; . . . for as a Courtier cannot hold the plough . . . so a Country-man cannot court it. . . . "

[49] *Essayes and Characters Ironical and Instructive,* the second impression (London, 1615), p. 415.

[50] In fact, the *reductio ad absurdam* of "pastoral cipher" found in Sidney's *Arcadia* and in Greene's *Menaphon* is here given to Touchstone (II. iv. 46 ff.) where it works to qualify idealistic love in *all* the lovers.

[51] *Le Jeu de Robin et Marion* in *Théâtre Français au Moyen Age,* ed. L. J. N. Monmerqué et Francisque Michel (Paris, 1842), p. 116.

[52] See Leo Marx, "Susan Sontag's 'New Left' Pastoral," p. 553.

THE ROLE OF WOMEN

Margaret Boerner Beckman (essay date 1978)

SOURCE: "The Figure of Rosalind in *As You Like It,*" in *Shakespeare Quarterly,* Vol. 29, No. 1, Winter, 1978, pp. 44-51.

[*In the following essay, Beckman describes Rosalind as a figure who personifies the reconciliation of opposites in* As You Like It.]

Toward the end of *As You Like It,* just before she resolves the plot, the disguised Rosalind tells Orlando:

> Believe then, if you please, that I can do strange things: I have, since I was three years old, conversed with a magician, most profound in his art and yet not damnable. If you do love Rosalind . . . it is not impossible to me, if it appear not inconvenient to you, to set her before your eyes tomorrow human as she is, and without any danger.[1]

Even if the play strains the bounds of probability, no magic has been worked in it before this scene. It therefore seems strange that Shakespeare has Rosalind resolve the plot by appearing to work magic rather than by simply stripping off her disguise—particularly if, as is usually asserted, she has disguised herself only because she must find out whether Orlando really loves her. The question, then, is why Rosalind's "strange things" constitute a proper end to the play.

I would like to suggest that Rosalind ends the play as a magician because throughout the whole play she has made extraordinary, seemingly impossible—and thus "magical"—conjunctions between contrary things. Her own person is a seemingly impossible reconciliation of opposites. The magic she performs brings contrarieties together and harmonizes them. The "strange things" she does, then, are not incidental to the play, but rather a logical development from what she has been doing all along.

Although there has been comparatively little analysis of the figure of Rosalind herself, a good deal has been made of the opposites in the play. The conclusion usually drawn is that one or another in a given pair of the play's opposites is the version we are finally to accept. Since the major opposition in *As You Like It* is generally understood to involve "realism" and "idealism," therefore, critics tend to view Shakespeare as ultimately choosing either idealism or realism and then subordinating its opposite.

The more usual—and perhaps more old-fashioned—view of the play has skeptical, melancholy, or sensual realism disappear by incorporation into a less extravagant final version of the play's depiction of romantic, honorable, love-at-first-sight idealism. For example, although he spends some time showing how one character's point of view contradicts or corrects another's, Harold Jenkins concludes his discussion of the play as follows:

> In *As You Like It* ideals, though always on the point of dissolving, are for ever recreating themselves.

They do not delude the eye of reason, yet faith in them is not extinguished in spite of all that reason can do. "I would not be cured, youth."[2]

Jenkins regards many of the oppositions in the play as never having been real. Thus, of Orlando's hanging verses on the trees, Jenkins says that "in so human a creature these love-gestures appear not as his *raison d'être,* but as an aberration." Similarly, Rosalind's mockery of Orlando is not truthful, but "only play at taunting her adorer while allowing her real woman's heart to be in love with him in earnest" (p. 47). For Jenkins, then, any hard opposition dissolves into general approval of an idealistic love that is not uncomfortably extravagant.

The most important dissenter from this view is C. L. Barber. His analysis of the oppositions in *As You Like It* points toward a *concordia discors.* But he is bound by his thesis to regard opposition as a means of comically presenting "what is not ideal in man." He therefore concludes that Shakespeare "represents or evokes ideal life, and then makes fun of it because it does not square with life as it ordinarily is."[3] Addressing himself to the social value of *As You Like It* and its effect on its contemporary audience, Barber reads the play as a conflict between "reality and the illusions . . . which love generates and by which it is expressed" (p. 230). The play offers the audience a "festive release" for its sentimental impulses, but controls those very impulses by "presenting what was sentimental extremity as impulsive extravagance and so leaving judgment free to mock what the heart embraces" (p. 223). Barber views Jaques and Touchstone as representatives of a final realism; their "real position is generally mediate between the audience and something in the play," and Touchstone embodies "in a character and his relations with other characters the comedy's purpose of maintaining objectivity" (p. 228).

To regard Jaques and Touchstone as having this position in *As You Like It* is, I would argue, to fail to come to terms with the real complexity of the play and in effect to make any real opposition disappear into a general approval of realistic "objectivity." In Shakespeare—and in Renaissance literature as a whole—opposition need not necessarily be resolved by taking one opposite as more "objective" than the other. Opposites were often balanced, if not "yoked," together to form a "new concoction."[4] Barber implies such a pattern in *As You Like It* when he says "romantic participation in love and humorous detachment from its follies, the two polar attitudes which are balanced against each other in the action as a whole, meet and are reconciled in Rosalind's personality" (p. 233). But Barber does not pursue this idea, possibly because such a conception of the figure of Rosalind does not seem to him to help argue "the comedy's purpose of maintaining objectivity."

The problem, as I see it, is that many critics wish to dissolve opposition in *As You Like It* because they do not conceive of opposition and ambivalence as offering a comedic resolution; to them, comedy is not an affirmation if it maintains alternative perspectives to its very end. But there is really no literary or dramatic reason why opposition, ambivalence, and alternative perspectives cannot work together to form an affirmative whole. If comedy presents a vision of life as "playing," there is no reason not to have opposed sides participating in it. Indeed, much play demands opposition. And opposition need not be overcome to be resolved. If comedy celebrates life, it may regard the rich contrariety of life as its particular vision.

The point I wish to argue is that in *As You Like It* Shakespeare shows man's "possible perfection" rather than his "certain imperfection," presenting that perfection as a reconciliation of opposites in which both members of the opposition are retained in the face of all temptation to choose one or the other. *As You Like It* invites us to conceive of the difficult "magic" of two opposites existing simultaneously, truly contrary and mutually exclusive, but bound together in a creative, if paradoxical, union—like man and wife.

For if the plot of this plotless play is about anything, it is about man and wife, about "getting married and living happily ever after." As Hymen, the god of marriage, says at the end of the play,

> Then is there mirth in heaven,
> When earthly things made even
>   Atone together.
>
> (V. iv. 114-16)

To make "earthly things . . . even" is not to make them the same or to make one subordinate to another; it is to reconcile them and make them one ("atone") in a creative relationship. The name for this kind of relationship is "harmony,"[5] and its central representative in *As You Like It* is Rosalind. She *is* harmony, a coincidence of opposites, promising to "make all this matter even" and to "make the doubts all even" (V. iv. 18, 25). Her "way is to conjure you," she says in the play's Epilogue, because *concordia discors* defies logic and seems impossible. But the "magic" she performs is not fearful. The opposites she represents are not "yoked by violence together"; her opposites are peacefully reconciled in the harmony of marriage.

Since marriage is a *concordia discors,*[6] Rosalind's image is a complex one. She starts out simply enough as a woman who "on such a sudden . . . fall[s] into so strong a liking with old Sir Rowland's youngest son" (I. iii. 28-29). She therefore first stands for "idealism." But when she later comes to "speak to [Orlando] like a saucy lackey and under that habit play the knave with him" (III. ii. 312-13), she stands for the "realism" that is opposed to Orlando's idealism. To her it is obvious that Orlando's verses are "a tedious homily" (III. ii. 163). But Rosalind is also "many fathom deep . . . in love" (IV. i. 210).

Maintaining these two alternative perspectives, she already represents a *concordia discors*. But Shakespeare heightens the paradox of her figure through a number of other devices. The most important one is that she is a *woman* presenting the voice of critical realism about love. Celia says, "You have simply misused our sex in your love-prate" (IV. i. 205-6). As this remark shows, women had been traditionally associated with the "heart" or emotions, men with the "head" or intellect. In *As You Like It,* however, it is Rosalind who intelligently and realistically speaks from the head, as when she tells Phebe, "Sell when you can: you are not for all markets" (III. iv. 60). And it is Orlando, the man, who speaks from the heart, responding to Ganymede's realism with "I would not be cured, youth" (III. ii. 444). As a couple, then, Orlando and Rosalind represent a coincidence of opposites, but the coincidence is made doubly paradoxical by the fact that the two lovers often switch traditional sexual characteristics.

A further intensification of the paradox is achieved by having Rosalind stand by herself for both opposites. She has a more complicated function in the play than Orlando, and in some sense she alone stands for the same thing that they stand for together as a couple. When Shakespeare presents Rosalind as a woman disguised as a man pretending to be a woman, then, he does more than merely "permit her to furnish the humorous commentary on her own ardent love affair" (Barber, p. 233). He offers us a symbolic image of "earthly things made even."

Rosalind's disguise is in fact even more complex, for on the stage she is actually a boy playing the part of a woman disguised as a man pretending to be a woman: the boy actor playing Rosalind disguised as Ganymede pretending to be Rosalind. (The boy actor is important enough to Shakespeare's conception of Rosalind's figure for him to have her make a clear reference to her masculine nature in the Epilogue, even though still maintaining that we see "the lady the epilogue.") Rosalind may thus be related to the Renaissance prototype of all combinations of male and female, the union of Mars and Venus. Erwin Panofsky reminds us that this union represents "the auspicious fusion of two cosmic forces begetting harmony."[7] And Edgar Wind has shown that there is an even deeper mystery: that "Venus is not only joined to Mars, but that his nature is an essential part of her own."[8]

But the union of male and female in Rosalind is not only shown physically and worked out in terms of the head and the heart; it is also presented in the plot line by certain of Rosalind's actions. We see her both as a protecting masculine figure and as a faint-hearted female figure. For example, Rosalind undertakes to protect Celia on their journey to Arden, but after they arrive she faints at the news of Orlando's wound. Each act is made a further *concordia discors* on its own through the device of implying its immediate opposite. Thus, when she proposes the disguise to Celia, Rosalind says,

> Were it not better,
> Because that I am more than common tall,
> That I did suit me all points like a man?
> A gallant curtle-axe upon my thigh,
> A boar-spear in my hand; and—in my heart
> Lie there what hidden woman's fear there
>   will—
> We'll have a swashing and a martial outside,
> As many other mannish cowards have
> That do outface it with their semblances.
>   (I. iii. 116-24)

Here Rosalind's outside depicts a man's readiness to fight, complete with sword and spear; on the inside she hides "woman's fear." Later, just the opposite physical effect occurs when she faints at the "napkin / Dyed in [Orlando's] blood" (IV. iii. 155-56). There a faint-hearted outside is passed off as a disguise: "Ah, sirrah, a body would think this was well counterfeited! I pray you, tell your brother how well I counterfeited. Heigh-ho!" (IV. iii. 167-69). In both instances the inner "reality"—the woman's fear and the man's courage—are, in a certain light, less real than the disguising outside. The external feigning reveals the internal truth. For Rosalind *is* taller, braver, and more aggressive than Celia, just as she is shorter, more fearful, and less physically aggressive than Orlando.

After she awakens, Rosalind assures her audience—even though the audience watching this audience knows better—that her faint was counterfeit. But she also admits that she "should have been a woman by right," since she "lacks a man's heart." Indeed, others can be more aggressive than Rosalind. It is Celia who first plans the escape to Arden. But others can also be more weak than Rosalind. It is Orlando who swoons so heavily (IV. iii) that he cannot rise at all. And it is only because Orlando's "masculine" anger at his evil brother has been overcome by "feminine" heartfelt pity that he tackles the lioness. In relation to both Orlando and Celia, then, Rosalind's position is a complex one, paradoxical both emotionally and physically.

Throughout the play we see a male/female coincidence in Rosalind's character. She follows Celia's first plans for their trip and depends on her for their purchase of the rural cottage. But she also organizes Celia's actions, protecting her and deciding the parts she and Celia will play in the forest. She is an attendant on the Duke, but she guides him to his daughter. She leads

Orlando into love-making, but must attend while he "break[s] an hour's promise in love" (IV. i. 44). She lacks a lover and father, acting only to bring others together, but she gains a lover and a father and comes together with them in the course of bringing others together. As a man, she swears she will marry no woman; but as a woman, she marries herself to the man she has rejected and marries the woman she has rejected to another. She is the chaste woman who does not tell her love and "will not have" (IV. i. 92) Orlando, but she is also the aggressive lover who forces Orlando's confessions.

Such a central figure is not unusual in Shakespeare: the "master-mistress of my passion" appears, *mutatis mutandis,* in Viola, Portia, Cleopatra, and Imogene. Shakespeare had a strong interest in the androgynous, but not epicene, sexual figure.[9] But it is important to note that his androgynous figure does more than set forth paradox for its own sake. Such a figure symbolizes the natural union of those opposites that are made for each other. Male and female are thus images for all reconcilable contraries. As concrete images, male and female help to demonstrate more abstract reconcilable contraries. That is, since we can readily assent that male and female are opposites that combine, we can be persuaded through such imagery that other opposites combine too. It is not that *As You Like It* allegorizes the coincidence of Mars and Venus. It is rather that such coincidences as those involving Mars and Venus or Rosalind and Ganymede can be used to symbolize that natural harmony of opposed forces that constitutes man's "possible perfection." And in comedy, man's perfection is epitomized in marriage.

When the figure of Rosalind is seen as in itself a *concordia discors,* her word-play reveals itself to be the rhetorical expression of her symbolic function. Her puns, witticisms, and paradoxes first of all show her as a "masculine" intelligence, not because Shakespeare thought women incapable of wit, but because to be witty is to be able to control others and to lead them, as Rosalind leads Orlando. Wit is therefore—as an image, not as a conclusion about women—active and "masculine" intellectual expression, as opposed to passive and "feminine" emotional expression. Celia is speaking of Rosalind's wit when she (wittily) says, "You have simply misused our sex in your love prate." And Orlando says, "A man that had a wife with such a wit, he might say 'Wit, whither wilt?'" (IV. i. 166-67). But Rosalind's wit is not held against her, no matter how "masculine" it is, for Shakespeare does not think it necessary that a female wit be epicene or bad-tempered. Like male compassion, female wit is part of a fully realized human character. Thus, although Shakespeare establishes clear differences between the "masculine" and the "feminine" in his plays, he often implies that characters who are totally one or the other are sterile.

Rosalind's wit presents in the mode of rhetoric the same coincidence of opposites that her disguise and actions present in other modes. Her wit is a necessary corollary of her function in the play. To play on words is, after all, to make unlikely connections and to bring together contrary meanings. In word-play what is said "is valid in, refers to, several modes of judgment or of feeling."[10] Thus when Rosalind says of Celia and Oliver, "They are in the very wrath of love, and they will together; clubs cannot part them" (V. ii. 43-45), her word-play brings together Jaques' melancholy, Touchstone's sensuality, Orlando's romanticism, and her own warm heart and sense of the ridiculous; the result is a complex total meaning that brings alternative perspectives into an organic relationship with each other. Rosalind here applies all of the play's attitudes about love toward a vision of Celia and Oliver getting married and living happily ever after. If "clubs cannot part them," no audience's sense of man's "certain imperfection" can part them. It is Rosalind's characterization of them as in "the very wrath of love," therefore, and not Jaques' realism, that truly embodies what Barber called "the comedy's purpose of maintaining objectivity."

The complex meaning of Rosalind's description of the love of Celia and Oliver can be built up by only such a person as Rosalind, for complex meaning cannot be constructed simply by adding together all the individual points of view in the play. As William Empson has pointed out,

> to say anything in two parts is different in incalculable ways from saying it as a unit. . . . the only way of forcing the reader to grasp your total meaning is to arrange that he can only feel satisfied if he is bearing all the elements in mind at the moment of conviction; the only way of not giving something heterogeneous is to give something which is at every point a compound.[11]

Rosalind's word-play serves as a necessary verbal imitation of "earthly things made even," bringing together in union things that are at odds. And her word-play in turn reinforces her magical power to bring about the unions at the end of the play.

Oppositions between melancholy and laughter, country-life and court-life, humble and high estate, danger and safety, time and timelessness, limit and freedom—all have been pointed out and explored by commentators on *As You Like It.*[12] But when one side of each pair is thought of as deposing the other, just as when realism is thought of as triumphant over idealism, only a partial view of the Shakespearean reality emerges.

Rosalind displays a Jaques-like melancholy when she tells Orlando that in this "poor world" there are no romantic love stories like those of Troilus or Leander:

"These are all lies: men have died from time to time and worms have eaten them, but not for love" (IV. i. 106-8). But when Jaques says to her, "I do love [melancholy] better than laughing," Rosalind replies with a condemnation of single-mindedness: "Those that are in extremity of either are abominable fellows and betray themselves to every modern censure worse than drunkards" (IV. i. 5-7). Throughout the play Rosalind's laughter implies a certain skeptical melancholy as well as a tolerant good humor.

Similarly, Rosalind is both a courtier and a country shepherd. Orlando has seen both in her, and at the end of the play he attempts to resolve the seeming contradiction when he says of her:

> My lord, the first time that I ever saw him
> Methought he was a brother to your daughter:
> But, my good lord, this boy is forest-born,
> And hath been tutor'd in the rudiments
> Of many desperate studies by his uncle,
> Whom he reports to be a great magician,
> Obscured in the circle of this forest.
>
> (V. iv. 28-34)

Closely related to the country-court combination is the way Rosalind combines the Arcadian lover with the rustic truth-teller. She is, as Rosalind, a golden figure to Orlando; she whiles away a golden-age time in the forest with the Duke; and she is an Arcadian lover to Phebe, who calls her a "god to shepherd turn'd." But she is also a country plain-speaker like Corin when she tells Silvius that Phebe is no Arcadian maid:

> Come, come, you are a fool
> And turn'd into the extremity of love.
> I saw her hand: she has a leathern hand,
> A freestone-coloured hand: I verily did think
> That her old gloves were on, but 'twas her
>   hands.
>
> (IV. iii. 23-27)

In like manner, Rosalind's estate comprises both extremes of the play. She has no father, depends on Celia, and is in some danger from Duke Frederick, who has told her:

> Within these ten days if that thou be'st found
> So near our public court as twenty miles,
> Thou diest for it.
>
> (I. iii. 44-46)

At the court she is in danger but of high estate; in Arden she is out of danger but of low estate, a simple country shepherd. But even in the forest she combines both low and high estate and both safety and danger, for she depends on others to protect her even as she protects them and unites them. While she passes time in the timeless forest of Arden, she is aware of time

(giving Orlando several analyses of it) and effects a realistic, as well as "magical," resolution to her own and others' love affairs. And while she seems as helpless as anyone in the play—under sentence of death, without a father or lover, without money—she also seems to have greater powers than anyone else in the play, directing others as she will and finally entering in Act V with the god of marriage himself.

To know Rosalind is to know that opposites can be reconciled.

Notes

[1] *The Complete Works of Shakespeare,* eds. Hardin Craig and David Bevington, rev. ed. (Glenview, Ill.: Scott Foresman, 1973), V. ii. 63-66. The Craig-Bevington edition will be used throughout.

[2] Harold Jenkins, *"As You Like It," Shakespeare Survey,* 8 (1955), 51.

[3] *Shakespeare's Festive Comedy: A Study of Dramatic Form and Its Relation to Social Custom* (Princeton: Princeton Univ. Press, 1959), pp. 228-29.

[4] See Frank L. Huntley, "Dr. Johnson and Metaphysical Wit: or, *Discordia Concors* Yoked and Balanced," *Papers of the Midwest Modern Language Association,* ed. Robert Scholes, 1 (1969), 103-12.

[5] See Brendan P. O. Hehir, "Balanced Opposites in the Poetry of Pope, and the Historical Evolution of the Concept," Diss. Johns Hopkins 1959, pp. 22-25.

[6] I use *"concordia discors"* throughout rather than the familiar *"discordia concors"* because, as O Hehir has pointed out, Dr. Johnson distinguished sharply between the two, "differentiat[ing] the forcible yoking together of the totally diverse (*discordia concors*) from the harmonious combination of the true opposites, the male and female (*concordia discors*)," p. 260. Although one cannot hope successfully to continue Johnson's essential distinction, *discordia concors* seems to me uncomfortably inappropriate to *As You Like It.*

[7] *Studies in Iconology: Humanistic Themes in the Art of the Renaissance,* rev. ed. (New York: Harper Torchbooks, 1962), p. 164.

[8] *Pagan Mysteries in the Renaissance,* rev. ed. (New York: Penguin, 1968), p. 94.

[9] See Barbara Everett, *"Much Ado About Nothing," Critical Quarterly,* 12 (1961), 319-35, and G. Wilson Knight, *The Mutual Flame* (New York: Macmillan, 1955).

[10] William Empson, *Seven Types of Ambiguity,* rev. ed. (London: Chatto and Windus, 1963), p. 129.

[11] Ibid., p. 269.

[12] See Jenkins and Barber; also see Helen Gardner, *"As You Like It,"* in *More Talking of Shakespeare,* ed. John Garrett (London: Longmans, 1959); James Smith, *"As You Like It,"* Scrutiny, 9 (1940); D. L. Stevenson, *The Love Game Comedy* (New York: Columbia Univ. Press, 1960); and Mark Van Doren, *Shakespeare* (New York: Holt, 1939).

Susan Carlson (essay date 1991)

SOURCE: "Shakespeare's Rosalind: The Strong Woman in the Comic Tradition," in *Women and Comedy: Rewriting the British Theatrical Tradition,* The University of Michigan Press, 1991, pp. 43-67.

[*In the following excerpt, Carlson observes the character of Rosalind in terms of gender roles, specifically as a temporary inversion of the patriarchal status quo in the play.*]

Women in British comedy have often been illusory, weak, or—to the feminist, at least—simply objectionable. In Shakespeare's *The Taming of the Shrew,* Kate's seeming capitulation plagues feminist critics who defend Shakespeare's women and creates problems for contemporary theater directors. In Jonson's plays, women either have minor roles *(Volpone)* or are most palatable when they are actually men in disguise *(Epicoene).* In Wycherley's cynical world, the women are present as either pure virtue or despicable weakness. And in the philosophical world of Stoppard's *Jumpers,* women are alternately romping acrobats or concupiscent wives. But my concern . . . is not plays in which women are either objectified or vilified. It is instead the many plays in which women are strong and central, in which comic inversion gives rise to vocal, active women. In other words, the focus of my study is the comic plays that have the most to offer women; for it is in such plays that the tension between powerful comic heroines and restrictive comic structures is most fully on display. . . .

. . . I begin with Shakespeare, the earliest British comic playwright to recognize and exploit the power comedy can offer women. In *As You Like It,* he creates a heroine, Rosalind, who sets the standard for the strong woman in comedy.

At the end of *As You Like It,* when Hymen teases Phebe with the notion that she cannot love Ganymede— "You to his [Silvius's] love must accord, / Or have a woman to your Lord" (5.4.127-28)—he recalls the comic advantage Shakespeare has found in Rosalind's disguise as Ganymede. Less obvious, however, is his implicit reference to the most steady love of the play, that between two women, Celia and Rosalind. His mockery of such love and the uncharacteristic silence of the women that accompanies it are two act 5 indications of the way women are represented in the play. *As You Like It* has been acclaimed as a play about the expansiveness of love, the graciousness of fate, and the inevitability of human foible. But it is also a play about women in the comic world.[1] And while Shakespeare's women claim control and voice in the play's long-celebrated inversion, they fail to transcend the limits a traditional comic ending imposes on them.

. . . Shakespeare's plays have elicited the most through critical analysis of women in British comedy. Such analysis offers an exemplary display of the paradoxes that accompany critical discussion of women in comedy. On the one hand, Charlton *(Skakespearian Comedy),* Nevo *(Comic Transformations),* Bamber *(Comic Women, Tragic Men),* and French *(Shakespeare's Division of Experience)* focus on the festive liberation of the plays to find that comic women benefit from their mid-play freedom. On the other hand, Park ("As We Like It"), Garner ("A Midsummer Night's Dream"), Parten ("Re-establishing Sexual Order"), Erickson ("Sexual Politics"), and Neely *(Broken Nuptials)* emphasize the power of the comic ending to defuse, even reverse, sexual revolution. Yet as Karen Newman has demonstrated, these opposing responses to Shakespeare's comic women are not strictly incompatible. In studying *The Merchant of Venice,* Newman argues that inversion is not always "simply a safety mechanism." On the contrary, she asserts, it can be an efficient intrusion on male "structures of exchange" ("Portia's Ring," 29). Thus Newman acknowledges the limitations of inversion but maintains that even a restricted inversion can establish irrevocable transformations. I sympathize with this attempt to hold the two accounts of comic inversion in critical tension. Yet with *As You Like It,* . . . I find even the most productive rebellion finally negated by comedy's multiple options for accommodation.

I can best explain the complicated position of this play's women by considering separately the play's status quo, its inversion of that standard order, and its return to order. What is important about the status quo in *As You Like It*'s duration is the fact that it never disappears. While the forest of Arden most obviously represents a rejection of the status quo, both the play's dependence on symmetry and its flirtation with androgyny prove strong indications of an uninterrupted status quo based on sexual double standards. In turn, this pervasive status quo affects the celebrated inversion that Arden represents. Thus my discussion of the play's inversion is focused on women's language and friendships, two areas in which the women's supposed liberation proves to be as qualified as it is empowering. My study of the play's conclusion, then, is a look at how the ending saturated with marriage completes this play's paradoxical foregrounding of women. A final section on contemporary production of the play takes note of recent attempts to secure the power this play offers women, but even these attempts to capitalize on Rosalind's strength prove the durability of comic structures that qualify comedy's women.

The Status Quo

The establishment of a status quo world is a routine feature in Shakespearean comedy. In *As You Like It,* the court of Duke Frederick is a predictable world governed by civil laws and stable mores. It is also standard in Shakespearean comedy, however, that the status quo world, when it proves hostile to changing conditions, is challenged by an alternate world—usually a different place (Arden)—where the norms are relaxed, even reversed. Ultimately *As You Like It,* like other Shakespearean comedies, ends with a return to the status quo, a return acceptable because of the modifications that have, supposedly, been negotiated in the alternate location. While critics disagree on the effects of this cycle—is there or is there not a new (or better or different) world at play's end?—they generally agree on its presence.

The special effect such circular motions have on the women of *As You Like It* has been most thoroughly studied by Peter Erickson. To reach his conclusion that "*As You Like It* is primarily a defensive action against female power rather than a celebration of it," Erickson compiles an extensive list of the signs of patriarchy present throughout the play ("Sexual Politics," 82). Most important, he shows that the altered world of Arden is only superficially a release from everyday, partiarchal norms, and that as a temporary *reversal* of the norms Arden is never a threat to them. Although Erickson never makes the connection explicitly, he bases this reading of *As You Like It*'s persistent everyday world on the presence of a sexual double standard. This double standard in Shakespeare's status quo world is not significant simply because it grants women less freedom and power than it does men. Rather, it is important because in the middle world of the play, when norms are reversed, the power and freedom women *do* gain is *still* based on the double standard. In other words, the middle world does not revoke the double standard, but only invokes a temporary criticism of it. While the social criticism of *As You Like It* is not negated by the play's cycle, it is continually undercut by the omnipresence of the play's double standard.

In my examination of *As You Like It*'s middle, I will study how the temporary nature of the play's reversal limits its rebellions. Rosalind's powerful language and close female friendships that flourish in Arden are, for example, muted by the influence of patriarchal norms. Her male dress, symbolically, preserves the male as dominant. As a continuation of my argument that mid-play challenges to order are qualified, my examination of the ending will point to Rosalind's inability *not* to choose marriage. I introduce these considerations of inversion and ending, however, with a closer look at ways in which the status quo and its sexual double standards establish (and ultimately qualify) the play's portraits of women. Both the play's general manifestations of equality and its specific connections with androgyny are undermined by enduring norms and their reflection of the status quo.

Equality informs language and structure alike. While the words "equal" and "equally" each occur only once in the course of the play, they are notations of a pattern present throughout the play. Celia and Rosalind, in 1.2, offer equality as a desirable goal and a standard of judgment, first when Celia finds that the ideal bestowal of Fortune's gifts must be an equal one—"Let us sit and mock the good housewife Fortune from her wheel, that her gifts may henceforth be bestowed equally" (1.2.29-31)—and later when she counsels Orlando to "a more equal enterprise" (1.2.161) than Charles the Wrestler appears to be. The construction of the play stands as the most striking example of the persistent valorization of symmetry and balance these comments hint at. For example, a standard of symmetry balances one action against another when a conversation on the killing of deer (2.1) is matched by the actual hunting of deer (4.2); when Rosalind's first wooing of Orlando (3.2) is mated to a second (4.1); when Orlando's triumphant dialogue with Jaques (3.2) is repeated in Rosalind's similar victory over the cynic (4.1). The significance of characters is likewise refined when they are considered in pairs—Jaques's cynicism is tempered by Touchstone's loving parody, Silvius's idealism is braced by Corin's realism, one bad brother (Oliver, Duke Frederick) is paired with one good one (Orlando, Duke Senior), and one unrequited love (Phebe's) is upstaged by another one, less vain (Silvius's).

Rosalind is the ultimate incarnation of all such equations, symmetries, and balances. For not only does she act as a matchmaker for others, but she is at the same time self-conscious of her own vacillations between the realistic and the idealistic. By the end of the play, when Silvius offers his litany of love in 5.2 and when Hymen and Jaques parcel out their verbal gifts of love in 5.4, the play's four marriages seem to be natural extensions of a play full of equations and balances. In the play's final scene, Celia's word "equal" has become "even"; first when Rosalind disappears "to make these doubts all even" (5.4.25) and second when Hymen elevates her "even" by rhyming it with heaven: "Then is there mirth in heaven / When earthly things made even / Atone together" (5.4.102-4). "Even," like the "equal" of 1.2, is meant to indicate that by the end of the play life is orderly and balanced.

While it has been common to link the play's balances to an idea of sexual equality, these formal and linguistic symmetries are better seen as reflections of the play's dependence on the status quo than as a guarantee of equitable relations between the sexes. In fact, the androgyny that critics have praised as the pinnacle of the play's many equalities is not a signpost of sexual liberation; instead, it is another signal of the play's foundation on inequitable norms.

In his study of the androgyny of the play, Erickson points out that a leveling of sexual differences is not possible, even in this play's measured world, because the basis for both of *As You Like It*'s worlds is patriarchy ("Sexual Politics," 77).[2] In the end, this limitation makes androgyny more meaningful to the men returning to power at the play's end than to the women about to give it up:

> However, the conservative counter-movement built into comic strategy applies exclusively to Rosalind. Her possession of the male costume and the power it symbolizes is only temporary. But Orlando does not have to give up the emotional enlargement he has experienced in the forest. Discussions of androgyny in *As You Like It* usually focus on Rosalind, whereas in fact it is the men rather than the women who are the lasting beneficiaries of androgyny. ("Sexual Politics," 77)

Androgyny is not a reality for the women in *As You Like It* in the same way it is for the men because the women are never equal to the men; the most that they gain is a reversal of an inequitable situation during the middle of the play. This temporary reversal ensures that while men learn their weaknesses and women their powers in the inversion of the play's middle world, norms do not change.[3] The status quo of male dominance that Duke Frederick's court represents thus remains present throughout the play. For the women of Shakespeare's comedy, then, the status quo conditions their extraordinary liberation as well as their ordinary endings.

The Inverted World of Arden

The play's inequitable status quo is tested by its free, leveling middle, though little altered by it. Nevertheless, the play's inverted world calls for careful scrutiny, scrutiny that seeks to identify not only the play's retention of standard norms but also its fierce battles against convention. In Shakespeare, as in Maugham, the position of women in the inverted world is marked by a tension between unconventional power and conventional standards. By first examining women's language and then their friendships, I can detail both where freedom manifests itself and how it is restricted.

Rosalind commands the rich linguistic world at the center of *As You Like It*, yet her mastery of language varies. Her language is, in other words, a clear indication of the power she alternately does and does not have in the play. In 1.2, Shakespeare establishes the contradictions of the women's linguistic patterns in the realm of the status quo by contrasting their verbal acuity with their acquiescence. In 1.3 also, as Rosalind confronts the censure of Duke Frederick, she displays her verbal skill, but learns that women's language skills carry little weight in the Duke's court. Only when Rosalind and Celia move to Arden—i.e., to a world where Rosalind herself establishes the limits on her own language—does she realize her full linguistic range. Inversion, in short, sets her linguistically free.

In 3.2, Rosalind blossoms as literary critic, witty conversationalist, and lover. She is clear-headed enough to recognize the inadequacies of Orlando's verbal celebrations of her, telling Celia of his verses, "some of them had in them more feet than the verses would bear" (159-60). She can then banter with Celia over the concrete image of "feet" she calls up. She further displays her versatility by matching witty analogies to nature with Touchstone (111-15) and by making more learned allusions at her leisure—calling up Pythagoras, for example (168). But her power and control are most obvious in her first conversation with Orlando. From the exit of Jaques in line 281 to Rosalind and Orlando's joint exit at the scene's end, a simple measure of her command of this conversation is the number of lines both characters speak: Rosalind has ninety-eight lines to Orlando's thirty. But even such lopsided numbers only begin to suggest her mastery of their interaction. Orlando, on the one hand, takes a passive role and feeds lines and questions to Rosalind. In addition, Orlando has brief speeches devoid of imagination or wit. Rosalind, on the other hand, is represented by a hearty prose in which the melodies of the language are the melodies of her love. Act 3, scene 2 is evidence that only in Arden does Rosalind use her masterful prose for both power and pleasure.

There continue to be moments later in the play when Rosalind's wit and verbal acuity command attention, as she chides Phebe in 3.4 or directs the others in the recitations of 5.2. But the depth and range of her linguistic skills are clearest when her heart is in them, in 3.2 and 4.1 especially. Rosalind reaches the height of her powers in 4.1. Here the gymnastic playfulness of 3.2 is transformed into heartfelt pronouncements on love and marriage. When Rosalind plays the realist in denying to Orlando that one could die from lack of love, the great love she feels for him softens her harsh statement and gives it its graceful rhythms:

> The poor world is almost six thousand years old, and in all this time there was not any man died in his own person, videlicet, in a love cause. Troilus

had his brains dashed out with a Grecian club; yet he did what he could to die before, and he is one of the patterns of love. Leander, he would have lived many a fair year though Hero had turned nun, if it had not been for a hot midsummer night; for good youth, he went but forth to wash him in the Hellespont, and being taken with the cramp, was drowned; and the foolish chroniclers of that age found it was 'Hero of Sestos.' But these are all lies. Men have died from time to time, and worms have eaten them, but not for love. (4.1.85-98)

When Rosalind gives up her language along with her disguise and is silent at the play's end, a gaping hole is left in the play. As ritual takes prominence in the play's final scene, the language of all the characters is diminished. But the loss is greatest for Rosalind. As the emotions and powers of Rosalind's language give way to the comparative shallowness of song and dance, Rosalind takes her silent place in the marriage ritual. Even the epilogue, in awarding the last words to Rosalind, does not make up for her silence in the last scene. Erickson points out that the epilogue, in fact, subverts the woman's world of this play by recalling the boy Rosalind-Ganymede and not the woman who has been the linguistic heart of the play ("Sexual Politics," 79-80). I would suggest, in addition, that Rosalind's return as an actor (whether male *or* female) reinforces the signal present all along that her power comes only from a suspension of the play's—and the world's—reality. The fact that she still must enact her last moment of power while in her male disguise only increases my suspicion that the Rosalind of the play's middle disappears because her linguistic command is as dangerous as it is endearing.

The epilogue and the silence that precede it are, in fact, only the last indications of the way the women's linguistic powers remain attached throughout the play to assumptions that undercut them. In considering the variations in Rosalind's linguistic command, two conclusions are unavoidable. First, Rosalind's verbal control increases in scope and power when she enters the play's inverted territory of Arden. Second, her linguistic power is always conditioned (even in her grandest moments) by the patriarchal assumptions encouraged by comic structures. In other words, Rosalind's language is never quite her own. A second look at her language in the play will corroborate that her command is always accompanied by a discrediting of women's linguistic power. The discrediting comes predominantly from Rosalind herself, although it has corollaries in the language and behavior of all the play's women.

In 1.3, Duke Frederick warns Celia of the deception in Rosalind's language:

> She is too subtle for thee; and the
>   smoothness,

> Her very silence and her patience,
> Speak to the people, and they pity her.
>
> (1.3.73-75)

His warning is dismissible since his character is suspect; yet Rosalind elsewhere voices similar reservations herself. For example, she prefaces her talk with Orlando in 3.2 by asking Celia the self-deprecating question, "Do you know I am a woman? When I think, I must speak" (3.2.237-38). She reconfirms her diagnosis of logorrhea by lacing the pyrotechnics of 4.1 with similar undercuttings of her skill. Here she warns her future husband Orlando that "certainly a woman's thought runs before her actions" (4.1.127-28) and counsels him, further, to be wary of his wife's wayward wit:

> Make the doors upon a woman's wit, and it will out at the casement; shut that, and 'twill out at the keyhold; stop that, 'twill fly with the smoke out at the chimney.
>
> (4.1.148-51)

Rosalind's comments are all tongue-in-cheek, but they cannot simply be dismissed as comic. Simply put, the direct discrediting of female language in these statements is of a piece with other subversive tactics that women have adopted.

Rosalind is responsible for the greatest share of such subversion and the self-deprecation it is linked to. Even as Ganymede, she accepts limiting stereotypes. One might speculate that Rosalind adopts her deferential behavior to preserve her male disguise. Yet she is similarly deferential in 1.2, before she adopts the guise of Ganymede. Of the disguise itself, Rosalind suggests in 1.3 that it will help her hide in her heart "what hidden woman's fear there will" (1.3.115). Later, while collapsing at the end of the journey into Arden, she blames the weak female in her: "I could find in my 2heart to disgrace my man's apparel and to cry like a woman; but I must comfort the weaker vessel, as doublet and hose ought to show itself courageous to petticoat" (2.4.4-7). She disdains the woman in herself at the same time that she feels an obligation to comfort Celia-Aliena. Even in 3.2, a scene enriched by her confidence and control, Rosalind's doubts about her female self loom large. She tells Celia that she retains the impatience of a woman (3.2.185-89). And later, after teasing Orlando with a catalogue of women's faults— "All like one another as halfpence are, every one fault seeming monstrous till his fellowfault came to match it" (3.2.334-36)—she paints a giddy picture of the female lover:

> At which time would I, being but a moonish youth, grieve, be effeminate, changeable, longing and liking, proud, fantastical, apish, shallow, inconstant, full of tears, full of smiles; for every passion truly

anything, as boys and women are for the most part cattle of this color; would now like him, now loathe him; then entertain him, then forswear him; now weep for him, then spit at him; that I drove my suitor from his mad humor of love to a living humor of madness, which was, to forswear the full stream of the world and to live in a nook merely monastic.

(3.2.384-94)

Rosalind's self-conscious mockery means that such comments are always devalued; yet I am inclined to agree with Celia in her charge to Rosalind, "You have simply misused our sex in your love prate" (4.1.185-86).

What Celia cannot realize, however, is how much the action in the play validates Rosalind's comments. Indeed, the subversion Rosalind vocalizes characterizes the behavior of all the play's women. For example, Rosalind, Celia, Phebe, and Audrey do become giddy and rash when in love, just as Rosalind has foretold. Rosalind herself presents the most severe case when, in 4.1, she demands a wedding ceremony one moment and warns of cuckolds the next. More numerically overwhelming are the many indirect actions of the women in the play. In her disguise, Rosalind gains strength and control, but her indirect expressions of love pale next to Orlando's direct confessions of being "love-shaked" (3.2.346). By the end of the play Rosalind has never once told Orlando she loves him. Phebe's description of her love for Ganymede similarly revolves around negations and contradictions:

Think not I love him, though I ask for him;
'Tis but a peevish boy; yet he talks well.
But what care I for words? Yet words do well
When he that speaks them pleases those that
    hear.
It is a pretty youth; not very pretty;
But sure he's proud; and yet his pride
    becomes him.

. . . . .

There be some women, Silvius, had they
    marked him
In parcels as I did, would have gone near
To fall in love with him; but, for my part,
I love him not nor hate him not; and yet
I have more cause to hate him than to love
    him;

(3.5.108-13, 123-27)

Audrey's nearly nonverbal reactions operate on the same principles. Her gross lack of understanding is only a less practiced indirection than the responses of the other women. Celia's love for and relationship with Oliver may be an exception to these female patterns of indirection; but since Oliver and Celia rarely interact,

speculation about how she may have avoided indirection is useless.

In studying the consequences of such indirection, linguistic and otherwise, Madelon Gohlke and Coppélia Kahn have found the language of such comic heroines as Rosalind to be the reflection of a patriarchal order. Though Gohlke's work is primarily on the language of tragedy, she connects the linguistic freedoms of comic heroines to the threat of infidelity the women pose for their mates. Arguing that the indirections of the women's langauge cannote infidelity for the men, she identifies the darkest threat implied in free female language such as Rosalind's:

Whereas "honesty" in relations among men may be perceived primarily as a matter of keeping one's word, in relations with women, it is clearly a sexual concern. For a woman to lie is to be unfaithful. For this reason the attribution of complex speech to female characters in the comedies in the form of lies, riddles, puns and statements made in the context of disguise, often involves sexual matters generally or specifically the threat of infidelity.

("'All That Is Spoke,'" 167-68)

While such sexual betrayal remains latent in most comedies, the threat is so real that the linguistic freedom women gain in the play's middle is suspended by the play's end. Touchstone's prolonged digression on lies in 5.4 (which appropriately coincides with Rosalind's silence) is symbolic of the male recapturing of playful language at the end of *As You Like It*. Discussing *The Taming of the Shrew*, Kahn uncovers similar consequences in the indirection of a comic heroine's language. She notes that language is Kate's only way of asserting herself and Shakespeare's only device for calling his male order into question. Even so, and despite her ironic reading of Kate's final speech, Kahn ultimately finds such language to be but one more measure of patriarchal control: "But on the deepest level, because the play depicts its heroine as outwardly compliant but inwardly independent, it represents possibly the most cherished male fantasy of all—that woman remain *un*tamed, even in her subjection" (*Man's Estate,* 117). I believe, with Gohlke and Kahn, that the language of the women in the play does double duty, acting both as a conduit for female power and as an automatic check on it. Through her language Rosalind creates a strong counteruniverse in the inverted world of *As You Like It,* and yet her power is as temporary as her stay in Arden.

Few playwrights can match Shakespeare in his linguistic richness; therefore, I will not repeat this concentration on women's language in my analyses of Congreve, Shaw, and Ayckbourn. Yet my argument based on the language of *As You Like It*—that the play's inversion but deceptively empowers women—is transferable (though less applicable) to other plays. The more important subsequent point, . . . is that women's language has become a major concern and tool in the comic world of contemporary women playwrights. But even in the theater of the last twenty years, language for the women of comedy remains simultaneously powerful and restrictive.

While Rosalind's most obvious source of power in the inverted world of the play is language, a second expression of her strength—as well as the limit to that strength—is her friendship with Celia. Not surprisingly, the friendship between the two women is as much affected by the cyclical patterns of the comedy as is the language.[4]

Initially, the court world of *As You Like It* seems hospitable to female attachments. Although Celia and Rosalind's bond is introduced in the hostile environment of 1.1, bone-breaker Charles softens while describing what is, even to him, a beautiful, strong, enviable attachment:

> The Duke's daughter her cousin so loves her, being ever from their cradles bred together, that she would have followed her exile, or have died to stay behind her. She is at the court, and no less beloved of her uncle than his own daughter, and never two ladies loved as they do.
>
> (1.1.100-105)

When Celia and Rosalind appear in 1.2, the love, trust, and intimacy of their woman's world mark a distinct difference from the combative male world of 1.1. In the second scene, another man—this time Le Beau—reveals the depth of the women's love for one another: "[Their] loves /Are dearer than the natural bond of sisters" (1.2.256-57). But more important, their love glows in the intimate word games that open the scene; here familiarity produces a conversation with two wits in league against the world, not in combat with one another. Such teamwork characterizes the women's verbal games with Touchstone, Le Beau, and even Orlando. Their pleas to Orlando to abstain from wrestling are best described as choric:

> *Rosalind:* The little strength that I have, I
> would it were with you.
> *Celia:* And mine to eke out hers.
> *Rosalind:* Fare you well. Pray heaven I be
> deceived in you!
> *Celia:* Your heart's desires be with you!
>
> . . . . .
>
> *Rosalind:* Now Hercules be thy speed, young
> man!
> *Celia:* I would I were invisible, to catch the
> strong fellow by the leg.

> *Wrestle.*
> *Rosalind:* O Excellent young man!
> *Celia:* If I had a thunderbolt in mine eye, I
> can tell who should down.
>
> (1.2.177-82; 192-97)

The third scene stands as the climax of the play's celebration of women's love. Significantly, it is Celia, not Rosalind, who gives voice to this celebration.[5] The two tributes she makes to their love become the touchstones by which the cousins' relationship in the rest of the play must be considered. First Celia pleads with her father to respect the women's mutual love:

> If she be a traitor,
> Why, so am I. We still have slept together,
> Rose at an instant, learned, played, eat
> together;
> And whereso'e'er we went, like Juno's swans,
> Still we went coupled and inseparable.
>
> (1.3.68-72)

That he cannot understand or respect their love is predictable. That Celia must repeat the same plea to Rosalind suggests less the depth of their bond than its precariousness:

> Rosalind lacks then the love
> Which teacheth thee that thou and I am one.
> Shall we be sund'red, shall we part, sweet
> girl?
> No, let my father seek another heir.
>
> (1.3.92-95)

The disguises the two women subsequently put on—one the garb of a man, one the skirts of a country woman—are obvious manifestations of the rift developing between them. This female-female couple must now become a female-male team to survive. The two can no longer appear (literally) "as one." Thus when Celia and Rosalind set off "to liberty," they set off without the full strength of the love that has previously sustained them. In the next four acts, a charting of their actions shows them moving progressively further apart. They never regain the closeness of act 1.

The forces that separate the two women include the subversion and self-deprecation I noted in my study of language, but most detrimental to their friendship is the assumption in the play that the natural, inevitable pairing is that of woman to man. In 2.2, for example, Duke Frederick assumes either that Celia and Rosalind must have run off with a man in their entourage or that a man is the cause of their running off. Yet as wrong as he is in assuming that they are chasing Orlando, he is only making the same assumption they have made in preparing their disguises—i.e., that two women could not take off on their own. The rest of act 2 reinforces such assumptions. Rosalind, dressed as a man, assumes a protective male role as she transacts the women's business with Corin in 2.4. Jaques, in his "seven ages of man" speech, does women the courtesy of inclusion when he speaks of "the men and women merely players," yet he mentions women again only as supernumeraries—nurses and mistresses. Although Celia and Rosalind temporarily gain power in Arden, they have only entered a different sort of man's world than the one they have left at the court, a world that forces one of them into dress as a man and prods both of them to marriage.

In the rich discussions of acts 3 and 4, further impositions on the women's friendship accumulate. In 3.2, the first scene in which the women are happily settled in Arden, Celia teases Rosalind with her (Celia's) knowledge of Orlando's presence in the forest. In a stressful moment, the two are refreshed and comforted by their well-known patterns of banter. Yet as soon as Rosalind begins to woo Orlando, Celia is silent. Her silence can be partially accounted for by the dynamics of the situation—it is Rosalind and Orlando who are in love, after all, not Celia. But Celia's presence as silent chaperon serves also as a strong visual reminder that her friendship with Rosalind is no longer Rosalind's primary concern. In 3.4, with the two women once again alone together, familiar patterns of conversation return. Celia provides the support Rosalind needs by echoing agreement to each outrageous statement Rosalind makes (3.4.1-23). She matches her praise for praise, complaint for complaint. But while Rosalind gets the support she needs, she can make no thankful acknowledgment of it. Her mind is all on Orlando, not Celia.

The two women continue to appear together in 3.5, 4.1, and 4.3. Yet there is no more linguistic evidence of the comfort and support the two women can provide for one another. While Celia participates in these scenes as a silent partner, Rosalind acts more and more on her own. In 3.5, for example, Rosalind handles Phebe and Silvius without a single word from Celia. In 4.1, at the height of Rosalind's linguistic control, Celia has only six short speeches. And finally, 4.3 is evidence that the two women, even in Arden, have come to face the world separately. The most convincing proof of Celia's sudden love for Oliver is the revival of her language in 4.3, the scene in which Oliver first appears in Arden. Earlier, in her six short speeches of 4.1, Celia had demonstrated a playful distaste for Rosalind's actions, charging her with the misuse of "our sex" (4.1.185), dismissing Rosalind's affections for Orlando as "bottomless" (4.1.193), and responding to Rosalind's announcement of her vigil for Orlando with an atypical lack of concern: "And I'll sleep" (4.1.202). So by 4.3 Celia is ready to focus her energy and concern elsewhere. In the early parts of that scene, she has only two short speeches; once Oliver enters, however, she explodes into speech, and it is Rosalind's turn to be

the bystander. In addition, 4.3 marks the first time Celia pays primary attention to someone other than Rosalind. Celia and Rosalind's exit with Oliver at the end of the scene also marks the last time the two women make their motions in tandem. When Rosalind re-enters in 5.2, she is without Celia for the first time in the play. When Celia next appears, at the opening of 5.4, she is similarly without Rosalind, who enters shortly after with Phebe and Silvius. By the end of the play, the dominant pairing for the women is not each other but Celia with her love Oliver and Rosalind with her love Orlando. Hymen's amusement at the coupling of women in his comment to Phebe adds a final, godly consent to the separation of the cousins (5.4.127-28).

Although Rosalind and Celia are the heart of the joyous woman's world, they are only half of the female population in the play. While the cousins are inseparable until the end of the play, Audrey and Phebe live isolated existences throughout. Their separate presences further accentuate the slimness of the possibilities for female community in this world. It is no accident that immediately after Rosalind's first show of power in 3.2 Audrey appears as an unforgettable reminder that few of the world's women are like Rosalind. Audrey is effectively speechless in response to Touchstone's verbal battering (3.3). And she is outnumbered three to one by men telling her what to do. Though she has been seen as a healthy reminder of sexuality in the play, by 5.1 she is no more than Touchstone's sexual possession. The choice of Audrey and Touchstone as the representatives of a lover and his lass in 5.3 is also revealing; instead of celebrating headstrong Rosalind and her lover, the two pages celebrate a more conventional couple, Audrey and her love. Finally, Audrey's fulfillment of expectations about conventional stereotypes of women is certified by her isolation. The only time she appears on stage with any other women is in 5.4, by which time the business of marriage assures she will be part of a married, heterosexual community, not a female one.

Phebe's journey through the inverted world of Rosalind's rule surpasses Audrey's in showing the play's restrictions on female community. Phebe appears first in 3.5 when Rosalind, Celia, and Corin are spying on her conversation with Silvius. For the first time, three women stand together on stage; and a potential expansion develops in that female community as Phebe is attracted to Rosalind-Ganymede. But Rosalind entertains Phebe's affection only as sport, and her decision ensures that Phebe's infatuation is cause for laughter—not for alarm or love. One might speculate, on the basis of her love for Celia, that Rosalind would show sympathy for Phebe. Instead, Rosalind shows disdain for her in 3.5 and belittles her love whenever possible throughout the rest of the play. In 4.3, for example, when Silvius carries Phebe's letter to Ganymede, Rosalind-Ganymede puts Phebe's love in the harshest terms, telling Silvius, "Wilt thou love such a woman? What, to make thee an instrument, and play false strains upon thee?" (4.3.68-69). And in 5.2, when Phebe tells Ganymede of her love, Phebe's desires become the comic link in Rosalind's love chain. In payment for her silly infatuation, Phebe is suitably embarrassed in the couplings of the final scene and must find her refuge in the man who has picked her. While both Phebe and Silvius are silly in their poses, Silvius, through his doggish sincerity earns a redemption Phebe cannot. There is no place in the play's final order for Phebe's attachment to Ganymede-Rosalind.

Audrey and Phebe serve double duty in the play. First they expose the isolation of the women in the play as Rosalind and Celia—with their long-standing love—cannot. In this way they defuse the threat of women that Shirley Nelson Garner finds responsible for similar isolations in *A Midsummer Night's Dream;* as Garner puts it, "the male characters think they can keep their women only if they divide and conquer them" (*"A Midsummer Night's Dream,"* 61). Second, Audrey and Phebe serve as a multipurpose counterpoint to Rosalind and Celia. The power, language, and love of Rosalind and Celia are undercut through the simplistic presences of Phebe and Audrey. What happens to Audrey and Phebe is especially important because they are women *only* of Arden. They, and not Rosalind and Celia, are the true representatives of Arden's inverted world. Most crucially, then, the presence of Phebe and Audrey assures that Rosalind and Celia are not the rule, that women can be separated, even in Arden. Or perhaps as a result of the underlying patriarchy, women are separated *especially* in Arden. In the end, the women in *As You Like It* are both without numbers (there are only four women in a cast of at least seventeen men) and without any effective claim to power and order.[6]

I have limited hope for the women of the play, partly because—as I have shown—the play limits female language and community and partly—and more basically—because in doing so it precludes change, especially a change for the women. While the inversion of the play allows the women primacy and control, that difference of status points not to change but to the return of convention. Individual change does occur in the play; the most obvious and important comes in Rosalind herself, who matures from a sharp and witty young woman into a loving, wise woman ready for the compromises of marriage. They giddy woman speculating about love in 1.2 becomes the magician of 5.4 and appears content to subordinate her own concerns to those she may share with Orlando. These personal changes, however, make no difference for the communal end of the play and may, in fact, simply allow for the group to take precedence. Rosalind has transformed herself, but the world of Arden (and, more important, the court world she is about to return to) remain firmly

patriarchal and able to absorb her personal brilliance. The world emerging at the end of the comedy is marked by four new couples, yet they have been accepted as representatives of a familiar ritual indoctrination. The corrupt rule of Duke Frederick will be replaced by the predictable, benign rule of Duke Senior, Oliver, and Orlando. And as the actions and cycles of the play have made clear, part of that predictability includes the necessity of traditional sexual stereotypes and a naturalization of the double standard. The characters' final acceptance of each other is an acceptance of the limits that the play has enforced, namely, limits on women's words, friendships, and power. To put it more precisely, the kinds of change possible for *As You Like It*'s women are as restricted as are their language and their friendships. In a play headed irrevocably toward marriage, which *As You Like It* is as soon as it begins, women, their changes, and their choices are from the first circumscribed by the overriding authority of men. There is no lasting change in women's status; there is no lasting challenge to the comic genre.

Based on her considerations of the comic genre, Bamber comes to a nearly opposite conclusion from mine: she finds that the dictates of comedy are so flexible that choice prevails, or more precisely, that the liberation of this world makes choice unnecessary (*Comic Women, Tragic Men,* 117-29). Catherine Belsey's Saussurian reading of Shakespearean comedy and Renaissance society also suggests a more optimistic possibility for the instabilities allowed in comedy's middle. Studying the structures of sexual identity, she argues that the plurality of the middle extends beyond its duration to offer a "radical challenge to patriarchal values by disrupting sexual difference itself" ("Disrupting Sexual Difference," 180). Yet after offering a dazzling account of the unfixing of social and sexual norms in both society and literature, even Belsey must conclude with qualifications. She ends her essay by retaining a hope for change in conventions and their interpretation while acknowledging that even in Shakespearean comedy the happy ending is not necessarily "happy" for the women (190). I am less optimistic about even the unfixed middle of traditional comedy (though, like Belsey, I see Shakespearean comedy as potentially revolutionary). Ultimately, I find that as Shakespeare guides his female characters through the Scylla and Charybdis of revolution and reaction, he offers at best limited change. In other words, intense experience doesn't yield appreciable change either in character or in genre.

The middle of Shakespeare's play presents possibilities for female linguistic power and community; but as I have shown, these possibilities exist side by side with strategies for disrupting them. Ultimately, the disruption of power, community, and autonomy for women is completed by the ending, in which marriage dissolves the temporary triumph of possibility.

The Return to Order

I argued in [an earlier] chapter that the comic ending is the most significant cause of women's compromised presence in traditional comedy. For Shakespeare, as for other writers who have shaped the British comic tradition, marriage determines the overtones of that ending.

In Shakespearean criticism, as in general criticism of comedy, marriage has been portrayed as everything from a "beneficent arrangement through which mankind achieves a maximum of human joy" (Charlton, *Shakespearian Comedy*, 117) to an imposition on comic characters, both male and female. Several recent feminist investigations of Shakespeare's portrayals of marriage in the context of Renaissance attitudes to marriage have added social scrutiny to such literary study. After suggesting that both patriarchy and mutuality were possible models for Renaissance marriage, Marianne Novy finds that in Shakespeare's comedies "mutuality," or the sharing of responsibility, respect, and love, is the general guide for defining romantic relations between men and women (*Love's Argument*, 21-44). Carol Thomas Neely also details conflicting opinions on the role of women in Renaissance marriage. Yet she concludes that despite the new egalitarian ideal of the compassionate marriage that arrived with the Reformation, "the woman had unequal status at every point in the process of wooing and wedding" (*Broken Nuptials*, 11). She adds, however, that a "continuing dialectic" between Renaissance women's gains in power and status and the restrictions such gains called up make definitive conclusions about Renaissance women and marriage "difficult" (19).[7] Thus, in each Renaissance comedy the actions offer but a single portrait of the complex social terrain of marriage. The marriages at the end of *As You Like It* are both defiant of and acquiescent to contemporary practice. They are also firmly dependent on generic convention. And they offer a final example of the intractable limitations to women's power in Shakespearean comedy.

In *As You Like It,* marriage is more an assumption than a visible institution. Although marriage is the goal of at least nine characters in the play (the four couples, plus William), no character is known to be married, though Duke Senior and Duke Frederick can be assumed to have been. Marriage, thus, exists as an abstract idea with the potential of becoming an ideal. Although the play is overflowing with critical evaluations of life in the country, life at the court, the age itself, and even love, marriage is rarely spoken of. In 3.3, as Touchstone's love for Audrey is to be translated into marriage by Sir Oliver Mar-Text, the first image of marriage is one Touchstone embellishes with a cuckold's horns (3.3.42-55). A brief exchange between Touchstone and Jaques adds to this a picture of marriage as a contest of animal desires (3.3.68-71).

Yet when Jaques refuses to let Touchstone's mockery of a wedding take place, the sanctity of the institution is preserved, curiously, by the biggest cynic in the play. Rosalind is the only other character to consider fully, before play's end, the transformation of love into marriage; and her view, like Touchstone's, is mockingly brutal. As she foretells her life as Orlando's wife in 4.1, her portrait of marriage promises little more than infidelity and animal passions. Orlando's firm response stands as proof against her changes, however, as do Rosalind's own pleas with Celia to "marry" her and Orlando. The play absorbs Rosalind's mockery as it absorbed Touchstone's cynicism. Marriage is rescued once by the realist Jaques and once by the idealist Orlando, and is, in both cases, preserved intact for the play's final scene where the would-be marriages of 3.3 and 4.1 are transformed into real marriages. Marriage remains an ideal unblemished by example.

The less obvious but more pervasive presence of marriage lies in the long-anticipated happy ending of the play. Familiarity with comic convention has led an audience to expect an ending in marriage, at least since Rosalind and Orlando fell in love in 1.2; and Shakespeare's only interference with such expectations comes in the teasing of his aborted marriages and in his omnipresent ironies. The drive toward marriage controls much action, as I have shown; friendship between women, for example, must finally take second place to the search for a mate and to the physical demands for regeneration. Comic endings in marriage are not simplistically happy—as even Shakespeare's array of comedies shows. And extensive criticism has confirmed that there can be no equation between marriage and a happy ending; yet the two remain, even if only ironically, attached and inseparable. The pressing question, however, is what marriage as the ending of comedy symbolizes for the women of *As You Like It*.

This brings me back to a consideration of convention and the power of an expected ending. Northrop Frye finds that the new society created in the marriages at the end of Shakespearean comedy is a changed one where a younger generation triumphs and gains the right to assert its fresh answers to life's dilemmas (*Natural Perspective*, 130). The joy of the comic ending is affixed to the promise of social renewal and regeneration. Both Rosalie Colie (*Resources of Kind*) and Heather Dubrow (*Genre*) extend the possibilities for some such sort of change, noting that because genres (such as comedy) create expectations, writers can use them to question those expectations and create a climate where actual change can occur. But the changes promoted by comedy are different for the women characters than they are for the men and for the society that these men control. The possibilities for change that do exist for women are severely reduced by an ending in marriage, in large part because comedy's reversals utilize a double standard, as I have previously argued.

Thus, the application of what Rosalind learns about love and self in the middle of the play is limited by the fact that she cannot choose to avoid marriage. Her choice is binary: either she retains the illusory power and freedom of a Ganymede, or she gains the love and predictable comfort of a married Rosalind. The comic genre as Shakespeare adopted it—*Love's Labor's Lost* notwithstanding—does not allow for the possibility of combining Rosalind's linguistic power, her friendship with Celia, *and* her marriage to Orlando. The play ends, rather, with her silence, her apparent distance from Celia, and her marriage to Orlando. Like many other comedies, *As You Like It* investigates the effect of changing power structures, gender structures, and even generic structures. But for Rosalind, Celia, Audrey, and Phebe, any participation in change will be funneled through marriage.

As You Like It *on the Contemporary Stage*

I conclude my study of Shakespeare's play and its women with an optimistic qualification. Although the women in *As You Like It* gain a circumscribed freedom, production of this and other Shakespearean comedies in recent years has offered enhanced possibilities for reducing the power of comedy's reversals and ending. The 1978 Ashland Festival Production of *The Taming of the Shrew* is a case in point. As Martha Andresen-Thom reports, the production placed great faith in the play's ability to counteract its own sexism. For instance, the action that preceded Kate's final treatise on marriage focused the audience on equality, not hierarchy:

> In tone and action she [Kate] conveys to us and to the incredulous audience on stage that her alliance is with Petruchio (Rich Hamilton) who attends to her, subdued and moved, until she starts to kneel so as to place her hand beneath his foot. He then goes to her and kneels too, catching her hand in his. Slowly they rise together, face to face, the bond between them enacted in this public ritual and soon to be consummated in the private domain of their bedchamber.

("Shrew-Taming," 123)

The 1983 Royal Shakespeare Company production of *Much Ado about Nothing* employed a similarly bold and unconventional ending to announce its refusal to accept wholeheartedly the final couplings that are part of the comic tradition. The expected male-female coupling of the festive ending was replaced with a series of circle dances where combinations of men, of women, and of men and women made male-female couples only a minor part of a spectrum. In this broadened range of relationships, the final focus on Beatrice and Benedick was placed in context, with the lovers' relationship retaining its romance not because of but in defiance of traditional assumptions.

The 1985-86 RSC production of *As You Like It* at the Barbican Theatre in London offers a translation of such feminist staging to *As You Like It* itself.[8] The production was an even more thorough attempt than those I have just mentioned to counteract the forces of traditional comedy. Most important, director Adrian Noble took great pains to imply not only that Duke Frederick's court never disappeared, but also that it was a *patriarchal* court from which the characters could not escape. Toward these ends, the roles of the two dukes were played by a single actor; he and his men simply covered the elegant tuxes of Duke Frederick's court with blankets to become Duke Senior and his banished men (the blankets later disappeared to reveal tattered tuxes). Visually, in other words, the audience was told that the court (and all it implies) is never really gone or forgotten. This compression of roles helped point to what one reviewer called the production's "consistently bleak view of the male competitive world" (Ratcliffe). Such a critique of the play's status quo world helped Noble and his actors strengthen the radical potential of the production's Arden. Orlando, for instance, was a very strong presence, stronger I would say, than his words. Not only was the actor physically muscular enough to make his wrestling victory in 1.2 more than convincing, but he also exuded during his discussions with Rosalind a strength of presence, an intelligence, that was a match for her powerful, controlling language. Orlando's strength challenged the simplistic sex-role reversals of the play. The treatment of the production's two main women—Rosalind and Celia—was, however, the most forceful attack on the traditional *As You Like It.*

Reviewer Irving Wardle connected the loss of a traditional pastoral world directly to the enlargement of Rosalind's presence—"Whatever pastoral elements this approach excludes, it is precisely in harmony with the heroine's line of development." I agree. As Rosalind exchanged her evening dress of act 1 for the white pants of Arden, actor Juliet Stevenson came into her own. It was immediately clear that the elaborate dress had physically inhibited her—she moved with energy and athleticism in Arden. As Stevenson puts it, "Literally and figuratively the disguise releases her [Rosalind]: you have to imagine her going into doublet and hose from Elizabethan petticoat and farthingale and a rib-cracking corset. . . . Rosalind can stretch her limbs, she can breathe properly, and so she's able to embark on increasingly long sweeps of thoughts and expression that take her ever deeper into new terrain" (Rutter, *Clamorous Voices,* 104). In addition to changing costumes, Stevenson completely discarded physical poses or mannerisms one might associate only with women. She seemed, indeed, a woman freed from confining gender roles. Yet despite the monumental efforts undertaken by Noble, Stevenson, and others to transcend traditional sexual roles and traditional genre expectations, this production too made its compromises.[9]

In the RSC program, for example, there appear four collections of quotations. One is entitled "In Search of Her Self." While this gesture toward the recuperation of a female subjectivity is laudable, the prose and poetry presented is all written by men and fails to approximate anything like a female point of view. A much more significant determinant of the production's compromises was the choice made about the play's ending. Surprisingly, the enlightened approach that characterized the early and middle portions of the production gave way to a very traditional happy ending. The physical onstage coupling, for example, was all heterosexual, with but a brief moment in which Rosalind and Celia confirmed the continuation of their bond. More surprisingly, Hymen took form as a disembodied, omnipresent voice; he commanded (and exacted) a reverence for marriage. Stevenson defends this production choice in arguing that the "miraculous" appearance of the god Hymen suggests Rosalind's "direct access to the gods" and thus confirms her power. Yet Stevenson also acknowledges that this celebration is a difficult one for Rosalind to take part in (Rutter, *Clamorous Voices,* 118-19). And indeed, the production's final gestures toward the preservation of convention allowed the audience to forget the careful construction of Rosalind's power. For example, reviewer John Barber admired Stevenson not for her challenge to but for her compliance with the traditional portrayal of Rosalind. As he put it, Stevenson "combines a handsome femininity with the leaping vitality of youth, but her 'sex and sexuality' are never in doubt." Stevenson's own comments, finally, suggest the perpetual tension involved in the project of bringing the women of comedy to fulfillment:

> The *frustration* of the play-endings in the comedies is a continuous one—with Isabella in "Measure for Measure" . . . we could never arrive at a solution and I don't believe we have on "As You Like It" either. I find myself constantly (and isolatedly) arguing in rehearsal *against* the Happy Ever After choices, because inevitably the heroine is left in a deeply compromised position in order that the status quo should be restored. Such arguments, on occasion, relate not just to the ending but to the whole play, in fact . . . for 18 months I played a Rosalind that I never felt I'd been allowed to make truly my own.
>
> (Letter, 20 July 1986)

Other recent productions of *As You Like It* have also stood as efforts to reclaim its strong women and disruptive potential. In the 1986 production at the Royal Exchange in Manchester, Janet McTeer apparently managed to create a Rosalind who was able to retain the affections of both Celia and Orlando (Coveney review). Yet even McTeer's Rosalind, whom most reviewers found refreshing and independent, was found by at least one reviewer to be nothing more than a predictable and risible female type: "It was an angular, archly-humourous portrait of a woman in love with her ability to manipulate men" (O'Neill). Taken together, both of these productions of *As You Like It* suggest first that performance offers a conduit for transcending the power of traditional comic structures and their effect on women, and second that even in contemporary production, the traditions so central to the play make such transcendence a slippery and illusory business.

As You Like It invites producers and scholars to question their own definitions of comedy and to grapple with the incongruities of women's place in the comic world. In her strength, Rosalind promises possibilities that critics, directors, and actors are struggling to realize.

Notes

[1] Not *As You Like It,* however, but *Love's Labor's Lost* offers the most substantial evidence of Shakespeare's inclination to center on women in an attempt to disrupt comic form. The collision of women and comedy in that play is highlighted by Berowne as he bemoans his still unmarried state at the play's end:

> Our wooing doth not end like an old play;
> Jack hath not Jill. These ladies' courtesy
> Might well have made our sport a comedy.
> (5.2.864-66)

While a study of *Love's Labor's Lost* would allow for a fruitful investigation of that play's renegade women, I turn to *As You Like It* instead, and to a collection of women both disruptive and accommodating. *As You Like It,* in the range of rebellion to be found in its women, offers a more complete portrait than *Love's Labor's Lost* of the paradoxes that attach to women in comedy.

[2] See also Jardine, who concurs that the gender swapping does not necessarily benefit women (*Still Harping,* 19-20). Kimbrough ("Androgyny") is among those who do find the play's androgyny a sign of sexual equality.

[3] See Montrose ("'The Place of a Brother'") for a similar view that the reversals of comedy operate as a "structure for her [Rosalind's] containment."

[4] See Rutter (*Clamorous Voices*) for a perceptive reading of the friendship between Rosalind and Celia. In Rutter's interview with actor Juliet Stevenson, they discuss the great feminist possibilities of the connection as well as the persistent difficulties the two cousins face in a patriarchal world.

[5] In their playing of the cousins in the 1985-86 RSC production, actors Fiona Shaw and Juliet Stevenson

attempted to transmit Celia's ascendancy in the early portions of the play (Rutter, *Clamorous Voices,* 103).

[6] Marjorie Garber (*Coming of Age,* 140-70) and George Gordon (*Shakespearian Comedy,* 31-32) read the movement of women away from each other in the play positively, each finding a psychic gain in such separation. Marilyn French (*Shakespeare's Division of Experience,* 79) and Carole McKewin ("Counsels of Gall") are even more optimistic: French refers to plays such as *As You Like It* as rare literary sites where female bondage is transformed to female bonding. Most recently, however, both Janet Adelman ("Male Bonding," 82-84) and Carol Neely (*Broken Nuptials*) have advanced the view that, like mine, finds the play's female friendships ultimately sacrificed by the women. In her book, Neely returns again and again to the conclusion that Shakespeare's plays consistently separate women. Thomas MacCary (*Friends and Lovers*) provides a complementary study of male friendship, finding that marriage is also often a deathblow to male bonds.

[7] Antonia Fraser offers an encyclopedia of specific examples on marriage and Renaissance women. Her study of women in all classes (*The Weaker Vessel*) suggests how the portrait of marriage varied from class to class and decade to decade.

[8] I am responding to the production that transferred from Stratford-upon-Avon to London. For a thorough description and feminist analysis of the original Stratford production, see Rutter, *Clamorous Voices,* 97-121.

[9] Stevenson's analysis of the production (and its feminist possibilities) is somewhat more optimistic than mine. See Rutter, *Clamorous Voices,* 95-121.

FURTHER READING

Bennett, Robert B. "The Reform of a Malcontent: Jaques and the Meaning of *As You Like It.*" *Shakespeare Studies* IX (1976): 183-204.

Regards Jaques as an essentially benign character whose presence in Arden provides both a needed balance in the forest-court debate and a cynicism to counter the preciousness of the pastoral setting.

Brissenden, Alan. "The Dance in *As You Like It* and *Twelfth Night.*" *Cahiers Elisabethains* No. 13 (April 1978): 25-34.

Examines Shakespeare's use of dance in *As You Like It.* Noticing the combination of joy and solemnity following the marriages in Act V, scene iv, Brissenden posits the likelihood of the couples dancing a patterned and harmonious pavan.

Brooks, Charles. "Shakespeare's Heroine-Actresses." *Shakespeare Jahrbuch* 60 (1960): 134-44.

Focuses on Rosalind's disguise role, and realates this device to Shakespeare's concern with themes of identity, self-knowledge, reality, and illusion.

Brown, John Russell. "*As You Like It.*" In *Shakespeare's Dramatic Style,* pp. 72-103. London: Heinemann, 1970.

Investigation of stagecraft in *As You Like It* that focuses on selected scenes in the play for purposes of analyzing language and elements of dramaturgy.

Carroll, William C. "'Forget to Be a Woman'." In *The Metamorphoses of Shakespearean Comedy,* pp. 103-37. Princeton: Princeton University Press, 1985.

Includes a discussion of "real and apparent" transformations in *As You Like It* based upon the direct and indirect influence of Ovid's *Metamorphoses.*

Cole, Howard C. "The Moral Vision of *As You Like It.*" *College Literature* III, No. 1 (Winter 1975): 17-32.

Argues that in *As You Like It* Shakespeare portrays the complexities of debates and oppositions without taking sides, and tests the conventions of the romance and pastoral genres.

Daley, A. Stuart. "Where Are the Woods in *As You Like It?*" *Shakespeare Quarterly* 34, No. 2 (Summer 1983): 172-80.

Warns that exaggerating the sylvan quality of *As You Like It* makes it difficult to understand the play as it was understood by its Elizabethan audience. Daley distinguishes between two Arden settings, one dark and perilous, the other characterized by sunny fields and a murmuring stream.

Doran, Madeleine. "'Yet am I inland Bred'." *Shakespeare Quarterly* 15, No. 2 (Spring 1964): 99-114.

Examines the theme of civilized man in *As You Like It,* allowing that Shakespeare presents a complex social picture in the play that does not favor any of the terms nature, art, or nurture to the expense of the others.

Draper, John W. "Country and Court in Shakespeare's Plays." In *Stratford to Dogberry: Studies in Shakespeare's Earlier Plays,* pp. 1-10. Pittsburgh: University of Pittsburgh Press, 1961.

Discusses *As You Like It* and other plays by Shakespeare in their historical contexts, particularly in the contrast between urban and rural life in Elizabethan England.

Forker, Charles R. "All the World's a Stage: Multiple Perspectives in Arden." *Iowa State Journal of Research* 54, No. 4 (May 1980): 421-30.

Describes tensions in *As You Like It* in terms of "Nature versus Grace, Life versus Art, Time versus

Timelessness, and Subjectivity versus Objectivity"; arguing that, though these remain unresolved in the play, they reach a synthesis in the character of Rosalind.

Fortin, René E. "'Tongues in Trees': Symbolic Patterns in *As You Like It*." *Texas Studies in Literature and Language* XIV, No. 4 (Winter 1973): 569-82.

Focusing on Act II, scene i and Act IV, scene iii, Fortin claims that Shakespeare has subtly transformed his sources to introduce classical and Christian images "that charge these key scenes with symbolic significance."

Hieatt, Charles W. "The Quality of Pastoral in *As You Like It*." *Genre* VII, No. 2 (June 1974): 164-82.

Identifies a variety of combinations of pastoral conventions in *As You Like It*, especially those involving the hero/shepherd motif, and determines that the irony of the Arden scenes is "alien to the pastoral mid-section of romance."

Kelly, Thomas. "Shakespeare's Romantic Heroes: Orlando Reconsidered." *Shakespeare Quarterly* XXIV, No. 1 (Winter 1973): 12-24.

Considers Orlando "a breed apart" from Shakespeare's usual romantic heroes, whom we are inclined to regard as peculiarly inept and slightly ridiculous.

Kuhn, Maura Slattery. "Much Virtue in *If*." *Shakespeare Quarterly* 28, No. 1 (Winter 1977): 40-50.

Close analysis of the staging, decorum, text, and dramatic recognition of Act V, scene iv of *As You Like It*.

Mares, F. H. "Viola and Other Transvestist Heroines in Shakespeare's Comedies." In *Stratford Papers, 1965-67*, edited by B. A. W. Jackson, pp. 96-109. Hamilton, Ontario: McMaster University Press, 1969.

Briefly compares Rosalind's empowering guise as a man in *As You Like It* to Viola's embarrassment and humiliation while disguised in *Twelfth Night*.

Martz, William J. "Rosalind and Incremental Development of Character in Comedy." In *Shakespeare's*

Universe of Comedy, pp. 84-99. New York: David Lewis, 1971.

Traces the evolution of Rosalind's experience from romantic to imaginative love, to loneliness and longing, to the wooing process as self-discovery, to the "lyric wonder of love," and finally to love as an earnest passion.

Nevo, Ruth. "Existence in Arden." In *Comic Transformations in Shakespeare*, pp. 180-99. London and New York: Methuen & Co., 1980.

Treats *As You Like It* as a "meta-comedy," in which the underlying principles of Shakespearean practice "are drawn out for all to see and turned into the comic material itself."

Traci, Philip. "*As You Like It*: Homosexuality in Shakespeare's Play." *CLA Journal* XXV, No. 1 (September 1981): 91-105.

Maintains that Rosalind's multiple identities— reinforced and enlarged by the fact that her original portrayal on stage was by a young, probably effeminate, boy—suggests that homosexuality and pederasty are among the diverse sexual preferences that Shakespeare explores in *As You Like It*.

Turner, Frederick. "*As You Like It*: 'Subjective', 'Objective', and 'Natural' Time." In *Shakespeare and the Nature of Time: Moral and Philosophical Themes in Some Plays and Poems of William Shakespeare*, pp. 28-44. London: Oxford University Press, 1971.

Comments on the subject of time in *As You Like It*, examining varied presentations of social time, historical time, and the timelessness of nature, along with their relation to the theme of love.

Wilson, Rawdon. "The Way to Arden: Attitudes Toward Time in *As You Like It*." *Shakespeare Quarterly* XXVI, No. 1 (Winter 1975): 16-24.

Discusses concepts of Aristotelian time in *As You Like It*, concluding that "the consciousness of time continues but is transferred to the interiority of the mind's aperception," causing the concern for "objective, public time" to be lost.

The Comedy of Errors

For further information on the critical and stage history of *The Comedy of Errors,* see *SC,* Volumes 1 and 26.

INTRODUCTION

Generations of critics considered *The Comedy of Errors* as mere farce, an apprentice work that gives no inkling of Shakespeare's mature achievements. But in the 1960s critics began re-examining the play as a highly accomplished, serious work that, for all its horseplay, adumbrates many of the central concerns of Shakespeare's oeuvre. Beginning with R. A. Foakes (1962), critics began to discuss the shaky sense of identity of all the major characters, but particularly of Antipholus of Syracuse. Another area of concern that has received sustained critical attention is the question of the play's generic identity—is *The Comedy of Errors* a farce, a comedy, a tragedy, a mixed-genre work, a problem play? The play's characterization and criticisms of gender relations have also gained increasing scrutiny, the critical literature being marked by a gradual but radical about-face in the interpretation of gender issues in *The Comedy of Errors.*

Despite ongoing differences and disagreements between critics of *The Comedy of Errors,* one question may be regarded as having been settled conclusively: the play goes far beyond its source material—the *Menaechmi* of the ancient Roman playwright Plautus— in its treatment of the theme of mistaken identity. Shakespeare exploits the dramatic potential of mistaken identity, and shows how being mistaken for someone else unsettles the various characters' own sense of identity. While R. A. Foakes was the first to draw attention to the way in which *The Comedy of Errors* connects a stable sense of self with social harmony and order, subsequent critics have further explored the idea in relation to various elements of the Elizabethan world view.

That Shakespeare also transforms his Plautine source material in his treatment of gender issues was a much later critical discovery. The crux, it would appear, lies in the evaluation of Adriana's character and conduct. She was initally taken to be a shrew—as her counterpart in Plautus *Menaechmi* clearly is—whose complaining and scolding is the cause of her husband's inconstancy. This view is represented by T. W. Baldwin (1962), who concludes that Luciana's speech on the just and inevitable inequality of the sexes is authoritative. The first major challenge to that position came from Marilyn French (1981), who argues that the play is highly critical of the male "establishment" of Ephesus, which is oppressive and much given to violence. Thomas Hennings (1986), reading *The Comedy of Errors* in light of the contemporary position on marriage of the Anglican Church, dealt another blow to the older reading, proposing that Antipholus of Syracuse's irresponsibility as a husband is the cause of Adriana's justified complaints. Joseph Candido (1990) reaches a similar conclusion by analyzing the characters' attitudes towards food and mealtimes as a social function that shores up both marriage and society in general. He also shows how Luciana's authority on the issue of gender relations—or any other subject, for that matter—is fatally undermined by her earnest arguments in favor of hypocrisy. By 1993, then, Adriana's exoneration was complete, and the critical evaluation of *The Comedy of Errors'* stance on gender issues had been completely reversed.

The question of the appropriate generic classification of *The Comedy of Errors* has occasioned less consensus. Since the critical community gave up the notion that the play is a farce, critics have argued for a variety of more just generic labels without being able to put the question to rest. Gwyn Williams (1964) made a case for the play as near-tragedy. Ruth Nevo (1980) argued that it has all the hallmarks of a Shakespearean comedy and should be labeled accordingly. Dorothea Kehler (1987) proposed that *The Comedy of Errors* is in fact a problem play. Arthur Kinney (1988) qualified these different views by showing the extent to which *The Comedy of Errors* is informed by mystery plays and other liturgical drama and texts. The debate concerning the genre to which the play belongs will undoubtedly continue in the future.

OVERVIEWS

C. L. Barber (essay date 1964)

SOURCE: "Shakespearian Comedy in *The Comedy of Errors,*" in *College English,* Vol. 25, No. 7, April, 1964, pp. 493-97.

[*In this essay, Barber discusses the nature of the comic elements in* The Comedy of Errors.]

Mr. R. A. Foakes, in his excellent Arden edition of the *Comedy of Errors,* remarks that producers of the play have too often regarded it "as a short apprentice work in need of improvement, or as mere farce, 'shamelessly trivial' as one reviewer in *The Times* put it." Accordingly they have usually adapted it, added to it, fancied it up. But in its own right, as its stage popularity attests, it is a delightful play. Shakespeare outdoes Plautus in brilliant, hilarious complication. He makes the arbitrary reign of universal delusion the occasion for a dazzling display of his dramatic control of his characters' separate perspectives, keeping track for our benefit of just what each participant has experienced and the conclusions he or she draws from it. One must admit that the way the confusion is elaborated by wrangling with words is sometimes tedious, especially on the stage, where the eye cannot assist the ear in following the young poet's fascination with manipulating language. But most of the time one can enjoy the wonderful verbal energy with which he endows his characters as they severally struggle to put together and express their baffling encounters. There is a great deal of good fun in seeing how each distorts and simplifies, and sometimes lies a little, to make sense of the crazy situation (and often to draw a little advantage from it on the side).

The use Shakespeare makes of Plautine models does involve a real limitation, for the plot is in effect imposed on the characters from outside, an arbitrary circumstance. As a result, too many of the errors are not meaningful in the way that errors become in the later comedies. We miss, as Professor Bertram Evans has pointed out in his *Shakespeare's Comedies,* people within the play who share in our superior awareness from outside it. The plot does not permit anyone to contrive the errors, tailor them to the particular follies of the victims, and share with the audience the relish of the folly brought out by the "practice"—a method which Mr. Evans has shown to be standard in the later comedies.

But the play is much better, much more meaningful, than the arbitrariness of its plot would lead one to expect. Shakespeare feeds Elizabethan life into the mill of Roman farce, life realized with his distinctively generous creativity, very different from Plautus' tough, narrow, resinous genius. And, although the mill grinds a good deal of chaff as well as wheat, he frequently makes the errors reveal fundamental human nature, especially human nature under the stress and tug of marriage. The tensions of marriage dramatized through Antipholus of Ephesus and his wife he relates to the very different tensions in the romantic tale of Egeon and Emilia with which he frames the Ephesian mix-ups. In the combination he makes of Gower's narrative with Roman dramatic form, we can see Shakespeare's sense of life and art asserting itself through relatively uncongenial materials.

There is more of daily, ordinary life in *The Comedy of Errors* than in any other of the comedies except *The Merry Wives of Windsor.* A mere machinery of mistakes is never enough even for the most mechanical comedy; the dramatist must be able to present particular lives being caught up in mistakes and carrying them onward. Something must be going on already— Antipholus of Ephesus late for dinner again, his wife in her usual rage ("Fie, how impatience loureth in your face!"). Shakespeare is marvelous at conveying a sense of a world already there, with its routine tensions:

> The capon burns, the pig falls from the spit;
> The clock hath strucken twelve upon the bell:
> My mistress made it one upon my cheek:
> She is so hot because the meat is cold . . .

He also creates a prosperous commercial town outside the domestic world of the jealous wife's household: its merchant-citizens are going about their individual business, well known to one another and comfortably combining business with pleasure—until the errors catch up with them.

To keep farce going also requires that each person involved be shown making *some* sort of sense out of it, while failing to see through it as the audience can. It would be fatal for one twin to conclude, "Why, I must have been mistaken for my long-lost brother!" So the dramatist must show each of his people taking what happens according to his own bent, explaining to himself as best he can what occurs when, for example, one of the twin masters meets the wrong slave and finds the fellow denying that he ever heard instructions received by the other slave a few moments before. Too often, the master concludes simply that the slave is lazy or impudent, and beats him; this constant thumping of the Dromios grows tedious and is out of key— the one instance where Roman plot has not been adapted to Elizabethan manners.

The idea that the mistakes must be sorcery goes much better. The traveling brothers have heard that Ephesus is full of "Dark-working sorcerers that change the mind." (The town was identified with sorcerers by Saint Paul's reference to their "curious arts" in his *Epistle to the Ephesians,* one reason perhaps for Shakespeare's choice of the town as a locale, as Geoffry Bullough has suggested in his *Narrative and Dramatic Sources of Shakespeare.*) The visitors decide that "This is the fairy land. O spite of spites! / We talk with goblins, owls and sprites." As the errors are wound up tighter and tighter, the wife and sister conclude that husband and slave must be mad, and bring on a real live exorcist, the absurd Dr. Pinch in a huge red wig and beard, to conjure the devil out of them. By the end, Adriana is calling on the whole company to witness that her husband "is born about invisible." We relish the elaboration of these factitious notions of magic to explain events that do indeed seem to "change the mind"; at the same time we enjoy the final return of all hands to the level of fact, where we have been situated all along. The end of the delusions is heralded by Dr. Pinch's being all but burned up by his outraged "patients." The Ephesian husband stubornly hangs onto his senses and his sense of outrage; he sets fire to the "doctor" as a comic effigy on whom to take vengeance for the notions of madness and magic to which almost everyone has given away:

> O mistress, mistress, shift and save yourself!
> My master and his man are both broke loose,
> Beaten the maids a-row, and bound the doctor,
> Whose beard they have singed off with brands
>   of fire,
> And ever, as it blaz'd, they threw on him
> Great pails of puddled mire to quench the hair:
> My master preaches patience to him and the
>   while
> His man with scissors nicks him like a fool . . .

The most interesting misinterpretations of the mistakes about identity are of course those where error feeds already existing passions—Adriana's jealousy, her husband's irritation—and leads finally to a kind of rhapsody exploding just before the final resolution. Adriana's self-defeating rage at her husband is particularly finely treated, especially in the moment when the traveling brother seems to provide her with the ultimate provocation, by making love to her sister. (Shakespeare added the charming, sensible sister, not in Plautus, as a foil and confidant for the shrewish wife.) After a frenzy of railing, the sister brings the wife up short by asking why she cares about her husband if he is so despicable, and she answers "Ah, but I think him better than I say, . . . My heart prays for him, though my tongue do curse." She is brought up short again, in a final tableau, when the Abbess traps her into betraying how she has made her husband's life miserable. The older woman delivers a splendid, formal rebuke:

> *Adriana.* Still did I tell him it was vile and
>   bad.
> *Abbess.* And therefore came it that the man
>   was mad.
> The venom clamors of a jealous woman
> Poisons more deadly than a mad dog's
>   tooth. . . .

Adriana is chastened: "She doth betray me to my own reproof." But her domineering bent is still there: she goes on insisting on her rights to manage her own husband's madness: "I will attend my husband, be his nurse, / Diet his sickness, for it is my office, / And will have no attorney but myself; . . ."

We can see a revealing contrast with Plautus in the handling of the Ephesian couple's relations. Shakespeare's husband and wife are more complex; they are also more decent. In *Menaechmi* the husband, at the opening of the play, is making off with a fine cloak of his wife's to give it to Erotium, the courtesan; he has already stolen for her a gold chain of his wife's. Shakespeare's Antipholus only decides to go elsewhere to dine in response to the incomprehensibly outrageous behavior of his wife in locking the doors (while *she* thinks she has at last got him home). It is in revenge for this that he decides to give the young "hostess" the necklace originally ordered for his wife. His eye has strayed, to be sure—"I know a wench of excellent discourse, / Pretty and witty; wild, and yet, too, gentle; . . . My wife . . . Has oftentimes upbraided me withal." In Plautus there is no ambiguity and no mixture of attitudes: from the outset it is "To hell with my wife, I'm going to have my fun." When in Plautus the visiting twin comes along, he has his unknown brother's good time with Erotium, gets the cloak and chain, and rejoices that it was all free. Shakespeare's twin, by contrast, falls romantically in love with the modest sister Shakespeare has provided, speaking some lovely poetry as he does so.

The difference reflects the difference in the two cultures, Roman and Elizabethan. It also reflects the different form of comedy which Shakespeare was beginning to work out, a comedy appropriate to the fullest potentialities of his culture. Roman comedy functioned as a special field-day for outrageousness; by and large, it fitted Aristotle's formula that comedy deals with characters who are worse than we are. Though there are some conventional, stock heroes and heroines, most of the stage people are meant to be fractions of human nature on its aggressive, libidinal side. The central characters in Shakespeare's comedies, on the other hand, are presented as total, not fractional: whatever their faults, they are conceived as whole people. His comedy dramatizes outrageousness, but usually it is presented as the product of special circumstances, or at least it is abetted by circumstances. Often the occasion is festivity, or a special situation like a holiday, a moment felt as a saturnalian exception to ordinary life, as I have stressed in writing about *Shakespeare's Festive Comedy*. Here the mistakes of identity bring the husband and wife to extremities on a day which is otherwise very much an "every day." Shakespeare however does frame the release of the animal or natural or foolish side of man by presentations of the normal and the ideal. Of course Roman comedy had its recognized place in the whole of life, its accepted fescennine function; but this was something implicit, understood by author, actors and audience. Shakespeare even in this early play makes the *placing* of the comic extremes part of the comedy itself.

The headlong day of errors is begun and ended by the story of Egeon, the bereft father of the twins, condemned to die in the morning, at evening pardoned and reunited with his long-lost wife and sons. It is a story of a very different tonality from the Plautine materials, derived as it is from Gower's Mediaeval handling of a late Greek romance. Shakespeare handled it again in *Pericles, Prince of Tyre,* where he realizes exquisitely the sense of life's mystery characteristic of the late romances, centering on precarious and sacred family relationships. In *The Comedy of Errors* the old tale is used only to sound a chord of grief at the outset (a somewhat blurred chord), then at the end a much fuller chord of joyful atonement. Yet the story of ocean voyages and long separations, so different from the busy, close-together bustle that comes between its exposition and conclusion, provides a meaningful finale.

That the ending does work, in spite of this difference and the utterly far-fetched coincidences involved, is largely thanks to Shakespeare's control of the rhythm of feeling. In the final farce scenes, feelings break loose, people are beside themselves; extras rush on the stage to bind struggling Antipholus and Dromio; a moment later the two are loose again, as it seems, with swords drawn, driving away all comers. Then suddenly, after this release of passion, the tone changes: the Abbess and the Duke, with aged Egeon, take over the stage, figures of authority and reverence. We hear poignant accents of family feeling in Egeon's:

Not know my voice! O time's extremity,
Hast thou so crack'd and splitted my poor
 tongue
In seven short years, that here my only son
Knows not my feeble key of untun'd cares?
Though now this grained face of mine be hid
In sap-consuming winter's drizzled snow,...
Tell me thou art my son Antipholus.

A moment later the Syracusian Antipholus, who does know his father, comes on stage; the doubles are visible together at last, and the plot is unsprung. But instead of ending there, we are lifted into a curiously serious final moment. The Abbess, now discovered as the wife, speaks of the moment as a new birth of her children:

Thirty-three years have I but gone in travail
Of you, my sons, and till this present hour
My heavy burthen ne'er delivered.

She invites all to "a gossips' feast"—a Christening party, "gossips" here being the old, Prayer-book word for godparents, "god-sibs," brothers and sisters in God of the parents. "After so long grief, such nativity!" the Abbess-wife exclaims. As all go out except the four brothers, the Duke sets his seal on the renewal of

community, centered in the family: he uses the word gossip in both its ceremonial sense of "sponsor" and its ordinary, neighborly sense:

With all my heart, I'll gossip at this feast.

One final goodhumored Error amongst masters and slaves, and the play ends gayly with the Dromios' joke about repeating *their* birth:

We came into this world like brother and
 brother;
And now let's go hand in hand, not one
 before another.

Shakespeare's sense of comedy as a moment in a larger cycle leads him to go out of his way, even in this early play, to frame farce with action which presents the weight of age and the threat of death, and to make the comic resolution a renewal of life, indeed explicitly a rebirth. One must admit, however, that he does rather go out of his way to do it: Egeon and Emilia are offstage and almost entirely out of mind in all but the first and last scenes. We can notice, however, that the bonds of marriage, broken in their case by romantic accident, are also very much at issue in the intervening scenes, where marriage is subjected to the very unromantic strains of temperament grinding on temperament in the setting of daily life. Moreover, Adriana and her Antipholus are both *in* their marriage (as wooing couples are in love); its hold on them comes out under the special stress of the presence of the twin doubles. The seriousness of the marriage, however trying, appears in Adriana's long speech rebuking and pleading with her husband when he seems at last to have come home to dinner (it is, of course, the wrong brother):

Ah, do not tear thyself away from me;
For know, my love, as easy mayst thou fall
A drop of water in the breaking gulf,
And take unmingled thence that drop again, . . .
As take from me thyself and not me too.
How dearly would it touch thee to the quick,
Shouldst thou but hear I were licentious . . .

That for her husband home and wife are really primary is made explicit even when he is most angry:

Since mine own doors refuse to entertain me,
I'll knock elsewhere, to see if they'll disdain
 me.

Shakespeare nowhere else deals with the daily substance of marriage, its irritations and its strong holding power (*The Merry Wives of Windsor* touches some of this, at a later stage of married life; the rest of the comedies are wooing and wedding). There *is* a deep logic, therefore, to merging, in the ending, the fulfillment of a long-stretched, romantic longing of husband and wife with the conclusion, in the household of Antipholus, of domestic peace after domestic frenzy. No doubt their peace is temporary, but for the moment all vexation is spent; and Adriana *may* have learned something from the Abbess' lecture, even though the Abbess turns out to be her mother-in-law!

APPEARANCE VS. REALITY

Sidney R. Homan (essay date 1984)

SOURCE: "*The Comedy of Errors* and Its Audience: 'And Here We Wander in Illusions'," in *The CEA Critic*, Vol. 47, Nos. 1/2, Fall-Winter, 1984, pp. 17-30.

[*In this essay, Homan discusses* The Comedy of Errors' *myriad collisions of reality with misleading or misunderstood appearances.*]

What we hear and see at the present moment constitutes an experience unique to the theater, one not shared by non-dramatic works that, operating by their own unique principles, must perforce have their own definitions of "experience"[1] This theatrical "presence" is especially ironic in *The Comedy of Errors,* given the significance of its past, that "history" extending from the birth of the twins, and from the coincidental birth of twin servants, to the accident at sea separating the family, to the separate lives led in Ephesus and Syracuse, with roughly seventeen years intervening before the Syracusian son and Egeon began the search for their family. No less ironic in terms of theatrical presence is the significance of the future, for there would be no play at all if the Duke had not extended Egeon's life until five that evening.

Given the improbabilities of its plot, what engages us in *Errors,* I believe, is not so much its mirror image of normal life but rather the gap in Shakespeare's theater of presence between our sense of the play's purpose and the perceptions of its characters who, until the very end, have no sense of their own play on that same stage we witness both aurally and visually. In seeing, at length, their whole play, they can be extricated not only from a comic dilemma but from the larger comedy itself, life's own comedy of errors. We are fixed; they are in error and are erring, in the older sense of "wandering." Our exit from the theater is therefore dependent on theirs.

I

As the "outside" audience, our first requirement, then, is that we all see the same thing: however confusing

they may be to the "onstage" audience, we recognize the two Antipholi as just that—as two. Conversely, the characters' inability to distinguish each other even finds precedent in the play's own prehistory: through Egeon's opening narrative one can imagine the scene where, their mast split in two, the divided family sees its other half in a progressively diminished perspective until even vision itself went blank. Egeon comments that the "sight" of the three being rescued by the fishermen of Corinth was only "as we thought" (1.1.110-111). We, however, see precisely what we need to see, and thus the implied stage set of Syracuse, actually inhabited for seven years by father, son, and servant, need not exist for us.

Hence, for "them" even the most basic object, a prop like the rope or chain so solid it can be seen and touched, cannot be seen for what it is. The Ephesian Antipholus requests money and is brought a rope by his "servant"; the Syracusian Antipholus finds his Dromio bringing not a rope as requested but gold, just as earlier he had received a chain without asking for one. For doing what one was told to do, as well as for not doing what one was told to do, a servant gets a beating. As several commentators have observed, Shakespeare quadruples the number of servant beatings from Plautus, but to the servants so consistently beaten they are literally receiving "something" for "nothing" (2.2.51-52).[2] The characters, of course, devise numerous interpretations for these strange events, even though all miss the mark.

And yet when we attach a meaning to such objects, if we see, as some critics have, a social or symbolic meaning to the chain, if we find in the composite gold-chain-rope an emblem of the play's dramatization of the tragicomedy of perception,[3] do we do anything less, however more consciously than the stage's confused characters? We ourselves thus "confuse" or exchange an object so that we can avoid mere spectacle, and thereby we sustain that delicate balance of the visual and the verbal essential to the theater. Like the primitive or the sophisticate with his fetishes, the characters also sense in this transformation of gold to rope or of nothing to a chain a mysterious force that denies the literal, that alternately explains or reduces what was assumed, literally, to be only itself. Consciousness of this force, of the playwright whose craft invites our own more productive interpretation, alone separates us from them; as long as they remain unconscious of the source of their confusion, they can see only conflicting purposes, or tragedies of adultery or comedies of enchantment and of windfalls.

Indeed, the visual without the signifying power of language risks losing even its own physical base; at one point the characters onstage can only "Witness" that Antipholus has vanished from the priory and been "borne about invisible" (5.1.187). But there is no magic here, no occult force performing vanishing acts. If

Ephesus in Saint Paul's *Letters* has associations with witchcraft and sorcery, we see no such city here, despite the supposition of the characters. The play is based on reality, a fact: the co-presence of twins.

This bare fact itself is paralleled by the single stage set, its unchanging presence in contrast to, say, the sweeping panorama—to use the movies' cliche—of *Antony and Cleopatra* or the spatial movement in *King Lear* from court to heath and back to court. In fact, while there is some debate as to the exact set,[4] we know that the bare stage itself served as the street or playing area, with three upstage exits signifying the house of Antipholus, Aemilia's abbey, and the Porpentine where the Courtesan lives. What appears to us, therefore, as a clear, contiguous playing area is not so for the characters who see it as an arena of "tricks" where people exit only to reappear suddenly with changed identities, where, as the Syracusian Dromio believes, the secular earth has been transformed to a "fairy land" (2.2.189).

II

Our identification with Shakespeare's characters through this need to interpret—and also, I might add here, through our ignorance of Aemilia's presence—is only a prelude to our larger identification when we acknowledge that their confusion both is and is not of their own making, and that this gamut effectively covers possibilities for disorder in our own world. In his first discourse on the inter-relation between time and baldness, Dromio rejects the Syracusian Antipholus's attempt to find something "sound" or "sure" or "certain" in time's assault on human existence (2.2.91-95), yet in the face of this same relative time the characters persist in trying to establish something certain, a source for or a way out of their confusion, whether it take the form of a psychological explanation of marriage problems or the practical strategy of adopting as a reality a role that everyone but the recipient thinks of as his own.

As we acknowledge the play's illusionary status, its being about "nothing," that concession is then undercut by the simple fact that both during and after the performance we share the same world as the characters. In a sense the ending or resolution is secondary, for *Errors,* as a piece for the theater, concerns more than the onstage family reunion. The title itself tells us, despite the somber opening, that this reunion is a foregone conclusion. Their piecing together of what was otherwise disparate yet autonomous, integral narratives is itself a sign of what we must do. We cannot help but be involved.

The theater is thus a community's attack on the obvious, no less than on narrowed vision; it insists on meaning because, at its core, it refuses to take the world, *any* world, as it is. What we see must admit a

discourse, and like the characters themselves we too must "entertain the offered fallacy" (2.2.186). Adriana demands to "know the truth hereof at large" (4.4.143). In searching for a truth (if not "the" truth) or in seeking an interpretation, we, as the united community of its audience, also *charge* the stage world with meaning, an action highly significant in a play that presents a fractured community, both in terms of its history and its present lack of a common understanding.

The literal play thus becomes a play of charged presence, and this succession in which an object is enhanced informs the conversation between the Ephesian Antipholus and Balthazar as they debate what determines good entertainment: the fare or the host, in effect, the dinner itself or the context of courtesy (3.1.19-30). Clearly in terms of the play, both are wrong individually and yet right collectively, and that the play at this point for those onstage cannot sustain such a union of existence and essence, if you will, is underscored when both would-be host and would-be guest are barred from the door. Those inside must come forth and join those outside so that outside/inside distinctions, a metaphor itself for the larger cleavage threatening the theater's community, can be dissolved. In terms of the play's visual core, the extremes to be avoided are what we might call the "reductively" physical (just before the act 5 reunions rapiers are drawn as the visitors threaten their hosts) and the "illusory" physical (Luciana is not a magician and, despite its reputation, there are no charlatans in Ephesus).

In point of fact, if the characters are not three-dimensional—and the mathematics of that phrase seems closer to the jargon of conventional theater reviewers—they are not without psychological traces of a malaise frustrating such unified vision.[5] We learn that the Ephesian Antipholus "hath been heavy, sour, sad" for a week before the day's actions, though Adriana herself cannot find the link between that condition and what appears to be his present "extremity of rage" (5.1.45-48). Egeon would have gladly embraced even "A doubtful warrant of immediate death" (1.1.168) if it had not been for the "incessant weepings" of his wife; significantly, he forgoes a death-wish for the sake of his mate and thereby allows the tragedy at sea to become a tragicomedy. Upon his entrances in Ephesus, Antipholus is in a state that can only be described as depressed: anyone commanding him to his "own content" commends him to "the thing [he] cannot get"; "unhappy" because of his separation from his family, he will efface himself, going about the town "Unseen," albeit "inquisitive" (1.2.33-40). Adriana is a creature of unfounded jealousy[6] and Luciana, otherwise clear-sighted, refrains from marriage and yet counsels Antipholus to conceal his adultery. Aemilia has withdrawn from the world into her convent, and the would-be nun in Shakespeare—witness Isabella—*must* be converted from such celibacy to marriage. In each case, there is evidence of retreat, regression, withdrawal, and such action goes against the play's own insistence, and that of Shakespeare's theater generally, on a community of unified vision as a defense against the randomness of fate.

The central characters are therefore incomplete, lacking wholeness, not the "formal" man (5.5.105) of which Aemilia speaks. This exile from their complete selves is echoed in the various images of division: a ship split on the rocks, with even its auxiliary mast, that for a time serves to unite the family, split in turn; the two towns of Ephesus and Syracuse now "adverse" (1.1.15) over an act of cruelty in which Ephesians lost their lives for the very same reason now threatening Egeon. If the play lacks "real" characters, the fact is that until the very end the real characters themselves are fractured, elsewhere.

III

Despite the duplication of the twins' first names, for the audience the play's verbal clarity is at one with its visual clarity; we can hear as ironic what the characters take as literal, and as untrue what they themselves take for the truth: Antipholus's confession of love for Luciana, for instance, is just that, and not the evidence of adulterous passion she imagines. We know whether a command given a servant can be fulfilled, and in a play where everyone accuses everyone else of lying, we know that no one lies. For us, then, words fix on their proper referents, and even when the characters consciously play with language, as in Dromio's punning, we can detect an irony behind the smaller irony intended by the punster. However, given the characters' visual confusion, their verbal confusion follows hard upon.

Egeon ironically opens the play with a request that the Duke speak, that he "Proceed" to "procure [his] fall."[7] What proceeds, of course, is not his immediate fall, since that is deferred until sundown, but rather Egeon's own narrative, and though the Duke orders him to "plead no more" (3), Egeon proceeds to do precisely that, his argument being that accident and not human design has cast him on these hostile shores. Egeon's speech, as many commentators have observed and as any actor charged with memorizing this lengthy narrative can attest, is the most sustained and eloquent piece of poetry in the play. Yet it is delivered against a political context in which language has become rigid, inflexible, unplayful. The Duke speaks of his countrymen as having "seal'd" the "rigorous statues" of Syracuse with "their blood" (9), and of Ephesus's counterlaw as being "decreed" in "solemn synods" (13). Egeon will die when the Duke's "words are done" (28), and in this fact he takes a certain morbid comfort. Without the inner play to follow, the narrative itself would be irrelevant, nothing but a dead man's ineffectual, albeit moving account of a family's history. Hearing Egeon's words, even acknowledging that his presence here in Ephesus is not a sin of commission, the Duke is still powerless to change his nation's decree. In terms of the reality assumed by the characters in the play's thematic world, the lengthy narrative, while it provides coherence to Egeon's own life, can therefore at best be gossip, at worst, a waste of speech itself. For his listeners in this opening scene, onstage as well as off, Egeon is indeed silenced until that final appearance where execution rather than explication will or should be the order of the day.

Only when our own view expands into the second scene can we admit some alleviation from the verbally moribund world of that opening scene. In his edition, R. A. Foakes observes that Egeon's poetry continues into this second scene,[8] and that with the entrance of the Syracusian Antipholus and the scenic link provided by the First Merchant when he refers to a "Syracusian merchant . . . not being able to buy out his life" (1.2.3-5), we know that the seemingly impossible, Egeon's ransom, is now within the bounds of possibility. If Egeon is ineffectively loquacious, his son vows to be effectively silent—and visually obscure. On the advice of the Merchant, Antipholus will deny his identity and spend his time viewing the town, rather than talking about his history, "Unseen," although "inquisitive." He promises to be as secondary as his father was central in the previous scene: "I to the world am like a drop of water, / That in the ocean seeks another drop" (35-36). We will realize later, of course, that Antipholus's desire for anonymity will be as unrealized as Egeon's commitment to death: the father will be granted life, and the moody son forced into dialogue against his will.

But for the characters, once the visual certainty breaks down—and this occurs a mere forty-two lines into scene 2 when the Ephesian Dromio returns in place of his twin with a reminder that the Ephesian Antipholus, also mistaken for his twin, is late for dinner—then verbal certainly also collapses. Word is literally divorced from object. Puns are sometimes unintentional and are not always playful, as when the Ephesian Dromio, locked out of his master's house, frustrates Antipholus when he translates the requested crow-bar to *crow* (3.1.80-84). Indeed, here for a time the pun almost threatens to run off with a scene whose pathos is as great for the participants, especially for the excluded husband, as it is comic from our perspective. At one point a character employs "wit" to scan "every word" of a dialogue, and yet he cannot understand a thing that is said (2.2.150-151), cannot fathom the "folded meaning of [the] word's deceit" (3.1.36). If the object so misunderstood threatens to lead to its extinction, then words here quickly degenerate to a glotal sound, then to wind itself, and, what is worse, wind as crude and as insignificant as a fart: "A man may break a word with you, sir, and words are but wind" (3.1.75).

In order to "speak" to a master who beats him without cause, the Ephesian Dromio resorts to a fantastic metaphor in which his skin becomes parchment and the blows from his master the ink (3.1.12-14). We will recall Hamlet's somber question to Horatio: "Is not parchment made of sheepskins?" (5.1.114). In his melancholy, Hamlet would trace even the paper used by the playwright to its source in the skin of a dead, or sacrificial animal. By the end of *Errors,* where the verbal confusion matches its ancestor in visual confusion, all dialogue is dismissed as "mad" (282). The Syracusian Antipholus would even stop his ears against the exquisite poetry of the women he loves. If one cannot close up the orifice of hearing, then the only alternative is taking the next ship out from Ephesus, removing oneself visually *and* aurally from this town where object and speech seem helplessly intertwined and contradictory.

IV

Such visual and verbal confusion, and the resulting disparity in perception between audience and characters, is inseparable from the problem of time in the play, both real time and theatrical time. As Gamini Salgado keenly observes, for the characters themselves the only sure time is that accounted for in Egeon's narrative; only the past, all that time antecedent to the actual events of the day spent in Ephesus, proves orderly.[9] The twins speak confidently of the Dromios as their "almanac" (1.2.41), the visible record of their birth date, and Dromio confirms the fact: from the "hour of [his] nativity to this instant" he has served Antipholus (4.4.30-31). Balthazar appeals to the Ephesian Antipholus's "long experience" of his wife's "wisdom" (3.1.89) in order to prevent him from being too hasty in censuring her when he is barred from the house. Adriana's reference to the previous week during which her husband's humor was "sour" later becomes part of Aemilia's diagnosis of the source of their marital conflict.

But this same past-tense order just barely manages to make its way from the "pre-play" or from Egeon's "induction" to the inner play. The Syracusian Antipholus is quite right when he designates his time spent in Ephesus as "two hours" (2.2. 148), but this will be the last temporal certainty he will know—until the closing moments. We realize, also, that Antipholus's present problems have very little to do with Aemelia's diagnosis, and if his longstanding service to the state prejudices the Duke to his cause, it alone cannot excuse his seemingly insane actions in the final scene.

Other characters, not at the center of the controversy, have a surer sense of time. The "wind and tide" (4.1.46) do indeed wait for the Second Merchant, though not for the Syracusian Antipholus; and for Angelo there is no confusion when he announces that he "gave [the chain to Antipholus] even now" (55). Yet as this recent, orderly past recedes and the play itself moves toward the moment of disclosure that will in turn allow debts to be paid and ships to depart with their intended cargo, such temporal sanity vanishes, and thus the "now" of the play, while still orderly for us, cannot be so for the participants. The Messenger declares that he has "not breath'd almost" (5.1.181) since he last saw the Ephesian Antipholus, but no one onstage can possibly believe him since before his entrance they have been audience to a raving Antipholus.

Soon time's deformed hand violates all temporal probability, rendering irrational both sight, as in the messenger's conflict with the onstage audience, and language, the latter anticipated when Dromio desperately wishes his master's "mouth" could be as accurate a clock as his own (1.1.66). The servant twin bears the bruises of such disordered time.

Indeed, the two discussions of time most relevant to the inner play come from Dromio: one, his paradox that time at once bestows hair on men even as in passing it renders them bald, both of hair and of wit (2.2.77-108); the other, equating time with a bankrout or thief (4.2.55-62). Even these two accounts of time, once collated, are right only in a negative sense, for in *Errors* there is, with time, not a diminishment of reason but its replenishment. Given the improbability of two sets of twins sharing the stage, there is, inevitably, a high probability that the coincidence will in time be disclosed. This latter chance, nourished by time, is anticipated by the hair-line coincidences in the play: consider the juxtaposition of the twins' exits and entrances within minutes and even lines of each other (for example, 1.2.18-40 or 4.2.66-4.3.11), and the previous discussed inside/outside scene (3.1). Linked to the play's visual and verbal "matings" (3.2.54; 5.1.282), time here stands as both the cause and the victim of their distortions. The audience, of course, accepts this arbitrary stage time, as well as the violation of the unity of place or plot. For us, therefore, "presence" embraces the fictive, perfectly ordered stage world, its bizarre doppleganger experienced by the characters (an absurd fiction born from an historical fact of births), and our own parallel reality offstage. For the characters, however, such presence can only be a cruel caricature.

V

The image of the actor is inseparable from this trinity of theatrical vision, language, and presence. Here we have actors from Shakespeare's company playing characters either forced into new roles or deprived of a past role, consciously trusting in what we ourselves admit as an impossibility in physics: that two people can occupy the same space. In effect, the play gives a comic, albeit revealing twist to Iago's observation, at once simple, complex, and potentially revealing: "Were I the Moor, I would not be Iago" (1.1.57). But a warning: if we would agree that the distorted onstage image of the audience is not without significance, then the same may apply, in reverse fashion, to the metadramatically confused actors onstage. To what degree are we, offstage, actors unconscious of that play that otherwise passes as life itself?

Again, for the Ephesian master and servant act 3, scene 1 marks the death of roles they thought were their own. In a parody of the Greek ideal of our own double identity, as private person at home and public person in the *polis,* they are unwillingly forced into a public sphere offering them a role at variance with, rather than complementary to that assumed indoors. The stage itself, with its public playing area downstage and three upstage doors leading to residences, silently underscores this double role. Luciana maintains that once outside his home, man is allowed a liberty—a field of play—that would be inappropriate indoors (2.1.1-43). Seeking to find his brother's home and, at the same time, to re-establish their common home, the Syracusian Antipholus unintentionally forces his brother to leave that house and "wander unknown fields" (3.2.38). Conversely, the women remain indoors and yet are responsible, in a sense, for the explusion of the men, whether that expulsion take the form of Luciana's argument for masculine liberty, Adriana's confusion between husbands, or Aemilia's understandable but fatal choice in accompanying her husband on the sea voyage. Thus, all three women serve not only as the home to which the men must return but also as their source of expulsion and thereby inspiration, offering each man a new identity, allowing the otherwise secure Ephesian Antipholus to play the role of his wandering brother, and the wanderer, the stranger, to fill the vacuum in becoming the domesticated spouse. As has been observed, the inner play in something of a dream world where one takes on—though here without much choice—a role either feared (the wanderer) or desired (the husband, complete with adoring wife, and with servants).[10] The twinship is thus both a fact and the grounds for translation to another identity.

Such playing, whether enforced or wished-for, is often terrifying, a displacement of reality—or of what was assumed to be reality—by relativity. The Syracusian Antipholus cries out "Am I in earth, in heaven, or in hell? / Sleeping or waking, mad or well-advised" (2.2.212-213), while his servant wonders, "Am I Dromio? . . . Am I myself?" (3.2.74). At one point his twin compares himself to a football thrown about by the winds of volition (2.1.83). Like that of Sly's when he is transformed from drunken tinker to aristocrat, the change is equally exhilarating: both "man and master" seem "possess'd" (4.4.92), their new roles assigned by "inspiration" (2.2.166-167), they themselves "transformed" (2.2.195). But for them, ultimately, the metamorphosis of roles constitutes a downward spiral, from secure man to ape to ass (2.2.198-199).

The actor's own conscious playing of a role is here distorted, for we are doubly aware that the "man" onstage has both consciously and unconsciously assumed a part. The Syracusian Antipholus thus says more than he knows when he wishes to "lose" himself in Ephesus, or on that stage before us. Perhaps, as has been suggested, this loss of the normal self and the subsequent assumption of a new role shows man as a divided being, *homo sapiens* turning here, unconsciously, into *homo ludens*—Huizinga with a twist. The two Antipholi and Egeon are like old Adam, the man before revelation whom Dromio purposely confuses with the sergeant (4.3.13-33): arrested, unable to function in a new role, no longer about to play an accustomed role, or like Egeon and Aemilia held in abeyance, hidden until the final scene. But given the playtime allowed by Shakespeare through the Duke, that working day otherwise so confused here, Egeon emerges at length not as victim but as restored and restoring husband. Likewise, the enforced playing time for the sons allows them, discomforts notwithstanding, time to "dally" (1.2.59), to abandon one's self but also to search for one's other half.

The characters themselves also seem to call for such playing, such stepping outside of an assumed role. The Syracusian Antipholus asks Luciana to "teach" him "how to think and speak" (2.2.3), and the first advice he is given, we will recall, is to "give out" (1.2.1) that he is from Epidamnum, in effect to counterfeit himself. In another sense, this "fairy land" (2.2.189) or "dream" (182) of multiple roles may be unconsciously wished for by the characters, and hence opposes the self-effacing mania of the Syracusian visitors. Or it may stem from an otherwise unfathomable discontent, such as the sour disposition of the Ephesian brother.

If playing a role has its ultimate source in the play's own masterplotter, that providential Shakespeare behind the scenery, its value is to be found in the play's playful servants, not free men but men already assigned a burdensome role, a "gentleman's gentleman" as the English would have it. Men suffering from often arbitrary masters, made even more arbitrary by the day's confusions, the Dromios are thus forced to adopt a sense of play for survival itself. The servants' humor is "merry" (1.2.21), and their ability to jest or play mitigates against the determinism otherwise implicit in the age's medical/psychological term "humor." Even the Ephesian Antipholus, though normally conservative or unplayful, vows to "jest" (3.1.123) in spite of the "expense" to himself. Adriana starves for a "merry look" (2.1.88) from her husband, and though he is in anything but a sportive humor, the Syracusian Antipholus chooses to adopt the fallacy offered by the strange events, to take part, in essence, in what he knows is a play, in something at variance with reality. If time is cruel here, that giver and taker as characterized by Dromio, there is still a "good time" in which to "jest" and hence a "time for all things" (2.2.64-65). Aemilia diagnoses the marital problems as caused by Adriana's inhibiting her husband's "sports" (5.1.77), while the Ephesian Antipholus "entertains" the arrest, despite his knowledge of his innocence, as a "sport" (4.1.81). In general, the play makes a clear distinction between an "ape" (one who consciously plays by imitation) and an "ass" (the helpless butt of humor, playful or cruel as the case may be).

Against the imposed plot, the cruel "mishaps" (1.1.120) that have separated the family, the terror in losing an identity or gaining one unsought, there stands this sense of playfulness that would wrest some of the power from time. Adriana asks the Syracusian Dromio to "play the porter" (2.2.211) and he does, violating his conscious knowledge to his role in a way that distinguishes him from *The Shrew*'s Sly. The otherwise sober Luciana calls on the Syracusian Antipholus to "Muffle [his] false love with some show of blindness" (3.2.8) so as to prevent her sister from—appropriately—reading in his "eyes" and "tongue" (9-10) his reality as an adulterer. To divert the tragedy that will itself be diverted once disclosures are made, he can, with her instruction, "apparel vice like virtue's harbinger" (3.2.12), playing "secret-false" (15). Even the sober Ephesian Antipholus will "play" the faithless husband, choosing the courtesan because she is "witty" and "wild" (3.1.140), the playful opposite of the stereotypical Elizabethan matron, Adriana. Antipholus, in fact, will play that role "Be it for nothing but in spite of my wife" (118). In a larger sense, each twin plays the other, and this applies to servants and masters. The Ephesian Dromio speaks to the issue when he asks his Syracusian counterpart, who is concealed indoors, to consider what it would be like "If thou hast been Dromio to-day in my place" (3.1.46).

Whatever the source of such playing—enforced, willed, chosen, or advised—it establishes a counterpoint to what the play itself had established in the opening scene, that moribund world, as I have called it, a scene caught in the past and promising nothing beyond a repetition with Egeon's death of a former act of political cruelty. Yet once these varied concepts of playing are established in the inner plot, the characters *stick* to the stage, the play's field of play, rather than fleeing, though the Syracusian Antipholus attempts to flee. Nor do they go mad beyond recovery, however sorely tempted, nor retreat to the abbey, as if such retreat were possible in a play forcing its characters together.

The very essence of comedy, that coming together after a breach in station or personality has been healed, is at one with the Plautine plot that Shakespeare complicates only to uncomplicate.

VI

For us the issue, comically tested in *Errors,* is how to see the world as it *is,* how by "computation" (2.2.4) of its various ingredients to come to some assessment of what it is to be human in the context of a world that at any moment can overwhelm the individual, how, in Dennis Huston's words, to live with the "potentially tragic problem of discontinuity in human experience."[11] Adriana claims to be "press'd down with conceit— / Conceit, my comfort and my injury" (4.2.65-66). She uses "conceit" here in two senses, as "understanding" and as "imagination," the latter alluding both to Shakespeare's talent and the art for which a taste must be acquired by the onstage participants. Though it would be absurd to imagine the characters coming to any other conclusion in act 5, the final scene does represent the application of conceit as *understanding* to a five-act play that has been sustained, consciously and unconsciously, by the characters' willingness to play. If fate or Shakespeare creates the play, the character-actors sustain that creation by remaining in Ephesus, even if forced to do so, here in the legendary home of illusions and illusion-makers. At length they are able to see what is, what we as audience see; and once this happens, then language, so deficient until that moment, blossoms in their own long speeches splicing together the earlier disjointed narratives of their one-day mating. If these final long speeches are dull, they are so only because the characters now tell us what we have known, and in language, now functioning as a mere recorder and at one with its object, that can no longer be playful. Like the four lovers of *A Midsummer Night's Dream,* they speak of events "strange" if not "admirable" (5.1.27), but, again, no magic is involved and here the doubting Theseus is replaced by a Duke who believes their common story precisely because "what is" has not been challenged but rather affirmed. There is no forest here, no separate world in contradistinction to reality or Athens. In Shakespeare's later comedy, the woman alone, Hippolyta, maintained the imaginative sympathy for the lovers in the face of Theseus's disclaimers; here in *Errors*—if I may borrow Hippolyta's line from *A Midsummer Night's Dream*—both men and women find the narrations growing to "something of great constancy."[12]

With this enforced play leading to the harmonious community of the final scene, the characters, without retreating to a forest, can also avoid worlds that have or should have no real existence. Persia (4.1.4)—anywhere but here and now—remains only a theoretical destination for the Second Merchant. Nor does Aemilia remain locked eternally in the abbey; nor does her Syracusian son stay forever the wanderer or her Ephesian son the smug husband. The equitable but cruel state law applied to Egeon never materializes. Like that opening scene of *A Midsummer Night's Dream* promising a tragedy on the lines of *Romeo and Juliet,* the opening scene here shows what can happen *without* play. But the stage, the arena of play, must "admit traffic" (1.1.15), and even as theater itself plays between the visual and verbal, *Errors* plays on its own seemingly inflexible opening situation. The family reunion in turn frees up both the state and those characters not part of the original accident yet affected by the family's separation. Without the "conceit" of act 5 and of the play generally, Angelo would face imprisonment and the Merchant, going unpaid, would have to change travel plans. Unjust or light penalities, to be sure, but indicating the potential replication when the eyes and ears of those most affected are not functioning properly.

Reality is thus not a constant in this play but rather a compromise between what is and how we perceive that "is." Again, the debate between Balthazar and Antipholus on what constitutes a good meal, the fare itself or the quality of the hosting, underlines this duality. Not to make dinner on time is both a temporal and a spatial fact, and yet at the same time a commentary on the mind-set of the "non-participant."

If man on the stage of both the theater and the encompassing world is at once actor and audience, he also must play both roles constantly, given the nature of dialogue and of the human community. The challenge then becomes: given the definition of reality as an ongoing compromise, can we agree on *one* counterfeit, with some room for difference, to be sure, but also with boundaries for difference? Can we see the *same thing,* albeit illusory in being not one thing but the product of a collective vision? Can the characters onstage and, by extension, on the world's stage do what those "characters" in Shakespeare's audience are assisted in doing by an onstage fiction balancing language and spectacle, all within the time-scheme of probability? Dromio cannot valorize such absolute words as *sound, sure,* and *certain,* despite his master's insistence; those onstage and off, therefore, must learn to see as one "this sure uncertainity" (2.2.185). To rework Adriana's marriage metaphor, if we are all "undividable incorporate" (2.2.122), individual drops that cannot be isolated from the sea of life, and if the audience offstage can identify with those onstage, then, being doubly so "undividable incorporate," can we still see and hear *roughly* the same thing?

VII

"Here we wander in illusions" (4.3.43), and the cry goes up for "Some blessed power [to] deliver us from hence" (44). Our human goal is to decipher the source, albeit manifold, of such illusions. Bottom's *Pyramus and Thisby* also rests on such illusions; for example, Pyramus takes the sight of Thisby's blood-stained mantle as proof that she has been devoured by a lion, but the results are doubly tragic precisely because the community so affected, the children and their parents, never comes together, as do their prototypes in *Romeo and Juliet.* That artistocratic Athenian audience, who fail to comprehend the parallel between Bottom's comic tragedy and what *A Midsummer Night's Dream* promises if Oberon and Puck had not intervened, is in *Errors* an all-knowing and harmonized audience. And while *Errors* is not blessed with strong, sentient characters—a Rosalind or a Prospero—it does show characters moving away from isolation, out of such "adversity"(4.4.20) whether imposed or self-imposed, whether it be Egeon's mishaps or Adriana's "Self-harming jealousy" (2.1.102). Forced to play, forced to confront a world of illusions, the stage itself taken to an extreme, they make such a movement. Now, acting out of love, Adriana will ransom her husband, even while acknowleding that her "heart prays for him, though [her] tongue do curse" (4.2.28); she will pay his debt no matter how it "grows" (4.4.121) or seems to grow. Similarly, the Duke, while at first upholding the barrier between the two cities, releases Egeon from the ransom; the play's imposed measure for measure is dissolved just as the play of that name, through the wisdom of its own Duke, dissolves judgment, with the exception of the penalty placed on Lucio. Here, even a son is eager to pay the ransom for a father whom he has not seen since his nativity.

In the final scene the characters, like us, see the events of the day *as* illusions, as *theater,* as comic errors in a comedy of errors. Having been forced to play actors and audience in that illusion, they are now at "liberty" (2.1.7) from illusions as well as from their otherwise incomplete selves. Similarly, the actor's own impersonation completes our selves, bridging the existential gap between what we do and our perception of ourselves as doers or actors. The world is no different from what it was at the start; the facts remain the same: on this given day are present four members plus servants of the same fractured family. Only the perception, the *naming* has been altered. Players on both sides of the stage now share the common emotion generated by such liberty, relief, and release. Everyone becomes a "formal" man again (5.1.105), discovering the self through playing (or seeing and hearing, in our case) its opposite, and then rediscovering the self as it is defined in the context of the family.

Allowing ourselves to be transformed from actor to audience, we too are complete, having achieved that completion by journeying into the play, hazarding our everyday concept of reality for this fictive, shaman-like journey, a journey taken both for the profit at its and for the pleasure when its parabolic curve returns us home. We can all go home now, for as we "came into the world" of the theater, we go out "hand in hand" (5.1.425-426), although the characters onstage and those characters offstage leave through opposing exits.

Notes

[1] My text for *The Comedy of Errors* is *The Riverside Shakespeare,* ed. G. Blakemore Evans (Boston, 1974).

[2] See John Arthos, "Shakespeare's Transformation of Plautus," *Comparative Drama 1* (Winter, 1967-1968): 239-253.

[3] See John Russell Brown, *Shakespeare and His Comedies* (London, 1964, reprint), pp. 54-57; and Richard Henze, *"The Comedy of Errors:* A Freely Binding Chain," *Shakespeare Quarterly* 22 (1971): 35-41.

[4] Anne Barton summarizes this debate nicely in her introduction to the play in *The Riverside Shakespeare,* pp. 79-80. And for some provocative comments on the staging, and other matters in the play, see Harry Levin, "Introduction to *The Comedy of Errors,*" *The Signet Classic Shakespeare,* gen. ed. Sylvan Barnet (New York, 1965), p. xxiii-xxxviii.

[5] The notion that this is a superficial play, its characters only types, is epitomized in Francis Fergusson's *"The Comedy of Errors* and *Much Ado about Nothing,*" *Sewanee Review* 62 (1954): 24-37. Larry Champion finds Adriana alone having something of a "psychology" and hence a subsequent character change in *The Evolution of Shakespeare's Comedy: A Study in Dramatic Perspective* (Cambridge, Mass., 1970), pp. 13-24. But Barbara Freedman, in two very insightful pieces, finds much more in the play. See her "Egeon's Debt: Self-Division and Self-Redemption in *The Comedy of Errors,*" *English Literary Renaissance* 10 (1980): 360-383; and "Errors in Comedy: A Psychoanalytic Theory of Farce," in the special edition on *Shakespearean Comedy* in *New York Literary Forum,* ed. Maurice Charney, 5-6 (1980): 233-243. In that same issue see Catherine M. Shaw, "The Conscious Art of *The Comedy of Errors,*" pp. 17-28. And see Ruth Nevo, "My Glass and Not My Brother," in *Comic Transformations in Shakespeare* (London, 1980), pp. 22-36.

[6] See Ralph Berry, *Shakespeare's Comedies: Explorations in Form* (Princeton, 1972), p. 32.

[7] I am especially indebted here to J. Dennis Huston for a series of perceptive remarks he made while this article was in manuscript, as well as for his commentary on Egeon and the play's "induction" scene in *Shakespeare's Comedies of Play* (New York, 1981), pp. 14-34.

[8] See R. A. Foakes's introduction to the Arden edition (London, 1963), p. 12.

[9] Gamini Salgado, "'Time's Deformed Hand': Sequence, Consequence, and Inconsequence in *The Comedy of Errors,*" *Shakespeare Survey* 22 (1972): 81-91.

[10] See Michel Grivelet's excellent "Shakespeare, Moliere, and the Comedy of Ambiguity," *Shakespeare Survey* 22 (1969): 15-26.

[11] Huston, *Comedies of Play,* pp. 32-33.

[12] For the significance of this phrase I am indebted to David Young, *Something of Great Constancy: The Art of "A Midsummer Night's Dream"* (New Haven, Conn.: Yale University Press, 1966).

Douglas Lanier (essay date 1993)

SOURCE: "'Stigmatical in Making': The Material Character of *The Comedy of Errors,*" in *English Literary Renaissance,* Vol. 23, No. 1, Winter, 1993, pp. 81-112.

[*In this excerpt, Lanier argues that the instability of the characters in* The Comedy of Errors *proceeds from disjunctions between apparent and actual identity.*]

[A cultural crisis of self-representation] clearly fascinated Shakespeare throughout his career.[1] Barry Weller's observation that "much of the action of Shakespearean drama [might be seen] as a struggle, not so much for self-awareness, as for self-representation" (p. 342) is particularly appropriate for the early comedies. Shakespeare's Plautine adaptation *The Comedy of Errors,* for example, takes as its focus the discontinuity between identities and the external marks that display, support, and confirm them. Despite the play's Christian overlay and its extensive references to witchcraft, what has impressed most critics is not its metaphysics so much as its physiques.[2] That is, *Errors* stresses the marks and rituals—faces, clothing, beatings, warts and moles, meals,[3] rings and gold chains— that make characters recognizable, and it demonstrates in copious variety how reliance upon this material evidence leads to unpredictable identity-effects. Like many commentators before and after him, Harold Brooks observes that the play's central issue is relentlessly "made visible, audible, and tangible by 'business' . . . the gold chain seen, the blows seen and heard, make double the effect they would in narrative."[4] Near its center is an emblem of the play's thoroughgoing focus on corporeality: the grotesquely fat kitchen wench Nell, whose sweating, greasy, swarthy body parts Dromio of Syracuse lavishly details and matches to appropriate countries on the globe.[5] And, as many commentators have noticed, Shakespeare has changed the setting to Ephesus, a commercial center, and obsessively returns to details of trade such as the ubiquitous mart, several merchants added as minor characters, the central place of exchanges of money and goods in nearly all relationships. Taken together, these changes mark the essentially materialist premises of this world.

Significantly, the plot is set in motion by the duplication of characterological marks, which Shakespeare foregrounds by doubling the single set of twins he found in Plautus's *Menaechmi*. The two Antipholi and Dromios pose a kind of limit case: how might identity be disrupted when the public marks of that identity are not merely counterfeited but *exactly duplicated and possessed by someone else?* Once doubled, those marks become nightmarishly iterable, physically the same but signifying differently, open to a wild variety of preposterous supposes and ultimately leading to near social breakdown. Out of that iterability springs the play's much-remarked imagery of shape-changing. Once Antipholus and Dromio's faces can point to identities not their own, the play breaks the seemingly necessary correspondence between outer and inner character; a certain self may not necessarily take a certain shape and form.[6] For a culture that places such weight on stable characterological display, the danger to selfhood registers in a threat both spiritual and physical.

In her introduction to *The Comedy of Errors,* Anne Barton raises the central "naive" question, largely dodged in critical discussions, that shapes a viewer's experience of this play: why don't these characters conclude that their myriad confusions are caused not by wandering affections, demons or madness, but by the presence of twins?[7] Their blindness points not, as Crewe has argued (p. 216), to a general failure of reason, nor is it, as Coleridge asserted, simply a *donnée* we must grant his farce. Rather, it makes palpable an ideological blind spot *within a particular kind of logic* that governs the construction of Elizabethan identity: these characters don't come up with the solution "twins" because, as Emilia notes, they all make the same "sympathisèd one day's error" (5.1.397). They assume that distinct identities are manifest in distinct marks. Crucial to this "local" logic is the role of the viewer, who recognizes those marks and upon whose recognition the character's sense of identity depends. Shakespeare signals the importance of this confirming gaze as early as Egeon's tragic tale of shipwreck in the opening scene, where Egeon tells us that in the midst of a tempest he and his wife Emilia tied their twin sons and servants to a mast:

> My wife, more careful for the latter-born,
> Had fasten'd him unto a small spare mast,
> Such as sea-faring men provide for storms;
> To him one of the other twins was bound,
> Whilst I had been like heedful of the other.

> The children thus dispos'd, my wife and I,
> Fixing our eyes on whom our care was fix'd,
> Fasten'd ourselves at either end the mast
>   (1.1.78-85)

Egeon and Emilia bind their twins in this way, it seems, so that each parent might gaze upon the child he or she loved better, "Fixing our eyes on whom our care was fix'd."[8] Presumably, each child might do likewise. This odd chiastic arrangement of parent and child is prompted by the logic of the reassuring, recognizing gaze, and it results, with just a little push from Fortune, in the potentially tragic "unjust divorce" of these three pairs. Without understanding their significance, Egeon underlines the importance of paired gazes when he goes on to describe the sun's gaze upon the earth, which literally changes the features of the obscured "face" it looks upon:

> At length the sun, gazing upon the earth,
> Dispers'd those vapours that offended us,
> And by benefit of his wished light
> The seas wax'd calm, and we discovered
> Two ships from far
>
>   (1.1.88-92)

The demand for another's gaze—for a constant witness—is not Egeon's alone. Antipholus of Syracuse underscores that his quest for his twin brother is motivated by a search for his confirming other:

> I to the world am like a drop of water
> That in the ocean seeks another drop,
> Who, falling there to find his fellow forth,
> (*Unseen,* inquisitive), confounds himself.
> So I, to find a mother and a brother,
> In quest of them, unhappy, lose myself.
>   (1.2.35-40, emphasis added)

Although critics have traditionally (and rightly) understood this passage as evincing a latent fear of self-dissolution (or "weak ego boundaries"), Antipholus' interjected "unseen" suggests a rather precise formulation: the single gaze of his "fellow," a gaze in which he might find himself, is set against the engulfing gaze of the world, a gaze that fails to *see him*.[9] (His musings, we might remember, follow his declaration that he intends to "view the manners of the town, / Peruse the traders, gaze upon the buildings" [1. 2. 12-13], pointedly as the viewer rather than the one viewed.) Only after recalling his lost brother does he designate Dromio "the almanac of my true date" (1.2.41), as if his servant were a text—the last he has left—in which he can confirm his being. As the confusions mount, Dromio of Ephesus too seeks to confirm who he is by pointing to his apparently rocky relationship with his master. His central exhibits are the bruise marks that function as Antipholus' characteristic signature: "That you beat me at the mart I have your hand to show. / If skin were parchment and the blows you gave were ink, / Your own hand-writing would show you what I think" (3.1.12-14). Here subjectivity ("what I think") becomes quite literally black-and-blue characters on the white flesh. The joke is that the wrong Antipholus does not recognize those "self-evident" marks and so ironically he adds a few of his own.

With Adriana, thoroughly changed from her Plautine source, our attention shifts to yet another mutual relationship. This time the focus falls upon how completely a wife's sense of self depends upon her husband's recognition of her beautiful features:

> His company must do his minions grace,
> Whilst I at home starve for a merry look.
> Hath homely age th'alluring beauty took
> From my poor cheek? then he hath wasted it.
> Are my discourses dull? barren my wit?. . . .
> What ruins are in me that can be found
> By him not ruin'd? Then is he the ground
> Of my defeatures: my decayed fair
> A sunny look of his would soon repair
>   (2.1.87-91, 96-99)

In a very important way his look constitutes her sense of identity. As she observes in a later comparison, the enamelled jewel, protected from another's gaze and touch, loses its beauty, yet "the gold bides still / That others touch, and often touching will / Wear gold" (2.1.109-11), a "wearing" that paradoxically produces gold's lustre.[10] With her husband's look and "touch" withdrawn, Adriana's physical features become "defeatures," suddenly susceptible to ruin and unrecognizability.[11] Her insistence upon the "undividable, incorporate" (2.2.122) union of husband and wife, imaged with talk of drops mingled in the ocean and the more traditional image of elms entwined with vines, derives less from the Plautine character-type of the shrew than from the self-presentational symbiosis Adriana needs. She tells Antipholus that he need only "look strange and frown" and "I am not Adriana, nor thy wife" (2.2.110, 112). Egeon, Antipholus, and Dromio have nearly identical moments. It would seem that supposedly self-evident physical distinctions (accounts of faces, warts, bruises, chains, rings) and events (dinners, promises, arrests, beatings) need constantly to be rehearsed and re-rehearsed in order to maintain who's who. Given such characterological instability, it is little wonder that well over a third of the play is taken up with narrating events that have already occurred before the audience's eyes.[12]

This logic of recognition leads to a further uncanny identity-effect: instead of the twins possessing their distinctive marks and thus their identities, those marks (and the identities they carve out) come to possess them. More precisely, because their outward characters are not exclusively their own, identities can be projected upon them from without, an operation that feels to the twins like being inhabited by a spirit. Dromio of Syracuse announces this ubiquitous link between being "defined" and being demonically possessed. When Nell (mis)recognizes the "privy marks I had about me, as the mark of my shoulder, the mole in my neck, the great wart on my left arm" (3.2.141-43), Dromio speaks of her as "one that claims me, one that haunts me, one that will have me" (3.2.80-81). And although he dashes onto the stage seeking confirmation from Antipholus that he is in fact Dromio—"Do you know me, sir? Am I Dromio? Am I your man? Am I myself?" (3.2.72-73)—he later claims that if he had not relied upon an unmanifest manly interiority (his breast of faith and heart of steel) Nell would have transformed him into a "curtal dog," her emasculated beast of burden. Through knowledge or possession of a self's outward marks, he fears, that self can be possessed, and so he urges his master not to give the courtesan the ring or chain she demands: "Some devils ask but the parings of one's nail, a rush, a hair, a drop of blood, a pin, a nut, a cherry-stone; but she, more covetous, would have a chain. Master, be wise; and if you give it her, the devil will shake her chain and fright us with it" (4.3.69-73). For Antipholus of Ephesus, this trope of possession is literalized to great comic effect. Observing "his heart's meteors tilting in his face" (4.2.6), fiery and sharp looks, ecstatic trembling and propensity to strike, all products of his considerable frustration, Adriana, Doctor Pinch and company all conclude that Satan is "hous'd within this man" (4.4.52). In fact, once Pinch's diagnosis takes hold, Antipholus' protests and grimaces only serve as further "objective" evidence of his demonic possession, a point stressed by Pinch's and Luciana's knowing comments about his "pale and deadly looks" (4.4.91, 106). Here we might notice that the "metaphysics" of this play emphatically does *not* establish some stable supernatural frame of reference. Rather, the allusions to demons, witchcraft, and God's protection are all part of yet another false supposition, generated by the desperate need for these characters to save appearances. In Ephesus the law of the characterological marketplace rules: "possess or be possessed." Indeed, because the twins do not own exclusive rights to the marks of their characters, or to the proliferating interpretations that become attached to those identical yet differing marks, they find themselves again and again self-*dis*possessed.

Given such premises and such unpredictable effects, what's a person to do? Antipholus of Ephesus's experience is that resisting only makes matters worse. Near the center of the play, Luciana voices a second and unexpectedly Machiavellian alternative: accept the identity others seek to project upon you and fashion from it a facade that serves your own interests. If Antipholus must carry on an affair (an erroneous supposition on Luciana's part), then, she declares, he should at least preserve the illusion of his fidelity by faking for Adriana the sunny looks she so craves:

> If you did wed my sister for her wealth,
> Then for her wealth's sake use her with more
>   kindness;
> Or if you like elsewhere, do it by stealth,
> Muffle your false love with some show of
>   blindness.
> Let not my sister read it in your eye;
> Be not thy tongue thy own shame's orator;
> Look sweet, speak fair, become disloyalty;
> Apparel vice like virtue's harbinger;
> Bear a fair presence, though your heart be
>   tainted;
> Teach sin the carriage of a holy saint;
> Be secret-false: what need she be
>   acquainted?. . . .
> 'Tis double wrong to truant with your bed,
> And let her read it in thy looks at board;
> Shame hath a bastard fame, well managed
>   (3.2.5-15, 17-19)

On its surface, especially considering its source, Luciana's advice has an unexpectedly moral ring: this *would* save Adriana's fragile sense of self. But the passage invokes the very distinctions that would thereby become erased, distinctions between false and true, becoming and being, bearing and heart, saints and sinners, virtue and vice. Such a world of well-managed simulacra, another version of Stubbes's "confuse mingle mangle," would obliterate the world she proffered earlier to Adriana, a world of "natural" distinctions and hierarchies where "there's nothing situate under heaven's eye / But hath his bound" (1.2.16-17). It is a world where, we should notice, those bounds are maintained by public rituals of obeisance. As the scene progresses, Shakespeare twice underscores the dangers of Luciana's counsel, first by having Antipholus misread it as a siren-like come-on to which he instantaneously succumbs, and, second by having Dromio rush onstage to recount his tale of Nell, a tale that terrifyingly illustrates the consequences of accepting a projected identity—castration, servility, beastliness. Just in the nick of time, Antipholus resists becoming "traitor to myself" (3.2.161). Yet Shakespeare cannot leave the scene without also returning our attention (and Antipholus') to the attractions of pretense for profit. For even as Antipholus utters his intention to "stop mine ears against the mermaid's song," Angelo the goldsmith enters and, mistaking him for the other Antipholus, hands him a gold chain. The central scene ends on a note of extraordinary ideological poise, suspended between rejecting and embracing this other-directed world gone wild.

Anxiety about the effacement of one's distinguishing features reaches a climax in the final scene. There Egeon, who has himself mistaken one Antipholus for another, seeks his son's recognition:

> I am sure you both of you remember me. . . .
> Why look you strange on me? you know me
>   well. . . .
> O! grief hath chang'd me since you saw me
>   last,
> And careful hours with time's deformed hand
> Have written strange defeatures in my face
>   (5.1.292, 296, 298-300)

Figuring his unrecognized face as a text rendered illegible by the ill-formed over-scribblings of Time, Egeon seeks desperately for some other distinctive mark of who he is, drawing attention next to his voice. When Dromio and Antipholus shrug that they still just don't recall him, Egeon is thrown into anguished self-doubt:

> Not know my voice? O time's extremity,
> Hast thou so crack'd and splitted my poor
>   tongue
> In seven short years, that here my only son
> Knows not my feeble key of untun'd cares?
> Though now this grained face of mine be hid
> In sap-consuming winter's drizzled snow,
> And all the conduits of my blood froze up,
> Yet hath my night of life some memory;
> My wasting lamps some fading glimmer left;
> My dull deaf ears a little use to hear—
> All the old witnesses, I cannot err,
> Tell me thou art my son Antipholus.
>   (5.1.308-17)

Here Egeon's unrecognized visage runs perilously close to extinguishing him, both figuratively ("all the conduits of my blood froze up") and literally (he can only be saved if his son recognizes him and pays his ransom). Egeon backs away from this death by unrecognition by entertaining an alternate possibility: "but perhaps, my son, / Thou sham'st to acknowledge me in misery" (5.1.321-22). Nonetheless, Egeon's persistent reliance upon "these old witnesses" fuels this crisis, for Antipholus can offer equally authoritative "witnesses": "The duke, and all that know me in the city, / Can witness with me that it is not so" (5.1.323-24). We see an earlier indication that these characters occupy different interpretive universes in this exchange between Dromio of Syracuse and Adriana:

> *Adr.* Tell me, was he arrested on a band?
> *Dro.* Not on a band, but on a stronger thing:
> A chain, a chain, do you not hear it ring?
> *Adr.* What, the chain?
> *Dro.*   No, no, the bell, 'tis time that I
>   were gone,
> It was two ere I left him, and now the clock
>   strikes one.

Adr. The hours come back; that did I never
    hear.

Dro. O yes, if any hour meet a sergeant, 'a
    turns back for very fear.

Adr. As if time were in debt; how fondly dost
    thou reason!

Dro. Time is a very bankrupt, and owes more
    than he's worth to season. . . .

If 'a be in debt and theft, and a sergeant in the
    way,

Hath he not reason to turn back an hour in a
    day?

                         (4.2.50-58, 61-62)

The puns on "band / bond," "on / one" and "hour
/ whore"—duplicated sounds, yet distinct meanings—and the confusion of referents such as the
ambiguous "it" in l.52 leads to a confusion about
objective clock time. By the end of the passage the
objective world seems to mime Dromio's final
punning line.[13] In the final scene of the *Menaechmi*,
one brother, despite the visible evidence before his
eyes, must be convinced in an extended comic
barrage of personal names and remembered details
that his twin brother stands before him; the interpretive universes are eased into synchronism. In
Errors, Shakespeare prunes this set piece. In this
case the recognition occurs nearly instantaneously,
in a glance rather than through persuasion. Only
when the two twins are seen standing side by side
is some normative frame of reference reestablished,
with all its reassuring social determinations of kinship and rank.

Or is it? Undeniably, the characters' "original" identities have snapped back into place but, I want to
argue, with a crucial difference. Especially noteworthy is the extent to which these characters' faith
in that final perspective has become much more
provisional. The Duke hardly supplies an authoritative perspective, for even his lordly eye cannot
sort out the myriad errors. Even after the twins
stand side by side before him, the Duke remains
confused: "One of these men is *genius* to the other:
/ And so of these, which is the natural man, / And
which the spirit? *Who deciphers them?*" (5.1.333-
35, emphasis added). The Duke does establish who's
who by publicly recalling the tale of Egeon's broken family, but he still continues to misidentify
Antipholus, and he has to command the twins to
"stand apart, I know not which is which" (5.1.364).
This touch of comic byplay offers a serious blow
to those readings that champion the Duke as an
agent and guarantor of order. As the remaining
characters unravel their tangle of misrecognitions,
their stress is on "if," "I think," and they entertain
the possibility that they are dreaming, echoing earlier moments of supposed transformation (for example, 2.2.195-96, 212-15):

Abbess. Speak old Egeon, *if* thou be'st the
    man
That hadst a wife once call'd Emilia,
That bore thee at a burden two fair sons?
                         (5.1.341-43)

Egeon. If I dream not, thou art Emilia;
If thou art she, tell me, where is that son
That floated with thee on the fatal raft?
                         (5.1.352-54)

Ant.S. [To Luciana.] What I told you then,
I hope I shall have leisure to make good,
If this be not a dream I see and hear.
Angelo. That is the chain, sir, which you had
    of me.
Ant.S. I think it be, sir, I deny it not.
Ant.E. And you, sir, for this chain arrested
    me.
Angelo. I think I did, sir, I deny it not.
                 (5.1.374-80, emphasis added)

The Abbess' conventional invitation to a feast signals,
as many have observed, the reestablishment of a community and, presumably, each person's place within it.
At the same time she signals a symbolic rebirth of her
sons: "After so long grief, such Nativity" (V.i.406).[14]
Particularly amplified by the context of Holy Innocents' Day (on which the play was twice staged, in
1594 and 1604),[15] the obvious resonance of the Nativity, that unique historical moment in which flesh and
ineffable spirit were mysteriously united, serves as an
absolute standard of presence. Measured against it, the
characters at the play's end come up short. The same
ideological poise that closes 3.2 also closes the play as
a whole.

As if to clarify this poise, *Errors* is rounded off
with a double coda that adds small but unmistakable
notes of irresolution to the play's very conventional
closure devices. In the first coda Dromio of Syracuse misrecognizes Antipholus of Ephesus. Like the
Duke's mistaking of Antipholus earlier in the scene,
this moment demonstrates how the characterological
conditions and logic that led to the errors in the first
place are still in force. Once again errors seem ready
to begin anew, implying that the "certainty" about
who's who established by this anagnorisis may be
less definitive than it first seems. The second coda,
a conversation between the Dromios, focuses at first
on the relational nature of character. Dromio of
Ephesus' comment about his brother underlines how
the other serves to verify and provide an ideal shape
for the I: "Methinks you are my glass, and not my
brother: / I see by you I am a sweet-fac'd youth"
(5.1.417-18). The conversation quickly turns to the
issue of natural rank, coordinates crucial to Renaissance identity that have supposedly just been
resecured:

Dro.E. Will you walk in to see their
   gossiping?

Dro.S. Not I, sir, you are my elder.

Dro.E. That's a question, how shall we try it?

Dro.S. We'll draw cuts for the senior; till
   then, lead thou first.

Dro.E. Nay then, thus:
We came into the world like brother and
   brother,
And now let's go hand in hand, not one
   before another.

                              (5.1.419-26)

The perspective offered here differs remarkably from that in the first act. There Egeon had distinguished between his sons apparently on the basis of order of birth, Antipholus of Syracuse had been incensed to blows when Dromio seemed to flout his superior rank, and Luciana could speak (however naively) of the natural pre-eminence of some creatures over others. As the play opens characters typically invoke fixed hierarchies of rank to chart their identities and actions. Here, however, hierarchy is invoked precisely so that it might be made a matter of chance, not of God or nature ("We'll draw cuts for the senior"), and then it is postponed ("*till then,* lead thou first"). For the moment at least, these twins dwell in a world where distinctions of degree have *not* yet been established *definitively:* "let's go hand in hand, *not* one before another" (emphasis added). In the opening scene the potentially tragic determinism of fate hung over events, a determinism signalled by Egeon's grim punning on "hap," "happy," and "hope," and his shaping of the narrative of shipwreck. Here in the final scene, it is as if "hap" has become the principle by which characters are (re)created, not destroyed.

My point here is not that the play adopts a kind of social egalitarianism in its final lines. After all, Shakespeare chooses not to use the two Antipholi for this exchange, where the drawing of lots for the senior among men of rank would imply profound, perhaps even revolutionary, social consequences. Rather, the play's final perspective and the identities it supports are subtly but persistently de-essentialized, made pointedly inconclusive and arbitrary. Chance and not any intentional action of the characters initiates the play's scene of recognition. Character, as it emerges from this play, is not co-extensive with its outward marks, but neither is it "that within that passes show." With something of the relentlessness of a nightmare, Shakespeare demonstrates that character is in effect an ongoing inference we make from outward marks, a hypothesis that demands constant interpretive support. And because the marks of character are multivalent, that hypothesis is always vulnerable to competing hypotheses. Of course, by play's end the characters no longer dwell in an *infinitely* mutable world where identity seems as it does to Antipholus of Syracuse, "Known

to these, and to myself disguis'd" (2.2.214). But neither, the Dromios stress, do they dwell in a fully stable world where distinctions of degree are conclusively God-given or where erroneous inferences about identity are no longer possible. Although Shakespeare does not yet locate character in interiority, he keeps before our eyes, even after the errors have been sorted out in the play's final scene, how the materiality of character troubles self-presence.

This conclusion may seem hard to accept, particularly since it would appear that the audience has had a privileged, indeed *the* definitive, frame of reference throughout the play. Jonathan Crewe, for example, stresses "the existence of an omniscient perspective on the action, a perspective that the audience is allowed to share up to the final moments and that confers upon the audience a happy invulnerability to the 'errors' by which those onstage are plagued. Only within such a perspective is it possible to characterize as *errors*— that is to say, as wholly illusory—the predicaments of those onstage.[16] This notion of an "omniscient perspective," which reduces onstage action to a kind of "pseudo-action"[17] dispelled in the final scene, accounts for one way the play has been seen: as "sterile," our sympathy or identification with the characters blunted by our God's-eye view. The final frame of reference— the doubled twins—seems all the more "solid" because we as an audience have accepted it as authoritative from the first and the characters have come to share it with us in the end. But there is, I think, reason to believe that this perspective is more complicated than Crewe and others have suggested. This is particularly so if we turn our attention to the most obvious staging problem this play presents: the doubled twins. If we can believe William Drummond's report, Ben Jonson refused to stage Plautus' *Amphitryo* because "he could never find two so like others that he could persuade the spectators they were one."[18] Even though we have no reason to believe that Jonson had *Errors* in mind when he made this observation,[19] it does make clear, even if we allow for his notorious critical idiosyncrasies, the special demands this play makes upon its audience's capacity for suspended disbelief. These demands Shakespeare deliberately exacerbated with his decision to double the twins. He could not dodge the problem of verisimilitude by having his actors wear masks (as would have been the case in Roman comedy or *commedia dell'arte*). It is extremely unlikely that he would have had access to *two* pairs of twins.[20] If the differences between the actors playing the twins were perceptible (and the relative intimacy of the Elizabethan stage almost assures that to be the case), then the problem of suspended disbelief, the gap between the visual evidence before us and the supposition we are encouraged to entertain about it, cannot help but constantly be before our eyes. And it is never more so than when the two sets of twins stand side by side at the play's end. As in the recent movie *Twins,* the obvious differences in appearance would be played for laughs, particularly when the Duke and Dromio continue to misrecognize the Antipholi or Dromio tells his brother "Methinks you are my glass."[21] This discrepancy, certainly significant in a play about mistaken appearances, works to distantiate the "authoritative" perspective from which we view the play's action. Although Crewe is correct that we need that perspective in order to judge the errors as errors, we are not as "happily invulnerable" to perceptual error as might first appear. For our "authoritative" perspective itself depends upon a provisional theatrical illusion particularly *visible* as an illusion. It is an error whose erroneousness the audience is simultaneously encouraged to forget and to recall. The gap between what we see and what we take it to mean draws attention to our own necessary engagement in "supposes" (at a different level of theatricality) and to the aleatory possibilities within the visual logic of character. In *Errors* Shakespeare powerfully interrogates the materiality of character by pushing its logic to its limits. He leaves the characters and the audience in what Peter Berger has called "ecstasy," a state of standing outside oneself looking at one's own social reality, knowing it is real, but knowing also that one has created it.[22] Certainly *Errors* is from first to last a "*play* of effects."[23] But it would nevertheless be an error to think that the effect of such an entertainment, for an audience that notoriously went to the theater to be seen as much as to see, was not also disturbing and profound.

Notes

[1] On conceptions of "crisis" in Renaissance culture, see Theodore K. Rabb's incisive summary in *The Struggle for Stability in Early Modern Europe* (Oxford, 1975), pp. 3-34.

[2] There are important exceptions, however. Exemplary of the metaphysical line of inquiry are Kinney, and Glyn Austen, "Ephesus Restored: Sacramentalism and Redemption in *The Comedy of Errors*," *Journal of Literature and Theology* 1 (1987), 54-69.

[3] See Joseph Candido's through and illuminating discussion of the importance of meals in defining Antipholus' identity as a respected citizen and respectful husband in "Dining Out in Ephesus: Food in *The Comedy of Errors*," *Studies in English Literature* 30 (1990), 217-41.

[4] "Theme and Structure in *The Comedy of Errors*," in *Early Shakespeare*, Stratford-Upon-Avon Studies III (New York, 1961), pp. 58, 60.

[5] Patricia Parker notes the linkage between Nell's "mountain of mad flesh" and the etymology of the term "farce," meaning "fattened, stuffed" (*Literary Fat Ladies: Rhetoric, Gender, Property* [New York, 1987], p. 18).

[6] The names of the two inns to which the Antipholi refer—the Centaur and the Phoenix—seem particularly meaningful in this context. Both are cases in which the creature's identity is indeterminate, the Centaur being visibly both man and beast, the Phoenix, because periodically reborn, being creatures both different and visibly the same. See Jonathan Crewe on "The Phoenix and the Turtle" in "God or the Good Physician: The Rational Playwright in *The Comedy of Errors*," *Genre* 15 (1982), 211.

[7] *The Riverside Shakespeare*, ed. G. Blakemore Evans et al. (Boston, 1974), p. 79.

[8] I here follow Parker's discussion of this crux (pp. 78-80). In 1.1. Egeon tells us that despite the fact that the two sons "could not be distinguish'd but by names" (52), his wife was "more careful for the latter-born," himself "like heedful of the other." Egeon ends up marooned with "my youngest boy, and yet my eldest care"(124), "sever'd from my bliss" (118). His greater care for the elder son no doubt springs from the demands of primogeniture: the elder son is the father's heir and substitute, an image of his authority. Parker notes that the issue of elder and younger returns in the play's final lines.

[9] See, for example, the discussion in Ruth Nevo, *Comic Transformations in Shakespeare* (New York, 1980), p. 26, of this passage and its matching counterpart, Adriana's speech in 2.2.125-29: "Neither sees him or herself as clearly and distinctly autonomous. Neither possesses the detachment of the drop, and both, in consequence, fear oceanic engulfment." Nevo assumes here, somewhat anachronistically, I believe, that such autonomy is possible and normative within Elizabethan culture.

[10] The linkage Foakes notes with the proverb "Gold by continual wearing wasteth" is potentially misleading, for the sense of the passage hinges on her paradoxical reversal of the adage: here the "wearing" clearly constitutes its beauty. See Gary Taylor, "Textual and Sexual Criticism: A Crux in *The Comedy of Errors*," *Renaissance Drama* 19 (1988), 195-225, for an extended discussion of this interpretive crux.

[11] Adriana's fear of the "defeaturing" action of aging finds its counterpart not only in Egeon's speeches in 5.1. about "time's deformed hand" but also in Dromio and Antipholus of Syracuse's witty exchange in 2.2.63-107 over male baldness. That exchange turns on the fact that the link between a man's hairiness and his wit is haphazard. Adriana's mention of Antipholus' "sunny look" unmistakably and suggestively echoes Egeon's

mention of the sun's gaze upon the obscured earth, a gaze that calms the seas and rescues his family at least momentarily from "unjust divorce."

12 Gamini Salgado, " 'Time's Deformed Hand': Sequence, Consequence, and Inconsequence in *The Comedy of Errors,*" *Shakespeare Survey* 25 (1972), 82.

13 See Salgado's discussion of time, as well as Eamon Grennon, "Arm and Sleeve: Nature and Custom in *The Comedy of Errors,*" *Philological Quarterly* 59 (1980), 159-60. Chmactic scenes of characters talking past one another are a staple of Plautine comedies.

14 I see no need to emend the Folio reading "Nativitie" to "felicity," as Foakes does. As others have noted in defense of the Folio reading, the repetition and capitalization of "Nativitie" in the Folio and its placement in the mouth of the Abbess draws attention to its scriptural connotations.

15 See Kinney for a full discussion of the linkages between the liturgical texts for Holy Innocents' Day and the play (pp. 44-51).

16 Crewe, "God," p. 204. This conception of *Errors* allows Crewe to argue elsewhere for "a certain canonical logic" at work in Shakespeare's earliest comedies, namely the demonstration of "almost alarmingly ostentatious early mastery—and masterfulness" (*Hidden Designs: The Critical Profession and Renaissance Literature* [New York, 1986], p. 134).

17 Crewe, "God," p. 204.

18 Jonson, *Works,* I, ll. 420-23.

19 Nonetheless, the possibility cannot be wholly discounted, for Shakespeare's name came up long enough for Jonson to insist, famously, that "Shakespeare wanted arte."

20 For a superb discussion of the issues raised by Jonson's comment, see Anne Barton, *Ben Jonson, Dramatist* (Cambridge, 1984), pp. 29-31. Discussions of the play's staging problems rarely focus on this issue: see, for example, Foakes's extensive discussion of staging, pp. xxxiv-xxxix.

21 In *Twins,* when Arnold Schwarzenegger's character declares that he is Danny DeVito's twin brother, DeVito declares, "The moment I saw you, it was like I was lookin' in a mirror."

22 Peter L. Berger, *Invitation to Sociology: A Humanist Perspective* (Garden City, 1963), pp. 136-38.

23 Kinney, p. 51, his emphasis.

IDENTITY

R. A. Foakes (essay date 1962)

SOURCE: An introduction to *The Comedy of Errors,* revised edition, edited by R. A. Foakes, Methuen & Co. Ltd., 1962, pp. xi-lv.

[*In this excerpt, Foakes argues that the chaotic situations engineered by the plot of* The Comedy of Errors *expose an underlying instability of the characters' sense of identity.*]

Shakespeare altered the tone of his immediate sources for the comedy, *Menaechmi* and *Amphitruo,* by introducing an element of romantic love in the jealousy of Adriana and in the passion of Antipholus of Syracuse for Luciana, and also by enclosing the comic plot within the story of the pathetic Egeon; he also enlarged and complicated the element of farce by giving the twin masters twin servants, so multiplying the possibilities of comic confusion. These two developments of source-material do not really tug in different directions, and Shakespeare had a larger purpose than merely to soften the harsh world of Plautine comedy, or exploit more fully the ancient comic device of mistaken identity. His modifications of the sources are used to develop a serious concern for the personal identity of each of the main characters, and for the relationships between them; and the jesting of the Dromios, and the "errors" or mistakes of the complicated action continually support this main development.[1]

So Antipholus of Syracuse arrives in Ephesus with a feeling that in searching for his mother and brother he has lost his identity, as if he will only find himself when he finds them:

> I to the world am like a drop of water
> That in the ocean seeks another drop,
> Who, falling there to find his fellow forth,
> (Unseen, inquisitive) confounds himself.
> So I, to find a mother and a brother,
> In quest of them, unhappy, lose myself.
>
> (I. ii. 35-40)

Ephesus holds a shock for him, mistaking him for his twin, and fastens an identity on him, so that he is invited to dine with Adriana as her husband, and feels that he is

> Known unto these, and to myself disguis'd.
>
> (II. ii. 214)

Here he seizes on the status of intimacy given to him in the household to make love to Luciana, and in her finds a new self, as he discovers a true passion for her. When he says,

> would you create me new?
> Transform me then, and to your power I'll
>　　yield,
>
> 　　　　　　　　　　　(III. ii. 39-40)

he is already transformed through love, in the recognition that she is

> 　　mine own self's better part,
> Mine eye's clear eye, my dear heart's dearer
>　　heart.
>
> 　　　　　　　　　　　(III. ii. 61-2)

Luciana thinks he is her brother-in-law gone mad, and, in the face of her inability to recognize him for what he is, he finally claims, "I am thee" (III. ii. 66).

Even as Antipholus of Syracuse discovers a new self, he is also bewildered by the assumptions of the people he meets, including Luciana, that they know him, that he is another person. Meanwhile, his brother, Antipholus of Ephesus, a more strongly determined character, more certain of himself, is angered when his wife refuses to acknowledge his identity; and Adriana, by nature jealous of him, and misled by his twin's attempt to woo Luciana, comes to think the worst of her husband, until she is ready to transform him in her mind[2]:

> He is deformed, crooked, old and sere,
> Ill-fac'd, worse bodied, shapeless everywhere;
> Vicious, ungentle, foolish, blunt, unkind,
> Stigmatical in making, worse in mind.
>
> 　　　　　　　　　　　(IV. ii. 19-22)

It is but a step from this for her to treat him as if he were mad or possessed, make him endure the ministrations of Doctor Pinch, and have him locked away in a dark cellar.

The serious force of the presentation of the Antipholus twins is paralleled by a more comic treatment of their servants. Each is puzzled at being mistaken for the other, and each comes to feel that he is being transformed—but into an ass, rather than another person. So Dromio of Ephesus suffers like an ass from the blows of his master (III. i. 18), and, finding that another has assumed his office and identity as servant in Adriana's household, and that for his service he is rewarded with still more blows as his master grows angrier, he resigns himself to his topsy-turvy world with a humorous acceptance of it:

> *Eph. Ant.* Thou art sensible in nothing but blows, and so is an ass.

> *Eph. Dro.* I am an ass indeed; you may prove it by my long ears. I have served him from the hour of my nativity to this instant, and have nothing at his hands for my service but blows . . .
>
> 　　　　　　　　　　　(IV. iv. 25-30)

At the same time, Dromio of Syracuse shares something of his master's sense of being subjected to witchcraft, and when Luciana, whom he has never seen before, addresses him by name, he speaks as if he has been "transformed":

> *Syr. Dro.* I am transformed, master, am I not?
> *Syr. Ant.* I think thou art in mind, and so am I.
> *Syr. Dro.* Nay, master, both in mind and in my shape.
> *Syr. Ant.* Thou hast thine own form.
> *Syr. Dro.* 　　　　　　　　　No, I am an ape.
> *Luc.* If thou art chang'd to aught, 'tis to an ass.
> *Syr. Dro.* 'Tis true, she rides me, and I long for grass;
> 'Tis so, I am an ass. . . .
>
> 　　　　　　　　　　　(II. ii. 195-201)

His sense of change or loss of identity is confirmed when the kitchen-maid Nell treats him as her man, and he bursts out, 'I am an ass, I am a woman's man, and besides myself' (III. ii. 76). Each Dromio applies the term 'ass' in relation to the beatings he is made to suffer, and to the way he is made to seem a fool; but the idea of being made a beast operates more generally in the play, reflecting the process of passion overcoming reason, as an animal rage, fear, or spite seizes on each of the main characters.[3]

For the sense of loss or change of identity in these figures goes together with a disruption of family, personal, and social relationships. Antipholus of Syracuse loses himself in the search for his mother and brother, but is hailed by all in Ephesus as if they knew him well; even as he thinks he is subject to "imaginary wiles" (IV. iii. 10), he is, unwittingly, causing a rift in the marriage of Adriana and his brother, and stirring discord between Antipholus of Ephesus and, on the one hand Angelo the goldsmith, on the other hand the Courtesan, over the matter of the chain. In the confusion which follows upon his dining with Adriana, the new self he had found in his passion for Luciana is frustrated; confirmed in his belief that he wanders in "illusions" (IV. iii. 41), he comes on at the end of Act IV, sword in hand, to drive her and Adriana off as 'witches'. At the same time, Antipholus of Ephesus, denied entry to his own house, comes to believe that he is the victim of a plot, and that his wife is a "strumpet" (IV. iv. 122). In addition, the normal relationship of master and servant is broken as each Antipholus meets the other's Dromio, and then beats his own servant for failing to carry out orders given to someone else. The normal intercourse of the city in its friendly, commercial relationships is also disturbed, to the extent that the Second Merchant, believing himself wronged, puts both Angelo and Antipholus under arrest, and the long-standing trust between these two is destroyed. The confusions of identity, involving for Antipholus of Syracuse and the two Dromios a sense especially of loss or transformation, and for Antipholus of Ephesus a need defiantly to assert his identity in a world that seems to go mad, thus lead to a breakdown of the social order through the frustration of normal relationships. Quarrels and arrests follow; Antipholus of Ephesus is bound and locked up; Doctor Pinch is harshly treated, and suffers the painful loss of a beard; the Dromios are mercilessly beaten[4]; and Antipholus of Syracuse and his Dromio usurp the office of the law when they rush in with 'naked swords'.

The growth of this disorder is reflected in two other strands in language and action which reinforce the serious undertones of the comedy. One is the establishment of Ephesus as a place associated with witchcraft. Antipholus of Syracuse arrives there with a prejudice about the city[5]:

> They say this town is full of cozenage,
> As nimble jugglers that deceive the eye,
> Dark-working sorcerers that change the mind,
> Soul-killing witches that deform the body,
> Disguised cheaters, prating mountebanks,
> And many such-like liberties of sin.
>
> (I. ii. 97-102)

As he becomes involved with the Merchant, Adriana, Luciana, and the Courtesan, so his belief that the city is a nest of sorcerers grows stronger. He wonders if his love for Luciana results from bewitchment, and calls her "mermaid" and "siren" (III. ii. 45, 47); soon he is ready to think "There's none but witches do inhabit here" (III. ii. 155), or "Lapland sorcerers" (IV. iii. 11); he comes to regard the Courtesan as a "fiend" and a "sorceress" (IV. iii. 63, 64), and finally achieves a state of mind so distraught that he feels safe only with a sword in his hand, and, pursued by Adriana's men, takes refuge in the priory. The prejudice which he has on reaching Ephesus provides a ready explanation for all the strange things that happen to him, and becomes a settled conviction; he is more and more disabled from distinguishing between what is real and what is not, until the whole city seems to him to be in the grip of an evil power:

> This fellow is distract, and so am I,
> And here we wander in illusions—
> Some blessed power deliver us from hence!
>
> (IV. iii. 40-2)

Antipholus of Ephesus, by contrast, regards himself as alone sane in a world gone mad. He is given some force of character, and a tendency to violence,[6] so that when he is shut out of his own house, he is driven to bewilderment and to passionate exclamation; though calmed for a moment by Balthasar, he thinks of punishing his wife by going at once to the Courtesan's, and by bestowing a "rope's end" (IV. i. 16), i.e. a whipping, upon Adriana and her "confederates." He invents an explanation of her treatment of him with this word; he decides he is the victim of a conspiracy. This private interpretation of his experience is confirmed for him when he is arrested in error, meets Dromio of Syracuse at cross-purposes, in his anger is himself regarded as mad, bewitched, or possessed, and is at last imprisoned in a "dark and dankish vault."

The confusions of identity and consequent disruptions of normal relationships force the characters to judge events according to their own private ordering of experience, as Adriana, too, is ready, at the suggestion of the Courtesan, to think her husband mad, and treat him as a dangerous lunatic. Out of the clashes of these private worlds of experience emerges another strand in language and action which is of some importance, a sense of evil at work in Ephesus. Dromio of Syracuse jests about the Officer who arrests Antipholus of Ephesus, calling him a devil,

> One that, before the judgment, carries poor
>   souls to hell;
>
> (IV. ii. 40)

he is quibbling on the last judgment, and on a common term for prison,[7] but his jest, as is characteristic of the word-play of the Dromios, quickly becomes earnest when he meets his own master in the next scene.[8] For Antipholus of Syracuse really thinks of the Courtesan as a "fiend," and uses to her Christ's words, "Satan, avoid," spoken in rejection of the devil's temptations in the wilderness[9]; and if the Officer was a "devil in an everlasting garment" to Dromio, the Courtesan now becomes "the devil's dam." A little later, Adriana puts her husband, as a man possessed by the "fiend," into the hands of an exorcist, who chants,

> I charge thee, Satan, hous'd within this man,
> To yield possession to my holy prayers.
>
> (IV. iv. 52-3)

These hints of the devil at work mark a stage in the play when the appearance of normal order breaks down, and the action erupts into violence, as one Antipholus is bound, and the other rushes in to attack a group he believes are 'witches'—a group that includes the Officer of the law.

In Act V the scene transfers to the Priory, which is the setting for the resolution of all difficulties, and which lends a faintly holy and redeeming colour to the end of the play. Here the enveloping action concerning Egeon is resumed. His hopeless condition, stranded friendless in a hostile city where the law condemned him to death, had been presented in a simple and dignified way in the opening scene. The Duke, representative of justice, had listened to the tale of his long search for his family, and had given him a day in which to seek, vainly as we see, for money to pay a ransom that would save him from execution. The end of the day comes just when one Antipholus lies bound as a madman, and the other has taken refuge in the Priory. At this point (V. i. 129), a solemn procession enters, headed by the Duke, and bringing on Egeon, bound, guarded, and accompanied by the executioner. Adriana, who is anxiously trying to persuade the Abbess to release the man she thinks to be her husband, stops the Duke to beg for "Justice, most sacred Duke, against the Abbess," and, shortly afterwards, Antipholus of Ephesus arrives to cry, "Justice, most gracious Duke, O, grant me justice," this time against Adriana. Each clamours for an idea of justice based on a private ordering of experience, and the conflicting evidence of witnesses and supporters sets a problem too difficult for the law to solve; the Duke cries,

> Why, what an intricate impeach is this?
> I think you all have drunk of Circe's cup.
>
> (V. i. 270-1)

His words nicely suggest the kind and degree of transformation that has taken place in the citizens of Ephesus; they are behaving madly, and there is no order or coherence in what they allege against one another.

To make matters worse, Egeon seizes the opportunity to appeal for help to the son he sees before him, but Antipholus of Ephesus does not know him. The law cannot deal with this situation, and it is time for the Abbess to reappear, with the second Antipholus; the twins are brought face to face for the first time, Adriana's mistake is revealed, and Egeon is saved as the Abbess turns out to be his long-lost wife Emilia. It is as if, through her intervention, the harsh justice embodied in the Duke is tempered by a Christian grace and mercy. Bitterness gives way to harmony, a harmony celebrated in a feast that marks a new beginning, a new life, a baptismal feast, from which Antipholus of Ephesus will not be excluded. Here the characters recover or discover their real identity, order is restored, and the two pairs of twins follow the others off stage, the masters embracing, the servants hand in hand. Violence is replaced by mildness and love, and the sense of witchcraft, evil, and Circean transformation is dispelled.

Notes

[1] See in the commentary the notes to I. ii. 40, II. ii. 142, III. ii. 45-66, 76, 161-6, IV. iii. 40-2, and V. i. 405.

[2] Adriana and her husband are alike in their proneness to anger, their "impatience," or lack of "patience," words used in relation to them several times; see II. i. 9ff., III. i. 85, IV. ii. 16, IV. iv. 18-19, 78-99 and notes.

[3] The process is summed up in the Duke's cry as he is faced with conflicting claims at the end, "I think you all have drunk of Circe's cup"; see below, p. xlviii, and see also III. ii. 39-40, 76, 145, IV. iv. 26-8 and notes. The same kind of process is at work in the transformation of the sergeant into a devil in Dromio's mind (IV. ii), and of the Courtesan into a fiend in the mind of Antipholus of Syracuse (IV. iii).

[4] It is true that Dromio of Ephesus says of his master, 'I have served him from the hour of my nativity to this instant, and have nothing at his hands for my service but blows' (IV. iv. 28-30), and both servants cheerfully expect beatings as part of their lot; at the same time, the anger of Antipholus of Ephesus is abnormal, and it is the sight of him beating Dromio in this scene that confirms Adriana in her belief that her husband is mad: 'His incivility confirms no less' (IV. iv. 44).

[5] See above, p. xxix; Shakespeare deliberately set the scene of his play in Ephesus because of the city's biblical associations with sorcery. *Menaechmi* has its setting in Epidamnum.

[6] As Erma Gill noted, 'A Comparison of the Characters in *The Comedy of Errors* with those in the *Menaechmi*', pp. 79ff., Shakespeare transferred this tendency to violence from the traveller brother in *Menaechmi* to the citizen Antipholus.

[7] See note to this line.

[8] Compare the jokes on mistiming (I. ii. 41ff., II. ii. 54ff.), which turn out to have a bearing on the disorder later in the play (see II. ii. 54-109 and n.; IV. i. 41-80 and n.), and the way in which Dromio of Syracuse both parodies and reinforces his master's prejudices in his account of the kitchen-wench, Nell (III. ii. 143 and n.).

[9] *Mathew,* iv. 10 (Geneva version).

John P. Cutts (essay date 1968)

SOURCE: *"The Comedy of Errors,"* in *The Shattered Glass: A Dramatic Pattern in Shakespeare's Early Plays,* Wayne State University Press, 1968, pp. 13-21.

[In this excerpt, Cutts maintains that the plot of The Comedy of Errors *hinges on the characters' failure to see beyond appearances, showing that they neither know themselves nor understand others.]*

The lasting interest of *The Comedy of Errors,* I suggest, lies in the inability of its dramatis personae to see beyond the mirror of identical twins, to see any further than outward semblances. Master and servant, husband and wife, tradesman and client know no more about each other than what mistakenly they *see* in a glass, nor do they realize they are seeing darkly. We may, of course, suggest that the characters are stock classical and / or commedia dell'arte representations, but whether we agree with this, there are good reasons for suggesting that the Dromios, the nearest counterparts to the classical and commedia forbears, are intrinsic to *The Comedy of Errors* not because they are *characters,* but because they make us see *double:* they make us see the problems at least twice over, and are indeed quite natural consequences of not seeing right the first time. The comedy of mistaken identity, brilliantly handled though it is with Shakespeare doubling the twins and manipulating far more skilfully than Lyly in *Mother Bombie,* is not just Shakespeare rehandling Plautine and Lylyan material and demonstrating how much better he can do the job than either of these dramatists. He is finding his way toward something that can be inimitably his own, not just in adaptation, but in the very framework and *structure* itself.

When the mistaken identities are cleared up there is little to suggest that any of the characters considers his "seeing" was at fault, though the nearest implication is that Adriana's shrewishness blinded her. The overall impression of the play is that man is *bewitched,* that uncanny powers are awake manipulating him. That the play is brilliant in this puppetry sense is glaringly patent; what is by no means so obvious is why man allows himself to be a puppet. And here the significance of the tragic note of Aegeon is indispensable when we consider that this failure to see right is not just a laughing matter but fraught with tragic propensities both for the unseers and for those within the immediate "unseeing" focus; that man's unseeing actions have repercussions far beyond his wildest dreams and fears. With Antipholus of Syracuse we ask, "was I married to her in my dream? / Or sleep I now and think I hear all this? / What error drives our eyes and ears amiss?" (II.ii.184-86).

How comes it that man "Smoth'red in errors, feeble, shallow, weak" (III.ii.35), estranged from his "dear self's better part" (II.ii.125), "transformed" both "in mind and in . . . shape" (II.ii.199) makes such a complete ass of himself? He is apparently "Known unto [others], and to [him] self disguis'd" (II.ii.216), because he has not taken anything like a good look at himself yet, though Antipholus of Syracuse's witty re-

joinder to the first merchant's commending him to his own content, "He that commends me to mine own content / Commends me to the thing I cannot get" (I.ii.33-34) has possible introspective overtones, however momentary. Man in *The Comedy of* [human] *Errors* is easily "lost," "perplexed" and "bewitched," played upon by external forces not necessarily puckish. For the most part he does not yet know whether the gods are just or no, or whether he should even know to ask the question.

With Antipholus of Syracuse we are sufficiently puzzled by the play's situations to ask "What error drives [men's] eyes and ears amiss?" (II.ii.186), but we are in a better position than he to estimate why he "entertain[s] the [offer'd] fallacy" (II.ii.188) in the hope of finding out more about "this sure uncertainty" (II.ii.187).

On one level it is obviously sheerly ludicrous that he should be greeted by Adriana, whom he has never in his life seen before, as husband, and chided for not giving her the assurance of the chain of fair marriage "quarter with his bed" (II.i.108). On another it is exceedingly appropriate that this marriage estrangement should reflect his own sense of loss "like a drop of water / That in the ocean seeks another drop" (I.ii.35-36). Adriana forcibly reminds him of the binding quality of the chain to her which to break is as difficult as to retrieve a "drop of water in the breaking gulf" unmingled and "[w]ithout addition or diminishing" (II.ii.128,130). Antipholus of Syracuse nominally in search of "a mother and a brother" (I.ii.39) does run the enormous risk of losing himself in the breaking gulf, of foundering his ship, Aegeon-wise, on the "mighty rock" of inquisitive unseeing (I.ii.38), because he hardly knows what he is looking for or "if that [he is he]" (III.ii.41).

His coming to Ephesus in one sense reflects his growing concern with the discontent which is himself, and in another his escape from self—his decision to "wander up and down" to weary his identity with restless motion and "in this mist at all adventures go" (II.ii.218). Not until his self is symbolically returned to him in the "glass" (V.i.417) of his image at the very end of the play is the dream texture of his existence shattered into something like reality, and he is in amity with his identity, but ironically he hardly knows how to accept it as reality since his happiness of discovery is concerned with Luciana, who would never have appeared to him if error had not driven his "eyes and ears amiss."

He literally recovers a mother, father and brother, and gains a wife as the play's comedy of errors rectifies its situational self, but the real significance is that he has found a rounded out complete family identity, and in a way that is "past thought of human reason" (V.i.189), not by "Fixing [his] eyes on whom [his] care was fix'd"

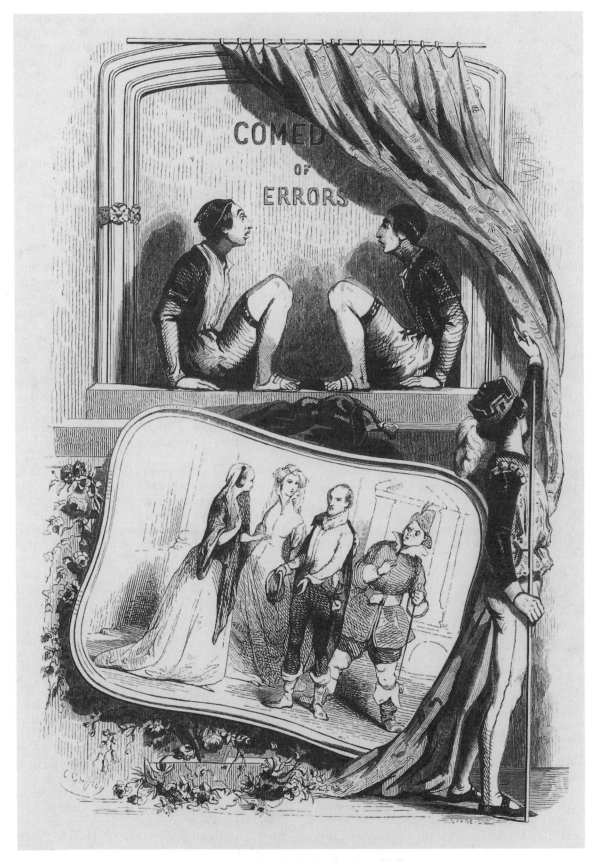

Engraving from the Verplanck edition (1847).

(I.i.85), but by losing himself "confound[ing] himself" (I.ii.38), in the serio-comic "stories of [his] own mishaps" (I.i.121).

It is a careful ironic stroke of juxtaposition to have his father under sentence of death exclaim at the very end of the first scene "Hopeless and helpless doth Aegeon wend" and then to have Antipholus enter immediately afterward, running the very same risk as his father—"if any Syracusian born / Come to the bay of Ephesus, he dies. . . . Unless a thousand marks be levied, / To quit the penalty and to ransom him" (I.i.18-20; 22-23), but with the "sure uncertainty" of his potential redemption money entrusted to a servant part of himself which he has not yet learnt to recognize, his Dromio, except to lighten his humor with his merry jests, and to be anchored at the Centaur where he can succumb to the lower part of his nature. It is only because either the presiding gods of the comedy of errors are benevolent or because stumbling man by rare accident somehow saves himself by stumbling that Antipholus's "Sleeping or waking? Mad or well-advis'd?" (II.ii.215) involvement in the banquet at Adriana's house does not transform him into the bestial victim of "Circe's cup" (V.i.270).

It is not merely coincidental that the dramatist has him describe Adriana's sister, Luciana, as a "siren" (III.ii.47) trying to drown him in her "sister's flood of tears" (III.ii.46), and call for her to "Transform [him] then" (III.ii.40) by singing for herself and by unfolding the meaning of her "words' deceit" (III.ii.36) to his "earthy, gross conceit" (III.ii.34). By this means he hopes to maintain his "soul's pure truth" (III.ii.37), for she is his own "self's better part" (III.ii.61), and yet the workaday rude mechanical servant part of himself, Syracusian Dromio, who has likewise been involved with a "very beastly creature, lay[ing] claim to [him]" (III.ii.88-89) mocks his involvement by reducing it to a consideration of physical geography, centaurishly bawdy at one level—"In what part of her body stands Ireland . . . Scotland . . . France" etc. (III.ii.118,122,125,etc.) and mentally assertive at another as Dromio flees from a Circean witch who would have "transform'd [him] to a curtal dog" (III.ii.151), and "almost made [him] traitor to [him]self . . . and guilty to self-wrong" (III.ii.167-68).

What irony it is that the putative Circean banquet takes place in the Phoenix, conducive to the regenerative image of the married calm of love. Antipholus of Syracuse anchors himself temporarily at the Centaur, financially and incognitoishly secure as he thinks, and flees from recognition where he imagines "every one knows [him] and [he] know[s] none" (III.ii.157) at the Phoenix. He mistakes the Centaur for the Phoenix and the Phoenix for the Centaur. What error drives his eyes and ears amiss.

His case is both closely paralleled and carefully complemented by his Ephesian self. Antipholus of Ephesus is escaping from his identity too. This is the pointed irony of his being faced with his own rude mechanical servant self, Ephesian Dromio, who charges that he "did deny [his] wife and house" (III.i.9). The humor of the error of Ephesian Dromio mistaking Syracusian Antipholus for his master obviously carries the moment in the comedy of errors, but the underlying reflection may be much more important. Ephesian Antipholus's "own handwriting would tell" (III.i.14) on the parchment of his own skin (III.i.13) what his servant sense would tell him if he knew how to recognize it. The metaphorical beating he gives this servant sense is a vain attempt to ignore its lesson.

The very first introduction of Antipholus of Ephesus in the play shows him trying to create the image of a displaced Antipholus, shut out from his house and from his marital bed by a shrewish wife. The jeweled necklace of a chain which he is commissioning at the goldsmith's, Angelo's, is ironically to afford him both an excuse for not having been at home—"Say that I linger'd with you at your shop" (III.i.3), and much more significantly a decoy of a "fair presence" (III.ii.13)—vice appareled "like virtue's harbinger" (III.ii.12), but its most serious significance lies in the fact that it is the symbol of the marriage chain he is trying to run away from and of the "unlawful love" (V.i.51) that he is running to link himself with.

But his unseduced servant self (Syracusian Dromio now within the Phoenix) belies him by asking, "Dost thou conjure for wenches, that thou calls't for such store / When one is one too many?" (III.i.34-35). It is exactly fitting that he should be literally shut out from the house and bed that he has obviously been neglecting. Adriana's fears that her husband's "company must do his minions grace, / Whilst [she] at home starve[s] for a merry look" (II.i.87-88) is hardly to be dismissed by her sister Luciana's charge that she is suffering from "Self-harming jealousy" (II.i.102), when so soon afterwards Luciana can plead with her brother-in-law to "if [he] like elsewhere, do it by stealth" (III.ii.7).

There is no doubt that Antipholus of Ephesus is attempting to escape from the chain of marriage. This is the force of his remark to Angelo for not having brought him the jeweled chain—"Belike you thought our love would last too long / If it were chain'd together, and therefore came not" (IV.i.25-26), and this the powerful significance of his not having "the present money" (IV.i.34) to pay for the chain and being arrested at Angelo's suit for denying receipt of the chain. It is doubly fitting that he thinks he has sent his servant self (Syracusian Dromio) home for money to buy off the arrest, and then is faced instead with the "rope's end" of his basic servant self (Ephesian Dromio). The rope's end had been ostensibly commissioned to "bestow /

Among [his] wife and [her] confederates / For locking [him] out of [his] doors by day" (IV.i.16-18), but Antipholus of Ephesus ends up beating his basic servant self.

The comedy, of course, is close to slapstick, master beating servant misunderstanding and misunderstood, but on a more solid level it points to the technique of punishing oneself at one remove, projecting one's guilt on the "obvious" target, until the "living dead" (V.i.241) pinch comes—the need to be "bound and laid in some dark room" (IV.iv.97) to "pluck out these false eyes" (IV.iv.107), not of the "Dissembling harlot" (IV.iv.104) of his wife's eyes, as he fondly imagines, but of his own, if only he could understand, for "his eye / Stray'd his affection in unlawful love" (V.i.50-51).

What irony it is that Antipholus of Syracuse has to gain his temporary freedom by "gnawing with [his] teeth [his] bonds in sunder" (V.i.249), and must attempt to gain his real freedom by appealing to the Duke on the grounds of erstwhile valiant military service when he "bestrid [him] in the wars, and took / Deep scars to save [his] life" (V.i.192-93) as if past service had anything to do with present misconduct. He is metaphorically fighting for his life as much as his father Aegeon, whom he now meets most appropriately for the first time in his life, and, of course, does not know how to recognize. His nonrecognition makes him a metamorphosed equivalent of one who has "drunk of Circe's cup" (V.i.270) and has become "mated or stark mad" (V.i.281).

"Hopeless and helpless" (I.i.158) Aegeon, Antipholus of Ephesus and Antipholus of Syracuse all wend, but fortunately their paths converge on the Abbey where the human solution to all their difficulties is to be found in Aemilia, who has "gone in travail" (V.i.400) of her own particular variety for thirty-three years, and has not been delivered of her identityless burden until now. Ironically Luciana accuses the Abbess of conduct ill beseeming her holiness by "separat[ing] the husband and the wife" (V.i.111), when in point of fact she herself was culpable in listening to the believed husband transferring his attention from Adriana to herself. And ironically, too, the Abbess is overhasty and unseeing in pronouncing judgment on Adriana "betray[ing] [her] to [her] own reproof" (V.i.90) of scaring her "husband from the use of wits" (V.i.86) by her "jealous fits" (V.i.85).

All of them, Aemilia, Adriana, Luciana, Aegeon, Antipholus of Syracuse, Antipholus of Ephesus, and the two Dromios need to "go hand in hand, not one before another" (V.i.425), so that their image in the "glass" (V.i.417) is "chained" beside them, forced on their recognition, not comfortably allowed to face them in a medium which *seems* to relieve them of any real necessity of looking.

The characters in *The Comedy of Errors* are fundamentally incapable of seeing beyond the outward appearances which serve to complicate and confuse the management of their affairs. Although dimly aware of a need for identity and a need to face their problems on a deeper level than the one of mere external manifestation, they lack the power to pursue this need for they are, after all, little more than puppets at the mercy of a master manipulator. The real dramatic significance of their presentation, however, lies in the fact that each is presented with the adumbrations of a solution to his problem in the existence of his alter ego, and his inability to profit thereby is the result of powers as yet unrecognized, which blind him to the importance of the image in the glass.

GENDER ISSUES

T. W. Baldwin (essay date 1962)

SOURCE: "Three Homilies in *The Comedy of Errors*," in *Essays on Shakespeare and Elizabethan Drama in Honor of Hardin Craig,* edited by Richard Hosley, University of Missouri Press, 1962, pp. 137-47.

[*In this essay, Baldwin discusses three speeches concerning the different moral standards applied to men and women in* The Comedy of Errors.]

1. Luciana's Homily on the 'Subjection' of the Wife's 'Stubborn Will,' 2.1.7-25

In *The Comedy of Errors,* Luciana is trying to impress upon her impatient sister the Christian duty of a wife, as stated typically in "An Homelie of the state of Matrimonie": wives "relinquish the lybertie of their owne rule" (*Certayn Sermons or Homilies,* ed. 1587, sig. 2G7). Luciana had said, "A man is Master of his libertie" (2.1.7). This Adriana resents: "Why should their libertie then ours be more?" (10).

> *Luciana.* Oh, know he is the bridle of your will.
> *Adriana.* There's none but asses will be bridled so.
> *Luciana.* Why, headstrong liberty is lasht with woe.
>
> (13-15)

This dialogue is partly in terms of *Proverbs,* 26.3 (Bishops' Bible, 1573): "Vnto the horse belongeth a whip, to the asse a bridle: and a rod to the fooles backe." The "headstrong liberty" of the ass gets not only the proverbial bridle for its "will" but is also "lasht with woe," as the horse is with a whip and the fool's back with a rod.[1] But the dialogue is also partly in terms of "An Homelie of the state of Matrimonie," which warns the wife against 'stubborn will': "That wicked vice of stubburne wyll and selfe-loue, is more meet to breake & to disseuer the loue of the heart, than to preserue concord" (*Homilies*, sig. 2G4v). Thus Shakespeare reproduces the 'official' position of the *Homilies* on the wife's will, combining it with the figure of the stubborn ass from *Proverbs*.

This prologue on the "headstrong liberty" of "will" introduces a homily on 'subjection' in an ordered Christian world. Noble (p. 107) quotes the Bishops' Bible (the Geneva Bible does not have "subjection"): "*Psalms*, 8.6-8: 'Thou makest him to have dominion of the works of thy hands: and thou hast put all things in subjection under his feet; All sheep and oxen: yea and the beasts of the field; The fowls of the air, and the fishes of the sea: and whatsoever walketh through the paths of the seas.' See also *Genesis*, 1.26 [Bishops' Bible: 'God sayde, Let vs make man in our image, after our lykenesse, & let them haue rule of the fishe of the sea, and of the foule of the ayre, and of cattel, & of al the earth, and of euery creepyng thyng that creepeth vpon the earth']. Cf. *Ecclesiastes*, 3.19B, 'a man hath no preeminence aboue a beast.'"

This biblical triplicity, "the beasts of the field; The fowls of the air, and the fishes of the sea," becomes the rhetorical framework for Luciana's homily on 'subjection':

> There's nothing situate vnder heauens eye,
> But hath his bound in earth, in sea, in skie.
>
> (16-17)

The corresponding animate creatures in these three divisions are "The beasts, the fishes, and the winged fowles" (18). All these "Are their males subiects, and at their controules" (19). Similarly for man:

> Man more diuine, the Master of all these,
> Lord of the wide world, and wilde watry seas.
>
> (20-21)

Here, to care for the triplicity, the "wide world" has to serve for the "winged fowles" (which are land-based) as well as for the "beasts." Then the reason for man's mastery is given: he is

> Indued with intellectuall sence and soules,
> Of more preheminence then fish and fowles, . . .
>
> (22-3)

According to the basic passage that is being echoed, "thou hast put all things in subjection under his feet." Here is the "subjection" (not in Geneva) of all things to man, under his "rule." But the word 'preheminence,' as Noble points out, is from the Bishops' Bible, *Ecclesiastes*, 3.19: "For it happeneth vnto menne as it

doth vnto beastes, euen one condition vnto them both: as the one dyeth, so dyeth the other: yea, they haue both one manner of breath: so that in this, a man hath no preeminence aboue a beast, but are al subdued vnto vanitie." The gloss is also reflected: "There is no difference betwixt a man and a beast, as touchyng the body, which of them both dyeth: but the soule of man lyueth immortally, and the body of man riseth vp agayne by the mighty power of the spirite of God." In his body, man has no "preeminence" over the beasts; the "preeminence" is in "the soule of man," because men are "Indued with intellectuall sence and soules." While the beast is not specifically mentioned here, nevertheless he is the basic member of the triplicity. The Geneva gloss plays down man's distinctive "reason, & iudgement" as ineffectual, as opposed to faith. While Shakespeare also refers to this difference of "intellectuall sence," he does so with a much different emphasis.

Shakespeare's phrase belongs to the psychological jargon of his time, being in terms of the three souls or parts of the soul, "vegetative, sensible or sensitive, rational or reasonable" (OED): "1398 Trevisa Barth., *De P. R.*, 3.7 (1495), 53. In dyuers bodyes ben thre manere soules: vegetabilis, that yeuyth lyfe and noo felinge, as in plantes and rootes; Sensibilis, that yeuyth lyfe and felynge and not reason in vnskylfull beestes; Racionalis, that yeuyth lyf, felyng and reason in men. . . . 1531 Elyot, *Gov.*, 3.24. The thirde parte of the soule is named the parte intellectuall or of understandynge." By virtue of the "intellectuall sence," the third of his souls, man is above all other creatures. So God has given him "preeminence" over them. The natural conclusion to this syllogism of analogy is that men also "Are masters to their females, and their Lords" (24). Shakespeare is here "varying" the current phrase of lord and master—"called their husbandes Lordes," says the homily. And so the necessary conclusion of the whole is: "Then let your will attend on their accords" (25). The Christian code does not tolerate for a wife "headstrong liberty" of "will." The statement of the Bishops' Bible is typical: "But as the Churche is subiecte vnto Christe, likewise the wiues to their owne husbandes in al thinges" (*Ephesians*, 5.24; cf. *1 Peter*, 3.1, *Colossions*, 3.18, etc.). While the theme of the 'subjection' of all to Christ is actually from the Bible, yet Luciana deduces it from the order of nature "vnder heauens eye," as given in the Bible, with all things under Heaven in subjection to man as the preeminent being in the lower hierarchy.

2. Adriana's First Homily on Adultery, 2.1.104-15

Twin homilies on adultery by Adriana have caused trouble in posing the major textual cruces of the play. In the first (2.1.104-15), she looks at the case of the adulterer and his "name" from the point of view of the effect upon the adulterer himself; in the second

(2.2.132-48), from the point of view of the effect upon the innocent wife and, through her, of the reflected effect upon the husband also.

The "matter" and the technical phraseology of Adriana's speeches come from the official homilies of the day, where "The second part of the Sermon against adultery" laments "what corruption commeth to mans soule thorough the sinne of adultery" (*Homilies*, sig. K6), and asks "Is not that treasure, which before all other is most regarded of honest persons, the good fame & name of man and woman, lost through whordome? . . . Come not the french-pocks, with diuers other diseases, of whoredome?" (sigs. K8-8v). Adriana expresses her fear to Luciana that her husband, because of his association with "minions" (2.1.87), will not "keepe faire quarter with his bed" (108); and she states her commonplace in aphoristic style worthy of grammar-school Cato himself: " . . . no man that hath a name, By falshood and corruption doth it shame" (112-13). The passage immediately in question runs as follows:

> I see the Iewell best enamaled
> Will loose his beautie: yet the gold bides still
> That others touch, and often touching will,
> Where gold and no man that hath a name,
> By falshood and corruption doth it shame: . . .
>
> (109-13)

Here we have the "good fame & name" of the homily, which will suffer "corruption," as indeed will even the soul itself, by whoredom, as is there stated repeatedly. In the homily, this "treasure" of "good fame & name" cannot be lost without defrauding Christ, who "hath bought vs from the seruitude of the diuell, not with corruptible golde and siluer, but with his most pretious & deare heart bloud" (*Homilies*, sig. K7). This phrase "golde and siluer" appeared prominently also in the original marriage ceremony (1549), along with "Iewels of golde." The wide use of "golde and siluer," "treasure," "Iewels," and so on, in Biblical and liturgical language aided in turn the promised chain in bringing on the figure of the corruptible jewel of enamel and gold, in which Adriana obscures her first homily. This gnomic commonplace, clinched with rhyme in a conventional form, is thus correctly stated, and its meaning is clear: No man of name (fame, reputation, honor)[2] should shame it with the falsehood of "company," as the husband is doing, which will occasion the corruption of whoredom, as the wife fears. The various suggested emendations of this aphorism, beginning with Theobald's (1733) of "By" to "But" (accepted by Malone, 1790), are certainly wrong.

It must be remembered that Adriana's complete simile grows out of a stated situation. She says of her husband that

> His company must do his minions grace,
> Whil'st I at home starue for a merrie looke. . . .
> I know his eye doth homage other-where. . . .
>
> (87-8, 104)

He has promised her a chain:

> Would that alone, a loue he would detaine,
> So he would keepe faire quarter with his
>   bed: . . .
>
> (107-8)

This promised chain then introduces the figure of "the Iewell best enamaled" (109), to rhyme with "bed." The falsehood to his marriage vow of company with, and eye-homage to, minions may be tolerated, if only the husband does not proceed to the actual corruption of whoredom. To achieve the comparison between the external of "company," involving the "homage" of the eye to "minions," contrasted with the fundamental of the marriage "bed," the subject of the simile is complicated from the usual gold of good name into a jewel of enamel and gold (109-10), a characteristic figure (see note 2). Stated directly instead of obliquely, the resultant simile becomes: touching will tarnish the beautifying enamel of a jewel, even if it does not affect its gold, "and" falsehood and corruption will shame a name (without reservation). The two parts of the simile are joined, not by "as . . . so," but by the conjunctive "and" (111), which is thus in rendition rhythmically emphatic (as is "man," which is the 'word' of the commonplace, and the contrast with "jewel"). Theobald emended line 112 by suggesting "so" to follow this conjunctive "and" ("and so no man"), in order to amend the meter. However, so far as the technical structure of the simile is concerned, such a "so" is wholly redundant. Logically, it could be used in the sense of 'consequently'; but it is not in the text, and there is nothing about the text itself to suggest that it should be there. The suggestion is a redundant addition by way of wrongly inferred improvement.

As to the alleged metrical irregularity of line 112, Malone objected to inserting either Theobald's "so" or Steevens's "though," since "Wear" or "Where" is "used as a dissyllable," a judgment that elicited from Chedworth (1805, p. 47) the pontifically damnatory pronouncement, "some commentators seem to have no ear." But even if a syllable should be missing, the technical structure clears the sense. A modern reader needs only suitable punctuation between "gold" and "and" (111) to set off the two halves of the simile. Failure to recognize this technical structure has been the cause of all our woe.

The "touching" here is stated as by "company" and by "homage" of the eye paid to "minions" (who occupy the place of the professional loose women of the *Menaechmi,* and get localized as the suspected Courtesan). This touching will spoil the beauty of the enamel, even if it does not affect the gold. Similarly, "falshood and corruption" tarnish a name (113). The husband is guilty of "falshood" in company and eye already, and the wife hopes only that he will not proceed to the "corruption" of whoredom against his "bed." For, as the homily warns, whoredom will not merely shame the name, the beautifying enamel; it will corrupt even the soul itself, the very gold of one's being. So in the conclusion no reservation is made for gold, such as had been made in the premise. The corruption of whoredom will be absolute.

The conjunctive "and" of line 112 is certainly correct, joining the two parts of the simile. This, as we have seen, in turn clears the conclusion of the simile. Most of the premise also falls naturally into place:

> I see the Iewell best enamaled
> Will loose his beautie: yet the gold bides still
> That others touch, . . .
>
>   (109-11)

The difficulty is in the immediately following lines:

>   . . . and often touching will,
> Where gold and no man that hath a name,
> By falshood and corruption doth it shame: . . .
>
>   (111-13)

As the text stands, "will" must be completed grammatically by the next precedent verb, "bides." In that case, "often touching" becomes the object, and the statement becomes, "gold will bide often touching." Then "Where gold" becomes the condition—"if it really is gold." The comma following "will" is in keeping with this interpretation, whereas if "often touching" is taken as the subject, and "Where" is replaced by "Wear," then the line should run on, without a comma, as does the preceding line, with which it rhymes. Theobald's suggested "Wear" (after Warburton) reverses the grammatical structure, which is bolstered by the punctuation.

Spence (1894) retained the folio reading "Where" but did not elucidate it or fit it into his freehand interpretation. Cuningham (1907) followed Theobald in reading "Wear gold; and so no man," and devoted an appendix to explanation of "this somewhat vexed and difficult passage." Apparently independently of Spence, J. Dover Wilson (1922) objected vigorously to Theobald's "Wear." "Theobald reads "wear" for "where," and all mod. edd. follow, ignoring the fact that "touching will wear gold" flatly contradicts 'the gold bides still that others touch.' " Dover Wilson prints "Where," though he obelizes the line and, postulating a cut of two or more rhyming lines, suggests that "the line is hopelessly corrupt." Analyzing the figure a few years later (1927), I argued that "Where" is the correct

word, a judgment which our fuller knowledge of the genetics of the figure now justifies. Kittredge (1936) read "Wear" for "Where" (112) and "But" for "By" (113). Hardin Craig (1951) accepts Theobald's "Wear" but obelizes the reading. Peter Alexander (1951) retains the folio text intact, adding only punctuation (most notably, a semicolon after "Where gold"). G. B. Harrison (1952) retains Theobald's "Wear" and interprets the basic figure as one of testing gold by means of a touchstone. C. J. Sisson (1953, and *New Readings in Shakespeare*, 1956, 1.91) breaks the basic structure of the simile to emend "the whole passage," reading "that" for "yet" (110), "yet" for "and" (111), and "Wear" for "Where" (112). It now appears, however, that the passage is not "hopelessly corrupt," even though we might well wish that Shakespeare had paid somewhat less attention to sentential profundity and a little more to sense.[3] But the common background of this bit of wisdom gave him and his contemporaries the sense. I hope they enjoyed and profited.

Adriana charges that her husband has already been false to the enamel of his name by "company" and the "homage" of his "eye," and hopes only that he will not proceed to corrupt the gold of his name and of his soul itself by unfaithfulness to his marriage bed. She laments that she cannot please even his eye, as his "minions" do:

> Since that my beautie cannot please his eie,
> Ile weepe (what's left away) and weeping die.
>
>   (114-15)

Proper sentimental self-pity from time immemorial!

3. Adriana's Second Homily on Adultery, 2.2.132-48

When Adriana thinks she has cornered her husband but has cornered Antipholus of Syracuse instead, she bestows on him a companion homily on the innocent wife adulterated by her husband, and the reflected effect upon him. The passage is built up as a thrice-stated figure in syllogistic sequence. In the first statement she poses the hypothetical case of her own infidelity:

> How deerely would it touch thee to the
>   quicke,
> Shouldst thou but heare I were licencious?
> And that this body consecrate to thee,
> By Ruffian Lust should be contaminate?
>
>   (2.2.132-5)

In the second statement she claims that, though innocent, she had been contaminated as though she were indeed guilty of adultery:

> I am possest with an adulterate blot,
> My bloud is mingled with the crime of lust: . . .
>
>   (142-3)

And in the third statement she accuses her husband of having effected this contamination:

> For if we two be one, and thou play false,
> I doe digest the poison of thy flesh,
> Being strumpeted by thy contagion: . . .
>
>   (144-6)

His "crime of lust" introduces a "poison" to his "flesh" (there is no "grime," as Dover Wilson and other editors would emend); and this in turn causes a "contamination," a "mingling," a "contagion" in her "bloud." Thus she is made into a "strumper"; his "crime of lust" results in her suffering the "stain" of an "adulterate blot."

It will be remembered that the homily on adultery had been quite specific as to the results of whoredom. "What gift of nature . . . is not corrupted with whoredome? Come not the french-pocks, with diuers other diseases, of whoredome?" (*Homilies,* sig. K8v); and are not wives also "corrupted . . . through whoredome?" The homily on matrimony gives as the first reasons for matrimony "to bring foorth fruit, and to auoide fornication. By which meane a good conscience might be preserued on both parties, in brideling the corrupt inclinations of the flesh, wythin the limits of honestie. For God hath straitly forbidden al whoredome and vncleannesse, and hath from time to time taken greeuous punishment of this inordinate lust, as all stories and ages have declared" (sig. 2G3v). (On the prohibition against "whoredome," see *Hebrews,* 13.4, *1 Corinthians,* 6.9, *Revelation,* 22.15, etc.) So, on the purely physical side, her husband will pass on to Adriana any "poison" of his "flesh," such as the "french-pocks" threatened by the homily; and he will do so because of his "crime of lust"—"inordinate lust," to use the language of the homily, for which God may mete out "greeuous punishment."

"The second part of the Sermon against adultery" says that the first part had shown "finally what corruption commeth to mans soule thorough the sinne of adultery." The second part then quotes various passages of Scripture (the principal being *1 Corinthians,* 6), and continues as follows: "he saith, do ye not know that your bodies are the members of Christ? shall I then take the members of Christe, and make them the members of an whore? God forbid. Do yee not knowe, that hee which cleaueth to an whore, is made one body with her? There shal be two in one fleshe (saith he) but he that cleaueth to the Lord, is one spirite" (*Homilies,* sig. K6v-7). Adriana therefore claims that, though she is innocent of adultery, her husband has, because man and wife are one flesh, made her into just such a strumpet as the Courtesan with whom she suspects him of having played her false. She concludes logically:

> Keepe then faire league and truce with thy
>   true bed,
> I liue distain'd, thou vndishonoured.
>
>   (147-8)

That is, if her husband does his duty by his "true bed," he will punish her as a strumpet, so that "I liue distain'd, thou vndishonoured." She will remain "distain'd" indeed, as he has unjustly made her, but he will have vindicated his honor and so will himself be "vndishonoured."

Both lines of this clinching gnomic distich are clear in their genetics. The underlying figure of the second line is of stained honor. This is the figure regularly used in Italian discussions of such cases of honor, and in these the ruling is the same as Adriana's. Annibale Romei in his *Courtiers Academie* (1596) twice rules that when a wife is unfaithful, "with her owne, shee also staineth the honour of her husband" (p. 97); "with her owne, she staineth also the honour of her husband" (p. 126). Benvenuto Italiano, in *The Passenger* (1612), has the same approximate phraseology: "she being marryed and accompanying with others, together with her owne, she staines her husbands honour also" (p. 609). Romei also rules typically that the husband "looseth not his honour, but when hee conuerseth with a married woman" (p. 97), though if he "falsifieth the oth of matrimony, frequenting with a loose woman," he is "worthy of some blame" (p. 96). But both writers agree that the wife stains both her own and her husband's honor by any deviation at all.

So the second line of the distich has been balanced on the "stain" and "honor" of this Italian ruling, which was a paradox. By any deviation the wife stained her honor, but the husband did not, unless with a married woman. But Adriana had been contending at length that husband and wife are one, and that consequently, if the husband goes a whoring, he makes a strumpet of his wife. So, in that case, "I liue distain'd, thou vndishonoured." Adriana has shaped the Italian phraseology correctly into her paradoxical line. Long before I knew the genetics of the line, I wrote: "Adriana points out to Antipholus that they two are undividably one, and that he would punish any erring on her part. But if so, he ought now to punish her, because he has sinned, and thus in their undividable oneness has made her guilty, without any act of her own. She again advises him therefore to keep fair league and truce with his bed by punishing or distaining her. So will he clear his own honor" (ed. 1927, p. 81). And Shakespeare himself did not change—or need to change—this original phraseology.

The first line of the distich, "Keepe then faire league and truce with thy true bed," is a restatement from Adriana's first homily, "would keepe faire quarter with his bed" (2.1.108). Thus "bed" has kept its place to become the rhyme to "vndishonoured," botched up with the inevitable epithet "true"; "with his" has been adapted as "with thy," and "would keepe" has been adapted to the sentence structure as "Keepe then"; "faire quarter" has become "faire league and truce," the word "truce" doubtless being suggested as balanced alliteration with "true." The two homilies have been tied together; the condition of the first has naturally become the exhortation of the second.

Each line of the distich is as Shakespeare wrote it, and each separately is quite correct. And each line separately states a correct conclusion for the preceding speech, as do the two together. It seems clear also that Shakespeare wrote the second line first, as a correct conclusion of his idea, and then adapted the first line of it from a line in the earlier homily to tie the two homilies together, and to make of the two lines a distich. So far as this text is concerned, then, any scholarly edition can only retain and explain the folio reading.

It seems clear that in Adriana's two homilies the printer accurately reproduced the copy that had been set before him; and thus we owe him a debt of gratitude. In these passages, and in Luciana's earlier homily, we are very close to Shakespeare's pen in the white heat of unblotted composition. The technical rhetorical forms, such as syllogistic reasoning, triplicity, sentential distich, and so on, are all readily at hand, well prepared for the heated flow. Considerable skill is already evident, awaiting that practice which sometimes makes perfect; but without evidence of that meticulous self-correction which is sometimes alleged to be necessary to attain complete perfection. "Would he had blotted a thousand," said the meticulous Ben, whose efforts were already too late; ours may well be more profitably expended upon our own miracles of composition.

Here we have watched the young Shakespeare applying his rhetorical skill to ideas from the official homilies of his day to produce three homilies for two of his characters, all centering on Adriana's problem husband. These homilies in turn throw light on what Shakespeare intended the positions and resultant emotions of those characters to be. Adriana has heard her Job's adviser Luciana, but like the stubborn ass she continues, with the most 'righteous' motives and on the basis of impeccable authority, to betray herself to her own eventual reproof. In doing so, she, like her sister, has been made by Shakespeare to think and speak in the official and conventional language of his day.

Notes

[1] Richmond Noble, in *Shakespeare's Biblical Knowledge* (1935), p. 237, sees a probable application of this passage in *Timon of Athens:* "Page. [*to the Fool*] Why, how now, captain? What do you in this wise company? How dost thou, Apemantus? *Apemantus.* Would I had a rod in my mouth, that I might answer thee profitably!" (2.2.77-80).

[2] For echoing statements on good name, reputation, honor, see *Richard II,* 1.1.177-8; *All's Well That Ends Well,* 4.2.45-51; *Othello,* 2.3.262-5, 3.3.155-61. With the last passage ("Who steals my purse steals trash") may be compared a passage in the *Homilies:* "many times cometh lesse hurt of a theefe, then of a rayling tongue: for the one taketh away a mans good name, the other taketh but his riches, which is of much lesse value and estimation, then is his good name" (sig. L8v). Compare also my *William Shakspere's Small Latine and Lesse Greeke* (1944), 2.275.

[3] In *Albions England* (ed. 1589) William Warner had admonished the English against the error of mixing similes and sententiousness: "Onely this error may be thought hatching in our English, that to runne on the Letter, we often runne from the Matter: and being ouer prodigall in Similes, wee become lesse profitable in Sentences, and more prolixious to Sense" (sig. ¶4).

Joseph Candido (essay date 1990)

SOURCE: "Dining Out in Ephesus: Food in *The Comedy of Errors,*" in *Studies in English Literature, 1500-1900,* Vol. 30, No. 2, Spring, 1990, pp. 217-41.

[*In this excerpt, Candido shows that characters' attitudes toward meals reveals their gendered understanding of marital social obligations.*]

C. L. Barber and Richard P. Wheeler observe shrewdly that in *The Comedy of Errors* "Shakespeare is marvelous at conveying a sense of a world already there," and cite Dromio of Ephesus's first words as illustrating the "routine tensions" of "daily, ordinary life" that pervade the play:[1]

> The capon burns, the pig falls from the spit;
> The clock hath strucken twelve upon the bell:
> My mistress made it one upon my cheek:
> She is so hot, because the meat is cold.
>
> (I.ii.44-47)

The passage is a fine indication of Shakespeare's early genius at dramatic economy, for not only does it catch effortlessly the rhythms of "a world already there," it also points to certain rhetorical and psychological traits that bind the parted Antipholuses and their Dromios together even as the two pairs of twins remain comically at odds throughout much of the play. Dromio's urgent concern over such matters as tardiness for dinner, the condition of food, household plans gone awry, and the anger of his mistress, is by no means exceptional in *The Comedy of Errors,* for voiced attention to the seemingly unremarkable events of day-to-day life occupy the two Antipholuses and their servants with striking regularity. Listen to Antipholus of Syracuse as he first sets foot in Ephesus:

> Within this hour it will be dinner-time;
> Till that, I'll view the manners of the town,
> Persue the traders, gaze upon the buildings,
> And then return and sleep within my inn,
> For with long travel I am stiff and weary.
>
> (I.ii.11-15)

The banal itinerary of the tourist tends not to be fit matter for Shakespearean romantic comedy, but in *The Comedy of Errors* bed and board often come abruptly to the forefront of the action. We are seldom unaware of people going to and from dinner or talking about the comforts of food and home. It is perhaps natural enough that the traveling Antipholus of Syracuse—whose sense of aimless nonattachment is so resonantly conveyed by the metaphor of the lone water drop seeking its fellow in the ocean (I.ii.35-38)—should be attracted to the security and solidity implied by the shared meal. He is, to be sure, an earnest seeker of dining companions, oddly receptive, for example, to the sudden feast thrust upon him by total strangers later in the play, and eager to make a dinner engagement with the first native Ephesian he meets. We miss much in the play if we ignore the tentative yet deep longing for connection behind his invitation to the anonymous Ephesian merchant:

> What, will you walk with me about the town,
> And then go to my inn and dine with me?
>
> (I.ii.22-23)

Coming as it does after Antipholus's admission of frequent "care and melancholy" (I.ii.20), the remark suggests a yearning for the personal and societal integration so sadly absent in the separated twin. Instructive in this regard are the concluding lines of the Ephesian Dromio's previously cited call to dinner, which both elaborate on the servant's urgent request and place the longings of the Syracusan visitor in a wider and more richly suggestive social context:

> The meat is cold, because you come not
>   home:
> You come not home, because you have no
>   stomach:
> You have no stomach, having broke your fast:
> But we that know what 'tis to fast and pray,
> Are penitent for your default to-day.
>
> (I.ii.48-52)

Dromio's witty admonition points to serious matters that go beyond a mere hunger for food and society; it posits a social reality in which a genuine and strongly felt causal relationship exists between the abandoned meal and intimate moral and marital concerns. The five lines that take us from cold meat to implied sinfulness ("your default to-day")[2] hinge on the assumption that Ephesus is a place where social ceremonies matter, where the wayward husband's suspected dining away ("having broke [his] fast") has serious consequences for his relationship to wife and home. Antipholus of Ephesus's absence has transformed his house into the social equivalent of a spiritually unprofitable Lent, imposing a penitential fasting on all its inhabitants and eliciting from his wife a resentment that manifests itself in violence to her servant and angry abstinence (I.ii.90).[3]

Before discussing the marital—and expressly sexual—implications of the Ephesian husband's absence from dinner at home, I should first like to review briefly the status of the midday meal for Shakespeare and his audience. William Harrison in his *Description of England* (1577, 1587) has much to say about the importance of the noon dinner for Elizabethans, particularly since this was the central and most elaborate meal of the day. Harrison's moralistic digression on dining habits, although not explicitly related to the action of Shakespeare's play, nonetheless indicates the close relationship between social mores and social morality. He disparages the frequent "odd repasts" of earlier times that included "breakfasts in the forenoon, beverages or nuncheons after dinner, and thereto reresuppers generally when it was time to go to rest,"[4] preferring instead the more enlightened modern habit of eating once, or at most twice, a day. Even this practice, however, is not without the gluttonous abuse of "long and stately sitting at meat" (p. 141): "For the nobility, gentlemen, and merchantmen, especially at great meetings, do sit commonly till two or three of the clock at afternoon, so that with many is an hard matter, to rise from the table to go to Evening Prayer and return from thence to come time enough to supper" (p. 141).

The "supper" to which Harrison alludes was a much lighter evening meal that carried little of the formal or symbolic character of the noon dinner. Lu Emily Pearson and Muriel St. Clare Byrne, both of whom examine in some detail the richly allusive meanings implicit in dinner at the home of a well-to-do Elizabethan, make this point persuasively.[5] Echoing Harrison, Pearson notes how the noon meal could drag on almost to supper with only time for evening prayer between; she then proceeds to underscore the personal and social symbolism implicit in the long repast: "cooking, like ornate architecture or elaborate dress or anything else that might impress one's acquaintants with a display of wealth, became a very important advertisement of a man's financial status. . . . No one was ever expected to partake of all the dishes but to eat and drink moderately by making a selection from the variety so bounteously offered" (pp. 556-57).

Although Pearson here is describing a somewhat more elaborate dinner than the family meal that Antipholus of Ephesus disregards so casually in *The Comedy of Errors,* even the ordinary dinner prepared for family alone was a matter of some culinary complexity for the housewife. (At least three main dishes were usually served, not including vegetables, bread, and drink, and Dromio mentions capon and pig specifically.) Moreover, Adriana's Elizabethan counterpart could have expected guests on short or no notice—witness the fact that Antipholus of Ephesus approaches his house with Angelo and Balthazar in tow—and her readiness in preparation would have been a sign of her domestic competence as well as her magnanimity as a hostess. Her social role—indeed her identity as wife—was linked in some measure to her success at entertaining, just as her husband's public reputation was linked to the affluence of his board.[6] Along these lines Pearson notes that "even everyday meals were served with due decorum in well-managed homes, and the table was carefully set" (p. 565). Byrne further elaborates on what she calls the "ceremony" observed for daily dinner in "a well-to-do townman's household":

> a cloth was laid upon the table, and at every place was set a trencher, a napkin, and a spoon. Wine, ale, and drinking vessels, Harrison tells us, stood on the buffet, and the servants filled a clean goblet or Venetian drinking glass when any guest called for liquor. In the kitchen quarters the butler took pains to chip the bread in order to remove any cinders from the crust, and he also squared each piece neatly before he set it on the board. Finally, the great salt-cellar would be placed on the table, and with basin,[7] ewer, and fine damask towel ready to hand for the diners' ablutions, all was prepared.
>
> (p. 30)

Clearly Antipholus of Ephesus's failure to come to dinner on time is a repudiation of more than mere food; his absence from home is the first step in the flouting of an accepted social ceremony that helps define his identity as respected citizen and respectful husband. It is surely no coincidence that in the course of the play he is threatened with the loss of both of these socially and emotionally vital aspects of the self. Reputation and marriage begin to dissolve together when the wrong brother dines at home.[8]

When viewed in this context Adriana's behavior assumes a deeper and more richly suggestive character than the mere ragings of a jealous housewife. Her determination to refrain from eating despite the fact that her husband is two hours late (II.i.3) indicates a serious attempt to maintain personal equilibrium and social bonds in the face of heavy pressures.[9] Adriana is no mere jealous shrew (her readiness to forgive later in the play is too often slighted); rather she is a fiercely combative woman confronting squarely the threat of an imperiled marriage and determined to sustain meaningful ties despite social and personal threats to her identity as wife and Lady. This is, oddly enough, a fact that her didactic and self-assured sister fails to recognize. Luciana's smug suggestion to "let us dine, and never fret" (II.i.6) implies an indifference to her sister's emotional plight that reveals the severe limitations of the unwedded woman's easy aphorisms about marriage (II.i.15-25). Adriana knows better; her rhetoric wisely acknowledges the heavy emotional tool exacted by her husband's absence in terms lost on her sister:

> His company must do his minions grace,
> Whilst I at home *starve* for a merry look:
>
> . . . . .
>
> But, too unruly deer, he breaks the pale,
> And *feeds from home;* poor I am but his stale.
> (II.i.87-101; emphasis added)

When Adriana finally locates the man she believes to be her Antipholus, her first instinct is to reestablish old connections by clarifying the proper relationship of husband to wife. Her moving speech on the mystical Christian notion that the married couple are one flesh evokes longingly an earlier stage of her marriage when identities were stable and rooted securely in the simple ceremonies of everyday life:

> The time was once, when thou unurg'd wouldst vow
> That never words were music to thine ear,
> That never object pleasing in thine eye,
> That never touch well welcome to thy hand,
> That never meat sweet-savor'd in thy taste,
> Unless I spake, or look'd, or touch'd, or carv'd to thee.
>
> (II.ii.113-18)

Adriana's suggestive use of the Syracusan brother's earlier image of "a drop of water in the breaking gulf" to define marital inseparability (II.ii.126) further implies her sense of identification with the man before her, particularly as he represents—in an almost literal sense—the younger and more innocent version of her husband.[10] Her urgent invitation to the Syracusan twin can thus be seen symbolically as a psychologically necessary act of marital renewal; Adriana's desire for the earlier and untainted version of her husband is symbolically fulfilled as she enacts with the younger twin the meaningful social ceremony that defines for her the basis of a stable marriage. Speaking, looking, and touching—the characteristic intimacies of romantic love—fuse curiously in her mind with carving. Moral realignment and marital recommitment both meet for the anxious wife in the ordered normalcy of the shared meal:

Come, come, no longer will I be a fool,
To put the finger in the eye and weep,
Whilst man and master laughs my woes to
　scorn.
Come, sir, to dinner. Dromio, keep the gate.
Husband, I'll dine above with you to-day,
And shrive you of a thousand idle pranks.
Sirrah, if any ask you for your master,
Say he dines forth, and let no creature enter.

　　　　　　　　　　　　　　(II.ii.203-10)

The episode is rich with implication. Anthropologists such as Mary Douglas and Claude Levi-Strauss have painstakingly detailed the close association of food with sexual longings and sexual identity.[11] Douglas, in particular, has probed how in various cultures "sexual and gastronomic consummation are made equivalents of one another by reasons of analogous restrictions applied to each" (p. 71), a phenomenon with obvious implications for the marital identity of the couple.[12] Similarly, Adriana's renewed enthusiasm for dinner with the man she thinks is her husband appears to include such psychological concerns. Despite the fact that Luciana will accompany the pair, theirs will be a rather private meal, "above," symbolically located in the living quarters upstairs rather than in the more public business quarters below. Moreover, the exclusivity of the meal is further underscored by Adriana's (unintentionally ironic) instructions to Dromio to tell all callers that her husband dines away, and by her explicit order to the servant to "play the porter well . . . let none enter, lest I break your pate" (II.ii.211, 218). Clearly there is more at stake here for Adriana than the rearrangement of a disturbed afternoon. Her private family meal serves as a convenient social vehicle for the larger issue of forgiveness, and her insistence on privacy metaphorically links confidential family matters with the equally confidential regenerative power of the confessional: "Husband, I'll . . . shrive you of a thousand idle pranks." Even Luciana seems to sense what the renewed meal means symbolically for her sister; there is a note of urgency as well as impatience in her enjoinder to the puzzled guest: "Come, come, Antipholus, we dine too late" (II.ii.219).

The arrival of the real husband, of course, throws all into confusion; but as is so often the case in *The Comedy of Errors*, it is a confusion that abruptly forces characters to clarify identities and locate priorities. As Antipholus of Ephesus approaches his house with Angelo and Balthazar, he exudes a settled complacency with the verities of his mercantile and male-oriented world. He is late for dinner, and although he knows that Adriana "is shrewish when I keep not hours" (III.i.2), he believes that the remedy for her discontent lies in the protective duplicity of his friend the goldsmith: "Say that I linger'd with you at your shop / To see the making of her carcanet, / And that to-morrow you will bring it home" (III.i.3-5). Antipholus's crass

gift of the necklace (which in anger he later transfers to the Courtesan) illustrates the immense psychological gap that separates his materialist notion of marriage from Adriana's loftier attitude of Christian idealism. For the inattentive husband, whose response to marital drift is to placate his wife with costly trinkets, the midday meal carries none of the deep-seated marital or sexual significance that it does for Adriana. Indeed, there is every indication that Antipholus sees the dinner as an *exclusively* male concern, an occasion for refined humanist discourse on the relationship of food to friendship, but little more. Any thought of the neglected wife disappears under the somewhat precious and over-embroidered male niceties that precede Antipholus's discovery of the locked door:

E. Ant. Y' are sad, Signior Balthazar, pray
　　God our cheer
May answer my good will and your good
　welcome here.
Balth. I hold your dainties cheap, sir, and
　your welcome dear.
E. Ant. O, Signior Balthazar, either at flesh or
　fish,
A table full of welcome makes scarce one
　dainty dish.
Balth. Good meat, sir, is common; that every
　churl affords.
E. Ant. And welcome more common, for that's
　nothing but words.
Balth. Small cheer and great welcome makes a
　merry feast.
E. Ant. Ay, to a niggardly host and more
　sparing guest:
But though my cates be mean, take them in
　good part;
Better cheer may you have, but not with better
　heart.
But soft, my door is lock'd; go bid them let
　us in.

　　　　　　　　　　　　　　(III.i. 19-30)

The stark reality of Adriana's shut door, carrying as it does the same sexual implications as that of the angry wife in *The Menaechmi*, turns Antipholus's dinner of male friendship and ostentation into a marital crisis. By virtue of his denied access to home and wife, the Ephesian brother comes to experience precisely the same feelings of alienation and sexual doubt that he has so casually inflicted upon his wife. But the confusion here produces more than mere psychological tit-for-tat. Antipholus's isolation outside the locked house functions symbolically to define the spiritual divorce he has already produced while at the same time literalizing ominously the ends to which his neglect will lead. In this sense the Ephesian brother joins Adriana, his twin, Egeon, and Aemelia in experiencing the anxieties of isolation and nonattachment, with the significant difference that in his case he alone is to blame.

There is a fine irony to the fact that while Antipholus suspects Adriana with another man, his real rival for his virtuous wife is the earlier and idealized image of himself as represented in his younger brother. Adriana *does* love another man—the Antipholus she so longingly evokes as she recalls what her husband once was, the Antipholus she believes she is restoring at dinner in her upstairs room. In an almost literal sense, then, the Ephesian brother is in conflict with himself, thus embodying, in another more resonantly suggestive form, the self-division that is everywhere in the play.[13] As Balthazar wisely points out, Antipholus's unseemly attempts to break into his own house in full view of others is really a senseless act of violence to self:

> Have patience, sir, O, let it not be so!
> Herein you war against your reputation,
> And draw within the compass of suspect
> Th' unviolated honor of your wife.
>
>   . . . . .
>
> If by strong hand you offer to break in
> Now in the stirring passage of the day,
> A vulgar comment will be made of it;
> And that supposed by the common rout
> Against your yet ungalled estimation,
> That may with foul intrusion enter in,
> And dwell upon your grave when you are
>   dead.
>
>   (III.i.85-104)

Although the irate husband finally departs "in quiet" (III.i.107), he hardly departs emotionally intact; self-rebellion and self-loathing, not just revenge, drive Antipholus to dinner at the Courtesan's.

The two separate dining experiences of the two identical twins stand in sharp contrast to each other; yet they also reflect each other in curious ways. For Antipholus of Ephesus the dinner with the Courtesan contains many of the same psychological elements as that planned by his Plautine counterpart in *The Menaechmi*. Just as Menaechmus of Epidamnum's choice of *Voluptas* over *Industria* involved a rejection of his wife for male companionship and dinner with Erotium, the Ephesian twin invites his male friends to dine with him at the Courtesan's where he will bestow the necklace "for nothing but to spite my wife" (III.i.118). Obviously Antipholus's rebellious dinner, at which the materialistic sign of his weak marital commitment is to change hands, represents the moral opposite of Adriana's feast of reconciliation. Perhaps less obvious, however, is the way in which the younger Antipholus's behavior at Adriana's dinner unwittingly parallels the unfaithfulness of his brother. As the symbolic embodiment of the younger version of his Ephesian twin, Antipholus of Syracuse reenacts his

brother's behavior by forsaking the woman who has welcomed him to the feast and turning his romantic attention to another. In professing love for Luciana he sounds strangely like an only slightly exaggerated version of his older brother:

> Your weeping sister is no wife of mine,
> Nor to her bed no homage do I owe:
> Far more, far more, to you do I decline.
>
>   (III.ii.41-43)

And later, when alone, he finds an even more distinctly "Antipholan" mode of expression:

> She that doth call me husband, even my soul
> Doth for a wife abhor. But her fair sister,
> Possess'd with such a gentle sovereign grace,
> Of such enchanting presence and discourse,
> Hath almost made me traitor to myself.
>
>   (III.ii.158-62)

Something very close to this attitude (expressed in strikingly similar rhetoric) lies behind the Ephesian brother's attraction to the "wench of excellent discourse, / Pretty and witty; wild, and yet, too, gentle" (III.i.109-10), at whose home he will dine and to whom he will give his wife's necklace. At both dinners Adriana is rejected by her husband.

Adriana's broken banquet fails to produce its desired ends, but it nonetheless sets in motion a process of moral and social realignment that continues to the end of the play. Critics have generally tended to overlook the rejected wife's response to her failed dinner, particularly her remarks upon hearing that at the meal her supposed husband has tried to woo Luciana:

> He is deformed, crooked, old, and sere,
> Ill-fac'd, worse bodied, shapeless every where;
> Vicious, ungentle, foolish, blunt, unkind,
> Stigmatical in making, worse in mind.
>
>   . . . . .
>
> Ah, but I think him better than I say,
> And yet would herein others' eyes were
>   worse:
> Far from her nest the lapwing cries away;
> My heart prays for him, though my tongue do
>   curse.
>
>   (IV.ii.19-28)

The division here between heart and tongue, feeling and saying, focuses upon yet another pair of forceful oppositions embedded in singleness. Adriana's acknowledgement of her inner divisions not only reflects the outer and more obvious tensions involved in relationships like twinship, sisterhood, marriage, and friendship; it also points implicitly to a means of finding concord in discord. Adriana is a frequent object of others' criticism—her husband, sister, and mother-in-law are only the most vocal examples—yet despite it all she remains the most fully responsive and synthetic character in the play, preferring finally in a crisis to labor at forgiveness rather than to ease into recrimination. If her first significant act of synthesis is her attempted dinner, her second is her readiness to forgive her husband despite its apparent failure. Her recognition of her own divided response to the supposed infidelity of her husband—outward rage and inward love—and her determination to act charitably in the face of it, implies the wise acceptance of a psychological duality in her self and in her husband that is symbolically represented in the two identical yet separate twins. The gold she gives to ransom her Antipholus is the surest sign of her clear-sighted resolve to meet rejection with forgiveness despite warring inner tensions: "Go Dromio . . . bring thy master home immediately. / Come, sister, I am press'd down with conceit— / Conceit, my comfort and my injury" (IV.ii.63-66). When the younger Antipholus rejects the Courtesan as his older brother should have ("I conjure thee to leave me and be gone" [IV.iii.67]), his behavior ratifies symbolically the process of marital reconciliation that Adriana's charity has begun. But the younger Antipholus's behavior is more than merely symbolic; it also has the practical effect of eroding the Ephesian brother's newly formed relationship with the Courtesan. After being turned away by Antipholus of Syracuse (whom she takes for the Ephesian twin), the Courtesan does an emotional about-face in order to recoup the day's financial losses. Her blatant self-concern—in clear contrast to Adriana's charity—only heightens the emotional poverty of her makeshift meal with the wayward husband:

> My way is now to hie home to his house,
> And tell his wife that, being lunatic,
> He rush'd into my house, and took perforce
> My ring away. This course I fittest choose,
> For forty ducats is too much to lose.
>
> (IV.iii.92-96)

But even Adriana, despite her strenuous attempts to sustain and revivify her marriage, is hardly guiltless of marital neglect. Like her husband, she must endure a harsh public embarrassment that airs private wrongs and forces her to confront squarely her share in the weakened relationship. Her sister's earnest yet commonplace strictures on the superiority of husband to wife (II.i.15-25) pale beside the withering—and more imperiously authoritative—criticism of the Abbess. Unlike Luciana, who relies on traditional and essentially Pauline notions of marriage to upbraid her sister, the Abbess turns her criticism inward to the intimate day-to-day activities of bedroom and kitchen that Adriana sees as her special province. The Abbess is, ironically, not nearly as concerned with theological and religious matters as she is with the practical goings-on inside Adriana's household. In this sense she sounds far less like a cloistered sister than like the concerned mother-in-law that she is. Here is the Abbess just after she learns, from Adriana herself, of the wife's frequent and public criticisms of her husband:

> And thereof came it that the man was mad.
> The venom clamors of a jealous woman
> Poisons more deadly than a mad dog's tooth.
> It seems his sleeps were hind'red by thy railing,
> And thereof comes it that his head is light.
> Thou say'st his meat was sauc'd with thy upbraidings:
> Unquiet meals make ill digestions,
> Thereof the raging fire of fever bred,
> And what's a fever but a fit of madness?
> Thou say'st his sports were hind'red by thy brawls:
> Sweet recreation barr'd, what doth ensue
> But moody and dull melancholy,
> Kinsman to grim and comfortless despair,
> And at her heels a huge infectious troop
> Of pale distemperatures and foes to life?
> In food, in sport, and life-preserving rest
> To be disturb'd, would mad or man or beast:
> The consequence is then, thy jealous fits
> Hath scar'd thy husband from the use of wits.
>
> (V.i.68-86)

The speech links two important domestic responsibilities that went hand-in-hand for the Elizabethan housewife, preparing food and ministering to the sick. Popular handbooks of the day such as Sir Hugh Plat's *Delightes for Ladies* (1608) repeatedly spelled out this dual responsibility.[14] Plat's four-part discourse takes up such matters as "The Arte of Preseruing," "Secrets in Distillation," and "Cookerie and Huswiferie," concluding with a detailed section on powders, ointments, and home cures that the good housewife would need to know in order to perform her domestic duties successfully. Here one can find remedies for problems such as yellow teeth, chilbains, pimpled or burned skin, bodily bruises of various sorts, and almost any other commonplace malady of the day. Implicit in Plat's book, particularly its final section, is a recognition of the important role of the housewife as custodian of domestic order and ease. In addition to her skill in the preparation of food (the largest part of the book consists of recipes), the resourceful mistress of an Elizabethan house was expected to produce medical results like that which relieved one "M. *Foster* an Essex man and an Atturney of the Common pleas" of an inflamed face: "Qvilt bay salt well dried & powdered, in double linnen sockes of a prettie bignesse, let the patient weare them in wide hose and shooes day and night, by the space of fourteene daies, or till he be well: euerie morning and euening let him dry his sockes by the fire and put them on againe" (p. 93). It is presumably Adriana's inattentiveness to details such as these to which the Abbess alludes when she speaks of the "huge infectious troop / Of pale distemperatures and foes to life" that characterize the wife's disordered household. Adriana should have paid more attention to Thomas Tusser, whose earnest *Points of Huswifery, United to the Comfort of Husbandry* (1573), also sees attention to food and physic as dual but hardly separate concerns for women like Adriana. Tusser's advice could almost serve as a shorthand introduction to some of the key critical issues in *The Comedy of Errors:*

> Good huswives provide, ere an' sickness do
> 　come,
> Of sundry good things, in her house to have
> 　some:
> Good *aqua composita,* and vinegar tart,
> Rose-water, and treacle, to comfort the heart.
> Cold herbs in her garden, for agues that burn,
> That over strong heat, to good temper may
> 　turn.
>
> 　　　　　　　　　　　　　　　(p. 274)

> 　　Use mirth and good word,
> 　　At bed and at board.
> Provide for thy husband, to make him good
> 　cheer,
> Make merry together, while time ye be here.
> At bed and at board, howsoever befall,
> Whatever God sendeth, be merry withall.
>
> 　　No brawling make,
> 　　No jealousy take.
> No taunts before servants, for hindering of
> 　fame,
> No jarring too loud, for avoiding of shame.
> 　　　　　　　　　　　　　　(p. 266)[15]

Tusser's cautionary advice could hardly be more apt in Adriana's case. The wife's defense of her jealous accusations is the virtual textbook antithesis of Tusser's admonitions:

> It [suspected philandering] was the copy of
> 　our conference:
> In bed he slept not for my urging it;
> At board he fed not for my urging it;
> Alone, it was the subject of my theme;
> In company I often glanced it;
> Still did I tell him it was vild and bad.
> 　　　　　　　　　　　　　　(V.i.62-67)

Adriana has indeed acted well in trying to refashion her broken noon meal into a dinner of forgiveness for her supposed husband, but absent from her notion of the shared meal is her own penitence for past wrongs. Now, for the first time, we sense why her husband may have been late for dinner in the first place, for

he had little reason to expect anything like the calm repast it was his wife's duty to supply. As the Abbess so pointedly says: "his meat was sauc'd with thy upbraidings: / Unquiet meals make ill digestions." Adriana's repeated unquiet meals have provided more sustenance for Antipholus's "raging fire of fever" and "moody and dull melancholy" than they have for his physical and emotional well-being. Adriana has, in short, forsaken the role of hostess and healer that it was her marital duty to perform. To her credit, however, she responds to this open exposé of her shortcomings, as she always does to a crisis, with admirable clear-sightedness. Her reaction to the Abbess's scathing public denunciation would have made Tusser proud:

> I will attend my husband, be his nurse,
> Diet his sickness, for it is my office,
> And will have no attorney but myself,
> And therefore let me have him home with me.
> 　　　　　　　　　　　　　　(V.i.98-101)

Adriana's suggestive "Diet his sickness" indicates a clear psychological commitment to her twin responsibilities as purveyor of meals and overseer of home remedies. Implicit in her response is the full acceptance of her role as custodian of the day-to-day activities that ensure marital harmony and household ease. In this sense Adriana becomes the willing secular equivalent of the Abbess, the mistress of a religious household, whose "wholesome syrups, drugs, and holy prayers" are "the charitable duty" of her order (V.i.104-107). Religious mother-in-law and secular wife merge psychologically in a mutual determination to ensure "food, sport, and life-preserving rest" for the separate Antipholuses in their care.

It is frequently observed that the last act of *The Comedy of Errors,* while suggesting some degree of familial reorientation and renewal, stops short of a full affirmation of marital harmony. This is essentially the view of Alexander Leggatt, who, in an allusive and sensitive essay on the play, points out that there is no explicit reconciliation between Adriana and her husband, leaving the final state of their marriage "an open question." For Leggatt the idea of reconciliation in marriage is not utterly dismissed "but it is quietly placed in the background, and no great hopes are pinned on it."[16] This is true enough, for at the end of the play we have no actual nuptial rite or even the symbolic evocation of one as we sometimes do in Shakespearean comedy. Instead the emphasis here is on the unification of an old family (even its younger members are old enough to have grown apart) rather than on the earnest hope for beginning a new one. But this is not to say that *The Comedy of Errors* is without its own significant—and characteristic—comic closure. When the multiple confusions are finally resolved, the Abbess invites the assembled company into *her* dwelling for a dining experience of a very different sort from those we have seen earlier in the play. This will be a "gossips' feast" (V.i.406), that is, a baptismal banquet at which the whole family assembles to welcome with joy a new member into a social and religious community. As such, it is a time for reestablishing old bonds and reaffirming one's commitment to a set of moral and religious values that impart spiritual significance to the activities of daily life.[17] It is a mended and more comprehensive version of the failed dinners of Adriana and the Courtesan, containing as it does the security and shared spiritual objectives theirs so obviously lack. At the Abbess's feast, in sharp contrast to the dinners planned by Adriana and the Courtesan, participants exist in a stable and recognizable relationship to each other. Indeed, the whole purpose of a baptismal gathering is to ratify collectively the stabilization of one's identity, for it is the baptismal act that fixes a new creature once and for all with a name that denotes both who he is and what one hopes he will become. The Abbess's feast is thus an attempt to reach backward—symbolically at least—to Egeon's and Aemelia's experience with their twin infants on the mast, to begin time again at the key moment when the sacramental stability of a double christening can cancel the psychological division of family shipwreck. Perhaps the surest sign of the need for such stability is the obvious personal and social chaos produced by twin brothers with *identical* names, a consequence that would have been impossible at their joint baptism. Aemelia is at some pains to rectify this problem, at least in psychological terms; and if we cannot see her insistence upon the banquet in the Abbey as a determination literally to re-name her sons, we surely recognize the event as a fit occasion for her to clarify (and codify) who and what they are.[18] Just as in sacramental terms baptism must precede marriage, so too a clear and secure notion of self must precede the hope of marital harmony. It is this process of reclamation that Aemelia begins at her gossips' feast inside the Abbey, a family banquet on which all other feasts—with whatever social, moral, or psychological meaning they may acquire—so heavily depend. After so long marital grief, Aemelia's family needs nothing more than the spiritual nativity and personal stability conferred by the sacrament. It is this need that they ratify in the play's final and most joyously comic banquet.

Notes

[1] C. L. Barber and Richard P. Wheeler, *The Whole Journey: Shakespeare's Power of Development* (Berkeley: Univ. of California Press, 1986), p. 68. See also E. M. W. Tillyard, *Shakespeare's Early Comedies* (New York: Barnes & Noble, 1965), pp. 54-55, and Marvin Felheim and Philip Traci, *Realism in Shakespeare's Romantic Comedies* (Washington: Univ. Press of America, 1980), pp. 14-15.

[2] So glossed in *The Riverside Shakespeare* (p. 85) and in other texts. However, some editors, like Foakes, gloss "default" simply as "offence" or "fault" (p. 15).

[3] For an impressive examination of the connection between food and sexual aggression in Shakespeare see Janet Adelman, " 'Anger's My Meat': Feeding, Dependency, and Aggression in *Coriolanus,*" in *Shakespeare: Pattern of Excelling Nature,* ed. David Bevington and Jay L. Halio (Newark: Univ. of Delaware Press, 1978), pp. 108-24. See also the Ephesian Dromio's remarks at I.ii.82-90.

[4] William Harrison, *The Description of England,* ed. Georges Edelen (Ithaca: Cornell Univ. Press, 1968), p. 140. Subsequent references to Harrison are noted parenthetically.

[5] Lu Emily Pearson, *Elizabethans at Home* (Stanford: Stanford Univ. Press, 1957); M. St. Clare Byrne, *Elizabethan Life in Town and Country* (Boston: Houghton Mifflin, 1926). Subsequent references to both works are noted parenthetically.

[6] Note, for example, the following lines from Ben Jonson's "To Penshurst," in which the poet praises the hospitality of Sir Robert Sidney, Viscount Lisle, and his wife Barbara Gamage:

> That found King James when, hunting late this way
> With his brave son, the Prince, they saw thy fires
> Shine bright on every hearth as the desires
> Of thy Penates had been set on flame
> To entertain them; or the country came
> With all their zeal to warm their welcome here.
> What (great, I will not say, but) sudden cheer
> Didst thou then make 'em! and what praise was heaped
> On thy good lady then! who therein reaped
> The just reward of her high housewifery;
> To have her linen, plate, and all things nigh,
> When she was far; and not a room but dressed
> As if it had expected such a guest!
> 　　　　　　　　　　　　　　　　(lines 76-88)

[7] Pearson discusses a further "ceremonial" aspect of Elizabethan dining regarding the basin: "If different ranks were not represented at table, one basin was frequently used for a small company, two or three washing their hands at the same time, but if guests of various ranks were present, there must be one basin for each rank, and music between courses. Sir Francis Drake, for example, liked to live up to his rank even at sea, and besides observing the usual decorum, he had his meals served with the sound of trumpets and other instruments" (p. 565).

[8] The confusion brought about by two sets of identical twins allows Shakespeare to enrich his play in subtly expressive ways. For example, when Antipholus of Syracuse is called to dinner (mistakenly) by the Ephesian Dromio, the Syracusan twin's reaction both expresses his own confusion and restates the *actual* attitude of the brother for whom he is mistaken: "Hang up thy mistress! I know not thy mistress, out on thy mistress!" (II.i.67-68), and "I know . . . no house, no wife, no mistress" (II.i.71). For an influential study of the way in which the Antipholan twins reflect psychological aspects of each other, see Barbara Freedman, "Egeon's Debt: Self-Division and Self-Redemption in *The Comedy of Errors,*" *English Literary Renaissance* 10 (1980):360-83.

[9] For a provocative study of the fasting of medieval women and its usefulness as a means of criticizing, manipulating, educating, or converting family members, see Caroline Walker Bynum, *Holy Feast and Holy Fast: The Religious Significance of Food to Medieval Women* (Berkeley: Univ. of California Press, 1987), particularly chapters 6 and 7 (pp. 189-244).

[10] The question of the relative ages of the two Antipholuses is a vexed one, since Egeon's comments in I.i on the issue seem to contradict each other. Many editors note Shakespeare's apparent confusion regarding which twin is the elder and, like Foakes, contend that "such conflict in details is not uncommon in Shakespeare and is not noticed on the stage" (p. 9). Addressing the problem critically, Patricia Parker has demonstrated how the "rhetorical crossing" in the relevant passage (I.i.78-85) indicates that the Syracusan twin is consistently referred to as the younger; see "Elder and Younger: The Opening Scene of *The Comedy of Errors,*" *Shakespeare Quarterly* 34 (1983):325-27. Parker's assumption is shared by most critics; see particularly Freedman (p. 368); Tillyard (p. 567); and Ralph Berry, *Shakespeare's Comedies: Explorations in Form* (Princeton: Princeton Univ. Press, 1972), pp. 28-29. The idea is implied if not expressly stated by Robert Ornstein, *Shakespeare's Comedies: From Roman Farce to Romantic Mystery* (Newark: Univ. of Delaware Press, 1986), p. 30; and by Alexander Leggatt, *Shakespeare's Comedy of Love* (London: Methuen, 1974), pp. 6-7.

[11] Mary Douglas, "Deciphering a Meal," *Daedalus* 101, 1 (Winter 1972):61-81; Levi-Strauss, *The Origins of Table Manners. Introduction to a Science of Mythology,* 3 vols., trans. John and Doreen Weightmann (New York: Harper & Row, 1978), *passim,* but particularly 3:54-59 where Levi-Strauss discusses the myth of the "clinging woman" which has certain curious analogies to the relationship between Antipholus of Ephesus and Adriana. See also, Kurt W. Back, "Food, Sex and Theory," *Nutrition and Anthropology in Action,* ed. Thomas K. Fitzgerald (Amsterdam: Van Gorcum,

1977), p. 31; and Peter Farb and George Armelagos, *Consuming Passions: The Anthropology of Eating* (Boston: Houghton Mifflin, 1980), pp. 4-5; 97-103.

[12] Farb and Armelagos note that "At marriage celebrations in northern Europe during the Middle Ages, it was considered an important moment when the couple ate together" (p. 5).

[13] See particularly Freedman's essay mentioned above, and Berry (p.176). Also of interest in this regard is William C. Carroll, *The Metamorphoses of Shakespearean Comedy* (Princeton: Princeton Univ. Press, 1985), pp. 68-77.

[14] Sir Hugh Plat, *Delightes for Ladies,* ed. G. E. Fussell and Kathleen Rosemary Fussell (London: Crosby Lockwood & Son, 1948); all references to Plat's work are to this edition and are noted parenthetically. See also Pearson, pp. 213, 403, 409, and 413. Of interest too are the remarks of George Herbert in *A Priest to the Temple or, The Country Parson* (1652) where the necessary characteristics of a good parson's wife are set forth in some detail. Herbert lists three separate qualities that such a woman must possess, among them expertise in "curing, and healing of all wounds and sores with her owne hands; which skill either she brought with her, or he [the parson] takes care she shall learn it of some religious neighbor." See *The Works of George Herbert,* ed. F. E. Hutchinson (Oxford: Clarendon Press, 1941), p. 239.

[15] References to Thomas Tusser are from *Five Hundred Points of Good Husbandry . . . together with A Book of Huswifery,* ed. William Mavor (London: Lackington, Allen, 1812). Also of interest is George Walton Williams, "Shakespeare's Metaphors of Health: Food, Sport, and Life-Preserving Rest," *JMRS* 14 (1984):187-202; and Owsei Temkin, "Nutrition from Classical Antiquity to the Baroque," in *Human Nutrition: Historic and Scientific,* ed. Iago Galdston (New York: International Univ. Press, 1960), pp. 78-97. Temkin points out that the concept of "diet" comprised not only food and drink "but also work, sleep, climate of the home, emotions, and sexual life, i.e., what the medieval doctors came to call the six *res non-naturales,* the six 'non-naturals'" (p. 83).

[16] Alexander Leggatt, *Shakespeare's Comedy of Love* (London: Methuen, 1974), pp. 9, 18.

[17] In *Action is Eloquence: Shakespeare's Language of Gesture* (Cambridge, MA: Harvard Univ. Press, 1984), David Bevington discusses the theatrical centrality of the banquet in several Shakespearean plays, most notably *Macbeth, Timon of Athens, Titus Andronicus,* and *Troilus and Cressida,* where the "ceremony of feasting represents not so much God's gift of charity" as a failed ritual of reincorporation that presents a "disillu-

sioned view of lifeless artificiality" (p. 159). As Bevington notes, the "violence and hypocrisy" underlying banqueting in these plays serves importantly to heighten its moral opposite—the "regular form and sense of hospitable order" that a communal feast implies (pp. 159-60). For an elaboration of the idea of inverted feasting in *Macbeth,* see G. Wilson Knight, *The Imperial Theme: Further Interpretations of Shakespeare's Tragedies Including the Roman Plays* (London: Methuen, 1951), ch. 5 (particularly pp. 134-41).

[18] Elizabethan and Jacobean comedies, of course, abound with concluding banquets (actual or proposed) as symbolic of social harmony and renewal. Shakespeare's *Taming of the Shrew* comes instantly to mind (but see Bevington's modifying remarks here [p. 159]), as do *The Two Gentlemen of Verona, A Midsummer Night's Dream,* and even the end of *The Merchant of Venice,* where, although "It is almost morning" Lorenzo sees Portia and Nerissa as dropping "manna in the way of starved people" (V.i.294-95). The disappearing banquet in *The Tempest* is far too richly allusive to be discussed here, but bears mentioning, as does the proposed feasting at the end of *Cymbeline* (V.v.483). All references to Shakespeare here are to *The Riverside Shakespeare.* Suffice it to say that the motif of the concluding harmonious banquet is so pervasive as to appear in plays as diverse as Peele's *Old Wives' Tale,* Dekker's *The Shoemaker's Holiday,* and Jonson's *Every Man in His Humor* and, most notably, *Bartholomew Fair.*

GENRE AND STRUCTURE

Gwyn Williams (essay date 1964)

SOURCE: "*The Comedy of Errors* Rescued from Tragedy," in *A Review of English Literature,* Vol. 5, No. 4, October, 1964, pp. 63-71.

[*In this essay, Williams discusses tragic elements of* The Comedy of Errors, *arguing that the play comes extremely close to being a tragedy.*]

There is no need to insist on or to exemplify the way in which *The Comedy of Errors* has until recently been considered a farce. Coleridge thought it so and on the stage the play has usually been taken as a romp.[1] (Shakespeare producers must have their secret list of comedies which may or may not be taken as pantomime.) A careful analysis of this play, however, shows that it might easily have worked out as a tragedy.

Shakespeare criticism has from Meres to the present day been misled by the pedantic division of drama into comedy or tragedy. Even Dr. Johnson, who admitted the appeal from criticism to nature, who observed the

mingling of the comic and the serious in everyday life and who said, "Shakespeare's plays are not in the rigorous sense either tragedies or comedies, but compositions of a distinct kind, exhibiting the real state of sublunary nature,"[2] even such a perceptive mind was too steeped in conventional ways of thinking not to protest occasionally against incongruities he found in Shakespeare's plays.

The incongruities in *The Comedy of Errors* have sidetracked the critics, who have preferred to consider the play as a farce which is spoilt by the injudicious introduction of serious material. Dowden was perhaps the most sympathetic in seeing the approach to tragedy in the play. For Quiller-Couch the play fell to the ground between farce and romance.[3] To H. B. Charlton the introduction of the serious characters, Egeon, Luciana and Emilia, brings in "a range of sentiment incompatible with the atmosphere of *The Comedy of Errors,*" where the general temper of life is "crude, coarse and brutal" in his opinion.[4] G. R. Elliott seems to have been nearer to full appreciation of the nature of the play in contrasting the comic horror of mistaken identity with "the real horror of the complete identity of two human beings,"[5] R. A. Foakes discusses more fully than has previously been done the serious elements in the play, the loss and rediscovery of identity, the idea of madness in this connection, the resulting "disruption of family, personal and social relationships,"[6] witchcraft, and concludes: "The fact is that the serious elements are in some danger of going unobserved, while no one is likely to miss the fun, especially in the distorted and jazzed-up versions of the play which are commonly staged."

Now that the Stratford production,[7] surely the gayest and most intelligent within living memory, is triumphantly touring the world, it may be the moment to look further into these serious elements and the apparent incongruity that has been seen in the play. A further analysis of the play seems called for, so that the reason may emerge for Shakespeare's addition of the two Dromios to the material he took from Plautus. This in turn may throw some light on the famous incongruities.

It will then appear that Shakespeare's purpose in making this duplication was not merely to increase the comic effect by repetition of a situation on a lower plane, a device he frequently used in comedy; it was not even to enhance the fun which could be elicited from the mistaking of identities. It was to save the play as comedy, to ensure, in fact, that there should be any fun at all.

As Shakespeare conceived the situation of Antipholus of Syracuse, the young man's bewilderment might well have made him desperate and against the solemn background of Egeon's predicament any act of violence could have carried Antipholus on to tragedy. On the other hand, this might have been precipitated by Antipholus of Ephesus, the more violent of the twins. The two Dromios, however, not only provide the low humour, the backchat, the healthy indecencies; not only is their predicament kept firmly comic, but the occasional contact with Dromio of Syracuse, the only person in the play (before the final recognition by Egeon) who recognizes him for what he is, clearly saves the sanity of Antipholus of Syracuse. It is true that his meetings with Dromio of Ephesus confuse him further but they do enable him to work off some of his mental anguish in the physical drubbings he administers.

Without the two Dromios the play would hardly have had any farcical elements, except for the late introduction of Dr. Pinch, who is apt to be blown up into a music-hall act, not entirely without justification from the text. Much less a farce, the play might not even have ended as a comedy. After all, Antipholus of Ephesus had much more to go on than Othello was to have.[8]

It may be worthwhile going quickly through the play once more, to follow this thread of concern with identity, to establish the seriousness of this thread and to observe how the two Dromios, more particularly Dromio of Syracuse, pull the play back from the brink of disaster.

Act I sc. i. Egeon's identification with Syracuse threatens to cause his death. (The dangers of peripheral aspects of identity.)

The Duke's sympathy is hamstrung by his own identity as ruler (*ll.* 142-5).

Act I sc. ii. Antipholus of Syracuse must deny one part of his identity, his Syracusan origin, to preserve his goods (*ll.* 1-2).

To the losses he has already suffered he now foresees the possible complete loss of his identity. This is expressed in the telling image of the drop of water:

> I to the world am like a drop of water
> That in the ocean seeks another drop,
> Who, falling there to find his fellow forth,
> Unseen, inquisitive, confounds himself.
> So I, to find a mother and a brother,
> In quest of them, unhappy, lose myself.
>
> (*ll.* 35-40)

Dromio of Ephesus now appears and confuses him. He puts this down to witchcraft.

Act II sc. i. According to Luciana, the personality and will of a woman should be subjugated to that of her husband. Men, she says,

> Are masters to their females, and their lords:
> Then let your will attend on their accords.
>
> (*ll.* 24-5)

(Katharina says something very similar at the end of *The Taming of the Shrew,* when she has become a quite different person from the girl everyone knew and whom we saw at the beginning of the play.)

Act II sc. ii. Antipholus of Syracuse desperately tries to find reasons for the new identity which is being thrust upon him. In Act I it was witchcraft; now it is dreams.

> What, was I married to her in my dream?
>
> (*l.* 182)

Antipholus and Dromio of Syracuse are forced to acknowledge that some change has come over them, but the similarity of their experience is a kind of comfort. A puzzling experience which is shared is not so alarming as one faced alone. Antipholus of Syracuse now sees the change as a mental one.

> *Syr. Dro.* I am transformed, master, am I not?
> *Syr. Ant.* I think thou art in mind, and so am I.
>
> (*ll.* 195-96)

A little later, as he goes in to dine with Adriana, Antipholus of Syracuse for the moment accepts his recognition by others as a person who is strange to himself. It may be worth while risking an adventure in another identity:

> Am I in earth, in heaven, or in hell?
> Sleeping or waking, mad or well advis'd?
> Known unto these, and to myself disguis'd,
> I'll say as they say, and persever so,
> And in this mist at all adventures go.
>
> (*ll.* 212-16)

Act III sc. i. It is now the turn of Antipholus of Ephesus; he is denied by his wife:

> *Adriana:* Your wife, sir knave? go, get you
>   from the door.
>
> (*l.* 64)

Dromio of Ephesus is similarly refused entrance and he also has a wife in the house. Antipholus of Ephesus is only restrained from immediate violence by the two puzzled merchants.

Act III sc. ii. Falling in love with Luciana creates a new human bond for Antipholus of Syracuse to replace those he has lost. The trouble is that this seems to involve the acceptance of a new identity and, still in the adventurous mood in which he went in to dine with his twin brother's wife, he invites Luciana to undertake his education as a new person.

Teach me, dear creature, how to think and
    speak;
Lay open to my earthy gross conceit,
Smother'd in errors, feeble, shallow, weak,
The folded meaning of your words' deceit. . . .
Are you a god? would you create me new?
Transform me then, and to your power I'll
    yield.

(*ll.* 33-6 and 39-40)

But he has not yet completely abandoned his personality, the identity he knows and clings to, and the use
of the word 'deceit' in reference to her words stresses
his awareness of the dangerous falsity of the situation.
The succeeding lines go,

But if that I am I, then well I know
Your weeping sister is no wife of mine.

(*ll.* 41-42)

Even to win this lovely girl he has no wish to lose his
identity. It is an extreme version of the surrender of
independence which to some extent love always demands. It is a tense situation for him and by no means
funny. Dromio of Syracuse also wonders whether he is
himself and is surprised to be recognized by his master:

Syr. Dro. Do you know me, sir? Am I
    Dromio? Am I your man? Am I myself?

(*l.* 72)

When his questions have been satisfactorily answered
by his master, Dromio can afford to be funny at the
expense of the fat wife who has been foisted on to
him. But no comedy, only a rather nasty situation,
sprang from Adriana's mistaking of Antipholus of
Syracuse for her husband.

At this point Antipholus and Dromio of Syracuse decide to leave Ephesus:

Syr. Ant. If everyone knows us and we know
    none,
'Tis time to trudge, pack and be gone.

(*ll.* 151-2)

For Antipholus the only temptation to remain is
Luciana, whom he now regards as a witch, relating her
to the Sirens of the *Odyssey*.

But her fair sister. . . .
Hath almost made me traitor to myself;
But lest myself be guilty to self-wrong,
I'll stop mine ears against the mermaid's song.

(*ll.* 158 and 161-3)

To love Luciana would be a form of suicide of the
identity, since it would involve acceptance of a new

one. At this point Angelo enters with the chain ordered
by Antipholus of Ephesus:

Angelo: Master Antipholus.
Syr. Ant. Ay, that's my name.

(*ll.* 163-4)

"That's my name," but not, "I'm the person you're
looking for." The name now seems to have no relation
to the person, a disturbing dissociation.

Act IV sc. iii. Antipholus of Syracuse, owing to the
confusion of the two Dromios, is still at Ephesus, show-
ered with gifts and compliments from people he does
not know, and still putting it all down to sorcery.

Syr. Ant. There's not a man I meet but doth
    salute me
As if I were their well-acquainted friend,
And every one doth call me by my name . . .
Sure these are but imaginary wiles,
And Lapland sorcerers inhabit here.

(*ll.* 1-3 and 10-11)

But he seems to be more confident of his identity now
and less fearful of losing it. It is a city of illusions, a
place notorious for witchcraft, and the sooner he and
his man are out of it the better.

And here we wander in illusions—
Some blessed power deliver us from hence!

(*ll.* 41-2)

Departure from the city would restore him to what he
was before the beginning of the play, but it would, of
course, mean death for his father. The other Antipholus's
violent attack upon his wife (Act IV sc. iv *ll.* 99-104)
shows how dangerous this confusion of identities has
become and how near to tragedy the central characters
are brought.

In Act V the explanation is unwound and all identities
are restored, but not before the Duke has commented:

I think you all have drunk of Circe's cup.

(*l.* 271)

The confusion of identity has been painful and potentially dangerous for the two Antipholuses. The denial
of identity has been most complete for Antipholus of
Syracuse, but he is in a foreign country, in a city renowned for witchcraft and sorcery, and he clings to his
reason by reminding himself of this fact. He can always get away and this he is always on the point of
doing. For Antipholus of Ephesus the case is very
different. He is in a town where he has been a person
of importance for twenty years. Quite suddenly to have
his orders disregarded by his servant, to be refused
admission to his own house and to be denied by his

own wife in broad daylight in the presence of others, to be arrested for debt and to be treated as a madman, all this makes a galling, infuriating experience for the Ephesian twin. He is a more violent character than his brother and he might quite easily have killed his wife.

It is significant that the character of Antipholus of Syracuse becomes much more important in Shakespeare's play than his counterpart in the source play by Plautus. Luciana is an addition to the story and so is the introduction of Egeon into the action. The possibilities of the story which interested Shakespeare, his recasting of it and the new elements he introduced, all led headlong towards tragedy, but he may not have felt sufficiently confident at this stage in his career as a dramatist to allow this to happen. It might have been thought too outrageous a flouting of a classical model at a time when Shakespeare was in open competition with university wits. (A similar hesitation, though in the reverse direction, is observable on Shakespeare's part in *Romeo and Juliet*, which has all the elements and atmosphere of comedy until the death of Mercutio, an event which the dramatist had reluctantly to bring about in order to give the play the promised tragic ending.)

The Comedy of Errors is an early study in the nature of personal identity. How soon does one's conception of oneself, the belief in one's own identity, break down before lack of recognition on the part of others? How far do we need others in order to have an identity at all? Is one's identity entirely dependent on the personal and social links and bonds, the ties of family, love, friendship and civic duty? In order that these questions might be tackled without in this case leading to madness and violent death, as they do in *King Lear*, Shakespeare added the twin servants. To condemn this on the grounds of improbability, as Quiller-Couch does, undersigned by Dover Wilson,[9] is to apply a standard which would not occur to one in the theatre, which is not relevant to drama or to great art of any kind. Shakespeare himself joked about this sort of criticism. "If this were play'd upon a stage now, I could condemn it as an improbable fiction."[10] It is curiously naïve to require more verisimilitude on the stage than is to be observed in life. Or perhaps absurdly sophisticated. The two Dromios of course provide a lot of fun, but this is not their main function. Whilst more often than not they unwittingly add to the confusion, they do sometimes recognize their true masters and the analysis made above shows this to be the only link that Antipholus of Syracuse has with his remembered identity, with reality. The fact that his servant is also taken for another person extends the predicament outside himself and makes it possible for him to hold the theory of witchcraft as a cause, thereby saving his reason. Antipholus of Ephesus, whom Shakespeare makes less interesting and sympathetic, is not given this comfort,

for there is little consolation for him in the fact that his servant is also refused admission to their house. This simply confirms the treachery of his wife to his mind.

There is an interesting ambivalence in the use made of Luciana. At a moment when Antipholus of Syracuse's identity seems to be disintegrating and he is in danger of losing all links with his past life, his new love for Luciana promises the building of a new bond, a new relationship to compensate for the loss of the old. But since a new identity is also involved, which is only viable in relation to her, this would be an act of treachery to his past and to the identity to which he is still clinging. Luciana is therefore a siren and a witch seducing him from his true self.

What seems to have happened in Shakespeare's handling of the story is this. He found the predicament of Antipholus of Syracuse far from farcical, but rather an opportunity to probe into the nature of personal identity. To provide another view of the problem he added to the story the ordeal of Egeon and his denial by Antipholus and Dromio of Ephesus, who of course do not know him but whom the old man takes to be those of Syracuse. The function of Luciana has already been discussed. The incongruities which have been seen in the play may be said to arise from Shakespeare's failure to accommodate the elements that really interested him in the play to a dramatic formula from which he could not yet quite escape. But since his additions to the story must indicate the nature and direction of his interest we should surely pay more attention to the serious elements in the play, without any risk, as R. A. Foakes points out, of surrendering any of the fun it offers. The Clowns in *Hamlet* are not the less funny for our considering the play to be in the main serious, nor would we enjoy the two Dromios and Dr. Pinch the less for a fuller realization of the significance of Antipholus of Syracuse.

This is not to read something into the play which is not there but to find conspicuously laid out in it a concern which is central to the writing and thought of our mid-twentieth century, the whole matter of the nature of personal identity, the study of which in *The Comedy of Errors* was kept by Shakespeare on a comic level only by the introduction of the two Dromios.

Notes

[1] For a summing up of views on the play see R. A. Foakes, *The Comedy of Errors*, Introduction, Arden edition (1962).

[2] *Johnson on Shakespeare,* ed. Raleigh (1908), p. 15.

[3] *The Comedy of Errors,* Introduction, New Cambridge edition (1962), p. xxiv.

[4] *Shakespearean Comedy* (1938), p. 70.

[5] Foakes, op. cit., p. xliii.

[6] Foakes op. cit., p. xlix.

[7] By Clifford Williams, first presented in Autumn 1962, revived in 1963 and 1964.

[8] J. R. Brown suggests in *Shakespeare and his Comedies* (1957) p. 57, another kind of seriousness, apart from considerations of identity. "No one would argue that *The Comedy of Errors* is a very profound play, but reference to Shakespeare's ideas about love's wealth and its difference from commercial wealth does suggest that its action is not merely that of a merry-go-round."

[9] *Errors,* Introduction (1962).

[10] *Twelfth Night,* III.iv. ll.127-8.

[11] Luciana is in a sense a step towards the heroines of the later romantic comedies, but she stands apart in the unusually equivocal situation Shakespeare gives her.

Vincent Petronella (essay date 1974)

SOURCE: "Structure and Theme Through Separation and Union in Shakespeare's *The Comedy of Errors,*" in *The Modern Language Review,* Vol. 69, No. 3, July, 1974, pp. 481-87.

[*In this essay, Petronella explores the structure of* The Comedy of Errors *by analyzing the dramatic function of the themes of separation and reunion.*]

Shakespeare's play of the twin Antipholuses and Dromios possesses a thematic impact that only in the last decade has been observed, measured, and enjoyed by scholars and critics who have gone further than merely discussing the play in the light of Plautus and Terence; and who, in turn, have gone beyond the question as to whether or not the play is really a farce.[1] Source-studies and genre-studies regarding *The Comedy of Errors* are indeed useful, but so much has been said about these matters that scholarly repetition has become obvious. In other words, the thematic substance of the play was not always given its due in the past; more recently, however, that substance has been shown to be sinewy enough to warrant critical analyses that clarify areas other than those related to the play's genre and sources. And just such areas do I wish to explore in the pages that follow.

It is my contention that this early Shakespearian comedy needs to be studied for the way it employs the structural pattern of separation and union—a pattern that is central to almost every comedy written, but one that informs the language, characterization, and action of *The Comedy of Errors* in a way that has not been explored in the past.[2] This basic structural pattern, moreover, underlies a complex of thematic statements and re-statements of ideas either closely or loosely related to separation and union. In *The Comedy of Errors* separation is represented by references to, and acts of, severing, untying, releasing, divorcing, freeing, and losing; these are balanced by different representations of union: binding, tying, fastening, uniting, confining, and finding. What is more, the implications of separation and union are profusely widespread. Separation, for example, becomes associated in the play with categories such as illogicality, chaos, and domestic dissolution; whereas union is linked with logic, order, and domestic stability. In the course of my discussion the dramatic polarities created by separation and union and the ramifications of such polarities within the framework of the play at hand will become clearer.

Before looking at the separation-union idea itself we should understand that another aspect of structure in *The Comedy of Errors* is the play's solid base made up of four interlocking levels of reality: family, commerce, state, and cosmos. The last of these does not have as prominent a role as do the first three; nevertheless, it *is* present; and, as we shall see, it does receive clear expression before the close of the play's third scene. In turn, the social situation (commerce and state) is not central to the play's meaning as is the domestic. Although the ties of family in the play are temporarily severed, causing, of course, separation, we see that those ties are actually extremely strong ones: brother seeks to be united with brother; son with mother; and father with son. The principal search is for the natural bonds that hold a family together as well as a search for individual members of that family. In a more general way all four levels are marked by a drive toward overcoming estrangement or division; and helping to underscore the importance of domestic, social, and cosmic ties (or the lack of them) is the separation-union antithesis, which helps to create ironies and ambiguities that make this play throb with dramatic and comic vigour. When in the denouement the ironies and ambiguities subside (meaning, of course, that the comic absurdities are at an end), a society and, more importantly, a family, are re-united. Happiness ultimately prevails in the world of the play. Just how Shakespeare effects this outcome with conviction is appreciated if we look at the separation-union pattern and its connexion with the four levels I have outlined.

Let us begin by considering the pattern on the level of state, for this situation immediately demands our attention as the play opens. Egeon, literally bound because he is under arrest, addresses the Duke of Ephesus with a couplet coloured by the tonality of tragic hopelessness:

Proceed, Solinus, to procure my fall,
And by the doom of death end woes and all.[3]

With language expressing eschatological sentiments the play begins. What sounds like a man's last words at the end of his life are actually his first words in a drama that will eventually culminate in freedom and a new lease of life. Here is Egeon, a prisoner of the state, bound by the dictates of the law of the land. Logic ties Egeon to the death-sentence that has been imposed upon him, and as the chief lawmaker and enforcer of order in Ephesus, Duke Solinus argues syllogistically in favour of that death-penalty:

. . . if any born at Ephesus
Be seen at Syracusian marts and fairs;
Again, if any Syracusian born
Come to the bay of Ephesus, he dies
His goods confiscate to the Duke's dispose,
Unless a thousand marks be levied
To quit the penalty and to ransom him.
Thy substance, valued at the highest rate,
Cannot amount unto a hundred marks;
Therefore by law thou art condemn'd to die.

(I.1.16)

Different commentators have spoken of Egeon's plight as a 'frame-story' that surrounds the frisky central action of *The Comedy of Errors*.[4] What has not been observed, however, is that Egeon is significantly bound when we first see him in the play (Act I) and when we see him again in Act V.[5] It is not only the presence of Egeon at the beginning and at the close of the play that makes him a framing figure; it is also his being seen as one tied by the legal demands of the state. In this way Egeon becomes an emblem for the idea of confinement, especially as it applies to the level of state.

Just as Egeon is put under arrest at one level of the play's action so is Angelo, the goldsmith, arrested at another. Angelo is part of the world of commerce. A bond has fallen due for the goldsmith; but because of the confusion involving the Antipholuses, Angelo cannot meet the bond. Therefore, the Second Merchant has him arrested (IV.1). This, in turn, leads to the arrest of the Ephesian Antipholus, who is held responsible for Angelo's never being paid for the gold chain. If we stop a moment to think of the thematic and symbolic complications at this point we shall see that they are real and appropriate.

At the level of commerce the word "bond" is obviously significant. But in the context of *The Comedy of Errors,* the word also suggests binding, arresting, or pulling together toward union. All of these suggestions are supported by two symbolic objects: the controversial gold chain that Antipholus of Ephesus ordered originally for his wife and the rope that the same Antipholus sends his Dromio to buy, presumably to spite Adriana.[6] Both items, the chain and the rope, become part of the general confusion at the same time that they signify the possibility of conjugal unity on the one hand and the reality of marital division on the other. Yet, although both the chain and the rope are instruments for binding, they do more to cause separation between characters. When Dromio of Syracuse comes to the wrong Antipholus bringing word of a ship sailing to Epidamnum (IV.1.86 ff.), the Ephesian scolds this Dromio for not bringing the desired rope. This friction between master and bondman comes on the heels of Angelo's being arrested for not meeting an overdue bond followed by the Ephesian Antipholus's being "attached" (IV.1.74) for not paying Angelo for the chain. Bond, bondman, legal arrests, a chain, and a rope are all of a piece when we realize that they are associated with the idea of one's being united or linked with legal responsibilities. The verbal exchange in Act IV, Scene 2 between the Syracusian Dromio and Adriana emphasizes this effectively:

Adriana What, is he [her husband] arrested?
    tell me at whose suit:
Dromio of Syracuse I know not at whose suit
    he is arrested well;
But is in a suit of buff which 'rested him, that
    can I tell:
Will you send him, mistress, redemption, the
    money in his desk?
Adriana Go, fetch it, sister; this I wonder at,
That he unknown to me should be in debt.
Tell me, was he arrested on a band?
Dromio of Syracuse Not on a band, but on a
    stronger thing;
A chain, a chain, do you not hear it ring?

(IV.2.43)

Hardin Craig points out that the words "bond" and "band" are interchangeable and that at line 50, the word 'band' also means manacle or dog-leash.[7] Being linked or united with legal responsibilities is made obviously stronger by such a pun drawn from the world of pets as well as from that of commerce.

The Courtesan is also a character who may be associated with commerce. In the past she was the subject of divisive altercations between Antipholus and his wife (III.1.111-13), and in the present action the spiteful Antipholus will use the Courtesan as a way of separating himself from Adriana, threatening to give the chain to the 'hostess' instead of to his wife.[8] The chain that was to unite husband and wife becomes symbolic of estrangement in marriage. Antipholus of Ephesus would substitute the rope for the chain, the cheaper object for the more valuable, the Courtesan for his wife. The figure of the Ephesian Antipholus positioned between the Courtesan and Adriana embodies a connexion between the level of commerce and that of family. State, commerce, and family are all

Act V, scene i. Egion, the Duke, Adriana, Dromio of Ephesus, Antipholus of Ephesus. Frontispiece to the Rowe edition (1709).

part of the action in Act IV, Scene 4. Here are an arresting Officer (representing the order of state), the Courtesan (representing her particular brand of commercial interests), and the two sisters, Adriana and Luciana. The Officer has Antipholus of Ephesus figuratively bound by legal arrest, Dromio of Ephesus comes in with the by now ridiculous rope, and the three women (Adriana, Luciana, and the Courtesan) bring in Doctor Pinch, the local conjurer, to separate Antipholus from the devil. If binding and separating were ever made farcical, here it is as robustly done as could be imagined. The outcome of the scene is the Ephesian Antipholus's and Dromio's being tied up and taken off stage. In the meantime the Syracusian Antipholus (with his repier drawn) and Dromio enjoy severed ties and are making ready to flee from the witchery of Ephesus.[9] The action of this bustling scene culminates in presenting the two sets of twins in situations that parallel their states at the outset of the drama. The Ephesian Antipholus and Dromio were bound to their domestic responsibilities when we first saw them; now they are literally bound by the state and by Pinch's would-be assistants in the absurd exorcism, which includes literal binding.[10] In the beginning the Syracusian Antipholus and Dromio were free wanderers; now they are again relatively free and desirous of getting out of Ephesus.[11] This situation acts as a frame within the more obvious frame-story of Egeon's legal difficulties.

Thus far we have observed separation or union operating on two levels: state and commerce. I have touched briefly on a third level, the family, and should like now to discuss it at greater length. To begin let us dwell for a moment on Egeon's fine expository speech in the opening scene of the play. I think it significant that the father of the Antipholuses has the opening lines of *The Comedy of Errors,* for his remarks are followed immediately by those of the 'father' of the dukedom, Solinus. The father of the Family and the father of the State are the only voices we hear throughout the first scene. Duke Solinus is interested in maintaining order and, therefore, is united—indeed equated—with the state as a responsible leader. Egeon, on the other hand, has been separated from his family and, as a result, searches desperately for the bonds of whatever family is left him. Egeon's family, as far as the old man knows, is made up of himself and the Syracusian Antipholus. Ironically his quest for his son will lead to his finding a complete family, but when we first see Egeon he is a man estranged from his loved ones. He is alone. And undergirding the sense of isolation is that wonderful description of what happened at sea many years ago (I.1.62-118). This is an extremely important passage, for it provides the basic dramatic setting and preparation for separation and union in the play. Egeon's speech, with its talk of retaining (line 65), embracing (69), fastening (79 and 85), binding (81), fixing (twice in 84), dispersing (89), meeting (100), splitting (103), divorcing (101), seizing

(112), and severing (118), is the dramatic generator that provides the strong alternating current of tying and untying that we detect flowing through *The Comedy of Errors*. Egeon's speech, for example, sets in motion the dramatic-thematic contrast between sets of characters such as the 'tied' Antipholus of Ephesus and the united Antipholus of Syracuse. The lengthy passage also prepares us for the contrast between Adriana, who is united in marriage with the Ephesian brother, and Luciana, who is single and united.

Ironically it is Luciana, the "free" sister, who speaks conservatively, rationally, and restrictively, as it were. This is to say that Luciana's general demeanour is united with reason, whereas Adriana's is separated from reason by the passions of jealousy and matrimonial despair.[12] Where Adriana represents a force that pushes domestic affairs toward separation and dissolution, Luciana embodies unifying Order. No other character (apart, perhaps, from Duke Solinus of Ephesus) speaks as does Luciana for the coherence attainable through order.[13] Her speech to Adriana in Act II is a clear indication of this:

> *Luciana* A man is master of his liberty;
> Time is their master, and when they see time,
> They'll go or come; if so, be patient, sister.
> *Adriana* Why should their liberty than ours
>   be more?
> *Luciana* Because their business still lies out
>   o'door.
> *Adriana* Look, when I serve him so, he takes
>   it ill.
> *Luciana* O, know he is the bridle of your
>   will.
> *Adriana* There's none but asses will be
>   bridled so.
> *Luciana* Why, headstrong liberty is lash'd
>   with woe.
> There's nothing situate under heaven's eye
> But hath his bound in earth, in sea, in sky.
> The beasts, the fishes, and the winged fowls
> Are their males' subjects, and at their
>   controls;
> Man, more divine, the master of all these,
> Lord of the wide world and wild wat'ry seas,
> Indued with intellectual sense and souls,
> Of more pre-eminence than fish and fowls,
> Are masters to their females, and their lords:
> Then let your will attend on their accords.
>
>   (II.1.7)

These lines by Luciana apply to the level of family, in particular to the relationship between man and wife. What is more, the passage is a brilliant statement of man's relationship to the order of nature or the cosmos. A man is unbound as far as his personal liberty is concerned, argues Luciana, but time binds man to the ever-turning wheel of things. Woman, like the beasts, fishes, and birds, is subservient to man in nature's cosmic plan. Luciana's speech on degree is spoken seriously and is to be taken as such. Shakespeare, at this early point in his play, aptly sketches in the Elizabethan world picture, which represents the greater logic to be contrasted with the absurd illogic that occurs in Ephesus during the course of several hours.

Luciana's sister characterizes herself through an even longer speech—one that also has a philosophical cast about it. Adriana's magnificent speech (II.2.113-46), a complaint to the Antipholus she mistakenly believes is her negligent husband, is filled with commentary on the discomfort of being separated from a loved one. And like the expository speech of Egeon in Act I, Adriana's lines here are packed with words and phrases sounding the separation-union motif: "touch" (line 116), "touch'd" (118), "estranged" (120), "strange" (121), "undividable" (122), "incorporate" (122), "tear away" (124), "the breaking gulf" (126), "unmingled" (127), "cut" (137), "deep-divorcing" (138), "mingled" (141), "keep . . . league and truce" (145). Through this juxtaposing of references to uniting and dividing, stylistic tension is made to carry emotional intensity. Adriana is pessimistic throughout this speech, but she uses the water-drop image (l. 127) not to speak hopelessly of separation (as does the Syracusian Antipholus in 1.2.35-40) but to emphasize the strength of the unifying bond that exists between man and wife. Therefore, as much as Adriana has to say about dissolution or the breaking of ties, she is at least very much aware of the cords that join two people in married love.

The bond between husband and wife is dramatized not only by what Luciana or Adriana says but also by what Egeon and Emilia experience at the end of the play.[14] After several years of separation they once again enjoy being together. Separation has given way to union in their fortunate case after Egeon is united by the state and Emilia leaves the confines of the priory. The Abbess says:

> Whoever bound him, I will loose his bonds,
> And gain a husband by his liberty.
>
> (V.1.339)

Similarly, Antipholus of Ephesus and Adriana are rebound after the husband is untied by the arresting Officer and the wife frees herself of stifling jealousy. And now for the Syracusian Antipholus and Luciana a presumably happy marriage is in the offing, especially in view of their freedom to marry, Antipholus's willingness to bind himself to "this fair gentlewoman" (V.1.373), and Luciana's outspoken advocacy of the binding doctrine of degree. Topping off the renewal of family ties between mother and father, husbands and wives, parents and children is the symbolic gesture of the two Dromios who leave the stage with the hand of

one brother bound to the hand of the other. A more effective parallel to the re-uniting of the Antipholuses as well as a more suitable conclusion to this drama would be hard to imagine.

Shakespeare's purpose, then, in using the separation-union idea is to establish a patterned structure that not only reflects but also becomes the overall plot-movement of the play. In addition, Shakespeare both fleshes out the fundamental separation-union pattern and communicates its archetypal comic value thematically through words, motifs, and visual action. *The Comedy of Errors* portrays relative confinement giving way to freedom and past separation being replaced by present reunion. The separation-union antithesis contributes to the play several pulsating and bewildering ironies; but fortunately these ironies are easy to live with, especially when, on the one hand, they are responsible for creating robust comedy and, on the other, they finally become subordinated to the preservation of cosmos, state, commerce, and family as well as to the attainment of the freedom to enjoy these same four levels of human reality. This is what *The Comedy of Errors* offers us through its rendering of the structural-thematic pattern I have analysed. The play does its work not by means of senseless antics and heavy-handed sentimentality but by producing clear-sighted comedy that is not afraid to enhance its vision with an occasional sojourn into farce.

Notes

[1] A brief account of recent criticism of the play appears in the note at the end of this article.

[2] In his posthumous *Shakespeare's Early Comedies* (London, 1965), E. M. W. Tillyard comes close to my view of the play (pp. 65-6), but he does not develop the idea beyond a single paragraph.

[3] All textual references are to the new Arden edition of the play edited by R. A. Foakes (London, 1962).

[4] See the following works cited in the note at the end of this article: the essay by C. L. Barber in *College English,* p. 496; Harold Brooks's article in *Early Shakespeare,* p. 56; and Tillyard's *Shakespeare's Early Comedies,* pp. 52-4. See also Bertrand Evans, *Shakespeare's Comedies* (Oxford, 1960), p. 8; Blaze O. Bonazza's *Shakespeare's Early Comedies* (The Hague, 1966), pp. 20-1; and especially Ernest W. Talbert's *Elizabethan Drama and Shakespeare's Early Plays* (Chapel Hill, North Carolina, 1963), pp. 144-9.

[5] In Act I, Egeon is presumably bound in the literal sense; in Act V, Dromio tells us that Egeon is literally bound (V.1.294).

[6] The fullest discussion to date of the chain and rope as symbols in the play is in Richard Henze's "*The Comedy of Errors:* 'A Freely Binding Chain' " *Shakespeare Quarterly,* 21 (1971), 35-41. For other comments on the chain as symbol in *The Comedy of Errors* see Cutts (pp. 15, 18-20), Bonazza (p. 31), and Tillyard (pp. 65-6). A negative and somewhat myopic observation comes from Mark Van Doren when he says that the chain "achieves no effect resembling that achieved by two plain words, 'the handkerchief', in a scene to come . . ." (*Shakespeare* (New York, 1939; reprinted 1953), p. 36).

[7] *The Complete Works of Shakespeare* (Chicago, 1961), p. 93, note 49.

[8] Some confusion exists as to whether the "hostess" of the Porpentine (III.1.116-19) and the Courtesan are indeed one and the same person. Balthasar suggests that Antipholus of Ephesus dine with him at the Tiger (111.1.95), and the Ephesian twin replies: "I know a wench of excellent discourse, Pretty and witty; wild and yet, too, gentle; There will we dine" (III.1.109). Does Antipholus mean that the "wench of excellent discourse" (clearly meaning the Courtesan) is available at the Tiger and not at the Porpentine? Or is he somewhat distracted at this point, thinking of the Courtesan and his plan to spite Adriana while he accepts the invitation to the Tiger, thereby juxtaposing the Tiger and the Courtesan in psychological confusion? I say no to the first question and yes to the second. The "hostess" and the Courtesan are the same person. For further substantiation, see the continuation of the chain incident (IV.3.43-5). There is no question as to the Courtesan's connexion with the world of commerce, which encompasses more obviously characters such as Egeon, Angelo the goldsmith, Balthasar, the First Merchant, and the Second Merchant. Interestingly, Egeon is a link between the levels of family, state, and commerce in that he is a father, a prisoner of the state, and a merchant.

[9] Foakes (pp. 113-15) offers a convenient tabulation of the relationship between Ephesian occultism, St Paul's account of it, and Shakespeare's apparent use of the relevant biblical passages.

[10] Doctor Pinch is himself forcibly subjected to binding, according to the Messenger (V.1.170).

[11] Significantly, the First Folio refers to the Syracusian Antipholus as "Erotes" (a possible corruption of *erraticus,* "wandering"). Foakes discusses this in his edition of the play (pp. xi-xxi and p. 12; see his opening notes to Act I, Scene 2).

[12] Especially relevant is II.1.86-116.

[13] Shakespeare gives Adriana's sister (a character not found in the Plautine source) the name Luciana, which derives from *lux.* This suits one so clear-sighted and high-principled. She is even called "fair sun" (III.2.56). Adriana's maid, Luce, also has a name that derives from *lux;* but this name becomes significant by way of pun (assuming an Anglicized pronunciation), not by way of association with the light of reason and virtue. Luce appears briefly in Act III, Scene 1, where she is twice called "minion" (here meaning hussy) and once "baggage" (ll. 54, 57, 59). And her reply to the Antipholus seeking entry into his house is coarse and bawdy: "Let him knock till it ache" (l. 58). In a dozen or so lines, then, Adriana's maid is linked with loose principles—hence her name. Whereas Luce is apparently separated from the moral norm, Luciana is bound to that norm. (Compare the looseness of Luce in this play with the far more fully realized looseness of Lucio in *Measure for Measure.*)

[14] In *A Natural Perspective: The Development of Shakespearean Comedy and Romance* (New York, 1965), Northrop Frye writes: "the central theme is the reunion, not of the twins, but of their father and mother" (p. 87). In this way *The Comedy of Errors* anticipates the dramatic romances at the close of Shakespeare's career. See also John Dover Wilson, *Shakespeare's Happy Comedies* (London, 1962), p. 40, and H. B. Charlton, *Shakespearian Comedy,* p. 72.

Eamon Grennan (essay date 1980)

SOURCE: "Arm and Sleeve: Nature and Custom in *The Comedy of Errors,*" in *Philological Quarterly,* Vol. 59, No. 2, Spring, 1980, pp. 150-64.

[*In this essay, Grennan argues that* The Comedy of Errors *is structured by a dialectic between the concepts of nature and custom.*]

In the midst of the comic jostling that gives life to "perhaps the most uncomplicatedly funny of all Shakespeare's plays,"[1] lurk a theme and a "structural idea"[2] serious enough to command attention not only for the light they cast on this play but for the first sight they give of a concern that was to persist throughout Shakespeare's work. The dialectic of nature and custom variously repeated in the theme, structure, and language of *The Comedy of Errors* offers, for all its sober overtones, a way into the play that is true to its textual and theatrical possibilities, and provides yet another hint of the integrity and continuity of Shakespeare's imaginative vision.

A brief example of the relationship may be found in the two speeches of Luciana. Since Adriana's sister is Shakespeare's most substantial single addition to his sources her very presence presumably betrays some important emphases this creative adaptation is designed to carry. When, further, the dramatist gives this invented character two dramatically important speeches containing contradictory views of the same subject, it is arguable that they reveal something of what he thought was central to the play's meaning. In fact, as far as the present argument is concerned, the ramifications of Luciana's opposed views of marriage leave few aspects of the play untouched.

To edify, indeed to pacify, her incensed sister, Luciana invokes the customary relationship between men and women in marriage as a manifestation of the cardinal law of nature. In doing so, she employs a traditionally sanctioned mode of analogy:

> There's nothing situate under heaven's eye
> But hath his bound in earth, in sea, in sky.
> The beasts, the fishes, and the winged fowls
> Are their males' subjects, and at their
>   controls;
> Man, more divine, the master of all these,
> Lord of the wide world and wild wat'ry
>   seas,
> Indued with intellectual sense and souls,
> Of more pre-eminence than fish and fowls,
> Are masters to their females, and their lords:
> Then let your will attend on their accords.
>
> (II.i.16-25)[3]

This eloquent secular sermon on degree paints in miniature what E. M. W. Tillyard has ensured will always be known as "the Elizabethan World Picture." It represents a world of meticulous symmetries, as esthetically rigid ("situate") as the solid couplets themselves. Fixture is the defining mark of this world. By insisting that nature possess the esthetic shapes it is the business of custom to impose upon the world, Luciana implicitly identifies customary truths and the laws of nature. The world and all that is in it run to the dictates of decorum, a single principle governing all aspects of reality. "Decorum," as a recent critic puts it, "was thought to be natural order as perceived by the senses or the aesthetic imagination."[4] The unitary mode of perception at work here subsumes the human order of custom into the more comprehensive, magisterial order of nature, "that manner of working which God hath set for each created thing to keepe."[5]

When Luciana later lectures the man she assumes to be the husband Antipholus on the same subject, however, the picture she provides is a radically different one (III.ii.1-28). Now what she calls "A husband's office" is a question less of cosmic determinism than circumstantial pragmatism. Hortatory piety cedes to practical considerations:

> If you did wed my sister for her wealth,
> Then for her wealth's sake use her with more
>   kindness;

> Or if you like elsewhere, do it by stealth,
> Muffle your false love with some show of
>   blindness.
>
> (4-7)

Mutability penetrates the fixed hierarchical picture of the world; marriage may suffer a seasonal fate ("shall, Antipholus, / Even in the spring of love, thy love-springs rot?" [2-3]). Without meaning to, Luciana severs the institution of marriage from all external supports and leaves it the naked human convention it is, a device to order in a decorous way, no matter what the inner truth, the surface appearances of sexual relationships:

> Look sweet, speak fair, become disloyalty;
> Apparel vice like virtue's harbinger;
> Bear a fair presence, though your heart be
>   tainted;
> Be secret false; what need she be acquainted?
> Though others have the arm, show us the
>   sleeve.
>
> (11-23)

The repeated use of clothes imagery stresses the emphatic superficiality of this custom: false love should be muffled, vice should be appareled as its opposite, and the "arm" of true love may be replaced in a way that is conventionally adequate by the pathetic "sleeve" of marital hypocrisy. Acceptable external show ought in such cases to misrepresent inner truth. Conventional appearances no longer reflect a natural design of universal nobility; instead, they are the decorous mask of human deceit, transforming the "Lord of the wide world" into a small-time Machiavel of marital politics. As the couplets of the earlier speech give way to the slightly more flexible quatrains of this one, a binary mode of perception capable of splitting custom irrevocably from nature replaces the unitary mode that identified them. Put more simply, the commonplaces of experience usurp the commonplaces of theory.

Between them these two speeches force us, it seems to me, to consider the relationship between nature and custom as it may appear elsewhere in the play, and to ask whether the play takes us beyond the unresolved dialectic with which this unit leaves us.

The theme of *The Comedy of Errors* has been variously described as "the loss of identity,"[6] the quest for identity,[7] the possessiveness of love,[8] and "Relationship between human beings, depending on their right relationship to truths and universal law."[9] These are all worthwhile, if partial, insights into the play. To them I would add my own claim, that the mainspring of the comic action is a conflict between what is customary (or, as I shall also call it, conventional) and what is natural. The very premise on which the comedy stands, for example, suggests no less. All the characters accept the truth of the assumption that identical appearances betoken identical realities. The facts as we know them, and they experience them, conventionally disprove this, however, and our amusement in part is a result of our witnessing such conventional assumptions short-circuited by factual truths. The play is punctuated by enough collisions to establish a structural rhythm, dividing the action into units that repeat this fundamental event.

The emblematic opening incident, for example, draws our attention insistently to two things: the arbitrary implacability of the law (custom carried to its dogmatic extremity), and the natural sympathy evoked by the pathetic figure of the condemned old man. It is, Solinus tells Egeon, "by law thou art condemn'd to die" (I.i.25); this law is itself the result of other "rigorous statutes" (9); the Duke would show clemency "were it not against our laws," and "passed sentence may not be recall'd" (142, 147). On the other hand, Egeon's long, woeful narrative, locked between the calculatedly "tragic" couplets with which he opens and closes the scene, is designed to move an audience to sympathetic grief. Like the Duke, the audience is compelled to experience in an almost ritualistic manner the tension between custom and nature. Abiding sorrowfully by the first all must nonetheless recognize the claims of the second, and grieve at how the pathetic fluency of the individual (externalized in the image of the quest) is subject to the ethic confinement of the law.

Other examples of this structural unit abound. Act I, Scene ii, for example, begins with an overtly civil conversation between Antipholus of Syracuse and the First Merchant. Their exchange is stuffed with social phenomena (mart, merchants, money, statutes, manners, buildings, inns, meal-times, masters and servants, a dinner invitation) and marked by the mannerly tone of polite social gesture ("I crave your pardon," "please you," "Sir, I commend you to your own content" [2-32]. Left alone, however, Antipholus utters a speech that unravels the tightly woven fabric of this secure social world, replacing its fixity, its confident conventional identity with his own mysterious sensation of non-being:

> I to the world am like a drop of water
> That in the ocean seeks another drop.
> Who, falling there to find his fellow forth,
> (Unseen, inquisitive) confounds himself.
>
>   (I.ii.35-38)

Such undermining of the customary world continues to the end of the scene. Dromio's breathless language and behavior must seem to Antipholus to be anarchic, 'natural.' They erode the conventional master-slave relationship ("these jests are out of season, / Reserve them till a merrier hour than this" 67-68) and in

Antipholus' baffled consciousness transform a solid, understandable environment of merchants, good manners, and fine buildings into a nightmare refuge of "jugglers that deceive the eye," sorcerers, witches, mountebanks, and cheats (95-105).

Act II, Scene i exemplifies the same structural pattern. There, in opposition to the custom-sanctioned picture of the world offered by Luciana (see above), Adriana asserts the nature of her own hurt self; the promptings of private pain force her to reject the fixed, public version of reality expressed by her sister: "They can be meek that have no other cause" (II.i.33). The first encounter between Adriana and Antipholus of Syracuse (II.ii.110 ff.) also confirms the operation of this structural paradigm. Antipholus' freshly restored confidence in the world's customary solidity (achieved by means of a word-game, a conventional way of relating with his slave, 70-109) is rudely shattered by the greeting of his supposed wife. His grasp on reality takes on the confused, fragmentary qualities of a dream (181-84); his servant imagines he has been dropped into a "fairy land"; and their perception of reality as ruled by transformation (nature run riot) is balanced by Adriana's opposite sense (seen in her repeated references to "husband") of reality restored to its norms. For her the world resumes its customary shape; for him it has become a region of dreadful obscurity (212), a place of mist and error where even his own condition ("Sleeping or waking, mad or well advis'd" [213]) must be doubted.

A variant of the same pattern appears in the first sequence concerning Antipholus of Ephesus. His conversation with Balthasar the Merchant is marked by super-polite platitudes, molded to a metric that augments our sense of the exchange as a procession of stylized social postures:

> *Bal.* Good meat, sir, is common; that every
> churl affords.
> *Ant.* And welcome more common, for that's
> nothing but words.
>
>   (III.i.24-25)

This calm social equilibrium is seriously (and hilariously) upset, however, when Antipholus is rejected by his own world. The natural violence of his response ("Go fetch me something, I'll break open the gate" [73]) is only mollified by Balthasar's reminder regarding all the conventional reasons (his reputation, his wife and honor, slander) for not resorting to such tactics (85-106). Even in the depths of the comic occasion, the dialectical tension between nature and custom endures.

The same tension marks the encounter between Antipholus of Syracuse and Luciana. To her conventional advice regarding how to fit the role of faithful husband (see above) he opposes his own natural passion ("Transform me, then, and to your power I'll yield" [III.ii.40]). In turn, even the conventional literary quality of his amorous assault is comically and almost immediately deflated by Dromio's description of Nell. Succeeding the conventional furniture of sirens, "silver waves," and "golden hairs," comes the grotesquely natural phenomenon of Nell, her body a cartographer's bad dream, with the bogs of Ireland in her buttocks, Spain in her hot breath, and the Indies "upon her nose, all o'er-embellished with rubies, carbuncles, sapphires," (80-145). It is true that, as Shakespeare's Sonnet 130 ("My mistress' eyes") and Donne's Elegy VIII ("The Comparison") show, the deflation of Petrarchan sentiment by underlining the woman's physical features is itself a recognizable convention. In the present case, however, what is on the aesthetic level a conflict between conventions (Petrarchism and anti-Petrarchism jostling one another) is on the substantial level a collision between the "natural" and "customary" in female beauty. It is true too that the use of geographical imagery at this point is also conventional (see Donne's Elegy XVIII, "Love's Progress"). But by its means the playwright instructs the audience in the opposition between conventionally elevating ways of perceiving the woman and her more naturally physical aspects.

As the play proceeds, the dialectic of custom and nature intensifies. By the fourth act the 'natural' side so threatens the whole world of the play that it must be opposed by the strictest of all social conventions, the law. Subject to the natural imperatives of weather and tide (IV.i.33, 46), the Second Merchant initiates a sequence in which Angelo and Antipholus of Ephesus are arrested for debt. In the course of this sequence (IV.i.1-85) the customary niceties of social behavior buckle under the pressures of natural belief and natural anger, as Antipholus' address of the Goldsmith declines from "good signior" through "sir" and "fellow" to "sirrah" (36, 43, 76, 82). Even the strictly conventional Luciana manifests one touch of nature, admitting that "in an honest suit" Antipholus' words "might move" (IV.ii.14). By this, while the structural pattern still operates, the relationship between its components has grown more complex, so that customary and conventional aspects of the world are themselves understood as natural deceptions. Antipholus of Syracuse, for example, in his description of how the Ephesians treat him, reveals the conventional life of the citizens:

> Some tender money to me, some invite me,
> Some other give me thanks for kindnesses,
> Some offer me commodities to buy.
>
> (IV:iii.4-6)

His fearful response to such behavior, however, immediately short-circuits its customary implications: he becomes the prey of natural confusion, convinced that such conventionality is mere deceit: "These are but

imaginary wiles, / And Lapland sorcerers inhabit here" (10-11). From the perspective of his terror, the conventional world he evokes is instantly devalued, a point made most explicit when, in a crowning touch to this sequence, his conventionally pious invocation "Some blessed power deliver us from hence" (42) is answered by the entrance of nature in the flesh—the Courtesan.

As the dialectic becomes more and more unbalanced in the direction of nature even that most conventional of men, Antipholus of Ephesus, must begin to lose his grip. At the beginning of IV.iv., however, he is still trying to explain the inexplicable in customary terms: the remarkable events are the result of his wife's "wayward mood" (his first words about her in the play are that she is "shrewish" [III.i.2]). However, when his servant, whom he "knows" has sent for redemption money returns instead with a rope, his threshold of conventionality is crossed and he gives in to his natural outrage by beating the unfortunate Dromio. With the entrance of his wife, her sister, the Courtesan, and Dr. Pinch, his outrage descends into what can only to the others appear natural madness: furiously he calls his wife "strumpet," strikes poor Pinch, struggles with his captors, and physically bound to a slave who is, as Dromio reminds us, bound to him by convention, is finally carried from the stage. In this welter of violent action (the women are driven from the stage by the "return" of the other Antipholus and Dromio) the calm assumptions of custom and convention seem incapable of being sustained for more than a moment or two. The dramatic rhythm, in other words (structure made manifest on the stage), corresponds to a thematic progression.

Finally, the opening of Act V contains a sequence that seems to shatter this structural organization on the comic disorder of events. First the conversation between Angelo and the Second Merchant about Antipholus of Ephesus evokes the conventional city we have already seen (V.i.1-9). With the entrance of Antipholus and Dromio of Syracuse, however, the mood shifts from such civility to the threat and counter-threat of incipient violence (29-32). This violence becomes even more spectacular when Adriana, Luciana, the Courtesan, and others dash on, and a frightened Antipholus and his man rush off. At this moment of furious action, through which the lineaments of the original paradigm still faintly glimmer, the structural unit that marks the play up to this seems to have been taken as far as it will go. What remains must be dissolution or resolution, chaos or synthesis. The dramatist can conclude his plot or abandon it.

As intimated earlier, the language of *The Comedy of Errors* mirrors its action, offering its own equivalent of the structural pattern. Even a superficial reading of the comedy immediately reveals how conventional its linguistic and poetic elements are. Repeatedly, our attention seems deliberately drawn to the care with which the dramatist observes contemporary literary conventions, as though this fact were itself the point. Egeon's protracted account of his miseries (I.i.32-140) is a strict version of conventional *narratio*.[10] Its verbal postures are those of a formal oration (e.g., 33, 94, 120), insisting, as any good production will see and exploit, upon an explicitly oratorical relationship between the speaker and his two audiences. That the speech is grounded in literary custom is revealed in its opening lines, which allude to the most famous prototype of such a tale as he is telling—Aeneas' account to Dido of his misfortunes—and by the fact that his whole narration bears some "general similarity" to Virgil's.[11] The verse is almost entirely regular,[12] and Egeon's three couplets, one at the opening, another after the Duke passes sentence, and the last to close the scene, frame his narration in an obvious way, underlining its conventionally static, tableau-like quality. The sequence as a whole fulfills the conventional function of a prologue or *argumentum* (as found in Plautus' *Menaechmi*, for example), composing a frame for the entire action and granting the audience a customary comic knowledge superior to that of any of the participants.

Similar observations are applicable to the language and verse of the other set-pieces salted at regular intervals through the play. The balance of the rhetorical units that make up Luciana's advice to Adriana (II.i.15-25) matches, as I remarked earlier, the universal equilibrium that is the speech's subject. No less regular is Adriana's more emotional reply, its decisively closed couplets as *formally* conventional as her sister's. Patently conventional too is Adriana's rhetoric of abuse and self-pity. Her speeches abound in extravagant imagery, rhetorical questions, and irritable logic (e.g., II.i.96-98), as well as in the conventionally pathetic diction and imagery of emotional appeal (e.g., 100-01, 114-15). Her direct verbal assault upon her husband (II.ii.110-16) is equally forthright in its rhetorical nature. She repeats the same phrase and employs a diction under the rhetorical influence of the sermon, using to pointed effect such latinate words as "licentious," "consecrate," "contaminate," as well as the more homely "spit," and "spurn," and employing phrases that edge into moral allegories ("ruffian lust," "harlot brow").

Apart from its interesting substance Luciana's advice to Antipholus (III.ii.1-28) also reveals an intensely conventional rhetorical organization. Composed of seven self-contained quatrains, and almost proverbial in its patness, its principal pattern is that of antithetical grouping ("Apparel vice like virtue's harbinger; / Bear a fair presence, though your heart be tainted; / Teach sin the carriage of a holy saint" [III.ii.12-14]), each of which possesses quasi-proverbial authority. Antipholus' lyrical reply is also extremely conventional, its rhetorical pattern traceable to Erasmus' advice on writing

love letters.[13] Calculated quatrains are its formal architecture, and its diction, imagery, and sentiments compose in their amalgam of Platonic, Petrarchan, and Ovidian elements what Samuel Johnson calls "the common cant of lovers," meaning the conventional rhetoric of love poets.[14]

Finally, the Abbess's chastisement of Adriana for jealousy (IV.i.58-86) bears all the marks of a conventional sermon against one of the seven deadly sins. "Thou sayest" is repeated with forensic exactitude and point; a sequence of cause and effect is developed with logical inevitability; and the sermon note is especially audible in the way a submerged personification surfaces to become a whole family of full-blown allegorical abstractions. As a result of jealousy, she asks rhetorically, "what doth ensue,"

> But moody and dull melancholy,
> Kinsman to grim and comfortless despair,
> And at her heel a huge infectious troop
> Of pale distemperatures and foes to life.
>
> (79-82)

Common to all these uses of language is an assumption that the forms employed and the statements made will immediately and in the way intended by the speakers be decipherable by the listeners. Even when the speakers are at odds with one another they use the language in essentially the same way. Both formally and substantively, therefore, language in such cases is being used according to custom and according to conventional shared beliefs about its secure relationship with non-linguistic reality—the world to which it refers.

Matching the structural pattern set up in dealing with the action, however, the play contains a further use of language that is the antithesis of the one I have just described. Thus at every turn we see the orderliness of conventional verbal forms sabotaged by the linguistic anarchy of the pun. For while the formal presence of the pun is a conventional comic device, its actual function within the fictional world is a reminder of the natural ambivalence inherent in experience. The implications of this fact, then, go deeper than language. For the pun, as Sigurd Burckhardt has remarked, "gives the lie direct to the social convention that is language," and by denying the meaningfulness of words it "calls into question the genuineness of the linguistic currency on which the social order depends."[15] The conflict between conventional uses of language and the pun re-enacts in linguistic terms the dialectical relationship of custom and nature observable in the action.

Since the play is built on a double pun, the two sets of twins being no less than the incarnation of this linguistic phenomenon, it is no accident that this is one of the drama's most frequently used literary devices.[16] The contrast between the two opposing uses of language is in the play from the very beginning. The stern conventionality of the legal and narrative language of the opening scene, briefly recalled by the first sixteen lines of Scene ii, collides in a remarkable way with the breathless barrage of puns launched against an astonished Antipholus of Syracuse by Dromio of Ephesus. Each mis-reads the other (beginning with Antipholus' "Here comes the almanac of my true date" [41]), and this mis-reading is given active body in the slave's puns on such innocent-seeming words as "stomach," "fast," and "marks" (11,94), all of which have for him, a natural, physical implication.

Such collisions punctuate the play's linguistic activity. In a flurry of puns Dromio of Ephesus interrupts the conventional language of the marriage debate between Luciana and Adriana (II.i.44ff.): physical and metaphysical meanings of a word, the one natural, the other customary or conventional, are divorced (so "at hand" becomes "at two hands," "Told" becomes "tolled," "feel" is given both its meanings). In each case the pun reveals a conventional (polite and almost abstract) meaning, and a physical (natural) one. As audience to this game we are obliged to attend to both, to hold both in an unresolved tension that provokes our comic response. As perpetrators of puns, the slaves repeatedly compensate for their social bondage by their linguistic freedom. Doing so they draw attention to the counterpoint between the conventional fixity of society, which victimizes them, and the natural fluidity of language, which is their weapon of comic revenge. Existing at a more physical level than the other characters (witness their incessant beatings which, while they belong to the dramatic convention that dictates this kind of master-slave relationship, are nonetheless a spectacular example of "natural" action), their language constantly reminds us of this anarchic realm. Thus, while Antipholus of Syracuse is transformed "in mind," his slave insists he himself is transformed "both in mind and in my shape" (II.ii.195-97), and translates the metaphorical "ass" he is called by Luciana into a literal one, " 'Tis true, she rides me, and I long for grass" (200). After his master's amorous siege of Luciana, Dromio counterpoints the conventional language of a lover with a blast of overt and covert puns in his description of Nell (III.ii.71-145). It is the same Dromio who in his account to Adriana of Antipholus' arrest perpetrates a flock of puns by converting such conventional legal terms as "case" and "suit" to their physical meanings, and quibbling on words like "redemption," "band," and "hour" (whore) (IV.ii.44-66).

The pun recognizes the refusal of language to be confined within its conventional borders. Such a deliberate emphasis upon the anarchic independence of language, its natural tendency to contrive a reality at odds with conventional, would-be objective truth best accounts for the extraordinary digressive descriptions Dromio of Syracuse gives of the Officer and of Time (IV.ii.32-40, 53-62; IV.iii.15-32). In a burst of what seems to be irrelevant creation (and to the utter confusion of Adriana) the ideas of "officer" and "Time" are subjected to a series of remarkable metamorphoses. The Officer becomes a devil, a fury, a wolf, "a fellow all in buff," "a back-fiend, a shoulder clapper," a hound, an avenging angel, Adam, the Prodigal son, a tempter, a bass-viol, and a bidder of kind good-nights. Less extravagantly, Time is turned into a guilty thief and a bankrupt, and made capable of moving backward. The sheer energy of these linguistic explosions, stuffed with puns, transforms their apparent irrelevance into an integral part of the drama. The natural anarchy of such verbal extravaganzas (anticipating Falstaff's splendid fustian) collides dialectically with the stiffest of all the play's conventions, those of law and time.

Marked as I have shown above by intensified confusion in the action, Act IV is also distinguished by an increase in linguistic chaos. First the entrance of the Courtesan causes Dromio of Syracuse to play in breathless terror on such words as "dam," "light," "burn," and "pride," whose inner meanings are all physical and sexual. In a snowball effect, then, puns are perpetrated by everyone, spilling out of such innocuous words as "end," "patient," "senseless," "sensible," "ears," "give," "feel," and "bond," (IV.iv.15-125). In such turmoil the conventional currency of language is devalued as soon as it is minted. And at this point, just as happened with the play's action, we have gone as far as possible while still retaining, in however unbalanced a way, the dialectic of custom and nature in language. The poet has stretched his language to its limits.

With the entrance of the Abbess at V.i.38, the dialectic of custom and nature in the language and the action of *Errors* achieves its synthesis. That the Abbess is a conventional figure of authority will immediately be suggested by the stage action, with the "people" growing silent and clustering round her. In questioning Adriana about her husband, however, she shows rich insight and an openness to natural feelings:

> Hath he not lost much wealth by wrack of
>   sea?
> Buried some dear friend? Hath not else his
>   eye
> Stray'd his affection in unlawful love,
> A sin prevailing much in youthful men,
> Who give their eyes the liberty of gazing?
> Which of these sorrows is he subject to?
>   (V.i.49-54)

Her tone throughout is humane and understanding; her authority, like her verse, is flexible in natural ways. Sin, the customary way of looking at Antipholus' behavior ("possession" in Pinch's terminology), is mitigated by a sorrow that speaks of her concern for a human being. In the same way her rebuke of Adriana's jealousy is not the reduction of a living woman to a conventional caricature (like her Plautine original, and as Luciana and Antipholus of Ephesus see her), but an accurate assessment of the pragmatic particulars. Unlike the conventional chiding of her sister (II.i.10-41), this assessment Adriana can accept: "She did betray me to mine own reproof" (90). As the sequence progresses we see that the Abbess combines unaffectedly the qualities of custom and nature. She refuses to submit to the wife's conventional priority when Adriana claims that the cure of her husband "is my office" (99), insisting instead that the higher law of 'sanctuary' be observed. She appeals to the "charitable duty of my order" to justify her taking care of Antipholus, showing the balance between humane and conventional in the conjunction of adjective and noun, while the means she will take to "make of him a formal man again" are likewise a combination of natural and customary, the physical and the spiritual, "wholesome syrups, drugs, and holy prayers" (104). In her speech and behavior she gathers conventional considerations into natural means and leads both into what can only be called the realm of "grace."[17]

It is at this tense moment that the play comes full circle, bringing not only its plot but also its structural, linguistic, and thematic dialectic to a satisfactory resolution. Egeon is led to execution. Appeals to the strictest conventionality of the law (in the person of the Duke) are made by Adriana against the Abbess and by Antipholus of Ephesus against his wife. As husband and wife narrate the day's occurrences from their opposite perspectives, nature and convention are oddly mingled—the discourse reasonable, the passions insoluble. The sudden appearance of both sets of twins baffles all customary assumptions: "who," asks the Duke, "deciphers them?" (334). It is at this *impasse* to conventional understanding, however, that the intractable knot is loosed by something beyond nature and custom in the person of Emilia: who is at once a part of this conflict and its proper resolution. In her various identity she belongs to and at the same time transcends both the orders of nature and of custom. By recognizing her husband she looses him from the law's conventional grasp, while she resolves the conventional dilemma of the identical twins by again going "in travail" of them and being at "this present hour" delivered of her "heavy burden" (400-02). Herself a perfect fusion of nature (mother) and custom (nun), it is appropriate that she bring the action to a concluding synthesis of the two. We may call that synthesis grace. That we will not take such grace too heavily, however, we have a lighter reflection of it in the final exit, reserved for the Dromios. Between them as they leave, they good-humoredly dissolve the social convention of precedence, and go off the stage

as they naturally came into the world, departing "like brother and brother, / . . . hand in hand, not one before another."

The scene has a linguistic development parallel to its action. Devoted to the untangling of errors the last act is almost entirely free of puns. Language is restored to its more normal usage: words for the most part bear only one meaning and that the conventionally appropriate one. In the Abbess's intention that all shall retire to the abbey (the house of truth) and there "hear at large discoursed all our fortunes" (395), language will be responsible for the restoration of an order that in part language has dislocated. The conventional meaning of words, like the relationships between those living puns, the twins, are sorted out. As the original shipwreck divided the brothers on a literal and then a metaphorical sea of formlessness and lost identity, the puns, splitting words into two identical but distinct elements, revealed the shape-shifting, uncertain nature of language itself. At the end, then, language is restored to a happy singularity, a sense of its own identity. But, as with the twins, it is an identity taught by experience to acknowledge its own implicit duality, its own dangerous power to shipwreck the conventional uses to which it is put. Such linguistic self-awareness I would call a synthesis of nature and convention, a grace of language proper to all of us, I suppose, but most proper to the poet, for whom inevitably it is not merely a fact but a subject. It is again the brothers Dromio, main agents of the pun, who give final expression to this awareness of the inherent duality of language, a duality that compels language beyond its customary boundaries and forces it to reflect a reality that itself cannot be contained by such conventional bonds. Finally language and reality are seen, quite simply, to have more than one meaning, and these multiple meanings are inseparable from one another. As far as language is concerned, this is the significance of the final couplet:

> We came into the world like brother and
> brother,
> And now let's go hand in hand, not one
> before another.

The simplicity of this, coming where it does, suggests a state of innocence after the experience of the fall. The couplet displays a linguistic grace that has the grace to be awkward, caught between and incorporating the convention of verse and the nature of prose. Aware of the experience of the fall, this new innocence instructs players and audience alike that the customary contours of their own experience are neither its final truth nor its substantial meaning.

To see the play as I have seen it in this essay is to locate certain preoccupations of the young dramatist. The relationship between custom and nature is the subject, in part, of *The Comedy of Errors*. Such a concern seems appropriate to an artist at the outset of his career. It is relevant to him as an individual talent coming to terms with the conventions of his art, and it concerns him as an observer of his world, coming to grips with its truths of theory and experience. Such preoccupations early establish contacts between the man and the artist that transform the making of plays into an activity that can re-enact in itself, whether in a comic or a tragic mask, the most important questions of existence. The relationship between nature and custom is an enduring concern of all of Shakespeare's work; his approach to it gains in richness of insight and complexity of meaning as he develops as a dramatist. To find it occupying such a central place in his earliest play is to suggest yet again the extraordinary coherence and integrity of the vision and the work.

Notes

1 David Bevington, Introduction to *The Comedy of Errors* in *The Complete Works of Shakespeare*, ed. Hardin Craig and David Bevington (rev. ed.; Glenview, Ill.: Scott, Foresman, 1973), p. 80.

2 The phrase is Ralph Berry's. See *Shakespeare's Comedies: Explorations in Form* (Princeton U. Press, 1972), p. 26.

3 *The Comedy of Errors,* ed. R. A. Foakes, New Arden Edition (Harvard U. Press, 1962). All textual references are to this edition. References cited as "Foakes" are to the editorial notes in this edition.

4 T. McAlindon, *Shakespeare and Decorum* (London: Macmillan, 1973), p. 8.

5 Richard Hooker, *Of the Laws of Ecclesiastical Polity,* in *The Folger Library Edition of the Works of Richard Hooker,* General Editor W. Speed Hill (Harvard U. Press, 1977), p. 64.

6 A. C. Hamilton, *The Early Shakespeare* (San Marino, California: Huntington Library, 1967), p. 90.

7 Foakes, pp. xliii-xlix.

8 John Russell Brown, *Shakespeare and His Comedies* (London: Methuen, 1957), p. 54.

9 Harold Brooks, "Themes and Structure in *The Comedy of Errors*," in *Early Shakespeare*, ed. John Russell Brown and Bernard Harris, Stratford-upon-Avon Studies III (London: Arnold, 1961), p. 67.

10 See Marvin T. Herrick, *Comic Theory in the Sixteenth Century* (U.of Illinois Press, 1950), p. 29.

11 See Foakes, p. 5 n.

12 Departures from the iambic norm occur at lines 3, 26, 42, 45, 82, non-pentameters are lines 38, 54, 61, 155.

13 See T. W. Baldwin, *William Shakspere's Small Latine and Lesse Greeke* (U. of Illinois Press, 1944), II, 282-84.

14 *Johnson on Shakespeare,* ed. Arthur Sherbo, Yale Edition of the Works of Samuel Johnson, VII (Yale U. Press, 1968), p. 356.

15 *Shakespearean Meanings* (Princeton U. Press, 1968), p. 25.

16 Bertrand Evans' claim that "the very pun . . . is scanted" (*Shakespeare's Comedies* [Oxford: Clarendon Press, 1960], p. 2), is difficult to reconcile with a close reading of the text.

17 It is significant that some undeniable Christian implications do appear not only in the Abbess's function, but in her speech: the "thirty-three years" she goes "in travail of her sons" reminds in a fairly arbitrary manner (since the computation of their years elsewhere does not give such an age) of the age of Christ, while the mention of "their nativity," as well as the overtones of baptism in "a gossips' feast" also contribute to a deliberately Christian sense of grace in this comic resolution. Development of this interesting point is not necessary to the present argument. See John Arthos, *Shakespeare: The Early Writings* (Totowa, N. J.: Rowan and Littlefield, 1972), pp. 36-37.

Ruth Nevo (essay date 1980)

SOURCE: "My Glass and Not My Brother," in *Comic Transformations in Shakespeare,* Methuen & Co. Ltd., 1980, pp. 22-36.

[*In this excerpt, Nevo analyzes* The Comedy of Errors *as a play that contains all the elements that mark Shakespeare's mature comedy.*]

If it were not so funny, Shakespeare's first comedy would read like a schizophrenic nightmare: identities are lost, split, engulfed, hallucinated, imploded.[1] Apparently solid citizens (solid at least to themselves) suffer "ontological uncertainty" in acute forms, wandering about unrecognized by all they encounter. During this chapter of accidents servants are subjected to assault and battery upon their persons and masters are subjected to the severest undermining of their sense of their own identity. A respectable citizen is shut out of his own house by his own wife and servants, abused by his merchant associates, arrested on charges of falsehood, taken for insane, given over for cure into the hands of a mountebank pedant and, in general, experiences the collapse of all the familiar social and cognitive foundations of his life and his sense of reality. At the same time a displaced, disorientated voyager is so alarmed by the inexplicable behaviour of all Ephesians, including the object of his new affections, that he becomes convinced he has taken leave of his senses, or is the victim of witchcraft. The disintegrating effects of this frenzy of errors are such as to cause one brother to be incarcerated as a raving lunatic and the other to take flight in panic.

These zany events are often dismissed as "farce", a youthful malady Shakespeare was to grow out of. The New Shakespeare editor says, "as yet, farce and romance were not one "form" but two separate stools; and between them in *The Comedy of Errors* he fell to the ground".[2] Quiller-Couch's half-truth misleads. As I have argued in the previous chapter, farce and romance appear, in varying proportions but indivisibly interlocked, in Shakespeare's New Comedy models; and while it would be simply foolish to deny the increasing refinement of artistry with which he manufactured "one form" out of his heterogeneous materials, nevertheless in *The Comedy of Errors,* I suggest, not only did he *not* fall between two stools, he laid the foundations for all his subsequent essays in the comic mode. It is precisely the farcical phase of *The Comedy of Errors* which, so far from requiring apology, confers upon it a genuine primacy.

I wish to argue that in this first of the comedies Shakespeare's fundamental, generating comic strategy is manifest, and that this is what we must seek if we are to understand the comicalness of Shakespearean comedy. The initiating privation is that created by the losses of the various limbs of a family body. A husband has lost a wife, a wife a husband, parents their children, children their parents, and brothers each other. At the immediate opening of the play we hear of poor Egeon's further loss of his one remaining son, and the threat of death by a harsh and retributive law. All that is required to save Egeon is a thousand marks but the extremity of his situation is the lack of anyone to pay it. Egeon's first speech, therefore is expressive of his total adversity, isolation and bereavement. He is a being so dispossessed that he welcomes his fate:

> Yet this my comfort, when your words are
> done,
> My woes end likewise with the evening sun.
> (I.i. 26-7)

The Comedy of Errors begins Shakespeare's long exploration of this danger zone with the issue which constitutes the basic condition of personal integrity, of personal identity: sameness and difference, pinpointed, in the doubleness of twins, in its most overt and pan-

tomimic form. The loading of the dice in this direction is made clear by a moment's glance at the *Menaechmi,* where the complete family plays no part, the likeness of the twins to each other is the occasion of merely technical errors, and the motivations of both sturdily pragmatic. Menaechmus I is engaged in keeping wife, mistress and parasite in that stage of tenuous equilibrium which makes life possible and Menaechmus II is speedily persuaded of the advantages of a courtesan's free hospitality however inexplicable. The climactically hilarious scene in which one twin simulates the madness everyone believes him to suffer from, in order to escape the attentions of a wife and a father-in-law, and the other *acts* madly out of the sheer fury and frustration induced by the unaccountable events, is totally devoid of reverberations which could suggest the dimension of inner experience. Compare the speech "He that commends me to mine own content" of the melancholy, voyaging Antipholus of Syracuse:

> He that commends me to mine own content,
> Commends me to the thing I cannot get:
> I to the world am like a drop of water,
> That in the ocean seeks another drop,
> Who, falling there to find his fellow forth
> (Unseen, inquisitive), confounds himself.
> So I, to find a mother and a brother,
> In quest of them (unhappy), ah, lose myself
> (I. ii. 33-40)

This is followed by the first *pas-de-deux* of mistaken identities—of being "unseen": he is called to a mysterious dinner by his servant who has unaccountably taken it into his head to chatter about mistresses and sisters instead of telling him where his money is bestowed.

When this same Dromio returns home to report to his mistress he does so with perhaps less than complete accuracy but with great pantomimic verve; and it so happens that his tale presents her with just what the feelings of a neglected wife need to inflame them:

> When I desir'd him to come home to dinner,
> He ask'd me for a [thousand] marks in gold;
> ' 'Tis dinner-time,' quoth I: 'My gold!' quoth
> he.
> 'Will you come?' quoth I: 'My gold!' quoth
> he;
> 'Where is the thousand marks I gave thee,
> villain?'
> 'The pig,' quoth I, 'is burn'd': 'My gold!'
> quoth he.
> 'My mistress, sir,' quoth I: 'Hang up thy
> mistress!
> I know not thy mistress, out on thy mistress!'
> (II. i. 60-8)

Adriana is a stout warrior against double standards ("Why should their liberty than ours be more?" and has tart replies to her sister's conservative pieties concerning women's place and the virtues of obedience, patience and meekness. But Dromio's tale confirms her worst suspicions, throws her into a paroxysm of self-pity and exacerbates the conjugal battle of the sexes between Adriana and her husband:

> His company must do his minions grace,
> Whilst I at home do starve for a merry look:
> Hath homely age th' alluring beauty took
> From my poor cheek? Then he hath wasted it.
>
> What ruins are in me that can be found,
> By him not ruin'd?
>
> (II. i. 87-90; 96-7)

When we hear her appeal to her once devoted, now (apparently) wayward husband it must come as something of a surprise that she uses the very language of the Antipholus she is in fact addressing in the belief that he is her husband:

> How comes it now, my husband, O how
>   comes it,
> That thou art then estranged from thyself?
> Thyself I call it, being strange to me,
> That, undividable incorporate,
> Am better than thy dear self's better part.
> Ah, do not tear away thyself from me;
> For know, my love, as easy mayst thou fall
> A drop of water in the breaking gulf,
> And take unmingled hence that drop again,
> Without addition or diminishing,
> As take from me thyself and not me too.
>
> (II. ii. 119-29)

Much has been made of the interesting recurrence, and interesting indeed it is. What I believe we are able to construct both from the recurrence as such and from the import of the ocean-waterdrop relation, is the restless, schizoid condition of Ephesians and Syracusans alike. Antipholus' baffled quest for himself—for the mother and the brother through whom he will realize himself—is the inverted mirror image of Adriana's almost rapacious "incorporation" of her husband into herself, a frantic, possessive dependence. What is lacking in both is self-possession. Neither is his own man, with a composed and secure sense of his own independent separate identity and, in consequence, of the boundaries between himself and others. She is estranged from her husband; he is a stranger in a strange land. Neither sees him or herself as clearly and distinctly autonomous. Neither possesses the detachment of the drop, and both, in consequence, fear oceanic engulfment.

The beautiful farcical point of the play's whole evolution is that precisely oceanic engulfment, the great dread, overcomes them and their fellow protagonists,

in the hyperbolic and comic-monstrous forms of fantasy. In the alien Antipholus, the tendency to be confused about who one is and where one is reaches a point where 'alienation' might well be a medical diagnosis. The disorientation and bewilderment of the Syracusan pair is referred to in terms which, while appropriate to the legendary Ephesus, transform the depth of their bafflement into a pathological paranoia: cozenage, sorcery, witchcraft, demonic possession; they are surrounded, so they believe, by cheats, mountebanks, "goblins", "owls", "sprites", "fiends", Satan himself, or "the devil's dam" in the shape of the comforting courtesan. The resident twin becomes "estranged from himself" in a sense no less radical.

The more they lose themselves in a spiralling whirligig of misapprehensions, the more their latent selves emerge, or are acted out. This is the fundamental Shakespearean discovery. The *processus turbarum* educes, brings out, exacerbates and enlarges the comic disposition, the maladies, frailties, fears and obsessions of the protagonists, and in so doing, brings remedy about. Both the comic fury of Ephesian Antipholus and the comic consternation of his twin illustrate the process. And when Adriana expresses her outrage in abuse of her errant husband:

> He is deformed, crooked, old, and sere,
> Ill-fac'd, worse-bodied, shapeless everywhere;
> Vicious, ungentle, foolish, blunt, unkind,
> Stigmatical in making, worse in mind.
>
> (IV. ii. 19-22)

and Luciana very sensibly enquires:

> Who would be jealous then of such a one?
> No evil lost is wail'd when it is gone.
>
> (IV. ii. 23-4)

Adriana's reply is significant:

> Ah, but I think him better than I say;
> And yet would herein other eyes were
>   worse.
> Far from her nest the lapwing cries away;
> My heart prays for him, though my tongue
>   do curse.
>
> (IV. ii. 25-8)

By the same token Adriana's simultaneous welcoming of one twin and rejection of the other can be seen as an externalization of the real ambivalence of her feelings. The knot of errors, the *processus turbarum,* turns the world of the protagonists upside down, and discovers them to us in all their comical, previously hidden ambivalences, violences and consternations. It also minimally, and as yet, inchoately, reveals them to themselves.

By the end of the play Antipholus will have found not only his mother, brother and father, but himself—a will and an orientation—through the familiar alchemy of romantic love; and Adriana, in the second plot, will have been neatly duped into a recognition of her own weaknesses and a capacity to realize her own genuine lovingness, through the cunning cross-examination of the Abbess. But for these bonuses of insight there is a price, the price of ridicule. Antipholus' courtship of Luciana is ridiculous because the lady in question is under the impression that he is her brother-in-law, who has taken leave of his morals as well as of his senses. It is one thing for a Petrarchan lover to find himself, his own self's better part, his eye's clear eye, his dear heart's dearer heart, his food, his fortune, his sweet hope's aim, his sole earth's heaven, and his heaven's claim in his mistress's visage, and quite another when the lady believes herself his sister-in-law and dashes off indignantly to fetch his wife to berate him.

Similarly, the Abbess's disguise (otherwise merely perfunctory) is made the means of the Abbess's tricky and therapeutic exposure of Adriana to herself. Trapped by the Abbess into a self-confession, Adriana recognizes as in a mirror her own face in the figure of the nagging wife. "She did betray me to my own reproof," she says, acknowledging the remedial, truth-producing power of benign deceit. We never hear whether her husband's solid bourgeois complacency and fiery temper have been in any way chastened by his experiences, but the lively account of Dr Pinch's drubbing provides, as we shall see, a ludicrous, safety-valve catharsis.

The play's comic device is not strictly a "device". It is not invented by anyone. The identicalness of two sets of twins—two different identities under one appearance—is a tricky stratagem at best on the part of nature, not art, and a device only in the sense that the comic dramatist exploits it for his comic purposes. It is, as Harry Levin puts it, "a practical joke conceived and executed by providence."[3] But the question of sibling doubles lies at the heart of much persistent human questioning of identities and essences and appearances; questioning which found expression in folklore and literature before the philosophers and anthropologists and psychologists made of it their special province. In *The Comedy of Errors* the matching of violently severed family bonds with the Dromios' burlesque imitation of their masters' consternations and perplexities: "Do you know me sir?" demands Syracusan Dromio of (this time!) Syracusan Antipholus. "Am I Dromio? Am I your man? Am I myself?" make problems of identity at the level of mere identification comment ironically upon, or wryly illuminate problems of identity at the level of personal ontology. The Dromios, as they march back and forth with their messages, and their missions, their rope ends and their masters' purses, fated to miscarry and constantly belaboured by their irate masters, function to defuse by laughter the dire personal threat of traumatic non-entity, or total chaotic non-being.

The *processus turbarum*, with its accelerating and cumulative whirl of errors, produces, in the fullness of time, its own remedies. It also produces most of the sheer risibility of Shakespeare's comedies. It will be statutory for the funniest, most farcical, most palpably ridiculous scenes in Shakespearean comedies to occur when the tumult of errors is at its "hiest and hottest", in Act III, and in IV, while the latter "begins to bring about the remedy". One of the funniest moments, for instance, occurs outside the Antipholus house when Ephesian Dromio yells for "Maude, Bridget, Marian, Cicely, Gillian, Ginn" and receives a mock echo from his mirror-image within: "Mome, malt-horse, capon, coxcomb, idiot, patch," (III. i. 31-2) and one radical source of comic pleasure—mimicry—is neatly yoked to the whole question of who's who in a name-calling pantomime of excess.

Freud's calculus of the comic economy explains why we find funny both over and under expenditure of physical (in relation to mental) energy.[4] The argument is well known and it will suffice to recall no more exacting instances than the routines of a country bumpkin armed with a sledgehammer lunging ponderously about after a fly, or a professor totally absorbed in the mental construction of a sophisticated electronic device for the undoing of the same vexing insect. What farce does is to multiply such situations and propel them, in a rhythm of increasing intensity, towards some point of explosion or collapse. I find in a recent study two excellently expressive terms for the double dynamic of farcical pleasure: riot and deadlock; riot for the hyperbolic whirl of comically excessive, usually disinhibitory actions, and deadlock for the no-exit *cul-de-sac* into which protagonists are manoeuvred and from which they must be extricated.[5] Farce, thus understood, may be instrumental in strategies of festive celebration, of satiric invective or of cathartic fantasy.

Farce is also, as its etymology tells us, stuffing;[6] and the structure of comic pleasure demands that a farce be stuffed indeed, to satiety, by its own exuberance. It is the achievement of Shakespeare's farce to exploit that exuberance for ends far beyond the immediate requirements of risibility, of celebration, or of satire. Ralph Berry has wittily summarized the relation between characters and situations in *The Comedy of Errors* as "a study of the reactions of people to the farce in which they find themselves."[7] But I would prefer to say, 'to the farce *through* which they find themselves', stressing therapy as final cause. Shakespeare's farcical *processus turbarum* is a working-out of psychic material—the obsessions, compulsions, fantasies which, unresolved, unremedied, would represent catastrophe.

Put in non-psychological terms, this is to say no more than that the *processus turbarum* exhibits and enacts the besetting errors of the *dramatis personae,* and that the play's real and formal remedy is the convergence of the entire family at the Abbey where Antipholus' and Egeon's recovery and all the reunions can take place. One pair of twins has taken refuge there, and is produced to confront the other pair upon their arrival, following the violent overthrow of Dr Pinch, and Adriana's hotfoot pursuit of her "poor distracted husband." Errors are unpeeled like onions as each plaintiff in turn appeals to the Duke, and he in turn to the Abbess. Then the fortuitous presence of the Abbess transforms loss into restoration, grief into joy, ignorance into knowledge, alienation into homecoming, and imminent death into metaphorical rebirth.

> Thirty-three years have I but gone in travail
> Of you, my sons, and till this present hour
> My heavy burthen [ne'er] delivered.
> The Duke, my husband, and my children both,
> And you the calendars of their nativity,
> Go to a gossip's feast, and go with me—
> After so long grief, such nativity!
>
> (V. i. 401-7)

She, the mother, is the matrix in which the whole family's individual identities are recovered; all are seen to be who they are, while the frontier between harm and remedy, the danger zone which is the territory of comedy, has been luridly marked by the doomed Egeon on his way to the nearby scaffold.

But, as I have indicated, Shakespeare proceeds consistently towards a conception of these follies and of their exhibition, as themselves remedial. His characters act out all manner of absurdities and these are, it turns out, the very stuff of human imperfection; the underside of the drama of psychic life. And the tumult they cause is at once expressive and therapeutic. By becoming absurd, the protagonists objectify their folly. Fooled, they become, to whatever degree, aware of themselves as selves and as fooled, and so have a basis for the regaining of control. And in this connection the episode of Dr Pinch is extremely interesting. Dr Pinch attempts to cure his client by the exorcism, in approved medieval mountebank manner, of the devils by whom he is, clearly, possessed. But since he is not in fact possessed by any devils at all, he turns the tables upon Dr Pinch and beats him prodigiously. The messenger's account of the breaking loose and the revenge of master and man, in V. i. 168-77, is uproariously comic, but what is of particular interest is the counterpoint treatment of remedy in this early comedy. Dr Pinch's cure for Antipholus' ills is a travesty of the true remedy which the play is enacting.

The complex and delicate transformation of perception, which lies at the heart of Shakespeare's comic method, is mediated by the Shakespearean fools, and is, indeed inconceivable without them. They are the common against which we measure the uncommon; they are the sense against which we measure nonsense; they are the natural against which we measure the unnatural; and they are the foolish against which we measure the wise.

Richard Levin, in his valuable study of multiple plots in Renaissance drama[8] provides useful categories for a theory of clowns. Clowns, he says, 'imitate' their betters, in actual practice or by formal analogy, giving a low comic version of what the serious, main protagonists are up to. But, as in any analogy, either difference or similarity can be stressed, or both, alternately. And it is in the play of complementaries, of difference and likeness, that the variety, interest and multiplicity of effect of Shakespeare's clowns lie. If, says Levin, it is the difference that is stressed, the ineptitude, rambunctiousness and amorality of, for instance, Pistol, Nym and Bardolph in *Henry V,* so that the skill, nobility and morality of the King's parallel activities are enhanced, then the clowns are acting as foils. If, on the other hand, it is the striking resemblance between the doings of the manifestly lower characters and the behaviour of the gentry that is stressed, then the higher characters will be disparaged, debased, assimilated and drawn down to the level of the foolish or ridiculous, and the clowns will have functioned as parodies. He quotes the Robin and Dick and Horse Courser episodes in *Dr Faustus* and notes that there will be differences in critical decision on whether their function is that of foil or parody according (mainly) to the reigning critical *zeitgeist.*

Two other possibilities are indicated by Levin. A clown's or clown plot's effect may function simultaneously in contrary directions with reference to two different higher characters. Pistol's cowardly bluster elevates Hal's soldiership by contrast, and ridicules the Dauphin's by similarity. And a clown or clownplot may function simultaneously in contrary directions with respect to the same higher character or group of characters. In this, the most complex case, the parody is only apparent; it is, in Empson's terms, "pseudoparody," which disarms anti-sentimental responses by taking them into account in anticipation.[9] Mercutio's bawdy in Act II of *Romeo and Juliet* would be an example, the result of which is to confirm the validity of Romeo's romantic passion, to enhance and not to debase it. Levin spells out the interesting resultant paradox: it is the foil clowns (Touchstone, for instance) not the parodic ones who are themselves literary, or literally, parodists—conscious and deliberate mockers. The further effect is that of a lighting conductor— "which works directly as a foil to set off an elevated main action, while it is working indirectly to attract and draw away those potential reactions hostile to that elevation." And this effect is what he calls magic, like a ritual mock curse to ward off the evil eye, or to reduce its powers by playing something of its part ahead of time.

> For the clown's roles as child-idiot-lout, as Saturnalian ruler, and as ritual mocker all seem to operate in this manner by sanctioning the release through the subplot of our anarchic impulses and feelings, under controls which prevent them from threatening the adult, civilized norms of the main plot.
>
> (p. 146)

The Dromios, unlike their masters, whose fate they share, keep their wits about them and are never without some impudent repartee or wry observation, thus making their master's plight even more ridiculous than their own. They are, therefore, like their Terentian prototypes, Eiron-Buffoons. In terms of the Shakespearean law of complementarity this makes the fooled Antipholuses a species of impostor. And so they are, indeed—the visiting Antipholus welcomed to bed and board none of his, and the resident Antipholus *treated* as an impostor by his frustrated creditors. The Dromios are the characteristic Shakespearean fools though the subtlety, obliquity and variety of the mimetic mockery deployed by later members of the class will grow immeasurably. In Syracusan Dromio's account of the "wondrous fat marriage" apparently in store for him, upon which he expatiates with an Aristophanic verve, there is a good early example of Levin's "lightning conductor" principle:

> Marry, sir, she's the kitchen wench and all grease, and I know not what use to put her to but to make a lamp of her and run from her by her own light. I warrant, her rags and the tallow in them will burn a Poland winter: if she lives till doomsday, she'll burn a week longer than the whole world.
>
> (III. ii. 95-100)

The analogy is to Adriana's claims upon Syracusan Antipholus as her supposed husband, and the similarity is certainly deflating. It has, moreover, an immediate absurd effect in that the dialogue precipitates Antipholus' beating of a retreat from a place apparently inhabited solely by comic-monstrous witches. But Dromio's diatribe, a ribald vilification of the fat wench's charms, is at the furthest possible remove downwards from the ambience of the relationship which has been developing between the peregrine Antipholus and his ostensible sister-in-law:

> It is thyself, mine own self's better part:
> Mine eye's clear eye, my dear heart's dearer heart
>
> (III. ii. 61-2)

and therefore functions as foil to the latter.

Luciana's "gentle sovereign grace," her 'enchanting presence and discourse' (III. ii. 160-1) is left not only intact but enhanced, while the abusive, wittily anti-erotic catalogue drains off a good measure of the sexual aggression triggered by the volatile situation which has been developing in Ephesus. Traversi says with caution:

> The introduction, through the twin Dromios, of a comic underplot, including a burlesque upon marriage itself in the pursuit of the Syracusan by the kitchen maid of Ephesus, presents yet another standpoint from which the central theme can be considered.[10]

The point at issue, however, is not the 'theme' of marriage but the dignity or absurdity of the protagonists, a matter which it is the function of Shakespearean comedy to place in exquisite and precarious poise.

Nothing is more revealing of his comic art, or of the directions it will take than the final moments of the play. The last words are, significantly, Dromio's. Says the Ephesian twin, complacently marching off with his brother: "Methinks you are my glass and not my brother: / I see by you I am a sweet-fac'd youth" (v. i. 418-19). The whole little episode is a deliciously comic forerunner of a Lacanian *stade du miroir*.[11] But it is also a parody of self-discovery. And it punctures the whole grand remedial idea of regenerated, enlightened, separate, complete and viable personalities with the impermeable lunatic logic of its narcissism. Punctures, and yet reaffirms, since the contentment of Dromio with his inability to acquire a separate self at all is, our laughter tells us, the most reassuring antidote to insanity Ephesus could possibly supply.

Shakespeare's next investigation into the acquiring of separate selves—*The Two Gentlemen*—both complicates and deepens the issues. But in the meantime there are rivalries afoot in Padua, the settling of which will forge a vital link in the dramatist's portrayal of the battle of the sexes.

Notes

[1] The terms are R. D. Laing's in his celebrated study of the structure and imagery of the schizophrenic personality, *The Divided Self* (London: Tavistock Publications, 1960; reprinted New York: Pantheon, 1965).

[2] The New Shakespeare edn (Cambridge: Cambridge University Press, 1922), p. xxii. A brilliant recent psychoanalytic study of *The Comedy of Errors* (Barbara Freedman, "Errors in Comedy: A Psychoanalytic Theory of Farce," Shakespearean Comedy issue of *New York Literary Forum,* ed. Maurice Charney, New York: Jeannine Plottel, 1980 [expected]), which came to my

attention too late to be fully taken into account, agrees in the defence of farce. It is "a strategic denial and displacement of meaning" through absurdity and the disjunction of cause and effect precisely in order for repressed libidinal material to find an acceptable outlet. "Farce enacts," says Freedman, "a primitive superego punishment for its characters' transgressions in the form of a maniacal plot which both arranges libidinal gratification and punishes for it." The initial transgression in the case of *The Comedy of Errors* is Egeon's abandonment of his wife, and the twins represent the consequent splitting up of his psychic personality into the restless wanderer and the delinquent stay-at-home. The play is obsessed with confronting, punishing and forgiving debts—Egeon's which is actual and monetary but meaningless, and the twins' which are basically marital, mistaken and meaningful. Barbara Freedman's richly suggestive study extends, and confirms, my own at many points; but in her emphasis upon the "one original, meaningful plot which can be retrieved" from the dispersions and denials of the farcical working through, that is, the plot of Egeon's rehabilitation or reintegration, she pays perhaps too little attention to the diversified, individualized dramatic material of the play.

[3] H. Levin, introduction to the Signet edn of *The Comedy of Errors* (New York: New American Library, 1965), p. xxvi.

[4] "Jokes and their Relation to the Unconscious," *The Standard Edition of the Complete Psychological Works of Sigmund Freud,* trans. James Strachey (London: Hogarth Press 1953-1966, vol. VIII, p. 236.

[5] Zvi Jagendorf, "Happy End." Unpublished Doctoral Dissertation, Hebrew University of Jerusalem (1977), pp. 16-20.

[6] See Robert C. Stephenson, "Farce as Method," *Tulane Drama Review,* vol. 5, no. 2 (1961), pp. 85-93; and Eric Bentley, "Farce" in *The Life of Drama* (New Jersey: Atheneum, 1964), pp. 219-56.

[7] Ralph Berry, *Shakespeare's Comedies* (New Jersey: Princeton University Press, 1972), p. 25.

[8] Richard Levin, *The Multiple Plot in English Renaissance Drama* (Chicago: University of Chicago Press, 1971), pp. 109-47.

[9] William Empson, *Seven Types of Ambiguity* (reprinted 1930; Penguin, 1961) p. 52.

[10] Derek Traversi, *Shakespeare: The Early Comedies* (London: Longman Green, 1960), p. 12.

[11] In the now famous article which heralded Parisian neo-Freudianism, *"Le Stade du Miroir"* (1949), Lacan writes of the child's experience of himself when placed in front of a mirror, compared with that of a monkey which does not recognize itself, as indicative of the fundamental "ontological structure of the human world." It suffices to comprehend the *stade du miroir* as an identification in the full sense of this term in analysis—that is, the transformation produced in the subject when he assumes an image. . . . The joyful assumption of his specular image of a being still unable to control his motor functions and still dependent on his mother to nurse him . . . therefore seems to me to reveal in an exemplary situation the symbolic matrix in which the *je* precipitates itself in a primordial form, before it becomes objectified in the dialectic of the identification with the other, and before language restores to it in the universal, its function as subject." Trans. Anthony Wilden, *The Language of the Self* (Baltimore: Johns Hopkins University Press, 1968), p. 135.

Dorothea Kehler (essay date 1987)

SOURCE: "*The Comedy of Errors* as Problem Comedy," in *Rocky Mountain Review,* Vol. 41, No. 4, 1987, pp. 229-40.

[*In this essay, Kehler argues that* The Comedy of Errors *is a problem play that has the appearance of a mixed-genre work.*]

Many elements combine in *The Comedy of Errors* to create a *genera mista:* the tragicomedy of the Egeon frame, the romantic comedy of S. Antipholus's love for Luciana, the predominant farce of a mistaken-identity plot with its knockabout humor. The plot develops out of a series of quests: Egeon seeks his son and finds his family; S. Antipholus seeks his brother and finds Luciana; Adriana seeks her husband's love and finds . . . what? Despite the last-act clarification of identities, we wonder if Adriana and E. Antipholus will be happier in an off-stage act 6 than they were in act 2; we also wonder if Luciana, whose most moving speech descants on not bringing trouble home (III.ii.1-28), is sufficiently convinced of her prospects for happiness with S. Antipholus to risk the "troubles of the marriage bed" (II.i.27) so amply illustrated in her sister's marriage. The play explores but does not answer a question answered emphatically in the negative throughout the Middle Ages: whether romantic love and marriage can coexist. However earnest the Elizabethan wish to fuse desire and morality, Shakespeare was too keen an observer of human nature to provide simplistic solutions to profound problems. *Errors,* transcending its time in the honesty of its depiction of the marital estate, adds yet another "kind" to its heterogeneous form—the problem play.

An awareness of Shakespeare's infinite generic variety exists among both past and present critics. Samuel Johnson observed that

> Shakespeare's plays are not in the rigorous and critical sense either tragedies or comedies, but compositions of a distinct kind; exhibiting the real state of sublunary nature, which partakes of good and evil, joy and sorrow, mingled with endless variety of proportion and innumerable modes of combination.
>
> (7:66)

Gwyn Williams, following Johnson's lead, asserts, "Shakespeare criticism has from Meres to the present day been misled by the pedantic division of drama into comedy or tragedy" (63). With regard to *The Comedy of Errors* Williams holds that "Without the two Dromios the play would hardly have had any farcical elements, except for the late introduction of Dr. Pinch. . . . Much less a farce, the play might not even have ended as a comedy" (65). W. Thomas MacCary sees *Errors* as pre-Menandrean or Aristophanic, a narcissistic or egocentric comedy taking as its goal the happiness of the self rather than the happiness of a heterosexual couple. Pointing out that "the marriage of Adriana to Antipholus of Ephesus is left unreconstructed," he urges a re-examination of genre: "this is a comedy of a different kind [from Menander's romantic New Comedy]. Its entire argument prepares us not for the union of man and wife—its view of marriage is especially pessimistic—but for the reunion of twins with each other and with their parents" (525).[1] With these critical statements in mind, I wish to consider the problem play elements in *The Comedy of Errors*.[2]

Both the final long silence between Adriana and her husband and the silence with which Luciana responds to her suitor's reiterated proposal produce an open ending that anticipates the problem plays *All's Well That Ends Well* and *Measure for Measure*. In the former, Bertram replies to the king rather than to his wife, who asks, "Will you be mine, now you are doubly won?" His answer is conditional: "*If* she, my liege, can make me know this clearly, / I'll love her dearly—ever, ever dearly" (V.iii.311-13, italics added). Bertram's silence toward Helena is underscored by Diana's silence toward the king. Disillusioned, Diana had declared, "Marry that will, I live and die a maid" (IV.ii.74); now the king offers her what earlier he had offered Helena: "Choose thou thy husband, and I'll pay thy dower" (V.iii.324). But she does not speak again. In *All's Well* we question whether the married couple will find love; whether the single woman will marry; and, if she does, whether she will be any happier than Helena. *Measure for Measure* also invites comparison with *Errors*, for both Luciana and Isabella have remained single out of choice[3]; in the final scenes neither encourages her suitor. Nor does the married

Angelo say a word to Mariana to indicate that they will be any happier than Lucio and his scorned punk. The similarity between the inconclusive conclusions of *Errors* and these later problem plays strongly suggests some commonality of generic elements.[4]

The specific problem Shakespeare explores through the relationship of Adriana and E. Antipholus is both timeless and peculiarly modern: can love survive marriage?[5] C. L. Barber notes that, unlike Plautus, Shakespeare "frequently makes the errors reveal fundamental human nature, especially human nature under the stress and tug of marriage" (493). Considering Shakespeare's depiction of a marriage "subjected to the very unromantic strains of temperament grinding on temperament in the setting of daily life," Barber concludes of Adriana and E. Antipholus, "No doubt their peace is temporary" (497). Certainly, despite their classical origin, Adriana and E. Antipholus could pass for a well-to-do modern couple headed for divorce. He, successful in business but bored at home, is ripe for more entertaining companionship; she, too much at home and insecure about his attachment to her, becomes impatient and demanding. Although a divorce in law may not be a customary Ephesian alternative, a divorce of hearts within a stifling marriage is universal. In *Errors,* Adriana and E. Antipholus enact that incipient emotional divorce as a psychodrama whose *anagnorisis,* if not to them, may yet be intelligible to us.

More than any other character in *Errors,* Adriana subverts farce. Because we know her more intimately than we do her husband, she lays first claim to our interest. Although most often described as a jealous and possessive shrew, of late she is not without defenders.[6] Marilyn French, in an illuminating reading, sees Adriana's problem as powerlessness created by economic, political, and social structures (72). But if the key to Adriana's personality and predicament is powerlessness, it is powerlessness of another sort as well. The play focuses on the *emotional* structure of a marriage, depicting the almost inevitable imbalance of love between spouses—an imbalance often aggravated to the woman's disadvantage by societal conditioning and restrictions—and the plight of a woman dependent on her husband for her sole identity as beloved wife. Byron knew the world's Adrianas: "Man's love is of man's life a thing apart, / 'Tis woman's whole existence" (*Don Juan* Canto I, st. 194). Edward Berry clarifies the generic issue raised by Adriana's emotional isolation and loss of identity, expressed in her neo-Platonic, Pauline speech (II.ii.119-29) on the melding of husband and wife into one soul:

> In their explorations of the self, the comedies are in some ways not unlike the tragedies, for in both genres Shakespeare consistently maneuvers his central characters into positions of psychological

isolation, leaving them exposed and vulnerable both within and without. While this kind of isolation is conventional in tragedy, in comedy it is unique to Shakespeare.

(49)

While a seminal model for the heroines of Shakespeare's romantic comedies (Charles Brooks 355), Adriana is also a precursor of Juliet and Desdemona. For all that Adriana is a character in a play long received as farce, her nature and situation are no less tragic than comic, and this duality creates yet another generic complication of *Errors*.

Powerless over her husband's heart, Adriana grows restive and irritable, questioning the restrictions on women's freedom: "Why should their [men's] liberty than ours be more?" (II.i.10). When Luciana replies that the husband is the bridle of the wife's will, Adriana asserts, "There's none but asses will be bridled so" (II.i.14). Male supremacy turns marriage into "servitude" (II.i.26). Although for the audience these lines imply a feminist manifesto, for Adriana they seem to hold no more lasting significance than does her threat to break Dromio's pate across. Tormented and confused, Adriana lashes out indiscriminately at all male authority, at E. Antipholus, and at an ineffectual slave; it is not sexual equality she seeks, however much she might profit from it, but only the husband she had in her spring of love:

> The time was once when thou unurg'd
> 　　wouldst vow
> That never words were music to thine ear,
> That never object pleasing in thine eye,
> That never touch well welcome to thy hand,
> That never meat sweet-savour'd in thy taste,
> Unless I spake, or look'd, or touch'd or carv'd
> 　　to thee.
>
> 　　　　　　　　　　(II.ii.113-18)

What Adriana cannot accept is that the honeymoon is over, that she is no longer all in all to her Antipholus. Institutionalizing desire within marriage frustrates this husband and this wife. While E. Antipholus wards off claustrophobia by lingering on the mart, despite his complaint that "My wife is shrewish when I keep not hours" (II.i.2), Adriana becomes obsessed with the conviction of her husband's infidelity, assured that to be excluded from two hours of his life is to be excluded from his heart forever. Unable to smile at grief, she becomes, in Luciana's words, one of the "many fond fools [who] serve mad jealousy" (II.i.116). In her company are Othello, Posthumus, and Leontes, who respond to suspected cuckoldry with privileged male fury. The jealous bourgeois wife merely nags, but her situation,[7] like that of her male counterparts, can be seen as the stuff of tragicomedy or tragedy rather than farce. Implicit in *Errors* is a transgression against the codified genre.

As Adriana's eloquent "nags" reveal her fierce hunger for a caring husband, Luciana's stilted set speech on male rule dwindles in importance, becoming, if not a non-sequitur, a red herring for which critics ill-advisedly have fished:

> There's nothing situate under heaven's eye
> But hath his bound, in earth, in sea, in sky.
> The beasts, the fishes, and the winged fowls
> Are their males' subjects, and at their
> 　　controls;
> Man, more divine, the master of all these,
> Lord of the wide world and wild wat'ry seas,
> Indued with intellectual sense and souls,
> Of more pre-eminence than fish and fowls,
> Are masters to their females, and their lords:
> Then let your will attend on their accords.
>
> 　　　　　　　　　　(II.i.16-25)

Just as Adriana's profound love for E. Antipholus undermines this speech's relevance, so the delineation of the male characters undermines its validity. "Man, more divine" is sadly represented in *Errors*. Most worthy are the loving but powerless Egeon, and Duke Solinus, who requires a miracle to enable him to tolerate foreign merchants as easily as he does native courtesans. The divinities with whom Adriana has more to do are even less awesome: the mountebank Pinch; the deluded, broken-pated Dromios; and their equally deluded, violent masters. Not surprisingly, Shakespeare bodies forth the principle of male supremacy through characters whose preeminence is dubious; Susan Snyder points out that the Elizabethan audience expected comedy to overturn accepted truths and customs (26-27), and Juliet Dusinberre points to those Elizabethan women who rejected the status quo, even to the extent of wearing men's clothes and weapons (7-8). Dusinberre notes that both liberated women and Humanist-influenced Puritans sympathetic to women comprised a significant part of Shakespeare's audience. For the more politically, intellectually, and theologically venturesome, Adriana must have evoked more compassion than amusement (11, 4-5, 15).

Nevertheless, the traditional interpretation of act 2, scene 1 reminds us that Adriana's emotional problems are compounded by her social situation: "revolt against a wife's place in the cosmic hierarchy," according to Harold Brooks, "is the original source of discord in Adriana's marriage" (67). In the cosmos as envisaged by men, woman is subordinate; hence, in the social system, she readily becomes a possession. At this Adriana has not balked. By marrying E. Antipholus, Adriana has accepted the authority of both the Duke and her husband, "who I made lord of me and all I had / At your important letters" (V.i.137-38). She revolts not against her place but against lack of love; her longing to be a vine to her husband's elm (II.ii.174-76) reveals her deepest desire: to subjugate herself in marriage. It is her misfortune that, in a male-dominated society, the possession who becomes possessive is regarded as a shrew.

Adriana's error is not refusal to accept male supremacy but the nagging tongue that provides her only relief. Even when she thinks E. Antipholus is courting her sister, she admits, "My heart prays for him, though my tongue do curse" (V.ii.28). She is trapped in a painful cycle. Feeling rejected, she desires her husband all the more desperately, but her incessant recriminations, later confessed to the abbess (V.i.62-67), elicit only further rejection from E. Antipholus. He lables her shrewish and "breaks the pale" (II.i.100), having found "a wench of excellent discourse, / Pretty and witty; wild and yet, too, gentle" (III.i.109-10). "Mad jealousy" prevents Adriana from realizing how self-defeating and absurd is the attempt to moralize another into love. Although a character's blindness is fundamental to farce, Adriana's pain is so keenly felt and lyrically expressed that sympathy undercuts laughter, and the problematic aspects of marriage—and genre—assert themselves.

Adriana's inability to comprehend the effect she produces upon E. Antipholus is the psychological reality behind the convention of indistinguishable twins in *Errors*. She is unable to distinguish her husband from his brother because she no longer knows her husband, having become totally engrossed in her own needs. Errors of physical identity aside, she speaks an emotional truth in her reply to Luciana:

> *Luc.* Then swore he that he was a stranger here.
> *Adr.* And true he swore, though yet forsworn he were.
>
> (IV.ii.9-10)

Adriana mistakes the newcomer for her husband because S. Antipholus is the honeymoon-lover of her heart's desire, like her husband in appearance, unlike him in spirit: sea-fresh, unspoiled by a stale marriage, trailing no minions in his wake. Most pitiful—and certainly at odds with *Errors'* farcical temper—is our realization, based on Adriana's intelligence, spirit, and capacity for love, that this out-of-control "shrew" must herself once have been "a wench of excellent discourse, / Pretty and witty; wild and yet, too, gentle"—another twin!

Despite her "venom clamours" (V.i.69), Adriana seems singularly restrained and chaste compared to her husband, a chief vehicle of farce in *Errors*. On stage, E. Antipholus strikes the Dromios (IV.iv.17,42) and Doctor Pinch (IV.iv.51), and attempts to pluck out Adriana's eyes (IV.iv.102). A messenger reports that E. Antipholus beats the maids, singes off Pinch's beard, throws pails of puddled mire on Pinch, encourages E. Dromio to nick Pinch with scissors

(V.i.169-77), and vows to scorch and disfigure Adriana's face (V.i.183). E. Antipholus compounds violence with insensitivity to his wife's feelings; by withholding love and attention he induces a jealousy that is not entirely paranoid. At his first entrance, he asks Angelo to assist him in deceiving Adriana as to his whereabouts (III.i.3-4); more important, his acquaintance with a courtesan would distress a wife as patient as Griselda. Although Luciana tries to allay her sister's fears, secretly she suspects that E. Antipholus wed Adriana for her wealth and that he likes "elsewhere" (III.ii.5-7). Although Shakespeare apparently departs from his sources, making E. Antipholus guilty of thoughtless or spiteful congeniality rather than adultery, French penetrates the underlying fable: "on the mythic level, the play deals with serious disruption: a man neglects his wife for his prostitute" (75). Matthew would have agreed: "whosoever looketh on a woman to lust after her hath committed adultery with her already in his heart" (5.28). In fact, Shakespeare does not rule out the possibility of E. Antipholus's having committed adultery. Edward Berry suggests that "The ring [which E. Antipholus receives from the courtesan] is an appropriate symbol of the sexual and economic ambiguities in Antipholus's extra-marital relationship" (183). In *Errors* the distinction between having the name without the game or the name with the game is not so much a matter of substantive moral difference as of genre: if E. Antipholus has fallen only in spirit but not in flesh, the sin is revocable, a comic rather than tragic error. A happy ending, or some semblance of one, remains a contingency.

Luciana's admonition and the intrigue plot collaborate to reveal a means of perhaps achieving that happy ending, if husband and wife allow themselves to be instructed. Luciana's speech on male supremacy misfires, but its introduction does not: "Why, headstrong liberty is lash'd with woe" (II.i.15). Directed at Adriana, this admonition applies with equal if not greater force to E. Antipholus. Adriana, awash in emotion, has only worsened her situation by abusing the liberty of her tongue as a quick-tempered mistress, contentious sister, and discontented wife. Her husband, abusing the liberty of his eye, has ravaged the marital peace; abusing the liberty of his hand, he is taken for mad. The woe such headstrong liberty has brought them could be alleviated through the self-government endlessly enjoined by Renaissance moralists, through the subjugation of our infected will to our erected wit.[8] To do other is mutual madness. During her exchange with the courtesan, Adriana finds a name for her husband's fault:

> *Cour.* How say you now? Is not your husband mad?
> *Adr.* His incivility confirms no less.
>
> (IV.iv.43-44)

Will she realize that she too is guilty of incivility, a concomitant of headstrong liberty, of the will's mastery? Erasmus can tell us whose fault is greater: "Of an evyll husbande (I wyll well) a good wyfe may be mard, but of a good the evyll is wont to be refourmed and mended. We blame wyves falsly. No man (if ye gyve any credence to me) had ever a shrewe to his wyfe but thrughe hus owne defaute" (sig. Dii^v). Nevertheless, both the unthinking husband and the neglected powerless wife suffer, having forfeited contentment by insisting on their own satisfactions.

The plot, undervalued for lacking an intriguer "to make the confusion delightfully purposeful" (Jorgensen 57), actually achieves the thematic purpose of forcing E. Antipholus to lose his identity and take on his wife's: serving mad jealousy, he feels what she feels. Thinking himself sexually betrayed—is he projecting his own guilty conscience onto her?—he discovers the pain of being "abused and dishonour'd / Even in the strength and height of injury" (V.i.199-200). In another comedy involving a shipwreck, tradewar, twins, jealousy, and madness, Malvolio, like E. Antipholus, is bound and imprisoned in darkness. The practical joke suits, for in the world of cakes and ale, Malvolio's confusion of ambition with love and his denial of harmless pleasure mark him as insane. Shakespeare first employs this jocular punishment in *Errors,* with himself, the playwright, rather than his characters, as intriguer. For his incivility E. Antipholus suffers the treatment of a madman. (Adriana is also punished for incivility: betrayed by the abbess to her own reproof and public embarrassment). The plot holds a mirror up to husband and wife, showing them how their headstrong liberty has guided time's deformed hand in writing strange defeatures on their marriage. Of course this couple may prove no more capable of profiting from their lessons than did Malvolio. The play remains curiously open-ended.[9]

Directors who impose a happy ending have a good case. Happiness being preferable to unhappiness, Adriana and E. Antipholus are likely to opt for it; theirs, after all, is a comic world. The audience also opts for the happy ending in comedy. Even in James Cellan Jones's BBC production, which stressed the non-farcical aspects of *Errors,* the beginning of a reconciliation is suggested as E. Antipholus places the chain about Adriana's neck. After all, Adriana and her husband have been party to a miracle, the reunion of a family sundered for a generation; to blast such unlooked for joy with self-indulgent discord touches upon sacrilege. Thanks to the miracle of reunion, their nuclear family is now extended[10]: Adriana's isolation turns to a gossips' feast, and E. Antipholus may find wholesome recreation within his enlarged family. Ironic as it is that the only incontrovertibly happy couple has been separated for thirty-three years, even so the advice and example of loving parents may foster civility in their children.

Perhaps most important as a persuader to civility is the future of S. Antipholus and Luciana. Luciana, who makes no reply to S. Antipholus's proposal (V.i.374-76), had indicated earlier, when she mistook him for her brother-in-law, only that his words "*might move*" (IV.ii.14, italics added). The psychological reality behind the convention of indistinguishable twins for Luciana—the reason she cannot tell her would-be husband from E. Antipholus—is that, expecting no more of men than that they be "secret false" (III.ii.15), she has little motivation to sift their appearance from their reality. Her commitment phobia, as it were, may be explained by a last act in which errors of identity are clarified but errors in love are not. Luciana's sixth-act response depends on the reflection of her own future that she sees in her sister's and brother-in-law's problematic marriage. Will brother and sister, for the sake of brother and sister, learn to curb their infected wills? After the players have left the stage, will problem comedy resolve to romantic comedy?

Whether Shakespeare's personal experience of marriage accounts for this novel admixture of genres in his first comedy is an intriguing but unanswerable question. His portraits of Kate, Emilia, and Paulina suggest, however, that the stock character of the shrew proved too narrow for Shakespeare's breadth of understanding. Adriana's uncomic potential is released as Shakespeare, unlike earlier writers of shrew plays, considers the causes of shrewishness and the ordeal of a shrew. Such considerations, dictating a more realistic view of personality and marriage, take us beyond the classical pale into something rich and strange.[11] (Later, Shakespeare's sensitivity to the stock Jew will change the generic coloration of *The Merchant of Venice.*) But whatever causes begot this generic experiment, *Errors* succeeds. The demons that frighten us the most evoke the most cathartic laughter. The difficulty of sustaining a loving relationship as nuances of feeling inexorably change is just such a demon. The farce of mistaken identities and hallucinatory situations creates the *verfremdungseffekt* that allows us to laugh when the pain of human isolation brings us closer to tears. Through generic disjunction, Shakespeare demonstrates how complex are the responses an audience can experience when Plautine intrigue bows to *genera mista,* creating, most notably, a timeless vision of dissonance in the comedy of errors we call marriage.

Notes

[1] According to MacCary, "the negative attitude toward marriage which spreads through Shakespeare's play derives from Plautus', where the local twin lies to his wife and steals from her, and finally deserts her entirely to go home with his brother" (530).

[2] Francis Fergusson is representative of another critical tradition. Although he notes that "there is one strand running through the whole *Comedy of Errors* which might seem, on a first reading, to break the mood of farce: the troubled adventures of Antipholus of Ephesus's long-suffering wife" and that Adriana "and her sister and her maid, and eventually her real husband's mistress, form a dreary female procession through the quick twists of the plot" (35), he relies on performance tempo to define genre. Competent production will defeat our human response: "We are not called upon for much sympathy or imagination: in fact we must not try to see through these characters' eyes, or feel what they feel. It would ruin everything to take the wife's troubles . . . at all seriously" (36). Fergusson justifies this reductive view by claiming that "The play belongs in the stream of popular comedy, from Menander to Minsky" (36).

[3] Although Alexander Leggatt draws a less precise parallel—between Adriana and Isabella—he observes that Adriana and E. Antipholus say nothing to suggest a reconciliation (9).

[4] The endings of *The Two Gentlemen of Verona, A Midsummer Night's Dream, The Winter's Tale,* and *The Tempest,* as Richard Levin observes in his argument for closure, also feature "silent women" (341, n.4). Not germane to my discussion are Hermia and Helena, who are granted the husbands they had originally desired and who ascribe their midsummer night's tribulations to an innocent dream rather than to fickle lovers. Neither is Miranda, who accepts the marriage Prospero has engineered for her, loving at first sight—of any man other than her father. But the endings of *Two Gentlemen* and *Winter's Tale* pose genuine problems if we accept Ralph Berry's premise that the behavior of the characters in Shakespeare's comedies (and by extension, in his romances) "is, or ought to be, explicable in terms of naturalistic psychology [since] Shakespeare's intuitive grasp of psychology is the foundation of his drama" (18). Silvia may well have second thoughts about the lover who so peremptorily makes a gift of her love to the man who had just attempted to rape her. And Paulina has suffered too much and lived too long to be "given" in marriage, no matter how well-intentioned the donor.

Taking issue with many readings of Shakespeare's endings as ironic or ambiguous, Levin attacks "refutation" (337) of Shakespeare's "real meaning" (349). Aside from the intentional fallacy, Levin's insistence that "Shakespeare did not wish to be misunderstood" (349) fosters a simplistic view of Shakespearean drama as straightforward movement on a depthless surface.

[5] Shakespeare's plays do not abound in happy marriages. Setting apart the generally dismal marriages in the histories and giving the benefit of the doubt to Kate and Petruchio (he likens her to a range of beasts of field and sky, and she finally learns to obey her "keeper" [V.ii.151]), to the Pages (each ready to deceive the other over Anne's marriage), and to Portia and Brutus (he confides in her only after she wounds herself), we are left with Paulina and Antigonus's doomed marriage and with unions in which one or both spouses is fatally headstrong or vicious: Dionyza and Cleon, the Queen and Cymbeline, Hermione and Leontes, the Capulets, Gertrude and Claudius, and of course the Macbeths!

[6] See, for example, Weiss 14-18 and Ralph Berry 31-33 (who are sympathetic to Adriana) as opposed to Charlton 68, Brown 54-57, and Evans 7. In the criticism much more is made of Adriana's shrewish possessiveness than of E. Antipholus's nascent philandering and full-blown violence. In an otherwise insightful discussion, Barber admits that Antipholus's "eye has strayed, to be sure," yet his emphasis is on Adriana's "usual rage" as "the jealous wife" (494), on "Adriana's jealousy," on her "self-defeating rage" as "the shrewish wife," on "her frenzy of railing," and on "her domineering bent" (495). Not only does Barber allocate the lion's share of the blame to Adriana, but he concludes his essay by making explicit a sexist joke that Shakespeare could easily have allowed to surface but significantly did not: "Adriana *may* have learned something from the Abbess' lecture, even though the Abbess turns out to be her mother-in-law!" (497).

[7] See Hupka's discussion of romantic jealousy as a culturally determined *situation* rather than an emotional aberration (313-16).

[8] James L. Sanderson emphasizes the need for patience:

> The characterization that Shakespeare gives the principles here may be somewhat "humorous," that is, limited to certain specific predispositions of character. . . . But it seems clear that Shakespeare also intends the audience to recognize certain traits of easy wrath, impetuosity in thought, and recklessness in conduct—in short, deficiencies in patience—and he dramatized the "errors" in the play as manifestations of such flaws of character.
>
> (609)

[9] Structuralists as well as genre critics are interested in the phenomenon of the side-stepped happy ending. The "meaningful absence" of the expected or the violation of a generic convention produces what Jurij Lotman refers to as a "minus device," whose importance should not be overlooked in the analysis of the text (51).

[10] With allowances for *Errors'* Ephesian setting, Adriana's and E. Antipholus's family corresponds closely to what Lawrence Stone calls "The Restricted Patriar-

chal Nuclear Family" that flourished in England between 1550 and 1700 (653-64).

[11] A major tenet of the hermeneuticist Hans-Georg Gadamer is that discovering new meaning in art is in fact discovering inherent potential meaning:

> the literary critic, who is dealing with poetic or philosophical texts, knows that they are inexhaustible. . . . Every actualisation in understanding can be regarded as an historical potentiality of what is understood. It is part of the historical finiteness of our being that we are aware that after us others will understand in a different way. And yet it is a fact equally well established that it remains the same work, the fullness of whose meaning is proved in the changing process of understanding, just as it is the same history whose meaning is constantly being further determined.
>
> (336)

Works Cited

Barber, C. L. "Shakespearian Comedy in *The Comedy of Errors.*" *College English* 25 (1964): 493-97.

Berry, Edward. *Shakespeare's Comic Rites.* Cambridge: Cambridge University Press, 1984.

Berry Ralph. *Shakespeare's Comedies: Explorations in Form.* Princeton: Princeton University Press, 1972.

Brooks, Charles. "Shakespeare's Romantic Shrews." *Shakespeare Quarterly* 11 (1960): 351-56.

Brooks, Harold. "Theme and Structure in *The Comedy of Errors.*" Early Shakespeare. Stratford-upon-Avon Studies 3. New York: St. Martin's, 1961. 55-71.

Brown, John Russell. *Shakespeare and His Comedies.* London: Methuen, 1957.

[Byron, George Gordon.] *Don Juan. Byron.* Ed. Jerome J. McGann. The Oxford Authors. Oxford: Oxford University Press, 1986. 373-879.

Charlton, H. B. *Shakespearian Comedy.* London: Methuen, 1938.

Dusinberre, Juliet. *Shakespeare and the Nature of Women.* London: Macmillan, 1975.

Erasmus, Desiderius. *In Laude and Prayse of Matrymony.* Trans. Richard Tavernour. [1532].

Evans, Bertrand. *Shakespeare's Comedies.* Oxford: Clarendon, 1960.

Fergusson, Francis. "Two Comedies: *The Comedy of Errors* and *Much Ado About Nothing.*" *Sewanee Review* 62 (1954): 24-37. Rpt. in *Shakespeare's Comedies: An Anthology of Modern Criticism.* Ed. Laurence Lerner. Baltimore: Penguin, 1967. 32-43.

French, Marilyn. *Shakespeare's Division of Experience.* New York: Ballantine, 1981.

Gadamer, Hans-Georg. *Truth and Method.* [*Wahrheit und Methode.* Tubingen: J. C. B. Mohr (Paul Siebeck), 1960.] Trans. of the 2nd 1965 ed. New York: Seabury, 1975.

Hupka, Ralph B. "Cultural Determinants of Jealousy." *Alternative Lifestyles* 4 (1981): 310-56.

[Johnson, Samuel.] Preface [to Shakespeare, 1765]. *The Yale Edition of the Works of Samuel Johnson.* 15 vols. New Haven: Yale University Press, 1958-85. 7: 59-113.

Jorgensen, Paul A. Introduction. *The Comedy of Errors.* Harbage, *William Shakespeare: The Complete Works.* 55-58.

Leggatt, Alexander. *Shakespeare's Comedy of Love.* London: Methuen, 1973.

Levin, Richard. "Refuting Shakespeare's Endings." *Modern Philology* 72 (1975): 337-49.

Lotman, Jurij. *The Structure of the Artistic Text.* Tr. Ronald Vroon. Michigan Slavic Contributions, 7. Ann Arbor: [University of Michigan Press,] 1977.

MacCary, W. Thomas. "*The Comedy of Errors:* A Different Kind of Comedy." *New Literary History* 9 (1978): 525-36.

Sanderson, James L. "Patience in *The Comedy of Errors.*" *Texas Studies in Literature and Language* 6 (1974): 604-18.

[Shakespeare, William.] *All's Well That Ends Well. William Shakespeare: The Complete Works.* Gen. ed. Alfred Harbage. 369-99.

———. *The Comedy of Errors.* Ed. R. A. Foakes. The Arden Edition of the Works of William Shakespeare. London: Methuen, 1962.

———. *William Shakespeare: The Complete Works.* Gen. ed. Alfred Harbage. The Pelican Text Revised. New York: Viking, 1977.

———. *The Taming of the Shrew. William Shakespeare: The Complete Works.* Gen. ed. Alfred Harbage. 84-114.

Snyder, Susan. *The Comic Matrix of Shakespeare's Tragedies.* Princeton: Princeton University Press, 1979.

Stone, Lawrence. *The Family, Sex and Marriage in England 1500-1800.* New York: Harper, 1977.

Weiss, Theodore. *The Breath of Clowns and Kings: Shakespeare's Early Comedies and Histories.* New York: Atheneum, 1971.

Williams, Gwyn. "'The Comedy of Errors' Rescued from Tragedy." *Review of English Literature* 5.4 (1964): 63-71.

Arthur F. Kinney (essay date 1988)

SOURCE: "Shakespeare's *Comedy of Errors* and the Nature of Kinds," in *Studies in Philology,* Vol. LXXXV, No. 1, Winter, 1988, pp. 29-52.

[*Discussing* The Comedy of Errors *in terms of dramatic genre, Kinney explores liturgical influences shaping the play.*]

In his extraordinarily helpful study, *Shakespeare and the Confines of Art,* Philip Edwards works from premises that may seem in the abstract not only potentially complex but paradoxical. One of them is this:

> The protean Shakespeare seems to change his being as he moves from the cosmos of *Hamlet* to that of *Othello,* of *Lear, Macbeth, Antony and Cleopatra.* Our attempts to synthesize and catch the common factors too often hide the more obvious and more important quality of dissimilarity. The characters speak different languages, were brought up in different moral worlds, face entirely new difficulties— just could not belong in the neighbouring play. In each play a different mind seems to be creating a different world.[1]

Yet earlier Edwards has also issued the cautionary observation that, unlike many great poets, "Shakespeare escaped public resistance: his work was not gradually mediated to the public by the discerning few" as we might expect art to be when it keeps changing from play to play; rather, "popular approval slowly moved him towards acceptance by the critics" (6). But to talk about any of Shakespeare's plays—and here I will concentrate on what is putatively his first play, *The Comedy of Errors*—as the Elizabethans would have seen and understood them, Edwards' sense of popular understanding, is to talk of the conventions for plays and entertainments which they had come through long training and experience to expect. It is to talk of the uniqueness of a Shakespearean play, what marks it off from the others, in light of its similarity to existing traditions. It is, as the Tudors would have us do, to speak of Shakespeare's works as redefining the nature of kinds.

For some time we have been doing just this with *The Comedy of Errors* more often perhaps than with any other of Shakespeare's plays. A quarter century ago, D. A. Traversi wrote that this play is "a farcical work completely in the manner of Plautus"; more recently, Joel Fineman confidently proclaims the play "purely a farce of twins, and a mechanical farce at that."[2] But it is not quite so simple as all that. Given the Tudor perspective, even the very title tells us it is not, for Shakespeare seems to signal his own design by putting *comedy* in the title as he does nowhere else. And, in fact, simply calling the play a farce has created difficulties in reading the text and in producing the play. If we read the play as a farce following such customary definitions and discussions as the well-known one by Eric Bentley, noticing the aggressive, hostile, and violent movement and sensing as a basic theme the destruction of the family and of family values,[3] we shall concentrate on the middle acts and ignore the beginning and ending of the play. Many directors do, and the result is something like *commedia dell' arte,* a contemporary form of comedy in Italy but one posterior to Shakespeare in England. Such productions not only skew meaning but fragment the play: in the New Arden edition, for example, R. A. Foakes cites the anonymous reviewer in the London *Times* who says of a 1905 production that

> We . . . find certain things in *The Comedy of Errors* out of place in what is mainly, after all, a farce— the impending death of Aegeon, for instance, the love-making of Antipholus of Syracuse to Luciana, and the scene between the Abbess and Adriana before the steps of the priory. These things are not of farce as we understand it. . . .[4]

Just so: the sharp juxtaposition of the play's title and its Plautine elements repeatedly asks us, as it must have asked the early Tudors, whether the play means to stress the absurdity of plot or the human need for family, whether it focuses on circumstances or on estrangement, whether it is controlled by incident or by theme, whether it means to arouse spontaneous laughter or quickened sympathy.

Our first reaction is to think that it means to do all of these things, to combine farce and comedy, yet so far only Alexander Leggatt has made much of this. "Shakespeare gives us a play in a more mixed dramatic idiom," he writes. "The market-place atmosphere of Plautus is still present, but it no longer monopolizes the play; it is varied by suggestions of fantasy and mystery, and the result is a mixture of styles."[5] Leggatt goes on to note the "collisions" (14) of farcical incident with comic themes to explain this "mystery," while others have turned to the exotic setting of Ephesus or the traditions of romance. But again the facts suggest that this is the wrong place to look: the initial staging of the play on Holy Innocents' Day (for a work dealing with innocents and innocence) and with consistent (and overt) Christian references (so that Ephesus takes on Pauline connotations) indicate, rather, that the "mystery" of this play is one shared with something like the *Secunda Pastorum,* the Second Shepherds Play of the "Wakefield Master," which sees something serious in the stolen sheep and something farcical in the act of discovering it. Shakespeare seems, that is, to have understood the ranging resources of kind to which Rosalie L. Colie and Alastair Fowler have called our attention even at the start of his long and varied career as playwright.

I

We *know* now *only* that *The Comedy of Errors* was produced twice, in 1594 at Gray's Inn and in 1604 at the court; *both* performances were on December 28, Holy Innocents' Day. That is no coincidence. This connection with an important feast day of the Elizabethan and Jacobean church—that church which required attendance and whose liturgy became second nature—points to a huge number of liturgical connections which, when pursued, reveal just how bold Shakespeare's brilliant and initial effort in combining Roman farce and Christian belief really was. In superseding the pagan world of Plautus with his own Christian one, Shakespeare emphasizes the precise moment of that catastrophic change as the Elizabethans always perceived it—at the moment of the Nativity. "At Christs birth all [pagan] Oracles were mute, / And put to lasting silence," Thomas Heywood writes,[6] pointing to the miracle of the Incarnation (or the re-incarnation, of and by God) that marked the Christmas seasons of joy and high spirits. The later John Selden is even more to the point: "Oracles ceas'd presently after Christ, as soon as no body believ'd them. Just as we have no Fortune-Tellers, nor wise Men, when no body cares for them."[7] In a play in which fortune-tellers are displaced by an Abbess, whose miraculous appearance seems permanently to defeat the devilish conjuring in newly holy Ephesus, she invites us to contemplate her "Thirty-three years . . . in travail" (V.i.400)[8] that by "the calendars of . . . nativity" can result in a "feast" (V.i.404-05) for "gossips"—that is, a time of baptizing, of "godparenting" (from the Anglo-Saxon *godsibb*). There is no more mistaking these references at the end of the play than the use of *comedy* rather than farce in the play's title. "After so long grief," the Abbess tells us, "such felicity" (V.i.406). This miracle which turns the holy Ephesus of the Holy Bible into a *proper* setting for this initially Plautine play—surely an act of felicity in Shakespeare as strong and as theatrically striking as any—is the mystery ("felicity") of birth, the sacred renewing in this play of the sense of Christ's birth. Indeed, it is the same mystery (and the same felicity) that we (and Shakespeare, drawing on native stage tradition as much as on his Plautine schoolbook tradition) found at the heart of the medieval cycles of

mystery plays, those other dramas of the Nativity and of Holy Innocents' Day when unbelievers (like Dr. Pinch in the witch-ridden state of Ephesus in *The Comedy of Errors*) would be replaced by those who had been informed by Christ (such as the Abbess in the newly holy city in the play).

Such hints of this native tradition of church plays and liturgical drama that surrounded Shakespeare as a boy in Warwickshire invoke not simply yet another possible genre in a play which deliberately mixes kinds to establish one of its own, but a tradition which invites us to some extremely helpful ideas about the play, ideas to which Shakespeare himself provides clues so as to direct (or redirect) meaning. *The Comedy of Errors* intends, with one reference following another, to direct us *away* from the farce of a world of men who are foolish in their pursuit of fortune and family when they forget about God and *toward* a sense of comedy such as that conceived by Dante in his own great *comedia* as providential confusion when wandering and bafflement invite man to contemplate wonder and grace—and achieve, through a kind of rebirth, a baptizing or godparenting, a restructuring of experience which takes the form not simply of union and transformation, but of reuniting, of making parts newly conceived into a whole which they had earlier enjoyed.

Moreover, this mixing of kinds is just what the Tudor imagination, at its best, was setting out to do—in the *Defense of Poesie* and *The Faerie Queene,* in *The Unfortunate Traveller* and in *Measure for Measure.* We should sense the need, furthermore, because the earlier frames of reference we have used, when pressed into the simplest sort of exacting service, simply will not do. Structurally, for example, *The Comedy of Errors* has no real basis, no deep structure in common with Roman Old Comedy. So, for instance, those plays in which a man and his wife plot against each other (as in *Casina*) or in which we observe the pranks of a parasite (*Curculio*) or a clever slave (*Epidicus*) depend on stories of intrigue and connivance. But there is no trickster in *The Comedy of Errors,* no deliberate intriguer; there is only Antipholus of Syracuse's suspicion of some, calling our attention to the fact that they are simply not there. The force of plot is, rather, the force of fate or providence, not the craftiness of wily man.[9] H. B. Charlton sees these Roman plays somewhat differently—"The outstanding feature of the whole body of Roman comedy is that whilst it is full of sex, it is almost entirely devoid of love. . . . the object is almost invariably illicit"[10]—yet this too points to the enormous gap between the intentions and acts of copulation in Roman plays and the discussions of love that saturate *The Comedy of Errors,* discussions (and definitions) by Egeon, Adriana, Luciana, the two Antipholi, and Emilia, the Abbess. The "hard fathers, foolish mothers, vnthrifty young men, craftie seruantes, [and] sotle bawdes" that Roger Ascham complains of in

Plautus, or the moral lessons the representative Tudor translator Richard Bernard finds in the New Roman Comedy of Terence, where we are to learn by knowing laughter "the nature of the fraudulent flatterer, the grimme and greedie old Sire, the roysting ruffian, the minsing mynion, and beastly baud,"[11] the stock stereotypes of farce, are simply not part of Shakespeare's play. Rather, "The study of Adriana's jealous love, the lyrical proposal of Antipholus of Syracuse to Luciana," says Kenneth Muir in his indispensable book on the sources of Shakespeare's plays, results in "bewilderment and horror."[12] Anne Barton agrees: "violence and disorder in Ephesus rise to a pitch that is both funny and frightening."[13] The emphasis on farce in Old Comedy, on plot in New Comedy, and on transformation in romance is replaced in *The Comedy of Errors* by a psychological portrayal of Antipholus of Syracuse and his servant Dromio acting out the fears that Egeon renounces at the beginning of the play, allowing Ruth Nevo, for one, to think of "a schizophrenic nightmare" in which "identities are lost, split, engulfed, hallucinated, imploded."[14]

Barton and Nevo are not merely two twentieth-century sensibilities looking back on Tudor times, but two critics profoundly engaged in the very process of Shakespeare's play when they see, from quite separate starting-points, how dangerously close this drama can seem to come to the apocalyptic. But it is precisely this scraping along the skin and bones of our psyches, this constant return to the basic themes and human fears of estrangement, solitude, and exile—of being alone without family or friend, or being (as one character puts it explicitly) partial, fragmentary, incomplete—that arises directly from the occasion at which it was first staged; for this sense of isolation, of incompleteness was precisely what the Nativity meant, both in simple narrative terms and in only somewhat more complicated liturgical terms, to the churchgoing Elizabethans. Men generally lost a sense of direction, they believed, and God, in order to call His family of man back to Himself, sent part of Himself, His Son, to reconstitute His larger and more complete family. The Nativity of Christ, which cuts like lightning through a moment in human history as the Tudors perceived and received it, awakens the pain of loss and at the same time offers hope of the end to exile. This is the force of the lessons at Christmas-tide, of the prescribed church homilies under Edward VI and Elizabeth I. Strangers made pilgrims in just this way is how Shakespeare's audience would have conceived of nativity and the Nativity on Holy Innocents' Day, and how they would have defined providence. The recent BBC production senses this too, for even among the mountebanks and harlequins of their initial *commedia dell' arte* production, the chief characters with whom we associate wear crosses and crucifixes and, whenever confused or distraught, persistently kneel and genuflect.

Just these concerns are what put us back in touch with Holy Innocents' Day, for which *The Comedy of Errors* was at least twice thought suitable. And so informed, we can see Egeon as the first innocent of many, yet one who seems remarkably, discordantly holy too: he would hazard all, he says, to find his sons. It is faith, rather than weariness, which prompts his acceptance of Ephesian justice at the hands of the Duke as the unexpected ways of a world governed by providence. Egeon's sense of "comfort" (I.i.26) at the threat of imminent death derives from the same sense of faith as Claudio's in *Measure for Measure*—"The words of heaven: on whom it will, it will; / On whom it will not, so. Yet still 'tis just" (I.ii. 125-26)—a play more openly Christian in setting, but a play also presented during the Christmas season of 1604, on St. Stephen's Day, two nights before *The Comedy of Errors*. As *Measure for Measure* has its pointer within the text in this early appeal of the Duke to heaven, so *The Comedy of Errors* also has its pointer at the outset of the play in the setting of Ephesus. It was Ephesus, in the Acts of the Apostles, where St. Paul "went into the Synagogue, & spake boldely for the space of thre moneths, disputing & exhorting to the things that *apperteine* to the kingdome of God" (Acts 19:8)[15] but where, as in Shakespeare's Ephesus, he seemed to meet only with witchcraft and sorcery "So that from his bodie were broght vnto the sicke, kerchefs or handkerchefs, and the diseases departed from them, and the euil spirits went out of them" (Acts 19:12). It is St. Paul as the more successive corrective to Dr. Pinch. But there is not only this early, itinerant preacher Paul but the letter-writer Paul, building the New Church: in Paul's other connection to Ephesus, his letter to the Ephesians.[16] Here we find in the Christian New Testament, rather than in Roman farce, the source that inspired *all* parts of *The Comedy of Errors*—that gives it its overall shape and significance, not only mixing with but embodying and transforming Plautine conventions. This summary comes not in the sermon on order and on the directions for husbands and wives, parents and children that has often been cited from Ephesians 6, although this has its part to play in Shakespeare's drama, but in the summary of life's experiences in Ephesians 2 (a text as popular with the Tudors as the later passage). This is a source which has never been cited in connection with *The Comedy of Errors,* but which proceeds from a statement on death not unlike Egeon's through the sin and confusion of the play's chief action and finally to the last transformation of spirit before the priory. "And you *hathe he quickened,*" Paul writes,

> according to the course of this worlde, & after
> the prince that ruleth in this aire, *euen* the
> spirit, that now worketh in the childr' of
> disobedience,

Among whome we also had our cōuersation in
time past, in the lustes of our flesh, in
fulfilling the wil of the flesh, & of the
minde, and were by nature the children of
wrath, as wel as others.

But God which is riche i mercie, through his
great loue wherewith he loued vs,

Euen when we were dead by sinnes, hathe
quickened vs together in Christ, *by whose*
grace ye are saued,

And hathe raised vs vp together, and made vs
sit together in the heauenlie *places* in Christ
Iesus,

That he might shew in the ages to come the
exceding riches of his grace, through his
kindnes towarde vs in Christ Iesus.

For by grace are ye saued through faith, and
that not of your selues: it *is* the gifte of
God,

Not of workes, lest any man shulde boaste
him self.

For we are his workemanship created in Christ
Iesus vnto good workes, which God hathe
ordeined, that we shulde walke in them.

(2:2-10)

This is the Ephesus the Elizabethans knew by trained
instinct, not Shakespeare's. The enforced segregation
of Syracusan and Ephesian in the play—like the separation of Jews from Gentiles and Christians from Phari-
sees in the Bible—results from human sin and hostility
which focus on the wrong kind of transgression of the
wrong kind of laws. The Elizabethans knew and understood that from childhood. Such divisive acts of
fallen men, spurred on by evil lust and Satanic intention in Shakespeare's play, were just those acts that
God, Jesus, and Paul meant to heal by *reunion*. Thus
the central theme of the letter to the Ephesians, and
one which Elizabethan preachers proclaimed with co-
gency and simplicity, is not only that of order but that
of a reuniting—we think of the speeches on reunion as
a kind of transformation back into the original state in
The Comedy of Errors[17]—and the same theme emphasized in the only drama written with Paul as its hero,
the non-cycle Digby play known as *The Conversion of
St. Paul*. This is a miracle play which has at each of
its three stations the story of the secular Saul and the
reformed—the transformed—Paul. Here too we are
taught that life is not a state of permanent separation
or loss ("I to the world am like a drop of water / That
in the ocean seeks another drop, / Who, falling there
to find his fellow forth, / [Unseen, inquisitive] confounds himself,") Shakespeare's Antipholus of Syracuse confesses early on (I.ii.35-38), but *of being found*.
Chaos and oblivion are destroyed, despite the immediate slaughter of some innocents, in the spreading need
and redemptive power of the Nativity ("here we wander in illusions—/ Some blessed power deliver us from
hence!" [IV.iii.41-42]). With the patience constantly

urged by such disparate characters as Adriana (II.i.32),
the Duke's officer (IV.iv.18), and the Abbess (V.i.102),
men learn to forget that "guilders . . . redeem their
lives" as the Duke's limited sense of law, of justice,
and of redemption has it (I.i.8), for his "law" condemns men "to die" (I.i.25). Rather, faith and "sanctuary" (V.i.94) "for God's sake" (V.i.36) are necessary
to bring a man "to his wits again" (V.i.96). Thus the
customary world of historic time, of farce—of assignations, wedlock, childbirth—is rescued, subsumed, and
eventually fulfilled in this play in providential time.[18]

Sensing this deeper organization in a play more integral and traditional than it is to us, the Tudors would
see the end of *The Comedy of Errors*, centered as it
is on the Abbess, as natural and fitting. Her powers,
A. P. Riemer reminds us, heralded by "elevated diction," are "beyond the ordinary through the holiness
and virtue conferred upon her by her 'order' " much as
Helena will claim all human powers are in *All's Well
That Ends Well* (II.i.147ff.).[19] The Abbess says, in Act
V of *The Comedy of Errors*,

Be patient, for I will not let him stir
Till I have us'd the approved means I have,
With wholesome syrups, drugs and holy
  prayers,
To make of him a formal man again.
It is a branch and parcel of mine oath,
A charitable duty of my order.

(V.i.102-07)

"The Abbess's powers are sanctioned by religion and
morality; she employs natural distillations—syrups,
wholesome drugs—accompanied by prayer. The phrase
'charitable duty of mine order' suggests that we have
here something other than merely practical, secular
medicine; the promise to make Antipholus a 'formal
man again' reinforces the particular nature of her skill,"
Riemer writes (113). But the Abbess, with all her
powers, is limited in her power: providence reminds us
of the true nature of providentiality. For the Abbess's
"control is merely emotional or theatrical: it is events
and circumstances that bring about the extraordinary
felicity of reunion and salvation," Riemer concludes
(114). Human expectations and tested beliefs can help
to save: it is a necessary cause in *The Comedy of Errors*,
most decidedly, but not an efficient one.

By changing the classical Epidamnum of Plautus'
Menaechmi, the Old Comedy of separated twins, to the
Christian Ephesus associated with Paul, then, Shakespeare decisively if subtly shifts the generic expectations of an Elizabethan audience steeped in Scripture
and the liturgical calendar from pure farce to something like a divine comedy in which emotional experiences and intellectual reflections portrayed by the
characters are shared simultaneously by the playgoers
despite their privileged knowledge of the twinned

Antipholi and their twinned Dromios. The comedy works, as Paul Ricoeur claims all comedies work, by moving "from what it says to that about which it speaks."[20] The shape of the travel undergone by Egeon and by Antipholus of Syracuse is like the progress of Pilgrim, but with a double pilgrimage. In both instances, "The pattern of man's individual life coincides with that of Christian history," as Richard Axton writes in reference to the earlier native drama:[21] both Egeon and Antipholus of Syracuse seek that they may find; they lose their present selves to find the fuller selves embodied in their reunited family; they hazard all that they may gain all in a new life that actually restores the old one but with the lessons brought about by faith and heralded by providence. That both characters openly declare this shared philosophy at the outset of the play, one in dialogue, the other in soliloquy, only secures it within the framework of Paul's letter, while the exorcism of Dr. Pinch and the imprisonment of Antipholus of Ephesus, with its allusions to the Harrowing of Hell, confirm, at the play's end, the need for conversion and the desire for salvation. The New Testament and its dramatic outgrowths, as in the *Conversion of St. Paul,* provide what Kenneth Burke calls the "frames of acceptance" of genres[22] in which, here, the past constantly informs the present while the present, in searching for the past, realizes the future. It is this simultaneity of two frames of time—both in the generations represented by Egeon and Antipholus of Syracuse and in the implied past and future—that *The Comedy of Errors* draws its confusion and its resolution. This it shares with the native English tradition of the miracle play, such as the Digby play of St. Paul, the Digby *Mary Magdalene,* and the Wakefield *Secunda Pastorum.*

II

Still this informing shape strikes us at first as startling—perhaps as ingenious—and certainly at some distance from the play as we have come to know it, on the stage or in the study. So much worldliness in the decidedly mercantile environment of Shakespeare's Ephesus, so many set-up scenes such as the confusion with the courtesan and the misunderstanding about dinner, and so many physical beatings and verbal brawls sound nothing at all like the miracle play of St. Paul—or of any of the other examples of the vibrant, abiding medieval drama that has come down to us. But in this instance, I think, our conventional expectations betray us. If we recall Mak and his farcical transformation of sheep for baby as a parallel to the Nativity in the *Secunda Pastorum,* or think of the brawling of Noah's wife or the double-dealing of Cain, events analogous to those in *The Comedy of Errors,* or the juxtaposition of Egeon's grief alongside the Dromios' antics with the mingling of potential tragedy and lively comedy in the Noah play and the Brome *Abraham and Isaac,* we will be closer to the expectations and realizations of the audiences to whom Shakespeare's first actors

played. Much like the language of the *Secunda Pastorum,* in fact, is the language of orthodox Christianity that *The Comedy of Errors* refuses to ignore. Adriana advises her sister, for example, that "A wretched soul bruis'd with adversity, / We bid be quiet when we hear it cry" (II.i.34-35); later she also senses of herself that as "I am possess'd with an adulterate blot, / My blood is mingled with the crime of lust" (II.ii.140-41). Insight, Antipholus of Syracuse tells Dromio elsewhere, is realized only "by inspiration" (II.ii.167).

Indeed, it is a peculiar critical myopia that with Shakespeare's apparent first play—closest in time and experience to the religious drama he saw in childhood—we have been blind to just the kind of influence which some of our best and shrewdest readers have found in much later Shakespearean plays—for the playwright, once launched on this sort of mixed reference (or mixed genres, mixed kinds) alluding to sacred plays even over secular influences, will do it again and again in the plays that follow. Hamlet can speak of out-Heroding Herod and Macbeth's porter can make passing but pointed reference to the Harrowing of Hell in plays written well after the dominance of mystery plays in England. There are numerous other, subtler instances. M. C. Bradbrook and somewhat later O. B. Hardison, Jr. were only the first to see in the tetralogy from *Richard II* to *Henry V* Shakespeare's own Protestant cycle. "When he wrote a cycle of secular history plays, depicting the Fall and Redemption of the English monarchy," Bradbrook comments in *The Growth and Structure of Elizabethan Comedy,*

> Shakespeare was adapting the forms of the old Faith to the glory of the new state, as any good Protestant would do. With the fall of Richard II, the Garden of England is despoiled. With the casting out of the diabolic Richard III, and the triumph of the angelically supported Henry, the ghosts are led out of hell and the curse is annealed. A divine comedy is re-enacted in political terms.[23]

In addition, Emrys Jones points to the Passion play in the mystery cycles as the pattern Shakespeare follows in the tragedy of Humphrey, Duke of Gloucester in *2 Henry VI,* and the play called *The Buffeting* (of Christ) behind the treatment of York in *3 Henry VI.*[24] Lear's humiliation, Coriolanus' exile, Timon's passion, and Caesar's assassination, he tells us, all deliberately hearken back to the plays of Christ's Passion (57, 59, 71-72) while Rosemary Woolf notes the *Massacre of Innocents* play—the true basis for Holy Innocents' Day where Herod ranted, as Hamlet knows—spelled out in Henry V's warning to the citizens of Harfleur regarding the carnage they will experience at England's hands if they do not yield:

> Your naked infants spitted upon pikes,
> Whiles the mad mothers with their howls
> confus'd

Do break the clouds, as did the wives of
  Jewry
At Herod's bloody-hunting slaughtermen.[25]
                                      (*Henry V,* III.iii.38-41)

Honor Matthews, whose entire book on Shakespeare deals with the marked and essential residue of medieval liturgical drama throughout all of his plays, finds pronounced verbal echoes of the *Ludus Coventriae*'s Cain and Abel in the speeches of Regan and Goneril, lines from *Nature* in Friar Laurence's speeches to Romeo and the *Coming of Antichrist* in the rise of Richard III, to name only three from hundreds of examples.[26] Richard S. Ide notes the slaughter of Duncan as the first of many slaughters of the innocents by Macbeth which lead, in time, to significant re-dramatizations in that play of the Last Supper, the Harrowing of Hell, and the Last Judgment.[27] Nor were such mystery plays at all remote. The Ashburnham MS of the York Cycle has notations for Elizabeth I by Archbishop Grindal, who examined the Papist script for its use of doctrine, while Matthews records a performance of the Coventry cycle at Kenilworth, neighboring Stratford, in 1575 and A. W. Pollard reports that miracle plays were performed at York at least through 1579, at Newcastle until at least 1589 and at Chester at least through 1600 (last copied in 1607).[28] As for Coventry, of the two extant plays surely from that cycle, one is the Coventry Nativity, performed by the Shearmen and Tailors' guild in Shakespeare's own day, covering the Biblical story from the Annunciation to the Massacre of Innocents, and staged at least until 1580. "As one whose boyhood was spent in Warwickshire," Emrys Jones reminds us, "Shakespeare was exceptionally well placed to catch by the tail the vanishing eel of medieval dramatic tradition" (33).

The form and features of the mystery cycles are pervasive in *The Comedy of Errors.* The cycles began with serious treatments of the fall (and "death") of Adam (needing, like Egeon, to be saved in the person or representative of Christ), moved into knockabout farce with plays on Cain and Abel (much as we witness with the treatment of the two Dromios), and then restored high seriousness in showing how Christ's love conquered travail and sin (as with the increasing seriousness of the final scenes of Shakespeare's play). Some works, like the *Secunda Pastorum,* even collapsed these stages into a single dramatic effort. Audiences expected to see such a varied narrative on a fixed platform with several *sedes* (mansions, rooms, doors) before an unlocalized *platea* or place on the ground swept clean for players to help them suggest and realize plot as pilgrimage. Thus the Digby *Conversion of St. Paul* seems to have been played on a platform which had Damascus at one side and Jerusalem at the other end and the road between a playing place before both, while the *Secunda Pastorum* showed both the shepherds' field and Mak's cottage simultaneously. Like the various "places" in the mystery plays, the moralities, too, had various locations which, if presented first with a kind of shared neutrality, soon took on moral signification as the play unfolded. Most of them, including *The Castle of Perseverance* with its considerable number of places preserved in a diagram in the Macro MS, shows at once both the Hell-mouth and the Hill of Salvation, allowing within the play the presentation of the four stages of the mystery cycle which is also apparent in Shakespeare's play: Innocence; Temptation and Fall; Life in Sin; Realization and Repentance.[29] Following these plays, *The Comedy of Errors* depicts a representative mankind falling into confusion; distracted by worldly things (like a cloak and a chain) of a mercantile world, such as the merchants of Ephesus whom St. Paul addresses; and vulnerable to desire (for an unnamed courtesan or for Luciana) as the witchcraft Paul sees in Ephesus marked the Ephesians. Like the near-contemporary *Everyman,* and like the portrayal of Ephesus in the Acts of the Apostles, *The Comedy of Errors* begins with the Summoning of Death. But like all these religious kinds too, Shakespeare's play shifts from a concern with *ars moriendi,* holy dying, to holy living, *ars vivendi.*[30] (The conclusion of *The Comedy of Errors,* in and before the priory, seems especially close to one of its predecessors, *The Play of the Sacrament,* which, embodying all of the Corpus Christi cycle in one emblematic play, also concludes its pageant of events before the church.) Thus the threatened death of Egeon, finding an early resonance in Herod's threatened slaughter of the innocents, also finds a grim model against which the miracles wrought by providence through the Abbess need to overcome.

Such church plays, acting as what Heather Dubrow suggestively calls "host genres"[31], transform not only the significance of the situation and the plot but even the borrowed doorways from the Roman stage. It is clear from the entrances, exits, stage directions, and stage business in *The Comedy of Errors* that the three doors are to the Porpentine (an animal known primarily for copulation in medieval bestiaries), the Centaur (the single animal in the bestiaries known for reason), and the Phoenix (a bird, capable of resurrection, that figures Christ).[32] In the play, these signs are for the house of assignation of the courtesan, the inn where Antipholus of Syracuse preserves his worldly goods, and the place where he discovers his "divine" Luciana, or the traditional stations of Hell, Earth, and Heaven of mystery and morality traditions here seen as humanly—as partially, even mistakenly—conceived by the wandering, fallen Antipholus.[33] Pointedly, Antipholus of Ephesus alone enters the Porpentine to conduct business, while Antipholus of Syracuse naturally seeks out the Centaur with his tendency to reason and to common sense. It is Antipholus of Syracuse who foregoes the physical satisfaction of a good dinner at the Phoenix, presumably a great attraction for Antipholus of Ephesus, for the satisfaction of love; and it is when he and his servant Dromio run away from this earthly site of resurrection that they come to the priory (stage direction at V.i.37) in a state of fear and in need of direction. He is explicit about his choices too: "Am I in earth, in heaven, or in hell?" he asks (II.ii.212), calling attention to the three doors of the Plautine stage transformed by Christianity early on in the play into a new set of stations, a new set of choices. And as in the miracle plays Hell here is called a "sty" or "pit" while the great "hall" of the priory suggests the setting of Heaven used in the N-Town cycle.[34] But the priory cannot be the same doorway as the Phoenix as previous critics claim, beginning with E. K. Chambers,[35] for Antipholus and Dromio of Syracuse are running *out* of that *to* the priory; nor can it be the door of the Centaur, for they are running away from their worldly goods to a place of holy sanctuary. The doorway of the priory, then, is the miraculously transformed doorway of the Porpentine; the Courtesan has been displaced, visually and on stage, by the Abbess, and through it she comes to conquer sin and commerce by calling forth the entire cast—the whole world of the play—and transforming them too. "Shakespeare's characters live," Harry Levin says tellingly, "in a Christian ethos."[36]

R. Chris Hassel, Jr. anticipates this understanding of the play when he remarks that "A glance at the liturgical tradition of Innocents' Day makes it even less likely that mere nostalgia or coincidence explains the dual performance of the play on that religious festival." He notes that the proper lesson prescribed for that feast day in the *Book of Common Prayer* is Jeremiah 31:1-17, concerned with "the dispersal and reunion of families. In fact, from such other prescribed passages as . . . Matt. 2:13-18, Rev. 14:1-5, and Isa. 60, we realize that this theme was a central motif of the liturgical festival." He notes further that

> Jeremiah 31 is insistently parallel to the first and final scene of *Errors*. After the Lord's several promises to gather the remnant of Israel from the coasts of the world, verses 15-17, on the ultimate deliverance of all innocents, seem particularly close to the situation and the sensibility of Egeon and Emilia, parents of their own lost children:
>
> 15 A voice was heard on hie, a mourning and bitter weping, Ra[c]hel weping for her children, . . . because thei were not.
>
> 16 Thus saith the Lord, Refraine thy voice from weping, and thine eyes from teares: for thy worke shalbe rewarded, saith ye Lord, and thei shal come againe from the land of the enemie.
>
> 17 And there is hope in thine end, saith the Lord, that thy children shal come againe to their owne borders.[37]

III

Shakespeare's characters, it would seem, like his audiences, could not escape the Christian ethos even if they wanted to.

So rhetorically this aporetic play, full of doubts, becomes at its conclusion ecphrastic in the forthright sermon of the Abbess, the overall structure resembling a renewed catechism. The stations derived from the miracle and morality plays are underscored by Christian references throughout the play—to the Dromios' twin births in an inn (I.i.53) following the example of the twin Antipholi (I.i.51), to Antipholus of Syracuse's admission that he is a Christian (I.ii.77) and to his Dromio's plea to his rosary (II.ii.188), to Luciana's litany of God's creatures derived from the Homily on Obedience as well as Acts 19 (II.i.15-25), while Act 4, opening with a reference to Pentecost, leads directly to Dr. Pinch's exorcism chanted in Christian terms (IV.iv.52-55), Antipholus' plea for deliverance (IV.iii.42) and Dromio of Syracuse's concern with Adam and his obsession with prodigality (IV.iii.16ff.),[38] and the Abbess' final speech on Pauline charity (V.i.102-08). Such open terms and echoes cast their light backward on the suggestive language which forms Egeon's autobiography as he reports it to the Duke. Egeon likens himself, it would seem, to the Adam of the Corpus Christi cycle: "Proceed, Solinus, to procure my fall, / And by the doom of death end woes and all" (I.i.1-2) by showing how his paradoxical response to say what passes the saying can give testimony to those who attend him:

> A heavier task could not have been impos'd,
> Than I to speak my griefs unspeakable;
> Yet that the world may witness that my end
> Was wrought by nature, not by vile offence,
> I'll utter what my sorrow gives me leave.
>
> (I.i.31-35)

His tale, then, is "what obscured light the heavens did grant" (I.i.66) while his problem, as he knows too well, is his lack of faith—he became "Hopeless to find" (I.i.135)—and his awareness of that very loss: "yet loth to leave unsought / Or that or any place that harbours men" (I.i.135-36). His need for mercy and for renewed belief is the occasion for mercy from the Duke, who anticipates the Abbess, and his words, like hers, are far more Christian than Plautine. Against his crown the Duke places his soul:

> Against my crown, my oath, my dignity,
> Which princes, would they, may not disannul,
> My soul should sue as advocate for thee;
> But though thou art adjudged to the death,
> And passed sentence may not be recall'd
> But to our honour's great disparagement,
> Yet will I favour thee in what I can;
> Therefore, merchant, I'll limit thee this day

To seek thy health by beneficial help;
Try all the friends thou hast in Ephesus,
Beg thou, or borrow, to make up the sum,
And live.

(I.i.143-54)

That such trust and faith has some possibility even in this atmosphere of crass materialism and of doom—one famous production featured a huge clock on stage—is made clear in the opening lines of the very next scene when a merchant tells Antipholus of Syracuse of his own fortune while warning him to keep his citizenship secret (I.ii.1-8). But he is his father's son, even through the most farcical of the scenes, and money and doom are abruptly transformed into something else: "I to find a mother and a brother, / In quest of them, unhappy, lose myself" (I.ii.39-40). What looks very much like the possibility of a coming act of providence, then, in a language popularized in the miracle and morality plays, seems assured when this Antipholus, lost in a new city and lost to himself, never loses sight of his faith.

They say this town is full of cozenage,
As nimble jugglers that deceive the eye,
Dark-working sorcerers that change the mind,
Soul-killing witches that deform the body,
Disguised cheaters, prating mountebanks,
And many such-like liberties of sin:
If it prove so, I will be gone the sooner.

(I.ii.97-103)

Attracted instead to Luciana, whose name means "light," he is always able to distinguish between women who are worthy and those who are not, as he has apparently taught his own Dromio. When he meets an Ephesian courtesan on the street, both he and his servant are aware of the temptation she represents, and in Christian terms.

Syr. Ant. Satan avoid, I charge thee tempt me
not.
Syr. Dro. Master, is this mistress Satan?
Syr. Ant. It is the devil.
Syr. Dro. Nay, she is worse, she is the devil's
dam;
And here she comes in the habit of a light
wench, and thereof comes that the wenches
say "God damn me," that's as much as to
say, "God make me a light wench." It is
written, they appear to men like angels of
light; light is an effect of fire, and fire will
burn; ergo, light wenches will burn; come
not near her.[39]

(IV.iii.46-55)

Both are tested here, and not found wanting, just as Antipholus of Ephesus will be tested by Dr. Pinch and again in the dungeon into which he is thrown. Such

temptations and trials here, as in the mystery plays, are what provide a blessed joy. "After so long grief," says the Abbess, "such felicity" (V.i.406),[40] figuring Mary as intercessor and as mother. At the end of the play, the law of the Duke is apparent with his reappearance—actually, only his second appearance—but he is soon made (eternally) subordinate to the Abbess, as Justice is made subordinate to Mercy in numerous scriptural plays.

So many punning and persistent words introduce us, at the end, to The Word. The final petition of the Great Litany in the *Book of Common Prayer* is strikingly appositive in thought and image: "Thoughe we be tyed and bounde with the chayne of our synnes, yet let the pitifulness of thy great mercy lose vs." The idea is reinforced in the general confession spoken each day at Morning Prayer: "We have erred and straied from thy waies, lyke lost shepe. . . . We have left vndone those thinges whiche we ought to have done, and we haue done those thinges which we ought not to have done, and there is no health in vs." "If we say that we haue no synne, we decyve ourselues, and there is no truthe in vs." But *The Comedy of Errors* does more than give rebirth to general doctrine; it also responds to—and is perhaps partly directed by—the liturgical text for Holy Innocents' Day, making the play a kind of parable for that occasion. The way in which Egeon and his sons seek their own salvation glosses the Scripture assigned that day for morning prayer and not noted by Hassel:

But this shalbe the couenant that I wil make with
the house of Israel. After those daies, saith the Lord,
I wil put my Law in their inwarde partes, & write
it in their hearts, & wil be their God, and thei shalbe
my people.

And thei shal teache nomore euerie ma his neighbour
and euerie man his brother, saying, Knowe the Lord:
for they shal all knowe me from the least of them
vnto the greatest of them, saith the Lord: for I wil
forgiue their iniquitie, and wil remember their sinnes
no more (Jeremiah 31:33-34)—

as well as the first and second lessons set for that day's evening prayer:

ARise, *o Ierusalem:* be bright, for thy light is
come, & the glorie of the Lord is risen
vpon thee.

For beholde, darkenes shal couer ye earth, and
grosse darkenes the people: but the Lord
shal arise vpon thee, and his glorie shalbe
sene vpon thee.

And the Gentiles shal walke in thy light, &
Kings at ye brightnes of thy rising vp
(Isaiah 60:1-3).

Babes, kepe your selues frō idoles, Amē (1
John 5:21).

The Abbess, like the play, draws into narrative those Scriptural passages which Elizabethans heard invariably, year in and year out, on the same day this play was presented, had perhaps just finished hearing that very morning or afternoon; and both move from the painful memory of a slaughter of innocents to the joy of the knowledge of providence which lies through and beyond such bloodshed during the celebration of Christ's birth, the Incarnation of God come to earth.

Such signs and symbols are captured in the *tableaux vivants,* the telling emblem scenes allegorically put forth in *The Comedy of Errors:* in the visual image of the bewildered Antipholus of Syracuse, the maddened (because uninstructed) Dr. Pinch, and, in the final moments, that scene on the steps of the priory that resembles, and is meant to re-embody, something like the Last Judgment. In this, too, *The Comedy of Errors* looks forward to *Macbeth* and especially to *Measure for Measure* where, Ide shows, Vincentio is heralded by trumpets and comes before the gates of the city to distribute rewards and punishments "much like his judicial model at the final compt before the gates of heaven."[41] But whereas that justice is purely retributive (and so goes awry), the judgment and justice of the Abbess are distributive (superbly informed by mercy): she displaces the justice of the Duke. This could not be clearer: "Justice, most sacred duke, against the abbess" (V.1.133) Adriana asks, insisting on the primacy of the law of Ephesus over the law of God, and her husband confirms this request: "Justice, most gracious Duke, O grant me justice" (V.i.190). But such law is at best imperfect; "Most mighty" but not sacred Duke, says the Abbess, "Most mighty duke, behold a man much wrong'd" (V.i.330). It is the Abbess' mercy overcoming human rule: "Whoever bound him, I will loose his bonds" (V.i.339), thereby gaining a husband (V.i.340) and sons (V.i.343, 401) whom she has "delivered" (V.i.402) with the help of God. Thus the Abbess reenacts the host of Judgment plays in the mystery cycles.

The wonders of the religious drama highlight the piling on of wonders that is the concluding movement of *The Comedy of Errors,* yet none is more wonderful than this: that so short a play—actually Shakespeare's briefest—moves all the way from the Nativity to the Last Judgment, spanning not only the life of the Christian but all of Christian history as well. That too is the essential idea behind Paul's letter to the Ephesians and so may also lie behind Shakespeare's choice of scene.

> 1 Therefore, *be§g* prisoner in ye Lord, praye you that ye walke worthie of the vocation whereunto ye are called,
>
> With all humblenes of minde, and mekenes, with long suffring, supporting one another through loue,

> Endeuoring to kepe the vnitie of the Spirit in the bonde of peace.
>
> There *is* one bodie, and one Spirit, euen as ye are called in one hope of your vocation.
>
> *There is* one Lord, one Faith, one Baptisme, One God & Father of all, which is aboue all, and through all, & in you all. . . .
>
> Til we all mete together (in the vnitie of faith & knowledge of the Sonne of God) vnto a perfite man, & vnto the measure of the age of the fulnes of Christ,
>
> That we hence forthe be no more children, wauering & caryed about with euerie winde of doctrine, by the deceit of m', and with craftines, whereby they laye in waite to deceiue.
>
> But let vs followe the trueth in loue. . . .
>
> Be angry, but sinne not: let not the sunne go downe vpon your wrath,
>
> Neither giue place to the deuil. . . .
>
> And grieue not the holie Spirit of God by whome ye are sealed vnto the day of redemption.
>
> Let all bitternes, and angre, and wrath, crying, and euil speaking be put away frō you, with all maliciousnes.
>
> Be ye courteous one to another, & tender hearted, forgiuing one another, euen as God for Christs sake forgaue you.
>
> BE ye therefore followers of God, as dere children,
>
> And walke in loue
>
>   (4:1-6, 13-15, 26-27, 30-32; 5:1-2).

The Comedy of Errors is also about the long suffering of those who face the deceit of men, temptations of the devil, bitterness and maliciousness in order to restore the one body of the family, as in one baptism, realizes this. His recognition ends the play: "We came into the world like brother and brother," he tells Dromio of Syracuse, "And now let's go hand in hand, not one before another" (V.i.425-26). "After so long grief, such felicity." So Hamner. But the Folio text does not say that. It reads, "After so long grief, such Natiuitie"—with a capital N, while Dyce, after Dr. Johnson, makes another choice still: "After so long grief, such festivity." He may not have the word quite right, but surely he has caught the sense of the play too. Seen thus in all its contexts, *The Comedy of Errors* is not merely a mechanical farce, a limp and imitative early play, or even a confusion of kinds, but an excellent play, well digested in the scenes, set down with as much modesty as cunning.

At the close, three couples stand with their servants united in one large family, presenting on stage the very heart of Christian theology in a living icon. It is a profound—and profoundly moving—effect, but actually it is only the last of many. For *The Comedy of*

Errors is, from first to last, a *play* of effects—the arrest of Egeon, the tardiness of Antipholus of Ephesus for dinner, the pursuit of Dromio of Syracuse by Nell, the sudden fascination of Antipholus of Syracuse for Luciana, the sudden appearance of the Abbess and her priory—that keeps us actively searching for causes, forcing us into the position of the characters who are likewise searching for causes, and, like them, frustrated, bewildered, and subject to wonder: open as they are to amazement and to grace.

And such searching by us before the play resembles that of Shakespeare behind it. "Shakespeare was not a system-builder: he was an artist, a dealer in dramatic fictions," Philip Edwards writes. "By adjusting the patterns of art, he would seem to be looking for that fictional ordering which could act as a powerful interpretive formula not only for the experience of his audience, but for his own" (14). Edwards has just cited *Twelfth Night, Henry V, All's Well That Ends Well, Antony and Cleopatra,* and *The Tempest,* but we do not need to seek for this motivating force, this secret of Shakespeare's power, in later or major works alone. It is there, coiled up, sprung, and in operation in the earliest of them, where the native, classical, Christian, and Pauline traditions of drama are first exploited and then, in turn, mingled, mixed, and metamorphosed. By bringing his powers of creativity and synthesis to the occasion of Holy Innocents' Day, Shakespeare's peculiar forms and powers of art are visible from the through love. Even the least of the characters, Dromio of Ephesus, first—and apparent for those of us who, like the early Elizabethans, can understand the signals, the allusions, and the significance of the various natures of kinds.

Notes

[1] Philip Edwards, *Shakespeare and the Confines of Art* (London: Methuen, 1968; rpt. 1981), 11.

[2] D. A. Traversi, *An Approach to Shakespeare,* 2nd ed. (London: Sands & Co., 1957), 14; Fineman, "Fratricide and Cuckoldry: Shakespeare's Doubles" in *Representing Shakespeare: New Psychoanalytic Essays,* ed. Murray M. Schwartz and Coppélia Kahn (Baltimore: Johns Hopkins University Press, 1980), 70. This line is the most traditional one. Cf. M. R. Ridley: "It is the best kind of slick prentice work. It is completely artificial, hard, glittering, and exact; but, of its kind, brilliant; it is completely mechanical, 'but it moves,' with the smoothness of well-oiled machinery" (*Shakespeare's Plays* [London: The Folcroft Press, Inc., 1937], 53). The most sympathetic and detailed of recent authorities is E. M. W. Tillyard, who writes, in his posthumous *Shakespeare's Early Comedies,* "The core of the *Comedy of Errors* is farce and it is derived from one play of Plautus and some scenes from another" (ed.

Stephen Tillyard [London: Chatto and Windus, 1965], 46). Harold Brooks, "Themes and Structure in 'The Comedy of Errors' " in *Early Shakespeare,* ed. John Russell Brown and Bernard Harris (London: Edward Arnold Ltd., 1961), 55-71, and Alexander Leggatt, *Shakespeare's Comedy of Love* (London: Methuen, 1974), chap. 1.

[3] Eric Bentley, *The Life of the Drama* (New York: Atheneum, 1964), chap. 7.

[4] Introduction to *The Comedy of Errors,* ed. R. A. Foakes (London: Methuen, 1962), liii-liv.

[5] Leggatt, *Shakespeare's Comedy of Love,* 3.

[6] Thomas Heywood, *The Hierarchie of the Blessed Angells* (1635), 24; quoted in C. A. Patrides, *Premises and Motifs in Renaissance Thought and Literature* (Princeton: Princeton Univ. Press, 1982), 116.

[7] John Selden, *Table-Talk,* 2nd ed. (1696), 139; quoted in Patrides, 118.

[8] Citations of this and other Shakespeare plays are to the New Arden texts.

[9] See the relevant discussion by Madeleine Doran in *Endeavors of Art: A study of form in Elizabethan drama* (Madison, Wisc.: Univ. of Wisconsin Press, 1964), 152ff.

[10] H. B. Charlton, *Shakespearian Comedy* (London: Methuen, 1966), 52.

[11] Quoted in Kenneth Muir, *Shakespeare's Comic Sequence* (Liverpool: Liverpool Univ. Press, 1979), 3-4.

[12] Kenneth Muir, *The Sources of Shakespeare's Plays* (New Haven: Yale Univ. Press, 1978), 16.

[13] Anne Barton, Introduction to *The Comedy of Errors in The Riverside Shakespeare,* ed. G. Blakemore Evans *et al.* (Boston: Houghton Mifflin, 1974), 81.

[14] Ruth Nevo, *Comic Transformations in Shakespeare* (London: Methuen, 1980), 22.

[15] My citations of Scripture are to *The Geneva Bible* (1560) in the facsimile ed. with an introduction by Lloyd E. Berry (Madison, Wisc.: Univ. of Wisconsin Press, 1969).

[16] Biblical scholars now doubt Paul's authorship of this letter, and assign it to the School of Paul; for Shakespeare, however, the letter was authentic.

[17] For example, at II.i.15ff.; II.ii.195-96; III.ii.39-40; IV.ii.19-22, 27-28; V.i.270-72.

[18] On these matters, see also Brooks, "Themes and Structure," 66.

[19] A. P. Riemer, *Antic Fables: Patterns of Evasion in Shakespeare's Comedies* (Manchester: Manchester Univ. Press, 1980), 113.

[20] Quoted in Nevo, 10.

[21] Richard Axton, "The Morality Tradition" in *Medieval Literature: Chaucer and the Alliterative Tradition,* New Pelican Guide to English Literature, ed. Boris Ford (Harmondsworth, Engl.: Penguin, 1982), I:347.

[22] Kenneth Burke, *Attitudes Toward History* (Los Altos, Calif.: Hermes Publications, 1959), 43ff.

[23] M. C. Bradbrook, *The Growth and Structure of Elizabethan Comedy* (London: Chatto and Windus, 1963), 21-22; cf. Hardison, *Christian Rite and Christian Drama in the Middle Ages: Essays in the Origin and Early History of Modern Drama* (Baltimore: Johns Hopkins University Press, 1965), 290.

[24] Emrys Jones, *The Origins of Shakespeare* (Oxford: Clarendon Press, 1977), 35-54.

[25] Rosemary Woolf, *The English Mystery Plays* (Berkeley: Univ. of California Press, 1972), 208.

[26] Honor Matthews, *Character & Symbol in Shakespeare's Plays* (Cambridge: Cambridge Univ. Press, 1969), 119. Surprisingly, she pays little attention to *The Comedy of Errors.* I am grateful to Raymond V. Utterback for directing me to Matthews' study.

[27] Richard S. Ide, "The Theatre of the Mind: An Essay on *Macbeth*" *English Literary History* 43 (1975): 338-61.

[28] Alfred W. Pollard, Introduction to *English Miracle Plays Moralities and Interludes,* 8th ed. (Oxford: Clarendon Press, 1927, 1965), lxvii.

[29] Such stations are diagrammatically shown for the Anglo-Norman *La Seinte Resureccion* and for *The Castle of Perseverance in Medieval Drama,* ed. David Bevington (Boston: Houghton Mifflin, 1975), 122, 796-97.

[30] Some of these remarks paraphrase V. A. Kolve, "*Everyman* and the Parable of the Talents," in *Medieval English Drama: Essays Critical and Contextual,* ed. Jerome Taylor and Alan H. Nelson (Chicago: Univ. of Chicago Press, 1972), 340.

[31] Heather Dubrow, *Genre* (London: Methuen, 1982), 116.

[32] Cf. T. H. White, *The Bestiary: A Book of Beasts,* a trans. of a Latin Bestiary of the twelfth century (New York: Putnam, 1954), 10n., 86, 125ff.

[33] The recent York presentation of the York cycle at the ruins of St. Mary's Abbey has such a stage which shows Hell-Mouth at one end, the Hill of Salvation at another location, and various stations along a front stage for various locations on earth.

[34] See Nelson, "Some Configurations of Staging in Medieval English Drama," in Taylor and Nelson, *Medieval English Drama,* 116-47, esp. 133ff.

[35] E. K. Chambers, *William Shakespeare: A Study of Facts and Problems* (Oxford: Clarendon Press, 1930), 1:307; the idea reappears (without source) in Stanley Wells, Introduction to *The Comedy of Errors,* New Penguin Shakespeare (Harmondsworth: Penguin, 1972), 25, and in Foakes, xxxiv-xxxv.

[36] Harry Levin, Introduction to *The Comedy of Errors,* The Signet Classic Shakespeare (New York: New Amerian Library, 1965), xxviii.

[37] Rudolph Chris Hassel, *Renaissance Drama & the English Church Year* (Lincoln, Neb.: Univ. of Nebraska Press, 1979), 40-41.

[38] In his edition of the play (Cambridge: Cambridge Univ. Press, 1962), 106, J. Dover Wilson notes that "Dromio's mind is full of images from the old miracle and morality plays." Also quoted in A. C. Hamilton, *The Early Shakespeare* (San Marino, Calif.: Huntington Library, 1967), 100n.

[39] For more discussion of this passage, see James H. Sims, *Dramatic Uses of Biblical Allusions in Marlowe and Shakespeare,* University of Florida Monographs, Humanities No. 24 (Gainesville, Fla.: Univ. of Florida Press, 1966), 30.

[40] "The celebration called for by Aemilia is properly a nativity feast because the central characters are truly reborn; each of them has gained new relationships and thus in the metaphysics of the play transformed his identity." Thomas F. Van Laan, *Role-playing in Shakespeare* (Toronto: Univ. of Toronto Press, 1978), 25.

[41] "Homiletic Tragicomedy and the Ending of *Measure for Measure,*" an unpublished essay Ide has shared with me, 10.

FURTHER READING

Arthos, John. "Shakespeare's Transformation of Plautus." *Comparative Drama* 1, No. 4 (Winter 1967-68): 239-53.

Discusses Shakespeare's substitution of a hierarchical social order for Plautus's disordered and confused collection of citizens, and asserts that such a change shows Shakespeare's predilection for just and ordered societies.

Baker, Susan. "Status and Space in *The Comedy of Errors.*" *Shakespeare Bulletin* 8, No. 2 (Spring 1990): 6-8.

Discusses various staging issues in *The Comedy of Errors* in light of the acting theories of Keith Johnstone, which highlight the play's emphasis on displacement, dislocation, and dispossession.

Clubb, Louise George. "Italian Comedy and *The Comedy of Errors.*" *Comparative Literature* XIX, No. 3 (Summer 1967): 240-51.

Relates *The Comedy of Errors* to the *commedia grave* of the Italian counter-reformation. Though no direct link can be found in the compositional genetics of *The Comedy of Errors,* Clubb cites certain features that distinguish the *Comedy* and the *commedia grave* from the medieval Italian comedies: the lesser role of the courtesan, the "addition of pathos," the theme of jealousy, the theme of madness and sorcery, and the reunification of the characters at the close of the play.

Grivelet, Michel. "Shakespeare, Molière, and the Comedy of Ambiguity." *Shakespeare Survey* 22 (1969): 15-26.

Develops a psychological theory of comedy and laughter and discusses the similarities and differences between Plautus's *Menaechmi* and its different adaptations in Shakespeare's *Comedy of Errors* and Molière's *Amphitryon.*

Hamilton, A. C. "The Early Comedies: *The Comedy of Errors.*" In *The Early Shakespeare,* pp. 90-108. San Marino, CA: Huntington Library, 1967.

Explores *The Comedy of Errors* as a harbinger of Shakespeare's mature work, discussing both the many strengths already present and the weaknesses that were later to be improved upon.

Levin, Harry. "Two Comedies of Errors." In *Refractions: Essays in Comparative Literature,* pp. 128-50. New York: Oxford University Press, 1966.

Reviews the similarities and differences between *The Comedy of Errors* and the *Menaechmi.* Levin concentrates on the problem of identity and demonstrates that Shakespeare deepened Plautus's two-dimensional play.

Marcotte, Paul J. "Luciana's Prothalamion: Comedy, Error, Domestic Tragedy." *College Literature* IX, No. 2 (Spring 1982): 147-49.

A defense of Adriana, which uses, virtually without comment, quotations from Shakespeare and other contemporary authors to show that women are as a matter of course very ill-treated by men in general and their husbands in particular.

Parker, Patricia. "Elder and Younger: The Opening Scene of *The Comedy of Errors.*" *Shakespeare Quarterly* 34, No. 3 (Autumn 1983): 325-27.

Explicates a textual point concerning the division of Egeon's family during the original shipwreck that prepares for the plot of *The Comedy of Errors.*

Slights, Camille Wells. "Time's Debt to Season: *The Comedy of Errors,* IV.ii.58." *English Language Notes* XXIV, No. 1 (Sept. 1986): 22-25.

Proposes an interpretation of what has been taken for a corrupted passage by most Shakespeare editors and connects it with an interpretation of the play's treatment of time as one of its structuring themes.

Weller, Barry. "Identity and Representation in Shakespeare." *English Literary History* 49, No. 2 (Summer 1982): 339-62.

Includes a brief discussion of *The Comedy of Errors* in the context of an analysis of Shakespeare's treatment of the theme of self-discovery.

Twelfth Night

For further information on the critical and stage history of *Twelfth Night*, see *SC*, Volumes 1 and 26.

INTRODUCTION

Written before the "problem comedies" such as *Troilus and Cressida* and *Measure for Measure*, *Twelfth Night* marks for many critics the most well-crafted of Shakespeare's "happy comedies," one rich in symbolism and complex in its exploration of love, its blurring of appearance and reality, its troubling of gender, and its portrayal of human psychology.

As in most of Shakespeare's romantic comedies from the 1590's, love motivates many of the characters' actions and attitudes. Some commentators, such as Peter G. Phialas (1966) and Charles Tyler Prouty (1966), have claimed that the characters interact in order to depict a Renaissance ideal of courtly love. Richard Henze (1975) has expanded this line of thought, arguing that Shakespeare resolves the play's contradictions through the interaction of characters, particularly through love-relationships. Similarly, Dennis R. Preston (1970) has asserted that the minor characters bind the seemingly disparate elements of the play, forming a unified whole. Other critics, including Terence Eagleton (1967), have contended that love in the play fuses language and reality, and thus questions the fixity of nature.

While some scholars have argued that love is the primary subject of *Twelfth Night* and have debated whether it has a unifying or dissembling effect on the dichotomy between appearance and reality, other commentators have identified this very dichotomy as the play's central theme. For example, Karen Greif (1981) has focused on Shakespeare's questioning of the nature of truth through the characters' "play," claiming that "*Twelfth Night* poses questions about 'the purpose of playing' and about whether illusion is perhaps too deeply embedded in human experience to be ever completely separated from reality." Other critics, including D. J. Palmer (1967), have contextualized Shakespeare within a tradition that conflates art and nature, and Walter N. King (1968), drawing on the history of philosophy, has considered Shakespeare to be consciously commenting on a Parmenidean approach to metaphysics. The resulting portrayal of nature has led commentators such as Karin S. Coddon (1993) to consider *Twelfth Night* as questioning the stability of so-

cial status by troubling a supposedly natural hierarchy in Elizabethan society.

In addition to Shakespeare's problematizing the fixity of nature, many feminist literary theorists have claimed that disorder in *Twelfth Night* also affects definitions of sex and gender, focusing primarily on the Viola/Cesario character. Scholars have extensively debated whether Shakespeare consciously or unconsciously uses Viola's role-playing to demonstrate the plasticity of socially constructed gender roles as well as whether the character calls supposedly fixed sexual differences into question. Stevie Davies (1993) and Nancy Hayles (1979), for example, have contended that Viola's role-playing questions the idea of a naturally determined gender. Others, such as Lorna Hutson (1996), have argued that Shakespeare affirms not only the plasticity of gender, but the rhetorical construction of sex as well.

Modern commentators have also studied the tenets of psychoanalysis to explore both the actions of the characters and the motivations of the author. Freudian and Jungian taxonomies have been used to dissect characters' actions (such as Viola's putting on the guise of a man) and their personification of psychological attributes. For example, Helene Moglen (1973) has contended that *Twelfth Night* portrays a psychological picture "strikingly similar to major aspects of Freud's own theory of psycho-sexual development." Critics such as Leonard F. Manheim (1964) have even applied psychoanalytic theory to Shakespeare himself, finding in *Twelfth Night* an expression of his unconscious attempt to enact an Oedipal fantasy.

Critical approaches to *Twelfth Night* have varied considerably, from strict examinations of the text alone to psychoanalytic evaluations of its author, from historical inquiries into Elizabethan love to feminist interpretations of sex and gender. Regardless, *Twelfth Night* continues to attract contemporary criticism, as commentators find in the play the height of Shakespeare's comedic art.

OVERVIEWS

Peter G. Phialas (essay date 1966)

SOURCE: "*Twelfth Night*," in *Shakespeare's Romantic Comedy: The Development of Their Form and*

Meaning, The University of North Carolina Press, 1966, pp. 256-305.

[*In the following essay, Phialas examines the elements of* Twelfth Night *that Shakespeare adapted from his earlier comedies, and he discerns in the play an ideal of love that emerges through the juxtaposition of Viola's selfless love and the self-indulgent love of Orsino and Olivia.*]

I

Twelfth Night has been called a masterpiece not of invention but recapitulation, a summing-up of the admirable features of the "joyous" comedies. It is certainly that and much more. Its connections with earlier Shakespearean comedies are many and they have to do with large elements of the plot, although of course we should bear in mind that some of these elements are present also in the sources of the play. In any case, it is clear that the confusion of twins goes back to *The Comedy of Errors.* The theme of a disguised lady serving the man she loves in his courtship of another woman, though present in the sources of *Twelfth Night,* had been employed in *The Two Gentlemen of Verona.* And here it may be worth mentioning that the disguised Julia in *The Two Gentlemen of Verona* calls herself Sebastian. Sebastian's devoted Antonio in *Twelfth Night* recalls Bassanio's equally devoted friend of the same name in *The Merchant of Venice.* With *Much Ado About Nothing,* as with other comedies, *Twelfth Night* has in common the motif of the disdainful lover, a motif it develops rather in the way of *As You Like It,* where Phoebe in some ways anticipates Olivia's fruitless love for a disguised lady. Another connection with *As You Like It* is an analogy in the roles of Viola and Silvius, both of whom undertake to advance rival love affairs of those they love themselves. Furthermore, and far more significant, is the fact that Feste, though of course a fresh, independent character, is a creation in the new manner of Touchstone, and he is intended to supply something like the latter's point of view and commentary.[1] These and other features of earlier comedies *Twelfth Night* employs in fresh combinations, in an action that, in spite of these borrowings, produces the impression of complete novelty. But although the story is fresh and although Shakespeare invents episodes and characters, the total effect of the play, its chief thematic concern, repeats the large meaning we have discovered in the earlier plays and particularly in the other two joyous comedies. If we accept as the play's chief theme the education in the ways of love of the disdainful as well as the romantic lover then it is clear that in this it repeats the central ideas of *As You Like It* and *Much Ado About Nothing.* And if in addition we accept Rosalind as the representative of the ideally balanced temperament and exemplar of the proper attitude toward love, then we shall conclude that Shakespeare intends something very

like that in his conception of Viola. This is not to say that the two heroines have the same temperament but rather that through them, in somewhat different ways, the dramatist defines the proper point of view towards life's processes. Through their intelligent, level-headed, and generous approach to the challenges of this "working-day world," they demonstrate the sure way to maximum happiness for themselves and those around them. Of this more presently.

In chronology *Twelfth Night* appears to have followed the other two joyous comedies, and its date can be fixed with fair accuracy. To begin with, the limits of that date are 1598, the year of Meres' *Palladis Tamia,* which fails to mention the play, and the first allusion to it on February 2, 1601/2 (Candlemas), in John Manningham's *Diary,* where he records that at "our feast wee had a play called 'Twelue Night or What you Will.'"[2] But before this performance of February, 1601/2, the play must have been acted in a private or public theatre or both. The title strongly suggests that it was first acted on Twelfth Night, and this would defeat Dover Wilson's view that it was originally drafted for the performance at the Inns of Court on February 2, 1601/2, to which Manningham alludes in his diary.[3] Two contemporary facts, though seeming to raise difficulties, ultimately contribute to a precise dating of the play. Shakespeare's company acted a play at court on Twelfth Night, January 6, 1600/1, and on that same day the Queen entertained Don Virginio Orsino, Duke of Bracciano, who was visiting her court. And what is even more tantalizing is his report in a letter to his Duchess that the Queen's entertainment had included *una commedia mescolata, con musiche e balli,* "a mingled comedy with bits of music and dances."[4] Unfortunately Don Virginio gives no further details but promises his Duchess to tell her more by word of mouth. From this and other contributory records Leslie Hotson has concluded that *Twelfth Night* was the play in question, that Shakespeare's Orsino is a graceful compliment to the visiting Duke, that Olivia is intended to suggest the Queen, and that Malvolio is indeed, as other critics had supposed, an audacious though by no means impudent satiric portrait of Sir William Knollys, the Queen's controller.[5] Some connection between the name of Shakespeare's Orsino and the Queen's royal visitor there must be, but it is scarcely possible that Shakespeare wrote the play especially for the Duke's entertainment. One reason is that he would have had scant time—just eleven days—to compose the comedy since firm news of the Duke's journey and of the probable date of his arrival reached Whitehall on Christmas Day, 1600.[6] It was thus on Christmas Day or shortly thereafter that the Queen gave detailed directions to her Lord Chamberlain which he was to follow in planning the grand entertainment. Among these directions occur the following: "To Confer with my Lord Admirall and the Master of the Revells for takeing order generally with the players to make choyse of [?the] play that shalbe best furnished with rich apparell, have great variety and change of Musicke and daunces, and of a Subject that may be most pleasing to her Majestie."[7] The probability is strong that "to make choyse" here means select a play in existence, not commission a new one, a play with music and dance and a theme pleasing to the Queen. The care and minuteness of detail in the royal directions suggest that the Queen was unwilling to allow chance and improvisation to detract from the splendor of the royal celebration, and it seems logical to conclude that she wished to present to her visitor a play known to possess the qualities she specified. Furthermore, it is not certain that Shakespeare's Orsino and Olivia would have been sufficiently flattering to Don Virginio and his imperial hostess. In all probability the play was written later in the year 1601, when the name Orsino could be employed with greater propriety and the character could be presented with greater freedom than would have been possible in 1600. Other evidence points to a date after 1600. The new map alluded to in III, ii, 66, is that in Hakluyt's *Voyages* which was printed in 1600. In addition, 1600 is the date of Robert Jones's *First Booke of Songs and Ayres* from which Shakespeare borrowed the song "Farewell, dear heart," which is sung alternately by Feste and Sir Toby Belch.[8] What all this does is to narrow the probable date of the play by placing it in or after 1600 and before Manningham's allusion on February 2, 1601/2. Since, as we have seen, 1600 will not do, the only Twelfth Night available was that of 1601, and this means that the play, the last of Shakespeare's romantic comedies, must have been acted for the first time a few weeks before Manningham's reference to it on February 2, 1601/2.

II

For the love story of the four chief characters in the play Shakespeare may have turned to a variety of sources, dramatic and non-dramatic. The chief of these seems to have been the story of Apolonius and Silla in Barnaby Riche's *Farewell to Militarie Profession,* first printed in 1581. Here Shakespeare found the story of twins of different sexes, which would admit a romantic treatment of the sort of confusion of identity which in a different context had formed the central theme of *The Comedy of Errors.* In addition he found a shipwreck on a strange coast which forces the heroine to take the sex and name of her brother. Thus disguised, Silla (Viola) seeks employment with Apolonius (Orsino), the man she loves, who sends her to court Juliana (Olivia) for him. The latter, rejecting Apolonius' suit, falls in love with the disguised Silla, who is later replaced by her long-absent twin brother, Silvio (Sebastian). Silvio's acceptance of Juliana's invitation, Juliana's revelation of her betrothal, her criticism of the page's refusal to acknowledge it, and the Duke's anger with his page—these matters are so close to the

corresponding episodes in *Twelfth Night* that Shakespeare must have known Riche's version of the tale.[9]

The alleged topicality of the conflict between Sir Toby and Malvolio has been the subject of much speculation. In addition to Leslie Hotson's theory alluded to above, it has been observed that another contemporary quarrel may have given Shakespeare the impetus and even details for the attack upon Malvolio. The quarrel was that between Sir Posthumus Hoby and two or three gentlemen, including Sir Richard Cholmley and William Eure, who, after a day's hunting in the country, invited themselves to spend the night in Hoby's house and proceeded to disturb that household with their boisterous drinking. The matter was brought to trial and seems to have been the talk of London during the years 1600-02.[10] Still another source for the Malvolio episodes has been found in Sidney's *Arcadia,* in the broad comedy dealing with Dametas and his family.[11] A more likely influence upon the episodes with Malvolio and his tormentors may have been the severe onslaught upon humour characters in Jonsonian comedy. Such influence may have been particularly strong in Shakespeare's conception of Malvolio and Sir Andrew Aguecheek. The latter may be seen in part as a composite of Matthew and Stephen, Jonson's city and country gulls in his *Every Man in His Humour.*[12]

III

The materials available to Shakespeare were, then, extensive; and it is possible that he was indebted to a good many of them. But what is of great interest is that the two chief actions in the play, the mistaking of twins and the service by a disguised lady of the man she loves in his courtship of another woman, had each been dramatized in different plays by Shakespeare at the very outset of his career. In *Twelfth Night,* where he combines these two actions, he seems to complete the circle. But the way the two themes are combined and the conception of the characters, especially the heroines, clearly give proof of the distance Shakespeare had measured since the composition of *The Comedy of Errors* and *The Two Gentlemen of Verona.* And thus the structure of *Twelfth Night,* the way its episodes are conceived and related, the re-creation of characters found in the sources, the invention of new episodes and characters, the function of music and song, and in general the mutual qualification of the play's several parts—these matters derive in great part from earlier comedies written in the long interval of nearly ten years. Whether Shakespeare was indebted to a contemporary quarrel or Sidney's *Arcadia* for a few details in the Malvolio episodes it is impossible to say.[13] What is clear is that those episodes owe their presence to Shakespeare's concern with different attitudes toward love. And it is equally clear that those episodes are presented in close relationship to the chief events in the comedy. Malvolio is not simply the butt of the inebriated Sir Toby and Andrew Aguecheek. He is conceived in terms which bear close relevance to the love theme of the play.[14] Malvolio is first and last one of Olivia's suitors, and his chief contribution to the play is in representing a particular attitude toward love as well as toward himself and his world. In this he recalls Jaques of *As You Like It,* and it is his peculiar response to love and his rigid objection to all indulgence which exclude him for a time from the happy and harmonious conclusion of the play. Malvolio's opposition to indulgence, in itself an important theme of the play, is the immediate cause of his undoing, but that undoing has to do with him as Olivia's suitor, one who represents a particular conception of love. Malvolio has clearly evolved out of Shakespeare's preoccupation, in his romantic comedies, with different and often conflicting conceptions of man's ideal relationship to woman.[15]

Malvolio's love for Olivia, or what he takes to be love, is limited or rather vitiated by his extreme and humorless self-love. But there is another side in Shakespeare's conception of the pompous steward. The complete absence of humor and self-awareness in him is coupled with a fierce indictment of all liberality and pleasure.[16] In this he stands for an extreme view which, by juxtaposition with its opposite, is intended to point to an ideal attitude. But the theme of indulgence is not a gratuitous adjunct to the main concern of *Twelfth Night*. It is instead a theme dramatized in analogical relationship to the theme of love. Thus Malvolio, involved in both themes, must be seen as a central character, and the dramatist's conception of him is clearly dictated by thematic considerations. He evolves in great part out of Shakespeare's choice to dramatize the analogy between romantic love and self-indulgence.[17]

Other features in the action of *Twelfth Night* which derive from earlier plays may be cited. The scene in which Orsino declares his love for Olivia in the hearing of the disguised Viola repeats in the main the action of a similar episode in *The Two Gentlemen of Verona*. There is of course an important difference, namely the fact that, unlike Proteus, Orsino is not violating any love vows made earlier to the disguised woman who loves him. And this difference is dictated by the dramatist's choice to stress different motifs in the two scenes. In the scene in *The Two Gentlemen of Verona* the emphasis is upon Proteus' violation of his vows and the effect of his action upon the disguised Julia. In *Twelfth Night* the stress is upon the Duke's manner of expressing his infatuation with Olivia, his hyperbolic romanticism, as well as upon its painful effect on the disguised Viola. Here there is no immediate question of fickleness on the part of Orsino in the sense of the episode in *The Two Gentlemen of Verona*.[18] Orsino's outpouring of what he considers his great passion for Olivia is of course undermined by his rhetoric, but it is also thrown into comic relief in retrospect

later on in the play by his all too sudden transference of that passion from Olivia to Viola.

Among the many links connecting the comedy with *Much Ado About Nothing* is the ruse employed in the intrigues aimed at the pair of reluctant lovers in the earlier play and at Malvolio in *Twelfth Night*. The ironic effect of the conversations which are intended to be overheard by Benedick and Beatrice is here repeated through the letter which Maria drops in Malvolio's path. Maria's letter is but a variation of Don Pedro's plan to bring Beatrice and Benedick together. There are of course the obvious differences in the circumstances of the ruse and its ultimate effects upon its "victims." But there are also certain striking correspondences of detail. Before he overhears talk of Beatrice's love for him, Benedick, it will be recalled, is shown in a long soliloquy attacking Claudio's recent transformation from soldier to lover. But at the conclusion of that passage Benedick asks if he, himself, could be changed by love in the same manner. The question and Benedick's uncertain answer reveal that he is vulnerable, indeed ready to receive the impact of Don Pedro's plan. In like manner Malvolio is shown in the act of revealing his own readiness to be duped by Maria's letter and its "revelations." He is presented in soliloquy imagining himself worthy of Olivia's love. Indeed he imagines himself married to her and in the act of making ready to deal rather severely with Sir Toby. And at that very moment his eye falls upon the letter. The episode is furthermore given a refinement which likewise recalls and surpasses something similar in the earlier play. Benedick is convinced that what he overhears is not counterfeited: the very thought that someone is trying to gull somebody is instantly rejected. And this is brought about by having that suspicion utterly demolished by the grave witness of the elderly Leonato. The words onstage merge into Benedick's own thoughts so imperceptibly that he would have thought "this a gull but that the white-bearded fellow speaks it." And later he concludes that "This can be no trick." In *Twelfth Night* Shakespeare in like manner provided a device by which Malvolio is tricked into the conviction that Maria's letter is genuine. What Malvolio reads in the letter are of course his own thoughts and most devout wishes, but there is more. When we consider the letter's style, particularly in the last long passage—"Let thy tongue tang arguments of state; put thyself into the trick of singularity"—we can see clearly that this is neither Olivia's style nor Maria's but Malvolio's own. It is a brilliant stroke. Both the thoughts and words in the letter are so expressive of Malvolio's being that they produce instant conviction.[19]

IV

Shakespeare's dependence on earlier comedies for certain elements of *Twelfth Night* ranged beyond his use in fresh combinations of certain episodes. As we have already noted, he repeats certain characters, though of course he recreates them in a fashion to fit the structural and thematic necessities of the story he is dramatizing. This is true in the creation or recreation of minor as well as major characters. Though lacking the brilliant virtuosity of Rosalind and her superior comic awareness, Viola is nevertheless meant to represent the same balance of sentiment with common sense, the same steady and level view of the world around her. In this she repeats Rosalind's function in the earlier play, a function made indispensable by the dramatist's chief concern in these plays. But of course the dramatic terms of her existence require individual features in Viola which are quite different from Rosalind's. Rosalind could not be repeated. Certainly in Viola's position Rosalind would never allow Orsino to maintain even a semblance of an initiative. But her general attitude towards love is repeated in Viola, though more profoundly, albeit more obliquely expressed in the latter. Rosalind's direct attempts to "cure" both Orlando and Phoebe, the one of his bookish Petrarchism and the other of disdain, are repeated by Viola in the later play. But a glance at her scenes with Orsino and Olivia will show how tentative Viola's approach is. She seldom opposes Orsino's whims, and when she differs with him, her comments are gentle and indirect. When she confronts Olivia in their initial meeting, her comment on the latter's disinterest in love is gentler than Rosalind's similar criticism of Phoebe. But Viola's words to Olivia carry greater significance, a maturer vision as befits her own temperament and also the character and position of Olivia. To Viola's inquiry if she is "the lady of the house," Olivia replies: "If I do not usurp myself, I am." Viola's comment on this expresses one of Shakespeare's favorite themes: "Most certain, if you are she, you do usurp yourself; for what is yours to bestow is not yours to reserve." The import of such a speech would have been beyond Phoebe, and perhaps it is beyond Olivia as well. But what is far more significant is that the speech could not have come from Rosalind, for the words proceed from the sort of stillness and reflection we would not associate with her temperament. The attitude expressed in the passage, though repeating Rosalind's general point of view concerning the rejection of love, is enriched by evidence of serious thought. It is an attitude presupposing Rosalind's and transcending it. Although rationality and incisive intellect combine to produce that most attractive quality in Rosalind which we identified with the comic spirit, it is also true that she is not innocent of emotion and the romantic attitude towards love and her lover. But with all this, it must be admitted that Rosalind is master of her emotions; she is in complete control of these as she is of her destiny. Though exiled and forced to disguise herself for safety, she is never in any danger. Rosalind is never in pain, and this is one of the chief points in which she differs from Viola. While Rosalind has "convers'd with a magician" and can do "strange

things"—she promises to unite all the lovers on the morrow—Viola is bewildered by her dilemma.[20]

> O time! thou must untangle this, not I.
> It is too hard a knot for me t' untie!
>
> (II, ii, 41-42)

It may be said of Rosalind that she controls not only her emotions and her destiny but also the action of the whole play. The same cannot be said of Viola, whose role is somewhat passive by comparison.

This general difference in the conception of Rosalind and Viola is to be found also in other characters. Feste, for instance, though he repeats in part Touchstone's function, achieves his ends by more oblique means. Like Touchstone, his chief role is to comment upon and thereby deflate the sentimental pretensions of such characters as Orsino and Olivia. But his comment upon Orsino's love-melancholy and Olivia's capriciously excessive mourning is both more oblique in manner and more serious in tone than Touchstone's had been in the earlier play. In both cases Feste addresses his reducing commentary in part through songs of time's passing and lovers' deaths and thereby implies at once a subtler attitude towards the aberrations of Orsino and Olivia as well as a measure of sympathy.[21] These features of Feste's character and function suggest greater reflection, perhaps we should say greater maturity, than is revealed in Touchstone.

This reflectiveness implied in the character of Viola and Feste accords with—and indeed generates—a sense of melancholy characteristic of the general mood of the play. In spite of much revelry in its action, *Twelfth Night* impresses one with a certain air of gravity which is quite different from the high spirits of *As You Like It*. The world of *Twelfth Night* appears a little more complex and thus more puzzling than that of the earlier comedies. And this complexity anticipates the greater seriousness not only of the tragedies which are soon to follow but also of the problem plays and the romances.

V

Another significant relationship between *Twelfth Night* and *As You Like It* has to do with an aspect of their structure, for here again Shakespeare presents the theme of love in analogical relationship with a secondary theme, the theme of indulgence. In an earlier section the point was made that Malvolio's role has to do with both love and the theme of indulgence which is presented in a special relationship to it. Malvolio is both a lover, one of Olivia's suitors, and also the exponent of opposition to all pleasure. His interest in Olivia, which he calls love, is vitiated by his self-love, and in this he is the antithesis of Viola, whose generous and self-sacrificing love of Orsino may be said to represent the opposite extreme. In his attitude toward indulgence, Malvolio is contrasted with Sir Toby Belch and Sir Andrew Aguecheek, whose overindulgence clearly throws into relief the steward's austerity. But although Malvolio rejects the kind of indulgence practiced by the other two, he overindulges in self-love, so surfeiting that in Olivia's words he becomes "sick of self-love." What is to be noted here is that Shakespeare presents extravagant attitudes toward the themes of love and indulgence, extremes which by juxtaposition tend toward mutual qualification. Malvolio is but one of the characters whose attitudes form the main action of the comedy. But he is central to that action in his double role of being both a lover, or would-be lover, and an exponent of a particular attitude toward indulgence.

The theme of indulgence, as we have said, is here presented in such a way that attitudes toward it are made to reflect upon analogous attitudes toward love. The relationship of the two themes can be seen as it affects other characters besides Malvolio. Orsino and Olivia are both gluttons in their way, both gorging themselves upon boundless sentiment: he upon extravagant passion (as he calls it) for Olivia, she upon equally excessive mourning for a dead brother. In effect he is overfond of love-melancholy, she of grief. Both, then, overindulge in certain emotions, and that extravagance, and especially the rhetoric of its expression, form yet another instance of comic reduction. And thus it may be said that Orsino, Olivia, Malvolio, Sir Toby, and Sir Andrew are presented in postures of overindulgence of one sort or another. Furthermore, that part of the plot which deals with Malvolio and his enemies dramatizes indulgence itself, that is, what in the main action is a metaphor here becomes a theme. And the comic reduction of excess in this part of the play, the comic comment upon extreme attitudes toward indulgence, reinforces the comic reduction of extreme attitudes toward love. And as we have seen, this last is accomplished in part by the metaphoric function of the term indulgence in the main action of the comedy. From the point of view of structure, this circumstance represents the highest point to which Shakespeare could raise the analogical relationship of the two themes.

The theme of indulgence, then, occupies an important position in the play, but we should remember that it is secondary to the theme of love, that it is employed in support of it. Because *Twelfth Night* is associated with revelry, it is quite possible to over-stress this element of the plot. Thus one critic has proposed that "*Twelfth Night* is a philosophical defence of a moderate indulgence in pleasure, in opposition on the one hand to an extreme hostility to pleasure and on the other hand to an extreme self-indulgence."[22] A related view finds that the play "develops an ethic of indulgence based on the notion that the personality of any individual is a function not of the static proportions of the humors within him, but of the dynamic appetites that may more pur-

posefully, as well as more pragmatically, be said to govern his behavior."[23] This is relevant and just so long as we do not raise the theme of indulgence to a position above that assigned to it by the dramatist. In a second and equally provocative essay on *Twelfth Night,* Professor Hollander sees the play as "representing the killing off of excessive appetite through indulgence of it, leading to the rebirth of the unencumbered self."[24] Though an exciting notion of comic catharsis, such a view lays undue stress on what we have called the play's chief metaphor at the expense of its central idea.[25]

In addition to the primary metaphor of indulgence, and most significantly associated with it, is the subsidiary concept of musical order and due proportion. Even as order and proportion are indispensable to harmony, whether musical, celestial, or political, so they are to the well-being and inner unity of the individual. Here music, which fills *Twelfth Night,* achieves the status of motif in the thought of the play. "The general concern of *Twelfth Night,*" says Professor Hollander, "is *musica humana,* the Boethian application of abstract order and proportion to human behavior."[26] This is unquestionably so, and what is said here of *Twelfth Night* applies with equal force to Shakespearean drama generally. But again it should be noted that the play is concerned with a particular application, an application to a particular aspect of human behavior. That *Twelfth Night* dramatizes the concept of proportion and moderation. there can be no question. We may go so far as to say that the play's chief theme has to do with proportion and moderation. But it is proportion and moderation neither in terms of general behavior nor of revelry, eating, and drinking, though these provide both metaphoric and thematic support. The play is primarily concerned with proportion and moderation in matters concerning romantic love, the general subject of all Shakespeare's romantic comedies.

VI

The chief idea of *Twelfth Night* has been variously identified. Some have argued that the leading note of the play is fun; others have held that the play's "lesson is . . . 'Sweet are the uses of adversity.'"[27] Unrequited love is another choice.[28] Still another is social security. According to this view *Twelfth Night* is not a story of love "but of the very realistic struggles and intrigues over the betrothal of a rich countess, whose selection of a mate determines the future of all the major and most of the minor characters."[29] Much closer to the mark than any of these is the view that *Twelfth Night* "exhibits in its action one of the fundamental motifs of comedy: the education of a man or woman."[30] What needs to be added here is that the motif exhibited in the action of the play has to do with the education of characters in matters of love. As in the comedies we have so far considered, so here the main action presents in juxtaposition attitudes toward love, with the result that such attitudes by mutual qualification point to the best attitude possible in the world created by the play, a world ultimately not different from our own.

The initial episode introduces the two contrasting attitudes toward love which we have found at the center of Shakespeare's other romantic comedies. Orsino in his opening lines reveals and exposes to the censure of the comic spirit his immoderately sentimental conception of what he thinks is his passion for Olivia. His fancy is, in his own words, "high fantastical," and the pain it causes him is insupportable. For that reason he calls for music as a way to relieve his passion.

> If music be the food of love, play on!
> Give me excess of it, that, surfeiting,
> The appetite may sicken, and so die.
>
> (I, i, 1-3)

Notwithstanding its "capacity," love may be so surfeited with music, he hopes, that its force will abate for a short while. It is all in excess, all expressed in one comic hyperbole after another.

> O, when mine eyes did see Olivia first,
> Methought she purg'd the air of pestilence!
> That instant was I turn'd into a hart;
>
> (ll. 19-21)

With the entrance of Valentine at line 23 and his report to the Duke, Shakespeare matches Orsino's hyperboles with Olivia's own extreme sentimentality in rejecting his suit in order to abandon herself to excessive grief over her brother's death. The extravagance of Olivia's mourning, like Orsino's passion, is given a comic note by the language in which it is expressed. Furthermore, Valentine's description tends to qualify the genuineness of the vow by the elaborate insistence on its austerity:

> The element itself, till seven years' heat,
> Shall not behold her face at ample view;
> But, like a cloistress, she will veiled walk,
> And water once a day her chamber round
> With eye-offending brine;
>
> (ll. 26-30)

The two attitudes toward love are here bound together more significantly than in earlier comedies. Orsino is the romantic lover who vaunts his alleged passion in hyperboles. And Olivia is the reluctant lover who rejects the Duke's addresses to her. But she is very different from such disdainful lovers as Phoebe of *As You Like It,* the king and his lords in *Love's Labour's Lost,* and Benedick and Beatrice. Like all these, Olivia rejects thoughts of love, but she does so in favor of something else, a passionate surrender to what seems to be her love of grief. In this, though she rejects Orsino,

she acts very much like him. Both exhibit excessive sentimentality which shows as folly, though the object of that folly is different in the two characters. Their attitudes toward love and grief are extreme and they are best expressed by the thematic metaphor of indulgence, the very image the Duke employs in the opening lines of the play. Orsino and Olivia overindulge their passions or what they consider their passions. And so in the initial episode Shakespeare briefly but pointedly defines the comic errors of these two, errors to be recognized before the conclusion of the play. But he does much more in these early lines. He binds Orsino's and Olivia's contrasting attitudes towards love by means of an identical attitude towards their respective passions, love and grief. And furthermore he relates all this to the idea of indulgence, the theme of the secondary action.

The opening scene, then, presents Orsino and Olivia in contrasting attitudes towards love but in identical attitudes towards themselves. In the second scene the two are contrasted with Viola, both in their attitudes towards themselves and towards love. From the first lines she speaks Viola reveals the absence in her of sentimentality and self-pity.

> *Viola.* What country, friends, is this?
> *Captain.* This is Illyria, lady.
> *Viola.* And what should I do in Illyria?
> My brother he is in Elysium.
> Perchance he is not drown'd. What think you, sailors?
>
> (I, ii, 1-5)

The captain encourages her to hope, for he saw her brother, "most provident in peril," "bind himself" to "a strong mast that liv'd upon the sea." Whereupon she turns to the present moment and demands to know who governs Illyria.

> *Captain.* A noble duke, in nature as in name.
> *Viola.* What is his name?
> *Captain.* Orsino.
> *Viola.* Orsino! I have heard my father name him.
> He was a bachelor then.
>
> (ll. 25-29)

Viola is as eager to know the Duke as she is unwilling to give herself over to excessive grief over her brother's feared death. Her feelings and the words expressing them are level and direct, avoiding the extremes we have noted in the alleged passions of Orsino and Olivia. In this she clearly presents a contrast to these two, and her role in the rest of the play will be to aid them in amending their ways. On the one hand, Viola essays to persuade Olivia that falling in love—with Orsino or another—is her unavoidable responsibility (else she usurps herself); on the other, she tells the Duke that he is not the only one who suffers from unrequited love. From the above we should conclude that Viola is intended to represent the norm, an attitude we might call ideal. And we may add that her words and acts are so aimed as to bring about comic recognition by Orsino and Olivia. In due course he learns that he was never in love with Olivia but someone else; and the latter soon discovers that far from being able to remain heart-whole she falls in love at first sight with Orsino's page, who she later finds is a lady in disguise. To such recognition and self-knowledge these two are led by the agency of Viola, by what she says and does, by what she is.

VII

But Viola is not the only character whose words and actions are employed to those ends. Feste, who as his name suggests occupies a significant position in the development of the theme of indulgence in the subplot, carries an equal responsibility in the conduct of the main action as well. In the subplot his chief purpose is to oppose Malvolio's austerity with the notion of revelry, though perhaps not in the extreme form practiced by Sir Andrew and Sir Toby.[31] When Sir Toby tells Malvolio that there shall be "cakes and ale" in spite of the steward's "virtuousness," Feste adds: "Yes, by Saint Anne, and ginger shall be hot i' th' mouth too." In addition, Feste helps bring about Malvolio's comic retribution. He defines both the steward's austerity and his presumption that Olivia could love him as a kind of madness and thus proves him a fool. In so doing Feste in his own way essays to lead Malvolio toward a recognition of his folly. This is especially clear in the scene wherein Feste, both in his own person and as Sir Topas, engages the steward in conversation while the latter is locked in the dark room.

Feste's allusion to Malvolio's folly in his notions about Olivia is made obliquely in the song he sings to him:

> *Clown.* "Hey, Robin, jolly Robin,
> Tell me how thy lady does."
> *Malvolio.* Fool!
> *Clown.* "My lady is unkind, perdy."
> *Malvolio.* Fool!
> *Clown.* "Alas, why is she so?"
> *Malvolio.* Fool, I say!
> *Clown.* "She loves another"—Who calls, ha?
> (IV, ii, 78-85)

The steward's persistent calling of "Fool!" points ironically to the very term most properly applying to himself in the scene. And this is followed by an even clearer allusion to his folly in the following exchange with Feste a few lines later.

> *Clown.* Alas, sir, how fell you besides your
> five wits?

> *Malvolio.* Fool, there was never man so
> notoriously abus'd. I am as well in my wits,
> fool, as thou art.
> *Clown.* But as well? Then you are mad
> indeed, if you be no better in your wits
> than a fool.

> (ll. 92-97)

Precisely the same purpose as shown here is to be seen in Feste's role in the main plot, that is, in the words he addresses to Orsino and Olivia. Again his most pregnant comments on the self-deception of those two are made through songs, that is, in the same oblique manner he employs in part in his treatment of Malvolio, for Orsino and Olivia in what they say and do enact extreme attitudes identical with those exhibited by the steward. Professor Dover Wilson is partly right in suggesting that Malvolio "reflects in a kind of distorting mirror the emotional situation of the main plot. For Malvolio is a dreamer, after his kind; like Orsino he aspires for the hand of Olivia; and like both Orsino and Olivia he mistakes dreams for realities."[32] It is certainly true that there is something of the dreamer in a steward who is so self-endeared that he supposes himself the object of Olivia's love. Malvolio does not merely aspire for the hand of Olivia; he believes that she has chosen him for her husband. But it can scarcely be said that Orsino and Olivia are dreamers unless by the term we mean persons who by their extravagant posturings reveal utter failure to understand themselves and their relationships with others. Such posturing is perhaps more vulnerable to the comic spirit than dreaming can ever be. What is accurate in Professor Wilson's comment is the notion that Malvolio's comic shortcomings in the subplot are a reflex of Orsino's and Olivia's shortcomings in the main action. Hence Feste's analogous comment, in matter and form, upon the aberrations of those two.

When first confronted with Olivia, Feste proceeds to "catechise" her, to demonstrate in playful fashion that she, instead of himself, is the fool. Her calling him a fool is, he instructs her, "Misprision in the highest degree!" In contrast, he adds, his mistress has been acting foolishly in the excessive show of grief, especially since she believes her brother's soul in heaven: "The more fool, madonna, to mourn for your brother's soul being in heaven." (I, v, 76-77) This initial comment upon Olivia's folly is followed shortly by another, this one in the form of the clown's first song. Although "O Mistress Mine" is ostensibly sung for the delectation of Sir Toby and Sir Andrew, it really concerns Olivia, though of course she is not present while it is sung. But the content, from the first line, "O mistress mine, where are you roaming," to the concluding invitation to love since "Youth's a stuff will not endure," has exclusive application to her, gently reprimanding her careless wasting, in Viola's phrase usurping, her own youth and beauty. The lines are in a sense addressed to Olivia, pointing gently to her folly in refusing love in favor of immoderate sorrow. Furthermore, the song anticipates her eventual capitulation and hints at the strange conjunction into which she will be thrown. For it announces that her "true love's coming / That can sing both high and low." Olivia will fall in love with Cesario-Sebastian, but in the end all will be well.[33]

Likewise the song Feste addresses to the Duke in the following scene serves the purpose of gently mocking his exaggerated sense of his own grief in love, a grief that could find release only in death. Because it expresses his love-melancholy as well as the self-pity occasioned by it Orsino prefers that song over all others. And he calls upon Cesario to heed its lines, little knowing that his page is the one who truly suffers genuine love-grief. In the lines following the song, Feste leaves no doubt as to its comic intention. For he adds to its mockery of the Duke's love melancholy his own direct comment. "Now, the melancholy god protect thee, and the tailor make thy doublet of changeable taffeta, for thy mind is a very opal." And he adds the further mocking note that he would have "men of such constancy put to sea, that their business might be everything and their intent everywhere." The gentle mockery of the Duke's inconstancy is resumed a few lines later when Orsino in conversation with Viola draws a distinction between the strength of his own passion for Olivia and a woman's love.

> There is no woman's sides
> Can bide the beating of so strong a passion
> As love doth give my heart; no woman's heart
> So big, to hold so much. They lack retention.
>   (II, iv, 96-99)

His insistence on his own steadfast passion in contrast to a woman's incapacity for such love not only anticipates ironically his swift transference of that passion from Olivia to Viola at the conclusion of the play but also points with equal irony to the latter's constancy and devotion throughout. And this difference between Orsino's extravagant protestations and her own reticence is further stressed by Viola in her allusion to her father's fictional daughter who, because of unrequited love,

>   sat, like Patience on a monument,
> Smiling at grief.
>   (ll. 117-18)

To which she adds:

>   Was not this love indeed?
> We men may say more, swear more; but
>   indeed
> Our shows are more than will, for still we
>   prove
> Much in our vows, but little in our love.
>   (ll. 118-21)

Both in the image of Patience smiling at grief and in the presence of rhyme in the second passage Shakespeare introduces a faint tinge of self-consciousness, perhaps even of self-pity, just sufficient to enrich Viola's attitude toward her dilemma.

VIII

The comic process of *Twelfth Night,* then, presents episodes which are intended to expose and reduce extravagant attitudes on the part of Orsino and Olivia as well as Malvolio. And the function of this comic reduction is carried out in the main by Viola and Feste. But there is a further action dealing with Sebastian, Sir Toby, Sir Andrew Aguecheek, and Fabian. Just as Maria initiates the intrigue against Malvolio, so Sir Toby puts into practice a second intrigue aimed at Sir Andrew Aguecheek and the disguised Viola. But Aguecheek is the main target. Sir Toby's purpose in forcing a duel upon those two is the sheer comedy of exposing Sir Andrew's pretensions to bravery. For some moments there is also the additional effect of Viola's discomfiture, perhaps intended as a comment upon the liability of her disguise. Structurally, the most significant effect of the intrigue is the challenge of the newly arrived Sebastian by Sir Andrew and Sir Toby. And the severe beating they receive at his hands is a kind of censure upon their overindulgence and boisterousness. But far more important, their challenge of Sebastian brings him into the action of the love-triangle so that his reunion with Viola resolves the lovers' dilemma.

As noted above, the action of *Twelfth Night* presents episodes which expose and reduce attitudes toward love and the related theme of indulgence. That reduction is brought about by direct statement, by the juxtaposition of opposed attitudes, by song. And out of such action there emerges a simple conception of the way to happiness, namely through individual as well as communal integration. That level and sensible way is the way we reach through experience, leading to both self-understanding and a clear awareness of one's role as a social being. And this simple wisdom is precisely the meaning of the song Feste sings at the conclusion of the play.

Most critics have expressed doubts concerning the authenticity and dramatic appropriateness of the song.[34] Among the very few who have defended it was A. C. Bradley, who thought it most appropriate to the singer, and even conceded that Shakespeare may have written the concluding stanza.[35] Richmond Noble also defends the song as Shakespearean, a song of wise nonsense, fitting commentary on the events of the play.[36] And he alludes to the following lines by John Weiss which he considers the most sensible interpretation of Feste's concluding song: "Then he sings a song which conveys to us his feeling of the world's impartiality: all things proceed according to law; nobody is humored; people must abide the consequences of their actions, 'for the rain it raineth every day.' A 'little tiny boy' may have his toy; but a man must guard against knavery and thieving: marriage itself cannot be sweetened by swaggering; whoso drinks with 'toss-pots' will get a 'drunken head:' it is a very old world, and began so long ago that no change in its habits can be looked for."[37] This is indeed the general meaning of the song, a crystallization of that simple wisdom to which the comic spirit is always pointing. Such wisdom is a fitting epilogue not only to this particular play but to the series of comedies it brings to a conclusion. Whether in childhood, adulthood, or old age, we find that certain things are constant; they have not changed and we cannot change them. Such changes are really what Orsino and Olivia and others like them would bring about, but in the end they are made to shed their aberrations. The sovereignty of nature asserts itself in Olivia's precipitous falling in love, even as it does in the case of Benedick and Beatrice and the rest. Nor are other pretensions less vulnerable as Malvolio and Sir Toby and Sir Andrew discover. "A great while ago the world began" and its laws, which are but the laws of nature, cannot change to accommodate some strange caprice or posturing. The individual, in these plays the lover, whether romantic or disdainful, must become a part of society, must be integrated into it. But the lover must first achieve an individual fulfillment, an inner integration. How fitting, then, that in the closing song of this last of his romantic comedies Shakespeare should express through the wise fool's seeming nonsense, and in the simplest terms, the comic vision he had been dramatizing during the last decade of the century.

In form *Twelfth Night* represents the ultimate plane to which Shakespeare could raise the structure of his romantic comedy. For here Shakespeare at last achieved a completely independent and fully unified romantic plot, a plot from which he eliminated the kind of external obstacle to love's fruition represented by Don John's machinations in *Much Ado* and by the conflict of the two pairs of brothers in *As You Like It*. Instead, *Twelfth Night* unites the romantic concerns of the two earlier plays, that is, the two aspects of the *internal* conflict which for a time delays love's fulfillment. It combines the disdain of love, which forms the most absorbing theme of *Much Ado,* with the education of a romantic lover, which is at the center of *As You Like It*. Orlando and Silvius are here replaced by Orsino, while Benedick and Beatrice are replaced by Olivia. And, as was shown above, the two attitudes toward love are related metaphorically by the idea of indulgence which forms the theme of the secondary action. It is, then, in this perfect combination of the two master-themes that *Twelfth Night* may be said to represent the final and near-pure form of Shakespearean romantic comedy. But the play marks also another milestone in Shakespeare's dramatic career. It is the last of his

romantic comedies. Having perfected a comic form through which he could reflect his responses to one aspect of human destiny, Shakespeare immediately turned away from romantic comedy and its theme of romantic love and proceeded to give dramatic expression to other responses by means of other modes.

This turn to other dramatic modes is anticipated perhaps in a special quality of *Twelfth Night*. Although it sums up and recapitulates the earlier comedies, the play differs from them in one particular. Its atmosphere, in spite of the play's revelry, is characterized by a reflectiveness which at moments tends towards gravity. This quality of the play is in great part associated with the temperament of Viola and Feste who, though deriving from earlier creations, prefigure later and greater studies to be placed in the graver air of the tragedies and the romances. Viola's character, though owing a good deal to earlier conceptions, really points to the heroines of the romances, particularly Hermione and Imogen. And Feste, though not unlike Touchstone in his function, is by temperament quite different. His individuality is to be seen especially in a certain quality of apartness which gives him a special perspective and also contributes to a measure of pathos in his relationships with others. In this and in the irony which plays about his name and circumstances Feste anticipates Lear's fool. If Feste's concluding song is by Shakespeare, it may well be that the dramatist thought of him and Lear's fool together, since the latter sings a stanza of the same song in *King Lear*. Indeed it appears that what is needed to draw from Feste the kind of devotion we see in the fool of the later play is a worthy object of such devotion, a great and greatly suffering nature such as Lear's.

In these matters *Twelfth Night* may be said to reflect, albeit distantly, Shakespeare's growing concern with those other aspects of human motive and destiny which were soon to fill the world of the later plays. But *Twelfth Night* is a romantic comedy, bringing to a brilliant conclusion Shakespeare's search for a comic structure which could treat most divertingly and significantly man's relationship to woman. Like its predecessors, and especially the other two "joyous" comedies, it projects a vision of the lovers' ideal, the best possible way to achieve inner as well as outer fulfillment, a unity within and a harmony with the world in which we live. That vision expresses man's longing for a state of being which transcends human limitation, the limitation against which it is here dramatized. And it is precisely in responding to and gratifying that longing by presenting the ideal as achievable that romantic comedy is so deeply satisfying.

Notes

[1] There are other similarities with earlier plays. Viola's disguise recalls that of Portia and Nerissa, of Jessica

and Rosalind. Sir Toby and Aguecheek recall Falstaff and Slender, and the trick played on Malvolio looks back to the trick played on Benedick and Beatrice.

[2] *A New Variorum Edition of Shakespeare,* ed. H. H. Furness (Philadelphia, 1901), p. xii.

[3] New Cambridge Shakespeare (Cambridge, 1939), pp. 100-1.

[4] Leslie Hotson, *The First Night of Twelfth Night* (New York, 1954), pp. 229-30.

[5] *Ibid., passim.*

[6] *Ibid.,* p. 63.

[7] *Ibid.,* p. 180.

[8] II. iii, 110-21. The song is to be found in Edward H. Fellowes' edition in *The English School of Lutenist song Writers,* Series II, Vol. IV (London, 1959), 24-25.

[9] Geoffrey Bullough, *Narrative and Dramatic Sources of Shakespeare* (London, 1961), II, 270-71. For minor details Shakespeare may be indebted to *Gl'Ingannati,* first performed in 1537, which is the ultimate source of all versions, including *Gl'Inganni* (1562) by Nicolò Secchi and Curzio Gonzaga's *Gl'Inganni* (1592). In the Induction to the play there is a Fabio and also a Malevolti, as well as a reference to *la notte di Beffana,* which some believe may have suggested the title of Shakespeare's play. Although *Gl'Ingannati* is closer to Shakespeare's play, it is nevertheless true that Curzio Gonzaga's *Gl'Inganni* gives Cesare (Cesario) as the name of the disguised heroine. In connection with the names of the chief characters it should be noted also that in Emanuel Forde's *Famous History of Parismus* (1598) there is a Viola who is shipwrecked while following her lover in the disguise of a page. See Bullough, *Narrative and Dramatic Sources,* II, 363-71. It has also been proposed that another play by Nicolò Secchi, *L'Interesse,* (c. 1547), may have suggested the duel between Sir Andrew and Viola. See Helen A. Kaufman, "Nicolò Secchi as a Source of *Twelfth Night,*" SQ V (1954), 271-80.

[10] See Violet A. Wilson, *Society Women of Shakespeare's Time* (New York, 1924), pp. 238-56.

[11] See Fitzroy Pyle, "*Twelfth Night, King Lear,* and *Arcadia,*" *MLR,* XLIII (1948), 449-55.

[12] See Oscar J. Campbell, *Shakespeare's Satire* (New York, 1943), p. 83. See also Paul Mueschke and Jeannette Fleisher, "Jonsonian Elements in the Comic Underplot of *Twelfth Night,*" *PMLA,* XLVIII (1933), 722-40.

[13] Even Malvolio's "examination" for diabolical possession cannot in any of its details be interpreted as a glance at public process of the law either in a particular case or general practice. See C. J. Sisson, "Tudor Intelligence Tests: Malvolio and Real Life," in *Essays on Shakespeare and Elizabethan Drama in Honor of Hardin Craig* (Columbia, Missouri, 1962), pp. 183-200.

[14] On the other hand it is perhaps going too far to say that Shakespeare "invented the story of Malvolio, and used it with rare skill as the foundation of the play." Milton Crane, "*Twelfth Night* and Shakespearean Comedy," *SQ* VI (1955), 7. Nor is it quite accurate to call Malvolio "the most comical and most ridiculous character in the play." Sen Gupta, *Shakespearian Comedy* (Oxford, 1950), p. 168. In Shakespearean romantic comedy the most comical characters are misguided or disdainful lovers, or the self-dramatizing lover whose language is fraught with hyperbole and his passion with sentimentality, the lover who believes himself a realist yet who all along responds to love in the romantic manner. The most comical characters in such comedy are the king and his lords in *Love's Labour's Lost,* Benedick and Beatrice, Orlando and Rosalind, Orsino and Olivia.

[15] It is interesting to note that his cross-gartered yellow stockings may be intended to show him as a lover and more particularly as a jealous one. See M. Channing Linthicum, "Malvolio's Cross-gartered Yellow Stockings," *MP,* XXV (1927), 87-93; also M. P. Tilley, "Malvolio's Yellow Stockings and Cross Garters," *SAB,* XII (1937), 54-55. Yellow is also the color of the narcissus, that is, a symbol of self-love. See Hotson, *The First Night of Twelfth Night,* p. 98.

[16] In his rigidity, his lack of self-awareness, and his obsessive concern with certain proprieties, malvolio approaches the Jonsonian humour character.

[17] His *raison d'être* is thus much more significant than might appear on the surface. His role in the play is not, for instance, "so that Shakespeare's lovers may preserve their status free from the nothing-if-not-critical comic scrutiny which would otherwise expose their romantic pretensions to the withering winds of laughter," Melvin Seiden, "Malvolio Reconsidered," *University of Kansas City Review,* XXVII (1961), 106-7. Incidentally, the lovers do not escape comic scrutiny in the play.

[18] Cf. Harold Jerking, "Shakespeare's *Twelfth Night,*" *Rice Institute Pamphlet,* XLV (1959), 28-29.

[19] Something like this takes place during the initial meeting of Touchstone and Jaques, reported by the latter, in which Touchstone tells him precisely what he wants to hear and in the terms he himself would have used.

[20] On this see pertinent comments in Gupta, *Shakespearian Comedy,* p. 165: and L. C. Salingar, "The Design of *Twelfth Night,*" *SQ,* IX (1958), 122.

[21] Cf. some relevant remarks in John R. Brown, *Shakespeare and His Comedies* (London, 1957), pp. 176-77.

[22] Morris P. Tilley, "The Organic Unity of *Twelfth Night,*" *PMLA,* XXIX (1914), 550-51.

[23] John Hollander, "Musica Mundana and *Twelfth Night,*" *Sound and Poetry* (English Institute Essays, 1956), pp. 73-74.

[24] John Hollander, "*Twelfth Night* and the Morality of Indulgence," *Sewanee Review,* LXVIII (1959), 234.

[25] This overstress on the play's metaphor can be seen in Professor Hollander's suggestion that Orsino's name reflects and defines his nature: "Orsino—the bear, the ravenous and clumsy devourer." *Ibid.,* p. 224.

[26] Hollander, "Musica Mundana and *Twelfth Night,*" p. 75.

[27] Furnivall, quoted in Furness, *Variorum,* p. 385.

[28] S. Nagarajan, "'What You Will': A Suggestion," *SQ,* X (1959), 61.

[29] J. W. Draper, *The Twelfth Night of Shakespeare's Audience* (Palo Alto, 1950), p. 249. This and other views of Professor Draper have been answered by N. A. Brittin in "The *Twelfth Night* of Shakespeare and Professor Draper," *SQ,* VII (1956), 211-16.

[30] Jerking, "Shakespeare's *Twelfth Night,*" p. 21.

[31] It has been suggested that Feste and Viola "represent the golden mean of temperance, in whom reason and emotion are at poise." Tilley, "The Organic Unity of *Twelfth Night,*" p. 558.

[32] John Dover Wilson, *Shakespeare's Happy Comedies* (London, 1962), p. 172.

[33] Whether written by Shakespeare or borrowed, the song illustrates his ability to endow complex function to music and song, both thematic and structural. For in addition to its obvious thematic meaning the song leads to more riotous singing which in turn brings the protesting Malvolio to the stage. And out of this emerges the conspiracy against him. In spite of this, some critics have failed to see the dramatic relevance of the song and its perfect blending with its context. See for instance L. B. Lathrop, "Shakespeare's Dramatic Use of Songs," *MLN,* XXIII (1908), 3; John H. Long, *Shakespeare's Use of Music: A study of Music and its Performance in the Original Production of Seven*

Comedies (Gainesville, Florida, 1955), I, 169. The authenticity of "O Mistress Mine" has been the subject of a long debate, dealing mainly with the relationship of the song in Shakespeare's play to a tune (without words) by the same title in Thomas Morley's *First Booke of Consort Lessons* (1599). Was the song, words and tune, an old one or did Shakespeare compose his own words, and if so did he employ Morley's tune? Did Shakespeare and Morley collaborate? Is there any connection between Shakespeare's song and Morley's tune? See E. Brennecke, Jr., "Shakespeare's Collaboration with Morley," *PMLA,* LIV (1939), 139-49; Sydney Beck, "The Case of 'O Mistress Mine,'" *Renaissance News,* VI (1953), 19-23. Edward H. Fellowes saw no connection between Morley's tune and Shakespeare's song and believed that the dramatist probably rewrote an old song. See Richmond Noble, *Shakespeare's Use of Song* (London, 1923), p. 82.

[34] Capell thought it was either a popular song of the day or it was composed by William Kempe, who, he believed, had played the part of Feste. Furness, *Variorum,* pp. 313-14. H. B. Lathrop considered the song extraneous and not by Shakespeare. "Shakespeare's Dramatic Use of Songs," p. 2. L. B. Wright insisted that the song "has no relation to the play." "Extraneous Song in Elizabethan Drama After the Advent of Shakespeare," *SP,* XXIV (1927), 263. John R. Moore thought it might have been an interpolation. "The Songs of the Public Theaters in the Time of Shakespeare," *JEGP,* XXVIII (1929), 182. And John Dover Wilson is convinced that the song was written by Robert Armin. New Cambridge Shakespeare, p. 170. Finally John H. Long follows L. B. Wright and H. B. Lathrop, saying that "there does not seem to be any reason to doubt their conclusions." *Shakespeare's Use of Music,* I, 180.

[35] "Feste the Jester," in *A Book of Homage to Shakespeare,* ed. I. Gollancz (Oxford, 1916), pp. 164-69.

[36] Noble, *Shakespeare's Use of Song,* p. 85.

[37] John Weiss, *Wit, Humor, and Shakespeare* (Boston, 1876), p. 204.

Dennis R. Preston (essay date 1970)

SOURCE: "The Minor Characters in *Twelfth Night,*" in *Shakespeare Quarterly,* Vol. XXI, No. 2, Spring, 1970, pp. 167-76.

[*In the following essay, Preston discusses the important functions of the minor characters in* Twelfth Night: *complementing prominent characters, maintaining the play's pace, and providing a complex of motivations for the action.*]

It is pretty well agreed upon that no matter what the central plot of *Twelfth Night* may be the total effect is musical, or, to make that flat analogy more descriptive, the characters of *Twelfth Night,* as disparate in function as the different instruments of an orchestra are, play in concert: Sir Toby's bass notes crash in on the lyric qualities established in the first two scenes of the play, only to be answered by Viola and Orsino, the soloists of those scenes, who "play" a duet in scene four. So the arrangement goes; never reaching symphonic heights until the denouement, but developing and introducing aspects of plot and character in short concerti which build to the final total chorus of voices. There are soloists in each scene in the sense that instruments of an orchestra are featured in concerto, but there are few truly *soli* passages.

The major characters—Orsino, Viola, Maria, Sir Toby, Sir Andrew, Feste, Olivia, Malvolio, and Sebastian—could not, by their interweaving of parts, maintain the pace which prevents any character from becoming a Hamlet or Macbeth. If the major figures attempted to accomplish this liveliness without assistance, the dramatic action would be thoroughly confused. The dramatic purpose is served, in keeping with the total musical effect of the play, and the confusion of the Italian *novella* avoided by the careful use of minor characters.

Unlike Shakespeare's other Italian romance comedies, where the minor characters make up a second or third plot which injects the play with native humor, *Twelfth Night* already has an Elizabethan plot involving major characters. The importance of the minor figures, then, does not rest in a single section of the play, nor do those characters act together as an example of a class or type. *Twelfth Night* demands, rather, a number of minor figures, coming from all of society and occurring throughout the play. Some of them fulfill such obvious functions as bringing a letter, performing a service, or announcing an arrival. Others, however, build contrasts, stand in for major players, further the action, or contribute a distinct character. None, even of the members of the first mentioned group, is left without sensible dramatic motivation.

I believe that a careful survey of the minor players of *Twelfth Night* can display how three common errors in the performance, reading, and criticism of lesser figures in Shakespearian drama may be avoided. The easiest way to deal with minor figures is to indicate their social standing. For many this method seems to be the final word in character analysis; however, a list of social "do's" and "don't's" coupled with a social rank supplies only a necessary and handy framework for further investigation. The character has yet the dramatic justification of his presence and his lines. More important, especially as a minor figure, he must be related to the structure, themes, action, and major characters of the play.

The other two faults are especially dramatic ones, though the first often asserts itself in reading as well. Minor characters are likely to be skipped over. In reading, their lines seem often to be mere transitional devices, hardly the words of real people. In performance, their presentation is often so flat that they conflict disastrously with the flesh-and-blood reality of the major players. The opposite of the fault is especially disastrous in performance, however. Often a minor player supplies a faulty motivation for his part or conceives of his part as being more important to the development of the plot than it really is. Therefore, in a play which, when performed well or read carefully, moves so quickly as *Twelfth Night* does and relies so obviously on small parts for a good deal of its chief effect, the minor figures must be given rather exacting interpretation. The reason for and explanation of their being should provide a rather detailed basis for the construction of their characters.

It is not necessary to prepare a set of director's notes to sketch in such a background of character. Characterization is not a question here, though, at times, it is necessary to indicate a particular rendering of a line, especially if the line is capable of diverse and conflicting deliveries. What can be made, however, is an indication of the role, in the broadest sense of that word, each figure is to play in the drama.

It is perhaps most difficult to deal with the really small members of the cast, for they usually take care of an immediate structural necessity and then disappear or remain silent. Whatever part of the action is moved by their message or appearance only reacts to a purely mechanical convenience, for what they have to say or do is more a total dependence on the demands of the action or a major character than a willful extension of their own reality.

This distinction between minor figures whose character is completely revealed by the immediate dramatic purpose and those whose character is further revealed in the outcome of some action or in their extended relation to other characters may be seen between the two officers who arrest Antonio in Act III.

The First Officer, evidently the superior, is not, as it might seem at first, only an identifier of Antonio and a bystander to the process of arrest:

> *1st Off.* This is the man. Do thy office.
> *2nd Off.* Antonio, I arrest thee at the suit
> Of Count Orsino.
> *Ant.* You do mistake me, sir.
> *1st Off.* No, sir, no jot. I know your favor well,
> Though now you have no sea cap on your head.
> Take him away. He knows I know him well.
> (III. iv. 359-365)[1]

Although, as he later explains to Orsino, the First Officer has fought against Antonio, this functionary now, perhaps due to times of peace or his advancing age, is a municipal officer in Illyria: "What's that to us? The time goes by—away!" And though it is the Second Officer's official duty to perform the actual arrest, the First, probably more familiar with military swiftness of procedure, is the one who finally demands Antonio's cooperation: "The man grows mad. Away with him! Come, come, sir."

Here, and later, when the First Officer tells Orsino of Antonio's crime against Illyria, the dramatic action depends upon and demands a specific individual with knowledge of specific details and events.

The Second Officer, no more than a type, meets only the dramatic necessity of number in handling the rough Antinio.[2] His concern is purely official: "Antonio, I arrest thee at the suit of Count Orsino." Without the First Officer this policeman might prove a poor adversary to the daring seaman. The officers are not, however, guards of Dogberry quality. In spite of Orsino's love-sickness, he has kept an efficient state.

Other characters who suffer the minute demands of dramatic or linguistic necessity are Curio, the Priest, and the Messenger. Curio, however, requires more than the Second Officer, even though the Duke's servant seems to serve the dramatic action less than the policeman does. Indeed, his presence seems purely linguistic; he is a "straight man" to Orsino's pun on "hart". But even though Curio's line seems only to fill this need in the dialogue and supply a transition between Orsino's two speeches, it must be given some dramatic quality or motivation. The Second Officer had a job to do and an obvious motivation. Curio is in a less revealing position; his line, nevertheless, must partake of the same real qualities that the Second Officer's does.

Two possibilities are apparent; perhaps both are there. Aside from providing Orsino with a character to feed him his cue, Shakespeare probably intended Curio's "Will you go hunt, my Lord?" to contrast humorously with Orsino's rhapsodic speech. However, this stylistic purpose cannot be extended to the character. If the pun on "hart" is first Curio's, then he must be allowed an unlikely license with his Duke's serious thoughts. Only a jester (witness Feste's "catechizing" of Olivia) could dare make fun of such emotions in the nobility, and there is nothing in Curio's name, lines, or behavior to indicate that he is the court fool. If he filled such a position, he certainly missed a professional opportunity to make a disparaging remark about Feste, whom he fetches to sing for the Duke.

It is most likely that Curio is a serving man to the Count, older than Velentine, perhaps a follower of Orsino's father. Since Curio is aware that Orsino is more in love with love than he is with Olivia, he suggests the traditional Elizabethan cure for love-melancholia—hunting.[3]

In spite of the fact that more can be said of Curio than of the Second Officer, the Count's man is really no more than a verbal functionary, and his character, even when infused with dramatic motivation, is no more than a broadly defined type.

Of Valentine, Curio's social counterpart, more can be said. His report to Orsino, though consisting of information he got from Olivia's handmaid, is not framed in language he heard from Maria:

> So please my lord, I might not be admitted,
> But from her handmaid do return this answer:
> The element itself, till seven years' heat,
> Shall not behold her face at ample view;
> But, like a cloistress, she will veiled walk
> And water once a day her chamber round
> With eye-offending brine—all this to season
> A brother's dead love, which she would keep
>   fresh
> And lasting in her sad remembrance.
>
> (I. i. 24-32)

In name and in speech Valentine seems well-suited to the task Orsino has set for him. Unlike Curio, whose character is formulated best by a reference to Elizabethan medical theory, Valentine is best understood in reference to the larger context of the play. He is called upon, as many minor Shakespearian figures are, to explain the first turn of the action: the love Orsino has described in the first lines of the play must go unrequited. Curio, on the other hand, speaks his lines before any plot has developed; his sole obligation is to Orsino's character. Valentine too contributes to the Count's character, but the contribution is by comparison rather than contrast. The love messenger continues the mood of Orsino's first two speeches. Like the Count's love, Olivia's rejection of it, as Valentine chooses to phrase it, is lengthy and descriptive. Furthermore, Valentine's speech, unlike Curio's brief cue, is one of the four poetic units which make up the first scene.

Curio's later lines, delivered when he is sent to summon Feste, tell nothing further about his character. Draper would say, however, that Valentine's gossipy remarks to Viola at the beginning of scene four are significant:

> *Val.* If the Duke continue these favors toward
>   you, Cesario, you are like to be much
>   advanced. He hath known you but three
>   days, and already you are no stranger.

Vio. You either fear his humor or my
    negligence that you call in question the
    continuance of his love. Is he inconstant,
    sir, in his favors?

Val. No, believe me.

(I. iv. 1-8)

Thus Viola takes over Valentine's thankless post. The older servingman is luckily not jealous, and kindly tells "Cesario" that she is like to be "much advanc'd," that Orsino is by nature constant in his favors; and with these felicitations, he seems to drop out of the play as if his task as unsuccessful intermediary had quite exhausted him. His magnanimity to Viola, without apparent motive, makes him seem a bit too good for this wicked world, for very few of us rejoice to be supplanted by others more successful.[4]

The problem here is that the lines quoted above and by Draper occur at the very beginning of scene four, and nothing has passed to indicate that Viola or anyone else has been chosen to supplant Valentine. By line thirteen the audience knows that Orsino has spoken to Viola of his love for Olivia: "I have unclasped / To thee the book even of my secret soul." But the Count's first speech of the scene was, "Stand you awhile aloof." His words to Viola are private, and when, in line fifteen, he instructs Viola to go to Olivia, there is no reason to assume that this commission had been arranged earlier. The line Draper uses to substantiate the contrast between Viola and Valentine does not occur until half the scene is played out: "She will attend it better in thy youth / Than in a nuncio's of more grave aspect."

Rather than being magnanimous, as Draper would have it, Valentine is only indulging in court talk with Viola. She misunderstands his remark, and, uncertain of her new position, questions Valentine about the constancy of the Count's affections. Viola probably observes in Valentine, as she did in the Captain who brought her to Illyria, a "fair behavior" and thus permits herself to ask the serving man a frank question about his master. Aside from this confidence that Valentine must have inspired in Viola, there is little in this repartee to define his character further.

The minor figures of Olivia's household, except for Fabian, are even less significant than the Duke's serving men. The servant who tells Olivia in Act III that "the young gentleman of the Count Orsino's is returned" is simply a stand-in for Malvolio who is parading on stage with his yellow stockings and ambition. He, as steward, would ordinarily bring such news, as he did at Viola's first arrival. If he were otherwise involved, Maria would serve in that capacity, as she does twice earlier. In this scene, since Malvolio and Maria are both on stage, another servant must be inserted for the announcement.

The Priest who marries Olivia and Sebastian has a little treatise on marriage to deliver when he is asked about Cesario. Perhaps H. B. Charlton is right when he asserts that the main problem in Elizabethan comedy is the fusion of comedy and romance.[5] Shakespeare has on stage an Italian delight: A woman disguised as a man is accused of courting her master's lady; the master is about to inflict a harsh punishment on the mistaken deceiver; she, all the while, loves the misguided master; the lady reveals that a marriage has already taken place; a formidable sea-pirate, whose case has been set aside, is, by association, kept on stage as a reminder of the real husband. Yet into this excellent comedy of romance Shakespeare chooses to insert a fatuous Priest whose lines could not have been taken seriously:

A contract of eternal bond of love,
Confirmed by mutual joindure of your hands,
Attested by the holy close of lips,
Strengthened by the interchangement of your
    rings.
And all the ceremony of this compact
Sealed in my function, by my testimony.
Since when, my watch hath told me, toward
    my grave
I have traveled but two hours.

(V. i. 159-166)

If the outline of the marriage ceremony does not make the Priest a marked man for a laugh, his notion of reckoning time will.

It is surely a mistake, though, to suggest that the Priest is comic relief for the potentially dangerous situation on stage, for romantic comedy thrives on such situations. The comic irony of differing levels of awareness, misunderstandings, and mistaken identities is the real basis of the romantic comedy. The Priest is an Elizabethan fault. Even in *Twelfth Night,* Shakespeare's greatest achievement in romance comedy, the dramatist did not pass by the chance to introduce one more genre figure. Instead of relying completely on the comic realization of the romantic plot, Shakespeare chose to add to an already complete situation. This is probably one of the few instances in Shakespeare where obtrusive lines should be delivered as unobtrusively as possible.

Two of the more important minor figures of the play have similar functions. The first duty of the two seamen, Antonio and the Captain who serves Viola, is to show by their attitudes and actions what attractive and likeable young people Viola and Sebastian are.

Viola's friend is agreeable at every turn. He gives Viola hope for Sebastian's safety, describes the situation in Illyria, and agrees to help Viola in her plan to serve the Count. Beyond this agreeableness, however, the Captain's character is something of a puzzle. It is difficult to draw the broad social boundaries necessary for a beginning. While Valentine's speeches show that he is on a plane of sophistication near the Duke's, the Captain's halting, overly-parenthetical speeches contrast sharply with Viola's flowing lines. However, his lines are set in poetic form, and, even though he admits that "what the great ones do the less will prattle of", he is well-informed about the situation in the Illyrian court. It is unlikely that he would knowingly classify himself a prattler. In spite of his halting lines, the Captain, instead of indulging in hearty sea-talk, alludes to court affairs and classical learning.

That he is not an ordinary seaman can be seen further in his gentle pun of Viola's "perchance", his attractive manner, and his ability to introduce Viola into the Illyrian court. Though M. St. Clare Byrne shows that accessibility to the great was unrealistically easy in Shakespeare's plays,[6] it is difficult to believe that Viola's friend is merely a mechant seaman. Perhaps he, like the First Officer, is a former defender of Illyria and has gained the respect and admiration of the Count through service in war. His readiness to take a "fearfull oath", familiarity with the ways of the sea, and courtly manner all indicate that he might have spent earlier years in the Count's military.

The second seafarer, Antonio, is the most completely developed minor character, though the honor of most useful must be reserved for Fabian. Although Antonio introduces Sebastian and helps reveal his likeable qualities in the same way the Captain does for Viola in Act I, the rough pirate does not disappear from the action. Perhaps there is some question about his identity, but it need not be so involved as Draper would have it. By narrowly interpreting "breach of the waves", from whence Antonio saved Sebastian, to mean "shore", Draper assumes that Antonio has a house by the seaside, was not a pirate or a seaman (since the boarding party onto the *Tiger* would probably have been led by a soldier), and entrusts too much friendship and money to Sebastian to be the "Notable Pyrate" he is called in Shakespeare's text.[7]

"Breach of the waves" is just as likely a reference to the break between the crests of the waves on the open sea. It is as well unlikely that Antonio, had he been a soldier serving a rival state, would choose not to reimburse Orsino had the government so demanded. He is most likely the commander of a privateer, where, as leader of a group of men necessarily fighters and sailors, he would have led the party that boarded the *Tiger*. The First Officer indicates that Antonio is a man of the sea: "I know your favor well, / Though now you wear no sea cap on your head." Orsino later explicitly states what Antonio's profession is: "A bawbling vessel he was captain of."

In Antonio's original motivation Shakespeare probably commits one error to gain several advantages. Sebastian directs his course to Orsino's court purely by chance. If a strong friendship had developed between the two men and Antonio sincerely wished to accompany Sebastian, the young man could surely have been persuaded to wander to less dangerous ground. That possibility is, of course, not open to the play, so Shakespeare must formulate Sebastian's hasty farewell and Antonio's decision to follow within the framework of strong friendship, hoping that that theme will dominate and Sebastian's illogical direction will pass unnoticed. Shakespeare uses this weakly motivated passage, however, to strengthen the two most important aspects of Antonio's character—daring and devotion:

> I have many enemies in Orsino's Court,
> Else would I very shortly see thee there.
> But, come what may, I do adore thee so
> That danger shall seem sport, and I will go.
> (II. i. 45-49)

Further corroboration for the likelihood of Antonio's seamanship and devotion comes from the highly suggestive parallel with Viola's Captain of Act I. Both are fatherly, though neither attempts to persuade his young charge to a different course of action. But, unlike the Captain's, Antonio's language is full of references to the sea: He has come far to find Sebastian, but his love "might have drawn one to a longer voyage"; Illyria, like the sea, may prove "rough and unhospitable to a stranger"; Antonio is in danger in Illyria because he has done service "in a sea fight, 'gainst the Count his galleys"; Sebastian, when pulled "from the rude sea's enraged and foamy mouth", was, like a ship in peril, "a wreck past hope". Thus in language alone Antonio does more than help define Sebastian's character.

This paradoxically gruff and doting seaman adds a distinct character to the already overflowing lists of *Twelfth Night*. He views the action from a completely different point of view, providing two excellent scenes of comic irony with Viola. In some sense he knows much less about the immediate situation than do the regular inhabitants of Illyria. On the other hand, his presence in the play is an added note of realistic awareness. At least his confusion involves Sebastian, a real person. All of Illyria, however, has been undermined by the Count's new favorite, "Cesario".[8] Antonio brings with him, as well, a note of honesty which imperils his life. All have lied in one way or another; even Viola's Captain is a partner to her disguise, but Antonio is unwilling to assume a mask in a world of pretenders.[9]

His presence on stage, especially in the last act, substitutes for the absent Sebastian and indicates the probable outcome of the confusion. At the same time his rough character announces the disorder of the final scene.[10] In other words, Antonio usurps the world of

Twelfth Night as he has usurped the Count's peace. Although his faith in Sebastian has been shattered, his truthfulness and courage make him a suitable symbol for the strength of the time which will undo the knot Viola has found too difficult to untie.

The man of all work in *Twelfth Night* is Fabian. Although his very presence in the play is questioned, since Maria tells Sir Toby and Sir Andrew to "let the fool make a third", Fabian becomes essential, performing services Feste could not. Fabian is probably the second son of a country gentleman, and, having no place in the inheritance, he seeks his fortune in service. His language is particularly rich in allusions to the country, though occasionally his wit sparkles with a new-learned reference to travel, money, or theater.

Only Hugh Hunt has called Fabian's identity into question. He suggests that the clever servant may be a second fool, younger than Feste and much more circumspect.[11] Hunt says that the actor who played Feste may have enjoyed too many liberties behind Malvolio's back during the letter scene, forcing the actor who did Malvolio to request a less ebullient background for his scene. Indeed, that segment of Feste's character which, especially in song, might be called melancholy would be given added significance if the old fool were about to be replaced by a youthful counterpart.[12]

Like Curio, however, there is nothing in Fabian's name or manner or speech to indicate that he is a professional jester. Sir Toby would not address a fool as "Signior Fabian"; Feste would not call a professional inferior "Master Fabian". It is much safer to assume that Fabian is a well-born servant of the type rendered completely useless in the overstaffed Elizabethan household. His affinity for good times has attracted him to Sir Toby, and the roaring knight no doubt looks on Fabian as a particular favorite. Although Fabian shows he is quick to pun by picking up many cues from Malvolio in the letter scene, he only once indulges in the counter-logical type of argument Feste is so fond of. He "proves" to Sir Andrew that Olivia's favors to Cesario in the orchard were directed subtly at the tall knight. Even this, however seems more like Sir Toby's proof that to be up late is to go to bed early than Feste's involved syllogisms.

Fabian enters the action of the play just in time to relieve the major players of their burden of contrapuntal effect. Only four scenes after the last major player has contributed his introduction to the speed of the play, Fabian appears. As if expecting disappointment or consternation at the absence of Feste, Shakespeare supplies an immediate motivation for Fabian's part in the device against Malvolio: "You know he brought me out o'favor with my lady about a bear-baiting here."

In the scene which follows Fabian restrains Sir Toby and Sir Andrew from giving away the plot and shows himself to be the quickest wit of the three. His role becomes increasingly important, however, when he is seen not only as an accomplice in the plot against Malvolio, but also as a confidante of Sir Toby's in the constant gulling of Sir Andrew. In the fourth scene of Act III Fabian supplies the necessary addition which prevents a simple two-part banter between Belch and Aguecheek. He moves the foolish knight as surely as Sir Toby does, and, since soliloquy is at a minimum in *Twelfth Night,* he allows Sir Toby to tell of his friendship for Sir Andrew: "I have been dear to him, lad, some two thousand strong or so."

In that scene Fabian is in and out, silent and witty as the action demands. He plays a minor role in the encounter with Malvolio but becomes a witty commentator when Sir Toby reads Aguecheek's challenge. In the duel he plays an even more important role, performing the service of "arrangement", a privilege Feste could not have aspired to.[13] Except for the final moments of the play, Fabian is most essential in this scene. He frightens Viola with reports of Sir Andrew's skill and ferocity, warns Sir Toby of the approaching officers, and becomes silent as other minor figures help distribute the action.

Fabian disappears when Feste enters into the trick against Malvolio. Perhaps the Fool was afraid earlier to be outrightly involved in the plot but now enters into the fun when his anonymity as a tormentor seems likely. This almost obvious substitution seems to further validate the necessity for a character of Fabian's social standing in such sequences as the duel. This is hardly necessary, however, if only Feste is to be considered as a major counterpart to Fabian, for Fabian relieves the necessity for constant reappearance and cross play of the entire range of major figures who infest Olivia's household.

When Fabian returns he is in hot pursuit of Feste, who is carrying Malvolio's letter. In Act V Fabian must become a real part of the background. The stage directions indicate that he is before Olivia's house while Feste jokes with the Count, Antonio is heard, Cesario is accused, the Priest verifies the marriage, and Sir Toby and Sir Andrew enter from their disastrous duel. All the while he must remain, like Antonio, an unobtrusive observer. He has wisely avoided the conflict with Sebastian, but he and Feste lead the wounded revellers off. Fabian returns with Feste (after Sebastian has entered and ended the chief masquerade of the play) in time to be present for the unfolding of Malvolio's plight. He reads the letter which Feste refuses to read except, allowing Vox, as a "madmans epistle", and goes off to fetch the imprisoned steward. It is indeed Fabian who knows more about the Malvolio plot than any other person on stage at the end of the drama. Although Feste is happy to disclose himself as Sir Topas, Fabian must tell his mistress the history of Malvolio's downfall. He takes away from any serious tone Malvolio might inject with his "revenge" by explaining that the foolery "may rather pluck on laughter than revenge." Though Orsino is to repeat his taking of Viola ("But when in other habits you are seen, / Orsino's mistress and his fancy's Queen"), Fabian discloses the last important turn of action in the play: "Maria writ / The letter at Sir Toby's great importance, / In recompense whereof he hath married her."

Each of *Twelfth Night*'s minor figures has been carefully employed for rather specific reasons, but the major effects of this conglomeration of individuals are speed and economy. The major characters have not been left alone to indulge in tiring repartee, but the play has never been crowded with unnecessary groups of hangers-on. The play has never been invaded meaninglessly as *Romeo and Juliet* is by the musicians, nor has it been left bare at any time.

Especially noticeable is the fact that the minor characters at the first of the play—the Captain, Curio, and Valentine—perform specific chores and, since the introduction of the major characters is performing the contrapuntal function, disappear or remain unheard. The speed in the first part of the play is almost entirely dependent on the introduction of the long list of major figures which is finally complete at the beginning of Act II. After that, except for the very specific jobs done by the Priest and the Messenger, two more important minor players—Antonio and Fabian—serve as reappearing aids in the pace of the drama. Their significantly different points of view and degrees of awareness produce involvements in the irony, structure, and information of the play.

Even though Antonio and Fabian play more significant parts both as characters and contributors to the action, all the minor figures perform essential services, all the speaking parts can be dramatically justified. Although at times some minor characters fall below the expected Shakespearian mark of characterization or consistency, all contribute vitally to the contrapuntal weaving of people, events, and ideas that is the basis of *Twelfth Night*.

Notes

1 *Shakespeare: The Complete Works,* ed. by G. B. Harrison (New York, 1952), p. 871.

2 John W. Draper, *The Twelfth Night of Shakespeare's Audience* (Stanford, 1950), p. 167.

3 Draper, p. 165.

4 Draper, p. 165.

5 H. B. Charlton, *Shakespearean Comedy* (London, 1938), p. 23.

6 M. St. Clare Byrne, "The Social Background", in *A Companion to Shakespeare Studies,* ed. by H. Granville-Barker and G. B. Harrison (Garden City, New York, 1960), pp. 196-200.

7 Draper, 158.

8 Bertrand Evans, *Shakespeare's Comedies* (Oxford, 1960), p. 137.

9 Joseph H. Summers, "The Masks of *Twelfth Night*", *Shakespeare: Modern Essays in Criticism,* ed. Leonard F. Dean (New York, 1957), p. 131.

10 John R. Brown, *Shakespeare and His Comedies* (London, 1957), p. 179.

11 Hugh Hunt, *Old Vic Prefaces* (London, 1954), p. 77.

12 Hunt, p. 78.

13 Draper, p. 163.

Richard Henze (essay date 1975)

SOURCE: "*Twelfth Night:* Free Disposition on the Sea of Love," in *The Sewanee Review,* Vol. LXXXIII, No. 2, Spring, 1975, pp. 267-83.

[*In this essay, Henze claims that the variety of seemingly contradictory interpretations of* Twelfth Night *result from Shakespeare's attempt to portray a "sea" of interacting opposites and their reconciliation.*]

Critical interpretations of *Twelfth Night* are notable for the variety of contradictory meanings that their makers attach to the play. The play has been called, among other things, a vindication of romance, a depreciation of romance, a realistic comment on economic security and practical marriage, an account of saturnalian festivity, a "subtle portrayal of the psychology of love," a play about "unrequital in love" because of self-deception, an account of love's wealth, a dramatic account of Epiphany and the gift of Divine Love, a moral comedy about the surfeiting of the appetite so that it "may sicken and so die" and allow "the rebirth of the unencumbered self." Various critics have variously described the chief character in the play to be Malvolio, Viola, Olivia, or even Feste. The complexity of the play is such that each of these opinions is supported by considerable textual evidence. The play is about the vindication of romance and the depreciation of romance, but the romance that is vindicated is that of Viola and

Sebastian reunited and chosen by love and not that of Orsino and his selfish, conventional, melancholic seclusion in a bower of flowers. The play does deal with both practicality and prudence—Viola tells us her very practical reasons for joining the duke's household, for example; but the play also shows saturnalian festivity in full sway under Sir Toby Belch, master of the holiday. The play shows Viola's epiphany of love and Toby's surfeit of the appetite—Viola's love fulfilled and Malvolio's love unrequited.

I should like to propose a solution to this puzzle of interpretations: that *Twelfth Night* is a play about opposites and that each of the interpretations above tends to treat just one of a pair of opposites in the play. The primary opposition in the play is the one implicit in the title, *Twelfth Night; or, What You Will:* epiphany and the divine gift of love or earthly appetite, desire, and choice. But as the play's action proceeds, oppositions become much more complicated and subtle than the single one in the title as they grow to include oppositions between characters, between actions, between images, and finally between the present mirth of the play and the continual indiscriminate rain of Feste's concluding song.

The most obvious opposition in the play is that between giving and taking: whether it is better to give or to receive is a question that the play continually poses and answers ambiguously. Viola gives freely, Sebastian takes unhesitantly. Maria gives, Toby takes. Orsino gives, Feste takes. Critics have described very well the giving side of the play, but not very fully at all its opposite—the constant taking of the play. The generosity is obvious: Viola gives freely of her money and herself; she even offers to give her life finally if Orsino will take it. Antonio, until he is captured, gives his money and himself for Sebastian; then he asks for his money back and regrets his generosity. Orsino gives money somewhat generously to the fool, himself very insistently to Olivia; Olivia matches Orsino by taking care to preserve Malvolio even while she forces herself upon Viola. Maria gives sport that delights Toby and deludes Malvolio. Sebastian gives himself to Olivia; Orsino finally gives himself to Viola. Gifts in the play are multiple even though giving is not always generous.

But taking is just as important in the play, and most evident in Feste's constant begging for tips and bribes, although Feste only begs so long as someone is bountiful toward him; he is never very insistent, but is often even hesitant in his pleas: as he says, "I would not have you to think that my desire of having is the sin of covetousness." Just as free from greed—and no beggar at all—is Sebastian in his acceptance of Olivia. Olivia and Orsino, on the other hand, lack full freedom from covetousness, although they covet persons rather than money. Less hesitant and more covetous still are

Toby in his attempts to get Andrew's money and horse, Andrew in his attempt to get Olivia, and Malvolio in his conceited assurance that Olivia loves him and that he will soon have power over Toby.

Feste describes in the play a norm for getting what he wills without taking what others would not have him take. He differs from Sebastian in that he does not repay what he gets with a like gift; he differs from the other takers in his lack of covetousness, even though his profession is to beg. He is the generous taker.

The other norm, that of generous giving, is defined by Viola as she gives herself and her services to Orsino, money to the fool, and half her purse to Antonio. The others in the play, with the exception of Sebastian, violate one or both of the norms established by Feste and Viola. Orsino gives himself to Olivia, but he also tries to claim her as Antonio did his ship. Olivia seems to be generous: "What shall you ask of me that I'll deny, / That honour, sav'd, may upon asking give?" Yet she tries to buy Viola-Cesario with a show of wealth. Antonio is extravagant in his generosity toward Sebastian, but he is also a "salt water pirate" and very concerned about his own safety in spite of his hazard of himself. Malvolio's offer of himself is gross conceit; Andrew's is gross foolishness. Maria gives Toby sport but seeks to end Malvolio's freedom. Only Viola consistently gives freely and graciously with no expectation of profit or power; only Feste consistently takes freely and graciously without disturbing another's bounty and without giving himself in return.

The range in the action of the play is suggested by the characterization of Viola and Feste. Viola becomes the embodiment of gracious, nearly divine Twelfth Night giving, Feste of festive Twelfth Night taking. Yet, though they seem to contradict each other, Viola and Feste are more alike than they are unlike, for they share the essential qualities of graciousness, civility, and free disposition; they are both careful not to intrude on someone else's free disposition.

Free disposition in the play involves two things: that one be generous with one's money and one's self where the money and self are freely desired—and that one graciously accept what one is freely offered if to accept the gift does not intrude on the free disposition of giver or recipient. To be simply generous is not enough, for generosity can become terribly selfish if it is imposed on one who does not desire it. Simply to take is likewise not enough, for graciousness requires that one take only what one is freely offered. Viola and Feste demonstrate the right kind of generosity and the right kind of graciousness; Malvolio, on the other hand, neither generous nor gracious, opposes both Feste and Viola. As the characters become more like Viola and Feste and less like Malvolio, they acquire generosity, graciousness, and true civility.

The freedom that Orsino and Olivia finally acquire, freedom to give where the gift is desired, is the true festivity that Feste himself tends to symbolize in the play. Here the distinction is between Feste's true festivity and the belching, oversatisfied, what-shall-we-do-else sport of Toby. There will be cakes and ale to be sure, but cakes and ale are not all that life is. Feste's sport inspires generosity without intruding on free disposition; he begs only as long as one is freely generous, then he allows bounty to sleep a while. Toby on the other hand has no concern whatever for others' freedom. His sport is terribly ungenerous, endangering even Viola—free disposition itself—as well as Andrew and Malvolio. His sport is too indiscriminate, too little inclined to take into account person, time, and circumstances. He, like Falstaff, has too little to do with the time of the day.

A proper attitude toward festivity, the play implies, is one that recommends Feste and his freedom even while it rejects the excess of Toby Belch. But one's choice is not always that simple. Maria, for example, has to choose between Malvolio and Toby: in that case Maria, the embodiment of wit, properly prefers Toby's freedom to Malvolio's self-love; but she recognizes, at the same time, that Toby is out of order. So does the fool he too prefers Toby's attitude to Malvolio's, but he sees Toby for the drunk that he is.

The names of the characters indicate their symbolic qualities. Viola is both musical and free in volition; her counterimage, Malvolio is the embodiment of ill will who intrudes on free disposition. Feste is festive; his counterimage, Belch, is surfeited. Toby Belch, until his marriage to Maria, threatens to replace Twelfth Night's generous festivity with uncivil sport. For what you will to be fully satisfactory, it must be Viola's what you will and not Malvolio's. For the festivity of Twelfth Night to be fully satisfactory, it must be Feste's graciousness, not Toby's rambunctiousness.

The movement of the play is from ill will to true festivity, generosity, and the harmonic feast of marriage and friendship. Sebastian's arrival signifies the approaching success of the characters in arriving at that point, for Sebastian is a compound of Feste and Viola, one who freely gives and just as freely takes. He furnishes the single embodiment of the Twelfth Night spirit that Viola and Feste together define, and the final opposition of the play is the thorough opposition between Sebastian and Malvolio rather than the superficial one between Feste and Viola. Twelfth Night becomes what you will; desire and generosity operate in accord.

The play begins with Orsino's attempt to force himself upon Olivia. Orsino wants an excess of music, as Toby wants an excess of cakes and ale, "that, surfeiting, /

The appetite may sicken, and so die." Such appetite hardly surfeits itself into correction, however; instead it threatens music, one of Viola's significances:

> for I can sing
> And speak to him in many sorts of music
> That will allow me very worth his service.

Like all false lovers Orsino considers himself like all true lovers, but in his demands on Olivia, his desire for solitude, his selfish submersion in melancholy, he is neither truly loving nor truly generous. While he "prizes not quantity of dirty lands," he demands the immediate surrender of Olivia, "that miracle and queen of gems," and thus shows himself to be more like witless Andrew and ill-willed Malvolio than like Viola.

Viola warns Orsino that Olivia may not wish to accept his gift:

> *Duke*. I cannot be so answer'd.
> *Vio*. Sooth, but you must.

Viola sees the threat to free disposition; the duke merely feels his appetite "all as hungry as the sea":

> Make no compare
> Between that love a woman can bear me
> And that I owe Olivia.

The woman is Viola and we do make compare.

The sea which Orsino is "as hungry as" is the sea of love that can either support or devour, but the ships upon it are responsible for its quality; they can support one another or they can prey upon one another. Orsino describes that sea:

> O spirit of love, how quick and fresh art thou,
> That notwithstanding thy capacity
> Receiveth as the sea, naught enters there,
> Of what validity and pitch soe'er
> But falls into abatement and low price
> Even in a minute.

This metaphor of ships sailing on an ocean of love becomes the most important image in the play. The sea begins as the great devouring element that almost drowns Viola and Sebastian when their ship is destroyed in a storm. But their voyage on a sometimes supporting, sometimes devouring sea does not end when they drift ashore from the literal sea, for, safely ashore they begin a dangerous voyage toward a journey's "end in lovers meeting" on a sea of love where they continually encounter pirates and rocks. With the lovers finally together, the salt waves have proved themselves kind, to Viola at least, and the collision that gets the ships together is a fortunate wreck.

Not all ships fall, as the duke complains, into "abatement and low price" The waves threaten worthy vessel and pirate ship alike, but the worthy ships get through on the strength of generosity and graciousness while the pirates either sink or surrender. The sea does devour, but it devours those who trust rotten timbers of self-conceit and greed, who seek profit from the other ships and not at the journey's end. The prime example, of course, is Malvolio, who, in spite of his high self-estimation, loses, even in a minute, his value on the sea. Orsino, in his warlike assault on Olivia, is likewise at first too much the pirate. He sends Viola to board and claim a prize: "Be clamorous, and leap all civil bonds, / Rather than make unprofited return." To demand profit is both uncivil and ungenerous, like the prospects of Malvolio instead of the generosity of Viola. Orsino promises Viola a share in the profits if she succeeds:

> Prosper well in this,
> And thou shalt live as freely as thy lord,
> To call his fortunes thine.

Orsino's promise is fulfilled in a fashion that he does not expect, and not because of any desire for profit on Viola's part.

In spite of Orsino's commission to her, Viola hoists her sail and accosts Olivia with "no overture of war, no taxation of homage; I hold the olive in my hand; my words are as full of peace as matter." Viola woos gently for Orsino, pities Olivia when she loves Cesario instead of Orsino, and finally leaves the whole problem up to time, the larger ocean that includes the sea of love and its coasts.

The difference between the generosity of Viola and Sebastian and that of Orsino is a difference in relationship to the sea of love. Orsino is himself as hungry as the sea, ready to devour Olivia. Viola and Sebastian, on the other hand, are provident and generous and able to survive misfortune on the sea. Viola has been saved by hanging "on our driving boat"; her brother, Sebastian, "most provident in peril" by binding himself (courage and hope both teaching him the practice) "to a strong mast that liv'd upon the sea." When Sebastian lands upon Illyria, and embarks on its sea of love, he proves himself just as provident in peril by binding himself to Olivia, another strong mast on the sea. Viola, on the other hand, hangs onto her driving boat, Orsino, until the wind calms on the sea and the preservation of Sebastian proves "salt waves fresh in love."

Olivia is not the pirate that Orsino is, but her generosity is hardly Viola's. She refuses to listen to Viola's suit for Orsino:

> But would you undertake another suit,
> I had rather hear you to solicit that
> Than music from the spheres.

Viola hopes that "grace and good disposition attend your ladyship!" Such good disposition should be freer than Olivia's is at the moment. That very loss of freedom involves, as it does with Malvolio and Orsino, delusion:

> *Oli.* I prithee tell me what thou think'st of
> me.
> *Vio.* That you do think you are not what you
> are.
> *Oli.* If I think so, I think the same of you.
> *Vio.* Then think you right: I am not what I
> am.

In her delusion Olivia is, as she admits, as mad as Malvolio, "if sad and merry madness equal be." As madness is delusion on a sea of love that leads one to become uncivil or ungenerous, Olivia's madness is like Malvolio's; for both she and Malvolio attempt to board and claim a prize. Toby's merry madness, as it leaps the confines of holiday freedom and threatens Viola, becomes likewise piratical. Malvolio's "very midsummer madness" is contagious as long as the ships encourage the sea to devour rather than support the vessels that sail on it.

Love given unsought is good, as Olivia says, but only if it does not compromise the loved one's free disposition. Olivia is neither truly generous nor truly gracious when she forces herself upon Viola-Cesario and even attempts to purchase love: "How shall I feast him? What bestow of him? / For youth is bought more oft than begg'd or borrow'd." Olivia wishes that Viola "were as I would have you be." That is the problem. What Olivia wills compromises Viola's capability to give freely of herself; the opposition is an improper one between Twelfth Night and what you will, between what is given and what is desired.

Orsino and Olivia are alike; Viola is the opposite. She asks only Olivia's "true love for my master," although she would like to be his bride herself. She refuses even to accept a trip from Olivia: "I am no fee'd post, lady; keep your purse; / My master, not myself, lacks recompense." Generosity to Viola requires, as it does for Antonio in *The Merchant of Venice,* the hazard of everything. With Orsino and Olivia, on the other hand, generosity is an uncivil attempt to seize power and profit on the sea of love. They are potentially generous; they indicate that by their treatment of the fool and Malvolio: Olivia would not have Malvolio "miscarry for the half of my dowry"; but until they both learn as Viola tells Olivia that "what is yours to bestow is not yours to reserve," and learn to bestow it without hope of power or profit where it is freely desired, they will both breathe "thriftless sighs."

While Viola opposes false generosity with true generosity, Feste opposes false festivity with true festivity. Feste takes graciously when Orsino pays him "for thy pains":

> *Clown.* No pains, sir, I take pleasure in
> singing, sir.
> *Duke.* I'll pay thy pleasure then.
> *Clown.* Truly, sir, and pleasure will be paid,
> one time or another.

As Viola tells him, he begs well. Of all the beggars in the play only Feste is capable of inspiring generosity without compromising his free disposition. Orsino and Olivia in contrast are both uncivil in their begging, while Sir Andrew has no manners or civility whatever. Only Feste, both wise and civil enough to play the fool, is able to "observe their mood on whom he jests, / The quality of persons, and the time"; and to practice foolery "full of labor as a wise man's art."

Toby's festivity and piracy lack such labor and wisdom. Where Feste does "care for something," Toby cares for nothing but his own enjoyment and profit, the food for his insatiable appetite. Like witless Andrew, Toby delights in "masques and revels sometimes altogether," because life "consists of eating and drinking":

> *And.* Shall we set about some revels?
> *Toby.* What shall we do else?

Toby's sport is sport, to be sure, holiday madness that gives plenty of matter for a May morning; but his sport is too much lacking in civility—as Maria points out: he has "no wit, manners, nor honesty, but to gabble like tinkers at this time of night." Cakes and ale are not enough. Civility, good manners, generosity are as important to the proper sport of life as eating and drinking. That Malvolio points out, although he is too much like Ophelia's preacher who "recks not his own rede": "Mistress Mary, if you priz'd my lady's favor at anything more than contempt, you would not give means for this uncivil rule." Toby's rule is uncivil and ungenerous toward Olivia and Viola; yet he lacks the ill will of Malvolio. Thus Maria, siding with Toby, chooses the lesser of two evils, even though she clearly recognizes Toby's fault.

Toby, however, does not operate alone; his cronies are careless Fabian and witless Andrew. The three together oppose Malvolio; even their excessive festivity may lessen the power of ill will; but their unconfined festivity becomes dangerous when Toby maneuvers his "dear minikin" Andrew into a duel that threatens free disposition and order. To oppose Malvolio, as Maria points out, is necessary; but to dismiss all restraint is not satisfactory. Toby, Fabian, and Andrew lack the moderation, grace, and wit that Feste has. The union

between Maria and Toby and the confession of Fabian at the end of the play indicate the movement of Toby and Fabian toward Viola and Feste. Andrew we can do little more with than we can Malvolio: absolute ill will and absolute witlessness are both impossible to reform.

Toby's appetite is excessive and threatens anarchy; Malvolio's is distempered and threatens tyranny. Olivia indicates her potential for clear sight by describing accurately the fault of Malvolio when he calls Feste "a barren rascal": "O, you are sick of self-love, Malvolio, and taste with a distemper'd appetite. To be generous, guiltless, and of free disposition, is to take those things for birdbolts that you deem cannon bullets." Malvolio, of all the ships that sail on the sea of love, is most nearly a self-contained pirate: "Nothing that can be can come between me and the full prospect of my hopes." Although he gives credit to Jove, Malvolio knows that he himself deserves full credit for his own success.

Maria, with her "sport royal," makes Malvolio, the "time pleaser," a "common recreation" by playing on his self-conceit that "all that look on him love him." The gulling of Malvolio is comically acceptable because he is ill will itself being downed by the holiday that he would prevent, even though the profit from the gulling is less satisfactory than Viola's final recompense from Orsino. But for the holiday to go further and become anarchy is not comically acceptable. When Toby begins to endanger Viola and Sebastian, he becomes too uncivil. Olivia's criticism is harsh but proper: "Ungracious wretch, / Fit for the mountains and the barbarous caves, / Where manners ne'er were preach'd!" Toby joins Malvolio in disgrace, to be redeemed only by the generous gift of himself to Maria. Malvolio, incapable to the end of such free disposition, remains unredeemed.

Feste, dressed as Sir Topas the curate, goes to Malvolio in his prison of darkness that symbolizes Malvolio himself and tries to arouse the spirit of holiday generosity in him. He points out to Malvolio that the mind can be its own place if it is free and generous: "I say there is no darkness but ignorance, in which thou art more puzzled than the Egyptians in their fog." The darkness of the room, like the rain that falls every day, may be penetrated by light and warmth if one generously wills to do so. Feste's insistence that the room is light and bright indicates Feste's ability to will it so; Malvolio's failure to consider it light signifies his ill will.

With ill will comes captivity; with free disposition comes security. In *The Comedy of Errors* true security, as Luciana says, lies in social bonds; by being bound one becomes truly free, by losing one's self in the ocean one attains the fullest and noblest individuality. The same kind of security is recommended in *Twelfth Night:* the hazard of self and free acceptance of restrictions. Sebastian finally embodies that combination of Feste and Viola that makes collision on the sea a happy wreck. Safely ashore from the literal sea, Sebastian embarks on a "determinate voyage" of "mere extravagancy." Although Sebastian does not wish to endanger Antonio ("It were a bad recompense for your love"), he does accept with grace Antonio's bounteously offered purse:

> I can no other answer make but thanks,
> And thanks; and ever oft good turns
> Are shuffled off with such uncurrent pay.

Sebastian most perfectly of all the characters in the play combines generosity, wit, and civility. He hazards himself, accepts support that he is freely offered, and recognizes, better than Viola, the possibility of delusion: "There's something in't / That is deceivable." He lacks Malvolio's self-conceited ability to think that his own worth is sufficient cause for everyone to love him, but he nevertheless accepts love that is offered:

> *Oli.* Nay, come I prithee. Would thou'dst be
> rul'd by me!
> *Seb.* Madam, I will.

He will be ruled; he voluntarily disposes himself to follow Olivia. Thus he is not a puppet, as Viola would have been had Olivia had her way, and as Andrew is to Toby. He retains his freedom to bestow himself where he will, chooses to bestow himself where he is desired, and thus forms, with Olivia, who is finally giving herself where she is desired, a free and mutually generous pair.

Antonio, like his namesake in *The Merchant of Venice,* demonstrates the hazard of self; he follows Sebastian even though great danger is present: "I do adore thee so / That danger shall seem sport, and I will go." "Willing love" and care, "as might have drawn one to a longer voyage," draw him after Sebastian. But Antonio's generosity, unlike Sebastian's, is modified by the fact that Antonio has been a pirate and may be again; he pirated a ship from Orsino:

> It might have since been answer'd in repaying
> What we took from them, which for traffic's
> sake
> Most of our city did. Only myself stood out,
> For which if I be lapsed in this place
> I shall pay dear.

Antonio's generosity, like Olivia's and Orsino's, is not absolute; thus when he is captured he begins to doubt that he should have been generous: "What will you do, now my necessity / Makes me to ask you for my purse?" Since he saved Sebastian from "the rude sea's enrag'd and foamy mouth," he expects Sebastian to repay his generosity freely. When Sebastian seems ungracious

and ungrateful, Antonio begins to fear for his own safety. The point is that safety on the sea from the rain that "raineth every day" requires human generosity, human civility. If people prey upon each other, the sea will accept the wrecks; if they support each other, even the accidents that do happen may be fortunate like the "happy wrack" that occurs in *Twelfth Night*.

Sebastian establishes the proper combination of the qualities of Feste and Viola to allow movement toward that happy wrack; the last-act accomplishes that combination in other characters. The act begins with Feste carrying Malvolio's letter to Olivia. Fabian asks to see it. Without violating generosity, in fact by encouraging generosity, Feste avoids showing the letter:

> *Fab.* Now as thou lov'st me, let me see his
> letter.
> *Clown.* Good Master Fabian, grant me another
> request.
> *Fab.* Anything.
> *Clown.* Do not desire to see this letter.
> *Fab.* This is to give a dog, and in recompense
> desire my dog again.

But that very return of the dog allows a double generosity without intruding on Feste's free disposition and desire. This interchange effectively emphasizes Feste's ability to inspire generosity in others without giving up his own freedom. Then Feste offers some wise foolishness which the duke rewards:

> *Duke.* Thou shalt not be the worse for me,
> there's gold.
> *Clown.* But that it would be double-dealing,
> sir, I would you could make it another.

The duke gives Feste a second coin. Feste suggests that "the third pays for all":

> *Duke.* You can fool no more money out of me
> at this throw. If you will let your lady
> know I am here to speak with her, and
> bring her along with you, it may awake my
> bounty further.
> *Clown.* Marry, sir, lullaby to your bounty till I
> come again!
> . . . But as you say, sir, let your bounty take
> a nap, I will awake it anon.

While the duke's bounty is asleep, the sea threatens to devour order and generosity as "blind waves and surges" wash the boats.

Antonio, brought in captive, accuses Viola once again of ingratitude. Then Olivia rejects Orsino's suit before he can speak, and the Duke accuses her of incivility:

You uncivil lady,
To whose ingrate and inauspicious altars
My soul the faithfull'st off'rings hath breath'd
    out
That e'er devotion tender'd!

Orsino even threatens to kill Olivia: "a savage jeal-ousy / That sometime savors nobly," and then Viola: "I'll sacrifice the lamb that I do love, / To spite a raven's heart within a dove." Viola goes "most jocund, apt, and willingly, / To do you rest." Olivia feels her-self beguiled and calls for the priest to confirm her marriage. Toby and Andrew come with broken heads. Finally Sebastian brings the proper combination of giving and taking, freedom and wit, to end the confu-sion. The duke, finally reawakened to generosity, asks a "share in this most happy wrack" and gives himself where he is desired, thus finally allowing free disposi-tion.

Malvolio is sent for. Olivia offers to bear the cost of a celebration, "here at my house and at my proper cost." Orsino generously and civilly agrees; then he gives Viola his hand and himself—the true generosity. All are generous but Malvolio; even he is given a chance. Fabian freely confesses his and Toby's "de-vice against Malvolio here, / Upon some stubborn and uncourteous parts / We had conceiv'd against him." The confession reaffirms the norm: Fabian is willing to forgive Malvolio; only Malvolio is obdurate in in-civility: "I'll be reveng'd on the whole pack of you!" Toby, appetite, can be tempered: he has, "in recom-pense" to Maria, married her; ill will can only be avoided.

The play ends, as Feste foretold, with the ships in harbor and lovers well-met: "Journeys end in lovers meeting, / Every wise man's son doth know"; but it ends too with the awareness that the rain will fall again, as Feste also foretold: "Present mirth hath present laugh-ter" and "Youth's a stuff will not endure." For finally there is Feste's song about the continual rain. We have seen the sunshine, now we see the rain; the final op-position seems to be one between Feste's conclusion and the play that we have just seen; but that opposition is not so abrupt, for the rain has been near throughout the play, in the death of Olivia's brother, in the near loss of Viola and Sebastian, in Feste's songs about life's melancholy, and most importantly in the ill will of Malvolio that appropriately is recognized but not reformed. The difference between this play and the comedies that precede it is finally the difference of Feste's song. The song is a description of the flow of time, of the dark strand in the weave, the dying fall, the deceit of disguise, the loss of the rose of beauty, the rain that raineth every day.

While the play does remain essentially a happy ac-count of Jack getting Jill, the implication is no longer so clear that the man shall get his mare again and all shall be well. Fortunate shipwrecks may occur, but drownings also occur, and the sun that brightly illumi-nates all *Twelfth Night* except Malvolio's dark room may be shining through a break in the clouds of storm. It has rained before; it will rain again; one cannot trust in the sunshine, but one can perhaps trust in generos-ity, grace, and free disposition, in the mind's ability to be its own place, to turn a dark, rainy, devouring ocean into a sunlit kind sea teeming with life.

Twelfth Night lacks much of the substantial security of the earlier comedies; Sir Topas replaces Aemilia; a devouring ocean replaces Arden; the rain partly ob-scures the feast. Order is possible, to be sure; the comic norm remains; but that order requires more than a walk in the fields or the arrival of Theseus in the woods. The ring that Bassanio must take great care to keep safe has now been replaced by larger relationships. The consequences of fault are not yet tragic; one does not lose Desdemona or Cordelia; one does not even lose the sixteen years, youth, and innocence that Leontes loses. But one does see the rain closing in and the waves rising.

APPEARANCE VS. REALITY

Terence Eagleton (essay date 1967)

SOURCE: "Language and Reality in *Twelfth Night*," in *Critical Quarterly,* Vol. 9, No. 3, Autumn, 1967, pp. 217-28.

[*In the essay that follows, Eagleton contends that the language of* Twelfth Night *melds with its reality and, through the central subject of love, collapses and con-fuses the social roles of the characters.*]

At the opening of *Twelfth Night,* Orsino describes his love for Olivia in terms which directly recall some of the paradoxes of language and illusion in other Shakespearian plays:

O spirit of love, how quick and fresh art thou!
That, notwithstanding thy capacity
Receiveth as the sea, nought enters there,
Of what validity and pitch soe'er,
But falls into abatement and low price
Even in a minute.

(1, 1)

Orsino's love has the destructively creative quality of the language of Richard II and the *Macbeth* witches, and the illusions of Puck: it absorbs and transforms reality into its own image, levelling its values to its own standard and thus rendering all experience arbitrary and interchangeable. The free-ranging, ocean-like quality of excessive love is the ground of its own negation: its capacity to receive all experience is equally its inability to discriminate between the intrinsic values of particular items. Excessive love, like disembodied or elaborate language, is a self-generating subjectivity detached from physical reality and therefore illusory; like the illusions of Oberon and Richard II it dominates reality, shaping it to its own form and granting it validity only within these terms, negating the experiences from which it draws positive substance. Unrequited, melancholic love intensifies this process: it is self-consuming, as Orsino is pursued and consumed by his own desires. When love, like language and created illusion, ceases to be closely structured by the physical situations which render it intelligible, its relation to these situations becomes paradoxically both parasitic and imperialist: it feeds off a real condition which it simultaneously creates, and can then be seen as an embodied contradiction, a self-cancelling encounter of negative and positive life.

The complex relations of language and reality is a common theme in *Twelfth Night*. Language in the play, as in Gaunt's use of metaphor in *Richard II*, can shape reality creatively, disclosing through linguistic connection a previously obscure truth:

> *Viola* And what should I do in Illyria?
> My brother he is in Elysium.
> Perchance he is not drown'd—what think you, sailors?
> *Captain* It is perchance that you yourself were saved.
> *Viola* O my poor brother! and so perchance may he be.
>
> (1, 2)

The Captain catches up Viola's use of 'perchance' and gives it a slightly different emphasis, which Viola then takes up with a sense of new insight, using the word a second time with both her own original emphasis and the Captain's new meaning in mind.

This creative-exploratory use of language can be contrasted with the verbal fencing of Sir Toby Belch and his companions. In these exchanges language constantly overrides reality, ceaselessly spawning new meanings which grow, not from the substance of an argument, but from previous verbal resonances themselves unrooted in reality. Language detaches itself from reality and takes flight as a self-creating force, controlling rather than articulating the course of a conversation until reality comes to exist almost wholly at a verbal level, only tenuously connected to actual experience:

> *Sir Andrew* Fair lady, do you think you have fools in hand?

> *Maria* Sir, I have not you by th' hand.
> *Sir Andrew* Marry, but you shall have; and here's my hand.
> *Maria* Now, sir, thought is free. I pray you, bring your hand to the butt'ry bar and let it drink.
> *Sir Andrew* Wherefore, sweetheart? What's your metaphor?
> *Maria* It's dry, sir.
> *Sir Andrew* Why, I think so; I am not such an ass but I can keep my hand dry. But what's your jest?
> *Maria* A dry jest, sir.
> *Sir Andrew* Are you full of them?
> *Maria* Ay, sir, I have them at my fingers' ends; marry, now I let go of your hand, I am barren.
>
> (1, 3)

The progress of this exchange is shaped wholly by verbal resonances, each giving rise to another. The puns and allusions collide, counter-cross and interact rapidly, and one significant element in the word-play is the quick, confusing switches from physical fact to metaphor. Maria converts Aguecheek's metaphor of 'hand' into fact, then unifies fact and metaphor in the image of the hand drinking at the buttery-bar; Aguecheek latches onto the metaphor and is then further confused by Maria's ambivalent use of 'dry' to apply both to her own language and Aguecheek's hand; when Augecheek settles on the first meaning at Maria's instigation, Maria reverts to applying the term to physical fact—his hand—but in a metaphorical way. Maria's language absorbs and appropriates reality for its own purpose, without ever submitting to the contours of fact itself: her speech is an area of free, fluid existence ('thought is free') beyond the rigidities of stable definition, an area within which elements of experience can be endlessly interchanged, combined and devalued to create fresh absurdities and arbitrary connections.[1]

Metaphor, then, can operate creatively or destructively: by breaking down the limits of settled definition it can extend one reality into illuminating connection with another; it can also break down defined reality into a purely negative freedom, disclosing insights and relations held at a sheerly verbal level beyond the boundaries of actuality and therefore incapable of interacting with known reality to reveal fresh truth. The breakdown of creative connection at the level of normal discourse is a corollary of this mode of communication:

> *Sir Toby* He's as tall a man as any's in Illyria.
> *Maria* What's that to th' purpose?
> *Sir Toby* Why, he has three thousand ducats a year.
>
> (1, 3)

Verbal dexterity is effective only at the level of its own self-generated illusion: brute reality can expose it for what it is, as an elaborate nothing, a substanceless patter:

> *Sir Toby* Approach, Sir Andrew. Not to be
>   abed after midnight is to be up betimes; and
>   'diluculo surgere' thou know'st—
> *Sir Andrew* Nay, by my troth, I know not; but
>   I know to be up late is to be up late.
> *Sir Toby* A false conclusion! I hate it as an
>   unfill'd can . . .
>
>   (2, 2)

For Belch, reality consists in proving contradiction and illusion, and Aguecheek's simple-minded assertion of the self-evident offends his sensibility. Yet Aguecheek's mode of discourse is paradoxically similar to Belch's: to affirm that things are what they are, to resist elaboration, is a tautology equivalent in its own realm to the contradictions which Sir Toby discerns. A tautology is as self-contained and self-created as Belch's own language: reality itself shares the quality of illusion.

The issue of language and reality emerges directly in Viola's conversation with the Clown in Act 3 Scene 1. The Clown acknowledges himself as a 'corrupter of words':

> To see this age! A sentence is but a chev'ril glove
> to a good wit. How quickly the wrong side may be
> turn'd outward! . . . I can yield you (no reason)
> without words, and words are grown so false I am
> loath to prove reason with them.

Reason—reality—can be expressed only in language and yet is falsified by language; without language there can be no reason yet with language there can be none either—to speak or keep silent is equally illusory. The Clown is aware that language and experience are so intertwined that to manipulate words is to distort reality:

> *Viola* . . . they that dally nicely with words
>   may quickly make them wanton.
> *Clown* I would, therefore, my sister had had
>   no name, sir.
> *Viola* Why, man?
> *Clown* Why, sir, her name's a word; and to
>   dally with that word might make my sister
>   wanton.

Yet the power of language to shape reality to itself, a power which involves the absorption of reality into speech, highlights paradoxically the distance of language from reality:

> . . . in my conscience, sir, I do not care for you. If
> that be to care for nothing, sir, I would it would
> make you invisible.
>
>   (3, 1)

Language draws real substance into itself and becomes a self-contained, substitute reality confronting a nothing—the vacuum left by the reality it has assimilated. Because it confronts nothing, and nothing cannot be changed, it is impotent to affect it: the Clown's rejection of Viola as nothing cannot in fact make her invisible.

Before the Clown leaves Viola he manages to extract from her two coins, and the connection of money and language is significant. The Clown's response to Viola's first coin is to ask for another:

> *Clown* Would not a pair of these have bred,
>   sir?
> *Viola* Yes, being kept together and put to use.
> *Clown* I would play Lord Pandarus of
>   Phrygia, sir, to bring a Cressida to this
>   Troilus.

The Clown personifies the coins, endowing them with real, generative life, reducing himself simultaneously to a neutral go-between, a mediating element. The relation of money (symbol) to human life (reality) is inverted, as it is in *Richard II*: the coins, like language, 'breed' by their own independent life, becoming the controlling masters of a human reality which exists as a parasite upon them. Human life is objectivised and inanimate life subjectivised in a single movement, as language, inanimate symbol, sucks life from real human existence and reduces it to a corpse, an inanimate nothing. In both cases, money and language control, and yet cannot control, reality: they dominate and determine it as a superior power, yet since their mode of domination is to absorb reality into themselves, they are merely regulating themselves.[2]

The duping of Malvolio is a similar instance of the controlling power of language. Malvolio is driven to false and illusory action which he believes real by a language-created illusion—the letter written by Toby and his friends—which has all the force of reality. Malvolio's laborious tracing out of letters, words and meanings is an image of a man falling under the false power of language, viewing language as a completely adequate motivation to action. His behaviour before Viola is purely linguistic and therefore illusory, with no ground in fact: the letter determines and controls his physical existence, as in the text of the letter itself Viola is presented as saying that 'M.O.A.I. doth sway my life', shown as under the power of inanimate strokes of the pen. As a result of the illusion, Malvolio the servant overreaches his role to become a self-created master, as language itself, the servant of human life, becomes its tyrant. The letter which Belch later presses Aguecheek to write, challenging Antonio to a duel, reveals a similar confusion of language and reality:

Taunt him with the license of ink; if thou thou'st him some thrice, it shall not be amiss; and as many lies as will lie in thy sheet of paper, although the sheet were big enough for the bed of Ware in England, set 'em down; go about it. Let there be gall enough in thy ink, though thou write with a goose-pen, no matter. About it.

(3, 2)

The interchange here of symbol and reality is parallel to the similar interchange in Maria's puns. The physical yet symbolic act of writing becomes itself a substitute for physical activity, so that metaphor constantly blurs into fact: the greater the physical size of the paper the greater the insults will be, the gall is almost literally in the pen despite the physical fact that the pen may be a goose-pen.[3]

The illusory, interchangeable quality of language in the play, its capacity to absorb and regulate the substance of human reality, has a direct parallel in the action of the drama itself: in the illusions, switchings and mistakes involved in the adoption of human roles. Throughout the play, roles adopted as conscious illusions backfire and begin to control reality itself, to a point where the frontier of reality and illusion is dangerously obscured. Olivia and Orsino are both 'actors', self-consciously fostering roles of lover and beloved which are objectively false but seen by the actors themselves as real; the roles, like language, actually regulate their owners' physical behaviour, providing them, as in a play, with strictly delimited 'texts', given functions and attitudes, from which their personal action must never deviate. Each character's role depends on the role of the other, in an act of collaborative illusion: Orsino's identity as a rejected lover feeds off Olivia's identity as the cold beloved, and vice versa, in a reciprocal movement of negative and positive creation. Viola is then drawn within this illusion, through her adoption of an illusion of disguise to further her real aim of serving Orsino; she is made to act the part of one actor (Orsino) to another actor (Olivia) in a way which conflicts with her own genuine identity (her love of Orsino). Viola, like the Clown with his coins, is reduced from real human existence to the status of a neutral mediator between two illusions: in the scene where she presents Orsino's claims to Olivia she operates merely as an embodied verbal message, a metaphor connecting two separate realities. Her role in this scene is to live at a sheerly linguistic level, eliminating her own authentic desires; she is an actor who must confine herself to a given text, with no reality beyond this:

Olivia Whence came you, sir?
Viola I can say little more than I have
    studied, and that question's out of my part.

(1, 5)

When Viola asks to see Olivia's face she is told that she is 'now out of (her) text'; the face which is then shown is equally a defined and static illusion, a 'picture' which can be itemised in mechanical detail, as Viola's set speeches are a similar categorisation of elements.

The consequence of Viola's entering the reciprocal illusion of Orsino and Olivia is the creation in Olivia of a reality—her love for Viola—which breaks beyond the illusion and yet is similarly illusory—she does not know that Viola is a woman. Both Viola and Olivia define themselves and each other in roles which contradict their personal reality, weaving a network of illusion which neither dare break: their conversation is false for each, yet each considers it real for the other. Viola's enforced role as mediator for Orsino is a kind of self-cancellation: she is placed in a 'double-bind' situation where to secure Orsino's love is to further his love for Olivia and therefore destroy his love for herself. Either way she will come to nothing: her original, conscious adoption of the illusion of disguise to win Orsino's love is turned against itself, controlling rather than nourishing her real aims. Viola's own substance of identity is at odds with her role as linguistic mediator in precisely the way that language, in the play, falsifies human reality. Olivia is placed in a similarly impossible position: in rejecting Viola at the level of linguistic mediator she must harm herself by rejecting her also as the 'man' she loves. Since Viola has fully assimilated this personal reality into her assumed role when she confronts Olivia, the language and substance cannot be separated out.

The story of Malvolio brings together similar themes and images into a significant pattern. Malvolio, like Macbeth, overreaches a defined social role at the instigation of inauthentic language and becomes himself inauthentic, illusory: his bid for a higher freedom is a self-enslavement, leading to physical imprisonment in a suffocatingly narrow dungeon which is at once materially cramping and, because pitch dark, a kind of nothingness, an absence of all material experience. By confining himself so strictly to the false role which Sir Toby creates for him, in order finally to overreach and negate it (he obeys 'every point of the letter', as Viola talks precisely within her text), he plunges himself into a prison which is a cynically apt image of his real condition: a space so narrow and enclosed that it is at once positively limiting and, in its darkness, a negation which allows his imagination free and impotent range beyond it. The prison, that is, is simply a grotesque intensification of Malvolio's previous existence, disclosing its deepest reality: his positive and pedantic self-confinement to a narrow social role—brought out in the solid, laborious quality of his language—and the self-negating, overreaching ambition which paradoxically accompanied it, are pressed in prison into caricatures of themselves, and the essential relation of these positive and negative aspects exposed within a single condition. Malvolio falls both below and above the level of true identity: he restricts himself inhumanly to a rigid social role, and simultaneously allows his imagination free and ludicrous range beyond it.

The scene where Sir Toby and the Clown visit Malvolio in his prison brings the confusions of illusion and reality to their highest peak. The Clown disguises himself as a curate, and in doing so exposes four levels of illusion: he is a Clown (and thus, as we shall see later, a kind of illusion) disguised in the illusion of a curate, a role itself often illusory ('I would I were the first that ever dissembled in such a gown'), visiting Malvolio in a prison whose darkness—itself a nothingness—renders the disguise superfluous, doubly unreal. This particular interaction of illusion and reality discloses the nature of the whole situation: Belch and his companions trap Malvolio in a created illusion aimed to reveal the reality of his character (a reality itself defined by illusory ambition), and then treat the illusion as real, bringing rational criteria to bear on it to torment Malvolio into a further sense of unreality. The Clown refuses to treat Malvolio's answers to his questions as 'real', attributing them to a devil inside the illusory facade of Malvolio's personality, treating Malvolio's physical reality as a disguise for a diabolic (and therefore illusory) reality behind it. Because Sir Toby and the Clown have themselves set, and can control, the terms of the illusory game in which Malvolio is trapped, they can turn any of his answers against him as proofs of his madness, offering a question or remark which he grasps as real and then withdrawing it as illusory:

> Clown What is the opinion of Pythagoras
>   concerning wild fowl?
> Malvolio That the soul of our grandam might
>   haply inhabit a bird.
> Clown What think'st thou of his opinion?
> Malvolio I think nobly of the soul, and no
>   way approve his opinion.
> Clown Fare thee well. Remain thou still in
>   darkness: thou shalt hold th' opinion of
>   Pythagoras ere I will allow of thy wits.
>
>   (4, 2)

Malvolio cannot win: whatever answers he advances will be absorbed, neutralised and turned against themselves by the rules of the illusion. It is his word against the Clown's, and because the Clown controls the conventions of the game Malvolio will always lose:

> Malvolio I am not mad, Sir Topas. I say to
>   you this house is dark.
> Clown Madman, thou errest. I say there is no
>   darkness but ignorance; in which thou art
>   more puzzled than the Egyptians in their
>   fog.

> Malvolio I say this house is as dark as
>   ignorance, though ignorance were as dark as
>   hell . . .

Within the framework of an illusion which has carefully excluded real fact, truth is a matter of who can destroy the other linguistically. The Clown frames his questions to create 'double-bind' situations for Malvolio, blocking off certain aspects of reality and loading his language to produce the replies he wants:[4]

> But tell me true, are you not mad indeed, or
>   do you but counterfeit?

The possibility that Malvolio is neither mad nor counterfeiting but sane and ill-treated is carefully excluded from the question; whatever Malvolio replies can then be used to his detriment. When Malvolio attempts to prove his sanity by comparison with the Clown's—'I am as well in my wits, fool, as thou art'—the Clown, by exploiting the ambiguity of 'fool', as both a social title and a character-description, denies his own sanity and therefore Malvolio's: 'Then you are mad indeed, if you be no better in your wits than a fool'.

Illusion, then, both defines a man falsely and negates as false any criterion beyond itself to which appeal can be made: it is a kind of language which, by collapsing and controlling reality within itself, can adjust it endlessly for its own purposes. Illusion and language create a structure whose roles operate to control, not only the experience within the structure, but any possible experience outside it. By setting up the language and the illusion in a particular way, all experience is controllable and any assault on the structure can be deflected, as Malvolio's answers are deflected and distorted. Language, money, illusion, are only parts of reality, but parts which can encompass and regulate the whole.

Just as, in *A Midsummer Night's Dream,* Titania, herself an illusion, is trapped by Oberon into the further illusion of loving Bottom, so in this play Andrew Aguecheek, who helps Belch to ensnare Malvolio, becomes himself the victim of a Belch-created illusion, when he is induced to duel with Viola. Belch's manipulation of the duel is a striking instance of illusion creating reality: by mediating illusory information about each other to Viola and Aguecheek, Belch creates a situation in which each of the duellers thinks himself unwilling and the other willing to fight. The supposed mediator is in fact the creator and controller of the event: by deluding each character about the other, Belch can make something from nothing, fashioning a positive—a fight—from two negatives.[5] By falsely defining each character to the other, Belch induces each to fight under the sway of this false image; by pretending to take his own created illusion as a real drama in which he is a minor participant, he produces a positive quarrel which is also a negation, one without cause or substance. In Viola's case, the illusion of the duel is simply a further illusion into which her original illusion of disguise has led her: it interlocks with the illusion brought about by the confusion of her with her brother Sebastian. In Aguecheek's case, the duel serves to expose the disparity evident throughout the play between his language and action, his real condition and his illusions about it:

> . . . besides that he's a fool, he's a great quarreller; and but that he hath the gift of a coward to allay the gusts he hath in quarrelling, 'tis thought among the prudent he would quickly have the gift of a grave.
>
> (1, 3)

Aguecheek's language and action are mutually cancelling: he is a contradictory embodiment of language and action, and the point of the duel is to bring him to recognition of this reality. Sir Toby persuades him first that language is an adequate substitute for reality:

> . . . so soon as ever thou seest him, draw; and as thou draw'st, swear horrible; for it comes to pass oft that a terrible oath, with a swaggering accent sharply twang'd off, gives manhood more approbation than ever proof itself would have earn'd him.
>
> (3, 4)

By creating this illusion, he can draw Aguecheek into the further falsity of the duel, a real action which reveals his negativity.

The positions of Belch and the Clown in this general confusion of reality and illusion, false role and language, are especially significant. Belch refuses all limit, all definition:

> *Maria* . . . you must confine yourself within the modest limits of order.
> *Sir Toby* Confine! I'll confine myself no finer than I am.
>
> (1, 3)

His rejection of definition is a refusal of external limit, of imposed convention; in a play where false versions of identity are being continually offered, he escapes relatively unscathed, defining others rather than suffering definition. Yet his rejection of restraint is not made in terms of an absolute freedom to become all, to appropriate all roles and experiences; it is made simply in terms of a freedom to be himself, to live within his own limits, confining himself to precisely what he is. His presentation in terms of physical sensuality, of the body, underlines this fact: like Falstaff, his overriding of social order springs from an achieved stasis, a bodily fullness which breaks order not by reaching beyond it

but by ignoring it in favour of a stolid self-containment, by falling below rather than above it.

The Clown is in some senses the opposite of Belch, in some ways a parallel figure: they are positively related as polarities. The Clown, like Puck, is roleless, a negative, disembodied presence within and yet beyond the conventions of human community, all-licensed and thus a limitless nothing, a merely linguistic mode of existence, fast-talking but inactive. He is beyond community-rules because he questions all codes, all definitions, dissolving them into the paradox and contradiction of his free, fluid speech; yet he is also within the community because this negativity is sanctioned by the social role of Clown. Like Puck, his role is to be roleless; his positive and defined function in society is to criticise all function, all positivity. Olivia's rebuke to Malvolio, whom the Clown's wit offends, suggests the degree to which the fooling is sanctioned:

> There is no slander in an allow'd fool, though he do nothing but rail; nor no railing in a known discreet man, though he do nothing but reprove.
>
> (1, 5)

The emphasis here is on 'allow'd' and 'known': once it is recognised that the fool's formal function is to rail—that he draws positive identity from this negativity—he can be tolerated: his social role both lends him defined reality and, by containing his wit, neutralises it to the level of play, of illusion. The Clown is himself aware of this process, as his ambivalent use of the word 'fool' signifies. As we have seen already in his taunting of Malvolio, the Clown creates paradox by using the word in two senses, as professional occupation and character-judgement:

> *Olivia* Take the fool away.
> *Clown* Do you not hear, fellows? Take away the lady . . . The lady bade take away the fool; therefore, I say again, take her away.
>
> (1, 5)

The Clown goes on to justify 'fool' as a judgement on Olivia, thus validating his reversal of her command. He dissolves the defined status of 'fool'—the social meaning—into the reality of human foolishness, thus showing the social status to be illusory—he, the Fool, has wisely revealed foolishness in what seemed reality—and therefore ironically exposing his own (illusory) role as more real than reality itself.

The truth implicit in his word-play is that to be a Clown is to be simultaneously real and illusory, positive and negative. The Clown is a 'corrupter of words' and as such the supreme focus of society's unreality, reflecting it back to them: he is thus both more real than others, disclosing what is ultimately true of them, and less real, since his own foolery is the function of an

Engraving from the Hanmer edition (1744).

arbitrary social role before it is a genuine personal characteristic. He exists in so far as he is 'allow'd', as Fool, by society, given a social function which, because the negation of all function, is self-cancelling and illusory. Yet he is more real than others because *consciously* a fool, adopting this negative role with grim and positive realism:

> Those wits that think they have (wit) do very oft prove fools; and I that am sure I lack thee may pass for a wise man.
>
> 　　　　　　　　　　　　　　　(1, 5)

Viola recognises this truth also:

> This fellow is wise enough to play the fool;
> And to do that well craves a kind of wit . . .
> 　　　　　This is a practice
> As full of labour as a wise man's art;
> For folly that he wisely shows is fit;
> But wise men, folly-fall'n, quite taint their
> 　　wit.
>
> 　　　　　　　　　　　　　　　(3, 1)

The Clown is therefore more real than Orsino and Olivia, who are fools without knowing it; he is a good actor who, like Viola herself, consciously adopts an illusory role and remains undeceived by his own acting. The Fool is thus wiser than the fool: the more of a fool he is, the better Fool he makes and thus the less foolish he becomes, the more he fulfils a particular, settled definition without overreaching it into absurdity. The greater his clowning, and thus his illusion, the more real a man he becomes. The Clown, unlike Macbeth and Malvolio, can combine a complete social definition with complete freedom: total linguistic liberty is the constitutive element of his sanctioned role. He fuses the self-containment of Olivia and Orsino with the self-squandering liberty of Sir Toby Belch, achieving that synthesis which is implicit in the ideal (rather than, in this play, the reality) of the *steward,* who preserves and dispenses in careful balance. The Clown's sanity—his reality—springs from the fact that he fulfils a settled role consistently, and it is the lack of such consistency in the play as a whole which suggests that illusion and insanity are general conditions. Consistent role-playing allows conjunction and communication, a reciprocal confirmation of identity and thus of sanity; inconsistent role-playing creates insanity, unreality, as the general confusion of identities at the end of the play suggests. In this situation, the Clown's ironic self-awareness, his insight into the confusion, is a negative mode of sanity.

In the whole action of the play, then, illusion, role and language connect into a single pattern. The switching and interchange of human roles is a kind of living pun and metaphor, a blurring of the symbols through which reality is expressed in a way which casts radical doubt on the consistency of that reality. Hamlet's advice to the Players, to suit the action to the word and the word to the action, cannot be sustained: language overwhelms and manipulates action, draining reality until it finds itself in danger of collapsing into nothing under the weight of its own excess. If language is in this sense articulate unreality, social role shares the same quality: they, too, define reality falsely, detaching themselves from the real purposes they were fashioned to sustain into a self-contained realm of illusion where they set up relations between themselves in isolation from real experience, thwarting and obscuring it. The final irony, as in *A Midsummer Night's Dream,* is that this whole process occurs within a play which is itself, as the subtitle suggests, a kind of illusion, a momentary sport; when Fabian remarks that he would condemn Malvolio's behaviour as 'an improbable fiction' if he were to see it on stage, the play pauses to reflect on its own illusory nature, becoming for a moment less real than the characters it presents. When Viola confronts Olivia with Orsino's love, the effect, once the illusion of the whole play is held in mind, is one of an overlapping series of unrealities: Viola, an actor playing an actor playing an actor, presents the case of one actor playing an actor to another actor playing an actor. The relations of illusion and reality touch a peak of complexity which is equalled only later, in some of the mature tragedies.

Notes

[1] c.f. Falstaff in *Henry IV Part II:* 'A good wit will make use of anything. I will turn diseases to commodity.' (1, 22).

[2] c.f. the Clown's own connection between language and money when he remarks that words have been disgraced by *bonds.* C.f. also the quarrel between Antonio and Sebastian in Act 3 Scene 4, which is created and controlled by money: the purse which Antonio gave to Sebastian as a symbol of trust and friendship becomes humanly divisive, as (from Antonio's mistaken viewpoint) the 'purse-bearer', the servant, becomes the master, overstepping his role.

[3] This interchange of animate and inanimate occurs in several minor images in the play. Physical objects are themselves symbolic—they have meaning, like signs, only in terms of what they do—but can be endowed with a constant human existence: Belch wishes that his boots should 'hang themselves in their own straps' (1, 3), Malvolio, at the moment he is endowing the symbolic shapes of written language with life, begs leave of the wax of the letter for breaking it.

[4] c.f. also the exchange between Fabian and the Clown, Act 5 Scene 1:

Fabian Now, as thouo lov'st me, let me see his letter.

Clown Good Master Fabian, grant me another request.

Fabian Anything.

Clown Do not desire to see this letter.

Fabian This is to give a dog, and in recompense desire my dog again.

The Clown frames his remark so that Fabian cancels out his own request: Fabian's generosity is turned against itself, by the Clown's verbal dexterity.

⁵ c.f. the Clown, Act 5 Scene 1: 'Marry, sir, (my friends) praise me and make an ass of me. Now my foes tell me plainly I am an ass; so that by my foes, sir, I profit in the knowledge of myself, and by my friends I am abused; so that, conclusions to be as kisses, if your four negatives make your two affirmatives, why then, (I am) the worse for my friends and the better for my foes.' Negative criticism induces by negation positive self-awareness.

Walter N. King (essay date 1968)

SOURCE: "Shakespeare and Parmenides: Metaphysics of *Twelfth Night*," in *Studies in English Literature, 1500-1900,* Vol. VIII, No. 2, Spring, 1968, pp. 283-306.

[*In the following excerpt, King focuses on the character of Feste, comparing his ambiguous comments to those made by the sixth-century Greek philosopher Parmenides regarding "what is" and "what is not."*]

Recurrent themes are by now such a recognized feature of Shakespearian drama that we are perhaps in danger of underrating them. And when one begins to reconsider Shakespeare's use of the most recurrent theme of them all, the contrast between the ideal and the real (between what the mind comprehends discursively or intuitively and what it apprehends by means of the senses), this caveat seems especially apropos. For everyone knows that Shakespeare manipulates this theme in play after play throughout his career, and it all begins to seem tediously old hat. One recollects the casket scene in *The Merchant of Venice,* the mirror scene in *Richard II,* and Falstaff's homily on honor in *1 Henry IV.* One thinks of Hamlet's bitter awareness of the discrepancy between what ought to be and what is (or appears to be), and of Lear's anguished realization that the ethics of quality (what ought to be) must not be confused with any plausible ethics of quantity (what appears to be or may be in a material sense). And one recalls the obvious differences between appearance and reality in the comedies, differences that ultimately take on the resonance of symbols: the mistaken identities in *The Comedy of Errors,* the costume

and sex disguise of Julia in *The Two Gentlemen of Verona,* and the misunderstandings that crop up in *Much Ado About Nothing* because at crucial moments different characters fail to see or hear distinctly.

Now a metaphysical view of things is at least implicit in all these scenes and situations, a metaphysic that is easier to get at, if not easy to define in any definitive way, in the tragedies. Lear, for instance, asks Edgar at a focal point in the play, "What is the cause of thunder?" (III.iv.160)¹—a question that remains unanswered, but implies a metaphysical force, or being, or what you will, that is responsible for both the physical and the moral universe. And Hamlet can return to the traditional Christian view that "there's a divinity that shapes our ends" and that "there's a special providence in the fall of a sparrow" (V.ii.10, 230-231). Even Coriolanus perceives at last that "nature" cannot be denied or made other than it is and that no man is "author of himself" (V.iii.25, 36).

But in which of the comedies are the metaphysical aspects of Shakespeare's near obsession with the antithesis between appearance and reality explored with any acuity? Perhaps in *As You Like It,* where the kaleidoscopic shifts from one possible center of values to another and the modification of values as episode comments upon preceding episode suggest a possible relativistic view of human experience. Or perhaps in *Much Ado,* where in the church scene the difference between what seems to be and what is receives a steady analytical treatment.² But more profoundly in *Twelfth Night* with its riddling sub-title, *What You Will,* and its holiday atmosphere that prompts commonsensical discrimination between the worlds of moral order and misrule, between the excess traditionally permissible to the Christmas season and the relaxed return to decorum with the arrival of Epiphany. In no other comedy of Shakespeare is delusion, self-induced or attributable to blameless misapprehension, so central, and in no other comedy is attention so consistently directed toward the ambiguities that play between "what is" and "what is not."

Yet even if this be so, what character in *Twelfth Night* is reflective enough to grapple with the contradictions inherent in the relationship of "seeming" to "being?" Viola will not do. Though intelligent enough to be attracted to the professional raillery of Feste, she is too much a part of the illusion that characterizes Illyria and too dependent upon the "whirligig of time" and its revenges to probe very far beneath the surface. There is only Feste, the one figure in all the comedies with a true gift for Socratic irony, and Socratic enough to know that he knows nothing: "Those wits that think they have thee [i.e., wit] do very oft prove fools; and I that am sure I lack thee may pass for a wise man" (I.v.36-38). And it is Feste who reappears as the Fool in *Lear* and sings another stanza to the nostalgic song, that elusive blend of sense and nonsense, with which *Twelfth Night* dissolves into conclusion.

But is there really a Shakespearian metaphysic for comedy, and can Feste actually be its spokesman? And doesn't the mere suggestion that there might be one trigger the warning that whatever Shakespeare's comedies are about, they are not dramatizations of philosophical systems? Are they not, as representative critics insist, just exuberant expressions of the here and now,[3] of the saturnalian claims of life,[4] of love and its fulfillment?[5] Shakespeare is, of course, extolling all these things; hence the difficulty of interpreting the comedies by means of any one critical standard. But it may be that by seeking some broad conceptual base we can discover a critical stance that permits us to do justice to at least the major comedies as a group—to their joyous acceptance of life and love, their social satire, their low comedy characters who are always more than mere clowns, their poignant songs that are always more than mere embellishments to the action, and their breathless cascades of wit that are surely something more than mere witticisms. What fashions these disparate elements into obvious comic wholes if it is not some philosophic vision pervasive through them all, something which Shakespeare was gradually coming to understand during the 1590's? And if there is such a vision—skeptics will assert at once that there is not—might it not be discoverable in *Twelfth Night,* the one comedy in which everyone agrees that Shakespeare recombines into a subtler, almost perfect whole everything (plot devices, character types, themes) to be found in more diluted combinations in the earlier comedies?

By its very nature the search I am undertaking in this essay will lead far into the critical area called by John Russell Brown that of the "implicit judgment."[6] For what I am suggesting is that through Feste Shakespeare is concerning himself in a teasing, yet finally serious way with the ontological postulates affirmed by Parmenides in his insistence upon the irreconcilable difference between "what is" and "what is not," and is implying a somewhat whimsical, but nevertheless penetrating criticism of it. Whether Shakespeare had any knowledge of the fragments of Parmenides's poem, *Nature,* I shall defer till the end of this essay, meanwhile citing and commenting upon the curious parallels between several of Feste's most cryptic statements and their counterparts in Parmenides.

I approach this possibility primarily in the spirit of play, on the assumption that without damaging the judgment we can, like equilibrists, balance these parallels against each other for a while and speculate about whether by means of them a rounded interpretation of *Twelfth Night* might not be possible. And if by this means light can be shed upon odd corners of the play usually bypassed by critics, it may then be profitable

to turn to the historical issue—could Shakespeare have known anything about Parmenides, and if so, what?—and debate it tranquilly. And then could we not conclude, if only tentatively, that there is a metaphysical basis for Shakespearian comedy—even if Shakespeare had no knowledge of Parmenides whatsoever?

II

Of all Feste's ambiguous comments, three seem to me to be tinged with something I tend to call Parmenidean:

1. The most elusive (usually dismissed as nonsense by editors if they annotate it at all) occurs immediately prior to Feste's masquerade as Sir Topas, the curate: "for, as the old hermit of Prague, that never saw pen and ink, very wittily said to a niece of King Gorboduc, 'That that is is'; so I, being Master Parson, am Master Parson; for what is 'that' but that, and 'is' but is?"

(IV.ii.14-19)

2. Almost as puzzling is the second, which occurs when Feste confuses Sebastian for Cesario and exclaims: "No, I do not know you; nor I am not sent to you by my lady, to bid you come speak with her; nor your name is not Master Cesario; nor this is not my nose neither. Nothing that is so is so"

(IV.i.5-9)

3. The third occurs somewhat earlier, when to Viola's joshing comment that he is "a merry fellow and car'st for nothing," Feste replies: "Not so, sir; I do care for something; but in my conscience, sir I do not care for you. If that be to care for nothing, sir, I would it would make you invisible" (III.i.30-35). And a few lines later Feste declares: "I am indeed not her [Olivia's] fool, but her corrupter of words"

(III.i.40-41)

When we place these passages, especially the first two, against one of the key passages from the first part of the body of Parmenides's poem, often called the *Way of Truth,* we find an odd correspondence:

Come now and I will tell thee—listen and lay my word to heart—the only ways of inquiry that are to be thought of: one, that [*That which is*] *is, and it is impossible for it not to be,* is the Way of Persuasion, for Persuasion attends on Truth.

Another, that *It is not, and must needs not be*—this I tell thee is a path that is utterly undiscernible: for thou couldst not know that which is not—for that is impossible—nor utter it.

For it is the same thing that can be thought and that can be.

What can be spoken of and thought must be: for it is possible for it to be, but it is not possible for "nothing" to be. These things I bid thee ponder; for this is the first Way of inquiry from which I hold thee back.[7]

The verbal parallels should be obvious between Feste's "that that is is" and Parmenides's "[*That which is*] *is*" in the first verse-paragraph; though perhaps I should state flatly that Feste's second comment, "Nothing that is so is so" I see as parallel to Parmenides's assertions in the second and fourth verse-paragraphs that not-being, or nothing, cannot be known. These assertions are also relevant to Feste's insistence in the third comment that he does care for "something"—"something" (left undefined) being balanced against "nothing" and "invisible."

But it is one thing to point out corresponding passages and another to interpret them; and since Parmenides's poem is not always immediately comprehensible to lay readers, it may not be amiss to quote at some length from F. M. Cornford's interpretation:

This first way of untruth directly contradicts the Way of Truth. The starting-point of the true Way is: *That which is is, and cannot not-be.* The starting-point of this false way is: *That which is, is not, and must not-be,* or *It is possible for 'nothing' to be.* Here is a flat contradiction; one or other of the starting-points must be completely dismissed before we can advance a step in any direction. The goddess accordingly condemns the false Way as 'utterly undiscernible': a Way starting from nonentity lies in total darkness and cannot be followed to any conclusions whatsoever. . . .

No advance can be made from the premise that all that exists was once in a state of non-existence, or that nonentity can exist. . . . Thought cannot pursue such a Way at all; there is no being for thought to think of or for language to describe significantly. This impassable Way may be called, for distinction, the Way of Notbeing. It is dismissed, once for all, in the above fragments.[8]

In short, Parmenides is drawing an absolute distinction between an intelligible world ("*that which is, is*") comprehensible to the mind and therefore called the Way of Truth, and its opposite ("*that which is, is not*"), totally incomprehensible to the mind and therefore logically absurd.

"But," Parmenides continues,

secondly (I hold thee back) from the Way whereon mortals who know nothing wander, two-headed; for perplexity guides the wandering thought in their breasts, and they are borne along, both deaf and blind, bemused, as undiscerning hordes, who have

determined to believe that *it is and it is not, the same and not the same,* and for whom there is a way of all things that turns back upon itself.

For never shall this be proved; that things that are not are; but do thou hold back thy thought from this Way of inquiry, nor let custom that comes of much experience force thee to cast along this Way an aimless eye and a droning ear and tongue, but judge by reasoning the much-debated proof I utter.[9]

Cornford's explanation:

I have called this second way of untruth the 'Way of Seeming' . . . because 'opinions' or 'beliefs' is too narrow a rendering. 'What seems to mortals' . . . includes (a) what *seems real* or appears to the senses; (b) what *seems true,* what all men, misled by the senses, believe and the dogmas taught by philosophers and poets on the same basis; and (c) what has *seemed right* to men, . . . the decision they have 'laid down' to recognize appearances and the beliefs founded on them in the conventional institution of language. . . .

Parmenides means that all men—common men and philosophers alike—are agreed to believe in the reality of the world our senses seem to show us. The premise they start from is neither the recognition of the One Being only (from which follows the Way of Truth and nothing more) nor the recognition of an original state of sheer nothingness (which would lead to the impassable Way of Not-being). What mortals do in fact accept as real and ultimate is a world of diversity, in which things 'both are and are not,' passing from non-existence to existence and back again in becoming and perishing, and from being *this* ('the same') to being *something else* ('not the same') in change.[10]

Whatever these passages from Parmenides and Cornford may lead to, it should at least be clear that Feste's ambiguous statements, cited earlier, ought not to be brushed aside as mere nonsense. Here we have, tucked into contexts tricked out as the usual pattern of the professional stage fool, statements that apparently do more than echo Parmenides (as we shall see shortly). And they are just the sort of metaphysical statements suitable to a play whose plot depends upon the confusions generated by self-deception, physical and psychological disguise, and mistaken identity—confusions that gradually become worse confounded until the shrewder characters begin to make sharp distinctions between "what is" and "what appears to be." But the critical problem itself is initially one of tone. Is Shakespeare mocking philosophical hair-splitting, or is he getting down to substantial metaphysical assumptions by adopting an oblique approach calculated not to disrupt the genial comic mood that pervades every scene? Or to put the question another way, is Feste in the most literal sense only a "corrupter of words," a clever professional entertainer acquainted only by hearsay with the philosophical slogans and catchwords of the age?

Persuasive answers to these questions depend upon the meanings implicit in Feste's statements and the degree to which they illuminate major themes. First: "'That that is is'; so I, being Master Parson, am Master Parson; for what is 'that' but that, and 'is' but is?" On the simplest level Feste is suggesting here the difference between what is indubitably real and what only appears to be so. Though dressed as Sir Topas, he is not really Sir Topas, either to Maria, Sir Toby, or himself, since all three know his real identity. Nevertheless he is "really" Sir Topas to Malvolio as long as he can play the role imaginatively enough for Malvolio to accept him as such. And this Malvolio does, partly because he cannot *see* Feste, partly because he is too confused, owing to the imputation of madness, to penetrate Feste's vocal disguise, and partly because, owing to delusions about himself (his own reality), he is incapable of recognizing reality of any sort. But the problem is more complex than this. There is the provocative possibility, as Feste hints, that so long as one plays a role to perfection, one *is* the role one plays: the mask one assumes can become oneself. But in this case "that" (one's former self) is no longer "that," but has become "this" (one's present self), so that "is" may not necessarily always be "is." Contrary to Parmenides's conviction, "the same" may not be easily distinguishable even on purely logical grounds from "not the same." And so appearance seems to possess some measure of reality.

But as Feste knows very well, he is not Master Parson. He is himself, a concrete entity that unquestionably *is* and about whom he can think clearly so long as he avoids self-delusion and is on guard against possible false appraisals of what is real. Such mistakes are common enough unless one evaluates sensory data according to rigorous logical standards. For though the effort to determine what "that that is" actually "is" may lead to bewilderment, nevertheless "that that is is." In sum, Shakespeare through Feste is suggesting obliquely both the strength of Parmenides's metaphysics, the need for absolute definition of the real; and its weakness, Parmenides's failure to credit the world of sensible objects with any reality whatsoever.

In addition, Feste is implicitly exposing the ambiguity of basing a metaphysic upon the meaning of the verb "to be." Unhappily, "to be" has three general meanings that breed confusion of thought by their tendency to elide into each other. (1) Identification—i.e., Feste can be named and thus is knowable in Parmenides's terms. (2) The existential—i.e., Feste "is," or has being, and so is again available to cognition. And (3) the copulative—i.e., Feste is equivalent to himself, yet paradoxically can assert, "so I, being Master Parson, am Master Parson." But as the ensuing scene with

Malvolio demonstrates, all three definitions point to involvement in the world of sensible, as well as of intelligible data, so that appearance cannot always be readily differentiated from reality (as Plato revealed to the disadvantage of Parmenides's system).[11]

The ambiguity implicit in "to be" is even more glaring in Feste's mistaken identification of Sebastian for Cesario: "No, I do not know you; nor I am not sent to you by my lady, to bid you come speak with her; nor your name is not Master Cesario; nor this is not my nose neither. Nothing that is so is so." Here Feste's position is reversed from what it is in the preceding instance. Not in control of all the facts, he is obliged like Malvolio to rely upon sensory impressions for the determination of what is real. Yet he has two advantages over Malvolio. He need not doubt his own sanity, nor is he suffering from self-delusion. It is noticeable that he depends, if only negatively, upon the meaning of "to be" as identification ("nor your name is not Master Cesario") and as the existential ("nor this is not my nose neither"). Sight is misleading him, but touch and his full awareness of his own body are not. He can therefore conclude, both logically and illogically (as well as ironically), that "nothing that is so is so." He can argue correctly by analogy that if his nose is still his nose, Cesario must still be Cesario (and can thus be named), not somebody else—and yet incorrectly, since Sebastian is not Cesario.

Furthermore, Feste's "nothing that is so is so" is curiously reminiscent of Parmenides's (1) *"It is not, and must needs not be"* (explicated by Cornford as *"That which is, is not, and must not-be"*), and (2) Parmenides's *"it is and it is not, the same and not the same."* Feste, then, in his confusion, yet in his certainty that he is right, is unwittingly undermining, we might say, the very keystone of Parmenides's metaphysic. By relying upon sensory evidence and past experience, the only raw materials for cognition he now possesses, Feste is pursuing the Way of Seeming; and to the degree that this Way supports his sound conclusion that his nose is his nose, the weakness of Parmenides's proposition that the Way of Seeming is a totally false way is strongly implied. But to the degree that sensory evidence and past experience lead Feste, however naturally, to a false conclusion, Parmenides's dogmatic dismissal of the Way of Seeming and his equally dogmatic insistence upon the Way of Truth as the only true way are affirmed.[12] "That that is is." Sebastian is plainly something, not nothing; yet just as plainly neither sensory evidence alone nor sound logic will ever lead to defining or naming correctly what and who he is. The unreliability of sensory data is further emphasized in the immediate and similar misapprehension of Sebastian's identity by Sir Toby, Sir Andrew, and Fabian, so that Sebastian begins to question the sanity of everyone in Illyria: "Are all the people mad?" (V.i.29)—a copulative use of "to be."

On the other hand, the conclusion is implied that nothing can come from nothing, a solidly Parmenidean doctrine. Thus it can be assumed that when Feste informs Viola he does "care for something," in reply to her good-natured assertion that he is a "merry fellow and car'st for nothing," he means what he says. What that something is can be conjectured after the remainder of his reply has been interpreted: "but in my conscience, sir, I do not care for you. If that be to care for nothing, sir, I would it would make you invisible." Kittredge's gloss seems only a good try: "to care for something is the same as not to care for nothing; then perhaps the fact that I do not care for you makes you equivalent to *nothing;* and, in that case, I wish you might be actually nothing, and so—invisible."[13] In the light of Parmenides's views upon nothing, a considerably more acute interpretation is possible.

To quote again from Cornford's analysis of the second passage from Parmenides: "No advance can be made from the premise that all that exists was once in a state of non-existence, or that nonentity can exist. . . . Thought cannot pursue such a Way at all; there is no being for thought to think of or for language to describe significantly."[14] Feste's rejoinder to Viola (phrased conditionally, be it noted) seems, then, to imply the Parmenidean doctrine of the non-existence of nothing and the consequent existence of something. To care for nothing would be tantamount to believing that nothing "is," and this would be a palpable absurdity. In such a case, Viola would indeed be invisible, just as is nothing. It would be impossible to think or say anything about Viola that would make logical sense. Feste would then be, what he knows he is not, a "corrupter of words."

But to care for something is to possess values, to be engaged in ethical measurements—to care for what is true. And this means to care for what is real, since, though in an ontological sense reality can be limited only to "what is," in an ethical sense it can be extended to cover "what ought to be" or "what is best," as Plato very well understood. When Feste insists that he does care for something, he means in all likelihood that he cares for reality in both these senses. What that something is, is the sum total of "what is" and "what ought to be" disclosed in the comic vision of life that is the play, and this vision is implied in Feste's ironic criticism of the false values of the various deluded characters.[15] But this is to move from metaphysics to ethics, which Parmenides was scrupulous not to do, but which Shakespeare as a comic dramatist could not have avoided doing, had he been minded to.[16]

III

Earlier I posed questions to which specific answers may now be offered. Let me repeat the questions here. "Is Shakespeare mocking philosophical hair-splitting, or is he getting down to substantial metaphysical assumptions by adopting an oblique approach calculated not to disrupt the genial comic mood that pervades every scene? Or to put the question another way, is Feste in the most literal sense only a 'corrupter of words,' a clever professional entertainer acquainted only by hearsay with the philosophical slogans and catchwords of the age?"

That Feste is not corrupting words, contrary to his own assertion, is evident throughout. Indeed, he implies broadly that the inhabitants of Illyria are the real corrupters of words. Early in the play he warns his auditors (and so us): "I wear not motley in my brain" (I.v.63); and midway in the play he points out the danger of mistaking words for things. (1) "A sentence is but a chev'ril glove to a good wit. How quickly the wrong side may be turn'd outward!" (III.i.13-15) (2) "But indeed words are very rascals since bonds disgrac'd them" (III.i.24-25). And (3) "Words are grown so false that I am loath to prove reason with them" (III.i.29-30). Are we not, then, committed to the working assumption that Feste's words are rich with implications, especially when he speaks most cryptically? For to be cryptic is not necessarily to be verbally corrupt.

It seems equally implausible to believe, after absorbing the range of implications in Feste's three "Parmenidean" statements, that Shakespeare's intention was to mock philosophical hair-splitting. Leaving aside the fact that this kind of mockery supplies only a limited comic mileage, one can remind oneself that all great comedy has for its *raison dêtre* the exposure of the difference between "what is" and "what appears to be," both being balanced, however gingerly, against "what ought to be." That this touchy contrast and balance are fundamental to all Shakespearian comedy no one would deny. Is it, then, unreasonable to assume that in the substratum of his maturest comedy, the one immediately preceding the great tragedies, Shakespeare was speculating upon the nature of reality and dramatizing how difficult it is to be certain of any type of reality? Furthermore, the parallels with Parmenides are too pronounced (still leaving aside the historical problem) to be ignored. One is at least driven to wonder where Shakespeare came upon the most telling phrase of Eleatic philosophy, "that that is is," and why he placed it in Feste's dialogue just at the point in the play where appearance and reality are being thoroughly confused by all the characters, and even by Feste. One cannot assume that Shakespeare, by this time an accomplished dramatist, would have thrust in this puzzling statement only for obscurantist reasons or only because it was part of the verbal rag-tag of the 1590's, as of course it may have been. Lastly, the metaphysical issues I have been sketching in permeate the entire play.

It has never been commented upon, to my knowledge, that *Twelfth Night* is very liberally sprinkled with questions. Numbering slightly over 300, their greatest incidence is in those scenes in which misunderstandings grounded in self-delusion or mistaken identity are most prevalent.[17] A fair number of questions simply promote plot movement or comic gags, but an impressively high total have to do with identification and motive—with what is materially and non-materially real. In fact, the characteristic questions turn upon the verbs "to be" and "to will" (i.e., to want, desire, or intend), as in Olivia's pointed questioning of Viola: "What are you? What would you?" (I.v.228-229).

Shakespeare's iteration of this kind of questioning reaches into every cranny of the play and every question devolves upon the proposition, "that that is is," or upon modifications of it. Hence, though cataloguing is a weariness to the critical soul, I shall give typical examples in this and the following paragraph, which readers are at liberty to skip or skim. In I.ii, Viola asks about Orsino and Olivia: "What is his name?" (26) and "What's she?" (35). In I.iii, Sir Toby asks about the detractors of Sir Andrew: "Who are they?" (37). In I.v, Olivia asks about Cesario, before Viola's entrance: "What kind o' man is he?" (159); "What manner of man?" (161); "Of what personage and years is he?" (164); and to Viola: "Are you a comedian?" (194); and "What is your parentage?" (296)—all of them questions dealing with identification. In this same scene Viola begs Olivia to remove her veil, a typical Shakespearian symbol of appearance masking reality. In II.iii, Malvolio asks Feste, Sir Andrew, and Sir Toby: "My masters, are you mad? or what are you? Have you not wit, manners, nor honesty, but to gabble like tinkers at this time of night? . . . Is there no respect of place, persons, nor time in you?" (93-99). To which Sir Toby replies: "Art any more than a steward? Dost thou think, because thou art virtuous, there shall be no more cakes and ale?" (122-125), and later with respect to Malvolio he asks Maria: "What, for being a Puritan?" (155). And in II.v, Malvolio's soliloquy upon the identity of the intended recipient of the forged letter, supposedly written by Olivia, is entirely consonant with the implied self-questioning: "Am I he?"

In III.i, Viola asks Feste: "Art thou a churchman?" (4); "Art not thou the Lady Olivia's fool?" (36); and Olivia bluntly asks Viola: "What is your name?" (107). And when Olivia hints: "I would you were as I would have you be!" Viola asks in return: "Would it be better, madam, than I am?" (154-155). In III.iv, Olivia asks Malvolio a series of questions about his ludicrous behavior, among them: "Why, how dost thou, man? What is the matter with thee?" (26-27); "Why dost thou smile so, and kiss thy hand so oft?" (35-36); to which Maria adds: "Why appear you with this ridiculous boldness before my lady?" (40-41). Somewhat later Viola inquires about Sir Andrew: "What is he?"

(256) and "What manner of man is he?" (288-289). Later yet Antonio is asked by Sir Toby: "Why, what are you?" (346). In IV.i, Sebastian wonders: "Are all the people mad?" (29) and shortly demands of Sir Toby: "What wouldst thou now?" (44). In IV.ii, all the questions Feste asks Malvolio concern the "is" and "is not" of his madness and culminate in: "But tell me true, are you not mad indeed? or do you but counterfeit?" (121-123). And in Act V the crucial questions follow the same pattern until mistakes have been rectified, true identities and motives have been confessed, and the need for such questions has disappeared.

The relevance of these questions to Feste's "that that is is" and "nothing that is so is so" hardly requires comment. Throughout the play one character after another attempts to ascertain the reality of other characters: their identity, their intentions, their being-ness—so that disguise and mistaken identity are not mechanical plot devices, as in the early comedies, but are symbolic figurations of the metaphysical problems of "seeming" and "being." The difference between inner and outer, already symbolized in the caskets in *The Merchant of Venice,* is developed in *Twelfth Night* to apply fully to the "knot intrinsicate" of human personality and the difficulty of defining or describing it accurately, all of which is revealed in the various forms of self-deception of Orsino, Olivia, Malvolio, and Sir Andrew, and of the bafflement consequent upon the mask of appearance worn by many of the characters.[18]

Viola's estimate of the Captain's character is an apt summary of the metaphysical and ethical situation: "And though that nature with a beauteous wall / Doth oft close in pollution, yet of thee / I will believe thou hast a mind that suits / With this thy fair and outward character" (I.ii.48-51). Indeed, the image of the beauteous wall incorporates both Parmenides's Way of Truth and Way of Seeming and makes concrete the ease with which "what appears" may be mistaken for "what is." Orsino and Olivia, handsome without, are sentimental within. Equally absurd discrepancies between "seeming" and "being" are burlesqued in the degraded gentility of Sir Andrew and the social climbing of Malvolio. And in time the image of the wall is applied to Viola herself, when upbraided by Antonio in words that echo her own judgment of the Captain (III.iv.400-404).[19]

This image works its way through the play submerged in turns of phrase, often paradoxical, that bear down hard upon Feste's "that that is is." In I.v, Viola tells Olivia: "I am not that I play" (196-197); and "I see you what you are" (269). In II.ii, Viola's "as I am man" and "as I am woman" (37 and 39) further the ambiguity, along with Orsino's egotistical observation in II.iv: "For such as I am all true lovers are" (17). In II.v, Malvolio is ironically bidden in the forged letter "to insure thyself to what thou are like to be, cast thy humble slough and appear fresh" (160-162); and in

III.i, Feste remarks to Viola: "Who you are and what you would are out of my welkin" (63-64). In the same scene Viola informs Olivia: "That you do think you are not what you are" (151) and "I am not what I am" (153). In III.iv, Sir Andrew addresses Viola in his inane letter of challenge: "Youth, whatsoever thou art, thou art but a scurvy fellow" (161-162); and in V.i, Olivia begs Viola, mistaking her for Sebastian: "Be that thou know'st thou art, and then thou art / As great as that thou fear'st" (152-153).[20]

This long sequence of interrogative, declarative, and imperative statements hinging on "to be" and "to will" heads up in Orsino's amazed reaction to the sight of Viola and Sebastian in Act V: "One face, one voice, one habit, and two persons! / A natural perspective, that is and is not!" (223-224). Here the Way of Truth ("that that is is") and the Way of Seeming or Not-Being merge in as subtle a criticism of Parmenides's metaphysics as Plato's more elaborate study of it in the *Parmenides* and the *Sophist*. "[That which is] is, and it is impossible for it not to be" appears less contradictory to "It is not, and must needs not be" (and to Parmenides's contempt for the "undiscerning hordes, who have determined to believe that *it is and it is not, the same and not the same*") than Parmenides had supposed. Whether Orsino's ironic echoing of Parmenides be deliberate or not, it is surely significant in any summing up of Shakespeare's own thinking. For it now appears that "what is" and "what is not" are not by necessity mutually exclusive, however illogical this conclusion seemed to Parmenides.[21]

But seemingly illogical conclusions need not be frightening so long as one faces squarely the possibility of deception and of lack of pertinent information, as Sebastian does in his soliloquy in III.iv. Here for the first time a character employs human reason as an instrument for probing beneath appearances. By carefully testing the reality of his situation through controlled analysis of the information provided by his senses of sight and touch, he concludes that his dreamlike relationship with Olivia is not delusion. "For though my soul disputes well with my sense / That this may be some error, but no madness," he is still "ready to distrust mine eyes / And wrangle with my reason" on the supposition that either he or Olivia might be mad (III.iv.9-16). Percept is mingling here with concept, which is to say that either without the other has pronounced limitations.

Thus Shakespeare's conclusion appears to be that to reach trustworthy conclusions about "seeming" and "being," neither logic alone (Parmenides's Way of Truth) nor thoughtless faith in the senses (Parmenides's Way of Seeming) are entirely reliable. They can be either singly or mutually misleading. In a play as steeped in deception and self-deception as *Twelfth Night* such a conclusion is, of course, rich in implications,

especially when extended into value judgments. For just as "seeming" and "being" need to be distinguished between in matters of identification and of existential and copulative relationships, so too must they be distinguished between when one is evaluating love and the legitimate and illegitimate claims of pleasure and of moral principle (the overt themes of the play).

But this is not to say that reliance upon logical thought and sensory perception should not be employed to the full, nor that, to weigh the scales again in Parmenides's favor, "that that is, is not." Viola turns out to be Viola, not Cesario: "that that is is." And so we can conclude with Feste, in the final song that touches upon every theme of the play, that "what you will" and "what is" mutually limit each other, owing to the nature of things and to human fallibility, though "what you will" and "what is" are both capable of a fair degree of descriptive definition.

IV

But did Shakespeare have any knowledge of Parmenides (a problem inevitably linked with his possible knowledge of Platonism)? And if not, or if we cannot be sure, does this fact militate against the metaphysical interpretation of *Twelfth Night* offered in this essay?

That Shakespeare had any direct acquaintance with Parmenides seems improbable. But that in the sixteenth century it would have been impossible to learn anything about Parmenides is simply not so. One must bear in mind that the fragments of Parmenides's poem survived for the most part in two sources; (1) the poem is quoted in full by Sextus Empiricus in his *Against the Logicians* and to this quotation he added a commentary; and (2) the major fragments from the body of the poem were preserved by Simplicius in his commentary on the *Physics* and the *de Caelo* of Aristotle.[22] That both Sextus and Simplicius were available to those who cared is certain (Sextus, in particular, in the Latin translation of Henri Estienne, Paris, 1562), though it is not easy or always possible to plot out with any certainty the spread of pre-Socratic philosophy during the Renaissance. We do know, for instance, that soon after his return from Italy, Thomas Linacre translated the commentary of Simplicius on the *Physics,* but did not publish it;[23] and we do know that some of the fragments of Parmenides were published in his *Poesis Philosophica* by Henri Estienne (Geneva, 1573) along with some doxography from Plato, Theophrastus, Plutarch, Clement, and Proclus.[24] But no one could have learned much from this collection, nor is there much likelihood that Shakespeare ever saw it. It is also true that prior to 1573 J. C. Scaliger had gathered together the verse of Parmenides and Empedocles, but his manuscript was not published.[25] In point of fact, no complete or even semi-complete edition of the fragments appeared until late in the eighteenth century.[26]

A possible Shakespearian source for information about Parmenides might have been Giordano Bruno, whose English sojourn extended from 1582 to 1585, and whose London circle included John Florio, Sir Philip Sidney (who alludes to Parmenides, as well as to Thales, Empedocles, Pythagoras, and Phocylides in the fourth paragraph of "The Defense of Poesy"), and Sir Fulke Greville. Two of Bruno's Italian works are dedicated to Sidney, and Greville appears as host in Bruno's *Ash Wednesday Supper.* Bruno apparently also knew Sir Thomas Sackville, Lord Buckhurst, later first Earl of Dorset, and perhaps Gabriel Harvey, who certainly knew about Bruno. It has even been suggested by Benedetto Croce that Berowne in *Love's Labor's Lost* is a portrait of Bruno himself. [27] That Bruno greatly admired the pre-Socratic philosophers there can be no doubt. Writes Dorothea Waley Singer: "Among many passages we may recall from the *De Immenso* Bruno's magnificent lines proclaiming that the potentiality of all parts is in the whole and in each ('All things are in all'). This is the real basis of his view of the Identity of Opposites, and he fortifies himself with the support of such names as Anaxagoras, Anaximenes and 'the divine Parmenides,' as well as of Plato's *Timaeus* and the neoplatonists." [28] But be this as it may, such allusions to the works of Bruno in Shakespeare's plays as have been alleged are far from convincing, nor can one accept without considerable skepticism the parallels, suggested by Frances A. Yates, between Italians living in London in the 1590's and some of the characters in *Love's Labor's Lost.* [29] On the whole, it seems fairly improbable that Shakespeare could have learned much about Parmenides via Bruno.

Of all the possible sources the most plausible appears to be the brief account of Parmenides in Diogenes Laertius's *Lives of Eminent Philosophers,* Latin translations of which were well-thumbed during the Renaissance. Here Shakespeare could have learned that Parmenides

> divided his philosophy into two parts dealing the one with truth, the other with opinion. Hence he somewhere says: Thou must needs learn all things, as well the unshakeable heart of well-rounded truth as the opinions of mortals in which there is no sure trust. . . . He made reason the standard and pronounced sensations to be inexact. At all events his words are: And let not long-practiced wont force thee to treat this path, to be governed by an aimless eye, and echoing ear and a tongue, but do thou with understanding bring the much-contested issue to decision. [30]

Here we have a good thumb-nail sketch of the conventional Renaissance view of Parmenides's metaphysics and his method, but even if Shakespeare had read it and had noted any of the other unelightening references to Parmenides scattered through the *Lives,* he would not have found Feste's "that that is is."

Were it certain that Shakespeare's acquaintance with Plato came directly from the dialogues, it might be conjectured that his source for Feste's phrase was either the *Parmenides* or the *Sophist,* in the Latin translation of Ficino, widely read in the Renaissance, wherein Parmenides's postulates are rigorously examined; or in the *Theaetetus,* the *Symposium,* or the *Euthydemus,* wherein Parmenides is either alluded to by name or certain of his doctrines, such as the nonexistence of nothing, are briefly mentioned. But no investigator of Shakespeare's learning has ever claimed that his knowledge of Plato was either scholarly or extensive. On the other hand, so authoritative a student of Greek philosophy as John Burnet has argued that in Lorenzo's rhapsodic lines upon the music of the spheres in *The Merchant of Venice* (V.i.59-65) "Shakespeare has given us the finest interpretation in any language of one of the central doctrines of Greek philosophy"—that the soul, imprisoned in the body, cannot hear the harmonies produced by the motion of celestial bodies—as stated in the *Timaeus.* [31] Burnet contends that Shakespeare's classical attainments were more considerable than are supposed and that he "was able to disentangle the essential meaning of the Pythagorean doctrines preserved in that dialogue [the *Timaeus*], though these were only known to him through a very distorted tradition." [32] This tradition Burnet traces with great care in order to support his belief that by the fifteenth century the principal ideas of the *Timaeus* were everybody's property, and that Shakespeare's knowledge of Plato came to him through a long line of sources whose fountainhead was the early medieval School of Chartres. [33] "It is certain, at any rate, that there was a vast mass of floating traditional lore, of Pythagorean and Platonic origin, in the England of Shakespeare's youth, and that he was just the man to be influenced by it." [34]

My own impression is that the best, and probably the only, case to be made for Shakespeare's possible knowledge of Parmenides is the kind Burnet makes for his knowledge of Plato and Pythagoras. (One should not forget that Feste "tests Malvolio's madness by quizzing him about Pythagoras's theory of metempsychosis"—IV.ii.55-65) When such scrupulous scholars as J. S. Smart, J. A. K. Thomson and T. W. Baldwin hesitate to claim much for Shakespeare's Latinity and classical learning, [35] it would be pointless to argue that Shakespeare possessed scholarly knowledge of Parmenides, especially when such knowledge was not widespread in his own age. All one can do is measure the degree of his knowledge against a representative text, as Burnet did with respect to the *Timaeus.* If such measurement leads to a more intensive reading of *Twelfth Night,* or to considerable portions of it, then one can suspect rather strongly that somewhere behind the play stands, *mirabile dictu,* the figure of Parmenides.

Certainly the postulate (and conclusion too, since Parmenides's thought is finally circular), "that that is is," is not original with Shakespeare. Just as certainly, so far as can now be known, it was original with Parmenides. And just as certainly the phrase is not meaningless jargon. Therefore it has meaning when Feste speaks it. Where Shakespeare found it I frankly do not know, nor do I know how we can find out for certain now. On the other hand, dangerous though it may be, we should not be afraid to assume that Shakespeare, like many other Renaissance writers with well stocked minds, had a broader knowledge about many things than scrupulous scholarly researchers can pin down precisely. The possibility is strong that "that that is is" had for some time been current as part of the stock phraseology of the age and was used commonly in certain contexts by the formally educated Elizabethan. I can imagine, then, that Shakespeare might have picked it up by ear and perhaps might never have associated it with any philosopher known to him. But that he would not have wondered what the phrase means, would not have worried it over in his own mind, would not have been attracted to it because of its succinctness and its cryptic quality I cannot imagine. Whatever kind of mind Shakespeare had, we can be certain that it was an inquisitive one, one given to intense speculative habits.[36] Consequently I cannot believe that he put this curious phrase into Feste's mouth fortuitously just when deception of every sort is most rampant in the play and when plot complications are maximal. By the time Shakespeare was writing *Twelfth Night* he was not composing plays by reliance only upon inspiration, and this play is one of Shakespeare's most intricately planned achievements. "That that is is" fits too snugly into the total pattern of the play to be only a lucky hit.

Indeed, once its full meaning is understood and applied back to puzzling passages in the play, everything in it begins to respond resonantly—so that one becomes convinced that the play has a metaphysical substratum. This resonance does not destroy, but rather harmonizes with and enhances the play's Twelfth Night gaiety and its curiously reserved, almost sad, yet always sympathetic feeling for the nature and quality of love, of moral order, and of human *joie de vivre*. These things have their own reality and their own appearances, neither precisely like those defined by Parmenides, nor yet precisely unlike them. Love both is and appears to be; so likewise with moral order and joy in being alive. Failure to perceive this ambiguity, which is fundamental to man's experience, leads to the folly of Orsino and Olivia, of Malvolio, and of the revelers who comprise Sir Toby's social intimates. For folly may be defined as failure to perceive the true nature of people, events, values, things, or as incapacity to separate words from things.

And so it can be argued that something like a Parmenidean metaphysics, with its Platonic qualifications, is singularly appropriate as a foundation for a metaphysic of Shakespearian comedy. The rigid simplicity of "that that is is" obliges us, as it apparently obliged Shakespeare, to speculate rigorously about what is permanent in a world of constant flux. This, too, is one of the obligations of the writer of comedy, plus the sensitivity not to draw too rigid distinctions. (I am not implying, of course, that Shakespeare had not speculated on the relationship of appearance to reality until he wrote *Twelfth Night*. His thinking on this issue began very early in his career and came to a rapid, but immature head in *The Rape of Lucrece*.) It is noteworthy that in *Twelfth Night* rigid distinctions are not drawn, yet neither are they blurred out. Rather, they are faced up to, and a process is covertly suggested whereby human beings, limited by nature, may intelligently face up to them; hence the iteration of characteristic questions and paradoxical answers that embrace both the sensible and the intelligible worlds.

Moreover, through understanding clearly the meaning of "that that is is," we can better understand Shakespeare's enormous advance in *Twelfth Night* as a craftsman: his movement away from the implausible use in the early comedies of conventional theatrical disguises, mistaken identities and the like into a more plausible use of them in the mature comedies (where misuse of the senses, especially of sight and hearing, become crucial), and finally into the fully symbolic use of disguise and mistaken identity in Edgar, for instance, in *King Lear*. And it is Lear far more even than Hamlet who struggles toward the rockbottom meaning of "that that is is" and learns through experiences of horrifying actuality the fallacy of Parmenides's doctrinaire belief that "nothing can come from nothing."

It ought not, then, to be considered heavy-handed or straw-clutching to seek out a metaphysic for *Twelfth Night* by way of Parmenides, even if, as may be the case, Shakespeare had no knowledge of Parmenides whatsoever. By juxtaposing this merriest, yet saddest of all Shakespeare's comedies against the rigors of Parmenidean thought, we can at least make use of a basic tool for thinking clearly about "seeming" and "being," a tool Shakespeare made use of, whether he understood its place in the history of ideas or not. It was a tool that Plato himself was happy to employ, though in time he forged a better one by developing Socratic dialectic. So also did Shakespeare. For the dialectic of speech and action typical of *Twelfth Night* prepared the way for the dialectic of thought and action Shakespeare developed as far as he could in the great tragedies that were on the horizon.

Notes

[1] Citations from any of Shakespeare's plays refer to the Kittredge *Complete Works* (Boston, 1936).

[2] See my essay, "Much Ado About *Something*," *Shakespeare Quarterly*, XV (Summer, 1964), 143-155.

[3] H. B. Charlton, "Shakespeare's Comedies: The Consummation," *Bulletin of the John Rylands Library*, XXI (1937), 345.

[4] C. L. Barber, "The Saturnalian Pattern in Shakespeare's Comedy," *The Sewanee Review*, LIX (1951), 594.

[5] Joseph H. Summers, "The Masks of *Twelfth Night*," *University of Kansas City Review*, XXII (1955), 25.

[6] *Shakespeare and His Comedies* (London, 1957), chap. I.

[7] Citations from Parmenides are from the translation by Francis MacDonald Cornford of those fragments upon which he comments in *Plato and Parmenides* (New York, 1939)—in this instance, pp. 30-31.

[8] Cornford's commentary, pp. 31-32.

[9] Cornford's translation, p. 32.

[10] Cornford's commentary, pp. 32-33.

[11] The complexities inherent in such a differentiation are explored in the *Theatetus* and in the two dialogues in which Plato submits the philosophy of Parmenides to rigorous dialectic, the *Parmenides* and the *Sophist*.

[12] See Plato's criticisms of Parmenides's metaphysics in the *Parmenides* and the *Sophist*.

[13] The one-volume edition of *Twelfth Night* (New York, 1941), p. 133.

[14] Cornford's commentary, p. 31.

[15] See especially Feste's subtle criticism of Orsino (II.iv.75-81). I cannot accept L. G. Salingar's interpretation of Feste as a skeptical moralist who finds a sanctuary in fantasies of pure nonsense: "what he sees at the bottom of the well is 'nothing.'" ("The Design of *Twelfth Night*," *Shakespeare Quarterly*, IX [Spring, 1958], 136.) Salingar's analysis of all the overt themes of the play is, however, acute and persuasive.

[16] I am assuming, of course, that metaphysics and ethics cannot be rigidly separated. What is real in an ethical sense is real only to the degree that behind it is an ontological reality of some sort.

[17] Altogether there are 314 questions: 92 in Act I; 67 in II; 76 in III; 26 in IV; and 51 in V. The greatest incidence occurs in I.iii.—32; I.v.—46; II.iii.—29; II.v.—21; III.i.—13; III.iv.—53; IV.ii.—15; and V.i.—51; i.e. in the eight crucial scenes out of the total eighteen.

[18] See Summers, *passim*.

[19]   Thou hast, Sebastian, done good feature shame.
    In nature there's no blemish but the mind;
    None can be call'd deform'd but the unkind.
    Virtue is beauty; but the beauteous evil
    Are empty trunks, o'erflourish'd by the devil."

[20] On the epistemological level *Twelfth Night* is not provocative. There is considerable iteration of forms of "to know," but questions and answers dealing with how one knows are too few to admit of a theory of knowledge.

[21] Plato argues somewhat similarly in the *Sophist*. See A. E. Taylor, *Plato, the Man and His Work*, 6th ed. (London, 1949), p. 389: "When we say that something 'is not so-and-so,' by the not-being here asserted we do not mean the 'opposite' . . . of what is but only something different from what is. '*A* is not *X*' does not mean that *A* is nothing at all, but only that it is something other than anything which is X. . . . We may say, then, that 'not-being' is as real and has as definite a character as being. This is our answer to Parmenides. We have not merely succeeded in doing what he forbade, asserting significantly that 'what is not, is': we have actually discovered *what* it is. It is 'the different.' . . . It is childishly easy to see that any thing is different from other things and so may be said to be 'what is not'; the true difficulty is to determine the precise limits of the identity and difference to be found among things. . . . "

[22] See the Loeb ed. of Sextus Empiricus, Vol. II, the trans. of R. G. Bury (Cambridge, Massachusetts, 1935), pp. 57-63; and Hermann Diels, *Die Fragmente des Vorsokratiker*, 5th ed., ed. Walther Kranz (Berlin, 1934), I.

[23] See John Edwin Sandys, *A History of Classical Scholarship* (Cambridge, 1908), II, 226.

[24] See pp. 41-46. Three Latin versions of Simplicius were published in the sixteenth century: Paris, 1544; Venice, 1551; and Venice, 1558. See *Simplicii In Aristotelis Physicorum Libros Quattuor Priores Commentaria*, ed. Hermann Diels (Berlin, 1882), pp. xxi-xxii.

[25] See Francis Riaux, *Essai sur Parménide d'Élée*, suivi du texte et de la *traduction des fragments* (Paris, 1840), p. 2.

[26] Francis Riaux, p. 2.

[27] Dorothea Waley Singer, *Giordano Bruno, His Life and Thought* (New York, 1950), pp. 34-41 and footnote 9, p. 30.

[28] Singer, pp. 84-85.

[29] See her *A Study of Love's Labour's Lost* (London, 1936).

[30] See the Loeb ed., trans. R. D. Hicks (Cambridge, Massachusetts, 1950), 11, 431. Sextus Empiricus in his commentary on Parmenides says much the same thing. See footnote 22.

[31] John Burnet, "Shakespeare and Greek Philosophy" in *A Book of Homage to Shakespeare,* ed. Israel Gollancz (Oxford, 1916), p. 58.

[32] *A Book of Homage to Shakespeare.* It is generally believed, however, that Shakespeare's specific knowledge of Pythagoras came from Ovid, *Metamorphoses,* XV.

[33] Burnet, pp. 59-60. See also Burnet, "How Platonism Came to England" in *Essays and Addresses* (London, 1924), pp. 267-276, an even more comprehensive survey than that in "Shakespeare and Greek Philosophy."

[34] Burnet, "Shakespeare and Greek Philosophy," p. 60.

[35] See J. S. Smart, *Shakespeare, Truth and Tradition* (London, 1928); J. A. K. Thomson, *Shakespeare and the Classics* (London, 1952); and T. W. Baldwin, *William Shakespeare's Small Latine & Less Greeke,* 2 vols. (Urbana, 1944). All these scholars agree that Shakespeare read no Greek; that his reading knowledge of Latin was sufficient to allow him to read Ovid in the original, though he appears to have read Golding's translation of the *Metamorphoses* through preference; and that his classical knowledge, though extensive in many ways, could not be called scholarly by Renaissance standards.

[36] Inasmuch as the approach to source studies employed in this essay will undoubtedly produce anguished reactions in some quarters, it may not be amiss to quote a somewhat similar defense, written by J. B. Leishman in support of his conviction that Shakespeare must have had a fair knowledge of Horace: "Was Shakespeare familiar with Horace's Odes? I can see no way of proving that he was, but on the other hand, it seems to me almost incredible that he should not have been. Almost all other great poets have learnt from their predecessors, either by way of a progressively unimitative imitation, or simply through an ever-renewed awareness of the infinite possibilities of expression and of what great poetry could and ought to be; but it seems to be generally assumed that, except for a few translations, Shakespeare, when he read at all, read chiefly almanacks, Fat Stock Prices, and whatever may have been the Elizabethan equivalent of a financial weekly. What I find so incredible about this is the lack of curiosity it presupposes. . . . No doubt the fact that he could write like Aeschylus without ever, perhaps, having even heard the name of Aeschylus, makes it not impossible to suppose that he could write like Horace without ever having read him. On the other hand, we cannot assume that Shakespeare had not read him simply because we cannot produce from his poems and plays such immediately recognisable imitations of variations of Horatian phrases and passages as we can produce from Petrarch or Ronsard or Ben Jonson." (*Themes and Variations in Shakespeare's Sonnets* [London, 1961], p. 36.)

Helene Moglen (essay date 1973)

SOURCE: "Disguise and Development: The Self and Society in *Twelfth Night*," in *Literature and Psychology,* Vol. XXIII, No. 1, 1973, pp. 13-20.

[*In this essay, Moglen postulates a set of Freudian psychological theses that underlie Shakespeare's portrayal of disguised characters in* Twelfth Night.]

Mistaken identity and sex disguise are familiar, rather hackneyed devices used with some regularity in romantic comedy. Critics of *Twelfth Night* have taken these conventions for granted and have been content simply to describe their use in the articulation of plot and character.[1] Surprisingly little allowance has been made for the possibility that Shakespeare might have defined quite differently, at different points in his career, the varying functions of devices as rich in implication as these. Because critics of the play have largely ignored the psychological premises of romance, they have not understood that Shakespeare, in the comic romances of this period, reinterpreted conventional techniques and incorporated them into an apparent theory of the development of personal and therefore sexual identity. It will be the purpose of this essay to indicate the ways in which these psychological premises are fundamental to the treatment of theme and character in *Twelfth Night,* basic to the relation of plot to subplot, and strikingly similar to major aspects of Freud's own theory of psycho-sexual development.

Illyria is a world of the dreaming mind: landscaped by wishes and fears, peopled by fragments of the self. Illyria is a world of symbols in which the face must be traced in the mask and the appearance is more real than reality. Here the dreaming heroes and heroines (Orsino, Sebastian, Olivia, Viola) explore the secrets of their own identities. The object of their quest is love: to recapture the unconscious unity of childhood in the integration of the self with another.

But Illyria is also a real world: comic and absurd. Here self-indulgence replaces self-involvement and hypocrisy is the primary disguise. The comic heroes (Sir Toby, Sir Andrew, Malvolio) move between freedom and rigidity. Their need to free themselves from restraint confronts their obligation to assume responsibility. In one world, the individual's self-definition is given a psychological reference. In the other, the process takes place within a social context.

In *Twelfth Night* the conditions of the romantic journey have been satisfied before the play begins. All authority figures have miraculously disappeared, external barriers are down, the self is thrust back upon itself.[2] As they undertake their quests, Orsino, Olivia and Viola seem to emerge from states of childish narcissism in which they are themselves objects of their own love: a beginning stage (as Freud was later to define it) of all normal sexual development.[3]

Thus, Orsino egotistically withdraws from society, neglecting the responsibilities of the dukedome ("For I myself am best / when least in company")[4] and giving himself instead to the sensation of sensation. It is not a woman he loves, but love itself—in the form of Olivia. It is the "food of love" he enjoys; his own capacity for love which he celebrates. His feeling is not part of a relationship. It is stimulated by appearance. Its source is visual.

> O' when mine eyes did see Olivia first,
> Methought she purged the air of pestilence.
>
> (I, i, 20-21)

As with many courtly lovers before him, Orsino is delighted by his own reflection—discovered in his mistress's eyes.

Olivia is a perfect object for Orsino's egotism. With her as his beloved, he can enjoy the experience of love without having to confront its reality. He can appreciate Olivia's capacity for sisterly affection while anticipating the passion which will eventually accompany her aroused sexuality:

> O' she that hath a heart of that fine frame
> To pay this debt of love but to a brother,
> How will she love when the rich golden shaft
> Hath killed the flock of all affections else
> That live in her . . .
>
> (I, i, 34-38)

And he is safe in the knowledge that for seven years nothing will disturb the sweetness of that anticipation. Olivia protects herself by carefully preserving and

savoring the subtly spiced sensations of the grief which is the condition of her celibacy:

> But like a cloistress she will veiled walk,
> And water once a day her chamber round
> With eye-offending brine: all this to season
> A brother's dead love, which she would keep
>   fresh
> And lasting in her sad remembrance.
>
> (I, i, 29-33)

Both Orsino and Olivia are locked within the prisons of their self-love. They progress from narcissism only insofar as they *define* their self-involvement as love for another. But their behavior belies the truth of their definitions and it remains for Viola to become the agency of their freedom, helping them progress through adolescent conflict to mature resolution.

Initially, Viola's own situation seems to parallel theirs, but her divergences prove more crucial than the similarities. With Orsino and Olivia, she is cut off from the familiar forms of her old life, but while the causes of change are, in their cases, largely specious and self-imposed, they are, for her, radical and decisive. She has undergone a long and dangerous sea-journey (a familiar metaphor for the romantic quest for self) and, at the end, she finds herself bereft—as is Olivia—of a brother. Almost drowned, on the shore of a strange country, she has been, in a sense, reborn; prepared for a new life which is, from another perspective, a new level of development.

Viola's spontaneous response to the information that Orsino rules the land to which she has come, implies that she, like Olivia and the Duke himself, is interested in the possibilities of courtship.

> Orsino! I have heard my father name him.
> He was a bachelor then.
>
> (I, ii, 28-29)

But her interest is not conscious. Viola, unlike the heroines upon whom she was modeled,[5] has no *particular* interest in the Duke. Her susceptibility to love is general: a stage in her development. And, quite typically, her curiosity is accompanied by fear and ambivalence. If she is attracted, she is also repelled by an environment that threatens her uncertain sexuality. The security of Olivia's household, the immediate sense of kinship, is tempting:

> O' that I served that lady,
> And might not be delivered to the world,
> Till I had made mine own occasion mellow.
> What my estate is.
>
> (I, ii, 41-44)

But she must and is prepared to play—as Olivia and Orsino are not—an active role. With a more sophisticated understanding of the dangers of disguise, the delusory quality of appearance (Nature with a beauteous wall / Doth oft close in pollution . . .) (I, iii, 48-9) she initiates the next stage of her development, deciding to become "the form of my intent," offering to serve the duke in the guise of a young man. The chosen disguise suggests that Viola's intent is to become that androgynous person who, in the Eden of childhood she was, and longs again to be. She is a boy-girl hovering precariously, if self-consciously, between the sexless child and the adult female. Her disguise is the adolescent confusion of identity made visible. It is a confusion of identity equally, if less consciously, shared by Olivia and Orsino.

Seen from this perspective, the loss of the brother represents for Viola and Olivia a denial of the primitive, infantile unity of the personality: a schism that necessarily accompanies self-awareness. Orsino's isolation implies a similar fragmentation. For all, the primary narcissism of childhood yields to the sexual ambiguity of adolescence which must be confronted before it can be resolved. The assumption of a male identity is essential to Viola's definition of herself as woman. It suggests the objectification of conflict, allows her to act out her ambivalence, and enables her ultimately to assume a role more appropriate to the demands of nature and society. Similarly, as they interact with the ambiguous sexuality of Viola-Cesario, Olivia and the Duke confront themselves in homoerotic relationships which allow them to achieve the security which is essential if they are to accept mature, heterosexual love. Freud remarked:

> It is well known that even in the normal person it takes a certain time before a decision in regard to the sex of the love-object is finally achieved. Homosexual enthusiasms, tinged with sensuality are common enough in both sexes during the first years after puberty.[6]

It is with this period of uncertainty and change that Shakespeare concerns himself. What Jan Kott calls, in another context, "the metamorphasis of sex," becomes the focus of the play.[7] Sexual roles are explored and defined, conflicts are resolved and Viola is the medium and the measure.

To Orsino, Viola offers the terms of a rather simple compromise. The security afforded by Cesario's masculine appearance allows the Duke to reveal himself to the receptive—albeit disguised—femininity of Viola:

> Thou know'st no less but all. Cesario, I have unclasped to thee the book even of my secret soul.
>
> (I, iv, 12-14)

From Cesario, the Duke (whose "mind is a very opal") learns the lesson of a constancy that creates meaning for the romantic songs that feed his fantasies. He has congratulated himself on the strength of his passion, "as hungry as the sea," and dotes on stories of lovers slain by the heartlessness of fair maidens. By his own admission:

> . . . however we do praise ourselves,
> our fancies are more giddy and unfirm
> more longing, wavering, sooner lost and worn,
> Than women's are.
>
> (II, iv, 33-36)

He is quick to deny the affection he has professed for his young page, when he suspects Cesario's involvement with Olivia:

> Come, boy, with me; my thoughts are
> ripe in mischief.
> I'll sacrifice the lamb that I do love,
> To spite a raven's heart within a dove.
>
> (V, i, 132-4)

Cesario remains steadfast, however, and offers himself lovingly and *in fact* to the cruelty of his sentimental wrath:

> And I, most jocund, apt and willingly,
> To do you rest a thousand deaths would die.
>
> (V, i, 112-3)

By affording him this transitional relationship, Viola forces Orsino to search out the truth of the disguise and provides him with a corrective to illusion.

In relating to Olivia, Viola must play a complex role. By avoiding contact with Orsino and removing herself from the temptation of a heterosexual love relationship, Olivia has revealed her fear of herself. An orphan, like Viola,[8] she will not jeopardize her newly won authority nor will she endanger the integrity of an identity already threatened by the symbolic loss of her brother. The efficient head of a complicated household, Olivia does not want to surrender her masculine dominance: "She'll not match above her degree, neither in estate, years, nor wit (I, iii, 106-7)." She is willing to speak with Cesario because he is unthreatening: his audacious wit as well as his commanding nobility which make her put aside her veil. Her ambivalence is betrayed. Her vulnerability is exposed. In admitting that "Ourselves we do not owe (I, v, 311)," she acknowledges herself to be part of a developmental process which she cannot control. It is the odd logic of this process which defines her actions, attracting her to Viola, attaching her to Cesario and leading her to accept quite readily the eventual substitution of Sebastian.

Viola, too, recognizes that she is not mistress of her situation:

> O Time, thou must entangle this, not I;
> It is too hard a knot for me t' untie.
>
> (II, ii, 40-1)

And she becomes aware of the dangers of the disguise which she has assumed:

> Disguise, I see thou art a wickedness
> Wherein the pregnant enemy does much.
>
> (II, ii, 27-8)

Still, to embrace illusion is to give oneself to a necessary madness. As Cesario, Viola is able to establish the meaning of her sexual identity. Although she enjoys her easy domination of Olivia, she prefers to subordinate herself to the Duke. In the process of convincing Olivia that it is appropriate for her to give freely of her love ("What is yours to bestow is not yours to preserve (I, v, 186-7).") she explores in herself a capacity for feeling which is profound. The security afforded by her disguise makes the exploration possible. She is an eloquent petitioner:

> Make me a willow cabin at your gate
> And call upon my soul within the house;
> Write loyal cantons of contemned love
> And sing them loud even in the dead of night;
> Hallo your name to the reverberate hills
> And make the babbling gossip of the air
> Cry out "Olivia." O you should not rest
> Between the elements of air and earth
> But you should pity me.
>
> (I, v, 269-277)

Her disguise makes her eloquence a mockery of romantic sentiment, but it also invests that mockery with the genuine feeling which is her love for the Duke.

Viola demonstrates the truth of the clown's assertion that: "A sentence is but a chev'ril glove to a good wit. How quickly the wrong side may be turned outward (III, i, 11-13)." Her language is as ambiguous as her disguise, and reveals as it hides. The game she plays enables her to test reality while only partially accepting it. Her ultimate readiness to confront herself is asserted by her confrontation with Sebastian. Aware of the nature of her femininity, she can encounter the masculine possibility: her brother externalized and experienced now as "the other." He is the form of her awareness and, on the level of plot, he makes it possible for that awareness to be activated. The mystery of their twinship solved, her separateness asserted, she is able to put on her "woman's weeds" and assume the role of wife.

Sebastian is, in every respect, an appropriate "double" for Viola. His experience parallels hers and his development is the same as Olivia's and Orsino's. Like Viola, Sebastian has endured an arduous sea-journey which deprives him of his twin and brings him to a new land. The images used to describe his experiences are symbolic of resurrection (he binds himself to a mast and rides upon it like Arion upon the Dolphin's back) and suggest that he has progressed from one level of development to another. In the crisis of identity, friend supplants sister (" . . . for some hour before you took me from the breach of the sea was my sister drown's (II, i, 22-24).") The fact that his relationship with Antonio is tinged by the same homoeroticism that distinguishes Olivia's attraction to Viola and Orsino's affection for Cesario, is suggested by the language that Antonio uses when he speaks of the depth and intensity of his attachment:

> If you will not murder me for my love,
> let me be your servant.
>
> (II, i, 36-37)

> . . . . .

> I have many enemies in Orsino's court,
> Else would I very shortly see thee there.
> But come what may, I do adore thee so
> That danger shall seem sport, and I will go.
>
> (II, i, 46-49)

When we are first introduced to Sebastian as he takes leave of Antonio, he seems slightly feminized.

> My bosom is full of kindness and
> I am yet so near the manners
> Of my mother that, upon the least
> Occasion more, mine eyes will tell
>   Tales of me.
>
> (II, i, 39-42)

But he hovers on the edge of manhood, anxious to separate himself from the domination of his older friend ("Therefore I shall crave of you your leave, that I may bear my evils alone (II, i, 5-6).") It is appropriate that he should now divest himself of his disguise, telling Antonio his name and describing to him his background. Having endured the loss of his sister, inviting a separation from Antonio, Sebastian seems in growing control of himself. He demonstrates his physical prowess when challenged by Sir Toby and Andrew and, more importantly, he welcomes with mature ease, the reality of the dream:

> What relish is in this? How runs the stream?
> Or I am mad, or else this is a dream,
> Let fancy still my sense in Lethe steep;
> If it be thus to dream, still let me sleep!
>
> (IV, i, 59-62)

When he explains to Olivia: "You are betrothed both to a maid and man (V, i, 263)," he reveals the truth of the illusion.

Through Sebastian the resolution of the romance is made possible. In their readiness for marriage all of the characters affirm their own sexual identities. In choosing a mate each of the characters confronts that part of the self which is subordinate but, nevertheless, essential to total definition. Courtship involves an awareness and externalization of conflict. Marriage is the promise of a higher unity. Explaining the need of the personality to move beyond its early narcissism, Freud wrote:

> . . . we are so impelled when the cathexis of the ego with libido exceeds a certain degree. A strong egoism is a protection against disease but in the last resort we must begin to love in order that we may not fall ill, and must fall ill if, in consequence of frustration, we cannot love.[9]

It is the illusion, the experimental assumption of roles, which allows the development here from the disease of self-involvement and fragmentation to the healthful state of love and self-definition.

II

In the sub-plot of *Twelfth Night* the same themes are explored, but the exploration is given a social focus. The romantic characters and situations have their comic counterparts. Self-revelation replaces self-recognition. Self-indulgence replaces narcissism and the absence of self-knowledge is expressed in hypocrisy. The conflict is one of social rather than sexual definition and the antithetical possibilities which must be resolved are personal freedom and expression on one hand, social formalism and responsibility on the other.

Sir Toby, the "Lord of Misrule" who "burlesques majesty by promoting license,"[10] occupies a key position, similar to Viola's. Viola, in her androgynous disguise, encourages Olivia and the Duke to project freely the selves submerged in the roles they play. Sir Toby, whose drunken revelry is another form of disguised freedom, manipulates Sir Andrew and Malvolio so that each betrays his true nature, hypocritically masked. Anti-social qualities are identified and purged. In Sir Andrew, the vanity of the courtly lover is revealed: recognition of his cowardice is a corrective to the absurdity of idealized romance. Ignorant of himself and the woman chosen to be his mistress, he is Orsino perceived through the lens of social comedy. Only ridiculous, he is not punished, for he does, after all, search for love remembering, with some nostalgia, that he "was adored once too."

Malvolio, alone of the Illyrians, does not share this capacity for affection. His narcissism is not an early

stage of a complex developmental process, but seems rather to be endemic. He is "sick of self-love" and "tastes with a distempered appetite (I, v, 90-91)." He is a man who "practises behavior to his own shadow (II, v, 16)." A precursor of the commercial revolution, as C. L. Barber suggests,[11] Malvolio translates all values into material terms. Love, for him, is power. To marry Olivia is to become Count Malvolio. It is to exercise control over the household, to claim the right to berate Sir Toby. In his pride he rejects the established order of society and believes that accepted hierarchies can be overturned. Most important of all, perhaps, Malvolio rejects the wisdom of the fool and refuses to accept the function of disguise:

> I protest I take these wise men
> that crow so at these set kind
> of fools no better than the fools' zanies.
>   (I, v, 87-9)

Paradoxically, it is because of his inflexibility that he alone is sealed into a disguise. Maria's plan offers him only the concrete, external form of his own self-deception. He belongs to the world of comic realism and aspires to the world of psychological romance. He is unable to use the freedom of either as part of his process of self-definition. He rejects the dream along with the cakes and ale. His journey into the self can be nothing more than what it, in fact, becomes: imprisonment in the pitch blackness of delusion.

Malvolio is representative of that egotism which is, in its extreme form, anti-social and self-destructive. His final threat of revenge makes this clear. Because he cannot progress to a state of knowledge which implies integration through the recognition of inner and outer order, he must himself be purged. His dismissal is the symbolic condition of the consolidation of the society and the integration of the individual which is represented by marriage.

It is in the atmosphere of freedom created by Sir Toby that Malvolio's unmasking is created by Maria. Only she is able to mediate between the two worlds of Illyria, while being part of their reality.[12] Moving between Olivia and Sir Toby, she maintains the structures of the household (a microcosmic version of Illyria) imposing order, meting out justice. Her wit, like Viola's, implies the flexibility requisite to personal maturity and social stability. In the parodic letter she writes to Malvolio and in her chiding of Sir Toby, she suggests the limitations of romantic idealism and comic freedom.

At first Sir Toby rejects those restrictions which her reason would impose upon him:

> MARIA: Ay, but you must confine yourself
> within the modest limits of order.

TOBY: Confine? I'll confine myself no finer
than I am. These cloths are good enough to
drink in, and so be these boots too. And
they be not, let them hang themselves in
their own straps.

(I, iii, 8-13)

but he recognizes the value of a wit that can conceive as the form of disguise the revelation of truth. Responding joyously to her ingenuity ("I could marry this wench for this device (II, v, 83)") he comes to respect the constructive intelligence which makes it possible. In this way Maria functions for him as Viola functions for Orsino and Olivia. And when Sir Toby does, in fact, decide to marry Maria, his decision implies his recognition of the limited and transitional value of disguise. Somewhat ruefully he puts aside his freedom ("I hate a drunken rogue (V, i, 200)") and accepts responsibility.

Feste's song places the action of the play in its final perspective. The inevitable movement from childhood to maturity is noted. The psychological and social resolutions once affected, are qualified. The play is, after all, only another kind of disguise which presents reality in a bearable form. The truth itself encompasses more than the image by which it is suggested. The ambivalent quest for self, the conflict between personal integrity and social definition: these are seldom resolved as happily as in Illyria. Freedoms claimed are easily lost, recognitions made are obscured and "the rain it raineth every day."

Notes

[1] See, for example, M. C. Bradbrook, *The Growth and Structure of Elizabethan Comedy* (London, 1955); John Hollander, "*Twelfth Night* and The Morality of Indulgence," *The Sewance Review,* LXVIII (1959); L. G. Salinger, "The Design of *Twelfth Night*," *Shakespeare Quarterly,* IX (1958); Porter Williams, Jr., "Mistakes in *Twelfth Night* and Their Resolution: A Study in some Relationships of Plot and Theme," *PMLA,* LXXVI (1961).

[2] Joseph H. Summers, "The Masks of Twelfth Night," *The University Review,* XXII (1955), p. 25.

[3] See Sigmund Freud, "On Narcissism: An Introduction," *Collected Papers,* trans. by Joan Riviere, Vol. IV, New York, Basic Books, p. 30. Freud describes narcissism as "the libidinal complement to the egosim of the instinct of self-preservation, a measure of which may justifiably be attributed to every living creature, p. 32."

[4] William Shakespeare, *Twelfth Night, Or What You Will,* ed. Charles T. Prouty, Penguin Books, Baltimore,

Maryland, 1958, I, iv, 36-37. All subsequent references will be to this edition and will be given in the text.

[5] L. G. Salinger, in "The Design of *Twelfth Night,* points out that in all four of the plays which served as probable or possible sources for *Twelfth Night,* the heroine knew previously the master whom she serves as page and, wanting to win his love, pursued him to his own country.

[6] Freud, "The Psychogenesis of a Case of Homosexuality in a Woman," *Collected Papers,* IV, p. 227.

[7] Jan Kott, *Shakespeare Our Contemporary,* New York, Anchor, 1961, p. 314. Kott suggests that the play deals with the ambiguity and impossibility of clear sexual definition and choice. His argument is stimulating and insightful, but seems to overlook the developmental aspect of the plot as well as the resolution of central conflicts. Shakespeare seems to express his point in Sebastian's words to Olivia:

So comes it, lady, you have been mistook;
But nature to her bias drew in that.

V, i, 266-7

[8] It is interesting to note, as L. G. Salinger points out in "The Design of *Twelfth Night,*" that the Italian authors who provided Shakespeare with his sources for the play, gave Viola both a domineering father and a foster mother, like Juliet's nurse. The effect of Shakespeare's change is not simply to make "the whole situation more romantically improbable, more melancholy at some points, more fantastic at others," as Salinger suggests, but to emphasize the psycho-sexual, developmental aspect of his characterization.

[9] Freud, "On Narcissism: An Introduction," p. 42.

[10] C. L. Barber, *Shakespeare's Festive Comedy,* New York, 1963, p. 25.

[11] Barber, p. 256.

[12] Feste also mediates between the comic and romantic sensibilities, but he remains, in the tradition of the jester, an outsider.

Karen Greif (essay date 1981)

SOURCE: "Plays and Players in *Twelfth Night,*" in *Shakespeare Survey: An Annual Survey of Shakespearian Study and Production,* Vol. 34, 1981, pp. 121-30.

[*In this essay, Greif claims that* Twelfth Night *views "playing" as a means both to conceal and to reveal truth.*]

'The purpose of playing,' says Hamlet, is 'to hold as 'twere the mirror up to nature: to show virtue her feature, scorn her own image, and the very age and body of the time his form and pressure.'[1] Hamlet himself employs 'playing', in various guises, as a means of penetrating false appearances to uncover hidden truths, but he also discovers how slippery illusions can be when their effects become entangled in the human world. Like *Hamlet,* but in a comic vein, *Twelfth Night* poses questions about 'the purpose of playing' and about whether illusion is perhaps too deeply embedded in human experience to be ever completely separated from reality.

Virtually every character in *Twelfth Night* is either an agent or a victim of illusion, and often a player will assume both these roles: as Viola is an impostor but also a prisoner of her own disguise, or as Sir Toby loses control of the deception he has contrived when he mistakes Sebastian for his twin. Illyria is a world populated by pretenders, which has led one critic to describe the action as 'a dance of maskers . . . for the assumption of the play is that no one is without a mask in the serio-comic business of the pursuit of happiness'.[2] In the course of the story, many of these masks are stripped away or willingly set aside; but illusion itself plays a pivotal yet somewhat ambiguous role in this process. While Viola's masquerade serves to redeem Orsino and Olivia from their romantic fantasies and ends in happiness with the final love-matches, the more negative aspects of deception are exposed in the trick played against Malvolio, which leads only to humiliation and deeper isolation.

Role-playing, deceptions, disguises, and comic manipulations provide the fabric of the entire action. So pervasive is the intermingling of illusion and reality in the play that it becomes impossible at times for the characters to distinguish between the two. This is not simply a case of illusion becoming a simulated version of reality. 'I am not that I play', Viola warns her fellow player (1.5.184); but, as the subtitle suggests, in *Twelfth Night* one discovers that 'what you will' may transform the ordinary shape of reality.

The fluidity of the relationship between 'being' and 'playing' is indirectly illuminated at the beginning of act 3, in the play's single face-to-face encounter between Viola and Feste, who share the distinction of being the only pretenders in Illyria who do not wear their motley in their brains. They match wits in a contest of wordplay, which moves the Fool to sermonize: 'To see this age! A sentence is but a chev'ril glove to a good wit. How quickly the wrong side may be turn'd outward!' (3.1.11-13). According to Feste, words have become like kidskin gloves, pliable outside coverings readily yielding to manipulation by a good wit. Viola's response echoes this sense; those who know how to play with words 'may quickly make them wanton' (l.

15). Men may expect words to operate as constant symbols of meaning, faithfully reflecting the concrete outlines of reality; but, in fact, words prove to be flighty, untrustworthy mediators between human beings and experience:

> *Clown.* But indeed, words are very rascals
>   since bonds disgrac'd them.
> *Viola.* Thy reason, man?
> *Clown.* Troth, sir, I can yield you none
>   without words, and words are grown so
>   false, I am loath to prove reason with them.
>
> (ll. 20-5)

Rather than serving as a medium for straightforward communication, words have become bent to the purposes of dissembling. Feste declares himself a 'corrupter of words' (l. 36), and throughout the play he demonstrates how chameleon-like words can become in the mouth of an expert dissembler like himself. Yet Feste is also recognized by his audience and many of his fellow players as a kind of truth-teller; under the guise of fooling and ingenious word-play, he reminds those around him of truths they have blocked out of their illusion-bound existences. The Fool's dialogue with Viola suggests that 'since bonds disgrac'd them', words have fallen under suspicion within the world of *Twelfth Night,* at least among those who admit their own dissembling. But for those who possess wit and imagination, the protean nature of words also affords an exhilarating form of release. Dexterity with language becomes a means of circumventing a world that is always shifting its outlines by exploiting that fluidity to the speaker's own advantage.

The same ambiguity that is characteristic of words pervades almost every aspect of human experience in *Twelfth Night.* Illyria is a world of deceptive surfaces, where appearances constantly fluctuate between what is real and what is illusory. Out of the sea, there comes into this unstable society a catalyst in the form of the disguised Viola, who becomes the agent required to free Orsino and Olivia from the bondage of their self-delusions. Equilibrium is finally attained, however, only after the presence of Viola and her separated twin has generated as much error and disturbance as Illyria could possibly contain.

Moreover, this resolution is achieved not by a straightforward injection of realism into this bemused dreamworld, but by further subterfuge. 'Conceal me what I am', Viola entreats the Sea Captain after the shipwreck (1.2.53), setting in motion the twin themes of identity and disguise that motivate so much of the action in *Twelfth Night.* Identity, it is important to bear in mind, includes both the identity that represents the essence of one's being, the 'what I am' that separates one individual from another, and also the identity that makes identical twins alike; and the comedy is concerned with the loss and the recovery of identity in both these senses.

Viola's plan to dissemble her true identity proves to be ironically in keeping with the milieu she has entered. But the fact that Viola, left stranded and unprotected by the wreck, assumes her guise as Cesario in response to a real predicament sets her apart from most of the pretenders already dwelling in Illyria. Surfeiting on fancy, they endlessly fabricate grounds for deceiving others or themselves. Orsino and Olivia are foolish, in part, because it is apparent that the roles of unrequited lover and grief-stricken lady they have chosen for themselves spring more from romantic conceits than from deep feeling or necessity. The games-playing mania of Sir Toby Belch and his cohorts carries to comic extremes the Illyrian penchant for playing make-believe. Just as words, in Sir Toby's hands, are rendered plastic by his Falstaffian talent for making their meaning suit his own convenience, so he manufactures circumstances to fit his will.

The kind of egotism that stamps Sir Toby's perpetual manipulation of words and appearances, or Orsino and Olivia's wilful insistence on their own way, is far removed from Viola's humility as a role-player. Although she shares Feste's zest for wordplay and improvisation, Viola never deludes herself into believing she has absolute control over either her own part or the actions of her fellow players. Musing over the complications of the love triangle into which her masculine disguise has thrust her, Viola wryly concedes 'O time, thou must untangle this, not I, / It is too hard a knot for me t'untie' (2.2.40-1). Viola's outlook is unaffectedly realistic without the need to reject imaginative possibilities. Her own miraculous escape encourages her to hope her brother has also survived the wreck, but throughout most of the play she must continue to act without any certainty he is still alive. She accepts the facts of her dilemma without self-pity and begins at once to improvise a new, more flexible role for herself in a difficult situation; but she also learns that the freedom playing permits her is only a circumscribed liberty. For as long as the role of Cesario conceals her real identity, Viola is free to move at will through Illyria, but not to reveal her true nature or her love for Orsino.

The first meeting between Cesario and Olivia creates one of the most demanding tests of Viola's ability to improvise. She meets the challenge with ingenuity, but Viola also insists, with deliberate theatricality, on the disparity between her true self and the role that she dissembles:

> *Viola.* I can say little more than I have
> studied, and that question's out of my part.
> Good gentle one, give me modest assurance
> if you be the lady of the house, that I may
> proceed in my speech.

> *Olivia.* Are you a comedian?
> *Viola.* No, my profound heart; and yet (by the
> very fangs of malice I swear) I am not that
> I play.
>
> (1.5.178-84)

In her exchanges with Olivia, Viola is able to treat the part she plays with comic detachment; but the somewhat rueful tone underlying her awareness of the ironies of her relation to Olivia turns to genuine heartache when this separation between her true identity and her assumed one comes into conflict with her growing love for Orsino.

Unable to reveal her love openly, Viola conjures for Orsino the imaginary history of a sister who

> lov'd a man
> As it might be perhaps, were I a woman,
> I should your lordship.
>
> (2.4.107-9)

As long as Orsino clings to his fancied passion for Olivia and she herself holds on to her disguise, Viola can vent her true feelings only by more dissembling, so she masks her secret love for the Duke with the sad tale of this lovelorn sister. Yet her fiction also serves to present her master with a portrait of genuine love against which to measure his own obsession for Olivia. 'Was this not love indeed?' she challenges him:

> We men may say more, swear more, but
> indeed
> Our shows are more than will; for still we
> prove
> Much in our vows, but little in our love.
>
> (ll. 116-18)

Her story is a touching one, and for once Orsino's blustering is stilled. He is moved to wonder 'But died thy sister of her love, my boy?'; but she offers only the cryptic answer 'I am all the daughters of my father's house, / And all the brothers too—and yet I know not' (ll. 119-21). Viola's veiled avowal of her love is perhaps the most delicate blend of imagination and truth in the play, and this fabrication will finally yield its reward when Cesario is free to disclose 'That I am Viola' (5.1.253).

Role-playing, whether it be a deliberate choice like Viola's disguise or the foolish self-delusions that Orsino, Olivia, and Malvolio all practise upon themselves, leads to a general confusion of identity within Illyria. In the second encounter between Olivia and Cesario, this tension between being and playing is given special resonance:

> *Olivia.* I prithee tell me what thou think'st of
> me.

Viola. That you do think you are not what
you are.

Olivia. If I think so, I think the same of you.

Viola. Then think you right: I am not what I
am.

Olivia. I would you were as I would have you
be.

Viola. Would it be better, madam, than I am?
I wish it might, for now I am your fool.

(3.1.138-44)

Like a tonic chord in a musical passage. Viola's riddles always come back to the idea of 'what you are' and 'what I am', the enduring truth of one's real identity. But this note of resolution is never a stable one. Viola warns Olivia that she has deluded herself into acting out fantasies with no basis in reality, first in her vow of celibacy to preserve her grief and then in her pursuit of the unattainable Cesario. In turn, she herself admits that 'I am not what I am.' Olivia, meanwhile, is obsessed with 'what thou think'st of me' and what 'I would have you be'. She is less interested in the truth about Cesario or her own nature than in making what is conform to what she would like it to be. On the one hand, the facts of nature ensure that she will be frustrated in her wooing, and yet her beloved will indeed be transformed into what she would have him be when the counterfeit Cesario is replaced by the real Sebastian.

The compression of so many levels of meaning within this passage suggests how complicated and paradoxical the relationship is in *Twelfth Night* between what actually is and what playing with reality can create. Viola's exchange with Olivia follows directly upon her encounter with Feste, and the second dialogue translates into terms of identity and role-playing the same attitudes towards words appearing in the first. The Fool claims that 'since bonds disgrac'd them', words have no static nature—that no unchanging identification between the-thing-itself and the word symbolizing it is ever possible—and the condition of being, the identity belonging to 'what I am', is in a comparable state of flux throughout most of the action.

The separation between being and playing, like the disjunction between words and concrete reality, may lead to a sense of disorientation closely akin to madness. This is the condition that the release of imagination creates in Malvolio. When he exchanges the reality of what he is for the make-believe part he dreams of becoming, he begins to act like a madman. Viola's charade as Cesario produces a welter of mistaken identities that so disorient her fellow players no one is quite certain of his or her sanity. Yet another variation of the madness which springs from unleashing the effects of imagination upon reality is seen in the escapades of Sir Toby Belch.

His reign of misrule is fuelled by his refusal to allow reality to interfere with his desires, and this unruliness drives his associates to wonder repeatedly if he is mad.

Yet, just as Feste finds means of communicating truth by playing with words, so does the unstable relationship between being and playing allow at least a few of the players in Illyria to discover a more flexible sense of identity that can accommodate both enduring truths and changing appearances. The same loosening of the bonds governing identity that can lead to bewildering confusion may also open up a fresh sense of freedom in shaping one's own nature. What you will may indeed transform what you are.

The point at which all these attitudes converge is in the recognition scene of the final act. At the moment when Viola and Sebastian finally come face to face upon the stage, the climactic note of this motif is sounded in Orsino's exclamation of wonder:

One face, one voice, one habit, and two
persons,
A natural perspective, that is and is not!

(5.1.216-17)

For the onlookers, who are still ignorant both of Viola's true identity and of the existence of her twin, the mirror image created by the twins' confrontation seems explicable only as an optical illusion of nature. Yet the illusion of nature. Yet the illusion proves to be real; this 'natural perspective' is the stable reality underlying the mirage of shifting appearances caused by mistaken identity.

This dramatic revelation of the identity that has been obscured by illusory appearances, but is now made visible in the mirror image of the twins, is deliberately prolonged as Viola and Sebastian exchange their tokens of recognition. Anne Barton has drawn attention to the fact that the recognition scene provides

a happy ending of an extraordinarily schematized and 'playlike' kind. Viola has already had virtual proof, in Act III, that her brother has survived the wreck. They have been separated for only three months. Yet the two of them put each other through a formal, intensely conventional question and answer test that comes straight out of Greek New Comedy.[3]

The recognition of identity is at first an experience involving only the reunited twins; but, as the facts of their kinship are brought forth, the circle of awareness expands to include Orsino and Olivia. They appreciate for the first time their shared folly in desiring the unobtainable and both discover true love in unexpected forms by sharing in the recognition of the twins' identities. As Orsino vows,

If this be so, as yet the glass seems true,
I shall have share in this most happy wrack.

                                        (5.1.265-6)

The reflections of identity that have been present throughout the play are now openly acknowledged and sealed by the bonds of marriage and kinship. The similarities between Viola and Olivia, for example—the lost brother, the unrequited love, the veiled identity—which are echoed in the names that are virtually anagrams, are now confirmed by the ties of sisterhood when each wins the husband she desires.

Paradoxically, what allows this dramatic moment of epiphany[4] to occur at all is the same loss and mistaking of identities that caused the original confusion. It is the separation of the twins and Viola's subsequent decision to 'Conceal me what I am' which gives emotional intensity to the moment when identity is recognized and regained. This final scene, moreover, makes it clear that the regaining of lost personal identity—the individuality that distinguishes Viola from Sebastian—is closely tied to the recognition of the likeness that makes the twins identical. The recognition scene, with its ritual-like ceremony of identification, suggests that men and women must recognize how much they are identical, how much alike in virtues and follies and in experiences and desires, before they can affirm the personal identities that make them unique.[5] These twin senses of identity converge in the final act, dramatically embodied in the reunited twins who share 'One face, one voice, one habit, and two persons'.

But at what point do the reflections stop? Beyond the onlookers upon the stage who behold this ceremony of recognition is the larger audience of the illusion that is *Twelfth Night*. The play itself is 'a natural perspective, that is and is not': a mirror held up to nature intended to reflect the contours of reality and simultaneously a work of imagination that incarnates the world of being in a world of playing. What the audience encounters in the mirror of the play is its own reflected identity in the characters who play out their experiences upon the stage. In sharing the experience of *Twelfth Night,* we come to recognize the ties of identity that link our own world of being to the imagined world of the play; and, on a more personal level, we identify our private follies and desires in our fictional counterparts upon the stage. In acknowledging this kinship of resemblance, we too gain a fresh awareness of the nature of 'what I am', the true self concealed beneath the surface level of appearances. Moreover, having witnessed how deeply life is ingrained with illusion within Illyria, we may awake from the dreamworld of the play to wonder if 'what we are' in the world outside the playhouse is perhaps less static and immutable than we once believed. At this point, imagination and truth may begin to merge in our own world: 'Prove true, imagination, O, prove true' (3.4.375).

If art possesses this creative power, however, there remains the problem of dealing with the more troubling issues raised by the gulling of Malvolio. The plot contrived to convince the steward of Olivia's passion for him is enacted with deliberately theatrical overtones, and the conspirators employ deception to feed and then expose Malvolio's folly in much the same way that a playwright manipulates illusion and reality upon the stage. Yet Malvolio's enforced immersion in the world of make-believe in no way reforms him. Nor does it enable him to gain a more positive understanding of either his own identity or the ties that bind him to his fellow men. Malvolio remains isolated and egotistical to the end. What is more, the mockers who have seen their own follies reflected in Malvolio's comic performance are no more altered by the experience than he is.

The plot against Malvolio is originally planned along the traditional lines of Jonsonian 'humour' comedy: the victim's folly is to be exposed and purged by comic ridicule to rid him of his humour. Maria explains the scheme in such terms to her fellow satirists:

> . . . it is his grounds of faith that all that look on him love him; and on that vice in him will my revenge find notable cause to work. . . . I know my physic will work with him.

                                        (2.3.151-3;172-3)

But there is also a strong dose of personal spite in their mockery. The pranksters are really more eager to be entertained by Malvolio's delusions of grandeur than they are to reform him. Maria guarantees her audience that 'If I do not gull him into an ayword, and make him a common recreation, do not think I have wit enough to lie straight in my bed' (ll. 134-7). It is certainly in this spirit that the revellers take the jest. 'If I lose a scruple of this sport', Fabian pledges as the game begins, 'let me be boil'd to death with melancholy' (2.5.2-3).

Maria plants the conspirators in the garden box-tree like spectators at a play, bidding them: 'Observe him, for the love of mocker y; for I know this letter will make a contemplative idiot of him' (ll. 18-20). Malvolio, who 'has been yonder i' the sun practising behavior to his own shadow this half hour' (ll. 16-18), is a natural play-actor; and he immediately takes the bait of this improvised comedy. The megalomania suppressed beneath his Puritan façade is comically set free by the discovery of Maria's forged letter, and he is soon persuaded to parade his folly publicly by donning the famous yellow stockings.

Maria's letter cleverly exploits Malvolio's conceit, but he himself manufactures his obsession. With only the flimsiest of clues to lead him on, Malvolio systematically construes every detail of the letter to fuel his newly liberated dreams of greatness, never pausing to consider how ludicrous the message really is:

> Why, this is evident to any formal capacity, there is no obstruction in this. And the end—what should that alphabetical position portend? If I could make that resemble something in me! . . . M.O.A.I. This simulation is not as the former; and yet, to crush this a little, it would bow to me, for every one of these letters are in my name.

(ll. 116-20; 139-41)

The deception deftly juggles appearances to prompt Malvolio to his own undoing, but there is always the danger inherent in such games of make-believe that the dupe will no longer be able to cope with reality once his self-fabricated fantasies are stripped away from him. 'Why, thou hast put him in such a dream', Sir Toby laughingly tells Maria, 'that when the image of it leaves him he must run mad' (ll. 193-4). But no such qualms disturb these puppet-masters. When Fabian echoes this warning, Maria replies 'The house will be the quieter' (3.4.134).

Although it is the letter that persuades Malvolio to play out his fantasies in public, his audience has already been treated to a display of his fondness for make-believe. While the conspirators impatiently wait for him to stumble on the letter, Malvolio muses on his dream of becoming the rich and powerful 'Count Malvolio'. As he paints the imaginary scene of Sir Toby's future humiliation and expulsion, the eavesdroppers find themselves unexpectedly drawn into the performance they are watching. Sir Toby, in particular, becomes so enraged at this 'overweening rogue' (l. 29) that Fabian must repeatedly warn him to control his outbursts: 'Nay, patience, or we break the sinews of our plot!' (ll. 75-6). Malvolio's audience prove to be as uncertain as their gull about the boundaries separating fiction from fact, as will be made comically evident in the miscalculations and confusions that result from the duel contrived between Sir Andrew and Cesario. Taken unawares by Malvolio's tableau of future triumph, the three spies inadvertently become participants in the comedy they are observing.

Malvolio's private playlet of revenge and his discovery of the letter are staged in a deliberately theatrical manner, played before the unruly audience of Sir Toby, Sir Andrew, and Fabian. His play-acting exposes Malvolio's folly to comic perfection; but it also, in its own topsy-turvy fashion, holds the mirror up to nature for both the spectators in the box-tree and the audience beyond the stage. It is a glass more like a funhouse mirror than the symmetry of a 'natural perspective', but in Malvolio's absurd performance the pranksters are presented with a comically distorted image of their own follies and delusions. Malvolio's folly is made more ludicrous by the charade that openly exposes the overweening ambition and conceit normally held within respectable bounds by the sanctimonious steward, but the difference between the performer and his audience is simply one of degree.

If Malvolio is treated by these practical jokers as a puppet on a string, a 'trout that must be caught with tickling' (2.5.22), Sir Andrew is no less Sir Toby's own 'dear manikin' (3.2.53). His auditors deride Malvolio's pretensions to his mistress's love; but Sir Andrew's wooing of Olivia is equally preposterous, and his hopes are based entirely on Sir Toby's counterfeit assurances. Sir Toby may ridicule Malvolio's determined efforts to 'crush' the letter's message to accommodate his own desires, but the assertion of imagination over concrete reality is no less a characteristic trait of Sir Toby himself, who has earlier insisted that 'Not to be a-bed after midnight is to be up betimes' (2.3.1-2). The only difference in their dealings with words is that Malvolio uses logic as a crowbar to twist and hammer meanings into a more gratifying form, while Sir Toby chooses to suspend logic altogether. The steward's obsessive instinct for order is simply the inverted image of Sir Toby's own mania for disorder. Even their plot to put an end to Malvolio's authority is dramatized for the spectators in a parody version supplied by Malvolio's own dream of revenge.

The spectators are in their own ways as much drowned in excesses of folly and imagination as their gull. But as they mock the woodcock nearing the gin, the onlookers fail to realize that the 'play' itself is an imaginary snare for the woodcocks in its audience. Sir Andrew's reaction to Malvolio's fictive dialogue with a humbled Sir Toby exemplifies the fatuity of his fellow auditors:

> *Malvolio.* 'Besides, you waste the treasure of your time with a foolish knight'—
> *Andrew.* That's me, I warrant you.
> *Malvolio.* 'One Sir Andrew'—
> *Andrew.* I knew 'twas I, for many do call me fool.

(2.5.77-81)

Sir Andrew makes the correct identification but remains oblivious to the intended reprimand. In the same fashion, all the members of Malvolio's audience observe their reflected images in the mirror of the comedy without recognition, thus comically fulfilling Jonathan Swift's famous dictum that 'Satyr is a sort of Glass, wherein Beholders do generally discover every body's Face but their own.'[6]

By the time Malvolio encounters Olivia again after reading her supposed declaration of love, his perceptions have become completely mastered by his delusions. To those around him who are unaware of the deception, Malvolio appears quite mad. 'Why, this is very midsummer madness', (3.4.56) cries Olivia in response to the incoherent ramblings of this smiling, cross-gartered apparition. From his own perspective, however, he is unquestionably sane, and it is the rest of the world that is behaving strangely. Unlike Viola or Feste, Malvolio has no talent for improvisation. His rejection of a rigidly defined identity, although it gives him a temporary release from social bonds, affords Malvolio no room for flexibility.

Faced with the fluidity of the world of playing in which he suddenly finds himself, Malvolio insists on trying to marshal shifting appearances back into regimented formation:

> Why, every thing adheres together, that no dram of a scruple, no scruple of a scruple, no obstacle, no incredulous or unsafe circumstance—What can be said?
>
> (3.4.78-81)

But Malvolio's efforts to control the flux are like trying to sculpt water into solid shapes; the material itself refuses static form. His obstinate insistence that the words and actions of those around him should conform to his will makes him appear mad to his fellow players, while they seem equally insane to him.

The quandary over who is mad and who is sane becomes even more entangled in the dialogue between the incarcerated steward and the Fool, disguised as Sir Topas. Malvolio is entirely just in his charge that 'never was man thus wrong'd. . . . they have laid me here in hideous darkness' (4.2.28-30). From his perspective, the darkness is tangible and his madness the fantasy of those around him. Yet it is also true, as 'Sir Topas' insists, that the darkness is symbolic of the shroud of ignorance and vanity through which Malvolio views the world:

> *Malvolio.* I am not mad, Sir Topas, I say to
>   you this house is dark.
> *Clown.* Madman, thou errest. I say there is no
>   darkness but ignorance, in which thou art
>   more puzzled than the Egyptians in their
>   fog.
> *Malvolio.* I say this house is as dark as
>   ignorance, though ignorance were as dark as
>   hell; and I say there was never man thus
>   abus'd. I am no more mad than you are.
>
>   (4.2.40-8)

His 'confessor's' riddles seem designed to force Malvolio to a new understanding of his identity as a fallible and often foolish human being. But 'Sir Topas' is himself a fake—a self-avowed corrupter of words whose disguised purpose is not to heal Malvolio's imagined lunacy, but to drive him deeper into madness. Feste juggles words with ease because he under-

stands that they are 'very rascals since bonds disgrac'd them', but Malvolio stubbornly insists on making rascal words behave with as much decorum as he believes they should. Throughout this scene, Malvolio returns to his claim 'I am not mad' with the same tonic emphasis as Viola reverts to 'what I am' in her dialogue with Olivia (act 3, scene 1). But being incapable of Viola's playful attitude, Malvolio rejects any imaginative interpretation of his dilemma.

His rigidity toward both language and experience leaves him incapable of comprehending any truth beyond the concrete limits of reality. 'I tell thee I am as well in my wits as any man in Illyria' (4.2.106-7), Malvolio insists with absolute justice; but how far from madness are the other inhabitants of Illyria? In a very ironic sense, Malvolio gets what he deserves when he is imprisoned in his cell. Having persisted in imposing his arbitrary order upon capricious words and appearances, he is himself confined in a guardhouse for his own caprices.

Whatever his deserts, there is nonetheless considerable justice to Malvolio's charge that he has been much abused by the deceivers who have made him 'the most notorious geck and gull / That e'er invention play'd on' (5.1.343-4). Ironically, Malvolio's absurdly inflated ego and his isolation are only hardened by his satiric treatment. Even in making his defence, Malvolio stubbornly maintains yet another delusion, that Olivia is personally responsible for his torment. Humiliated beyond endurance, Malvolio stalks off the stage with a final ringing assertion of his vanity and alienation: 'I'll be reveng'd on the whole pack of you' (l. 378). Malvolio stands as an isolated figure in a festive world from beginning to end because never once does he honestly perceive his own nature, the true identity of 'what I am', or the corresponding ties of identity that bind him to his fellow players.

The pranksters, in spite of their fondness for 'fellowship', do not fare much better. They have already demonstrated a failure to detect their own follies in Malvolio's pretensions, and it is therefore appropriate that the beguilers as well as their gull should be missing from the witnesses at the recognition scene and the subsequent revelations. Sir Toby, in particular, suffers for his failures of identification. After having challenged Sebastian to a fight in the mistaken belief he was the timorous Cesario, Sir Toby rages onto the stage with a bloody head, angrily spurning the comfort of his friend Sir Andrew: 'Will you help?—an ass-head and a coxcomb and a knave, a thin-fac'd knave, a gull!' (5.1.206-7).

Whereas the mistaken identities and role-playing in the romantic plot centring on Viola ultimately lead, in the recognition scene, to a renewal of identity and the human bonds of kinship and marriage, Malvolio's immersion in a world of make-believe yields no such beneficial rewards. The ironic counterpart to the recognition scene with its unravelling of identities is Malvolio's dungeon scene. There, Malvolio is literally enclosed in darkness in a cell cutting him off from all direct human contact, and he is bedevilled by tricksters who would like to drive him into deeper confusion. Nor does his audience there or in the garden scene gain any greater insight into their own characters. This failure of imagination, set against Viola's own miraculous success, reflects ironically on the supposedly therapeutic value of 'playing' and the dubious morality of the would-be satirists as much as it does on Malvolio's own recalcitrance. Malvolio's final words and his incensed departure add a discordant note to the gracefully orchestrated harmonies of the final act.

Malvolio's response to his comic purgatory stirs unresolved questions about the value of playing with reality. Whereas Viola's part in the comedy reveals how the release that playing allows can lead to a renewed sense of identity and human bonds, Malvolio's role exposes the other side of the coin, the realm in which release of imagination leads only to greater isolation and imperception. Fabian's jest about Malvolio's absurd play-acting, 'If this were play'd upon a stage now, I could condemn it as an improbable fiction' (3.4.127-8), like the theatrical overtones of Viola's improvisations and the playlike quality of the recognition scene, deliberately opens up the vistas of the play by reminding us that we are witnesses of a play, 'a natural perspective, that is and is not'. But amusing as Malvolio's surrender to playing is, it raises the most disturbing questions in the play. Can men, in fact, ever perfectly distinguish what is real from what is imagined or intentionally spurious? Can they ever come to know the truth about themselves, the identity appearances have concealed from them?

Twelfth Night itself offers no pat solutions. In a comic world devoted to playing and yet mirroring the actual world of being, in which identities are both mistaken and revealed, in which deception can both conceal truths and expose them, and in which bonds have disgraced the words on which men are dependent for communication, no permanent resolution of these ambiguities is ever possible. Shakespeare himself shrugs off the task of providing any final illumination with delightful finesse. As the play draws to a close with Feste's epilogue song and the world of playing begins to dissolve back into the world of being, the Fool concludes:

> A great while ago the world begun,
>   With hey ho, the wind and the rain,
> But that's all one, our play is done,
>   And we'll strive to please you every day.

RELATION TO ELIZABETHAN CULTURE

Charles Tyler Prouty (lecture date 1966)

SOURCE: "*Twelfth Night*," in *Stratford Papers: 1965-67*, edited by B. A. W. Jackson, McMaster University Library Press, 1969, pp. 110-28.

[*In the following essay first delivered at the 1966 Shakespeare Seminar, Prouty positions* Twelfth Night *with regard to Shakespeare's source materials, focusing specifically on his interpretation of Renaissance notions of courtly love.*]

In some thirty years of teaching it has been my experience that of all the plays in the Shakespeare canon the comedies are the most difficult to teach. The Joyous Comedies in particular require so much explanation that we are in danger of losing the play in establishing what I regard as the essential details. The reason is very simply that these are sophisticated plays based on a complex of social and literary conventions that were well known to the Renaissance world in general and the Elizabethan world in particular but are almost unknown to our world. In *Twelfth Night* we are dealing almost exclusively with the conventions of love and the behaviour of lovers—conventions which are completely alien to our world. The important thing, however, is Shakespeare's reaction to these conventions, which controls the nature of his play and makes it, therefore, peculiarly his own. In the social world of the Renaissance the traditions of the Middle Ages which we call Courtly Love flourished, and these conventions were incredibly sophisticated; they are not certainly, to be seen in the context of the banal sexuality of our times.

For example, in the 1570s a *novella* by George Whetstone entitled 'Rinaldo and Giletta' tells us a lovely story. An aged man by the name of Frizaldo is in love with the fair Giletta, but Giletta is not in love with him. Rather she is in love with Rinaldo, a handsome but poor young man who is, of course, in love with her. On a specific occasion Frizaldo has entered Giletta's chamber while Rinaldo is outside underneath the balcony singing a love song. Frizaldo, recognizing the voice, pretends ignorance as far as Giletta is concerned, and so he addresses her with the term of 'Mistress'. Giletta, in order to conceal her knowledge of the singer outside, is forced to use the appropriate reply: she addresses Frizaldo as 'Servant'. These words, 'Servant' and 'Mistress', are conventional words and do not necessarily imply a sexual relationship; but the implication is enough for the wretched Rinaldo, who flees the scene and jumps into the river, ostensibly to die. But, perhaps because of the temperature of the water or for some other reason, he has second thoughts, swims to the farthest shore, returns in the nick of time to rescue the fair Giletta, and all ends happily! The conventions in this kind of story are typical, and, for example, we see in the second scene of *Twelfth Night,* where the ship captain tells Viola, 'What great ones do, the less will prattle of,' that the types of behaviour reflected here were not exclusively the property of the great; while the great had established the game, the game itself was known through all strata of society. However by the 1590s the game had become the subject of witty scoffing. For example, in Greene's *Menaphon,* first published in 1589, we find these lines from 'Doron's Eclogue ioynd with Carmela's'. Doron addresses Carmela:

> Carmela *deare, euen as the golden ball*
> *That* Venus *got, such are thy goodly eyes,*
> *When cherries iuice is iumbled therewithall,*
> *Thy breath is like the steeme of apple pies.*
>
> *Thy lippes resemble Two Cowcumbers faire,*
> *Thy teeth like to the tuskes of fattest swine,*
> *Thy speach is like the thunder in the aire:*
> *Would God thy toes, thy lips and all were*
>   *mine.*

Here we can see how the conventional epithets of 'ruby lips' and 'pearl-like teeth' have been reduced to rustic figures, and thus how the whole game is deliberately undercut and becomes the subject of laughter. The same kind of thing occurs in *As You Like It* when Rosalind tells Orlando, 'Men have died from time to time and worms have eaten them but not for love.' This, of course, is a great blow to the over-serious Orlando because he really does believe that he would die from love, even though he fails to keep his appointments with Rosalind in spite of all his oaths. And Rosalind has played with the conventions still further with her references to Troilus's having his brains dashed out with a Grecian club and Leander's being drowned by catching a cramp on a hot summer's night. The whole set of conventions was understood by the Elizabethans (and as a matter of fact it was still understood in pre-war England as we can see in such a play as Noel Coward's *Private Lives* or in the popular press. Such periodicals as the *Tatler* were filled with pictures of the 'great ones' at balls, at hunts, at race meetings and all that sort of thing, and these were largely seized upon by the middle and lower classes as subjects for conversation and objects of admiration.)

The conventions are clearly indicated in the source materials of *Twelfth Night* so we must know about these materials and must try to ascertain Shakespeare's comprehension of them, what he read and also what he knew about the intellectual milieu in which these conventions operated and out of which the written materials came.

The first mention of *Twelfth Night,* in John Manningham's *Diary,* is in the entry for 2 February 1602. At the Middle Temple the Candlemas Feast was celebrated by a performance which Manningham describes as 'a play called Twelve Night or What You Will, much like the Commedy of Errores, or Menechmi in Plautus, but most like and neere to that in Italian called *Inganni.*'

The latter play to which Manningham refers is an Italian play of 1562 written by one Nicolo Secchi. More important for our purposes, however, is the earliest known play dealing with the theme of separated twins; this, *Gl'Ingannati,* first printed in 1537, was presented by the Academy of the Intronnati of Siena—Intronnati, of course, means 'Thunderstruck'. In its printed form it was preceded by another play, a comedy entitled the *Comedia del Sacrificio,* which was also a presentation of the Thunderstruck Ones. Here the members all appear as rebels against the tyranny of love. In the centre of the stage is a large urn with a fire burning inside and each member of the Academy in turn makes his way forward to cast into the urn some token of his erstwhile beloved so that it is consumed by the flames and thus symbolizes his rejection of love. He, of course, speaks appropriate lines to indicate what he is doing and why he is doing it.

Now this Academy is not something unusual. It was one of many that spread all over Italy during the late fifteenth and early sixteenth century, and these derived from the fifteenth-century Platonic Academy in Florence which was a very serious Academy (for example, Ficino's Commentary on Plato's *Symposium* was only one of the works that came out of it). The serious purpose was, however, very soon lost and the jesting spirit took over. Practically every city in Italy had an Academy by the sixteenth century, and the custom of such academies spread to even France and Germany. The aim had now become one of producing courtiers in imitation of *Il Cortegiano,* polished and refined gentlemen. The names of the societies and of the individual members became wittily allegorical or symbolic. Wit was prized above all, everything was a subject for jesting.

It is just such an academy as this that we find in Shakespeare's *Love's Labour's Lost* or in the festivities at Gray's Inn, entitled *Gesta Grayorum.* Now let us turn to the play of the 'Thunderstruck Ones'. It's a typical Italian comedy of plot, the Commedia Erudita. There is no attention paid to character or morality; the play is amoral. Most important there is no tone except the tone of jesting and a complete lack of seriousness. This is the most important aspect that we have to consider in *Twelfth Night*—the whole aspect of tone.

Specifically the immediate English source is a short story by Barnaby Riche, 'Apollonius and Scilla', contained in a collection which Riche wrote and entitled *Riche His Farewell to the Militarie profession,* printed in 1581. Riche's point of view is quite different from that of the Italians and, of course, from that of Shakespeare. He has gathered together these stories, according to his own word, for 'the onely delight of the courteous Gentlewomen bothe of England and Ireland'. Riche is, in short, a bourgeois moralist who, as a very moral gentleman, takes a very dim view of the whole game of Love. In his own preface to the volume he speaks of the poisoned cup of error, love being madness, wickedness, etc., etc. But we do not need to labour that point, it will appear later.

Exactly as Riche began his story with comments on love in general so did Shakespeare, but with what a difference: 'If music be the food of love, play on, Give me excess of it . . . ' (It's interesting that Kemble transposed this scene, made it the second scene, and made Viola's appearance, which we find in scene two of modern editions, the first—Sir Tyrone Guthrie did the same thing in his production at this Stratford.) This is, of course, a gross misunderstanding of the play because one needs this first scene to set the tone of the whole play. The problem is, of course, how we are to read this soliloquy of Orsino's. It can be read as 'big' lyric poetry, with high soaring gestures, and so on, or perhaps, more wisely, it can be read with a certain degree of archness which will give the audience an idea of a slight undercutting. As a matter of fact, the whole show is given away by the Duke's final lines, 'So full of shapes is fancy / That it alone is high fantastical,' which are immediately followed by Curio's inquiry, 'Will you go hunt, my lord?'

> DUKE: What, Curio?
> CURIO: The hart.
> DUKE: Why, so I do, the noblest that I have.
> O, when mine eyes did see Olivia first,
> Methought she purged the air of pestilence.
> That instant was I turned into a hart,
> And my desires, like fell and cruel hounds,
> E'er since pursue me.

The reference was obvious to anybody in Shakespeare's audience because even the middle classes would have read Ovid in school. They would have known that the learned Duke was referring to the myth of Actaeon who gazed upon Diana bathing and was punished by being pursued by his own hounds after a vengeful Diana metamorphosed him into a stag.

The same kind of learned reference is found in the ensuing dialogue when Valentine reports about Olivia's reaction to the Duke's suit. The key here is, of course, in the language and the way it is used. Valentine knows the proper words: 'And water once a day her chamber round with high offending brine.' But the Duke does even better:

> O, she that hath a heart of that fine frame
> To pay this debt of love but to a brother,
> How will she love when the rich golden shaft
> Hath killed the flock of all affections else
> That live in her; when liver, brain, and heart,
> These sovereign thrones, are all supplied and
>   filled,
> Her sweet perfections, with one self king.
> A way before me to sweet beds of flow'rs;
> Love-thoughts lie rich when canopied with
>   bow'rs.

In other words, Orsino has read all the right books. The 'rich golden shaft' is, of course, Cupid's arrow. He has two sets of arrows, gold and lead; the gold inspires love, the lead inspires dislike, or to use the Elizabethan word, disdain. Furthermore, it is not just a golden arrow, it is a rich, golden shaft. And Orsino continues to demonstrate his knowledge as well as his imaginative powers. The seats of her affections are thoroughly described, 'liver, brain, and heart'—the 'sovereign thrones'.

Now according to various theories of love, the seat of the affections could be any one of these three parts of the body—usually the heart, though of course the liver and brain figured too. But Orsino has to get them all in just to prove how learned he really is. Here then is a key to the whole play. The use of language, the words, the conceits, the figures, the references, but most important the way in which these are used and the tone in which they are spoken, is exemplified for us quite clearly, I think, by what I have said about Curio's entry, the Ovid reference, Cupid's arrows and the seats of the affections.

We find the same tone in Viola's first appearance in the second scene:

> VIOLA: What country, friends, is this?
> CAPTAIN: This is Illyria, lady.
> VIOLA: And what should I do in Illyria?
> My brother he is in Elysium.

Having consigned her brother to the other world, Viola at once imagines that he is not dead. 'Perchance he is not drowned. What think you, sailors?' One notes the three 'perchances' in three successive lines: 'perchance he is not drowned'; the captain replies that it is 'perchance' she was saved; Viola replies, 'O my poor brother, and so perchance may he be.' This is no accident; this is another perfectly clear clue to an Elizabethan audience, as it should be to us, that games are going on. The game continues with the Captain, who refers to her brother whom he had seen clinging to a mast

> Where like Arion on the dolphin's back,
> I saw him hold acquaintance with the waves
> So long as I could see.

The Captain is learned, he knows his classical mythology too. The story of Arion and the dolphin was well known. This matter of tone is further evidenced by the way in which coincidence now takes over. It just so happens that the Captain was born near where they have been cast up on the seacoast and he knows all about Orsino. So, too, does Viola. 'Orsino! I have heard my father name him. He was a bachelor then.' (One notices Viola's first reference, 'He was a bachelor then.' Her 'fell and cruel' intent is quite clear!)

Following the Captain's reference to Olivia and his description of her, Viola momentarily forgets about the bachelor. Now she is going to serve this lady who has retired from the world and whose sad condition suits with Viola's. However, she immediately changes her mind again and decides to serve Orsino, of course in disguise. She is going to be a eunuch to account for her voice, and the Captain is to introduce her and to secure her a position in Orsino's service. As far as this matter of tone is concerned, the exit line is interesting. Viola says, 'I thank thee. Lead me on.' Well, what a way to end the scene!

Let us follow this whole matter of tone in the main plot. Viola next appears in Act I, Scene iv, where she is going under the assumed masculine name of Cesario. She is very high in the Duke's favour, so high in fact that she is to go a-wooing for him: 'I'll do my best to woo your lady.' But suddenly we are struck over the head by her concluding lines, with their nice use of couplet, in an aside, 'Yet a barful strife! Whoe'er I woo, myself would be his wife.'

In all the typical Elizabethan romances this is the way they fall in love. It is a *coup de foudre*—all of a sudden they are in love. This is the first we have heard of Viola's love. We might have anticipated it, but the way in which it is delivered to us gives us the tone of the play and the tone with which we are expected to approach the love portions of the play.

But it most certainly should be noted that, although we are dealing with a convention, the language of Viola here, and of other characters in similar situations, is not stylized, not a language of conventions. Here we have a plain style, with a simple, bare, statement of fact. Elsewhere when Viola is dealing with other conventions she can use an imaginative language, a poetic language, but here in her declaration of love, she does not.

The next time we meet Viola is toward the end of the first act. Here she has come a-wooing for Orsino, but the scene has begun with our introduction to the lady Olivia whose first line, to us, is 'Take the fool away' (referring, of course, to the Clown, Feste), In the ensuing dialogue with Feste and Malvolio there is no evidence whatsoever of Olivia's great sorrow of which

we have heard so much but which she never displays. Feste does ask her why she mourns, but she makes merely a brief and undeveloped factual response to this. Olivia ticks off Malvolio, she greets the drunken Sir Toby rather easily and her big moment comes, as I have said, when Viola comes a-wooing for Orsino.

This encounter between Viola (Cesario) and Olivia is what I choose to call the 'Big Game' scene, because in this scene both Viola and Olivia know that each is playing a game and each one of them knows that the other knows that respective roles are being performed. Just to make sure that we do not miss the point Viola begins by referring to herself as an actor: 'I would be loath to cast away my speech; for, besides that it is excellently well penned, I have taken great pains to con it.' In other words, she has a set speech which she has ostensibly written herself and which she has learned by heart. The same figure of an actor is carried on in the ensuing dialogue when Olivia inquires, 'Are you a comedian?' 'No', says Viola, 'no, my profound heart; and yet (by the very fangs of malice I swear) I am not that I play.' A few lines later she again refers to her speech, 'Alas, I took great pains to study it, and 'tis poetical.' An actual definition of her role is found when she says, 'I am a messenger.' She subsequently uses, of course, the language of heraldry, as does Olivia. And here the dialogue gives a clear indication of the nature and intention of the scene, when Olivia says, 'Sure you have some hideous matter to deliver, when the courtesy of it is so fearful. Speak your office' (the office of herald). One notes the adjectives 'hideous' and 'fearful'; such matters, of course, are not for everyone's ears, and so Viola makes it quite clear that she will only speak to Olivia: 'It alone concerns your ear. I bring no overture of war, no taxation of homage. I hold the olive in my hand. My words are as full of peace as matter.' These are the phrases, the conventional phrases, of a herald.

Olivia opens the next gambit by inquiring, 'Now, sir, what is your text?', to which Viola replies, 'Most sweet lady—'. Olivia: 'A most comfortable doctrine, and much may be said of it. Where lies your text?' Now the use of this word 'text' is a definite reminder of the language of love, which is part of the amalgamation of the Petrarchan tradition with that of Courtly Love in which the lover becomes an almost religious figure and the lady, of course, a saint. (Near the beginning of his career in *The Two Gentlemen of Verona* Shakespeare uses this religious conceit in connection with love in the dialogue in the very first scene between Valentine and Proteus.) The conceits continue. In answer to the inquiry, 'Where lies your text?' Viola replies, 'In Orsino's bosom.' Olivia asks, 'In his bosom? In what chapter of his bosom?' To which Viola replies, 'To answer by the method, in the first of his heart.' Thus the figure of the 'text' of her message has been related to Orsino's heart. Olivia is playing along and uses the word 'chapter', referring, of course, to 'text'; one is curious as to just what Viola means by the 'method'. Certainly she doesn't mean 'method' in the modern sense of 'mumble and scratch'; she means 'method' in following the conventions. This is the way you play the Game; this is what you ought to say.

Viola's next move is to ask to see Olivia's face, and Viola can be a little bit arch or, to some people's tastes, almost cruel. When she comments on the vision of Olivia's beauty, 'Excellently done, if God did all,' Olivia insists, ''Tis in grain sir; 'twill endure wind and weather.' Says Viola,

> 'Tis beauty truly blent, whose red and white
> Nature's own sweet and cunning hand laid on.
> Lady, you are the cruell'st she alive
> If you will lead these graces to the grave,
> And leave the world no copy.

(We are at once reminded of similar ideas in Shakespeare's *Sonnets* where the friend is urged to marry so that his beauty may be passed on through his children to subsequent generations and thus not be lost to the world.) Well, this is rather old stuff by about 1600, the probable date of *Twelfth Night*. Olivia is not going to have much more of this, and solves the problem of preserving her beauty by saying,

> O, sir, I will not be so hard-hearted. I will give out divers schedules of my beauty. It shall be inventoried, and every particle and utensil labelled to my will: as, item, two lips, indifferent red; item, two grey eyes, with lids to them; item, one neck, one chin, and so forth. Were you sent hither to praise me?

Beauty has thus been reduced to an inventory such as one might find appended to an *inquisition post mortem* or in a testamentary paper such as a will. The conceit that Olivia is here employing punctures, of course, any idealization of love. It completely destroys the traditional description of a beautiful woman derived from Ariosto's description of Alcina, one that begins at the forehead and proceeds down to the eyebrows, the eyes, the nose, the lips, the teeth, the throat and so on.

Olivia thinks rather well of Orsino:

> Yet I suppose him virtuous, know him noble,
> Of great estate, of fresh and stainless youth;
> In voices well divulged, free, learned, and
>   valiant,
> And in dimension and the shape of nature
> A gracious person. But yet I cannot love him.
> He might have took his answer long ago.

At this point Viola remembers her speech and launches into it when Olivia inquires, 'Why, what would you?'

> Make me a willow cabin at your gate
> And call upon my soul within the house;
> Write loyal cantons of contemned love
> And sing them loud even in the dead of night;
> Halloe your name to the reverberate hills
> And make the babbling gossip of the air
> Cry out 'Olivia!' O, you should not rest
> Between the elements of air and earth
> But you should pity me.

This lyric strain is soon ended by Olivia whose only comment is, 'You might do much. What is your parentage?'

> VIOLA: Above my fortunes, yet my state is
>   well.
> I am a gentleman.
> OLIVIA: Get you to your lord.
> I cannot love him. Let him send no more.

Viola does her best to preserve the traditional love strain:

> Love makes his heart of flint that you shall
>   love;
> And let your fervor, like my master's, be
> Placed in contempt. Farewell, fair cruelty.

And with only a few more words than Viola has used to inform us of her love for Orsino, Olivia tells us that she has fallen in love with Viola in her guise of Cesario:

>   Not too fast; soft, soft,
> Unless the master were the man. How now?
> Even so quickly may one catch the plague?
> Methinks I feel this youth's perfections
> With an invisible and subtle stealth
> To creep in at mine eyes.

And, at the conclusion, 'Well, let it be.' This is all we hear. She has fallen love; there is nothing much to be done about it. Well, let it be.

The ring episode concludes this part of our study. Olivia has sent Malvolio in pursuit of Viola-Cesario, telling him that the ring had been left with her by Cesario, presumably as a gift from Orsino. Of course, no such ring has appeared. This is simply a device of Olivia's, and Viola quite understands what's going on when she encounters Malvolio. Here again the language is very important. Viola says:

> She loves me sure; the cunning of her passion
> Invites me in this churlish messenger.
> None of my lord's ring? Why he sent her
>   none.
> I am the man. If it be so, as 'tis,
> Poor lady, she were better love a dream.
> Disguise, I see thou art a wickedness

Wherein the pregnant enemy does much.
How easy is it for the proper false
In women's waxen hearts to set their forms!
Alas, our frailty is the cause, not we,
For such as we are made of, such we be.

There can be no question that in the terms 'pregnant enemy' and 'proper false' we have a reference to Satan, but what is such a serious reference doing in such a context? Well, very simply in my view it emphasizes the whole artificiality of the episode that we have witnessed—the game that Olivia and Viola have been playing with one another. And this artificiality is, of course, emphasized by the couplet with which Viola ends the scene:

O Time, thou must untangle this, not I;
It is too hard a knot for me t' untie.

Again the couplet rhyme, again the bald statement of fact—nothing much can be done about it, time just has to work it out somehow or other. This final couplet, like Viola's couplet announcing her love for Orsino, is in the best tradition of the romances, exactly the sort of thing that we find in *Two Gentlemen of Verona* over and over again. The point is that we are laughing at, or are amused by, the whole business. The ultimate absurdity in this play is found in the denouement. The Duke learning of Olivia's love, is ready to kill Cesario. He breaks forth:

O thou dissembling cub, what wilt thou be
When time hath sowed a grizzle on thy case?
Or will not else thy craft so quickly grow
That thine own trip shall be thine overthrow?
Farewell, and take her; but direct thy feet
Where thou and I, henceforth, may never
    meet.

About a hundred lines later, after Sebastian has appeared and the mystery of the identity has cleared up, the Duke is very anxious to marry Viola:

Give me thy hand,
And let me see thee in thy woman's weeds.

Here again a declaration of love is couched in very, very simple language, lacking ornamentation or imagery of any sort: 'Let me see thee in thy woman's weeds.' This is no 'big' confession of love, no 'big lyric love stuff' whatsoever. In fact, the nearest we come to any traditional language is found when the Duke says,

Here is my hand; you shall from this time be
Your master's mistress.

We may now, I think, briefly summarize the main plot. We have been operating in a world of artificiality. The whole question of reality has been raised by Viola. The business of falling in love is completely artificial. The switch of the Duke is completely artificial. The characters themselves are not, in the accepted sense of the word, rounded, three-dimensional characters. They are, in essence, flat, but this does not mean that Shakespeare has lacked dramatic skill—far from it. He is using these characters for his own purposes. He is playing games with us, and, by playing games, he convinces us of the reality of the characters. Of course we like Viola. She is a very sweet girl, but there is no depth to the character, no dimension to it beyond the purely theatrical. In other words, we are dealing here with theatrical truth as opposed to the truth of the printed page. The illusion in the theatre will hold us, will captivate us, and, in the theatre, no more is needed for this artificial love. It's exactly the sort of thing that Noel Coward does to perfection. In other words, I am suggesting that we treat the play as a play and examine it on the basis of its theatrical premises. Here these premises are the artificial world of lovers as exemplified over and over again in the world of Queen Elizabeth's court where such games were played, such lines spoken, such attitudes taken; and everything turns out all right, of course.

As we turn to the subplot we find ourselves in a very real world indeed. Sir Toby and Sir Andrew are drunk every night. Toby is, of course, urging Sir Andrew on, ostensibly to woo Olivia, but mainly because Sir Andrew has three thousand ducats a year. The hypocrisy of Toby's attitude toward Sir Andrew and his possible wooing of Olivia is found in his description of Sir Andrew: 'He's as tall a man as any's in Illyria'—'tall' suggesting a 'fine, upstanding noble fellow'. Furthermore, according to Toby, Sir Andrew has other gifts: 'He plays o' th' viol-de-gamboys, and speaks three or four languages word for word without book, and hath all the good gifts of nature.' But immediately Sir Andrew appears his stupidity is apparent in his misunderstanding of Toby's simple injunction, 'Accost', which he takes to be Maria's name. As far as being a musician or having other talents, as far as languages go, Sir Andrew denies them specifically in his own words. For example, he says, 'Methinks sometimes I have no more with than a Christian or an ordinary man has. But I am a great eater of beef, and I believe that does harm to my wit.' A few lines later he demonstrates his complete ignorance of foreign languages when Toby inquires, 'Pourquoi, my dear knight?' 'What is pourquoi?' asks Andrew, 'Do, or not do? I would I had bestowed that time in the tongues that I have in fencing, dancing, and bear-baiting. O, had I but followed the arts!' Sir Toby's original description of Andrew in terms of the courtier, the gentleman, is completely invalidated by Andrew himself. He is rather the exact opposite of the ideal courtier, the ideal courtly gentleman. When describing his abilities in dancing, in response to Toby's inquiry, 'What is thy excellence in a galliard, knight?' 'Faith, I can cut a caper,' says Sir

Viola, Olivia, and Malvolio (Cheri Lunghi, Kate Nicholls, and John Woodvine) in the Royal Shakespeare Company's 1979 production of Twelfth Night.

Malvolio is the enemy of joy, of cakes and ale, of pleasure in life. This has tempted some to press, I think, just a bit too hard on Malvolio as a portrait of a Puritan. No, no! Olivia is much more accurate when, earlier in the play, she has told Malvolio, 'You are sick of self-love.'

And it is this very state of mind, this being sick of self-love, that motivates the action of the subplot. Here we note that in contrast with the main plot we do have specific motivation. Things happen now for a reason. The letter is planted in order to gull and trick Malvolio. The characters involved are in a sense lowlife and quite realistic. Thus we have the artificial world of Orsino and Olivia and Viola, in contrast with the world in the servants' hall. In both plots we see foolish love, but in the artificial world everything works out all right. We need a bit of machinery to get Antonio out of trouble. And, obviously, there has got to be some machinery to get Malvolio out of gaol. But it cannot be too strongly emphasized that there is no machinery of this nature in the main plot; there we have simply the *deus ex machina* appearance of Sebastian to resolve the question of identity and all is well.

We must not leave the play without some mention of the note of sadness which has received so much comment. Reviewing a recent performance at Stratford-upon-Avon, Harold Hobson of the *Sunday Times* described *Twelfth Night* as Shakespeare's most melancholy play and also as his most wittily written.

The melancholy is found exclusively in Feste's songs, in the first:

> O mistress mine, where are you roaming?
> O, stay and hear! your true-love's coming,
> 　　That can sing both high and low.
> Trip no further, pretty sweeting;
> 　　Journeys end in lovers meeting,
> 　　Every wise man's son doth know;

and the conclusion of the second verse,

> Then come kiss me, sweet and twenty,
> 　　Youth's a stuff will not endure.

To suit the Duke's melancholy of love Feste produces another famous song:

> 　Come away, come away, death,
> And in sad cypress let me be laid.

And, of course, perhaps the most famous song is that which concludes the play when Feste sings:

> When that I was and a little tiny boy,
> 　With hey, ho, the wind and the rain,

Andrew; and he goes on, 'And I think I have the back-trick simply as strong as any man in Illyria.' Toby hits back very, very hard: 'Wherefore are these things hid?' These things are, of course, not assets; they are not recommendations for Sir Andrew as a potential suitor for the fair Olivia—far from it.

If Sir Andrew is a caricature, so too is Malvolio. But Malvolio has the further distinction of being rather unpleasant. We see this unpleasantness quite clearly in the later scene when Sir Toby and the others are having a good time drinking and singing and eating:

> My masters, are you mad? Or what are you? Have you no wit, manners, nor honesty, but to gabble like tinkers at this time of night? Do ye make an alehouse of my lady's house, that ye squeak out your coziers' catches without any mitigation or remorse of voice? Is there no respect of place, persons, nor time in you?

Here Malvolio's attitude is well described in Toby's line, 'Dost thou think, because thou art virtuous, there shall be no more cakes and ale?'

A foolish thing was but a toy,
　For the rain it raineth every day.

I think we should, perhaps, temper our attitude towards this note of sadness with reference to the title of the play, *Twelfth Night or What You Will*. Twelfth Night, the Feast of the Epiphany, marked the end of the Christmas festivities and, as a general rule, there was no more playing of plays at Court until the Sunday before the beginning of Lent or on Shrove Tuesday itself. Thus very simply Twelfth Night marks the end of the festivities of the Christmas season. In that sense it is not too difficult to understand that final stanza of the last song.

　A great while ago the world begun,
　　With hey, ho, the wind and the rain;
　But that's all one, our play is done,
　　And we'll strive to please you every day.

The fun and the games are over and we will have one last fling, a sort of carnival time before Lent—but that is still some weeks away. In other words, I don't think we need to be any more seriously concerned about it than I have indicated. The title—The End of the Christmas Revelry. Yes, yes. It's all over—the fun and games are ended. And so Adieu.

Notes

[1] 3.2.20-4. Quotations from Shakespeare are from *The Riverside Shakespeare*, ed. G. Blakemore Evans *et al.* (Boston, 1974).

[2] Joseph H. Summers, 'The Masks of *Twelfth Night*', *The University Review*, 22 (1955), 26.

[3] '"As You Like It" and "Twelfth Night": Shakespeare's Sense of an Ending', in *Shakespearian Comedy*, ed. Malcolm Bradbury and David Palmer, Straford-upon-Avon Studies, 14 (1972), p. 175.

[4] It is relevant to recall that the festival of Twelfth Night, in addition to its popular associations with the holiday release of Misrule festivities, was also a religious celebration of the Feast of Epiphany.

[5] Discussing the use of identical twins in *The Comedy of Errors*, Northrop Frye argues: ' . . . I feel that one reason for the use of two sets of twins in this play is that identical twins are not really identical (the same person) but merely similar, and when they meet they are delivered, in comic fashion, from the fear of the loss of identity, the primitive horror of the döppelganger which is an element in nearly all forms of insanity, something of which they feel as long as they are being mistaken for each other.' (*A Natural Perspective* (New York, 1965), p. 78)

[6] *A Tale of a Tub, With Other Early Works, 1696-1707,* ed. Herbert Davis (Oxford, 1957), p. 140.

Karin S. Coddon (essay date 1993)

SOURCE: "Slander in and Allow'd Fool: *Twelfth Night*'s Crisis of the Aristocracy," in *Studies in English Literature, 1500-1900,* Vol. 33, No. 2, Spring, 1993, pp. 309-25.

[*In this essay, Coddon claims that the closing of* Twelfth Night *emphasizes disorder over natural order, seeming "less than a wholesale endorsement of the privileges of rank and hierarchy."*]

In *Twelfth Night* demarcations between male and female, master and servant, libertine and moralist come into festive—and not so festive—collision. Typical readings of the play have focused on its misrule and topsy-turvy as serving ultimately to reaffirm the dominant, aristocratic values against which the ostensible "puritan," Malvolio, stands as a scorn-worthy scapegoat.[1] By this reasoning, the play may be seen as a comedy in which insubordination, cross-dressing, and unruly "license" are, in the final analysis, contained in the rites of unmasking and marriage. The play's notably troubled closure—Malvolio's vow of revenge, the Captain's imprisonment, and Feste's strangely inappropriate closing dirge—has been given its due only insofar as it contributes to the comedy's "dark outline."[2] But the problem of closure also aligns *Twelfth Night* with *Hamlet* and *King Lear,* plays in which the apparent "restoration of order" is countered by the excesses of precedent *dis*order that have been repressed, perhaps, but not entirely effaced.[3] If in *Twelfth Night* the aristocratic order is ostensibly reasserted in the pairings of Orsino/Viola and Oliva/Sebastian, the refusal of the play's closing to recuperate two of its most disorderly subjects—Malvolio and Feste—suggests rather less than a wholesale endorsement of the privileges of rank and hierarchy. For by mockingly disclosing the mutability and contingency of social rank, *Twelfth Night* demystifies one of Elizabethan authority's central political fictions. In the process, the play tests the precarious limits of theatrical "license," as festivity itself exceeds the containment of mere "fantasy inversion" to take on a markedly historical, even contestatory dimension.

Elizabethan and Jacobean culture is commonly characterized by an overwhelming obsession with "good order and obedience." Copious propaganda exhorted a minutely classified, divinely ordained social hierarchy:

　Everye degre of people in theyr vocation, callyng, and office hath appointed to them, theyr duty and ordre. Some are in hyghe degree, some in lowe, some kynges and prynces, some inferiors and subjectes, priestes, and layemenne, Maysters and Servauntes, Fathers and chyldren, husbandes and wives, riche and poore, and everyone hath nede of other: so that in all thynges is to be lauded and praysed the goodly order of god, wythoute the whiche, no house, no citie, no commonwealth can continue and indure or laste.[4]

Yet Keith Wrightson has suggested that the promulgators of this rigidly organic paradigm "knew very well that it was an ideal, an aspiration," a response to increased opportunities for social mobility rather than a reflection of universal belief or practice.[5] As Wrightson has demonstrated, while the foremost status of the titular nobility remained a constant, there was notable slippage throughout the entire social hierarchy between supposedly rigid "degrees of people":

gentle status itself could be achieved as well as inherited; by obtaining a university degree, by appointment to governmental or military office, or by any man who "can live without manuell labour, and thereto is able and will beare the port, charge and countenance of a gentleman."[6]

The Elizabethan propensity for classifying and even legislating (e.g., via sumptuary laws) a fixed and self-evident social hierarchy was belied by actual social practice; under James the First, rampant title-mongering would further erode the primacy of blood and birth as sole determinants of social rank.[7] Jacobean indiscretions aside, the official propaganda chiefly served the interests of the uppermost social echelon, not the least of which was a crown intent on absolutism but without a standing militia to enforce it. For the primacy of blood, after all, lay at the core of the divine-right ideology so dear to both Elizabeth and James.

The theater, of course, already occupied the most equivocal of situations toward the aristocratic and nonaristocratic, even antiaristocratic factions. As Michael Bristol has remarked, "The social position of the players and of their work was based on two contradictory presuppositions—that they were engaged in a business or industry, and that they were engaged in 'service' to their aristocratic patrons."[8] Government licensing and courtly patronage do not necessarily imply the theater's ideological alignment with the court, especially given the apparent, remarkable social heterogeneity of Elizabethan and Jacobean audiences. Comedy in particular tended to foster heterogeneity, as Robert Weimann has noted:

In matters of social custom and dramatic taste there was as yet no clear division between the rural *plebs* and the London middle classes. This meant that there was little difference between the middle class and the plebeian reception of the Morris dance, the jig, clowning, and the like. The middle strata of these

craftsmen and the more wealthy dealers and retailers enjoyed these entertainments just as did the lower strata, the laborer, carriers, servants.[9]

Similarly, the very nature of theatrical representation defied "official" positions on rank and degree, as common players personated princes, male actors "boyed" females.[10] If Malvolio, like such antitheatrical polemicists as Phillip Stubbes, disapproves of festive misrule in principle, the government's regulation of the theater testifies to its own anxieties about the drama's potential to produce (and reproduce) fictions contesting Tudor and Stuart official ideologies. The theater, like the "all-licens'd fool," was to an extent authorized to enact a degree of insubordination, apparently on the thought that it would thus function as a sort of safety valve for discontent that might otherwise seek less indirect forms of expression. But as Natalie Zemon Davis has argued, festive misrule need not be conceived as either wholly contestatory or wholly conservative:

It is an exaggeration to view the carnival and Misrule as merely a "safety valve," as merely a primitive, prepolitical form of recreation. . . . the structure of the carnival form can evolve so that it can act both to reinforce order and to suggest alternatives to that existing order.[11]

My suggestion, then, is that *Twelfth Night* pointedly reinforces neither aristocratic nor anticourt values; rather, by exploding the kinds of social classifications propounded by contemporary theorists into a multiplicity of slippery, contingent positions, the play subversively confounds holiday and history, festive "license" and contestation. Officially controlled by the government and increasingly subjected to virulent antitheatrical attacks, the theater was positioned as much in a site of limited resistance as of limited allegiance. The opening—and closing—resistance of Feste the clown to narrative recuperation suggests not only the possibility of theatrical *evasion* of order, but also a material if limited autonomy from the institutional structures seemingly acknowledged in the reversions of the young nobles and the overreaching Malvolio to their proper places and degrees.

Lawrence Stone's argument for a "crisis of the aristocracy" as a major precipitant of the 1642 revolution has been roundly criticized by a number of social historians.[12] It has been suggested, for example, that radical social change in seventeenth-century England was due more to the emergence of landed and professional "middle classes" than to a decline in the aristocracy's prestige.[13] Yet without asserting a direct causality between aristocratic excesses and the development of a revolutionary movement, it seems clear that the nobility's profligate expenditures and conspicuous consumption served to weaken the aristocracy both economically and in terms of popular perception.[14] The latter is evidenced in mocking gallows derision through-out Jacobean tragedy; Shakespeare's *Lear* and Tourneur's *Revenger's Tragedy* offer bitter critiques of courtly extravagances. Even so worldly a blade as John Harington remarked upon the libertinism of the Jacobean court, where

> those, whom I never coud get to taste good liquor, now follow the fashion and wallow in beastly delights. The Ladies abandon their sobriety, and are seen to roll about in intoxication. . . . I do often say (but not aloud) that the Danes have again conquered the Britains, for I see no man, or woman either, that can now command himself or herself.[15]

But the court of James Stuart hardly introduced excess into the early modern English aristocracy. *Twelfth Night,* with its elaborate imagery of appetite and satiety, seems to draw upon contemporary notions, by no means hyperbolic, about the consumption habits of an aristocratic household. In fact, the supposed "morality of indulgence" John Hollander attributes to aristocratic excess and satiety in the play becomes a bit incongruous in light of Stone's catalogues of noble gluttony.[16] According to Stone, even conservative, prudent Lord Burghley indulged in the extravagant gormandizing of aristocratic "festive" entertainments:

> The £363 [Burghley] spent on a feast to the French Commissioners in 1581 might perhaps be explained on grounds of public policy. But what are we to make of the £629 spent in three days' junketing at the marriage of his daughter a year later? At this vast party there were consumed, among other things, about 1,000 gallons of wine, 6 veals, 26 deer, 15 pigs, 14 sheep, 16 lambs, 4 kids, 6 hares, 36 swans, 2 storks, 41 turkeys, over 370 poultry, 49 curlews, 135 mallards, 354 teals, 1,049 plovers, 124 knotts, 280 stints, 109 pheasants, 277 partridges, 615 cocks, 485 snipe, 840 larks, 21 gulls, 71 rabbits, 21 pigeons, and 2 sturgeons.[17]

If music be the food of love, play on, indeed; Orsino's elaborate tropes of appetite and satiety might well have prompted a subversive laughter, given the mind-boggling extravagances of the Elizabethan aristocrat's table. On the other hand, certain factions were less likely to find such gluttony a laughing matter in the inflation- and famine-plagued 1590s. For the commoner and particularly the poor, the 1590s were years of economic hardship and deprivation. Four consecutive failed harvests between 1594 and 1597 contributed to rampant food shortages;[18] authorities greatly feared the possibility of large-scale social disorder, and in fact, a number of food riots occurred in both the countryside and London.[19] As Buchanan Sharp has shown, the privileged were frequently the focus of the rioters' deepest resentments: "The reported poor of Somerset who in 1596 seized a load of cheese were reported to be animated by a hatred of all gentlemen because they

believed 'that the rich men had gotten all into their hands, and will starve the poor.'"[20] Civil discontent over food shortages bore the threat of an attack on the entire social order, as the Privy Council itself recognized.[21] Indeed, in the aftermath of the abortive Oxfordshire Rising of 1596, Attorney-General Coke insisted that "[t]he real purpose of Bartholomew Stere [one of the Oxfordshire conspirators] was 'to kill the gentlemen of that countrie and to take the spoile of them, affirming that the commons, long sithens in Spaine did rise and kill all the gentlemen in Spain and sithens that time have lyved merrily there.'"[22] Thus historicized, *Twelfth Night's* mockery of noble excesses may be seen as homologous to the rather less playful sentiments of another Oxfordshire conspirator, James Bradshaw, who asked "Whether there were not certaine good fellowes in Witney that wold ryse & knock down the gentlemen & riche men that take in the comons, and made corne so deare?"[23]

It is worth noting, however, that the play's lone vocal critic of profligacy, Malvolio, is held up to even greater derision than the extravagant nobles. As Elliot Krieger has noted, Malvolio "actually threatens the social order much less than he seems to. . . . [H]e has the greatest respect for all the accoutrements of aristocratic rank."[24] Malvolio, "sick of self-love,"[25] covets the very privilege he seems to criticize, as is borne out by his desire to transcend his social rank by marrying Olivia. Far from a radical social critic, Malvolio is more reminiscent of the antitheatricalists[26] who lambasted playgoers for their own variety of moral gluttony. Phillip Stubbes claimed that playgoers "are alwaies eating, & neuer satisfied; euer seeing, & neuer contented; continualie hearing, & neuer wearied; they are greedie of wickednes."[27] That Malvolio's threat of revenge troubles the play's comic ending suggests less an endorsement of the legitimacy of his grievances than an ironic acknowledgment of the strident persistence of antitheatricalism.

Orsino's opening trope, then—

> If music be the food of love, play on,
> Give me excess of it, that, surfeiting,
> The appetite may sicken, and so die
>
> (I.i.1-3)

—lends to his lyric self-indulgence a material marker of social privilege and its excesses. It serves to yoke together the amorous appetites of the relatively decorous Orsino and the more grotesque, "carnivalesque" appetites of Sir Toby Belch.[28] For Sir Toby is, of course, the play's most comical—and most pointed—travesty of aristocratic self-indulgence. His revels are informed by the popular tradition of "seasonal misrule," a tradition already suspect for its violations of class and gender boundaries.[29] Sir Toby cavorts not only with his fellow titled tosspot Sir Andrew Aguecheek, but also with his social inferiors—Feste, Fabian, and Maria, the last of whom he marries.[30] The deflation of Malvolio's ambition to wed into the aristocracy is countered by the marriage of Olivia's uncle to her serving-woman. The play's fantasy transgressions typical of festive misrule—Olivia's infatuation with a disguised woman, "Cesario's" with Orsino—are ostensibly contained as gender stability is restored. Like Malvolio's vow of revenge, however, Sir Toby's offstage marriage to Maria is a reminder of the instability of rank and order that persists outside the world of the play. Far from being merely a temporary and cathartic release from social order, festivity intervenes to alter that order. Sir Toby's marriage to Maria makes explicit the identification of festivity with social fluidity, despite the play's apparent recuperation of transvestism and homoerotic desire.

But Sir Toby's marriage is not the play's sole—or most significant—offstage social transgression. Feste's first appearance in I.v. aligns the clown with insubordination, with the equivocal boundaries between licensed and unlicensed foolery.

> MARIA. Nay, either tell me where thou hast
> been, or I will open my lips so wide as a
> bristle may enter, in way of thy excuse: my
> lady will hang thee for thy absence.
>
> CLOWN. Let her hang me: he that is well
> hanged in this world needs to fear no
> colours.
>
>   (I.v.1-5)

As has been frequently noted, Feste's entrance is marked by an emphatic lacuna;[31] his introduction is colored not only by the unauthorized absence from Olivia's household, but also by his defiant resistance ("Let her hang me") to Maria's interrogations about his whereabouts, even under the threat of hanging or unemployment. The clown's unlicensed insubordination lies less in the nature of his absence than in his refusal to represent a "subjectivity" to his interrogator. This is not to claim that Feste's uncooperation is akin to Hamlet's "I have that within which passes show" (I.ii.85), but rather, that theatricality constitutes a site of evasion from subjectification, i.e., the strategies of surveillance and interrogation that comprise, as Michel Foucault has written, "a ritual of discourse in which the speaking subject is also the subject of the statement . . . a ritual that unfolds within a power relationship."[32] An actor does not speak a "self"—he impersonates; his social identity is not metaphysical but infinitely manipulable, as was recognized, however disapprovingly, by the theater's critics. For

> unlike the consecrated minister of God's word or the political orator, an actor is a man whose public utterance does not represent what he feels or thinks, although it is said with full conviction and the sound of authority. An actor is not just someone whose

speech is "dissembling": the deeper problem is that he is most valued for his ability to dissemble convincingly.[33]

That virtually the first thing we learn about Feste is that he has been somewhere offstage, outside of representation and vigilance, suggests not a Derridean aporia so much as the theater's potential to exceed its carefully, officially delimited boundaries, to collapse the distinction between "festivity" and history. As Bristol notes of Feste, "[the clown] traverses the boundary between a represented world and the here-and-now world he shares with the audience."[34] Earlier clowns like Richard Tarlton commonly interacted directly with the audience as well as with other characters in the play;[35] though Feste embodies the sophistication and intellectualism of the later Elizabethan jester, he is as much of the world outside the play as of the fictive world within.

Despite its comic word-play, Feste's exchange with Maria has somewhat grave undertones. The threat of hanging seems hyperbolic, though as Maria notes, "to be turned away" would be "as good as a hanging" (I.v.18); a fool without a post would be "voiceless," indeed. The refusal of interrogation risks a coerced expulsion from discourse entirely. The Elizabethan theater, like Feste testing the limits of licensed foolery, was subject to an authority that could—and occasionally, did—impose silence. But also like Feste, the theater deftly confounds the boundaries between festive misrule and unruly license. Not the least of the Elizabethan clown's functions is to mediate between audience and play; with Feste, the mediation takes on, however playfully, a dimension of conspiracy.

Upon Olivia's appearance, the clown launches into what is ostensibly the licensed insubordination allowed his function by his patroness and superior. Feste's witty impertinence reestablishes his "allow'd," public role as jester. Though he effectively proves her a fool, Olivia concedes, "There is no slander in an allow'd fool" (I.v.94). Yet because Feste's cheeky demonstration of his mistress's foolishness has been preceded by his *un*licensed absence, Olivia's authority here seems superfluous, even specious, as though Feste is but humoring her by playing the prescribed role of servant. Typically mistrustful of festive insubordination and frivolity, Malvolio, rather than Olivia, takes offense at the fool's impudence. But Olivia's rejoinder—"O, you are sick of self-love, Malvolio, and taste with a distempered appetite" (lines 90-91)—tacitly accuses the steward of the very ills he claims to disdain. For Malvolio's "self-love" is pointedly not the absence of appetite but merely a "distempered" one. That Olivia's reprimand of Malvolio is shortly followed by the reappearance of Sir Toby "in the third degree of drink" (line 136) marks a less festive variety of inversion: Malvolio is not so much the antithesis of Sir Toby as he is the reversed mirror-image.

Feste, then, is far more than merely the "spirit of festivity"; he is also an ironic commentator upon the discrepancies between aristocratic myth and the material circumstances that contradict it. The clown's consistent gulling of his social superiors has been frequently noted,[36] but it is a mistake to view Feste as simply a protocapitalist "service professional."[37] The emphasis on payment serves to remind the spectator that this is not the mythic, feudal world of loyal, ideal service, "The constant service of the antique world, / When service sweat for duty, not for meed!"[38] but rather one in which festivity itself is purchased at the same outlandishly inflated rate that swells Orsino's plaints of love or Olivia's grandiloquent self-denial. The contrast between the bawdy knights' boisterous entreaties for a song and the melancholy "O Mistress Mine" with which the clown responds points up the distance between mythic *carpe diem* romance and the almost indiscriminate, self-indulgent appetites that govern not only Sir Toby and Sir Andrew but Orsino and Malvolio as well. Hollander's suggestion that the song is a reflection upon the various lovers' romantic foibles[39] does not take into account either the inappropriate audience or the closing allusion to an uncertain future outside of the festive present: "Youth's a stuff will not endure" (II.iii.53). *Twelfth Night*'s nominal situation in a particular, finite time not only evokes traditional, popular festivity organized around the church calendar;[40] it also foregrounds the play's precarious temporality. The Epiphany functions as a temporal trope much as the Forest of Arden, in *As You Like It,* functions as a spatial one: the time of carefree, aristocratic festivity is gone, and between nostalgia for an idealized past and uncertainty about the historical time beyond holiday is the tenuous and hence ironic celebration of the present.

As Feste willingly joins Sir Toby and Sir Andrew for a merry round, he playfully reminds the latter that his own cooperation in the song entails a transgression of rank: "'Hold thy peace, then, knave,' knight? I shall be constrained in it to call thee knave, knight" (II.iii.66-67); Feste subtly remarks upon the knights' complicity in the deconstruction of social order. Akin to government licensing of the theater, the nobles' authorization of "benign" festive subversion enables the terms by which institutional authority may be mocked and questioned. The ostensibly vast social distinction between gentleman and common player is elided. Just as Feste has previously "proven" Olivia a fool, his observation that Sir Toby is "in admirable fooling" (line 81) places his social superior in the role of servant, jester, *player*— the very kind of class "mingle-mangle" so mistrusted by the antitheatricalists.[41] Interestingly, it is Malvolio who scolds the revelers for their violation of good order:

> My masters, are you mad? Or what are you? Have you no wit, manners, nor honesty, but to gabble like tinkers at this time of night? Do ye make an ale-house of my lady's house, that ye squeak out your coziers' catches without any mitigation or remorse of voice? Is there no respect of place, persons, nor time in you?
>
> (II.iii.84-93)

Malvolio objects to the revelry explicitly on grounds of its disorderliness of "place, persons, [and] time"; once more, the critic of aristocratic "uncivil rule" is the play's most vehement proponent of a stable, orderly social structure. But Sir Toby, thus chided for transgression of his degree, picks up the gauntlet with a peculiarly bitter rejoinder to Malvolio: "Art any more than a steward? Dost thou think because thou art virtuous, there shall be no more cakes and ale?" (lines 113-15). The question, of course, is rhetorical, though like Malvolio's threat of revenge, in retrospect rather eerily prophetic.

There is some suggestion, once again, that the festive interval—as *interval*—itself is already anachronistic, that the revels have, if not ended, become embedded in historical rather than holiday matters. Orsino, in II.iv once more caught in the throes of a language of amorous appetite, requests "that old and antic song" (line 3) performed the night before. Curio's response to this is, interestingly, the first and only time Olivia's clown is named, and, additionally, given a history: he is "a fool that the Lady Olivia's father took much delight in" (lines 11-12). The introduction of Feste's name in this context seems appropriate; for the festivity with which Orsino identifies him is indeed a thing of the past, when festive rites were bound up in a popular, material marking of time:

> Mark it, Cesario, it [the song] is old and
>   plain;
> The spinsters and the knitters in the sun,
> And the free maids that weave their thread
>   with bones,
> Do use to chant it: it is silly sooth,
> And dallies with the innocence of love,
> Like the old age.
>
> (lines 43-48)

Given Orsino's own penchant for florid, hyperbolic love talk, his paean to the "silly" song is noteworthy. And yet the song, when it does come, seems less a rustic lay than a pensive Elizabethan lyric telling of a lady's disdain and a "dying," unrequited lover's lonely fate. Like "O Mistress Mine," "Come Away, Death" is touched by Petrarchan conventions of female resistance and frustrated male desire. The song's melancholy, along with its identification with an idealized past, contrasts strikingly with the language of self-indulgent appetite and desire that characterizes its context. The sad song is unsuited to its setting, but not solely because of the play's comic aims. It is a performance whose signification has been rendered specious by the play's own ironization of desire; the song, like the one preceding, is merely the "food of love" for the nobleman's appetite. Indeed, Orsino follows with two more elaborate speeches of quantification and appetite to "Cesario," in blatant contradiction of his prior homage to the simplicity of the old love song. The disembodied metaphoric trappings of petrarchan love become in *Twelfth Night* parodically reconstituted as crassly material, even gluttonous.

Similarly, Feste's refusal, to Viola, of the "licensed" title of fool, and his claim that he is, rather, Olivia's "corrupter of words" (III.i.36-37), acknowledge the degeneration of language, the discrepancy between the anachronistic idiom of lyric love and the actual amorous discourses marked by consumption and excess. As Terry Eagleton has observed, "What has discredited language in Feste's view is commerce, the breaking of bonds. . . . Bonds—written commercial contracts—have rendered signs valueless, since too often they are not backed up by the physical actions they promise."[42] Feste is Olivia's "corrupter of words," but after the fact: language is no more innocent than love. Feste's corruption of language, however, is of a different and more equivocal variety than Orsino's or Malvolio's, for he consistently takes the words of his noble superiors—much as he does their money—and destabilizes them, exposing the semiotic and political slipperiness of ostensibly stable categories and values. Thus he responds to Viola's characterization of him as "a merry fellow, [who] car'st for nothing" (III.i.26-27) with what may seem like an inexplicably surly rejoinder: "Not so, sir, I do care for something; but in my conscience, sir, I do not care for you" (lines 27-28). Like Orsino before her, Viola attempts to constitute Feste as merely the embodiment of the mirthful court jester, the abstract spirit of song and festivity. But the clown, as in his initial exchange with Maria, at once resists the fixity of his prescribed role and pointedly refuses to invest "corrupt" words with any kind of truth value. What that "something" may be for which he cares is less significant than the refusal of explication.

When Feste accepts Viola's money, he also accepts his function as servant, but not without a saucy allusion to her complicity in the crassest variety of commerce: "I would play Lord Pandarus of Phrygia, sir, to bring a Cressida to this Troilus" (III.i.51). Pandarus, of course, evokes the activity for which Orsino has engaged "Cesario"; like Feste, Viola is playing the role of servant, and her actual social superiority is undercut by the clown's suggestion of a kind of material equivalence between them. Viola apparently recognizes her error in labeling Feste merely a merry madcap, and characterizes him as, like herself, one playing a part:

This fellow is wise enough to play the fool,
And to do that well, craves a kind of wit:
He must observe their mood on whom he
    jests,

The quality of persons, and the time,
And like the haggard, check at every feather
That comes before his eye. This is a practice
As full of labour as a wise man's art.
For folly that he wisely shows is fit;
But wise men, folly-fall'n, quite taint their
    wit.

                                        (lines 60-68)

This speech is commonly taken as the playwright's homage to the art of theater, or even as a tribute to Robert Armin.[43] But while it is an oversimplification to read Feste's function as strictly metadramatic, Viola's words indeed testify to the "labour" and intellection of playing, as if to counter antitheatricalist accusations of wantonness and idleness. Indeed, one of Armin's own *Quips upon Questions* articulates a similar theme:

True it is, he plays the Foole indeed;
But in the Play he plays it as he must:
Yet when the play is ended, then his speed
Is better than the pleasure of thy trust.
For he shall have what thou that time has
    spent,
Playing the foole, thy folly to consent.

He plays the Wise man then, and not the
    Foole,
That wisely for his lyving so can do;
So doth the Carpenter with his sharpe tool,
Cut his owne finger oft, yet lives by't to.
He is a foole to cut his limbe say I
But not so with his toole to live thereby.[44]

The notion of fooling as professional, intellectual labor at once responds to and significantly revises such suspicions as those of Stephen Gosson regarding the actor's equivocal identity: "There is more in [Players] than we perceive."[45] The comic actor is thus transformed from diabolically Protean hypocrite to expertly skilled craftsman, a keen observer of social practices shrewd enough to play fool "for his lyving."

In fact, Feste corrupts words chiefly to expose the corruption of others by them, and for them. To this extent, the clown embodies the instructive model of comedy extolled by Thomas Heywood in *An Apologie for Actors* (1612):

And what is then the subject of this harmlesse mirth?
either in the shape of a clowne to shew others their
slovenly and unhandsome behaviour, that they may
reforme that simplicity in themselves which others
make their sport, lest they happen to become the
like subject of generall scorne to an auditory; else
it intreates of love, deriding foolish inamorates, who
spend their ages, their spirits, nay themselves, in
the servile and ridiculous imployments of their
mistresses.[46]

In IV.ii, wherein "Sir Topas" interrogates Malvolio, Feste both exemplifies and parodies the didactic dimension of foolery. Again, the scene owes a debt to the festive tradition of "misrule," in which, as Stuart Clark has noted, typically "clerical parodies of divine service substituted the profane for the sacred, and low for high office."[47] But Feste is doing more than mocking Malvolio with his travesty of a Puritan curate. With his emphatic, ludicrous "testing" of Malvolio's sanity, Feste parodies the discourse of interrogation he has himself consistently eluded. The clown uses the guise of authority to mock authority, a strategy manifest not only in "Sir Topas's" worrying of the "madman," but also in Feste's assumption of the voices of both the curate and the servant: "Maintain no words with him, good fellow!—Who, I, sir? not I, sir! God buy you, good Sir Topas!—Marry, amen!—I will, sir, I will" (lines 102-105). As Maria has pointed out, the clown's costume is superfluous (lines 64-65); language itself enables dissemblance. In theater, subjectivity is no more than a habit that aptly is put on. Feste's trick question to Malvolio—"But tell me true, are you not mad indeed, or do you but counterfeit?" (lines 117-18)—mockingly discloses the equivocal nature of playing itself. Neither madness nor sanity has any ontological status in the realm of theatricality, for the "counterfeit" is at once as true—and as false—as the thing itself. Stable distinctions between licensed and unlicensed foolery then, are radically problematic, Heywood's "harmlesse mirth" perhaps not as socially benign as the term suggests.

Not surprisingly, the play's final act, with its various unmaskings and revelations, yet falls short of the thorough restoration of order that the plot and genre seem to dictate. V.i begins with an almost uncanny echo of I.v, as Fabian beseeches the clown to show him Malvolio's letter, only to be enigmatically refused (lines 1-6). Feste's resistance to Fabian's entreaty is narratively inexplicable, since the latter has been in on the trick all along and the former at least attempts to read the letter publicly. Feste's refusal appears motivated simply by a characteristic deflection of interrogation for its own sake. But it is also in the last act that Feste is silenced, as Olivia objects to his "mad" reading of Malvolio's letter, despite his protests, and orders Fabian to deliver the missive instead. It is a significant moment, not the least because Olivia, the clown's employer, here disdains his foolery on grounds that its theatricality is an apparent obstacle to discerning the truth. This momentary suppression of theatricality serves to refigure—temporarily, at any rate—the intractable lines of social hierarchy heretofore overturned by playing. Malvolio, upon appearing, issues a proclamation whose very tenor is one of "unseemly" entitlement: "Madam, you have done me wrong. Notorious wrong" (lines 327-28). But the ensuing explanation merely reiterates the steward's subordinate position, as Olivia remarks, "Alas, poor fool, how they have baffled

thee!" (line 368). Malvolio, the overreacher, is now reduced to the lowly status of one whose function he has previously scorned, as Feste promptly reminds him, concluding "thus the whirligig of time brings in his revenges" (lines 375-76). But just as Feste has taken his cue to speak from Olivia's epithet "poor fool," so does Malvolio take his from the clown's gloating last words. "I'll be reveng'd on the whole pack of you(!)" Malvolio warns (line 378), the "whole pack" evidently including not only the pranksters (the two chiefest of whom—Sir Toby and Maria—are not present) but the nobles as well. The so-called "festive comedy" concludes rather ominously; if indeed "the whirligig of time brings in his revenges," it is difficult to dismiss Malvolio's parting threat as merely one sour note troubling an otherwise stable social hierarchy.

Significantly, the clown's closing song seems to take its uncertain, melancholy tone not from the promised (though deferred) wedding and "golden time" of Orsino's last speech, but from the bitter note of Malvolio's final words. Far from heralding a "golden time," a term that itself evokes the pastoral myths of idyllic, benevolent relations between masters and servants,[48] the haunting song marks the end of holiday time and takes the play back into history, into materiality. Not just the wind and rain, but their inexorability against the festive vices of lust and drunkenness, the harshness of "man's estate" wherein gates are shut against foolery, call attention to the illusory nature of comic resolution and to the uncertain world to which actor and spectator alike must return. The final line, "And we'll strive to please you every day" (line 407), is a reminder that playing itself, while trafficking in illusion, is historically embedded, materially reproducible in time and space, and thus vulnerable as well to "wind and rain," to the threats that escape narrative closure. But like Malvolio's threat, Feste too is outside the narrative here, his song not mediated by the now-vanished illusory world of Illyria. It is a moment that keenly demonstrates Weimann's assertion that "the comic actor . . . does not merely play *to* the audience: to a certain degree he still plays *with* the audience."[49] If Malvolio's evasion of closure deflates the ideal of a "golden time," Feste's signifies a resonant deconstruction of the boundaries between festivity and history. He stands as an emblem of the theater's capacity to intervene in lived experience. This gesture of *self-licensed* foolery figures the theater's testimonial to a limited institutional autonomy, even while the melancholy song discloses the material terms of those limitations.[50]

Notes

[1] See, e.g., John Hollander, "*Twelfth Night* and the Morality of Indulgence," in *Modern Shakespearean Criticism: Essays on Style, Dramaturgy, and the Ma-*

jor Plays, ed. Alvin B. Kernan (New York: Harcourt, Brace, and World, 1970), pp. 228-41.

[2] The phrase is C.L. Barber's. See *Shakespeare's Festive Comedy: A Study of Dramatic Form and Its Relation to Social Custom* (Princeton: Princeton Univ. Press, 1959), p. 259.

[3] For a consideration of the problematics of disorder and closure in *Hamlet,* see my essay "'Suche Strange Desygns': Madness, Subjectivity, and Treason in *Hamlet* and Elizabethan Culture," *Renaissance Drama* n.s. 20 (1989): 51-76.

[4] From *Homily on Obedience* (1559), quoted in *Elizabethan Backgrounds: Historical Documents of the Age of Elizabeth I,* ed. Arthur F. Kinney (Hamden, CT: Archon, 1975), p. 60.

[5] Keith Wrightson, *English Society, 1580-1680* (London: Hutchinson, 1982), p. 19.

[6] Wrightson, p. 20.

[7] See Lawrence Stone, *The Crisis of the Aristocracy,* abridged edn. (New York: Galaxy, 1967), pp. 37-61.

[8] Michael Bristol, *Carnival and Theater: Plebeian Culture and the Structure of Authoritarian Renaissance England* (London: Routledge, 1985), p. 112.

[9] Robert Weimann, *Shakespeare and the Popular Tradition in the Theater: Studies in the Social Dimension of Dramatic Form and Function,* ed. Robert Schwartz (Baltimore: Johns Hopkins Univ. Press, 1978), p. 185.

[10] For an insightful discussion of Renaissance theatrical transvestism, see Jyotsna Singh, "Renaissance Antitheatricality, Antifeminism, and Shakespeare's *Antony and Cleopatra,*" *Renaissance Drama* n.s. 20 (1989): 99-122.

[11] Natalie Zemon Davis, *Society and Culture in Early Modern France: Eight Essays* (Stanford: Stanford Univ. Press, 1975), pp. 122-23.

[12] Stone essentially defends his thesis in a later essay, "The Bourgeois Revolution of Seventeenth-Century England Revisited," *Past and Present* 109 (November 1985): 44-54.

[13] See, e.g., D.M. Palliser, *The Age of Elizabeth: England under the Later Tudors, 1547-1603* (London: Longman, 1983), p. 76; Derek Hirst, *Authority and Conflict: England, 1603-1638* (London: Edward Arnold, 1986), p. 13.

[14] Stone, pp. 249-67.

[15] John Harington, *Nugae Antiquae,* vol. 2 (1779; rprt. Hildesheim: Georg Olms, 1968), pp. 126-27, 130.

[16] See note 1.

[17] Stone, p. 256.

[18] Buchanan Sharp, *In Contempt of All Authority: Rural Artisans and the Riot in the West of England, 1586-1660* (Berkeley and Los Angeles: Univ. of California Press, 1980), p. 17; see also Palliser, pp. 27-28.

[19] John Walter, "A 'Rising of the People'? The Oxfordshire Rising of 1596," *Past and Present* 107 (May 1985): 90-143.

[20] Sharp, p. 36.

[21] Walter, pp. 96-99.

[22] Sharp, p. 39.

[23] Quoted in Walter, p. 99.

[24] Elliot Krieger, *A Marxist Study of Shakespeare's Comedies* (New York: Barnes and Noble, 1979), p. 129.

[25] William Shakespeare, *Twelfth Night,* Arden edn., ed. J.M. Lothian and T. W. Craik (London and New York: Routledge, 1988), I.v.90. Further references will be to this edition and included in the text.

[26] I am deliberately avoiding the term "puritan" in reference to Malvolio, not only because I do not believe he is explicitly a satirical Puritan in the sense, e.g., of Jonson's Zeal-of-the-Land Busy, but also because, as Palliser observes, "'Puritan' has proven almost impossible to define, both at the time and since, and some historians are now tempted to abandon the term altogether" (p. 347; see also pp. 346-51).

[27] Quoted in Weimann, p. 171.

[28] Cf. Terry Eagleton: "Like Falstaff [Sir Toby] . . . is a rampant hedonist, complacently anchored in his body, falling at once 'beyond' the symbolic order of society in his verbal anarchy, and 'below' it in his carnivalesque refusal to submit his body to social control" (*William Shakespeare* [London: Basil Blackwell, 1986], p. 32).

[29] On "seasonal misrule," see Stuart Clark, "Inversion, Misrule, and the Meaning of Witchcraft," *Past and Present* 87 (May 1980): 98-127.

[30] Ralph Berry remarks that Maria's exact social status is somewhat unclear, though he observes that other characters frequently address her as a menial servant (*Shakespeare and Social Class* [Atlantic Highlands, NJ: Humanities Press International, 1988], pp. 70-71).

[31] I still think that C.L. Barber says it best: "the fool in *Twelfth Night* has been over the garden wall into some such world as the Vienna of *Measure for Measure*. He never tells where he has been, gives no details. But he has an air of knowing more of life than anyone else—too much, in fact" (p. 259).

[32] Michael Foucault, *History of Sexuality,* vol. 1, trans. Robert Hurley (New York: Pantheon Books, 1978), pp. 61-62.

[33] Bristol, p. 113.

[34] Bristol, p. 140.

[35] See Weimann, p. 213.

[36] Eagleton, pp. 28-29; Krieger, p. 116.

[37] The term may be found in Berry, p. 74.

[38] William Shakespeare, *As You Like It, The Riverside Shakespeare,* ed. Blakemore Evans (Boston: Houghton Mifflin, 1974), II.iii.57-58.

[39] Hollander, p. 237.

[40] On the relation of festivity and the old church calendar, see Leah S. Marcus, *The Politics of Mirth: Jonson, Herrick, Milton, Marvell and the Defense of Old Holiday Pastimes* (Chicago: Univ. of Chicago Press, 1986), p. 1.

[41] See Weimann, pp. 23-25; Marcus, p. 27.

[42] Eagleton, p. 28.

[43] The suggestion that the speech may refer specifically to Armin may be found in the Arden Edition of *Twelfth Night,* p. 27, nn. 61-69.

[44] In Robert Armin, *The Collected Works* (New York and London: Johnson Reprint Corporation, 1972).

[45] Stephen Gosson, *The Schoole of Abuse* (1579; rprt. London: The Shakespeare Society, 1841), p. 27.

[46] Thomas Heywood, *An Apologie For Actors* (1612; rprt. London: The Shakespeare Society, 1841), p. 54.

[47] Clark, p. 101.

[48] On the pastoral and its mythologizing of master-servant relations, see Louis A. Montrose, "'Eliza, Queene of shepheardes' and the Pastoral of Power," *ELR* 10, 2 (Spring 1980): 153-82 (see esp. pp. 157-59).

[49] Weimann, p. 257.

[50] I would like to thank Don Wayne and Louis Montrose for their generous suggestions.

SEXUAL AMBIGUITY

Leonard F. Manheim (essay date 1964)

SOURCE: "The Mythical Joys of Shakespeare, or, What You Will," in *Shakespeare Encomium,* edited by Anne Paolucci, The City College, 1964, pp. 100-12.

[*In the following essay, Manheim gives a psychoanalytic treatment of* Twelfth Night, *contending that the play is "an oedipal comedy written from the viewpoint of the father."*]

> Such tricks hath strong imagination,
> That if it would but apprehend some joy,
> It comprehends some bringer of that joy.
> *A Midsummer Night's Dream* V.i.18-20

> *Will* will fulfill the treasure of thy love . . .
> Sonnet 136

I offer an interpretation of *Twelfth Night* based on accepted Shakespearean scholarship plus the data of psychoanalysis. I shall extrapolate beyond the words assigned to the characters in the play and shall consider these characters as "persons" known to me (and, in all truth, there are few persons whom I meet in the ordinary intercourse of life whom I know as well as I know these characters), and capable of having a former and a future existence of their own, all, of course, wholly within the bounds of the play's basic structure and development. In the same way, and using the same data, I shall attempt to read *out of* (not into) the text evidence of the author's own fears, hopes, and wishes, none of which will at any time contradict or attenuate any accepted biographical facts and documented material. I know that in accepting Freud, Jones, and their school, and rejecting that of Stool and Sisson, I run the risk of critical condemnation, including the risk of being belabored with the cudgel of Professor Sisson's animadversions on "The Mythical Sorrows of Shakespeare."[1]

I know this so well that I have run to meet it by basing my title on Sisson's. But the reading is different. By "mythical" I mean not that which is mendacious, factitious, untrue, consciously conceived by an irresponsible critic; but rather that which is the product of a non-conscious, "mythopoeic" drive to explain phenomena which are not rationally understood, or which are so understood but are not, on the psychodynamic level, acceptable to the conscious mind.[2] I substitute "joys" for "sorrows," and I mean by "joy" just what Shakespeare meant by the word in his treatise on the ways of the mind which is embodied in the colloquy between Theseus and Hippolyta in the fifth act of *A Midsummer Night's Dream.* As is apparent, I agree with Freud that "Story-tellers are valuable allies, [whose] testimony is to be rated high, for they usually know many things between heaven and earth that our academic wisdom does not even dream of."[3] But I am concerned not only with the intuitions of Shakespeare the creative artist, but with the wish-fulfilling fantasies of Shakespeare the man, and I imply this by adopting, with a possible change of emphasis, his sub-title for *Twelfth Night,* indicating that by the fantasy of this piece of joyous entertainment he is flying in the teeth of certain painful but unalterable facts, giving himself through this fantasy grounds for (irrational) joy. In other words, "What You Will" implies the phenomenon of "the omnipotence of thought"; it means not (or not only) "whatever you prefer" but "that which you *will* into being," "that which you attempt to bring about as a wish-fulfillment."[4] I contend that in *Twelfth Night* Shakespeare was freely expressing a number of such wish-fulfillments, some of them conscious, some of them possibly preconscious (that is, not within the area of awareness but capable of being understood directly when they are brought into that area), but most of them completely unconscious; that these wish-fulfillments had indeed grown out of the private and personal experience of the author but were also projected into the personal and private experience of the "persons" introduced as characters in the play.

The more conventional Shakespearean critic, apprehensive—not without cause—of the excesses committed by some psychoanalytic investigators (I hesitate to call them "critics"), will ask, "How much do we really know of Shakespeare's private and personal experience?" and "What does that private and personal experience have to do with his works of art?" To the first question I respond that I shall imply nothing concerning Shakespeare's private life which is not in complete harmony with evidence which is acceptable to the most traditional critic; *viz.,* the Shakespearean documents gathered and published by J. O. Halliwell-Phillips,[5] D. H. Lambert,[6] E. K. Chambers,[7] and B. Roland Lewis.[8] Nor do I intend to imply a one-to-one relationship between documented events and works produced; that, for instance, a shocking event will necessarily be reflected in an attitude or tone in the next succeeding play. I do imply, however, that once an event of importance has been established in point of time, it must be considered as having some influence on some work which follows it, closely or at farther remove. And this makes plain my reply to the second question, for I firmly believe that Shakespeare was a man as well as an artist, and that no man can do, say, or write anything (even—or, rather, particularly—a work of art) that does not reflect his own experience directly or indirectly. The real difficulty is not in finding evidence in a work of art that points clearly to the influence of private experience; on the contrary, the difficulty lies in the fact that created material has its roots in many, seemingly unrelated, elements of personal experience, much of it, I must repeat, unconscious; in other words, much of that material is, as the psychoanalyst puts it, "overdetermined," requiring investigation into many, often inconsistent and seemingly irreconcilable, sources.

The preliminaries thus disposed of, I proceed to my basic contention: *Twelfth Night* is an oedipal comedy written from the viewpoint of the father, just as *Hamlet* is an oedipal tragedy written from the viewpoint of the son. The comedy was written between 1598 and 1601; so was the tragedy.[9] Shakespeare's son, Hamnet, died in August of 1596, at the age of eleven, and was survived by his twin sister Judith.[10] In *Twelfth Night* the twin son and daughter are separated by the primal power of the sea, each considering the other dead. The living daughter takes upon herself the sex and appearance of the dead twin son and is so successful in passing for him that the sea-captain Antonio, who has enacted the role of father-substitute to the son, can say when he sees the two of them together,

> How have you made division of yourself?
> An apple, left in two, is not more twin
> Than these two creatures. Which is
>   Sebastian?[11]

It need not be pointed out (and it could hardly have been unknown to the Elizabethans) that whatever might have been the confusion between male twins in *The Comedy of Errors,* brother-and-sister twins are fraternal, not identical; they do not resemble each other more than ordinary brothers and sisters do.[12]

Here, then, is the first and fundamental wish-fulfillment of the play. The dead son can be replaced by the living daughter, who gives up her own sex in order to obtain access, by appearing as a man, or at least "an eunuch," to the bachelor who must be considerably older than she is, for she has "heard [her] father name him" (I.ii.28), and that father "died that day when Viola from her birth / Had number'd thirteen years" (V.i.251-252). The Duke, when informed by Cesario that "he" has been attracted to a woman of about the Duke's age, exclaims,

> Too old, by heaven; let still the woman take
> An elder than herself . . .
>
> (II.iv.30-31)

and stresses the persistent fantasy that women, on losing their virginity, are thereby rendered less attractive to their lovers, a doctrine to which Viola will, of course, not wholly assent:

Duke: Then let thy love be younger than
  thyself,
Or thy affection cannot hold the bent;
For women are as roses, whose fair flower
Being once display'd, doth fall that very hour.
Viola: And so they are: alas, that they are so;
To die, even when they to perfection grow!

                                   (II.iv.37-42)

The Duke's attitude toward Viola's masculinity seems to me to be rather ambivalent, and Cesario clearly runs the risk of being accused of a homosexual attachment to the bachelor Orsino. Even in the opening scenes, Valentine comments, "If the Duke continue these favours towards you, Cesario, you are like to be much advanced: he hath known you but three days and already you are no stranger" (I.iv.1-4). And the Duke himself displaces and condenses his emotional attachments by insisting that Cesario-Viola is the best possible bearer of the tale of his love for Olivia:

For they shall yet belie thy happy years,
That say thou art a man: Diana's lip
Is not more smooth and rubious; thy small
  pipe
Is as the maiden's organ, shrill of sound;
And all is semblative a woman's part.

              . . . . .

    . . . Prosper well in this,
And thou shalt live as freely as thy lord,
To call his fortunes thine.

                          (I.v.29-34,37-39)

Orsino reveals even more when he loses his temper, for he reproaches both Cesario and Olivia when he refers to the former as "this your minion, whom I know you love, / And whom, by heaven I swear, I tender dearly" (V.i.128-129), an obvious projection, for if Cesario is anyone's "minion" it will have to be Orsino's who tenders him dearly rather than Olivia's. And this ambivalence of Orsino is embedded in the speech in which Italianate sadism for once rears its ugly head in the fantasy-land of Illyria:

Why should I not, had I the heart to do it,
Like to the Egyptian thief at point of death,
Kill what I love?—a savage jealousy
That sometimes savours nobly. . . .

              . . . . .

Come, boy, with me; my thoughts are ripe in
  mischief:
I'll sacrifice the lamb that I do love,
To spite a raven's heart within a dove.
                    (V.i.120-123,133-134)

For a moment it seems that the pattern of Fletcher's *Philaster* and Bellario is about to be enacted, when Olivia sets matters right by calling in the euphuistic priest to testify to the marriage. But I wonder how many readers and viewers of the play have not suspected, as I did years ago, that Orsino was aware of Viola's secret on some level of marginal consciousness.

But no such logical inference is necessary, for there is no logic in the wish-fulfilling Unconscious, and Viola can be both the lost twin-brother and the surviving twin-sister, who will provide the mourning dramatist with the male heir he so greatly desires and at the same time be the solacing daughter who will unwaveringly prefer the father-figure in spite of all the enticements of normal heterosexual adjustment.[13] In the blithe irrationality of the Unconscious, Viola comes back to life once as her own twin brother, the sea-devoured Hamnet-Sebastian, and then Sebastian (the beautiful martyr, the "hanging god," let it be remembered, of medieval and Renaissance art) also returns to life to wed with most precipitate haste the other virginal figure who is, as we shall note more fully in a moment, another projection of the beloved daughter, leaving the first daughter-image, the inviolate Viola, free to devote herself wholly to her beloved father-Duke. And all this happens in Illyria, a fantasy-land like the later Bohemia which had a seacoast for the same reason that Illyria does; i.e., in order that the sea may both engulf and give up its dead. The word-play "Illyria-Elysium" is made at the very outset of the play (I.ii.3-4). In this country of the fulfilled wishes of fantasy it is possible for a sister not only to take the place of her dead brother and thus restore him to life, but also to be, in one guise, a loving daughter to her mourning father, while her *alter ego* is recompensed for the loss of one brother by finding another who is permitted to be her sexual mate.

Note how the legitimized incest-fantasies become more and more apparent as we examine the ambivalent intricacies imposed by the plot. Manningham was able to gloss over the implications of an underlying incest-theme by forgetting (or never realizing) the occasion of Olivia's mourning and referring to her as the "lady widowe," even though Viola's seacaptain says at the very outset that she is

A virtuous maid, the daughter of a count
That died some twelvemonth since; then
  leaving her
To the protection of his son, her brother,
Who shortly also died; for whose dear love,
They say, she hath abjured the company
And sight of man.

                                   (I.ii.36-41)

to which Viola quite naturally responds,

O that I served that lady,
And might not be delivered to the world,
Till I had made mine own occasion mellow,
What my estate is!

(I.ii.41-4)

But Viola is not to be allowed to join her lot with that of her sister in misfortune; instead she goes to serve a living lord and master who "knows her not." And the father-daughter incest theme is betrayed in lines which through their insistent poetic beauty, have obscured their revealing ambiguity.

Viola: My father had a daughter loved a man,
As it might be, perhaps, were I a woman,
I should your lordship.
Duke: And what's her history?
Viola: A blank, my lord. She never told her love,
But let concealment, like a worm i' the bud,
Feed on her damask cheek: she pined in thought
And with a green and yellow melancholy,
She sat like patience on a monument,
Smiling at grief. Was not this love indeed?

. . . . .

Duke: But died thy sister of her love, my boy?
Viola: I am all the daughters of my father's house,
And all the brothers too: and yet I know not.

(II.iv.110-118,122-124)

A moment ago I spoke of Olivia as Viola's *alter ego*. The point might be made without more painstaking demonstration, but there is a pattern in the play which blurts out the secret that even he who runs may read. Let us look for a moment at a piece of deliberate mystification concocted by Maria for the humbling of Malvolio and the delectation of Toby and his companions. In the forged letter which Malvolio believes to have been written by Olivia, there are two sets of verses, the second of which is to convey to the hapless steward, who hardly needs the additional assurance, that it is he and he alone who is the object of his mistress' love:

I may command where I adore;
    But silence, like a Lucrece knife,
With bloodless stroke my heart doth gore:
    M, O, I, A, doth sway my life.

(II.v.115-118)

Neither Malvolio nor the audience needs much prompting that the code points to him. "M,—Malvolio," he says; "M,—why that begins my name" (II.v.137-138). But he is concerned because "A should follow, but O

does" (II.v.142-143). Apart from his reading, we may want to make one of our own, for the letters contribute to a pervasive anagram. The vowels are to be found in the name of every character in the romantic (incest-ridden) plot. All three are to be found in "Viola" and "Olivia" as well as in "Malvolio." Two are to be found in the lesser figures, "Orsino" and "Maria." In the gulled steward whose name furnishes the first clue to the anagram, the "mal-" element points clearly to the "evil" in the presumption of the Puritanical steward who should be the protector of the virginity of his lady-mistress, but instead raises his eyes in unholy desire for her. This is emphasized by the "will" element in "-volio" (*voglio*), substituted in place of the original letters in the "Malevolti" of the source-material. All three vowels are to be found in his name, the "o" being used twice, to establish a masculine ending to a rearrangement of both "Viola" and "Olivia." And these two are obvious anagrams for each other, with the latter name carrying a second "i." And, as I have suggested above, she is indeed a second "I" to Viola. As double, therefore, she rejects the substitute father whom her counterpart adores, thus rejecting but also achieving the implied incest. She loses one brother but is recompensed for the loss by her marriage to Sebastian, just as the first "I" loses a brother and finds a father.

The incest-taboo is also avoided by what we might term a "purloined letter" technique; the relationships, real and substitute, are made so obvious, so oft-repeated, that they are accepted as innocent, since nothing forbidden could be so patently presented. This is, of course, a pattern not uncommon in Shakespeare, as in other Elizabethan dramatists. Viola and Sebastian, the fatherless twins, each have their respective father-protectors, the sea-captains who rescue them from the sea of death and watch over them even after bringing them to rebirth in the land of Illyria-Elysium. Viola's unnamed captain is the sole custodian of her secret, as well as of her "maiden weeds" (V.i.262), but his possible protection for the daughter who turns out to need none is frustrated by the evil "father" Malvolio, who keeps him "in durance" (V.i.281-284). Antonio, Sebastian's faithful father-protector, fares worse, for he is in mortal danger in Illyria (in which he resembles father Aegeon in *The Comedy of Errors*) but braves all dangers for the son who proves to be (or at least seems to be) ungrateful and unfilial. He is saved only by the intervention of the father-paramount, the Duke.

To the fathers who serve, or are served by the twins (the reversal is a dynamic equivalence in the pattern of the Unconscious, in which there is no such word as "not"), there must be added the congeries of fathers who cluster about the second "I." With her real father and brother gone, she avows her intention of remaining unseen—veiled—for seven years, the appropriate period of biblical servitude. She casts aside that veil, however, both literally and symbolically, when brother

Cesario makes his appearance and saucily commands her to do so. In the meantime, and until her deliverance by Cesario-Sebastian, she is surrounded by a grotesque set of "protectors," only one of whom, Sir Toby, has designs on her fortune which do not also include threats to her virginity. But they cannot prevail, for if Viola-Cesario has not the swordsman's skill to defend her against the witless Sir Andrew, Sebastian is waiting to act as substitute in the nick of time, and to give Sir Toby a bloody coxcomb (or to make it plain that that is what each of the two false knights really is) and break Sir Andrew's head as well, thus rescuing the virgin "I" from all her unworthy "protectors."

Before concluding, let me repeat my words of warning. I am not describing or attempting to describe the conscious, intentional devices of an artist, appealing to the conscious awareness of the reader or spectator. Any such appeal would arouse anxiety rather than pleasure in both; whereas such anxiety is avoided when "deep calleth unto deep." The analytic critic, like the anlaytic therapist, avoids this anxiety by a process which I cannot undertake to explain here. In any case, it has become apparent in the years since psychoanalytic criticism first began to function (as criticism, I repeat, not as clinical analysis) that analysis does not "reduce" the work of art nor militate against its full enjoyment; rather, the contrary is true: we perceive in depth what we had formerly missed superficially. In our play we see the disarming nature of the approach through comedy summed up in the song of Feste as epilogue:

> When that I was and a little tiny boy,
>   With hey, ho, the wind and the rain:
> A foolish thing was but a toy,
>   For the rain it raineth every day.

A profound but unacceptable psychodynamic drive is presented as "a foolish thing," "a toy"; indeed, nothing more than a Twelfth-Night frolic. It could have been masked in the form of tragedy; perhaps the self-same drive would reappear some years later in *King Lear*. But now, at the end of *Twelfth Night; or, What You Will* we rest content, for

> A great while ago the world begun,
>   With hey, ho, the wind and the rain:
> But that's all one, our play is done,
>   And we'll strive to please you every day.

Notes

[1] The 1934 Annual Shakespeare Lecture of the British Academy (*Proceedings of the British Academy,* Vol. XX; London: Humphrey Milford). Actually, Professor Sisson's fire is not directed against the psychoanalytic critic. The immediate cause of his irritation was Nazi propaganda in the guise of criticism, ". . . by dint of which there arises, as from a trap-door at Bayreuth, a dour heroic figure of pure Nordic ancestry, the enemy of all Southern decadences, faithful to his Leader, the prophet of the new Germany of today" (pp. 3-4). These excesses Professor Sisson ascribes not to the influence of psychoanalysis (under the circumstances, he could hardly do so) but to the example of Coleridge, carried over into the nineteenth-century German criticism of the brothers Schlegel and their followers, and back into *their* British successors in the later nineteenth and early twentieth centuries.

Not that there is a lack of evidence of Professor Sisson's animosity toward psychoanalytic criticism *per se*. See, for example, his introduction to *Hamlet* in his edition of the *Complete Works* (New York: Harper & Bros., [1953]):

> There has been altogether too much throwing about of brains concerning the character of Hamlet himself, both analytic and psycho-analytic. We would do better to consider Hamlet according to his own words, and against the contemporary background of the writings of Thomas More or of John Donne on the problems of his state of mind.
>
> (p. 997)

The psychoanalytic critic—need it be said?—does consider the character "according to his own words," and he does not deny the influence of Shakespeare's contemporary background; he does, however, insist on his right and duty to consider the author first as a *man,* then as a Western man, and then as an Elizabethan man.

[2] When we consider how much more prevalent the latter meaning of "mythical" has become, it is at least remarkable that the critic who used the word in "mythical sorrows" should not have chosen some expression which is unequivocally indicative of "non-existent" or "grossly exaggerated."

[3] *Delusions and Dreams in Jensen's "Gradiva"* (1893-1895), *Standard Edition of the Works of Sigmund Freud* (London: Hogarth Press, (1953)), IX, 8. See also Norman N. Holland, "Freud and the Poet's Eye," *Literature and Psychology,* XI, 2 (Spring 1961), 37 (n. 5), and *passim*.

[4] "The omnipotence of thoughts, or, more accurately speaking, of wishes, has since been recognized as an essential element in the mental life of primitive people." This is Freud's additional (1923) note to "A Case of Obsessional Neurosis" (1909) in *Collected Papers* (London: Hogarth Press), IV (1953), 370n. The play on "will" is, of course, closely allied to Shakespeare's wordplay on his own name, as, for example, in the "Will" sonnets (135, 136, 143).

[5] *Outlines of the Life of Shakespeare* (London: Longmans, Green, 1898).

[6] *Cartae Shakespeareanae: Shakespeare Documents* (London: George Bell & Sons, 1904).

[7] *William Shakespeare: A Study of Facts and Problems* (Oxford: The Clarendon Press, 1930), 2 vols.

[8] *The Shakespeare Documents* (Stanford University Press, 1940-41), 2 vols.

[9] Israel Gollancz, preface to the Temple edition of *Twelfth Night* (London: J. M. Dent & Sons, 1923; first issued in 1894), pp. v-vi; and Sisson, *Complete Works,* pp. 336 and 997. Harold Jenkins, "William Shakespeare: A Biographical Essay," in Sisson, *Complete Works,* stresses the probable alternation of comedy and tragedy: "As far as one can tell in ignorance of precise dating, *Julius Caesar* and *Hamlet* alternated with *As You Like It* and *Twelfth Night*" (p. xiii). Wright and LaMar in the *Folger Library General Reader's Shakespeare* edition of *Hamlet* (New York: Washington Square Press, 1957) state that " . . . it was performed, probably about 1600," and G. B. Harrison in *Introducing Shakespeare* (London: Pelican Books, 1939), p. 121, lists both plays in the canon as of the year 1601. For my purposes, I am content with any dating after, but probably not long after, 1596.

[10] Much of the biographical information concerning births, marriages, and deaths is taken by the authorities named in notes 5-8 from entries in the parish Register of the Church of the Holy Trinity, Stratford-upon-Avon. This gives 2 February 1585 as the date of the christening of Hamnet and Judith, son and daughter of William Shakespeare, and 11 August 1596 as the date of Hamnet's funeral.

[11] *TN,* V.i.229-231. I use the Temple edition (see note 9), and I see no need to reproduce old spelling and punctuation. Act, scene, and line numbers are hereafter indicated in the text.,

[12] It may be argued that the identical appearance of the twins is inherent in Shakespeare's sources. Whether this is so or not is not decisive in the matter of psychodynamic interpretation, for what Shakespeare invented and what Shakespeare adopted by selection from his source material are both indicative of at least some personal predilection on his part for a particular dramatic device. Still, it may be appropriate to glance at the scholarly data concerning the sources. Manningham's diary entry for 2 February 1601 (-2) describes the play as "Much like the Comedy of Errors, or Menechmi in Plautus; but most like and near to that in Italian called Inganni" (Gollancz, p. v). "The source for the main plot," writes Sisson (*Complete Works,* p. 356), "is apparently *Riche his Farewell to Militarie Profession* (1581) in which he tells the tale of *Apolonius and Sila,* Apolonius being Orsino and Sila Viola. . . . The story came to Riche from Bandello's Italian *novella,* and to him from an Italian play *Gli Ingannati* (The deceived ones) dating from 1531. . . . " The identity of the Italian source is not particularly clarified by the fact that "there are at least two Italian plays called *Gl'Inganni* (The Cheats), to which Manningham may have referred in his entry as containing incidents resembling those of *Twelfth Night;* one of these plays, by Nicolo Secchi, was printed in 1562; another by Curzio Ganzalo, was first published [in Italian?] in 1592. In the latter play the sister, who dresses as a man and is mistaken for her brother, gives herself the name of Cesare. . . . A third play, however, entitled *Gl'Ingannati* (Venice 1537), . . . bears a much stronger resemblance to *Twelfth Night;* in its poetical induction, *Il Sacrificio,* occurs the name 'Malevolti,' which is at least suggestive of the name 'Malvolio'" (Gollancz, pp. vi-vii). To dispose of matters of source and origin, it seems generally agreed that Malvolio (except for the suggestion of the name), Sir Toby. Sir Andrew, Fabian, Feste, Maria, and (at least as far as her name is concerned) Olivia are all wholly Shakespeare's.

[13] I for my part, have forsworn all temptation to speculative biographical inferences, but I cannot refrain from marshalling a few of the well-attested facts. leaving the inferences to the reader.

Both of Shakespeare's daughters were unmarried at the time *Twelfth Night* was probably written, Susanna being no more than eighteen years old and Judith no more than sixteen (if we take the *terminus ad quem,* 1601, as the date of the play; it seems more probable that they were both several years younger). Susanna married on 5 June 1607, at the age of twenty-one, and the marriage seems to have been considered a good one; at all events, William Shakespeare named John and Susanna Hall the residuary legatees in his Will, in addition to indicating other marked signs of confidence in them. Judith did not marry until 10 February 1616, being then thirty-one years of age.

Judith's marriage was followed soon after (25 March 1616) by the execution of Shakespeare's Will, and about a month after that by Shakespeare's death. A few words of comment on some of the less familiar provisions of the Will. (I think I may make them on the strength of the text of the Will alone, for I claim some familiarity with the Anglo-American law of wills, since I was admitted to the New York Bar in 1925.) I have already commented on the special favor shown to John and Susanna Hall. In the Will Judith receives £100 "in discharge of her marriage porcion" (the words quoted were added to the original draft of the Will), plus £50 in return for her surrender of her rights as heir-at-law of certain real property left to Susanna; plus another

£150, which is attributable to her only if she survives the testator's death by three years, and which is then to be held in trust with the income alone payable to her "soe long as she shalbe married and covert baron" (a familiar device to prevent a husband's getting his hands on his wife's property), with a gift over to her children, "if she have anie, and if not, to her executors or assignes, she lyving the saied term after my deceas."

It is plain that the elder daughter was preferred to the younger, even though the latter had remained unmarried and faithful to the father for so many years. The very close order in which her marriage, her father's Will, and his death followed one another seems to me most interesting,—but I have sworn to let the reader do the speculating, and I say no more.

Lorna Hutson (essay date 1996)

SOURCE: "On Not Being Deceived: Rhetoric and the Body in *Twelfth Night*," in *Texas Studies in Literature and Language,* Vol. XXXVIII, No. 2, Summer, 1996, pp. 140-73.

[*In the excerpt that follows, Hutson contends that in* Twelfth Night *Shakespeare questions natural sexual differences, blurs sex and gender, and explores sex through rhetorical deception.*]

> *Elder Loveless*. Mistres, your wil leads my
>   speeches from the purpose. But as a man—
> *Lady*. A *Simile* servant? This room was built
>   for honest meaners, that deliver themselves
>   hastily and plainely, and are gone. Is this a
>   time or place for *Exordiums*, and *Similes*,
>   and *metaphors*?[1]

"Shakespearean comedy," writes Stephen Greenblatt, "constantly appeals to the body and to sexuality as the heart of its theatrical magic."[2] Without wishing to disparage the enterprise of writing histories of the body, or indeed to underestimate what such histories have accomplished in terms of enhancing our understanding of early modern culture[3], I would like in the following pages to challenge the operation of a certain kind of "body history" within recent Shakespeare criticism. I do not so much want to disagree with Greenblatt's statement as it stands, as to argue that our understanding of how Shakespeare's comedy intervened, both in its own time and subsequently, to modify attitudes to sexuality and to gender has been more obscured than enlightened by the obsession with the "body" as Greenblatt here understands it, and with the kind of body history to which he and others have prompted us to turn.

1. Circulating Arguments: The "Single Sex" Body

I shall focus my argument on Shakespeare's *Twelfth Night,* a play which, for all the curiously metaphoric, even disembodied nature of the language in which it articulates the desires of its protagonists, has nevertheless become the touchstone of this "body" criticism within Shakespeare studies. Yet it is worth remarking that the current critical interest in *Twelfth Night* as a play about the indeterminacy of gender and the arbitrary nature of sexual desire actually began with the contemplation not of the materiality of the body, but with that of the signifier. In much earlier twentieth-century criticism, Shakespeare's comedies have been appreciated as temporary aberrations from an established sexual and social order for the purposes of a thoroughly conservative "self-discovery" and return to the *status quo*.[4] Saussurian linguistics, alerting critics to the way in which meaning in language is always the effect of a play of differences, enabled them to challenge such interpretations on their own terms by arguing that the conservative denouement was inadequate to contain and fix the meanings released by the play of differences. This was especially the case in comedies such as *As You Like It* and *Twelfth Night,* in which the fiction of a woman's successful masquerade of masculinity is complicated by the understanding of its having been originally composed for performance by a boy. Suddenly, instead of being about the discovery of one's "true" identity, or a "natural" social and sexual order, it seemed that what the comedies were about was the ease with which systems of sexual difference could be dismantled, and the notion of gendered identity itself called into question. This was important when it happened—the mid-1980s—because at the same time feminist critics were beginning to draw attention to the misogynistic implications of the transvestite theater, thereby throwing into confusion that venerable tradition of critical delight in the sprightliness of Shakespeare's girls-dressed-as-boys. How could we go on liking Rosalind and Viola in the knowledge that what they really represented was the denial to women of access to the histrionic exchanges in which they excelled and we took pleasure?[5] Just in time poststructuralist criticism saved us from the agony of this dilemma by recuperating the double transvestitism of the comedies as a calling into question of the "fully unified, gendered subject," thereby producing, instead of a patriarchal Shakespeare, a Shakespeare, who, in the words of Catherine Belsey, offered "a radical challenge to patriarchal values by disrupting sexual difference itself."[6]

Subsequently, the notion that what the comedies were about was really the indeterminacy of gender was given a new and historically authenticating twist by investigations into the history of biological definitions of gender which seemed to prove that, in the minds of Shakespeare's contemporaries, gender itself was a kind of comic plot, the happy denouement of which could only be masculinity. A special issue of *Representations* on "Sexuality and the social body in the nineteenth century" contained an article by Thomas Laqueur which, though primarily concerned with the politics of nineteenth-century reproductive biology, was nevertheless to have a considerable impact on Renaissance literary studies as a result of what its findings implied about the biological construction of gender in the early modern period. Laqueur drew our attention to a momentous, but overlooked event in the history of sexuality. Sometime in the late eighteenth century, the old belief that women needed to experience orgasm in order to conceive was abandoned. Women were henceforward to be thought of as properly passionless, because passive, participants in the act of sexual reproduction. What this implied was nothing less than a change in the existing physiology of sexual difference: the ancient Galenic model, according to which the hidden reproductive organs of women were merely a colder, imperfectly developed, and introverted type of the penis and testicles, requiring to be chafed into producing their seed, was replaced by the modern notion of the incommensurability of male and female reproductive organs. Laqueur's crucial point, however, was that the need to replace the old Galenic "metaphysics of hierarchy" between the sexes with an "anatomy and physiology of incommensurability" actually anticipated any real scientific understanding of women's reproductive makeup, and must therefore have been motivated not by scientific discovery, but by the need to find a new rationale for the exclusion of women from Enlightenment claims for the equality of men.[7]

I am ignorant of the effect of Laqueur's argument on nineteenth-century criticism, but the impact on Renaissance studies has been considerable. Writing in 1986 Laqueur cites, in a footnote, a paper on Shakespeare's *Twelfth Night* by Stephen Greenblatt, which was first published in 1985 in a collection called *Reconstructing Individualism*[8] and subsequently included in Greenblatt's 1988 *Shakespearean Negotiations* as the essay, "Fiction and Friction." Both authors evince exactly the same ancient and sixteenth- and seventeenth-century medical texts—first and foremost, Galen on the exact parity between male and female reproductive organs ("think of the 'uterus turned outward and projecting': Would not the testes [ovaries] then necessarily be inside it? Would it not contain them like a scrotum? Would not the neck [the cervix], hitherto concealed . . . be made into the male member?"[9]) and then Galen's sixteenth- and seventeenth-century readers, Ambroise Paré, Jacques Duval, Thomas Vicary, Helkiah Croke, and Jane Sharp.[10] They also both cite Montaigne, who twice refers to a story also told by Ambroise Paré about the sex-change of Marie-Germaine, a contemporary inhabitant of Vitry-le-François, who had the misfortune or good fortune to realize her manhood by jumping too energetically over a stream, thus prompting the eruption of the appropriate genitals[11].

Where Laqueur expounded the Galenic model of woman as introverted man in order to expose the politics of nineteenth-century reproductive biology and its denial of female orgasm, Stephen Greenblatt's identical quotations employ the model's stress on the defective "heat" of female reproductive organs, and the "friction" required to activate them, as an allegory for the "theatrical representation of individuality in Shakespeare." "Erotic chafing" writes Greenblatt, "is the central means by which characters in plays like *The Taming of the Shrew, A Midsummer Night's Dream, Much Ado About Nothing, As You Like It,* and *Twelfth Night* realize their identities and form loving unions."[12] One might be forgiven for balking at the definition of *The Taming of the Shrew* as a fiction of "identity," or at the naturalization of its highly pragmatic argument of husbandry as a form of "erotic chafing"; Greenblatt, however, refrains from pursuing his argument in relation to this or indeed any of Shakespeare's comedies other than *Twelfth Night*. He puts the question of the relation of identity to erotic chafing—of fiction to friction—more persuasively by asking, "how does a play come to possess sexual energy?"[13]. The answer is supplied by a reading of *Twelfth Night,* the crux of which is a short speech made by the male twin, Sebastian, after Olivia has realized that his double, with whom she was in love, is a woman and his sister. "So comes it, lady," says Sebastian, "you have been mistook,"

> But nature to her bias drew in that.
> You would have been contracted to a maid;
> Nor are you therein, by my life, deceiv'd:
> You are betroth'd both to a maid and man.[14]

According to Greenblatt, the "nature" to which Sebastian refers is, precisely, the Galenic discourse of the one-gender body. Sebastian's reference to himself as "both a maid and man" consequently invokes the inherent instability of gender as construed by this model, which in turn enables a good, radical-sounding assault on more comfortable readings which essentialize sexual difference. Thus, Greenblatt quotes C. L. Barber's argument that, "the most fundamental distinction that the play brings home to us . . . is the difference between men and women" in order to reinforce, by contrast, the persuasiveness of his view that the fundamental physiological distinction between men and women is precisely what the play can't "bring home," historically speaking. At the end of *Twelfth Night,* as he points out, "Viola is still Cesario—'For so you shall be,' says Orsino, 'while you are a man' (5.1.386)— and Olivia, strong-willed as ever, is betrothed to one who is, by his own account, both 'a maid and a man.'"[15] Notice just how closely this conclusion resembles the poststructuralist reading which found *Twelfth Night* calling into question, "the possibility of a fully unified, gendered subject." And, as with the poststructuralist argument, a crucial legacy of this reading is its obscuring of the need to account, in feminist terms, for the historical fact of the absence of women's bodies from the Renaissance stage. In the light of the Galenic theory of reproduction, concludes Greenblatt, it is easy to see that transvestitism actually "*represents* a structural identity between men and women—an identity revealed in the dramatic disclosure of the penis concealed behind the labia."[16] And the dramatic fiction—an outrage to belief which is nevertheless endowed with generative because persuasive power—becomes analogous to the friction or chafing required, according to this Galenic model, both to warm women into conception, and to stimulate their reticent reproductive organs into realizing their latent virility.

Two years after Greenblatt's "Fiction and Friction" was published, Laqueur's thesis on the political and cultural investments of reproductive biology was published in book form as, *Making Sex: Body and Gender from the Greeks to Freud*. The chapter on the pervasiveness of the Galenic model in Renaissance thought and culture carries an epigraph from *Twelfth Night*:

> *Sebastian* [To Olivia]
> So comes it, lady, you have been mistook.
> But nature to her bias drew in that.
> You would have been contracted to a maid;
> Nor are you therein, by my life, deceived:
> You are betrothed both to a maid and man.[17]

And he goes on to introduce the substance of his chapter thus:

> Somehow if Olivia—played by a boy, of course—is not to marry the maid with whom she has fallen in love, but the girl's twin brother Sebastian; if Orsino's intimacy with "Cesario" is to go beyond male bonding to marriage with Viola, "masculine usurped attire" must be thrown off and woman linked to man. Nature must "to her bias" be drawn, that is, deflected from the straight path. "Something off center, then, is implanted in nature," as Stephen Greenblatt puts it, which "deflects men and women from their ostensible desires and toward the pairings for which they are destined." But if that "something" is not the opposition of two sexes that naturally attract one another—as it came to be construed in the eighteenth century—then what is it?[18]

The answer, of course, is the one-gender body according to Galen, with all its micro- and macrocosmic correspondences. The reading of a single Shakespeare play—or rather, the reading of *five lines* from a single Shakespeare play—seems to be doing a lot of work in supporting a circular argument about the relevance of body history to the question of how the magic of theater relates to the early modern conception of the body.

In the last five years, Laqueur's and Greenblatt's arguments and examples—Galen, Ambroise Paré, Jacques Duval, Helkiah Crooke, Jane Sharp, and (especially, perhaps) Montaigne—have been repeatedly invoked and quoted to support arguments about the pervasiveness of sixteenth-century fears that women might turn into men and men into women. Stephen Orgel thus accounts for the practice of having boys play women on the English stage by means of a complex argument whereby pathological fears about the chastity of women are weighed against equally pathological "fantas[ies] of a reversal from the natural transition from woman to man," which "are clearly related to anatomical theories of the essential homology of male and female." "Many cases," he writes, "were recorded of women becoming men through the pressure of some great activity."[19] The endnote to this large claim refers not to women, but to alligators, but as the previous note referred the reader to Laqueur's *Representations* article and to Greenblatt's "Fiction and Friction," we can be reasonably sure that the "many cases" in question are in fact the single case of Marie-Germaine, cited by both Paré and Montaigne. It is true that both Montaigne and Paré liken the case of Marie-Germaine to other examples; these, however, being drawn from such authors as Pliny and Ovid, scarcely seem to constitute "many cases being recorded" in the times of the authors concerned.[20] Judith Brown's well-researched *Immodest Acts: The Life of a Lesbian Nun in Renaissance Italy* exaggerates less, but still enlarges the evidence: "in a few cases women did not just imitate men, but actually became men," she writes, citing Greenblatt.[21] More recently, Valerie Traub's *Desire and Anxiety: Circulations of Sexuality in Shakespearean Drama*—which contains an interesting and persuasive account of *Twelfth Night*—claims, citing both Greenblatt and Laqueur, that fear of turning into a woman "may have been a common masculine fantasy" in the sixteenth and seventeenth centuries.[22] Traub's critical project involves enlarging Orgel's contention that the homoerotics of the Renaissance stage enabled "fantasies of freedom" for women as well as men[23] by deconstructing the hierarchy of hetero- over homo-erotic readings of the plays, and revealing, as she puts it, "the polymorphous potential of desire itself, which Shakespeare so assiduously evokes and controls." Though such potential might not seem to have much to do with women in an exclusively male theater, Traub argues that boys were available to women as objects of fantasy, and in rejecting what she characterizes as the "feminist" interpretation of the boy player's significance (that is, the boy-player as instrument of the patriarchal control of female chastity) reveals her indebtedness to Greenblatt in preferring to argue that the boy-player represented, "an embodiment of the metadramatic theme of identity itself: always a charade, a masquerade, other." Laqueur provides further support for Traub's rejection of the idea that an all-male theater in itself argues either indifference to women's intelligent participation, or fear of the effects of such participation upon the reputation of women and their families. On Laqueur's evidence Traub proposes that in spite of patriarchal control of female sexuality through the ideology of chastity and the laws regarding marriage, there seems to have been a high cultural investment in female erotic pleasure—not because women's pleasure was intrinsically desirable, but because it was thought necessary for conception to occur.[24]

Once again, as in Greenblatt and in Orgel, the focus on a medical discourse about the body enables a way of speaking of sixteenth- and seventeenth-century dramatic discourse, and of the position that it offered women in the audience, as exhaustively signified by its analogue, erotic arousal.

What bothers me most about these arguments is that while they seem to be historicizing and de-essentializing our ideas about the relationship of gender to sexuality, the "fantasies" and "anxieties" that they identify in early modern dramatic texts take no account at all of the way in which, in sixteenth-century society, a woman's sexual behavior was perceived to affect the honor and therefore the credit and economic power of her kinsmen.[25] Nor do they consider the way in which such traditional conceptions of sexual honor, credit, and wealth were themselves being rapidly transformed by the technology of persuasion—or "credit"—that such dramatic texts as Shakespeare's represented. None of these critics appear to entertain the possibility that the capacity to plot, write, and *be able to make use* of the erudition and wit of a comedy such as *Twelfth Night* might in itself be more central to sixteenth- and seventeenth-century conceptions of what it meant to "be a man" than any theory derived from Galen. Moreover, for all the emphasis on plurality, the "polymorphous potential" and the "unmooring of desire" released by the comedies, there still seems to be a commitment to the twentieth-century "lit-crit" notion that what the comedies are really all about is individual identity. Traub explores how characters negotiate their individual desires in the plays as if they were real people and not even partly figures in a persuasive discourse or agents of a plot, while Greenblatt celebrates "the emergence of identity through the experience of erotic heat" as "this Shakespearean discovery, perfected over a six- or seven- year period from *Taming* to *Twelfth Night*."[26] It seems that where literary criticism, as it was once conceived, celebrated the saturnalian energies of Shakespeare's comedies for returning us to a "natural" social and sexual order, these theorists of desire want to find a historically specific concept of "nature"—the Galenic one-sex body—that mimics what is actually their essentialized notion of culture as something which is always preoccupied with the theatrical destabilization of "identities"—identity is "always a masquerade, a charade, other." But what if the errors, confusions, and masquerades of comedy were not, in their own time, thought of as dramas of identity? And what if the way in which the plays construct sexual difference in

relation to the audience crucially concerned not the sexual object-choice of men or women in the audience[27], but whether or not they were able to make use of the play as a discourse, an argument, to enhance their own agency? When James Shirley wrote the preface to an edition of Beaumont and Fletcher's comedies, published in 1647, he called it the collection of

> the Authentick Witt that hath made Blackfriers an Academy, where the three howers spectacle while *Beaumont* and *Fletcher* were presented, were usually of more advantage to the hopefull young Heire, then a costly, dangerous, forraine Travell . . . And it cannot be denied but that the young spirits of the Time, whose Birth and Quality made them impatient of the sowrer ways of education, have from the attentive hearing of these pieces, got ground in point of wit and carriage of the most severely employed students . . . How many passable discoursing dining witts stand yet in good credit upon the bare stock of two or three of these single scenes![28]

I'd like to suggest that Shirley's final metaphor of young men as prodigals, living on the "credit" of an ability to recommend themselves to strangers, a "stock" of wit which they have learned from plays, might tell us something about the way in which Shakespeare's plays, for all that they invoke the magic of the reproductive body, nevertheless construct sexual difference by appealing to the male (because formally educated) mind.

2. "Nor are you therein, by my life, deceiv'd":
Twelfth Night and Gl'Ingannati

My counter-argument depends on the claim that the kind of comic plot from which Shakespeare never wavered—the five-act plot derived from Terence and Plautus—was perceived in his own time to be concerned, not with the emergence of identity, but with men's discursive ability to improvise social credit, or credibility. For all its popular appeal, Shakespeare's drama had a rigorous intellectual basis in the deliberative or hypothetical structure of Terentian comedy as it was rhetorically analyzed in every grammar school.[29] The rhetorical analysis of Terentian comedy, far from being a rigid intellectual straightjacket (as I was implicitly taught at school, where I learned that Shakespeare transcended his contemporaries by ignoring the classical unities) enabled the achievement of a drama that carried emotional conviction as an unfolding narrative of events—"a kind of history," as Shakespeare himself called it—by investing the representation of those events with the impression of an intelligible combination of causality and fortuitousness.[30] Not only were Terentian plots themselves examples of how one might dispose an argument probably; they also offered images of male protagonists who were themselves able, in moments of crisis, to improvise a temporary source of credit (perhaps a disguise, or a fiction of being related to someone rich) that could defer disaster until the terms of the crisis had altered to bring in a fortunate conclusion. The commentaries of the fourth-century grammarian, Donatus, together with those of Melanchthon and other sixteenth-century humanists, were appended to every edition of Terence, with the effect that no schoolboy could escape noticing how the plays demonstrated that uncertain or conjectural arguments were more productive in social exchanges—because more productive of emotional credibility—than the traditional means of assuring of good faith by oaths or other tokens.[31]

The Terentian plot characteristically concerned an illicit sexual union between a well born young man and a prostitute, which in turn betrayed a promise made between his father and neighbor that the son should unite their houses by marrying the neighbor's daughter. Characteristically, too, the plot managed to lend emotional credibility to the highly improbable argument that the prostitute in question was, in fact, the long lost daughter of the neighbor, thereby reconciling in her person the laws of desire and those of social exchange. Dontaus's commentary on Terence was discovered in 1433, and its impact on the composition of European drama evident by the early sixteenth century.

Formal effects upon sixteenth-century vernacular drama, however, were complicated by the ideological impacts of the Reformation and Counter-Reformation, both of which revolutionized attitudes to sex, marriage, and the conjugal household in Europe. For example: Terentian comedy articulates a sense in which the space of prostitution is prophylactic; a household of male, citizen relatives is not dishonored by the entry of the heroine whose desirability was initially associated with her marginal status and sexual accessibility to the young hero. The plays therefore represent a society in which official tolerance of prostitution first sanctions the initial violation of chastity and ensures that, once attached to a citizen household, the woman will be protected by the very institution that once made her vulnerable. The Reformation and the Counter-Reformation, however, brought with them an end to ideologically sanctioned prostitution, so that, as Lyndal Roper writes of Augburg, "any sexual relationship outside marriage, and any occasion on which the sexes mingled . . . might lead to sin."[32] The marginal status once overtly allocated to prostitutes became a covertly allocated category of suspicion embracing all women.

Nevertheless, there were differences in the way in which Catholic and Protestant Europe acknowledged this and reacted to the sexual mores of the Terentian plot. While the writers of Italian *commedia erudita* cynically substituted citizens' wives and daughters for the prostitutes of Roman comedy, northern humanists tempered their enthusiasm for New Comedy as a model of Latinity and eloquence with a distaste for its evident authorization of illicit financial and sexual transactions, that is, clandestine marriages and rhetorical and sartorial impostures of credit. Thus, while Ariosto was claiming to outdo Terence and Plautus with his brilliant *I Suppositi* in which conjectural arguments ("supposes") are manipulated by the dramatist and the heroes to facilitate and subsequently legitimize the defloration of a citizen's daughter, German and Dutch humanists were redeeming the Terentian plot of sexual and financial deception by adapting it to the New Testament parable of the talents and that of the prodigal son.[33] The waste of money and dissipation of male sexual energy, became, in these reforming "Christian Terence" plays, analogous to the danger posed to civil society by the abuse of conjectural argument in what we might call the "technology of credit" represented by the Terentian plot.[34]

I use the word "technology" here to stress the material impact of the pedagogic dissemination of Terentian rhetoric. A pre-capitalist society necessarily guarantees its economic exchanges—exchanges of honor and wealth—by such instruments as oaths, which bind the faith of the contracting parties. The Terentian plot dramatizes a situation in which oaths and gestures of good faith bring about such an impasse as can only be resolved by exploiting the "error" or uncertainty about motive and intention which obtains between the participants in any social transaction. At a formal level, this very exploitation of error or uncertainty was the basis of the Terentian achievement of dramatic verisimilitude. Reformation dramatists were, therefore, concerned to appropriate the power of the Terentian formula to grant verisimilitude to dramatic fantasy, or to bestow credibility upon outrageous hypotheses, without endorsing the suggestion that this rhetorical "technology of credit" be exploited to facilitate deceptive sexual and financial exchanges in real life.

Much has been made, in recent discussions of "desire" on the English Renaissance stage, of the anti-theater writers' objections to the eroticized body of the boy player. These discussions evidently misunderstand the relationship of anti-theater writing to sixteenth-century neo-Terentian drama, with disastrously simplifying effects. Thus, for example, the title of one polemic against the stage, Stephen Gosson's *Playes Confuted in Five Actions* does not go unnoticed, but its relevance is missed; Laura Levine calls Gosson's conception of his attack as a five-act play "confused," while Jean Howard simply notes that Gosson "uses the five-act structure of classical drama to wage war on theatre."[35] The point is that the five act Terentian argument represented, for educated sixteenth-century men, a technology of credit or of probability which, in its dramatic form, was perceived to be implicated in an ethos of betrayal, sexual and otherwise. Gosson's title indicates a need to appropriate dramatic probability for the cause of reform, as it moves from mocking native English drama's ignorance of verisimilitude to condemning the probable arguments of Italian *commedia erudita* for their thematic endorsement of sexual and financial deception:

> When the soule of your playes is . . . Italian baudery, or the wooing of gentlewomen, what are we taught? . . . the discipline we gette by these playes is like to the justice that a certaine Schoolmaster taught in *Persia,* which taught his schollers to lye, and not to lye, to deceive, and not to deceive, with a distinction how they might do it to their friends, & how to their enemies; to their friends, for exercise; to their foes, in earnest. Wherein many of his pupils became so skillful by practise, by custome so bolde, that their dearest friendes payde more for their learning than their enemies. I would wish the Players to beware of this kinde of schooling . . . whilst they teach youthfull gentlemen how to love, and not to love . . . As the mischiefe that followed that discipline of *Persia* enforced them to make a lawe, that young men should ever after, as householders use to instruct their families: so I trust, that when the Londoners are sufficiently beaten with the hurte of suche lessons that are learned at Plaies, *if not for conscience sake, yet for shunning the mischief that may privately breake into every mans house,* this methode of teaching will become so hateful, that even worldly pollicy . . . shal be driven to banish it.[36]
>
> [my italics]

Gosson, of course, had himself been a dramatist; English playwrights were not ideologically immune to the effects of the Reformation, and were themselves torn between admiration for the rhetorical proficiency of Italian *commedia erudita,* and unease at its explicit promotion of an ethos of imposture and deception.

George Gascoigne thus produced an exuberant translation of Ariosto's irrepressible *I Suppositi* but followed it with the composition of an exceptionally harsh prodigal son play in which he argued that he would henceforth be guilty of "no Terence phrase," since "Reformed speech doth now become us best."[37] George Whetstone's two five-act plays concerning the exposition and punishment of illicit sex and the abuse of financial credit in a city like London were prefaced by an acknowledgment of the need for English dramatists to heed the Terentian rhetoric of probability, for the English playwright "grounds his work on impossibilities." The problem, argued Whetstone, was that the available Continental models of a probable drama— *commedia erudita* and "Christian Terence"—were no use to the English dramatist: "at this daye, the *Italian* is so lascivious in his commedies that the worst hearers are greeved at his actions," while "the *German* is too holye: for he presentes on every common Stage, what Preachers should pronounce in Pulpets."[38] As Shakespeare paid both Gascoigne and Whetstone the

compliment of rewriting the plays in question, we may reasonably infer that he was aware of the difficulty of dissociating the productivity of the Terentian technology of probability from its implicit endorsement of violations of chastity and betrayals of household honor.[39]

Shakespeare's *Twelfth Night,* for all its currency as a drama of the body and sexual desire, is in fact so remarkably chaste that Elizabeth Barrett Browning's friend, Anna Jameson, writing a political and feminist criticism of Shakespeare in 1832 could exclaim, "how exquisitely is the character of Viola fitted to her part, carrying through her ordeal with all inward grace and modesty!"[40] Jameson was not being naive or repressed about the sexual content of the play: a glance at the Italian or Roman models of any comedy by Shakespeare will reveal how consistently he chastened their arguments, displacing deep into his depiction of female "character" the signs of an inclination towards sexual betrayal that in his originals were explicit sexual acts. The lawyer John Manningham, seeing a performance of *Twelfth Night* at the Middle Temple in February 1601, noted that it was "much like the commedy of errors or Menachmi in Plautus, but most like and neere to that in Italian called Inganni."[41] Although there is a play called "Inganni," Manningham was almost certainly thinking of *Gl'Ingannati* or "The Deceived," a play by the Accademia degli Intronati di Siena, written as an apology to the ladies for a sketch performed the previous evening, which was Twelfth Night, 1531.[42] *Gl'Ingannati* seems to have enjoyed a reputation for formal excellence only second, or perhaps not even that, to Ariosto. If Machiavelli (who himself translated Terence's *Andria,* the play central to Donatus's analysis) could urge the Tuscans to forget their prejudice against Ferarese Ariosto, for his "gentil composizione," the French Charles Estienne, dedicating his translation of *Gl'Ingannati* to the Dauphin in 1549, argued that this Sienese play surpassed even Ariosto, giving the reader the impression "que si Terence mesmes l'eust composé en Italien, à peine mieux l'eust il sceu diter, inventer ou deduyer."[43] [That if Terence himself had composed it in Italian, he would hardly have known better how to express, invent or handle it.] English readers were probably aware of the play's high literary reputation; the scholarly publisher, Girolamo Ruscelli, included a collection of Italian comedies "buone degne di legersi, & d'imitarsi," [well worthy of being read and imitated] to which he appended a critical apparatus "de' modi osservati in esse da gli antichi, cosi Greci come Latini" [in the manner observed in the case of ancient authors, both Greek and Latin] so as to make them into a book of "eloquentia."[44]

Behind the central plot device of both Ariosto's *I Suppositi* and *Gl'ingannati* (and remotely, therefore, behind Shakespeare's *Taming of the Shrew* and *Twelfth Night*) lay the notorious play by Terence called

Eunuchus, which concerns a young man's gaining access, on the pretext of being a eunuch, to the house in which a virgin is being kept, whom he proceeds to rape[45]. The subsequent predictable discovery of her citizenship makes her eligible for marriage without making him guilty of the rape of a citizen's daughter, since the house where he performed the rape was a brothel. Renaissance versions of the plot, of course, have to deal with what we might call the "homosocial" aspect of the crime—that is, the outrage to fathers and kinsmen—since the virgin is no longer found in a house of courtesans. Thus, Polinesta's father in *I Suppositi* lifts the genre into pathos with his sorrow at the loss of his daughter's honor in his own house. And in *Gl'Ingannati,* though there is less pathos, the scandal of the daughter's seduction is perhaps even greater, due to the bizarre means by which she is left alone with a man in her bedroom (her father assumed the man was a woman dressed up; maybe it is a reminiscence of this scandalous plot that has Viola asking to be presented "as an eunch" to Orsino's court at the beginning of *Twelfth Night*[46]).

Gl'Ingannati begins with a contract between two old men, Virginio and Gherardo, whereby Gherardo is to marry Virginio's daughter, Lelia; "Ne pensar ch'io mi sia permutare di quel ch'io t'ho promesso" [Don't think I'll go back on what I've promised] says Virginio; a merchant's credit depends on keeping his word.[47] But his daughter, Lelia—Shakespeare's Viola—has slipped away from her convent and, disguised as a page, has entered the service of Flammineo, with whom she is in love, but who is himself besotted with another, namely Gherardo's daughter, Isabella, the equivalent of Shakespeare's Olivia. Isabella receives letters and "embassies" [imbasciati] from Flammineo by means of his cute page, Fabio (Lelia in disguise) with whom she, of course, falls in love.

It is worth pointing out how much more explicit than *Twelfth Night* this play is about the fact that sexual desire is not gender specific. Indeed, it becomes very clear that what counts, in distinguishing those who may desire and ask, and those who must be passive, is not gender but social status.[48] Thus, when Lelia's nurse, Clemenzia, finds out that, as Flammineo's page, she has been sleeping in the antechamber of his bedroom, she assumes he will ask her to sleep with him.[49] And later, when Isabella's maid, Pasquella, asks Lelia, disguised as Fabio, why on earth "he" doesn't want to sleep with her mistress, Lelia-as-Fabio replies: "a me bisogna servire il padrone, intendi, Pasquella?" [I have to serve the master, you know what I mean, Pasquella?] and Pasquella does understand: "O io so ben che a tu padron non faresti dispiacere a venirci, non dormi forse con lui?" [Oh, I know very well that you don't displease your master by coming here; but you don't, by any chance, sleep with him?]. When Lelia replies, "Dio il volesse ch'io fosse tanto in gratia sua" [I wish I

were so much in his favor] Pasquella is puzzled; "Oh non dormiresti piu volentieri con Isabella?" [Wouldn't you rather sleep with Isabella?], she asks. And she makes it clear, in an ensuing speech on the ephemerality of Fabio's good looks, that (as a fellow dependent herself) she regards the arrangement of sleeping with Isabella not so much as more "natural" than simply as more stable, practical, and fortunate in the long term for Fabio.[50]

In good Terentian fashion, the denouement of the play proves that the contract between the old men is not broken, though both are fortunately deceived; their houses are united not by the impotent old Gherardo's marrying Lelia, but by the passionately consummated union of Isabella with Lelia's long-lost twin bother, Fabrizio, who, like Shakespeare's Sebastian, doesn't question his good fortune in happening accidentally upon a rich woman who ardently desires him. But where Shakespeare's Olivia finds out who her lover really is by means of the words he speaks (which, as we've seen, have been recently been read as proof of the inherent instability of gender in sixteenth-century thinking about the body), Isabella and the audience of *Gl'Ingannati* discover who *her* lover is in a speech which is more explicitly designed to "appeal to the body." Pasquella, Isabella's maid, emerges from the room in which the two old men have locked Isabella and someone who they think is the truant Lelia, in boy's clothes:

> *Pasquella:*
> those two old sheep insisted that young man was a woman, and shut him in the room with Isabella, my mistress, and gave me the key. I wanted to go in and see what they were doing, and, finding them embracing and kissing together, I had to satisfy myself as to whether the other[51] was male or female. The mistress had him stretched out on her bed, and was asking me to help her, while she held him by the hands. He allowed himself to be overcome, and I undid him in front, and in one pull, I felt something hit my hand; I couldn't tell whether it was a pestle, or a carrot, or indeed something else, but whatever it was, it hadn't suffered from hailstones. When I saw how it was, girls, I fled, and locked the exit! And I know that as far as I'm concerned, I won't go back in alone, and if one of you doesn't believe me, and wants to satisfy herself, I'll lend her the key.[52]

Pasquella then tries to persuade the distraught Gherardo that it isn't true—his daughter isn't really embracing a man: "vedeste voi ogni cosa, e miraste che gli è femina" [Did you see everything? Well, then you can see she's a woman]. But Gherardo is not to be appeased: "svergognato a me," he says, "I am dishonoured."[53] Gherardo has been deceived, despite his own sharp awareness of the nebulous quality of sexual honor and its susceptibility to gossip.

Precisely because they involve citizens' wives and daughters rather than courtesans, Renaissance imitations of Terentian comedy exhibit a strong awareness of the resemblance of the Terentian technology of probability—the uncertain, or conjectural argument—to the everyday gossip that destroys female sexual honor. Ariosto makes this a theme in *I Suppositi,* where the nurse comes out of her house, onto the stage, anxious to avoid the spread of rumor within the walls, and proceeds to announce to the theatre at large that her charge has (probably) been sleeping with a household servant. But here in *Gl'Ingannati* the joke turns on the way that Gherardo's cautious calculations on the risks of mere probability, uncertainty, and conjecture—calculations as to whether an association with the transvestite (and hence probably promiscuous) Lelia would call Isabella's own sexual innocence into question—are overthrown, by the substitution of Fabrizio for Lelia in Isabella's bedroom, which ensures an unequivocally penetrative defloration. "L'ho veduto con questi occhi," says Gherado, "egli s'era spogliato in giubbone, et non hebbe tempo a corprisi . . . Io dico che gli e maschio, e bastarebbe a far due maschi" [I saw it with these eyes . . . he was undressed to his shirt and didn't have time to cover himself . . . I tell you he was a man, and had enough for two men].[54]

The rhetorical deceptions by means of which the play's argument attains its probability—"la gaçon de disposer & pursuyure leur sens & argumens en icelles, pour donner recreation aux auditeurs" that Charles Estienne so admired[55]—thus come to be associated with this act of penetrative sex. To the ladies in the audience, the prologue comments,

> As far I understand it, they've called this comedy "The Deceived" not because they were ever deceived by you, oh no, . . . but they've called it so because there aren't many characters in the plot (favola) who don't, in the end, find themselves deceived. But there is among these deceptions one particular sort which makes me wish (for the malice I bear you) that you might be often deceived, if I were the deceiver . . . the plot is a new one . . . and is extracted from no other source than their busy pumpkin heads, from whence also came the fortunes you were allotted on Twelfth Night.[56]

In this context, it looks as if the most significant single departure from the Italian variants on the plot of *The Eunuch* in *Twelfth Night* is its dissociation of the effectiveness of the original imposture of credit—the original pretense of androgyny or emasculation which effectively gains access to both to the person and to the heart of the wealthy Olivia—from the identification of its triumph as explicitly sexual (Fabrizio proving his virility with Isabella), rather than chastely marital (Sebastian contracted to Olivia). To a chance member of the audience of *Twelfth Night* in the Middle Temple in 1601 who saw the resemblance of

Shakespeare's play to *Gl'Inganni* or *Gl'Ingannati,* meaning respectively "the deceits" and "the deceived," Sebastian's speech at the end might well recall these plays' themes and titles:

> So comes it, lady, you have been mistook.
> But nature to her bias drew in that.
> You would have been contracted to a maid;
> *Nor are you therein, by my life, deceiv'd:*
> You are betroth'd both to a maid and man.
>
> (V.i.257-61)

"Deceiv'd" surely here recalls its Italian translation, "ingannata," and no less surely, there is an ethical distinction being made here between being "mistook" and being "deceiv'd" that turns on the question of whether or not Sebastian is a "maid." His affirmation before the audience that he is both "a maid and man" is less a signal of his inherent androgyny than an assurance that Olivia, not having experienced the same "inganno" as Isabella, remains chaste, honorable, and a prize worthy his, Sebastian's, having.

To the argument implied here—namely, that the explicit eroticism of *Gl'Ingannati* makes interpretations of *Twelfth Night* that focus exclusively on the body and sexuality look a little contrived—it could be objected that I am being literal-minded about the theatrical representation of desire. It could be argued (and I would agree) that the very reticence and fantasticality of the amorous language of *Twelfth Night* ensures the "circulation" of desire or of sexual energy more effectively than the gleeful voyeurism of *Gl'Ingannati*. If this is so, however, it must also be acknowledged that the same linguistic reticence and latency of meaning which allows us, in the 1990s, to read *Twelfth Night* as a celebration of the polymorphous potential of desire, equally enabled Anna Jameson in 1832 to find in Viola a paradigm of the sexual self-control that qualified women for access to education and political life. For, within Laqueur's argument, Jameson belongs to that category of nineteenth-century women who based their claims for the recognition of women's political capacity on arguments proving their inherent moral strength.[57] If the rest of Laqueur's argument for the importance of the eighteenth-century transition from the endorsement to the denial of female orgasm has substance, then it must follow that Shakespeare's own texts belong among the discourses that have, historically, helped to construct the moral characteristics felt to be appropriate to a biology of *incommensurability*—sexual difference—between the male and female. And this in turn would imply that, in their own time, Shakespeare's comedies were not just—in Stephen Greenblatt's words—fictions which "participated in a larger field of sexual discourses" but were fictions of the Reformation—that is, they were actively transformative of existing sexual discourses, tending to substitute the intimation of female sexual intention for the representation of the act which would implicate both sexes equally.[58]

It is, in fact, possible to trace through Shakespeare's plays a consistency of strategy (though not, of course, of effect) in his chastening of the roles and language of women. Whereas in his Italian and Roman sources, the significance of the "woman's part" to the resolution of the dilemma depends upon her having had sex, in Shakespeare this significance is translated into an implicit, or uncertain argument involving her *disposition* to have sex, or her "sexuality." To modern readers this can give the impression of a more complex "interiority" or "character" because its doubtfulness requires our interpretation. In the fraught context of the emergent commercial theatre of sixteenth-century England, however, Shakespeare's chastening of Italian and Roman dramatic models was motivated by the need to prove that the productively deceptive arguments of a Terentian-style theatre need not, as its enemies suggested, necessarily advocate the breakdown of trust and honor by endorsing every kind of sexual and financial deception in contemporary society.[59]

To attempt a reading of *Twelfth Night* that would seriously try to take account of the play's place in the history of sex and gender would require some elaboration of how, in common with other Shakespeare plays, this comedy makes a theme of being implicated in a humanistic literary culture which, through its privileging of skill in persuasive argument, was in the process of transforming relations of economic and social dependency. Current discussions of the subversive erotics of the Renaissance stage trivialize the economic and social issues at stake in *Twelfth Night* and similar plays by reducing the whole of the humanist literary culture of which the theatre was a product to the most banal version of Greenblatt's "self-fashioning"—a mere "increased self-consciousness about the fashioning of human identity as a manipulable, artful process."[60] "Self-fashioning" thereby becomes synonymous with a quite unspecific notion of "theatricality," which in turn is easily assimilated to the concept of "performativity" articulated by Judith Butler in relation to the category of gender.[61] The sixteenth-century investment in masculine education, which crucially enabled the very instances of "self-fashioning" or of "theatricality" so beloved of current criticism—an education which privileged the dialectical and analysis and imitation of classical texts—is simply left out of the discussion. What we have as a result is a criticism of Shakespeare, Jonson and others that is incapable of accounting for the rhetorical and affective excess distinguishing this drama of the English Renaissance from its Continental antecedents; an excess which, in the case of *Twelfth Night*, permits interpretations as widely divergent as those of Greenblatt, Barber, and Jameson, and which therefore (because of its contribution to the historical "instability" of the play's "identity") surely begs to be interpreted as a thematic aspect of the play's concern with disguise, deception, and "theatricality."

For an example of how even good contemporary criticism effaces the rhetorical content of the play I want to turn to Valerie Traub's argument that the meaning of Viola/Cesario resides principally in the "dual erotic investment" that the play establishes in order to "elicit the similarly polymorphous desires of the audience, whose spectator pleasure would be at least partly derived from a transgressive glimpse of multiple erotic possibilities." In order to "substantiate the play's investment in erotic duality," she continues,

> one can compare the language used in Viola/Cesario's two avowals of love: the first as Orsino's wooer of Olivia, and the second as s/he attempts to communicate love to Orsino. In both avowals, Viola/Cesario *theatricalizes desire*, using a similar language of conditionals toward both erotic objects . . ."If I did love you with my master's flame, / With such a suff'ring, such a deadly life, / In your denial I would find no sense; / I would not understand it." . . ."My father had a daughter love'd a man, / As it might be, perhaps, were I a woman, I should your lordship." (my italics)[62]

I would not for a moment deny the existence of the "dual erotic investment" which Traub does well to point out. However, another brief glance at *Gl'Ingannati* will show that Shakespeare's text is more remarkable for resisting than exploiting the considerable dramatic potential of any such investment.

Reading *Gl'Ingannati,* Shakespeare would have come across a model for a scene between Olivia and Viola/Cesario. The scene in question requires the audience to share the voyeuristic position of Flammineo's servants who stumble across Isabella and Lelia/Fabio during an intimate exchange of words and caresses. The audience, however, knows that "Fabio" is, for the purposes of the play, a woman (though the part was probably played by a boy).[63] For the servants, then, the scene arouses sexual feeling and a sense of scandal at the betrayal of Flammineo by the "boy" whom he loved and trusted so much; the audience, however, freed from any sense of the latter, is invited to enjoy the transgression of the scene as if it were a kind of affluence; in Traub's words, it becomes "a transgressive glimpse of multiple erotic possibilities."

Isa. Do you know what I'd like?
Lel. What would you like?
Isa. I'd like you to come closer.
Sca. Get closer, you bumpkin.
Isa. Listen, do you want to go?
Sca. Kiss her, for Christ's sake.
Cri. She's afraid of being seen.
Isa. Come into the doorway a little.
Sca. The thing is done.
Cri. Alas, alas, I'm dry and thirsty—do it to me!
Sca. Didn't I tell you he'd kiss her?[64]

Without denying the possibility of performing the equivalent scene between Olivia and Viola/Cesario in such a way as to maximize its erotic possibilities, I would want to argue that the rhetorical excess which distinguishes Shakespeare's text from the Italian model insists on a far higher level of engagement from the audience *as auditors*. This, in turn, reorients the dramatic meaning of the scene from pleasure in the spectacle of erotic possibility towards complicity in the act of *interpretation* by means of which a reader or auditor lends credibility to the figures, tropes, and fictions in the discourse of another.

Such audience complicity in the bestowal of credibility through interpretation replicates what the scene offers by way of a narrative of "desire." Olivia's desire for Viola/Cesario must become intelligible (unless we ignore the text altogether) through Viola/Cesario's progression away from formal literary models of courtship towards the affective intimacy of a more familiar mode of address, exemplified in the deservedly famous speech which begins, "Make me a willow cabin at your gate" (1.5.273). At this point we have already witnessed Olivia's unenchanted exposure of the economics of the Petrarchan argument, her parody of its facile and opportunistic movement from the praise of natural beauty to the imperatives of husbandry and reproduction: "O sir, I will not be so hard-hearted, I will give out divers schedules of my beauty" (1.5.247-48). Cesario's subsequent readiness to improvise a first-person fiction of abandonment in love represents an ability to extemporize, to seize "the gifts of moment" and so illustrate the crowning glory of classical rhetorical education.[65]

The speech's most obvious analogue in the schoolboy literature which prepared men for such improvisations is that of the impassioned epistolary rhetoric of the women of Ovid's *Heroides,* whose vivid evocations of their writing, and of the cries that echo through the wild and lonely places to which they are abandoned, resemble (in their simultaneous acknowledgment of hopelessness and its contradiction by the emotions aroused in the reader) the curious emotional power tapped by Cesario's entry into a hypothetical desolation of ineffectual texts that nevertheless defy the premise of their ineffectuality. Like Dido writing "without hope to move you," or Oenone, telling Paris how she made Ida resound with howls ("uluati") at his desertion, Viola/Cesario imagines filling the vacant times and spaces of rejection with "cantons of contemned love" and "halloos" of Olivia's name, suddenly evoking a geography of loneliness in a play otherwise suggestive of houses, estates, and urbanity.[66] The implied femininity of Cesario's hypothetically assumed persona here, however, merely complicates the already problematic dramatic hypothesis of a female "Viola" inasmuch as the prominence of Ovid's *Heroides* within the education syllabus for boys implied, as Warren Boutcher has noted,

a relationship between the path to knowledge and . . . the mastery of the heroical *genus familiare,* with its base in epistolary stories which involve— both in the telling and in the action—intimate access to and power over feminine sensibility.[67]

The "femininity" of the genre, then, is inseparable from its implication in a plot of seduction not unlike that of Petrarchism, except that in this version "femininity" itself—understood as a peculiar susceptibility to artificially induced compassion—is the emotional catalyst of masculine rhetorical success.

Olivia's desire for Viola/Cesario becomes apparent as a response to this speech and is inseparable, in its articulation, from the material expression of belief ("credit") that would exempt the unknown stranger from providing the heraldic display (the "blazon") that would put "his" gentility beyond doubt:

"What is my parentage?"
"Above my fortunes, yet my state is well,
I am a gentleman." I'll be sworn thou art;
Thy tongue, thy face, thy limbs, actions and
   spirit
Do give thee five-fold blazon. Not too fast:
   soft! soft!
Unless the master were the man . . .
                                        (1.5.293-98)

Olivia's desire motivates her affirmation of Cesario's somewhat evasive protestation of gentility on the grounds of "his" exceptional beauty, eloquence, and presence of mind. What this implies, then, is that the capacity to arouse desire resides less in the androgynous beauty of the body, than in the body conceived as the medium of *elocutio* ("tongue . . . face . . . limbs . . . actions . . . spirit"); that is, the apt delivery of the mind's invention. Viola/ Cesario *embodies* the capacity of timely and well expressed speech to compel for a mere fiction *credit,* that is the kind of materially consequential belief (in this case, belief in matrimonial eligibility) that is rarely afforded to the "real thing."

The transgressive "glimpse" being offered to a seventeenth-century audience here, I would suggest, is less that of lesbian desire than that of the opportunity for social advancement and erotic gratification afforded by education for any servant of ability entrusted with missions of such intimate familiarity. That the entertainment of such a possibility is necessarily transgressive (though here held at bay from full recognition by the "femininity" of Viola) is evident from the care taken in the Malvolio plot to exploit the audience's revulsion at the very same idea. As a steward, Malvolio shares with Viola/Cesario the distinction of being a household servant whose "civility" of manner is qualification for a position of exceptional trust in the intimate affairs of the household. Olivia's musing, "unless the master were the man," touches the center of the play's concern with the question of social advancement by means of skills and attractions "blazoned" in the execution of service rather than properly inhering in nobility. How can such social advancement be imagined except as an individualistic pursuit of gain, a betrayal of trust, sexual honor, economic dependency, and love?

Leo Salingar and Emrys Jones have shown how comedies of the late 1590s and early 1600s are concerned with establishing the credentials of a notion of "gentility" that operates independently of the feudal structures of lineage and affinity. "The king might create a duke, but not even he could create a gentleman," writes Jones, echoing a sentiment expressed in plays of this period.[68] Gentility thus conceived is less the effect of lineage than of a certain affluence—freedom from manual labor—combined with the type of liberal education that might contribute a civil demeanor in social exchange. The arguments of such comedies therefore require that the discursively and morally cumbersome aspects of the humanist education bequeathed by Erasmus and the grammar schools be adapted to requirements of a style and *habitus* such as Viola/Cesario exhibits: a non-pedantic conversational facility appropriate to the modest enterprises of urban social encounter.

Salingar sees the conflicts played out through this redefinition of humanistic "wit" in terms of an attempt to distinguish between money values and "the values of a leisure class" whose social and financial ambitions are subliminally expressed as the civilized pleasures of courtship. Jones notes in the early 1600s the "crystallisation of a new theatrical formula":

> The plays in question are comedies, usually set in some fictitious vaguely foreign court, often with a double-plot of which one part may be romantic and the other more frankly comic. The comic action sometimes takes the form of a persecution, a "baiting" extended through several episodes.[69]

About the same time as the Chamberlain's men performed *Twelfth Night,* the children of the Chapel staged one of the plays to which Jones here refers, *The Gentleman Usher.*[70] In the predicament of its eponymous antihero, Bassiolo, the play comments interestingly on *Twelfth Night,* condensing different aspects of the situations in which Viola/Cesario and Malvolio find themselves. Bassiolo is, like Malvolio, the most trusted servant in the household of Count Lasso, but, like Viola/Cesario, his being familiarly confided in and befriended by a nobleman for whom he undertakes to woo Margaret, Count Lasso's daughter, immediately puts him in a position of both actual and potential betrayal of trust: Vincentio accuses him of behaving, "as if the master were the man" in an erotic sense, but he has

already done so in the sense that in his contract of friendship with Vincentio, he is wooing for himself.

Chapman's is, however, a far more conservative play than Shakespeare's. Whereas Viola/Cesario's inspired improvisation on the model of the Ovidian heroic epistle actually gains the sympathetic ear and the heart of Olivia, Bassiolo's verbose and cumbersome attempt at amorous epistles merely earns him the noble lovers' contempt, serving to prove that the adaptation of a liberal education to civilized wooing can only be managed by one whose gentleness of birth is beyond dispute. The play is nevertheless concerned to argue the necessity of complementing the hunting and riding skills traditionally definitive of nobility with "wits and paper learning"[71] of a non-pedantic kind; the Duke's ennobling of his illiterate minion, Medice, proves disastrous, arguing against the social advancement of servants who are unable to acquit themselves plausibly in noble society. At the same time, however, the play finds, in Bassiolo's dilemma between fidelity to his master, and the opportunity offered by Vincentio's pretended confidence in his rhetorical ability, that any servant so accomplished and entrusted is liable to deceive.

The fantastic unlikelihood of the plot of *Twelfth Night* and its apparent preoccupation with issues of gender have distracted critical attention from the play's affinity with such contemporary comedies of civility and social advancement. Yet it might well be argued that the very fantasticality of the fiction of gender in *Twelfth Night* constitutes the play's strategy of engagement with contemporary debates on the legitimacy of the individualistic exploitation of service in order, in Viola's own words, to "make occasion mellow."[72]

Twelfth Night endorses the notion of rhetorical opportunism, or individual enterprise insofar as it expresses the mastery of fortune and of the occasions of civil life as the metaphorical equivalent of heroic enterprise on the high seas. Thus, for example, the rivalry between Viola and Aguecheek for the favor of Olivia is recurrently expressed in a nautical idiom. Viola is spoken of as having "trade" (3.1.76) and "commerce" (3.4.175) with Olivia, "she is the list of my voyage" says Viola (3.1.77). The hapless Aguecheek, for lack of Viola's witty invention and attractive presence, is berated for having "sailed into the north of my lady's opinion, where you will hang, like an icicle on a Dutchman's beard, unless you redeem it by some laudable attempt, either of valor or policy" (3.3.24-28). Fabian's reference here—to a 1598 translation of Gerrit de Veer's report of the ordeal of Dutch explorers trapped for ten months in Nova Zembla, where they "never saw, nor heard of any man"[73]—comically imagines Aguecheek's conversational failure both as a failure to prove his masculinity and as meriting exile altogether from the new medium of masculine self-assertion—the profitable commerce of sociability.

The sociability thus defined as heroically masculine, however, must be purposeful as well as facile; Orsino, as Feste says, is insufficiently discriminating in the object of his discourse: "I would have men of such constancy put to sea that their business might be everywhere and there intent nowhere, for that's it always makes a good voyage of nothing" (2.4.75-78). The pervasiveness of such oceanic metaphors, as well as references to maps and narratives of discovery (Malvolio's smiling face is likened to the 1599 map which displayed the new world "as revealed by actual voyages of discovery"[74]) invests the Renaissance synonymity of "tempest" and "fortune" with specifically economic resonances.[75] From the analogy developed between drinking and the hazards of navigation (Feste tells Olivia that a drunken man is like a drowned man—1.5.132) there emerges a chiastic narrative of rhetorical *oikonomia,* in which the eloquent and beautiful twins exchange near-drowning for domestic security, while the drunken and inept or irresponsible Toby and Aguecheek—initially comfortable with cakes and ale in Olivia's buttery—are finally banished, like the "knaves and fools" they prove to be, to the "wind and the rain" of Feste's song, beyond Olivia's gates.

Oikonomia is rhetorical because linguistic ability is identified with the ability to manage wealth. Maria declares of the wealthy Aguecheek that he is incompetent with his resources, he will "have but a year to all those ducats. He's a very fool, and a prodigal" (1.3.22); this failure in husbandry is then discovered at intervals during the play as Aguecheek's recurrent inability to invent plausible arguments or "reasons" for his words or actions. Aguecheek's companions are always teasing him for the reasons he cannot give; *"Pourquoi?"* asks Toby when Aguecheek declares his intention to leave at once, but the question bewilders the knight (1.3.89). In a later exchange Fabian joins Toby in demanding evidence of plausibility: "You must needs yield your reason, Sir Andrew" (3.2.2). The letter which Toby urges him to make "eloquent and full of invention" (3.2.41-43) turns out to be as barren as his speech: *"Wonder not . . . why I do call thee [a scurvy fellow] for I will show thee no reason for't"* (3.4.152-53).[76]

When Anna Jameson praised Viola for the moral sensibility she displayed both in the propriety of her fidelity to Orsino, and in "her generous feeling for her rival Olivia," she appropriated for nineteenth-century feminism a seventeenth-century play's concern with calling into question the assumption that eloquent servants, accomplished in the provision of reasons, and entrusted with the intimate affairs of the household, are necessarily opportunists, people who *deceive.*[77] The narrative rationale of the scene I have already remarked upon in *Gl'Ingannati,* in which Flammineo's servants spy upon Isabella and Lelia's kiss, is to enrage Flammineo against the deceitfulness of his favorite, Fabio; a hilarious scene ensues in which the probability of the kiss is itself called into doubt by the incompetence of the servants in relaying to Flammineo their evidence of Fabio's perfidy.[78] The point here, however, is that Lelia/Fabio *has* kissed Isabella; one deceit leads to another, and Lelia finds herself explaining her refusal of further favors to Isabella on the grounds that "too much love" for Isabella has already led her to deceive ("ingannare") her lord.[79] Earlier, however, Lelia/Fabio showed a singular lack of regard for Flammineo's suit, attempting by means of Pasquella to ensure that Isabella would never respond to his affections; Viola, as Jameson notes, is remarkable for resisting the temptation to do this. In Chapman's *Gentleman Usher,* Bassiolo, also in the position of a go-between or an ambassador between lovers, is tempted not only into exploitation of his position of trust, but into presumptions of equality and friendship with the nobleman who employs him, which the play then ridicules with all the fervor of profound social anxiety.

It becomes clear that the twinning of Sebastian and Viola, and the femininity of the latter, occurs in Shakespeare's play not simply (as in other derivatives of Terence's *Eunuch*) for the sake of resolving an erotic impasse by offering a means of gaining access to the cloistered woman, but for the sake of foregrounding an outrageously improbable *hypothesis* about the possibility of combining fidelity in service with rhetorical *oikonomia*—that is, the heroic exploitation of rhetorical opportunity, which typically achieves both economic security and erotic gratification. Terence Cave has noted that the final revelation of "Viola's" identity remains merely hypothetical, contingent on an accumulation of probabilities beyond the scope of the play: "Do not embrace me till each circumstance / Of place, time, fortune do cohere and jump / *That* I am Viola."[80] It could be said that the femininity of Viola is the grounds upon which the fiction of the servant Cesario can prove the success of eloquence in the narrative of social advancement that Sebastian fulfills, while at the same time ensuring this narrative remains quite untainted by what would otherwise be its precondition—the betrayal of the master by his "man." Viola/Cesario, then, represents more than the "dual erotic investment" that exhausts the meaning of Lelia/Fabio, for s/he is the means by which a seventeenth-century audience could be seduced into entertaining unawares the possibility of a positive version of Malvolio, a servant able to exploit the civility that earns the trust and favor of noblewomen to the extent of achieving the "love" that promises contractual equality. When Fabian imagines himself condemning the crossgartered Malvolio as an "improbable fiction" on the stage, he draws attention to the self-consciousness that marks the play's violation of the Terentian rhetoric of probability, which remains so near the textual surface of *Gl'Ingannati.* Any audience hearing Fabian, however, must feel that the primary violation of probability lies not in the outrageousness of Malvolio's behavior, but in the very existence of the person called Viola, who represents, as Terence Cave has written, "a particularly fruitful violation of the laws of rational discourse no less than sexual decorum," and whose name performs a number of associative tricks, as it "echoes the erotic flowers and music of the opening scene, insidiously rearranges the letters of Olivia's name, and comes close to naming violation itself."[81]

The play's erotic investment in Viola/Cesario is less, I would argue, than its investment in the violation of probability constituted by the twinship of Viola and Sebastian, which first casts the desire and emotion aroused by Cesario into extremity, and then resolves that extremity as a miraculous disproof of the betrayal of trust that would, in the ordinary circumstances of daily life, be its explanation. Thus, for example, where the sodomitic behavior of Fabrizio's traveling companion, the pedant in *Gl'Ingannati,* merely fuels the sexual comedy of that play,[82] the love Antonio feels for Sebastian, while equally open to homoerotic interpretation, is not sidelined by mockery, but rendered able to share on equal terms in a dramatic climax which turns less on the nuptials that unite the two houses than on the proof that not one of the lovers of a beautiful "boy"—neither his wife, nor his master, nor his friend in need—is "therein, by my life, deceiv'd." The "hints of corruption and aggression," which, as Cave notes, recur in the play, accumulate around the common sense perception that the youthful beauty of a stranger is *probably* as deceitful as it is irresistibly attractive.[83]

Certainly Orsino, having charged his lovely ambassador with the ethically problematic obligation to make "discourse" of his "dear faith" and "act" his woes, reads the apparent consequence—Cesario's contract to Olivia—as presaging the youth's career in similar deceptions: "thou dissembling cub! What wilt thou be / When time hath sown a grizzle on thy case?" (5.1.162-63). The pathos of Olivia's case is more marked, as she interprets Viola/Cesario's love for Orsino as the "fear" rightfully aroused by the consciousness of having betrayed his master. In attempting to prevent Viola/Cesario's protestation of innocence, she exposes the instability of her own grounds for belief in the youth's continued fidelity to her. "Oh, do not swear!" she begs, "Hold little faith, though thou hast too much fear" (5.1.169-170). Most moving of all, however, is Antonio's apology for being obliged by love into an extremity that makes demands of the one he loves. "What will you do, now my necessity / Makes me to ask you for my purse?" he gently enquires (3.4.342-43), only to be moved by Viola/Cesario's non-recognition, into an outburst against the deceptiveness of the "promise" that was the boy's manner and looks (3.4.369-79).

A contemporary reader, perusing a popular anthology of the period known as *The Paradyse of daynty deuises,* found one poem entitled thus: "Who mindes to bring

his ship to happy shore / Must care to know the lawes of wisdomes lore." By this poem he wrote, "rules of wary life," bracketing off for particular annotation a verse referring to trust in friendship. Do not bestow credit on boys, the verse advised, for, "Ful soone the boy thy freendship will despyse / And him for loue thou shalt ungrateful find."[84] As Erica Sheen has pointed out, the protracted denouement of *Cymbeline* features a "boy" called Imogen who refuses to plead for the life of her savior and friend, Lucentio. His moralizing comment, "briefly die their joys / that place them on the truth of girls and boys" does nothing to assuage the audience's impatient desire to resolve his mistake, proving the "truth" that probability and versified common sense would deny.[85] Just so here, in *Twelfth Night,* Antonio's sententious conclusions on beauty and deceit merely fuel the audience's desire to relieve him of the pain of believing he has loved a "most ingrateful boy" (5.1.75). In view of this, Greenblatt's observation that, at the end of the play, "Viola is still Cesario," seems not so much to argue for any specific beliefs about instability of gender, as to be a part of that complex affective structure by means of which a boy proves, most improbably, to be "true" to all the kinds of lovers he might have—right up until the end of the play.

What, then, of the play's place in a history of sex and gender? The least that should be said is that any attempt to de-essentialize and historicize gender by appealing to a Galenic theory of men and women differentiated only by degrees of body heat is of strictly limited value in the analysis of a complicated tradition of comic writing in which what distinguishes men is their privileged access to allusive and intertextual levels of meaning—in other words, their access to active participation in the historical and discursive process of defining the social roles and characteristics of either sex. But something rather more positive may be said about *Twelfth Night* in particular. For here once again Shakespeare has chastened the argument of a neo-Terentian play in such a way as to maximize the interpretative possibilities, and consequently the historical tenacity, of the English dramatic text.

That the meaning of the Viola/Olivia courtship for a seventeenth-century audience resided at least partly in its capacity to seduce them into condoning the social (rather than sexual) transgression elsewhere reviled by the play's mockery of Malvolio is suggested by the history of critical reaction to Shakespeare's conception of Viola. The probability of Lelia's dressing up as Fabio is established in *Gl'Ingannati* in an exchange with her nurse during which she admits that since being kept prisoner by soldiers, she has become sexually suspect irrespective of her conduct: ever since the sack of Rome, she says, "ne credevo poter vivere sí honestamente, che bastasse a far che la gente non havesse che dire" [I didn't see how I could live honestly enough to stop them gossiping].[86] In 1753 Charlotte Lennox, writing a criticism of Shakespeare, objected to the want of any similar argument of probability in relation to Viola's decision to dress as a man:

> A very natural scheme, this for a beautiful and virtuous young Lady, to throw off all the modesty and Reservedness of her Sex, mix among men, herself disguised as one; and prest by no Necessity; influenced by no Passion, expose herself to all the dangerous consequences of so unworthy and shameful a Situation.

The Italian source, she notes, "is much more careful to preserve Probability" than "the Poet Shakespeare."[87]

However, by 1832 the very want of any "probable" argument for Viola's behavior (since any such would reflect upon Viola's modesty) enabled Anna Jameson to celebrate her femininity as the source of the peculiar integrity which characterizes her relations to both master and mistress.[88] The very improbability of Viola, then, serves to break down the identification of rhetorical virtuosity (the capacity to make things probable) *with the sexual conquest of women* that marks the plot of the Italian play. The literal intertwining of the names of Malvolio, Olivia, and Viola has often been pointed out, but it many not be entirely fanciful to recall that the identification of "inganni" (deceptions, probable arguments) with the sexual deception that makes Isabella unchaste is signaled in the prologue of *Gl'Ingannati* with following innuendo:

> But there is among these deceptions one particular sort which makes me wish, *for the malice I bear you,* that you might be often deceived, if I were the deceiver.[89]

Here "il mal ch'io vi voglio" is a kind of flirtatious joke on the euphemism for fancying someone, "ti voglio bene." In entertaining ambitious fantasies which suddenly and indecorously make the audience aware that these are also sexual fantasies about Olivia (2.5.47-48), Shakespeare's Malvolio bears the trace of the erotic "mal . . . voglio" by which Fabrizio's economic success is identified as a sexual conquest and extended through innuendo to characterize the terms upon which a female audience may be imagined capable of enjoying the argument of the play.

What was positive for seventeenth-century women about the way in which *Twelfth Night* addressed them, then, was due less to the "high cultural investment in female erotic pleasure . . . because it was thought necessary for conception to occur" than to its opposite:[90] the extent to which, by refusing to subject Olivia to the "mal . . . voglio" of an explicitly sexual encounter with Sebastian on the model of Isabella's with Fabrizio, Shakespeare manages to portray a heroine whose prudence, good judgment, and ability to govern

others remain uncompromised even by her contract with the beautiful youth. For in marrying Sebastian, Olivia has arguably yielded to no whim, but carried out the strategic plan first made known to us by Sir Toby Belch: "she'll not match above her degree, neither in estate, years, nor wit" (1.3.106-108). Olivia never wavers from this purpose, and in providing the precedent that it elsewhere pretends to deny—marriage between a noblewoman and one beneath her—the play endorses the real-life example of the highly intelligent Katherine Brandon, Duchess of Suffolk, who, after having been married at fourteen to her forty-nine-year-old noble guardian, later decided to marry none other then her gentleman usher, who was "an accomplished gentleman, well versed in the study of the languages . . . bold in discourse, quick in repartee." There were, as Katherine Brandon's biographer commented, "many reasons why the clever and serviceable gentleman usher who conducted her business . . . should seem to the Duchess a more desirable husband than an ambitious noble."[91] Shakespeare's play, around 1602, contributed to the undoing of the social and sexual stereotyping that would make of that last statement nothing but a dirty joke.

Notes

[1] Francis Beaumont and John Fletcher, *The Scornful Lady, The Dramatic Works in the Beaumont and Fletcher Canon,* ed. Fredson Bowers (Cambridge: Cambridge UP, 1970), 2: I.i.82-86. This paper was first written for a seminar led by Alison Brown at the Institute of Historical Research; see Alison Brown, "Renaissance Bodies: A New Seminar on the Renaissance," *Bulletin for the Society of Renaissance Studies* 12 (1994): 20-22. I would like to thank Pamela Benson, Alan Bray, Terence Cave, Helen Hackett, David Norbrook, Diane Purkiss, and Erica Sheen for their helpful criticisms and comments.

[2] Stephen Greenblatt, "Fiction and Friction," *Shakespearean Negotiations* (Oxford: Clarendon, 1988), 86, quoted by Valerie Traub, *Desire and Anxiety: Circulations of Sexuality in Shakespearean Drama* (London: Routledge, 1992), 119.

[3] I should acknowledge here my gratitude to Gayle Kern Paster, who, on reading a version of this paper, pointed out that my concern here is more with textual cirticism's historicizing of erotic desire rather than with body history *per se.*

[4] For example, see C. L. Barber's still very interesting *Shakespeare's Festive Comedy* (Princeton: Princeton UP, 1959).

[5] See Lisa Jardine, *Still Harping on Daughters* (London: Harvester, 1983), 9-36.

[6] Catherine Belsey, "Disrupting sexual difference: meaning and gender in the comedies," *Alternative Shakespeares,* ed. John Drakkakis (London: Methuen, 1985), 180. For another poststructuralist challenge to traditional readings of the comedies, see Malcolm Evans, "Deconstructing Shakespeare's Comedies" in the same volume.

[7] Thomas Laqueur, "Orgasm, Generation and the Politics of Reproductive Biology," *Representations* 14 (1986), 3.

[8] See Stephen Greenblatt, "Fiction and Friction," *Reconstructing Individualism,* ed. Thomas C. Heller, Morton Sosna, and David E. Wellbery (California: Stanford UP, 1986), 30-52.

[9] Greenblatt 80; Laqueur 4-5.

[10] Greenblatt 74-75, 79, 85, 181; Laqueur 12-16.

[11] Greenblatt 81; Laqueur 13.

[12] Greenblatt, 88.

[13] Greenblatt, 87.

[14] William Shakespeare, *Twelfth Night,* ed. J. M. Lothian and T. W. Craik (London: Methuen, 1975), 5.1.257-61. Further references to this edition will appear in the text.

[15] Greenblatt, 72.

[16] Greenblatt, 82.

[17] Thomas Laqueur, *Making Sex: Body and Gender from the Greeks to Freud* (Cambridge, MA: Harvard UP), 114.

[18] Laqueur, 115.

[19] Stephen Orgel, "Nobody's Perfect: Or Why Did the English Stage Take Boys for Women?" *South Atalantic Quarterly* 88.1 (1989), 13.

[20] The examples Montaigne cites are those of Iphis, from Ovid, *Metamorphoses* IX, 793ff, and of Lucius Constitus, from Pliny, *Naturalis Historia* VII, iv. See Michel de Montaigne, *The Complete Essays,* trans. M. A. Screech (London: Penguin, 1991), 110. In his chapter of "histoires memorables de certains femmes qui sont degenerees en hommes," Ambroise Paré, *Des Monstres et Prodiges,* ed. Jean Céard (Geneva: Libraire Droz, 1971), includes the same example from Pliny, the story of Marie Germaine, and the example of Maria Pateca, told by João Rodrigues in *Amati Lusitani Medici Physici Praestantissimi, Curationum medicinalium centuriae quatuor* (Froben: Basel, 1567), 168. Need-

less to say, Rodrigues also cites Pliny, confirming a certain sense of circularity and repetition in the gathering of such instances. One might want to argue for a belief in the frequency of the phenomenon from Montaigne's comment, "Ce n'est pas tant de merveille que cette sort d'accident se rencontre frequent" [It isn't surprising that this sort of accident occurs frequently]. However, as Montaigne attributes the "accident" in question to the power of the imagination, which elsewhere in the same essay becomes responsible for unfounded beliefs in the magic that causes impotence, it is not clear how sceptically he means this. In any case, Montaigne's version of Marie-Germaine's accident does not conform to Paré's analysis, since Montaigne attributes to the power of the imagination the capacity to satisfy itself a sexual longing by producing the desired genitals of the (opposite?) sex—"si l'imagination peut en telles choses, elle est si continuellement et si vigoureusement attaché à ce sujet, que, pour n'avoir si souvent à rechoir en même pensée et âpreté de désir, elle a meilleur compte d'incorporer une fois pour toutes cette virile partie aux filles." This would seem to argue that girls did not already possess "cette virile partie." See Michel Eyquem de Montaigne, *Oeuvres Complètes,* ed. R. Barral (Paris: du Seuil, 1967), 54. An excellent article by Patricia Parker, which came to my notice after I had written this article, criticizes both the functioning of medical discourse and the teleology of masculinity as a "reassuringly stable ground" in the arguments of Laqueur and Greenblatt and points to the preoccupation of Montaigne's essay with the anxiety that masculinity itself requires supplementation, to repair the "defect in sex" which is impotence. See Patricia Parker, "Gender Ideology, Gender Change: The Case of Marie Germaine," *Critical Inquiry* 19 (Winter, 1993), 335-64.

[21] Judith C. Bown, *Immodest Acts: the Life of a Lesbian Nun in Renaissance Italy* (Oxford: Oxford UP, 1986), 12, 169.

[22] Traub, 51. This seems unlikely, since Paré explicitly says that the mutation can only go one way: "nous ne trouvons jamais en histoire veritable que d'homme aucun soit devenu femme, pour-ce que Nature tend tousjours à ce qui est le plus parfaict, et non au contraire faire ce qui est parfaict devienne imparfaict" [we never find in any true history that any man whatsoever became a woman, because Nature always tends towards that which is the most perfect, and does not on the contrary make what is perfect become imperfect].

[23] Orgel, 10.

[24] Traub, 103, 117, 141.

[25] Thus, Traub, in her concern to refute or modify Orgel's argument that the transvestite theatre was at least in part motivated by a recognition of the value

represented by female chastity, misleadingly represents the arguments as being about "the fantasized dangers posed by women" (121), which obscures beyond recovery the notion that women's chastity was valuable because it affected *male* honor and, therefore, economic power. The latter argument has been well made in relation to "desire" in the ancient world by John Winkler, *The Constraints of Desire: The Anthropology of Sex and Gender in Ancient Greece* (London: Routledge, 1990), 74-75.

[26] Greenblatt, 88.

[27] The idea that women in the audience fell in love with the players seems to have been common enough; see Beaumont and Fletcher 1.1.46-48, of a waiting maid: "She lov'd all the Players in the last Queenes time once over: she was strook when they acted lovers, and forsook some when they plaid murtherers." Women's susceptibility to the fiction, then, seems to have been laughed at, whereas the ridicule of men turns on the degree of aptitude or otherwise with which they make use of the wit they have heard at plays.

[28] James Shirley, "To the Reader," *Comedies and Tragedies Never Printed before and now published by the Authours Orginall Copies,* Francis Beaumont and John Fletcher (London: Humphrey Moseley, 1647), sig. A3ʳ.

[29] T. W. Baldwin, *Shakespeare's Five Act Structure* (Urbana: U of Illinois P, 1947); Marvin T. Herrick, *Comic Theory in the Renaissance* (Urbana: U of Illinois P, 1950); Georgia S. Nugent, *Ancient Theories of Comedy: The Treatises of Evanthius and Donatus, Shakespearean Comedy,* ed. Maurice Charney (New York: Literary Forum, 1980); Emrys Jones has pointed out how easily Shakespeare's accessibility becomes an argument for his comparative lack of learning, *The Origins of Shakespeare* (Oxford: Clarendon, 1977), 2-4. In this part of my argument, I draw on evidence represented more fully in my book, *The Usurer's Daughter,* (London: Routledge, 1994) chs. 5 and 6.

[30] William Shakespeare, *The Taming of the Shrew,* ed. Brian Morris (London: Methuen, 1981) Induction, line 140.

[31] For Donatus and Melanchthon see note 29, and Joel Altman, *The Tudor Play of Mind* (Berkeley: U of California P, 1978).

[32] Lyndal Roper, *The Holy Household* (Oxford: Oxford UP, 1989), 112.

[33] "E vi confessa in questo l'Autore avere e Plauto e Terenzio seguitato, . . . non solo ne li costumi, ma ne li argumenti ancora de le fabule vuole essere de li antiche . . . imitatore" [And the Author confesses that in this he has followed Plautus and Terence . . . be-

cause he wants to be an imitator of the ancients not just in their customs, but in their arguments and plots]: *Tutte le Opere di Ludovico Ariosto,* ed. Cesare Segre (Milan: Mondadori, 1974), 197.

[34] See Marvin T. Herrick, *Tragicomedy, Its Origins and Development in Italy and France* (Urbana: U of Illinois P, 1962), 17-46; John Palsgrave, *The Comedy of Acolastus translated in oure englysshe tongue after such maner as children are taught in grammar schoole,* ed. P. L. Carver (London: EETS, 1937); M. Christopherus Stummelius, *Studentes, comoedia de vita studiosorum* (Frankfurt: 1550).

[35] Laura Levine, *Men in Women's Clothing: Antitheatricality and Effeminization, 1579-1642* (Cambridge UP, 1994), 2; Jean E. Howard, *The Stage and Social Struggle in Early Modern England* (London: Routledge, 1994), 40.

[36] Stephen Gosson, *Plays Confuted in Five Actions* (London: T. Gosson, n.d.) sigs. C6ʳ-7ʳ. Gosson's example of the schoolmaster is taken from Xenophon, *Cyropaedia* I.6.26-39. The example is used to caution against fraud in civil life but to justify fraud in hunting and war, an argument Machiavelli refers to in *Discorsi sopra la prima deca di Tito Livio, Il Principe e altre opere Politiche,* ed. D. Cantimori (Milan, 1976) III. 39, 455-56.

[37] George Gascoigne, *The Complete Works,* 2 vols., ed. John W. Cunliffe (Cambridge UP, 1910) II. 6.

[38] George Whetstone, *The Right Excellent and Famous History of Promos and Cassandra: Devided into Two Commical Discourses, Shakespeare's Narrative and Dramatic Sources,* ed. Geoffrey Bullough (London: Routledge and Kegan Paul, 1968), 2: 443.

[39] Gascoigne's *Supposes* as *The Taming of the Shrew* and Whetstone's *Promos and Cassandra* as *Measure for Measure.*

[40] Anna Jameson, *Shakespeare's Heroines: Characteristics of Women, Moral, Poetical and Historical* (London: George Newnes Hd., 1897), 130. The first edition was published in 1832; see Clara Thomas, *Love and Work Enough: The Life of Anna Jameson* (London: Macdonald, 1967).

[41] See Shakespeare, *Twelfth Night* xxvi-liii.

[42] See Guido Bonino, "Introduzione: Il teatro a Siena tra Rozzi e Intronati," *Il Teatro Italiano,* 6 vols. (Milan: Einaudi, 1977), II. xxxvi-xliii, 87.

[43] *Les Abusez, comedie faite à la mode des anciens comiques . . . traduit en Françoys par Charles Estienne* (Paris: Estienne Grouleau, 1549), sig. A4ᵛ. On the

supremacy of Ariosto, and for Machiavelli's estimation of him, see Aulo Greco, *L'Istituzione del teatro comico al rinascimento* (Naples: Liguri, 1976), 10 and Machiavelli, *Discorso o dialogo intorno alla nostra lingua* in *Tutte le Opere di Machaivelli* a cura di F. Flora e di C. Cordie (Milano, 1950) II. 816.

⁴⁴ *Delle Comedie Elette Novamente raccolte insieme, con le correttioni, & annotationi di Girolamo Ruscelli* (Venetia, 1554), 164. Unfortunately, there are few annotations after Bibiena and Machiavelli, and there is nothing interesting on *Gl'Ingannati*.

⁴⁵ See Terence, *The Eunuch, Terence,* 2 vols., trans. J. Sergeant (London: Heinemann, 1912). Arisoto explicitly derives his seduction plot from *The Eunuch* (*Opere,* IV.197), but mitigates its scandalous effect by crossing it with Plautus' highminded *Captivi.* Shakespeare in *The Taming of the Shrew* makes several references to *The Eunuch,* which assimilate it to the humanist debate about the ethics of teaching schoolboys the classics, and to the anti-theatre argument that theatre works like pornography, to arouse men to commit sexual crimes. For the centrality of *The Eunuch* to sixteenth-century debates about art and pornography, see Carlo Ginzburg, "Titian, Ovid and Erotic Illustration," *Myths, Emblems, Clues,* trans. John and Anne Tedeschi (London: Hutchinson, 1986), 77-95.

⁴⁶ 1.3.56; "Thou shalt present me as an eunuch to him"; compare Terence, "*Chaerea.* o fortunatem istum eunuchum qui quidem inhanc detur domum! . . . *Parmeno.* pro illo te deducam" [*Chaerea.* o what a lucky eunuch to be made a present for that house! . . . *Parmeno.* I could take you instead], *The Eunuch,* in *Terence,* II. 270-71.

⁴⁷ *Il Sacrificio, Gl'ingannati, Comedia degli Intronati celebrato nei Giuochi d'un Carnovale di Siena* (Venetia: Altobello Salicero, 1569) 1.1, fol. 18ᵛ. There is a translation of this play by Geoffrey Bullough in *Narrative and Dramatic Sources of Shakespeare* (London: Routledge, 1958), 2:286-339, but it omits or censors a fair amount.

⁴⁸ On this topic in relation to *Twelfth Night,* see Lisa Jardine, "Twins and Travesties: gender, dependency and sexual availability," *Erotic Politics: Desire on the Renaissance Stage,* ed. Susan Zimmerman (London: Routledge, 1992), 27-38.

⁴⁹ "*Clem.* Dimmi un poco, & dove dormi tu? / *Lelia.* In una sua anticamera sola. / *Celm.* Se una notte tentato dalla maladetta tentatione ti chiamasse che tu dormisse con lui, come andrebbe? / *Lelia.* Io non voglio pensare al male prima che venga" 1.3, fol. 26ʳ.

⁵⁰ *Gl'Ingannati,* 2.2, fols. 32ᵛ-33ʳ.

⁵¹ This isn't quite accurate as a rendering of "s'era maschio o femina," but any other way would announce the gender of Isabella's partner too soon by assigning a pronoun.

⁵² *Gl'Ingannati,* 4.4, fol. 58ᵛ. This is one of the passages that Bullough omits in his translation.

⁵³ *Gl'Ingannati,* 4.8, fol. 62ᵛ.

⁵⁴ *Gl'Ingannati,* 4.8, fol. 62ᵛ.

⁵⁵ Estienne, *Les Abusez,* sig. A3ʳ.

⁵⁶ *Gl'Ingannati,* "Prologo," fol. 15ʳ.

⁵⁷ See Laqueur, *Making Sex,* 194-205 and Barbara Taylor, *Eve and the New Jerusalem* (Virago, 1983), 28. Laqueur and Taylor both refer to the use made by feminists like Jameson of texts such as John Millar's *The Origin of the Distinction of Ranks* (Basel, 1793), which suggested that position of women in any society might be taken as a measurement of its civility and well being. Millar's influence is certainly traceable in Anna Jameson's *Sketches in Canada, or Rambles among the Red Men* (London: Longman, 1852), and is compatible with the project of *The Characteristics of Women* as outlined in the introductory dialogue, 20-31.

⁵⁸ Greenblatt, *Fiction and Friction,* 75.

⁵⁹ For an account of how this happens in *The Comedy of Errors* and *The Taming of the Shrew,* see "Why do Shakespeare's women have 'characters'?" *The Usurer's Daughter,* 178-213.

⁶⁰ Levine, *Men in Women's Clothing,* 11; see also Howard, *Stage and Social Struggle,* 35. Both Levine and Howard reduce the meaning of "theatricality" to the subversions, sexual and social, effected by the assumption of *disguise,* as if clothes themselves made the theatrical fiction credible and powerful.

⁶¹ Levine, *Men in Women's Clothes,* 8.

⁶² Traub, *Desire and Anxiety,* 131.

⁶³ None of the authorities on sixteenth-century Italian drama that I consulted [Mario Baratto, *La Commedia del Cinquecento* (Venice, 1975); Nino Borsellino, *Rozzie Intronati* (Rome, 1974); Aulo Greceo, *L'Istituzione del teatro comico nel rinascimento* (Naples, 1976); Marvin Herrick, *Italian Comedy in the Renaissance* (Urbana: U of Illinois P, 1960); Louise Clubb, *Italian Drama in Shakespeare's Time* (New Haven: Yale UP, 1989)] could inform me on this question of staging. However, Pamela Benson very kindly consulted the current expert on Italian theatrical pro-

duction, Richard Andrews, whose reply suggested that although plays in convents had all female casts, courtesans were famous for improvising scenes in their salons, and there is some evidence that women did play at court and in some touring companies, they were unlikely to have taken parts in a play put on by a learned academy, such as the Intronati di Siena. I would like to thank Pamela Benson and Richard Andrews for this information.

[64] *Gl'Ingannati,* 2: 6, fol. 37[v].

[65] See Terence Cave, *The Cornucopian Text* (Oxford: Clarendon, 1979), 127.

[66] See Ovid, *Heroides and Amores,* trans. Grant Showerman (London: Heineman, 1977), 62-63, 82-83. *Twelfth Night* is implicitly urban, by virtue of the stress placed throughout on "civility"; Olivia, for example, berates Toby as an "ungracious wretch, / Fit for the mountains and barbarous caves, / Where manners were ne'er preach'd" before begging Sebastian to forgive the "uncivil" injury he has sustained at the hands of her kinsman. *Twelfth Night* IV.i.46-52.

[67] Warren Boutcher, "Catching the Court Ear in Sixteenth Century Europe," *The Cambridge Companion to Renaissance Humanism,* ed. Jill Kraye (Cambridge: Cambridge UP, 1995). For the centrality of Ovid's *Heroides* to the sixteenth-century grammar school syllabus, especially as practice in letter writing, see T. W. Baldwin, *William Shakespeare's Small Latine and Lesse Greeke,* 2 vols. (Urbana, 1944), 1: 119, 148, 157; 2: 239. See also Erasmus, "De Conscribendi Epistolis," *The Collected Works of Erasmus,* ed. J. K. Sowards (Toronto: U of Toronto P, 1985), 25: 22-25.

[68] Emrys Jones, "The First West End Comedy," *Proceedings of the British Academy,* LXVIII (1982), 215-58, 232.

[69] Jones, "The First West End Comedy" 233. See also Leo Salingar, "Wit in Jacobean Comedy," *Dramatic Form in Shakespeare and the Elizabethans* (Cambridge: Cambridge UP, 1986), 150.

[70] The date of *Twelfth Night* is established by Manningham's *Diary* as being before February 1602; see *Twelfth Night* xxvi. Champman's *The Gentleman Usher* was printed in 1606, and the date of first performance is conjectured to be between 1601 and 1604. See "Textual Introduction," *The Gentleman Usher,* ed. Robert Ornstein, *The Plays of George Chapman: The Comedies,* ed. Allan Holaday (Urbana: U of Illinois P, 1970), 131.

[71] Chapman, *The Gentleman Usher,* 2.1.58.

[72] Charlotte Lennox complains of the improbability of Shakespeare's plots in *Shakespeare Illustrated . . . by*

the author of the Female Quixote (London: 1753), 244. That Lennox's response was still commonplace in the nineteenth criticism is suggested by Jameson's comment, "The situation and character of Viola have been censured for their want of consistency and probability," *Shakespeare's Heroines* 130.

[73] Gerrit de Veer, *The True and Perfect Description of Three Voyages by the Ships of Holland and Zeland* [1609] (Amsterdam: Theatrum Orbis Terrarum, 1970), sig. A2[r]. The account was entered on the Stationers' Register in 1598; see *Twelfth Night* xxxii.

[74] Helen Wallis, "Edward Wright and the 1599 world map," *The Hakluyt Handbook,* ed. D. B. Quinn (London: Hakluyt Society, 1974), 73.

[75] See Jones, *The Origins of Shakespeare,* 209-10.

[76] Chapman, in *The Gentleman Usher,* also assumes a relationship between rhetorical skill, household management, and the favour of noblewomen: "You are not knowne to speak well? You haue wonne direction of the Earl and all his house, / The fauour of his daughter, and all Dames / That euer I sawe, come within your sight," Vincentio flatters the steward (3.2.167-70).

[77] Jameson, *Shakespeare's Heroines,* 33.

[78] *Gl'Ingannati,* 2: 8, fol. 40[v].

[79] *Gl'Ingannati,* 2: 8, fol. 38[r].

[80] Terence Cave, *Recognitions: A Study in Poetics* (Oxford: Clarendon, 1988), 279.

[81] Cave, 280.

[82] *Gl'Ingannati,* fol. 53[v], Stragualcia, the pedant's servant, rails, "che voi sete . . . un sodomito, un tristo, posso dire" [I could say you were a sodomite, a miserable specimen].

[83] Cave, *Recognitions,* 280.

[84] Richard Edwardes, *The Paradyse of daynty deuises* (London: Henry Disle, 1578) Bodleian Library Pressmark: Wood 482 (6), fols. 5[r]-6[v].

[85] *Cymbeline,* ed. J. M. Nosworthy (London: Methuen, 1969) 5.5.106-108. I would like to thank Erica Sheen for pointing out the similarity of this affective moment to that in *Twelfth Night.*

[86] *Gl'Ingannati,* I.ii., fol. 23[v].

[87] Charlotte Lennox, *Shakespear Illustrated . . . by the author of the Female Quixote* (London: 1753), 244.

[88] See above, note 72; Jameson observes that "The situation and character of Viola have been censured for their want . . . of probability," *Shakespeare's Heroines,* 130.

[89] *Gl'Ingannati,* "Prologo," fol. 15ʳ.

[90] Traub, *Desire and Anxiety,* 141.

[91] Lady Cecilie Goff, *A Woman of the Tudor Age* (London: John Murray, 1930), 213.

FURTHER READING

Berry, Ralph. "*Twelfth Night*: The Experience of the Audience." *Shakespeare Survey* XXXIV (1981): 111-19.

> Argues that, during the course of the play, *Twelfth Night* transforms the audience's perception of the performance, portraying "theatre as blood sport, theatre that celebrates its own dark origins."

Brown, John Russell. "*Twelfth Night*." In *Shakespeare's Dramatic Style,* pp. 132-59. New York: Barnes & Noble, 1971.

> Explores the syntax and diction in three extracts from *Twelfth Night* and how they contribute to characterization.

Champion, Larry S. "The Perspective of Comedy: Shakespeare's Pointers in *Twelfth Night*." *Genre* I, No. 4 (October 1968): 269-89.

> Considers *Twelfth Night* to be one of the richest of Shakespeare's comedies in terms of its characterization, moving beyond farce to a consideration of unique and complex identities and motivations.

Davies, Stevie. "Boy-girls and Girl-boys: Sexual Indeterminacy." In *Twelfth Night,* pp. 113-35. London and New York: Penguin Books, 1993.

> Contends that the figure of Viola/Cesario defies natural sexual categories by affirming the plasticity of gender.

Gérard, Albert. "Shipload of Fools: A Note on *Twelfth Night*." *English Studies* XLV, No. 2 (April 1964): 109-15.

> Asserts that *Twelfth Night* contains disturbing elements that prefigure the bleak worlds of such plays as *Hamlet* and *Troilus and Cressida,* because in *Twelfth Night* "Shakespeare was beginning to outgrow the pure mirth of the comic vision."

Hassel, R. Chris, Jr. "Malvolio's Dark Concupiscence." *Cahiers Elisabethains* No. 43 (April 1993): 1-11.

> Interprets Malvolio's imprisonment according to the religious teachings of Martin Luther.

Levin, Richard A. "Viola: Dr Johnson's 'Excellent Schemer'." *Durham University Journal* LXXI, No. 2 (June 1979): 213-22.

> Reviews Samuel Johnson's interpretation of Viola.

Markels, Julian. "Shakespeare's Confluence of Tragedy and Comedy: *Twelfth Night* and *King Lear*." In *Shakespeare 400: Essays by American Scholars on the Anniversary of the Poet's Birth,* edited by James G. McManaway, pp. 75-88. New York: Holt, Rinehart and Winston, 1964.

> Explores the plot elements and characterizations (especially of Malvolio and Lear) shared by *Twelfth Night* and *King Lear,* and what distinguishes them as comedy and tragedy, respectively.

Nagarajan, S. "'What You Will': A Suggestion." *Shakespeare Quarterly* X, No. 1 (Winter 1959): 61-67.

> Argues that the source of the comedy in *Twelfth Night* is "self-deception as it manifests itself in love."

Willbern, David. "Malvolio's Fall." *Shakespeare Quarterly* XXIX, No. 1 (Winter 1978): 85-90.

> Considers Malvolio to be essential to the "merriment" of *Twelfth Night,* especially in his expression of repressed sexual desires.

Wilson, John Dover. "*Twelfth Night*." *Shakespeare's Happy Comedies,* pp. 163-83. Evanston: Northwestern University Press, 1962.

> Provides an overview of *Twelfth Night,* comparing it to the comedies that preceded it.

Cumulative Index to Topics

The Cumulative Index to Topics identifies the principal topics of discussion in the criticism of each play and non-dramatic poem. The topics are arranged alphabetically. Page references indicate the beginning page number of each essay containing substantial commentary on that topic.

Topic Index

348, 373, 387, 393, 411, 418, 424

comparison **1:** 290, 295, 329, 348, 358, 393, 411, 419, 429, 431, 441

unity of both parts **1:** 286, 290, 309, 314, 317, 329, 365, 373, 374, 396, 402, 404, 419

relationship to other Shakespearean plays **1:** 286, 290, 309, 329, 365, 396; **28:** 101

religious or mythic content **1:** 314, 374, 414, 421, 429, 431, 434

staging issues **32:** 212

textual issues **22:** 114

time and change, motif of **1:** 372, 393, 411

Turkish elements **19:** 170

two fathers **14:** 86, 101, 105, 108

violence **25:** 109

Henry V

battle of Agincourt **5:** 197, 199, 213, 246, 257, 281, 287, 289, 293, 310, 318; **19:** 217; **30:** 181

Canterbury and churchmen **5:** 193, 203, 205, 213, 219, 225, 252, 260; **22:** 137; **30:** 215, 262

characterization **5:** 186, 189, 192, 193, 199, 219, 230, 233, 252, 276, 293; **30:** 227, 278

Chorus, role of **5:** 186, 192, 226, 228, 230, 252, 264, 269, 281, 293; **14:** 301, 319, 336; **19:** 133; **25:** 116, 131; **30:** 163, 202, 220

class relations **28:** 146

comic elements **5:** 185, 188, 191, 192, 217, 230, 233, 241, 252, 260, 276; **19:** 217; **28:** 121; **30:** 193, 202,

colonialism **22:** 103

economic relations **13:** 213

Elizabethan culture, relation to **5:** 210, 213, 217, 223, 257, 299, 310; **16:** 202; **19:** 133, 233; **28:** 121, 159; **30:** 215, 262

English language and colonialism **22:** 103; **28:** 159

epic elements **5:** 192, 197, 246, 257, 314; **30:** 181, 220, 237, 252

Falstaff **5:** 185, 186, 187, 189, 192, 195, 198, 210, 226, 257, 269, 271, 276, 293, 299; **28:** 146

Fluellen **30:** 278

French aristocrats and the Dauphin **5:** 188, 191, 199, 205, 213, 281; **22:** 137; **28: 121**

French language, Shakespeare's use of **5:** 186, 188, 190; **25:** 131

gender issues **13:** 183; **28:** 121, 146, 159

Henry

brutality and cunning **5:** 193, 203, 209, 210, 213, 219, 233, 239, 252, 260, 271, 287, 293, 302, 304; **30:** 159,

characterization in *1* and *2 Henry IV* contrasted **5:** 189, 190, 241, 304, 310; **19:** 133; **25:** 131; **32:** 157

courage **5:** 191, 195, 210, 213, 228, 246, 257, 267

disguise **30:** 169, 259

education **5:** 246, 267, 271, 289; **14:** 297, 328, 342; **30:** 259

emotion, lack of **5:** 209, 212, 233, 244, 264, 267, 287, 293, 310

as heroic figure **5:** 192, 205, 209, 223, 244, 252, 257, 260, 269, 271, 299, 304; **28:** 121, 146; **30:** 237, 244, 252,

humor **5:** 189, 191, 212, 217, 239, 240, 276

intellectual and social limitations **5:** 189, 191,

203, 209, 210, 225, 226, 230, 293; **30:** 220

interpersonal relations **5:** 209, 233, 267, 269, 276, 287, 293, 302, 318; **19:** 133; **28:** 146

mercy **5:** 213, 267, 289, 293

mixture of good and bad qualities **5:** 199, 205, 209, 210, 213, 244, 260, 304, 314; **30:** 262, 273

piety **5:** 191, 199, 209, 217, 223, 239, 257, 260, 271, 289, 310, 318; **30:** 244; **32:** 126

public vs. private selves **22:** 137; **30:** 169, 207

self-doubt **5:** 281, 310

slaughter of prisoners **5:** 189, 205, 246, 293, 318; **28:** 146

speech **5:** 212, 230, 233, 246, 264, 276, 287, 302; **28:** 146; **30:** 163, 227

historical content **5:** 185, 188, 190, 192, 193, 198, 246, 314; **13:** 201; **19:** 133; **25:** 131; **30:** 193, 202, 207, 215, 252

homoerotic elements **16:** 202

Hotspur **5:** 189, 199, 228, 271, 302

hypocrisy **5:** 203, 213, 219, 223, 233, 260, 271, 302

imperialism **22:** 103; **28:** 159

Irish affairs **22:** 103; **28:** 159

irony **5:** 192, 210, 213, 219, 223, 226, 233, 252, 260, 269, 281, 299, 304; **14:** 336; **30:** 159, 193

Katherine **5:** 186, 188, 189, 190, 192, 260, 269, 299, 302; **13:** 183; **19:** 217; **30:** 278

kingship **5:** 205, 223, 225, 233, 239, 244, 257, 264, 267, 271, 287, 289, 299, 302, 304, 314, 318; **16:** 202; **22:** 137; **30:** 169, 202, 259, 273

language and imagery **5:** 188, 230, 233, 241, 264, 276; **9:** 203; **19:** 203; **25:** 131; **30:** 159, 181, 207, 234 **30:** 159, 181, 207, 234

Machiavellianism **5:** 203, 225, 233, 252, 287, 304; **25:** 131; **30:** 273

MacMorris **22:** 103; **28:** 159; **30:** 278

Marlowe's works, compared with **19:** 233

metadramatic elements **13:** 194; **30:** 181,

Mistress Quickly **5:** 186, 187, 210, 276, 293; **30:** 278

morality **5:** 195, 203, 213, 223, 225, 239, 246, 260, 271, 293

obscenity **5:** 188, 190, 260

order **5:** 205, 257, 264, 310, 314; **30:** 193,

patriotism **5:** 198, 205, 209, 210, 213, 219, 223, 233, 246, 252, 257, 269, 299; **19:** 133, 217; **30:** 227, 262

Pistol **28:** 146

psychoanalytic interpretation **13:** 457

relation to tetralogy **5:** 195, 198, 205, 212, 225, 241, 244, 287, 304, 310; **14:** 337, 342; **30:** 215

religious or mythic content **25:** 116; **32:** 126

Salic Law **5:** 219, 252, 260; **28:** 121

self-interest or expediency **5:** 189, 193, 205, 213, 217, 233, 260, 287, 302, 304; **30:** 273

soldiers **5:** 203, 239, 267, 276, 281, 287, 293, 318; **28:** 146; **30:** 169,

staging issues **5:** 186, 189, 192, 193, 198, 205, 226, 230, 241, 281, 314; **13:** 194, 502; **14:** 293, 295, 297, 301, 310, 319, 328, 334, 336, 342; **19:** 217; **32:** 185

structure **5:** 186, 189, 205, 213, 230, 241, 264, 289, 310, 314; **30:** 220, 227, 234, 244

textual problems **5:** 187, 189, 190; **13:** 201

topical allusions **5:** 185, 186; **13:** 201

tragic elements **5:** 228, 233, 267, 269, 271

traitors (Scroop, Grey, and Cambridge) **16:** 202;

30: 220, 278

Turkish elements **19:** 170

war **5:** 193, 195, 197, 198, 210, 213, 219, 230, 233, 246, 281, 293; **28:** 121, 146; **30:** 262; **32:** 126

Williams **13:** 502; **16:** 183; **28:** 146; **30:** 169, 259, 278

wooing scene (Act V, scene ii) **5:** 186, 188, 189, 191, 193, 195, 260, 276, 299, 302; **14:** 297; **28:** 121, 159; **30:** 163, 207

Henry VI, Parts 1, 2, and 3

ambivalent or ironic elements **3:** 69, 151, 154

authorship, question of **3:** 16, 18, 19, 20, 21, 26, 27, 29, 31, 35, 39, 41, 55, 66; **24:** 51

autobiographical elements **3:** 41, 55

Cade scenes **3:** 35, 67, 92, 97, 109; **16:** 183; **22:** 156; **25:** 102; **28:** 112

carnival elements **22:** 156

characterization **3:** 18, 20, 24, 25, 31, 57, 64, 73, 77, 109, 119, 151; **24:** 22, 28, 38, 42, 45, 47

dance **22:** 156

decay of heroic ideals **3:** 119, 126

disorder and civil dissension **3:** 59, 67, 76, 92, 103, 126; **13:** 131; **16:** 183; **24:** 11, 17, 28, 31, 47; **25:** 102; **28:** 112

Elizabethan literary and cultural influences **3:** 75, 97, 100, 119, 143; **22:** 156; **28:** 112

Henry

characterization **3:** 64, 77, 151

source of social disorder **3:** 25, 31, 41, 115

as sympathetic figure **3:** 73, 143, 154; **24:** 32

historical accuracy **3:** 18, 21, 35, 46, 51; **16:** 217; **24:** 16, 18, 25, 31, 45, 48

as humanistic play **3:** 83, 92, 109, 115, 119, 131, 136, 143

Humphrey **13:** 131

as inferior Shakespearean work **3:** 20, 21, 25, 26, 35

Joan of Arc **16:** 131; **32:** 212

kingship **3:** 69, 73, 77, 109, 115, 136, 143; **24:** 32

language and imagery **3:** 21, 50, 52, 55, 57, 66, 67, 71, 75, 76, 97, 105, 109, 119, 126, 131; **24:** 28

legitimacy **3:** 89, 157

Margaret

characterization **3:** 18, 26, 35, 51, 103, 109, 140, 157; **24:** 48

Suffolk, relationship with **3:** 18, 24, 26, 157

Machiavellianism **22:** 193

Marlowe's works, compared with **19:** 233

medieval literary elements **3:** 59, 67, 75, 100, 109, 136, 151; **13:** 131

molehill scene (*3 Henry VI*, Act III, scene ii) **3:** 75, 97, 126, 149

moral inheritance **3:** 89, 126

multiple perspectives of characters **3:** 69, 154

Neoclassical rules **3:** 17, 18

patriarchal claims **16:** 131 **25:** 102

patriotism **24:** 25, 45, 47

place in Shakespeare's historical epic **3:** 24, 59; **24:** 51

play-within-the-play, convention of **3:** 75, 149

retribution **3:** 27, 42, 51, 59, 77, 83, 92, 100, 109, 115, 119, 131, 136, 151

Topic Index

Topic Index

Richard II

Richard III

Topic Index

ISBN 0-8103-9980-6

90000

9 780810 399808